THIS HOLY BIBLE

Presented to

_____

_____

BY _____

_____

DATE_____

OCCASION_____

For the faithful in all English-speaking countries the publication of <u>The New American Bible</u> represents a notable achievement. Its pages contain a new Catholic version of the Bible in English, along with illustrations and explanations that facilitate the understanding of the text.

For more than a quarter of a century, members of the Catholic Biblical Association of America, sponsored by the Bishops' Committee of the Confraternity of Christian Doctrine, have labored to create this new translation of the Scriptures from the original languages or from the oldest extant form in which the texts exist.

In so doing, the translators have carried out the directive of our predecessor, Pius XII, in his famous Encyclical <u>Divino Afflante Spiritu</u>, and the decree of the Second Vatican Council (<u>Dei Verbum</u>), which prescribed that "up-to-date and appropriate translations be made in the various languages, by preference from the original texts of the sacred books," and that "with the approval of Church authority, these translations may be produced in cooperation with our separated brethren" so that "all Christians may be able to use them."

The holy task of spreading God's word to the widest possible readership has a special urgency today. Despite all his material achievements, man still struggles with the age-old problems of how to order his life for the glory of God, for the welfare of his fellows and the salvation of his soul. Therefore we are gratified to find in this new translation of the Scriptures a new opportunity for men to give themselves to frequent reading of, and meditation on, the living Word of God. In its pages we recognize His voice, we hear a message of deep significance for every one of us. Through the spiritual dynamism and prophetic force of the Bible, the Holy Spirit spreads his light and his warmth over all men, in whatever historical or sociological situation they find themselves.

On all who have contributed to this translation, and all who seek in its pages the sacred teaching and the promise of salvation of Jesus Christ our Lord, we gladly bestow our paternal Apostolic Blessing.

From the Vatican, September 18, 1970

Paulus PP. VI-

THE
NEW
AMERICAN
BIBLE

*Translated from the Original Languages
with Critical Use
of All the Ancient Sources*

AND

THE REVISED NEW TESTAMENT
AUTHORIZED BY THE BOARD OF TRUSTEES
OF THE
CONFRATERNITY OF CHRISTIAN DOCTRINE
AND
APPROVED BY THE ADMINISTRATIVE COMMITTEE/BOARD
OF THE
NATIONAL CONFERENCE OF CATHOLIC BISHOPS
AND THE
UNITED STATES CATHOLIC CONFERENCE

FIRESIDE BIBLE PUBLISHERS
WICHITA, KANSAS

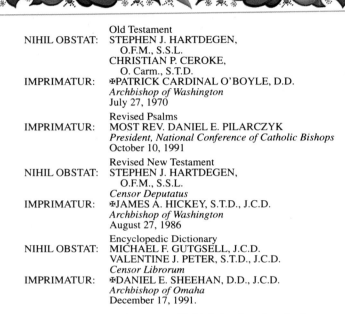

	Old Testament
NIHIL OBSTAT:	STEPHEN J. HARTDEGEN, O.F.M., S.S.L.
	CHRISTIAN P. CEROKE, O. Carm., S.T.D.
IMPRIMATUR:	✠PATRICK CARDINAL O'BOYLE, D.D.
	Archbishop of Washington
	July 27, 1970

	Revised Psalms
IMPRIMATUR:	MOST REV. DANIEL E. PILARCZYK
	President, National Conference of Catholic Bishops
	October 10, 1991

	Revised New Testament
NIHIL OBSTAT:	STEPHEN J. HARTDEGEN, O.F.M., S.S.L.
	Censor Deputatus
IMPRIMATUR:	✠JAMES A. HICKEY, S.T.D., J.C.D.
	Archbishop of Washington
	August 27, 1986

	Encyclopedic Dictionary
NIHIL OBSTAT:	MICHAEL F. GUTGSELL, J.C.D.
	VALENTINE J. PETER, S.T.D., J.C.D.
	Censor Librorum
IMPRIMATUR:	✠DANIEL E. SHEEHAN, D.D., J.C.D.
	Archbishop of Omaha
	December 17, 1991.

The Nihil Obstat and Imprimatur are official declarations that a book or pamphlet is free of doctrinal or moral error. No implication is contained therein that those who have granted the Nihil Obstat and Imprimatur agree with the content, opinions or statements expressed.

COPYRIGHT, 1987 AND 1981, BY DEVORE & SONS, INC.
WICHITA, KANSAS 67201
COPYRIGHT, 1970, BY CATHOLIC BIBLE PUBLISHERS
WICHITA, KANSAS 67201
PRINTED IN THE UNITED STATES OF AMERICA
1996-1997 EDITION

Pope John Paul II

Pope John Paul II

MEETING in secret conclave for the second time in less than two months, the College of Cardinals on October 16, 1978, elected a new Pope to succeed the late Pope John Paul I. In accepting the position, Karol Cardinal Wojtyla, Archbishop of Cracow, took the name of John Paul II and succeeded St. Peter as the 265th Supreme Pontiff. Ceremonies on October 22 marked the inauguration of his pontificate.

Pope John Paul II was born on May 18, 1920, in Wadowice, Poland. After ordination in 1946, he went to Rome, receiving a doctorate in ethics at the Angelicum University. Upon returning to Poland, he continued studies for a doctorate in theology at the Catholic University of Lublin, where he also served on the faculty. During this time, he also assumed pastoral duties in Cracow and was named Auxiliary Bishop of Cracow in 1958. In this capacity he attended all of the sessions of Vatican II, making several noteworthy contributions to the work of the Council. Named Archbishop of Cracow on January 13, 1964, and a cardinal on June 26, 1967, he maintained close ties with the Vatican and wrote extensively on many subjects. He traveled twice to the United States in 1969 and 1976, making special visits to Polish Catholic communities.

The Succession of Popes

St. Peter (-67)
St. Linus (67-76)
St. Anacletus (76-88)
St. Clement (88-97)
St. Evaristus (97-105)
St. Alexander I (105-115)
St. Sixtus I (115-125)
St. Telesphorus (125-136)
St. Hyginus (136-140)
St. Pius I (140-155)
St. Anicetus (155-166)
St. Soter (166-175)
St. Eleutherius (175-189)
St. Victor I (189-199)
St. Zephyrinus (199-217)
St. Callistus I (217-222)
St. Urban I (222-230)
St. Pontian (230-235)
St. Anterus (235-236)
St. Fabian (236-250)
St. Cornelius (251-253)
St. Lucius I (253-254)
St. Stephen I (254-257)
St. Sixtus II (257-258)
St. Dionysius (259-268)
St. Felix I (269-274)
St. Eutychian (275-283)
St. Caius (283-296)
St. Marcellinus (296-304)
St. Marcellus I (308-309)
St. Eusebius (309?-310?)
St. Meltiades (311-314)
St. Sylvester I (314-335)
St. Marcus (336-336)
St. Julius I (337-352)
Liberius (352-366)
St. Damasus I (366-384)

St. Siricius (384-399)
St. Anastasius I (399-401)
St. Innocent I (401-417)
St. Zozimus (417-418)
St. Boniface I (418-422)
St. Celestine I (422-432)
St. Sixtus III (432-440)
St. Leo I (440-461)
St. Hilary (461-468)
St. Simplicius (468-483)
St. Felix III (II) (483-492)
St. Gelasius I (492-496)
Anastasius II (496-498)
St. Symmachus (498-514)
St. Hormisdas (514-523)
St. John I (523-526)
St. Felix IV (III) (526-530)
Boniface II (530-532)
John II (533-535)
St. Agapitus I (535-536)
St. Silverius (536-537)
Vigilius (537-555)
Pelagius I (556-561)
John III (561-574)
Benedict I (575-579)
Pelagius II (579-590)
St. Gregory I (590-604)
Sabinianus (604-606)
Boniface III (607-607)
St. Boniface IV (608-615)
St. Deusdedit (Adeodatus I) (615-618)
Boniface V (619-625)
Honorius I (625-638)
Severinus (640-640)
John IV (640-642)
Theodore I (642-649)

St. Martin I (649-655)
St. Eugene I (654-657)
St. Vitalian (657-672)
Adeodatus II (672-676)
Donus (676-678)
St. Agatho (678-681)
St. Leo II (682-683)
St. Benedict II (684-685)
John V (685-686)
Conon (686-687)
St. Sergius I (687-701)
John VI (701-705)
John VII (705-707)
Sisinnius (708-708)
Constantine (708-715)
St. Gregory II (715-731)
St. Gregory III (731-741)
St. Zachary (741-752)
St. Stephen II (752-752)
Stephen II (III) (752-757)
St. Paul I (757-767)
Stephen III (IV) (768-772)
Adrian I (772-795)
St. Leo III (795-816)
Stephen IV (V) (816-817)
St. Paschal I (817-824)
Eugene II (824-827)
Valentine (827-827)
Gregory IV (827-844)
Sergius II (844-847)
St. Leo IV (847-855)
Benedict III (855-858)
St. Nicholas I (858-867)
Adrian II (867-872)
John VIII (872-882)
Marinus I (882-884)
St. Adrian III (884-885)

Stephen V (VI) (885-891)
Formosus (891-896)
Boniface VI (896-896)
Stephen VI (VII) (896-897)
Romanus (897-897)
Theodore II (897-897)
John IX (898-900)
Benedict IV (900-903)
Leo V (903-903)
Sergius III (904-911)
Anastasius III (911-913)
Landus (913-914)
John X (914-928)
Leo VI (928-928)
Stephen VII (VIII) (928-931)
John XI (931-935)
Leo VII (936-939)
Stephen VIII (IX) (939-942)
Marinus II (942-946)
Agapitus II (946-955)
John XII (955-964)
Leo VIII (963-965)
Benedict V (964-966)
John XIII (965-972)
Benedict VI (973-974)
Benedict VII (974-983)
John XIV (983-984)
John XV (985-996)
Gregory V (996-999)
Sylvester II (999-1003)
John XVII (1003-1003)
John XVIII (1004-1009)
Sergius IV (1009-1012)
Benedict VIII (1012-1024)
John XIX (1024-1032)
Benedict IX (1032-1044)
Sylvester III (1045-1045)
Benedict IX (1045-1045)
Gregory VI (1045-1046)
Clement II (1046-1047)
Benedict IX (1047-1048)
Damasus II (1048-1048)
St. Leo IX (1049-1054)
Victor II (1055-1057)
Stephen IX (X) (1057-1058)
Nicholas II (1059-1061)
Alexander II (1061-1073)
St. Gregory VII (1073-1085)
Bl. Victor III (1086-1087)
Bl. Urban II (1088-1099)
Paschal II (1099-1118)
Gelasius II (1118-1119)

Callistus II (1119-1124)
Honorius II (1124-1130)
Innocent II (1130-1143)
Celestine II (1143-1144)
Lucius II (1144-1145)
Bl. Eugene III (1145-1153)
Anastasius IV (1153-1154)
Adrian IV (1154-1159)
Alexander III (1159-1181)
Lucius III (1181-1185)
Urban III (1185-1187)
Gregory VIII (1187-1187)
Clement III (1187-1191)
Celestine III (1191-1198)
Innocent III (1198-1216)
Honorius III (1216-1227)
Gregory IX (1227-1241)
Celestine IV (1241-1241)
Innocent IV (1243-1254)
Alexander IV (1254-1261)
Urban IV (1261-1264)
Clement IV (1265-1268)
Bl. Gregory X (1271-1276)
Bl. Innocent V (1276-1276)
Adrian V (1276-1276)
John XXI (1276-1277)
Nicholas III (1277-1280)
Martin IV (1281-1285)
Honorius IV (1285-1287)
Nicholas IV (1288-1292)
St. Celestine V (1294-1294)
Boniface VIII (1294-1303)
Bl. Benedict XI (1303-1304)
Clement V (1305-1314)
John XXII (1316-1334)
Benedict XII (1334-1342)
Clement VI (1342-1352)
Innocent VI (1352-1362)
Bl. Urban V (1362-1370)
Gregory XI (1370-1378)
Urban VI (1378-1389)
Boniface IX (1389-1404)
Innocent VII (1404-1406)
Gregory XII (1406-1415)
Martin V (1417-1431)
Eugene IV (1431-1447)
Nicholas V (1447-1455)
Callistus III (1455-1458)
Pius II (1458-1464)
Paul II (1464-1471)
Sixtus IV (1471-1484)

Innocent VIII (1484-1492)
Alexander VI (1492-1503)
Pius III (1503-1503)
Julius II (1503-1513)
Leo X (1513-1521)
Adrian VI (1522-1523)
Clement VII (1523-1534)
Paul III (1534-1549)
Julius III (1550-1555)
Marcellus II (1555-1555)
Paul IV (1555-1559)
Pius IV (1559-1565)
St. Pius V (1566-1572)
Gregory XIII (1572-1585)
Sixtus V (1585-1590)
Urban VII (1590-1590)
Gregory XIV (1590-1591)
Innocent IX (1591-1591)
Clement VIII (1592-1605)
Leo XI (1605-1605)
Paul V (1605-1621)
Gregory XV (1621-1623)
Urban VIII (1623-1644)
Innocent X (1644-1655)
Alexander VII (1655-1667)
Clement IX (1667-1669)
Clement X (1670-1676)
Bl. Innocent XI (1676-1689)
Alexander VIII (1689-1691)
Innocent XII (1691-1700)
Clement XI (1700-1721)
Innocent XIII (1721-1724)
Benedict XIII (1724-1730)
Clement XII (1730-1740)
Benedict XIV (1740-1758)
Clement XIII (1758-1769)
Clement XIV (1769-1774)
Pius VI (1775-1799)
Pius VII (1800-1823)
Leo XII (1823-1829)
Pius VIII (1829-1830)
Gregory XVI (1831-1846)
Pius IX (1846-1878)
Leo XIII (1878-1903)
St. Pius X (1903-1914)
Benedict XV (1914-1922)
Pius XI (1922-1939)
Pius XII (1939-1958)
John XXIII (1958-1963)
Paul VI (1963-1978)
John Paul I (1978-1978)

TABLE OF CONTENTS

Introductory Matter

Presentation Page
Letter from Pope Paul VI
Title Page
Imprimatur
Copyrights
Picture of Pope John Paul II
The Succession of Popes

Reference Aids

The Old Testament Section

The New Testament Section

Additional Reference Aids in Studying the Bible

PAUL, BISHOP,
SERVANT OF THE SERVANTS OF GOD
TOGETHER WITH THE
FATHERS OF THE SACRED
COUNCIL

FOR EVERLASTING MEMORY

DOGMATIC
CONSTITUTION
ON DIVINE REVELATION

PREFACE

1. Hearing the Word of God with reverence and proclaiming it with faith, the sacred Synod takes its direction from these words of St. John: "We announce to you the eternal life which dwelt with the Father and was made visible to us. What we have seen and heard we announce to you, so that you may have fellowship with us and our common fellowship be with the Father and His Son Jesus Christ" (1 John 1; 2-3). Therefore, following in the footsteps of the Council of Trent and of the First Vatican Council, this present Council wishes to set forth authentic doctrine on divine revelation and how it is handed on, so that by hearing the message of salvation the whole world may believe, by believing it may hope, and by hoping it may love.[1]

CHAPTER 1

REVELATION ITSELF

2. In His goodness and wisdom God chose to reveal Himself and to make known to us the hidden purpose of His will (see Eph. 1: 9) by which through Christ, the Word made flesh, man might in the Holy Spirit have access to the Father and come to share in the divine nature (see Eph. 2: 18; 2 Peter 1: 4). Through this revelation, therefore, the invisible God (see Col. 1: 15; 1 Tim. 1: 17) out of the abundance of His love speaks to men as friends (see Ex. 33: 11; John 15: 14-15) and lives among them (see Bar. 3: 38), so that He may invite and take them into fellowship with Himself. This plan of revelation is realized by deeds and words having an inner unity: the deeds wrought by God in the history of salvation manifest and confirm the teaching and realities signified by the words, while the words proclaim the deeds and clarify the mystery contained in them. By this revelation then, the

deepest truth about God and the salvation of man shines out for our sake in Christ, who is both the mediator and the fullness of all revelation.[2]

3. God, who through the Word creates all things (see John 1: 3) and keeps them in existence, gives men an enduring witness to Himself in created realities (see Rom. 1: 19-20). Planning to make known the way of heavenly salvation, He went further and from the start manifested Himself to our first parents. Then after their fall His promise of redemption aroused in them the hope of being saved (see Gen. 3: 15) and from that time on He ceaselessly kept the human race in His care, to give eternal life to those who perseveringly do good in search of salvation (see Rom. 2: 6-7). Then, at the time He had appointed He called Abraham in order to make of him a great nation (see Gen. 12:2). Through the patriarchs, and after them through Moses and the prophets, He taught this people to acknowledge Himself the one living and true God, provident father and just judge, and to wait for the Saviour promised by Him, and in this manner prepared the way for the Gospel down through the centuries.

4. Then, after speaking in many and varied ways through the prophets, "now at last in these days God has spoken to us in His Son" (Heb. 1: 1-2). For He sent His Son, the eternal Word, who enlightens all men, so that He might dwell among men and tell them of the innermost being of God (see John 1: 1-18). Jesus Christ, therefore, the Word made flesh, was sent as "a man to men."[3] He "speaks the words of God" (John 3: 34), and completes the work of salvation which His Father gave Him to do (see John 5: 36, 17: 4). To see Jesus is to see His Father (see John 14: 9). For this reason Jesus perfected revelation by fulfilling it through His whole work of making Himself present and manifesting Himself: through His

---

[1]Cf. St. Augustine, *De Catechizandis Rudibus*, C, IV, 8: PL. 40, 316.

[2]Cf. Mt. 11: 27; Jn. 1: 14 and 17; 14: 6; 17: 1-3; 2 Cor. 3: 16 and 4: 6; Eph. 1: 3-14.

[3]*Epistle to Diognetus*, c. VII, 4: Funk, *Apostolic Fathers*, I, p. 403.

words and deeds, His signs and wonders, but especially through His death and glorious resurrection from the dead and final sending of the Spirit of truth. Moreover He confirmed with divine testimony what revelation proclaimed, that God is with us to free us from the darkness of sin and death, and to raise us up to life eternal.

The Christian dispensation, therefore, as the new and definitive covenant, will never pass away and we now await no further new public revelation before the glorious manifestation of our Lord Jesus Christ (see 1 Tim. 6: 14 and Tit. 2: 13).

5. "The obedience of faith" (Rom. 16: 26; see Rom. 1: 5; 2 Cor. 10: 5-6) "is to be given to God who reveals, an obedience by which man commits his whole self freely to God, offering the full submission of intellect and will to God who reveals,"[4] and freely assenting to the truth revealed by Him. To make this act of faith, the grace of God and the interior help of the Holy Spirit must precede and assist, moving the heart and turning it to God, opening the eyes of the mind and giving "joy and ease to everyone in assenting to the truth and believing it."[5] To bring about an ever deeper understanding of revelation the same Holy Spirit constantly brings faith to completion by His gifts.

6. Through divine revelation, God chose to show forth and communicate Himself and the eternal decisions of His will regarding the salvation of men. That is to say, He chose to share with them those divine treasures which totally transcend the understanding of the human mind.[6]

As a sacred Synod has affirmed, God, the beginning and end of all things, can be known with certainty from created reality by light of human reason (see Rom. 1: 20); but it teaches that it is through His revelation "that those religious truths which are by their nature accessible to human reason can be known by all men with ease, with solid certitude and with no trace of error, even in this present state of the human race."[7]

CHAPTER II

HANDING ON DIVINE REVELATION

7. In His gracious goodness, God has seen to it that what He had revealed for the salvation of all nations would abide perpetually in its full integrity and be handed on to all generations. Therefore Christ the Lord in whom the full revelation of the supreme God is brought to completion (see 2 Cor. 1: 20; 3: 16; 4: 6), commissioned the Apostles to preach to all men that Gospel which is the source of all saving truth and moral teaching,[8] and to impart to them heavenly gifts. This Gospel had been promised in former times through the prophets, and Christ Himself had fulfilled it and promulgated it with His lips. This commission was faithfully fulfilled by the Apostles who, by their oral preaching, by example, and by observances handed on what they had received from the lips of Christ, from living with Him, and from what He did, or what they had learned through the prompting of the Holy Spirit. The commission was fulfilled, too, by those Apostles and apostolic men who under the inspiration of the same Holy Spirit committed the message of salvation to writing.[9]

But in order to keep the Gospel forever whole and alive within the Church, the Apostles left bishops as their successors, "handing over" to them "the authority to teach in their own place."[10] This sacred tradition, therefore, and Sacred Scripture of both the Old and New Testaments are like a mirror in which the pilgrim Church on earth looks at God, from whom she has received everything, until she is brought finally to see Him as He is, face to face (see 1 John 3: 2).

8. And so the apostolic preaching, which is expressed in a special way in the inspired books, was to be preserved by an unending succession of preachers until the end of time. Therefore the Apostles, handing on what they themselves had received, warn the faithful to hold fast to the traditions which they have learned either by word of mouth or by letter (see 2 Thess. 2: 15), and to fight in defense of the faith handed on once and for all (see Jud. 3).[11] Now what was handed on by the Apostles includes everything which contributes toward the holiness of life and increase in faith of the People of God; and so the Church, in her teaching, life and worship, perpetuates and hands on to all generations all that she herself is, all that she believes.

This tradition which comes from the Apostles develops in the Church with the help of

---

[4]First Vatican Council, *Dogmatic Constitution on the Catholic Faith,* Chap. 3, "On Faith:" Denzinger 1789 (3008).

[5]–Second Council of Orange, Canon 7: Denzinger 180 (377); First Vatican Council, *loc. cit.:* Denzinger 1791 (3010).

[6]First Vatican Council, *Dogmatic Constitution on the Catholic Faith,* Chap. 2, "On Revelation:" Denzinger 1786 (3005).

[7]*Ibid:* Denzinger 1785 and 1786 (3004 and 3005).

[8]Cf. Matt. 28: 19-20, and Mark 16: 15; Council of Trent, session IV, *Decree on Scriptural Canons:* Denzinger 783 (1501).

[9]Cf. Council of Trent, *loc. cit.;* First Vatican Council, session III, *Dogmatic Constitution on the Catholic Faith,* Chap. 2, "On revelation:" Denzinger 1787 (3006).

[10]St. Irenaeus, *Against Heretics* III, 3, 1: PG 7, 848; Harvey, 2, p. 9.

[11]Cf. Second Council of Nicea: Denzinger 303 (602); Fourth Council of Constance, session X, Canon 1: Denzinger 336 (650-652).

the Holy Spirit.[12] For there is a growth in the understanding of the realities and the words which have been handed down. This happens through the contemplation and study made by believers, who treasure these things in their hearts (see Luke 2: 19, 51), through a penetrating understanding of the spiritual realities which they experience, and through the preaching of those who have received through episcopal succession the sure gift of truth. For as the centuries succeed one another, the Church constantly moves forward toward the fullness of divine truth until the words of God reach their complete fulfillment in her.

The words of the holy Fathers witness to the presence of this living tradition, whose wealth is poured into the practice and life of the believing and praying Church. Through the same tradition the Church's full canon of the sacred books is known, and the sacred writings themselves are more profoundly understood and unceasingly made active in her; and thus God, who spoke of old, uninterruptedly converses with the bride of His beloved Son; and the Holy Spirit, through whom the living voice of the Gospel resounds in the Church, and through her, in the world, leads unto all truth those who believe and makes the Word of Christ dwell abundantly in them (see Col. 3: 16).

9. Hence there exists a close connection and communication between sacred tradition and sacred Scripture. For both of them, flowing from the same divine wellspring, in a certain way merge into a unity and tend toward the same end. For sacred Scripture is the Word of God inasmuch as it is consigned to writing under the inspiration of the divine Spirit, while sacred tradition takes the Word of God entrusted by Christ the Lord and the Holy Spirit to the Apostles, and hands it on to their successors in its full purity, so that led by the light of the Spirit of truth, they may in proclaiming it preserve this Word of God faithfully, explain it, and make it more widely known. Consequently it is not from sacred Scripture alone that the Church draws her certainty about everything which has been revealed. Therefore both sacred tradition and sacred Scripture are to be accepted and venerated with the same sense of loyalty and reverence.[13]

10. Sacred tradition and sacred Scripture form one sacred deposit of the Word of God, committed to the Church. Holding fast to this deposit the entire holy people united with their shepherds remain always steadfast in the teaching of the Apostles, in the common life, in the breaking of the bread and in prayers (see

Acts 8: 42, Greek text), so that holding to, practicing and professing the heritage of the faith, it becomes on the part of the bishops and faithful a single common effort.[14]

But the task of authentically interpreting the Word of God, whether written or handed on,[15] has been entrusted exclusively to the living teaching office of the Church,[16] whose authority is exercised in the name of Jesus Christ. This teaching office is not above the Word of God, but serves it, teaching only what has been handed on, listening to it devoutly, guarding it scrupulously and explaining it faithfully in accord with a divine commission and with the help of the Holy Spirit; it draws from this one deposit of faith everything which it presents for belief as divinely revealed.

It is clear, therefore, that sacred tradition, sacred Scripture and the teaching authority of the Church, in accord with God's most wise design, are so linked and joined together that one cannot stand without the others, and that all together and each in its own way under the action of the one Holy Spirit contribute effectively to the salvation of souls.

CHAPTER III

SACRED SCRIPTURE, ITS INSPIRATION AND DIVINE INTERPRETATION

11. Those divinely revealed realities which are contained and presented in sacred Scripture have been committed to writing under the inspiration of the Holy Spirit. For holy mother Church, relying on the belief of the Apostles (see John 20: 31; 2 Tim. 3: 16; 2 Peter 1: 19-21; 3: 15-16), holds that the books of both the Old and New Testaments in their entirety, with all their parts, are sacred and canonical because written under the inspiration of the Holy Spirit, they have God as their author and have been handed on as such to the Church herself.[17] In composing the sacred books, God chose men and while employed by Him[18] they made use of their powers and abil-

---

[12]Cf. First Vatican Council, *Dogmatic Constitution on the Catholic Faith*, Chap. 4, "On Faith and Reason:" Denzinger 1800 (3020).

[13]Cf. Council of Trent, session IV, *loc. cit.*: Denzinger 783 (1501).

[14]Cf. Pius XII, apostolic constitution, *Munificentissimus Deus*, Nov. 1, 1950: AAS 42 (1950) p. 756; Collected Writings of St. Cyprian, Letter 66, 8: Hartel, III B, p. 733: "The Church [is] people united with the priest and the pastor together with his flock."

[15]Cf. First Vatican Council, *Dogmatic Constitution on the Catholic Faith*, Chap. 3 "On Faith:" Denzinger 1792 (3011).

[16]Cf. Pius XII, Encyclical Letter *Humani Generis*, Aug. 12, 1950: AAS 42 (1950) pp. 568-69: Denzinger 2314 (3886).

[17]Cf. First Vatican Council, *Dogmatic Constitution on the Catholic Faith*, Chap. 2 "On Revelation:" Denzinger 1787 (3006); Biblical Commission, *Decree* of June 18, 1915: Denzinger 2180 (3629): EB 420; Holy Office, *Epistle* of Dec. 22, 1923: EB 499.

[18]Cf. Pius XII, Encyclical Letter *Divino Afflante Spiritu*, Sept. 30, 1943: AAS 35 (1943) p. 314; Enchiridion Biblic. (EB) 556.

ities, so that with Him acting in them and through them,[19] they, as true authors, consigned to writing everything and only those things which He wanted.[20]

Therefore since everything asserted by the inspired authors or sacred writers must be held to be asserted by the Holy Spirit, it follows that the books of Scripture must be acknowledged as teaching solidly, faithfully and without error that truth which God wanted put into the sacred writings[21] for the sake of our salvation. Therefore "all Scripture is divinely inspired and has its use for teaching the truth and refuting error, for reformation of manners and discipline in right living, so that the man who belongs to God may be efficient and equipped for good work of every kind" (2 Tim. 3: 16-17, Greek text).

12. However, since God speaks in sacred Scripture through men in human fashion,[22] the interpreter of sacred Scripture, in order to see clearly what God wanted to communicate to us, should carefully investigate what meaning the sacred writers really intended, and what God wanted to manifest by means of their words.

To search out the intention of the sacred writers, attention should be given, among other things, to "literary forms." For truth is set forth and expressed differently in texts which are variously historical, prophetic, poetic, or of other forms of discourse. The interpreter must investigate what meaning the sacred writer intended to express and actually expressed in particular circumstances by using contemporary literary forms in accordance with the situation of his own time and culture.[23] For the correct understanding of what the sacred author wanted to assert, due attention must be paid to the customary and characteristic styles of feeling, speaking and narrating which prevailed at the time of the sacred writer, and to the patterns men normally employed at that period in their everyday dealings with one another.[24]

But, since holy Scripture must be read and interpreted in the same spirit in which it was written,[25] no less serious attention must be given to the content and unity of the whole of Scripture if the meaning of the sacred texts is to be correctly worked out. The living tradition of the whole Church must be taken into account along with the harmony which exists between elements of the faith. It is the task of exegetes to work according to these rules toward a better understanding and explanation of the meaning of sacred Scripture, so that through preparatory study the judgment of the Church may mature. For all of what has been said about the way of interpreting Scripture is subject finally to the judgment of the Church, which carries out the divine commission and ministry of guarding and interpreting the Word of God.[26]

13. In sacred Scripture, therefore while the truth and holiness of God always remains intact, the marvelous "condescension" of eternal wisdom is clearly shown, "that we may learn the gentle kindness of God, which words cannot express, and how far He has gone in adapting His language with thoughtful concern for our weak human nature."[27] For the words of God, expressed in human language, have been made like human discourse, just as the word of the eternal Father, when He took to Himself the flesh of human weakness, was in every way made like men.

CHAPTER IV

THE OLD TESTAMENT

14. In carefully planning and preparing the salvation of the whole human race the God of infinite love, by a special dispensation, chose for Himself a people to whom He would entrust His promises. First He entered into a covenant with Abraham (see Gen. 15: 18) and, through Moses, with the people of Israel (see Ex. 24: 8). To this people which He had acquired for Himself, He so manifested Himself through words and deeds as the one true and living God that Israel came to know by experience the ways of God with men. Then, too, when God Himself spoke to them through the mouth of the prophets, Israel daily gained a deeper and clearer understanding of His ways and made them more widely known among the nations (see Ps. 21: 29; 95: 1-3; Is. 2: 1-4; Jer. 3: 17). The plan of salvation foretold by the sacred authors, recounted and explained by them, is found as the true Word of God in the

---

[19]"In" and "for" man: cf. Heb. 1: 1 and 4: 7; ("in"): 2 Sm. 23: 2; Mt. 1: 22 and various places; ("for"): First Vatican Council, *Schema on Catholic Doctrine,* note 9: Coll. Lac. VII, 522.

[20]Leo XIII, Encyclical Letter *Providentissimus Deus,* Nov. 18, 1893: Denzinger 1952 (3293); EB 125.

[21]Cf. St. Augustine, *Gen. ad Litt.* 2, 9, 20: PL 34, 270-271; Epistle 82, 3: PL 33, 277: CSEL 34, 2, p. 354.
—St. Thomas, "On Truth," Q. 12, A. 2, C.
—Council of Trent, session IV, *Scriptural Canons:* Denzinger 783 (1501).
Leo XIII, Encyclical Letter *Providentissimus Deus:* EB 121, 124, 126-127.
—Pius XII, Encyclical Letter *Divino Afflante Spiritu:* EB 539.

[22]St. Augustine, *City of God,* XVII, 6, 2: PL 41, 537: CSEL XL, 2, 228.

[23]St. Augustine, *On Christian Doctrine* III, 18, 26; PL 34, 75-76.

[24]Pius XII, *Loc. cit.:* Denzinger 2294 (3829-3830); EB 557-562.

[25]Cf. Benedict XV, Encyclical Letter *Spiritus Paraclitus,* Sept. 15, 1920: EB 469. St. Jerome, "In Galatians" 5, 19-20: PL 26, 417 A.

[26]Cf. First Vatican Council, *Dogmatic Constitution on the Catholic Faith,* Chapter 2, "On Revelation:" Denzinger 1788 (3007).

[27]St. John Chrysostom *In Genesis* 3, 8 (Homily 17, 1): PG 53, 134; "Attemperatio" [in English "Suitable adjustment"] in Greek "synkatabasis."

books of the Old Testament: these books, therefore, written under divine inspiration, remain permanently valuable. "For all that was written for our instruction, so that by steadfastness and the encouragement of the Scriptures we might have hope" (Rom. 15: 4).

15. The principal purpose to which the plan of the old covenant was directed was to prepare for the coming of Christ, the redeemer of all and of the messianic kingdom, to announce this coming by prophecy (see Luke 24: 44; John 5: 39; 1 Peter 1: 10), and to indicate its meaning through various types (see 1 Cor. 10: 11). Now the books of the Old Testament, in accordance with the state of mankind before the time of salvation established by Christ, reveal to all men the knowledge of God and of man and the ways in which God, just and merciful, deals with men. These books, though they also contain some things which are incomplete and temporary, nevertheless show us true divine pedagogy.[28] These same books, then, give expression to a lively sense of God, contain a store of sublime teachings about God, sound wisdom about human life, and a wonderful treasury of prayers, and in them the mystery of our salvation is present in a hidden way. Christians should receive them with reverence.

16. God, the inspirer and author of both Testaments, wisely arranged that the New Testament be hidden in the Old and the Old be made manifest in the New.[29] For, though Christ established the new covenant in His blood (see Luke 22: 20; 1 Cor. 11: 25), still the books of the Old Testament with all their parts, caught up into the proclamation of the Gospel,[30] acquire and show forth their full meaning in the New Testament (see Matt. 5: 17; Luke 24: 27; Rom. 16: 25-26; 2 Cor. 3: 14-16) and in turn shed light on it and explain it.

CHAPTER V

THE NEW TESTAMENT

17. The Word of God, which is the power of God for the salvation of all who believe (see Rom. 1: 16), is set forth and shows its power in a most excellent way in the writings of the New Testament. For when the fullness of time arrived (see Gal. 4: 4), the Word was made flesh and dwelt among us in His fullness of graces and truth (see John 1: 14). Christ established the Kingdom of God on earth, manifested His Father and Himself by deeds and

words, and completed His work by His death, resurrection and glorious ascension and by the sending of the Holy Spirit. Having been lifted up from the earth, He draws all men to Himself (see John 12: 32, Greek text), He who alone has the words of eternal life (see John 6: 68). This mystery had not been manifested to other generations as it was now revealed to His holy Apostles and prophets in the Holy Spirit (see Eph. 3: 4-6, Greek text), so that they might preach the Gospel, stir up faith in Jesus, Christ and Lord, and gather together the Church. Now the writings of the New Testament stand as a perpetual and divine witness to these realities.

18. It is common knowledge that among all the Scriptures, even those of the New Testament, the Gospels have a special preeminence, and rightly so, for they are the principal witness for the life and teaching of the Incarnate Word, our Savior.

The Church has always and everywhere held and continues to hold that the four Gospels are of apostolic origin. For what the Apostles preached in fulfillment of the commission of Christ, afterwards they themselves and apostolic men, under the inspiration of the divine Spirit, handed on to us in writing: the foundation of faith, namely, the fourfold Gospel, according to Matthew, Mark, Luke and John.[31]

19. Holy Mother Church has firmly and with absolute constancy held, and continues to hold, that the four Gospels just named, whose historical character the Church unhesitatingly asserts, faithfully hand on what Jesus Christ, while living among men, really did and taught for their eternal salvation until the day He was taken up into heaven (see Acts 1: 1-2). Indeed, after the ascension of the Lord the Apostles handed on to their hearers what He had said and done. This they did with that clearer understanding which they enjoyed[32] after they had been instructed by the glorious events of Christ's life and taught by the light of the Spirit of truth.[33] The sacred authors wrote the four Gospels, selecting some things from the many which had been handed on by word of mouth or in writing, reducing some of them to a synthesis, explaining some things in view of the situation of their churches, and preserving the form of proclamation but always in such fashion that they told us the honest truth about Jesus.[34] For their intention in writing was that either from their own memory and recollections, or from the witness of those who "themselves from the beginning were eyewit-

---

[28] Pius XI Encyclical Epistle *Mit Brennender Sorge,* March 14, 1937: AAS 29 (1937) p. 51.

[29] St. Augustine, *Quest in Hept.* 2, 73: PL 34, 623.

[30] St. Irenaeus, *Against Heretics* III, 21, 3: PG 7, 950; (Same as 25, 1: Harvey 2, p. 115). St. Cyril of Jerusalem, *Catech.* 4, 35; PG 33, 497. Theodore of Mopsuestia, *In Soph.* 1, 4-6: PG 66, 452D-453A.

[31] Cf. St. Irenaeus, *Against Heretics* III, 11, 8: PG 7, 885; Sagnard Edition, p. 194.

[32] John 2: 22; 12: 16; Cf. 14: 26; 16: 12-13; 7: 39.

[33] Cf. John 14: 26; 16: 13.

[34] Cf. instruction *Holy Mother Church* edited by Pontifical Consilium for Promotion of Bible Studies: AAS 56 (1964) p. 715.

nesses and ministers of the Word'' we might know ''the truth'' concerning those matters about which we have been instructed (see Luke 1: 2-4).

20. Besides the four Gospels, the canon of the New Testament also contains the epistles of St. Paul and other apostolic writings, composed under the inspiration of the Holy Spirit, by which according to the wise plan of God, those matters which concern Christ the Lord are confirmed, His true teaching is more and more fully stated, the saving power of the divine work of Christ is preached, the story is told of the beginnings of the Church and its marvelous growth, and its glorious fulfillment is foretold.

For the Lord Jesus was with His Apostles as He had promised (see Matt. 28: 20) and sent them the advocate Spirit who would lead them into the fullness of truth (see John 16: 13).

CHAPTER VI

SACRED SCRIPTURE IN THE LIFE OF THE CHURCH

21. The Church has always venerated the divine Scriptures just as she venerates the body of the Lord, since, especially in the sacred liturgy, she unceasingly receives and offers to the faithful the bread of life from the table both of God's Word and of Christ's Body. She has always maintained them, and continues to do so, together with sacred tradition, as the supreme rule of faith, since, as inspired by God and committed once and for all to writing, they impart the Word of God Himself without change, and make the voice of the Holy Spirit resound in the words of the prophets and Apostles. Therefore, like the Christian religion itself, all the preaching of the Church must be nourished and regulated by sacred Scripture. For in the sacred books, the Father who is in heaven meets His children with great love and speaks with them; and the force and power in the word of God is so great that it stands as the support and energy of the Church, the strength of faith for her sons, the food of the soul, the pure and everlasting source of spiritual life. Consequently these words are perfectly applicable to sacred Scripture: ''For the word of God is living and active'' (Heb. 4: 12) and ''it has power to build you up and give you your heritage among all those who are sanctified'' (Acts 20: 32; see 1 Thess. 2: 13).

22. Easy access to sacred Scripture should be provided for all the Christian faithful. That is why the Church from the very beginning accepted as her own that very ancient Greek translation of the Old Testament which is called the septuagint; and she has always given a place of honor to other Eastern translations

and Latin ones, especially the Latin translation known as the vulgate. But since the Word of God should be accessible at all times, the Church by her authority and with maternal concern sees to it that suitable and correct translations are made into different languages, especially from the original texts of the sacred books. And should the opportunity arise and the Church authorities approve, if these translations are produced in cooperation with the separated brethren as well, all Christians will be able to use them.

23. The bride of the Incarnate Word, the Church taught by the Holy Spirit, is concerned to move ahead toward a deeper understanding of the sacred Scriptures so that she may increasingly feed her sons with the divine words. Therefore, she also encourages the study of the holy Fathers of both East and West and of sacred liturgies. Catholic exegetes then and other students of sacred theology, working diligently together and using appropriate means, should devote their energies, under the watchful care of the sacred teaching office of the Church, to an exploration and exposition of the divine writings. This should be so done that as many ministers of the divine word as possible will be able effectively to provide the nourishment of the Scriptures for the People of God, to enlighten their minds, strengthen their wills, and set men's hearts on fire with the love of God.[35] The sacred Synod encourages the sons of the Church and Biblical scholars to continue energetically, following the mind of the Church, with the work they have so well begun, with a constant renewal of vigor.[36]

24. Sacred theology rests on the written Word of God, together with sacred tradition, as its primary and perpetual foundation. By scrutinizing in the light of faith all truth stored up in the mystery of Christ, theology is most powerfully strengthened and constantly rejuvenated by that Word. For the sacred Scriptures contain the Word of God and since they are inspired really are the Word of God; and so the study of the sacred page is, as it were, the soul of sacred theology.[37] By the same word of Scripture the ministry of the Word also, that is, pastoral preaching, catechetics and all Christian instruction, in which the liturgical homily must hold the foremost place, is nourished in a healthy way and flourishes in a holy way.

25. Therefore, all the clergy must hold fast to the sacred Scriptures through diligent

---

[35]Cf. Pius XII, Encyclical Letter *Divino Afflante Spiritu:* EB 551, 553, 567.
–Pontifical Biblical Commission, *Instruction on Proper Teaching of Sacred Scripture in Seminaries and Religious Colleges,* May 13, 1950: AAS 42 (1950) pp. 495-505.
[36]Cf. Pius XII, *ibid:* EB 569.
[37]Cf. Leo XIII, Encyclical Letter *Providentissimus Deus:* EB 114; Benedict XV, Encyclical Letter *Spiritus paraclitus:* EB 483.

sacred reading and careful study, especially the priests of Christ and others, such as deacons and catechists who are legitimately active in the ministry of the Word. This is to be done so that none of them will become "an empty preacher of the word of God outwardly, who is not a listener to it inwardly"[38] since they must share the abundant wealth of the divine Word with the faithful committed to them, especially in the sacred liturgy. The sacred Synod also earnestly and especially urges all the Christian faithful, especially Religious, to learn by frequent reading of the divine Scriptures the "excellent knowledge of Jesus Christ" (Phil. 3: 8). "For ignorance of the Scriptures is ignorance of Christ."[39] Therefore, they should gladly put themselves in touch with the sacred text itself, whether it be through the liturgy, rich in the divine Word or through devotional reading, or through instructions suitable for the purpose and other aids which, in our time, with approval and active support of the shepherds of the Church, are commendably spread everywhere. And let them remember that prayer should accompany the reading of the sacred Scripture, so that God and man may talk together; for "we speak to Him when we pray; we hear Him when we read the divine saying."[40]

It devolves on sacred bishops "who have the apostolic teaching"[41] to give the faithful entrusted to them suitable instruction in the right use of the divine books, especially the New Testament and above all the Gospels.

---

[38]St. Augustine, *Sermons,* 179, 1: PL 38, 966.

[39]St. Jerome, *Commentary on Isaiah,* Prol: PL 24, 17.

Cf. Benedict XV, Encyclical Letter *Spiritus paraclitus:* EB 475-480; Pius XII, Encyclical Letter *Divino Afflante Spiritu:* EB 544.

[40]St. Ambrose, *On the Duties of Ministers* I, 20, 88: PL 16, 50.

[41]St. Irenaeus, *Against Heretics* IV, 32, 1: PG 7, 1071; (Same as 49, 2) Harvey, 2, p. 255.

This can be done through translations of the sacred texts, which are to be provided with the necessary and really adequate explanations so that the children of the Church may safely and profitably become conversant with the sacred Scriptures and be penetrated with their spirit.

Furthermore, editions of the sacred Scriptures, provided with suitable footnotes, should be prepared also for the use of non-Christians and adapted to their situation. Both pastors of souls and Christians generally should see to the wise distribution of these in one way or another.

26. In this way, therefore, through the reading and study of the sacred books "the word of God may spread rapidly and be glorified" (2 Thess. 3: 1) and the treasure of revelation, entrusted to the Church, may more and more fill the hearts of men. Just as the life of the Church is strengthened through more frequent celebration of the Eucharistic mystery, similarly we may hope for a new stimulus for the life of the Spirit from a growing reverence for the word of God, which "lasts forever" (Is. 40: 8, see 1 Peter 1: 23-25).

‡ ‡ ‡ ‡

The entire text and all the individual elements which have been set forth in this Constitution have pleased the Fathers. And by the Apostolic power conferred on us by Christ, we, together with the Venerable Fathers, in the Holy Spirit, approve, decree and enact them; and we order that what has been thus enacted in Council be promulgated, to the glory of God.

Rome, at St. Peter's 18 November, 1965

I, PAUL, Bishop of the Catholic Church

There follow the signatures of the Fathers.

Translation of the Second Vatican Council's "Dogmatic Constitution on Divine Revelation" reprinted by permission of the Publications Office, United States Catholic Conference, Washington, D.C.

THE BOOKS OF THE BIBLE

THE OLD TESTAMENT

THE NEW TESTAMENT

THE BOOKS OF THE
OLD AND NEW TESTAMENTS
AND THEIR ABBREVIATIONS

THE OLD TESTAMENT

Book	Abbrev.	Page	Book	Abbrev.	Page
Genesis	Gn	6	Proverbs	Prv	634
Exodus	Ex	58	Ecclesiastes	Eccl	664
Leviticus	Lv	95	Song of Songs	Sg	673
Numbers	Nm	122	Wisdom	Wis	680
Deuteronomy	Dt	161	Sirach	Sir	699
Joshua	Jos	195	Isaiah	Is	746
Judges	Jgs	217	Jeremiah	Jer	803
Ruth	Ru	238	Lamentations	Lam	859
1 Samuel	1 Sm	243	Baruch	Bar	866
2 Samuel	2 Sm	272	Ezekiel	Ez	874
1 Kings	1 Kgs	295	Daniel	Dn	917
2 Kings	2 Kgs	321	Hosea	Hos	936
1 Chronicles	1 Chr	347	Joel	Jl	947
2 Chronicles	2 Chr	374	Amos	Am	951
Ezra	Ezr	404	Obadiah	Ob	959
Nehemiah	Neh	414	Jonah	Jon	961
Tobit	Tb	428	Micah	Mi	964
Judith	Jdt	442	Nahum	Na	970
Esther	Est	456	Habakkuk	Hb	973
1 Maccabees	1 Mc	468	Zephaniah	Zep	976
2 Maccabees	2 Mc	497	Haggai	Hg	979
Job	Jb	519	Zechariah	Zec	982
Psalms	Ps(s)	547	Malachi	Mal	991

THE NEW TESTAMENT

Book	Abbrev.	Page	Book	Abbrev.	Page
Matthew	Mt	1005	1 Timothy	1 Tm	1306
Mark	Mk	1063	2 Timothy	2 Tm	1313
Luke	Lk	1090	Titus	Ti	1318
John	Jn	1135	Philemon	Phlm	1321
Acts of the Apostles	Acts	1169	Hebrews	Heb	1323
Romans	Rom	1208	James	Jas	1341
1 Corinthians	1 Cor	1229	1 Peter	1 Pt	1347
2 Corinthians	2 Cor	1251	2 Peter	2 Pt	1354
Galatians	Gal	1268	1 John	1 Jn	1359
Ephesians	Eph	1277	2 John	2 Jn	1365
Philippians	Phil	1285	3 John	3 Jn	1367
Colossians	Col	1292	Jude	Jude	1369
1 Thessalonians	1 Thes	1298	Revelation	Rv	1372
2 Thessalonians	2 Thes	1302			

The Names and Order of All the

BOOKS OF THE OLD AND NEW TESTAMENTS

Alphabetically Arranged

Book	Abbrev.		Page	Book	Abbrev.		Page
Acts of the Apostles	Acts	NT†	1169	2 Kings	2 Kgs	OT	321
Amos	Am	OT*	951	Lamentations	Lam	OT	859
Baruch	Bar	OT	866	Leviticus	Lv	OT	95
1 Chronicles	1 Chr	OT	347	Luke	Lk	NT	1090
2 Chronicles	2 Chr	OT	374	1 Maccabees	1 Mc	OT	468
Colossians	Col	NT	1292	2 Maccabees	2 Mc	OT	497
1 Corinthians	1 Cor	NT	1229	Malachi	Mal	OT	991
2 Corinthians	2 Cor	NT	1251	Mark	Mk	NT	1063
Daniel	Dn	OT	917	Matthew	Mt	NT	1005
Deuteronomy	Dt	OT	161	Micah	Mi	OT	964
Ecclesiastes	Eccl	OT	664	Nahum	Na	OT	970
Ephesians	Eph	NT	1277	Nehemiah	Neh	OT	414
Esther	Est	OT	456	Numbers	Nm	OT	122
Exodus	Ex	OT	58	Obadiah	Ob	OT	959
Ezekiel	Ez	OT	874	1 Peter	1 Pt	NT	1347
Ezra *Esdras*	Ezr	OT	404	2 Peter	2 Pt	NT	1354
Galatians	Gal	NT	1268	Philemon	Phlm	NT	1321
Genesis	Gn	OT	6	Philippians	Phil	NT	1285
Habakkuk	Hb	OT	973	Proverbs	Prv	OT	634
Haggai	Hg	OT	979	Psalms	Ps(s)	OT	547
Hebrews	Heb	NT	1323	Revelation	Rv	NT	1372
Hosea	Hos	OT	936	Romans	Rom	NT	1208
Isaiah	Is	OT	746	Ruth	Ru	OT	238
James	Jas	NT	1341	1 Samuel	1 Sm	OT	243
Jeremiah	Jer	OT	803	2 Samuel	2 Sm	OT	272
Job	Jb	OT	519	Sirach	Sir	OT	699
Joel	Jl	OT	947	Song of Songs	Sg	OT	673
John	Jn	NT	1135	1 Thessalonians	1 Thes	NT	1298
1 John	1 Jn	NT	1359	2 Thessalonians	2 Thes	NT	1302
2 John	2 Jn	NT	1365	1 Timothy	1 Tm	NT	1306
3 John	3 Jn	NT	1367	2 Timothy	2 Tm	NT	1313
Jonah	Jon	OT	961	Titus	Ti	NT	1318
Joshua	Jos	OT	195	Tobit	Tb	OT	428
Jude	Jude	NT	1369	Wisdom	Wis	OT	680
Judges	Jgs	OT	217	Zechariah	Zec	OT	982
Judith	Jdt	OT	442	Zephaniah	Zep	OT	976
1 Kings	1 Kgs	OT	295				

* OT—Old Testament † NT—New Testament

BOOKS OF THE OLD AND NEW TESTAMENTS

Alphabetically Arranged

Book	Abbrev.	Test.	Page	Book	Abbrev.	Test.	Page
Acts of the Apostles	Acts	NT	1169	2 Kings	2 Kgs	OT	331
Amos	Am	OT	951	Lamentations	Lam	OT	858
Baruch	Bar	OT	866	Leviticus	Lv	OT	95
1 Chronicles	1 Chr	OT	364	Luke	Lk	NT	1090
2 Chronicles	2 Chr	OT	371	1 Maccabees	1 Mc	OT	568
Colossians	Col	NT	1292	2 Maccabees	2 Mc	OT	597
1 Corinthians	1 Cor	NT	1239	Malachi	Mal	OT	991
2 Corinthians	2 Cor	NT	1251	Mark	Mk	NT	1063
Daniel	Dan	OT	917	Matthew	Mt	NT	1005
Deuteronomy	Dt	OT	161	Micah	Mi	OT	964
Ecclesiastes	Eccl	OT	664	Nahum	Na	OT	971
Ephesians	Eph	NT	1277	Nehemiah	Neh	OT	414
Esther	Est	OT	535	Numbers	Nm	OT	122
Exodus	Ex	OT	58	Obadiah	Ob	OT	959
Ezekiel	Ez	OT	834	1 Peter	1 Pt	NT	1347
Ezra	Ezr	OT	404	2 Peter	2 Pt	NT	1354
Galatians	Gal	NT	1268	Philemon	Phlm	NT	1321
Genesis	Gn	OT	1	Philippians	Phil	NT	1285
Habakkuk	Hb	OT	974	Proverbs	Prv	OT	624
Haggai	Hg	OT	979	Psalms	Ps(s)	OT	567
Hebrews	Heb	NT	1322	Revelation	Rv	NT	1373
Hosea	Hos	OT	936	Romans	Rom	NT	1208
Isaiah	Is	OT	706	Ruth	Ru	OT	238
James	Jas	NT	1341	1 Samuel	1 Sm	OT	243
Jeremiah	Jer	OT	803	2 Samuel	2 Sm	OT	279
Job	Jb	OT	549	Sirach	Sir	OT	691
Joel	Jl	OT	947	Song of Songs	Sg	OT	673
John	Jn	NT	1185	1 Thessalonians	1 Thes	NT	1298
1 John	1 Jn	NT	1356	2 Thessalonians	2 Thes	NT	1302
2 John	2 Jn	NT	1361	1 Timothy	1 Tm	NT	1306
3 John	3 Jn	NT	1362	2 Timothy	2 Tm	NT	1313
Jonah	Jon	OT	969	Titus	Ti	NT	1318
Joshua	Jos	OT	195	Tobit	Tb	OT	428
Jude	Jude	NT	1363	Wisdom	Wis	OT	640
Judges	Jgs	OT	218	Zechariah	Zec	OT	982
Judith	Jdt	OT	512	Zephaniah	Zep	OT	976
1 Kings	1 Kgs	OT	305				

*OT—Old Testament †NT—New Testament

COLLABORATORS ON THE OLD TESTAMENT
THE NEW AMERICAN BIBLE

Bishops' Committee
The Confraternity of Christian Doctrine

Most Rev. Charles P. Greco, D.D., Chairman

Most Rev. Joseph T. McGucken, S.T.D.   Most Rev. Romeo Blanchette, D.D.

Most Rev. Vincent S. Waters, D.D.   Most Rev. Christopher J. Weldon, D.D.

Editors in Chief

Rev. Louis F. Hartman, C.SS.R., S.S.L., Ling. Or. L., Chairman
Rev. Msgr. Patrick W. Skehan, S.T.D., LL.D., Vice Chairman
Rev. Stephen J. Hartdegen, O.F.M., S.S.L., Secretary

Associate Editors and Translators

Rev. Edward P. Arbez, S.S., S.T.D.

Rev. Msgr. Edward J. Byrne, Ph.D., S.T.D.

Rev. Edward A. Cerny, S.S., S.T.D.

Rev. James E. Coleran, S.J., S.T.L., S.S.L.

Rev. John J. Collins, S.J., M.A., S.S.L.

Sr. M. Emmanuel Collins, O.S.F., Ph.D.

Prof. Frank M. Cross, Jr., Ph.D.

Rev. Patrick Cummins, O.S.B., S.T.D.

Rev. Antonine A. De Guglielmo, O.F.M., S.T.D., S.S.L., S.S. Lect. Gen.

Rev. Alexander A. Di Lella, O.F.M., S.T.L., S.S.L., Ph.D.

Most Rev. John J. Dougherty, S.T.L., S.S.D.

Rev. William A. Dowd, S.J., S.T.D., S.S.L.

Prof. David Noel Freedman, Ph.D.

Rev. Michael J. Gruenthaner, S.J., S.T.D., S.S.D.

Rev. Msgr. Maurice A. Hofer, S.S.L.

Rev. Justin Krellner, O.S.B., S.T.D.

Rev. Jospeh L. Lilly, C.M., S.T.D., S.S.L.

Rev. Roderick F. MacKenzie, S.J., M.A., S.S.D.

Rev. Edward A. Mangan, C.SS.R., S.S.L.

Rev. Daniel W. Martin, C.M., S.T.L., S.S.L.

Rev. William H. McClellan, S.J.

Rev. James McGlinchey, C.M., S.T.D.

Rev. Frederick Moriarty, S.J., S.S.L., S.T.D.

Rev. Richard T. Murphy, O.P., S.T.D., S.S.D.

Rev. Roland E. Murphy, O. Carm., M.A., S.T.D., S.S.L.

Rev. Msgr. William R. Newton, M.S., S.S.D.

Rev. Eberhard Olinger, O.S.B.

Rev. Charles H. Pickar, O.S.A., S.T.L., S.S.L.

Rev. Christopher Rehwinkel, O.F.M., S.T.D., S.S. Lect. Gen.

Rev. Msgr. John R. Rowan, S.T.D., S.S.L.

Prof. J.A. Sanders, Ph.D.

Rev. Edward F. Siegman, C.PP.S., S.T.D., S.S.L.

Rev. Msgr. Matthew P. Stapleton, S.T.D., S.S.L.

Rev. Msgr. John E. Steinmueller, S.T.D., S.S.L.

Rev. John Ujlaki, O.S.B., Litt. D.

Rev. Bruce Vawter, C.M., S.T.L., S.S.D.

Rev. John B. Weisengoff, S.T.D., S.S.L.

COLLABORATORS ON THE REVISED EDITION
THE NEW TESTAMENT
THE NEW AMERICAN BIBLE

Bishops' Ad Hoc Committee

Most Rev. Theodore E. McCarrick, D.D.
Most Rev. Richard J. Sklba, D.D.
Most Rev. J. Francis Stafford, D.D.
Most Rev. John F. Whealon, D.D., Chairman

Board of Editors

Rev. Msgr. Myles M. Bourke
Rev. Francis T. Gignac, S.J., Chairman
Rev. Stephen J. Hartdegen, O.F.M., Secretary
Rev. Claude J. Peifer, O.S.B.
Rev. John H. Reumann

Revisers

Rev. Msgr. Myles M. Bourke
Rev. Frederick W. Danker
Rev. Alexander A. Di Lella, O.F.M.
Rev. Charles H. Giblin, S.J.
Rev. Francis T. Gignac, S.J.
Rev. Stephen J. Hartdegen, O.F.M.
Dr. Maurya P. Horgan

Rev. John R. Keating, S.J.
Rev. John Knox
Dr. Paul J. Kobelski
Dr. J. Rebecca Lyman
Bro. Elliott C. Maloney, O.S.B.
Dr. Janet A. Timbie

Consultants

Rev. Joseph Jensen, O.S.B.
Rev. Aidan Kavanagh, O.S.B.
Dr. Marianne Sawicki

Business Manager

Charles A. Buggé

Word Processor

Suzanna Jordan

ORIGIN, INSPIRATION, AND HISTORY OF THE BIBLE

ORIGIN OF THE BIBLE

No Book in the history of the world has wielded as much influence on civilization as the Holy Bible. The Bible is unique in that it had God as its Author, while all other books were composed by human beings. It is indeed, the Book of Books.

THE DEPOSIT OF FAITH

The Catholic Church derives all of its teaching authority from its tradition, the doctrine which has come down to it from Christ. This tradition is preserved in written form in the "Bible" which contains the principle truths of faith taught to the Apostles by Christ.

Inspired men were moved by the Spirit of God to commit these matters to writing in the early church. Only a short time after Christ's Ascension, perhaps within twenty years, the need to preserve these truths in a permanent form was recognized. Before any book was accepted as "authentic" however, the authority of an Apostle was demanded by the early Christian communities. Mark's Gospel was accepted because he was Peter's companion. Similarly, though Luke was a man who had not seen Christ, his book gained acceptance through St. Paul's authority.

The Church has protected and guarded these books which contained the revelations of Christ to His disciples and their testimony concerning Him.

THE BIBLE DEFINED

The other source of supernatural knowledge is the Bible. In the words of the Council of Trent, which enumerated the books of the Bible under their proper titles, the Church declares that she receives: "All the books of the Testaments, Old and New, since the one God is the Author of both." The Vatican Council is more explicit: "The Church holds those books as sacred and canonical, not because, having been composed by human industry, they were afterwards approved by her authority, nor merely because they contain revelation without error, but because having been written under the inspiration of the Holy Spirit, they have God as their Author."

The word "Bible" comes from the Greek *biblion* meaning "the book;" the plural is *ta biblia*, "the books." In the Greek the word is a neuter, but later on the word *biblia* was taken for a feminine singular, "the book." Taken in this sense, it refers to all the books of both Testaments. The Bible is the Book par excellence.

THE BIBLE NEEDS AN INTERPRETER

The Bible is extremely difficult to understand, even by Bible scholars. It was written in languages long dead, and in the manner and idiom of the time. To interpret the Bible, it is not only necessary to understand the languages in which the Bible was written, but to understand the meanings that the words of the Bible had at the time they were written. The Bible, therefore, has to be interpreted to be understood, and for Catholics, the Church, guided by the Holy Spirit, is the official guardian and infallible interpreter of the Bible.

CANON OF THE BIBLE

The Bible contains 72 books (or 73, depending on whether the Book of Lamentations is listed as a separate book and not as a part of Jeremiah), varying in length from a few hundred words to many thousands. Together, these books comprise the official list or canon of the Bible. Of these books, 45 were written before the time of Christ and are called the books of the Old Testament. The other 27 books were written after the time of Christ and are called the books of the New Testament.

MEANING OF THE WORD "TESTAMENT"

The meaning of the word "testament" as used here is that of a pact, an agreement, or a covenant. The Old Testament is the pact or alliance that God made first with the Patriarchs and then with the Jewish people through Moses; a Saviour is promised and a Law is proclaimed, and salvation is through the Law.

The New Testament is the covenant or the alliance that God made with all men whereby, through the mediatorship of His Son, Jesus Christ, all men can be saved.

DETERMINATION OF THE BIBLE CANON

At the time the books of the New Testament were written, many other pious stories and legends relating to Christ and His times were also widely circulated. As a result, in the early centuries of the Church, there was some confusion and doubt as to which books were inspired and biblical, and which were not. As far as is known, it was the Council of Hippo in A.D. 393 which first determined which books were inspired and were to be included in the Bible canon, a canon in every respect identical with the canon of the Council of Trent. Subsequent Councils confirmed this decision, and the Council of Trent, in 1546, formally canonized all the traditional books of the Bible. These books comprise the Old and the New Testaments, and it is a matter of faith for Catholics to believe that all passages of all books are equally inspired.

THE APOCRYPHA

Those books which were rejected by the Council of Hippo as being non-biblical belong to what is called the Apocrypha. These books treat largely of the incidents and events during the life of Christ not related in the books of the Bible. They are often well worth reading, as they offer much historical information not otherwise available. However, some of these stories have slightly heretical tendencies.

The Catholic use of the word "Apocrypha," as defined above, should be distinguished from the incorrect Protestant use of the word. Protestants use this term to designate the seven books of the Bible included in the Catholic Bible canon, but not accepted or found in Protestant Bibles. These seven books are: Tobit, Judith, Wisdom, Sirach, Baruch, 1 and 2 Maccabees, and parts of Esther and Daniel. Protestants call the books found in the Catholic Apocrypha the Pseudepigraphal books.

HISTORY OF THE PROTESTANT CANON

The difference in the Catholic and Protestant Bibles arose in the following manner. The Jews living in the few centuries before Christ were divided into two groups — the Jews dwelling in Palestine and speaking Hebrew, and the large number of Jews scattered throughout the Roman Empire and speaking the Greek language, a consequence of the conquest of Alexander the Great of Greece.

CRITERIA OF THE JEWISH CANON

In the several centuries before the coming of Christ, the Jews in Palestine re-examined and eliminated some of the books from the existing collection as not in harmony with the Law of Moses and as of doubtful inspiration. The Pharisees set up four criteria which their sacred books had to pass in order to be included in the revised Jewish canon: (1) They had to be in harmony with the Pentateuch (Torah or Law); (2) They had to have been written before the time of Ezra; (3) They had to be written in Hebrew; (4) They had to have been written in Palestine.

BIBLE BOOKS ELIMINATED BY THE JEWS

The application of these arbitrary criteria eliminated Judith, probably written in Aramaic; Wisdom and 2 Maccabees, written in Greek; Tobit and parts of Daniel and Esther, written in Aramaic and probably outside of Palestine; Baruch, written outside of Palestine; and Sirach and 1 Maccabees, written after the time of Ezra. By the 1st Century after Christ, this revised canon was generally accepted by all Jews.

THE CHURCH RECOGNIZES
THE ALEXANDRINE CANON

From the earliest times, the Christian Church recognized the Jewish canon of the Greek-Roman tradition, or Alexandrine canon, as being the true Bible. Jesus Himself quoted from this Bible, and not until the Reformation was this canon seriously challenged.

These seven disputed books are also called the deuterocanonical books, while the rest of the books of the Old Testament comprise the protocanonical books. By protocanonical books is meant the "books of the first canon," books of the Old Testament accepted by both Christians and Jews. The deuterocanonical books, "books of the second canon," are those seven books found only in the Catholic canon.

Luther rejected the deuterocanonical books of the Old Testament. At one time he also eliminated Hebrews, James, Jude, and the Apocalypse from the New Testament, but later Protestants reinserted them. Today the Catholic and Protestant New Testament books are identical.

LANGUAGES OF THE BIBLE

The books of the Bible were originally written in three languages: Hebrew, Aramaic, and Greek. Aramaic is a branch of the Semitic languages, and was the language used in Palestine in the time of Christ. It is the language Christ spoke. Hebrew is a Semitic language which originated in Canaan and which was passed on by Abraham and his descendants, reaching its greatest glory in the reigns of David and Solomon. It was the language of the Holy Land until about the 3rd

Century B.C., when it was supplanted by Aramaic. The Greek language as used in the Bible is not the classical Greek as we know it today, but a dialect spread throughout the known world of the time by conquests of Alexander the Great.

Most of the books of the Old Testament were written in Hebrew, while all of the New Testament, excepting Matthew, was written in Greek. The Book of Wisdom and 2 Maccabees were also written in Greek. Portions of the Book of Daniel, Ezra, Jeremiah, and Esther, and all of Tobit, Judith, and the Gospel of St. Matthew were written in Aramaic.

TEXTUAL DIVISION OF THE BIBLE

The Bible as originally set down was not divided into chapter and verse as we know it today. Stephen Langton, Archbishop of Canterbury in the 13th Century, first divided the Bible text into Chapters. Santes Pagninus divided the Old Testament chapters into verses in 1528, and Robert Etienne, a printer in Paris, did the same for the New Testament in 1551.

THE OLD TESTAMENT

In the past we have tended to think of the books of the Bible as historical (such as Genesis, Exodus, Kings, and Maccabees); legal (Leviticus, Deuteronomy, etc.); prophetic (predicting the future); and so on.

An appreciation of the Jewish method of dividing the books (given on the previous page) may be a more helpful method. The first five books of the Bible (Genesis, Exodus, Leviticus, Numbers and Deuteronomy) were considered the books central to their faith. They were called Torah in Hebrew. The word Torah means an "instruction" not just a lesson but the kind of instruction a parent gives to a child when he wants him to obey.

Many of the books which we think of as historical (Joshua, Judges, Samuel and Kings) were considered "prophetic" by the Jews. By prophetic they meant an inspired sermon. These books recounted events from their history in order to moralize. They were sermons from history. In these books we may find prophets appearing but they are prophets who act. They leave us no long sermons. They are part of the rough and tumble of life. Important Kings may hardly be mentioned simply because they offered few examples to be imitated. Unimportant kings may receive more attention because they were good men. This is not our modern way of writing history, of course. Even for them it was not primarily history. It was rather religious editorializing. We may err by thinking of them as history. They are that but they are much more. The Jews called them the "former" prophets not because they came earlier in time but because they were bound into the Bible first.

The Prophetical books, the "latter prophets," whether written by the prophet himself or by a disciple, are inspired sermons. A prophet is a man who speaks for God and to his own times. He is a man concerned about his own world. He sometimes predicts the future. More frequently it is the immediate future. When he does so he is exercising a power that is not, strictly speaking, prophetic. It is an additional power from God. We tend to be led astray if we think of them primarily as predictors of the future.

The "Writings" are a catch-all for other books. Chronicles, which we think of as history, is a many-faceted book. To call it history is to miss many of its qualities. The poetry of Psalms and Wisdom-literature such as Proverbs is also included in this section. Daniel, which is a special kind of literature known as "apocalyptic" is included here though in the past we thought of it as among the Prophetic books.

Those books accepted by the Septuagint or Greek version of the Hebrew Bible but which the Jews rejected after the time of Christ are called "Deutero-Canonical" books. They, together with parts of Daniel and Esther, are not accepted as part of the Bible by Protestants or Jews. Catholics have always revered them as such since the earliest days of the church.

THE NEW TESTAMENT

In the New Testament we think of the "four gospels" of Matthew, Mark, Luke and John. These are the Gospels (or "good news") of Jesus Christ. But Acts of Apostles is the same kind of book. It is the "gospel of the Holy Spirit" and depicts the work of Christ continued in the early Church.

Though none of the "four gospels" are a "Life of Christ" for they tell us very little about most of His life, they do use incidents from the life of Christ to illustrate His teaching. Primarily then, the Gospels and Acts (also written by Luke) present us with the message, mission, and works of Christ. Every man who saw Christ saw him from a unique perspective. These four men we call Evangelists saw him from their own particular points of view.

"Epistles" are letters of various kinds. Some are like "letters to the editor" that were intended to be widely circulated, not only in the church to which they were sent but throughout the territory. Others were quite private. Charming little "Philemon" is a short note of Paul to a convert. Still others were written in the style of a letter as a style of literature. The Epistles of James and Peter are really treatises on doctrine.

The last book of the Bible, "Revelations" (or Apocalypse) is the only New Testament book written in a very popular style of the day. As with Daniel and Ezekiel in the Old Testament it was written in a kind of code of persecuted members of God's people recounting God's saving acts in the past in the face of present trials. They look forward, also, to saving acts in the future based on their faith in Him.

INSPIRATION OF THE BIBLE

THE BOOKS of the Bible have as their principal author the Holy Spirit, although He Himself did not write them. The Holy Spirit inspired the human authors of the Bible to write down in their own words, and in the manner and style of the day, what He wanted them to write, and He guided them to the extent that they wrote faithfully what they had been taught. This working together of God and man in the writing of the Bible is called inspiration. This inspiration covers not only matters of faith and morals, but extends as well to the facts of history as related, and to the whole Bible.

BIBLICAL INSPIRATION DEFINED

Pope Leo XIII, in his encyclical *Providentissimus Deus,* explains how inspiration affected the biblical writers. "By supernatural power God so moved and impelled them to write. He was so present to them, that they first rightly understood, then willed faithfully to write down, and finally expressed in apt words and with infallible truth the things which He ordered, and those only."

BIBLICAL REFERENCES TO ITS INSPIRATION

Besides the infallible teaching of the Church as to the inspiration of the Bible, we have reliable historical evidence as well. Many indirect passages in the Old Testament refer to its inspiration (Isaiah 8, 1; Wisdom 7, 15), and in the New Testament St. Peter refers to it in 2 Peter 1, 20-21.

TRADITION CONFIRMS BIBLICAL INSPIRATION

Tradition, too, provides overwhelming proof that from the earliest days of the Church it was believed that the Bible was inspired. The Fathers of the Church allude to it in many passages, stating variously that the books were inspired, that God is the Author of the Bible, and that the sacred writers were the instruments of God. Throughout its history, the Church has made many official pronouncements in ecclesiastical documents reaffirming the fact of inspiration.

EXTENT OF INSPIRATION

The Council of Trent on April 8, 1546, decreed that "those entire books with all their parts as have been accustomed to be read in the Catholic Church" must be considered as sacred and canonical. This was reaffirmed by the Council of the Vatican in 1870. In the centuries since this decree, Catholic theologians differed on two points of interpretation, as to whether matters of faith and morals alone were to be considered inspired or to whether inspiration extended just to important matters. These questions were settled by Pope Leo XIII in his encyclical *Providentissimus Deus,* in which he reaffirmed the decisions of the Council of Trent and emphasized that the Bible in all its parts was inspired and that a stated fact must be accepted as falling under inspiration, down to the most insignificant item; that is, *the whole Bible is the Word of God*.

HISTORY OF THE BIBLE

NO ORIGINAL MANUSCRIPTS of the Bible have come down to us, due to the perishable material upon which they were written and the fact that the Roman emperors decreed the destruction of the manuscripts during the Christian persecutions. While none of the original manuscripts are known to exist, some very ancient transcriptions have survived the years.

ANCIENT MANUSCRIPTS OF THE BIBLE

The oldest Hebrew manuscript known is a copy of the Book of Isaiah, written in Hebrew in the 2nd Century. It was found in 1947 in a cave near Jericho. The oldest Greek fragment known to exist is in the John Ryland Library in Manchester, England. This fragment is from the 2nd Century A.D. Several thousand other ancient Greek manuscripts have been found, the three most complete and important being the Codex Sinaiticus, Codex Vaticanus, and the Codex Alexandrinus, all probably of the 4th and 5th Century after Christ. The Codex Vaticanus is in the Vatican library.

EARLY TRANSLATIONS OF THE BIBLE

The most important early translations of the Bible were the Septuagint and the Vulgate. The Septuagint, a Greek translation of the Old Testament, was begun about 250 B.C. and completed about 100 B.C. This translation was made for the Jews of Egypt so that they could read their sacred books in Greek, the only language that most of them understood at that time. Before long, the Septuagint was widely used in Palestine and distributed throughout the Greek-speaking peoples of the Mediterranean world during the time of Christ and for the 1st Century or longer of the Christian era. The Apostles of Christ used this translation in their teaching.

THE BIBLE IN THE FIRST
TWO CENTURIES AFTER CHRIST

In the early days of the Church, the Scriptures were read at divine services in Greek. An early translation from Greek to Latin was needed for many of the Christians in the West could not understand Greek. Such translations, gathered together, made up the first Latin Bible. Prepared by so many different people of varying education, the translations were uneven and inaccurate. By the 2nd Century, there were a number of Latin translations, the most widely circulated being the *Old Latin,* or *Itala.*

ST. JEROME AND THE VULGATE TRANSLATION

Because of the numerous variant readings of the *Itala,* due to the copyists, revisers, or translators, Pope Damasus requested St. Jerome to revise and correct the New Testament. St. Jerome began his revision with the four Gospels and then revised the remaining books of the New Testament, but more hurriedly. The work was completed at Rome about A.D. 383-4. After the death of Pope Damasus, St. Jerome went to the Holy Land. He spent 34 years there, devoting his time to revising the Bible, to exegetical works, but mainly to the great work of his life — the translation of the protocanonical books of the Old Testament from Hebrew into Latin. This work extended over a period of fifteen years and it was a prodigious task, for the modern Vulgate is made up of: (a) the protocanonical books of the Old Testament, with the exception of the Psalter, translated from the Hebrew by St. Jerome; (b) the deuterocanonical books of Tobit and Judith from the Aramaic by St. Jerome; (c) the deuterocanonical books of Wisdom, Sirach, Baruch, and 1 and 2 Maccabees from the Old Latin unrevised by St. Jerome; (d) the deuterocanonical parts of Daniel from the Greek of Theodotion and of

Esther from the Septuagint; and (e) the New Testament revised from the Old Latin by St. Jerome.

THE VULGATE SUPERSEDES
ALL OTHER VERSIONS

As St. Jerome's work on the Old Testament was a work of private enterprise, it met great opposition. He was accused of changing the text of the Bible, which was familiar to the people in the *Itala* or Old Latin. However, as time went on, the great merits of his work were recognized. By the 9th Century, Jerome's version was universally accepted. In view of its general adoption, it gradually assumed the name of "Vulgate," the "disseminated" or people's Bible.

THE CHURCH APPROVES THE VULGATE

On April 8, 1546, the Church, in the Council of Trent, designated the Vulgate as the official Church translation. To this day the Vulgate remains the official version of the Church, and translations of it are found in practically every language in the world. However, it does not mean that it is to be preferred over the Septuagint or over original manuscripts, or that it was entirely free from error. On the contrary, the Church recognized certain limitations in the translations from the beginning, and ordered a revision. This revised version was published in 1592 under Pope Clement VIII.

THE VULGATE FROM JEROME TO GUTENBERG

Jerome's text suffered many vicissitudes throughout the ages. In assembling a complete Bible, copyists would take some of their readings, by misadventure, from the old Latin texts and some from the Vulgate; both texts were in circulation. A monk might have memorized several passages from the old version in school, then, in writing a copy of the Vulgate, subconsciously lapse into the old phrasing so familiar to him. Some of the transcribers were not exercising a critical sense and would incorporate texts from other manuscripts, parallel passages, and texts from the liturgy.

The invention of printing only multiplied these problems for a time, but eventually scholars were able to print a text near to the text as it came from the hands of St. Jerome. While the Vulgate became the official version of the Western Church, it did not prevent other translations from being made. A Coptic version appeared in the 2nd Century; Ulfilas, an Arian bishop, made a Gothic translation in the 4th Century, and there were numerous Syrian, Armenian, Georgian, Arabic, and Slavonic versions in the early centuries.

GUTENBERG AND THE FIRST PRINTED BIBLE

The invention and development of a practical printing process by Gutenberg in the 15th Century did more to revolutionize and modernize the world than any other invention. Prior to this, all manuscripts and books had to be copied by hand and only the very wealthy could ever afford to have one. At once the tedious work of the professional copyist was ended. Not only did it do away with the copyist, it eliminated the many human errors made in copying.

By 1450 Gutenberg had developed the art of printing so well that he was ready to print his first book; the first book printed was the Bible, in the Latin Vulgate translation. About two years were spent in printing and binding the Bible, and it was completed in 1452. Over 200 copies were printed in the first edition.

THE BIBLE IN PRINT

With the invention of printing, the Bible ran through edition after edition — 124 in the first 50 years, all sponsored by the Catholic Church. By the time Luther's New Testament appeared in 1522 there were 14 complete editions in German. Parallel with this in time was the appearance of 11 Italian translations, 10 French, 2 Bohemian, one Flemish, and one Russian.

THE BIBLE IN ENGLISH

The first complete English translation of the Bible appeared relatively late, probably not until the 14th Century. However, the English people were not without the Bible in those early years, as the Latin Vulgate was widely disseminated and in daily use. In addition, numerous paraphrases, translations, and commentaries of various Bible stories were well known through scop and gleeman, the popular storytellers of their day.

EARLY HISTORY NOT DEFINITELY KNOWN

Much of the earlier history of the Bible in English still remains a mystery. Tradition holds that Aidan, Bishop of Landisfarne, who died in 651, encouraged his followers to read the Scriptures in their own tongue. Aldhelm, Bishop of Sherborne until his death in 709, is said to have translated the Psalms into the Saxon language. Between 721 and

901 various writers, including the Venerable Bede, Eadfrith, Alcuin, and King Alfred, are believed to have translated parts or all of the Bible stories into Old English. In the 10th Century, a translation of the first seven books of the Bible and the Book of Job made by Aelfric, Archbishop of Canterbury from 994 to 1005, was in circulation.

During the time between the death of Aelfric and the reputed work of Wyclif in 1380, other translations are reported to have existed. However, this was a period of great transition in the English language, and practically nothing remains of these writings. It was not until the 15th Century that English as we know it today emerged as a definite language.

WYCLIF'S TRANSLATION

The next important English version is the so-called Wyclif translation, of which over 150 manuscripts are extant. It is taken indirectly from the Vulgate. Much doubt has been cast recently on the theory that Wyclif was responsible for this pre-Reformation Bible in recent years, since the translation is largely Catholic in tone and diction and since most of the manuscripts of this version were found in the possession of notably Catholic families.

THE DOUAY-RHEIMS TRANSLATION.

The first complete and printed Catholic English translation that is definitely known appeared rather late, at the turn of the 16th Century. This is known as the Douay-Rheims version. It was a translation of the Latin Vulgate and was produced in France by English scholars who had fled the Catholic persecutions in England. The New Testament was published in Rheims in 1582 and the Old Testament in Douay in 1610.

Since the Douay-Rheims translation, the English language has undergone continuous changes. It was necessary, therefore, to revise and bring the Bible up to date from time to time. Bishop Challoner of England undertook and published a complete revision of the Douay-Rheims in 1750, and several less successful revisions appeared between that time and the 20th Century.

PROTESTANT BIBLICAL SCHOLARSHIP

Besides the Catholic versions of the Bible mentioned above, numerous Protestant versions of the Bible in English have appeared since the Reformation. William Tyndale (1484-1536) was one of the first Protestant translators of the Bible. His translation is especially noteworthy because he translated from the original Greek versions then available to him rather than from the traditional Vulgate.

Miles Coverdale translated and printed a complete English Bible in 1535. Coverdale's translation was the first English edition of the Bible to separate the deuterocanonical books from the protocanonical books. The deuterocanonical books were put in the back of the regular Bible text.

Between the publication of Coverdale's Bible and the King James or Authorized Version, other less important translations took place. Noteworthy among these were the Taverner's Bible, the Great Bible, Cranmer's Bible, the Geneva Bible, and the Bishop's Bible.

THE KING JAMES BIBLE

When James I ascended the throne of England in 1603, numerous and variant Protestant Bibles were in circulation. In 1604 preparations were, therefore, made to undertake a revision of the Protestant Bible. A group of scholars was organized, and using the Bishop's Bible as the basis for their new translation, produced the King James Version, which was published in 1611.

While of great literary merit, Protestants themselves recognized many serious defects in the translation. In 1881-1885 a revision was made, and this is popularly known as the Revised Version. Many other modern versions are also published today, the most important, perhaps, being the Revised Standard Version published in 1952. More recently the New English Version, among others have been published.

PRESENT CATHOLIC BIBLICAL SCHOLARSHIP

Pope Leo XIII gave the modern impetus to Bible study when he issued his famous encyclical, *Providentissimus Deus*, which set up standards for all future Bible scholarship. In addition, he established the Biblical Commission in 1902 to study and to give answers to biblical questions. In 1890 M. J. Lagrange, O. P., founded the Ecole Biblique at Jerusalem and also established the periodical, *Revue Biblique*. The Biblical Institute was established in Rome in 1908 by Pius X to give advanced training to biblical scholars.

In 1907 the Biblical Commission asked the Benedictine Order to undertake the task of revising the Vulgate, and this translation is still in process. Under the direction of the English Jesuit, Reverend Cuthbert Lattey, English and American scholars produced the Westminster edition of the Sacred Scriptures directly from the Greek and Hebrew texts. Other modern versions include a translation of the New Testament from the original languages by Fr. F. Spencer, O. P., and this was published in 1937. A complete translation of the Bible was made by Msgr. Ronald Knox of England in 1950 and has attained wide popularity because of the modernness and clarity of its language.

CONFRATERNITY TRANSLATION OF THE BIBLE

In the United States in the last 40 years, there has been a general revival of religion and the hierarchy felt a great need for an accurate modern translation of the Bible. Out of this has developed a new translation of the Bible by American Scripture scholars, sponsored by the Confraternity of Christian Doctrine.

The first task of this group was to prepare a modern edition of the Challoner revision of the Douay-Rheims English translation of the Bible. Proceeding with this, they published the New Testament in 1941, and then began the translation of the Old Testament. However, Pope Pius XII issued his Encyclical, *Divino Afflante Spiritu,* in 1943 which dealt with, among other things, the need for a new translation of the Bible directly from the original languages of the sacred authors. For this reason, the further revision of the Challoner-Douay-Rheims Version was abandoned.

The Confraternity then began the new translation of the Old Testament directly from the original Hebrew and of the New Testament from the original languages. The New American Bible is a culmination of their efforts.

REVISED NEW TESTAMENT TRANSLATION

Since the introduction of the New American Bible in 1970, interest and participation in Bible study has increased rapidly. Awareness of this trend combined with the experience of its actual use (especially in oral proclamation) provided a basis for a revision of the original New Testament text.

Begun in 1978 and completed in 1986, the threefold purpose of this revision (also expressed in the preface of the first edition) was: "to provide a version suitable for liturgical proclamation, for private reading and for purposes of study."

An additional concern of the editors was the production of a version as accurate and faithful to the original Greek text as possible. At the same time, special attention was paid to ensure that the language chosen not only reflected contemporary American usage, but eliminated all discrimination (especially against women) whenever possible.

More abundant introductions, footnotes and explanatory material were also added to facilitate devotional reading and make the revision more suitable for purposes of study.

The New American Bible is a Roman Catholic translation. This revision, however, like the first edition, is the result of collaboration with scholars from other Christian Churches, both among the revisors and members of the editorial board.

THE OLD
TESTAMENT

Preface to
THE NEW AMERICAN BIBLE
Old Testament

On September 30, 1943, His Holiness Pope Pius XII issued his now famous encyclical on scripture studies, *Divino afflante Spiritu*. He wrote: "We ought to explain the original text which was written by the inspired author himself and has more authority and greater weight than any, even the very best, translation whether ancient or modern. This can be done all the more easily and fruitfully if to the knowledge of languages be joined a real skill in literary criticism of the same text."

Early in 1944, in conformity with the spirit of the encyclical, and with the encouragement of Archbishop Cicognani, Apostolic Delegate to the United States, the Bishops' Committee of the Confraternity of Christian Doctrine requested members of The Catholic Biblical Association of America to translate the sacred scriptures from the original languages or from the oldest extant form of the text, and to present the sense of the biblical text in as correct a form as possible.

The first English Catholic version of the Bible, the Douay-Rheims (1582–1609/10), and its revision by Bishop Challoner (1750) were based on the Latin Vulgate. In view of the relative certainties more recently attained by textual and higher criticism, it has become increasingly desirable that contemporary translations of the sacred books into English be prepared in which due reverence for the text and strict observance of the rules of criticism would be combined.

THE NEW AMERICAN BIBLE has accomplished this in response to the need of the church in America today. It is the achievement of some fifty biblical scholars, the greater number of whom, though not all, are Catholics. In particular, the editors-in-chief have devoted twenty-five years to this work. The collaboration of scholars who are not Catholic fulfills the directive of the Second Vatican Council, not only that "correct translations be made into different languages especially from the original texts of the sacred books," but that, "with the approval of the church authority, these translations be produced in cooperation with separated brothers" so that "all Christians may be able to use them."

The text of the books contained in THE NEW AMERICAN BIBLE is a completely new translation throughout. From the original and the oldest available texts of the sacred books, it aims to convey as directly as possible the thought and individual style of the inspired writers. The better understanding of Hebrew and Greek, and the steady development of the science of textual criticism, the fruit of patient study since the time of St. Jerome, have allowed the translators and editors in their use of all available materials to approach more closely than ever before the sense of what the sacred authors actually wrote.

Where the translation supposes the received text—Hebrew, Aramaic, or Greek, as the case may be—ordinarily contained in the best-known editions, as the original or the oldest extant form, no additional remarks are necessary. But for those who are happily able to study the original text of the scriptures at first-hand, a supplementary series of textual notes pertaining to the Old Testament was added originally in an appendix to the typical edition. (It is now obtainable in a separate booklet from The Catholic Biblical Association of America, The Catholic University of America, Washington, DC 20064.) These notes furnish a guide in those cases in which the editorial board judges that the manuscripts in the original languages, or the evidence of the ancient versions, or some similar source, furnish the correct reading of a passage, or at least a reading more true to the original than that customarily printed in the available editions.

The Massoretic text of 1 and 2 Samuel has in numerous instances been corrected by the more ancient manuscripts Samuel a, b, and c from Cave 4 of Qumran, with the aid of important evidence from the Septuagint in both its oldest form and its Lucianic recension. Fragments of the lost Book of Tobit in Aramaic and in Hebrew, recovered from Cave 4 of Qumran, are in substantial agreement with the Sinaiticus Greek recension used for the translation of this book. The lost original Hebrew text of 1 Maccabees is replaced by its oldest extant form in Greek. Judith, 2 Maccabees, and parts of Esther are also translated from the Greek.

The basic text for the Psalms is not the Massoretic but one which the editors considered closer to the original inspired form, namely the Hebrew text underlying the new Latin Psalter of the Church, the *Liber Psalmorum* (1944[1],

1945²). Nevertheless they retained full liberty to establish the reading of the original text on sound critical principles.

The translation of Sirach, based on the original Hebrew as far as it is preserved and corrected from the ancient versions, is often interpreted in the light of the traditional Greek text. In the Book of Baruch the basic text is the Greek of the Septuagint, with some readings derived from an underlying Hebrew form no longer extant. In the deuterocanonical sections of Daniel (3, 24–90; 13, 1–14, 42), the basic text is the Greek text of Theodotion, occasionally revised according to the Greek text of the Septuagint.

In some instances in the Book of Job, in Proverbs, Sirach, Isaiah, Jeremiah, Ezekiel, Hosea, Amos, Micah, Nahum, Habakkuk, and Zechariah there is good reason to believe that the original order of lines was accidentally disturbed in the transmission of the text. The verse numbers given in such cases are always those of the current Hebrew text, though the arrangement differs. In these instances the textual notes advise the reader of the difficulty. Cases of exceptional dislocation are called to the reader's attention by footnotes.

The Books of *Genesis to Ruth* were first published in 1952; the Wisdom Books, *Job to Sirach,* in 1955; the Prophetic Books, *Isaiah to Malachi,* in 1961; and the Books of *Samuel to Maccabees,* in 1969. In the present edition of *Genesis to Ruth* there are certain new features: a general introduction to the Pentateuch, a retranslation of the text of Genesis with an introduction, cross-references, and revised textual notes, besides new and expanded exegetical notes which take into consideration the various sources or literary traditions.

The revision of *Job to Sirach* includes changes in strophe division in Job and Proverbs and in titles of principal parts and sections of Wisdom and Ecclesiastes. Corrections in the text of Sirach are made in 39, 27–44, 17 on the basis of the Masada text, and in 51, 13–30 on the basis of the occurrence of this canticle in the Psalms scroll from Qumran Cave 11. In this typical edition, new corrections are reflected in the textual notes of Job, Proverbs, Wisdom, and Sirach. In the Psalms, the enumeration found in the Hebrew text is followed instead of the double enumeration, according to both the Hebrew and the Latin Vulgate texts, contained in the previous edition of this book.

In the Prophetic Books *Isaiah to Malachi,* only minor revisions have been made in the structure and wording of the texts, and in the textual notes.

The spelling of proper names in THE NEW AMERICAN BIBLE follows the customary forms found in most English Bibles since the Authorized Version.

The work of translating the Bible has been characterized as "the sacred and apostolic work of interpreting the word of God and of presenting it to the laity in translations as clear as the difficulty of the matter and the limitations of human knowledge permit" (A. G. Cicognani, Apostolic Delegate, in *The Catholic Biblical Quarterly,* 6, [1944], 389–90). In the appraisal of the present work, it is hoped that the words of the encyclical *Divino afflante Spiritu* will serve as a guide: "Let all the sons of the church bear in mind that the efforts of these resolute laborers in the vineyard of the Lord should be judged not only with equity and justice but also with the greatest charity; all moreover should abhor that intemperate zeal which imagines that whatever is new should for that very reason be opposed or suspected."

Conscious of their personal limitations for the task thus defined, those who have prepared this text cannot expect that it will be considered perfect; but they can hope that it may deepen in its readers "the right understanding of the divinely given Scriptures," and awaken in them "that piety by which it behooves us to be grateful to the God of all providence, who from the throne of his majesty has sent these books as so many personal letters to his own children" (*Divino afflante Spiritu*).

THE PENTATEUCH

The Pentateuch, which consists of the first five books of the Bible (Genesis, Exodus, Leviticus, Numbers, Deuteronomy), enjoys particular prestige among the Jews as the "Law," or "Torah," the concrete expression of God's will in their regard. It is more than a body of legal doctrine, even though such material occupies many chapters, for it contains the story of the formation of the People of God: Abraham and the patriarchs, Moses and the oppressed Hebrews in Egypt, the birth of Israel in the Sinai covenant, the journey to the threshold of the Promised Land, and the "discourses" of Moses.

The grandeur of this historic sweep is the result of a careful and complex joining of several historical traditions, or sources. These are primarily four: the so-called Yahwist, Elohist, Priestly and Deuteronomic strands that run through the Pentateuch. (They are conveniently abbreviated as J, E, P and D.) Each brings to the Torah its own characteristics, its own theological viewpoint—a rich variety of interpretation that the sensitive reader will take pains to appreciate. A superficial difference between two of these sources is responsible for their names: the Yahwist prefers the name Yahweh (represented in translation as Lord) by which God revealed himself to Israel; the Elohist prefers the generic name for God, Elohim. The Yahwist is concrete, imaginative, using many anthropomorphisms in its theological approach, as seen, e.g., in the narrative of creation in Gn 2, compared with the Priestly version in Gn 1. The Elohist is more sober, moralistic. The Priestly strand, which emphasizes genealogies, is more severely theological in tone. The Deuteronomic approach is characterized by the intense hortatory style of Dt 5–11, and by certain principles from which it works, such as the centralization of worship in the Jerusalem temple.

However, even this analysis of the Pentateuch is an over-simplification, for it is not always possible to distinguish with certainty among the various sources. The fact is that each of these individual traditions incorporates much older material. The Yahwist was himself a collector and adapter. His narrative is made up of many disparate stories that have been reoriented, and given a meaning within the context in which they now stand; e.g., the story of Abraham and Isaac in Gn 22. Within the J and P traditions one has to reckon with many individual units; these had their own history and life-setting before they were brought together into the present more or less connected narrative.

This is not to deny the role of Moses in the development of the Pentateuch. It is true we do not conceive of him as the author of the books in the modern sense. But there is no reason to doubt that, in the events described in these traditions, he had a uniquely important role, especially as lawgiver. Even the later laws which have been added in P and D are presented as a Mosaic heritage. Moses is the lawgiver par excellence, and all later legislation is conceived in his spirit, and therefore attributed to him. Hence, the reader is not held to undeviating literalness in interpreting the words, "the LORD said to Moses." One must keep in mind that the Pentateuch is the crystallization of Israel's age-old relationship with God.

In presenting the story of the birth of the People of God, the Pentateuch looks back to the promises made to the patriarchs, and forward to the continuing fulfillment of these promises in later books of the Bible. The promises find their classic expression in Gn 12, 1ff. The "God of the Fathers" challenges Abraham to believe: the patriarch is to receive a people, a land, and through him the nations will somehow be blessed.

The mysterious and tortuous way in which this people is brought into being is described: Despite Sarah's sterility, Isaac is finally born—to be offered in sacrifice! The promises are renewed to him eventually, and also to the devious Jacob, as if to show that the divine design will be effected, with or without human cunning. The magnificent story of Joseph is highlighted by the theme of Providence; the promise of a people is taking shape.

Israel is not formed in a vacuum, but amid the age-old civilization of Mesopotamia and the Nile. Oppression in Egypt provokes a striking intervention of God.

Yahweh reveals himself to Moses as a savior, and the epic story of deliverance is told in Exodus. This book also tells of the Sinai covenant, which is rightfully regarded as the key to the Old Testament. Through the covenant Israel becomes

Yahweh's people, and Yahweh becomes Israel's God. This act of grace marks the fulfillment of the first promise; that Abraham will be the father of a great nation, God's special possession. The laws in Exodus and Leviticus (P tradition) are both early and late. They spell out the proper relationship of the federation of the Twelve tribes with the LORD. He is a jealous God, demanding exclusive allegiance; he cannot be imaged; he takes vengeance upon the wicked, and shows mercy to the good. Slowly the LORD reveals himself to his people; with remarkable honesty, Israel records the unsteady response—the murmurings and rebellions and infidelities through the desert wanderings up to the plain of Moab.

This sacred history was formed within the bosom of early Israel, guided by the spirit of God. It was sung beside the desert campfires; it was commemorated in the liturgical feasts, such as Passover; it was transmitted by word of mouth from generation to generation—until all was brought together in writing, about the sixth century B.C., when the literary formation of the Pentateuch came to an end.

The Book of Deuteronomy has a history quite peculiar to itself. Its old traditions and law code (12–26) are put forth in the form of "discourses" of Moses before his death. The extraordinarily intense and hortatory tone fits the mood of a discourse. The book contains possibly the preaching of the Levites in the northern kingdom of Israel before its fall in 721 B.C. If this book is situated in its proper historical perspective, its true impact is more vividly appreciated. It is the blueprint of the great "Deuteronomic" reform under King Josiah (640–609 B.C.). This was an attempt to galvanize the people into a wholehearted commitment to the covenant ideals, into an obedience motivated by the great commandment of love (Dt 6, 4ff). Israel has yet another chance, if it obeys. The people are poised between life and death; and they are exhorted to choose life—today (26, 16–19; 30, 15–20).

The Book of

GENESIS

Genesis, the first book of the Bible, opens with the Hebrew word bereshit, which means "in the beginning." The title "Genesis" was given to the Septuagint (Greek) translation of the book, because of its concern with the origin of the world (Gn 1, 1; 2, 4), of the human race, and, in particular, of the Hebrew people.

Eleven structural units (toledoth), of unequal length and importance, present the unity and purpose of the books in terms of God's universal sovereignty, his dealings with men, and his choice and formation of a special people to be the instrument of his plan of salvation.

The tracing of the direct descendance from Adam to Jacob constitutes the major part of the book, while the genealogical tables of lateral branches are not so developed nor of such interest as those that pertain to the story of the Israelite people. In fact, these lateral branches gradually disappear from the narrative. And with the introduction of Abraham and his covenant with God, the history of humanity as such becomes contracted to the story of the descendants of Abraham through Isaac and Jacob—the chosen people.

Despite its unity of plan and purpose, the book is a complex work, not to be attributed to a single original author. Several sources, or literary traditions, that the final redactor used in his composition are discernible. These are the Yahwist (J), Elohist (E) and Priestly (P) sources, which in turn reflect older oral traditions (see Introduction to the Pentateuch).

In Genesis, the Yahwist source is the most important by reason of its teaching, its antiquity, and the continuity it gives the book. It constitutes a sacred history, continually drawing attention to the working out of God's design through his interventions in the affairs of men. The Elohist source, less well preserved, is found in fragmentary form only, depicting God's manifestations through visions and dreams rather than theophanies. Angels are God's intermediaries with men. Moreover, there is a solicitude for the divine transcendence and greater sensitivity toward the moral order. The Priestly source contains those elements—chronological data, lists, genealogies—that construct the framework of Genesis and bind its contents together. To the J and E sources it adds such legal institutions as the sabbath rest, circumcision and the alliances between God and Noah and God and Abraham.

The interpreter of Genesis will recognize at once the distinct object that sets chapters 1–11 apart: the recounting of the origin of the world and of man (primeval history). To make the truths contained in these chapters intelligible to the Israelite people destined to preserve them, they needed to be expressed through elements prevailing among that people at that time. For this reason, the truths themselves must therefore be clearly distinguished from their literary garb.

With the story of the patriarchs Abraham, Isaac and Jacob (Gn 11, 27–50, 26), the character of the narrative changes. While we do not view the account of the patriarchs as history in the strict sense, nevertheless certain of the matters recounted from the time of Abraham onward can be placed in the actual historical and social framework of the Near East in the early part of the second millennium B.C. (2000–1500), and documented by non-biblical sources.

Genesis contains many religious teachings of basic importance: the preexistence and transcendence of God, his wisdom and goodness, his power through which all things are made and on which they all depend; the special creation of man in God's image and likeness, and of woman from the substance of man; the institution of marriage as the union of one man with one woman; man's original state of innocence; man's sin of pride and disobedience, its consequences for the protoparents and their posterity. Despite the severity of their punishment, hope of reconciliation is offered by God through the first as well as the subsequent promises of salvation and blessing. Abraham is blessed for his faith and obedience, and he is to be a blessing for all nations through his offspring, Isaac, Jacob, and Jacob's *sons (Gn 12, 3; 18, 18; 22, 18), of whom the Messiah, mankind's greatest blessing, will eventually be born (Gal 3, 8).*

Frequent references to Genesis are found in the New Testament. Christ becomes the antithesis of Adam: sin and death comes to mankind through Adam, justification and life through Jesus Christ (Rom 5, 12. 17ff). Noah's ark becomes the symbol of the church, by which men are saved from destruction through the waters of baptism (1 Pt 3, 20ff); Abraham's faith is the model for all believers; the sacrifice of his son Isaac typifies the sacrifice of Christ, Son of the Father. The liturgy, too, relates the persons of Abel, Abraham and Melchizedek to Christ in his act of sacrifice.

The Book of Genesis is divided as follows:
I. The Primeval History (1, 1–11, 26).
II. The Patriarch Abraham (11, 27–25, 18).
III. The Patriarchs Isaac and Jacob (25, 19–36, 43).
IV. Joseph and His Brothers (37, 1–50, 26).

1: The Primeval History

CHAPTER 1

First Story of Creation.*   **1** In the beginning, when God created the heavens and the earth,ᵃ **2** the earth was a formless wasteland, and darkness covered the abyss,* while a mighty wind swept over the waters.ᵇ

3 Then God said, "Let there be light," and there was light.ᶜ **4** God saw how good the light was. God then separated the light from the darkness. **5** God called the light "day," and the darkness he called "night." Thus evening came, and morning followed—the first day.*

6 Then God said, "Let there be a dome in the middle of the waters, to separate one body of water from the other." And so it happened: **7** God made the dome, and it separated the water above the dome from the water below it. ᵈ **8** God called the dome "the sky." Evening came, and morning followed—the second day.

9 Then God said, "Let the water under the sky be gathered into a single basin, so that the dry land may appear." And so it happened: the water under the sky was gathered into its basin, and the dry land appeared.ᵉ **10** God called the dry land "the earth," and the basin of the water he called "the sea." God saw how good it was. **11** ᶠThen God said, "Let the earth bring forth vegetation: every kind of plant that bears seed and every kind of fruit tree on earth that bears fruit with its seed in it." And so it happened: **12** the earth brought forth every kind of plant that bears seed and every kind of fruit tree on earth that bears fruit with its seed in it. God saw how good it was. **13** Evening came, and morning followed—the third day.

14 Then God said: "Let there be lights in the dome of the sky, to separate day from night. Let them mark the fixed times, the days and the years,ᵍ **15** and serve as luminaries in the dome

of the sky, to shed light upon the earth." And so it happened: **16** God made the two great lights, the greater one to govern the day, and the lesser one to govern the night; and he made the stars.ʰ **17** God set them in the dome of the sky, to shed light upon the earth, **18** to govern the day and the night, and to separate the light from the darkness. God saw how good it was. **19** Evening came, and morning followed—the fourth day.

20 ⁱThen God said, "Let the water teem with an abundance of living creatures, and on the earth let birds fly beneath the dome of the sky." And so it happened: **21** God created the great sea monsters and all kinds of swimming creatures with which the water teems, and all kinds of winged birds. God saw how good it was, **22** and God blessed them, saying, "Be fertile, multiply, and fill the water of the seas; and let

---

a Gn 2, 1.4; Pss 8, 4; 38—39; 90, 2; Wis 11, 17; Sir 16, 24; Jer 10, 12; 2 Mc 7, 28; Acts 14, 15; Col 1, 16f; Heb 1, 2f; 3, 4; 11, 3; Rv 4, 11.
b Jer 4, 23.
c 2 Cor 4, 6.
d Prv 8, 27f; 2 Pt 3, 5.
e Jb 38, 8; Ps 33, 7; Jer 5, 22.
f Ps 104, 14.
g Jb 26, 10; Ps 19, 1f; Bar 3, 33.
h Dt 4, 19; Ps 136, 7ff; Wis 13, 2ff; Jer 31, 35.
i Jb 12, 7-10.
j Gn 8, 17.

---

*

1, 1—2, 4a: This section introduces the whole Pentateuch. It shows how God brought an orderly universe out of primordial chaos.

1, 2: The abyss: the primordial ocean according to the ancient Semitic cosmogony. After God's creative activity, part of this vast body forms the salt-water seas (vv 9f); part of it is the fresh water under the earth (Ps 33, 7; Ez 31, 4), which wells forth on the earth as springs and fountains (Gn 7, 11; 8, 2; Prv 3, 20). Part of it, "the upper water" (Ps 148, 4; Dn 3, 60), is held up by the dome of the sky (Gn 1, 6f) from which rain descends on the earth (Gn 7, 11; 2 Kgs 7, 2. 19; Ps 104, 13). A mighty wind: Literally, "a wind of God," or "a spirit of God"; cf Gn 8 1.

1, 5: In ancient Israel a day was considered to begin at sunset. According to the highly artificial literary structure of Gn 1, 1—2, 4a, God's creative activity is divided into six days to teach the sacredness of the sabbath rest on the seventh day in the Israelite religion (Gn 2, 2f).

the birds multiply on the earth."[j] **23** Evening came, and morning followed—the fifth day.

24 [k]Then God said, "Let the earth bring forth all kinds of living creatures: cattle, creeping things, and wild animals of all kinds." And so it happened: **25** God made all kinds of wild animals, all kinds of cattle, and all kinds of creeping things of the earth. God saw how good it was. **26** [l]Then God said: "Let us make man in our image, after our likeness. Let them have dominion over the fish of the sea, the birds of the air, and the cattle, and over all the wild animals and all the creatures that crawl on the ground."*

27 God created man in his image;
   in the divine image he created him;
   male and female he created them.

28 God blessed them, saying: "Be fertile and multiply; fill the earth and subdue it. Have dominion over the fish of the sea, the birds of the air, and all the living things that move on the earth."[m] **29** [n]God also said: "See, I give you every seed-bearing plant all over the earth and every tree that has seed-bearing fruit on it to be your food; **30** and to all the animals of the land, all the birds of the air, and all the living creatures that crawl on the ground, I give all the green plants for food." And so it happened. **31** God looked at everything he had made, and he found it very good. Evening came, and morning followed—the sixth day.[o]

CHAPTER 2

1 Thus the heavens and the earth and all their array were completed.[p] **2** Since on the seventh day God was finished with the work he had been doing, he rested on the seventh day from all the work he had undertaken.[q] **3** So God blessed the seventh day and made it holy, because on it he rested from all the work he had done in creation.[r]

4 Such is the story of the heavens and the earth at their creation.

Second Story of Creation.*

At the time when the LORD God made the earth and the heavens— **5** while as yet there was no field shrub on earth and no grass of the field had sprouted, for the LORD God had sent no rain upon the earth and there was no man to till the soil, **6** but a stream was welling up out of the earth and was watering all the surface of the ground—**7** the LORD God formed man out of the clay of the ground* and blew into his nostrils the breath of life, and so man became a living being.[s]

8 Then the LORD God planted a garden in Eden,* in the east, and he placed there the man whom he had formed.[t] **9** Out of the ground the LORD God made various trees grow that were

delightful to look at and good for food, with the tree of life in the middle of the garden and the tree of the knowledge of good and bad.[u]

10 A river rises* in Eden to water the garden; beyond there it divides and becomes four branches. **11** The name of the first is the Pishon; it is the one that winds through the whole land of Havilah, where there is gold. **12** The gold of that land is excellent; bdellium and lapis lazuli are also there. **13** The name of the second river is the Gihon; it is the one that winds all through the land of Cush.[v] **14** The name of the third river is the Tigris; it is the one that flows east of Asshur. The fourth river is the Euphrates.

15 The LORD God then took the man and settled him in the garden of Eden, to cultivate and care for it.[w] **16** The LORD God gave man this order: "You are free to eat from any of the trees of the garden[x] **17** except the tree of knowledge of good and bad. From that tree you shall not eat; the moment you eat from it you are surely doomed to die."[y]

18 The LORD God said: "It is not good for the man to be alone. I will make a suitable partner for him."[z] **19** So the LORD God formed out of the ground various wild animals and various birds of the air, and he brought them to the

k Sir 16, 27f; Bar 3, 32.
l 26f: Gn 5, 1. 3; 9, 6; Ps 8, 5f; Wis 2, 23; 10, 2; Sir 17, 1. 3f; Jas 3, 7; 1 Cor 11, 7; Eph 4, 24; Col 3, 10; Mt 19, 4; Mk 10, 6.
m Gn 8, 17; 9, 1; Pss 8, 6-9; 115, 16; Wis 9, 2.
n 29f: Gn 9, 3; Ps 104, 14f.
o 1 Tm 4, 4.
p Is 45, 12; Jn 1, 3.
q Ex 20, 9ff; 31, 17; Heb 4, 4. 10.
r Ex 20, 11; Dt 5, 14; Neh 9, 14.
s Gn 3, 19; 18, 27; Tb 8, 6; Jb 34, 15; Pss 103, 14; 104, 29; Eccl 3, 20; 12, 7; Wis 7, 1; Sir 33, 10; 1 Cor 15, 45.
t Is 51, 3; Ez 31, 9.
u Gn 3, 22; Prv 3, 18; Rv 2, 7; 22, 2. 14.
v Sir 24, 25.
w Sir 7, 15.
x Ps 104, 14.
y Gn 3, 2f; Rom 6, 23.
z Tb 8, 6; Sir 36, 24; 1 Cor 11, 9; 1 Tm 2, 13.

*

1, 26: Man is here presented as the climax of God's creative activity; he resembles God primarily because of the dominion God gives him over the rest of creation.

2, 4b–25: This section is chiefly concerned with the creation of man. It is much older than the narrative of Gn 1, 1—2, 4a. Here God is depicted as creating man before the rest of his creatures, which are made for man's sake.

2, 7: God is portrayed as a potter molding man's body out of clay. There is a play on words in Hebrew between adam ("man") and adama ("ground"). Being: literally, "soul."

2, 8: Eden: used here as the name of a region in southern Mesopotamia; the term is derived from the Sumerian word eden, "fertile plain." A similar-sounding Hebrew word means "delight"; the garden in Eden could therefore be understood as the "garden of delight," so that, through the Greek version, it is now known also as "paradise," literally, a "pleasure park."

2, 10–14: Rises: in flood to overflow its banks. Beyond there: as one travels upstream. Branches: literally, "heads," i.e., upper courses. Eden is near the head of the Persian Gulf, where the Tigris and the Euphrates join with two other streams to form a single river. The land of Cush here and in Gn 10, 8, is not Ethiopia (Nubia) as elsewhere, but the region of the Kassites east of Mesopotamia.

man to see what he would call them; whatever the man called each of them would be its name. **20** The man gave names to all the cattle, all the birds of the air, and all the wild animals; but none proved to be the suitable partner for the man.

21 So the LORD God cast a deep sleep on the man, and while he was asleep, he took out one of his ribs and closed up its place with flesh.*a* **22** The LORD God then built up into a woman the rib that he had taken from the man. When he brought her to the man, **23** the man said:

"This one, at last, is bone of my bones
    and flesh of my flesh;
This one shall be called 'woman,'
    for out of 'her man' this one has been
       taken."*

24 *b*That is why a man leaves his father and mother and clings to his wife, and the two of them become one body.*

    25 The man and his wife were both naked, yet they felt no shame.

CHAPTER 3

The Fall of Man.   **1** Now the serpent was the most cunning of all the animals that the LORD God had made. The serpent asked the woman, "Did God really tell you not to eat from any of the trees in the garden?" **2** The woman answered the serpent: "We may eat of the fruit of the trees in the garden; **3** *c*it is only about the fruit of the tree in the middle of the garden that God said, 'You shall not eat it or even touch it, lest you die.'" **4** But the serpent said to the woman: "You certainly will not die!*d* **5** No, God knows well that the moment you eat of it your eyes will be opened and you will be like gods who know* what is good and what is bad." **6** The woman saw that the tree was good for food, pleasing to the eyes, and desirable for gaining wisdom. So she took some of its fruit and ate it; and she also gave some to her husband, who was with her, and he ate it.*e* **7** Then the eyes of both of them were opened, and they realized that they were naked; so they sewed fig leaves together and made loincloths for themselves.

  8 When they heard the sound of the LORD God moving about in the garden at the breezy time of the day,* the man and his wife hid themselves from the LORD God among the trees of the garden.*f* **9** The LORD God then called to the man and asked him, "Where are you?" **10** He answered, "I heard you in the garden; but I was afraid, because I was naked, so I hid myself." **11** Then he asked, "Who told you that you were naked? You have eaten, then, from the tree of which I had forbidden you to eat!" **12** The man replied, "The woman whom

you put here with me—she gave me fruit from the tree, so I ate it." **13** The LORD God then asked the woman, "Why did you do such a thing?" The woman answered, "The serpent tricked me into it, so I ate it."*g*

  14 Then the LORD God said to the serpent:

"Because you have done this, you shall be
    banned
  from all the animals
  and from all the wild creatures;
On your belly shall you crawl,
  and dirt shall you eat
  all the days of your life.*h*
15 I will put enmity between you and the
    woman,
  and between your offspring and hers;
He will strike at your head,
  while you strike at his heel."*i*
16 To the woman he said:
"I will intensify the pangs of your
    childbearing;
  in pain shall you bring forth children.
Yet your urge shall be for your husband,
  and he shall be your master."*j*

17 To the man he said: "Because you listened to your wife and ate from the tree of which I had forbidden you to eat,

"Cursed be the ground because of you!
In toil shall you eat its yield
  all the days of your life.*k*
18 Thorns and thistles shall it bring forth to
    you,
  as you eat of the plants of the field.

---

a Sir 17, 1; 1 Cor 11, 8f;
  1 Tm 2, 13.
b Mt 19, 5; Mk 10, 7;
  1 Cor 7, 10f; Eph 5,
  31.
c Gn 2, 17; Rom 6, 23.
d 4f: Wis 2, 24; Sir 25,
  14; Is 14, 14; Jn 8, 44;
  2 Cor 11, 3.
e Gn 3, 22; 1 Tm 2, 14.
f Jer 23, 24.

g 2 Cor 11, 3.
h Is 65, 25; Mi 7, 17; Rv
  12, 9.
i Is 7, 14; 9, 5; Rom 16,
  20; 1 Jn 3, 8; Rv 12,
  17.
j 1 Cor 11, 3; Eph 5, 22f;
  1 Tm 2, 12.
k Gn 5, 29; Rom 5, 12;
  8, 20; Heb 6, 8.

*

2, 23: There is a play on the similar-sounding Hebrew words ishsha ("woman") and ishah ("her man, her husband").

2, 24: One body: literally "one flesh"; classical Hebrew has no specific word for "body." The sacred writer stresses the fact that conjugal union is willed by God.

3, 5: Like gods who know: or "like God who knows."

3, 8: The breezy time of the day: literally "the wind of the day." On most days in Palestine a cooling breeze blows from the sea shortly before sunset.

3, 15: He will strike . . . at his heel: since the antecedent for he and his is the collective noun offspring, i.e., all the descendants of the woman, a more exact rendering of the sacred writer's words would be, "They will strike . . . at their heels." However, later theology saw in this passage more than unending hostility between snakes and men. The serpent was regarded as the devil (Wis 2, 24; Jn 8, 44; Rv 12, 9; 20, 2), whose eventual defeat seems implied in the contrast between head and heel. Because "the Son of God appeared that he might destroy the works of the devil" (1 Jn 3, 8), the passage can be understood as the first promise of a Redeemer for fallen mankind. The woman's offspring then is primarily Jesus Christ.

19 By the sweat of your face
    shall you get bread to eat,
Until you return to the ground,
    from which you were taken;
For you are dirt,
    and to dirt you shall return.''*l*

20 The man called his wife Eve, because she became the mother of all the living.*

21 For the man and his wife the LORD God made leather garments, with which he clothed them. 22 Then the LORD God said: "See! The man has become like one of us, knowing what is good and what is bad! Therefore, he must not be allowed to put out his hand to take fruit from the tree of life also, and thus eat of it and live forever.''*m* 23 The LORD God therefore banished him from the garden of Eden, to till the ground from which he had been taken. 24 When he expelled the man, he settled him east of the garden of Eden; and he stationed the cherubim and the fiery revolving sword, to guard the way to the tree of life.*

CHAPTER 4

Cain and Abel.   1 The man had relations with his wife Eve, and she conceived and bore Cain, saying, "I have produced a man with the help of the LORD.''* 2 Next she bore his brother Abel. Abel became a keeper of flocks, and Cain a tiller of the soil. 3 In the course of time Cain brought an offering to the LORD from the fruit of the soil, 4 while Abel, for his part, brought one of the best firstlings of his flock.*n* The LORD looked with favor on Abel and his offering, 5 but on Cain and his offering he did not. Cain greatly resented this and was crestfallen. 6 So the LORD said to Cain: "Why are you so resentful and crestfallen? 7 If you do well, you can hold up your head; but if not, sin is a demon lurking* at the door: his urge is toward you, yet you can be his master.''*o*

8 Cain said to his brother Abel, "Let us go out in the field." When they were in the field, Cain attacked his brother Abel and killed him.*p* 9 Then the LORD asked Cain, "Where is your brother Abel?" He answered, "I do not know. Am I my brother's keeper?" 10 The LORD then said: "What have you done! Listen: Your brother's blood cries out to me from the soil! 11 Therefore you shall be banned from the soil that opened its mouth to receive your brother's blood from your hand.*q* 12 If you till the soil, it shall no longer give you its produce. You shall become a restless wanderer on the earth." 13 Cain said to the LORD: "My punishment is too great to bear. 14 Since you have now banished me from the soil, and I must avoid your presence and become a restless wanderer on the earth, anyone may kill me at sight." 15 "Not so!" the LORD said to him. "If anyone kills

Cain, Cain shall be avenged sevenfold.'' So the LORD put a mark* on Cain, lest anyone should kill him at sight. 16 Cain then left the LORD's presence and settled in the land of Nod,* east of Eden.

Descendants of Cain and Seth.

17 *Cain had relations with his wife, and she conceived and bore Enoch. Cain also became the founder of a city, which he named after his son Enoch. 18 To Enoch was born Irad, and Irad became the father of Mehujael; Mehujael became the father of Metusael, and Methusael became the father of Lamech. 19 Lamech took two wives; the name of the first was Adah, and the name of the second Zillah. 20 Adah gave birth to Jabal, the ancestor of all who dwell in tents and keep cattle. 21 His brother's name was Jubal; he was the ancestor of all who play the lyre and the pipe. 22 Zillah, on her part, gave birth to Tubalcain, the ancestor of all who forge instruments of bronze and iron. The sister of Tubalcain was Naamah. 23 Lamech said to his wives:

"Adah and Zillah, hear my voice;
    wives of Lamech, listen to my utterance:
I have killed a man for wounding me,
    a boy for bruising me.
24 If Cain is avenged sevenfold,
    then Lamech seventy-sevenfold.''

25 Adam again had relations with his wife, and

---

l Gn 2, 7; Jb 10, 9; 34,
  15; Pss 90, 3; 103, 14;
  Eccl 3, 20; 12, 7; Wis
  15, 8; Sir 10, 9; 17, 2;
  Rom 5, 12; 1 Cor 15,
  21; Heb 9, 27.
m Gn 2, 9; Rv 22, 2. 14.

n Ex 34, 19; Heb 11, 4.
o Sir 7, 1; Jude 11.
p Wis 10, 3; Mt 23, 35;
  Lk 11, 51; 1 Jn 3, 12;
  Jude 11.
q Dt 27, 24.

---

*

3, 20: This verse seems to be out of place; it would fit better after v 24. The Hebrew name hawwa ("Eve") is related to the Hebrew word hay ("living").

3, 24: The above rendering is based on the ancient Greek version; that of the current Hebrew is, When he expelled the man, he settled east of the garden of Eden, the cherubim.

4, 1: The Hebrew name qayin ("Cain") and the term qaniti ("I have produced") present another play on words.

4, 7: Demon lurking: in Hebrew, robes, literally "croucher," is used here, like the similar Akkadian term rabisu, to designate a certain kind of evil spirit.

4, 15: A mark: probably a tattoo. The use of tattooing for tribal marks has always been common among the nomads of the Near Eastern deserts.

4, 16: The land of Nod: not a definite geographic region. The term merely means "the land of nomads."

4, 17–22: In vv 12–16 Cain was presented as the archetype of nomadic peoples. The sacred author in this section follows another ancient tradition that makes Cain the prototype of sedentary peoples with higher material culture.

4, 25f: Has granted: Hebrew shat, a wordplay on the name shet ("Seth"). Enosh: in Hebrew, a synonym of adam ("man"). At the time . . . name: men began to call God by his personal name, Yahweh, rendered as "the Lord" in this version of the Bible. The ancient, so-called Yahwist source used here employs the name Yahweh long before the time of Moses. Another ancient source, the Elohist (from its use of the term Elohim,

she gave birth to a son whom she called Seth. ''God has granted* me more offspring in place of Abel,'' she said, ''because Cain slew him.'' **26** To Seth, in turn, a son was born, and he named him Enosh.

At that time men began to invoke the LORD by name.*r*

CHAPTER 5

Generations: Adam to Noah.*   **1** *s*This is the record of the descendants of Adam. When God created man, he made him in the likeness of God; **2** he created them male and female. When they were created, he blessed them and named them ''man.''

3 *t*Adam was one hundred and thirty years old when he begot a son in his likeness, after his image; and he named him Seth.*u* **4** Adam lived eight hundred years after the birth of Seth, and he had other sons and daughters. **5** The whole lifetime of Adam was nine hundred and thirty years; then he died.

6 When Seth was one hundred and five years old, he became the father of Enosh. **7** Seth lived eight hundred and seven years after birth of Enosh, and he had other sons and daughters. **8** The whole lifetime of Seth was nine hundred and twelve years; then he died.

9 When Enosh was ninety years old, he became the father of Kenan. **10** Enosh lived eight hundred and fifteen years after the birth of Kenan, and he had other sons and daughters. **11** The whole lifetime of Enosh was nine hundred and five years; then he died.

12 When Kenan was seventy years old, he became the father of Mahalalel. **13** Kenan lived eight hundred and forty years after the birth of Mahalalel, and he had other sons and daughters. **14** The whole lifetime of Kenan was nine hundred and ten years; then he died.

15 When Mahalalel was sixty-five years old, he became the father of Jared. **16** Mahalalel lived eight hundred and thirty years after the birth of Jared, and he had other sons and daughters. **17** The whole lifetime of Mahalalel was eight hundred and ninety-five years; then he died.

18 When Jared was one hundred and sixty-two years old, he became the father of Enoch. **19** Jared lived eight hundred years after the birth of Enoch, and he had other sons and daughters. **20** The whole lifetime of Jared was nine hundred and sixty-two years; then he died.

21 When Enoch was sixty-five years old, he became the father of Methuselah. **22** Enoch lived three hundred years after the birth of Methuselah, and he had other sons and daughters. **23** The whole lifetime of Enoch was three hundred and sixty-five years. **24** Then Enoch walked with God,* and he was no longer here, for God took him.*v*

25 When Methuselah was one hundred and eighty-seven years old, he became the father of Lamech. **26** Methuselah lived seven hundred and eighty-two years after the birth of Lamech, and he had other sons and daughters. **27** The whole lifetime of Methuselah was nine hundred and sixty-nine years; then he died.

28 When Lamech was one hundred and eighty-two years old, he begot a son **29** *w*and named him Noah, saying, ''Out of the very ground that the LORD has put under a curse, this one shall bring us relief from our work and the toil of our hands.''* **30** Lamech lived five hundred and ninety-five years after the birth of Noah, and he had other sons and daughters. **31** The whole lifetime of Lamech was seven hundred and seventy-seven years; then he died.

32 When Noah was five hundred years old, he became the father of Shem, Ham and Japheth.*x*

CHAPTER 6

Origin of the Nephilim.*   **1** When men began to multiply on earth and daughters were

---

r 1 Chr 1, 1; Lk 3, 38.
s Gn 1, 27; Wis 2, 23;
  Sir 17, 1; 1 Cor 11, 7;
  Jas 3, 9.
t Gn 4, 25.
u 3-32: 1 Chr 1, 1-4; Lk

3, 36ff.
v Wis 4, 10f; Sir 44, 16;
  49, 14; Heb 11, 5.
w Gn 3, 17ff.
x Gn 6, 10; 10, 1.

---

*

''God,'' instead of Yahweh, ''Lord,'' for the pre-Mosaic period), makes Moses the first to use Yahweh as the proper name of Israel's God, previously known by other names as well; cf Ex 3, 13ff.

5, 1–32: Although this chapter, with its highly schematic form, belongs to the relatively late ''Priestly document,'' it is based on very ancient traditions. Together with Gn 11, 10–26, its primary purpose is to bridge the genealogical gap between Adam and Abraham. Adam's line is traced through Seth, but several names in the series are the same as, or similar to, certain names in Cain's line (Gn 4, 17ff). The long lifespans attributed to these ten antediluvian patriarchs have a symbolic rather than a historical value. Babylonian tradition also recorded ten kings with fantastically high ages who reigned successively before the flood.

5, 24: In place of the usual formula, Then he died, the change to Enoch walked with God clearly implies that he did not die, but like Elijah (2 Kgs 2, 11f) was taken alive to God's abode.

5, 29: There is a similarity in sound between the Hebrew word noah, ''Noah,'' and the verbal phrase yenahamenu, ''he will bring us relief''; this latter refers both to the curse put on the soil because of the fall of man (Gn 3, 17ff) and to Noah's success in agriculture, especially in raising grapes for wine (Gn 9, 20f).

6, 1–4: This is apparently a fragment of an old legend that had borrowed much from ancient mythology. The sacred author incorporates it here, not only in order to account for the prehistoric giants of Palestine, whom the Israelites called the Nephilim, but also to introduce the story of the flood with a moral orientation—the constantly increasing wickedness of mankind.

born to them, **2** the sons of heaven* saw how beautiful the daughters of man were, and so they took for their wives as many of them as they chose.*y* **3** Then the LORD said: "My spirit* shall not remain in man forever, since he is but flesh. His days shall comprise one hundred and twenty years."

4 At that time the Nephilim appeared on earth (as well as later*), after the sons of heaven had intercourse with the daughters of man, who bore them sons. They were the heroes of old, the men of renown.*z*

Warning of the Flood.

5 *When the LORD saw how great was man's wickedness on earth, and how no desire that his heart conceived was ever anything but evil,*a* **6** he regretted that he had made man on the earth, and his heart was grieved.

7 So the LORD said: "I will wipe out from the earth the men whom I have created, and not only the men, but also the beasts and the creeping things and the birds of the air, for I am sorry that I made them." **8** But Noah found favor with the LORD.

9 These are the descendants of Noah. Noah, a good man and blameless in that age,*b* **10** for he walked with God, begot three sons: Shem, Ham and Japheth.

11 In the eyes of God the earth was corrupt and full of lawlessness.*c* **12** When God saw how corrupt the earth had become, since all mortals led depraved lives on earth,*d* **13** he said to Noah: "I have decided to put an end to all mortals on earth; the earth is full of lawlessness because of them. So I will destroy them and all life on earth.*e*

Preparation for the Flood.

14 "Make yourself an ark of gopherwood,* put various compartments in it, and cover it inside and out with pitch. **15** This is how you shall build it: the length of the ark shall be three hundred cubits, its width fifty cubits, and its height thirty cubits.* **16** Make an opening for daylight* in the ark, and finish the ark a cubit above it. Put an entrance in the side of the ark, which you shall make with bottom, second and third decks. **17** I, on my part, am about to bring the flood [waters] on the earth, to destroy everywhere all creatures in which there is the breath of life; everything on earth shall perish.*f* **18** But with you I will establish my covenant; you and your sons, your wife and your sons' wives, shall go into the ark.*g* **19** Of all other living creatures you shall bring two into the ark, one male and one female, that you may keep them alive with you. **20** Of all kinds of birds, of all kinds of beasts, and of all kinds of creeping things, two of each shall come into the ark with you, to stay alive. **21** Moreover, you are to provide yourself

with all the food that is to be eaten, and store it away, that it may serve as provisions for you and for them." **22** This Noah did; he carried out all the commands that God gave him.

CHAPTER 7

1 Then the LORD said to Noah: "Go into the ark, you and all your household, for you alone in this age have I found to be truly just.*h* **2** Of every clean animal, take with you seven pairs, a male and its mate; and of the unclean animals, one pair, a male and its mate; **3** likewise, of every clean bird of the air, seven pairs, a male and a female, and of all the unclean birds, one pair, a male and a female. Thus you will keep their issue alive over all the earth. **4** Seven days from now I will bring rain down on the earth for forty days and forty nights, and so I will wipe

y Mt 24, 38; Lk 17, 26f.   24, 37ff.
z Wis 14, 6; Bar 3, 26.   f Gn 7, 4. 21; 2 Pt 2, 5.
a Ps 14, 2f.   g Gn 9, 9; Wis 14, 6;
b Wis 10, 4; Sir 44, 17.   Heb 11, 7; 1 Pt 3, 20.
c Jb 22, 15ff.   h Wis 10, 4; Sir 44, 17;
d Ps 14, 2.   2 Pt 2, 5.
e Sir 40, 9f; 44, 17; Mt   i Gn 6, 17; 2 Pt 2, 5.

*

6, 2: The sons of heaven: literally "the sons of the gods" or "the sons of God," i.e., the celestial beings of mythology.

6, 3: My spirit: the breath of life referred to in Gn 2, 7. His days . . . years: probably the time God would still let men live on earth before destroying them with the flood, rather than the maximum span of life God would allot to individual men in the future.

6, 4: As well as later: According to Nm 13, 33, when the Israelites invaded Palestine and found there the tall aboriginal Anakim, they likened them to the Nephilim; cf Dt 2, 10f. Perhaps the huge megalithic structures in Palestine were thought to have been built by a race of giants, whose superhuman strength was attributed to semi-divine origin. The heroes of old: the legendary worthies of ancient mythology.

6, 5—8, 22: The story of the great flood here recorded is a composite narrative based on two separate sources interwoven into an intricate patchwork. To the Yahwist source, with some later editorial additions, are usually assigned 6, 5–8; 7, 1–5. 7–10. 12. 16b. 17b. 22–23; 8, 2b–3a. 6–12. 13b. 20–22. The other sections come from the "Priestly document." The combination of the two sources produced certain duplications (e.g., 6, 13–22 of the Yahwist source, beside 7, 1–5 of the Priestly source); also certain inconsistencies, such as the number of the various animals taken into the ark (6, 19f; 7, 14f of the Priestly source, beside 7, 2f of the Yahwist source), and the timetable of the flood (8, 3–5. 13f of the Priestly source, beside 7, 4. 10. 12. 17b; 8, 6. 10. 12 of the Yahwist source). Both biblical sources go back ultimately to an ancient Mesopotamian story of a great flood, preserved in the eleventh tablet of the Gilgamesh Epic. The latter account, in some respects remarkably similar to the biblical account, is in others very different from it.

6, 14: Gopherwood: an unidentified wood not mentioned elsewhere; gopher is merely the Hebrew word for it.

6, 15: The dimensions of Noah's ark were approximately 440 × 73 × 44 feet, a foot and a half to the cubit. The ark of the Babylonian flood story was an exact cube, 120 cubits in length, width, and height.

6, 16: Opening for daylight: a conjectural rendering of the Hebrew word sohar, occurring only here. The reference is probably to an open space on all sides near the top of the ark to admit light and air. The ark also had a window or hatch, which could be opened and closed (Gn 8. 6).

out from the surface of the earth every moving creature that I have made."[i] 5 Noah did just as the LORD had commanded him.

The Great Flood. 6 Noah was six hundred years old when the flood waters came upon the earth. 7 Together with his sons, his wife, and his sons' wives, Noah went into the ark because of the waters of the flood.[j] 8 Of the clean animals and the unclean, of the birds, and of everything that creeps on the ground, 9 [two by two] male and female entered the ark with Noah, just as the LORD had commanded him.[k] 10 As soon as the seven days were over, the waters of the flood came upon the earth.

11 In the six hundredth year of Noah's life, in the second month, on the seventeenth day of the month: it was on that day that

> All the fountains of the great abyss* burst forth,
> and the floodgates of the sky were opened.

12 For forty days and forty nights heavy rain poured down on the earth.

13 On the precise day named, Noah and his sons Shem, Ham and Japheth, and Noah's wife, and the three wives of Noah's sons had entered the ark, 14 together with every kind of wild beast, every kind of domestic animal, every kind of creeping thing of the earth, and every kind of bird. 15 Pairs of all creatures in which there was the breath of life entered the ark with Noah. 16 Those that entered were male and female, and of all species they came, as God had commanded Noah. Then the LORD shut him in.

17 The flood continued upon the earth for forty days. As the waters increased, they lifted the ark, so that it rose above the earth. 18 The swelling waters increased greatly, but the ark floated on the surface of the waters. 19 Higher and higher above the earth rose the waters, until all the highest mountains everywhere were submerged, 20 the crest rising fifteen cubits higher than the submerged mountains. 21 All creatures that stirred on earth perished: birds, cattle, wild animals, and all that swarmed on the earth, as well as all mankind.[l] 22 Everything on dry land with the faintest breath of life in its nostrils died out. 23 The LORD wiped out every living thing on earth: man and cattle, the creeping things and the birds of the air; all were wiped out from the earth. Only Noah and those with him in the ark were left.

CHAPTER 8

7, 24 *The waters maintained their crest over the earth for one hundred and fifty days, 1 and then God remembered Noah and all the animals, wild and tame, that were with him in

the ark. So God made a wind sweep over the earth, and the waters began to subside. 2 The fountains of the abyss and the floodgates of the sky were closed, and the downpour from the sky was held back. 3 Gradually the waters receded from the earth. At the end of one hundred and fifty days, the waters had so diminished 4 that, in the seventh month, on the seventeenth day of the month, the ark came to rest on the mountains of Ararat.* 5 The waters continued to diminish until the tenth month, and on the first day of the tenth month the tops of the mountains appeared.

6 At the end of forty days Noah opened the hatch he had made in the ark,* 7 and he sent out a raven, to see if the waters had lessened on the earth. It flew back and forth until the waters dried off from the earth. 8 Then he sent out a dove, to see if the waters had lessened on the earth. 9 But the dove could find no place to alight and perch, and it returned to him in the ark, for there was water all over the earth. Putting out his hand, he caught the dove and drew it back to him inside the ark. 10 He waited seven days more and again sent the dove out from the ark. 11 In the evening the dove came back to him, and there in its bill was a plucked-off olive leaf! So Noah knew that the waters had lessened on the earth. 12 He waited still another seven days and then released the dove once more; and this time it did not come back.

13 In the six hundred and first year of Noah's life, in the first month, on the first day of the month, the water began to dry up on the earth. Noah then removed the covering of the ark and saw that the surface of the ground was drying up. 14 In the second month, on the twenty-seventh day of the month, the earth was dry.

15 Then God said to Noah: 16 "Go out of the ark, together with your wife and your sons and your sons' wives. 17 Bring out with you every living thing that is with you—all bodily creatures, be they birds or animals or creeping things of the earth—and let them abound on the earth, breeding and multiplying on it."[m] 18 So Noah came out, together with his wife and his sons and his sons' wives; 19 and all the ani-

---

j Wis 14, 6; 1 Pt 3, 20;   39; Lk 17, 27; 2 Pt 3,
  2 Pt 2, 5.   6.
k Gn 6, 19.   m Gn 1, 22. 28.
l 21ff; Jb 22, 16; Mt 24,

*

7, 11: Abyss: the subterranean ocean; see note on Gn 1, 2.

7, 24: This verse belongs to chapter 7 but its contents properly introduce chapter 8.

8, 4: Ararat: ancient Urartu, north of the Mesopotamian plain, part of modern Armenia.

8, 6: In the original Yahwist source, from which this verse is taken, the forty days refer to the full period of the flood itself (cf Gn 7, 4. 17); in the present context, however, they seem to refer to a period following the date just given in v 5 from the Priestly source.

mals, wild and tame, all the birds, and all the creeping creatures of the earth left the ark, one kind after another.

20 Then Noah built an altar to the LORD, and choosing from every clean animal and every clean bird, he offered holocausts on the altar. **21** When the LORD smelled the sweet odor, he said to himself: "Never again will I doom the earth because of man, since the desires of man's heart are evil from the start;* nor will I ever again strike down all living beings, as I have done. [n]

22 As long as the earth lasts,
     seedtime and harvest,
        cold and heat,
     Summer and winter,
        and day and night
        shall not cease." [o]

CHAPTER 9

Covenant with Noah. **1** God blessed Noah and his sons and said to them: "Be fertile and multiply and fill the earth. [p] **2** Dread fear of you shall come upon all the animals of the earth and all the birds of the air, upon all the creatures that move about on the ground and all the fishes of the sea; into your power they are delivered. **3** [q]Every creature that is alive shall be yours to eat; I give them all to you as I did the green plants.* **4** [r]Only flesh with its lifeblood still in it you shall not eat.* **5** For your own lifeblood, too, I will demand an accounting: from every animal I will demand it, and from man in regard to his fellow man I will demand an accounting for human life. [s]

6 If anyone sheds the blood of man,
     by man shall his blood be shed;
  For in the image of God
     has man been made. [t]

7 Be fertile, then, and multiply; abound on earth and subdue it." [u]

8 God said to Noah and to his sons with him: **9** "See, I am now establishing my covenant with you and your descendants after you [v] **10** and with every living creature that was with you: all the birds, and the various tame and wild animals that were with you and came out of the ark. **11** I will establish my covenant with you, that never again shall all bodily creatures be destroyed by the waters of a flood; there shall not be another flood to devastate the earth." [w] **12** God added: "This is the sign that I am giving for all ages to come, of the covenant between me and you and every living creature with you: **13** [x]I set my bow in the clouds to serve as a sign of the covenant between me and the earth. **14** When I bring clouds over the earth, and the bow appears in the clouds, **15** I will recall the covenant I have made between me and you and

all living beings, so that the waters shall never again become a flood to destroy all mortal beings. [y] **16** As the bow appears in the clouds, I will see it and recall the everlasting covenant that I have established between God and all living beings—all mortal creatures that are on earth." **17** God told Noah: "This is the sign of the covenant I have established between me and all mortal creatures that are on earth."

Noah and His Sons. **18** *The sons of Noah who came out of the ark were Shem, Ham and Japheth. (Ham was the father of Canaan.) [z] **19** These three were the sons of Noah, and from them the whole earth was peopled.

20 Now Noah, a man of the soil, was the first to plant a vineyard. **21** When he drank some of the wine, he became drunk and lay naked inside his tent. [a] **22** Ham, the father of Canaan, saw his father's nakedness, and he told his two brothers outside about it. **23** Shem and Japheth, however, took a robe, and holding it on their backs, they walked backward and covered their father's nakedness; since their faces were turned the other way, they did not see their father's nakedness. **24** When Noah woke up from his drunkenness and learned what his youngest son had done to him, **25** he said:

  "Cursed be Canaan!
     The lowest of slaves
        shall he be to his brothers." [b]

---

n Sir 44, 18; Is 54, 9;
  Rom 7, 18.
o Jer 33, 20. 25.
p Gn 1, 22, 28; 8, 17;
  Jas 3, 7.
q Gn 1, 29f; Dt 12, 15.
r Lv 7, 26f; 17, 4; Dt 12,
  16. 23; 1 Sm 14, 33;
  Acts 15, 20.
s Gn 4, 10f; Ex 21, 12.

t Gn 1, 26f; Lv 24, 17;
  Nm 35, 33; Jas 3, 9.
u Gn 1, 28; 8, 17; 9, 2.
v Gn 6, 18.
w Sir 44, 18; Is 54, 9.
x Sir 43, 12.
y Is 54, 9.
z Gn 5, 32; 10, 1.
a Lam 4, 21; Heb 2, 15.
b Dt 27, 16; Wis 12, 11.

*

8, 21: From the start: literally "from his youth." It is uncertain whether this means from the beginning of the human race or from the early years of the individual.

9, 3: Antediluvian creatures, including man, are depicted as vegetarians (Gn 1, 29f), becoming carnivorous only after the flood.

9, 4: Because a living being dies when it loses most of its blood, the ancients regarded blood as the seat of life, and therefore as sacred. Although in itself the prohibition against eating meat with blood in it is comparable to the ritual laws of the Mosaic code, the Jews considered it binding on all men, because it was given by God to Noah, the new ancestor of all mankind; therefore the early Christian Church retained it for a time (Acts 15, 20. 29).

9, 18–27: This story seems to be a composite of two earlier accounts; in the one, Ham was guilty, whereas in the other, it was Canaan. One purpose of the story is to justify the Israelites' enslavement of the Canaanites because of certain indecent sexual practices in the Canaanite religion. Obviously the story offers no justification for enslaving African Negroes, even though Canaan is presented as a "son" of Ham because the land of Canaan belonged to Hamitic Egypt at the time of the Israelite invasion.

26 He also said:

"Blessed be the LORD, the God of Shem!*
Let Canaan be his slave.
27 May God expand Japheth,*
so that he dwells among the tents of
Shem;
and let Canaan be his slave."

28 Noah lived three hundred and fifty years after the flood. **29** The whole lifetime of Noah was nine hundred and fifty years; then he died.

CHAPTER 10

Table of the Nations.* **1** These are the descendants of Noah's sons, Shem, Ham and Japheth, to whom sons were born after the flood.

2 cThe descendants of Japheth:
Gomer,* Magog, Madai, Javan, Tubal,
Meschech and Tiras. d
3 The descendants of Gomer:
Ashkenaz,* Riphath and Togarmah.
4 The descendants of Javan:
Elishah,* Tarshish, the Kittim and the
Rodanim.

5 These are the descendants of Japheth, and from them sprang the maritime nations, in their respective lands—each with its own language —by their clans within their nations.

6 The descendants of Ham:
Cush,* Mizraim, Put and Canaan.
7 The descendants of Cush:
Seba, Havilah, Sabtah, Raamah and
Sabteca.
The descendants of Raamah: Sheba and
Dedan.

8 Cush* became the father of Nimrod, who was the first potentate on earth. **9** He was a mighty hunter by the grace of the LORD; hence the saying, "Like Nimrod, a mighty hunter by the grace of the LORD." **10** The chief cities of his kingdom were Babylon, Erech and Accad, all of them in the land of Shinar.* **11** From that land he went forth to Asshur,* where he built Nineveh, Rehoboth-Ir and Calah, **12** as well as Resen, between Nineveh and Calah,* the latter being the principal city.

13 eMizraim became the father of the Ludim, the Anamim, the Lehabim, the Naphtuhim, **14** the Pathrusim,* the Casluhim, and the Caphtorim from whom the Philistines sprang.

15 Canaan became the father of Sidon, his first-born, and of Heth;* **16** also of the Jebusites, the Amorites, the Girgashites, **17** the Hivites, the Arkites, the Sinites, **18** the Arvadites, the Zemarites and the Hamathites. Afterward, the clans of the Canaanites spread out, **19** so that the Canaanite borders extended from Sidon all the way to Gerar, near Gaza, and all the way to Sodom, Gomorrah, Admah and Zeboiim, near Lasha.*

20 These are the descendants of Ham, according to their clans and languages, by their lands and nations.

21 To Shem also, Japheth's oldest brother and the ancestor of all the children of Eber, sons were born.

22 fThe descendants of Shem:
Elam, Asshur, Arpachshad, Lud and
Aram.
23 The descendants of Aram:
Uz, Hul, Gether and Mash.

24 Arpachshad became the father of Shelah,

---

c 2-8: 1 Chr 1, 5-10.   e 13-18: 1 Chr 1, 11-16.
d Ez 38, 2.   f 22-29: 1 Chr 1, 17-23.

*

9, 26: Blessed . . . Shem: perhaps the text read originally, "Blessed of the Lord be Shem," which would be expected in the context.

9, 27: In the Hebrew text there is a play on the words yapt ("expand") and yepet ("Japheth").

10, 1-32: This chapter presents a remarkably good classification of the various peoples known to the ancient Israelites; it is theologically important as stressing the basic family unity of all men on earth. The relationship between the various peoples is based partly on linguistic, partly on geographic, and partly on political grounds according to their . . . languages, . . . lands and nations: (v 31). In general, the descendants of Japheth (vv 2–5) are the peoples of the Indo-European languages to the north and west of Mesopotamia and Syria; the descendants of Ham (vv 6–20) are the Hamitic-speaking peoples of northern Africa; and the descendants of Shem (vv 21–31) are the Semitic-speaking peoples of Mesopotamia, Syria and Arabia. But there are many exceptions to this rule; the Semitic-speaking peoples of Canaan, for instance, are considered descendants of Ham, because at the time they were subject to Hamitic Egypt (vv 6. 15–19). This chapter is a composite from the Yahwist source (vv 8–19. 21. 24–30) of about the ninth century B.C., and the Priestly source (vv 1–7. 20. 22f. 31f) of a few centuries later. That is why certain tribes of Arabia are listed under both Ham (v 7) and Shem (vv 26ff).

10, 2: Gomer: the Cimmerians; Madai: the Medes; Javan: the Greeks.

10, 3: Ashkenaz: the Scythians.

10, 4: Elishah: Cyprus; the Kittim: certain inhabitants of Cyprus; the Rodanim: the inhabitants of Rhodes.

10, 6: Cush: Biblical Ethiopia, modern Nubia. Mizraim: Egypt; Put: either Punt in East Africa or Libya.

10, 8: Cush: here, the Kassites; see note on Gn 2, 10–14. Nimrod: probably Tukulti-Ninurta I (thirteenth century B.C.), the first Assyrian conqueror of Babylonia and a famous city-builder at home.

10, 10: Shinar: ancient Sumer in southern Mesopotamia, mentioned also in Gn 11, 2; 14, 1.

10, 11: Asshur: Assyria. Rehoboth-Ir: literally "wide-streets city," was probably not the name of another city, but an epithet of Nineveh; cf Jon 3, 3.

10, 12: Calah: Assyrian Kalhu, the capital of Assyria in the ninth century B.C.

10, 14: The Pathrusim: the people of upper (southern) Egypt; cf Is 11, 11; Jer 44, 1; Ez 29, 14; 30, 14. Caphtorim: Crete; for Caphtor as the place of origin of the Philistines, cf Dt 2, 23; Am 9, 7; Jer 47, 4.

10, 15: Heth: the biblical Hittites; see note on Gn 23, 3.

10, 19: Lasha: the reading of this name is uncertain; perhaps it should be "Bela"; cf Gn 14, 2.

and Shelah became the father of Eber. **25** To Eber two sons were born: the name of the first was Peleg, for in his time the world was divided;* and the name of his brother was Joktan.

26 Joktan became the father of Almodad, Sheleph, Hazarmaveth, Jerah, **27** Hadoram, Uzal, Diklah, **28** Obal, Abimael, Sheba **29** Ophir, Havilah and Jobab. All these were descendants of Joktan. **30** Their settlements extended all the way to Sephar, the eastern hill country.

31 These are the descendants of Shem, according to their clans and languages, by their lands and nations.

32 These are the groupings of Noah's sons, according to their origins and by their nations. From these the other nations of the earth branched out after the flood.

CHAPTER 11

The Tower of Babel.*   1 The whole world spoke the same language, using the same words. **2** While men were migrating in the east, they came upon a valley in the land of Shinar* and settled there. **3** They said to one another, "Come, let us mold bricks and harden them with fire." They used bricks for stone, and bitumen for mortar. **4** Then they said, "Come, let us build ourselves a city and a tower with its top in the sky,* and so make a name for ourselves; otherwise we shall be scattered all over the earth."

5 The LORD came down to see the city and the tower that the men had built. **6** Then the LORD said: "If now, while they are one people, all speaking the same language, they have started to do this, nothing will later stop them from doing whatever they presume to do. **7** Let us then go down and there confuse their language, so that one will not understand what another says." **8** Thus the LORD scattered them from there all over the earth, and they stopped building the city. **9** That is why it was called Babel,* because there the LORD confused the speech of all the world. It was from that place that he scattered them all over the earth.

The Line from Shem to Abraham.*

10 *g*This is the record of the descendants of Shem. When Shem was one hundred years old, he became the father of Arpachshad, two years after the flood. **11** Shem lived five hundred years after the birth of Arpachshad, and he had other sons and daughters.

12 When Arpachshad was thirty-five years old, he became the father of Shelah.* **13** Arpachshad lived four hundred and three years after the birth of Shelah, and he had other sons and daughters.

14 When Shelah was thirty years old, he be-

came the father of Eber. **15** Shelah lived four hundred and three years after the birth of Eber, and he had other sons and daughters.

16 When Eber* was thirty-four years old, he became the father of Peleg. **17** Eber lived four hundred and thirty years after the birth of Peleg, and he had other sons and daughters.

18 When Peleg was thirty years old, he became the father of Reu. **19** Peleg lived two hundred and nine years after the birth of Reu, and he had other sons and daughters.

20 When Reu was thirty-two years old, he became the father of Serug. **21** Reu lived two hundred and seven years after the birth of Serug, and he had other sons and daughters.

22 When Serug was thirty years old, he became the father of Nahor. **23** Serug lived two hundred years after the birth of Nahor, and he had other sons and daughters.

24 When Nahor was twenty-nine years old, he became the father of Terah. **25** Nahor lived one hundred and nineteen years after the birth of Terah, and he had other sons and daughters.

26 When Terah was seventy years old, he became the father of Abram, Nahor and Haran. *h*

---

g 10-26: 1 Chr 1, 24-27;   h Jos 24, 2; 1 Chr 1, 27.
Lk 3, 34ff.

* ———————————

10, 25: In the Hebrew text there is a play on the name Peleg and the word niplega, "was divided."

11, 1–9: This story, based on traditions about the temple towers or ziggurats of Babylonia, is used by the sacred writer primarily to illustrate man's increasing wickedness, shown here in his presumptuous effort to create an urban culture apart from God. The secondary motive in the story is to present an imaginative origin of the diversity of the languages among the various peoples inhabiting the earth, as well as an artificial explanation of the name "Babylon."

11, 2: Shinar: see note on Gn 10, 10.

11, 4: Tower with its top in the sky: a direct reference to the chief ziggurat of Babylon, the E-sag-ila, signifying "the house that raises high its head." Babylonian ziggurats were the earliest skyscrapers.

11, 9: Babel: the Hebrew form of the name "Babylon"; the native name, Bab-ili, means "gate of the gods." The Hebrew word balil, "he confused," has a similar sound. Apparently the name referred originally only to a certain part of the city, the district near the gate that led to the temple area.

11, 10–26: This section is a continuation of the genealogical record given in Gn 5, 1–32; see note there. Although the ages of the patriarchs in this list are much lower than those of the antediluvian patriarchs, they are still artificial and devoid of historical value. The ages given here are from the current Hebrew text; the Samaritan and Greek texts have divergent sets of numbers in most cases.

11, 12: The Greek text has a certain Kenan (cf Gn 5, 9f) between Arpachshad and Shelah. The text is followed in Lk 3, 36.

11, 16: Eber: the eponymous ancestor of the Hebrews, "descendants of Eber" (Gn 10, 21. 24–30); see note on Gn 14, 13.

II: The Patriarch Abraham

Terah.   **27** This is the record of the descendants of Terah. Terah became the father of Abram, Nahor and Haran, and Haran became the father of Lot. **28** Haran died before his father Terah, in his native land, in Ur of the Chaldeans.* **29** Abram and Nahor took wives; the name of Abram's wife was Sarai, and the name of Nahor's wife was Milcah, daughter of Haran, the father of Milcah and Iscah.[i] **30** Sarai was barren; she had no child.

31 Terah took his son Abram, his grandson Lot, son of Haran, and his daughter-in-law Sarai, the wife of his son Abram, and brought them out of Ur of the Chaldeans, to go to the land of Canaan.* But when they reached Haran, they settled there.[j] **32** The lifetime of Terah was two hundred and five years; then Terah died in Haran.*

CHAPTER 12

Abram's Call and Migration.   **1** The LORD said to Abram: ''Go forth from the land of your kinsfolk and from your father's house to a land that I will show you.[k]

2 ''I will make of you a great nation,
    and I will bless you;
I will make your name great,
    so that you will be a blessing.[l]
3 [m]I will bless those who bless you
    and curse those who curse you.
All the communities of the earth
    shall find blessing in you.''*

4 [n]Abram went as the LORD directed him, and Lot went with him. Abram was seventy-five years old when he left Haran. **5** Abram took his wife Sarai, his brother's son Lot, all the possessions that they had accumulated, and the persons* they had acquired in Haran, and they set out for the land of Canaan. When they came to the land of Canaan, **6** Abram passed through the land as far as the sacred place at Shechem, by the terebinth of Moreh. (The Canaanites were then in the land.)

7 The LORD appeared to Abram and said, ''To your descendants I will give this land.'' So Abram built an altar there to the LORD who had appeared to him.[o] **8** From there he moved on to the hill country east of Bethel, pitching his tent with Bethel to the west and Ai to the east. He built an altar there to the LORD and invoked the LORD by name. **9** Then Abram journeyed on by stages to the Negeb.*

Abram and Sarai in Egypt.   **10** There was famine in the land; so Abram went down to Egypt to sojourn there, since the famine in the land was severe.[p] **11** When he was about to enter Egypt, he said to his wife Sarai: ''I know well how beautiful a woman you are. **12** When the Egyptians see you, they will say, 'She is his wife'; then they will kill me, but let you live. **13** Please say, therefore, that you are my sister,* so that it may go well with me on your account and my life may be spared for your sake.''[q] **14** When Abram came to Egypt, the Egyptians saw how beautiful the woman was; **15** and when Pharaoh's courtiers saw her, they praised her to Pharaoh. So she was taken into Pharaoh's palace. **16** On her account it went very well with Abram, and he received flocks and herds, male and female slaves, male and female asses, and camels.*

---

i Gn 17, 15; 20, 12.
j Jos 24, 3; Neh 9, 7; Jdt
  5, 6-9; Acts 7, 4.
k Acts 7, 3; Heb 11, 8.
l Gn 17, 6; Sir 44, 20;
  Rom 4, 17-22.
m Gn 18, 18; 22, 18;

n 4f: Gn 11, 31; Jos 24,
  3; Acts 7, 4.
o Ex 33, 1; Dt 34, 4;
  Acts 7, 5.
p Gn 26, 1.
q Gn 20, 12f; 26, 7.

*

11, 28: Ur of the Chaldeans: Ur was an extremely ancient city of the Sumerians (later, of the Babylonians) in southern Mesopotamia. The Greek text has ''the land of the Chaldeans.'' In either case, the term Chaldeans is an anachronism, because the Chaldeans were not known to history until approximately a thousand years after Abraham's time.

11, 31: The Samaritan and Greek texts include Nahor and his wife in Terah's migration to Haran. Although this is probably due to scribal harmonization, Nahor's family actually did migrate to Haran; cf Gn 24, 10; 27, 43.

11, 32: Since Terah was seventy years old when his son Abraham was born (v 26), and Abraham was seventy-five when he left Haran (Gn 12, 4), Terah lived in Haran for sixty years after Abraham's departure. According to the tradition in the Samaritan text, Terah died when he was one hundred and forty-five years old, therefore, in the same year in which Abraham left Haran. This is the tradition followed in St. Stephen's speech: Abraham left Haran ''after his father's death'' (Acts 7, 4).

12, 3: Shall find blessing in you: the sense of the Hebrew expression is probably reflexive, ''shall bless themselves through you'' (i.e., in giving a blessing they shall say, ''May you be as blessed as Abraham''), rather than passive, ''shall be blessed in you.'' Since the term is understood in a passive sense in the New Testament (Acts 3, 25; Gal 3, 8), it is rendered here by a neutral expression that admits of both meanings. So also in the blessings given by God to Isaac (Gn 26, 4) and Jacob (Gn 28, 14).

12, 5: Persons: slaves and retainers that formed the social aggregate under the leadership of Abraham; cf Gn 14, 14.

12, 9: The Negeb: the semidesert land of southern Palestine.

12, 13: You are my sister: although Abraham's deceit may not be fully defensible, his statement was at least a half-truth; Sarah was indeed his relative, called ''a sister'' in Hebrew; cf Gn 20, 12. Moreover, the ancient traditions on which this story and the parallel ones in Gn 20, 1–18 and 26, 6–11 are based, probably come from the Hurrian custom of wife-sister marriage. Among the Hurrians, with whom Abraham's clan lived in close contact at Haran, a man could adopt his wife as his sister and thus give her higher status.

12, 16: Camels: domesticated camels probably did not come into common use in the ancient Near East until the end of the 2nd millennium B.C. Thus the mention of camels at the time of the patriarchs (Gn 24, 11–64; 30, 43; 31, 17. 34; 32, 8. 16; 37, 25) is seemingly an anachronism.

17 But the LORD struck Pharaoh and his household with severe plagues because of Abram's wife Sarai.ʳ **18** Then Pharaoh summoned Abram and said to him: "How could you do this to me! Why didn't you tell me she was your wife? **19** Why did you say, 'She is my sister,' so that I took her for my wife? Here, then, is your wife. Take her and be gone!"

20 Then Pharaoh gave men orders concerning him, and they sent him on his way, with his wife and all that belonged to him.

CHAPTER 13

Abram and Lot Part.   **1** From Egypt Abram went up to the Negeb with his wife and all that belonged to him, and Lot accompanied him.ˢ **2** Now Abram was very rich in livestock, silver and gold.ᵗ **3** From the Negeb he traveled by stages toward Bethel, to the place between Bethel and Ai where his tent had formerly stood, **4** The site where he had first built the altar; and there he invoked the LORD by name.ᵘ

5 Lot, who went with Abram, also had flocks and herds and tents, **6** so that the land could not support them if they stayed together; their possessions were so great that they could not dwell together. **7** There were quarrels between the herdsmen of Abram's livestock and those of Lot's. (At this time the Canaanites and the Perizzites were occupying the land.)

8 So Abram said to Lot: "Let there be no strife between you and me, or between your herdsmen and mine, for we are kinsmen. **9** Is not the whole land at your disposal? Please separate from me. If you prefer the left, I will go to the right; if you prefer the right, I will go to the left." **10** Lot looked about and saw how well watered the whole Jordan Plain was as far as Zoar, like the LORD'S own garden, or like Egypt. (This was before the LORD had destroyed Sodom and Gomorrah.) **11** Lot, therefore, chose for himself the whole Jordan Plain and set out eastward. Thus they separated from each other; **12** Abram stayed in the land of Canaan, while Lot settled among the cities of the Plain, pitching his tents near Sodom. **13** Now the inhabitants of Sodom were very wicked in the sins they committed against the LORD.ᵛ

14 After Lot had left, the LORD said to Abram: "Look about you, and from where you are, gaze to the north and south, east and west;ʷ **15** all the land that you see I will give to you and your descendants forever.ˣ **16** I will make your descendants like the dust of the earth; if anyone could count the dust of the earth, your descendants too might be counted.ʸ **17** Set forth and walk about in the land, through its length and breadth, for to you I will give it." **18** Abram moved his tents and went on to settle near the terebinth of Mamre, which is at Hebron. There he built an altar to the LORD.ᶻ

CHAPTER 14

The Four Kings.   **1** In the days of . . . ,* Amraphel king of Shinar, Arioch king of Ellasar, Chedorlaomer king of Elam, and Tidal king of Goiim **2** made war on Bera king of Sodom, Birsha king of Gomorrah, Shinab king of Admah, Shemeber king of Zeboiim, and the king of Bela (that is, Zoar). **3** All the latter kings joined forces in the Valley of Siddim (that is, the Salt Sea*). **4** For twelve years they had been subject to Chedorlaomer, but in the thirteenth year they rebelled. **5** *In the fourteenth year Chedorlaomer and the kings allied with him came and defeated the Rephaim in Ashteroth-karnaim, the Zuzim in Ham, the Emim in Shaveh-kiriathaim, **6** and the Horites in the hill country of Seir, as far as Elparan, close by the wilderness.ᵃ **7** They then turned back and came to Enmishpat (that is, Kadesh), and they subdued the whole country both of the Amalekites and of the Amorites who dwelt in Hazazon-tamar. **8** Thereupon the king of Sodom, the king of Gomorrah, the king of Admah, the king of Zeboiim, and the king of Bela (that is, Zoar) marched out, and in the Valley of Siddim they went into battle against them: **9** against Chedorlaomer king of Elam, Tidal king of Goiim, Amraphel king of Shinar, and Arioch king of Ellasar—four kings against five. **10** Now the Valley of Siddim was full of bitumen pits; and as the kings of Sodom and Gomorrah fled, they fell into these, while the rest fled to the mountains. **11** The victors seized all the possessions and food supplies of Sodom and Gomorrah and then went their way, **12** taking with them Abram's nephew Lot, who had been living in Sodom, as well as his possessions.ᵇ

13 A fugitive came and brought the news to Abram the Hebrew,* who was camping at the terebinth of Mamre the Amorite, a kinsman of Eshcol and Aner; these were in league with Abram. **14** When Abram heard that his nephew

---

r Ps 105, 14.
s Gn 12, 9.
t Ps 112, 1ff; Prv 10, 22.
u Gn 12, 8.
v Gn 18, 20; Ez 16, 49; 2 Pt 2, 6ff; Jude 1, 7.
w Gn 28, 14.

x Gn 12, 7; Mt 5, 4; Lk 1, 55; Acts 7, 5; Gal 3, 16.
y Gn 22, 17; Nm 23, 10.
z Gn 14, 13.
a Dt 2, 12.
b Gn 13, 10ff.

---

*

14, 1: In the days of . . . : the personal name by which the event is dated has not been preserved.

14, 3: The Salt Sea: now known as the Dead Sea.

14, 5f: The five kings came from north to south through the land east of the Jordan.

14, 13: Abram the Hebrew: elsewhere in the Old Testament, until the last pre-Christian centuries, the term "Hebrew" is used only by non-Israelites, or by Israelites in speaking to foreigners, since it evidently had a disparaging connotation —something like "immigrant." The account in this chapter may, therefore, have been taken originally from a non-Israelite source, in which Abraham, a warlike sheik of Palestine, appears as a truly historical figure of profane history.

had been captured, he mustered three hundred and eighteen of his retainers, born in his house, and went in pursuit as far as Dan. **15** He and his party deployed against them at night, defeated them, and pursued them as far as Hobah, which is north of Damascus. **16** He recovered all the possessions, besides bringing back his kinsman Lot and his possessions, along with the women and the other captives.

17 When Abram returned from his victory over Chedorlaomer and the kings who were allied with him, the king of Sodom went out to greet him in the Valley of Shaveh (that is, the King's Valley).

18 Melchizedek, king of Salem,* brought out bread and wine, and being a priest of God Most High,* he blessed Abram with these words: c

19 "Blessed be Abram by God Most High,*
the creator of heaven and earth;
20 And blessed be God Most High,
who delivered your foes into your hand."

Then Abram gave him* a tenth of everything.

21 The king of Sodom said to Abram, "Give me the people; the goods you may keep." **22** But Abram replied to the king of Sodom: "I have sworn to the LORD, God Most High,* the creator of heaven and earth, **23** that I would not take so much as a thread or a sandal strap from anything that is yours, lest you should say, 'I made Abram rich.' **24** Nothing for me except what my servants have used up and the share that is due to the men who joined me—Aner, Eshcol and Mamre; let them take their share."

CHAPTER 15

The Covenant with Abram.   **1** Some time after these events, this word of the LORD came to Abram in a vision:

"Fear not, Abram!
I am your shield;
I will make your reward very great."

2 But Abram said, "O Lord GOD, what good will your gifts be, if I keep on being childless and have as my heir the steward of my house, Eliezer?" **3** Abram continued, "See, you have given me no offspring, and so one of my servants will be my heir." **4** Then the word of the LORD came to him: "No, that one shall not be your heir; your own issue shall be your heir." d **5** He took him outside and said, "Look up at the sky and count the stars, if you can. Just so," he added, "shall your descendants be." e **6** f Abram put his faith in the LORD, who credited it to him as an act of righteousness.*

7 He then said to him, "I am the LORD who brought you from Ur of the Chaldeans to give you this land as a possession." g **8** "O Lord GOD," he asked, "how am I to know that I shall possess it?" **9** He answered him, "Bring me a three-year-old heifer, a three-year-old she-goat, a three-year-old* ram, a turtle-dove, and a young pigeon." h **10** He brought him all these, split them in two, and placed each half opposite the other; but the birds he did not cut up. **11** Birds of prey swooped down on the carcasses, but Abram stayed with them. **12** As the sun was about to set, a trance fell upon Abram, and a deep, terrifying darkness enveloped him.

13 Then the LORD said to Abram: "Know for certain that your descendants shall be aliens in a land not their own, where they shall be enslaved and oppressed for four hundred years. i **14** But I will bring judgment on the nation they must serve, and in the end they will depart with great wealth. j **15** You, however, shall join your forefathers in peace; you shall be buried at a contented old age. **16** In the fourth time-span* the others shall come back here; the wickedness of the Amorites will not have reached its full measure until then." k

17 When the sun had set and it was dark,

---

c Ps 110, 4; Heb 5, 6.
10; 7, 1.
d Gn 17, 16.
e Gn 22, 17; 28, 14; Ex
32, 13; Dt 1, 10; Sir
44, 21; Rom 4, 18;
Heb 11, 12.
f 1 Mc 2, 52; Rom 4, 3.
9. 22; Gal 3, 6f; Jas
2, 23.
g Gn 11, 31; 12, 1; Ex
32, 13; Neh 9, 7f;
Acts 7, 2f.
h Lv 1, 14.
i Ex 12, 40; Nm 20, 15;
Jdt 5, 9f; Is 52, 4;
Acts 13, 20; Gal 3, 17.
j Ex 3, 8. 21f.
k 1 Kgs 21, 26.

*

14, 18: Salem: traditionally identified with Jerusalem (Ps 76, 3), but the Hebrew text is not certain; instead of the present melek shalem ("king of Salem") the original may have been melek shelomo ("a king allied to him"). In Heb 7, 2, "king of Salem" is interpreted as "king of peace" (shalom).

14, 19: God most High: in Hebrew, el-elyon. In Canaanite texts, each element may occur separately as the name of a specific deity, or they may be applied together to a single deity, as is done here by the Canaanite priest Melchizedek. For the Israelites, el became a poetic synonym for elohim ("God"); elyon ("Most High") became one of the titles of their God Yahweh.

14, 20: Abram gave him: literally "he gave him"; but Abram is to be understood as the subject of the sentence, for the tithes were the tenth part assigned to priests; cf Heb 7, 4–10.

14, 22: Abraham uses the name of the Canaanite god el-elyon ("God, the Most High") in apposition to the name of his God, yahweh ("the Lord").

15, 6: Abraham's faith in God's promises was regarded as an act of righteousness, i.e., as expressing the "right" attitude of man toward God. In turn, God credited this to Abraham, i.e., gave him title to the fulfillment of God's promises. St. Paul (Rom 4, 1–25; Gal 3, 6–9) makes Abraham's faith a model for that of Christians.

15, 9: Three-year-old: ritually mature.

15, 16: Time-span: the Hebrew term dor is commonly rendered as "generation," but it may signify a period of varying length. Neither this passage nor the statement about the four hundred years has any value for determining how long the Israelites were in Egypt.

15, 17: Brazier: literally "oven"; a portable one is meant here. The smoke and fire represent God's presence. Although the text does not mention it, Abraham no doubt also walked between the split carcasses. For the meaning of this strange

there appeared a smoking brazier* and a flaming torch, which passed between those pieces. **18** It was on that occasion that the LORD made a covenant* with Abram, saying: "To your descendants I give this land, from the Wadi of Egypt to the Great River [the Euphrates], *l* **19** *m*the land of the Kenites, the Kenizzites, the Kadmonites, **20** the Hittites, the Perizzites, the Rephaim, **21** the Amorites, the Canaanites, the Girgashites, and the Jebusites."

CHAPTER 16

Birth of Ishmael. **1** *Abram's wife Sarai had borne him no children. She had, however, an Egyptian maidservant named Hagar. *n* **2** Sarai said to Abram: "The LORD has kept me from bearing children. Have intercourse, then, with my maid; perhaps I shall have sons through her." Abram heeded Sarai's request. *o* **3** Thus, after Abram had lived ten years in the land of Canaan, his wife Sarai took her maid, Hagar the Egyptian, and gave her to her husband Abram to be his concubine. **4** He had intercourse with her, and she became pregnant. When she became aware of her pregnancy, she looked on her mistress with disdain. *p* **5** *q*So Sarai said to Abram: "You are responsible for this outrage against me. I myself gave my maid to your embrace; but ever since she became aware of her pregnancy, she has been looking on me with disdain. May the LORD decide between you and me!" **6** Abram told Sarai: "Your maid is in your power. Do to her whatever you please." Sarai then abused her so much that Hagar ran away from her.

7 The LORD's messenger* found her by a spring in the wilderness, the spring on the road to Shur, *r* **8** and he asked, "Hagar, maid of Sarai, where have you come from and where are you going?" She answered, "I am running away from my mistress, Sarai." **9** But the LORD's messenger told her: "Go back to your mistress and submit to her abusive treatment. **10** I will make your descendants so numerous," added the LORD's messenger, "that they will be too many to count. *s* **11** Besides," the LORD's messenger said to her:

"You are now pregnant and shall bear a son;
you shall name him Ishmael,*
For the LORD has heard you,
God has answered you.

12 He shall be a wild ass of a man,
his hand against everyone,
and everyone's hand against him;
In opposition to all his kin
shall he encamp." *t*

13 To the LORD who spoke to her she gave

a name, saying, "You are the God of Vision";* she meant, "Have I really seen God and remained alive after my vision?" *u* **14** That is why the well is called Beer-lahai-roi.* It is between Kadesh and Bered.

15 Hagar bore Abram a son, and Abram named the son whom Hagar bore him Ishmael. *v* **16** Abram was eighty-six years old when Hagar bore him Ishmael.

CHAPTER 17

Covenant of Circumcision. **1** When Abram was ninety-nine years old, the LORD appeared to him and said: "I am God the Almighty.* Walk in my presence and be blameless. *w* **2** Between you and me I will establish my covenant, and I will multiply you exceedingly." *x*

3 When Abram prostrated himself, God continued to speak to him: **4** "My covenant with you is this: you are to become the father of a host of nations. *y* **5** No longer shall you be called Abram; your name shall be Abraham,* for I am making you the father of a host of nations. *z* **6** I will render you exceedingly fertile; I will make nations of you; kings shall stem from you. **7** I will maintain my covenant with you and your descendants after you throughout the ages as an everlasting pact, to be your God and the God of your descendants after you. *a* **8** I will give to

---

l Ex 32, 13; Neh 9, 8; Ps 105, 11; Sir 44, 21.
m 19f: Dt 7, 1.
n Gn 11, 30.
o Gn 21, 8f; Gal 4, 22.
p 1 Sm 1, 6; Prv 30, 23.
q 5-16: Gn 21, 10-19.
r Ex 15, 22.
s Gn 17, 20; 21, 13. 18; 25, 12-18.
t Gn 21, 20; 25, 18.

u Gn 24, 62.
v Gn 16, 2; Gal 4, 22.
w Gn 35, 11; Ex 6, 3.
x Gn 12, 2; 13, 16; Ex 32, 13.
y Sir 44, 21; Rom 4, 17.
z Neh 9, 7.
a Ps 105, 42; Lk 1, 72f; Gal 3, 16.
b Ex 32, 13; Dt 1, 8; 14, 2; Lk 1, 55; Acts 7, 5.

---

* ceremony, see note on Jer 34, 18ff.

15, 18: Made a covenant: literally "cut a covenant"; the expression derives from the ceremony of cutting the animals in two.

16, 1–6: Sarah's actions are all in keeping with the laws of the time, as known from ancient extra-biblical sources.

16, 7: The Lord's messenger: a manifestation of God in human form; therefore in v 13 the messenger is identified with the Lord himself.

16, 11: Ishmael: in Hebrew the name means "God has heard."

16, 13: The God of Vision: in Hebrew, el-roi; hence the name of the spring. Remained alive: for the ancient notion that a person died on seeing God, cf Gn 32, 31; Ex 20, 19; Dt 4, 33; Jgs 13, 22.

16, 14: Beer-lahai-roi: probably "the well of living sight," i.e., the well where one can see (God) and yet live.

17, 1: The Almighty: traditional but incorrect rendering of the divine title shaddai, of uncertain meaning.

17, 5: Abram and Abraham are merely two forms of the same name, both meaning "the father is exalted"; another variant form is Abiram (Nm 16, 1; 1 Kgs 16, 34). The additional -ha- in the form Abraham is explained by folk etymology as coming from ab-hamon goyim, "father of a host of nations."

you and to your descendants after you the land in which you are now staying, the whole land of Canaan, as a permanent possession; and I will be their God.''[b]

9 God also said to Abraham: ''On your part, you and your descendants after you must keep my covenant throughout the ages. **10** This is my covenant with you and your descendants after you that you must keep: every male among you shall be circumcised.[c] **11** Circumcise the flesh of your foreskin, and that shall be the mark of the covenant between you and me.[d] **12** Throughout the ages, every male among you, when he is eight days old, shall be circumcised, including houseborn slaves and those acquired with money from any foreigner who is not of your blood.[e] **13** Yes, both the houseborn slaves and those acquired with money must be circumcised. Thus my covenant shall be in your flesh as an everlasting pact. **14** If a male is uncircumcised, that is, if the flesh of his foreskin has not been cut away, such a one shall be cut off from his people; he has broken my covenant.''

15 God further said to Abraham: ''As for your wife Sarai, do not call her Sarai; her name shall be Sarah.* **16** I will bless her, and I will give you a son by her. Him also will I bless; he shall give rise to nations, and rulers of peoples shall issue from him.''[f] **17** Abraham prostrated himself and laughed* as he said to himself, ''Can a child be born to a man who is a hundred years old? Or can Sarah give birth at ninety?''[g] **18** Then Abraham said to God, ''Let but Ishmael live on by your favor!'' **19** God replied: ''Nevertheless, your wife Sarah is to bear you a son, and you shall call him Isaac. I will maintain my covenant with him as an everlasting pact, to be his God and the God of his descendants after him.[h] **20** As for Ishmael, I am heeding you: I hereby bless him. I will make him fertile and will multiply him exceedingly. He shall become the father of twelve chieftains, and I will make of him a great nation.[i] **21** But my covenant I will maintain with Isaac, whom Sarah shall bear to you by this time next year.''[j] **22** When he had finished speaking with him, God departed from Abraham.

23 Then Abraham took his son Ishmael and all his slaves, whether born in his house or acquired with his money—every male among the members of Abraham's household—and he circumcised the flesh of their foreskins on that same day, as God had told him to do. **24** Abraham was ninety-nine years old when the flesh of his foreskin was circumcised,[k] **25** and his son Ishmael was thirteen years old when the flesh of his foreskin was circumcised. **26** Thus, on that same day Abraham and his son Ishmael were circumcised; **27** and all the male members of his household, including the slaves born in his

house or acquired with his money from foreigners, were circumcised with him.

CHAPTER 18

Abraham's Visitors.   **1** The LORD appeared to Abraham by the terebinth of Mamre, as he sat in the entrance of his tent, while the day was growing hot. **2** Looking up, he saw three men standing nearby. When he saw them, he ran from the entrance of the tent to greet them; and bowing to the ground,[l] **3** he said: ''Sir,* if I may ask you this favor, please do not go on past your servant. **4** Let some water be brought, that you may bathe your feet, and then rest yourselves under the tree. **5** Now that you have come this close to your servant, let me bring you a little food, that you may refresh yourselves; and afterward you may go on your way.'' ''Very well,'' they replied, ''do as you have said.''

6 Abraham hastened into the tent and told Sarah, ''Quick, three seahs* of fine flour! Knead it and make rolls.'' **7** He ran to the herd, picked out a tender, choice steer, and gave it to a servant, who quickly prepared it. **8** Then he got some curds* and milk, as well as the steer that had been prepared, and set these before them; and he waited on them under the tree while they ate.

9 ''Where is your wife Sarah?'' they asked him. ''There in the tent,'' he replied. **10** One of them* said, ''I will surely return to you about this time next year, and Sarah will then have a son.'' Sarah was listening at the entrance of the tent, just behind him.[m] **11** Now Abraham and Sarah were old, advanced in years, and Sarah had stopped having her womanly periods.[n]

---

c Jn 7, 22; Acts 7, 8; Rom 4, 11.
d Sir 44, 21.
e Lv 12, 3; Lk 1, 59; 2, 21.
f Gn 18, 10; Gal 4, 23.
g Rom 4, 19; Heb 11, 11f.
h Gn 11, 30; 21, 2; Ex 32, 13; Sir 44, 22.
i Gn 16, 10; 21, 13. 18; 25, 12-16.
j Gn 18, 14; 21, 2; 26, 2-5; Rom 9, 7.
k Gn 17, 10; Rom 4, 11.
l Heb 13, 1f.
m Gn 17, 19; 21, 1; 2 Kgs 4, 16; Rom 9, 9.
n Gn 17, 17; Rom 4, 19; Heb 11, 11f.

---
*

17, 15: Sarai and Sarah are variant forms of the same name, both meaning ''princess.''

17, 17: Laughed: yishaq, which is the Hebrew form of the name ''Isaac''; other similar explanations of the name are given in Gn 18, 12 and 21, 6.

18, 3: Abraham addresses the leader of the group, whom he does not yet recognize as Yahweh; in the next two verses he speaks to all three men. The other two are later (Gn 19, 1) identified as messengers.

18, 6: Three seahs: one ephah, about half a bushel.

18, 8: Curds: a type of soft cheese or yoghurt.

18, 10: One of them: i.e., the Lord. Abraham now realizes this for the first time when he hears the prediction of a miraculous birth. About this time next year: literally ''when the time becomes alive,'' i.e., at the time when birth is due after the period of gestation; the conception is understood as taking place soon after the prediction.

12 So Sarah laughed* to herself and said, "Now that I am so withered and my husband is so old, am I still to have sexual pleasure?" 13 But the LORD said to Abraham: "Why did Sarah laugh and say, 'Shall I really bear a child, old as I am?' 14 Is anything too marvelous for the LORD to do? At the appointed time, about this time next year, I will return to you, and Sarah will have a son."*o* 15 Because she was afraid, Sarah dissembled, saying, "I didn't laugh." But he said, "Yes you did."

Abraham Intercedes for Sodom 16 The men set out from there and looked down toward Sodom; Abraham was walking with them, to see them on their way. 17 The LORD reflected: "Shall I hide from Abraham what I am about to do, 18 now that he is to become a great and populous nation, and all the nations of the earth are to find blessing in him? *p* 19 Indeed, I have singled him out that he may direct his sons and his posterity to keep the way of the LORD by doing what is right and just, so that the LORD may carry into effect for Abraham the promises he made about him." 20 *q*Then the LORD said: "The outcry against Sodom and Gomorrah is so great, and their sin so grave,* 21 that I must go down and see whether or not their actions fully correspond to the cry against them that comes to me. I mean to find out."

22 While the two men walked on farther toward Sodom, the LORD remained standing before Abraham. 23 Then Abraham drew nearer to him and said: "Will you sweep away the innocent with the guilty? 24 Suppose there were fifty innocent people in the city; would you wipe out the place, rather than spare it for the sake of the fifty innocent people within it? 25 Far be it from you to do such a thing, to make the innocent die with the guilty, so that the innocent and the guilty would be treated alike! Should not the judge of all the world act with justice?"*r* 26 The LORD replied, "If I find fifty innocent people in the city of Sodom, I will spare the whole place for their sake." 27 Abraham spoke up again: "See how I am presuming to speak to my Lord, though I am but dust and ashes!*s* 28 What if there are five less than fifty innocent people? Will you destroy the whole city because of those five?" "I will not destroy it," he answered, "if I find forty-five there." 29 But Abraham persisted, saying, "What if only forty are found there?" He replied, "I will forbear doing it for the sake of the forty." 30 Then he said, "Let not my Lord grow impatient if I go on. What if only thirty are found there?" He replied, "I will forbear doing it if I can find but thirty there." 31 Still he went on, "Since I have thus dared to speak to my Lord, what if there are no more than twenty?" "I will not destroy it," he answered, "for the sake of the twenty." 32 But he still persisted, "Please, let not my Lord grow angry if I speak up this last time. What if there are at least ten there?" "For the sake of those ten," he replied, "I will not destroy it."*t*

33 The LORD departed as soon as he had finished speaking with Abraham, and Abraham returned home.

CHAPTER 19

Destruction of Sodom and Gomorrah.
1 The two angels reached Sodom in the evening, as Lot was sitting at the gate of Sodom. When Lot saw them, he got up to greet them; and bowing down with his face to the ground, 2 he said, "Please, gentlemen,* come aside into your servant's house for the night, and bathe your feet; you can get up early to continue your journey." But they replied, "No, we shall pass the night in the town square."*u* 3 He urged them so strongly, however, that they turned aside to his place and entered his house. He prepared a meal for them, baking cakes without leaven, and they dined.

4 *v*Before they went to bed, all the townsmen of Sodom, both young and old—all the people to the last man—closed in on the house. 5 They called to Lot and said to him, "Where are the men who came to your house tonight? Bring them out to us that we may have intimacies with them." 6 Lot went out to meet them at the entrance. When he had shut the door behind him, 7 he said, "I beg you, my brothers, not to do this wicked thing. 8 I have two daughters who have never had intercourse with men. Let me bring them out to you, and you may do to them as you please. But don't do anything to these men, for you know they have come under the shelter of my roof." 9 They replied, "Stand back! This fellow," they sneered, "came here as an immigrant, and now he dares to give orders! We'll treat you worse than them!" With

o Mt 19, 26; Mk 10, 27; Lk 1, 37; 18, 27; Rom 4, 21.
p Lk 1, 55.
q Gn 19, 13; Is 3, 9; Lk 17, 28; Jude 1, 7.
r Dt 32, 4; Jb 8, 3. 20; Wis 12, 15.
s Sir 10, 9; 17, 27.
t Jer 5, 1; Ez 22, 30.
u Wis 10, 6; Sir 16, 8; Ez 16, 50; Heb 13, 1f.
v 4-9; Jgs 19, 22-25; Jude 1, 7.
w Gn 13, 12; 2 Pt 2, 7f.

*

18, 12: Sarah laughed: see note on Gn 17, 17.

18, 20: Israelite tradition was unanimous in ascribing the destruction of Sodom and Gomorrah to the wickedness of these cities, but tradition varied in regard to the nature of this wickedness. According to the present account of the Yahwist, the sin of Sodom was homosexuality (Gn 19, 4f), which is therefore also known as sodomy; but according to Isaiah (1, 9f; 3, 9), it was a lack of social justice; Ezekiel (16, 46–51) described it as a disregard for the poor, whereas Jeremiah (23, 14) saw it as general immorality.

19, 2: Gentlemen: Lot does not yet know that the distinguished-looking men are God's messengers; cf Gn 18, 3.

that, they pressed hard against Lot, moving in closer to break down the door.ʷ **10** But his guests put out their hands, pulled Lot inside with them, and closed the door; **11** at the same time they struck the men at the entrance of the house, one and all, with such a blinding light* that they were utterly unable to reach the doorway.

12 Then the angels said to Lot: "Who else belongs to you here? Your sons [sons-in-law]* and your daughters and all who belong to you in the city—take them away from it!ˣ **13** We are about to destroy this place, for the outcry reaching the LORD against those in the city is so great that he has sent us to destroy it."ʸ **14** So Lot went out and spoke to his sons-in-law, who had contracted marriage with his daughters.* "Get up and leave this place," he told them; "the LORD is about to destroy the city." But his sons-in-law thought he was joking.

15 As dawn was breaking, the angels urged Lot on, saying, "On your way! Take with you your wife and your two daughters who are here, or you will be swept away in the punishment of the city." **16** When he hesitated, the men, by the LORD's mercy, seized his hand and the hands of his wife and his two daughters and led them to safety outside the city. **17** As soon as they had been brought outside, he was told: "Flee for your life! Don't look back or stop anywhere on the Plain. Get off to the hills at once, or you will be swept away."ᶻ **18** "Oh, no, my lord!" replied Lot. **19** "You have already thought enough of your servant to do me the great kindness of intervening to save my life. But I cannot flee to the hills to keep the disaster from overtaking me, and so I shall die. **20** Look, this town ahead is near enough to escape to. It's only a small place.* Let me flee there—it's a small place, isn't it?—that my life may be saved." **21** "Well, then," he replied, "I will also grant you the favor you now ask. I will not overthrow the town you speak of. **22** Hurry, escape there! I cannot do anything until you arrive there." That is why the town is called Zoar.ᵃ

23 The sun was just rising over the earth as Lot arrived in Zoar;ᵇ **24** at the same time the LORD rained down sulphurous fire upon Sodom and Gomorrah [from the LORD out of heaven].ᶜ **25** He overthrew* those cities and the whole Plain, together with the inhabitants of the cities and the produce of the soil.ᵈ **26** But Lot's wife looked back, and she was turned into a pillar of salt.ᵉ

27 Early the next morning Abraham went to the place where he had stood in the LORD's presence. **28** As he looked down toward Sodom and Gomorrah and the whole region of the Plain,* he saw dense smoke over the land rising like fumes from a furnace.ᶠ

29 Thus it came to pass: when God destroyed the Cities of the Plain, he was mindful of Abraham by sending Lot away from the upheaval by which God overthrew the cities where Lot had been living.

Moabites and Ammonites.*

30 Since Lot was afraid to stay in Zoar, he and his two daughters went up from Zoar and settled in the hill country, where he lived with his two daughters in a cave. **31** The older one said to the younger: "Our father is getting old, and there is not a man on earth to unite with us as was the custom everywhere. **32** Come, let us ply our father with wine and then lie with him, that we may have offspring by our father." **33** So that night they plied their father with wine, and the older one went in and lay with her father; but he was not aware of her lying down or her getting up. **34** Next day the older one said to the younger: "Last night it was I who lay with my father. Let us ply him with wine again tonight, and then you go in and lie with him, that we may both have offspring by our father." **35** So that night, too, they plied their father with wine, and then the younger one went in and lay with him; but again he was not aware of her lying down or her getting up.

36 Thus both of Lot's daughters became pregnant by their father. **37** The older one gave

---

x 2 Pt 7, 9.
y Is 1, 7. 9; Zep 2, 9; Lk 17, 29.
z Wis 10, 6.
a Wis 10, 6.
b Pss 9, 6; 11, 6; 107, 34.
c Wis 10, 7; Is 1, 9; 13,

19; Lam 4, 6; 17, 29;
2 Pt 2, 6.
d Dt 29, 22; Jer 50, 40;
Am 4, 11.
e Wis 10, 7; Lk 17, 32.
f Rv 9, 2; 14, 10f.
g Dt 2, 9.

---

*

19, 11: Blinding light: a preternatural flash that temporarily dazed the wicked men and revealed to Lot the true nature of his guests.

19, 12: Since Lot apparently had no sons, a glossator interpreted the term to mean sons-in-law.

19, 14: It is uncertain whether Lot's sons-in-law were fully married to his daughters or only "engaged" to them (Israelite "engagement" was the first part of the marriage ceremony), or even whether the daughters involved were the same as, or different from, the two daughters who were still in their father's house.

19, 20: A small place: the Hebrew word misar, literally "a little thing," has the same root consonants as the name of the town Zoar in v 22.

19, 25: Overthrew: the consistent use of this term, literally "turned upside down," to describe the destruction of the Cities of the Plain seems to imply that their upheaval (v 29) was caused primarily by an earthquake; this would naturally be accompanied by a disastrous fire, especially in a region containing bitumen (Gn 14, 10) and its accompanying gases.

19, 28f: From the height east of Hebron, Abraham could easily see the region at the southern end of the Dead Sea, where the Cities of the Plain were probably located.

19, 30–38: This Israelite tale about the origin of Israel's neighbors east of the Jordan and the Dead Sea was told partly to ridicule these racially related but rival nations and partly to give folk etymologies for their names.

19, 37: From my father: in Hebrew, meabi, similar in sound

birth to a son whom she named Moab, saying, "From my father."* He is the ancestor of the Moabites of today.ᵍ **38** The younger one, too, gave birth to a son, and she named him Ammon, saying, "The son of my kin."* He is the ancestor of the Ammonites of today.ʰ

CHAPTER 20

Abraham at Gerar.* **1** Abraham journeyed on to the region of the Negeb, where he settled between Kadesh and Shur. While he stayed in Gerar, **2** he said of his wife Sarah, "She is my sister." So Abimelech, king of Gerar, sent and took Sarah. **3** But God came to Abimelech in a dream one night and said to him, "You are about to die because of the woman you have taken, for she has a husband." **4** Abimelech, who had not approached her, said: "O Lord, would you slay a man even though he is innocent? **5** He himself told me, 'She is my sister,' and she herself also stated, 'He is my brother.' I did it in good faith and with clean hands." **6** God answered him in the dream: "Yes, I know you did it in good faith. In fact, it was I who kept you from sinning against me; that is why I did not let you touch her. **7** Therefore, return the man's wife—as a spokesman* he will intercede for you—that your life may be saved. If you do not return her, you can be sure that you and all who are yours will certainly die."

8 Early the next morning Abimelech called all his court officials and informed them of everything that had happened, and the men were horrified. **9** Then Abimelech summoned Abraham and said to him: "How could you do this to us! What wrong did I do to you that you should have brought such monstrous guilt on me and my kingdom? You have treated me in an intolerable way. **10** What were you afraid of," he asked him, "that you should have done such a thing?" **11** "I was afraid," answered Abraham, "because I thought there would surely be no fear of God in this place, and so they would kill me on account of my wife. **12** Besides, she is in truth my sister, but only my father's daughter, not my mother's; and so she became my wife.ⁱ **13** When God sent me wandering from my father's house, I asked her: 'Would you do me this favor? In whatever place we come to, say that I am your brother.'"

14 Then Abimelech took flocks and herds and male and female slaves and gave them to Abraham; and after he restored his wife Sarah to him, **15** he said, "Here, my land lies at your disposal; settle wherever you please." **16** To Sarah he said: "See, I have given your brother a thousand shekels of silver.* Let that serve you as a vindication before all who are with you; your honor has been preserved with everyone." **17** Abraham then interceded with God, and

God restored health to Abimelech, that is, to his wife and his maidservants, so that they could bear children; **18** for God had tightly closed every womb in Abimelech's household on account of Abraham's wife Sarah.

CHAPTER 21

Birth of Isaac. **1** The LORD took note of Sarah as he had said he would; he did for her as he had promised.ʲ **2** Sarah became pregnant and bore Abraham a son in his old age, at the set time that God had stated.ᵏ **3** Abraham gave the name Isaac to this son of his whom Sarah bore him.ˡ **4** When his son Isaac was eight days old, Abraham circumcised him, as God had commanded.ᵐ **5** Abraham was a hundred years old when his son Isaac was born to him. **6** Sarah then said, "God has given me cause to laugh, and all who hear of it will laugh with me.ⁿ **7** Who would have told Abraham," she added, "that Sarah would nurse children! Yet I have borne him a son in his old age." **8** Isaac grew, and on the day of the child's weaning Abraham held a great feast.

9 *Sarah noticed the son whom Hagar the Egyptian had borne to Abraham playing with her son Isaac; **10** so she demanded of Abraham: "Drive out that slave and her son! No son of that slave is going to share the inheritance with my son Isaac!"ᵒ **11** Abraham was greatly distressed, especially on account of his son Ishmael. **12** But God said to Abraham: "Do not be distressed about the boy or about your slave woman. Heed the demands of Sarah, no matter what she is asking of you; for it is through Isaac that descendants shall bear your name.ᵖ **13** As for the son of the slave woman, I will make a great nation of him also, since he too is your offspring."

---

h Dt 2, 19.
i Gn 12, 13.
j Gn 17, 19; 18, 10.
k Gal 4, 23; Heb 11, 11.
l Mt 1, 2; Lk 3, 34.

m Gn 17, 10ff; Acts 7, 8.
n Gn 17, 17.
o Jgs 11, 2; Gal 4, 30.
p Rom 9, 7; Heb 11, 18.

---

*
to the name "Moab."

19, 38: The son of my kin: in Hebrew, ben-ammi, similar in sound to the name "Ammonites."

20, 1–18: This story from the Elohist source (see note on Gn 4, 25) combines elements found in the two very similar but distinct stories of the Yahwist source in Gn 12, 10–20 and 26, 6–11.

20, 7: Spokesman: the Hebrew term nabi used here is regularly translated as "prophet," but it simply means "one who speaks on behalf of another," whether the latter is God, as in almost all cases, or another man, as in Ex 4, 16.

20, 16: A thousand shekels of silver: not a gift distinct from that of the animals and the slaves (v 14), but the monetary value of these.

21, 9–19: This story of Hagar's expulsion, in the Elohist source, is in general a duplicate of the one from the Yahwist source in Gn 16, 5–14; but the two stories differ greatly in detail.

14 Early the next morning Abraham got some bread and a skin of water and gave them to Hagar. Then, placing the child on her back,* he sent her away. As she roamed aimlessly in the wilderness of Beer-sheba, **15** the water in the skin was used up. So she put the child down under a shrub, **16** and then went and sat down opposite him, about a bowshot away; for she said to herself, "Let me not watch to see the child die." As she sat opposite him, he began to cry. **17** God heard the boy's cry, and God's messenger called to Hagar from heaven: "What is the matter, Hagar? Don't be afraid; God has heard the boy's cry in this plight of his.q **18** Arise, lift up the boy and hold him by the hand; for I will make of him a great nation." **19** Then God opened her eyes, and she saw a well of water. She went and filled the skin with water, and then let the boy drink.

20 God was with the boy as he grew up. He lived in the wilderness and became an expert bowman, **21** with his home in the wilderness of Paran. His mother got a wife for him from the land of Egypt.

The Pact at Beer-sheba.   **22** About that time Abimelech, accompanied by Phicol, the commander of his army,* said to Abraham: "God is with you in everything you do. **23** Therefore, swear to me by God at this place* that you will not deal falsely with me or with my progeny and posterity, but will act as loyally toward me and the land in which you stay as I have acted toward you." **24** To this Abraham replied, "I so swear."

25 Abraham, however, reproached Abimelech about a well that Abimelech's men had seized by force. **26** "I have no idea who did that," Abimelech replied. "In fact, you never told me about it, nor did I ever hear of it until now."

27 Then Abraham took sheep and cattle and gave them to Abimelech and the two made a pact. **28** Abraham also set apart seven ewe lambs of the flock, **29** and Abimelech asked him, "What is the purpose of these seven ewe lambs that you have set apart?" **30** Abraham answered, "The seven ewe lambs you shall accept from me that thus I may have your acknowledgment that the well was dug by me." **31** This is why the place is called Beer-sheba;* the two of them took an oath there. **32** When they had thus made the pact in Beer-sheba, Abimelech, along with Phicol, the commander of his army, left and returned to the land of the Philistines.

33 Abraham planted a tamarisk at Beer-sheba, and there he invoked by name the LORD, God the Eternal.* **34** Abraham resided in the land of the Philistines for many years.

CHAPTER 22

The Testing of Abraham.   **1** Some time after these events, God put Abraham to the test.* He called to him, "Abraham!" "Ready!" he replied.r **2** Then God said: "Take your son Isaac, your only one,* whom you love, and go to the land of Moriah. There you shall offer him up as a holocaust on a height that I will point out to you."s **3** Early the next morning Abraham saddled his donkey, took with him his son Isaac, and two of his servants as well, and with the wood that he had cut for the holocaust, set out for the place of which God had told him.

4 On the third day Abraham got sight of the place from afar. **5** Then he said to his servants: "Both of you stay here with the donkey, while the boy and I go on over yonder. We will worship and then come back to you." **6** Thereupon Abraham took the wood for the holocaust and laid it on his son Isaac's shoulders, while he himself carried the fire and the knife. **7** As the two walked on together, Isaac spoke to his father Abraham: "Father!" he said. "Yes, son," he replied. Isaac continued, "Here are the fire and the wood, but where is the sheep for the holocaust?" **8** "Son," Abraham answered, "God himself will provide the sheep for the holocaust." Then the two continued going forward.

9 When they came to the place of which God

---

q Gn 16, 7.   Heb 11, 17.
r Sir 44, 20.   t Jas 2, 21.
s 2 Chr 3, 1; 1 Mc 2, 52;

---

*

21, 14: Placing the child on her back: the phrase is translated from an emended form of the Hebrew text. In the current faulty Hebrew text, Abraham put the bread and the waterskin on Hagar's back, while her son apparently walked beside her. This reading seems to be a scribal attempt at harmonizing the present passage with the data of the Priestly source, in which Ishmael would have been at least fourteen years old when Isaac was born; compare Gn 16, 16 with 21, 5; cf 17, 25. But in the present Elohist story Ishmael is obviously a little boy, not much older than Isaac; cf vv 15, 18.

21, 22: Here and in v 32 the Greek text has ". . . Abimelech, accompanied by Ahuzzath, his councilor, and Phicol . . ."; but this is probably a secondary harmonization with Gn 26, 26. Abimelech took Phicol with him in order to intimidate Abraham by a show of strength.

21, 23: This place: Beer-sheba (v 31). Abimelech had come from Gerar (Gn 20, 2), about thirty miles west of Beer-sheba.

21, 31: Beer-sheba: the Hebrew name really means "the well of the seven," i.e., the place where there are seven wells, alluded to in the episode of the seven ewe lambs, vv 28ff; but it can also be interpreted to mean "the well of the oath."

21, 33: God the Eternal: in Hebrew, el olam, perhaps the name of the deity of the pre-Israelite sanctuary at Beer-sheba, but used by Abraham merely as a title of Yahweh; cf Is 40, 28.

22, 1: God put Abraham to the test: to prove the firmness of Abraham's faith in God's promise that through Isaac all the nations of the earth would find blessing; cf Gn 18, 10. 18; 21, 12.

22, 2: Only one: uniquely precious, especially loved; therefore the same term is rendered in vv 12. 17 as "beloved."

had told him, Abraham built an altar there and arranged the wood on it. Next he tied up his son Isaac, and put him on top of the wood on the altar.[t] **10** Then he reached out and took the knife to slaughter his son.[u] **11** But the LORD's messenger called to him from heaven, "Abraham, Abraham!" "Yes, Lord," he answered. **12** "Do not lay your hand on the boy," said the messenger. "Do not do the least thing to him. I know now how devoted you are to God, since you did not withhold from me your own beloved son."[v] **13** As Abraham looked about, he spied a ram caught by its horns in the thicket. So he went and took the ram and offered it up as a holocaust in place of his son. **14** Abraham named the site Yahweh-yireh;* hence people now say, "On the mountain the LORD will see."

15 Again the LORD's messenger called to Abraham from heaven **16** [w]and said: "I swear by myself, declares the LORD, that because you acted as you did in not withholding from me your beloved son, **17** I will bless you abundantly and make your descendants as countless as the stars of the sky and the sands of the seashore; your descendants shall take possession of the gates of their enemies,[x] **18** and in your descendants all the nations of the earth shall find blessing—all this because you obeyed my command."[y]

19 Abraham then returned to his servants, and they set out together for Beer-sheba, where Abraham made his home.

Nahor's Descendants.*

20 Some time afterward, the news came to Abraham: "Milcah too has borne sons, to your brother Nahor: **21** Uz, his first-born, his brother Buz, Kemuel (the father of Aram), **22** Chesed, Hazo, Pildash, Jidlaph and Bethuel." **23** Bethuel became the father of Rebekah. These eight Milcah bore to Abraham's brother Nahor. **24** His concubine, whose name was Reumah, also bore children: Tebah, Gaham, Tahash and Maacah.

CHAPTER 23

Purchase of a Burial Place. **1** The span of Sarah's life was one hundred and twenty-seven years. **2** She died in Kiriatharba (that is, Hebron) in the land of Canaan, and Abraham performed the customary mourning rites for her. **3** Then he left the side of his dead one and addressed the Hittites:* **4** "Although I am a resident alien* among you, sell me from your holdings a piece of property for a burial ground, that I may bury my dead wife."[z] **5** The Hittites answered Abraham: "Please, sir, **6** listen to us! You are an elect of God among us. Bury your dead in the choicest of our burial sites. None of us would deny you his burial ground for the burial of your dead." **7** Abraham, however,

began to bow low before the local citizens, the Hittites, **8** while he appealed to them: "If you will allow me room for burial of my dead, listen to me! Intercede for me with Ephron, son of Zohar, asking him **9** to sell me the cave of Machpelah that he owns; it is at the edge of his field. Let him sell it to me in your presence, at its full price, for a burial place."

10 Now Ephron was present with the Hittites. So Ephron the Hittite replied to Abraham in the hearing of the Hittites who sat on his town council:* **11** "Please, sir, listen to me! I give you both the field and the cave in it; in the presence of my kinsmen I make this gift. Bury your dead!" **12** But Abraham, after bowing low before the local citizens, addressed Ephron in the hearing of these men: **13** "Ah, if only you would please listen to me! I will pay you the price of the field. Accept it from me, that I may bury my dead there." **14** Ephron replied to Abraham, "Please, **15** sir, listen to me! A piece of land worth four hundred shekels* of silver —what is that between you and me, as long as you can bury your dead?" **16** [a]Abraham accepted Ephron's terms; he weighed out to him the silver that Ephron had stipulated in the hearing of the Hittites, four hundred shekels of silver at the current market value.*

17 [b]Thus Ephron's field in Machpelah, facing Mamre, together with its cave and all the trees anywhere within its limits, was conveyed

u Wis 10, 5.
v Rom 8, 32; 1 Jn 4, 9.
w 16f: Gn 15, 5; Ex 32, 13; Lk 1, 73; Rom 4, 13; Heb 6, 13f; 11, 12.
x Gn 24, 60.
y Gn 12, 3; 18, 18; 26, 4;

Sir 44, 21; Acts 3, 25; Gal 3, 16.
z Gn 33, 19; Acts 7, 16; Heb 11, 9.
a Acts 7, 16.
b 17f: Gn 49, 29f.

*

23, 14: Yahweh-yireh: a Hebrew expression meaning "the Lord will see"; the reference is to the words in v 8, "God himself will see to it."

22, 20–24: A list of Aramean tribes who lived to the east and northeast of Israel, twelve in number, like the twelve tribes of Israel (Gn 35, 23) and the twelve tribes of Ishmael (Gn 25, 12–16).

23, 3: The Hittites: a non-Semitic people in Canaan; their relationship to the well-known Hittites of Asia Minor is uncertain.

23, 4: A resident alien: literally "a sojourner and a settler," i.e., a long-term resident alien. Such a one would normally not have the right to own property. The importance of Abraham's purchase of the field in Machpelah, which is worded in technical legal terms, lies in the fact that it gave his descendants their first, though small, land rights in the country that God had promised the patriarch they would one day inherit as their own. Abraham therefore insists on purchasing the field and not receiving it as a gift.

23, 10: Who sat on his town council: probable meaning of the literal translation, "who came in at the gate of his city"; so also in v 18.

23, 15: Four hundred shekels: probably an exorbitant sum; Jeremiah (32, 9) paid only seventeen shekels for his field in Anathoth, though the Babylonian invasion no doubt helped to reduce the price.

23, 16: The current market values: the standard weight called a shekel varied according to time and place.

18 to Abraham by purchase in the presence of all the Hittites who sat on Ephron's town council. **19** After this transaction, Abraham buried his wife Sarah in the cave of the field of Machpelah, facing Mamre (that is, Hebron) in the land of Canaan. **20** Thus the field with its cave was transferred from the Hittites to Abraham as a burial place.

CHAPTER 24

Isaac and Rebekah.   **1** Abraham had now reached a ripe old age, and the LORD had blessed him in every way. **2** *c*Abraham said to the senior servant of his household, who had charge of all his possessions: "Put your hand under my thigh,* **3** and I will make you swear by the LORD, the God of heaven and the God of earth, that you will not procure a wife for my son from the daughters of the Canaanites among whom I live, *d* **4** but that you will go to my own land and to my kindred to get a wife for my son Isaac." **5** The servant asked him: "What if the woman is unwilling to follow me to this land? Should I then take your son back to the land from which you migrated?" **6** "Never take my son back there for any reason," Abraham told him. **7** "The LORD, the God of heaven, who took me from my father's house and the land of my kin, and who confirmed by oath the promise he then made to me, 'I will give this land to your descendants,—he will send his messenger before you, and you will obtain a wife for my son there. *e* **8** If the woman is unwilling to follow you, you will be released from this oath. But never take my son back there!" **9** So the servant put his hand under the thigh of his master Abraham and swore to him in this undertaking.

10 The servant then took ten of his master's camels, and bearing all kinds of gifts from his master, he made his way to the city of Nahor* in Aram Naharaim. **11** Near evening, at the time when women go out to draw water, he made the camels kneel by the well outside the city. **12** Then he prayed: "LORD, God of my master Abraham, let it turn out favorably for me* today and thus deal graciously with my master Abraham. **13** While I stand here at the spring and the daughters of the townsmen are coming out to draw water, **14** if I say to a girl, 'Please lower your jug, that I may drink,' and she answers, 'Take a drink, and let me give water to your camels, too,' let her be the one whom you have decided upon for your servant Isaac. In this way I shall know that you have dealt graciously with my master."

15 *f*He had scarcely finished these words when Rebekah (who was born to Bethuel, son of Milcah, the wife of Abraham's brother Nahor) came out with a jug on her shoulder. **16** The girl was very beautiful, a virgin, untouched by man. She went down to the spring and filled her jug. As she came up, **17** the servant ran toward her and said, "Please give me a sip of water from your jug." **18** "Take a drink, sir," she replied, and quickly lowering the jug onto her hand, she gave him a drink. **19** When she had let him drink his fill, she said, "I will draw water for your camels, too, until they have drunk their fill." **20** With that, she quickly emptied her jug into the drinking trough and ran back to the well to draw more water, until she had drawn enough for all the camels. **21** The man watched her the whole time, silently waiting to learn whether or not the LORD had made his errand successful. **22** When the camels had finished drinking, the man took out a gold ring weighing half a shekel, which he fastened on her nose, and two gold bracelets weighing ten shekels, which he put on her wrists. **23** Then he asked her: "Whose daughter are you? Tell me, please. And is there room in your father's house for us to spend the night?" **24** She answered: "I am the daughter of Bethuel the son of Milcah, whom she bore to Nahor. **25** There is plenty of straw and fodder at our place," she added, "and room to spend the night." **26** The man then bowed down in worship to the LORD, **27** saying: "Blessed be the LORD, the God of my master Abraham, who has not let his constant kindness toward my master fail. As for myself also, the LORD has led me straight to the house of my master's brother."

28 Then the girl ran off and told her mother's household about it. **29** *g*Now Rebekah had a brother named Laban. **30** As soon as he saw the ring and the bracelets on his sister Rebekah and heard her words about what the man had said to her, Laban rushed outside to the man at the spring. When he reached him, he was still standing by the camels at the spring. **31** So he said to him: "Come, blessed of the LORD! Why are you staying outside when I have made the house ready for you, as well as a place for the

---

c 2f: Gn 47, 29.
d Gn 24, 37; 28, 1f; Jgs
   14, 3; Tb 4, 12.
e Gn 12, 7; Ex 6, 8; Tb
5, 17; Gal 3, 16.
f Gn 22, 23.
g Gn 27, 43.

*

24, 2:   Put your hand under my thigh: the symbolism of this act was apparently connected with the Hebrew concept of children issuing from their father's "thigh" (Gn 46, 26; Ex 1, 5). Perhaps the man who took such an oath was thought to bring the curse of sterility on himself if he did not fulfill his sworn promise. Jacob made Joseph swear in the same way (Gn 47, 29). In both these instances, the oath was taken to carry out the last request of a man upon his death.

24, 10:   Nahor: it is uncertain whether this is to be understood as the name of Abraham's brother (Gn 11, 27), Rebekah's grandfather (Gn 24, 15), or the city of the same name (as known from the Mari documents); Aram Naharaim, situated near Haran (Gn 11, 31) in northern Mesopotamia.

24, 12:   Let it turn out favorably for me: let me have a favorable omen; cf end of v 14.

camels?'' **32** The man then went inside; and while the camels were being unloaded and provided with straw and fodder, water was brought to bathe his feet and the feet of the men who were with him. **33** But when the table was set for him, he said, ''I will not eat until I have told my tale.'' ''Do so,'' they replied.

34 ''I am Abraham's servant,'' he began. **35** ''The LORD has blessed my master so abundantly that he has become a wealthy man; he has given him flocks and herds, silver and gold, male and female slaves, and camels and asses. **36** My master's wife Sarah bore a son to my master in her old age, and he has given him everything he owns. **37** My master put me under oath, saying: 'You shall not procure a wife for my son among the daughters of the Canaanites in whose land I live; **38** instead, you shall go to my father's house, to my own relatives, to get a wife for my son.' **39** When I asked my master, 'What if the woman will not follow me?' **40** he replied: 'The LORD, in whose presence I have always walked, will send his messenger with you and make your errand successful, and so you will get a wife for my son from my own kindred of my father's house.[h] **41** Then you shall be released from my ban. If you visit my kindred and they refuse you, then, too, you shall be released from my ban.'

42 ''When I came to the spring today, I prayed: 'LORD, God of my master Abraham, may it be your will to make successful the errand I am engaged on! **43** While I stand here at the spring, if I say to a young woman who comes out to draw water, Please give me a little water from your jug, **44** and she answers, Not only may you have a drink, but I will give water to your camels, too—let her be the woman whom the LORD has decided upon for my master's son.'

45 ''I had scarcely finished saying this prayer to myself when Rebekah came out with a jug on her shoulder. After she went down to the spring and drew water, I said to her, 'Please let me have a drink.' **46** She quickly lowered the jug she was carrying and said, 'Take a drink, and let me bring water for your camels, too.' So I drank, and she watered the camels also. **47** When I asked her, 'Whose daughter are you?' she answered, 'The daughter of Bethuel, son of Nahor, born to Nahor by Milcah.' So I put the ring on her nose and the bracelets on her wrists. **48** Then I bowed down in worship to the LORD, blessing the LORD, the God of my master Abraham, who had led me on the right road to obtain the daughter of my master's kinsman for his son. **49** If, therefore, you have in mind to show true loyalty to my master, let me know; but if not, let me know that, too. I can then proceed accordingly.''

50 [i]Laban and his household said in reply:

''This thing comes from the LORD; we can say nothing to you either for or against it. **51** Here is Rebekah, ready for you; take her with you, that she may become the wife of your master's son, as the LORD has said.'' **52** When Abraham's servant heard their answer, he bowed to the ground before the LORD. **53** Then he brought out objects of silver and gold and articles of clothing and presented them to Rebekah; he also gave costly presents to her brother and mother. **54** After he and the men with him had eaten and drunk, they spent the night there.

When they were up the next morning, he said, ''Give me leave to return to my master.''[j] **55** Her brother and mother replied, ''Let the girl stay with us a short while, say ten days; after that she may go.'' **56** But he said to them, ''Do not detain me, now that the LORD has made my errand successful; let me go back to my master.'' **57** They answered, ''Let us call the girl and see what she herself has to say about it.'' **58** So they called Rebekah and asked her, ''Do you wish to go with this man?'' She answered, ''I do.'' **59** At this they allowed their sister Rebekah and her nurse to take leave, along with Abraham's servant and his men. **60** Invoking a blessing on Rebekah, they said:

''Sister, may you grow
   into thousands of myriads;
And may your descendants gain possession
   of the gates of their enemies!''[k]

61 Then Rebekah and her maids started out; they mounted their camels and followed the man. So the servant took Rebekah and went on his way.

62 Meanwhile Isaac had gone from Beer-lahai-roi and was living in the region of the Negeb.[l] **63** One day toward evening he went out . . .* in the field, and as he looked around, he noticed that camels were approaching. **64** Rebekah, too, was looking about, and when she saw him, she alighted from her camel **65** and asked the servant, ''Who is the man out there, walking through the fields toward us?'' ''That is my master,'' replied the servant. Then she covered herself with her veil.

66 The servant recounted to Isaac all the things he had done. **67** Then Isaac took Rebekah into his tent; he married her, and thus she became his wife. In his love for her Isaac found solace after the death of his mother Sarah.

---

h Tb 5, 17; 10, 13.   k Gn 22, 17.
i 50f; Tb 7, 12.   l Gn 16, 13f; 25, 11.
j Tb 7, 14; 8, 20.

24, 63: He went out: the meaning of the Hebrew term that follows this is obscure.

CHAPTER 25

Abraham's Sons by Keturah.

1 *m**Abraham married another wife, whose name was Keturah. 2 She bore him Zimran, Jokshan, Medan, Midian, Ishbak and Shuah. 3 Jokshan became the father of Sheba and Dedan. The descendants of Dedan were the Asshurim, the Letushim, and the Leummim.*n* 4 The descendants of Midian were Ephah, Epher, Hanoch, Abida and Eldaah. All of these were descendants of Keturah.

5 Abraham deeded everything that he owned to his son Isaac. 6 To his sons by concubinage, however, he made grants while he was still living, as he sent them away eastward, to the land of Kedem,* away from his son Isaac.

Death of Abraham.

7 The whole span of Abraham's life was one hundred and seventy-five years. 8 Then he breathed his last, dying at a ripe old age, grown old after a full life; and he was taken to his kinsmen. 9 *o*His sons Isaac and Ishmael buried him in the cave of Machpelah, in the field of Ephron, son of Zohar the Hittite, which faces Mamre, 10 the field that Abraham had bought from the Hittites; there he was buried next to his wife Sarah. 11 After the death of Abraham, God blessed his son Isaac, who made his home near Beer-lahai-roi.

Descendants of Ishmael.

12 These are the descendants of Abraham's son Ishmael, whom Hagar the Egyptian, Sarah's slave, bore to Abraham. 13 *p*These are the names of Ismael's sons, listed in the order of their birth: Nebaioth (Ishmael's firstborn), Kedar, Adbeel, Mibsam,*q* 14 Mishma, Dumah, Massa, 15 Hadad, Tema, Jetur, Naphish and Kedemah, 16 These are the sons of Ishmael, their names by their villages and encampments; twelve chieftains of as many tribal groups.*r*

17 The span of Ishmael's life was one hundred and thirty-seven years. After he had breathed his last and died, he was taken to his kinsmen. 18 The Ishmaelites ranged from Havilah-by-Shur, which is on the border of Egypt, all the way to Asshur; and each of them pitched camp* in opposition to his various kinsmen.*s*

III: The Patriarchs Isaac and Jacob

Birth of Esau and Jacob.

19 This is the family history of Isaac, son of Abraham; Abraham had begotten Isaac. 20 Isaac was forty years old when he married Rebekah, the daughter of Bethuel the Aramean of Paddan-aram and the sister of Laban the Aramean.*t* 21 Isaac entreated the LORD on behalf of his wife, since she was sterile. The LORD heard his entreaty, and

Rebekah became pregnant. 22 But the children in her womb jostled each other so much that she exclaimed, "If this is to be so, what good will it do me!" She went to consult the LORD, 23 and he answered her:

"Two nations are in your womb,
    two peoples are quarreling while still
        within you;
But one shall surpass the other,
    and the older shall serve the younger.*u*

24 When the time of her delivery came, there were twins in her womb.*v* 25 The first to emerge was reddish,* and his whole body was like a hairy mantle; so they named him Esau. 26 His brother came out next, gripping Esau's heel;* so they named him Jacob. Isaac was sixty years old when they were born.*w*

27 As the boys grew up, Esau became a skillful hunter, a man who lived in the open; whereas Jacob was a simple man, who kept to his tents.*x* 28 Isaac preferred Esau, because he was fond of game; but Rebekah preferred Jacob. 29 Once, when Jacob was cooking a stew, Esau came in from the open, famished. 30 He said to Jacob, "Let me gulp down some of that red stuff;* I'm starving." (That is why he was called Edom.) 31 But Jacob replied, "First

m 1-4; 1 Chr 1, 32f.
n Is 21, 13.
o 9f: Gn 23, 3-20.
p 13-16: 1 Chr 1, 29ff.
q Is 60, 7.
r Gn 17, 20.
s Gn 16, 12.
t Gn 24, 66.

u Gn 27, 29; Nm 24, 18; Mal 1, 2-5; Rom 9, 11f.
v Hos 12, 3.
w Mt 1, 2
x Gn 27, 6f.
y Dt 21, 17.

*

25, 1–11: Though mentioned here, Abraham's marriage to a "concubine," or wife of secondary rank, and his death are not to be understood as happening chronologically after the events narrated in the preceding chapter.

25, 6: The land of Kedem: or "the country of the East," the region inhabited by the Kedemites or Easterners (Gn 29, 1; Jgs 6, 3. 33; Jb 1, 3; Is 11, 14). The names mentioned in vv 2ff, as far as they can be identified, are those of tribes in the Arabian desert.

25, 18: Pitched camp: literally "fell"; the same Hebrew verb is used in Jgs 7, 12 in regard to the hostile encampment of Bedouin tribes. The present passage shows the fulfillment of the prediction contained in Gn 16, 12.

25, 25: Reddish: in Hebrew, admoni, a reference to Edom, another name for Esau (v 30; 36, 1). Edom, however, was really the name of the country south of Moab where the descendants of Esau lived. It was called the "red" country because of its reddish sandstone. Hairy: in Hebrew, sear, a reference to Seir, another name for Edom (Gn 36, 8). One might expect the text to say, "So they named him Seir"; but Esau (esaw) also means "hairy."

25, 26: Esau's heel: the Hebrew is baaqeb esaw, a reference to the name Jacob; cf Gn 27, 36. Probably, however, the name Jacob has no true etymological connection with the Hebrew word for "heel" (aqeb), but is instead a shortened form of some such name as yaaqob-el ("may God protect").

25, 30: Red stuff: in Hebrew, adom; another play on the word Edom, the "red" land.

25, 31: Birthright: the privilege that entitled the first-born son to a position of honor in the family and to a double share in the possessions inherited from the father.

give me your birthright* in exchange for it."*y* 32 "Look," said Esau, "I'm on the point of dying. What good will any birthright do me?" 33 But Jacob insisted, "Swear to me first!" So he sold Jacob his birthright under oath.*z* 34 Jacob then gave him some bread and the lentil stew; and Esau ate, drank, got up, and went his way. Esau cared little for his birthright.

CHAPTER 26

Isaac and Abimelech. 1 *a*There was a famine in the land (distinct from the earlier one that had occurred in the days of Abraham), and Isaac went down to Abimelech, king of the Philistines in Gerar.*b* 2 The LORD appeared to him and said: "Do not go down to Egypt, but continue to camp wherever in this land I tell you. 3 Stay in this land, and I will be with you and bless you; for to you and your descendants I will give all these lands, in fulfillment of the oath that I swore to your father Abraham.*c* 4 I will make your descendants as numerous as the stars in the sky and give them all these lands, and in your descendants all the nations of the earth shall find blessing—*d* 5 this because Abraham obeyed me, keeping my mandate (my commandments, my ordinances and my instructions)."

6 *So Isaac settled in Gerar. 7 When the men of the place asked questions about his wife, he answered, "She is my sister." He was afraid, if he called her his wife, the men of the place would kill him on account of Rebekah, since she was very beautiful. 8 But when he had been there for a long time, Abimelech, king of the Philistines, happened to look out of a window and was surprised to see Isaac fondling his wife Rebekah. 9 He called for Isaac and said: "She must certainly be your wife! How could you have said, 'She is my sister'?" Isaac replied, "I thought I might lose my life on her account." 10 "How could you do this to us!" exclaimed Abimelech. "It would have taken very little for one of the men to lie with your wife, and you would have thus brought guilt upon us!" 11 Abimelech therefore gave this warning to all his men: "Anyone who molests this man or his wife shall forthwith be put to death."

12 *Isaac sowed a crop in that region and reaped a hundredfold the same year. Since the LORD blessed him, 13 *e*he became richer and richer all the time, until he was very wealthy indeed. 14 He acquired such flocks and herds, and so many work animals, that the Philistines became envious of him. (15 *f*The Philistines had stopped up and filled with dirt all the wells that his father's servants had dug back in the days of his father Abraham.) 16 So Abimelech said to Isaac, "Go away from us; you have

become far too numerous for us." 17 Isaac left there and made the Wadi Gerar his regular campsite. (18 Isaac reopened the wells which his father's servants had dug back in the days of his father Abraham and which the Philistines had stopped up after Abraham's death; he gave them the same names that his father had given them.) 19 But when Isaac's servants dug in the wadi and reached spring water in their well, 20 the shepherds of Gerar quarreled with Isaac's servants, saying, "The water belongs to us!" So the well was called Esek,* because they had challenged him there. 21 Then they dug another well, and they quarreled over that one too; so it was called Sitnah.* 22 When he had moved on from there, he dug still another well; but over this one they did not quarrel. It was called Rehoboth, because he said, "The LORD has now given us ample room, and we shall flourish in the land."

23 From there Isaac went up to Beer-sheba. 24 The same night the LORD appeared to him and said: "I am the God of your father Abraham. You have no need to fear, since I am with you. I will bless you and multiply your descendants for the sake of my servant Abraham."*g* 25 So he built an altar there and invoked the LORD by name. After he had pitched his tent there, his servants began to dig a well nearby.

26 *h*Abimelech had meanwhile come to him from Gerar, accompanied by Ahuzzath, his councilor, and Phicol, the general of his army. 27 Isaac asked them, "Why have you come to me, seeing that you hate me and have driven me away from you?" 28 They answered: "We are convinced that the LORD is with you, so we propose that there be a sworn agreement between our two sides—between you and us. Let us make a pact with you: 29 you shall not act unkindly toward us, just as we have not molested you, but have always acted kindly toward you and have let you depart in peace. Henceforth, 'The LORD's blessing be upon you!'" 30 Isaac then made a feast for them, and they ate and drank. 31 Early the next morning they

---

z Heb 12, 16.
a 1-14: Gn 12, 10-20.
b Gn 12, 1.
c Gn 12, 7; 15, 18; Ex 32, 13; Ps 105, 9; Sir 44, 22; Heb 11, 9.
d Gn 12, 3; 22, 17f; 28,

14; Ex 32, 13.
e 13f: Jb 1, 3.
f 15-24: Gn 21, 25-31.
g Gn 46, 3.
h 26-33: Gn 21, 22-31; Prv 16, 7.

26, 6–11: The Yahwist's version of the wife-sister episode at Gerar; the Elohist's version (Gn 20, 1–18) is connected with Abraham and Sarah.

26, 12–33: The Yahwist's version of the story about the wells at Beer-sheba; again, the Elohist's version (Gn 21, 22f) is connected with Abraham. A redactor joined the two accounts by means of the parenthetical verses 15 and 18.

26, 20: Esek: "challenge."

26, 21: Sitnah: "opposition"; one might expect the text to be continued by some such words as "because they were in opposition there."

exchanged oaths. Then Isaac bade them farewell, and they departed from him in peace.

32 That same day Isaac's servants came and brought him news about the well they had been digging; they told him, "We have reached water!" **33** He called it Shibah;* hence the name of the city, Beer-sheba, to this day.

34 *When Esau was forty years old, he married Judith, daughter of Beeri the Hittite, and Basemath, daughter of Elon the Hivite.*[i]* **35** But they became a source of embitterment to Isaac and Rebekah.

CHAPTER 27

Jacob's Deception.* **1** When Isaac was so old that his eyesight had failed him, he called his older son Esau and said to him, "Son!" "Yes, father!" he replied. **2** Isaac then said, "As you can see, I am so old that I may now die at any time. **3** Take your gear, therefore—your quiver and bow—and go out into the country to hunt some game for me. **4** With your catch prepare an appetizing dish for me to eat, such as I like, and bring it to me to eat, so that I may give you my special blessing* before I die."

5 Rebekah had been listening while Isaac was speaking to his son Esau. So when Esau went out into the country to hunt some game for his father,*[j]* **6** Rebekah said to her son Jacob, "Listen! I overheard your father tell your brother Esau, **7** 'Bring me some game and with it prepare an appetizing dish for me to eat, that I may give you my blessing with the LORD's approval before I die.' **8** Now, son, listen carefully to what I tell you. **9** Go to the flock and get me two choice kids. With these I will prepare an appetizing dish for your father, such as he likes. **10** Then bring it to your father to eat, that he may bless you before he dies." **11** "But my brother Esau is a hairy man," said Jacob to his mother Rebekah, "and I am smooth-skinned!*[k]* **12** Suppose my father feels me? He will think I am making sport of him, and I shall bring on myself a curse instead of a blessing." **13** His mother, however, replied: "Let any curse against you, son, fall on me! Just do as I say. Go and get me the kids."

14 So Jacob went and got them and brought them to his mother; and with them she prepared an appetizing dish, such as his father liked. **15** Rebekah then took the best clothes of her older son Esau that she had in the house, and gave them to her younger son Jacob to wear; **16** and with the skins of the kids she covered up his hands and the hairless parts of his neck. **17** Then she handed her son Jacob the appetizing dish and the bread she had prepared.

18 Bringing them to his father, Jacob said, "Father!" "Yes?" replied Isaac. "Which of my sons are you?" **19** Jacob answered his father: "I am Esau, your first-born. I did as you told me. Please sit up and eat some of my game, so that you may give me your special blessing." **20** But Isaac asked, "How did you succeed so quickly, son?" He answered, "The LORD, your God, let things turn out well with me." **21** Isaac then said to Jacob, "Come closer, son, that I may feel you, to learn whether you really are my son Esau or not." **22** So Jacob moved up closer to his father. When Isaac felt him, he said, "Although the voice is Jacob's, the hands are Esau's." **23** (He failed to identify him because his hands were hairy, like those of his brother Esau; so in the end he gave him his blessing.) **24** Again he asked him, "Are you really my son Esau?" "Certainly," he replied. **25** Then Isaac said, "Serve me your game, son, that I may eat of it and then give you my blessing." Jacob served it to him, and Isaac ate; he brought him wine, and he drank. **26** Finally his father Isaac said to him, "Come closer, son, and kiss me." **27** As Jacob went up and kissed him, Isaac smelled the fragrance of his clothes. With that, he blessed him, saying,

"Ah, the fragrance of my son
    is like the fragrance of a field
    that the LORD has blessed!*[l]*

28 "May God give to you
    of the dew of the heavens
And of the fertility of the earth
    abundance of grain and wine.

29 *[m]*"Let peoples serve you,
    and nations pay you homage;
Be master of your brothers,

---

i 34f: Gn 27, 46.   l Gn 22, 17f; Heb 11, 20.
j Gn 25, 28.   m Gn 25, 23; 49, 8; Nm
k Gn 25, 25.   24, 9.

---

*

26, 33: Shibah: "seven," for the sake of a closer assonance with Beer-sheba; but the present version of the story says nothing about there being seven wells there as implied in Gn 21, 28–31. The Greek version understood the Hebrew text more logically as shebua, "oath," in keeping with the present story.

26, 34f: These verses from the Priestly source, which have no logical connection with the preceding stories, serve as an introduction to the following section on Esau's loss of his birthright by suggesting a motivation for this in Isaac's and Rebekah's dislike for Esau's Canaanite wives.

27, 1–45: What Jacob did in deceiving his father and thereby cheating Esau out of Isaac's deathbed blessing is condemned as blameworthy, not only by Hosea (12, 4) and Jeremiah (9, 3), but also, indirectly, by the Yahwist narrator of the present story, who makes the reader sympathize with Esau as the innocent victim of a cruel plot, and shows that Jacob and his mother, the instigator of the plot, paid for it by a lifelong separation from each other. The story was told because it was part of the mystery of God's ways in salvation history—his use of weak, sinful men to achieve his own ultimate purpose.

27, 4: My special blessing: "the blessing of my soul." The same expression is used also in vv 19. 25. 31. In the context it must mean something like a solemn deathbed blessing, believed to be especially efficacious.

and may your mother's sons bow down to
you.

Cursed be those who curse you,
and blessed be those who bless you.''

30 Jacob had scarcely left his father, just
after Isaac had finished blessing him, when his
brother Esau came back from his hunt. **31** Then
he too prepared an appetizing dish with his
game, and bringing it to his father, he said,
"Please, father, eat some of your son's game,
that you may then give me your special blessing." **32** "Who are you?" his father Isaac
asked him. "I am Esau," he replied, "your
first-born son." **33** With that, Isaac was seized
with a fit of uncontrollable trembling. "Who
was it, then," he asked, "that hunted game and
brought it to me? I finished eating it just before
you came, and I blessed him. Now he must
remain blessed!" **34** On hearing his father's
words, Esau burst into loud, bitter sobbing.
"Father, bless me too!" he begged. **35** When
Isaac explained, "Your brother came here by a
ruse and carried off your blessing," **36** Esau
exclaimed, "He has been well named Jacob! He
has now supplanted me* twice! First he took
away my birthright, and now he has taken away
my blessing." Then he pleaded, "Haven't you
saved a blessing for me?"[n] **37** Isaac replied: "I
have already appointed him your master, and I
have assigned to him all his kinsmen as his
slaves; besides, I have enriched him with grain
and wine. What then can I do for you, son?"
38 But Esau urged his father, "Have you only
that one blessing, father? Bless me too!" Isaac,
however, made no reply; and Esau wept aloud.[o]
39 Finally Isaac spoke again and said to him:

"Ah, far from the fertile earth
shall be your dwelling;
far from the dew of the heavens above![p]
40 "By your sword you shall live,
and your brother you shall serve;
But when you become restive,
you shall throw off his yoke from your
neck."[q]

41 Esau bore Jacob a grudge because of the
blessing his father had given him. He said to
himself, "When the time of mourning for my
father comes, I will kill my brother Jacob."[r]
42 When Rebekah got news of what her older
son Esau had in mind, she called her younger
son Jacob and said to him: "Listen! Your brother Esau intends to settle accounts with you by
killing you. **43** Therefore, son, do what I tell
you: flee at once to my brother Laban in Haran,
44 and stay with him a while until your brother's fury subsides **45** [until your brother's anger
against you subsides] and he forgets what you
did to him. Then I will send for you and bring
you back. Must I lose both of you in a single
day?"

Jacob Sent to Laban. **46** *Rebekah said
to Isaac: "I am disgusted with life because of
the Hittite women. If Jacob also should marry
a Hittite woman, a native of the land, like these
women, what good would life be to me?"[s]

CHAPTER 28

1 Isaac therefore called Jacob, greeted him
with a blessing, and charged him: "You shall
not marry a Canaanite woman![t] **2** Go now to
Paddan-aram, to the home of your mother's
father Bethuel, and there choose a wife for yourself from among the daughters of your uncle
Laban.[u] **3** May God Almighty bless you and
make you fertile, multiply you that you may
become an assembly of peoples. **4** May he extend to you and your descendants the blessing
he gave to Abraham, so that you may gain possession of the land where you are staying, which
he assigned to Abraham."[v] **5** Then Isaac sent
Jacob on his way; he went to Paddan-aram, to
Laban, son of Bethuel, the Aramean, and brother of Rebekah, the mother of Jacob and Esau.[w]
6 Esau noted that Isaac had blessed Jacob
when he sent him to Paddan-aram to get himself
a wife there, charging him, as he gave him his
blessing, not to marry a Canaanite woman,
7 and that Jacob had obeyed his father and
mother and gone to Paddan-aram. **8** Esau realized how displeasing the Canaanite women
were to his father Isaac, **9** so he went to Ishmael, and in addition to the wives he had, married
Mahalath, the daughter of Abraham's son Ishmael and sister of Nebaioth.[x]

Jacob's Dream at Bethel. **10** Jacob departed from Beer-sheba and proceeded toward
Haran. **11** When he came upon a certain

n Gn 25, 26. 29-34; Hos 12, 4.
o Heb 12, 17.
p Heb 11, 20.
q 2 Kgs 8, 20. 22; 2 Chr 21, 8.
r Wis 10, 10; Ob 1, 10.
s Gn 26, 34f.
t Gn 24, 3f; 26, 35.
u Gn 22, 22; 17, 1f. 4f.
v Ex 32, 13.
w Jdt 8, 26.
x Gn 36, 2f.

*

27, 36: He has now supplanted me: in Hebrew, wayyaqebeni, a wordplay on the name Jacob, yaaqob; see Jer 9, 3 and note, as well as Gn 25, 26. There is also a play between the Hebrew words bekora ("birthright") and beraka ("blessing").

27, 46—28, 9: This section, which is from the Priestly source and a direct sequel of Gn 26, 34f, presents a different, though not contradictory, reason for Jacob's going to Paddan-aram: namely, to preserve racial purity among the chosen people. The account of Esau's marriages is given for the purpose of explaining the racial mixture of the Edomites, who were descended in part from tribes related to Israel, in part from older peoples in Edom called Hittites, Horites or Hivites, and in part from the Ishmaelite (Arabian) tribes who later invaded the region.

28, 11: Shrine: literally "place," often used specifically of a

shrine,* as the sun had already set, he stopped there for the night. Taking one of the stones at the shrine, he put it under his head and lay down to sleep at that spot. **12** Then he had a dream: a stairway* rested on the ground, with its top reaching to the heavens; and God's messengers were going up and down on it. *y* **13** And there was the LORD standing beside him and saying: "I, the LORD, am the God of your forefather Abraham and the God of Isaac; the land on which you are lying I will give to you and your descendants. *z* **14** These shall be as plentiful as the dust of the earth, and through them you shall spread out east and west, north and south. In you and your descendants all the nations of the earth shall find blessing. *a* **15** Know that I am with you; I will protect you wherever you go, and bring you back to this land. I will never leave you until I have done what I promised you." *b*

16 When Jacob awoke from his sleep, he exclaimed, "Truly, the LORD is in this spot, although I did not know it!" **17** In solemn wonder he cried out: "How awesome is this shrine! This* is nothing else but an abode of God, and that is the gateway to heaven!" **18** Early the next morning Jacob took the stone that he had put under his head, set it up as a memorial stone,* and poured oil on top if it. *c* **19** He called that site Bethel,* whereas the former name of the town had been Luz. *d*

20 Jacob then made this vow: "If God remains with me, to protect me on this journey I am making and to give me enough bread to eat and clothing to wear, **21** and I come back safe to my father's house, the LORD shall be my God. **22** This stone that I have set up as a memorial stone shall be God's abode. Of everything you give me, I will faithfully return a tenth part to you."

CHAPTER 29

Arrival in Haran.   **1** *e* After Jacob resumed his journey, he came to the land of the Easterners.* **2** Looking about, he saw a well in the open country, with three droves of sheep huddled near it, for droves were watered from that well. *f* **3** Only when all the shepherds were assembled there could they roll the stone away from the mouth of the well and water the flocks. Then they would put the stone back again over the mouth of the well.

4 Jacob said to them, "Friends, where are you from?" "We are from Haran," they replied. **5** Then he asked them, "Do you know Laban, son of Nahor?" "We do," they answered. *g* **6** He inquired further, "Is he well?" "He is," they answered; "and here comes his daughter Rachel with his flock." **7** Then he

said: "There is still much daylight left; it is hardly the time to bring the animals home. Why don't you water the flocks now, and then continue pasturing them?" **8** "We cannot," they replied, "until all the shepherds are here to roll the stone away from the mouth of the well; only then can we water the flocks."

9 While he was still talking with them, Rachel arrived with her father's sheep; she was the one who tended them. **10** As soon as Jacob saw Rachel, the daughter of his uncle Laban, with the sheep of his uncle Laban, he went up, rolled the stone away from the mouth of the well, and watered his uncle's sheep. **11** Then Jacob kissed Rachel and burst into tears.* **12** He told her that he was her father's relative, Rebekah's son, and she ran to tell her father. **13** When Laban heard the news about his sister's son Jacob, he hurried out to meet him. After embracing and kissing him, he brought him to his house. Jacob then recounted to Laban all that had happened, **14** and Laban said to him, "You are indeed my flesh and blood."*

Marriage to Leah and Rachel.   After Jacob had stayed with him a full month, **15** Laban said to him: "Should you serve me for nothing just because you are a relative of mine? Tell me what your wages should be." **16** Now Laban had two daughters; the older was called Leah, the younger Rachel. **17** Leah had lovely eyes,*

---

y Jn 1, 51.
z Dt 1, 8; Mi 7, 28.
a Gn 12, 3; 13, 14f; 15, 5f; 18, 18; 22, 17f; 26, 4; Dt 19, 8; Sir 44, 21.
b Gn 31, 3.
c Gn 31, 13; 35, 14f.
d Gn 35, 6; 48, 3; Jos 18, 13; Jgs 1, 23; Hos 12, 4.
e Wis 10, 10.
f Gn 24, 11f.
g Tb 7, 4.

---

* sacred site. Here the place was Bethel (v 19), a sacred site as early as the time of Abraham (Gn 12, 8).

28, 12: Stairway: in Hebrew, sullam, traditionally but inaccurately, translated as "ladder." The corresponding verb, sal-al, means "to heap up" something, such as dirt for a highway or ramp. The imagery in Jacob's dream is derived from the Babylonian ziggurat or temple tower, "with its top in the sky" (Gn 11, 4), and with brick steps leading up to a small temple at the top.

28, 17: This: the stone Jacob used as a headrest; cf v 22. That: the stairway Jacob saw in his dream.

28, 18: Memorial stone: in Hebrew, masseba, a stone which might vary in shape and size, set upright and usually intended for some religious purpose. Since the custom of erecting such "sacred pillars" in Palestine went back to its pre-Israelite period, their pagan associations were often retained; therefore, later Israelite religion forbade their erection (Lv 26, 1; Dt 16, 22) and ordered the destruction of those that were associated with paganism (Ex 34, 31; Dt 12, 3).

28, 19: Bethel: i.e., "house of God"; the reference is to the abode of God in v 17.

29, 1: Easterners: see note on Gn 25, 6.

29, 11: Burst into tears: literally "raised his voice and wept," i.e., for joy.

29, 14: Flesh and blood: literally "bone and flesh," i.e., a close relative; on the Hebrew idiom, see Gn 2, 23.

29, 17: Lovely eyes: The adjective modifying eyes is often translated as "weak," but "lovely" is the more probable word.

but Rachel was well formed and beautiful. **18** Since Jacob had fallen in love with Rachel, he answered Laban, "I will serve you seven years for your younger daughter Rachel."* **19** Laban replied, "I prefer to give her to you rather than to an outsider. Stay with me." **20** So Jacob served seven years for Rachel, yet they seemed to him but a few days because of his love for her.[h]

21 Then Jacob said to Laban, "Give me my wife, that I may consummate my marriage with her, for my term is now completed." **22** So Laban invited all the local inhabitants and gave a feast. **23** At the nightfall he took his daughter Leah and brought her to Jacob, and Jacob consummated the marriage with her. **24** (Laban assigned his slave girl Zilpah to his daughter Leah as her maidservant.) **25** In the morning Jacob was amazed:* it was Leah! So he cried out to Laban: "How could you do this to me! Was it not for Rachel that I served you? Why did you dupe me?" **26** "It is not the custom in our country," Laban replied, "to marry off a younger daughter before an older one. **27** Finish the bridal week* for this one, and then I will give you the other too, in return for another seven years of service with me."[i]

28 Jacob agreed. He finished the bridal week for Leah, and then Laban gave him his daughter Rachel in marriage. **29** (Laban assigned his slave girl Bilhah to his daughter Rachel as her maidservant.) **30** Jacob then consummated his marriage with Rachel also, and he loved her more than Leah. Thus he remained in Laban's service another seven years.[j]

Jacob's Children.   31 When the LORD saw that Leah was unloved, he made her fruitful, while Rachel remained barren. **32** Leah conceived and bore a son, and she named him Reuben;* for she said, "It means, 'The LORD saw my misery; now my husband will love me.'"[k] **33** She conceived again and bore a son, and said, "It means, 'The LORD heard that I was unloved,' and therefore he has given me this one also"; so she named him Simeon.* **34** Again she conceived and bore a son, and she said, "Now at last my husband will become attached to me, since I have now borne him three sons"; that is why she has named him Levi.* **35** Once more she conceived and bore a son, and she said, "This time I will give grateful praise to the LORD"; therefore she named him Judah.* Then she stopped bearing children.[l]

CHAPTER 30

1 When Rachel saw that she failed to bear children to Jacob, she became envious of her sister. She said to Jacob, "Give me children or I shall die!"[m] **2** In anger Jacob retorted, "Can I take the place of God, who has denied you the fruit of the womb?"[n] **3** She replied, "Here is my maidservant Bilhah. Have intercourse with her, and let her give birth on my knees,* so that I too may have offspring, at least through her."[o] **4** So she gave him her maidservant Bilhah as a consort,* and Jacob had intercourse with her. **5** When Bilhah conceived and bore a son, **6** Rachel said, "God has vindicated me; indeed he has heeded my plea and given me a son." Therefore she named him Dan.* **7** Rachel's maidservant Bilhah conceived again and bore a second son, **8** and Rachel said, "I engaged in a fateful struggle with my sister, and I prevailed." So she named him Naphtali.*

9 When Leah saw that she had ceased to bear children, she gave her maidservant Zilpah to Jacob as a consort. **10** So Jacob had intercourse with Zilpah, and she conceived and bore a son. **11** Leah then said, "What good luck!" So she named him Gad.* **12** Then Leah's maidservant Zilpah bore a second son to Jacob; **13** and Leah said, "What good fortune!"—meaning, "Women call me fortunate." So she named him Asher.*

---

h Hos 12, 13.
i Hos 12, 13.
j Dt 21, 15ff.
k Gn 49, 3.
l Mt 1, 2; Lk 3, 33.
m Prv 30, 16.
n 2 Kgs 5, 7.
o Gn 16, 2ff.

---

*

29, 18: Jacob offers to render service (Jos 15, 16f; 1 Sm 17, 25; 18, 17) in lieu of the customary bridal price (Ex 22, 16f; Dt 22, 29).

29, 25: Jacob was amazed: he had not recognized Leah because a bride was veiled when she was brought to her bridegroom; cf Gn 24, 65.

29, 27: The bridal week: an ancient wedding lasted for seven days of festivities; cf Jgs 14, 12.

29, 32: Reuben: the literal meaning of the Hebrew name is "look, a son!" But in this case, as also with the names of all the other sons of Jacob, a symbolic rather than an etymological interpretation of the name is given, because the name and the persons were regarded as closely interrelated. The symbolic interpretation of Reuben's name, according to the Yahwist source, is based on the similar-sounding, raa beonyi, "he saw my misery." In the Elohist source, the name is explained by the similar-sounding yeehabani, "he will love me."

29, 33: Simeon: in popular etymology, related to shama, "he heard."

29, 34: Levi: related to yillaweh, "he will become attached."

29, 35: Judah: related to odeh, "I will give grateful praise."

30, 3: On my knees: in the ancient Near East, a father would take a newborn child in his lap to signify that he acknowledged it as his own; Rachel uses the ceremony in order to adopt the child and establish her legal rights to it.

30, 4: Consort: the Hebrew word normally means "wife," but here it refers to a wife of secondary rank, who did not have the full legal rights of an ordinary wife.

30, 6: Dan: explained by the term dannanni, "he has vindicated me."

30, 8: Naphtali: explained by the phrase "naptule elohim niptalti, literally, "in a divine wrestling match I have wrestled," perhaps implying the concept of an ordeal; hence the above rendering, I engaged in a fateful struggle.

30, 11: Gad: explained by the Hebrew term begad, literally "in luck," i.e., what good luck!

30, 13: Asher: explained by the term beoshri, literally "in my good fortune, i.e., what good fortune, and by the term ish-sheruni, "they call me fortunate."

14 One day, during the wheat harvest, when Reuben was out in the field, he came upon some mandrakes* which he brought home to his mother Leah. Rachel asked Leah, "Please let me have some of your son's mandrakes." **15** Leah replied, "Was it not enough for you to take away my husband, that you must now take my son's mandrakes too?" "Very well, then!" Rachel answered. "In exchange for your son's mandrakes, Jacob may lie with you tonight." **16** That evening, when Jacob came home from the fields, Leah went out to meet him. "You are now to come in with me," she told him, "because I have paid for you with my son's mandrakes." So that night he slept with her, **17** and God heard her prayer; she conceived and bore a fifth son to Jacob. **18** Leah then said, "God has given me my reward for having let my husband have my maidservant"; so she named him Issachar.* **19** Leah conceived again and bore a sixth son to Jacob; **20** and she said, "God has brought me a precious gift. This time my husband will offer me presents, now that I have borne him six sons"; so she named him Zebulun.* **21** Finally, she gave birth to a daughter, and she named her Dinah.

22 Then God remembered Rachel; he heard her prayer and made her fruitful. **23** She conceived and bore a son, and she said, "God has removed my disgrace."*p* **24** So she named him Joseph,* meaning, "May the LORD add another son to this one for me!"

Jacob Outwits Laban. **25** After Rachel gave birth to Joseph, Jacob said to Laban: "Give me leave to go to my homeland. **26** Let me have my wives, for whom I served you, and my children, too, that I may depart. You know very well the service that I have rendered you." **27** Laban answered him: "If you will please. . . .

"I have learned through divination that it is because of you that God has blessed me. **28** So," he continued, "state what wages you want from me, and I will pay them." **29** Jacob replied: "You know what work I did for you and how well your livestock fared under my care; **30** the little you had before I came has grown into very much, since the LORD's blessings came upon you in my company. Therefore I should now do something for my own household as well." **31** "What should I pay you?" Laban asked. Jacob answered: "You do not have to pay me anything outright. I will again pasture and tend your flock, if you do this one thing for me: **32** go through your whole flock today and remove from it every dark animal among the sheep and every spotted or speckled one among the goats.* Only such animals shall be my wages. **33** In the future, whenever you check on these wages of mine, let my honesty testify against me: any animal in my possession that is not a speckled or spotted goat, or a dark sheep, got there by theft!" **34** "Very well," agreed Laban. "Let it be as you say."

35 That same day Laban removed the streaked and spotted he-goats and all the speckled and spotted she-goats, all those with some white on them, as well as the fully dark-colored sheep; these he left . . . in charge of his sons.* **36** Then he put a three days' journey between himself and Jacob, while Jacob continued to pasture the rest of Laban's flock.

37 Jacob, however, got some fresh shoots of poplar, almond and plane trees, and he made white stripes in them by peeling off the bark down to the white core of the shoots. **38** The rods that he had thus peeled he then set upright in the watering troughs, so that they would be in front of the animals that drank from the troughs. When the animals were in heat and came to drink, **39** *the goats mated by the rods, and so they brought forth streaked, speckled and spotted kids. **40** The sheep, on the other hand, Jacob kept apart, and he set these animals to face the streaked or fully dark-colored animals of Laban. Thus he produced special flocks of his own, which he did not put with Laban's flock. **41** Moreover, whenever the hardier animals were in heat, Jacob would set the rods in the troughs in full view of these animals, so that they mated by the rods; **42** but with the weaker animals he would not put the rods there. So the feeble animals would go to Laban, but the stur-

---

p Lk 1, 25.

30, 14: Mandrakes: an herb whose root was anciently thought to promote conception. The Hebrew word for mandrakes, dudaim, has erotic connotations, since it sounds like the words daddayim ("breasts") and dodim ("sexual pleasure").

30, 18: Issachar: explained by the terms, sekari, "my reward," and in v 16, sakor sekartika, literally "I have hired you," i.e., I have paid for you.

30, 20: Zebulun: related to the Akkadian word zubullum, "bridegroom's gift," is explained by the terms, zebadani . . . zebed tob, "he has brought me a precious gift," and yizbeleni, "he will offer me presents."

30, 24: Joseph: explained by the words yosep, "may he add," and in v 23, asap, "he has removed."

30, 32: Dark . . . sheep . . . spotted or speckled goats: In the Near East the normal color of sheep is light gray, whereas that of goats is uniform dark brown or black. Ordinarily, therefore, Jacob would have received but few animals.

30, 35: By giving the abnormally colored animals to his sons, Laban not only deprived Jacob of his first small wages, but he also designed to prevent in this way the future breeding of such animals in the part of his flock entrusted to Jacob.

30, 39–42: Jacob's stratagem was based on the widespread notion among simple people that visual stimuli can have prenatal effects on the offspring of breeding animals. Thus, the rods on which Jacob had whittled stripes or bands or chevron marks were thought to cause the female goats that looked at them to bear kids with lighter-colored marks on their dark hair, while the gray ewes were thought to bear lambs with dark marks on them simply by visual cross-breeding with the dark goats.

dy ones to Jacob. **43** Thus the man grew increasingly prosperous, and he came to own not only large flocks but also male and female servants and camels and asses.

CHAPTER 31

Flight from Laban. **1** Jacob learned that Laban's sons were saying, "Jacob has taken everything that belonged to our father, and he has accumulated all this wealth of his by using our father's property." **2** Jacob perceived, too, that Laban's attitude toward him was not what it had previously been. **3** Then the LORD said to Jacob, "Return to the land of your fathers, where you were born, and I will be with you."[q]

4 So Jacob sent for Rachel and Leah to meet him where he was in the field with his flock. **5** There he said to them: "I have noticed that your father's attitude toward me is not as it was in the past; but the God of my father has been with me. **6** You well know what effort I put into serving your father; **7** yet your father cheated me and changed my wages time after time. God, however, did not let him do me any harm.[r] **8** *Whenever your father said, 'The speckled animals shall be your wages,' the entire flock would bear speckled young; whenever he said, 'The streaked animals shall be your wages,' the entire flock would bear streaked young. **9** Thus God reclaimed your father's livestock and gave it to me. **10** Once, in the breeding season, I had a dream in which I saw mating he-goats that were streaked, speckled and mottled. **11** In the dream God's messenger called to me, 'Jacob!' 'Here!' I replied. **12** Then he said. 'Note well. All the he-goats in the flock, as they mate, are streaked, speckled and mottled, for I have seen all the things that Laban has been doing to you. **13** I am the God who appeared to you in Bethel, where you anointed a memorial stone and made a vow to me. Up, then! Leave this land and return to the land of your birth.' "[s]

14 Rachel and Leah answered him: "Have we still an heir's portion in our father's house? **15** Are we not regarded by him as outsiders?* He not only sold us; he has even used up the money that he got for us! **16** All the wealth that God reclaimed from our father really belongs to us and our children. Therefore, do just as God has told you."[t] **17** Jacob proceeded to put his children and wives on camels, **18** and he drove off with all his livestock and all the property he had acquired in Paddanaram, to go to his father Isaac in the land of Canaan.

19 Now Laban had gone away to shear his sheep, and Rachel had meanwhile appropriated her father's household idols.[u] * **20** Jacob had hoodwinked* Laban the Aramean by not telling him of his intended flight. **21** Thus he made his escape with all that he had. Once he was across the Euphrates, he headed for the highlands of Gilead.

22 On the third day, word came to Laban that Jacob had fled. **23** Taking his kinsmen with him, he pursued him for seven days* until he caught up with him in the hill country of Gilead. **24** But that night God appeared to Laban the Aramean in a dream and warned him. "Take care not to threaten Jacob with any harm."[v]

Jacob and Laban in Gilead. **25** When Laban overtook Jacob, Jacob's tents were pitched in the highlands; Laban also pitched his tents there, on Mount Gilead. **26** "What do you mean," Laban demanded of Jacob, "by hoodwinking me and carrying off my daughters like war captives?* **27** Why did you dupe me by stealing away secretly? You should have told me, and I would have sent you off with merry singing to the sound of tambourines and harps. **28** You did not even allow me a parting kiss to my daughters and grandchildren! What you have now done is a senseless thing. **29** I have it in my power to harm all of you; but last night the God of your father said to me, 'Take care not to threaten Jacob with any harm!' **30** Granted that you had to leave because you were desperately homesick for your father's house, why did you steal my gods?" **31** "I was frightened," Jacob replied to Laban, "at the thought that you might take your daughters away from me by force. **32** But as for your gods, the one you find them with shall not remain alive! If, with my kinsmen looking on, you identify anything here as belonging to you, take it." Jacob, of course, had no idea that Rachel had stolen the idols.

33 Laban then went in and searched Jacob's

---

q Gn 26, 3; 28, 15; 32, 10.
r Jdt 8, 26.
s Gn 28, 18.

t Wis 10, 10f.
u Gn 19, 34; 1 Sm 19, 13.
v Wis 10, 12.

*

31, 8–12: This Elohist account of the miraculous increase in Jacob's flock differs somewhat from the Yahwist account given in Gn 30, 32–42.

31, 15: Outsiders: literally "foreign women"; they lacked the favored legal status of native women. Used up: literally "eaten, consumed"; the bridal price that a man received for giving his daughter in marriage was legally reserved as her inalienable dowry.

31, 19: Household idols: in Hebrew, teraphim, figurines used in divination (Ez 21, 26; Zec 10, 2). Laban calls them his "gods" (v 30).

31, 20: Hoodwinked: literally "stolen the heart of," i.e., lulled the mind of. Aramean: The earliest extra-biblical references to the Arameans date from several centuries after the time of Jacob; to call Laban an Aramean and to have him speak Aramaic (v 47) would seem to be an anachronism.

31, 23: For seven days: literally "a way of seven days," a general term to designate a long distance; it would have taken a camel caravan many more days to travel from Haran to Gilead, the region east of the northern half of the Jordan.

31, 26: War captives: literally "women captured by the sword"; the women of a conquered people were treated as part of the victor's booty; cf 1 Sm 30, 2; 2 Kgs 5, 2.

tent and Leah's tent, as well as the tents of the two maidservants; but he did not find the idols. Leaving Leah's tent, he went into Rachel's. **34** Now Rachel had taken the idols, put them inside a camel cushion, and seated herself upon them. When Laban had rummaged through the rest of her tent without finding them,[w] **35** Rachel said to her father, "Let not my lord feel offended that I cannot rise in your presence; a woman's period is upon me." So, despite his search, he did not find his idols.

36 Jacob, now enraged, upbraided Laban. "What crime or offense have I committed," he demanded, "that you should hound me so fiercely? **37** Now that you have ransacked all my things, have you found a single object taken from your belongings? If so, produce it here before your kinsmen and mine, and let them decide between us two.

38 "In the twenty years that I was under you, no ewe or she-goat of yours ever miscarried, and I have never feasted on a ram of your flock. **39** [x]I never brought you an animal torn by wild beasts; I made good the loss myself. You held me responsible for anything stolen by day or night.* **40** How often the scorching heat ravaged me by day, and the frost by night, while sleep fled from my eyes! **41** Of the twenty years that I have now spent in your household, I slaved fourteen years for your two daughters and six years for your flock, while you changed my wages time after time. **42** If my ancestral God, the God of Abraham and the Awesome One of Isaac, had not been on my side, you would now have sent me away empty-handed. But God saw my plight and the fruits of my toil, and last night he gave judgment."[y]

43 *Laban replied to Jacob: "The women are mine, their children are mine, and the flocks are mine; everything you see belongs to me. But since these women are my daughters, I will now do something for them and for the children they have borne. **44** Come, then, we will make a pact, you and I; the LORD shall be a witness between us."

45 Then Jacob took a stone and set it up as a memorial stone.[z] **46** Jacob said to his kinsmen, "Gather some stones." So they got some stones and made a mound; and they had a meal there at the mound. **47** Laban called it Jegar-sahadutha,* but Jacob named it Galeed. **48** "This mound," said Laban, "shall be a witness from now on between you and me." That is why it was named Galeed— **49** and also Mizpah,* for he said: "May the LORD keep watch between you and me when we are out of each other's sight. **50** If you mistreat my daughters, or take other wives besides my daughters, remember that even though no one else is about, God will be witness between you and me."

51 Laban said further to Jacob: "Here is this mound, and here is the memorial stone that I have set up between you and me. **52** This mound shall be witness, and this memorial stone shall be witness, that, with hostile intent, neither may I pass beyond this mound into your territory nor may you pass beyond it into mine. **53** May the God of Abraham and the god of Nahor [their ancestral deities] maintain justice between us!" Jacob took the oath by the Awesome One of Issac. **54** He then offered a sacrifice on the mountain and invited his kinsmen to share in the meal. When they had eaten, they passed the night on the mountain.

CHAPTER 32

1 Early the next morning, Laban kissed his grandchildren and his daughters goodbye; then he set out on his journey back home, **2** while Jacob continued on his own way. Then God's messengers encountered Jacob. **3** When he saw them he said, "This is God's encampment." So he named that place Mahanaim.*

Embassy to Esau.   **4** Jacob sent messengers ahead to his brother Esau in the land of Seir, the country of Edom,[a] **5** with this message: "Thus shall you say to my lord Esau: 'Your servant Jacob speaks as follows: I have been staying with Laban and have been detained there until now. **6** I own cattle, asses and sheep, as well as male and female servants. I am sending my lord this information in the hope of gaining my lord's favor.' " **7** When the messengers returned to Jacob, they said, "We reached your brother Esau. He is now coming to meet you, accompanied by four hundred men."

8 Jacob was very much frightened. In his anxiety, he divided the people who were with

---

w Gn 31, 19.
x Ex 22, 12.
y Gn 19, 24. 29.
z Gn 28, 18; 35, 14.
a Gn 36, 6.

*

31, 39: Laban's actions were contrary to the customs of the ancient Near East, as recorded in the Code of Hammurabi: "If in a sheepfold an act of god has occurred, or a lion has made a kill, the shepherd shall clear himself before the deity, and the owner of the fold must accept the loss" (par. 266); cf Ex 22, 12.

31, 43–54: In this account of the treaty between Laban and Jacob, the Yahwist and Elohist sources are closely interwoven. The mound or cairn of stones comes from the Yahwist source, the memorial stone or stele comes from the Elohist one.

31, 47: Jegar-sahadutha: an Aramaic term meaning "mound of witness." Galeed: in Hebrew, galed, with the same meaning; also offers an explanation of the regional name Gilead.

31, 49: Mizpah: a town in Gilead; cf Jgs. 10, 17; 11, 11. 34; Hos 5, 1. The Hebrew name mispa ("lookout") is allied to yisep yhwh ("may the Lord keep watch"), and also echoes the word masseba ("memorial pillar").

32, 3: Mahanaim: a town in Gilead (Jos 13, 26. 30; 21, 38; 2 Sm 2, 8; etc.). The Hebrew name means "two camps." There are other allusions to the name in vv 8. 11.

him, as well as his flocks, herds, and camels, into two camps. **9** "If Esau should attack and overwhelm one camp," he reasoned, "the remaining camp may still survive." **10** Then he prayed, "O God of my father Abraham and God of my father Isaac! You told me, O LORD, 'Go back to the land of your birth, and I will be good to you.'[b] **11** I am unworthy of all the acts of kindness that you have loyally performed for your servant: although I crossed the Jordan here with nothing but my staff, I have now grown into two companies. **12** Save me, I pray, from the hand of my brother Esau! Otherwise I fear that when he comes he will strike me down and slay the mothers and children.[c] **13** You yourself said, 'I will be very good to you, and I will make your descendants like the sands of the sea, which are too numerous to count.'"

14 After passing the night there, Jacob selected from what he had with him the following presents for his brother Esau: **15** two hundred she-goats and twenty he-goats; two hundred ewes and twenty rams; **16** thirty milch camels and their young; forty cows and ten bulls; twenty she-asses and ten he-asses. **17** He put these animals in charge of his servants, in separate droves, and he told the servants, "Go on ahead of me, but keep a space between one drove and the next." **18** To the servant in the lead he gave this instruction: "When my brother Esau meets you, he may ask you, 'Whose man are you? Where are you going? To whom do these animals ahead of you belong?' **19** Then you shall answer, 'They belong to your brother Jacob, but they have been sent as a gift to my lord Esau; and Jacob himself is right behind us.'" **20** He gave similar instructions to the second servant and the third and to all the others who followed behind the droves, namely: "Thus and thus shall you say to Esau, when you reach him; **21** and be sure to add, 'Your servant Jacob is right behind us.'" For Jacob reasoned, "If I first appease him with gifts that precede me, then later, when I face him, perhaps he will forgive me." **22** So the gifts went on ahead of him, while he stayed that night in the camp.

Struggle with the Angel.   **23** In the course of that night, however, Jacob arose, took his two wives, with the two maidservants and his eleven children, and crossed the ford of the Jabbok. **24** After he had taken them across the stream and had brought over all his possessions, **25** Jacob was left there alone. Then some man* wrestled with him until the break of dawn. **26** When the man saw that he could not prevail over him, he struck Jacob's hip at its socket, so that the hip socket was wrenched as they wrestled.[d] **27** The man then said, "Let me go, for it is daybreak." But Jacob said, "I will not let you go until you bless me." **28** "What is your

name?" the man asked. He answered, "Jacob."[e] **29** Then the man said, "You shall no longer be spoken of as Jacob, but as Israel,* because you have contended with divine and human beings and have prevailed." **30** Jacob then asked him, "Do tell me your name, please." He answered, "Why should you want to know my name?" With that, he bade him farewell. **31** Jacob named the place Peniel,* "Because I have seen God face to face," he said, "yet my life has been spared."[f]

32 At sunrise, as he left Penuel, Jacob limped along because of his hip. **33** That is why, to this day, the Israelites do not eat the sciatic muscle that is on the hip socket, inasmuch as Jacob's hip socket was struck at the sciatic muscle.

CHAPTER 33

Jacob and Esau Meet.   **1** Jacob looked up and saw Esau coming, accompanied by four hundred men. So he divided his children among Leah, Rachel and the two maidservants, **2** putting the maids and their children first, Leah and her children next, and Rachel and Joseph last. **3** He himself went on ahead of them, bowing to the ground seven times, until he reached his brother. **4** Esau ran to meet him, embraced him, and flinging himself on his neck, kissed him as he wept.

5 When Esau looked about, he saw the women and children. "Who are these with you?" he asked. Jacob answered, "They are the children whom God has graciously bestowed on your servant." **6** Then the maidservants and their children came forward and bowed low; **7** next, Leah and her children came forward and bowed low; lastly, Rachel and her children came forward and bowed low. **8** Then Esau asked, "What did you intend with all those droves that I encountered?" Jacob answered, "It was to gain my lord's favor." **9** "I have plenty," replied Esau; "you should keep what is yours, brother." **10** "No, I beg you!" said Jacob. "If

---

b Gn 31, 3.
c Gn 28, 14; 48, 16; Ex 32, 13; Heb 11, 12.
d Hos 12, 4.

e Gn 35, 10; 1 Kgs 18, 31; 2 Kgs 17, 34.
f Jgs 13, 22.

*

32, 25: Some man: a messenger of the Lord in human form, as is clear from vv 29ff.

32, 29: Israel: the first part of the Hebrew name Yisrael is given a popular explanation in the word sarita, "you contended"; the second part is the first syllable of elohim, "divine beings." The present incident, with a similar allusion to the name Israel, is referred to in Hos 12, 5, where the mysterious wrestler is explicitly called an angel.

32, 31: Peniel: a variant of the word Penuel (v 32), the name of a town on the north bank of the Jabbok in Gilead (Jgs 8, 8f. 17; 1 Kgs 12, 25). The name is explained as meaning "the face of God," peni-el. Yet my life has been spared: see note on Gn 16, 13.

you will do me the favor, please accept this gift from me, since to come into your presence is for me like coming into the presence of God, now that you have received me so kindly. **11** Do accept the present I have brought you; God has been generous toward me, and I have an abundance.'' Since he so urged him, Esau accepted.

12 Then Esau said, ''Let us break camp and be on our way; I will travel alongside you.'' **13** But Jacob replied: ''As my lord can see, the children are frail. Besides, I am encumbered with the flocks and herds, which now have sucklings; if overdriven for a single day, the whole flock will die. **14** Let my lord, then, go on ahead of me, while I proceed more slowly at the pace of the livestock before me and at the pace of my children, until I join my lord in Seir.'' **15** Esau replied, ''Let me at least put at your disposal some of the men who are with me.'' But Jacob said, ''For what reason? Please indulge me in this, my lord.'' **16** So on the same day that Esau began his journey back to Seir, **17** Jacob journeyed to Succoth. There he built a home for himself and made booths for his livestock. That is why the place was called Succoth.*

18 Having thus come from Paddan-aram, Jacob arrived safely at the city of Shechem, which is in the land of Canaan, and he encamped in sight of the city. *g* **19** The plot of ground on which he had pitched his tent he bought for a hundred pieces of bullion* from the descendants of Hamor, the founder of Shechem. *h* **20** He set up a memorial stone there and invoked ''El, the God of Israel.'' *i*

CHAPTER 34

The Rape of Dinah.   **1** *Dinah, the daughter whom Leah had borne to Jacob, went out to visit some of the women of the land. **2** When Shechem, son of Hamor the Hivite,* who was chief of the region, saw her, he seized her and lay with her by force. **3** Since he was strongly attracted to Dinah, daughter of Jacob, indeed was really in love with the girl, he endeavored to win her affection. **4** Shechem also asked his father Hamor, ''Get me this girl for a wife.''

5 Meanwhile, Jacob heard that Shechem had defiled his daughter Dinah; but since his sons were out in the fields with his livestock, he held his peace until they came home. **6** Now Hamor, the father of Shechem, went out to discuss the matter with Jacob, **7** just as Jacob's sons were coming in from the fields. When they heard the news, the men were shocked and seethed with indignation. What Shechem had done was an outrage in Israel; such a thing could not be tolerated. *j*

8 Hamor appealed to them, saying, ''My son Shechem has his heart set on your daughter.

Please give her to him in marriage. **9** Intermarry with us; give your daughters to us, and take our daughters for yourselves. **10** Thus you can live among us. The land is open before you; you can settle and move about freely in it, and acquire landed property here.'' **11** Then Shechem, too, appealed to Dinah's father and brothers: ''Do me this favor, and I will pay whatever you demand of me. **12** No matter how high you set the bridal price, I will pay you whatever you ask; only give me the maiden in marriage.''

Revenge of Jacob's Sons.   **13** Jacob's sons replied to Shechem and his father Hamor with guile, speaking as they did because their sister Dinah had been defiled. **14** ''We could not do such a thing,'' they said, ''as to give our sister to an uncircumcised man; that would be a disgrace for us. **15** We will agree with you only on this condition, that you become like us by having every male among you circumcised. **16** Then we will give you our daughters and take yours in marriage; we will settle among you and become one kindred people with you. **17** But if you do not comply with our terms regarding circumcision, we will take our daughter and go away.''

18 Their proposal seemed fair to Hamor and his son Shechem. **19** The young man lost no time in acting in the matter, since he was deeply in love with Jacob's daughter. Moreover, he was more highly respected than anyone else in his clan. **20** So Hamor and his son Shechem went to their town council and thus presented the matter to their fellow townsmen: **21** ''These men are friendly toward us. Let them settle in the land and move about in it freely; there is ample room in the country for them. We can marry their daughters and give our daughters to them in marriage. **22** But the men will agree to live with us and form one kindred people with

g Gn 12, 6; Jn 4, 6.   i Jgs 6, 24.
h Jos 24, 32; Jn 4. 5;   j 2 Sm 13, 12.
     Acts 7, 16.

33, 17: Succoth: an important town near the confluence of the Jabbok and the Jordan (Jos 13, 27; Jgs 8, 5–16; 1 Kgs 7, 46). Booths: in Hebrew, sukkot, of the same sound as the name of the town.

33, 19: Pieces of bullion: in Hebrew, kesita, a monetary unit of which the value is now unknown. Descendants of Hamor: Hamorites, ''the men of Hamor''; cf Jgs 9, 28. Hamor was regarded as the eponymous ancestor of the pre-Israelite inhabitants of Shechem.

34, 1–31: Behind the story of the rape of Dinah and the revenge of Jacob's sons on the men of the city of Shechem there probably lies a dimly recollected historical event connected with an armed conflict between the earliest Israelite tribes invading central Canaan and the Hurrian inhabitants of the Shechem region.

34, 2: Hivite: The Greek text has ''Horite''; the terms were apparently used indiscriminately to designate the Hurrian or other non-Semitic elements in Palestine.

us only on this condition, that every male among us be circumcised as they themselves are. **23** Would not the livestock they have acquired—all their animals—then be ours? Let us, therefore, give in to them, so that they may settle among us.''

24 All the able-bodied men of the town* agreed with Hamor and his son Shechem, and all the males, including every able-bodied man in the community, were circumcised. **25** On the third day, while they were still in pain, Dinah's full brothers Simeon and Levi, two of Jacob's sons, took their swords, advanced against the city without any trouble, and massacred all the males. *k* **26** After they had put Hamor and his son Shechem to the sword, they took Dinah from Shechem's house and left. *l* **27** Then the other sons of Jacob followed up the slaughter and sacked the city in reprisal for their sister Dinah's defilement. **28** They seized their flocks, herds and asses, whatever was in the city and in the country around. **29** They carried off all their wealth, their women, and their children, and took for loot whatever was in the houses. *m*

30 Jacob said to Simeon and Levi: ''You have brought trouble upon me by making me loathsome to the inhabitants of the land, the Canaanites and the Perizzites. I have so few men that, if these people unite against me and attack me, I and my family will be wiped out.'' **31** But they retorted, ''Should our sister have been treated like a harlot?''

CHAPTER 35

Bethel Revisited.   **1** God said to Jacob: ''Go up now to Bethel. Settle there and build an altar there to the God who appeared to you while you were fleeing from your brother Esau.'' *n* **2** So Jacob told his family and all the others who were with him: ''Get rid of the foreign gods* that you have among you; then, purify yourselves and put on fresh clothes. **3** We are now to go up to Bethel, and I will build an altar there to the God who answered me in my hour of distress and who has been with me wherever I have gone.'' **4** They therefore handed over to Jacob all the foreign gods in their possession and also the rings* they had in their ears. **5** Then, as they set out, a terror from God fell upon the towns round about, so that no one pursued the sons of Jacob.

6 Thus Jacob and all the people who were with him arrived in Luz [that is, Bethel] in the land of Canaan. *o* **7** There he built an altar and named the place Bethel, for it was there that God had revealed himself to him when he was fleeing from his brother. *p*

8 Death came to Rebekah's nurse Deborah;

she was buried under the oak below Bethel, and so it was called Allonbacuth.*

9 On Jacob's arrival from Paddan-aram, God appeared to him again and blessed him. **10** God said to him:

''You whose name is Jacob
    shall no longer be called Jacob,
    but Israel shall be your name.'' *q*

Thus he was named Israel. **11** God also said to him:

''I am God Almighty;
    be fruitful and multiply.
A nation, indeed an assembly of nations,
    shall stem from you,
    and kings shall issue from your loins.
12 The land I once gave
    to Abraham and Isaac
    I now give to you;
And to your descendants after you
    will I give this land.'' *r*

13 Then God departed from him. **14** On the site where God had spoken with him, Jacob set up a memorial stone, and upon it he made a libation and poured out oil. *s* **15** Jacob named the site Bethel, because God had spoken with him there.

Jacob's Family.   **16** Then they departed from Bethel; but while they still had some distance to go on the way to Ephrath, Rachel began to be in labor and to suffer great distress. **17** When her pangs were most severe, her midwife said to her, ''Have no fear! This time, too, you have a son.'' **18** With her last breath—for she was at the point of death—she called him Ben-oni;* his father, however, named him Ben-

---

k Gn 49, 6.
l Jdt 9, 2.
m Jdt 9, 3f.
n Gn 28, 12f.
o Gn 28, 19; Jos 18, 13;
   Jgs 1, 22f.
p Gn 28, 12f.
q 1 Kgs 18, 31; 2 Kgs
   17, 34.
r Ex 32, 13; Heb 11, 9.
s Gn 28, 18; 31, 45.

34, 24: Every able-bodied man in the community: literally ''all those who go out at the gate of the city,'' apparently meaning the men who go out to war. By temporarily crippling them through circumcision, Jacob's sons deprived the city of its defenders.

35, 2: Foreign gods: pagan images, including household idols (see note on Gn 31, 19), that Jacob's people brought with them from Paddan-aram.

35, 4: Rings: Earrings were often worn as amulets connected with pagan magic.

35, 8: This verse may have stood originally in some other context. Rebekah's nurse is spoken of without a name, in Gn 24, 59. Allon-bacuth: the Hebrew name means ''oak of weeping.''

35, 18: Ben-oni: means either ''son of my vigor'' or, more likely in the context, ''son of affliction.'' Benjamin: ''son of the right hand.'' This may be interpreted to signify a son who is his father's help and support, but more likely its original meaning was ''southerner.'' In the Hebrew idiom, the south lies to one's right hand, and Benjamin was the southernmost of the Rachel tribes.

jamin. **19** ʳThus Rachel died; and she was buried on the road to Ephrath [that is, Bethlehem].* **20** Jacob set up a memorial stone on her grave, and the same monument marks Rachel's grave to this day.

21 Israel moved on and pitched his tent beyond Migdal-eder. **22** While Israel was encamped in that region, Reuben went and lay with Bilhah, his father's concubine. When Israel heard of it, he was greatly offended. ᵘ

The sons of Jacob were now twelve. **23** The sons of Leah: Reuben, Jacob's first-born, Simeon, Levi, Judah, Issachar, and Zebulun; **24** *the sons of Rachel: Joseph and Benjamin; **25** the sons of Rachel's maid Bilhah: Dan and Naphtali; **26** the sons of Leah's maid Zilpah: Gad and Asher. These are the sons of Jacob who were born to him in Paddan-aram.

27 Jacob went home to his father Isaac at Mamre, in Kiriath-arba [that is, Hebron], where Abraham and Isaac had stayed. **28** The lifetime of Isaac was one hundred and eighty years; **29** then he breathed his last. After a full life, he died as an old man and was taken to his kinsmen. His sons Esau and Jacob buried him.

CHAPTER 36

Edomite Lists. **1** These are the descendants of Esau [that is, Edom]. **2** *Esau took his wives from among the Canaanite women: Adah, daughter of Elon the Hittite; Oholibamah, granddaughter through Anah of Zibeon the Hivite;ᵛ **3** and Basemath, daughter of Ishmael and sister of Nebaioth. **4** Adah bore Eliphaz to Esau; Basemath bore Reuel;ʷ **5** and Oholibamah bore Jeush, Jalam and Korah. These are the sons of Esau who were born to him in the land of Cannan.ˣ

6 Esau took his wives, his sons, his daughters, and all the members of his household, as well as his livestock comprising various animals and all the property he had acquired in the land of Canaan, and went to the land of Seir, out of the way of his brother Jacob.ʸ **7** Their possessions had become too great for them to dwell together, and the land in which they were staying could not support them because of their livestock. **8** So Esau settled in the highlands of Seir. [Esau is Edom.]ᶻ **9** These are the descendants of Esau, ancestor of the Edomites, in the highlands of Seir.

10 These are the names of Esau's sons: Eliphaz, son of Esau's wife Adah; and Reuel, son of Esau's wife Basemath. **11** ᵃThe sons of Eliphaz were Teman, Omar, Zepho, Gatam and Kenaz. **12** (Esau's son Eliphaz had a concubine Timna, and she bore Amalek to Eliphaz.) These are the descendants of Esau's wife Adah. **13** The sons of Reuel were Nahath, Zerah, Shammah and Mizzah. These are the descend-

ants of Esau's wife Basemath.ᵇ **14** The descendants of Esau's wife Oholibamah—granddaughter through Anah of Zibeon—whom she bore to Esau were Jeush, Jalam and Korah.ᶜ

15 The following are the clans of Esau's descendants. The descendants of Eliphaz, Esau's first-born: the clans of Teman, Omar, Zepho, Kenaz, **16** Korah, Gatam and Amalek. These are the clans of Eliphaz in the land of Edom; they are descended from Adah. **17** The descendants of Esau's son Reuel: the clans of Nahath, Zerah, Shammah and Mizzah. These are the clans of Reuel in the land of Edom; they are descended from Esau's wife Basemath. **18** The descendants of Esau's wife Oholibamah: the clans of Jeush, Jalam and Korah. These are the clans of Esau's wife Oholibamah, daughter of Anah. **19** Such are the descendants of Esau [that is, Edom] according to their clans.

20 The following are the descendants of Seir the Horite,* the original settlers in the land: Lotan, Shobal, Zibeon, Anah,ᵈ **21** Dishon, Ezer and Dishan; they are the Horite clans descended from Seir, in the land of Edom. **22** ᵉLotan's descendants were Hori and Hemam, and Lotan's sister was Timna. **23** Shobal's descendants were Alvan, Mahanath, Ebal, Shepho and Onam. **24** Zibeon's descendants were Aiah and Anah. (He is the Anah who found water in the desert while he was pasturing the asses of his father Zibeon.) **25** The descendants of Anah were Dishon and Oholibamah, daughter of Anah. **26** The descendants of Dishon were Hemdan, Eshban, Ithran and Cheran. **27** The descendants of Ezer were Bilhan, Zaavan and Akan. **28** The descendants of Dishan were Uz and Aran. **29** These are the Horite clans: the clans of Lotan, Shobal, Zibeon, Anah, **30** Dishon, Ezer

---

t Gn 48, 7; 1 Sm 10, 2; Mi 5, 2.	z Dt 2, 4f; Jos 24, 4.
	a 11f: 1 Chr 1, 36.
u Gn 49, 4; 1 Chr 5, 1.	b 1 Chr 1, 37.
v Gn 26, 34.	c 1 Chr 1, 35.
w 1 Chr 1, 35.	d 20f: 1 Chr 1, 38.
x 1 Chr 1, 35.	e 22-28: 1 Chr 1, 39-42.
y Gn 32, 4.	

*

35, 19: Bethlehem: the gloss comes from a later tradition that identified the site with Bethlehem, also called Ephrath or Ephratha (Jos 15, 59; Ru 4, 11; Mi 5, 1). But Rachel's grave was actually near Ramah (Jer 31, 15), a few miles north of Jerusalem, in the territory of Benjamin (1 Sm 20, 2).

35, 24ff: Benjamin is here said to have been born in Paddanaram, either because all twelve sons of Jacob are considered as a unit, or because the Priestly source, from which vv 23–29 are taken, follows a tradition different from that of the Elohistic source found in vv 16–20.

36, 2–14: The names of Esau's wives and of their fathers given here differ considerably from their names cited from other old sources in Gn 26, 34 and 28, 9. Zibeon the Hivite: In v 20 he is called a "Horite"; see note on Gn 34, 2.

36, 20: Seir the Horite: According to Dt 2, 12, the highlands of Seir were inhabited by Horites before they were occupied by the Edomites.

and Dishan; they were the clans of the Horites, clan by clan, in the land of Seir.

31 *f*The following are the kings who reigned in the land of Edom before any king reigned over the Israelites.* **32** Bela, son of Beor, became king in Edom; the name of his city was Dinhabah. **33** When Bela died, Jobab, son of Zerah, from Bozrah, succeeded him as king. **34** When Jobab died, Husham, from the land of the Temanites, succeeded him as king. He defeated the Midianites in the country of Moab; the name of his city was Avith. **35** When Husham died, Hadad, son of Bedad, succeeded him as king. **36** When Hadad died, Samlah, from Masrekah, succeeded him as king. **37** When Samlah died, Shaul, from Rehoboth-on-the-River, succeeded him as king. **38** When Shaul died, Baal-hanan, son of Achbor, succeeded him as king. **39** When Baal-Hanan died, Hadar succeeded him as king; the name of his city was Pau. (His wife's name was Mehetabel; she was the daughter of Matred, son of Mezahab.)

40 The following are the names of the clans of Esau individually according to their subdivisions and localities: the clans of Timna, Alvah, Jetheth, **41** Oholibamah, Elah, Pinon, **42** Kenaz, Teman, Mibzar, **43** Magdiel and Iram. These are the clans of the Edomites, according to their settlements in their territorial holdings. [Esau was the father of the Edomites.]

IV.: *Joseph and His Brothers*

CHAPTER 37

Joseph Sold into Egypt. **1** Jacob settled in the land where his father had stayed, the land of Canaan. **2** This is his family history. When Joseph was seventeen years old, he was tending the flocks with his brothers; he was an assistant to the sons of his father's wives Bilhah and Zilpah, and he brought his father bad reports about them.

3 Israel loved Joseph best of all his sons, for he was the child of his old age; and he had made him a long tunic. **4** When his brothers saw that their father loved him best of all his sons, they hated him so much that they would not even greet him.

5 Once Joseph had a dream, which he told to his brothers:*g* **6** "Listen to this dream I had. **7** There we were, binding sheaves in the field, when suddenly my sheaf rose to an upright position, and your sheaves formed a ring around my sheaf and bowed down to it." **8** "Are you really going to make yourself king over us?" his brothers asked him. "Or impose your rule on us?" So they hated him all the more because of his talk about his dreams.*h*

9 Then he had another dream, and this one, too, he told to his brothers. "I had another dream," he said; "this time, the sun and the moon and eleven stars were bowing down to me." **10** When he also told it to his father, his father reproved him. "What is the meaning of this dream of yours?" he asked, "Can it be that I and your mother and your brothers are to come and bow to the ground before you?" **11** So his brothers were wrought up against him but his father pondered the matter.

12 One day, when his brothers had gone to pasture their father's flocks at Shechem, **13** Israel said to Joseph, "Your brothers, you know, are tending our flocks at Shechem. Get ready; I will send you to them." "I am ready," Joseph answered. **14** "Go then," he replied; "see if all is well with your brothers and the flocks, and bring back word." So he sent him off from the valley of Hebron. When Joseph reached Shechem, **15** a man met him as he was wandering about in the fields. "What are you looking for?" the man asked him. **16** "I am looking for my brothers," he answered. "Could you please tell me where they are tending the flocks?" **17** The man told him, "They have moved on from here; in fact, I heard them say, 'Let us go on to Dothan.'" So Joseph went after his brothers and caught up with them in Dothan. **18** They noticed him from a distance, and before he came up to them, they plotted to kill him. **19** They said to one another: "Here comes that master dreamer! **20** Come on, let us kill him and throw him into one of the cisterns here; we could say that a wild beast devoured him. We shall then see what comes of his dreams."*i*

21 *When Reuben heard this, he tried to save him from their hands, saying, "We must not take his life. **22** Instead of shedding blood," he continued, "just throw him into that cistern there in the desert; but don't kill him outright." His purpose was to rescue him from their hands and restore him to his father.*j* **23** So when Joseph came up to them, they stripped him of the long tunic he had on; **24** then they took him and

---

f 31-43: 1 Chr 1, 45-54.
g Gn 42, 9.
h Gn 50, 17.
i Gn 44, 28.
j Gn 42, 22.

*

36, 31: Before any king reigned over the Israelites: obviously this statement was written after the time of Saul, Israel's first king.

37, 21-36: The chapter thus far is from the Yahwist source, as are also vv 25-28a. But vv 21-24 and 28b-36 are from the Elohist source. In the latter, Reuben tries to rescue Joseph, who is taken in Reuben's absence by certain Midianites; in the Yahwist source, it is Judah who saves Joseph's life by having him sold to certain Ishmaelites. Although the two variant forms in which the story was handed down in early oral tradition differ in these minor points, they agree on the essential fact that Joseph was brought as a slave into Egypt because of the jealousy of his brothers.

threw him into the cistern, which was empty and dry.

25 They then sat down to their meal. Looking up, they saw a caravan of Ishmaelites coming from Gilead, their camels laden with gum, balm and resin to be taken down to Egypt.[k] **26** Judah said to his brothers: "What is to be gained by killing our brother and concealing his blood?[l] **27** Rather, let us sell him to these Ishmaelites, instead of doing away with him ourselves. After all, he is our brother, our own flesh." His brothers agreed. **28** They sold Joseph to the Ishmaelites for twenty pieces of silver.*

Some Midianite traders passed by, and they pulled Joseph up out of the cistern and took him to Egypt.[m] **29** When Reuben went back to the cistern and saw that Joseph was not in it, he tore his clothes, **30** and returning to his brothers, he exclaimed: "The boy is gone! And I—where can I turn?" **31** They took Joseph's tunic, and after slaughtering a goat, dipped the tunic in its blood. **32** They then sent someone to bring the long tunic to their father, with the message: "We found this. See whether it is your son's tunic or not." **33** He recognized it and exclaimed: "My son's tunic! A wild beast has devoured him! Joseph has been torn to pieces!"[n] **34** Then Jacob rent his clothes, put sackcloth on his loins, and mourned his son many days. **35** Though his sons and daughters tried to console him, he refused all consolation, saying, "No, I will go down mourning to my son in the nether world." Thus did his father lament him.[o]

36 The Midianites, meanwhile, sold Joseph in Egypt to Potiphar, a courtier of Pharaoh and his chief steward.[p]

CHAPTER 38*

Judah and Tamar. **1** About that time Judah parted from his brothers and pitched his tent near a certain Adullamite named Hirah. **2** There he met the daughter of a Canaanite named Shua, married her, and had relations with her.[q] **3** She conceived and bore a son, whom she named Er. **4** Again she conceived and bore a son, whom she named Onan. **5** Then she bore still another son, whom she named Shelah. They were in Chezib* when he was born.[r]

6 Judah got a wife named Tamar for his first-born, Er. **7** But Er, Judah's first-born, greatly offended the LORD; so the LORD took his life.[s] **8** Then Judah said to Onan, "Unite with your brother's widow, in fulfillment of your duty as brother-in-law, and thus preserve your brother's line."* **9** Onan, however, knew that the descendants would not be counted as his; so whenever he had relations with his brother's

widow, he wasted his seed on the ground, to avoid contributing offspring for his brother. **10** What he did greatly offended the LORD, and the LORD took his life too. **11** Thereupon Judah said to his daughter-in-law Tamar, "Stay as a widow in your father's house until my son Shelah grows up"—for he feared that Shelah also might die like his brothers. So Tamar went to live in her father's house.

12 Years passed, and Judah's wife, the daughter of Shua, died. After Judah completed the period of mourning, he went up to Timnah for the shearing of his sheep, in company with his friend Hirah the Adullamite. **13** When Tamar was told that her father-in-law was on his way up to Timnah to shear his sheep, **14** she took off her widow's garb, veiled her face by covering herself with a shawl, and sat down at the entrance to Enaim, which is on the way to Timnah; for she was aware that, although Shelah was now grown up, she had not been given to him in marriage.[u] **15** When Judah saw her, he mistook her for a harlot, since she had covered her face. **16** So he went over to her at the roadside, and not realizing that she was his daughter-in-law, he said, "Come, let me have intercourse with you." She replied, "What will you pay me for letting you have intercourse with me?" **17** He answered, "I will send you a kid from the flock." "Very well," she said, "provided you leave a pledge until you send it." **18** Judah asked, "What pledge am I to give you?" She answered, "Your seal and cord,*

---

k Gn 43, 11.
l Jb 16, 18.
m Ps 105, 17; Wis 10, 13; Acts 7, 9.
n Gn 44, 28.
o Gn 42, 38.
p Ps 105, 17.
q 1 Chr 2, 3.
r 1 Chr 4, 21.
s 1 Chr 2, 3.
t Dt 25, 5; Mt 22, 24; Mk 12, 19; Lk 20, 28.
u Prv 7, 10.

*

37, 28: They sold Joseph . . . silver: in the Hebrew text, these words occur between out of the cistern and (they) took him to Egypt at the end of the verse.

38, 1–30: This chapter, from the Yahwist source, has nothing to do with the Joseph story in which Judah is still living with his father and brothers. The sacred author inserted this independent account from the life of Judah at this place to mark the long lapse of time during which Joseph's family knew nothing of his life in Egypt. This is apparently a personalized history of the early days of the tribe of Judah, which interbred with several Canaanite clans, though some of these soon became extinct.

38, 5: Chezib: a variant form of Achzib (Jos 15, 44; Mi 1, 14), a town in the Judean Shephelah.

38, 8: Preserve your brother's line: literally, "raise up seed for your brother." The ancient Israelites regarded as very important their law of levirate, or "brother-in-law" marriage; see notes on Dt 25, 5; Ru 2, 20. In the present story, it is primarily Onan's violation of this law, rather than the means he used to circumvent it, that brought on him God's displeasure (vv 9f).

38, 18: Seal and cord: the cylinder seal, through which a hole was bored lengthwise so that it could be worn from the neck by a cord, was a distinctive means of identification. Apparently a man's staff was also marked with his name (Nm 17, 16f) or other sign of identification.

and the staff you carry." So he gave them to her and had intercourse with her, and she conceived by him. **19** When she went away, she took off her shawl and put on her widow's garb again.

20 Judah sent the kid by his friend the Adullamite to recover the pledge from the woman; but he could not find her. **21** So he asked the men of the place, "Where is the temple prostitute,* the one by the roadside in Enaim?" But they answered, "There has never been a temple prostitute here." **22** He went back to Judah and told him, "I could not find her; and besides, the men of the place said there was no temple prostitute there." **23** "Let her keep the things," Judah replied; "otherwise we shall become a laughingstock. After all, I did send her the kid, even though you were unable to find her."

24 About three months later, Judah was told that his daughter-in-law Tamar had played the harlot and was then with child from her harlotry. "Bring her out," cried Judah; "she shall be burned." **25** But as they were bringing her out, she sent word to her father-in-law, "It is by the man to whom these things belong that I am with child. Please verify," she added, "whose seal and cord and whose staff these are." **26** Judah recognized them and said, "She is more in the right than I am, since I did not give her to my son Shelah." But he had no further relations with her.

27 When the time of her delivery came, she was found to have twins in her womb.ᵛ **28** While she was giving birth, one infant put out his hand; and the midwife, taking a crimson thread, tied it on his hand, to note that this one came out fiřst. **29** ʷBut as he withdrew his hand, his brother came out; and she said, "What a breach you have made for yourself!" So he was called Perez.* **30** Afterward his brother came out; he was called Zerah.ˣ *

CHAPTER 39

Joseph's Temptation. **1** When Joseph was taken down to Egypt, a certain Egyptian (Potiphar, a courtier of Pharoah and his chief steward*) bought him from the Ishmaelites who had brought him there. **2** ʸBut since the LORD was with him, Joseph got on very well and was assigned to the household of his Egyptian master. **3** When his master saw that the LORD was with him and brought him success in whatever he did, **4** he took a liking to Joseph and made him his personal attendant; he put him in charge of his household and entrusted to him all his possessions.ᶻ **5** From the moment that he put him in charge of his household and all his possessions, the LORD blessed the Egyptian's house for Joseph's sake; in fact, the LORD's blessing was on everything he owned, both inside the house and out. **6** Having left everything he owned in Joseph's charge, he gave no thought, with Joseph there, to anything but the food he ate.

Now Joseph was strikingly handsome in countenance and body. **7** After a time, his master's wife began to look fondly at him and said, "Lie with me." **8** But he refused. "As long as I am here," he told her, "my master does not concern himself with anything in the house, but has entrusted to me all he owns. **9** He wields no more authority in this house than I do, and he has withheld from me nothing but yourself, since you are his wife. How, then, could I commit so great a wrong and thus stand condemned before God?" **10** Although she tried to entice him day after day, he would not agree to lie beside her, or even stay near her.ᵃ

11 One such day, when Joseph came into the house to do his work, and none of the household servants were then in the house, **12** she laid hold of him by his cloak, saying, "Lie with me!" But leaving the cloak in her hand, he got away from her and ran outside. **13** When she saw that he had left his cloak in her hand as he fled outside, **14** she screamed for her household servants and told them, "Look! my husband has brought in a Hebrew slave to make sport of us! He came in here to lie with me, but I cried out as loud as I could. **15** When he heard me scream for help, he left his cloak beside me and ran away outside."

16 She kept the cloak with her until his master came home. **17** Then she told him the same story: "The Hebrew slave whom you brought here broke in on me, to make sport of me. **18** But when I screamed for help, he left his cloak beside me and fled outside." **19** As soon as the master heard his wife's story about how his slave had treated her, he became enraged.

---

v 1 Chr 2, 4.
w Rv 4, 12; Mt 1, 3; Lk 3, 33.
x Nm 26, 20; 1 Chr 2, 4; Mt 1, 3.
y 1 Sm 3, 19; 10, 7; 18, 14; 2 Sm 5, 10; 2 Kgs 18, 7; Acts 7, 9.
z Dn 1, 9.
a 1 Mc 2, 53.

*

38, 21: Temple prostitute: the Hebrew term qedesha, literally "consecrated woman," designates a woman who had ritual intercourse with men in pagan fertility rites; cf Dt 23, 18; Hos 4, 14, where the same Hebrew word is used. Hirah the Adullamite uses a word that refers to a higher social class than that designated by the term zona, common "harlot," used in vv 15. 24.

38, 29: He was called Perez: the Hebrew word means "breach."

38, 30: He was called Zerah: a name connected here by popular etymology with a Hebrew verb for the red light of dawn, alluding apparently to the crimson thread.

39, 1: (Potiphar . . . chief steward): These words in the text serve to harmonize ch 39 from the Yahwist source, with Gn 37, 36, and 40, 1–23, from the Elohist. In the former, the Ishmaelites who bought Joseph from his brothers (Gn 37, 28) sold him to the unnamed "Egyptian master" of ch 39. In the latter, the Midianites who kidnaped Joseph (Gn 37, 28; 40, 15) sold him to Potiphar, Paraoh's chief steward (Gn 37, 36), whose house was used as a royal prison (Gn 40, 2f).

20 He seized Joseph and threw him into the jail where the royal prisoners were confined. [b]

But even while he was in prison, **21** the LORD remained with Joseph; he showed him kindness by making the chief jailer well-disposed toward him. [c] **22** The chief jailer put Joseph in charge of all the prisoners in the jail, and everything that had to be done there was done under his management. **23** The chief jailer did not concern himself with anything at all that was in Joseph's charge, since the LORD was with him and brought success to all he did.

CHAPTER 40

The Dreams Interpreted.   **1** Some time afterward, the royal cupbearer and baker gave offense to their lord, the king of Egypt. **2** Pharaoh was angry with his two courtiers, the chief cupbearer and the chief baker, **3** and he put them in custody in the house of the chief steward (the same jail where Joseph was confined). **4** The chief steward assigned Joseph to them, and he became their attendant.

After they had been in custody for some time, **5** the cupbearer and the baker of the king of Egypt who were confined in the jail both had dreams on the same night, each dream with its own meaning. **6** When Joseph came to them in the morning, he noticed that they looked disturbed. **7** So he asked Pharaoh's courtiers who were with him in custody in his master's house, "Why do you look so sad today?" **8** They answered him, "We have had dreams, but there is no one to interpret them for us." Joseph said to them, "Surely, interpretations come from God. Please tell the dreams to me." [d]

9 Then the chief cupbearer told Joseph his dream. "In my dream," he said, "I saw a vine in front of me, **10** and on the vine were three branches. It had barely budded when its blossoms came out, and its clusters ripened into grapes. **11** Pharaoh's cup was in my hand; so I took the grapes, pressed them out into his cup, and put it in Pharaoh's hand." **12** Joseph said to him: "This is what it means. The three branches are three days; **13** within three days Pharaoh will lift up your head* and restore you to your post. You will be handing Pharaoh his cup as you formerly used to do when you were his cupbearer. **14** So if you will still remember, when all is well with you, that I was here with you, please do me the favor of mentioning me to Pharaoh, to get me out of this place. **15** The truth is that I was kidnaped from the land of the Hebrews, and here I have not done anything for which I should have been put into a dungeon."

16 When the chief baker saw that Joseph had given this favorable interpretation, he said to him: "I too had a dream. In it I had three wicker baskets on my head; **17** in the top one were all kinds of bakery products for Pharaoh, but the birds were pecking at them out of the basket on my head." **18** Joseph said to him in reply: "This is what it means. The three baskets are three days; **19** within three days Pharaoh will lift up your head and have you impaled on a stake, and the birds will be pecking the flesh from your body."

20 And in fact, on the third day, which was Pharaoh's birthday, when he gave a banquet to all his staff, with his courtiers around him, he lifted up the heads of the chief cupbearer and chief baker. **21** He restored the chief cupbearer to his office, so that he again handed the cup to Pharaoh; **22** but the chief baker he impaled—just as Joseph had told them in his interpretation. **23** Yet the chief cupbearer gave no thought to Joseph; he had forgotten him.

CHAPTER 41

Pharaoh's Dream.   **1** After a lapse of two years, Pharaoh had a dream. He saw himself standing by the Nile, **2** when up out of the Nile came seven cows, handsome and fat; they grazed in the reed grass. **3** Behind them seven other cows, ugly and gaunt, came up out of the Nile; and standing on the bank of the Nile beside the others, **4** the ugly, gaunt cows ate up the seven handsome, fat cows. Then Pharaoh woke up.

5 He fell asleep again and had another dream. He saw seven ears of grain, fat and healthy, growing on a single stalk. **6** Behind them sprouted seven ears of grain, thin and blasted by the east wind; **7** and the seven thin ears swallowed up the seven fat, healthy ears. Then Pharaoh woke up, to find it was only a dream.

8 Next morning his spirit was agitated. So he summoned all the magicians and sages of Egypt and recounted his dreams to them; but no one could interpret his dreams for him. **9** Then the chief cupbearer spoke up and said to Pharaoh: "On this occasion I am reminded of my negligence. **10** Once, when Pharaoh was angry, he put me and the chief baker in custody in the house of the chief steward. **11** Later, we both had dreams on the same night, and each of our dreams had its own meaning. **12** There with us was a Hebrew youth, a slave of the chief steward; and when we told him our dreams, he interpreted them for us and explained for each of us

---

b Ps 105, 18.   d Gn 41, 16.
c Acts 7, 9f.   e Dn 1, 17.
*

40, 13: Lift up your head: signifying "pardon you." In v 19 "to lift up the head" means "to behead"; and finally, in v 20, the same expression means "to review the case (of someone)." Joseph couches his interpretation of the dreams in equivocal terms.

the meaning of his dream. *e* **13** And it turned out just as he had told us: I was restored to my post, but the other man was impaled.''

14 Pharaoh therefore had Joseph summoned, and they hurriedly brought him from the dungeon. After he shaved and changed his clothes, he came into Pharaoh's presence. *f* **15** Pharaoh then said to him: ''I had certain dreams that no one can interpret. But I hear it said of you that the moment you are told a dream you can interpret it.'' **16** ''It is not I,'' Joseph replied to Pharaoh, ''but God who will give Pharaoh the right answer.'' *g*

17 Then Pharaoh said to Joseph: ''In my dream, I was standing on the bank of the Nile, **18** when up from the Nile came seven cows, fat and well-formed; they grazed in the reed grass. **19** Behind them came seven other cows, scrawny, most ill-formed and gaunt. Never have I seen such ugly specimens as these in all the land of Egypt! **20** The gaunt, ugly cows ate up the first seven fat cows. **21** But when they had consumed them, no one could tell that they had done so, because they looked as ugly as before. Then I woke up. **22** In another dream, I saw seven ears of grain, fat and healthy, growing on a single stalk. **23** Behind them sprouted seven ears of grain, shriveled and thin and blasted by the east wind; **24** and the seven thin ears swallowed up the seven healthy ears. I have spoken to the magicians, but none of them can give me an explanation.''

25 Joseph said to Pharaoh: ''Both of Pharaoh's dreams have the same meaning. God has thus foretold to Pharaoh what he is about to do. **26** The seven healthy cows are seven years, and the seven healthy ears are seven years—the same in each dream. **27** So also, the seven thin, ugly cows that came up after them are seven years, as are the seven thin, wind-blasted ears; they are seven years of famine. **28** It is just as I told Pharaoh: God has revealed to Pharaoh what he is about to do. **29** Seven years of great abundance are now coming throughout the land of Egypt; **30** but these will be followed by seven years of famine, when all the abundance in the land of Egypt will be forgotten. When the famine has ravaged the land, **31** no trace of the abundance will be found in the land because of the famine that follows it—so utterly severe will that famine be. **32** That Pharaoh had the same dream twice means that the matter has been reaffirmed by God and that God will soon bring it about.

33 ''Therefore, let Pharaoh seek out a wise and discerning man and put him in charge of the land of Egypt. **34** Pharaoh should also take action to appoint overseers, so as to regiment the land during the seven years of abundance. **35** They should husband all the food of the coming good years, collecting the grain under

Pharaoh's authority, to be stored in the towns for food. **36** This food will serve as a reserve for the country against the seven years of famine that are to follow in the land of Egypt, so that the land may not perish in the famine.''

37 This advice pleased Pharaoh and all his officials. *h* **38** ''Could we find another like him,'' Pharaoh asked his officials, ''a man so endowed with the spirit of God?'' **39** So Pharaoh said to Joseph: ''Since God has made all this known to you, no one can be as wise and discerning as you are. **40** You shall be in charge of my palace, and all my people shall dart at your command. Only in respect to the throne shall I outrank you. *i* **41** Herewith,'' Pharaoh told Joseph, ''I place you in charge of the whole land of Egypt.'' **42** With that, Pharaoh took off his signet ring* and put it on Joseph's finger. He had him dressed in robes of fine linen and put a gold chain about his neck. **43** He then had him ride in the chariot of his vizier, and they shouted ''Abrek!''* before him.

Thus was Joseph installed over the whole land of Egypt. **44** ''I, Pharaoh, proclaim,'' he told Joseph, ''that without your approval no one shall move hand or foot in all the land of Egypt.'' **45** Pharaoh also bestowed the name of Zaphnath-paneah* on Joseph, and he gave him in marriage Asenath, the daughter of Potiphera, priest of Heliopolis. **46** Joseph was thirty years old when he entered the service of Pharaoh, king of Egypt.

After Joseph left Pharaoh's presence, he traveled throughout the land of Egypt. **47** During the seven years of plenty, when the land produced abundant crops, **48** he husbanded all the food of these years of plenty that the land of Egypt was enjoying and stored it in the towns, placing in each town the crops of the fields around it. **49** Joseph garnered grain in quantities like the sands of the sea, so vast that at last

---

f Ps 105, 20.
g Gn 40, 8.
h Acts 7, 10.

i Ps 105, 21; Wis 10, 14;
1 Mc 2, 53; Acts 7, 10.

*

41, 42: Signet ring: a finger ring in which was set a stamp seal, different from the cylinder seal such as Judah wore; see note on Gn 38, 18. This is an authentic detail. By receiving Pharaoh's signet ring, Joseph was made vizier of Egypt (v 43); the vizier was known as ''seal-bearer of the king of Lower Egypt.'' Another authentic detail is the gold chain, a symbol of high office in ancient Egypt.

41, 43: Abrek: apparently a cry of homage, though the word's derivation and actual meaning are uncertain.

41, 45: Zaphenath-paneah: a Hebrew transcription of an Egyptian name meaning ''the god speaks and he (the newborn child) lives.'' Asenath: means ''belonging to (the Egyptian goddess) Neith.'' Potiphera: means ''he whom Ra (the Egyptian god) gave''; a shorter form of the same name was borne by Joseph's master (Gn 37, 36). Heliopolis: in Hebrew, On, a city seven miles northeast of modern Cairo, site of the chief temple of the sun god; it is mentioned also in v 50; Gn 46, 20; Ez 30, 17.

he stopped measuring it, for it was beyond measure.

50 Before the famine years set in, Joseph became the father of two sons, born to him by Asenath, daughter of Potiphera, priest of Heliopolis.[j] **51** He named his first-born Manasseh,* meaning, "God has made me forget entirely the sufferings I endured at the hands of my family"; **52** and the second he named Ephraim,* meaning, "God has made me fruitful in the land of my affliction."

53 When the seven years of abundance enjoyed by the land of Egypt came to an end, **54** the seven years of famine set in, just as Joseph had predicted. Although there was famine in all the other countries, food was available throughout the land of Egypt.[k] **55** When hunger came to be felt throughout the land of Egypt and the people cried to Pharaoh for bread, Pharaoh directed all the Egyptians to go to Joseph and do whatever he told them. **56** When the famine had spread throughout the land, Joseph opened all the cities that had grain and rationed it to the Egyptians, since the famine had gripped the land of Egypt. **57** In fact, all the world came to Joseph to obtain rations of grain, for famine had gripped the whole world.

CHAPTER 42

The Brothers' First Journey to Egypt.

1 When Jacob learned that grain rations were available in Egypt, he said to his sons: "Why do you keep gaping at one another? **2** I hear," he went on, "that rations of grain are available in Egypt. Go down there and buy some for us, that we may stay alive rather than die of hunger."[l] **3** So ten of Joseph's brothers went down to buy an emergency supply of grain from Egypt. **4** It was only Joseph's full brother Benjamin that Jacob did not send with the rest, for he thought some disaster might befall him. **5** Thus, since there was famine in the land of Canaan also, the sons of Israel were among those who came to procure rations.[m]

6 It was Joseph, as governor of the country, who dispensed the rations to all the people. When Joseph's brothers came and knelt down before him with their faces to the ground,[n] **7** he recognized them as soon as he saw them. But he concealed his own identity from them and spoke sternly to them. "Where do you come from?" he asked them. They answered, "From the land of Canaan, to procure food."

8 When Joseph recognized his brothers, although they did not recognize him, **9** he was reminded of the dreams he had about them. He said to them: "You are spies.[o] You have come to see the nakedness of the land."* **10** "No, my lord," they replied. "On the contrary, your servants have come to procure food. **11** All of us are sons of the same man. We are honest men; your servants have never been spies." **12** But he answered them: "Not so! You have come to see the nakedness of the land." **13** "We your servants," they said, "were twelve brothers, sons of a certain man in Canaan; but the youngest one is at present with our father, and the other one is gone."[p] **14** "It is just as I said," Joseph persisted; "you are spies. **15** This is how you shall be tested: unless your youngest brother comes here, I swear by the life of Pharaoh that you shall not leave here. **16** So send one of your number to get your brother, while the rest of you stay here under arrest. Thus shall your words be tested for their truth; if they are untrue, as Pharaoh lives, you are spies!" **17** With that, he locked them up in the guardhouse for three days.

18 On the third day Joseph said to them: "Do this, and you shall live; for I am a God-fearing man. **19** If you have been honest, only one of your brothers need be confined in this prison, while the rest of you may go and take home provisions for your starving families. **20** But you must come back to me with your youngest brother. Your words will thus be verified, and you will not die." To this they agreed.[q] **21** To one another, however, they said: "Alas, we are being punished because of our brother. We saw the anguish of his heart when he pleaded with us, yet we paid no heed; that is why this anguish has now come upon us."[r] **22** "Didn't I tell you," broke in Reuben, "not to do wrong to the boy? But you wouldn't listen! Now comes the reckoning for his blood."[s] **23** They did not know, of course, that Joseph understood what they said, since he spoke with them through an interpreter. **24** But turning away from them, he wept. When he was able to speak to them again, he had Simeon taken from them and bound before their eyes. **25** Then Joseph gave orders to have their containers filled with grain, their money replaced in each one's sack, and provisions given them for their journey. After this had been done for them, **26** they loaded their donkeys with the rations and departed.

27 *At the night encampment, when one of

j Gn 46, 20; 48, 5.
k Ps 105, 16; Acts 7, 11.
l Acts 7, 12.
m Jdt 5, 10; Acts 7, 11.
n Ps 105, 21.
o Gn 37, 5.
p Gn 44, 20.
q Gn 43, 5.
r Gn 37, 18-27.
s Gn 37, 22.

*

41, 51: Manasseh: allusion to this name is in the Hebrew expression, nishshani, "he made me forget."

41, 52: Ephraim: related to the Hebrew expression hiphrani, "(God) has made me fruitful."

42, 9. 12: The nakedness of the land: the military weakness of the land, like human nakedness, should not be seen by strangers.

42, 27-28: These two verses are from the Yahwist source, whereas the rest of the chapter is from the Elohist source, in which the men find the money in their sacks (not "bags"—a

them opened his bag to give his donkey some fodder, he was surprised to see his money in the mouth of his bag. **28** "My money has been returned!" he cried out to his brothers. "Here it is in my bag!" At that their hearts sank. Trembling, they asked one another, "What is this that God has done to us?"

29 When they got back to their father Jacob in the land of Canaan, they told him all that had happened to them. **30** "The man who is lord of the country," they said, "spoke to us sternly and put us in custody as if we were spying on the land. **31** But we said to him: 'We are honest men; we have never been spies. **32** There were twelve of us brothers, sons of the same father; but one is gone, and the youngest one is at present with our father in the land of Canaan.' **33** Then the man who is lord of the country said to us: 'This is how I shall know if you are honest men: leave one of your brothers with me, while the rest of you go home with rations for your starving families. **34** When you come back to me with your youngest brother, and I know that you are honest men and not spies, I will restore your brother to you, and you may move about freely in the land.' "

35 When they were emptying their sacks, there in each one's sack was his moneybag! At the sight of their moneybags, they and their father were dismayed. **36** Their father Jacob said to them: "Must you make me childless? Joseph is gone, and Simeon is gone, and now you would take away Benjamin! Why must such things always happen to me!" **37** Then Reuben told his father: "Put him in my care, and I will bring him back to you. You may kill my own two sons if I do not return him to you." **38** But Jacob replied: "My son shall not go down with you. Now that his full brother is dead, he is the only one left. If some disaster should befall him on the journey you must make, you would send my white head down to the nether world in grief."[t]

CHAPTER 43*

The Second Journey to Egypt. **1** Now the famine in the land grew more severe. **2** So when they had used up all the rations they had brought from Egypt, their father said to them, "Go back and procure us a little more food." **3** But Judah replied: "The man strictly warned us, 'You shall not appear in my presence unless your brother is with you.'[u] **4** If you are willing to let our brother go with us, we will go down to procure food for you. **5** But if you are not willing, we will not go down, because the man told us, 'You shall not appear in my presence unless your brother is with you.' "[v] **6** Israel demanded, "Why did you bring this trouble on me by telling the man that you had another

brother?" **7** They answered: "The man kept asking about ourselves and our family: 'Is your father still living? Do you have another brother?' We had to answer his questions. How could we know that he would say, 'Bring your brother down here'?"

8 Then Judah urged his father Israel: "Let the boy go with me, that we may be off and on our way if you and we and our children are to keep from starving to death.[w] **9** I myself will stand surety for him. You can hold me responsible for him. If I fail to bring him back, to set him in your presence, you can hold it against me forever.[x] **10** Had we not dilly-dallied, we could have been there and back twice by now!"

11 Their father Israel then told them: "If it must be so, then do this: Put some of the land's best products in your baggage and take them down to the man as gifts: some balm and honey, gum and resin, and pistachios and almonds.[y] **12** Also take extra money along, for you must return the amount that was put back in the mouths of your bags; it may have been a mistake. **13** Take your brother, too, and be off on your way back to the man. **14** May God Almighty dispose the man to be merciful toward you, so that he may let your other brother go, as well as Benjamin. As for me, if I am to suffer bereavement, I shall suffer it."

15 So the men got the gifts, took double the amount of money with them, and, accompanied by Benjamin, were off on their way down to Egypt to present themselves to Joseph. **16** When Joseph saw Benjamin with them, he told his head steward, "Take these men into the house, and have an animal slaughtered and prepared, for they are to dine with me at noon." **17** Doing as Joseph had ordered, the steward conducted the men to Joseph's house. **18** But on being led to his house, they became apprehensive. "It must be," they thought, "on account of the money put back in our bags the first time, that we are taken inside; they want to use it as a pretext to attack us and take our donkeys and seize us as slaves." **19** So they went up to Joseph's head steward and talked to him at the entrance of the house. **20** "If you please, sir," they said, "we came down here once before to procure food.[z] **21** But when we arrived at a night's encampment and opened our bags, there was each man's money in the mouth of his bag—our money in the full amount! We have

t Gn 37, 35.
u Gn 44, 23.
v Gn 42, 20.
w Gn 42, 37.

x Gn 44, 32.
y Gn 45, 23.
z Gn 42, 3.
a Gn 42, 27f.

*————————

different Hebrew word) only when they arrive home (v 35); cf Gn 43, 21.

43, 1–34: This chapter and the following one are from the Yahwist source, in which Judah, not Reuben as in the Elohist source, volunteers to go surety for Benjamin.

now brought it back.*a* **22** We have brought other money to procure food with. We do not know who put the first money in our bags.'' **23** ''Be at ease,'' he replied; ''you have no need to fear. Your God and the God of your father must have put treasures in your bags for you. As for your money, I received it.'' With that, he led Simeon out to them.

24 The steward then brought the men inside Joseph's house. He gave them water to bathe their feet, and got fodder for their donkeys. **25** Then they set out their gifts to await Joseph's arrival at noon, for they had heard that they were to dine there. **26** When Joseph came home, they presented him with the gifts they had brought inside, while they bowed down before him to the ground. **27** After inquiring how they were, he asked them, ''And how is your aged father, of whom you spoke? Is he still in good health?''*b* **28** ''Your servant our father is thriving and still in good health,'' they said, as they bowed respectfully. **29** When Joseph's eye fell on his full brother Benjamin, he asked, ''Is this your youngest brother, of whom you told me?'' Then he said to him, ''May God be gracious to you, my boy!''*c* **30** With that, Joseph had to hurry out, for he was so overcome with affection for his brother that he was on the verge of tears. He went into a private room and wept there.

31 After washing his face, he reappeared and, now in control of himself, gave the order, ''Serve the meal.'' **32** It was served separately to him,* to the brothers, and to the Egyptians who partook of his board. (Egyptians may not eat with Hebrews; that is abhorrent to them.) **33** When they were seated by his directions according to their age, from the oldest to the youngest, they looked at one another in amazement; **34** and as portions were brought to them from Joseph's table, Benjamin's portion was five times as large as* anyone else's. So they drank freely and made merry with him.

CHAPTER 44

Final Test.   **1** *Then Joseph gave his head steward these instructions: ''Fill the men's bags with as much food as they can carry, and put each man's money in the mouth of his bag. **2** In the mouth of the youngest one's bag put also my silver goblet, together with the money for his rations.'' The steward carried out Joseph's instructions. **3** At daybreak the men and their donkeys were sent off. **4** They had not gone far out of the city when Joseph said to his head steward: ''Go at once after the men! When you overtake them, say to them, 'Why did you repay good with evil? Why did you steal the silver goblet from me? **5** It is the very one from which

my master drinks and which he uses for divination.* What you have done is wrong.' ''

6 When the steward overtook them and repeated these words to them, **7** they remonstrated with him: ''How can my lord say such things? Far be it from your servants to do such a thing! **8** We even brought back to you from the land of Canaan the money that we found in the mouths of our bags. Why, then, would we steal silver or gold from your master's house? **9** If any of your servants is found to have the goblet, he shall die, and as for the rest of us, we shall become my lord's slaves.'' **10** But he replied, ''Even though it ought to be as you propose, only the one who is found to have it shall become my slave, and the rest of you shall be exonerated.'' **11** Then each of them eagerly lowered his bag to the ground and opened it; **12** and when a search was made, starting with the oldest and ending with the youngest, the goblet turned up in Benjamin's bag. **13** At this, they tore their clothes. Then, when each man had reloaded his donkey, they returned to the city.

14 As Judah and his brothers reentered Joseph's house, he was still there; so they flung themselves on the ground before him. **15** ''How could you do such a thing?'' Joseph asked them. ''You should have known that such a man as I could discover by divination what happened.'' **16** Judah replied: ''What can we say to my lord? How can we plead or how try to prove our innocence? God has uncovered your servant's guilt.* Here we are, then, the slaves of my lord—the rest of us no less than the one in whose possession the goblet was found.'' **17** ''Far be it from me to act thus!'' said Joseph. ''Only the one in whose possession the goblet was found shall become my slave; the rest of you may go back safe and sound to your father.'' *18-21 wk. 14 thurs july 9, '15* **18** Judah then stepped up to him and said: ''I beg you, my lord, let your servant speak earnestly to my lord, and do not become angry with

---

b Tb 7, 4.   c Gn 42, 13.

43, 32: Separately to him: that Joseph did not eat with the other Egyptians was apparently a matter of rank.

43, 34: Five times as large as: probably an idiomatic expression for "much larger than."

44, 1f: Replacement of the money in the men's bags is probably a redactional addition here, taken from the Yahwist account of the first visit. It is only the goblet in Benjamin's bag, not any replaced money, that plays a part in the rest of the chapter.

44, 5: Divination: seeking omens through liquids poured into a cup or bowl was a common practice in the ancient Near East; cf v 15. Even though divination was frowned on in later Israel (Lv 19, 31), it is in this place an authentic touch which the sacred author does not hesitate to ascribe to Joseph, the wisest man in Egypt.

44, 16: Guilt: in trying to do away with Joseph when he was young.

your servant, for you are the equal of Pharaoh. **19** *My lord asked your servants, 'Have you a father, or another brother?' **20** So we said to my lord, 'We have an aged father, and a young brother, the child of his old age. This one's full brother is dead, and since he is the only one by that mother who is left, his father dotes on him.'[d] **21** Then you told your servants, 'Bring him down to me that my eyes may look on him.' **22** We replied to my lord, 'The boy cannot leave his father; his father would die if he were to leave him.' **23** But you told your servants, 'Unless your youngest brother comes back with you, you shall not come into my presence again.'[e] **24** When we returned to your servant our father, we reported to him the words of my lord.

25 "Later, our father told us to come back and buy some food for the family. **26** So we reminded him, 'We cannot go down there; only if our youngest brother is with us can we go, for we may not see the man if our youngest brother is not with us.' **27** Then your servant our father said to us, 'As you know, my wife bore me two sons. **28** One of them, however, disappeared, and I had to conclude that he must have been torn to pieces by wild beasts; I have not seen him since.'[f] **29** If you now take this one away from me, too, and some disaster befalls him, you will send my white head down to the nether world in grief.'

30 "If then the boy is not with us when I go back to your servant my father, whose very life is bound up with his, he will die as soon as he sees that the boy is missing; **31** and your servants will thus send the white head of our father down to the nether world in grief. **32** Besides, I, your servant, got the boy from his father by going surety for him, saying, 'If I fail to bring him back to you, father, you can hold it against me forever.'[g] **33** Let me, your servant, therefore, remain in place of the boy as the slave of my lord, and let the boy go back with his brothers. **34** How could I go back to my father if the boy were not with me? I could not bear to see the anguish that would overcome my father.''

CHAPTER 45

The Truth Revealed. **1** Joseph could no longer control himself in the presence of all his attendants, so he cried out, "Have everyone withdraw from me!" Thus no one else was about when he made himself known to his brothers. **2** But his sobs were so loud that the Egyptians heard him, and so the news reached Pharaoh's palace. **3** [h]"I am Joseph," he said to his brothers. "Is my father still in good health?" But his brothers could give him no answer, so dumbfounded were they at him.

4 "Come closer to me," he told his brothers.

When they had done so, he said: "I am your brother Joseph, whom you once sold into Egypt. **5** But now do not be distressed, and do not reproach yourselves for having sold me here. It was really for the sake of saving lives that God sent me here ahead of you.[†] **6** For two years now the famine has been in the land, and for five more years tillage will yield no harvest. **7** God, therefore, sent me on ahead of you to ensure for you a remnant on earth and to save your lives in an extraordinary deliverance. **8** So it was not really you but God who had me come here; and he has made of me a father to Pharaoh,* lord of all his household, and ruler over the whole land of Egypt.

9 *"Hurry back, then, to my father and tell him: 'Thus says your son Joseph: God has made me lord of all Egypt; come to me without delay.[j] **10** You will settle in the region of Goshen,* where you will be near me—you and your children and grandchildren, your flocks and herds, and everything that you own. **11** Since five years of famine still lie ahead, I will provide for you there, so that you and your family and all that are yours may not suffer want.' **12** Surely, you can see for yourselves, and Benjamin can see for himself, that it is I, Joseph, who am speaking to you. **13** Tell my father all about my high position in Egypt and what you have seen. But hurry and bring my father down here." **14** Thereupon he flung himself on the neck of his brother Benjamin and wept, and Benjamin wept in his arms. **15** Joseph then kissed all his brothers, crying over each of them; and only then were his brothers able to talk with him.

16 When the news reached Pharaoh's palace that Joseph's brothers had come, Pharaoh and his courtiers were pleased. **17** So Pharaoh told Joseph: "Say to your brothers: 'This is what you shall do: Load up your animals and go without delay to the land of Canaan. **18** There get your father and your families, and then come back here to me; I will assign you the best land in Egypt, where you will live off the fat of the

d Gn 42, 13.
e Gn 43, 3.
f Gn 37, 20. 33.
g Gn 43, 9.
h 3f: Acts 7, 13.
i Gn 50, 20; Sir 49, 15.
j Acts 7, 14.
k Acts 7, 14.

*

44, 19: My lord . . . your servants: such frequently repeated expressions in Judah's speech show the formal court style used by a subject in speaking to a high official.

45, 8: Father to Pharaoh: a term applied to a vizier in ancient Egypt.

45, 9–15: In these verses, as in Gn 46, 31–47, 5a, all from the Yahwist source, Joseph in his own name invites his father and brothers to come to Egypt. Only after their arrival is Pharaoh informed of the fact. On the other hand, in 45, 16–20 from the Elohist source, it is Pharaoh himself who invites Joseph's kinsmen to migrate to his dominion.

45, 10: The region of Goshen: modern Wadi Tumilat in the eastern part of the Nile Delta.

land.'[k] **19** Instruct them further: 'Do this. Take wagons from the land of Egypt for your children and your wives and to transport your father on your way back here. **20** Do not be concerned about your belongings, for the best in the whole land of Egypt shall be yours.' "

21 The sons of Israel acted accordingly. Joseph gave them the wagons, as Pharaoh had ordered, and he supplied them with provisions for the journey. **22** He also gave to each of them fresh clothing, but to Benjamin he gave three hundred shekels of silver and five sets of garments. **23** Moreover, what he sent to his father was ten jackasses loaded with the finest products of Egypt and ten jennies loaded with grain and bread and other provisions for his journey. **24** As he sent his brothers on their way, he told them, "Let there be no recriminations on the way."

25 So they left Egypt and made their way to their father Jacob in the land of Canaan. **26** When they told him, "Joseph is still alive—in fact, it is he who is ruler of all the land of Egypt," he was dumbfounded; he could not believe them. **27** But when they recounted to him all that Joseph had told them, and when he saw the wagons that Joseph had sent for his transport, the spirit of their father Jacob revived. **28** "It is enough," said Israel. "My son Joseph is still alive! I must go and see him before I die."

CHAPTER 46

Migration to Egypt. **1** Israel set out with all that was his. When he arrived at Beer-sheba, he offered sacrifices to the God of his father Isaac. **2** There God, speaking to Israel in a vision by night, called, "Jacob! Jacob!" "Here I am," he answered. **3** Then he said: "I am God,* the God of your father. Do not be afraid to go down to Egypt, for there I will make you a great nation. **4** Not only will I go down to Egypt with you; I will also bring you back here, after Joseph has closed your eyes."

5 So Jacob departed from Beer-sheba, and the sons of Israel put their father and their wives and children on the wagons that Pharaoh had sent for his transport. **6** They took with them their livestock and the possessions they had acquired in the land of Canaan. Thus Jacob and all his descendants migrated to Egypt.[l] **7** His sons and his grandsons, his daughters and his granddaughters—all his descendants—he took with him to Egypt.

8 These are the names of the Israelites, Jacob and his descendants, who migrated to Egypt. Reuben, Jacob's first-born,[m] **9** *and the sons of Reuben: Hanoch, Pallu, Hezron and Carmi.[n] **10** The sons of Simeon: Nemuel, Jamin, Ohad, Jachin, Zohar, and Shaul, son of a Canaanite woman.[o] **11** The sons of Levi: Gershon, Kohath and Merari.[p] **12** The sons of Judah: Er, Onan, Shelah, Perez and Zerah—but Er and Onan had died in the land of Canaan; and the sons of Perez were Hezron and Hamul.[q] **13** The sons of Issachar: Tola Puah, Jashub and Shimron.[r] **14** The sons of Zebulun: Sered, Elon and Jahleel.[s] **15** These were the sons whom Leah bore to Jacob in Paddan-aram, along with his daughter Dinah—thirty-three persons in all, male and female.

16 The sons of Gad: Zephon, Haggi, Shuni, Ezbon, Eri, Arod and Areli.[t] **17** The sons of Asher: Imnah, Ishvah, Ishvi and Beriah, with their sister Serah; and the sons of Beriah: Heber and Malchiel.[u] **18** These were the descendants of Zilpah, whom Laban had given to his daughter Leah; these she bore to Jacob—sixteen persons in all.

19 The sons of Jacob's wife Rachel: Joseph and Benjamin. **20** In the land of Egypt Joseph became the father of Manasseh and Ephraim, whom Asenath, daughter of Potiphera, priest of Heliopolis, bore to him.[v] **21** The sons of Benjamin: Bela, Becher, Ashbel, Gera, Naaman, Ahiram, Shupham, Hupham and Ard.[w] **22** These were the sons whom Rachel bore to Jacob—fourteen persons in all.

23 The sons of Dan: Hushim.[x] **24** The sons of Naphtali: Jahzeel, Guni, Jezer and Shillem.[y] **25** These were the sons of Bilhah, whom Laban had given to his daughter Rachel; these she bore to Jacob—seven persons in all.

26 Jacob's people who migrated to Egypt—his direct descendants, not counting the wives of Jacob's sons—numbered sixty-six persons in all.[z] **27** Together with Joseph's sons who were born to him in Egypt—two persons—all the people comprising Jacob's family who

l Ex 1, 1; Jos 24, 4; Jdt 5, 10; Acts 7, 15.
m Ex 1, 2.
n Ex 6, 14; Nm 26, 5; 1 Chr 5, 3.
o Ex 6, 15; Nm 26, 12; 1 Chr 4, 24.
p Ex 6, 16; Nm 3, 17; 26, 57; 1 Chr 6, 1.
q Gn 38, 3-10. 29f; Nm 26, 19; Rv 4, 18-22; 1 Chr 2, 5.
r Nm 26, 23f; 1 Chr 7, 1.
s Nm 26, 26.
t Nm 26, 15f.
u Nm 26, 44; 1 Chr 7, 30f.
v Gn 41, 50; Nm 26, 28. 35.
w Nm 26, 38; 1 Chr 7, 6; 8, 1-4.
x Nm 26, 42.
y Nm 26, 48f; 1 Chr 7, 13.
z Ex 1, 5.
a Ex 1, 5; Dt 10, 22; Acts 7, 14.

*

46, 3: I am God: more precisely according to the Hebrew text, "I am El." "El" is here a divine name, not the common noun "god."

46, 9–27: This genealogical list has here been inserted by a redactor who based it on the clan lists (Nm 26, 5–50) at the time of Moses. Therefore it includes some of Jacob's grandchildren, who would hardly have been born when Joseph was still a relatively young man. The number fourteen (v 22) is based on a garbled version of the genealogical list.

46, 27: Seventy persons: either to be understood as a round number, or arrived at by including Jacob and Joseph with the preceding persons, who add up to sixty-eight.

had come to Egypt amounted to seventy persons* in all.[a]

28 Israel had sent Judah ahead to Joseph, so that he might meet him in Goshen. On his arrival in the region of Goshen, **29** Joseph hitched the horses to his chariot and rode to meet his father Israel in Goshen. As soon as he saw him, he flung himself on his neck and wept a long time in his arms. **30** And Israel said to Joseph, "At last I can die, now that I have seen for myself that Joseph is still alive."

31 Joseph then said to his brothers and his father's household: "I will go and inform Pharaoh, telling him: 'My brothers and my father's household, whose home is in the land of Canaan, have come to me. **32** The men are shepherds, having long been keepers of livestock; and they have brought with them their flocks and herds, as well as everything else they own.' **33** So when Pharaoh summons you and asks what your occupation is, **34** you must answer. 'We your servants, like our ancestors, have been keepers of livestock from the beginning until now,' in order that you may stay in the region of Goshen, since all shepherds are abhorrent to the Egyptians."

CHAPTER 47

Settlement in Goshen. **1** Joseph went and told Pharaoh, "My father and my brothers have come from the land of Canaan, with their flocks and herds and everything else they own; and they are now in the region of Goshen." **2** He then presented to Pharaoh five of his brothers whom he had selected from their full number. **3** When Pharaoh asked them what their occupation was, they answered, "We, your servants, like our ancestors, are shepherds. **4** We have come," they continued, "in order to stay in this country, for there is no pasture for your servants' flocks in the land of Canaan, so severe has the famine been there. Please, therefore, let your servants settle in the region of Goshen."[b] **5** Pharaoh said to Joseph, "They may settle in the region of Goshen; and if you know any of them to be qualified, you may put them in charge of my own livestock."

Thus, when Jacob and his sons came to Joseph in Egypt, and Pharaoh, king of Egypt, heard about it, Pharaoh said to Joseph, "Now that your father and brothers have come to you, **6** the land of Egypt is at your disposal; settle your father and brothers in the pick of the land." **7** Then Joseph brought his father Jacob and presented him to Pharaoh. After Jacob had paid his respects to Pharaoh, **8** Pharaoh asked him, "How many years have you lived?" **9** Jacob replied: "The years I have lived as a wayfarer amount to a hundred and thirty. Few and hard have been these years of my life, and they do not

compare with the years that my ancestors lived as wayfarers."* **10** Then Jacob bade Pharaoh farewell and withdrew from his presence.

11 As Pharaoh had ordered, Joseph settled his father and brothers and gave them holdings in Egypt on the pick of the land, in the region of Rameses.* **12** And Joseph sustained his father and brothers and his father's whole household, down to the youngest, with food.

Joseph's Land Policy. **13** Since there was no food in any country because of the extreme severity of the famine, and the lands of Egypt and Canaan were languishing from hunger, **14** Joseph gathered in, as payment for the rations that were being dispensed, all the money that was to be found in Egypt and Canaan, and he put it in Pharaoh's palace. **15** When all the money in Egypt and Canaan was spent, all the Egyptians came to Joseph, pleading, "Give us food or we shall perish under your eyes; for our money is gone." **16** "Since your money is gone," replied Joseph, "give me your livestock, and I will sell you bread in return for your livestock." **17** So they brought their livestock to Joseph, and he sold them food in return for their horses, their flocks of sheep and herds of cattle, and their donkeys. Thus he got them through that year with bread in exchange for all their livestock. **18** When that year ended, they came to him in the following one and said: "We cannot hide from my lord that, with our money spent and our livestock made over to my lord, there is nothing left to put at my lord's disposal except our bodies and our farm land. **19** Why should we and our land perish before your very eyes? Take us and our land in exchange for food, and we will become Pharaoh's slaves and our land his property; only give us seed, that we may survive and not perish, and that our land may not turn into a waste."

20 Thus Joseph acquired all the farm land of Egypt for Pharaoh, since with the famine too much for them to bear, every Egyptian sold his field; so the land passed over to Pharaoh, **21** and the people were reduced to slavery, from one end of Egypt's territory to the other. **22** Only the priests' lands Joseph did not take over. Since the priests had a fixed allowance from Pharaoh and lived off the allowance Pharaoh had granted them, they did not have to sell their land.

---

b Ex 23, 9; Dt 23, 8.

*

47, 9: Wayfarer ... wayfarers: man is merely a sojourner on earth; cf Ps 39, 13.

47, 11: The region of Rameses: same as the region of Goshen; see note on Gn 45, 10. The name Rameses, however, is an anachronism, since this royal name did not come into use before the end of the fourteenth century B.C., long after the time of Joseph.

23 Joseph told the people: "Now that I have acquired you and your land for Pharaoh, here is your seed for sowing the land. **24** But when the harvest is in, you must give a fifth of it to Pharaoh, while you keep four-fifths as seed for your fields, and as food for yourselves and your families [and as food for your children]." **25** "You have saved our lives!" they answered. "We are grateful to my lord that we can be Pharaoh's slaves." **26** Thus Joseph made it a law for the land in Egypt, which is still in force, that a fifth of its produce should go to Pharaoh. Only the land of the priests did not pass over to Pharaoh.

Jacob Blesses Ephraim and Manasseh.

27 Thus Israel settled in the land of Egypt, in the region of Goshen. There they acquired property, were fertile, and increased greatly.[c] **28** Jacob lived in the land of Egypt for seventeen years; the span of his life came to a hundred and forty-seven years. **29** When the time approached for Israel to die, he called his son Joseph and said to him: "If you really wish to please me, put your hand under my thigh as a sign of your constant loyalty to me; do not let me be buried in Egypt. **30** When I lie down with my ancestors, have me taken out of Egypt and buried in their burial place."[d] **31** "I will do as you say," he replied. But his father demanded, "Swear it to me!" So Joseph swore to him. Then Israel bowed at the head of the bed.*

CHAPTER 48

1 Some time afterward, Joseph was informed, "Your father is failing." So he took along with him his two sons, Manasseh and Ephraim. **2** When Jacob was told, "Your son Joseph has come to you," he rallied his strength and sat up in bed.

3 [e]Jacob then said to Joseph: "God Almighty appeared to me at Luz* in the land of Canaan, and blessing me, **4** he said, 'I will make you fertile and numerous and raise you into an assembly of tribes, and I will give this land to your descendants after you as a permanent possession.' **5** Your two sons, therefore, who were born to you in the land of Egypt before I joined you here, shall be mine; Ephraim and Manasseh shall be mine as much as Reuben and Simeon are mine. **6** Progeny born to you after them shall remain yours; but their heritage shall be recorded in the names of their two brothers. **7** [f]I do this because, when I was returning from Paddan, your mother Rachel died, to my sorrow, during the journey in Canaan, while we were still a short distance from Ephrath; and I buried her there on the way to Ephrath [that is, Bethlehem]."*

8 When Israel saw Joseph's sons, he asked, "Who are these?" **9** "They are my sons," Joseph answered his father, "whom God has given me here." "Bring them to me," said his father, "that I may bless them." **10** (Now Israel's eyes were dim from age, and he could not see well.) When Joseph brought his sons close to him, he kissed and embraced them. **11** Then Israel said to Joseph, "I never expected to see your face again, and now God has allowed me to see your descendants as well!"

12 Joseph removed them from his father's knees and bowed down before him with his face to the ground. **13** Then Joseph took the two, Ephraim with his right hand, to Israel's left, and Manasseh with his left hand, to Israel's right, and led them to him. **14** But Israel, crossing his hands, put out his right hand and laid it on the head of Ephraim, although he was the younger, and his left hand on the head of Manasseh, although he was the first-born. **15** Then he blessed them with these words:

"May the God in whose ways
  my fathers Abraham and Isaac walked,
The God who has been my shepherd
  from my birth to this day,[g]
16 The Angel who has delivered me from all
    harm,
  bless these boys
That in them my name be recalled,
  and the names of my fathers, Abraham
    and Isaac,
And they may become teeming multitudes
  upon the earth!"

17 When Joseph saw that his father had laid his right hand on Ephraim's head, this seemed wrong to him; so he took hold of his father's hand, to remove it from Ephraim's head to Manasseh's, **18** saying, "That is not right, father; the other one is the first-born; lay your right hand on his head!" **19** But his father resisted. "I know it, son," he said, "I know. That one too shall become a tribe, and he too shall be great. Nevertheless, his younger brother shall surpass him, and his descendants shall become a multitude of nations." **20** So when he blessed them that day and said, "By you shall the people of Israel pronounce blessings; may they say,

---

c Ex 1, 7.   f Gn 35, 19.
d Gn 50, 5.   g Heb 11, 21.
e 3f: Gn 28, 12-15; 35, 6.   h Heb 11, 21.

*

47, 31: Israel bowed at the head of the bed: meaning perhaps that he gave a nod of assent and appreciation as he lay on his bed. By reading with different vowels the Hebrew word for "bed," the Greek version translated it as "staff," and understood the phrase to mean that he bowed in worship, leaning on the top of his staff; it is thus quoted in Heb 11, 21.

48, 3: Luz: an older name of Bethel (Gn 28, 19).

48, 7: Since her early death prevented Rachel from bearing more than two sons, Jacob feels justified in treating her two grandsons as if they were her own offspring.

'God make you like Ephraim and Manasseh,' ''
he placed Ephraim before Manasseh.[h]

21 Then Israel said to Joseph: ''I am about to
die. But God will be with you and will restore
you to the land of your fathers. **22** [i]As for me,
I give to you, as to the one above his brothers,
Shechem, which I captured from the Amorites
with my sword and bow.''*

CHAPTER 49

Jacob's Testament. **1** Jacob called his
sons and said: ''Gather around, that I may tell
you what is to happen to you in days to come.

2 ''Assemble and listen, sons of Jacob,
    listen to Israel, your father.

3 ''You, Reuben, my first-born,
    my strength and the first fruit of my
       manhood,
    excelling in rank and excelling in power!
4 Unruly as water, you shall no longer excel,
    for you climbed into your father's bed
    and defiled my couch to my sorrow.[j]

5 ''Simeon and Levi, brothers indeed,
    weapons of violence are their knives.*
6 Let not my soul enter their council,
    or my spirit be joined with their company;
For in their fury they slew men,
    in their willfulness they maimed oxen.[k]
7 Cursed be their fury so fierce,
    and their rage so cruel!
I will scatter them in Jacob,
    disperse them throughout Israel.

8 ''You, Judah, shall your brothers praise
    —your hand on the neck of your enemies;
    the sons of your father shall bow down to
       you.
9 Judah, like a lion's whelp,
    you have grown up on prey, my son.
He crouches like a lion recumbent,
    the king of beasts—who would dare rouse
       him?[l]
10 The scepter shall never depart from Judah,
    or the mace from between his legs,
While tribute is brought to him,*
    and he receives the people's homage.
11 He tethers his donkey to the vine,
    his purebred ass to the choicest stem.
In wine he washes his garments,
    his robe in the blood of grapes.*
12 His eyes are darker than wine,
    and his teeth are whiter than milk.
13 ''Zebulun shall dwell by the seashore
    [This means a shore for ships],
    and his flank shall be based on Sidon.

14 ''Issachar is a rawboned ass,
    crouching between the saddlebags.
15 When he saw how good a settled life was,
    and how pleasant the country,

He bent his shoulder to the burden
    and became a toiling serf.

16 ''Dan shall achieve justice* for his kindred
    like any other tribe of Israel.
17 Let Dan be a serpent by the roadside,
    a horned viper by the path,
That bites the horse's heel,
    so that the rider tumbles backward.

18 ''[I long for your deliverance, O LORD!]

19 ''Gad shall be raided by raiders,
    but he shall raid at their heels.*

20 ''Asher's produce is rich,
    and he shall furnish dainties for kings.

21 ''Naphtali is a hind let loose,
    which brings forth lovely fawns.

22 ''Joseph is a wild colt,
    a wild colt by a spring,
    a wild ass on a hillside.
23 Harrying and attacking,
    the archers opposed him;
24 But each one's bow remained stiff,
    as their arms were unsteady,
By the power of the Mighty One of Jacob,
    because of the Shepherd, the Rock of
       Israel,
25 The God of your father, who helps you,*
    God Almighty, who blesses you,
With the blessings of the heavens above,

---

i Jos 17, 14. 17f; Jn 4.   k Gn 34, 25.
  5.   l 1 Chr 5, 2.
j Gn 35, 22; 1 Chr 5, 1f.

---
*

48, 22: Both the meaning of the Hebrew and the historical
reference in this verse are obscure. By taking the Hebrew word
for Shechem as a common noun meaning shoulder or mountain slope, some translators render the verse, ''I give you one
portion more than your brothers, which I captured . . .'' The
reference may be to the capture of Shechem by the sons of
Jacob (Gn 34, 24–29). Shechem lay near the border separating the tribal territory of Manasseh from that of Ephraim (Jos
16, 4–9; 17, 1f. 7).
    49, 5: Knives: if this is the meaning of the obscure Hebrew
word here, the reference may be to the knives used in circum-
cising the men of Shechem (Gn 34, 24; cf Jos 5, 2).
    49, 10: While tribute is brought to him: this translation is
based on a slight change in the Hebrew text, which, as it
stands would seem to mean, ''until he comes to Shiloh.'' A
somewhat different reading of the Hebrew text would be, ''until
he comes to whom it belongs.'' This last has been traditionally
understood in a Messianic sense. In any case, the passage
foretells the supremacy of the tribe of Judah, which found its
fulfillment in the Davidic dynasty and ultimately in the Messianic Son of David, Jesus Christ.
    49, 11: In Wine . . . the blood of grapes: Judah's clothes are
poetically pictured as soaked with grape juice from trampling
in the wine press, the rich vintage of his land; cf Is 63, 2.
    49, 16: In Hebrew the verb for achieve justice is from the
same root as the name Dan.
    49, 19: In Hebrew there is a certain assonance between the
name Gad and the words for ''raided,'' raiders'' and ''raid.''
    49, 25f: A very similar description of the agricultural riches
of the tribal land of Joseph is given in Dt 33, 13–16.

the blessings of the abyss that crouches
below,
The blessings of breasts and womb,
26   the blessings of fresh grain and blossoms,
The blessings of the everlasting mountains,
the delights of the eternal hills.
May they rest on the head of Joseph,
on the brow of the prince among his
brothers.

27 "Benjamin is a ravenous wolf;
mornings he devours the prey,
and evenings he distributes the spoils."

Farewell and Death.   28 All these are the
twelve tribes of Israel, and this is what their
father said about them, as he bade them farewell
and gave to each of them an appropriate message. **29** Then he gave them this charge: "Since
I am about to be taken to my kindred, bury me
with my fathers in the cave that lies in the field
of Ephron the Hittite, **30** the cave in the field
of Machpelah, facing on Mamre, in the land of
Canaan, the field that Abraham bought from
Ephron the Hittite for a burial ground. *m*
31 There Abraham and his wife Sarah are buried, and so are Isaac and his wife Rebekah, and
there, too, I buried Leah— **32** the field and the
cave in it that had been purchased from the
Hittites."
33 When Jacob had finished giving these instructions to his sons, he drew his feet into the
bed, breathed his last, and was taken to his
kindred.

CHAPTER 50

Jacob's Funeral.   1 Joseph threw himself
on his father's face and wept over him as he
kissed him. **2** Then he ordered the physicians in
his service to embalm his father. When they
embalmed Israel, **3** they spent forty days at it,
for that is the full period of embalming; and the
Egyptians mourned him for seventy days.
4 When that period of mourning was over, Joseph spoke to Pharaoh's courtiers. "Please do
me this favor," he said, "and convey to Pharaoh this request of mine. **5** Since my father, at
the point of death, made me promise on oath to
bury him in the tomb that he had prepared for
himself in the land of Canaan, may I go up there
to bury my father and then come back?" *n*
6 Pharaoh replied, "Go and bury your father,
as he made you promise on oath."
7 So Joseph left to bury his father; and with
him went all of Pharaoh's officials who were
senior members of his court and all the other
dignitaries of Egypt, **8** as well as Joseph's
whole household, his brothers, and his father's
household; only their children and their flocks
and herds were left in the region of Goshen.

9 Chariots, too, and charioteers went up with
him; it was a very large retinue.
10 When they arrived at Goren-ha-atad,*
which is beyond the Jordan, they held there a
very great and solemn memorial service; and
Joseph observed seven days of mourning for his
father. **11** When the Canaanites who inhabited
the land saw the mourning at Goren-ha-atad,
they said, "This is a solemn funeral the Egyptians are having." That is why the place was
named Abel-mizraim. It is beyond the Jordan.
12 Thus Jacob's sons did for him as he had
instructed them. **13** They carried him to the
land of Canaan and buried him in the cave in the
field of Machpelah, facing on Mamre, the field
that Abraham had bought for a burial ground
from Ephron the Hittite. *o*
14 After Joseph had buried his father he returned to Egypt, together with his brothers and
all who had gone up with him for the burial of
his father.

Plea for Forgiveness.   15 Now that their
father was dead, Joseph's brothers became fearful and thought, "Suppose Joseph has been
nursing a grudge against us and now plans to
pay us back in full for all the wrong we did
him!" **16** So they approached Joseph and said:
"Before your father died, he gave us these instructions: **17** 'You shall say to Joseph, Jacob
begs you to forgive the criminal wrongdoing of
your brothers, who treated you so cruelly.'
Please, therefore, forgive the crime that we, the
servants of your father's God, committed."
When they spoke these words to him, Joseph
broke into tears. **18** Then his brothers proceeded to fling themselves down before him and
said, "Let us be your slaves!" **19** But Joseph
replied to them: "Have no fear. Can I take the
place of God? **20** Even though you meant harm
to me, God meant it for good, to achieve his
present end, the survival of many people. *p*
21 Therefore have no fear. I will provide for
you and for your children." By thus speaking
kindly to them, he reassured them. *q*
22 Joseph remained in Egypt, together with
his father's family. He lived a hundred and ten
years. **23** He saw Ephraim's children to the

---

m Gn 23, 17.   p Gn 45, 5; Sir 49, 15.
n Gn 47, 30.   q Gn 47, 12.
o Gn 23, 16; Acts 7, 16.   r Nm 32, 39; Jos 17, 1.
*

50, 10f: Goren-ha-atad: "Threshing Floor of the Brambles."
Abel-mizraim: although the name really means "watercourse
of the Egyptians," it is understood here, by a play on the first
part of the term, to mean "mourning of the Egyptians." The site
has not been identified through either reading of the name. But
it is difficult to see why the mourning rites should have been
held in the land beyond the Jordan when the burial was at
Hebron. Perhaps an earlier form of the story placed the mourning rites beyond the Wadi of Egypt, the traditional boundary
between Canaan and Egypt (Nm 34, 5; Jos 15, 4. 47).

third generation, and the children of Manasseh's son Machir were also born on Joseph's knees. *r*

Death of Joseph.   **24** Joseph said to his brothers: "I am about to die. God will surely take care of you and lead you out of this land to the land that he promised on oath to Abraham, Isaac and Jacob."*s* **25** Then, putting the sons of Israel under oath, he continued, "When God thus takes care of you, you must bring my bones up with you from this place."*t* **26** Joseph died at the age of a hundred and ten. He was embalmed and laid to rest in a coffin in Egypt. *u*

s Ex 3, 8; Jos 24, 32;   t Ex 13, 19; Heb 11, 22.
  Heb 11, 22.   u Sir 49, 15.

The Book of

EXODUS

The second book of the Pentateuch is called Exodus from the Greek word for "departure," because the central event narrated in it is the departure of the Israelites from Egypt. It continues the history of the chosen people from the point where the Book of Genesis leaves off. It recounts the oppression by the Egyptians of the ever-increasing descendants of Jacob and their miraculous deliverance by God through Moses, who led them across the Red Sea to Mount Sinai where they entered into a special covenant with the Lord.

These events were of prime importance to the chosen people, for they became thereby an independent nation and enjoyed a unique relationship with God. Through Moses God gave to the Israelites at Mount Sinai the "law": the moral, civil and ritual legislation by which they were to become a holy people, in whom the promise of a Savior for all mankind would be fulfilled.

The principal divisions of Exodus are:
  I. The Israelites in Egypt (Ex 1, 1—12, 36).
  II. The Exodus from Egypt and the Journey to Sinai (Ex 12, 37—18, 27).
  III. The Covenant at Mount Sinai (Ex 19, 1—24, 18).
  IV. The Dwelling and Its Furnishings (Ex 25, 1—40, 38).

I: The Israelites In Egypt

CHAPTER 1

Jacob's Descendants in Egypt. **1** These are the names of the sons of Israel* who, accompanied by their households, migrated with Jacob into Egypt: **2** *Reuben, Simeon, Levi and Judah; **3** Issachar, Zebulun and Benjamin; **4** Dan and Naphtali; Gad and Asher. **5** The total number of the direct descendants* of Jacob was seventy.*a* Joseph was already in Egypt.

6 Now Joseph and all his brothers and that whole generation died.*b* **7** But the Israelites were fruitful and prolific. They became so numerous and strong that the land was filled with them.

The Oppression. **8** Then a new king, who knew nothing of Joseph,* came to power in Egypt.*c* **9** He said to his subjects, "Look how numerous and powerful the Israelite people are growing, more so than we ourselves! **10** Come, let us deal shrewdly with them to stop their increase; otherwise, in time of war they too may join our enemies to fight against us, and so leave our country."

11 Accordingly, taskmasters were set over the Israelites to oppress them with forced labor.*d* Thus they had to build for Pharaoh* the supply cities of Pithom and Raamses. **12** Yet the more they were oppressed, the more they multiplied and spread. The Egyptians, then,

dreaded the Israelites **13** and reduced them to cruel slavery, **14** making life bitter for them with hard work in mortar* and brick and all kinds of field work—the whole cruel fate of slaves.

Command to the Midwives. **15** The king of Egypt told the Hebrew midwives, one of whom was called Shiphrah and the other Puah, **16** "When you act as midwives for the Hebrew women and see them giving birth,* if it is a boy, kill him; but if it is a girl, she may live."

---

a Gn 46, 27; Dt 10, 22;   c 8ff: Acts 7, 18.
  Acts 7, 14.   d Dt 26, 6.
b Gn 50, 26.

*

1, 1: Sons of Israel: here literally the first-generation sons of Jacob. Cf v 5. However, beginning with Ex 1, 7 the same Hebrew phrase refers to the more remote descendants of Jacob; hence, from there on, it is ordinarily rendered as "the Israelites." Households: the family in its fullest sense, including wives, children and servants.

1, 2: The sons of Jacob are listed here according to the respective mothers. Cf Gn 29, 31; 30, 30; 35, 16—26.

1, 5: Direct descendants: literally, persons coming from the loins of Jacob; hence, wives and servants are here excluded. Cf Gn 46, 26.

1, 8: Who knew nothing of Joseph: this king ignored the services that Joseph had rendered to Egypt.

1, 11: Pharaoh: not a personal name, but a title common to all the kings of Egypt.

1, 14: Mortar: either the wet clay with which the bricks were made, as in Na 3, 14, or the cement used between the bricks in building, as in Gn 11, 3.

1, 16: And see them giving birth: the Hebrew text is uncertain.

17 The midwives, however, feared God; they did not do as the king of Egypt had ordered them, but let the boys live. **18** So the king summoned the midwives and asked. them, "Why have you acted thus, allowing the boys to live?" **19** The midwives answered Pharaoh, "The Hebrew women are not like the Egyptian women. They are robust and give birth before the midwife arrives." **20** Therefore God dealt well with the midwives. The people, too, increased and grew strong. **21** And because the midwives feared God, he built up families for them. **22** Pharaoh then commanded all his subjects, "Throw into the river* every boy that is born to the Hebrews,e but you may let all the girls live."

CHAPTER 2

Birth and Adoption of Moses.   **1** Now a certain man of the house of Levi married a Levite woman,f **2** who conceived and bore a son. Seeing that he was a goodly child, she hid him for three months.g **3** When she could hide him no longer, she took a papyrus basket,* daubed it with bitumen and pitch, and putting the child in it, placed it among the reeds on the river bank. **4** His sister stationed herself at a distance to find out what would happen to him.

5 Pharaoh's daughter came down to the river to bathe, while her maids walked along the river bank. Noticing the basket among the reeds, she sent her handmaid to fetch it. **6** On opening it, she looked, and lo, there was a baby boy, crying! She was moved with pity for him and said, "It is one of the Hebrews' children." **7** Then his sister asked Pharaoh's daughter, "Shall I go and call one of the Hebrew women to nurse the child for you?" **8** "Yes, do so," she answered. So the maiden went and called the child's own mother. **9** Pharaoh's daughter said to her, "Take this child and nurse it for me, and I will repay you." The woman therefore took the child and nursed it. **10** When the child grew,* she brought him to Pharaoh's daughter, who adopted him as her sonh and called him Moses; for she said, "I drew him out of the water."

Moses' Flight to Midian.   **11** On one occasion, after Moses had grown up,* when he visited his kinsmeni and witnessed their forced labor, he saw an Egyptian striking a Hebrew, one of his own kinsmen. **12** Looking about and seeing no one, he slew the Egyptian and hid him in the sand. **13** The next day he went out again, and now two Hebrews were fighting! So he asked the culprit, "Why are you striking your fellow Hebrew?" **14** But he replied, "Who has appointed you ruler and judge over us? Are you thinking of killing me as you killed the Egyp-

tian?" Then Moses became afraid and thought, "The affair must certainly be known."

15 Pharaoh, too, heard of the affair and sought to put him to death. But Moses fled from him and stayed in the land of Midian.j As he was seated there by a well, **16** seven daughters of a priest of Midian came to draw water and fill the troughs to water their father's flock. **17** But some shepherds came and drove them away. Then Moses got up and defended them and watered their flock. **18** When they returned to their father Reuel,* he said to them, "How is it you have returned so soon today?" **19** They answered, "An Egyptian* saved us from the interference of the shepherds. He even drew water for us and watered the flock!" **20** "Where is the man?" he asked his daughters. "Why did you leave him there? Invite him to have something to eat." **21** Moses agreed to live with him, and the man gave him his daughter Zipporah in marriage. **22** She bore him a son, whom he named Gershom;* for he said, "I am a stranger in a foreign land."k

The Burning Bush.   **23** A long time passed, during which the king of Egypt died. Still the Israelites groaned and cried out because of their slavery. As their cry for release went up to God,l **24** he heard their groaning and was mindful of his covenantm with Abraham, Isaac and Jacob. **25** He saw the Israelites and knew. . . .

---

e Acts 7, 19.
f Ex 6, 20; Nm 26, 59.
g Acts 7, 20; Heb 11, 23.
h Acts 7, 21; Heb 11, 24.
i 11-14: Acts 7, 23-28.
j Acts 7, 29; Heb 11, 27.
k Ex 18, 3.
l Ex 3, 7. 9; Dt 26. 7.
m Ex 6, 5; Pss 105, 8f; 106, 44f.

*

1, 22: The river: the Nile, which was "the" river for the Egyptians.

2, 3: Basket: literally, "chest" or "ark"; the same Hebrew word is used in Gn 6, 14 for Noah's ark. Here, however, the chest was made of papyrus stalks.

2, 10: When the child grew: probably when he was weaned or a little later. Moses: in Hebrew, Mosheh; the Hebrew word for "draw out" is mashah. The explanation of the name is not intended as a scientific etymology but as a play on words. The name is probably derived from an Egyptian word for "has been born," referring the birth to a god thought to be its sponsor.

2, 11: After Moses had grown up: Acts 7, 23 indicates that this was after an interval of nearly forty years. Cf Ex 7, 7. Striking: probably in the sense of "flogging"; according to some, "slaying."

2, 18: Reuel: he was also called Jethro. Cf Ex 3, 1; 4, 18; 18, 1.

2, 19: An Egyptian: Moses was probably wearing Egyptian dress, or spoke Egyptian to Reuel's daughters.

2, 22: Gershom: the name is explained as if it came from the Hebrew word ger, "stranger," joined to the Hebrew word sham, "there." Some Greek and Latin manuscripts add here a passage taken from Ex 18, 4.

(handwritten margin notes: "III Sun Lent 'e'", "1-8", "13-15")

CHAPTER 3

1 Meanwhile Moses was tending the flock of his father-in-law Jethro, the priest of Midian. Leading the flock across the desert, he came to Horeb, the mountain of God.* **2** There an angel of the LORD* appeared to him in fire flaming out of a bush.[n] As he looked on, he was surprised to see that the bush, though on fire, was not consumed. **3** So Moses decided, "I must go over to look at this remarkable sight, and see why the bush is not burned."

The Call of Moses. **4** When the LORD saw him coming over to look at it more closely, God called out to him from the bush, "Moses! Moses!" He answered, "Here I am." **5** God said, "Come no nearer![o] Remove the sandals from your feet, for the place where you stand is holy ground. **6** [p]I am the God of your father," he continued, "the God of Abraham, the God of Isaac, the God of Jacob."* Moses hid his face, for he was afraid to look at God. **7** But the LORD said, "I have witnessed the affliction of my people in Egypt and have heard their cry of complaint against their slave drivers, so I know well what they are suffering. **8** Therefore I have come down* to rescue them from the hands of the Egyptians and lead them out of that land into a good and spacious land, a land flowing with milk and honey, the country of the Canaanites, Hittites, Amorites, Perizzites, Hivites and Jebusites.[q] **9** So indeed the cry of the Israelites has reached me, and I have truly noted that the Egyptians are oppressing them. **10** Come, now! I will send you to Pharaoh to lead my people, the Israelites, out of Egypt."

11 But Moses said to God, "Who am I* that I should go to Pharaoh and lead the Israelites out of Egypt?" **12** He answered, "I will be with you; and this shall be your proof that it is I who have sent you: when you bring my people out of Egypt, you will worship God on this very mountain." **13** "But," said Moses to God, "when I go to the Israelites and say to them, 'The God of your fathers has sent me to you,' if they ask me, 'What is his name?' what am I to tell them?" **14** God replied, "I am who am."* Then he added, "This is what you shall tell the Israelites: I AM sent me to you."

15 God spoke further to Moses, "Thus shall you say to the Israelites: The LORD, the God of your fathers, the God of Abraham, the God of Isaac, the God of Jacob, has sent me to you.

"This is my name forever;[r]
   this is my title for all generations:

16 "Go and assemble the elders* of the Israelites, and tell them: The LORD, the God of your fathers, the God of Abraham, Isaac and Jacob, has appeared to me and said: I am concerned about you and about the way you are being treated in Egypt; **17** so I have decided to lead you up out of the misery of Egypt into the land of the Canaanites, Hittites, Amorites, Perizzites, Hivites and Jebusites, a land flowing with milk and honey.

18 "Thus they will heed your message. Then you and the elders of Israel shall go to the king of Egypt and say to him:[s] The LORD, the God of the Hebrews, has sent us word. Permit us, then, to go a three-days' journey in the desert, that we may offer sacrifice to the LORD, our God.

19 "Yet I know that the king of Egypt will not allow you to go unless he is forced. **20** I will stretch out my hand, therefore, and smite Egypt by doing all kinds of wondrous deeds there. After that he will send you away. **21** I will even make the Egyptians so well-disposed toward this people that, when you leave, you will not go empty-handed. **22** [t]Every woman shall ask her neighbor and her house guest for silver and gold articles* and for clothing to put on your

---

n 2-10; Acts 7, 30-35.
o Jos 5, 15.
p Ex 4, 5; Mt 22, 32; Mk 12, 36; Lk 20, 37.
q 8f: Gn 15, 19ff.
r Ps 135, 13.
s Ex 5, 3.
t 21f: Ex 11, 2f; 12, 35f.

---

*

3, 1: The mountain of God: probably given this designation because of the divine apparitions which took place there, such as on this occasion and when the Israelites were there after the departure from Egypt.

3, 2: An angel of the Lord: the visual form under which God appeared and spoke to men is referred to indifferently in some Old Testament texts either as God's angel or as God himself. Cf Gn 16, 7. 13; Ex 14, 19. 24f; Nm 22, 22–35; Jgs 6, 11–18.

3, 6: The appearance of God caused fear of death, since it was believed that no one could see God and live; cf Gn 32, 30. The God of Abraham . . . Jacob: cited by Christ in proof of the resurrection since the patriarchs, long dead, live on in God who is the God of the living. Cf Mt 22, 32; Mk 12, 26; Lk 20, 37.

3, 8: I have come down: a figure of speech signifying an extraordinary divine intervention in human affairs. Cf Gn 11, 5. 7. Flowing with milk and honey: an expression denoting agricultural prosperity, which seems to have been proverbial in its application to Palestine. Cf Ex 13, 5; Nm 13, 27; Jos 5, 6; Jer 11, 5; 32, 22; Ez 20, 6. 15.

3, 11: Who am I: besides naturally shrinking from such a tremendous undertaking, Moses realized that, as a fugitive from Pharaoh, he could hardly hope to carry out a mission to him. Perhaps he also recalled that on one occasion even his own kinsmen questioned his authority. Cf Ex 2, 14.

3, 14: I am who am: apparently this utterance is the source of the word Yahweh, the proper personal name of the God of Israel. It is commonly explained in reference to God as the absolute and necessary Being. It may be understood of God as the Source of all created beings. Out of reverence for this name, the term Adonai, "my Lord," was later used as a substitute. The word Lord in the present version represents this traditional usage. The word "Jehovah" arose from a false reading of this name as it is written in the current Hebrew text.

3, 16: Elders: the Israelite leaders, who were usually older men. They were representatives of the people.

3, 22: Articles: probably jewelry. Despoil: this was permissible, that the Israelites might compensate themselves for their many years of servitude; besides, the Egyptians would give these things willingly, Cf Ex 12, 33–36.

sons and daughters. Thus you will despoil the Egyptians.''

CHAPTER 4

Confirmation of Moses' Mission.

1 "But," objected Moses, "suppose they will not believe me, nor listen to my plea? For they may say, 'The LORD did not appear to you.' " **2** The LORD therefore asked him, "What is that in your hand?" "A staff," he answered. **3** The LORD then said, "Throw it on the ground." When he threw it on the ground it was changed into a serpent, [u] and Moses shied away from it. **4** "Now, put out your hand," the LORD said to him, "and take hold of its tail." So he put out his hand and laid hold of it, and it became a staff in his hand. **5** "This will take place so that they may believe," he continued, "that the LORD, the God of their fathers, the God of Abraham, the God of Isaac, the God of Jacob, did appear to you."

6 Again the LORD said to him, "Put your hand in your bosom." He put it in his bosom, and when he withdrew it, to his surprise his hand was leprous, like snow. **7** The LORD then said, "Now, put your hand back in your bosom." Moses put his hand back in his bosom, and when he withdrew it, to his surprise it was again like the rest of his body. **8** "If they will not believe you, nor heed the message of the first sign, they should believe the message of the second. **9** And if they will not believe even these two signs, nor heed your plea, take some water from the river and pour it on the dry land. The water you take from the river will become blood on the dry land." [v]

Aaron's Office as Assistant.

10 Moses, however, said to the LORD, "If you please, Lord, I have never been eloquent, neither in the past, nor recently, nor now that you have spoken to your servant; but I am slow of speech and tongue." [w] **11** The LORD said to him, "Who gives one man speech and makes another deaf and dumb? Or who gives sight to one and makes another blind? Is it not I, the LORD? **12** Go, then! It is I who will assist you in speaking and will teach you what you are to say." **13** Yet he insisted, "If you please, Lord, send someone else!"* **14** Then the LORD became angry with Moses and said, "Have you not your brother, Aaron the Levite? I know that he is an eloquent speaker. Besides, he is now on his way to meet you. **15** When he sees you, his heart will be glad. You are to speak to him, then, and put the words in his mouth. I will assist both you and him in speaking and will teach the two of you what you are to do. **16** He shall speak to the people for you: he shall be your spokesman,* and you shall be as God to him. [x] **17** Take this staff* in your hand; with it you are to perform the signs."

Moses' Return to Egypt.

18 After this Moses returned to his father-in-law Jethro and said to him, "Let me go back, please, to my kinsmen in Egypt, to see whether they are still living." Jethro replied, "Go in peace."* **19** In Midian [y] the LORD said to Moses, "Go back to Egypt, for all the men who sought your life are dead." **20** So Moses took his wife and his sons, and started back to the land of Egypt, with them riding the ass. The staff of God he carried with him. **21** The LORD said to him, "On your return to Egypt, see that you perform before Pharaoh all the wonders I have put in your power. I will make him obstinate,* however, so that he will not let the people go. **22** [z] So you shall say to Pharaoh: Thus says the LORD: Israel is my son, my first-born. **23** Hence I tell you: Let my son go, that he may serve me. If you refuse to let him go, I warn you, I will kill your son, your first-born." [a]

24 *On the journey, at a place where they spent the night, the Lord came upon Moses and would have killed him. **25** [b] But Zipporah took a piece of flint and cut off her son's foreskin and, touching his person, she said, "You are a spouse of blood to me." **26** Then God let Moses go. At that time she said, "A spouse of blood," in regard to the circumcision.

27 The LORD said to Aaron, "Go into the desert to meet Moses." So he went, and when they met at the mountain of God, Aaron kissed him. **28** Moses informed him of all the LORD had said in sending him, and of the various signs he had enjoined upon him. **29** Then Moses and Aaron went and assembled all the elders of the Israelites. **30** Aaron told them everything the LORD had said to Moses, and he performed the signs before the people. **31** The people be-

---

u Ex 7, 10.	y Ex 2, 15, 23.
v Ex 7, 17. 19f.	z Sir 36, 11.
w Ex 6, 12.	a Ex 11, 5; 12, 29.
x 15f: Ex 7, 1.	b Is 6, 2; 7, 20.

*

4, 13: Send someone else: literally, "Send by means of him whom you will send," that is, "Send whom you will."

4, 16: Spokesman: literally, "mouth"; Aaron was to serve as a mouthpiece for Moses, as a prophet does for God; hence the relation between Moses and Aaron is compared to that between God and his prophet. Cf Ex 7, 1.

4, 17: This staff: probably the same as that of vv 2ff; but some understand it here of a new staff now given by God to Moses.

4, 18: Moses did not tell his father-in-law his main reason for returning to Egypt, but this secondary motive which he offered was also true.

4, 21: Make him obstinate: literally, "harden his heart." God permitted Pharaoh to be stubborn in his opposition to the departure of the Israelites. Cf Rom 9, 17f.

4, 24ff: Apparently God was angry with Moses for having failed to keep the divine command given to Abraham in Gn 17, 10ff. Moses' life is spared when his wife circumcises their son.

lieved, and when they heard that the LORD was concerned about them and had seen their affliction, they bowed down in worship.

CHAPTER 5

Pharaoh's Obduracy. 1 After that, Moses and Aaron went to Pharaoh and said, "Thus says the LORD, the God of Israel: Let my people go, that they may celebrate a feast to me in the desert." 2 Pharaoh answered, "Who is the LORD, that I should heed his plea to let Israel go? I do not know the LORD; even if I did, I would not let Israel go." 3 They replied, "The God of the Hebrews has sent us word. Let us go a three days' journey in the desert, that we may offer sacrifice to the LORD, our God;*c* otherwise he will punish us with pestilence or the sword."

4 The king of Egypt answered them, "What do you mean, Moses and Aaron, by taking the people away from their work? Off to your labor! 5 Look how numerous the people of the land are already," continued Pharaoh, "and yet you would give them rest from their labor!"

6 That very day Pharaoh gave the taskmasters and foremen* of the people this order: 7 "You shall no longer supply the people with straw for their brickmaking* as you have previously done. Let them go and gather straw themselves! 8 Yet you shall levy upon them the same quota of bricks as they have previously made. Do not reduce it. They are lazy; that is why they are crying, 'Let us go to offer sacrifice to our God.' 9 Increase the work for the men, so that they keep their mind on it and pay no attention to lying words."

10 So the taskmasters and foremen of the people went out and told them, "Thus says Pharaoh: I will not provide you with straw. 11 Go and gather the straw yourselves, wherever you can find it. Yet there must not be the slightest reduction in your work." 12 The people, then, scattered throughout the land of Egypt to gather stubble for straw, 13 while the taskmasters kept driving them on, saying, "Finish your work, the same daily amount as when your straw was supplied."

Complaint of the Foremen. 14 The foremen of the Israelites, whom the taskmasters of Pharaoh had placed over them, were beaten, and were asked, "Why have you not completed your prescribed amount of bricks yesterday and today, as before?"

15 Then the Israelite foremen came and made this appeal to Pharaoh: "Why do you treat your servants in this manner? 16 No straw is supplied to your servants, and still we are told to make bricks. Look how your servants are beaten! It is you who are at fault." 17 Pharaoh answered, "It is just because you are lazy that

you keep saying, 'Let us go and offer sacrifice to the LORD.' 18 Off to work, then! Straw shall not be provided for you, but you must still deliver your quota of bricks."

19 The Israelite foremen knew they were in a sorry plight, having been told not to reduce the daily amount of bricks. 20 When, therefore, they left Pharaoh and came upon Moses and Aaron, who were waiting to meet them, 21 they said to them, "The LORD look upon you and judge! You have brought us into bad odor with Pharaoh and his servants and have put a sword in their hands to slay us."

Renewal of God's Promise. 22 Moses again had recourse to the LORD and said, "Lord, why do you treat this people so badly? And why did you send me on such a mission? 23 Ever since I went to Pharaoh to speak in your name, he has maltreated this people of yours, and you have done nothing to rescue them."

CHAPTER 6

1 Then the LORD answered Moses, "Now you shall see what I will do to Pharaoh. Forced by my mighty hand, he will send them away; compelled by my outstretched arm, he will drive them from his land."

2 God also said to Moses, "I am the LORD. 3 As God the Almighty I appeared*d* to Abraham, Isaac and Jacob, but my name, LORD, I did not make known to them. 4 I also established my covenant with them, to give them the land of Canaan, the land in which they were living as aliens.*e* 5 And now that I have heard the groaning of the Israelites, whom the Egyptians are treating as slaves, I am mindful of my covenant.*f* 6 Therefore, say to the Israelites: I am the LORD. I will free you from the forced labor of the Egyptians and will deliver you from their slavery. I will rescue you by my outstretched arm and with mighty acts of judgment. 7 I will take you as my own people, and you shall have me as your God.*g* You will know that I, the LORD, am your God when I free you from the labor of the Egyptians 8 and bring you into the land which I swore to give to Abraham, Isaac and Jacob. I will give it to you as your own possession—I, the LORD!" 9 But when Moses told this to the Israelites, they would not listen to him because of their dejection and hard slavery.

---

c Ex 3, 18.
d Gn 17, 1; 35, 11.
e Gn 15, 18; 17, 4-8.

f Ex 2, 24.
g Lv 26, 12.

*

5, 6: The taskmasters and foremen: the former were higher officials and probably Egyptians; the latter were lower officials, chosen from the Israelites themselves. Cf v 14.

5, 7: Straw was mixed with the clay to give the sun-dried bricks greater consistency.

10 Then the LORD said to Moses, **11** "Go and tell Pharaoh, king of Egypt, to let the Israelites leave his land." **12** But Moses protested to the LORD, "If the Israelites would not listen to me, how can it be that Pharaoh will listen to me, poor speaker[h] that I am!" **13** Still, the LORD, to bring the Israelites out of Egypt, spoke to Moses and Aaron and gave them his orders regarding both the Israelites and Pharaoh, king of Egypt.

Genealogy of Moses and Aaron.

14 These are the heads of the ancestral houses.* The sons of Reuben,[i] the first-born of Israel, were Hanoch, Pallu, Hezron and Carmi; these are the clans of Reuben. **15** The sons of Simeon[j] were Jemuel, Jamin, Ohad, Jachin, Zohar and Shaul, who was the son of a Canaanite woman; these are the clans of Simeon. **16** The names of the sons of Levi,[k] in their genealogical order, are Gershon, Kohath and Merari. Levi lived one hundred and thirty-seven years.

17 The sons of Gershon,[l] as heads of clans, were Libni and Shimei. **18** The sons of Kohath[m] were Amram, Izhar, Hebron and Uzziel. Kohath lived one hundred and thirty-three years. **19** The sons of Merari[n] were Mahli and Mushi. These are the clans of Levi in their genealogical order.

20 Amram married his aunt* Jochebed,[o] who bore him Aaron, Moses and Miriam. Amram lived one hundred and thirty-seven years. **21** The sons of Izhar were Korah, Nepheg and Zichri. **22** The sons of Uzziel were Mishael, Elzaphan and Sithri. **23** Aaron married Amminadab's[p] daughter, Elisheba, the sister of Nahshon; she bore him Nadab, Abihu, Eleazar and Ithamar. **24** The sons of Korah were Assir, Elkanah and Abiasaph. These are the clans of the Korahites. **25** Aaron's son, Eleazar, married one of Putiel's daughters, who bore him Phinehas. These are the heads of the ancestral clans of the Levites. **26** This is the Aaron and this the Moses to whom the LORD said, "Lead the Israelites from the land of Egypt, company by company." **27** These are the ones who spoke to Pharaoh, king of Egypt, to bring the Israelites out of Egypt—the same Moses and Aaron.

Moses and Aaron before Pharaoh.

28 On the day the LORD spoke to Moses in Egypt **29** he said, "I am the LORD. Repeat to Pharaoh, king of Egypt, all that I tell you." **30** But Moses protested to the LORD, "Since I am a poor speaker,[q] how can it be that Pharaoh will listen to me?"

CHAPTER 7

1 The LORD answered him, "See! I have made you as God to Pharaoh,[r] and Aaron your brother shall act as your prophet.* **2** You shall tell him all that I command you. In turn, your brother Aaron shall tell Pharaoh to let the Israelites leave his land. **3** Yet I will make Pharaoh so obstinate that, despite the many signs and wonders that I will work in the land of Egypt, **4** he will not listen to you. Therefore I will lay my hand on Egypt and by great acts of judgment I will bring the hosts of my people, the Israelites, out of the land of Egypt, **5** so that the Egyptians may learn that I am the LORD, as I stretch out my hand against Egypt and lead the Israelites out of their midst."

6 Moses and Aaron did as the LORD had commanded them. **7** Moses was eighty years old and Aaron eighty-three when they spoke to Pharaoh.

The Staff Turned into a Snake.

8 The LORD told Moses and Aaron, **9** "If Pharaoh demands that you work a sign or wonder, you shall say to Aaron: Take your staff and throw it down before Pharaoh, and it will be changed into a snake."[s] **10** Then Moses and Aaron went to Pharaoh and did as the LORD had commanded. Aaron threw his staff down before Pharaoh and his servants, and it was changed into a snake. **11** Pharaoh, in turn, summoned wise men and sorcerers, and they also, the magicians[t] of Egypt, did likewise by their magic arts. **12** Each one threw down his staff, and it was changed into a snake. But Aaron's staff swallowed their staffs. **13** Pharaoh, however, was obstinate and would not listen to them, just as the LORD had foretold.

First Plague: Water Turned into Blood.

14 *Then the LORD said to Moses, "Pharaoh is obdurate in refusing to let the people go. **15** Tomorrow morning, when he sets out for the water, go and present yourself by the river bank,

---

h Ex 6, 30.
i Nm 26. 5f; 1 Chr 5, 3
j Nm 26, 12; 1 Chr 4, 24.
k Nm 3, 17; 1 Chr 6, 1.
  16; 23, 6.
l Nm 3, 21; 1 Chr 6, 17;
  23, 7.
m Nm 3, 27; 1 Chr 6, 2.
  18.

n Nm 3, 20; 1 Chr 6, 19;
  23, 21.
o Nm 26, 59.
p Ru 4, 19f; 1 Chr 2, 10.
q Ex 6, 12.
r Ex 4, 15f.
s Ex 4, 3.
t 2 Tm 3, 8.

*

6, 14: The purpose of the genealogy here is to give the line from which Moses and Aaron sprang. Reuben and Simeon are first mentioned because, as older brothers of Levi, their names occur before his in the genealogy.

6, 20: His aunt: more exactly, "his father's sister." Later on such a marriage was forbidden. Cf Lv 18, 12. Hence, the Greek and Latin versions render here, "his cousin."

7, 1: Just as God had his prophets to speak to men in his name, so Moses had Aaron as his "prophet" to speak to Pharaoh. Cf Ex 4, 16.

7, 14: Most of the ten plagues of Egypt seem to be similar to certain natural phenomena of that country; but they are represented as supernatural at least in their greater intensity and in their occurring exactly to Moses' commands.

holding in your hand the staff that turned into a serpent. **16** Say to him: The LORD, the God of the Hebrews, sent me to you with the message: Let my people go to worship me in the desert. But as yet you have not listened. **17** The LORD now says: This is how you shall know that I am the LORD. I will strike the water of the river with the staff I hold, and it shall be changed into blood.ᵘ **18** The fish in the river shall die, and the river itself shall become so polluted that the Egyptians will be unable to drink its water.''

19 The LORD then said to Moses, ''Say to Aaron: Take your staff and stretch out your hand over the waters of Egypt—their streams and canals and pools, all their supplies of water —that they may become blood. Throughout the land of Egypt there shall be blood, even in the wooden pails and stone jars.''

20 Moses and Aaron did as the LORD had commanded. Aaron raised his staff and struck the waters of the river in full view of Pharaoh and his servants, and all the water of the river was changed into blood. **21** The fish in the river died, and the river itself became so polluted that the Egyptians could not drink its water. There was blood throughout the land of Egypt. **22** But the Egyptian magicians did the same by their magic arts. So Pharaoh remained obstinate and would not listen to Moses and Aaron, just as the LORD had foretold. **23** He turned away and went into his house, with no concern even for this. **24** All the Egyptians had to dig in the neighborhood of the river for drinking water, since they could not drink the river water.

Second Plague: the Frogs.   **25** Seven days passed after the LORD had struck the river. **26** *Then the LORD said to Moses, ''Go to Pharaoh and tell him:ᵛ Thus says the LORD: Let my people go to worship me. **27** If you refuse to let them go, I warn you, I will send a plague of frogs over all your territory. **28** The river will teem with frogs. They will come up into your palace and into your bedroom and onto your bed, into the houses of your servants, too, and your subjects, even into your ovens and your kneeding bowls. **29** The frogs will swarm all over you and your subjects and your servant.''

CHAPTER 8

1 The LORD then told Moses, ''Say to Aaron: Stretch out your hand and your staff over the streams and canals and pools, to make frogs overrun the land of Egypt.'' **2** Aaron stretched out his hand over the waters of Egypt, and the frogs came up and covered the land of Egypt. **3** But the magicians did the same by their magic arts. They, too, made frogs overrun the land of Egypt. **4** Then Pharaoh summoned Moses and Aar-

on and said, ''Pray the LORD to remove the frogs from me and my subjects, and I will let the people go to offer sacrifice to the LORD.'' **5** Moses answered Pharaoh, ''Do me the favor of appointing the time when I am to pray for you and your servants and your subjects, that the frogs may be taken away from you and your houses and be left only in the river.'' **6** ''Tomorrow,'' said Pharaoh. Then Moses replied, ''It shall be as you have said, so that you may learn that there is none like the LORD, our God. **7** The frogs shall leave you and your houses, your servants and your subjects; only in the river shall they be left.''

8 After Moses and Aaron left Pharaoh's presence, Moses implored the LORD to fulfill the promise he had made to Pharaoh about the frogs; **9** and the LORD did as Moses had asked. The frogs in the houses and courtyards* and fields died off. **10** Heaps and heaps of them were gathered up, and there was a stench in the land. **11** But when Pharaoh saw that there was a respite, he became obdurate and would not listen to them, just as the LORD had foretold.

Third Plague: the Gnats.   **12** Thereupon the LORD said to Moses, ''Tell Aaron to stretch out his staff and strike the dust of the earth, that it may be turned into gnatsʷ throughout the land of Egypt.''* **13** They did so. Aaron stretched out his hand, and with his staff he struck the dust of the earth, and gnats came upon man and beast. The dust of the earth was turned into gnats throughout the land of Egypt. **14** Though the magicians tried to bring forth gnats by their magic arts, they could not do so.ˣ As the gnats infested man and beast, **15** the magicians said to Pharaoh, ''This is the finger of God.''* Yet Pharaoh remained obstinate and would not listen to them, just as the LORD had foretold.

Fourth Plague: the Flies.   **16** Again the LORD told Moses, ''Early tomorrow morning present yourself to Pharaoh when he goes forth to the water, and say to him: Thus says the LORD: Let my people go to worship me. **17** If you will not let my people go, I warn you, I will loose swarms of flies upon you and your servants and your subjects and your houses. The houses of the Egyptians and the very ground on

---

u 17-21: Ex 4, 9; Pss   105, 30.
    78, 44; 105, 29; Wis   w 12f: Ps 105, 31.
    11, 5-7.   x Wis 17, 7.
v 26-29: Pss 78, 45;

*

7, 26—8, 28: This is Ex 8, 1–32 in the verse enumeration of the Vulgate.

8, 9: Courtyards: some render ''farmhouses.''

8, 12. 17: Gnats, flies: it is uncertain what species of troublesome insects are here meant.

8, 15: The finger of God: understood by the magicians as the staff mentioned in Ex 8, 13. Cf Lk 11, 20.

which they stand shall be filled with swarms of flies. **18** But on that day I will make an exception of the land of Goshen: there shall be no flies where my people dwell, that you may know that I am the LORD in the midst of the earth. **19** I will make this distinction between my people and your people. This sign shall take place tomorrow.'' **20** This the LORD did. Thick swarms of flies entered the house of Pharaoh and houses of his servants; throughout Egypt the land was infested with flies.*y*

21 Then Pharaoh summoned Moses and Aaron and said to them, ''Go and offer sacrifice to your God in this land.'' **22** But Moses replied, ''It is not right to do so, for the sacrifices we offer to the LORD, our God, are an abomination to the Egyptians.* If before their very eyes we offer sacrifices which are an abomination to them, will not the Egyptians stone us? **23** We must go a three days' journey in the desert to offer sacrifice to the LORD, our God, as he commands us.'' **24** ''Well, then,'' said Pharaoh, ''I will let you go to offer sacrifice to the LORD, your God, in the desert, provided that you do not go too far away and that you pray for me.'' **25** Moses answered, ''As soon as I leave your presence I will pray to the LORD that the flies may depart tomorrow from Pharaoh and his servants and his subjects. Pharaoh, however, must not play false again by refusing to let the people go to offer sacrifice to the LORD.'' **26** When Moses left Pharaoh's presence, he prayed to the LORD; **27** and the LORD did as Moses had asked. He removed the flies from Pharaoh and his servants and subjects. Not one remained. **28** But once more Pharaoh became obdurate and would not let the people go.

CHAPTER 9

Fifth Plague: the Pestilence.   **1** Then the LORD said to Moses, ''Go to Pharaoh and tell him: Thus says the LORD, the God of the Hebrews: Let my people go to worship me. **2** If you refuse to let them go and persist in holding them, **3** I warn you, the LORD will afflict all your livestock in the field—your horses, asses, camels, herds and flocks—with a very severe pestilence. **4** But the LORD will distinguish between the livestock of Israel and that of Egypt, so that none belonging to the Israelites will die.'' **5** And setting a definite time, the LORD added, ''Tomorrow the LORD shall do this in the land.'' **6** And on the next day the LORD did so. All the livestock of the Egyptians died,*z* but not one beast belonging to the Israelites. **7** But though Pharaoh's messengers informed him that not even one beast belonging to the Israelites had died, he still remained obdurate and would not let the people go.

Sixth Plague: the Boils.   **8** Then the LORD said to Moses and Aaron, ''Take a double handful of soot from a furnace, and in the presence of Pharaoh let Moses scatter it toward the sky. **9** It will then turn into fine dust over the whole land of Egypt and cause festering boils on man and beast throughout the land.''

10 So they took soot from a furnace and stood in the presence of Pharaoh. Moses scattered it toward the sky, and it caused festering boils on man and beast. **11** The magicians could not stand in Moses' presence, for there were boils on the magicians no less than on the rest of the Egyptians. **12** But the LORD made Pharaoh obstinate, and he would not listen to them, just as the LORD had foretold to Moses.

Seventh Plague: the Hail.   **13** Then the LORD told Moses, ''Early tomorrow morning present yourself to Pharaoh and say to him: Thus says the LORD, the God of the Hebrews: Let my people go to worship me, **14** or this time I will hurl all my blows upon you and your servants and your subjects, that you may know that there is none like me anywhere on earth. **15** For by now I would have stretched out my hand and struck you and your subjects with such pestilence as would wipe you from the earth. **16** But this is why I have spared you: to show you* my power and to make my name resound throughout the earth!*a* **17** Will you still block the way for my people by refusing to let them go? **18** I warn you, then, tomorrow at this hour I will rain down such fierce hail as there has never been in Egypt from the day the nation was founded up to the present. **19** Therefore, order all your livestock and whatever else you have in the open fields to be brought to a place of safety. Whatever man or beast remains in the fields and is not brought to shelter shall die when the hail comes upon them.'' **20** Some of Pharaoh's servants feared the warning of the LORD and hurried their servants and livestock off to shelter. **21** Others, however, did not take the warning of the LORD to heart and left their servants and livestock in the fields.

22 The LORD then said to Moses, ''Stretch out your hand toward the sky, that hail may fall upon the entire land of Egypt, on man and beast and every growing thing in the land of Egypt.'' **23** When Moses stretched out his staff toward the sky, the LORD sent forth hail*b* and peals of thunder. Lightning flashed toward the earth,

---

y Pss 78, 45; 105, 31;
   Wis 16, 9.
z Ps 78, 48.

a Rom 9, 17.
b 23f: Pss 78, 47; 105,
   32f.

*

8, 22: The Egyptians would fiercely resent the sacrifice of any animal they considered sacred. Certain animals were worshiped in Egypt, at least as the symbols of various deities.
  9, 16: To show you: some ancient versions read, ''to show through you.'' Cf Rom 9, 17.

and the LORD rained down hail upon the land of Egypt; **24** and lightning constantly flashed through the hail, such fierce hail as had never been seen in the land since Egypt became a nation. **25** It struck down every man and beast that was in the open throughout the land of Egypt; it beat down every growing thing and splintered every tree in the fields. **26** Only in the land of Goshen, where the Israelites dwelt, was there no hail.

27 Then Pharaoh summoned Moses and Aaron and said to them, "I have sinned again! The LORD is just; it is I and my subjects who are at fault. **28** Pray to the LORD, for we have had enough of God's thunder and hail. Then I will let you go; you need stay no longer." **29** Moses replied, "As soon as I leave the city I will extend my hands to the LORD; the thunder will cease, and there will be no more hail. Thus you shall learn that the earth is the LORD's. **30** But you and your servants, I know, do not yet fear the LORD God."

31 Now the flax and the barley were ruined, because the barley was in ear and the flax in bud. **32** But the wheat and the spelt were not ruined, for they grow later.

33 When Moses had left Pharaoh's presence and had gone out of the city, he extended his hands to the LORD. Then the thunder and the hail ceased, and the rain no longer poured down upon the earth. **34** But Pharaoh, seeing that the rain and hail and thunder had ceased, sinned again: he with his servants became obdurate, **35** and in his obstinacy he would not let the Israelites go, as the LORD had foretold through Moses.

CHAPTER 10

Eighth Plague: the Locusts.   **1** Then the LORD said to Moses, "Go to Pharaoh, for I have made him and his servants obdurate in order that I may perform these signs of mine among them **2** and that you may recount to your son and grandson how ruthlessly I dealt with the Egyptians and what signs I wrought among them, so that you may know that I am the LORD."[c]

3 So Moses and Aaron went to Pharaoh and told him, "Thus says the LORD, the God of the Hebrews: How long will you refuse to submit to me? Let my people go to worship me. **4** If you refuse to let my people go, I warn you, tomorrow I will bring locusts into your country. **5** They shall cover the ground, so that the ground itself will not be visible. They shall eat up the remnant you saved unhurt from the hail, as well as the foliage that has since sprouted in your fields. **6** They shall fill your houses and the houses of your servants and of all the Egyptians; such a sight your fathers or grandfathers have not seen from the day they first settled on

this soil up to the present day." With that he turned and left Pharaoh.

7 But Pharaoh's servants said to him, "How long must he be a menace to us? Let the men go to worship the LORD, their God. Do you not yet realize that Egypt is being destroyed?" **8** So Moses and Aaron were brought back to Pharaoh, who said to them, "You may go and worship the LORD, your God. But how many of you will go?" **9** "Young and old must go with us," Moses answered, "our sons and daughters as well as our flocks and herds must accompany us. That is what a feast of the LORD means to us." **10** "The LORD help you,"* Pharaoh replied, "if I ever let your little ones go with you! Clearly, you have some evil in mind. **11** No, no! Just you men can go and worship the LORD.* After all, that is what you want." With that they were driven from Pharaoh's presence.

12 The LORD then said to Moses, "Stretch out your hand over the land of Egypt, that locusts[d] may swarm over it and eat up all the vegetation and whatever the hail has left." **13** So Moses stretched out his staff over the land of Egypt, and the LORD sent an east wind* blowing over the land all that day and all that night. At dawn the east wind brought the locusts. **14** They swarmed over the whole land of Egypt and settled down on every part of it. Never before had there been such a fierce swarm of locusts, nor will there ever be. **15** They covered the surface of the whole land, till it was black with them. They ate up all the vegetation in the land and the fruit of whatever trees the hail had spared. Nothing green was left on any tree or plant throughout the land of Egypt.

16 Hastily Pharaoh summoned Moses and Aaron and said, "I have sinned against the LORD, your God, and against you. **17** But now, do forgive me my sin once more, and pray the LORD, your God, to take at least this deadly pest from me." **18** When Moses left the presence of Pharaoh, he prayed to the LORD, **19** and the LORD changed the wind to a very strong west wind, which took up the locusts and hurled them into the Red Sea.* But though not a single locust remained within the confines of Egypt, **20** the

---

c Dt 6, 20ff.   34f.
d 12ff: Pss 78, 46; 105,

*

10, 10:   The Lord help you . . . : literally, "May the LORD be with you in the same way as I let you . . ."; a sarcastic blessing intended as a curse.

10, 11:   Pharaoh realized that if the men alone went they would have to return to their families. He suspected that the Hebrews had no intention of returning.

10, 13:   East wind: coming across the desert from Arabia, the strong east wind brings Egypt the burning sirocco and, at times, locusts. Cf Ex 14, 21.

10, 19:   The Red Sea: according to the traditional translation, but the Hebrew is literally, "the Reed Sea"; hence the Red Sea of Exodus was probably a body of shallow water somewhat to the north of the present deep Red Sea.

LORD made Pharaoh obstinate, and he would not let the Israelites go.

Ninth Plague: the Darkness.

21 Then the LORD said to Moses, "Stretch out your hand toward the sky, that over the land of Egypt there may be such intense darkness* that one can feel it." **22** So Moses stretched out his hand toward the sky, and there was dense darkness*e* throughout the land of Egypt for three days. **23** Men could not see one another, nor could they move from where they were, for three days. But all the Israelites had light where they dwelt.

24 Pharaoh then summoned Moses and Aaron and said, "Go and worship the LORD. Your little ones, too, may go with you. But your flocks and herds must remain." **25** Moses replied, "You must also grant us sacrifices and holocausts to offer up to the LORD, our God. **26** Hence, our livestock also must go with us. Not an animal must be left behind. Some of them we must sacrifice to the LORD, our God, but we ourselves shall not know which ones we must sacrifice to him until we arrive at the place itself." **27** But the LORD made Pharaoh obstinate, and he would not let them go. **28** "Leave my presence," Pharaoh said to him, "and see to it that you do not appear before me again! The day you appear before me you shall die!" **29** Moses replied, "Well said! I will never appear before you again."

CHAPTER 11

Tenth Plague: the Death of the First-born.

1 Then the LORD told Moses, "One more plague will I bring upon Pharaoh and upon Egypt. After that he will let you depart. In fact, he will not merely let you go; he will drive you away. **2** Instruct your people that every man is to ask his neighbor, and every woman her neighbor, for silver and gold articles and for clothing."*f* **3** The LORD indeed made the Egyptians well-disposed toward the people; Moses himself was very highly regarded by Pharaoh's servants and the people in the land of Egypt.

4 Moses then said, "Thus says the LORD: At midnight I will go forth through Egypt.*g* **5** Every first-born in this land shall die,*h* from the first-born of Pharaoh on the throne to the first-born of the slave-girl at the handmill, as well as all the first-born of the animals. **6** Then there shall be loud wailing throughout the land of Egypt, such as has never been, nor will ever be again. **7** But among the Israelites and their animals not even a dog shall growl, so that you may know how the LORD distinguishes between the Egyptians and the Israelites. **8** *i*All these servants of yours shall then come down to me, and prostrate before me, they shall beg me, 'Leave us, you and all your followers!' Only

then will I depart." With that he left Pharaoh's presence in hot anger.

9 The LORD said to Moses, "Pharaoh refuses to listen to you that my wonders may be multiplied in the land of Egypt." **10** Thus, although Moses and Aaron performed these various wonders in Pharaoh's presence, the LORD made Pharaoh obstinate, and he would not let the Israelites leave his land.

CHAPTER 12

The Passover Ritual Prescribed.

1 The LORD said to Moses and Aaron in the land of Egypt, **2** "This month* shall stand at the head of your calendar; you shall reckon it the first month of the year.*j* **3** Tell the whole community of Israel: On the tenth of this month every one of your families must procure for itself a lamb, one apiece for each household. **4** If a family is too small for a whole lamb, it shall join the nearest household in procuring one and shall share in the lamb* in proportion to the number of persons who partake of it. **5** The lamb must be a year-old male and without blemish. You may take it from either the sheep or the goats. **6** You shall keep it until the fourteenth day of this month, and then, with the whole assembly of Israel present, it shall be slaughtered during the evening twilight. **7** They shall take some of its blood and apply it to the two doorposts and the lintel of every house in which they partake of the lamb. **8** That same night they shall eat its roasted flesh with unleavened bread and bitter herbs. **9** It shall not be eaten raw or boiled, but roasted whole, with its head and shanks and inner organs. **10** None of it must be kept beyond the next morning; whatever is left over in the morning shall be burned up.

11 "This is how you are to eat it: with your loins girt, sandals on your feet and your staff in hand, you shall eat like those who are in flight. It is the Passover* of the LORD. **12** For on this

---

e Ps 105, 28.
f 2f: Ex 3, 21f; 12, 35f.
g Ex 12, 12.
h 5f: Ex 12, 29f.
i Ex 12, 31ff.
j 2-20: Lv 23, 5-8; Nm 9, 2-5; 28, 16ff; Dt 16, 1-8.

*

10, 21: Darkness: at times a storm from the south, called the khamsin, blackens the sky of Egypt with sand from the Sahara; the dust in the air is then so thick that the darkness can, in a sense, "be felt."

12, 2: This month: Abib, the month of "ripe grain." Cf Ex 13, 4; 23, 15; 34, 18; Dt 16, 1. It occurred near the vernal equinox, March-April. Later it was known by the Babylonian name of Nisan. Cf Neh 2, 1; Est 3, 7.

12, 4: Share in the lamb: probably, in the expenses of its purchase. Some explain, "reckon for the lamb the number of persons required to eat it." Cf Ex 12, 10.

12, 11: Passover: in Hebrew, pesach, in Aramaic, pascha. In the following verses the same root is used in the verb "to pass over." The word may be originally Egyptian, pesach, "the blow," i.e., the final plague which destroyed the Egyptian first-born.

same night I will go through Egypt, striking down every first-born of the land, both man and beast, and executing judgment on all the gods of Egypt—I, the LORD! **13** But the blood will mark the houses where you are. Seeing the blood, I will pass over you; thus, when I strike the land of Egypt, no destructive blow will come upon you. *k*

14 "This day shall be a memorial feast for you, which all your generations shall celebrate with pilgrimage to the LORD, as a perpetual institution. **15** For seven days you must eat unleavened bread. From the very first day you shall have your houses clear of all leaven. Whoever eats leavened bread from the first day to the seventh shall be cut off from Israel. **16** On the first day you shall hold a sacred assembly, and likewise on the seventh. On these days you shall not do any sort of work, except to prepare the food that everyone needs.

17 "Keep, then, this custom of the unleavened bread. *l* Since it was on this very day that I brought your ranks out of the land of Egypt, you must celebrate this day throughout your generations as a perpetual institution. **18** From the evening of the fourteenth day of the first month until the evening of the twenty-first day of this month you shall eat unleavened bread. **19** For seven days no leaven may be found in your houses. Anyone, be he a resident alien or a native, who eats leavened food shall be cut off from the community of Israel. **20** Nothing leavened may you eat; wherever you dwell you may eat only unleavened bread.''

Promulgation of the Passover. **21** Moses called all the elders of Israel and said to them, ''Go and procure lambs for your families, and slaughter them as Passover victims. **22** Then take a bunch of hyssop,* and dipping it in the blood that is in the basin, sprinkle the lintel and the two doorposts with this blood. *m* But none of you shall go outdoors until morning. **23** For the LORD will go by, striking down the Egyptians. Seeing the blood on the lintel and the two doorposts, the LORD will pass over that door and not let the destroyer come into your houses to strike you down.

24 "You shall observe this as a perpetual ordinance for yourselves and your descendants. **25** Thus, you must also observe this rite when you have entered the land which the LORD will give you as he promised. **26** When your children ask you, 'What does this rite of yours mean?' *n* **27** you shall reply, 'This is the Passover sacrifice of the LORD, who passed over the houses of the Israelites in Egypt; when he struck down the Egyptians, he spared our houses.' ''

Then the people bowed down in worship, **28** and the Israelites went and did as the LORD had commanded Moses and Aaron.

Death of the First-born. **29** At midnight the LORD slew every first-born in the land of Egypt, *o* from the first-born of Pharaoh on the throne to the first-born of the prisoner in the dungeon, as well as all the first-born of the animals. **30** Pharaoh arose in the night, he and all his servants and all the Egyptians; and there was loud wailing throughout Egypt, for there was not a house without its dead.

Permission To Depart. **31** During the night Pharaoh summoned Moses and Aaron and said, ''Leave my people at once, you and the Israelites with you! Go and worship the LORD as you said. **32** Take your flocks, too, and your herds, as you demanded, and begone; and you will be doing me a favor.''

33 The Egyptians likewise urged the people on, to hasten their departure from the land; they thought that otherwise they would all die. **34** The people, therefore, took their dough before it was leavened, in their kneading bowls wrapped in their cloaks on their shoulders. **35** The Israelites did as Moses had commanded: they asked the Egyptians for articles of silver and gold and for clothing. *p* **36** The LORD indeed had made the Egyptians so well-disposed toward the people that they let them have whatever they asked for. Thus did they despoil the Egyptians.

II: The Exodus From Egypt and the Journey to Sinai

Departure from Egypt. **37** The Israelites set out from Rameses *q* for Succoth, about six hundred thousand men on foot, not counting the children. **38** A crowd of mixed ancestry* also went up with them, besides their livestock, very numerous flocks and herds. **39** Since the dough they had brought out of Egypt was not leavened, they baked it into unleavened loaves. They had been rushed out of Egypt and had no opportunity even to prepare food for the journey.

40 The time the Israelites had stayed in Egypt* was four hundred and thirty years. *r* **41** At the end of four hundred and thirty years, all the hosts of the LORD left the land of Egypt

---

k Heb 11, 28.
l Ex 13, 3.
m 22f: Ex 12, 7. 13.
n 26f: Ex 13, 8. 14; Dt 6, 20f.
o 29f: Ex 11, 4ff; Pss 78, 51; 105, 36; 136, 10;

Wis 18, 10-16.
p 35f: Ex 3, 21f; 11, 2f; Ps 105, 37f.
q Nm 33, 3ff.
r Gn 15, 13; Acts 7, 6; Gal 3, 17.

*

12, 22: Hyssop: a plant with many woody branchlets that make a convenient sprinkler.

12, 38: Mixed ancestry: half-Hebrew and half-Egyptian. Cf Nm 11, 4; Lv 24, 10f.

12, 40: In Egypt: according to some ancient sources, "in Canaan and Egypt," thus reckoning from the time of Abraham. Cf Gal 3, 17.

on this very date. **42** This was a night of vigil for the LORD, as he led them out of the land of Egypt; so on this same night all the Israelites must keep a vigil for the LORD throughout their generations.

Passover Regulations. **43** The LORD said to Moses and Aaron, "These are the regulations for the Passover. No foreigner may partake of it. **44** However, any slave who has been bought for money may partake of it, provided you have first circumcised him. **45** But no transient alien or hired servant may partake of it. **46** It must be eaten in one and the same house; you may not take any of its flesh outside the house.ˢ You shall not break any of its bones.* **47** The whole community of Israel must keep this feast. **48** If any aliensᵗ living among you wish to celebrate the Passover of the LORD, all the males among them must first be circumcised, and then they may join in its observance just like the natives. But no man who is uncircumcised may partake of it. **49** The law shall be the same for the resident alien as for the native."

50 All the Israelites did just as the LORD had commanded Moses and Aaron. **51** On that same day the LORD brought the Israelites out of Egypt company by company.

CHAPTER 13

Consecration of First-born. **1** The LORD spoke to Moses and said, **2** "Consecrate to me every first-born that opens the womb among the Israelites,ᵘ both of man and beast, for it belongs to me."

3 Moses said to the people, "Remember this day on which you came out of Egypt, that place of slavery.ᵛ It was with a strong hand that the LORD brought you away. Nothing made with leaven must be eaten. **4** This day of your departure is in the month of Abib. **5** Therefore, it is in this month that you must celebrate this rite, after the LORD, your God, has brought you into the land of the Canaanites, Hittites, Amorites, Hivites and Jebusites, which he swore to your fathers he would give you, a land flowing with milk and honey. **6** For seven days you shall eat unleavened bread, and the seventh day shall also be a festival to the LORD. **7** Only unleavened bread may be eaten during the seven days; no leaven and nothing leavened may be found in all your territory. **8** On this day you shall explain to your son, 'This is because of what the LORD did for me when I came out of Egypt.' **9** It shall be as a sign on your hand and as a reminder on your forehead;ʷ thus the law of the LORD will ever be on your lips, because with a strong hand the LORD brought you out of Egypt. **10** Therefore, you shall keep this prescribed rite at its appointed time from year to year.

11 "When the LORD, your God, has brought you into the land of the Canaanites, which he swore to you and your fathers he would give you, **12** you shall dedicate to the LORD every son that opens the womb;ˣ and all the male firstlings of your animals shall belong to the LORD. **13** Every first-born of an ass you shall redeem with a sheep. If you do not redeem it, you shall break its neck. Every first-born son you must redeem. **14** If your son should ask you later on, 'What does this mean?' you shall tell him, 'With a strong hand the LORD brought us out of Egypt, that place of slavery. **15** When Pharaoh stubbornly refused to let us go, the LORD killed every first-born in the land of Egypt, every first-born of man and of beast. This is why I sacrifice to the LORD everything of the male sex that opens the womb, and why I redeem every first-born of my sons.' **16** Let this, then, be as a sign on your hand and as a pendant on your forehead: with a strong hand the LORD brought us out of Egypt."ʸ

Toward the Red Sea. **17** Now, when Pharaoh let the people go, God did not lead them by way of the Philistines' land,* though this was the nearest; for he thought, should the people see that they would have to fight, they might change their minds and return to Egypt. **18** Instead, he rerouted them toward the Red Sea by way of the desert road. In battle array the Israelites marched out of Egypt. **19** Moses also took Joseph's bonesᶻ along, for Joseph had made the Israelites swear solemnly that, when God should come to them, they would carry his bones away with them.

20 Setting out from Succoth, they camped at Ethamᵃ near the edge of the desert.

21 The Lord preceded them, in the daytime by means of a column of cloud to show them the way, and at night by means of a column of fire* to give them light.ᵇ Thus they could travel both day and night. **22** Neither the column of cloud

---

s Nm 9, 12; Jn 19, 36.
t 47f: Nm 9, 14.
u Ex 13, 12-15.
v 3-10: Ex 12, 2-20.
w Ex 13, 16; Dt 6, 8; 11, 18.
x 12-15; Ex 13, 2; 22, 29f; 34, 19f: Nm 3, 12f; 8, 16; 18, 15; Dt
15, 19.
y Ex 13, 9.
z Gn 50, 25; Jos 24, 32.
a Nm 33, 6.
b 21f: Ex 40, 38; Nm 9, 15-22; Dt 1, 33; Neh 9, 19; Pss 78, 14; 105, 39; Wis 10, 17.

*

12, 46: You shall not break any of its bones: the application of these words to our Lord on the cross shows that the Paschal lamb was a prophetic type of Christ, immolated to free men from the bondage of sin. Cf also 1 Cor 5, 7; 1 Pt 1, 19.

13, 17: By way of the Philistines' land: the most direct route from Egypt to Palestine, along the shore of the Mediterranean.

13, 21: A column of cloud . . . a column of fire: probably one and the same preternatural phenomenon, a central nucleus of fire surrounded by smoke; only at night was its luminous nature visible. Cf Ex 40, 38.

by day nor the column of fire by night ever left its place in front of the people.

CHAPTER 14

1 Then the LORD said to Moses, **2** *"Tell the Israelites to turn about and camp before Pi-hahiroth, between Migdol and the sea. *c* You shall camp in front of Baal-zephon, just opposite, by the sea. **3** Pharaoh will then say, 'The Israelites are wandering about aimlessly in the land. The desert has closed in on them.' **4** Thus will I make Pharaoh so obstinate that he will pursue them. Then I will receive glory through Pharaoh and all his army, and the Egyptians will know that I am the LORD.''

This the Israelites did. **5** When it was reported to the king of Egypt that the people had fled, Pharaoh and his servants changed their minds about them. "What have we done!" they exclaimed. "Why, we have released Israel from our service!" **6** So Pharaoh made his chariots ready and mustered his soldiers— **7** six hundred first-class chariots and all the other chariots of Egypt, with warriors on them all. **8** So obstinate had the LORD made Pharaoh that he pursued *d* the Israelites even while they were marching away in triumph. **9** The Egyptians, then, pursued them; Pharaoh's whole army, his horses, chariots and charioteers, caught up with them as they lay encamped by the sea, at Pi-hahiroth, in front of Baal-zephon.

Crossing of the Red Sea. 10 Pharaoh

was already near when the Israelites looked up and saw that the Egyptians were on the march in pursuit of them. In great fright they cried out to the LORD. **11** And they complained to Moses, "Were there no burial places in Egypt that you had to bring us out here to die in the desert? Why did you do this to us? Why did you bring us out of Egypt? **12** Did we not tell you this in Egypt, when we said, 'Leave us alone. Let us serve the Egyptians'? Far better for us to be the slaves of the Egyptians than to die in the desert.'' **13** But Moses answered the people, "Fear not! Stand your ground, and you will see the victory the LORD will win for you today. These Egyptians whom you see today you will never see again. **14** The LORD himself will fight for you; you have only to keep still.''

15 Then the LORD said to Moses, "Why are you crying out to me? Tell the Israelites to go forward. **16** And you, lift up your staff and, with hand outstretched over the sea, split the sea in two, that the Israelites may pass through it on dry land. **17** But I will make the Egyptians so obstinate that they will go in after them. Then I will receive glory through Pharaoh and all his army, his chariots and charioteers. **18** The Egyptians shall know that I am the LORD, when

I receive glory through Pharaoh and his chariots and charioteers.''

19 The angel of God, who had been leading Israel's camp, now moved and went around behind them. The column of cloud also, leaving the front, took up its place behind them, **20** so that it came between the camp of the Egyptians and that of Israel. But the cloud now became dark,* and thus the night passed without the rival camps coming any closer together all night long. **21** Then Moses stretched out his hand over the sea, and the LORD swept the sea with a strong east wind throughout the night and so turned it into dry land. *e* When the water was thus divided, **22** the Israelites marched into the midst of the sea on dry land, with the water like a wall to their right and to their left.

Destruction of the Egyptians. 23 The

Egyptians followed in pursuit; all Pharaoh's horses and chariots and charioteers went after them right into the midst of the sea. **24** In the night watch just before dawn the LORD cast through the column of the fiery cloud upon the Egyptian force a glance that threw it into panic; **25** and he so clogged their chariot wheels that they could hardly drive. With that the Egyptians sounded the retreat before Israel, because the LORD was fighting for them against the Egyptians.

26 Then the LORD told Moses, "Stretch out your hand over the sea, that the water may flow back upon the Egyptians, upon their chariots and their charioteers.'' **27** So Moses stretched out his hand over the sea, and at dawn the sea flowed back to its normal depth. The Egyptians were fleeing head on toward the sea, when the LORD hurled them into its midst. **28** As the water flowed back, it covered the chariots and the charioteers of Pharaoh's whole army *f* which had followed the Israelites into the sea. Not a single one of them escaped. **29** But the Israelites had marched on dry land through the midst of the sea, with the water like a wall to their right and to their left. **30** Thus the LORD saved Israel on that day from the power of the Egyptians. When Israel saw the Egyptians lying dead

---

c Nm 33, 7f.
d 5-8: Wis 19, 3; 1 Mc 4, 9.
e 21f: Ex 15, 19; Pss 66, 6; 78, 13; 136, 13f;

Wis 10, 18; 19, 7f; Is 63, 12f; Heb 11, 29.
f 28f: Dt 11, 4; Ps 106, 11.

---

*

14, 2: These places have not been definitively identified. Even the relative position of Pi-hahiroth and Baal-zephon is not clear; perhaps the former was on the west shore of the sea, where the Israelites were, and the latter on the opposite shore.

14, 20: The cloud now became dark: the light which it ordinarily cast at night would now have been a help to the Egyptians; its present obscurity serves as a shield for the Israelites. However, the reading of the original text here is not quite certain.

on the seashore **31** and beheld the great power that the LORD had shown against the Egyptians, they feared the LORD and believed in him*g* and in his servant Moses.

CHAPTER 15

1 Then Moses and the Israelites sang*h* this song to the LORD:*

I will sing to the LORD, for he is gloriously
   triumphant;
   horse and chariot he has cast into the sea.
2 My strength and my courage is the LORD,
   and he has been my savior.
He is my God, I praise him;
   the God of my father, I extol him.*i*
3 The LORD is a warrior,
   LORD is his name!
4 Pharaoh's chariots and army he hurled into
      the sea;
   the elite of his officers were submerged in
      the Red Sea.

5 The flood waters covered them,
   they sank into the depths like a stone.*j*

6 Your right hand, O LORD, magnificent in
      power,
   your right hand, O LORD, has shattered
      the enemy.
7 In your great majesty you overthrew your
      adversaries;
   you loosed your wrath to consume them
      like stubble.
8 At a breath of your anger the waters piled
      up,
   the flowing waters stood like a mound,
   the flood waters congealed in the midst of
      the sea.

9 The enemy boasted, ''I will pursue and
      overtake them;
   I will divide the spoils and have my fill of
      them;
   I will draw my sword; my hand shall
      despoil them!''
10 When your wind blew, the sea covered
      them;
   like lead they sank in the mighty waters.

11 Who is like to you among the gods, O
      LORD?
   Who is like to you, magnificent in
      holiness?
   O terrible in renown, worker of wonders,
12   when you stretched out your right hand,
      the earth swallowed them!
13 In your mercy you led the people you
      redeemed;
   in your strength you guided them to your
      holy dwelling.
14 The nations heard and quaked:
   anguish gripped the dwellers in Philistia.
15 Then were the princes of Edom dismayed;

trembling seized the chieftains of Moab;
   All the dwellers in Canaan melted away;
16   terror and dread fell upon them.*k*
By the might of your arm they were frozen
      like stone,
   while your people, O LORD, passed over,
   while the people you had made your own
      passed over.

17 And you brought them in and planted them
      on the mountain of your inheritance—
   the place where you made your seat, O
      LORD,
   the sanctuary, O LORD, which your hands
      established.

18 The LORD shall reign forever and ever.

19 They sang thus because Pharaoh's horses and chariots and charioteers had gone into the sea, and the LORD made the waters of the sea flow back upon them, though the Israelites had marched on dry land through the midst of the sea.*l* **20** The prophetess Miriam, Aaron's sister, took a tambourine in her hand, while all the women went out after her with tambourines, dancing; **21** and she led them* in the refrain:

Sing to the LORD, for he is gloriously
   triumphant;
   horse and chariot he has cast into the
      sea.*m*

At Marah and Elim. **22** *n*Then Moses led Israel forward from the Red Sea, and they marched out to the desert of Shur. After traveling for three days through the desert without finding water, **23** they arrived at Marah, where they could not drink the water, because it was too bitter. Hence this place was called Marah. **24** As the people grumbled against Moses, saying, ''What are we to drink?'' **25** he appealed to the LORD, who pointed out to him a certain piece of wood. When he threw this into the water, the water became fresh.*o*

It was here that the LORD, in making rules and regulations for them, put them to the test. **26** ''If you really listen to the voice of the LORD, your God,'' he told them, ''and do what is right in his eyes: if you heed his commandments and keep all his precepts, I will not afflict

g 31f: Ps 106, 12; Wis
   10, 20.
h Ex 15, 21.
i Ps 118, 14; Is 12, 2.
j Neh 9, 11.
k 16f: Ps 78, 53ff.
l Ex 14, 21-29.
m Ex 15, 1.
n 22f: Nm 33, 8.
o Sir 38, 5.
p Dt 7, 15.
*

15, 1–21: This canticle (used in Christian liturgy) celebrates God's saving power, miraculously delivering his people from their enemies, and leading them to the victorious conquest of the Promised Land.

15, 21: She led them: Miriam's refrain re-echoes the first verse of this song and was probably sung as an antiphon after each verse.

you with any of the diseases with which I afflicted the Egyptians;*p* for I, the LORD, am your healer.''

27 Then they came to Elim, where there were twelve springs of water and seventy palm trees, and they camped there near the water.*q*

CHAPTER 16

The Desert of Sin. **1** Having set out from Elim, the whole Israelite community came into the desert of Sin, which is between Elim and Sinai, on the fifteenth day of the second month* after their departure from the land of Egypt. **2** Here in the desert the whole Israelite community grumbled against Moses and Aaron. **3** The Israelites said to them, ''Would that we had died at the LORD's hand in the land of Egypt, as we sat by our fleshpots and ate our fill of bread! But you had to lead us into this desert to make the whole community die of famine!''

The Quail and Manna. **4** Then the LORD said to Moses,*r* ''I will now rain down bread from heaven* for you. Each day the people are to go out and gather their daily portion; thus will I test them, to see whether they follow my instructions or not. **5** On the sixth day, however, when they prepare what they bring in, let it be twice as much as they gather on the other days.'' **6** So Moses and Aaron told all the Israelites, ''At evening you will know that it was the LORD who brought you out of the land of Egypt; **7** and in the morning you will see the glory of the LORD, as he heeds your grumbling against him.*s* But what are we that you should grumble against us? **8** When the LORD gives you flesh to eat in the evening,'' continued Moses, ''and in the morning your fill of bread, as he heeds the grumbling you utter against him, what then are we? Your grumbling is not against us, but against the LORD.''

9 Then Moses said to Aaron, ''Tell the whole Israelite community: Present yourselves before the LORD, for he has heard your grumbling.'' **10** When Aaron announced this to the whole Israelite community, they turned toward the desert, and lo, the glory of the LORD appeared in the cloud! **11** The LORD spoke to Moses and said, **12** ''I have heard the grumbling of the Israelites. Tell them: In the evening twilight you shall eat flesh, and in the morning you shall have your fill of bread, so that you may know that I, the LORD, am your God.''

13 In the evening quail*t* came up and covered the camp. In the morning a dew lay all about the camp, **14** and when the dew evaporated, there on the surface of the desert were fine flakes like hoarfrost on the ground. **15** On seeing it, the Israelites asked one another, ''What is this?''* for they did not know what it was.

But Moses told them, ''This is the bread which the LORD has given you to eat.*u*

Regulations Regarding the Manna.

16 ''Now, this is what the LORD has commanded. So gather it that everyone has enough to eat, an omer for each person, as many of you as there are, each man providing for those of his own tent.'' **17** The Israelites did so. Some gathered a large and some a small amount. **18** *But when they measured it out by the omer, he who had gathered a large amount did not have too much, and he who had gathered a small amount did not have too little.*v* They so gathered that everyone had enough to eat. **19** Moses also told them, ''Let no one keep any of it over until tomorrow morning.'' **20** But they would not listen to him. When some kept a part of it over until the following morning, it became wormy and rotten. Therefore Moses was displeased with them.

21 Morning after morning they gathered it, till each had enough to eat; but when the sun grew hot, the manna melted away. **22** On the sixth day they gathered twice as much food, two omers for each person. When all the leaders of the community came and reported this to Moses, **23** he told them, ''That is what the LORD prescribed. Tomorrow is a day of complete rest, the sabbath, sacred to the LORD. You may either bake or boil the manna, as you please; but whatever is left put away and keep for the morrow.'' **24** When they put it away for the morrow, as Moses commanded, it did not become rotten or wormy. **25** Moses then said, ''Eat it today, for today is the sabbath of the LORD. On this day you will not find any of it on the ground. **26** On the other six days you can gather it, but on the seventh day, the sabbath, none of it will be there.'' **27** Still, on the seventh day some of the people went out to gather it, although they did

---

q Nm 33, 9.
r Pss 78, 24f; 105, 40; Jn 6, 31f; 1 Cor 10, 3.
s 6f: Ex 16, 12.
t Nm 11, 31; Ps 78, 27f.
u Dt 8, 3.
v 2 Cor 8, 15.

*

16, 1: On the fifteenth day of the second month: just one full month after their departure from Egypt. Cf Ex 12, 2. 51; Nm 33, 3f They encamped in the desert of Sin on a Friday; the murmuring (vv 2f) occurred on the sabbath, the arrival of the quail (v 13) the evening before Sunday, followed by six mornings (vv 14–27) of collecting manna before the next sabbath.

16, 4: Bread from heaven: as a gift from God, the manna is said to come down from the sky. Cf Ps 78, 25; Wis 16, 20. Perhaps it was similar to a natural substance that is still found in small quantities on the Sinai peninsula, but here it is, at least in part, clearly miraculous. Our Lord referred to the manna as a type of the Blessed Eucharist. Cf Jn 6, 32. 49–52.

16, 15: What is this: the original man hu is thus rendered by the ancient versions, which understood the phrase as a popular etymology of the Hebrew word man, "manna"; some render, "This is manna."

16, 18: St. Paul cites this passage as an example of equitable sharing. Cf 2 Cor 8, 15.

not find any. **28** Then the LORD said to Moses, "How long will you refuse to keep my commandments and laws? **29** Take note! The LORD has given you the sabbath. That is why on the sixth day he gives you food for two days. On the seventh day everyone is to stay home and no one is to go out." **30** After that the people rested on the seventh day.

31 The Israelites called this food manna.ʷ It was like coriander seed,* but white, and it tasted like wafers made with honey.

32 Moses said, "This is what the LORD has commanded. Keep an omerful of manna for your descendants, that they may see what food I gave you to eat in the desert when I brought you out of the land of Egypt." **33** Moses then told Aaron, "Take an urn* and put an omer of manna in it. Then place it before the LORD in safekeeping for your descendants."ˣ **34** So Aaron placed it in front of the commandments* for safekeeping, as the LORD had commanded Moses.

35 The Israelites ate this manna for forty years, until they came to settled land;ʸ they ate manna until they reached the borders of Canaan. **36** [An omer is one tenth of an ephah.]

CHAPTER 17

Water from the Rock.

1 From the desert of Sin the whole Israelite community journeyed by stages, as the LORD directed, and encamped at Rephidim.ᶻ

Here there was no water for the people to drink. **2** They quarreled, therefore, with Moses and said, "Give us water to drink."ᵃ Moses replied, "Why do you quarrel with me? Why do you put the LORD to a test?" **3** Here, then, in their thirst for water, the people grumbled against Moses, saying, "Why did you ever make us leave Egypt? Was it just to have us die here of thirst with our children and our livestock?" **4** So Moses cried out to the LORD, "What shall I do with this people? A little more and they will stone me!" **5** The LORD answered Moses, "Go over there in front of the people, along with some of the elders of Israel, holding in your hand, as you go, the staff with which you struck the river. **6** I will be standing there in front of you on the rock in Horeb. Strike the rock, and the water will flow from it for the people to drink."ᵇ This Moses did, in the presence of the elders of Israel. **7** The place was called Massah and Meribah,* because the Israelites quarreled there and tested the LORD, saying, "Is the LORD in our midst or not?"ᶜ

Battle with Amalek.

8 At Rephidim, Amalek* came and waged war against Israel.ᵈ **9** Moses, therefore, said to Joshua, "Pick out certain men, and tomorrow go out and engage Amalek in battle. I will be standing on top of the hill with the staff of God in my hand." **10** So Joshua did as Moses told him: he engaged Amalek in battle after Moses had climbed to the top of the hill with Aaron and Hur. **11** As long as Moses kept his hands raised up, Israel had the better of the fight, but when he let his hands rest, Amalek had the better of the fight. **12** Moses' hands, however, grew tired; so they put a rock in place for him to sit on. Meanwhile Aaron and Hur supported his hands, one on one side and one on the other, so that his hands remained steady till sunset. **13** And Joshua mowed down Amalek and his people with the edge of the sword.

14 Then the LORD said to Moses, "Write this down in a document as something to be remembered, and recite it in the ears of Joshua.ᵉ I will completely blot out the memory of Amalek from under the heavens." **15** Moses also built an altar there, which he called Yahweh-nissi;* **16** for he said, "The LORD takes in hand his banner; the LORD will war against Amalek through the centuries."

CHAPTER 18

Meeting with Jethro.

1 Now Moses' father-in-law Jethro, the priest of Midian, heard of all that God had done for Moses and for his people Israel: how the LORD had brought Israel out of Egypt. **2** So his father-in-law Jethro took along Zipporah, Moses' wife, whom Moses had sent back to him, **3** and her two sons. One of these was called Gershom;ᶠ for he said, "I am a stranger in a foreign land." **4** The other was called Eliezer; for he said, "My father's God is my helper; he has rescued me from Pharaoh's sword." **5** Together with Moses' wife and sons, then, his father-in-law Jethro came to him in the desert where he was encamped near the mountain of God, **6** and he sent word to Moses, "I, Jethro, your father-in-law, am coming to

---

w Nm 11, 7.
x Heb 9, 4.
y Jos 5, 12.
z Nm 33, 12ff.
a 2-7: Nm 20, 2-13.
b 5f: Dt 8, 15; Pss 78,
 15f; 105, 41; Wis 11,

4; Is 43, 20; 48, 21.
c Ps 95, 8f.
d Dt 25, 17; 1 Sm 15, 2.
e Nm 24, 20; 1 Sm 15, 3.
 20.
f Ex 2, 22.

*

16, 31: Coriander seed: small, round, aromatic seeds of bright brown color; the comparison, therefore, refers merely to the size and shape, not to the taste or color of the manna.

16, 33: Urn: according to the Greek translation, which is followed in Heb 9, 4, this was a golden vessel.

16, 34: The commandments: the two tablets of the ten commandments, which were kept in the ark. Cf Ex 25, 16. 21f.

17, 7: Massah . . . Meribah: Hebrew words meaning respectively, "the (place of the) test," and "the (place of the) quarreling."

17, 8: Amalek: the Amalekites were an aboriginal people of southern Palestine and the Sinai peninsula. Cf Nm 24, 20.

17, 15: Yahweh-nissi: meaning, "the LORD is my banner."

you, along with your wife and her two sons.''

7 Moses went out to meet his father-in-law, bowed down before him, and kissed him. Having greeted each other, they went into the tent. **8** Moses then told his father-in-law of all that the LORD had done to Pharaoh and the Egyptians for the sake of Israel, and of all the hardships they had had to endure on their journey, and how the LORD had come to their rescue. **9** Jethro rejoiced over all the goodness that the LORD had shown Israel in rescuing them from the hands of the Egyptians. **10** "Blessed be the LORD," he said, "who has rescued his people from the hands of Pharaoh and the Egyptians. **11** Now I know that the LORD is a deity great beyond any other; for he took occasion of their being dealt with insolently to deliver the people from the power of the Egyptians.'' **12** Then Jethro, the father-in-law of Moses, brought a holocaust and other sacrifices to God, and Aaron came with all the elders of Israel to participate with Moses' father-in-law in the meal before God.

Appointment of Minor Judges.   **13** The next day Moses sat in judgment for the people, who waited about him from morning until evening. **14** When his father-in-law saw all that he was doing for the people, he inquired, "What sort of thing is this that you are doing for the people? Why do you sit alone while all the people have to stand about you from morning till evening?'' **15** Moses answered his father-in-law, "The people come to me to consult God. **16** Whenever they have a disagreement, they come to me to have me settle the matter between them and make known to them God's decisions and regulations.''

17 "You are not acting wisely,'' his father-in-law replied. **18** "You will surely wear yourself out, and not only yourself but also these people with you. The task is too heavy for you;g you cannot do it alone. **19** Now, listen to me, and I will give you some advice, that God may be with you. Act as the people's representative before God, bringing to him whatever they have to say. **20** Enlighten them in regard to the decisions and regulations, showing them how they are to live and what they are to do. **21** But you should also look among all the people for able and God-fearing men, trustworthy men who hate dishonest gain, and set them as officers over groups of thousands, of hundreds, of fifties, and of tens. h **22** Let these men render decisions for the people in all ordinary cases. More important cases they should refer to you, but all the lesser cases they can settle themselves. Thus, your burden will be lightened, since they will bear it with you. **23** If you do this, when God gives you orders you will be

able to stand the strain, and all these people will go home satisfied.''

24 Moses followed the advice of his father-in-law and did all that he had suggested. **25** He picked out able men from all Israel and put them in charge of the people as officers over groups of thousands, of hundreds, of fifties, and of tens. **26** They rendered decisions for the people in all ordinary cases. The more difficult cases they referred to Moses, but all the lesser cases they settled themselves. **27** Then Moses bade farewell to his father-in-law, who went off to his own country.

III: *The Covenant at Mount Sinai*

CHAPTER 19

Arrival at Sinai.   **1** iIn the third month after their departure from the land of Egypt, on its first day, the Israelites came to the desert of Sinai. **2** After the journey from Rephidim to the desert of Sinai, they pitched camp.

While Israel was encamped here in front of the mountain, **3** Moses went up the mountain to God. Then the LORD called to him and said, "Thus shall you say to the house of Jacob; **4** tell the Israelites: You have seen for yourselves how I treated the Egyptians and how I bore you up on eagle wings and brought you here to myself.j **5** Therefore, if you hearken to my voice and keep my covenant, you shall be my special possession, dearer to me than all other people,k though all the earth is mine. **6** You shall be to me a kingdom of priests,* a holy nation.l That is what you must tell the Israelites.'' **7** So Moses went and summoned the elders of the people. When he set before them all that the LORD had ordered him to tell them, **8** the people all answered together, "Everything the LORD has said, we will do.'' Then Moses brought back to the LORD the response of the people.

9 The LORD also told him, "I am coming to you in a dense cloud,m so that when the people hear me speaking with you, they may always have faith in you also.'' When Moses, then, had reported to the LORD the response of the people, **10** the LORD added, "Go to the people and have

---

g Nm 11, 14.
h 21. 25: Dt 1, 15; 16, 18.
i 1f: Nm 33, 15.
j Dt 32, 11.

k Dt 7, 6; 14, 2; 26, 18f; 32, 8f.
l 1 Pt 2, 9.
m Ex 20, 21; 24, 15-18.

---

*

19, 6: *Kingdom of priests:* inasmuch as the whole Israelite nation was consecrated to God in a special way, it formed a race of royal priests who participated in the liturgical sacrifices, even though the actual offering of the sacrifices was the exclusive prerogative of the Aaronic priesthood. The same condition exists in the New Dispensation as regards the whole Christian people and the Christian priesthood in the strict sense. Cf Is 61, 6; 1 Pt 2, 5. 9.

them sanctify themselves today and tomorrow. Make them wash their garments **11** and be ready for the third day; for on the third day the LORD will come down on Mount Sinai before the eyes of all the people. **12** Set limits for the people all around the mountain,[n] and tell them: Take care not to go up the mountain, or even to touch its base. If anyone touches the mountain he must be put to death. **13** No hand shall touch him; he must be stoned to death or killed with arrows. Such a one, man or beast, must not be allowed to live. Only when the ram's horn resounds may they go up to the mountain.'' **14** Then Moses came down from the mountain to the people and had them sanctify themselves and wash their garments. **15** He warned them, ''Be ready for the third day. Have no intercourse with any woman.''

The Great Theophany. **16** On the morning of the third day there were peals of thunder and lightning, and a heavy cloud over the mountain, and a very loud trumpet blast, so that all the people in the camp trembled. **17** But Moses let the people out of the camp to meet God, and they stationed themselves at the foot of the mountain.[o] **18** Mount Sinai was all wrapped in smoke, for the LORD came down upon it in fire. The smoke rose from it as though from a furnace, and the whole mountain trembled violently. **19** The trumpet blast grew louder and louder, while Moses was speaking and God answering him with thunder.

20 When the LORD came down to the top of Mount Sinai, he summoned Moses to the top of the mountain, and Moses went up to him. **21** Then the LORD told Moses, ''Go down and warn the people not to break through toward the LORD in order to see him; otherwise many of them will be struck down. **22** The priests, too, who approach the LORD must sanctify themselves; else he will vent his anger upon them.'' **23** Moses said to the LORD, ''The people cannot go up to Mount Sinai, for you yourself warned us to set limits around the mountain to make it sacred.'' **24** The LORD repeated, ''Go down now! Then come up again along with Aaron. But the priests and the people must not break through to come up to the LORD; else he will vent his anger upon them.'' **25** So Moses went down to the people and told them this.

1-17 Sunday B-1 Lent (3)

CHAPTER 20

The Ten Commandments. **1** Then God delivered all these commandments:*

2 [p]''I, the LORD, am your God, who brought you out of the land of Egypt,[q] that place of slavery. **3** You shall not have other gods besides me. **4** You shall not carve idols[r] for yourselves in the shape of anything in the sky above or on the earth below or in the waters beneath the earth; **5** you shall not bow down before them or worship them.[s] For I, the LORD, your God, am a jealous* God, inflicting punishment for their fathers' wickedness on the children of those who hate me, down to the third and fourth generation; **6** but bestowing mercy down to the thousandth generation, on the children of those who love me and keep my commandments.

7 ''You shall not take the name of the LORD, your God, in vain.[t] For the LORD will not leave unpunished him who takes his name in vain.

8 ''Remember to keep holy the sabbath day. **9** Six days you may labor and do all your work, **10** but the seventh day is the sabbath of the LORD, your God.[u] No work may be done then either by you, or your son or daughter, or your male or female slave, or your beast, or by the alien who lives with you. **11** In six days the LORD made the heavens and the earth, the sea and all that is in them; but on the seventh day he rested.[v] That is why the LORD has blessed the sabbath day and made it holy.

12 [w]''Honor your father and your mother, that you may have a long life in the land which the Lord, your God, is giving you.[x]

13 ''You shall not kill.[y]

14 ''You shall not commit adultery.[z]

15 ''You shall not steal.[a]

16 ''You shall not bear false witness against your neighbor.[b]

17 ''You shall not covet your neighbor's house. You shall not covet your neighbor's wife, nor his male or female slave, nor his ox or ass, nor anything else that belongs to him.''[c]

The Fear of God. **18** When the people witnessed the thunder and lightning, the trumpet blast and the mountain smoking, they all feared and trembled.[d] So they took up a position much farther away **19** and said to Moses, ''You speak to us, and we will listen; but let not God speak to us, or we shall die.'' **20** Moses answered the

n 12f: Ex 34, 3; Heb 12, 18f.
o 16ff: Dt 4, 10ff.
p 2-17; Dt 5, 6-21.
q Lv 26, 13; Ps 81, 10; Hos 13, 4.
r Ex 34, 17; Lv 26, 1; Dt 4, 15-19; 27, 15.
s Ex 34, 7. 14; Nm 14, 18; Dt 4, 24; 6, 15.
t Lv 19, 12; 24, 16.
u 8ff: Ex 23, 12; 31, 13-16; 34, 21; 35, 2; Lv 23, 3.
v Ex 31, 17; Gn 2, 2f.
w 12-16: Mt 19, 18f; Mk 10, 19; Lk 18, 20; Rom 13, 9.
x Mt 15, 4; Mk 7, 10; Eph 6, 2f.
y Mt 5, 21.
z Lv 18, 20; 20, 10; Dt 22, 22; Mt 5, 27.
a Lv 19, 11.
b Ex 23, 1; Dt 19, 16ff; Prv 19, 5. 9; 24, 28.
c Rom 7, 7.
d 18-21: Dt 4, 11; 5, 22-27; 18, 16; Heb 12, 18f.

*

20, 1–17: the precise division of these precepts into "ten commandments" is somewhat uncertain. Traditionally among Catholics vv 1–6 are considered as only one commandment, and v 17 as two. Cf Dt 5, 6–21.

20, 5: Jealous: demanding exclusive allegiance, such as a wife must have for her husband.

people, "Do not be afraid, for God has come to you only to test you and put his fear upon you, lest you should sin." **21** Still the people remained at a distance, while Moses approached the cloud where God was.

22 The LORD told Moses, "Thus shall you speak to the Israelites: You have seen for yourselves that I have spoken to you from heaven. **23** Do not make anything to rank with me; neither gods of silver nor gods of gold shall you make for yourselves.*e*

24 "An altar of earth you shall make for me, and upon it you shall sacrifice your holocausts and peace offerings, your sheep and your oxen.*f* In whatever place I choose for the remembrance of my name* I will come to you and bless you. **25** If you make an altar of stone for me,*g* do not build it of cut stone, for by putting a tool to it you desecrate it. **26** You shall not go up by steps to my altar, on which you must not be indecently uncovered.

CHAPTER 21

Laws Regarding Slaves. **1** "These are the rules* you shall lay before them. **2** *h*When you purchase a Hebrew slave, he is to serve you for six years, but in the seventh year he shall be given his freedom without cost. **3** If he comes into service alone, he shall leave alone; if he comes with a wife, his wife shall leave with him. **4** But if his master gives him a wife and she bears him sons or daughters, the woman and her children shall remain the master's property and the man shall leave alone. **5** If, however, the slave declares, 'I am devoted to my master and my wife and children; I will not go free,' **6** his master shall bring him to God* and there, at the door or doorpost, he shall pierce his ear with an awl, thus keeping him as his slave forever.

7 "When a man sells his daughter as a slave, she shall not go free as male slaves do. **8** But if her master, who had destined her* for himself, dislikes her, he shall let her be redeemed. He has no right to sell her to a foreigner, since he has broken faith with her. **9** If he destines her for his son, he shall treat her like a daughter. **10** If he takes another wife, he shall not withhold her food, her clothing, or her conjugal rights. **11** If he does not grant her these three things, she shall be given her freedom absolutely, without cost to her.

Personal Injury. **12** "Whoever strikes a man a mortal blow must be put to death.*i* **13** He, however, who did not hunt a man down, but caused his death by an act of God, may flee to a place which I will set apart for this purpose. **14** But when a man kills another after maliciously scheming to do so, you must take him

even from my altar and put him to death. **15** Whoever strikes his father or mother shall be put to death.

16 "A kidnaper, whether he sells his victim or still has him when caught, shall be put to death.*j*

17 "Whoever curses his father or mother shall be put to death.*k*

18 "When men quarrel and one strikes the other with a stone or with his fist, not mortally, but enough to put him in bed, **19** the one who struck the blow shall be acquitted, provided the other can get up and walk around with the help of his staff. Still, he must compensate him for his enforced idleness and provide for his complete cure.

20 "When a man strikes his male or female slave with a rod so hard that the slave dies under his hand, he shall be punished. **21** If, however, the slave survives for a day or two, he is not to be punished, since the slave is his own property.

22 "When men have a fight and hurt a pregnant woman, so that she suffers a miscarriage, but no further injury, the guilty one shall be fined as much as the woman's husband demands of him, and he shall pay in the presence of the judges.*l* **23** *But if injury ensues, you shall give life for life, **24** eye for eye, tooth for tooth, hand for hand, foot for foot, **25** burn for burn, wound for wound, stripe for stripe.

26 "When a man strikes his male or female slave in the eye and destroys the use of the eye, he shall let the slave go free in compensation for the eye. **27** If he knocks out a tooth of his male or female slave, he shall let the slave go free in compensation for the tooth.

28 "When an ox gores a man or a woman to

---

e Ex 20, 3f.
f Dt 12, 5. 11; 14, 23; 16, 6.
g Dt 27, 5; Jos 8, 31.
h 2-6: Lv 25, 39ff; Dt 15, 12-18; Jer 34, 14.
i 12ff: Lv 24, 17; Nm 35, 15-29; Dt 4, 41f; 19, 2-5.
j Dt 24, 7.
k Lv 20, 9; Prv 20, 20; Mt 15, 4; Mk 7, 10.
l 22-25: Lv 24, 18-21; Dt 19, 21; Mt 5, 38.

*

20, 24: I choose for the remembrance of my name: literally, "where I make my name to be remembered": at the sacred site where God wishes to be worshiped and his name revered.

21, 1: Rules: judicial precedents to be used in settling questions of law and custom. This introductory phrase serves as the title of the following collection of civil and religious laws (chapters 21–23) which is called in Ex 24, 7, the book of the covenant.

21, 6: To God: to the sanctuary; or perhaps the phrase is to be rendered, "to the gods," in the sense of "to the judges." Cf Ps 82, 1. Since the expression "to have an open ear" meant to "obey," a pierced ear lobe was an ancient symbol of obedience. Cf Ps 40, 7.

21, 8: Destined her: intended her as a wife of second rank.

21, 23ff: This section is known as the lex talionis, the law of tit for tat. The purpose of this law was not merely the enforcement of rigorous justice, but also the prevention of greater penalties than would be just. Christ refers to this passage when he exhorts Christians to cede their lawful rights for the sake of charity. Cf Mt 5, 38ff.

death, the ox must be stoned; its flesh may not be eaten. The owner of the ox, however, shall go unpunished. **29** But if an ox was previously in the habit of goring people and its owner, though warned, would not keep it in; should it then kill a man or a woman, not only must the ox be stoned, but its owner also must be put to death. **30** If, however, a fine is imposed on him, he must pay in ransom for his life whatever amount is imposed on him. **31** This law applies if it is a boy or a girl that the ox gores. **32** But if it is a male or a female slave that it gores, he must pay the owner of the slave thirty shekels of silver, and the ox must be stoned.

Property Damage.

33 "When a man uncovers or digs a cistern and does not cover it over again, should an ox or an ass fall into it, **34** the owner of the cistern must make good by restoring the value of the animal to its owner; the dead animal, however, he may keep.

35 "When one man's ox hurts another's ox so badly that it dies, they shall sell the live ox and divide this money as well as the dead animal equally between them. **36** But if it was known that the ox was previously in the habit of goring and its owner would not keep it in, he must make full restitution, an ox for an ox; but the dead animal he may keep.

37 *"When a man steals an ox or a sheep and slaughters or sells it, he shall restore five oxen for the one ox, and four sheep for the one sheep. [m]

CHAPTER 22

1 "[If a thief is caught* in the act of housebreaking and beaten to death, there is no bloodguilt involved. **2** But if after sunrise he is thus beaten, there is bloodguilt.] He must make full restitution. If he has nothing, he shall be sold to pay for his theft. **3** If what he stole is found alive in his possession, be it an ox, an ass or a sheep, he shall restore two animals for each one stolen.

4 *"When a man is burning over a field or a vineyard, if he lets the fires spread so that it burns in another's field, he must make restitution with the best produce of his own field or vineyard. **5** If the fire spreads further, and catches on to thorn bushes, so that shocked grain or standing grain or the field itself is burned up, the one who started the fire must make full restitution.

Trusts and Loans.

6 "When a man gives money or any article to another for safekeeping and it is stolen from the latter's house, the thief, if caught, must make twofold restitution. **7** If the thief is not caught, the owner of the house shall be brought to God,* to swear that he himself did not lay hands on his neighbor's proper-

ty. **8** In every question of dishonest appropriation, whether it be about an ox, or an ass, or a sheep, or a garment, or anything else that has disappeared, where another claims that the thing is his, both parties shall present their case before God; the one whom God convicts must make two-fold restitution to the other.

9 "When a man gives an ass, or an ox, or a sheep, or any other animal to another for safekeeping, if it dies, or is maimed or snatched away, without anyone witnessing the fact, **10** the custodian shall swear by the LORD that he did not lay hands on his neighbor's property; the owner must accept the oath, and no restitution is to be made. **11** But if the custodian is really guilty of theft, he must make restitution to the owner. **12** If it has been killed by a wild beast, let him bring it as evidence, and he need not make restitution for the mangled animal. [n]

13 "When a man borrows an animal from his neighbor, if it is maimed or dies while the owner is not present, the man must make restitution. **14** But if the owner is present, he need not make restitution. If it was hired, this was covered by the price of its hire.

Social Laws.

15 "When a man seduces a virgin who is not betrothed, and lies with her, he shall pay her marriage price and marry her. [o] **16** If her father refuses to give her to him, he must still pay him the customary marriage price for virgins.*

17 "You shall not let a sorceress live. [p]

18 "Anyone who lies with an animal shall be put to death. [q]

19 "Whoever sacrifices to any god, except to the LORD alone, shall be doomed. [r]

20 "You shall not molest or oppress an alien, for you were once aliens yourselves in the land of Egypt. [s] **21** You shall not wrong any widow or orphan. **22** If ever you wrong them and they cry out to me, I will surely hear their cry. **23** My wrath will flare up, and I will kill

---

m 2 Sm 12, 6.
n Gn 31, 39.
o 15f: Dt 22, 28f.
p Lv 19, 26. 31; 20. 6.
q Lv 18, 23; Dt 27, 21.
r Dt 13; 17, 2-7.
s 20-23: Ex 23, 9; Lv 19, 33f; Dt 10, 18f; 24, 27; Dt 18, 10f. 17f; 27, 19; Zec 7, 10.

---

*

21, 37—22, 30: In the Vulgate, 22, 1–31.

22, 1f: If a thief is caught: this seems to be a fragment of what was once a longer law on housebreaking, which has been inserted here into the middle of a law on stealing animals. At night the householder would be justified in killing a burglar outright, but not so in the daytime, when the burglar could more easily be caught alive. He must make full restitution: this stood originally immediately after 21, 37.

22, 4: The Greek and Latin versions understood this verse as a prohibition against allowing one's cattle to graze in the field of another.

22, 7: Brought to God: see note on Ex 21, 6. Cf also Ex 22, 10.

22, 16: The customary marriage price for virgins: fifty shekels according to Dt 22, 29.

you with the sword; then your own wives will be widows, and your children orphans.

24 ᵗ"If you lend money to one of your poor neighbors among my people, you shall not act like an extortioner toward him by demanding interest from him. **25** If you take your neighbor's cloak as a pledge, you shall return it to him before sunset; **26** for this cloak of his is the only covering he has for his body. What else has he to sleep in? If he cries out to me, I will hear him; for I am compassionate.

27 "You shall not revile God,* nor curse a prince of your people.ᵘ

28 "You shall not delay the offering of your harvest and your press. You shall give me the first-born of your sons. **29** You must do the same with your oxen and your sheep; for seven days the firstling may stay with its mother, but on the eighth day you must give it to me.ᵛ

30 "You shall be men sacred to me. Flesh torn to pieces in the field you shall not eat; throw it to the dogs.ʷ

CHAPTER 23

1 "You shall not repeat a false report. Do not join the wicked in putting your hand, as an unjust witness, upon anyone.ˣ **2** Neither shall you allege the example of the many as an excuse for doing wrong, nor shall you, when testifying in a lawsuit, side with the many in perverting justice. **3** You shall not favor a poor man in his lawsuit.ʸ

4 "When you come upon your enemy's ox or ass going astray, see to it that it is returned to him.ᶻ **5** When you notice the ass of one who hates you lying prostrate under its burden, by no means desert him; help him, rather, to raise it up.

6 "You shall not deny one of your needy fellow men his rights in his lawsuit. **7** You shall keep away from anything dishonest. The innocent and the just you shall not put to death, nor shall you acquit the guilty. **8** Never take a bribe, for a bribe blinds even the most clear-sighted and twists the words even of the just.ᵃ **9** You shall not oppress an alien; you well know how it feels to be an alien, since you were once aliens yourselves in the land of Egypt.ᵇ

Religious Laws.   **10** ᶜ"For six years you may sow your land and gather in its produce. **11** But the seventh year you shall let the land lie untilled and unharvested, that the poor among you may eat of it and the beasts of the field may eat what the poor leave. So also shall you do in regard to your vineyard and your olive grove.

12 "For six days you may do your work, but on the seventh day you must rest,ᵈ that your ox and your ass may also have rest, and that the son of your maidservant and the alien may be re-

freshed. **13** Give heed to all that I have told you.

"Never mention the name of any other god; it shall not be heard from your lips.

14 ᵉ"Three times a year you shall celebrate a pilgrim feast to me.* **15** You shall keep the feast of Unleavened Bread. As I have commanded you, you must eat unleavened bread for seven days at the prescribed time in the month of Abib, for it was then that you came out of Egypt. No one shall appear before me* empty-handed. **16** You shall also keep the feast of the grain harvest with the first of the crop that you have sown in the field; and finally, the feast at the fruit harvest at the end of the year, when you gather in the produce from the fields. **17** Thrice a year shall all your men appear before the LORD God.

18 "You shall not offer the blood of my sacrifice with leavened bread;ᶠ nor shall the fat of my feast be kept overnight till the next day. **19** The choicest first fruits of your soil you shall bring to the house of the LORD, your God.

"You shall not boil a kid in its mother's milk.*

Reward of Fidelity.   **20** "See, I am sending an angelᵍ before you, to guard you on the way and bring you to the place I have prepared. **21** Be attentive to him and heed his voice. Do not rebel against him, for he will not forgive your sin. My authority resides in him.* **22** If you heed his voice and carry out all I tell you, I will be an enemy to your enemies and a foe to your foes.

23 "My angel will go before you and bring you to the Amorites, Hittites, Perizzites, Canaanites, Hivites and Jebusites; and I will wipe them out. **24** Therefore, you shall not bow

---

t 24-26: Lv 25, 35-38; Dt 23, 19f; 24, 10-13; Ez 18, 7f. 17f.
u Acts 23, 5.
v Ex 13, 2; 34, 19; Lv 22, 27; Dt 15, 19.
w Lv 7, 24; 17, 15; 22, 8.
x 1f: Dt 19, 16ff.
y Lv 19, 15.
z Dt 22, 1ff.
a Dt 16, 19; 27, 25; Sir 20, 28.
b Ex 22, 21.
c 10f: Lv 25, 3-7.
d Ex 20, 8.
e 14-17: Ex 34, 18. 22ff; Lv 23; Dt 16, 1-17.
f 18f: Ex 34, 25f.
g Ex 14, 19; 32, 34; 33, 2.
h 23f: Ex 34, 10-16; Nm 33, 51f; Dt 7, 24ff.

22, 27: God: or perhaps "the gods," in the sense of "the judges," as the parallel with a price of your people suggests.

23, 14: These three feasts are elsewhere called the Passover, Pentecost and Booths. Cf Ex 34, 18–26; Lv 23; Dt 16.

23, 15: Appear before me: the original expression was "see my face"; so also in several other places, as Ex 23, 17; 34, 23f; Dt 16, 16; 31, 11.

23, 19: Boil a kid in its mother's milk: this was part of a Canaanite ritual; hence it is forbidden here as a pagan ceremony.

23, 21: My authority resides in him: literally, "My name is within him."

23, 24: Make anything like them: some render, "act according to their conduct." Sacred pillars: objects of religious veneration at Canaanite sanctuaries.

down in worship before their gods, nor shall you make anything like them;* rather, you must demolish them and smash their sacred pillars.[h] **25** The LORD, your God, you shall worship; then I will bless your food and drink, and I will remove all sickness from your midst; **26** no woman in your land will be barren or miscarry; and I will give you a full span of life.

27 "I will have the fear of me precede you, so that I will throw into panic every nation you reach.[i] I will make all your enemies turn from you in flight, **28** and ahead of you I will send hornets* to drive the Hivites, Canaanites and Hittites out of your way. **29** But not in one year will I drive them all out before you; else the land will become so desolate that the wild beasts will multiply against you. **30** Instead, I will drive them out little by little before you, until you have grown numerous enough to take possession of the land. **31** [j]I will set your boundaries from the Red Sea to the sea of the Philistines,* and from the desert to the River; all who dwell in this land I will hand over to you to be driven out of your way. **32** You shall not make a covenant with them or their gods. **33** They must not abide in your land, lest they make you sin against me by ensnaring you into worshiping their gods."[k]

CHAPTER 24

Ratification of the Covenant. **1** Moses himself was told, "Come up to the LORD, you and Aaron, with Nadab, Abihu, and seventy of the elders of Israel. You shall all worship at some distance, **2** but Moses alone is to come close to the LORD; the others shall not come too near, and the people shall not come up at all with Moses."

3 When Moses came to the people and related all the words and ordinances of the LORD, they all answered with one voice, "We will do everything that the LORD has told us."[l] **4** Moses then wrote down all the words of the LORD and, rising early the next day, he erected at the foot of the mountain an altar and twelve pillars* for the twelve tribes of Israel. **5** Then, having sent certain young men of the Israelites to offer holocausts and sacrifice young bulls as peace offerings to the LORD, **6** Moses took half of the blood and put it in large bowls; the other half he splashed on the altar. **7** Taking the book of the covenant, he read it aloud to the people, who answered, "All that the LORD has said, we will heed and do." **8** Then he took the blood and sprinkled it on the people, saying, "This is the blood of the covenant which the LORD has made with you in accordance with all these words of his."[m]

9 Moses then went up with Aaron, Nadab, Abihu, and seventy elders of Israel, **10** and they beheld the God of Israel. Under his feet there appeared to be sapphire tilework, as clear as the sky itself. **11** Yet he did not smite these chosen Israelites. After gazing on God,* they could still eat and drink.

Moses on the Mountain. **12** The LORD said to Moses, "Come up to me on the mountain and, while you are there, I will give you the stone tablets[n] on which I have written the commandments intended for their instruction." **13** So Moses set out with Joshua, his aide, and went up to the mountain of God. **14** The elders, however, had been told by him, "Wait here for us until we return to you. Aaron and Hur are staying with you. If anyone has a complaint, let him refer the matter to them." **15** After Moses had gone up, a cloud covered the mountain. **16** The glory of the LORD settled upon Mount Sinai. The cloud covered it for six days, and on the seventh day he called to Moses from the midst of the cloud.[o] **17** To the Israelites the glory of the LORD was seen as a consuming fire on the mountaintop.[p] **18** But Moses passed into the midst of the cloud as he went up on the mountain; and there he stayed for forty days and forty nights.[q]

IV: The Dwelling and Its Furnishings

CHAPTER 25

Collection of Materials. **1** This is what the LORD then said to Moses:[r] **2** "Tell the Israelites to take up a collection for me. From every man you shall accept the contribution that his heart prompts him to give me. **3** These are the contributions you shall accept from them: gold, silver and bronze;[s] **4** violet, purple and scarlet

---

i 27ff: Dt 2, 25; 7, 20ff.
j Gn 15, 18; Dt 11, 24; Jos 1, 4.
k 32f: Ex 34, 12-16; Dt 7, 2ff.
l Ex 19, 8.
m 5-8: Heb 9, 18ff.
n Ex 31, 18; 32, 15f; Dt 5, 22.
o Sir 45, 4.
p Ex 19, 18; Heb 12, 18.
q Ex 34, 28; Dt 9, 9.
r 1-7: Ex 35, 4-9. 20-29.
s Ex 35, 4-9.

23, 28: Hornets: some understand this figuratively of various troublesome afflictions; others translate the Hebrew word as "leprosy." Cf Dt 7, 20; Jos 24, 12; Wis 12, 8.

23, 31: The sea of the Philistines: the Mediterranean. The River: the Euphrates. Only in the time of David and Solomon did the territory of Israel come near to reaching such distant borders.

24, 4: Pillars: stone shafts or slabs, erected as symbols of the fact that each of the twelve tribes had entered into this covenant with God; not idolatrous as in Ex 23, 24, although the same Hebrew word is used in both passages. See note on Gn 28, 18.

24, 11: After gazing on God: the ancients thought that the sight of God would bring instantaneous death. Cf Ex 33, 20; Gn 16, 13; 32, 31; Jgs 6, 22f; 13, 22. Eat and drink: partake of the sacrificial meal.

yarn; fine linen and goat hair; **5** rams' skins
dyed red, and tahash* skins; acacia wood; **6** oil
for the light; spices for the anointing oil and for
the fragrant incense; **7** onyx stones and other
gems for mounting on the ephod and the breastpiece.

8 "They shall make a sanctuary for me, that
I may dwell in their midst.ᵗ **9** This Dwelling
and all its furnishings you shall make exactly
according to the pattern that I will now show
you.ᵘ

Plan of the Ark. **10** "You shall make an
ark of acacia wood,ᵛ two and a half cubits long,
one and a half cubits wide, and one and a half
cubits high. **11** Plate it inside and outside with
pure gold, and put a molding of gold around the
top of it. **12** Cast four gold rings and fasten
them on the four supports of the ark, two rings
on one side and two on the opposite side.
13 Then make poles of acacia wood and plate
them with gold. **14** These poles you are to put
through the rings on the sides of the ark, for
carrying it; **15** they must remain in the rings of
the ark and never be withdrawn. **16** In the ark
you are to put the commandments which I will
give you.

17 "You shall then make a propitiatory* of
pure gold, two cubits and a half long, and one
and a half cubits wide. **18** Make two cherubim*
of beaten gold for the two ends of the propitiatory, **19** fastening them so that one cherub springs
direct from each end. **20** The cherubim shall
have their wings spread out above, covering the
propitiatory with them; they shall be turned toward each other, but with their faces looking
toward the propitiatory. **21** This propitiatory
you shall then place on top of the ark. In the ark
itself you are to put the commandments which
I will give you. **22** There I will meet you and
there, from above the propitiatory, between the
two cherubim on the ark of the commandments,
I will tell you all the commands that I wish you
to give the Israelites.

The Table. **23** "You shall also make a table
of acaciaʷ wood, two cubits long, a cubit wide,
and a cubit and a half high. **24** Plate it with pure
gold and make a molding of gold around it.
25 Surround it with a frame,* a hand-breadth
high, with a molding of gold around the frame.
26 You shall also make four rings of gold for
it and fasten them at the four corners, one at
each leg, **27** on two opposite sides of the frame
as holders for the poles to carry the table.
28 These poles for carrying the table you shall
make of acacia wood and plate with gold. **29** Of
pure gold you shall make its plates* and cups,
as well as its pitchers and bowls for pouring
libations. **30** On the table you shall always keep
showbread set before me.ˣ

The Lampstand. **31** "You shall make a
lampstand of pure beaten goldʸ —its shaft and
branches—with its cups and knobs and petals
springing directly from it. **32** Six branches are
to extend from the sides of the lampstand, three
branches on one side, and three on the other.
33 *On one branch there are to be three cups,
shaped like almond blossoms, each with its
knob and petals; on the opposite branch there
are to be three cups, shaped like almond blossoms, each with its knob and petals; and so for
the six branches that extend from the lampstand.
34 On the shaft there are to be four cups,*
shaped like almond blossoms, with their knobs
and petals, **35** including a knob below each of
the three pairs of branches that extend from the
lampstand. **36** Their knobs and branches shall
so spring from it that the whole will form but a
single piece of pure beaten gold. **37** *You shall
then make seven lampsᶻ for it and so set up the
lamps that they shed their light on the space in
front of the lampstand. **38** These, as well as the
trimming shears and trays,* must be of pure
gold. **39** Use a talent of pure gold for the lampstand and all its appurtenances. **40** See that you
make them according to the pattern shown you
on the mountain.ᵃ

---

t 8f: Ex 26, 1-30; 36,　　w 23-30: Ex 37, 10-16.
　8-38.　　　　　　　　　x Lv 24, 5ff.
u Acts 7, 44.　　　　　　 y 31-40: Ex 37, 17-24.
v 10-22: Ex 37, 1-9; Heb　z Lv 24, 2ff; Nm 8, 2.
　9, 1-5.　　　　　　　　　a Heb 8, 5.

25, 5: Tahash: perhaps the name of a marine animal, such
as the dugong or the porpoise. The Greek and Latin versions
took it for the color hyacinth.

25, 17: Propitiatory: this traditional rendering of the Hebrew
term, which may mean merely "cover," is derived from its
connection with the ceremony of the Day of Atonement
whereby God was rendered "propitious." Cf Lv 16, 14ff.

25, 18ff: Cherubim: probably in the form of human-headed
winged lions. The cherubim over the ark formed the throne for
the invisible Lord. Cf Ps 80, 2. For a more detailed description
of the somewhat different cherubim in the temple of Solomon,
see 1 Kgs 6, 23–28; 2 Chr 3, 10–13.

25, 25: A frame: probably placed near the bottom of the
legs to keep them steady. The golden table of Herod's temple
is pictured thus on the Arch of Titus.

25, 29f: The plates held the showbread, that is, the holy
bread which was placed upon the table every sabbath as an
offering to God, and was later eaten by the priests. The cups
held the incense which was strewn upon the bread. Cf Lv 24,
5–9. The libation wine was poured from the pitchers into the
bowls. All these vessels were kept on the golden table.

25, 33: In keeping with the arrangement of the ornaments
on the shaft, the three sets of ornaments on each branch were
probably so placed that one was at the top and the other two
equally spaced along the length of the branch. Knob: the
cup-shaped seed capsule at the base of a flower.

25, 34f: Of the four ornaments on the shaft, one was at the
top and one was below each of the three sets of side branches.

25, 37: The lamps were probably shaped like small boats,
with the wick at one end; the end with the wick was turned
toward the front of the lampstand.

25, 38: Trays: small receptacles for the burnt-out wicks.

CHAPTER 26

The Tent Cloth. 1 "The Dwelling itself you shall make out of sheets* woven of fine linen twined and of violet, purple and scarlet yarn, with cherubim embroidered on them. *b* 2 The length of each shall be twenty-eight cubits, and the width four cubits; all the sheets shall be of the same size. 3 Five of the sheets are to be sewed together, edge to edge; and the same for the other five. 4 Make loops of violet yarn along the edge of the end sheet in one set, and the same along the edge of the end sheet in the other set. 5 There are to be fifty loops along the edge of the end sheet in the first set, and fifty loops along the edge of the corresponding sheet in the second set, and so placed that the loops are directly opposite each other. 6 Then make fifty clasps of gold, with which to join the two sets of sheets, so that the Dwelling forms one whole.

7 "Also make sheets woven of goat hair, to be used as a tent covering* over the Dwelling. 8 Eleven such sheets are to be made; the length of each shall be thirty cubits, and the width four cubits: all eleven sheets shall be of the same size. 9 Sew five of the sheets, edge to edge, into one set, and the other six sheets into another set. Use the sixth sheet double at the front of the tent.* 10 Make fifty loops along the edge of the end sheet in one set, and fifty loops along the edge of the end sheet in the second set. 11 Also make fifty bronze clasps and put them into the loops, to join the tent into one whole. 12 There will be an extra half sheet of tent covering, which shall be allowed to hang down over the rear of the Dwelling. 13 Likewise, the sheets of the tent will have an extra cubit's length to be left hanging down on either side of the Dwelling to protect it. 14 Over the tent itself you shall make a covering of rams' skins dyed red, and above that, a covering of tahash skins.

The Wooden Walls. 15 *c*"You shall make boards of acacia wood as walls for the Dwelling. 16 The length of each board is to be ten cubits, and its width one and a half cubits. 17 Each board shall have two arms* that shall serve to fasten the boards in line. In this way all the boards of the Dwelling are to be made. 18 Set up the boards of the Dwelling as follows: twenty boards on the south side, 19 with forty silver pedestals under the twenty boards, so that there are two pedestals under each board, at its two arms; 20 twenty boards on the other side of the Dwelling, the north side, 21 with their forty silver pedestals, two under each board; 22 six boards for the rear of the Dwelling, to the west; 23 and two boards for the corners at the rear of the Dwelling. 24 These two shall be double at the bottom, and likewise double at the top, to

the first ring. That is how both boards in the corners are to be made. 25 Thus, there shall be in the rear eight boards, with their sixteen silver pedestals, two pedestals under each board. 26 Also make bars of acacia wood: five for the boards on one side of the Dwelling, 27 five for those on the other side, and five for those at the rear, toward the west. 28 The center bar, at the middle of the boards, shall reach across from end to end. 29 Plate the boards with gold, and make gold rings on them as holders for the bars, which are also to be plated with gold. 30 You shall erect the Dwelling according to the pattern shown you on the mountain.

The Veils. 31 "You shall have a veil woven of violet, purple and scarlet yarn, *d* and of fine linen twined, with cherubim embroidered on it. *e* 32 It is to be hung on four gold-plated columns of acacia wood, which shall have hooks* of gold and shall rest on four silver pedestals. 33 Hang the veil from clasps. The ark of the commandments you shall bring inside, behind this veil which divides the holy place from the holy of holies. 34 Set the propitiatory on the ark of the commandments in the holy of holies.

35 "Outside the veil you shall place the table and the lampstand, the latter on the south side of the Dwelling, opposite the table, which is to be put on the north side. 36 For the entrance of the tent make a variegated* curtain of violet, purple and scarlet yarn and of fine linen twined. 37 Make five columns of acacia wood for this curtain; have them plated with gold, with their hooks of gold; and cast five bronze pedestals for them.

CHAPTER 27

The Altar of Holocausts. 1 "You shall make an altar *f* of acacia wood, on a square, five

---

b 1-14: Ex 36, 8-19.   e 31-37: Ex 36, 35-38.
c 15-30: Ex 36, 20-34.   f 1-8: Ex 38, 1-7.
d 2 Chr 3, 14.

26, 1: Sheets: strips of tapestry, woven of white linen, the colored threads being used for the cherubim which were embroidered on them. These sheets were stretched across the top of the Dwelling to form a roof, their free ends hanging down inside the boards which formed walls.

26, 7: Tent covering: the cloth made of sheets of goat hair to cover the Dwelling.

26, 9: Half the width of the end strip was folded back at the front of the Dwelling, thus leaving another half-strip to hang down at the rear. Cf v 12.

26, 17: Arms: literally, "hands." According to some, they served as "tongue and groove" to mortise the boards together; according to others, they were pegs at the bottom of the boards and fitted into sockets in the pedestals.

26, 32: Hooks: probably placed near the tops of the columns, to hold the rope from which the veils and curtains hung.

26, 36: Variegated: without definite designs such as the cherubim on the inner veil.

cubits long and five cubits wide; it shall be three cubits high. **2** At the four corners there are to be horns, so made that they spring directly from the altar. You shall then plate it with bronze. **3** Make pots for removing the ashes, as well as shovels, basins, forks and fire pans, all of which shall be of bronze. **4** Make a grating* of bronze network for it; this to have four bronze rings, one at each of its four corners. **5** Put it down around the altar, on the ground. This network is to be half as high as the altar. **6** You shall also make poles of acacia wood for the altar, and plate them with bronze. **7** These poles are to be put through the rings, so that they are on either side of the altar when it is carried. **8** Make the altar itself in the form of a hollow* box, just as it was shown you on the mountain.

Court of the Dwelling.

9 g "You shall also make a court for the Dwelling. On the south side the court shall have hangings a hundred cubits long, woven of fine linen twined, **10** with twenty columns and twenty pedestals of bronze; the hooks and bands on the columns shall be of silver. **11** On the north side there shall be similar hangings, a hundred cubits long, with twenty columns and twenty pedestals of bronze; the hooks and bands on the columns shall be of silver. **12** On the west side, across the width of the court, there shall be hangings, fifty cubits long, with ten columns and ten pedestals. **13** The width of the court on the east side shall be fifty cubits. **14** On one side there shall be hangings to the extent of fifteen cubits, with three columns and three pedestals; **15** On the other side there shall be hangings to the extent of fifteen cubits, with three columns and three pedestals.

16 "At the entrance of the court there shall be a variegated curtain, twenty cubits long, woven of violet, purple and scarlet yarn and of fine linen twined. It shall have four columns and four pedestals.

17 "All the columns around the court shall have bands and hooks of silver, and pedestals of bronze. **18** The enclosure of the court is to be one hundred cubits long, fifty cubits wide, and five cubits high. Fine linen twined must be used, and the pedestals must be of bronze.

19 All the fittings of the Dwelling, whatever be their use, as well as all its tent pegs and all the tent pegs of the court, must be of bronze.

Oil for the Lamps.

20 "You shall order the Israelites to bring you clear oil of crushed olives, to be used for the light, so that you may keep lamps burning regularly. h **21** From evening to morning Aaron and his sons shall maintain them before the LORD in the meeting tent, outside the veil which hangs in front of the commandments. This shall be a perpetual ordi-

nance for the Israelites throughout their generations.

CHAPTER 28

The Priestly Vestments.

1 i "From among the Israelites have your brother Aaron, together with his sons Nadab, Abihu, Eleazar and Ithamar, brought to you, that they may be my priests. **2** For the glorious adornment of your brother Aaron you shall have sacred vestments made. **3** Therefore, to the various expert workmen whom I have endowed with skill, you shall give instructions to make such vestments for Aaron as will set him apart for his sacred service as my priest. **4** These are the vestments they shall make: a breastpiece, an ephod, a robe, a brocaded tunic, a miter and a sash. In making these sacred vestments which your brother Aaron and his sons are to wear in serving as my priests, **5** they shall use gold, violet, purple and scarlet yarn and fine linen.

The Ephod and Breastpiece.

6 "The ephod* they shall make of gold thread and of violet, purple and scarlet yarn, embroidered on cloth of fine linen twined. j **7** It shall have a pair of shoulder straps joined to its two upper ends. **8** The embroidered belt on the ephod shall extend out from it and, like it, be made of gold thread, of violet, purple and scarlet yarn, and of fine linen twined.

9 "Get two onyx stones and engrave on them the names of the sons of Israel: **10** six of their names on one stone, and the other six on the other stone, in the order of their birth. **11** As a gem-cutter engraves a seal, so shall you have the two stones engraved with the names of the sons of Israel and then mounted in gold filigree work. **12** Set these two stones on the shoulder straps of the ephod as memorial stones of the sons of Israel. Thus Aaron shall bear their names on his shoulders as a reminder before the LORD. **13** Make filigree rosettes of gold, k **14** as well as two chains of pure gold, twisted

---

g 9-19: Ex 38, 9-20.   45, 8-14.
h 20f: Lv 24, 1-4.   k 13f: Ex 28, 22. 25; 39,
i 1-5: Ex 39, 1; Sir 45, 7.   15. 18.
j 6-12: Ex 39, 2-7; Sir

*

27, 4: Grating: it is not clear whether this was flush with the altar or at some small distance from it; in the latter case the space between the altar and the grating would be filled with stones and serve as a platform around the altar, which would otherwise be too high for the priest to reach conveniently.

27, 8: Hollow: probably filled with earth or stones when in use. Cf Ex 20, 24f.

28, 6: Ephod: this Hebrew word is retained in the translation because it is the technical term for a peculiar piece of the priestly vestments, the exact nature of which is uncertain. It seems to have been a sort of apron that hung from the shoulders of the priest by shoulder straps (v 7) and was tied around his waist by the loose ends of the attached belt (v 8).

like cords, and fasten the cordlike chains to the filigree rosettes.

15 *l*"The breastpiece* of decision you shall also have made, embroidered like the ephod with gold thread and violet, purple and scarlet yarn on cloth of fine linen twined. **16** It is to be square when folded double, a span high and a span wide. **17** *On it you shall mount four rows of precious stones: in the first row, a carnelian, a topaz and an emerald; **18** in the second row, a garnet, a sapphire and a beryl; **19** in the third row, a jacinth, an agate and an amethyst; **20** in the fourth row, a chrysolite, an onyx and a jasper. These stones are to be mounted in gold filigree work, **21** twelve of them to match the names of the sons of Israel, each stone engraved like a seal with the name of one of the twelve tribes.

22 "When the chains of pure gold, twisted like cords, have been made for the breastpiece, **23** you shall then make two rings of gold for it and fasten them to the two upper ends of the breastpiece. **24** The gold cords are then to be fastened to two rings at the upper ends of the breastpiece, **25** the other two ends of the cords being fastened in front to the two filigree rosettes which are attached to the shoulder straps of the ephod. **26** Make two other rings of gold and put them on the two lower ends of the breastpiece, on its edge that faces the ephod. **27** Then make two more rings of gold and fasten them to the bottom of the shoulder straps next to where they join the ephod in front, just above its embroidered belt. **28** Violet ribbons shall bind the rings of the breastpiece to the rings of the ephod, so that the breastpiece will stay right above the embroidered belt of the ephod and not swing loose from it.

29 "Whenever Aaron enters the sanctuary, he will thus bear the names of the sons of Israel on the breastpiece of decision over his heart as a constant reminder before the LORD. **30** In this breastpiece of decision*m* you shall put the Urim and Thummim,* that they may be over Aaron's heart whenever he enters the presence of the LORD. Thus he shall always bear the decisions for the Israelites over his heart in the LORD's presence.

Other Vestments.   **31** "The robe of the ephod*n* you shall make entirely of violet material. **32** It shall have an opening for the head in the center, and around this opening there shall be a selvage, woven as at the opening of a shirt, to keep it from being torn. **33** All around the hem at the bottom you shall make pomegranates, woven of violet, purple and scarlet yarn and fine linen twined, with gold bells between them; **34** first a gold bell, then a pomegranate, and thus alternating all around the hem of the robe. **35** Aaron shall wear it when ministering,

that its tinkling may be heard as he enters and leaves the LORD's presence in the sanctuary; else he will die.

36 "You shall also make a plate of pure gold and engrave on it, as on a seal engraving, "Sacred to the LORD." **37** This plate is to be tied over the miter with a violet ribbon in such a way that it rests on the front of the miter,*o* **38** over Aaron's forehead. Since Aaron bears whatever guilt the Israelites may incur in consecrating any of their sacred gifts, this plate must always be over his forehead, so that they may find favor with the LORD.

39 *p*"The tunic of fine linen shall be brocaded. The miter shall be made of fine linen. The sash shall be of variegated work.

40 "Likewise, for the glorious adornment of Aaron's sons you shall have tunics and sashes and turbans made. **41** With these you shall clothe your brother Aaron and his sons. Anoint and ordain them,* consecrating them as my priests. **42** You must also make linen drawers for them, to cover their naked flesh from their loins to their thighs.*q* **43** Aaron and his sons shall wear them whenever they go into the meeting tent or approach the altar to minister in the sanctuary, lest they incur guilt and die. This shall be a perpetual ordinance for him and for his descendants.

CHAPTER 29

Consecration of the Priests.   **1** "This is the rite you shall perform in consecrating them as my priests.*r* Procure a young bull and two unblemished rams. **2** With fine wheat flour make unleavened cakes mixed with oil, and unleavened wafers spread with oil, **3** and put them in a basket. Take the basket of them along with the bullock and the two rams. **4** Aaron and

---

l 15-21: Ex 39, 15-21.
m Lv 8, 8; Sir 45, 11.
n 31-35: Ex 39, 20ff; Lv 8, 9; Sir 45, 10.
o Ex 39, 31; Lv 8, 9.
p 39-43: Ex 39, 27ff.
q Ez 44, 18.
r 1-8: Lv 8, 1-9.

*

28, 15–30: Breastpiece: in shape like a modern altar burse, it was a pocketlike receptacle for holding the Urim and Thummim (v 30), and formed an integral part of the ephod, to which it was attached by an elaborate system of rings and chains. Both the ephod and its breastpiece were made of brocaded linen.

28, 17–20: The translation of the Hebrew names of some of these gems is quite conjectural.

28, 30: Urim and Thummim: both the meaning of these Hebrew words and the exact nature of the objects so designated are uncertain. They were apparently lots of some kind which were drawn or cast by the priest to ascertain God's decision in doubtful matters. Hence, the burse in which they were kept was called "the breastpiece of decision."

28, 41: Ordain them: literally, "fill their hands," a technical expression used solely for the installation of priests. The phrase probably originated in the custom of placing in the priests' hands the instruments or other symbols of the sacerdotal office.

his sons you shall also bring to the entrance of the meeting tent, and there wash them with water. **5** Take the vestments and clothe Aaron with the tunic, the robe of the ephod, the ephod itself, and the breastpiece, fastening the embroidered belt of the ephod around him. **6** Put the miter on his head, the sacred diadem on the miter. **7** Then take the anointing oil and anoint him with it, pouring it on his head. **8** Bring forward his sons also and clothe them with the tunics, **9** gird them with the sashes, and tie the turbans on them.ˢ Thus shall the priesthood be theirs by perpetual law, and thus shall you ordain Aaron and his sons.

Ordination Sacrifices.

10 ᵗ"Now bring forward the bullock in front of the meeting tent. There Aaron and his sons shall lay their hands on its head. **11** Then slaughter the bullock before the LORD, at the entrance of the meeting tent. **12** Take some of its blood and with your finger put it on the horns of the altar. All the rest of the blood you shall pour out at the base of the altar. **13** All the fat that covers its inner organs, as well as the lobe of its liver and its two kidneys, together with the fat that is on them, you shall take and burn on the altar. **14** But the flesh and hide and offal of the bullock you must burn up outside the camp, since this is a sin offering.ᵘ

15 "Then take one of the rams, and after Aaron and his sons have laid their hands on its head, **16** slaughter it. The blood you shall take and splash on all the sides of the altar. **17** Cut the ram into pieces; its inner organs and shanks you shall first wash, and then put them with the pieces and with the head. **18** The entire ram shall then be burned on the altar, since it is a holocaust, a sweet-smelling oblation to the LORD.

19 "After this take the other ram, and when Aaron and his sons have laid their hands on its head, **20** slaughter it. Some of its blood you shall take and put on the tip of Aaron's right ear and on the tips of his sons' right ears and on the thumbs of their right hands and the great toes of their right feet. Splash the rest of the blood on all the sides of the altar. **21** Then take some of the blood that is on the altar, together with some of the anointing oil, and sprinkle this on Aaron and his vestments, as well as on his sons and their vestments, that his sons and their vestments may be sacred.

22 "Now, from this ram you shall take its fat: its fatty tail,* the fat that covers its inner organs, the lobe of its liver, its two kidneys with the fat that is on them, and its right thigh, since this is the ordination ram; **23** then, out of the basket of unleavened food that you have set before the LORD, you shall take one of the loaves of bread, one of the cakes made with oil,

and one of the wafers. **24** All these things you shall put into the hands of Aaron and his sons, so that they may wave them as a wave offering* before the LORD. **25** After you have received them back from their hands, you shall burn them on top of the holocaust on the altar as a sweet-smelling oblation to the LORD. **26** Finally, take the breast of Aaron's ordination ram and wave it as a wave offering before the LORD; this is to be your own portion.

27 *"Thus shall you set aside the breast of whatever wave offering is waved,ᵛ as well as the thigh of whatever raised offering is raised up, whether this be the ordination ram or anything else belonging to Aaron or to his sons. **28** Such things are due to Aaron and his sons from the Israelites by a perpetual ordinance as a contribution. From their peace offerings, too, the Israelites shall make a contribution, their contribution to the LORD.

29 "The sacred vestmentsʷ of Aaron shall be passed down to his descendants, that in them they may be anointed and ordained. **30** The descendant who succeeds him as priest and who is to enter the meeting tent to minister in the sanctuary shall be clothed with them for seven days.

31 ˣ"You shall take the flesh of the ordination ram and boil it in a holy place. **32** At the entrance of the meeting tent Aaron and his sons shall eat the flesh of the ram and the bread that is in the basket. **33** They themselves are to eat of these things by which atonement was made at their ordination and consecration; but no layman may eat of them, since they are sacred. **34** If some of the flesh of the ordination sacrifice or some of the bread remains over on the next day, this remnant must be burned up; it is not to be eaten, since it is sacred. **35** Carry out all these orders in regard to Aaron and his sons just as I have given them to you.ʸ

"Seven days you shall spend in ordaining them, **36** ᶻsacrificing a bullock each day as a sin offering, to make atonement. Thus also shall you purge the altar* in making atonement for it;

---

s Lv 8, 13.　　　　　　　　18, 3.
t 10-26: Lv 8, 14-30.　　　w Nm 20, 26. 28.
u Heb 13, 11.　　　　　　　x 31-34: Lv 8, 31f.
v 27f: Lv 7, 31-34; 10,　　y Lv 8, 36.
　14f; Nm 18, 18f; Dt　　　z 36f: Lv 8, 33ff.

29, 22: Fatty tail: the thick layer of fat surrounding the tails of sheep and rams bred in Palestine even today. It is regarded as a choice food. Cf Lv 3, 9.

29, 24–26: Wave offering: the portions of a peace offering, breast and right thigh, which the officiating priest moved to and fro (waved) in the presence of the Lord. They were reserved for Aaron and his sons.

29, 27–30: These verses are a parenthetical interruption of the ordination ritual; v 31 belongs logically immediately after v 26.

29, 36f: Purge the altar: the construction of an altar by profane hands rendered it impure. The anointing and consecration of the altar purified it and made it sacred.

you shall anoint it in order to consecrate it. **37** Seven days you shall spend in making atonement for the altar and in consecrating it. Then the altar will be most sacred, and whatever touches it will become sacred.

38 *"Now, this is what you shall offer on the altar: two yearling lambs[a] as the sacrifice established for each day; **39** one lamb in the morning and the other lamb at the evening twilight. **40** With the first lamb there shall be a tenth of an ephah of fine flour mixed with a fourth of a hin of oil of crushed olives and, as its libation, a fourth of a hin of wine. **41** The other lamb you shall offer at the evening twilight, with the same cereal offering and libation as in the morning. You shall offer this as a sweet-smelling oblation to the LORD. **42** Throughout your generations this established holocaust shall be offered before the LORD at the entrance of the meeting tent, where I will meet you and speak to you.

43 "There, at the altar, I will meet the Israelites; hence, it will be made sacred by my glory.[b] **44** Thus I will consecrate the meeting tent and the altar, just as I also consecrate Aaron and his sons to be my priests. **45** I will dwell in the midst of the Israelites and will be their God. **46** They shall know that I, the LORD, am their God who brought them out of the land of Egypt, so that I, the LORD, their God, might dwell among them.

CHAPTER 30

Altar of Incense.   **1** "For burning incense you shall make an altar of acacia wood,[c] **2** with a square surface, a cubit long, a cubit wide, and two cubits high, with horns that spring directly from it. **3** Its grate on top, its walls on all four sides, and its horns you shall plate with pure gold. Put a gold molding around it. **4** Underneath the molding you shall put gold rings, two on one side and two on the opposite side, as holders for the poles used in carrying it. **5** Make the poles, too, of acacia wood and plate them with gold. **6** This altar you are to place in front of the veil that hangs before the ark of the commandments where I will meet you.[d]

7 "On it Aaron shall burn fragrant incense. Morning after morning, when he prepares the lamps, **8** and again in the evening twilight, when he lights the lamps, he shall burn incense. Throughout your generations this shall be the established incense offering before the LORD. **9** On this altar you shall not offer up any profane incense, or any holocaust or cereal offering; nor shall you pour out a libation upon it. **10** Once a year Aaron shall perform the atonement rite on its horns.[e] Throughout your generations this atonement is to be made once a year with the blood of the atoning sin offering. This altar is most sacred to the LORD."

Census Tax.   **11** The LORD also said to Moses, **12** "When you take a census[f] of the Israelites who are to be registered, each one, as he is enrolled, shall give the LORD a forfeit for his life, so that no plague may come upon them for being registered. **13** Everyone who enters the registered group must pay a half-shekel, according to the standard of the sanctuary shekel, twenty gerahs to the shekel. This payment of a half-shekel is a contribution to the LORD.[g] **14** Everyone of twenty years or more who enters the registered group must give this contribution to the LORD. **15** The rich need not give more, nor shall the poor give less, than a half-shekel in this contribution to the LORD to pay the forfeit for their lives. **16** [h]When you receive this forfeit money from the Israelites, you shall donate it to the service of the meeting tent, that there it may be the Israelites' reminder, before the LORD, of the forfeit paid for their lives."

The Laver.   **17** The LORD said to Moses, **18** "For ablutions you shall make a bronze laver with a bronze base. Place it between the meeting tent and the altar, and put water in it.[i] **19** Aaron and his sons shall use it in washing their hands and feet.[j] **20** When they are about to enter the meeting tent, they must wash with water, lest they die. Likewise when they approach the altar in their ministry, to offer an oblation to the LORD, **21** they must wash their hands and feet, lest they die. This shall be a perpetual ordinance for him and his descendants throughout their generations."

The Anointing Oil.   **22** The LORD said to Moses, **23** "Take the finest spices: five hundred shekels of free-flowing myrrh; half that amount, that is, two hundred and fifty shekels, of fragrant cinnamon; two hundred and fifty shekels of fragrant cane; **24** five hundred shekels of cassia—all according to the standard of the sanctuary shekel; together with a hin of olive oil; **25** and blend them into sacred anointing oil,[k] perfumed ointment expertly prepared. **26** [l]With this sacred anointing oil you shall anoint the meeting tent and the ark of the commandments, **27** the table and all its appurtenances, the lampstand and its appurtenances, the altar of incense **28** and the altar of holocausts with all its appurtenances, and the laver

---

a 38-42: Nm 28, 3-8.   h Ex 38, 25.
b Ex 25, 22.   i Ex 38, 8; 40, 7. 30.
c 1-5; Ex 37, 25-28.   j 19ff: Ex 40, 31f.
d Ex 40, 26.   k Ex 37, 29.
e Lv 16, 18.   l 26-29: Ex 40, 9ff; Lv 8,
f Nm 1, 2f; 26, 2.   10; Nm 7, 1.
g Mt 17, 24-27.

*

29, 38–42: A parenthesis inserted into the rubrics for consecrating the altar; v 43 belongs directly after v 37.

with its base. **29** When you have consecrated them, they shall be most sacred; whatever touches them shall be sacred. **30** Aaron and his sons you shall also anoint and consecrate as my priests.*m* **31** To the Israelites you shall say: As sacred anointing oil this shall belong to me throughout your generations. **32** It may not be used in any ordinary anointing of the body, nor may you make any other oil of a like mixture. It is sacred, and shall be treated as sacred by you. **33** Whoever prepares a perfume like this, or whoever puts any of this on a layman, shall be cut off from his kinsmen.''

The Incense.　34 *n*The LORD told Moses, ''Take these aromatic substances: storax and onycha and galbanum, these and pure frankincense in equal parts; **35** and blend them into incense. This fragrant powder, expertly prepared, is to be salted and so kept pure and sacred. **36** Grind some of it into fine dust and put this before the commandments in the meeting tent where I will meet you. This incense shall be treated as most sacred by you. **37** You may not make incense of a like mixture for yourselves; you must treat it as sacred to the LORD. **38** Whoever makes an incense like this for his own enjoyment of its fragrance, shall be cut off from his kinsmen.''

CHAPTER 31

Choice of Artisans.　1 *o*The LORD said to Moses, **2** ''See, I have chosen Bezalel, son of Uri, son of Hur, of the tribe of Judah, **3** and I have filled him with a divine spirit of skill and understanding and knowledge in every craft: **4** in the production of embroidery, in making things of gold, silver or bronze, **5** in cutting and mounting precious stones, in carving wood, and in every other craft. **6** As his assistant I have appointed Oholiab, son of Ahisamach, of the tribe of Dan. I have also endowed all the experts with the necessary skill to make all the things I have ordered you to make: **7** *p*the meeting tent, the ark of the commandments with the propitiatory on top of it, all the furnishings of the tent, **8** the table with its appurtenances, the pure gold lampstand with all its appurtenances, the altar of incense, **9** the altar of holocausts with all its appurtenances, the laver with its base, **10** the service cloths,* the sacred vestments for Aaron the priest, the vestments for his sons in their ministry, **11** the anointing oil, and the fragrant incense for the sanctuary. All these things they shall make just as I have commanded you.''

Sabbath Laws.　12 *q*The LORD said to Moses, **13** ''You must also tell the Israelites: Take care to keep my sabbaths, for that is to be the token between you and me throughout the gen-

erations, to show that it is I, the LORD, who make you holy. **14** Therefore, you must keep the sabbath as something sacred. Whoever desecrates it shall be put to death. If anyone does work on that day, he must be rooted out of his people. **15** Six days there are for doing work, but the seventh day is the sabbath of complete rest, sacred to the LORD. Anyone who does work on the sabbath day shall be put to death. **16** So shall the Israelites observe the sabbath, keeping it throughout their generations as a perpetual covenant. **17** Between me and the Israelites it is to be an everlasting token; for in six days the LORD made the heavens and the earth, but on the seventh day he rested at his ease.''

18 When the LORD had finished speaking to Moses on Mount Sinai, he gave him the two tablets of the commandments, the stone tablets inscribed by God's own finger.*r*

CHAPTER 32

The Golden Calf.　1 When the people became aware of Moses' delay in coming down from the mountain, they gathered around Aaron and said to him, ''Come, make us a god who will be our leader; as for the man Moses who brought us out of the land of Egypt, we do not know what has happened to him.''*s* **2** Aaron replied, ''Have your wives and sons and daughters take off the golden earrings they are wearing, and bring them to me.'' **3** So all the people took off their earrings and brought them to Aaron, **4** who accepted their offering, and fashioning this gold with a graving tool, made a molten calf. Then they cried out, ''This is your God, O Israel, who brought you out of the land of Egypt.''*t* **5** On seeing this, Aaron built an altar before the calf and proclaimed, ''Tomorrow is a feast of the LORD.''* **6** Early the next day the people offered holocausts and brought peace offerings. Then they sat down to eat and drink, and rose up to revel.*u*

7 With that, the LORD said to Moses, ''Go down at once to your people, whom you brought out of the land of Egypt, for they have become depraved. **8** *v*They have soon turned aside from the way I pointed out to them, making for them-

---

m Ex 29, 7; Lv 8, 12.
n 34ff: Ex 25, 6; 37, 29.
o 1-6: Ex 35, 30-35.
p 7-11: Ex 35, 10-19.
q 12-17: Ex 20, 8-11; 35, 1-3.

r Ex 24, 12; 32, 15f; Dt 5, 22.
s Ex 32, 23; Acts 7, 40.
t Ex 32, 8; 1 Kgs 12, 28.
u 1 Cor 10, 7.
v 7f: Dt 9, 12. 16.

*

31, 10: The service cloths: so the Greek. They were perhaps the colored cloths mentioned in Nm 4, 4–15.

32, 5: The calf . . . a feast of the Lord: from this it is clear that the golden calf was intended as an image, not of a false god, but of the Lord himself, his strength being symbolized by the strength of a young bull. The Israelites, however, had been forbidden to represent the Lord under any visible form. Cf Ex 20, 4.

selves a molten calf and worshiping it, sacrificing to it and crying out, 'This is your God, O Israel, who brought you out of the land of Egypt!' **9** I see how stiff-necked this people is,''*w* continued the Lord to Moses. **10** "Let me alone, then, that my wrath may blaze up against them to consume them. Then I will make of you a great nation."

11 But Moses implored the Lord, his God, saying,*x* "Why, O Lord, should your wrath blaze up against your own people, whom you brought out of the land of Egypt with such great power and with so strong a hand? **12** Why should the Egyptians say, 'With evil intent he brought them out, that he might kill them in the mountains and exterminate them from the face of the earth'? Let your blazing wrath die down; relent in punishing your people. **13** Remember your servants Abraham, Isaac and Israel, and how you swore to them by your own self, saying,*y* 'I will make your descendants as numerous as the stars in the sky; and all this land that I promised, I will give your descendants as their perpetual heritage.' " **14** So the Lord relented in the punishment he had threatened to inflict on his people.

15 Moses then turned and came down the mountain with the two tablets of the commandments in his hands,*z* tablets that were written on both sides, front and back; **16** tablets that were made by God, having inscriptions on them that were engraved by God himself.*a* **17** Now, when Joshua heard the noise of the people shouting, he said to Moses, "That sounds like a battle in the camp." **18** But Moses answered, "It does not sound like cries of victory, nor does it sound like cries of defeat; the sounds that I hear are cries of revelry." **19** As he drew near the camp, he saw the calf and the dancing. With that, Moses' wrath flared up, so that he threw the tablets down and broke them on the base of the mountain.*b* **20** Taking the calf they had made, he fused it in the fire and then ground it down to powder, which he scattered on the water* and made the Israelites drink.*c*

21 Moses asked Aaron, "What did this people ever do to you that you should lead them into so grave a sin?" Aaron replied, "Let not my lord be angry. **22** You know well enough how prone the people are to evil. **23** They said to me, 'Make us a god to be our leader; as for the man Moses who brought us out of the land of Egypt, we do not know what has happened to him.' **24** So I told them, 'Let anyone who has gold jewelry take it off.' They gave it to me, and I threw it into the fire, and this calf came out."

25 When Moses realized that, to the scornful joy of their foes, Aaron had let the people run wild, **26** he stood at the gate of the camp and cried, "Whoever is for the Lord, let him come to me!" All the Levites*d* then rallied to him,

27 and he told them, "Thus says the Lord, the God of Israel: Put your sword on your hip, every one of you! Now go up and down the camp, from gate to gate, and slay your own kinsmen,* your friends and neighbors!" **28** The Levites carried out the command of Moses, and that day there fell about three thousand of the people. **29** Then Moses said, "Today you have been dedicated to the Lord,* for you were against your own sons and kinsmen, to bring a blessing upon yourselves this day."

The Atonement. **30** On the next day Moses said to the people,*e* "You have committed a grave sin. I will go up to the Lord, then; perhaps I may be able to make atonement for your sin." **31** So Moses went back to the Lord and said, "Ah, this people has indeed committed a grave sin in making a god of gold for themselves! **32** If you would only forgive their sin! If you will not, then strike me out of the book that you have written."* **33** The Lord answered, "Him only who has sinned against me will I strike out of my book. **34** Now, go and lead the people whither I have told you. My angel will go before you. When it is time for me to punish, I will punish them for their sin."

35 Thus the Lord smote the people for having had Aaron make the calf for them.

CHAPTER 33

1 The Lord told Moses, "You and the people whom you have brought up from the land of Egypt, are to go up from here to the land which I swore to Abraham, Isaac and Jacob I would give to their descendants.*f* **2** Driving out the Canaanites, Amorites, Hittites, Perizzites, Hivites and Jebusites, I will send an angel before you*g* **3** to the land flowing with milk and honey. But I myself will not go up in your company, because you are a stiff-necked people; otherwise I might exterminate you on the way." **4** When the people heard this bad news, they

---

w 9f: Dt 9, 13; Ps 106, 23.
x 11f: Nm 14, 13ff; Dt 9, 28.
y Gn 22, 16f.
z Dt 9, 15.
a Ex 31, 18.

b Dt 9, 16f.
c Dt 9, 21.
d 26-29: Dt 33, 8f.
e 30-34: Dt 9, 18ff.
f Gn 12, 7.
g Ex 23, 23.

*

32, 20: The water: the stream that flowed down Mount Sinai. Cf Dt 9, 21.

32, 27: Slay your own kinsmen: those who were especially guilty of the idolatry.

32, 29: Dedicated to the Lord: because of their zeal for the true worship of the Lord, the Levites were chosen to be special ministers of the ritual service. However, the meaning of the Hebrew here is somewhat disputed.

32, 32: The book that you have written: the list of God's intimate friends. In a similar sense St. Paul wished to be anathema from Christ for the sake of his brethren. Cf Rom 9, 3.

went into mourning, and no one wore his ornaments.

5 The LORD said to Moses, "Tell the Israelites: You are a stiff-necked people. Were I to go up in your company even for a moment, I would exterminate you. Take off your ornaments, therefore; I will then see what I am to do with you." **6** So, from Mount Horeb onward, the Israelites laid aside their ornaments.

Moses' Intimacy with God. **7** The tent,[h] which was called the meeting tent,* Moses used to pitch at some distance away, outside the camp. Anyone who wished to consult the LORD would go to this meeting tent outside the camp. **8** Whenever Moses went out to the tent, the people would all rise and stand at the entrance of their own tents, watching Moses until he entered the tent. **9** As Moses entered the tent, the column of cloud would come down and stand at its entrance while the LORD spoke with Moses. **10** On seeing the column of cloud stand at the entrance of the tent, all the people would rise and worship at the entrance of their own tents. **11** The LORD used to speak to Moses face to face,[i] as one man speaks to another. Moses would then return to the camp, but his young assistant, Joshua, son of Nun, would not move out of the tent.

12 Moses said to the LORD, "You, indeed, are telling me to lead this people on;[j] but you have not let me know whom you will send with me. Yet you have said, 'You are my intimate friend,' and also, 'You have found favor with me.' **13** Now, if I have found favor with you, do let me know your ways so that, in knowing you, I may continue to find favor with you. Then, too, this nation is, after all, your own people." **14** "I myself,"* the LORD answered, "will go along, to give you rest." **15** Moses replied, "If you are not going yourself, do not make us go up from here. **16** For how can it be known that we, your people and I, have found favor with you, except by your going with us? Then we, your people and I, will be singled out from every other people on the earth." **17** The LORD said to Moses, "This request, too, which you have just made, I will carry out, because you have found favor with me and you are my intimate friend."

18 Then Moses said, "Do let me see your glory!" **19** He answered, "I will make all my beauty pass before you, and in your presence I will pronounce my name, 'LORD'; I who show favors to whom I will, I who grant mercy to whom I will.[k] **20** But my face you cannot see,[l] for no man sees me and still lives. **21** Here," continued the LORD, "is a place near me where you shall station yourself on the rock. **22** When my glory passes I will set you in the hollow of the rock and will cover you with my hand until

I have passed by. **23** Then I will remove my hand, so that you may see my back;* but my face is not to be seen."

CHAPTER 34

Renewal of the Tablets. **1** The LORD said to Moses, "Cut two stone tablets like the former,[m] that I may write on them the commandments which were on the former tablets that you broke. **2** Get ready for tomorrow morning, when you are to go up Mount Sinai and there present yourself to me on the top of the mountain. **3** No one shall come up with you, and no one is even to be seen on any part of the mountain;[n] even the flocks and the herds are not to go grazing toward this mountain." **4** Moses then cut two stone tablets like the former, and early the next morning he went up Mount Sinai as the LORD had commanded him, taking along the two stone tablets.

5 Having come down in a cloud, the LORD stood with him there and proclaimed his name, "LORD." **6** Thus the LORD passed before him and cried out, "The LORD, the LORD, a merciful and gracious God, slow to anger and rich in kindness and fidelity, **7** continuing his kindness for a thousand generations, and forgiving wickedness and crime and sin; yet not declaring the guilty guiltless, but punishing children and grandchildren to the third and fourth generation for their fathers' wickedness!"[o] **8** Moses at once bowed down to the ground in worship. **9** Then he said, "If I find favor with you, O LORD, do come along in our company. This is indeed a stiff-necked people; yet pardon our wickedness and sins, and receive us as your own."

Religious Laws. **10** "Here, then," said the LORD, "is the covenant I will make. Before the eyes of all your people I will work such marvels as have never been wrought in any nation anywhere on earth, so that this people among whom you live may see how awe-inspiring are the deeds which I, the LORD, will do at

h Ex 29, 42f.
i Nm 12, 8; Dt 34, 10; Sir 45, 4-6.
j Ex 32, 34.
k Rom 9, 15.
l Jn 1, 18; 1 Tm 6, 16.
m Dt 10, 1f.
n Ex 19, 12f. 21.
o 6f: Ex 20, 5f; Nm 14, 18; Dt 5, 9f; Jer 32, 18.

*

33, 7–11: The meeting tent is mentioned here by anticipation; its actual construction is described in the following chapters.

33, 14: I myself: literally, "my face," that is, "my presence." To give you rest: in the Promised Land; some understand, "to put your mind at rest"; others, by a slight emendation in the text, render, "to lead you."

33, 23: You may see my back: man can see God's glory as reflected in creation, but his "face," that is, God as he is in himself, mortal man cannot behold. Cf 1 Cor 13, 12.

fine linen twined, having cherubim embroidered on them with violet, purple and scarlet yarn. **9** The length of each sheet was twenty-eight cubits, and the width four cubits; all the sheets were of the same size. **10** Five of the sheets were sewed together, edge to edge; and the same for the other five. **11** Loops of violet yarn were made along the edge of the end sheet in the first set, and the same along the edge of the end sheet in the second set. **12** Fifty loops were thus put on one inner sheet, and fifty loops on the inner sheet in the other set, with the loops directly opposite each other. **13** Then fifty clasps of gold were made, with which the sheets were joined so that the Dwelling formed one whole.

14 Sheets of goat hair were also woven as a tent over the Dwelling. Eleven such sheets were made. **15** The length of each sheet was thirty cubits and the width four cubits; all eleven sheets were of the same size. **16** Five of these sheets were sewed edge to edge into one set; and the other six sheets into another set. **17** Fifty loops were made along the edge of the end sheet in one set, and fifty loops along the edge of the corresponding sheet in the other set. **18** Fifty bronze clasps were made with which the tent was joined so that it formed one whole. **19** A covering for the tent was made of rams' skins dyed red, and above that, a covering of tahash skins.

The Boards.   **20** *g* Boards of acacia wood were made as walls for the Dwelling. **21** The length of each board was ten cubits, and the width one and a half cubits. **22** Each board had two arms, fastening them in line. In this way all the boards of the Dwelling were made. **23** They were set up as follows: twenty boards on the south side, **24** with forty silver pedestals under the twenty boards, so that there were two pedestals under each board, at its two arms; **25** twenty boards on the other side of the Dwelling, the north side, **26** with their forty silver pedestals, two under each board; **27** six boards at the rear of the Dwelling, to the west; **28** and two boards at the corners in the rear of the Dwelling. **29** These were double at the bottom, and likewise double at the top, to the first ring. That is how both boards in the corners were made. **30** Thus, there were in the rear eight boards, with their sixteen silver pedestals, two pedestals under each board. **31** Bars of acacia wood were also made, five for the boards on one side of the Dwelling, **32** five for those on the other side, and five for those at the rear, to the west. **33** The center bar, at the middle of the boards, was made to reach across from end to end. **34** The boards were plated with gold, and gold rings were made on them as holders for the bars, which were also plated with gold.

The Veil.   **35** *h* The veil was woven of violet, purple and scarlet yarn, and of fine linen twined, with cherubim embroidered on it. **36** Four gold-plated columns of acacia wood, with gold hooks, were made for it, and four silver pedestals were cast for them.

37 The curtain for the entrance of the tent was made of violet, purple and scarlet yarn, and of fine linen twined, woven in a variegated manner. **38** Its five columns, with their hooks as well as their capitals and bands, were plated with gold; their five pedestals were of bronze.

CHAPTER 37

The Ark.   **1** Bezalel made the ark of acacia wood, two and a half cubits long, one and a half cubits wide, and one and a half cubits high. **2** The inside and outside were plated with gold, and a molding of gold was put around it. **3** Four gold rings were cast and put on its four supports, two rings for one side and two for the opposite side. **4** Poles of acacia wood were made and plated with gold; **5** these were put through the rings on the sides of the ark, for carrying it.

6 The propitiatory was made of pure gold, two and a half cubits long and one and a half cubits wide. **7** Two cherubim of beaten gold were made for the two ends of the propitiatory, **8** one cherub fastened at one end, the other at the other end, springing directly from the propitiatory at its two ends. **9** The cherubim had their wings spread out above, covering the propitiatory with them. They were turned toward each other, but with their faces looking toward the propitiatory. *i*

The Table.   **10** *j* The table was made of acacia wood, two cubits long, one cubit wide, and one and a half cubits high. **11** It was plated with pure gold, and a molding of gold was put around it. **12** A frame a handbreadth high was also put around it, with a molding of gold around the frame. **13** Four rings of gold were cast for it and fastened, one at each of the four corners. **14** The rings were alongside the frame as holders for the poles to carry the table. **15** These poles were made of acacia wood and plated with gold. **16** The vessels that were set on the table, its plates and cups, as well as its pitchers and bowls for pouring libations, were of pure gold.

The Lampstand.   **17** *k* The lampstand was made of pure beaten gold—its shaft and branches as well as its cups and knobs and petals springing directly from it. **18** Six branches extended from its sides, three branches on one side and three on the other. **19** On one branch there

---

g 20-34: Ex 26, 15-29.   j 10-16: Ex 25, 23-30.
h 35-38: Ex 26, 31-37.   k 17-24: Ex 25, 31-39.
i 1-9: Ex 25, 10-22.

were three cups, shaped like almond blossoms, each with its knob and petals; on the opposite branch there were three cups, shaped like almond blossoms, each with its knob and petals; and so for the six branches that extended from the lampstand. **20** On the shaft there were four cups, shaped like almond blossoms, with their knobs and petals, **21** including a knob below each of the three pairs of branches that extended from the lampstand. **22** The knobs and branches sprang so directly from it that the whole formed but a single piece of pure beaten gold. **23** Its seven lamps, as well as its trimming shears and trays, were made of pure gold. **24** A talent of pure gold was used for the lampstand and its various appurtenances.

The Altar of Incense. **25** *l*The altar of incense was made of acacia wood, on a square, a cubit long, a cubit wide, and two cubits high, having horns that sprang directly from it. **26** Its grate on top, its walls on all four sides, and its horns were plated with pure gold; and a molding of gold was put around it. **27** Underneath the molding gold rings were placed, two on one side and two on the opposite side, as holders for the poles to carry it. **28** The poles, too, were made of acacia wood and plated with gold.

29 The sacred anointing oil and the fragrant incense were prepared in their pure form by a perfumer. *m*

CHAPTER 38

The Altar of Holocausts. **1** The altar of holocausts*n* was made of acacia wood, on a square, five cubits long and five cubits wide; its height was three cubits. **2** At the four corners horns were made that sprang directly from the altar. The whole was plated with bronze. **3** All the utensils of the altar, the pots, shovels, basins, forks and fire pans, were likewise made of bronze. **4** A grating of bronze network was made for the altar and placed round it, on the ground, half as high as the altar itself. **5** Four rings were cast for the four corners of the bronze grating, as holders for the poles, **6** which were made of acacia wood and plated with bronze. **7** The poles were put through the rings on the sides of the altar for carrying it. The altar was made in the form of a hollow box.

8 The bronze laver, *o* with its bronze base, was made from the mirrors of the women who served* at the entrance of the meeting tent.

The Court. **9** *p*The court was made as follows. On the south side of the court there were hangings, woven of fine linen twined, a hundred cubits long, **10** with twenty columns and twenty pedestals of bronze, the hooks and bands of the columns being of silver. **11** On the north

side there were similar hangings, one hundred cubits long, with twenty columns and twenty pedestals of bronze, the hooks and bands of the columns being of silver. **12** On the west side there were hangings, fifty cubits long, with ten columns and ten pedestals, the hooks and bands of the columns being of silver. **13** On the east side the court was fifty cubits long. **14** Toward one side there were hangings to the extent of fifteen cubits, with three columns and three pedestals; **15** toward the other side, beyond the entrance of the court, there were likewise hangings to the extent of fifteen cubits, with three columns and three pedestals. **16** The hangings on all sides of the court were woven of fine linen twined. **17** The pedestals of the columns were of bronze, while the hooks and bands of the columns were of silver; the capitals were silver-plated, and all the columns of the court were banded with silver.

18 At the entrance of the court there was a variegated curtain, woven of violet, purple and scarlet yarn and of fine linen twined, twenty cubits long and five cubits wide, in keeping with the hangings of the court. **19** There were four columns and four pedestals of bronze for it, while their hooks were of silver. **20** All the tent pegs for the Dwelling and for the court around it were of bronze.

Amount of Metal Used. **21** The following is an account of the various amounts used on the Dwelling, the Dwelling of the commandments, drawn up at the command of Moses by the Levites under the direction of Ithamar, son of Aaron the priest. **22** However, it was Bezalel, son of Uri, *q* son of Hur, of the tribe of Judah, who made all that the Lord commanded Moses, **23** and he was assisted by Oholiab, son of Ahisamach, of the tribe of Dan, who was an engraver, an embroiderer, and a weaver of variegated cloth of violet, purple and scarlet yarn and of fine linen.

24 All the gold used in the entire construction of the sanctuary, having previously been given as an offering, amounted to twenty-nine talents and seven hundred and thirty shekels, according to the standard of the sanctuary shekel. **25** The amount of the silver received from the community was one hundred talents and one thousand seven hundred and seventy-five shekels, according to the standard of the sanctuary shekel; **26** one bekah apiece, that is, a half-shekel apiece, according to the standard of the

---

l 25-28: Ex 30, 1-5.
m Ex 30, 23ff. 34ff.
n 1-7: Ex 27, 1-8; 2 Chr 1, 5.
o Ex 30, 18-21.

p 9-20: Ex 27, 9-19.
q 22f: Ex 31, 2. 6; 35, 30. 34; 36, 1.
r Nm 1, 46.

*

38, 8: The reflecting surface of ancient mirrors was usually of polished bronze. The women who served: cf 1 Sm 2, 22.

sanctuary shekel, was received from every man of twenty years or more who entered the registered group; the number of these was six hundred and three thousand five hundred and fifty men.ʳ **27** One hundred talents of silver were used for casting the pedestals of the sanctuary and the pedestals of the veil, one talent for each pedestal, or one hundred talents for the one hundred pedestals. **28** The remaining one thousand seven hundred and seventy-five shekels were used for making the hooks on the columns, for plating the capitals, and for banding them with silver. **29** The bronze, given as an offering, amounted to seventy talents and two thousand four hundred shekels. **30** With this were made the pedestals at the entrance of the meeting tent, the bronze altar with its bronze gratings and all the appurtenances of the altar, **31** the pedestals around the court, the pedestals at the entrance of the court, and all the tent pegs for the Dwelling and for the court around it.

CHAPTER 39

The Vestments. **1** With violet, purple and scarlet yarn were woven the service cloths for use in the sanctuary, as well as the sacred vestmentsˢ for Aaron, as the LORD had commanded Moses.

2 ᵗThe ephod was woven of gold thread and of violet, purple and scarlet yarn and of fine linen twined. **3** Gold was first hammered into gold leaf and then cut up into threads, which were woven with the violet, purple and scarlet yarn into an embroidered pattern on the fine linen. **4** Shoulder straps were made for it and joined to its two upper ends. **5** The embroidered belt on the ephod extended out from it, and like it, was made of gold thread, of violet, purple and scarlet yarn, and of fine linen twined, as the LORD had commanded Moses. **6** The onyx stones were prepared and mounted in gold filigree work; they were engraved like seal engravings with the names of the sons of Israel. **7** These stones were set on the shoulder straps of the ephod as memorial stones of the sons of Israel, just as the LORD had commanded Moses.

8 ᵘThe breastpiece was embroidered like the ephod, with gold thread and violet, purple and scarlet yarn on cloth of fine linen twined. **9** It was square and folded double, a span high and a span wide in its folded form. **10** Four rows of precious stones were mounted on it: in the first row a carnelian, a topaz and an emerald; **11** in the second row, a garnet, a sapphire and a beryl; **12** in the third row a jacinth, an agate and an amethyst; **13** in the fourth row a chrysolite, an onyx and a jasper. They were mounted in gold filigree work. **14** These stones were twelve, to match the names of the sons of Israel, and each

stone was engraved like a seal with the name of one of the twelve tribes.

15 ᵛChains of pure gold, twisted like cords, were made for the breastpiece, **16** together with two gold filigree rosettes and two gold rings. The two rings were fastened to the two upper ends of the breastpiece. **17** The two gold chains were then fastened to the two rings at the ends of the breastpiece. **18** The other two ends of the two chains were fastened in front to the two filigree rosettes, which were attached to the shoulder straps of the ephod. **19** Two other gold rings were made and put on the two lower ends of the breastpiece, on the edge facing the ephod. **20** Two more gold rings were made and fastened to the bottom of the two shoulder straps next to where they joined the ephod in front, just above its embroidered belt. **21** Violet ribbons bound the rings of the breastpiece to the rings of the ephod, so that the breastpiece stayed right above the embroidered belt of the ephod and did not swing loose from it. All this was just as the LORD had commanded Moses.

The Other Vestments. **22** The robe of the ephod was woven entirely of violet yarn, **23** with an opening in its center like the opening of a shirt, with selvage around the opening to keep it from being torn. **24** At the hem of the robe pomegranates were made of violet, purple and scarlet yarn and of fine linen twined; **25** bells of pure gold were also made and put between the pomegranates all around the hem of the robe: **26** first a bell, then a pomegranate, and thus alternating all around the hem of the robe which was to be worn in performing the ministry—all this, just as the LORD had commanded Moses.

27 For Aaron and his sons there were also woven tunics of fine linen;ʷ **28** the miter of fine linen; the ornate turbans of fine linen; drawers of linen [of fine linen twined]; **29** and sashes of variegated work made of fine linen twined and of violet, purple and scarlet yarn, as the LORD had commanded Moses. **30** The plate of the sacred diadem was made of pure goldˣ and inscribed, as on a seal engraving: "Sacred to the LORD." **31** It was tied over the miter with a violet ribbon, as the LORD had commanded Moses.

Presentation of the Work to Moses. **32** Thus the entire work of the Dwelling of the meeting tent was completed. The Israelites did the work just as the LORD had commanded Moses. **33** They then brought to Moses the Dwelling, the tent with all its appurtenances, the clasps, the boards, the bars, the columns, the

s Ex 31, 10.
t 2-10: Ex 28, 6-12.
u 8-14: Ex 28, 15-21.
v 15-21: Ex 28, 31-35.
w 27ff: Ex 28, 39-42.
x 30f: Ex 28, 36f.

pedestals, **34** the covering of rams' skins dyed red, the covering of tahash skins, the curtain veil; **35** the ark of the commandments with its poles, the propitiatory, **36** the table with all its appurtenances and the showbread, **37** the pure gold lampstand with its lamps set up on it and with all its appurtenances, the oil for the light, **38** the golden altar, the anointing oil, the fragrant incense; the curtain for the entrance of the tent, **39** the altar of bronze with its bronze grating, its poles and all its appurtenances, the laver with its base, **40** the hangings of the court with their columns and pedestals, the curtain for the entrance of the court with its ropes and tent pegs, all the equipment for the service of the Dwelling of the meeting tent; **41** the service cloths for use in the sanctuary, the sacred vestments for Aaron the priest, and the vestments to be worn by his sons in their ministry. **42** The Israelites had carried out all the work just as the LORD had commanded Moses. **43** So when Moses saw that all the work was done just as the LORD had commanded, he blessed them.

CHAPTER 40

Erection of the Dwelling.

1 Then the LORD said to Moses, **2** *y*"On the first day of the first month* you shall erect the Dwelling of the meeting tent.*z* **3** Put the ark of the commandments in it, and screen off the ark with the veil.*a* **4** Bring in the table and set it. Then bring in the lampstand and set up the lamps on it. **5** Put the golden altar of incense in front of the ark of the commandments, and hang the curtain at the entrance of the Dwelling. **6** Put the altar of holocausts in front of the entrance of the Dwelling of the meeting tent. **7** Place the laver between the meeting tent and the altar, and put water in it. **8** Set up the court round about, and put the curtain at the entrance of the court.

9 *b*"Take the anointing oil and anoint the Dwelling and everything in it, consecrating it and all its furnishings, so that it will be sacred. **10** Anoint the altar of holocausts and all its appurtenances, consecrating it, so that it will be most sacred. **11** Likewise, anoint the laver with its base, and thus consecrate it.

12 *c*"Then bring Aaron and his sons to the entrance of the meeting tent, and there wash them with water. **13** Clothe Aaron with the sacred vestments and anoint him, thus consecrating him as my priest. **14** Bring forward his sons also, and clothe them with the tunics. **15** As you have anointed their father, anoint them also as my priests. Thus, by being anointed, they shall receive a perpetual priesthood throughout all future generations."

16 Moses did exactly as the LORD had commanded him. **17** On the first day of the first month of the second year the Dwelling was erected. **18** It was Moses who erected the Dwelling. He placed its pedestals, set up its boards, put in its bars, and set up its columns. **19** He spread the tent over the Dwelling and put the covering on top of the tent, as the LORD had commanded him. **20** *d*He took the commandments and put them in the ark; he placed poles alongside the ark and set the propitiatory upon it. **21** He brought the ark into the Dwelling and hung the curtain veil, thus screening off the ark of the commandments, as the LORD had commanded him. **22** He put the table in the meeting tent, on the north side of the Dwelling, outside the veil, **23** and arranged the bread on it before the LORD, as the LORD had commanded him.*e* **24** He placed the lampstand in the meeting tent, opposite the table, on the south side of the Dwelling, **25** and he set up the lamps before the LORD, as the LORD had commanded him. **26** He placed the golden altar in the meeting tent, in front of the veil, **27** and on it he burned fragrant incense, as the LORD had commanded him. **28** He hung the curtain at the entrance of the Dwelling. **29** He put the altar of holocausts in front of the entrance of the Dwelling of the meeting tent, and offered holocausts and cereal offerings on it, as the LORD had commanded him. **30** *f*He placed the laver between the meeting tent and the altar, and put water in it for washing. **31** Moses and Aaron and his sons used to wash their hands and feet there, **32** for they washed themselves whenever they went into the meeting tent or approached the altar, as the LORD commanded Moses. **33** Finally, he set up the court around the Dwelling and the altar and hung the curtain at the entrance of the court. Thus Moses finished all the work.

God's Presence in the Dwelling.

34 *g*Then the cloud covered the meeting tent, and the glory of the LORD filled the Dwelling. **35** Moses could not enter the meeting tent, because the cloud settled down upon it and the glory of the LORD filled the Dwelling. **36** Whenever the cloud rose from the Dwelling, the Israelites would set out on their journey. **37** But if the cloud did not lift, they would not go forward; only when it lifted did they go forward. **38** In the daytime the cloud of the LORD was seen over the Dwelling; whereas at night, fire was seen in the cloud by the whole house of Israel in all the stages of their journey.

---

y 2-8: Ex 40, 16-33.
z Ex 26, 30.
a 3ff: Ex 26, 33ff.
b 9ff: Ex 30, 26-29.
c 12-15: Ex 28, 41; 29, 4-9; Lv 8, 1-13.
d 20ff: Ex 25, 16, 21; 26, 33ff.
e Ex 25, 30.
f 30ff: Ex 30, 18ff.
g 34-38; Nm 9, 15-22.

40, 2: On the first day of the first month: almost a year after the departure of the Israelites from Egypt, Cf v 17.

The Book of
LEVITICUS

The name "Leviticus" was bestowed on the third book of the Pentateuch by the ancient Greek translators because a good part of this book consists of sacrificial and other ritual laws prescribed for the priests of the tribe of Levi.

Continuing the legislation given by God to Moses at Mount Sinai, Leviticus is almost entirely legislative in character; the rare narrative portions are subordinate to the main legislative theme. Generally speaking, the laws contained in this book serve to teach the Israelites that they should always keep themselves in a state of legal purity, or external sanctity, as a sign of their intimate union with the Lord. Accordingly, the central idea of Leviticus is contained in its oft-repeated injunction: "You shall be holy, because I, the LORD, am holy."

The main divisions of Leviticus are:
    I. Ritual of Sacrifices (Lv 1—7).
    II. Ceremony of Ordination (Lv 8—10).
    III. Laws regarding Legal Purity (Lv 11—16).
    IV. Code of Legal Holiness (Lv 17—26).
    V. Redemption of Offerings (Lv 27).

I: Ritual of Sacrifices

CHAPTER 1

Holocausts. 1 The LORD called Moses, and from the meeting tent gave him this message: 2 *a*"Speak to the Israelites and tell them: When any one of you wishes to bring an offering to the LORD, such an offering must be from the herd or from the flock.*

3 "If his holocaust* offering is from the herd, it must be a male without blemish.*b* To find favor with the LORD, he shall bring it to the entrance of the meeting tent 4 and there lay his hand on the head of the holocaust, so that it may be acceptable to make atonement for him.*c* 5 He shall then slaughter the bull before the LORD, but Aaron's sons, the priests, shall offer up its blood by splashing it on the sides of the altar which is at the entrance of the meeting tent.*d* 6 Then he shall skin the holocaust and cut it up into pieces. 7 After Aaron's sons, the priests, have put some burning embers on the altar and laid some wood on them, 8 they shall lay the pieces of meat, together with the head and the suet, on top of the wood and embers on the altar. 9 The inner organs and the shanks, however, the offerer shall first wash with water. The priest shall then burn the whole offering on the altar as a holocaust, a sweet-smelling oblation to the LORD.*e*

10 "If his holocaust offering is from the flock, that is, a sheep or a goat, he must bring a male without blemish. 11 This he shall slaughter before the LORD at the north side of the altar. Then Aaron's sons, the priests, shall splash its blood on the sides of the altar. 12 When the offerer has cut it up into pieces, the priest shall lay these, together with the head and suet, on top of the wood and the fire on the altar. 13 The inner organs and the shanks, however, the offerer shall first wash with water. The priest shall offer them up and then burn the whole offering on the altar as a holocaust, a sweet-smelling oblation to the LORD.

14 "If he offers a bird as a holocaust to the LORD, he shall choose a turtledove or a pigeon as his offering.*f* 15 Having brought it to the altar where it is to be burned, the priest shall snap its head loose and squeeze out its blood against the side of the altar.*g* 16 Its crop and feathers shall be removed and thrown on the ash heap at the east side of the altar. 17 Then, having split the bird down the middle without sepa-

---

a Lv 22, 18. 19.
b Ex 12, 5.
c Lv 3, 2. 8. 13; 4, 15; 8,
   14. 22; 16, 21; Ex 29,
   10. 15.
d Lv 3, 8.
e Lv 3, 5. 16; Ex 29, 18.
f Lv 5, 7; 12, 8; Lk 2, 24.
g Lv 5, 8.

---

*

1, 2: From the herd or from the flock: the only animals which could be used as sacrificial victims were either of the bovine class (bulls, cows and calves) or the ovine class (sheep and lambs, goats and kids). Excluded, therefore, were not only all wild animals, but also such "unclean" domestic animals as the camel and the ass. See note on Lv 11, 1ff.

1, 3: Holocaust: from the Greek word meaning "wholly burned," this is the technical term for the special type of sacrifice in which an entire animal except its hide was consumed in the fire on the altar. The primary purpose of this complete gift was to render glory and praise to God.

rating the halves, the priest shall burn it on the altar, over the wood on the fire, as a holocaust, a sweet-smelling oblation to the LORD.

CHAPTER 2

Cereal Offerings. 1 "When anyone wishes to bring a cereal offering to the LORD, his offering must consist of fine flour. He shall pour oil on it and put frankincense over it.*h* 2 When he has brought it to Aaron's sons, the priests, one of them shall take a handful of this fine flour and oil, together with all the frankincense, and this he shall burn on the altar as a token offering,* a sweet-smelling oblation to the LORD.*i* 3 The rest of the cereal offering belongs to Aaron and his sons. It is a most sacred oblation to the LORD.*j*

4 "When the cereal offering you present is baked in an oven, it must be in the form of unleavened cakes made of fine flour mixed with oil, or of unleavened wafers spread with oil. 5 If you present a cereal offering that is fried on a griddle, it must be of fine flour mixed with oil and unleavened.*k* 6 Such a cereal offering must be broken into pieces, and oil must be poured over it. 7 If you present a cereal offering that is prepared in a pot, it must be of fine flour, deep-fried in oil. 8 A cereal offering that is made in any of these ways you shall bring to the LORD, offering it to the priest, who shall take it to the altar. 9 Its token offering the priest shall then lift from the cereal offering and burn on the altar as a sweet-smelling oblation to the LORD. 10 The rest of the cereal offering belongs to Aaron and his sons. It is a most sacred oblation to the LORD.

11 "Every cereal offering that you present to the LORD shall be unleavened, for you shall not burn any leaven or honey as an oblation to the LORD.*l* 12 Such you may indeed present to the LORD in the offering of first fruits, but they are not to be placed on the altar for a pleasing odor. 13 However, every cereal offering that you present to the LORD shall be seasoned with salt.*m* Do not let the salt of the covenant of your God* be lacking from your cereal offering. On every offering you shall offer salt.

14 "If you present a cereal offering of first fruits to the LORD, you shall offer it in the form of fresh grits of new ears of grain, roasted by fire. 15 On this cereal offering you shall put oil and frankincense. 16 For its token offering the priest shall then burn some of the grits and oil, together with all the frankincense, as an oblation to the LORD.

CHAPTER 3

Peace Offerings. 1 "If someone in presenting a peace offering* makes his offering

from the herd, he may offer before the LORD either a male or a female animal, but it must be without blemish.*n* 2 He shall lay his hand on the head of his offering,*o* and then slaughter it at the entrance of the meeting tent; but Aaron's sons, the priests, shall splash its blood on the sides of the altar. 3 From the peace offering he shall offer as an oblation to the LORD the fatty membrane over the inner organs, and all the fat that adheres to them,*p* 4 as well as the two kidneys, with the fat on them near the loins, and the lobe of the liver,* which he shall sever above the kidneys. 5 All this Aaron's sons shall then burn on the altar with the holocaust,*q* on the wood over the fire, as a sweet-smelling oblation to the LORD.

6 "If the peace offering he presents to the LORD is from the flock, he may offer either a male or a female animal, but it must be without blemish. 7 If he presents a lamb as his offering, he shall bring it before the LORD, 8 and after laying his hand on the head of his offering, he shall slaughter it before the meeting tent; but Aaron's sons shall splash its blood on the sides of the altar. 9 As an oblation to the LORD he shall present the fat of the peace offering: the whole fatty tail,* which he must sever close to the spine, the fatty membrane over the inner organs, and all the fat that adheres to them,*r* 10 as well as the two kidneys, with the fat on them near the loins, and the lobe of the liver, which he must sever above the kidneys. 11 All this the priest shall burn on the altar as the food of the LORD's oblation.

12 "If he presents a goat, he shall bring it before the LORD, 13 and after laying his hand on its head, he shall slaughter it before the meeting tent; but Aaron's sons shall splash its blood on the sides of the altar. 14 From it he shall offer as an oblation to the LORD the fatty mem-

h Nm 15, 4.
i Lv 6, 15.
j Lv 7, 9f; Sir 7, 31; 1 Cor 5, 13.
k 1 Chr 23, 29.
l Lv 6, 16f; Mt 16, 12; Mk 8, 15; Lk 12, 1;
1 Cor 5, 7; Gal 5, 9.
m Ez 43, 24.
n Lv 22, 21.
o Lv 1, 4.
p Ex 29, 13. 22.
q Lv 6, 12.
r Lv 9, 19.

2, 2: Token offering: literally, "reminder." Instead of burning the whole cereal offering, they burned only this part of it on the altar; it thus corresponded to the fat of the peace offering. See note on Lv 3, 1.

2, 13: The salt of the covenant of your God: the partaking in common of salt by those seated together at table was an ancient symbol of friendship and alliance. Cf Mk 9, 49 and Col 4, 6; and see note on Nm 18, 19.

3, 1: Peace offering: thus the ancient versions have rendered the Hebrew word, which perhaps means more exactly, "fulfillment sacrifice," offered up in fulfillment of a vow. Cf Prv 7, 14. Its characteristic feature was the sacred banquet at which the offerer and his guests partook of the meat of the sacrificed animal. Cf Lv 7, 11–21.

3, 4: The lobe of the liver: some render, "the fatty covering of the liver."

3, 9: The whole fatty tail: see note on Ex 29, 22.

brane over the inner organs, and all the fat that adheres to them, **15** as well as the two kidneys, with the fat on them near the loins, and the lobe of the liver, which he must sever above the kidneys. **16** All this the priest shall burn on the altar as the food of the sweet-smelling oblation. All the fat belongs to the LORD. **17** This shall be a perpetual ordinance for your descendants wherever they may dwell. You shall not partake of any fat* or any blood.''^s

CHAPTER 4

Sin Offerings: For Priests.   **1** The LORD said to Moses, **2** "Tell the Israelites: When a person inadvertently commits a sin* against some command of the LORD by doing one of the forbidden things,^t **3** if it is the anointed priest* who thus sins and thereby makes the people also become guilty, he shall present to the LORD a young, unblemished bull as a sin offering for the sin he committed.^u **4** Bringing the bullock to the entrance of the meeting tent, before the LORD, he shall lay his hand on its head and slaughter it before the LORD.^v **5** The anointed priest shall then take some of the bullock's blood and bring it into the meeting tent, **6** where, dipping his finger in the blood, he shall sprinkle it seven times before the LORD, toward the veil of the sanctuary.^w **7** The priest shall also put some of the blood on the horns of the altar^x of fragrant incense which is before the LORD in the meeting tent. The rest of the bullock's blood he shall pour out at the base of the altar of holocausts which is at the entrance of the meeting tent. **8** From the sin-offering bullock he shall remove all the fat: the fatty membrane over the inner organs, and all the fat that adheres to them, **9** as well as the two kidneys, with the fat on them near the loins, and the lobe of the liver, which he must sever above the kidneys. **10** This is the same as is removed from the ox of the peace offering; and the priest shall burn it on the altar of holocausts. **11** The hide of the bullock and all its flesh, with its head, legs, inner organs and offal,^y **12** in short, the whole bullock, shall be brought outside the camp to a clean place where the ashes are deposited and there be burned up in a wood fire. At the place of the ash heap, there it must be burned.

For the Community.   **13** "If the whole community of Israel inadvertently and without even being aware of it does something that the LORD has forbidden and thus makes itself guilty,^z **14** should it later on become known that the sin was committed, the community shall present a young bull as a sin offering. They shall bring it before the meeting tent, **15** and here, before the LORD, the elders of the community shall lay their hands on the bullock's head.^a

When the bullock has been slaughtered before the LORD, **16** the anointed priest shall bring some of its blood into the meeting tent, **17** and dipping his finger in the blood, he shall sprinkle it seven times before the LORD, toward the veil. **18** He shall also put some of the blood on the horns of the altar of fragrant incense which is before the LORD in the meeting tent. The rest of the blood he shall pour out at the base of the altar of holocausts which is at the entrance of the meeting tent. **19** All of its fat he shall take from it and burn on the altar, **20** doing with this bullock just as he did with the other sin-offering bullock. Thus the priest shall make atonement for them, and they will be forgiven. **21** This bullock must also be brought outside the camp and burned, just as has been prescribed for the other one. This is the sin offering for the community.

For the Princes.   **22** "Should a prince commit a sin inadvertently by doing one of the things which are forbidden by some commandment of the LORD, his God, and thus become guilty, **23** if later on he learns of the sin he committed, he shall bring as his offering an unblemished male goat. **24** Having laid his hands on its head, he shall slaughter the goat as a sin offering before the LORD, in the place where the holocausts are slaughtered. **25** The priest shall then take some of the blood of the sin offering on his finger and put it on the horns of the altar of holocausts. The rest of the blood he shall pour out at the base of this altar. **26** All of the fat he shall burn on the altar like the fat of the peace offering.^b Thus the priest shall make atonement for the prince's sin, and it will be forgiven.

For Private Persons.   **27** "If a private person commits a sin inadvertently^c by doing one of the things which are forbidden by the commandments of the LORD, and thus becomes guilty, **28** should he later on learn of the sin he committed, he shall bring an unblemished

---

s Lv 17, 10-14; Gn 9, 4; Dt 12, 16. 23; 15, 23.
t Lv 5, 15. 17; Nm 15, 22-29.
u Heb 7, 27.
v Lv 1, 3f.
w Lv 8, 11.
x Lv 8, 15; 9, 9; 16, 18;

Ex 29, 12.
y Lv 8, 17; 9, 11; Ex 29, 14; Nm 19, 5.
z Lv 5, 2-4; Nm 15, 24-26.
a Lv 1, 4.
b Lv 3, 3-5.
c Nm 15, 27.

*

3, 17: Any fat: only the fat mentioned in vv 9f. 14f is meant; other fat could be eaten by the Israelites.

4, 2: A sin: not necessarily a moral fault; included are all the cases of ritual uncleanness which people necessarily incurred in certain unavoidable circumstances.

4, 3: The anointed priest: his violation of the ceremonial law brought a sort of collective guilt on all the people whom he represented before God. Sin offering: more exactly, "sacrifice for remitting sin"; sin is here understood as explained above.

she-goat as the offering for his sin. **29** Having laid his hand on the head of the sin offering,[d] he shall slaughter it at the place of the holocausts. **30** The priest shall then take some of its blood on his finger and put it on the horns of the altar of holocausts. The rest of the blood he shall pour out at the base of the altar. **31** All the fat shall be removed, just as the fat is removed from the peace offering, and the priest shall burn it on the altar for an odor pleasing to the LORD.[e] Thus the priest shall make atonement for him, and he will be forgiven.

32 "If, however, for his sin offering he presents a lamb, he shall bring an unblemished female. **33** Having laid his hand on its head, he shall slaughter this sin offering in the place where the holocausts are slaughtered. **34** The priest shall then take some of the blood of the sin offering on his finger and put it on the horns of the altar of holocausts. The rest of the blood he shall pour out at the base of the altar. **35** All the fat shall be removed, just as the fat is removed from the peace-offering lamb,[f] and the priest shall burn it on the altar with the other oblations of the LORD. Thus the priest shall make atonement for the man's sin, and it will be forgiven.

CHAPTER 5

For Special Cases.   **1** "If any person refuses to give the information which, as a witness of something he has seen or learned, he has been adjured to give, and thus commits a sin and has guilt to bear;[g] **2** or if someone, without being aware of it, touches any unclean thing, as the carcass of an unclean wild animal,[h] or that of an unclean domestic animal, or that of an unclean swarming creature, and thus becomes unclean and guilty; **3** or if someone, without being aware of it, touches some human uncleanness, whatever kind of uncleanness this may be, and then recognizes his guilt; **4** or if someone, without being aware of it, rashly utters an oath[i] to do good or evil, such as men are accustomed to utter rashly, and then recognizes that he is guilty of such an oath; **5** then whoever is guilty in any of these cases shall confess the sin he has incurred,[j] **6** and as his sin offering for the sin he has committed he shall bring to the LORD a female animal from the flock, a ewe lamb or a she-goat. The priest shall then make atonement for his sin.

7 "If, however, he cannot afford an animal of the flock, he shall bring to the LORD as the sin offering for his sin two turtledoves or two pigeons, one for a sin offering and the other for a holocaust.[k] **8** He shall bring them to the priest, who shall offer the one for the sin offering first. Snapping its head loose at the neck, yet without breaking it off completely,[l] **9** he shall

sprinkle some of the blood of the sin offering against the side of the altar.[m] The rest of the blood shall be squeezed out against the base of the altar. Such is the offering for sin. **10** The other bird shall be offered as a holocaust in the usual way. Thus the priest shall make atonement for the sin the man committed, and it will be forgiven.

11 "If he is unable to afford even two turtledoves or two pigeons, he shall present as a sin offering for his sin one tenth of an ephah of fine flour. He shall not put oil or frankincense on it, because it is a sin offering. **12** When he has brought it to the priest, the latter shall take a handful of this flour as a token offering, and this he shall burn as a sin offering on the altar with the other oblations of the LORD. **13** Thus the priest shall make atonement for the sin that the man committed in any of the above cases, and it will be forgiven.[n] The rest of the flour, like the cereal offerings, shall belong to the priest."

Guilt Offerings.   **14** The LORD said to Moses, **15** "If someone commits a sin by inadvertently cheating* in the LORD's sacred dues, he shall bring to the LORD as his guilt offering an unblemished ram from the flock, valued at two silver shekels according to the standard of the sanctuary shekel. **16** He shall also restore what he has sinfully withheld from the sanctuary, adding to it a fifth of its value.[o] This is to be given to the priest, who shall then make atonement for him with the guilt-offering ram, and he will be forgiven.

17 [p]"If someone, without being aware of it,* commits such a sin by doing one of the things which are forbidden by some commandment of the LORD, that he incurs guilt for which he must answer, **18** he shall bring as a guilt offering to the priest an unblemished ram of the flock of the established value. The priest shall then make atonement for the fault which was unwittingly committed, and it will be forgiven. **19** Such is the offering for guilt; the penalty of the guilt must be paid to the LORD."

---

d Lv 1, 4.
e Lv 1, 9; 3, 3-5.
f Lv 3, 3. 9.
g Prv 29, 24.
h Lv 11, 24. 31. 39; 12; 13; 15.
i Jgs 11, 30f; 1 Sm 14, 24; Mk 6, 23; Acts 23, 12.
j Lv 26, 40; Nm 5, 7.
k Lv 12, 8; Lk 2, 24.
l Lv 1, 15. 17.
m Lv 1, 15.
n Lv 4, 26. 35.
o Lv 22, 14.
p Lv 4, 2.

5, 15: Cheating: not offering the full amount in tithes, first fruits, etc. Guilt offering: its characteristic was a certain additional penalty imposed as reparation for the injustice involved in the fault which was atoned for by this sacrifice. However, in certain passages, e.g., Lv 14, 12f; Nm 6, 12; Ezr 10, 19, the term "guilt offering" is used for more important cases of "sin offerings" where no apparent injustice is involved.

5, 17: Without being aware of it: the case naturally presupposes that later on the offender learns of his mistake. Cf Lv 4, 13f.

20 The LORD said to Moses, **21** "If someone commits a sin of dishonesty against the LORD by denying his neighbor a deposit or a pledge for a stolen article, or by otherwise retaining his neighbor's goods unjustly, **22** or if, having found a lost article, he denies the fact and swears falsely about it with any of the sinful oaths that men make in such cases, **23** he shall therefore, since he has incurred guilt by his sin, restore the thing that was stolen or unjustly retained by him or the deposit left with him or the lost article he found **24** or whatever else he swore falsely about; on the day of his guilt offering he shall make full restitution of the thing itself, and in addition, give the owner one fifth of its value. **25** As his guilt offering he shall bring to the LORD an unblemished ram of the flock of the established value. When he has presented this as his guilt offering to the priest, **26** the latter shall make atonement for him before the LORD, and he will be forgiven whatever guilt he may have incurred."

CHAPTER 6

The Daily Holocaust. **1** The LORD said to Moses, **2** "Give Aaron and his sons the following command: This is the ritual* for holocausts. The holocaust is to remain on the hearth of the altar all night until the next morning, and the fire is to be kept burning on the altar. **3** The priest, clothed in his linen robe and wearing linen drawers on his body, shall take away the ashes to which the fire has reduced the holocaust on the altar, and lay them at the side of the altar. **4** Then, having taken off these garments and put on other garments, he shall carry the ashes to a clean place outside the camp. **5** The fire on the altar is to be kept burning; it must not go out. Every morning the priest shall put firewood on it. On this he shall lay out the holocaust and burn the fat of the peace offerings. **6** The fire is to be kept burning continuously on the altar; it must not go out.

Daily Cereal Offering. **7** "This is the ritual of the cereal offering. One of Aaron's sons shall first present it before the LORD, in front of the altar. **8** Then he shall take from it a handful of its fine flour and oil, together with all the frankincense that is on it, and this he shall burn on the altar as its token offering, a sweet-smelling oblation to the LORD. **9** The rest of it Aaron and his sons may eat; but it must be eaten in the form of unleavened cakes and in a sacred place: in the court of the meeting tent they shall eat it. **10** It shall not be baked with leaven. I have given it to them as their portion from the oblations of the LORD; it is most sacred, like the sin offering and the guilt offering. **11** All the male descendants of Aaron may partake of it as their rightful share in the oblations of the LORD perpetually throughout your generations. Whatever touches the oblations becomes sacred."

12 *The LORD said to Moses, **13** "This is the offering that Aaron and his sons shall present to the LORD [on the day he is anointed]: one tenth of a ephah of fine flour for the established cereal offering, half in the morning and half in the evening. **14** It shall be well kneaded and fried in oil on a griddle when you bring it in. Having broken the offering into pieces, you shall present it as a sweet-smelling oblation to the LORD. **15** Aaron's descendant who succeeds him as the anointed priest shall do likewise. This is a perpetual ordinance: for the Lord the whole offering shall be burned. **16** Every cereal offering of a priest shall be a whole burnt offering; it may not be eaten."

Sin Offerings. **17** The LORD said to Moses, **18** "Tell Aaron and his sons: This is the ritual for sin offerings. At the place where holocausts are slaughtered, there also, before the LORD, shall the sin offering be slaughtered. ^q It is most sacred. **19** The priest who presents the sin offering may partake of it; but it must be eaten in a sacred place, ^r in the court of the meeting tent. **20** Whatever touches its flesh shall become sacred. If any of its blood is spilled on a garment, the stained part must be washed in a sacred place. **21** A clay vessel in which it has been cooked shall thereafter be broken; ^s if it is cooked in a bronze vessel, this shall be scoured afterward and rinsed with water. **22** All the males of the priestly line may partake of the sin offering, since it is most sacred. ^t **23** But no one may partake of any sin offering of which some blood has been brought into the meeting tent ^u to make atonement in the sanctuary; such an offering must be burned up in the fire.

CHAPTER 7

Guilt Offerings. **1** "This is the ritual for guilt offerings, which are most sacred. **2** At the place where the holocausts are slaughtered, there also shall the guilt offering be slaughtered. ^v Its blood shall be splashed on the sides

---

q Lv 7, 2.
r Lv 10, 17.
s Lv 11, 33; 15, 12.

t Lv 7, 6; Nm 18, 10.
u Lv 4, 5; Heb 13, 11.
v Lv 6, 18.

*

6, 2: Ritual: literally, "law, instruction." Here, and in the following paragraphs, are given additional prescriptions for various kinds of sacrifices which were, in part, treated of in the preceding chapters.

6, 12–16: This is another law about the daily or "established" cereal offering. It differs in some respects from the preceding law (vv 7–11) and also from the law in Ex 29, 38–42. Hence, the words on the day he is anointed were probably added by some later scribe in order to avoid the difficulty of harmonizing this law with the other two laws on the same matter.

of the altar. **3** ʷAll of its fat shall be taken from it and offered up: the fatty tail, the fatty membrane over the inner organs, **4** as well as the two kidneys with the fat on them near the loins, and the lobe of the liver, which must be severed above the kidneys. **5** All this the priest shall burn on the altar as an oblation to the LORD. This is the guilt offering. **6** All the males of the priestly line may partake of it; but it must be eaten in a sacred place, since it is most sacred.ˣ

7 "Because the sin offering and the guilt offering are alike, both having the same ritual, the guilt offering likewise belongs to the priest who makes atonement with it. **8** Similarly, the priest who offers a holocaust for someone may keep for himself the hide of the holocaust that he has offered. **9** ʸAlso, every cereal offering that is baked in an oven or deep-fried in a pot or fried on a griddle shall belong to the priest who offers it, **10** whereas all cereal offeringsᶻ that are offered up dry or mixed with oil shall belong to all of Aaron's sons without distinction.

Peace Offerings. **11** "This is the ritual for the peace offerings that are presented to the LORD. **12** When anyone makes a peace offering in thanksgiving, together with his thanksgiving sacrifice he shall offer unleavened cakes mixed with oil, unleavened wafers spread with oil, and cakes made of fine flour mixed with oil and well kneaded. **13** His offering shall also include loaves of leavened bread* along with the victim of his peace offering for thanksgiving. **14** From each of his offerings he shall present one portion as a contribution to the LORD; this shall belong to the priest who splashes the blood of the peace offering.

15 ᵃ"The flesh of the thanksgiving sacrifice shall be eaten on the day it is offered; none of it may be kept till the next day. **16** However, if the sacrifice is a votive or a free-will offering, it should indeed be eaten on the day the sacrifice is offered, but what is left over may be eaten on the next day. **17** Should any flesh from the sacrifice be left over on the third day, it must be burned up in the fire. **18** If, therefore, any of the flesh of the peace offering is eaten on the third day, it shall not win favor for him nor shall it be reckoned to his credit; rather, it shall be considered as refuse, and anyone who eats of it shall have his guilt to bear. **19** Should the flesh touch anything unclean, it may not be eaten, but shall be burned up in the fire.

"All who are clean may partake of this flesh. **20** If, however, someone while in a state of uncleanness eats any of the flesh of a peace offering belonging to the LORD, that person shall be cut off from his people. **21** Likewise, if someone touches anything unclean, whether the uncleanness be of human or of animal origin

or from some loathsome crawling creature, and then eats of a peace offering belonging to the LORD, that person, too, shall be cut off from his people."

Prohibition against Blood and Fat.
22 The LORD said to Moses, **23** "Tell the Israelites: You shall not eat the fat* of any ox or sheep or goat.ᵇ **24** Although the fat of an animal that has died a natural death or has been killed by wild beasts may be put to any other use, you may not eat it.ᶜ **25** If anyone eats the fat of an animal from which an oblation is made to the LORD, such a one shall be cut off from his people. **26** Wherever you dwell, you shall not partake of any blood, be it of bird or of animal. **27** Every person who partakes of any blood shall be cut off from his people."ᵈ

The Portions for Priests. **28** The LORD said to Moses, **29** "Tell the Israelites: He who presents a peace offering to the LORD shall bring a part of it as his special offering to him, **30** carrying in with his own hands the oblations to the LORD. The fat is to be brought in, together with the breast, which is to be waved as a wave offering* before the LORD. **31** The priest shall burn the fat on the altar,ᵉ but the breast belongs to Aaron and his sons. **32** Moreover, from your peace offering you shall give to the priest the right leg as a raised offering. **33** The descendant of Aaron who offers up the blood and fat of the peace offering shall have the right leg as his portion, **34** for from the peace offerings of the Israelites I have taken the breast that is waved and the leg that is raised up, and I have given them to Aaron, the priest, and to his sons by a perpetual ordinance as a contribution from the Israelites."ᶠ

35 This is the priestly share* from the oblations of the LORD, allotted to Aaron and his sons on the day he called them to be the priests of the LORD; **36** on the day he anointed them the LORD ordered the Israelites to give them this share by

---

w 3-5: Lv 3, 4. 9f. 14-16; 4, 8f.
x Lv 6, 22.
y Lv 2, 3-10; Nm 18, 9; Ez 44, 29.
z Lv 2, 14f.
a 15-18: Lv 19, 6f.
b Lv 3, 17.
c Lv 22, 8.
d Lv 17, 10.
e Lv 3, 11. 16.
f Ex 29, 27f.

*

7, 13: Leavened bread: these loaves were not burned on the altar (cf Lv 2, 11), but were eaten at the "communion" meal which followed the sacrifice. See note on Lv 3, 1.

7, 23: The fat: only the particular portions specified in Lv 3, 9f. 14f are meant. Ox or sheep or goat: such animals as could be sacrificed; the fat of other clean animals could be eaten.

7, 30–34: A wave offering . . . a raised offering: these ceremonies are described in Ex 29, 24–28. The Hebrew word for "raised offering" is also rendered, in certain contexts, as "contribution."

7, 35: The priestly share: literally, "the anointed part."

a perpetual ordinance throughout their generations.

37 This is the ritual for holocausts, cereal offerings, sin offerings, guilt offerings, [ordination offerings] and peace offerings, **38** which the LORD enjoined on Moses at Mount Sinai at the time when he commanded the Israelites in the wilderness of Sinai to bring their offerings to the LORD.

II: Ceremony of Ordination

CHAPTER 8

Ordination of Aaron and His Sons.

1 The LORD[g] said to Moses,* **2** "Take Aaron and his sons, together with the vestments,* the anointing oil, the bullock for a sin offering, the two rams, and the basket of unleavened food. **3** Then assemble the whole community at the entrance of the meeting tent." **4** And Moses did as the LORD had commanded. When the community had assembled at the entrance of the meeting tent, **5** Moses told them what the LORD had ordered to be done. **6** Bringing forward Aaron and his sons, he first washed them with water.[h] **7** Then he put the tunic on Aaron,[i] girded him with the sash, clothed him with the robe, placed the ephod on him, and girded him with the embroidered belt of the ephod, fastening it around him. **8** [j]He then set the breastpiece on him, with the Urim and Thummim* in it, **9** [k]and put the miter on his head, attaching the gold plate, the sacred diadem, over the front of the miter, at his forehead, as the LORD had commanded him to do.

10 Taking the anointing oil, Moses anointed and consecrated the Dwelling, with all that was in it.[l] **11** Then he sprinkled some of this oil seven times on the altar, and anointed the altar, with all its appurtenances, and the laver, with its base, thus consecrating them. **12** He also poured some of the anointing oil on Aaron's head, thus consecrating him.[m] **13** Moses likewise brought forward Aaron's sons, clothed them with tunics, girded them with sashes, and put turbans on them, as the LORD had commanded him to do.

Ordination Sacrifices.

14 When he had brought forward the bullock for a sin offering, Aaron and his sons laid their hands on its head. **15** Then Moses slaughtered it, and taking some of its blood, with his finger he put it on the horns around the altar, thus purifying the altar. He also made atonement for the altar by pouring out the blood at its base when he consecrated it.[n] **16** Taking all the fat that was over the inner organs, as well as the lobe of the liver and the two kidneys with their fat,[o] Moses burned them on the altar. **17** The bullock, however, with its

hide and flesh and offal he burned in the fire outside the camp, as the LORD had commanded him to do.

18 He next brought forward the holocaust ram, and Aaron and his sons laid their hands on its head. **19** When he had slaughtered it, Moses splashed its blood on all sides of the altar. **20** After cutting up the ram into pieces, he burned the head, the cut-up pieces and the suet; **21** then, having washed the inner organs and the shanks with water, he also burned these remaining parts of the ram on the altar as a holocaust, a sweet-smelling oblation to the LORD, as the LORD had commanded him to do.

22 Then he brought forward the second ram, the ordination ram, and Aaron and his sons laid their hands on its head. **23** When he had slaughtered it, Moses took some of its blood and put it on the tip of Aaron's right ear, on the thumb of his right hand, and on the big toe of his right foot.[p] **24** Moses had the sons of Aaron also come forward, and he put some of the blood on the tips of their right ears, on the thumbs of their right hands, and on the big toes of their right feet. The rest of the blood he splashed on the sides of the altar. **25** He then took the fat: the fatty tail and all the fat over the inner organs, the lobe of the liver and the two kidneys with their fat, and likewise the right leg; **26** from the basket of unleavened food that was set before the LORD he took one unleavened cake, one loaf of bread made with oil, and one wafer; these he placed on top of the portions of fat and the right leg. **27** He then put all these things into the hands of Aaron and his sons, whom he had wave them as a wave offering before the LORD. **28** When he had received them back, Moses burned them with the holocaust on the altar as the ordination offering, a sweet-smelling oblation to the LORD. **29** He then took the breast and waved it as a wave offering before the LORD; this was Moses' own portion of the ordination ram. All this was in keeping with the LORD's command to Moses. **30** Taking some of the anointing oil and some of the blood that was on the altar, Moses sprinkled with it Aaron and his vestments, as well as his sons and their vestments, thus consecrating both Aaron and his vestments and his sons and their vestments.

31 Finally, Moses said to Aaron and his sons, "Boil the flesh at the entrance of the

---

g 1-36: cf Ex 29.   l Ex 30, 26.
h 6f: Ex 40, 12f.   m Sir 45, 15.
i 7ff: Ex 45, 8-13.   n Lv 4, 7; Heb 9, 22.
j Ex 28, 30.   o 16f: Lv 3, 4; 4, 8-11.
k Ex 28, 36.   p Lv 14, 14.

*

8, 1–9, 21: Though presented in the form of a narrative, this description of Aaron's ordination was intended to serve as a guide for all future ordinations.

8, 2: The vestments, etc.: already described in Ex 28–29.

8, 8: The Urim and Thummim: see note on Ex 28, 30.

meeting tent, and there eat it with the bread that is in the basket of the ordination offering, in keeping with the command I have received: 'Aaron and his sons shall eat of it.' **32** What is left over of the flesh and the bread you shall burn up in the fire. **33** Moreover, you are not to depart from the entrance of the meeting tent for seven days, until the days of your ordination are completed; for your ordination is to last for seven days. **34** *The LORD has commanded that what has been done today be done to make atonement for you. **35** Hence you must remain at the entrance of the meeting tent day and night for seven days, carrying out the prescriptions of the LORD; otherwise you shall die; for this is the command I have received." **36** So Aaron and his sons did all that the LORD had commanded through Moses.

CHAPTER 9

Octave of the Ordination. **1** On the eighth day Moses summoned Aaron and his sons, together with the elders of Israel, **2** and said to Aaron, "Take a calf for a sin offering and a ram for a holocaust, both without blemish, and offer them before the LORD. **3** Tell the elders of Israel, too: Take a he-goat for a sin offering, a calf and a lamb, both unblemished yearlings, for a holocaust, **4** and an ox and a ram for a peace offering, to sacrifice them before the LORD, along with a cereal offering mixed with oil; for today he LORD will reveal himself to you." **5** So they brought what Moses had ordered. When the whole community had come forward and stood before the LORD, **6** Moses said, "This is what the LORD orders you to do, that the glory of the LORD may be revealed to you. **7** Come up to the altar," Moses then told Aaron, "and offer your sin offering and your holocaust in atonement for yourself and for your family; then present the offering of the people in atonement for them, as the LORD has commanded."

8 Going up to the altar, Aaron first slaughtered the calf that was his own sin offering. **9** When his sons presented the blood to him, he dipped his finger in the blood and put it on the horns of the altar. The rest of the blood he poured out at the base of the altar. **10** He then burned on the altar the fat, the kidneys and the lobe of the liver that were taken from the sin offering, as the LORD had commanded Moses; **11** but the flesh and the hide he burned up in the fire outside the camp. **12** Then Aaron slaughtered his holocaust. When his sons brought him the blood, he splashed it on all sides of the altar. **13** They then brought him the pieces and the head of the holocaust, and he burned them on the altar. **14** Having washed the inner organs

and the shanks, he burned these also with the holocaust on the altar.

15 Thereupon he had the people's offering brought up. Taking the goat that was for the people's sin offering, he slaughtered it and offered it up for sin as before. **16** Then he brought forward the holocaust, other than the morning holocaust, and offered it in the usual manner. **17** He then presented the cereal offering; taking a handful of it, he burned it on the altar. **18** Finally he slaughtered the ox and the ram, the peace offering of the people. When his sons brought him the blood, Aaron splashed it on all sides of the altar. **19** The portions of fat from the ox and from the ram, the fatty tail, the fatty membrane over the inner organs, the two kidneys, with the fat that is on them, and the lobe of the liver, *q* **20** he placed on top of the breasts and burned them on the altar, **21** *r*having first waved the breasts and the right legs as a wave offering before the LORD, in keeping with the LORD's command to Moses.

Revelation of the Lord Glory. **22** Aaron then raised his hands over the people and blessed them. When he came down from offering the sin offering and holocaust and peace offering, **23** Moses and Aaron went into the meeting tent.*s* On coming out they again blessed the people. Then the glory of the LORD was revealed to all the people. **24** Fire came forth from the LORD's presence*t* and consumed the holocaust and the remnants of the fat on the altar. Seeing this, all the people cried out and fell prostrate.

CHAPTER 10

Nadab and Abihu. **1** During this time Aaron's sons Nadab and Abihu* took their censers and, strewing incense on the fire they had put in them,*u* they offered up before the LORD profane fire, such as he had not authorized. **2** Fire* therefore came forth from the LORD's presence and consumed them,*v* so that they died in his presence. **3** Moses then said to Aaron, "This is as the LORD said:

---

q 19f: Lv 3, 3ff.
r Lv 7, 31f.
s Nm 6, 23-26.
t 1 Kgs 18, 38; 2 Chr 7, 1.

u Lv 16, 1; Nm 3, 4; 26, 61; 1 Chr 24, 2.
v Nm 16, 35.
w Lv 21, 17. 21.

*———————

8, 34: The sense is not quite clear. Either the verse gives merely the reason why God ordered this ceremony, or it contains God's command that the same ceremony be used in all future ordinations, or it decrees a repetition of the entire ceremony on each of the seven days. At least a sin offering for atonement was made on each of these days. Cf Ex 29, 29–36.

10, 1: Nadab and Abihu: the older sons of Aaron. Cf Ex 6, 23f.

10, 2: Fire: perhaps after the manner of lightning.

10, 3: I will manifest my sacredness: the presence of God

Through those who approach me I will
   manifest my sacredness;*
   In the sight of all the people I will reveal
   my glory.''[w]

But Aaron said nothing. **4** Then Moses summoned Mishael and Elzaphan, the sons of Aaron's uncle Uzziel, with the order, ''Come, remove your kinsmen from the sanctuary and carry them to a place outside the camp.'' **5** So they went in and took them, in their tunics,* outside the camp, as Moses had commanded.

Conduct of the Priests.

6 Moses said to Aaron and his sons Eleazar and Ithamar, ''Do not bare your heads* or tear your garments,[x] lest you bring not only death on yourselves but God's wrath also on the whole community. Your kinsmen, the rest of the house of Israel, shall mourn for those whom the LORD's fire has smitten; **7** but do not you go beyond the entry of the meeting tent, else you shall die; for the anointing oil of the LORD is upon you.'' So they did as Moses told them.

8 The LORD said to Aaron, **9** ''When you are to go to the meeting tent, you and your sons are forbidden under pain of death, by a perpetual ordinance throughout your generations, to drink any wine or strong drink.[y] **10** You must be able to distinguish between what is sacred and what is profane, between what is clean and what is unclean;[z] **11** you must teach the Israelites all the laws that the LORD has given them through Moses.''[a]

The Eating of the Priestly Portions.

12 Moses said to Aaron and his surviving sons, Eleazar and Ithamar, ''Take the cereal offering left over from the oblations of the LORD, and eat it beside the altar in the form of unleavened cakes.[b] Since it is most sacred, **13** you must eat it in a sacred place. This is your due from the oblations of the LORD, and that of your sons; such is the command I have received. **14** [c]With your sons and daughters you shall also eat the breast of the wave offering and the leg of the raised offering, in a clean place; for these have been assigned to you and your children as your due from the peace offerings of the Israelites. **15** The leg of the raised offering and the breast of the wave offering shall first be brought in with the oblations, the fatty portions, that are to be waved as a wave offering before the LORD. Then they shall belong to you and your children by a perpetual ordinance, as the LORD has commanded.''

16 *When Moses inquired about the goat of the sin offering, he discovered that it had all been burned. So he was angry with the surviving sons of Aaron, Eleazar and Ithamar, and said, **17** [d]''Why did you not eat the sin offering in the sacred place, since it is most sacred? It has

been given to you that you might bear the guilt of the community and make atonement for them before the LORD. **18** If its blood was not brought into the inmost part of the sanctuary, you should certainly have eaten the offering in the sanctuary, in keeping with the command I had received.'' **19** Aaron answered Moses, ''Even though they presented their sin offering and holocaust before the LORD today, yet this misfortune has befallen me. Had I then eaten of the sin offering today, would it have been pleasing to the LORD?'' **20** On hearing this, Moses was satisfied.

III: Laws Regarding Legal Purity

CHAPTER 11

Clean and Unclean Food.

1 The LORD said to Moses and Aaron,* **2** ''Speak to the Israelites and tell them: Of all land animals these are the ones you may eat: **3** any animal that has hoofs you may eat, provided it is cloven-footed and chews the cud. **4** But you shall not eat any of the following that only chew the cud or only have hoofs: the camel, which indeed chews the cud, but does not have hoofs and is therefore unclean for you; **5** the rock badger,* which indeed chews the cud, but does not have hoofs and is therefore unclean for you; **6** the hare, which indeed chews the cud, but does not have hoofs and is therefore unclean for you; and the pig,

---

x Lv 21, 10.
y Ez 44, 21.
z Lv 11, 47; 20, 25; Ez 22, 26; 44, 23.

a Sir 45, 16.
b Lv 6, 16.
c 14f: Lv 7, 34.
d Lv 6, 18f.

---

*

is so sacred that it strikes dead those who approach him without the proper holiness. Cf Nm 20, 13; Ez 28, 22.

10, 5: In their tunics: they were buried just as they were, with no shroud or funeral solemnities.

10, 6: Bare your heads: go without the customary head covering, as a sign of mourning. Some interpreters, however, understand it as the cutting off of one's hair, which ordinarily all the Israelites, men as well as women, let grow long. Cf Is 15, 2; Jer 7, 29. Still others understand the verb to mean ''to let one's hair hang loose and wild.'' Cf Lv 13, 45; 21, 10, where the same phrase is used.

10, 16–19: Eleazar and Ithamar burned the entire goat of the sin offering (Lv 9, 15) instead of eating it in a sacred place (Lv 6, 19) to bear the guilt of the community. Aaron defends this action of his sons against Moses' displeasure by implying that they did not have sufficient sanctity to eat the flesh of the victim and thus perform the expiation of the people. They themselves still labored under the blow of the divine anger which struck their brothers Nadab and Abihu.

11, 1ff: These distinctions between edible and inedible meats were probably based on traditional ideas of hygiene, but they are here given a moral, religious basis: the inedible varieties are classified as ''unclean'' to remind the Israelites that they are to be a pure and holy people, dedicated to the Lord.

11, 5f: According to modern zoology, the rock badger (hyrax Syriacus) is classified as an ungulate, and the hare as a rodent; neither is a ruminant. They appear to chew their food as the true ruminants do, and it is upon this appearance that the classification in the text is based.

7 which does indeed have hoofs and is cloven-footed, but does not chew the cud and is therefore unclean for you. **8** Their flesh you shall not eat, and their dead bodies you shall not touch; they are unclean for you.

9 "Of the various creatures that live in the water, you may eat the following: whatever in the seas or in river waters has both fins and scales you may eat. **10** But of the various creatures that crawl or swim in the water, whether in the sea or in the rivers, all those that lack either fins or scales are loathsome for you, **11** and you shall treat them as loathsome. Their flesh you shall not eat, and their dead bodies you shall loathe. **12** Every water creature that lacks fins or scales is loathsome for you.

13 "Of the birds, these you shall loathe and, as loathsome, they shall not be eaten:* the eagle, the vulture, the osprey, **14** the kite, the various species of falcons, **15** the various species of crows, **16** the ostrich, the nightjar, the gull, the various species of hawks, **17** the owl, the cormorant, the screech owl, **18** the barn owl, the desert owl, the buzzard, **19** the stork, the various species of herons, the hoopoe, and the bat.*

20 "The various winged insects that walk on all fours are loathsome for you. **21** But of the various winged insects that walk on all fours you may eat those that have jointed legs for leaping on the ground; **22** hence of these you may eat the following: the various kinds of locusts,* the various kinds of grasshoppers, the various kinds of katydids, and the various kinds of crickets. **23** All other winged insects that have four legs are loathsome for you.

24 *"Such is the uncleanness that you contract, that everyone who touches their dead bodies shall be unclean until evening, **25** and everyone who picks up any part of their dead bodies shall wash his garments and be unclean until evening. **26** All hoofed animals that are not cloven-footed* or do not chew the cud are unclean for you; everyone who touches them becomes unclean. **27** Of the various quadrupeds, all those that walk on paws* are unclean for you; everyone who touches their dead bodies shall be unclean until evening, **28** and everyone who picks up their dead bodies shall wash his garments and be unclean until evening. Such is their uncleanness for you.

29 "Of the creatures that swarm on the ground, the following are unclean for you: the rat, the mouse, the various kinds of lizards, **30** the gecko, the chameleon, the agama, the skink, and the mole. **31** Among the various swarming creatures, these are unclean for you. Everyone who touches them when they are dead shall be unclean until evening. **32** Everything on which one of them falls when dead becomes unclean. Any such article that men use, whether

it be an article of wood, cloth, leather or goat hair, must be put in water and remain unclean until evening, when it again becomes clean. **33** Should any of these creatures fall into a clay vessel, everything in it becomes unclean, and the vessel itself you must break. **34** Any solid food that was in contact with water, and any liquid that men drink, in any such vessel become unclean. **35** Any object on which one of their dead bodies falls, becomes unclean; if it is an oven or a jar-stand, this must be broken to pieces; they are unclean and shall be treated as unclean by you. **36** However, a spring or a cistern for collecting water remains clean; but whoever touches the dead body* becomes unclean. **37** Any sort of cultivated grain remains clean even though one of their dead bodies falls on it; **38** but if the grain has become moistened, it becomes unclean when one of these falls on it.

39 "When one of the animals that you could otherwise eat, dies of itself, anyone who touches its dead body shall be unclean until evening; **40** and anyone who eats of its dead body shall wash his garments and be unclean until evening;*ᵉ* so also, anyone who removes its dead body shall wash his garments and be unclean until evening.

41 "All the creatures that swarm on the ground are loathsome and shall not be eaten. **42** Whether it crawls on its belly, goes on all fours, or has many legs, you shall eat no swarming creature: they are loathsome. **43** Do not make yourselves loathsome or unclean with any swarming creature through being contaminated by them.*ᶠ* **44** For I, the LORD, am your God; and you shall make and keep yourselves holy, because I am holy.*ᵍ* You shall not make yourselves unclean, then, by any swarming creature that crawls on the ground. **45** Since I, the LORD, brought you up from the land of Egypt that I might be your God, you shall be holy, because I am holy.

46 "This is the law for animals and birds and

---

e Lv 17, 15; 22, 8.　　　　g Lv 19, 2; 20, 7. 26; Mt
f 43f: Lv 20, 25f.　　　　　　5, 48; 1 Pt 1, 16.

*

11, 13–19. 30: The identification of the various Hebrew names for these birds and reptiles is in many cases uncertain.

11, 19: The bat: actually a mammal, but listed here with the birds because of its wings.

11, 22: The Hebrew distinguishes four classes of edible locust-like insects, but the difference between them is quite uncertain. Cf Mt 3, 4.

11, 24–28: This paragraph sharpens the prohibition against unclean animals: not only is their meat unfit for food, but contact with their dead bodies makes a person ritually unclean.

11, 26: All hoofed animals that are not cloven-footed: such as the horse and the ass.

11, 27: All those that walk on paws: such as dogs and cats.

11, 36: Whoever touches the dead body: to remove the dead insect from the water supply.

for all the creatures that move about in the water or swarm on the ground, **47** that you may distinguish between the clean and the unclean, between creatures that may be eaten and those that may not be eaten.''[h]

CHAPTER 12

Uncleanness of Childbirth. **1** The LORD said to Moses, **2** ''Tell the Israelites: When a woman has conceived and gives birth to a boy, she shall be unclean* for seven days, with the same uncleanness as at her menstrual period.[i] **3** On the eighth day, the flesh of the boy's foreskin shall be circumcised,[j] **4** and then she shall spend thirty-three days more in becoming purified of her blood; she shall not touch anything sacred nor enter the sanctuary till the days of her purification are fulfilled. **5** If she gives birth to a girl, for fourteen days she shall be as unclean as at her menstruation, after which she shall spend sixty-six days in becoming purified of her blood.

6 ''When the days of her purification for a son or for a daughter are fulfilled,[k] she shall bring to the priest at the entrance of the meeting tent a yearling lamb for a holocaust and a pigeon or a turtledove for a sin offering. **7** The priest shall offer them up before the LORD to make atonement for her, and thus she will be clean again after her flow of blood. Such is the law for the woman who gives birth to a boy or a girl child. **8** *If, however, she cannot afford a lamb, she may take two turtledoves or two pigeons,[l] the one for a holocaust and the other for a sin offering. The priest shall make atonement for her, and thus she will again be clean.''

CHAPTER 13

Leprosy. **1** The LORD said to Moses and Aaron, **2** [m]''If someone has on his skin* a scab or pustule or blotch which appears to be the sore of leprosy, he shall be brought to Aaron, the priest, or to one of the priests among his descendants, **3** who shall examine the sore on his skin. If the hair on the sore has turned white and the sore itself shows that it has penetrated below the skin, it is indeed the sore of leprosy; the priest, on seeing this, shall declare the man unclean. **4** If, however, the blotch on the skin is white, but does not seem to have penetrated below the skin, nor has the hair turned white, the priest shall quarantine the stricken man for seven days. **5** On the seventh day the priest shall again examine him. If he judges that the sore has remained unchanged and has not spread on the skin, the priest shall quarantine him for another seven days, **6** and once more examine him on the seventh day. If the sore is now dying out and has not spread on the skin, the priest

shall declare the man clean; it was merely eczema. The man shall wash his garments and so become clean. **7** But if, after he has shown himself to the priest to be declared clean, the eczema spreads at all on his skin, he shall once more show himself to the priest. **8** Should the priest, on examining it, find that the eczema has indeed spread on the skin, he shall declare the man unclean; it is leprosy.

9 ''When someone is stricken with leprosy, he shall be brought to the priest. **10** Should the priest, on examining him, find that there is a white scab on the skin which has turned the hair white and that there is raw flesh in it, **11** it is skin leprosy that has long developed. The priest shall declare the man unclean without first quarantining him, since he is certainly unclean. **12** If leprosy breaks out on the skin* and, as far as the priest can see, covers all the skin of the stricken man from head to foot, **13** should the priest then, on examining him, find that the leprosy does cover his whole body, he shall declare the stricken man clean; since it has all turned white, the man is clean. **14** But as soon as raw flesh appears on him, he is unclean; **15** on observing the raw flesh, the priest shall declare him unclean, because raw flesh is unclean; it is leprosy. **16** If, however, the raw flesh again turns white, he shall return to the priest; **17** should the latter, on examining him, find that the sore has indeed turned white, he shall declare the stricken man clean, and thus he will be clean.

18 ''If a man who had a boil on his skin which later healed, **19** should now in the place of the boil have a white scab or a pink blotch, he shall show himself to the priest. **20** If the latter, on examination, sees that it is deeper than the skin and that the hair has turned white, he shall declare the man unclean: it is the sore of leprosy that has broken out in the boil. **21** But if the priest, on examining him, finds that there

---

h Lv 10, 10.   k Lk 2, 22.
i Lv 15, 19.   l Lv 1, 14; Lk 2, 24.
j Gn 17, 12; Jn 7, 22.   m Dt 24, 8.

---

*

12, 2f: The uncleanness of the woman was more serious during the first period, the seven days after the birth of a boy or the fourteen days after the birth of a girl; only during this period would the rules given in Lv 15, 19–24 apply.

12, 8: Forty days after the birth of Jesus, his Virgin Mother made this offering of the poor (Lk 2, 22. 24); since the holocaust was offered in thanksgiving for the birth of the child, this was most fittingly offered by Mary. However, because of her miraculous delivery, she was not really obliged to make the sin offering of purification.

13, 2ff: Various kinds of skin blemishes are treated here which were not contagious but simply disqualified their subjects from association with others, especially in public worship, until they were declared ritually clean. The Hebrew term used does not refer to Hansen's disease, currently called leprosy.

13, 12ff: If leprosy breaks out on the skin: the symptoms described here point to a form of skin disease which is merely on the surface and therefore easily cured.

is no white hair in it and that it is not deeper than the skin and is already dying out, the priest shall quarantine him for seven days. **22** If it has then spread on the skin, the priest shall declare him unclean; the man is stricken. **23** But if the blotch remains in its place without spreading, it is merely the scar of the boil; the priest shall therefore declare him clean.

24 "If a man had a burn on his skin, and the proud flesh of the burn now becomes a pink or a white blotch, **25** the priest shall examine it. If the hair has turned white on the blotch and this seems to have penetrated below the skin, it is leprosy that has broken out in the burn; the priest shall therefore declare him unclean and stricken with leprosy. **26** But if the priest, on examining it, finds that there is no white hair on the blotch and that this is not deeper than the skin and is already dying out, the priest shall quarantine him for seven days. **27** Should the priest, when examining it on the seventh day, find that it has spread at all on the skin, he shall declare the man unclean and stricken with leprosy. **28** But if the blotch remains in its place without spreading on the skin and is already dying out, it is merely the scab of the burn; the priest shall therefore declare the man clean, since it is only the scar of the burn.

29 "When a man or a woman has a sore on the head or cheek, **30** should the priest, on examining it, find that the sore has penetrated below the skin and that there is fine yellow hair on it, the priest shall declare the person unclean, for this is scall,* a leprous disease of the head or cheek. **31** But if the priest, on examining the scall sore, finds that it has not penetrated below the skin, though the hair on it may not be black, the priest shall quarantine the person with scall sore for seven days, **32** and on the seventh day again examine the sore. If the scall has not spread and has no yellow hair on it and does not seem to have penetrated below the skin, **33** the man shall shave himself, but not on the diseased spot. Then the priest shall quarantine him for another seven days. **34** If the priest, when examining the scall on the seventh day, finds that it has not spread on the skin and that it has not penetrated below the skin, he shall declare the man clean; the latter shall wash his garments, and thus he will be clean. **35** But if the scall spreads at all on his skin after he has been declared clean, **36** the priest shall again examine it. If the scall has indeed spread on the skin, he need not look for yellow hair; the man is surely unclean. **37** If, however, he judges that the scall has remained in its place and that black hair has grown on it, the disease has been healed; the man is clean, and the priest shall declare him clean.

38 "When the skin of a man or a woman is spotted with white blotches, **39** the priest shall make an examination. If the blotches on the skin are white and already dying out, it is only tetter* that has broken out on the skin, and the person therefore is clean.

40 "When a man loses the hair of his head, he is not unclean merely because of his bald crown. **41** So too, if he loses the hair on the front of his head, he is not unclean merely because of his bald forehead. **42** But when there is a pink sore on his bald crown or bald forehead, it is leprosy that is breaking out there. **43** The priest shall examine him; and if the scab on the sore of the bald spot has the same pink appearance as that of skin leprosy of the fleshy part of the body, **44** the man is leprous and unclean, and the priest shall declare him unclean by reason of the sore on his head.

45 "The one who bears the sore of leprosy shall keep his garments rent and his head bare, and shall muffle his beard; he shall cry out, 'Unclean, unclean!' **46** As long as the sore is on him he shall declare himself unclean, since he is in fact unclean. *n* He shall dwell apart, making his abode outside the camp.

Leprosy of Clothes.   **47** "When a leprous infection* is on a garment of wool or of linen, **48** or on woven or knitted material of linen or wool, or on a hide or anything made of leather, **49** if the infection on the garment or hide, or on the woven or knitted material, or on any leather article is greenish or reddish, the thing is indeed infected with leprosy and must be shown to the priest. **50** Having examined the infection, the priest shall quarantine the infected article for seven days.

51 "On the seventh day the priest shall again examine the infection. If it has spread on the garment, or on the woven or knitted material, or on the leather, whatever be its use, the infection is malignant leprosy, and the article is unclean. **52** He shall therefore burn up the garment, or the woven or knitted material of wool or linen, or the leather article, whatever it may be, which is infected; since it has malignant leprosy, it must be destroyed by fire. **53** But if the priest, on examining the infection, finds that it has not spread on the garment, or on the woven or knitted material, or on the leather article, **54** he shall give orders to have the infected article washed and then quarantined for another seven days.

55 "Then the priest shall again examine the infected article after it has been washed. If the

---

n Nm 5, 2; 12, 14f;   2 Kgs 15, 5; Lk 17, 12.

*

13, 30:   Scall: a scabby or scaly eruption of the scalp. According to some, "ringworm."

13, 39:   Tetter: vitiligo, a harmless form of skin disease.

13, 47:   A leprous infection: some mold or fungus growth resembling human leprosy.

infection has not changed its appearance, even
though it may not have spread, the article is
unclean and shall be destroyed by fire. **56** But
if the priest, on examining the infection, finds
that it is dying out after the washing, he shall
tear the infected part out of the garment, or the
leather, or the woven or knitted material. **57** If,
however, the infection again appears on the garment, or on the woven or knitted material, or on
the leather article, it is still virulent and the thing
infected shall be destroyed by fire. **58** But if,
after the washing, the infection has left the garment, or the woven or knitted material, or the
leather article, the thing shall be washed a second time, and thus it will be clean. **59** This is
the law for leprous infection[o] on a garment of
wool or linen, or on woven or knitted material,
or on any leather article, to determine whether
it is clean or unclean.''

CHAPTER 14

Purification after Leprosy. 1 The LORD
said to Moses, **2** [p]''This is the law for the victim of leprosy at the time of his purification. He
shall be brought to the priest, **3** who is to go
outside the camp to examine him. If the priest
finds that the sore of leprosy has healed in the
leper, **4** he shall order the man who is to be
purified, to get two live, clean birds, as well as
some cedar wood, scarlet yarn,* and hyssop.
5 The priest shall then order him to slay one of
the birds over an earthen vessel with spring
water* in it. **6** Taking the living bird with the
cedar wood, the scarlet yarn and the hyssop, the
priest shall dip them all in the blood of the bird
that was slain over the spring water, **7** and then
sprinkle seven times the man to be purified from
his leprosy. When he has thus purified him, he
shall let the living bird fly away over the countryside. **8** The man being purified shall then
wash his garments and shave off all his hair and
bathe in water; only when he is thus made clean
may he come inside the camp; but he shall still
remain outside his tent for seven days. **9** On the
seventh day he shall again shave off all the hair
of his head, his beard, his eyebrows, and any
other hair he may have, and also wash his garments and bathe his body in water; and so he
will be clean.

Purification Sacrifices. **10** ''On the
eighth day he shall take two unblemished male
lambs, one unblemished yearling ewe lamb,
three tenths of an ephah of fine flour mixed with
oil for a cereal offering, and one log of oil.
11 The priest who performs the purification
ceremony shall place the man who is being purified, as well as all these offerings, before the
LORD at the entrance of the meeting tent.
12 Taking one of the male lambs, the priest
shall present it as a guilt offering, along with the
log of oil, waving them as a wave offering
before the LORD. **13** (This lamb he shall slaughter in the sacred place where the sin offering and
the holocaust are slaughtered; because, like the
sin offering, the guilt offering belongs to the
priest and is most sacred.) **14** Then the priest
shall take some of the blood of the guilt offering
and put it on the tip of the man's right ear, the
thumb of his right hand, and the big toe of his
right foot.[q] **15** The priest shall also take the log
of oil and pour some of it into the palm of his
own left hand; **16** then, dipping his right forefinger in it, he shall sprinkle it seven times
before the LORD. **17** Of the oil left in his hand
the priest shall put some on the tip of the man's
right ear, the thumb of his right hand, and the
big toe of his right foot, over the blood of the
guilt offering. **18** The rest of the oil in his hand
the priest shall put on the head of the man being
purified. Thus shall the priest make atonement
for him before the LORD. **19** Only after he has
offered the sin offering in atonement for the
man's uncleanness shall the priest slaughter the
holocaust **20** and offer it, together with the cereal offering, on the altar before the LORD.
When the priest has thus made atonement for
him, the man will be clean.

Poor Leper's Sacrifice. **21** ''If a man is
poor and cannot afford so much, he shall take
one male lamb for a guilt offering, to be used
as a wave offering in atonement for himself, one
tenth of an ephah of fine flour mixed with oil for
a cereal offering, a log of oil, **22** and two turtledoves* or pigeons, which he can more easily
afford, the one as a sin offering and the other as
a holocaust. **23** On the eighth day of his purification he shall bring them to the priest, at the
entrance of the meeting tent before the LORD.
24 Taking the guilt-offering lamb, along with
the log of oil, the priest shall wave them as a
wave offering before the LORD. **25** When he
has slaughtered the guilt-offering lamb, he shall
take some of its blood, and put it on the tip of
the right ear of the man being purified, on the
thumb of his right hand, and on the big toe of
his right foot. **26** The priest shall then pour
some of the oil into the palm of his own left hand
27 and with his right forefinger sprinkle it sev-
en times before the LORD. **28** Some of the oil
in his hand the priest shall also put on the tip of

---

o Lv 14, 54. 5, 14.
p Mt 8, 4; Mk 1, 44; Lk q Lv 8, 23f.

*

14, 4: Scarlet yarn: probably used for tying the hyssop sprig to the cedar branchlet.

14, 5: Spring water: literally, "living water," taken from some source of running water, not from a cistern.

14, 22: Two turtledoves: substitutes for the two additional lambs, similar to the offering of a poor woman after childbirth. Cf Lv 12, 8.

the man's right ear, the thumb of his right hand, and the big toe of his right foot, over the blood of the guilt offering. **29** The rest of the oil in his hand the priest shall put on the man's head. Thus shall he make atonement for him before the LORD. **30** Then, of the turtledoves or pigeons, such as the man can afford, **31** the priest shall offer up one as a sin offering and the other as a holocaust, along with the cereal offering. Thus shall the priest make atonement before the LORD for the man who is to be purified. **32** This is the law for one afflicted with leprosy who has insufficient means for his purification.''

Leprosy of Houses.   **33** The LORD said to Moses and Aaron, **34** "When you come into the land of Canaan, which I am giving you to possess, if I put a leprous infection on any house of the land you occupy, **35** the owner of the house shall come and report to the priest, 'It looks to me as if my house were infected.' **36** The priest shall then order the house to be cleared out before he goes in to examine the infection, lest everything in the house become unclean. Only after this is he to go in to examine the house. **37** If the priest, on examining it, finds that the infection on the walls of the house consists of greenish or reddish depressions which seem to go deeper than the surface of the wall, **38** he shall close the door of the house behind him and quarantine the house for seven days. **39** On the seventh day the priest shall return to examine the house again. If he finds that the infection has spread on the walls, **40** he shall order the infected stones to be pulled out and cast in an unclean place outside the city. **41** The whole inside of the house shall then be scraped, and the mortar that has been scraped off shall be dumped in an unclean place outside the city. **42** Then new stones shall be brought and put in the place of the old stones, and new mortar shall be made and plastered on the house.

43 "If the infection breaks out once more after the stones have been pulled out and the house has been scraped and replastered, **44** the priest shall come again; and if he finds that the infection has spread in the house, it is corrosive leprosy, and the house is unclean. **45** It shall be pulled down, and all its stones, beams and mortar shall be hauled away to an unclean place outside the city. **46** Whoever enters a house while it is quarantined shall be unclean until evening. **47** Whoever sleeps or eats in such a house shall also wash his garments. **48** If the priest finds, when he comes to examine the house, that the infection has in fact not spread after the plastering, he shall declare the house clean, since the infection has been healed. **49** To purify the house, he shall take two birds, as well as cedar wood, scarlet yarn, and hyssop.

50 One of the birds he shall slay over an earthen vessel with spring water in it. **51** Then, taking the cedar wood, the hyssop and the scarlet yarn, together with the living bird, he shall dip them all in the blood of the slain bird and the spring water, and sprinkle the house seven times. **52** Thus shall he purify the house with the bird's blood and the spring water, along with the living bird, the cedar wood, the hyssop, and the scarlet yarn. **53** He shall then let the living bird fly away over the countryside outside the city. When he has thus made atonement for it, the house will be clean.

54 "This is the law for every kind of human leprosy and scall, **55** *r* for leprosy of garments and houses, **56** as well as for scabs, pustules and blotches, **57** so that it may be manifest when there is a state of uncleanness and when a state of cleanness. This is the law for leprosy."

CHAPTER 15

Personal Uncleanness.   **1** The LORD said to Moses and Aaron, **2** "Speak to the Israelites and tell them: Every man who is afflicted with a chronic flow from his private parts is thereby unclean.*s* **3** Such is his uncleanness from this flow that it makes no difference whether the flow drains off or is blocked up; his uncleanness remains. **4** Any bed on which the man afflicted with the flow lies, is unclean, and any piece of furniture on which he sits, is unclean. **5** Anyone who touches his bed shall wash his garments, bathe in water, and be unclean until evening. **6** Whoever sits on a piece of furniture on which the afflicted man was sitting, shall wash his garments, bathe in water, and be unclean until evening. **7** Whoever touches the body of the afflicted man shall wash his garments, bathe in water, and be unclean until evening. **8** If the afflicted man spits on a clean man, the latter shall wash his garments, bathe in water, and be unclean until evening. **9** Any saddle on which the afflicted man rides, is unclean. **10** Whoever touches anything that was under him shall be unclean until evening; whoever lifts up any such thing shall wash his garments, bathe in water, and be unclean until evening. **11** Anyone whom the afflicted man touches with unrinsed hands shall wash his garments, bathe in water, and be unclean until evening. **12** Earthenware touched by the afflicted man shall be broken; and every wooden article shall be rinsed with water.

13 "When a man who has been afflicted with a flow becomes free of his affliction, he shall wait seven days for his purification. Then he shall wash his garments and bathe his body in

---

r Lv 13, 47-58.   s Nm 5, 2.

fresh water, and so he will be clean. **14** On the eighth day he shall take two turtledoves or two pigeons, and going before the LORD, to the entrance of the meeting tent, he shall give them to the priest, **15** who shall offer them up, the one as a sin offering and the other as a holocaust. Thus shall the priest make atonement before the LORD for the man's flow.

16 "When a man has an emission of seed, he shall bathe his whole body in water and be unclean until evening. **17** Any piece of cloth or leather with seed on it shall be washed with water and be unclean until evening.

18 "If a man lies carnally with a woman, they shall both bathe in water and be unclean until evening.

19 "When a woman has her menstrual flow, she shall be in a state of impurity for seven days.ᵗ Anyone who touches her shall be unclean until evening. **20** Anything on which she lies or sits during her impurity shall be unclean. **21** Anyone who touches her bed shall wash his garments, bathe in water, and be unclean until evening. **22** Whoever touches any article of furniture on which she was sitting, shall wash his garments, bathe in water, and be unclean until evening. **23** *But if she is on the bed or on the seat when he touches it, he shall be unclean until evening. **24** If a man dares to lie with her, he contracts her impurity and shall be unclean for seven days;ᵘ every bed on which he then lies also becomes unclean.

25 "When a woman is afflicted with a flow of blood for several days outside her menstrual period, or when her flow continues beyond the ordinary period,ᵛ as long as she suffers this unclean flow she shall be unclean, just as during her menstrual period. **26** Any bed on which she lies during such a flow becomes unclean, as it would during her menstruation, and any article of furniture on which she sits becomes unclean just as during her menstruation. **27** Anyone who touches them becomes unclean; he shall wash his garments, bathe in water, and be unclean until evening.

28 "If she becomes freed from her affliction, she shall wait seven days, and only then is she to be purified. **29** On the eighth day she shall take two turtledoves or two pigeons and bring them to the priest at the entrance of the meeting tent. **30** The priest shall offer up one of them as a sin offering and the other as a holocaust. Thus shall the priest make atonement before the LORD for her unclean flow.

31 "You shall warn the Israelites of their uncleanness, lest by defiling my Dwelling, which is in their midst, their uncleanness be the cause of their death.

32 "This is the law for the man who is afflicted with a chronic flow, or who has an emission of seed, and thereby becomes unclean;

33 as well as for the woman who has her menstrual period, or who is afflicted with a chronic flow; the law for male and female; and also for the man who lies with an unclean woman.''

CHAPTER 16

The Day of Atonement.   **1** After the death of Aaron's two sons, who died when they approached the LORD's presence, the LORD spoke to Moses **2** and said to him,ʷ "Tell your brother Aaron that he is not to come whenever he pleases into the sanctuary, inside the veil,* in front of the propitiatory on the ark; otherwise, when I reveal myself in a cloud above the propitiatory, he will die. **3** Only in this way may Aaron enter the sanctuary. He shall bring a young bullock for a sin offering and a ram for a holocaust. **4** He shall wear the sacred linen tunic, with the linen drawers next his flesh, gird himself with the linen sash and put on the linen miter. But since these vestments are sacred, he shall not put them on until he has first bathed his body in water. **5** From the Israelite community he shall receive two male goats for a sin offering and one ram for a holocaust.ˣ

6 "Aaron shall bring in the bullock, his sin offering to atone for himself and for his household. **7** Taking the two male goats, and setting them before the LORD at the entrance of the meeting tent, **8** he shall cast lots to determine which one is for the LORD and which for Azazel.* **9** The goat that is determined by lot for the LORD, Aaron shall bring in and offer up as a sin offering. **10** But the goat determined by lot for Azazel he shall set alive before the LORD, so that with it he may make atonement by sending it off to Azazel in the desert.

11 "Thus shall Aaron offer up the bullock, his sin offering, to atone for himself and for his family. When he has slaughtered it, **12** he shall take a censer full of glowing embers from the altar before the LORD, as well as a double handful of finely ground fragrant incense, and bringing them inside the veil, **13** there before

---

t Lv 12, 2. 5.   8, 43.
u Lv 18, 19.   w Heb 9, 6-12.
v Mt 9, 20; Mk 5, 25; Lk   x Nm 29, 11.

---

*

15, 23: What is added to the legislation by this verse is uncertain in both the Hebrew and the Greek.

16, 2: The sanctuary, inside the veil: the innermost part of the sanctuary, known also as "the holy of holies." Cf Ex 26, 33f. Here the high priest was allowed to enter only once a year, on Yom Kippur, the Day of Atonement. In Heb 9, 3–12 this ceremony is applied to Christ's single act of Redemption, whereby he won for us an everlasting atonement, Propitiatory: see note on Ex 25, 17.

16, 8: Azazel: perhaps a name of Satan, used only in this chapter. The ancient versions translated this word as "the escaping goat," whence the English word "scapegoat."

16, 13: Else he will die: the smoke is to conceal the resplendent majesty of God, the sight of which would strike any man

the LORD he shall put incense on the fire, so that a cloud of incense may cover the propitiatory over the commandments; else he will die.* **14** Taking some of the bullock's blood, he shall sprinkle it with his finger on the fore part of the propitiatory and likewise sprinkle some of the blood with his finger seven times in front of the propitiatory.*y*

15 "Then he shall slaughter the people's sin-offering goat, and bringing its blood inside the veil, he shall do with it as he did with the bullock's blood, sprinkling it on the propitiatory and before it.*z* **16** Thus he shall make atonement for the sanctuary because of all the sinful defilements and faults of the Israelites. He shall do the same for the meeting tent, which is set up among them in the midst of their uncleanness. **17** No one else may be in the meeting tent from the time he enters the sanctuary to make atonement until he departs. When he has made atonement for himself and his household, as well as for the whole Israelite community, **18** he shall come out to the altar before the LORD and make atonement for it also. Taking some of the bullock's and the goat's blood, he shall put it on the horns around the altar,*a* **19** and with his finger sprinkle some of the blood on it seven times. Thus he shall render it clean and holy, purged of the defilements of the Israelites.

The Scapegoat.   **20** "When he has completed the atonement rite for the sanctuary, the meeting tent and the altar, Aaron shall bring forward the live goat. **21** Laying both hands on its head, he shall confess over it all the sinful faults and transgressions of the Israelites, and so put them on the goat's head.*b* He shall then have it led into the desert by an attendant. **22** Since the goat is to carry off their iniquities to an isolated region, it must be sent away into the desert.*c*

23 *"After Aaron has again gone into the meeting tent, he shall strip off and leave in the sanctuary the linen vestments he had put on when he entered there. **24** After bathing his body with water in a sacred place, he shall put on his vestments, and then come out and offer his own and the people's holocaust, in atonement for himself and for the people, **25** and also burn the fat of the sin offering on the altar.

26 "The man who has led away the goat for Azazel shall wash his garments and bathe his body in water; only then may he enter the camp. **27** The sin-offering bullock and goat whose blood was brought into the sanctuary to make atonement, shall be taken outside the camp,*d* where their hides and flesh and offal shall be burned up in the fire. **28** The one who burns them shall wash his garments and bathe his body in water; only then may he enter the camp.

The Fast.   **29** *e*"This shall be an everlasting ordinance for you: on the tenth day of the seventh month every one of you, whether a native or a resident alien, shall mortify himself* and shall do no work. **30** Since on this day atonement is made for you to make you clean, so that you may be cleansed of all your sins before the LORD, **31** by everlasting ordinance it shall be a most solemn sabbath for you, on which you must mortify yourselves.

32 "This atonement is to be made by the priest who has been anointed and ordained to the priesthood in succession to his father. He shall wear the linen garments, the sacred vestments, **33** and make atonement for the sacred sanctuary, the meeting tent and the altar, as well as for the priests and all the people of the community. **34** This, then, shall be an everlasting ordinance for you: once a year atonement shall be made for all the sins of the Israelites."*f*

Thus was it done, as the LORD had commanded Moses.

IV: Code of Legal Holiness

CHAPTER 17

Sacredness of Blood.   **1** The LORD said to Moses, **2** "Speak to Aaron and his sons, as well as to all the Israelites, and tell them: This is what the LORD has commanded. **3** *Any Israelite who slaughters an ox or a sheep or a goat, whether in the camp or outside of it, **4** without first bringing it to the entrance of the meeting tent to present it as an offering to the LORD in front of his Dwelling, shall be judged guilty of bloodshed; and for this, such a man shall be cut off from among his people. **5** Therefore, such sacrifices as they used to offer up in the open field the Israelites shall henceforth offer to the LORD, bringing them to the priest at the entrance of the meeting tent and sacrificing them there as

---

y Heb 9, 13. 25.   1 Pt 2, 24.
z Heb 5, 1; 6, 19.   d Heb 13, 11.
a Ex 30, 12.   e Lv 23, 27. 32; Nm 29,
b Is 53, 6; 2 Cor 5, 21.   7.
c Is 53, 11. 12; Jn 1, 29;   f Heb 9, 7. 25.

*

dead.

16, 23: This verse is best read after v 25. According to later Jewish practice the high priest again went into the holy of holies to remove the censer.

16, 29: Mortify himself: literally, "afflict his soul"; traditionally understood by the Jews as signifying abstinence from all food. This is the only fast day prescribed in the Mosaic law.

17, 3ff: The ancients considered blood the seat and sign of life, and therefore something sacred, even in animals. Cf Gn 9, 4f. Hence, even the ordinary butchering of an animal for meat was looked upon as having a sacrificial character, so that it should be performed at the sanctuary. This law, however, could not be carried out without great difficulty when the Israelites were scattered throughout Palestine, and so was modified in Dt 12, 20ff.

peace offerings to the LORD. **6** The priest shall splash the blood on the altar of the LORD at the entrance of the meeting tent and there burn the fat for an odor pleasing to the LORD. **7** No longer shall they offer their sacrifices to the satyrs to whom they used to render their wanton worship.*g* This shall be an everlasting ordinance for them and their descendants.

8 "Tell them, therefore: Anyone, whether of the house of Israel or of the aliens residing among them, who offers a holocaust or sacrifice **9** without bringing it to the entrance of the meeting tent to offer it to the LORD, shall be cut off from his kinsmen. **10** And if anyone, whether of the house of Israel or of the aliens residing among them, partakes of any blood, I will set myself against that one who partakes of blood and will cut him off from among his people.*h* **11** *i*Since the life of a living body is in its blood, I have made you put it on the altar, so that atonement may thereby be made for your own lives,* because it is the blood, as the seat of life, that makes atonement. **12** That is why I have told the Israelites: No one among you, not even a resident alien, may partake of blood.

13 "Anyone hunting, whether of the Israelites or of the aliens residing among them, who catches an animal or a bird that may be eaten, shall pour out its blood and cover it with earth. **14** Since the life of every living body is its blood, I have told the Israelites: You shall not partake of the blood of any meat.*j* Since the life of every living body is its blood, anyone who partakes of it shall be cut off.

15 *k*Everyone, whether a native or an alien, who eats of an animal that died of itself or was killed by a wild beast, shall wash his garments, bathe in water, and be unclean until evening, and then he will be clean. **16** If he does not wash or does not bathe his body, he shall have the guilt to bear."

CHAPTER 18

The Sanctity of Sex. **1** The LORD said to Moses, **2** "Speak to the Israelites and tell them: I, the LORD, am your God. **3** You shall not do as they do in the land of Egypt, where you once lived, nor shall you do as they do in the land of Canaan, where I am bringing you; do not conform to their customs. **4** My decrees you shall carry out, and my statutes you shall take care to follow. I, the LORD, am your God. **5** Keep, then, my statutes and decrees, for the man who carries them out will find life through them. I am the LORD.*l*

6 *"None of you shall approach a close relative to have sexual intercourse with her. I am the LORD. **7** *m*You shall not disgrace your father by having intercourse with your mother. Besides, since she is your own mother, you shall not have

intercourse with her. **8** You shall not have intercourse with your father's wife,*n* for that would be a disgrace to your father. **9** You shall not have intercourse with your sister, your father's daughter or your mother's daughter, whether she was born in your own household or born elsewhere. **10** You shall not have intercourse with your son's daughter or with your daughter's daughter, for that would be a disgrace to your own family. **11** You shall not have intercourse with the daughter whom your father's wife bore to him, since she, too, is your sister. **12** *o*You shall not have intercourse with your father's sister, since she is your father's relative. **13** You shall not have intercourse with your mother's sister, since she is your mother's relative. **14** You shall not disgrace your father's brother by being intimate with his wife,*p* since she, too, is your aunt. **15** You shall not have intercourse with your daughter-in-law; she is your son's wife, and therefore you shall not disgrace her. **16** You shall not have intercourse with your brother's wife,* for that would be a disgrace to your brother.*q* **17** You shall not have intercourse with a woman and also with her daughter, nor shall you marry and have intercourse with her son's daughter or her daughter's daughter; this would be shameful, because they are related to her. **18** While your wife is still living you shall not marry her sister as her rival; for thus you would disgrace your first wife.

19 "You shall not approach a woman to have intercourse with her while she is unclean from menstruation. **20** You shall not have carnal relations with your neighbor's wife, defiling yourself with her. **21** *r*You shall not offer any of

---

g Ex 34, 15; Dt 32, 17;
  2 Chr 11, 15; 1 Cor
  10, 20.
h Lv 3, 17.
i Gn 9, 4.
j Lv 7, 26f.
k Lv 11, 39f; 22, 8.
l Gal 3, 12.
m 7-16: Lv 20, 11-21.

n Dt 23, 1; 27, 20; 1 Cor
  5, 1.
o 12f: Lv 20, 19.
p Lv 20, 20.
q Lv 20, 21; Mt 14, 3f;
  Mk 6, 18.
r Lv 20, 2-5; Dt 18, 10;
  2 Kgs 16, 3; 21, 6.

*

17, 11: That atonement may thereby be made for your own lives: hence, the sacrifice of an animal was a symbolic act which substituted the victim's life for the life of the offerer, who thus acknowledged that he deserved God's punishments for his sins. This idea of sacrifice is applied in Heb 9–10 to the death of Christ, inasmuch as "without the shedding of blood there is no forgiveness" (Heb 9, 22).

18, 6–18: These laws are formulated as directed to the male Israelites only, but naturally the same norms of consanguinity and affinity would apply to the women as well. Marriage, as well as casual intercourse, is here forbidden between men and women of the specified degrees of relationship.

18, 16: With your brother's wife: it was the violation of this law which aroused the wrath of John the Baptist against Herod Antipas. Cf Mk 6, 18. An exception to this law is made in Dt 25, 5.

18, 21: Immolated to Molech: the reference is to the Canaanite custom of sacrificing children to the god Molech. The little victims were first slain and then cremated. Cf Ez 16, 20ff;

your offspring to be immolated to Molech,* thus profaning the name of your God. I am the LORD. 22 You shall not lie with a male as with a woman; such a thing is an abomination.*s* 23 You shall not have carnal relations with an animal, defiling yourself with it; nor shall a woman set herself in front of an animal to mate with it; such things are abhorrent.*t*

24 "Do not defile yourselves by any of these things by which the nations whom I am driving out of your way have defiled themselves. 25 Because their land has become defiled, I am punishing it for its wickedness, by making it vomit out its inhabitants. 26 You, however, whether natives or resident aliens, must keep my statutes and decrees forbidding all such abominations 27 by which the previous inhabitants defiled the land; 28 otherwise the land will vomit you out also for having defiled it, just as it vomited out the nations before you. 29 Everyone who does any of these abominations shall be cut off from among his people. 30 Heed my charge, then, not to defile yourselves by observing the abominable customs that have been observed before you.*u* I, the LORD, am your God.''

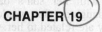

CHAPTER 19

Various Rules of Conduct. 1 The LORD said to Moses, 2 "Speak to the whole Israelite community and tell them: Be holy, for I, the LORD, your God, am holy.*v* 3 Revere your mother and father,*w* and keep my sabbaths. I, the LORD, am your God.

4 "Do not turn aside to idols, nor make molten gods for yourselves.*x* I, the LORD, am your God.

5 "When you sacrifice your peace offering to the LORD, if you wish it to be acceptable, 6 it must be eaten on the very day of your sacrifice or on the following day. Whatever is left over until the third day shall be burned up in the fire. 7 If any of it is eaten on the third day, the sacrifice will be unacceptable as refuse;*y* 8 whoever eats of it then shall pay the penalty for having profaned what is sacred to the LORD. Such a one shall be cut off from his people.

9 "When you reap the harvest of your land, you shall not be so thorough that you reap the field to its very edge, nor shall you glean the stray ears of grain.*z* 10 Likewise, you shall not pick your vineyard bare, nor gather up the grapes that have fallen. These things you shall leave for the poor and the alien. I, the LORD, am your God.

11 "You shall not steal. You shall not lie or speak falsely to one another.*a* 12 You shall not swear falsely by my name, thus profaning the name of your God.*b* I am the LORD.

13 "You shall not defraud or rob your neighbor. You shall not withhold overnight the wages of your day laborer.*c* 14 You shall not curse the deaf, or put a stumbling block in front of the blind, but you shall fear your God. I am the LORD.

15 "You shall not act dishonestly in rendering judgment. Show neither partiality to the weak nor deference to the mighty, but judge your fellow men justly.*d* 16 You shall not go about spreading slander among your kinsmen; nor shall you stand by idly when your neighbor's life is at stake. I am the LORD.

17 "You shall not bear hatred for your brother in your heart.*e* Though you may have to reprove your fellow man, do not incur sin because of him. 18 Take no revenge and cherish no grudge against your fellow countrymen. You shall love your neighbor as yourself.* I am the LORD.*f*

19 "Keep my statutes: do not breed any of your domestic animals with others of a different species; do not sow a field of yours with two different kinds of seed; and do not put on a garment woven with two different kinds of thread.

20 *"If a man has carnal relations with a female slave who has already been living with another man but has not yet been redeemed or given her freedom, they shall be punished but not put to death, because she is not free. 21 The man, moreover, shall bring to the entrance of the meeting tent a ram as his guilt offering to the LORD. 22 With this ram the priest shall make atonement before the LORD for the sin he has committed, and it will be forgiven him.

23 *"When you come into the land and plant any fruit tree there, first look upon its fruit as if it were uncircumcised. For three years, while its fruit remains uncircumcised, it may not be eat-

---

s Lv 20, 13; Rom 1, 27;
    1 Cor 6, 9f.
t Lv 20, 15f; Ex 22, 18.
u Lv 20, 23; Dt 18, 9.
v Lv 11, 44; Mt 5, 48;
    1 Pt 1, 16.
w Ex 20, 12.
x Lv 26, 1; Ex 20, 3-5;
    34, 17; Dt 27, 15.
y Lv 7, 18.
z Lv 23, 22; Dt 24, 19ff.

a Ex 20, 15f.
b Ex 20, 7; Mt 5, 33.
c Dt 24, 14f.
d Ex 23, 2f; Dt 1, 17; 16,
    19; Ps 82, 2; Prv 24,
    23.
e Mt 18, 15; Lk 17, 3;
    Gal 6, 1; 1 Jn 3, 14.
f Mt 5, 43; 19, 19; 22, 39;
    Mk 12, 31; Rom 13, 9;
    Gal 5, 14; Jas 2, 8.

*

20, 26. 31; 23, 37.

19, 18: You shall love your neighbor as yourself: cited by our Lord as the second of the two most important commandments of God. Cf Mt 22, 39; Mk 12, 31. Although in the present context the word "neighbor" is restricted to "fellow countrymen," in Lk 10, 29–37 Christ extends its meaning to embrace all men, even enemies. Cf also Mt 5. 43ff.

19, 20ff: This law seems out of its proper context here; perhaps it stood originally after Lv 20, 12. Female slave . . . given her freedom: reference is to the case treated of in Ex 21, 7–11.

19, 23ff: Uncircumcised: by analogy with a newborn boy, the newly planted tree was considered impure until "circumcised" by offering to the Lord all the fruit it bore in the fourth year.

en. **24** In the fourth year, however, all of its fruit shall be sacred to the LORD as a thanksgiving feast to him. **25** Not until the fifth year may you eat its fruit. Thus it will continue its yield for you. I, the LORD, am your God.

26 "Do not eat meat with the blood still in it. *g* Do not practice divination or soothsaying. **27** *Do not clip your hair at the temples, nor trim the edges of your beard. *h* **28** Do not lacerate your bodies for the dead, and do not tattoo yourselves. I am the LORD.

29 "You shall not degrade your daughter by making a prostitute of her; else the land will become corrupt and full of lewdness. **30** Keep my sabbaths, and reverence my sanctuary. *i* I am the LORD.

31 "Do not go to mediums or consult fortune-tellers, for you will be defiled by them. *j* I, the LORD, am your God.

32 "Stand up in the presence of the aged, and show respect for the old; thus shall you fear your God. I am the LORD.

33 "When an alien resides with you in your land, do not molest him. *k* **34** You shall treat the alien who resides with you no differently than the natives born among you; have the same love for him as for yourself; for you too were once aliens in the land of Egypt. *l* I, the LORD, am your God.

35 "Do not act dishonestly in using measures of length or weight or capacity. **36** You shall have a true scale and true weights, an honest ephah and an honest hin. *m* I, the LORD, am your God, who brought you out of the land of Egypt. **37** Be careful, then, to observe all my statutes and decrees. I am the LORD."

CHAPTER 20

Penalties for Various Sins. **1** The LORD said to Moses, **2** "Tell the Israelites: Anyone, whether an Israelite or an alien residing in Israel, who gives any of his offspring to Molech shall be put to death. *n* Let his fellow citizens stone him. **3** *o* I myself will turn against such a man and cut him off from the body of his people; for in giving his offspring to Molech, he has defiled my sanctuary and profaned my holy name. **4** Even if his fellow citizens connive at such a man's crime of giving his offspring to Molech, and fail to put him to death, **5** I myself will set my face against that man and his family and will cut off from their people both him and all who join him in his wanton worship of Molech. **6** Should anyone turn to mediums and fortune-tellers and follow their wanton ways, *p* I will turn against such a one and cut him off from his people. **7** Sanctify yourselves, then, and be holy; for I, the LORD, your God, am holy. *q* **8** Be careful, therefore, to observe what

I, the LORD, who make you holy, have prescribed.

9 "Anyone who curses his father or mother shall be put to death; *r* since he has cursed his father or mother, he has forfeited his life. **10** If a man commits adultery with his neighbor's wife, both the adulterer and the adulteress shall be put to death. *s* **11** If a man disgraces his father *t* by lying with his father's wife, both the man and his stepmother shall be put to death; they have forfeited their lives. **12** If a man lies with his daughter-in-law, *u* both of them shall be put to death; since they have committed an abhorrent deed, they have forfeited their lives. **13** If a man lies with a male as with a woman, *v* both of them shall be put to death for their abominable deed; they have forfeited their lives. **14** If a man marries a woman and her mother also, *w* the man and the two women as well shall be burned to death for their shameful conduct, so that such shamefulness may not be found among you. **15** If a man has carnal relations with an animal, the man shall be put to death, *x* and the animal shall be slain. **16** If a woman goes up to any animal to mate with it, *y* the woman and the animal shall be slain; let them both be put to death; their lives are forfeit. **17** If a man consummates marriage with his sister or his half-sister, *z* they shall be publicly cut off from their people for this shameful deed; the man shall pay the penalty of having had intercourse with his own sister. **18** If a man lies in sexual intercourse with a woman during her menstrual period, *a* both of them shall be cut off from their people, because they have laid bare the flowing fountain of her blood. **19** You shall not have intercourse with your mother's sister or your father's sister; *b* whoever does so shall pay the penalty of incest. **20** If a man disgraces his uncle by having intercourse with his uncle's wife, the man and his aunt shall pay the penalty by dying childless. **21** If a man marries his brother's wife and thus disgraces his brother, they shall be childless because of this incest.

22 "Be careful to observe all my statutes and all my decrees; otherwise the land where I am bringing you to dwell will vomit you out.

g Lv 3, 17; Dt 18, 10; 2 Kgs 17, 17; 21, 6; 2 Chr 33, 6.
h Lv 21, 5.
i Lv 26, 2; Ex 20, 8.
j Lv 20, 6. 27; Dt 18, 11; Is 8, 19.
k Ex 22, 20; 23, 9; Jer 22, 3; Mal 3, 5.
l Dt 10, 19.
m Dt 25, 13. 15; Prv 11, 1; 16, 11; 20, 10; Ez 45, 10.
n Lv 18, 21.
o Ez 23, 39.
p Lv 19, 31.

q Lv 11, 44; 19, 2; 1 Pt 1, 16.
r Ex 21, 17; Prv 20, 20; Mt 15, 4; Mk 7, 10.
s Lv 18, 20; Dt 22, 22; Jn 8, 5.
t Lv 18, 7f.
u Lv 18, 15.
v Lv 18, 22.
w Lv 18, 17; Dt 27, 23.
x Ex 22, 18; Dt 27, 21.
y Lv 18, 23.
z Lv 18, 9; Dt 27, 22.
a Lv 18, 19.
b Lv 18, 12f.

19, 27: See note on Lv 21, 5.

23 Do not conform, therefore, to the customs of the nations^c whom I am driving out of your way, because all these things that they have done have filled me with disgust for them. **24** But to you I have said:^d Their land shall be your possession, a land flowing with milk and honey. I am giving it to you as your own, I, the LORD, your God, who have set you apart from the other nations. **25** ^eYou, too, must set apart, then, the clean animals from the unclean, and the clean birds from the unclean, so that you may not be contaminated with the uncleanness of any beast or bird or of any swarming creature in the land that I have set apart for you. **26** To me, therefore, you shall be sacred; for I, the LORD, am sacred,^f I, who have set you apart from the other nations to be my own.

27 *"A man or a woman who acts as a medium or fortune-teller^g shall be put to death by stoning; they have no one but themselves to blame for their death."

CHAPTER 21

Sanctity of the Priesthood. **1** The LORD said to Moses, "Speak to Aaron's sons, the priests, and tell them: None of you shall make himself unclean for any dead person* among his people,^h **2** except for his nearest relatives, his mother or father, his son or daughter, his brother **3** or his maiden sister, who is of his own family while she remains unmarried; for these he may make himself unclean. **4** But for a sister who has married out of his family he shall not make himself unclean; this would be a profanation.

5 *"The priests shall not make bare the crown of the head, nor shave the edges of the beard,ⁱ nor lacerate the body. **6** To their God they shall be sacred,* and not profane his name; since they offer up the oblations of the LORD, the food of their God, they must be holy.

7 "A priest shall not marry a woman who has been a prostitute or has lost her honor, nor a woman who has been divorced by her husband; for the priest is sacred to his God.^j **8** Honor him as sacred who offers up the food of your God; treat him as sacred, because I, the LORD, who have consecrated him, am sacred.

9 "A priest's daughter who loses her honor by committing fornication and thereby dishonors her father also, shall be burned to death.

10 "The most exalted of the priests, upon whose head the anointing oil has been poured and who has been ordained to wear the special vestments, shall not bare his head* or rend his garments, **11** nor shall he go near any dead person. Not even for his father or mother may he thus become unclean **12** or leave the sanctuary;^k otherwise he will profane the sanctuary of

his God, for with the anointing oil upon him, he is dedicated to his God, to me, the LORD.

13 "The priest shall marry a virgin. **14** Not a widow or a woman who has been divorced or a woman who has lost her honor as a prostitute, but a virgin, taken from his own people, shall he marry;^l **15** otherwise he will have base offspring among his people. I, the LORD, have made him sacred."

Irregularities. **16** The LORD said to Moses, **17** "Speak to Aaron and tell him: None of your descendants, of whatever generation, who has any defect shall come forward to offer up the food of his God. **18** Therefore, he who has any of the following defects may not come forward: he who is blind, or lame, or who has any disfigurement or malformation, **19** or a crippled foot or hand, **20** or who is hump-backed or weakly or walleyed, or who is afflicted with eczema, ringworm or hernia. **21** No descendant of Aaron the priest who has any such defect may draw near to offer up the oblations of the LORD; on account of his defect he may not draw near to offer up the food of his God. **22** He may, however, partake of the food of his God: of what is most sacred as well as of what is sacred. **23** Only, he may not approach the veil nor go up to the altar on account of his defect; he shall not profane these things that are sacred to me, for it is I, the LORD, who make them sacred."

24 Moses, therefore, told this to Aaron and his sons and to all the Israelites.

CHAPTER 22

Sacrificial Banquets. **1** The LORD said to Moses, **2** "Tell Aaron and his sons to respect the sacred offerings which the Israelites consecrate to me; else they will profane my holy name. I am the LORD.

3 "Tell them: If any one of you, or of your descendants in any future generation, dares, while he is in a state of uncleanness, to draw

c Lv 18, 30.
d Ex 3, 8. 17; 6, 8.
e Lv 11, 2-47; Dt 14, 4-20.
f Lv 11, 44; Ex 19, 6; 1 Pt 1, 16.
g Lv 19, 31; Ex 22, 17;

Dt 18, 11.
h Ez 44, 25.
i Ez 44, 20.
j Ez 44, 22.
k Lv 10, 7.
l Ez 44, 22.

*

20, 27: This verse is best read immediately after v 6.

21, 1: Unclean for any dead person: by preparing the corpse for burial. Cf Nm 6, 6; 19, 11–19.

21, 5: Such mourning customs of the Canaanites were forbidden to all the Israelites, but especially to the priests. Cf Lv 19, 27f.

21, 6: Sacred: the same Hebrew word has both the active meaning of "holy," that is, keeping oneself free from profane impurities, and the passive meaning of "sacred," that is, set apart from what is profane and therefore treated with religious reverence.

21, 10: Bare his head: see note on Lv 10, 6.

near the sacred offerings which the Israelites consecrate to the LORD, such a one shall be cut off from my presence. I am the LORD.

4 "No descendant of Aaron who is stricken with leprosy, or who suffers from a flow, may eat of these sacred offerings, unless he again becomes clean. *m* Moreover, if anyone touches a person who has become unclean by contact with a corpse, or if anyone has had an emission of seed, **5** or if anyone touches *n* any swarming creature or any man whose uncleanness, of whatever kind it may be, is contagious, **6** the one who touches such as these shall be unclean until evening and may not eat of the sacred portions until he has first bathed his body in water; *o* **7** then, when the sun sets, he again becomes clean. Only then may he eat of the sacred offerings, which are his food. **8** He shall not make himself unclean by eating of any animal that has died of itself or has been killed by wild beasts. *p* I am the LORD.

9 "They shall keep my charge and not do wrong in this matter; else they will die for their profanation. I am the LORD who have consecrated them.

10 "Neither a lay person nor a priest's tenant or hired servant may eat of any sacred offering. *q* **11** But a slave whom a priest acquires by purchase or who is born in his house may eat of his food. **12** A priest's daughter who is married to a layman may not eat of the sacred contributions. **13** But if a priest's daughter is widowed or divorced and, having no children, returns to her father's house, she may then eat of her father's food as in her youth. No layman, however, may eat of it. **14** *r* If such a one eats of a sacred offering through inadvertence, he shall make restitution to the priest for the sacred offering, with an increment of one fifth of the amount. **15** The sacred offerings which the Israelites contribute to the LORD the priests shall not allow to be profaned *s* **16** nor in the eating of the sacred offering shall they bring down guilt that must be punished; it is I, the LORD, who make them sacred."

Unacceptable Victims. **17** The LORD said to Moses, **18** "Speak to Aaron and his sons and to all the Israelites, and tell them: When anyone of the house of Israel, or any alien residing in Israel, who wishes to offer a sacrifice, brings a holocaust as a votive offering or as a free-will offering to the LORD, **19** if it is to be acceptable, the ox or sheep or goat that he offers must be an unblemished male. *t* **20** You shall not offer one that has any defect, for such a one would not be acceptable for you. *u* **21** When anyone presents a peace offering *v* to the LORD from the herd or the flock in fulfillment of a vow, or as a free-will offering, if it is to find acceptance, it must be unblemished; it shall not have any

defect. **22** One that is blind or crippled or maimed, or one that has a running sore or mange or ringworm, you shall not offer to the LORD; do not put such an animal on the altar as an oblation to the LORD. **23** An ox or a sheep that is in any way ill-proportioned or stunted you may indeed present as a free-will offering, but it will not be acceptable as a votive offering. **24** One that has its testicles bruised or crushed or torn out or cut off you shall not offer to the LORD. You shall neither do this in your own land **25** nor receive from a foreigner any such animals to offer up as the food of your God; since they are deformed or defective, *w* they will not be acceptable for you."

26 The LORD said to Moses, **27** "When an ox or a lamb or a goat is born, it shall remain with its mother for seven days; only from the eighth day onward will it be acceptable, to be offered as an oblation to the LORD. *x* **28** You shall not slaughter an ox or a sheep on one and the same day with its young. **29** Whenever you offer a thanksgiving sacrifice to the LORD, so offer it that it may be acceptable for you; **30** it must, therefore, be eaten on the same day; none of it shall be left over until the next day. *y* I am the LORD.

31 "Be careful to observe the commandments which I, the LORD, give you, **32** and do not profane my holy name; in the midst of the Israelites I, the LORD, must be held as sacred. It is I who made you sacred **33** and led you out of the land of Egypt, that I, the LORD, might be your God."

CHAPTER 23

Holy Days. **1** The LORD said to Moses, **2** "Speak to the Israelites and tell them: The following are the festivals of the LORD, my feast days, which you shall celebrate with a sacred assembly.

3 "For six days work may be done; but the seventh day is the sabbath rest, a day for sacred assembly, on which you shall do no work. The sabbath shall belong to the LORD wherever you dwell. *z*

Passover. **4** "These, then, are the festivals of the LORD which you shall celebrate at their proper time with a sacred assembly. *a* **5** The Passover of the LORD falls on the fourteenth day

---

m Lv 7, 20; 15, 16.
n Lv 11, 24. 43.
o Heb 10, 22.
p Lv 17, 15; Dt 14, 21; Ez 44, 31.
q 1 Sm 21, 6; Mt 12, 4.
r Lv 5, 16; 27, 13. 15. 19.
s Lv 19, 8; Nm 18, 32.
t Lv 1, 3. 10.
u Dt 15, 21; 17, 1; Mal 1, 8. 14.
v Lv 3, 1. 6.
w Mal 1, 14.
x Ex 22, 29.
y Lv 7, 15.
z Ex 20, 8-11; 23, 12; 31, 14f; 34, 21; Dt 5, 12-15; Lk 13, 14.
a Ex 23, 14-19.
b Nm 9, 2f; 28, 16.

of the first month, at the evening twilight.*b* **6** The fifteenth day of this month is the LORD's feast of Unleavened Bread. For seven days you shall eat unleavened bread.*c* **7** On the first of these days you shall hold a sacred assembly and do no sort of work.*d* **8** On each of the seven days you shall offer an oblation to the LORD. Then on the seventh day you shall again hold a sacred assembly and do no sort of work."

9 The LORD said to Moses, **10** "Speak to the Israelites and tell them: When you come into the land which I am giving you, and reap your harvest, you shall bring a sheaf of the first fruits of your harvest to the priest, **11** who shall wave the sheaf before the LORD that it may be acceptable for you. On the day after the sabbath* the priest shall do this. **12** On this day, when your sheaf is waved, you shall offer to the LORD for a holocaust an unblemished yearling lamb. **13** Its cereal offering shall be two tenths of an ephah of fine flour mixed with oil, as a sweet-smelling oblation to the LORD; and its libation shall be a fourth of a hin of wine. **14** Until this day, when you bring your God this offering, you shall not eat any bread* or roasted grain or fresh kernels. This shall be a perpetual statute for you and your descendants wherever you dwell.

Pentecost.   **15** "Beginning with the day after the sabbath, the day on which you bring the wave-offering sheaf, you shall count seven full weeks,*e* **16** and then on the day after the seventh week, the fiftieth* day,*f* you shall present the new cereal offering to the LORD. **17** For the wave offering of your first fruits to the LORD, you shall bring with you from wherever you live two loaves of bread made of two tenths of an ephah of fine flour and baked with leaven. **18** Besides the bread, you shall offer to the LORD a holocaust of seven unblemished yearling lambs, one young bull, and two rams, along with their cereal offering and libations, as a sweet-smelling oblation to the LORD. **19** One male goat shall be sacrificed as a sin offering, and two yearling lambs as a peace offering.*g* **20** The priest shall wave the bread of the first fruits and the two lambs as a wave offering before the LORD; these shall be sacred to the LORD and belong to the priest. **21** On this same day you shall by proclamation have a sacred assembly, and no sort of work may be done. This shall be a perpetual statute for you and your descendants wherever you dwell.

22 "When you reap the harvest of your land, you shall not be so thorough that you reap the field to its very edge, nor shall you glean the stray ears of your grain. These things you shall leave for the poor and the alien. I, the LORD, am your God."

New Year's Day.   **23** The LORD said to Moses, **24** "Tell the Israelites: On the first day of the seventh month you shall keep a sabbath rest, with a sacred assembly and with the trumpet blasts as a reminder; **25** you shall then do no sort of work, and you shall offer an oblation to the LORD."

The Day of Atonement.   **26** *h*The LORD said to Moses, **27** "The tenth of this seventh month is the Day of Atonement,*i* when you shall hold a sacred assembly and mortify yourselves and offer an oblation to the LORD. **28** On this day you shall not do any work, because it is the Day of Atonement, when atonement is made for you before the LORD, your God. **29** Anyone who does not mortify himself on this day shall be cut off from his people; **30** and if anyone does any work on this day, I will remove him from the midst of his people. **31** This is a perpetual statute for you and your descendants wherever you dwell: you shall do no work, **32** but shall keep a sabbath of complete rest and mortify yourselves. Beginning on the evening of the ninth of the month, you shall keep this sabbath of yours from evening to evening."

The Feast of Booths.   **33** The LORD said to Moses, **34** "Tell the Israelites: The fifteenth day of this seventh month*j* is the LORD's feast of Booths,* which shall continue for seven days. **35** On the first day there shall be a sacred assembly, and you shall do no sort of work. **36** For seven days you shall offer an oblation to the LORD, and on the eighth day you shall again hold a sacred assembly and offer an oblation to

---

c Ex 12, 18; 13, 3. 10;
  23, 15; 34, 18.
d Ex 12, 15; Nm 28, 18.
  25.
e Ex 34, 22; Nm 28, 26;
  Dt 16, 9.

f Acts 2, 1.
g Nm 28, 30.
h Lv 25, 9.
i Lv 16, 29f; Nm 29, 7.
j Nm 29, 12; Dt 16, 13;
  2 Mc 1, 9. 18; Jn 7, 2.

23, 11: The sabbath: according to the Jewish tradition this was the feast day itself, the fifteenth of Nisan, which was a special day of rest. Cf v 7. However, some understand here the Saturday of the Passover week, or even the Saturday following it; cf Jn 19, 31.

23, 14: Any bread: made from the new grain. The harvest had first to be sanctified for man's use by this offering to God.

23, 16: The fiftieth: from the Greek word for this we have the name "Pentecost." Cf 2 Mc 12, 31; Acts 2, 1. It was also called "the feast of the Seven Weeks," or simply "the feast of Weeks" (Nm 28, 26; Dt 16, 10; Tb 2, 1). The new cereal offering: of flour made from the new grain. Pentecost was the thanksgiving feast at the end of the grain harvest, which began after Passover. Later tradition made it a commemoration of the giving of the law at Sinai.

23, 34: Feast of Booths: the joyful observance of the vintage and fruit harvest. Cf Dt 16, 13. During the seven days of the feast the Israelites camped in booths of branches erected on the roofs of their houses or in the streets in commemoration of their wanderings in the desert, where they dwelt in booths.

the LORD. On that solemn closing you shall do no sort of work.

37 "These, therefore, are the festivals of the LORD on which you shall proclaim a sacred assembly, and offer as an oblation to the LORD holocausts and cereal offerings, sacrifices and libations, as prescribed for each day, **38** in addition to those of the LORD's sabbaths, your donations, your various votive offerings and the free-will offerings that you present to the LORD.

39 "On the fifteenth day, then, of the seventh month, when you have gathered in the produce of the land,[k] you shall celebrate a pilgrim feast of the LORD for a whole week. The first and the eighth day shall be days of complete rest. **40** On the first day you shall gather foliage* from majestic trees, branches of palms and boughs of myrtles and of valley poplars, and then for a week you shall make merry before the LORD, your God. **41** By perpetual statute for you and your descendants you shall keep this pilgrim feast of the LORD for one whole week[l] in the seventh month of the year. **42** During this week every native Israelite among you shall dwell in booths, **43** that your descendants[m] may realize that, when I led the Israelites out of the land of Egypt, I made them dwell in booths. I, the LORD, am your God."

44 Thus did Moses announce to the Israelites the festivals of the LORD.

CHAPTER 24

The Sanctuary Light. **1** The LORD said to Moses, **2** "Order the Israelites to bring you clear oil of crushed olives for the light, so that you may keep lamps burning regularly.[n] **3** In the meeting tent, outside the veil that hangs in front of the commandments, Aaron shall set up the lamps to burn before the LORD regularly, from evening till morning. Thus, by a perpetual statute for you and your descendants, **4** the lamps shall be set up on the pure gold lampstand,[o] to burn regularly before the LORD.

The Showbread. **5** "You shall take fine flour and bake it[p] into twelve cakes, using two tenths of an ephah of flour for each cake. **6** These you shall place in two piles, six in each pile, on the pure gold table before the LORD. **7** On each pile put some pure frankincense, which shall serve as an oblation to the LORD, a token offering for the bread. **8** Regularly on each sabbath day this bread shall be set out afresh[q] before the LORD, offered on the part of the Israelites by an everlasting agreement. **9** It shall belong to Aaron and his sons, who must eat it in a sacred place, since, as something most sacred among the various oblations to the LORD, it is his by perpetual right."

Punishment of Blasphemy. **10** Among the Israelites there was a man born of an Israelite mother (Shelomith, daughter of Dibri, of the tribe of Dan) and an Egyptian father. **11** This man quarreled publicly with another Israelite and cursed and blasphemed the LORD's name. So the people brought him to Moses, **12** who kept him in custody till a decision from the LORD should settle the case for them. **13** The LORD then said to Moses, **14** "Take the blasphemer outside the camp, and when all who heard him have laid their hands on his head, let the whole community stone him. **15** Tell the Israelites: Anyone who curses his God shall bear the penalty of his sin; **16** whoever blasphemes the name of the LORD shall be put to death.[r] The whole community shall stone him; alien and native alike must be put to death for blaspheming the LORD's name.

17 "Whoever takes the life of any human being shall be put to death;[s] **18** whoever takes the life of an animal shall make restitution of another animal. A life for a life![t] **19** Anyone who inflicts an injury on his neighbor shall receive the same in return. **20** Limb for limb, eye for eye, tooth for tooth! The same injury that a man gives another shall be inflicted on him in return.[u] **21** Whoever slays an animal shall make restitution, but whoever slays a man shall be put to death. **22** You shall have but one rule, for alien and native alike.[v] I, the LORD, am your God."

23 When Moses told this to the Israelites, they took the blasphemer outside the camp and stoned him;[w] they carried out the command that the LORD had given Moses.

CHAPTER 25

The Sabbatical Year. **1** The LORD said to Moses on Mount Sinai, **2** "Speak to the Israelites and tell them: When you enter the land that I am giving you, let the land, too, keep a sabbath for the LORD. **3** For six years you may sow your field, and for six years prune your vineyard, gathering in their produce.[x] **4** But during

---

k Ex 23, 16; Dt 16, 13.
l Nm 29, 12-38.
m Dt 31, 10-13.
n Ex 27. 20f.
o Ex 25, 31.
p Ex 25, 30; 1 Kgs 7, 48; 2 Chr 4, 19; 13, 11; Heb 9, 2.
q 1 Chr 9, 32.
r 1 Kgs 21, 10. 13; Mt

26, 65f; Jn 10, 33.
s Gn 9, 5f; Ex 21, 12; Nm 35, 31; Dt 19, 11f.
t Ex 21, 33f.
u Dt 19, 21; Mt 5, 38.
v Lv 19, 34; Ex 12, 49; Nm 15, 16.
w Acts 7, 57f.
x Ex 23, 10f.
y 1 Mc 6, 49. 53.

*

23, 40: Foliage: literally, "fruit," but here probably used in the general sense of "produce, growth." These branches were used for constructing the "booths" or huts in which the people lived during the feast. Cf Neh 8, 15. However, from about the time of Christ on, the Jews have understood this of "fruit" in the strict sense; hence, branches of lemons and oranges were carried with the other branches in joyous procession.

the seventh year the land shall have a complete rest, a sabbath for the LORD,[y] when you may neither sow your field nor prune your vineyard. **5** *The aftergrowth of your harvest you shall not reap, nor shall you pick the grapes of your untrimmed vines in this year of sabbath rest for the land. **6** While the land has its sabbath, all its produce will be food equally for you yourself and for your male and female slaves, for your hired help and the tenants who live with you, **7** and likewise for your livestock and for the wild animals on your land.

The Jubilee Year.

8 "Seven weeks of years shall you count—seven times seven years—so that the seven cycles amount to forty-nine years. **9** Then, on the tenth day of the seventh month let the trumpet resound; on this, the Day of Atonement, the trumpet blast shall re-echo throughout your land. **10** This fiftieth year* you shall make sacred by proclaiming liberty in the land for all its inhabitants.[z] It shall be a jubilee for you, when every one of you shall return to his own property, every one to his own family estate. **11** In this fiftieth year, your year of jubilee, you shall not sow, nor shall you reap the aftergrowth or pick the grapes from the untrimmed vines. **12** Since this is the jubilee, which shall be sacred for you, you may not eat of its produce, except as taken directly from the field.

13 "In this year of jubilee, then, every one of you shall return to his own property. **14** Therefore, when you sell any land to your neighbor or buy any from him, do not deal unfairly. **15** On the basis of the number of years since the last jubilee shall you purchase the land from him;[a] and so also, on the basis of the number of years for crops, shall he sell it to you. **16** When the years are many, the price shall be so much the more; when the years are few, the price shall be so much the less. For it is really the number of crops that he sells you. **17** Do not deal unfairly, then; but stand in fear of your god. I, the LORD, am your God.

18 "Observe my precepts and be careful to keep my regulations, for then you will dwell securely in the land. **19** The land will yield its fruit and you will have food in abundance, so that you may live there without worry.[b] **20** Therefore, do not say, 'What shall we eat in the seventh year, if we do not then sow or reap our crop?'[c] **21** I will bestow such blessings on you in the sixth year that there will then be crop enough for three years. **22** When you sow in the eighth year, you will continue to eat from the old crop; and even into the ninth year, when the crop comes in, you will still have the old to eat from.[d]

Redemption of Property.

23 [e]"The land shall not be sold in perpetuity; for the land is mine, and you are but aliens who have become my tenants. **24** Therefore, in every part of the country that you occupy, you must permit the land to be redeemed. **25** When one of your countrymen is reduced to poverty and has to sell some of his property, his closest relative, who has the right to redeem it, may go and buy back what his kinsman has sold.[f] **26** If, however, the man has no relative to redeem his land, but later on acquires sufficient means to buy it back in his own name, **27** he shall make a deduction from the price in proportion to the number of years since the sale, and then pay back the balance to the one to whom he sold it, so that he may thus regain his own property. **28** But if he does not acquire sufficient means to buy back his land, what he has sold shall remain in the possession of the purchaser until the jubilee, when it must be released and returned to its original owner.[g]

29 "When someone sells a dwelling in a walled town, he has the right to buy it back during the time of one full year from its sale. **30** But if such a house in a walled town has not been redeemed at the end of a full year, it shall belong in perpetuity to the purchaser and his descendants; nor shall it be released in the jubilee. **31** However, houses in villages that are not encircled by walls shall be considered as belonging to the surrounding farm land; they may be redeemed at any time, and in the jubilee they must be released.

32 "In levitical cities the Levites shall always have the right to redeem the town houses that are their property. **33** Any town house of the Levites in their cities that had been sold and not redeemed, shall be released in the jubilee; for the town houses of the Levites are their hereditary property in the midst of the Israelites. **34** Moreover, the pasture land belonging to their cities shall not be sold at all;[h] it must always remain their hereditary property.

35 "When one of your fellow countrymen is

---

z Nm 36, 4; Is 61, 2; Ez
   46, 17; Lk 4, 19.
a Lv 27, 18. 23.
b Lv 26, 5.
c Mt 6, 25. 31; Lk 12, 22.
   29.
d Lv 26, 10.

e 1 Pt 2, 11.
f Ru 2, 20; 4, 4. 6; Jer
   32, 7f.
g Lv 27, 24.
h Nm 35, 3.
i Dt 15, 7. 8.

*

25, 5ff: As long as the produce of the sabbatical year remains on the field, it remains available to everyone; cf v 12. In Ex 23, 10f the poor and the wild beasts that have no other source of nourishment are alone mentioned.

25, 10: Fiftieth year: to arrive at this number, the preceding year of jubilee is included in the count, and therefore this is more exactly the forty-ninth year, the seventh sabbatical year. Liberty: Israelite slaves were set free (v 50) and landed property was returned to its original owner (v 13): two important laws for preserving the social and economic equilibrium. Jubilee: derived from the Hebrew word yobel, "ram's horn," which was blown on this occasion.

reduced to poverty and is unable to hold out beside you, extend to him the privileges of an alien or a tenant, so that he may continue to live with you.ⁱ **36** Do not exact interest from your countryman either in money or in kind, but out of fear of God let him live with you. **37** ^jYou are to lend him neither money at interest nor food at a profit. **38** I, the LORD, am your God, who brought you out of the land of Egypt to give you the land of Canaan and to be your God.

39 "When, then, your countryman becomes so impoverished beside you that he sells you his services, do not make him work as a slave.^k **40** Rather, let him be like a hired servant or like your tenant, working with you until the jubilee year, **41** when he, together with his children, shall be released from your service and return to his kindred and to the property of his ancestors. **42** Since those whom I brought out of the land of Egypt are servants of mine, they shall not be sold as slaves to any man. **43** Do not lord it over them harshly, but stand in fear of your God.

44 "Slaves, male and female, you may indeed possess, provided you buy them from among the neighboring nations. **45** You may also buy them from among the aliens who reside with you and from their children who are born and reared in your land. Such slaves you may own as chattels, **46** and leave to your sons as their hereditary property, making them perpetual slaves. But you shall not lord it harshly over any of the Israelites, your kinsmen.^l

47 "When one of your countrymen is reduced to such poverty that he sells himself to a wealthy alien who has a permanent or a temporary residence among you, or to one of the descendants of an immigrant family, **48** even after he has thus sold his services he still has the right of redemption; he may be redeemed by one of his own brothers, **49** or by his uncle or cousin, or by some other relative or fellow clansman; or, if he acquires the means, he may redeem himself. **50** With his purchaser he shall compute the years from the sale to the jubilee, distributing the sale price over these years as though he had been hired as a day laborer. **51** The more such years there are, the more of the sale price he shall pay back as ransom; **52** the fewer years there are left before the jubilee year, the more he has to his credit; in proportion to his years of service shall he pay his ransom. **53** The alien shall treat him as a servant hired on an annual basis, and he shall not lord it over him harshly under your very eyes. **54** If he is not thus redeemed, he shall nevertheless be released, together with his children, in the jubilee year.^m **55** For to me the Israelites belong as servants; they are servants of mine, because I brought them out of the land of Egypt, I, the LORD, your God.

CHAPTER 26

The Reward of Obedience. **1** "Do not make false gods for yourselves. You shall not erect an idol or a sacred pillar for yourselves, nor shall you set up a stone figure for worship in your land;ⁿ for I, the LORD, am your God. **2** Keep my sabbaths,^o and reverence my sanctuary. I am the LORD.

3 *"If you live in accordance with my precepts and are careful to observe my commandments, **4** I will give you rain in due season, so that the land will bear its crops, and the trees their fruit;^p **5** your threshing will last till vintage time, and your vintage till the time for sowing, and you will have food to eat in abundance, so that you may dwell securely in your land. **6** I will establish peace in the land, that you may lie down to rest without anxiety. I will rid the country of ravenous beasts, and keep the sword of war from sweeping across your land. **7** You will rout your enemies and lay them low with your sword. **8** Five of you will put a hundred of your foes to flight, and a hundred of you will chase ten thousand of them, till they are cut down by your sword. **9** I will look with favor upon you, and make you fruitful and numerous, as I carry out my covenant with you. **10** So much of the old crops will you have stored up for food that you will have to discard them to make room for the new.^q **11** ^rI will set my Dwelling among you, and will not disdain you. **12** Ever present in your midst, I will be your God, and you will be my people; **13** for it is I, the LORD, your God, who brought you out of the land of the Egyptians and freed you from their slavery, breaking the yoke they had laid upon you and letting you walk erect.

Punishment of Disobedience. **14** "But if you do not heed me and do not keep all these commandments, **15** if you reject my precepts and spurn my decrees, refusing to obey all my commandments and breaking my covenant, **16** then I, in turn, will give you your deserts. I will punish you with terrible woes—with wasting and fever to dim the eyes and sap the life. You will sow your seed in vain, for your enemies will consume the crop. **17** I will turn against you, till you are beaten down before your enemies and lorded over by your foes. You

j Dt 23, 19.
k 1 Kgs 9, 22.
l Is 14, 1f.
m Ex 21, 2f.
n Lv 19, 4; Ex 20, 4; Nm 33, 52; Dt 5, 8.
o Ex 20, 8.
p Ps 85, 13.
q Lv 25, 22.
r 11f: Ex 29, 45; Ez 39, 26ff; 2 Cor 6, 16.
s Dt 28, 25.

*

26, 3–45: Since God's covenant was with the Israelite nation as a whole, these promises and threats are made primarily to the entire community. The rewards and punishments are of a temporal nature because the community as such exists only here on earth, not in the hereafter.

will take to flight though no one pursues you.[s]

18 "If even after this you do not obey me, I will increase the chastisement for your sins sevenfold, **19** to break your haughty confidence. I will make the sky above you as hard as iron, and your soil as hard as bronze, **20** so that your strength will be spent in vain; your land will bear no crops, and its trees no fruit.

21 "If then you become defiant in your unwillingness to obey me, I will multiply my blows another sevenfold, as your sins deserve. **22** I will unleash the wild beasts against you, to rob you of your children and wipe out your livestock, till your population dwindles away and your roads become deserted.

23 "If, with all this, you still refuse to be chastened by me and continue to defy me, **24** I, too, will defy you and will smite you for your sins seven times harder than before.[t] **25** I will make the sword, the avenger of my covenant, sweep over you. Though you then huddle together in your walled cities, I will send in pestilence among you, till you are forced to surrender to the enemy. **26** And as I cut off your supply of bread, ten women will need but one oven for baking all the bread they dole out to you in rations[u] —not enough food to still your hunger.

27 "If, despite all this, you still persist in disobeying and defying me, **28** I, also, will meet you with fiery defiance and will chastise you with sevenfold fiercer punishment for your sins, **29** [v]till you begin to eat the flesh of your own sons and daughters.* **30** I will demolish your high places,[w] overthrow your incense stands, and cast your corpses on those of your idols. In my abhorrence of you, **31** I will lay waste your cities and devastate your sanctuaries, refusing to accept your sweet-smelling offerings. **32** So devastated will I leave the land that your very enemies who come to live there will stand aghast at the sight of it.[x] **33** You yourselves I will scatter among the nations[y] at the point of my drawn sword, leaving your countryside desolate and your cities deserted. **34** Then shall the land retrieve its lost sabbaths during all the time it lies waste, while you are in the land of your enemies; then shall the land have rest and make up for its sabbaths[z] **35** during all the time that it lies desolate, enjoying the rest that you would not let it have on the sabbaths when you lived there.

36 "Those of you who survive in the lands of their enemies I will make so fainthearted that, if leaves rustle behind them, they will flee headlong, as if from the sword, though no one pursues them; **37** stumbling over one another as if to escape a weapon, while no one is after them—so helpless will you be to take a stand against your foes! **38** You will be lost among the Gentiles, swallowed up in your enemies'

country. **39** Those of you who survive in the lands of their enemies will waste away for their own and their fathers' guilt.[a]

40 "Thus they will have to confess that they and their fathers were guilty of having rebelled against me and of having defied me, **41** so that I, too, had to defy them and bring them into their enemies' land. Then, when their uncircumcised hearts are humbled and they make amends for their guilt, **42** I will remember my covenant with Jacob, my covenant with Isaac, and my covenant with Abraham;[b] and of the land, too, I will be mindful. **43** But the land must first be rid of them, that in its desolation it may make up its lost sabbaths, and that they, too, may make good the debt of their guilt for having spurned my precepts and abhorred my statutes. **44** Yet even so, even while they are in their enemies' land, I will not reject or spurn them, lest, by wiping them out, I make void my covenant with them; for I, the LORD, am their God. **45** I will remember them because of the covenant I made with their forefathers, whom I brought out of the land of Egypt under the very eyes of the Gentiles,[c] that I, the LORD, might be their God."

46 *These are the precepts, decrees and laws which the LORD had Moses promulgate on Mount Sinai in the pact between himself and the Israelites.

V: Redemption of Offerings

CHAPTER 27

Redemption of Votive Offerings. **1** The LORD said to Moses, **2** "Speak to the Israelites and tell them: When anyone fulfills a vow of offering one or more persons to the LORD, who are to be ransomed at a fixed sum of money, **3** for persons between the ages of twenty and sixty, the fixed sum, in sanctuary shekels, shall be fifty silver shekels for a man, **4** and thirty shekels for a woman; **5** for persons between the ages of five and twenty, the fixed sum shall be twenty shekels for a youth, and ten for a maiden; **6** for persons between the ages of one month

---

t 24f; Jer 2, 30; Ez 5, 17; 14, 17.
u Is 9, 19; Ez 4, 16; 5, 16; 14, 13; Mi 6, 14.
v Is 9, 18.
w 2 Chr 14, 5; 34, 3. 4. 7; Ez 6, 3-6.
x 1 Kgs 9, 8; Jer 9, 11; 18, 16; 19, 8; 25, 18;

Ez 5, 15.
y Jer 9, 16; Zec 7, 14.
z Lv 25, 2; 2 Chr 36, 21.
a Ez 4, 17; 24, 23; 33, 10.
b Ex 6, 5; 2 Kgs 13, 23; Ps 106, 45; Ez 16, 60.
c Ex 12, 51.

*

26, 29: Eat the flesh of your own sons and daughters: extreme famine in cities under siege often forced their inhabitants to such dire means of subsistence. Cf Dt 28, 53; Jer 19, 9; Ez 5, 10; 2 Kgs 6, 28f.

26, 46: The Book of Leviticus seems originally to have ended here; the following chapter is an appendix.

and five years, the fixed sum shall be five silver shekels for a boy, and three for a girl; **7** for persons of sixty or more, the fixed sum shall be fifteen shekels for a man, and ten for a woman. **8** However, if the one who took the vow is too poor to meet the fixed sum, the person must be set before the priest, who shall determine the sum for his ransom in keeping with the means of the one who made the vow.

9 "If the offering vowed to the LORD is an animal that may be sacrificed, every such animal, when vowed to the LORD, becomes sacred. **10** The offerer shall not present a substitute for it by exchanging either a better for a worse one or a worse for a better one. If he attempts to offer one animal in place of another, both the original and its substitute shall be treated as sacred. **11** If the animal vowed to the LORD is unclean and therefore unfit for sacrifice, it must be set before the priest, **12** who shall determine its value* in keeping with its good or bad qualities, and the value set by the priest shall stand. **13** If the offerer wishes to redeem the animal, he shall pay one fifth more than this valuation. *d*

14 "When someone dedicates his house as sacred to the LORD, the priest shall determine its value in keeping with its good or bad points, and the value set by the priest shall stand. **15** If the one who dedicated his house wishes to redeem it, he shall pay one fifth more than the price thus established, and then it will again be his.

16 "If the object which someone dedicates to the LORD is a piece of his hereditary land, its valuation shall be made according to the amount of seed required to sow it, the acreage sown with a homer of barley seed being valued at fifty silver shekels. **17** If the dedication of a field is made at the beginning of a jubilee period, the full valuation shall hold; **18** but if it is some time after this, the priest shall estimate its money value according to the number of years left until the next jubilee year, with a corresponding rebate on the valuation. *e* **19** If the one who dedicated his field wishes to redeem it, he shall pay one fifth more than the price thus established, and so reclaim it. **20** If, instead of redeeming such a field, he sells it to someone else, it may no longer be redeemed; **21** but at the jubilee it shall be released as sacred to the LORD; like a field that is doomed, it shall become priestly property.

22 "If the field that some man dedicates to the LORD is one he had purchased and not a part of his hereditary property, **23** the priest shall compute its value in proportion to the number of years until the next jubilee, and on the same day the price thus established shall be given as sacred to the LORD; **24** at the jubilee, *f* however, the field shall revert to the hereditary owner of this land from whom it had been purchased.

25 "Every valuation shall be made accord-

ing to the standard of the sanctuary shekel. There are twenty gerahs to the shekel.

Offerings Not To Be Redeemed.

26 "Note that a first-born animal, *g* which as such already belongs to the LORD, may not be dedicated by vow to him. If it is an ox or a sheep, it shall be ceded to the LORD; **27** but if it is an unclean animal,* it may be redeemed by paying one fifth more than its fixed value. If it is not redeemed, it shall be sold at its fixed value.

28 "Note, also, that any one of his possessions which a man vows as doomed to the LORD, whether it is a human being or an animal or a hereditary field, shall be neither sold nor ransomed; everything that is thus doomed becomes most sacred to the LORD. *h* **29** All human beings that are doomed* lose the right to be redeemed; they must be put to death.

30 "All tithes of the land, whether in grain from the fields or in fruit from the trees, belong to the LORD, as sacred to him. *i* **31** If someone wishes to buy back any of his tithes, he shall pay one fifth more than their value. **32** The tithes of the herd and the flock shall be determined by ceding to the LORD as sacred every tenth animal as they are counted by the herdsman's rod. **33** It shall not matter whether good ones or bad ones are thus chosen, and no exchange may be made. If any exchange is attempted, both the original animal and its substitute shall be treated as sacred, without the right of being bought back."

34 These are the commandments which the LORD gave Moses on Mount Sinai for the Israelites.

---

d Lv 22, 14.
e Lv 25, 15f.
f Lv 25, 10. 28. 41.
g Ex 13, 2.

h 1 Sm 15, 21.
i Nm 18, 21. 24; 2 Chr 31, 5f. 12; Mal 3, 8.
10.

---

*

27, 12: Determine its value: fix the price at which the animal may be sold to someone else. Only the original owner must pay the twenty percent tax, as a penalty for buying back what he had vowed to God. So also for houses and fields that are vowed to the Lord, as treated of in the following verses. The money from the sale or from the redemption of such vowed property naturally goes to the sanctuary.

27, 27: An unclean animal: such as the first-born of an ass, which was unfit for sacrifice. According to Ex 13, 13; 34, 20, a first-born ass was to be redeemed by offering a sheep in its stead, or was to have its neck broken. The present law is probably a later modification of the earlier one.

27, 29: All human beings that are doomed: according to some interpreters, this signifies the idolatrous Canaanites, who were doomed to destruction by divine authority; according to others, this drastic law was enacted for the purpose of discouraging private persons from rashly vowing their slaves or other dependents as offerings to God. Cf Ex 22, 19; Dt 13, 13–19.

The Book of

NUMBERS

The Book of Numbers derives its name from the account of the two censuses of the Hebrew people taken, one near the beginning and the other toward the end of the journey in the desert (chapters 1 and 26). It continues the story of that journey, begun in Exodus, and describes briefly the experiences of the Israelites for a period of thirty-eight years, from the end of their encampment at Sinai to their arrival at the border of the Promised Land. Numerous legal ordinances are interspersed in the account, making the book a combination of law and history.

The various events described clearly indicate the action of God, who punishes the murmuring of the people by prolonging their stay in the desert, at the same time preparing them by this discipline to be his witnesses among the nations.

In the New Testament Christ and the Apostles derive useful lessons from such events in the Book of Numbers as the brazen serpent (Jn 3, 14f), the sedition of Korah and its consequences (1 Cor 10, 10), the prophecies of Balaam (2 Pt 2, 15f), and the water gushing from the rock (1 Cor 10, 4).

The chief divisions of the Book of Numbers are as follows:
I. Preparation for the Departure from Sinai (Nm 1, 1–10, 10).
II. From Sinai to the Plains of Moab (Nm 10, 11–22, 1).
III. On the Plains of Moab (Nm 22, 2–36, 13).

I: Preparation for the Departure from Sinai

CHAPTER 1

The Census. 1 In the year following that of the Israelites' departure from the land of Egypt, on the first day of the second month, the LORD said to Moses in the meeting tent in the desert of Sinai: 2 *"Take a census of the whole community of the Israelites,[a] by clans and ancestral houses, registering each male individually. 3 You and Aaron shall enroll in companies all the men in Israel of twenty years or more who are fit for military service.

Moses' Assistants. 4 "To assist you there shall be a man from each tribe, the head of his ancestral house. 5 [b]These are the names of those who are to assist you:

from Reuben: Elizur, son of Shedeur;
6 from Simeon: Shelumiel, son of Zurishaddai;
7 from Judah: Nahshon, son of Amminadab;
8 from Issachar: Nethanel, son of Zuar;
9 from Zebulun: Eliab, son of Helon;
10 from Ephraim: Elishama, son of Ammihud, and from Manasseh: Gamaliel, son of Pedahzur, for the descendants of Joseph;
11 from Benjamin: Abidan, son of Gideoni;
12 from Dan: Ahiezer, son of Ammishaddai;
13 from Asher: Pagiel, son of Ochran;

14 from Gad: Eliasaph, son of Reuel;
15 from Naphtali: Ahira, son of Enan.''

16 [c]These were councilors of the community, princes of their ancestral tribes, chiefs of the troops* of Israel. 17 So Moses and Aaron took these men who had been designated, 18 and assembled the whole community on the first day of the second month. Every man of twenty years or more then declared his name and lineage according to clan and ancestral house, 19 as the LORD had commanded Moses.

Count of the Twelve Tribes. This is their census as taken in the desert of Sinai. 20 Of the descendants of Reuben, the first-born of Israel, registered by lineage in clans and ancestral houses: when all the males of twenty years or more who were fit for military service were polled, 21 forty-six thousand five hundred were enrolled in the tribe of Reuben.

22 Of the descendants of Simeon, registered by lineage in clans and ancestral houses: when all the males of twenty years or more who were

---

a 2f: Nm 14, 29; 26,   b 5-15: Nm 10, 14-27.
  2-51.   c Ex 18, 21. 25.

1, 2: All Israel was divided into tribes, each tribe into clans, and each clan into ancestral houses.

1, 16: Troops: literally "thousands"; this division of the Israelites, with its subdivisions of "hundreds, fifties and tens," was primarily for military and judicial purposes. Ct Ex 18, 21: 2 Sm 18, 1.

fit for military service were polled, **23** fifty-nine thousand three hundred were enrolled in the tribe of Simeon.

24 Of the descendants of Gad, registered by lineage in clans and ancestral houses: when all the males of twenty years or more who were fit for military service were polled, **25** forty-five thousand six hundred and fifty were enrolled in the tribe of Gad.

26 Of the descendants of Judah, registered by lineage in clans and ancestral houses: when all the males of twenty years or more who were fit for military service were polled, **27** seventy-four thousand six hundred were enrolled in the tribe of Judah.

28 Of the descendants of Issachar, registered by lineage in clans and ancestral houses: when all the males of twenty years or more who were fit for military service were polled, **29** fifty-four thousand four hundred were enrolled in the tribe of Issachar.

30 Of the descendants of Zebulun, registered by lineage in clans and ancestral houses: when all the males of twenty years or more who were fit for military service were polled, **31** fifty-seven thousand four hundred were enrolled in the tribe of Zebulun.

32 Of the descendants of Joseph—

Of the descendants of Ephraim, registered by lineage in clans and ancestral houses: when all the males of twenty years or more who were fit for military service were polled, **33** forty thousand five hundred were enrolled in the tribe of Ephraim.

34 Of the descendants of Manasseh, registered by lineage in clans and ancestral houses: when all the males of twenty years or more who were fit for military service were polled, **35** thirty-two thousand two hundred were enrolled in the tribe of Manasseh.

36 Of the descendants of Benjamin, registered by lineage in clans and ancestral houses: when all the males of twenty years or more who were fit for military service were polled, **37** thirty-five thousand two hundred were enrolled in the tribe of Benjamin.

38 Of the descendants of Dan, registered by lineage in clans and ancestral houses: when all the males of twenty years or more who were fit for military service were polled, **39** sixty-two thousand seven hundred were enrolled in the tribe of Dan.

40 Of the descendants of Asher, registered by lineage in clans and ancestral houses: when all the males of twenty years or more who were fit for military service were polled, **41** forty-one thousand five hundred were enrolled in the tribe of Asher.

42 Of the descendants of Naphtali, registered by lineage in clans and ancestral houses: when all the males of twenty years or more who

were fit for military service were polled, **43** fifty-three thousand four hundred were enrolled in the tribe of Naphtali.

44 It was these who were registered, each according to his ancestral house, in the census taken by Moses and Aaron and the twelve princes of Israel. **45** The total number of the Israelites of twenty years or more who were fit for military service, registered by ancestral houses, **46** was six hundred and three thousand five hundred and fifty.

Levites Omitted in the Census. **47** The Levites, however, were not registered[d] by ancestral tribe with the others.* **48** For the LORD had told Moses, **49** "The tribe of Levi alone you shall not enroll nor include in the census along with the other Israelites. **50** You are to give the Levites charge of the Dwelling of the commandments with all its equipment and all that belongs to it. It is they who shall carry the Dwelling with all its equipment and who shall be its ministers.[e] They shall therefore camp around the Dwelling. **51** When the Dwelling is to move on, the Levites shall take it down; when the Dwelling is to be pitched, it is the Levites who shall set it up.[f] Any layman who comes near it shall be put to death. **52** While the other Israelites shall camp by companies, each in his own division of the camp,[g] **53** the Levites shall camp around the Dwelling of the commandments.[h] Otherwise God's wrath will strike the Israelite community. The Levites, then, shall have charge of the Dwelling of the commandments." **54** All this the Israelites fulfilled as the LORD had commanded Moses.

CHAPTER 2

Arrangement of the Tribes. **1** The LORD said to Moses and Aaron: **2** "The Israelites shall camp, each in his own division, under the ensigns of their ancestral houses.[i] They shall camp around the meeting tent, but at some distance from it.

3 *"Encamped on the east side, toward the sunrise, shall be the divisional camp of Judah, arranged in companies. [The prince of the Judahites was Nahshon, son of Amminadab, **4** and his soldiers amounted in the census to

---

d Nm 2, 33; 3, 14-39; 26, 57-62.
e Nm 3, 7f; 4, 2-49; 1 Chr 6, 48.
f Nm 3, 10. 38; 18, 7; 2 Sm 6, 6f; 1 Chr 13,
g Nm 2, 2. 34.
h Nm 3, 7f. 38; 8, 19; 18, 4f.
i Nm 1. 52.

*

1, 47: The Levites were not enrolled in this census, which was principally for military purposes, but a separate census was made of them. Cf Nm 3, 15f. 39.

2, 3–31: A similar arrangement of the tribes around the central sanctuary in the ideal Israelite state is given in Ez 48.

seventy-four thousand six hundred.] **5** With Judah shall camp the tribe of Issachar [their prince was Nethanel, son of Zuar, **6** and his soldiers amounted in the census to fifty-four thousand four hundred] **7** and the tribe of Zebulun. [Their prince was Eliab, son of Helon, **8** and his soldiers amounted in the census to fifty-seven thousand four hundred. **9** The total number of those registered by companies in the camp of Judah was one hundred and eighty-six thousand four hundred.] These shall be first on the march.

10 "On the south side shall be the divisional camp of Reuben, arranged in companies. [Their prince was Elizur, son of Shedeur, **11** and his soldiers amounted in the census to forty-six thousand five hundred.] **12** Beside them shall camp the tribe of Simeon [their prince was Shelumiel, son of Zurishaddai, **13** and his soldiers amounted in the census to fifty-nine thousand three hundred] **14** and next the tribe of Gad. [Their prince was Eliasaph, son of Reuel, **15** and his soldiers amounted in the census to forty-five thousand six hundred and fifty. **16** The total number of those registered by companies in the camp of Reuben was one hundred and fifty-one thousand four hundred and fifty.] These shall be second on the march.

17 "Then the meeting tent and the camp of the Levites shall set out in the middle of the line. As in camp, so also on the march, every man shall be in his proper place, with his own division.

18 "On the west side shall be the divisional camp of Ephraim, arranged in companies. [Their prince was Elishama, son of Ammihud, **19** and his soldiers amounted in the census to forty thousand five hundred.] **20** Beside them shall camp the tribe of Manasseh [their prince was Gamaliel, son of Pedahzur, **21** and his soldiers amounted in the census to thirty-two thousand two hundred] **22** and the tribe of Benjamin. [Their prince was Abidan, son of Gideoni, **23** and his soldiers amounted in the census to thirty-five thousand four hundred. **24** The total number of those registered by companies in the camp of Ephraim was one hundred and eight thousand one hundred.] These shall be third on the march.

25 "On the north side shall be the divisional camp of Dan, arranged in companies. [Their prince was Ahiezer, son of Ammishaddai, **26** and his soldiers amounted in the census to sixty-two thousand seven hundred.] **27** Beside them shall camp the tribe of Asher [their prince was Pagiel, son of Ochran, **28** and his soldiers amounted in the census to forty-one thousand five hundred] **29** and next the tribe of Naphtali. [Their prince was Ahira, son of Enan, **30** and his soldiers amounted in the census to fifty-three thousand four hundred. **31** The total number of those registered by companies in the camp of Dan was one hundred and fifty-seven thousand six hundred.] These shall be the last of the divisions on the march."

32 [j]This was the census of the Israelites taken by ancestral houses. The total number of those registered by companies in the camps was six hundred and three thousand five hundred and fifty. **33** The Levites, however, were not registered with the other Israelites, for so the LORD had commanded Moses. **34** The Israelites did just as the LORD had commanded Moses; both in camp and on the march they were in their own divisions, every man according to his clan and his ancestral house.

CHAPTER 3

The Sons of Aaron. **1** The following were the descendants of Aaron and Moses at the time that the LORD spoke to Moses on Mount Sinai. **2** The sons of Aaron were Nadab his first-born, Abihu, Eleazar, and Ithamar.[k] **3** These are the names of the sons of Aaron, the anointed priests who were ordained to exercise the priesthood. **4** But when Nadab and Abihu offered profane fire before the LORD in the desert of Sinai, they met death[l] in the presence of the LORD, and left no sons. Thereafter only Eleazar and Ithamar performed the priestly functions under the direction of their father Aaron.

Levites in Place of the First-born.

5 Now the LORD said to Moses: **6** "Summon the tribe of Levi and present them to Aaron the priest, as his assistants.[m] **7** They shall discharge his obligations and those of the whole community before the meeting tent[n] by serving at the Dwelling. **8** They shall have custody of all the furnishings of the meeting tent and discharge the duties of the Israelites in the service of the Dwelling. **9** You shall give the Levites to Aaron and his sons;[o] they have been set aside from among the Israelites as dedicated to me. **10** But only Aaron and his descendants shall you appoint to have charge of the priestly functions.[p] Any layman who comes near shall be put to death."

11 The LORD said to Moses, **12** "It is I who have chosen the Levites from the Israelites in place of every first-born that opens the womb among the Israelites.[q] The Levites, therefore, are mine, **13** because every first-born is mine. When I slew all the first-born in the land of Egypt, I made all the first-born in Israel sacred to me, both of man and of beast. They belong to me; I am the LORD."

---

j 32-33: Nm 1, 46-49.
k Ex 6, 23.
l Nm 26, 61; Lv 10, 1f; 1 Chr 24, 2.
m Nm 18, 2.
n Nm 8, 24.
o Nm 8, 19.
p Nm 1, 51; 18, 7.
q 12f: Nm 3, 41; 8, 16f; Ex 13, 2. 12. 15.

Census of the Levites.

14 The LORD said to Moses in the desert of Sinai, 15 "Take a census of the Levites by ancestral houses and clans, registering every male of a month or more."r 16 Moses, therefore, took their census in accordance with the command the LORD had given him.

17 sThe sons of Levi were named Gershon, Kohath and Merari. 18 The descendants of Gershon, by clans, were named Libni and Shimei. 19 The descendants of Kohath, by clans, were Amram, Izhar, Hebron and Uzziel. 20 The descendants of Merari, by clans, were Mahli and Mushi. These were the clans of the Levites by ancestral houses.

Duties of the Levitical Clans.

21 To Gershon belonged the clan of the Libnites and the clan of the Shimeites; these were the clans of the Gershonites. 22 When all their males of a month or more were registered, they numbered seven thousand five hundred. 23 The clans of the Gershonites camped behind the Dwelling, to the west. 24 The prince of their ancestral house was Eliasaph, son of Lael. 25 tAt the meeting tent they had charge of whatever pertained to the Dwelling,* the tent and its covering, the curtain at the entrance of the meeting tent, 26 the hangings of the court, the curtain at the entrance of the court enclosing both the Dwelling and the altar, and the ropes.

27 To Kohath belonged the clans of the Amramites, the Izharites, the Hebronites, and the Uzzielites; these were the clans of the Kohathites. 28 When all their males of a month or more were registered, they numbered eight thousand three hundred. They had charge of the sanctuary. 29 The clans of the Kohathites camped at the south side of the Dwelling. 30 The prince of their ancestral house was Elizaphan, son of Uzziel. 31 They had charge of whatever pertained to the ark, the table, the lampstand, the altars, the utensils with which the ministry of the sanctuary was exercised, and the veil.* 32 The chief prince of the Levites, however, was Eleazar, son of Aaron the priest; he was supervisor over those who had charge of the sanctuary.

33 To Merari belonged the clans of the Mahlites and the Mushites; these were the clans of Merari. 34 When all their males of a month or more were registered, they numbered six thousand two hundred. 35 The prince of the ancestral house of the clans of Merari was Zuriel, son of Abihail. They camped at the north side of the Dwelling. 36 *The Merarites were charged with the care of whatever pertained to the boards of the Dwelling, its bars, columns, pedestals, and all its fittings, 37 as well as the columns of the surrounding court with their pedestals, pegs and ropes.

38 East of the Dwelling, that is, in front of the meeting tent, toward the sunrise, were camped Moses and Aaron and the latter's sons. They discharged the obligations of the sanctuary for the Israelites. Any layman who came near was to be put to death.

39 The total number of male Levites a month old or more whom Moses had registered by clans in keeping with the LORD's command, was twenty-two thousand.

Census and Ransom of First-born.

40 The LORD then said to Moses, "Take a census of all the first-born males of the Israelites a month old or more, and compute their total number. 41 Then assign the Levites to me, the LORD, in place of all the first-born of the Israelites, as well as their cattle in place of all the first-born among the cattle of the Israelites." 42 So Moses took a census of all the first-born of the Israelites, as the LORD had commanded him. 43 When all the first-born males of a month or more were registered, they numbered twenty-two thousand two hundred and seventy-three.

44 The LORD said to Moses: 45 "Take the Levites in place of all the first-born of the Israelites, and the Levites' cattle in place of their cattle, that the Levites may belong to me. I am the LORD. 46 As ransom for the two hundred and seventy-three first-born of the Israelites who outnumber the Levites, 47 you shall take five shekels for each individual, according to the standard of the sanctuary shekel, twenty gerahs to the shekel.u 48 Give this silver to Aaron and his sons as ransom for the extra number." 49 So Moses took the silver as ransom from those who were left when the rest had been redeemed by the Levites. 50 From the first-born of the Israelites he received in silver one thousand three hundred and sixty-five shekels according to the sanctuary standard. 51 He then gave this ransom silver to Aaron and his sons, as the LORD had commanded him.

---

r Nm 3, 39; 26, 62.
s 17-20: Nm 26, 57; Gn 46, 11; Ex 6, 16-19; 1 Chr 6, 1f. 16-19.
t 25-26: Ex 26, 7. 14. 36; 36, 14.
u Nm 18, 16; Ex 30, 13; Lv 27, 25; Ez 45, 12.

---

*

3, 25f: The Gershonites had two wagons for transporting these things; cf Nm 7, 7. For a description of the Dwelling, see Ex 26, 1–6; the tent, Ex 26, 7–13; its covering, Ex 26, 14; the curtain at the entrance, Ex 26, 36; the hangings of the court, Ex 27, 9–15; the curtain at the entrance of the court, Ex 27, 16; the ropes of the Dwelling, Ex 35, 18.

3, 31: The Kohathites had to carry these sacred objects on their shoulders; cf Nm 7, 9. For a description of the ark, see Ex 25, 10–22; the table, Ex 25, 23–30; the lampstand, Ex 25, 31–40; the altars, Ex 27, 1–8; 30, 1–10.

3, 36f: The Merarites had four wagons for transporting this heavy material; cf Nm 7, 8. For a description of the boards, bars, etc., of the Dwelling, see Ex 26, 15–30; the columns, pedestals, etc., of the court, Ex 27, 9–19.

CHAPTER 4

Duties Further Defined. 1 The LORD said to Moses and Aaron: 2 "Among the Levites take a total of the Kohathites, by clans and ancestral houses, all the men of the Kohathites 3 between thirty* and fifty years of age; these are to undertake obligatory tasks in the meeting tent. *v*

4 "The service of the Kohathites in the meeting tent concerns the most sacred objects. 5 In breaking camp, Aaron and his sons shall go in and take down the screening curtain* and cover the ark of the commandments with it. 6 Over these they shall put a cover of tahash skin, and on top of this spread an all-violet cloth. They shall then put the poles in place. 7 On the table of the Presence they shall spread a violet cloth and put on it the plates and cups, as well as the bowls and pitchers for libations; the established bread offering shall remain on the table. 8 Over these they shall spread a scarlet cloth and cover all this with tahash skin. They shall then put the poles in place. 9 They shall use a violet cloth to cover the lampstand with its lamps, trimming shears, and trays, as well as the various containers of oil from which it is supplied. 10 The lampstand with all its utensils they shall then enclose in a covering of tahash skin, and place on a litter. 11 Over the golden altar* they shall spread a violet cloth, and cover this also with a covering of tahash skin. They shall then put the poles in place. 12 Taking the utensils of the sanctuary service, they shall wrap them all in violet cloth and cover them with tahash skin. They shall then place them on a litter. 13 After cleansing the altar* of its ashes, they shall spread a purple cloth over it. 14 On this they shall put all the utensils with which it is served: the fire pans, forks,* shovels, basins, and all the utensils of the altar. They shall then spread a covering of tahash skin over this, and put the poles in place.

15 "Only after Aaron and his sons have finished covering the sacred objects and all their utensils on breaking camp, shall the Kohathites enter to carry them. But they shall not touch the sacred objects; if they do they will die. *w* These, then, are the objects in the meeting tent that the Kohathites shall carry.

16 "Eleazar, son of Aaron the priest, shall be in charge of the oil for the light, the fragrant incense, the established cereal offering, and the anointing oil. He shall be in charge of the whole Dwelling with all the sacred objects and utensils that are in it."

17 The LORD said to Moses and Aaron: 18 "Do not let the group of Kohathite clans perish from the body of the Levites. 19 That they may live and not die when they approach the most sacred objects, this is what you shall do for them: Aaron and his sons shall go in and assign to each of them his task and what he must carry; 20 but the Kohathites shall not go in to look upon the sacred objects, even for an instant; if they do, they will die." *x*

21 The LORD said to Moses, 22 "Take a total among the Gershonites also, by ancestral houses and clans, 23 of all the men between thirty and fifty years of age; these are to undertake obligatory tasks in the meeting tent. 24 This is the task of the clans of the Gershonites, what they must do and what they must carry: 25 they shall carry the sheets of the Dwelling, the meeting tent with its covering and the outer wrapping of tahash skin, the curtain at the entrance of the meeting tent, 26 the hangings of the court, the curtain at the entrance of the court that encloses both the Dwelling and the altar, together with their ropes and all other objects necessary in their use. Whatever is to be done with these things shall be their task. 27 The service of the Gershonites shall be entirely under the direction of Aaron and his sons, with regard to what they must do and what they must carry; you shall make each man of them responsible for what he is to carry. 28 This, then, is the task of the Gershonites in the meeting tent; and they shall be under the supervision of Ithamar, son of Aaron the priest.

29 "Among the Merarites, too, you shall enroll by clans and ancestral houses 30 all their men between thirty and fifty years of age; these are to undertake obligatory tasks in the meeting tent. 31 *y* This is what they shall be responsible for carrying, all the years of their service in the meeting tent: the boards of the Dwelling with its bars, columns and pedestals, 32 and the columns of the surrounding court with their pedestals, pegs and ropes. You shall designate for each man of them all the objects connected with his service, which he shall be responsible for carrying. 33 This, then, is the task of the clans of the Merarites during all their service in the meeting tent under the supervision of Ithamar, son of Aaron the priest."

---

v Nm 8, 24; 1 Chr 23, 24-27.
w 2 Sm 6, 6f; 1 Chr 13,
9f.
x 1 Sm 6, 19.
y Nm 3, 36f.

---

*

4, 3: Thirty: at a later period the Levites began to serve when they were twenty-five (Nm 8, 24) or even only twenty years old (1 Chr 23, 24. 27; 2 Chr 31, 17; Ezr 3, 8; but cf 1 Chr 23, 3).

4, 5: The screening curtain: the veil between the inner and the outer rooms of the sanctuary. Cf Ex 26, 31–33.

4, 11: The golden altar: the altar of incense. Cf Ex 30, 1–6.

4, 13: The altar: the bronze altar of holocausts. Cf Ex 27, 1–8.

4, 14: Forks: used in turning over the sacrificed animal on the fire of the altar. Basins: to receive the sacrificial blood; cf Zec 9, 15.

Number of Adult Levites. 34 So Moses and Aaron and the princes of the community made a registration among the Kohathites, by clans and ancestral houses, 35 of all the men between thirty and fifty years of age. These were to undertake obligatory tasks in the meeting tent; 36 as registered by clans, they numbered two thousand seven hundred and fifty. 37 Such was the census of all the men of the Kohathite clans who were to serve in the meeting tent, which Moses took, together with Aaron, as the LORD bade him.

38 The registration was then made among the Gershonites, by clans and ancestral houses, 39 of all the men between thirty and fifty years of age. These were to undertake obligatory tasks in the meeting tent; 40 as registered by clans and ancestral houses, they numbered two thousand six hundred and thirty. 41 Such was the census of all the men of the Gershonite clans who were to serve in the meeting tent, which Moses took, together with Aaron, at the LORD's bidding.

42 Then the registration was made among the Merarites, by clans and ancestral houses, 43 of all the men from thirty up to fifty years of age. These were to undertake obligatory tasks in the meeting tent; 44 as registered by clans, they numbered three thousand two hundred. 45 Such was the census of the men of the Merarite clans which Moses took, together with Aaron, as the LORD bade him.

46 Therefore, when Moses and Aaron and the Israelite princes had completed the registration among the Levites, by clans and ancestral houses, 47 of all the men between thirty and fifty years of age who were to undertake tasks of service or transport of the meeting tent, 48 the total number registered was eight thousand five hundred and eighty. 49 According to the LORD's bidding to Moses, they gave them their individual assignments for service and for transport; so the LORD had commanded Moses.

CHAPTER 5

The Unclean Expelled. 1 The LORD said to Moses: 2 "Order the Israelites to expel from camp every leper, and everyone suffering from a discharge, and everyone who has become unclean by contact with a corpse.*z 3 Male and female alike, you shall compel them to go out of the camp; they are not to defile the camp in which I dwell."a 4 The Israelites obeyed the command that the LORD had given Moses; they expelled them from the camp.

Unjust Possession. 5 *The LORD said to Moses, 6 b"Tell the Israelites: If a man (or woman) commits a fault against his fellow man and wrongs him, thus breaking faith with the

LORD, 7 he shall confess the wrong he has done, restore his ill-gotten goods in full, and in addition give one fifth of their value to the one he has wronged. 8 However, if the latter has no next of kin* to whom restoration of the ill-gotten goods can be made, the goods to be restored shall be the LORD's and shall fall to the priest; this is apart from the atonement ram with which the priest makes amends for the guilty man. 9 Likewise, every sacred contribution that the Israelites are bound to make shall fall to the priest.c 10 Each Israelite man may dispose of his own sacred contributions; they become the property of the priest to whom he gives them."d

Ordeal for a Suspected Adulteress. 11 The LORD said to Moses, 12 "Speak to the Israelites and tell them: If a man's wife goes astray and becomes unfaithful to him 13 by having intercourse with another man,e though her husband has not sufficient evidence of the fact, so that her impurity remains unproved for lack of a witness who might have caught her in the act; 14 or if a man is overcome by a feeling of jealousy that makes him suspect his wife, whether she was actually impure or not: 15 he shall bring his wife to the priest and shall take along as an offering for her a tenth of an ephah of barley meal. However, he shall not pour oil on it nor put frankincense over it, since it is a cereal offering of jealousy, a cereal offering for an appeal in a question of guilt.

16 "The priest shall first have the woman come forward and stand before the LORD. 17 In an earthen vessel he shall meanwhile put some holy water,* as well as some dust that he has taken from the floor of the Dwelling.f 18 Then, as the woman stands before the LORD, the priest shall uncover her head and place in her hands the cereal offering of her appeal,* that is, the cereal offering of jealousy, while he himself shall hold the bitter water that brings a curse. 19 Then he shall adjure the woman, saying to her, 'If no other man has had intercourse with

---

z Nm 19, 11. 13; Lv 13, 46; 21, 1; 22, 4.
a Nm 35, 34.
b 6ff; Lv 5, 21-25.
c Dt 18, 3f; Ex 44, 29f.
d Lv 10, 12-15.
e Lv 18, 20; Jn 8, 4.
f Nm 19, 17.

*

5, 2: For the laws regarding victims of leprosy, see Lv 13–14; those suffering from a discharge, Lv 15; the unclean by contact with a corpse, Nm 19, 11–22; Lv 21, 1–4.

5, 5–10: The basic law on unjust possession is given in Lv 5, 14–26. The new item here concerns the case where the injured party has died and left no heirs, in which case the restitution must be made to the priest.

5, 8: Next of kin: literally, "redeemer," a technical term denoting the nearest relative, upon whom devolved the obligation of "redeeming" the family property, in order to keep it within the family. Cf Lv 25, 25; Ru 4, 1–6.

5, 17: Holy water: water from the laver that stood in the court of the Dwelling.

5, 18: Appeal: by which she invokes the Lord and refers her case to his decision.

you, and you have not gone astray by impurity while under the authority of your husband, be immune to the curse brought by this bitter water. **20** But if you have gone astray while under the authority of your husband and have acted impurely by letting a man other than your husband have intercourse with you'—; **21** so shall the priest adjure the woman with this oath of imprecation—'may the LORD make you an example of malediction and imprecation* among your people by causing your thighs to waste away and your belly to swell! **22** May this water, then, that brings a curse, enter your body to make your belly swell and your thighs waste away!'g And the woman shall say, 'Amen, amen!'* **23** The priest shall put these imprecations in writing and shall then wash them off into the bitter water, **24** which he is to have the woman drink, so that it may go into her with all its bitter curse. **25** But first he shall take the cereal offering of jealousy from the woman's hand, and having waved this offering before the LORD, shall put it near the altar, **26** where he shall take a handful of the cereal offering as its token offering and burn it on the altar.h Only then shall he have the woman drink the water. **27** Once she has done so, if she has been impure and unfaithful to her husband, this bitter water that brings a curse will go into her, and her belly will swell and her thighs will waste away, so that she will become an example of imprecation among her people. **28** If, however, the woman has not defiled herself, but is still pure, she will be immune and will still be able to bear children.

29 "This, then, is the law for jealousy: When a woman goes astray while under the authority of her husband and acts impurely, **30** or when such a feeling of jealousy comes over a man that he becomes suspicious of his wife, he shall have her stand before the LORD, and the priest shall apply this law in full to her. **31** The man shall be free from guilt,* but the woman shall bear such guilt as she may have."

CHAPTER 6

Laws Concerning Nazirites. **1** The LORD said to Moses: **2** "Speak to the Israelites and tell them: When a man (or a woman) solemnly takes the nazirite* vow to dedicate himself to the LORD, **3** he shall abstain from wine and strong drink;i he may neither drink wine vinegar, other vinegar, or any kind of grape juice, nor eat either fresh or dried grapes. **4** As long as he is a nazirite he shall not eat anything of the produce of the vine; not even unripe grapes or grapeskins. **5** While he is under the nazirite vow, no razar shall touch his hair.j Until the period of his dedication to the LORD is over, he shall be sacred, and shall let the hair of his head

grow freely. **6** As long as he is dedicated to the LORD, he shall not enter where a dead person is.k **7** Not even for his father or mother, his sister or brother, should they die, may he become unclean, since his head bears his dedication to God. **8** As long as he is a nazirite he is sacred to the LORD.

9 "If someone dies very suddenly in his presence, so that his dedicated head becomes unclean, he shall shave his head on the day of his purification, that is, on the seventh day. **10** On the eighth day he shall bring two turtledoves or two pigeons to the priest at the entrance of the meeting tent. **11** The priest shall offer up the one as a sin offering and the other as a holocaust, thus making atonement for him for the sin he has committed by reason of the dead person. On the same day he shall reconsecrate his head **12** and begin anew the period of his dedication to the LORD as a nazirite, bringing a yearling lamb as a guilt offering. The previous period is not valid, because his dedicated head became unclean.

13 "This is the ritual for the nazirite:l On the day he completes the period of his dedication he shall go to the entrance of the meeting tent, **14** bringing as his offering to the LORD one unblemished yearling lamb for a holocaust, one unblemished yearling ewe lamb for a sin offering, one unblemished ram as a peace offering, along with their cereal offerings and libations, **15** and a basket of unleavened cakes of fine flour mixed with oil and of unleavened wafers spread with oil. **16** The priest shall present them before the LORD, and shall offer up the sin offering and the holocaust for him. **17** He shall then offer up the ram as a peace offering to the LORD, with its cereal offering and libation, and

---

g Ps 109, 18.
h Lv 5, 12.
i 3f: Jgs 13, 7. 14.
j Jgs 13, 5; 16, 17; 1 Sm

1, 11.
k Nm 19, 11. 16; Lv 21, 11.
l Acts 21, 24, 26.

*

5, 21: An example of malediction and imprecation: the woman's name would be used in curses and oaths to invoke a similar misfortune on another person or on oneself. Cf Is 65, 15; Jer 29, 22.

5, 22: Amen: a Hebrew word meaning, "certainly, truly," used to give assent to a statement, a curse, a blessing, a prayer, or the like; in this sense of "so be it," the Christian liturgy also uses it after prayers and blessings.

5, 31: Free from guilt: by fulfilling his obligation of obtaining a decision in the matter.

6, 1ff: Nazirite: from the Hebrew word nazir, meaning "set apart as sacred, dedicated, vowed." The nazirite vow could be either for a limited period or for life. Those bound by this vow had to abstain from all the products of the grapevine, from cutting or shaving their hair, and from contact with a corpse. They were regarded as men of God like the prophets; cf Am 2, 11f. Examples of lifelong nazirites were Samson (Jgs 13, 4f. 7; 16, 17), Samuel (1 Sm 1, 11), and John the Baptizer (Lk 1, 15). At the time of Christ the practice of taking the nazirite vow for a limited period seems to have been quite common, even among the early Christians; cf Acts 18, 18; 21, 23f. 26.

the basket of unleavened cakes. **18** Then at the entrance of the meeting tent the nazirite shall shave his dedicated head,*m* collect the hair, and put it in the fire that is under the peace offering. **19** After the nazirite has shaved off his dedicated hair, the priest shall take a boiled shoulder of the ram, as well as one unleavened cake and one unleavened wafer from the basket, and shall place them in the hands of the nazirite. **20** The priest shall then wave them as a wave offering before the LORD. They become sacred and shall belong to the priest, along with the breast of the wave offering and the leg of the raised offering. Only after this may the nazirite drink wine.

21 "This, then, is the law for the nazarite; this is the offering to the LORD which is included in his vow of dedication apart from anything else which his means may allow. Thus shall he carry out the law of his dedication in keeping with the vow he has taken."

The Priestly Blessing. **22** The LORD said to Moses: **23** "Speak to Aaron and his sons and tell them: This is how you shall bless the Israelites. Say to them:

24 The LORD bless you and keep you!
25 The LORD let his face shine* upon you, and be gracious to you!
26 The LORD look upon you kindly and give you peace!*

27 So shall they invoke my name upon the Israelites, and I will bless them."

CHAPTER 7

Offerings of Princes. **1** Now, when Moses had completed the erection of the Dwelling and had anointed and consecrated it with all its equipment*n* (as well as the altar with all its equipment), **2** an offering was made by the princes of Israel, who were heads of ancestral houses; the same princes of the tribes who supervised the census. **3** The offering they brought before the LORD consisted of six baggage wagons and twelve oxen, that is, a wagon for every two princes, and an ox for every prince. These they presented as their offering before the Dwelling.

4 The LORD then said to Moses, **5** "Accept their offering, that these things may be put to use in the service of the meeting tent. Assign them to the Levites, to each group in proportion to its duties." **6** So Moses accepted the wagons and oxen, and assigned them to the Levites. **7** He gave two wagons and four oxen to the Gershonites*o* in proportion to their duties, **8** and four wagons and eight oxen to the Merarites in proportion to their duties, under the supervision of Ithamar, son of Aaron the priest. **9** He gave none to the Kohathites, because they

had to carry on their shoulders the sacred objects which were their charge.*p*

10 For the dedication of the altar also, the princes brought offerings before the altar on the day it was anointed.*q* **11** But the LORD said to Moses, "Let one prince a day present his offering for the dedication of the altar."

12 *The one who presented his offering on the first day was Nahshon, son of Amminadab, prince of the tribe of Judah. **13** His offering consisted of one silver plate weighing a hundred and thirty shekels according to the sanctuary standard and one silver basin weighing seventy shekels, both filled with fine flour mixed with oil for a cereal offering; **14** one gold cup of ten shekels' weight filled with incense; **15** one young bull, one ram, and one yearling lamb for a holocaust; **16** one goat for a sin offering; **17** and two oxen, five rams, five goats, and five yearling lambs for a peace offering. This was the offering of Nahshon, son of Amminadab.

18 On the second day Nethanel, son of Zuar, prince of Issachar, made his offering. **19** He presented as his offering one silver plate weighing a hundred and thirty shekels according to the sanctuary standard and one silver basin weighing seventy shekels, both filled with fine flour mixed with oil for a cereal offering; **20** one gold cup of ten shekels' weight filled with incense; **21** one young bull, one ram, and one yearling lamb for a holocaust; **22** one goat for a sin offering; **23** and two oxen, five rams, five goats, and five yearling lambs for a peace offering. This was the offering of Nethanel, son of Zuar.

24 On the third day it was the turn of Eliab, son of Helon, prince of the Zebulunites. **25** His offering consisted of one silver plate weighing a hundred and thirty shekels according to the sanctuary standard and one silver basin weighing seventy shekels, both filled with fine flour mixed with oil for a cereal offering; **26** one gold cup of ten shekels' weight filled with incense; **27** one young bull, one ram, and one yearling lamb for a holocaust; **28** one goat for a sin offering; **29** and two oxen, five rams, five goats, and five yearling lambs for a peace offering. This was the offering of Eliab, son of Helon.

30 On the fourth day it was the turn of Elizur, son of Shedeur, prince of the Reubenites. **31** His offering consisted of one silver plate

---

m Acts 18, 18; 21, 24.   p Nm 3, 31; 4, 4-15.
n Ex 40, 17.   q Nm 7, 84.
o 7f: Nm 4, 24-33.

---

*

6, 25: Let his face shine: a Hebrew idiom for "smile."
6, 26: Peace: the Hebrew word includes the idea of "prosperity, happiness."
7, 12–88: The repetitious account of the same offerings brought by each of the twelve tribal princes and the summary of them are characteristic of an official registration.

weighing a hundred and thirty shekels according to the sanctuary standard and one silver basin weighing seventy shekels, both filled with fine flour mixed with oil for a cereal offering; **32** one gold cup of ten shekels' weight filled with incense; **33** one young bull, one ram, and one yearling lamb for a holocaust; **34** one goat for a sin offering; **35** and two oxen, five rams, five goats, and five yearling lambs for a peace offering. This was the offering of Elizur, son of Shedeur.

36 On the fifth day it was the turn of Shelumiel, son of Zurishaddai, prince of the Simeonites. **37** His offering consisted of one silver plate weighing a hundred and thirty shekels according to the sanctuary standard and one silver basin weighing seventy shekels, both filled with fine flour mixed with oil for a cereal offering; **38** one gold cup of ten shekels' weight filled with incense; **39** one young bull, one ram, and one yearling lamb for a holocaust; **40** one goat for a sin offering; **41** and two oxen, five rams, five goats, and five yearling lambs for a peace offering. This was the offering of Shelumiel, son of Zurishaddai.

42 On the sixth day it was the turn of Eliasaph, son of Reuel, prince of the Gadites. **43** His offering consisted of one silver plate weighing a hundred and thirty shekels according to the sanctuary standard and one silver basin weighing seventy shekels, both filled with fine flour mixed with oil for a cereal offering; **44** one gold cup of ten shekels' weight filled with incense; **45** one young bull, one ram, and one yearling lamb for a holocaust; **46** one goat for a sin offering; **47** and two oxen, five rams, five goats, and five yearling lambs for a peace offering. This was the offering of Eliasaph, son of Reuel.

48 On the seventh day it was the turn of Elishama, son of Ammihud, prince of the Ephraimites. **49** His offering consisted of one silver plate weighing a hundred and thirty shekels according to the sanctuary standard and one silver basin weighing seventy shekels, both filled with fine flour mixed with oil for a cereal offering; **50** one gold cup of ten shekels' weight filled with incense; **51** one young bull, one ram, and one yearling lamb for a holocaust; **52** one goat for a sin offering; **53** and two oxen, five rams, five goats, and five yearling lambs for a peace offering. This was the offering of Elishama, son of Ammihud.

54 On the eighth day it was the turn of Gamaliel, son of Pedahzur, prince of the Manassehites. **55** His offering consisted of one silver plate weighing a hundred and thirty shekels according to the sanctuary standard and one silver basin weighing seventy shekels, both filled with fine flour mixed with oil for a cereal offering; **56** one gold cup of ten shekels' weight filled

with incense; **57** one young bull, one ram, and one yearling lamb for a holocaust; **58** one goat for a sin offering; **59** and two oxen, five rams, five goats, and five yearling lambs for a peace offering. This was the offering of Gamaliel, son of Pedahzur.

60 On the ninth day it was the turn of Abidan, son of Gideoni, prince of the Benjaminites. **61** His offering consisted of one silver plate weighing a hundred and thirty shekels according to the sanctuary standard and one silver basin weighing seventy shekels, both filled with fine flour mixed with oil for a cereal offering; **62** one gold cup of ten shekels' weight filled with incense; **63** one young bull, one ram, and one yearling lamb for a holocaust; **64** one goat for a sin offering; **65** and two oxen, five rams, five goats, and five yearling lambs for a peace offering. This was the offering of Abidan, son of Gideoni.

66 On the tenth day it was the turn of Ahiezer, son of Ammishaddai, prince of the Danites. **67** His offering consisted of one silver plate weighing a hundred and thirty shekels according to the sanctuary standard and one silver basin weighing seventy shekels, both filled with fine flour mixed with oil for a cereal offering; **68** one gold cup of ten shekels' weight filled with incense; **69** one young bull, one ram, and one yearling lamb for a holocaust; **70** one goat for a sin offering; **71** and two oxen, five rams, five goats, and five yearling lambs for a peace offering. This was the offering of Ahiezer, son of Ammishaddai.

72 On the eleventh day it was the turn of Pagiel, son of Ochran, prince of the Asherites. **73** His offering consisted of one silver plate weighing a hundred and thirty shekels according to the sanctuary standard and one silver basin weighing seventy shekels, both filled with fine flour mixed with oil for a cereal offering; **74** one gold cup of ten shekels' weight filled with incense; **75** one young bull, one ram, and one yearling lamb for a holocaust; **76** one goat for a sin offering; **77** and two oxen, five rams, five goats, and five yearling lambs for a peace offering. This was the offering of Pagiel, son of Ochran.

78 On the twelfth day it was the turn of Ahira, son of Enan, prince of the Naphtalites. **79** His offering consisted of one silver plate weighing a hundred and thirty shekels according to the sanctuary standard and one silver basin weighing seventy shekels, both filled with fine flour mixed with oil for a cereal offering; **80** one gold cup of ten shekels' weight filled with incense; **81** one young bull, one ram, and one yearling lamb for a holocaust; **82** one goat for a sin offering; **83** and two oxen, five rams, five goats, and five yearling lambs for a peace offering. This was the offering of Ahira, son of Enan.

84 These were the offerings for the dedication of the altar, given by the princes of Israel on the occasion of its anointing: twelve silver plates, twelve silver basins, and twelve gold cups. **85** Each silver plate weighed a hundred and thirty shekels, and each silver basin seventy, so that all the silver of these vessels amounted to two thousand four hundred shekels, according to the sanctuary standard. **86** The twelve gold cups that were filled with incense weighed ten shekels apiece, according to the sanctuary standard, so that all the gold of the cups amounted to one hundred and twenty shekels. **87** The animals for the holocausts were, in all, twelve young bulls, twelve rams, and twelve yearling lambs, with their cereal offerings; those for the sin offerings were twelve goats. **88** The animals for the peace offerings were, in all, twenty-four oxen, sixty rams, sixty goats, and sixty yearling lambs. These, then, were the offerings for the dedication of the altar after it was anointed.

The Voice.   **89** When Moses entered the meeting tent to speak with him, he heard the voice addressing him from above the propitiatory[r] on the ark of the commandments, from between the two cherubim; and it spoke to him. . . .

CHAPTER 8

The Lamps Set Up.   **1** The LORD spoke to Moses, and said, **2** "Give Aaron this command: When you set up the seven lamps,[s] have them throw their light toward the front of the lampstand." **3** Aaron did so, setting up the lamps to face toward the front of the lampstand, just as the LORD had commanded Moses. **4** The lampstand was made of beaten gold[t] in both its shaft and its branches, according to the pattern which the LORD had shown Moses.

Purification of the Levites.   **5** The LORD said to Moses: **6** "Take the Levites from among the Israelites and purify them.* **7** This is what you shall do to them to purify them. Sprinkle them with the water of remission;* then have them shave their whole bodies and wash their clothes, and so purify themselves. **8** They shall take a young bull, along with its cereal offering of fine flour mixed with oil; you shall take another young bull for a sin offering. **9** Then have the Levites come forward in front of the meeting tent, where you shall assemble also the whole community of the Israelites. **10** While the Levites are present before the LORD, the Israelites shall lay their hands upon them. **11** Let Aaron then offer the Levites before the LORD as a wave

offering from the Israelites, thus devoting them to the service of the LORD. **12** The Levites in turn shall lay their hands on the heads of the bullocks, which shall then be immolated, the one as a sin offering and the other as a holocaust to the LORD, in atonement for the Levites. **13** Thus, then, shall you have the Levites stand before Aaron and his sons, to be offered as a wave offering to the LORD; **14** and thus shall you set aside the Levites from the rest of the Israelites, that they may be mine.[u]

15 "Only then shall the Levites enter upon their service in the meeting tent. You shall purify them and offer them as a wave offering; **16** because they, among the Israelites, are strictly dedicated to me; I have taken them for myself in place of every first-born that opens the womb among the Israelites.[v] **17** Indeed, all the first-born among the Israelites, both of man and of beast, belong to me; I consecrated them to myself on the day I slew all the first-born in the land of Egypt.[w] **18** But in place of all the first-born Israelites I have taken the Levites; **19** and I have given these dedicated Israelites to Aaron and his sons[x] to discharge the duties of the Israelites in the meeting tent and to make atonement for them, so that no plague may strike among the Israelites should they come near the sanctuary."

20 Thus, then, did Moses and Aaron and the whole community of the Israelites deal with the Levites, carrying out exactly the command which the LORD had given Moses concerning them. **21** When the Levites had cleansed themselves of sin* and washed their clothes, Aaron offered them as a wave offering before the LORD, and made atonement for them to purify them. **22** Only then did they enter upon their service in the meeting tent under the supervision of Aaron and his sons. The command which the LORD had given Moses concerning the Levites was carried out.

Age Limits for Levitical Service.   **23** The LORD said to Moses: **24** "This is the rule for the Levites. Each from his twenty-fifth year onward shall perform the required service in the meeting tent.[y] **25** When he is fifty years old, he shall

---

r Ex 25, 22.
s Ex 25, 37.
t Ex 25, 31. 40.
u Nm 3, 45.
v Nm 3, 12. 45.
w Nm 3, 13; 13, 2; Lk 2, 23.
x Nm 3, 9f.
y Nm 4, 3. 23.

8, 6: Purify them: in the language of the Pentateuch only the priests were "consecrated," that is, made sacred or set aside for the Lord, in an elaborate ceremony described in Ex 29; Lv 8. The Levites were merely "purified," that is, made ritually clean for their special work.

8, 7: Water of remission: literally, "water of sin," that is, for the remission of sin.

8, 21: Cleansed themselves of sin: by having the "water of remission" sprinkled on them as prescribed in v 7.

retire from the required service and work no longer. **26** His service with his fellow Levites shall consist in sharing their responsibilities in the meeting tent, but he shall not do the work. This, then, is how you are to regulate the duties of the Levites.''

CHAPTER 9

Second Passover.   **1** In the first month of the year following their departure from the land of Egypt, the LORD said to Moses in the desert of Sinai, **2** ''Tell the Israelites to celebrate the Passover at the prescribed time. **3** The evening twilight of the fourteenth day of this month*z* is the prescribed time when you shall celebrate it, observing all its rules and regulations.'' **4** Moses, therefore, told the Israelites to celebrate the Passover. **5** And they did so, celebrating the Passover in the desert of Sinai during the evening twilight of the fourteenth day of the first month, just as the LORD had commanded Moses.

6 There were some, however, who were unclean because of a human corpse and so could not keep the Passover that day. These men came up to Moses and Aaron that same day **7** and said, ''Although we are unclean because of a corpse, why should we be deprived of presenting the LORD's offering at its proper time along with the other Israelites?'' **8** Moses answered them, ''Wait until I learn what the LORD will command in your regard.''

9 The LORD then said to Moses: **10** ''Speak to the Israelites and say: If any one of you or of your descendants is unclean because of a corpse, or if he is absent on a journey, he may still keep the LORD's Passover. **11** But he shall keep it in the second month,*a* during the evening twilight of the fourteenth day of that month, eating it with unleavened bread and bitter herbs, **12** and not leaving any of it over till morning, nor breaking any of its bones,*b* but observing all the rules of the Passover. **13** However, anyone who is clean and not away on a journey, who yet fails to keep the Passover, shall be cut off from his people, because he did not present the LORD's offering at the prescribed time. That man shall bear the consequences of his sin.

14 ''If an alien* who lives among you wishes to keep the LORD's Passover, he too shall observe the rules and regulations for the Passover. You shall have the same law for the resident alien as for the native of the land.''*c*

The Fiery Cloud.   **15** On the day when the Dwelling was erected, the cloud* covered the Dwelling, the tent of the commandments; but from evening until morning it took on the appearance of fire over the Dwelling.*d* **16** It was

always so: during the day the Dwelling was covered by the cloud, which at night had the appearance of fire. **17** Whenever the cloud rose from the tent, the Israelites would break camp; wherever the cloud came to rest, they would pitch camp.*e* **18** At the bidding of the LORD the Israelites moved on, and at his bidding they encamped.*f* As long as the cloud stayed over the Dwelling, they remained in camp.

19 Even when the cloud tarried many days over the Dwelling, the Israelites obeyed the LORD and would not move on; **20** yet sometimes the cloud was over the Dwelling only for a few days. It was at the bidding of the LORD that they stayed in camp, and it was at his bidding that they departed. **21** Sometimes the cloud remained there only from evening until morning; and when it rose in the morning, they would depart. Or if the cloud lifted during the day, or even at night, they would then set out. **22** Whether the cloud tarried over the Dwelling for two days or for a month or longer, the Israelites remained in camp and did not depart; but when it lifted, they moved on. **23** Thus, it was always at the bidding of the LORD that they encamped, and at his bidding that they set out; ever heeding the charge of the LORD, as he had bidden them through Moses.

CHAPTER 10

The Silver Trumpets.   **1** The LORD said to Moses: **2** ''Make two trumpets of beaten silver, which you shall use in assembling the community and in breaking camp. **3** When both are blown, the whole community shall gather round you at the entrance of the meeting tent; **4** but when one of them is blown, only the princes, the chiefs of the troops of Israel, shall gather round you. **5** When you sound the first alarm, those encamped on the east side shall set out; **6** when you sound the second alarm, those encamped on the south side shall set out; when you sound the third alarm, those encamped on the West side shall set out; when you sound the fourth alarm, those encamped on the north side shall set out. Thus shall the alarm be sounded for them to depart. **7** But in calling forth an assembly you are to blow an ordinary blast, without sounding the alarm.

8 ''It is the sons of Aaron, the priests, who shall blow the trumpets; and the use of them is prescribed by perpetual statute for you and your

---

z Ex 12, 6; Lv 23, 5.   d Ex 13, 21.
a 2 Chr 30, 2-15.   e Wis 18, 3.
b Ex 12, 46; Jn 19, 36.   f 1 Cor 10, 1.
c Ex 12, 48f.

*

9, 14: An alien: this passage presupposes that he is already circumcised as prescribed in Ex 12, 48.

9, 15: The cloud: already mentioned at the departure from Egypt; cf Ex 13, 21f.

descendants. **9** ᵍWhen in your own land you go to war against an enemy that is attacking you, you shall sound the alarm on the trumpets, and the LORD, your God, will remember you and save you from your foes. **10** On your days of celebration,* your festivals, and your new-moon feasts, you shall blow the trumpets over your holocausts and your peace offerings;ʰ this will serve as a reminder of you before your God. I, the LORD, am your God."

II: From Sinai to the Plains of Moab

Departure from Sinai. **11** In the second year, on the twentieth day of the second month, the cloud rose from the Dwelling of the commandments. **12** The Israelites moved on from the desert of Sinai by stages, until the cloud came to rest in the desert of Paran.

13 The first time that they broke camp at the bidding of the LORD through Moses, **14** ⁱthe camp of the Judahites, under its own standard and arranged in companies, was the first to set out. Nahshon, son of Amminadab, was over their host, **15** and Nethanel, son of Zuar, over the host of the tribe of Issachar, **16** and Eliab, son of Helon, over the host of the tribe of Zebulun. **17** Then, after the Dwelling was dismantled, the clans of Gershon and Merari set out, carrying the Dwelling. **18** The camp of the Reubenites, under its own standard and arranged in companies, was the next to set out, with Elizur, son of Shedeur, over their host, **19** and Shelumiel, son of Zurishaddai, over the host of the tribe of Simeon, **20** and Eliasaph, son of Reuel, over the host of the tribe of Gad. **21** The clan of Kohath then set out, carrying the sacred objects for the Dwelling, which was to be erected before their arrival. **22** The camp of the Ephraimites next set out, under its own standard and arranged in companies, with Elishama, son of Ammihud, over their host, **23** and Gamaliel, son of Pedahzur, over the host of the tribe of Manasseh, **24** and Abidan, son of Gideoni, over the host of the tribe of Benjamin. **25** Finally, as rear guard for all the camps, the camp of the Danites set out, under its own standard and arranged in companies, with Ahiezer, son of Amishaddai, over their host, **26** and Pagiel, son of Ochran, over the host of the tribe of Asher, **27** and Ahira, son of Enan, over the host of the tribe of Naphtali. **28** This was the order of departure for the Israelites, company by company.

Hobab as Guide. As they were setting out, **29** Moses said to his brother-in-law Hobab, son of Reuel the Midianite, "We are setting out for the place which the LORD has promised to give us. Come with us, and we will be generous

toward you, for the LORD has promised, prosperity to Israel." **30** *But he answered, "No, I will not come. I am going instead to my own country and to my own kindred." **31** Moses said, "Please, do not leave us; you know where we can camp in the desert, and you will serve as eyes for us. **32** If you come with us, we will share with you the prosperity the LORD will bestow on us."

Into the Desert. **33** ʲThey moved on from the mountain of the LORD,* a three days' journey, and the ark of the covenant of the LORD which was to seek out their resting place went the three days' journey with them. **34** And when they set out from camp, the cloud of the LORD was over them by day.

35 Whenever the ark set out, Moses would say,

> "Arise, O LORD, that your enemies may be scattered,
> and those who hate you may flee before you."

36 And when it came to rest, he would say,

> "Return, O LORD, you who ride upon the clouds,
> to the troops of Israel."

CHAPTER 11

Discontent of the People. **1** Now the people complained in the hearing of the LORD;ᵏ and when he heard it his wrath flared up so that the fire of the LORD burned among them and consumed the outskirts of the camp. **2** But when the people cried out to Moses, he prayed to the LORD and the fire died out. **3** Hence that place was called Taberah,* because there the fire of the LORD burned among them.

4 The foreign elements among them were so greedy for meat that even the Israelites lamented again,ˡ "Would that we had meat for food! **5** We remember the fish we used to eat without cost in Egypt, and the cucumbers, the melons, the leeks, the onions, and the garlic. **6** But now

g 2 Chr 13, 14.
h Nm 29, 1; 2 Chr 29, 26ff.
i 14ff: Nm 2, 3. 5. 7.
j Dt 1, 33.
k Dt 9, 22.
l Ps 78, 18.
m 5f: Nm 21, 5; Ex 16, 3; Acts 7, 39.

*

10, 10: Days of celebration: special holidays, such as the occasion of a victory. Festivals: the great annual feasts of the Passover, Pentecost and Booths described in Lv 23; Nm 28–29.

10, 30ff: Hobab wished to be coaxed before granting the favor. From Jgs 1, 16 it seems probable that he did accede to Moses' request.

10, 33: The mountain of the Lord: Sinai (Horeb), elsewhere always called "the mountain of God."

11, 3: Taberah: means "the burning."

we are famished; we see nothing before us but this manna.''[m]

7 [n]Manna was like coriander seed* and had the appearance of bdellium. 8 When they had gone about and gathered it up, the people would grind it between millstones or pound it in a mortar, then cook it in a pot and make it into loaves, which tasted like cakes made with oil. 9 At night, when the dew fell upon the camp, the manna also fell.[o]

10 When Moses heard the people, family after family, crying at the entrance of their tents, so that the LORD became very angry, he was grieved. 11 ''Why do you treat your servant so badly?'' Moses asked the LORD. ''Why are you so displeased with me that you burden me with all this people? 12 Was it I who conceived all this people? or was it I who gave them birth, that you tell me to carry them at my bosom, like a foster father carrying an infant, to the land you have promised under oath to their fathers? 13 Where can I get meat to give to all this people? For they are crying to me, 'Give us meat for our food.' 14 I cannot carry all this people by myself, for they are too heavy for me. 15 If this is the way you will deal with me, then please do me the favor of killing me at once, so that I need no longer face this distress.''

The Seventy Elders. 16 Then the LORD said to Moses, ''Assemble for me seventy of the elders of Israel, men you know for true elders and authorities among the people, and bring them to the meeting tent. When they are in place beside you, 17 I will come down and speak with you there. I will also take some of the spirit that is on you and will bestow it on them, that they may share the burden of the people with you. You will then not have to bear it by yourself.

18 ''To the people, however, you shall say: Sanctify yourselves for tomorrow, when you shall have meat to eat. For in the hearing of the LORD you have cried, 'Would that we had meat for food! Oh, how well off we were in Egypt!' Therefore the LORD will give you meat for food, 19 and you will eat it, not for one day, or two days, or five, or ten, or twenty days, 20 but for a whole month—until it comes out of your very nostrils and becomes loathsome to you. For you have spurned the LORD who is in your midst, and in his presence you have wailed, 'Why did we ever leave Egypt?' ''

21 But Moses said, ''The people around me include six hundred thousand soldiers; yet you say, 'I will give them meat to eat for a whole month.' 22 Can enough sheep and cattle be slaughtered for them? If all the fish of the sea were caught for them, would they have enough?'' 23 The LORD answered Moses, ''Is this beyond the LORD's reach? You shall see

now whether or not what I have promised you takes place.''

The Spirit on the Elders. 24 So Moses went out and told the people what the LORD had said. Gathering seventy elders of the people, he had them stand around the tent. 25 The LORD then came down in the cloud and spoke to him. Taking some of the spirit that was on Moses, he bestowed it on the seventy elders; and as the spirit came to rest on them, they prophesied.*

26 Now two men, one named Eldad and the other Medad, were not in the gathering but had been left in the camp. They too had been on the list, but had not gone out to the tent; yet the spirit came to rest on them also, and they prophesied in the camp. 27 So, when a young man quickly told Moses, ''Eldad and Medad are prophesying in the camp,'' 28 Joshua, son on Nun, who from his youth had been Moses' aide, said, ''Moses, my lord, stop them.'' 29 But Moses answered him, ''Are you jealous for my sake? Would that all the people of the LORD were prophets! Would that the LORD might bestow his spirit on them all!'' 30 Then Moses retired to the camp, along with the elders of Israel.

The Quail. 31 There arose a wind[p] sent by the LORD, that drove in quail from the sea and brought them down over the camp site at a height of two cubits from the ground* for a distance of a day's journey all around the camp. 32 [q]All that day, all night, and all the next day the people gathered in the quail. Even the one who got the least gathered ten homers of them. Then they spread them out* all around the camp. 33 But while the meat was still between their teeth, before it could be consumed, the LORD's wrath flared up against the people, and

---

n 7f: Ex 16, 14f. 31; Ps 78, 24; Wis 16, 20; Jn 6, 31.
o Ex 16, 14f.
p Ps 78, 26ff.
q 32f: 78, 26-31; 1 Cor 10, 6-7.

11, 7: Coriander seed: see note on Ex 16, 31. Bdellium: a transparent, amber-colored gum resin, which is also mentioned in Gn 2, 12.

11, 25: They prophesied: in the sense, not of foretelling the future, but of speaking in enraptured enthusiasm. Such manifestations of mystic exaltation occurred in the early days of Hebrew prophecy (1 Sm 10, 10ff; 19, 20ff) and in the first years of the Church (Acts 2, 6-II. 17; 19, 6; 1 Cor 12–14).

11, 31: At a height of two cubits from the ground: exhausted by the storm, the quail could take but short, low flights, so that they were easily captured. To give food to the hungry people, God may have used the natural phenomenon of the annual migration of quail across the Sinai Peninsula. In the spring large flocks of these birds cross the Gulf of Aqabah flying toward the west; in the fall they fly back eastward from the Mediterranean. The sea mentioned here probably refers to the former body of water.

11, 32: They spread them out: to cure by drying.

he struck them with a very great plague. **34** So that place was named Kibroth-hattaavah,* because it was there that the greedy people were buried.

35 From Kibroth-hattaavah the people set out for Hazeroth.

CHAPTER 12

Jealousy of Aaron and Miriam. While they were in Hazeroth, **1** Miriam and Aaron spoke against Moses on the pretext of the marriage he had contracted with a Cushite woman.* **2** They complained,* "Is it through Moses alone that the LORD speaks? Does he not speak through us also?" And the LORD heard this. **3** rNow, Moses himself was by far the meekest man on the face of the earth. **4** So at once the LORD said to Moses and Aaron and Miriam, "Come out, you three, to the meeting tent." And the three of them went. **5** Then the LORD came down in the column of cloud, and standing at the entrance of the tent, called Aaron and Miriam. When both came forward, **6** he said, "Now listen to the words of the LORD:

Should there be a prophet among you,
in visions will I reveal myself to him,
in dreams will I speak to him;
7 Not so with my Servant Moses!
Throughout my house he bears my trust:s
8 face to face I speak to him,t
plainly and not in riddles.
The presence of the LORD he beholds.

Why, then, did you not fear to speak against my servant Moses?"

Miriam's Leprosy. **9** So angry was the Lord against them that when he departed, **10** and the cloud withdrew from the tent, there was Miriam,u a snow-white leper!* When Aaron turned and saw her a leper, **11** "Ah, my lord!" he said to Moses, "please do not charge us with the sin that we have foolishly committed! **12** Let her not thus be like the stillborn babe that comes forth from its mother's womb with its flesh half consumed." **13** Then Moses cried to the LORD, "Please, not this! Pray, heal her!" **14** But the LORD answered Moses, "Suppose her father had spit in her face, would she not hide in shame for seven days? Let her be confined outside the camp for seven days; only then may she be brought back." **15** So Miriam was confined outside the camp for seven days, and the people did not start out again until she was brought back.

16 After that the people set out from Hazeroth and encamped in the desert of Paran.

CHAPTER 13

The Twelve Scouts. **1** The LORD said to Moses, **2** "Send men to reconnoiter the land of Canaan, which I am giving the Israelites. You shall send one man from each ancestral tribe, all of them princes." **3** vSo Moses dispatched them from the desert of Paran, as the LORD had ordered. All of them were leaders among the Israelites; **4** by name they were:

Shammua, son of Zaccur, of the tribe of Reuben;
5 Shaphat, son of Hori, of the tribe of Simeon;
6 Caleb, son of Jephunneh, of the tribe of Judah;
7 Igal [son of Joseph] of the tribe of Issachar;
10 Gaddiel, son of Sodi, of the tribe of Zebulun;
11 Gaddi, son of Susi, of the tribe of Manasseh, for the Josephites, with
8 Hoshea, son of Nun, of the tribe of Ephraim;
9 Palti, son of Raphu, of the tribe of Benjamin;
12 Ammiel, son of Gemalli, of the tribe of Dan;
13 Sethur, son of Michael, of the tribe of Asher;
14 Nahbi, son of Vophsi, of the tribe of Naphtali;
15 Geuel, son of Machi, of the tribe of Gad.

16 These are the names of the men whom Moses sent out to reconnoiter the land. But Hoshea, son of Nun, Moses called Joshua.*

17 In sending them to reconnoiter the land of Canaan, Moses said to them, "Go up here in the Negeb, up into the highlands, **18** and see what kind of land it is. Are the people living there strong or weak, few or many? **19** Is the country in which they live good or bad? Are the towns in which they dwell open or fortified? **20** Is the soil fertile or barren, wooded or clear? And do

r Sir 45, 1f.   u Dt 24, 9.
s Sir 45, 3; Heb 3, 2. 5.   v 3-33: Dt 1, 22-28.
t Ex 33, 11; Dt 34, 10.

*

11, 34: Kibroth-hattaavah: means "graves of greed."

12, 1: Cushite woman: apparently Zipporah, the Midianitess, is meant; cf Ex 2, 21. Perhaps the term is used here merely in the sense of "despised foreigner."

12, 2: The real reason for Miriam's quarrel with her brother Moses was her jealousy of his superior position; his Cushite wife served only as an occasion for the dispute. Aaron merely followed his sister in her rebellion; hence she alone was punished.

12, 10: A snow-white leper: afflicted with "white leprosy," a skin disease that generally is not serious or of long duration. Cf Lv 13, 3–6.

13, 16: Joshua: in Hebrew, "Jehoshua," which was later modified to "Jeshua," the Hebrew pronunciation of the name "Jesus." Hoshea and Joshua are variants of one original name meaning "the LORD saves." Cf Mt 1, 21.

your best to get some of the fruit of the land.''
It was then the season for early grapes.

21 So they went up and reconnoitered the land from the desert of Zin* as far as where Rehob adjoins Labo of Hamath. **22** ʷGoing up by way of the Negeb, they reached Hebron, where Ahiman, Sheshai and Talmai, descendants of the Anakim,* were living. [Hebron had been built seven years before Zoan in Egypt.] **23** They also reached the Wadi Eshcol,* where they cut down a branch with a single cluster of grapes on it, which two of them carried on a pole, as well as some pomegranates and figs. **24** It was because of the cluster the Israelites cut there that they called the place Wadi Eshcol.ˣ

Their Return. **25** After reconnoitering the land for forty days they returned, **26** ʸmet Moses and Aaron and the whole community of the Israelites in the desert of Paran at Kadesh, made a report to them all, and showed them the fruit of the country. **27** They told Moses: "We went into the land to which you sent us. It does indeed flow with milk and honey, and here is its fruit. **28** However, the people who are living in the land are fierce, and the towns are fortified and very strong.ᶻ Besides, we saw descendants of the Anakim there. **29** Amalekites live in the region of the Negeb; Hittites, Jebusites and Amorites dwell in the highlands, and Canaanites along the seacoast and the banks of the Jordan.''

30 Caleb, however, to quiet the people toward Moses, said, "We ought to go up and seize the land, for we can certainly do so.'' **31** But the men who had gone up with him said, "We cannot attack these people; they are too strong for us.'' **32** So they spread discouraging reportsᵃ among the Israelites about the land they had scouted, saying, "The land that we explored is a country and consumes its inhabitants. And all the people we saw there are huge men, **33** ᵇveritable giants* [the Anakim were a race of giants]; we felt like mere grasshoppers, and so we must have seemed to them.''

CHAPTER 14

Threats of Revolt. **1** At this, the whole community broke out with loud cries, and even in the night the people wailed. **2** ᶜAll the Israelites grumbled against Moses and Aaron, the whole community saying to them, "Would that we had died in the land of Egypt, or that here in the desert we were dead! **3** Why is the LORD bringing us into this land only to have us fall by the sword? Our wives and little ones will be taken as booty. Would it not be better for us to return to Egypt?'' **4** So they said to one another, "Let us appoint a leader and go back to Egypt.''

5 But Moses and Aaron fell prostrate before the whole assembled community of the Israelites; **6** while Joshua, son of Nun, and Caleb, son of Jephunneh, who had been in the party that scouted the land, tore their garments **7** and said to the whole community of the Israelites,ᵈ "The country which we went through and explored is a fine, rich land. **8** If the LORD is pleased with us, he will bring us in and give us that land, a land flowing with milk and honey. **9** ᵉBut do not rebel against the LORD! You need not be afraid of the people of that land; they are but food for us!* Their defense has left them, but the LORD is with us. Therefore, do not be afraid of them.'' **10** In answer, the whole community threatened to stone them.

The Lord's Sentence. But then the glory of the LORD appeared at the meeting tent to all the Israelites. **11** And the LORD said to Moses, "How long will this people spurn me? How long will they refuse to believe in me, despite all the signs I have performed among them?ᶠ **12** I will strike them with pestilence and wipe them out. Then I will make of you a nation greater and mightier than they.''ᵍ

13 ʰBut Moses said to the LORD: "Are the Egyptians to hear of this? For by your power you brought out this people from among them. **14** And are they to tell of it to the inhabitants of this land? It has been heard that you, O LORD, are in the midst of this people; you, LORD, who plainly reveal yourself! Your cloud stands over them, and you go before them by day in a column of cloud and by night in a column of fire.ⁱ **15** If now you slay this whole people, the nations who have heard such reports of you will

---

w Jos 11, 21f.
x Nm 32, 9; Dt 1, 24f.
y 26f: Ex 3, 8. 17.
z 28f: Dt 9, 1f.
a Nm 32, 9; Jos 14, 8.
b Dt 2, 10.
c Ex 16, 3; Ps 106, 25.

d 7f: Dt 1, 25.
e Dt 7, 18.
f Ps 78, 22. 32.
g Ex 32, 10.
h 13-16: Ex 32, 12; Dt 9, 26ff; Ps 106, 23.
i Ex 13, 21; Jos 2, 9f.

---

*

13, 21: The desert of Zin: north of Paran and southwest of the Dead Sea. It is quite distinct from "the desert of Sin" near the border of Egypt (Ex 16, 1; 17, 1; Nm 33, 11). Labo of Hamath: a town near Riblah (Jer 39, 5f) at the southern border of Hamath, an independent kingdom in southern Syria. David's conquests extended as far as Hamath (2 Sm 8, 9ff), and Labo thus formed the northern border of the ideal extent of Israel's possessions (Nm 34, 7ff; Ez 47, 15; 48, 1). Some commentators think that this verse is a later addition to the text; cf Dt 1, 24.

13, 22. 28: Anakim: an aboriginal race in southern Palestine, largely absorbed by the Canaanites before the Israelite invasion. Either because of their tall stature or because of the massive stone structures left by them the Israelites regarded them as giants.

13, 23: Eshcol: means "cluster."

13, 33: Giants: in Hebrew, "nephilim." Cf Gn 6, 4.

14, 9: They are but food for us: that is, "we can easily consume and destroy them." This is the answer to the pessimistic report that this land "consumes its inhabitants" (Nm 13, 32).

say, **16** 'The LORD was not able to bring this people into the land he swore to give them; that is why he slaughtered them in the desert.'*j* **17** Now then, let the power of my Lord be displayed in its greatness, even as you have said, **18** *k*'The LORD is slow to anger and rich in kindness, forgiving wickedness and crime; yet not declaring the guiltless guilty, but punishing children to the third and fourth generation for their fathers' wickedness.' **19** Pardon, then, the wickedness of this people in keeping with your great kindness, even as you have forgiven them from Egypt until now.''*l*

20 The LORD answered: "I pardon them as you have asked. **21** Yet, by my life and the LORD's glory that fills the whole earth, **22** of all the men who have seen my glory and the signs I worked in Egypt and in the desert,*m* and who nevertheless have put me to the test ten times already and have failed to heed my voice, **23** not one shall see the land which I promised on oath to their fathers. None of these who have spurned me shall see it. **24** But because my servant Caleb has a different spirit and follows me unreservedly,*n* I will bring him into the land where he has just been, and his descendants shall possess it. **25** But now, since the Amalekites and Canaanites are living in the valleys,* turn away tomorrow and set out in the desert on the Red Sea road.''

26 The LORD also said to Moses and Aaron: **27** "How long will this wicked community grumble against me?*o* I have heard the grumblings of the Israelites against me. **28** Tell them:* By my life, says the LORD, I will do to you just what I have heard you say. **29** Here in the desert*p* shall your dead bodies fall. Of all your men of twenty years or more, registered in the census, who grumbled against me, **30** not one shall enter the land where I solemnly swore to settle you, except Caleb, son of Jephunneh, and Joshua, son of Nun. **31** Your little ones, however, who you said would be taken as booty, I will bring in, and they shall appreciate the land you spurned.*q* **32** But as for you, your bodies shall fall here in the desert, **33** here where your children must wander for forty years, suffering for your faithlessness, till the last of you lies dead in the desert.*r* **34** Forty days you spent in scouting the land; forty years shall you suffer for your crimes: one year for each day. Thus you will realize what it means to oppose me. **35** I, the LORD, have sworn to do this to all this wicked community that conspired against me: here in the desert they shall die to the last man.''

36 And so it happened to the men whom Moses had sent to reconnoiter the land*s* and who on returning had set the whole community grumbling against him by spreading discouraging reports about the land; **37** these men who

had given out the bad report about the land were struck down by the LORD had died. **38** Of all the men who had gone to reconnoiter the land, only Joshua, son of Nun, and Caleb, son of Jephunneh, survived.*t*

Unsuccessful Invasion. **39** When Moses repeated these words to all the Israelites, the people felt great remorse. **40** Early the next morning they started up into the foothills, saying, "Here we are, ready to go up to the place that the LORD spoke of:*u* for we were indeed doing wrong." **41** But Moses said, "Why are you again disobeying the LORD's orders? This cannot succeed. **42** Do not go up, because the LORD is not in your midst; if you go, you will be beaten down before your enemies.*v* **43** For there the Amalekites and Canaanites face you, and you will fall by the sword. You have turned back from following the LORD; therefore the LORD will not be with you.''

44 Yet they dared to go up into the foothills,*w* even though neither the ark of the covenant of the LORD nor Moses left the camp. **45** And the Amalekites and Canaanites who dwelt in that hill country came down and defeated them, beating them back as far as Hormah.*

CHAPTER 15

Secondary Offerings. **1** The LORD said to Moses, **2** *"Give the Israelites these instructions: When you have entered the land that I will give you for your homesteads, **3** if you make to the LORD a sweet-smelling oblation from the herd or from the flock, in holocaust, in fulfillment of a vow, or as a freewill offering, or for one of your festivals, **4** whoever does so shall also present to the LORD a cereal offering consisting of a tenth of an ephah of fine flour mixed with a fourth of a hin of oil, **5** as well as a

j Ex 32, 12; Dt 9, 28.
k Ex 20, 5; 34, 6f; Pss 103, 8; 145, 8.
l Ps 78, 38.
m 22f; Dt 1, 35.
n Jos 14, 8f.
o Ex 16, 7. 12.
p Dt 1, 35; Heb 3, 17.
q Dt 1, 39.
r 33f: Nm 13, 26; 32, 13; Ps 95, 10; Ez 4, 6.
s 36f: Nm 13, 17. 32f; 1 Cor 10, 10.
t Nm 26, 65.
u Nm 13, 18; Dt 1, 42.
v Dt 1, 42.
w Dt 1, 43.

*

14, 25: The valleys: the low-lying plains in the Negeb and along the seacoast and in the Jordan depression as well as the higher valleys in the mountains farther north; cf Nm 14, 45.

14, 28f: God punished the malcontents by giving them their wish; cf v 2. Their lack of faith and of confidence in God is cited in 1 Cor 10, 10, and Heb 3, 12–18, as a warning for Christians.

14, 45: Hormah: one of the Canaanite royal cities in southern Judea (Jos 12, 14), known at this time as "Zephath"; the origin of the later name is told in Nm 21, 3; Jgs 1, 17.

15, 2–16: These laws on sacrifice are complementary to those of Lv 1–3. Since the food of the Israelites consisted not only of bread but also of meat and wine, so, besides the animal oblations, they offered flour, wine and oil in sacrifice to the Lord.

libation of a fourth of a hin of wine, with each lamb sacrificed in holocaust or otherwise. **6** With each sacrifice of a ram you shall present a cereal offering of two tenths of an ephah of fine flour mixed with a third of a hin of oil, **7** and a libation of a third of a hin of wine, thus making a sweet-smelling offering to the LORD. **8** When you sacrifice an ox as a holocaust, or in fulfillment of a vow, or as a peace offering to the LORD, **9** with it you shall present a cereal offering of three tenths of an ephah of fine flour mixed with half a hin of oil, **10** and a libation of half a hin of wine, as a sweet-smelling oblation to the LORD. **11** The same is to be done for each ox, ram, lamb or goat. **12** Whatever the number you offer, do the same for each of them.

13 "All the native-born shall make these offerings in the same way, whenever they present a sweet-smelling oblation to the LORD. **14** Likewise, in any future generation, any alien residing with you permanently or for a time, who presents a sweet-smelling oblation to the LORD, shall do as you do. **15** There is but one rule for you and for the resident alien, a perpetual rule for all your descendants. Before the LORD you and the alien are alike, **16** with the same law and the same application of it for the alien residing among you as for yourselves."

17 The LORD said to Moses, **18** "Speak to the Israelites and tell them: When you enter the land into which I will bring you **19** and begin to eat of the food of that land, you shall offer the LORD a contribution **20** consisting of a cake of your first batch of dough.* You shall offer it just as you offer a contribution from the threshing floor.*x* **21** Throughout your generations you shall give a contribution to the LORD from your first batch of dough.

Sin Offerings.   22 *"When through inadvertence you fail to carry out any of these commandments which the LORD gives to Moses,*y* **23** and through Moses to you, from the time the LORD first issues the commandment down through your generations: **24** if the community itself unwittingly becomes guilty of the fault of inadvertence, the whole community shall offer the holocaust of one young bull as a sweet-smelling oblation pleasing to the LORD, along with its prescribed cereal offering and libation, as well as one he-goat as a sin offering. **25** *z*Then the priest shall make atonement for the whole Israelite community; thus they will be forgiven the inadvertence for which they have brought their holocaust as an oblation to the LORD. **26** Not only the whole Israelite community, but also the aliens residing among you, shall be forgiven, since the fault of inadvertence affects all the people.

27 "However, if it is an individual who sins

inadvertently,*a* he shall bring a yearling she-goat as a sin offering, **28** and the priest shall make atonement before the LORD for him who sinned inadvertently; when atonement has been made for him, he will be forgiven. **29** You shall have but one law for him who sins inadvertently, whether he be a native Israelite or an alien residing with you.

30 "But anyone who sins defiantly,*b* whether he be a native or an alien, insults the LORD, and shall be cut off from among his people. **31** *c*Since he has despised the word of the LORD and has broken his commandment, he must be cut off. He has only himself to blame."

The Sabbath-breaker.   32 While the Israelites were in the desert, a man was discovered gathering wood on the sabbath day. **33** Those who caught him at it brought him to Moses and Aaron and the whole assembly. **34** But they kept him in custody, for there was no clear decision* as to what should be done with him.*d* **35** Then the LORD said to Moses, "This man shall be put to death; let the whole community stone him outside the camp." **36** So the whole community led him outside the camp and stoned him to death, as the LORD had commanded Moses.

Tassels on the Cloak.   37 The LORD said to Moses, **38** "Speak to the Israelites and tell them that they and their descendants must put tassels* on the corners of their garments, fastening each corner tassel with a violet cord.*e* **39** When you use these tassels, let the sight of them remind you to keep all the commandments of the LORD, without going wantonly astray after the desires of your hearts and eyes. **40** Thus you will remember to keep all my commandments and be holy to your God. **41** I, the LORD, am your God who, as God, brought you out of Egypt that I, the LORD, may be your God."*f*

---

x 19-20: Ez 44, 30.   c Prv 13, 13.
y 22f: Lv 4, 13f.   d Lv 24, 12.
z Lv 4, 20.   e Dt 22, 12.
a 27f: Lv 4, 27f.   f Lv 22, 32f.
b Dt 17, 12.

---

*

15, 20: Dough: some render, "barley grits." This word is used elsewhere only in Ez 44, 30 and Neh 10, 33; a related Hebrew word is used in Lv 2, 14.

15, 22ff: Although no moral guilt is incurred by an inadvertent violation of God's commandments, the sanctity of the law can require some reparation even for such violations.

15, 34: No clear decision: they already knew that a willful violation of the sabbath was a capital offense, but they did not yet know how the death penalty was to be inflicted.

15, 38: Tassels: at the time of Christ these tassels were worn by all pious Jews, including our Lord (Mt 9, 20f; Mk 6, 56); the Pharisees wore very large ones in ostentation of their zeal for the law (Mt 23, 5).

CHAPTER 16

Rebellion of Korah.   1 Korah, son of Izhar, son of Kohath, son of Levi,* [and Dathan
and Abiram, sons of Eliab, son of Pallu, son of
Reuben] took 2 two hundred and fifty Israelites
who were leaders in the community, members of the council and men of note. They
stood before Moses, 3 and held an assembly
against Moses and Aaron, to whom they
said,*g* "Enough from you! The whole community, all of them, are holy; the LORD is in their
midst. Why then should you set yourselves over
the LORD's congregation?"

4 When Moses heard this, he fell prostrate.
5 Then he said to Korah and to all his band,
"May the LORD make known tomorrow morning who belongs to him and who is the holy one
and whom he will have draw near to him!
Whom he chooses, he will have draw near him.
6 Do this: take your censers [Korah and all his
band] 7 and put fire in them and place incense
in them before the LORD tomorrow. He whom
the LORD then chooses is the holy one. Enough
from you Levites!"

8 Moses also said to Korah, "Listen to me,
you Levites! 9 *h*Is it too little for you that the
God of Israel has singled you out from the community of Israel, to have you draw near him for
the service of the LORD's Dwelling and to stand
before the community to minister for them?
10 He has allowed you and your kinsmen, the
descendants of Levi, to approach him, and yet
you now seek the priesthood too. 11 It is therefore against the LORD that you and all your band
are conspiring. For what has Aaron done that
you should grumble against him?"

Rebellion of Dathan and Abiram.
12 Moses summoned Dathan and Abiram, sons
of Eliab, but they answered, "We will not go.*
13 Are you not satisfied with having led us here
away from a land flowing with milk and honey,
to make us perish in the desert, that you must
now lord it over us? 14 Far from bringing us to
a land flowing with milk and honey, or giving
us fields and vineyards for our inheritance, will
you also gouge out our eyes?* No, we will not
go."

15 Then Moses became very angry and said
to the LORD, "Pay no heed to their offering. I
have never taken a single ass from them, nor
have I wronged any one of them."*i*

Korah.   16 Moses said to Korah, "You and
all your band shall appear before the LORD tomorrow—you and they and Aaron too. 17 Then
each of your two hundred and fifty followers
shall take his own censer, put incense in it, and
offer it to the LORD; and you and Aaron, each
with his own censer, shall do the same." 18 So

they all took their censers, and laying incense on
the fire they had put in them, they took their
stand by the entrance of the meeting tent along
with Moses and Aaron. 19 Then, when Korah
had assembled all his band against them at the
entrance of the meeting tent, the glory of the
LORD appeared to the entire community, 20 and
the LORD said to Moses and Aaron, 21 "Stand
apart from this band, that I may consume them
at once." 22 But they fell prostrate and cried
out, "O God, God of the spirits of all mankind,
will one man's sin make you angry with the
whole community?" 23 The LORD answered
Moses, 24 "Speak to the community and tell
them: Withdraw from the space around the
Dwelling" [of Korah, Dathan and Abiram].

Punishment of Dathan and Abiram.
25 Moses, followed by the elders of Israel,
arose and went to Dathan and Abiram.*
26 Then he warned the community, "Keep
away from the tents of these wicked men and do
not touch anything that is theirs: otherwise you
too will be swept away because of all their
sins." 27 When Dathan and Abiram had come
out and were standing at the entrances of their
tents with their wives and sons and little ones,
28 Moses said, "This is how you shall know
that it was the LORD who sent me to do all I have
done, and that it was not I who planned it: 29 if
these men die an ordinary death, merely suffering the fate common to all mankind, then it was
not the LORD who sent me. 30 But if the LORD
does something entirely new, and the ground
opens its mouth and swallows them alive down
into the nether world, with all belonging to
them, then you will know that these men have
defied the LORD." 31 *j*No sooner had he finished saying all this than the ground beneath

---

g Ps 106, 16ff; Sir 45, 19;   i I Sm 12, 3.
   1 Cor 10, 10.   j 31ff: Nm 26, 10; Lv 10,
h Dt 10, 8.   2; Dt 11, 6; Ps 106, 7f.

---

*

16, 1ff: The evidence seems to show that there were two
distinct rebellions: one of Korah and his band (Nm 27, 3) and
the other of Dathan and Abiram (Dt 11, 6); cf Ps 106. The
present account combines both events into one narrative; but
even here it is rather easy to separate the two, once certain
proper names (vv 1. 6. 24. 32. 35) have been identified as
glosses. The rebellion of the Reubenites, Dathan and Abiram,
was of a political nature, against Moses alone as the civil
leader; these rebels were punished by being swallowed alive
in an earthquake. The rebellion of Korah was of a religious
nature, against the religious leadership of both Moses and
Aaron; about two hundred and fifty malcontents joined Korah's
band; they were punished by fire. The parts of the present
section which refer to the rebellion of Dathan and Abiram are
vv 12–15 and vv 25–34 of chapter 16; the rest of chapter 16
and all of chapter 17 concern the rebellion of Korah.

16, 12: We will not go: to appear before Moses' tribunal.

16, 14: Gouge out your eyes: blind us to the real state of
affairs.

16, 25: Since Dathan and Abiram had refused to go to
Moses (vv 12ff), he, with the elders as witnesses, was obliged
to go to their tent.

them split open, **32** and the earth opened its mouth and swallowed them and their families [and all of Korah's men] and all their possessions. **33** They went down alive to the nether world with all belonging to them; the earth closed over them, and they perished from the community. **34** But all the Israelites near them fled at their shrieks, saying, "The earth might swallow us too!"

Punishment of Korah.　**35** So they withdrew from the space around the Dwelling [of Korah,* Dathan and Abiram]. And fire from the LORD came forth which consumed the two hundred and fifty men who were offering the incense.

CHAPTER 17

1 The LORD said to Moses, **2** "Tell Eleazar, son of Aaron the priest, to remove the censers from the embers; and scatter the fire some distance away, **3** *for these sinners have consecrated the censers at the cost of their lives. Have them hammered into plates to cover the altar, because in being presented before the LORD they have become sacred. In this way they shall serve as a sign to the Israelites." **4** So Eleazar the priest had the bronze censers of those burned during the offering hammered into a covering for the altar, **5** in keeping with the orders which the LORD had given him through Moses. This cover was to be a reminder to the Israelites that no layman, no one who was not a descendant of Aaron, should approach the altar to offer incense before the LORD, lest he meet the fate of Korah and his band.

6 The next day the whole Israelite community grumbled against Moses and Aaron, saying, "It is you who have slain the LORD's people." **7** But while the community was deliberating against them, Moses and Aaron turned toward the meeting tent, and the cloud now covered it and the glory of the LORD appeared. **8** Then Moses and Aaron came to the front of the meeting tent, **9** and the LORD said to Moses and Aaron, **10** "Depart from this community, that I may consume them at once." But they fell prostrate.

11 Then Moses said to Aaron, "Take your censer, put fire from the altar in it, lay incense on it, and bring it quickly to the community to make atonement for them; for wrath has come forth from the LORD and the blow is falling."[k] **12** Obeying the orders of Moses, Aaron took his censer and ran in among the community, where the blow was already falling on the people. Then, as he offered the incense and made atonement for the people, **13** standing there between the living and the dead, the scourge was checked. **14** Yet fourteen thousand seven hundred died from the scourge, in addition to those

who died because of Korah. **15** When the scourge had been checked, Aaron returned to Moses at the entrance of the meeting tent.

Aaron's Staff.　**16** The LORD now said to Moses, **17** "Speak to the Israelites and get one staff* from them for each ancestral house, twelve staffs in all, one from each of their tribal princes. Mark each man's name on his staff; **18** and mark Aaron's name on Levi's staff,* for the head of Levi's ancestral house shall also have a staff. **19** Then lay them down in the meeting tent, in front of the commandments, where I meet you. **20** There the staff of the man of my choice shall sprout. Thus will I suppress from my presence the Israelites' grumbling against you."

21 So Moses spoke to the Israelites, and their princes gave him staffs, twelve in all, one from each tribal prince; and Aaron's staff was with them. **22** Then Moses laid the staffs down before the LORD in the tent of the commandments. **23** The next day, when Moses entered the tent, Aaron's staff, representing the house of Levi, had sprouted and put forth not only shoots, but blossoms as well, and even bore ripe almonds! **24** Moses thereupon brought out all the staffs from the LORD's presence to the Israelites. After each prince identified his own staff and took it, **25** the LORD said to Moses, "Put back Aaron's staff in front of the commandments, to be kept there as a warning to the rebellious, so that their grumbling may cease before me; if it does not, they will die." **26** And Moses did as the LORD had commanded him.

Charge of the Sacred Things.　**27** *Then the Israelites cried out to Moses, "We are perishing; we are lost, we are all lost! **28** Every time anyone approaches the Dwelling of the

---

k Wis 18, 20f.

*

16, 35: This verse continues v 24; the first sentence is transposed from v 27.

17, 3: Whatever was brought into intimate contact with something sacred shared in its sacredness. See note on Nm 19, 20.

17, 17: The staff was not merely an article of practical use, but also a symbol of authority; cf Gn 49, 10; Nm 24, 17; Jer 48, 17. Hence, the staff of a leader of a tribe was considered the emblem of his tribe; in fact, certain Hebrew words for "staff" also means "tribe." Perhaps for this reason, to avoid confusion, the author here uses the term "ancestral house" instead of the ordinary word for "tribe."

17, 18: Levi's staff: it is not clear whether this is considered as one of the twelve mentioned in the preceding verse, or as a thirteenth staff. Sometimes Levi is reckoned as one of the twelve tribes (e.g., Dt 27, 12f); but more often the number twelve is arrived at by counting the two sub-tribes of Joseph, i.e., Ephraim and Manasseh, as distinct tribes. In this passage also it seems probable that the tribe of Levi is considered apart from the other twelve.

17, 27f: Logically these two verses belong immediately after Nm 16, 35.

LORD, he dies! Are we to perish to the last man?''

CHAPTER 18

1 The LORD said to Aaron,* ''You and your sons as well as the other members of your ancestral house shall be responsible for the sanctuary; but the responsibility of the priesthood shall rest on you and your sons alone. 2 Bring with you also your other kinsmen of the tribe of Levi, your ancestral tribe, as your associates* and assistants, while you and your sons are in front of the tent of the commandments. 3 They shall look after your persons and the whole tent; however, they shall not come near the sacred vessels or the altar, lest both they and you die. 4 As your associates they shall have charge of all the work connected with the meeting tent. But no layman* shall come near you. 5 You shall have charge of the sanctuary and of the altar, that wrath may not fall again upon the Israelites.

6 ''Remember, it is I who have taken your kinsmen, the Levites, from the body of the Israelites; they are a gift to you,[l] dedicated to the LORD for the service of the meeting tent. 7 [m]But only you and your sons are to have charge of performing the priestly functions in whatever concerns the altar and the room within the veil.* I give you the priesthood as a gift. Any layman who draws near shall be put to death.''

The Priests' Share of the Sacrifices.

8 The LORD said to Aaron,* ''I myself have given you charge of the contributions made to me in the various sacred offerings of the Israelites;[n] by perpetual ordinance I have assigned them to you and to your sons as your priestly share. 9 You shall have the right to share in the oblations that are most sacred, in whatever they offer me as cereal offerings or sin offerings or guilt offerings; these shares shall accrue to you and to your sons. 10 In eating them you shall treat them as most sacred; every male among you may partake of them. As sacred, they belong to you.

11 ''You shall also have what is removed from the gift in every wave offering* of the Israelites; by perpetual ordinance I have assigned it to you and to your sons and daughters.[o] All in your family who are clean may partake of it. 12 I have also assigned to you all the best[p] of the new oil and of the new wine and grain that they give to the LORD as their first fruits; 13 and likewise, of whatever grows on their land, the first products that they bring in to the LORD shall be yours; all of your family who are clean may partake of them. 14 Whatever is doomed* in Israel shall be yours. 15 Every living thing that opens the womb, whether of man or of beast, such as are to be offered to

the LORD, shall be yours;[q] but you must let the first-born of man, as well as of unclean animals, be redeemed. 16 The ransom for a boy is to be paid when he is a month old; it is fixed at five silver shekels according to the sanctuary standard, twenty gerahs to the shekel. 17 But the first-born of cattle, sheep or goats shall not be redeemed; they are sacred. Their blood you must splash on the altar and their fat you must burn as a sweet-smelling oblation to the LORD. 18 [r]Their meat, however, shall be yours, just as the breast and the right leg of the wave offering belong to you. 19 By perpetual ordinance I have assigned to you and to your sons and daughters all the contributions from the sacred gifts which the Israelites make to the LORD; this is an inviolable covenant* to last forever before the LORD, for you and for your descendants.'' 20 [s]Then the LORD said to Aaron,* ''You shall not have any heritage in the land of the Israelites nor hold any portion among them; I will be your portion and your heritage among them.

Tithes Due the Levites.

21 ''To the Levites, however, I hereby assign all tithes in Israel as their heritage in recompense for the service they perform in the meeting tent.[t] 22 The Israelites may no longer approach the meeting tent; else they will incur guilt deserving death.

---

l Nm 3, 9; 8, 19.
m Nm 3, 10.
n Nm 5, 9.
o Ex 29, 27f; Lv 7, 34; 10, 14.
p 12f; Dt 18, 4; 26, 2.
q Ex 13, 2.
r Lv 7, 31-34.
s Dt 10, 9; 18, 1f; Jos 13, 33; Ez 44, 28.
t Heb 7, 5.

*

18, 1ff: This law, which kept unqualified persons from contact with sacred things, is the answer to the Israelites' cry in Nm 17, 28. It is followed by other laws concerning priests and Levites.

18, 2: Associates: in Hebrew this word alludes to the popular etymology of the name ''Levi.'' Cf Gn 29, 34.

18, 4: Layman: here, ''one who is not a Levite''; in v 7, ''one who is not a priest.''

18, 7: Veil: the outer veil, or ''curtain,'' is probably meant.

18, 8ff: Two classes of offerings are here distinguished: the most sacred offering, which only the male members of the priestly families could eat (vv 8ff), and the other offerings, which even the women of the priestly families could eat (vv 11-19).

18, 11: Wave offering: this included the breast and right leg (v 18), the shoulder of the peace offering (Lv 7, 30-34), and portions of the nazirite sacrifice (Nm 6, 19f).

18, 14: Doomed: in Hebrew, herem, which means here ''set aside from profane use and made sacred to the Lord.'' Cf Lv 27, 21. 28.

18, 19: An inviolable covenant: literally, ''a covenant of salt.'' Cf 2 Chr 13, 5. The reference may perhaps be to the preservative power of salt (cf Mt 5, 13); but more likely the phrase refers to the custom of partaking of the same salt in common to render a contract unbreakable. See note on Lv 2, 13.

18, 20: The priests and Levites were forbidden to own hereditary land such as the other Israelites possessed; therefore in the allotment of the land they were not to receive any portion of it. Certain cities, however, were assigned to them for their residence; cf Nm 35, 1-8.

23 Only the Levites are to perform the service of the meeting tent, and they alone shall be held responsible; this is a perpetual ordinance for all your generations. The Levites, therefore, shall not have any heritage among the Israelites, 24 for I have assigned to them as their heritage the tithes which the Israelites give as a contribution to the LORD. That is why I have ordered that they are not to have any heritage among the Israelites.''

Tithes Paid by the Levites. 25 The LORD said to Moses, 26 ''Give the Levites these instructions: When you receive from the Israelites the tithes I have assigned you from them as your heritage, you are to make a contribution from them to the LORD, a tithe of the tithes; 27 and your contribution will be credited to you as if it were grain from the threshing floor or new wine from the press. 28 Thus you too shall make a contribution from all the tithes you receive from the Israelites, handing over to Aaron the priest the part to be contributed to the LORD. 29 From all the gifts that you receive, and from the best parts, you are to consecrate to the LORD your own full contribution.

30 ''Tell them also: Once you have made your contribution from the best part, the rest of the tithes will be credited to you Levites as if it were produce of the threshing floor or of the wine press. 31 Your families, as well as you, may eat them anywhere, since they are your recompense for service at the meeting tent. 32 You will incur no guilt so long as you make a contribution of the best part. Do not profane the sacred gifts of the Israelites and so bring death on yourselves.''

CHAPTER 19

Ashes of the Red Heifer. 1 The LORD said to Moses and Aaron: 2 ''This is the regulation which the law of the LORD prescribes. Tell the Israelites to procure for you a red heifer that is free from every blemish and defect and on which no yoke has ever been laid. 3 This is to be given to Eleazar the priest, to be led outside the camp* and slaughtered in his presence. 4 Eleazar the priest shall take some of its blood on his finger and sprinkle it seven times toward the front of the meeting tent.* 5 Then the heifer shall be burned in his sight, with its hide and flesh, its blood and offal; 6 and the priest shall take some cedar wood, hyssop and scarlet yarn and throw them into the fire in which the heifer is being burned. 7 The priest shall then wash his garments and bathe his body in water. He remains unclean until the evening, and only afterward may he return to the camp. 8 Likewise, he who burned the heifer shall wash his garments, bathe his body in water, and be un-

clean until evening. 9 Finally, a man who is clean shall gather up the ashes of the heifer and deposit them in a clean place outside the camp. There they are to be kept for preparing lustral water for the Israelite community. The heifer is a sin offering. 10 He who has gathered up the ashes of the heifer shall also wash his garments and be unclean until evening. This is a perpetual ordinance, both for the Israelites and for the aliens residing among them.

Use of the Ashes. 11 ''Whoever touches the dead body of any human being shall be unclean for seven days; 12 he shall purify himself with the water on the third and on the seventh day, and then he will be clean again. But if he fails to purify himself on the third and on the seventh day, he will not become clean. 13 ᵘEveryone who fails to purify himself after touching the body of any deceased person, defiles the Dwelling of the LORD and shall be cut off from Israel. Since the lustral water has not been splashed over him, he remains unclean; his uncleanness still clings to him.

14 ''This is the law: When a man dies in a tent, everyone who enters the tent, as well as everyone already in it, shall be unclean for seven days; 15 likewise, every vessel that is open, or with its lid unfastened, shall be unclean. 16 Moreover, everyone who in the open country touches a dead person, whether he was slain by the sword or died naturally, or who touches a human bone or a grave, shall be unclean for seven days. 17 *For anyone who is thus unclean, ashes from the sin offering shall be put in a vessel, and spring water shall be poured on them. 18 Then a man who is clean shall take some hyssop, dip it in this water, and sprinkle it on the tent and on all the vessels and persons that were in it, or on him who touched a bone, a slain person or other dead body, or a grave. 19 The clean man shall sprinkle the unclean on the third and on the seventh day; thus purified on the seventh day, he shall wash his garments and bathe his body in water, and in the evening he will be clean again. 20 *Any unclean man

---

u Lv 15, 31.

*

19, 3: Outside the camp: several Fathers of the Church saw in this a prefiguring of the sacrificial death of Christ outside the walls of Jerusalem; cf Jn 19, 20; Heb 13, 12; in the purifying water, into which the ashes of the red heifer were put, they saw a type of the water of Baptism.

19, 4: Toward the front of the meeting tent: since the tabernacle faced the east (Ex 26, 15–30), the killing of the heifer took place east of the camp; in later times it was done on the Mount of Olives, east of the Temple.

19, 17ff: ''If . . . the sprinkled ashes of a heifer sanctify the unclean unto the cleansing of the flesh, how much more will the blood of Christ . . . cleanse your conscience from dead works?'' (Heb 9, 13f).

19, 20: Ritual uncleanness is, as it were, contagious; so also sacredness; see note on Nm 17, 3.

who fails to have himself purified shall be cut off from the community, because he defiles the sanctuary of the LORD. As long as the lustral water has not been splashed over him, he remains unclean. **21** This shall be a perpetual ordinance for you.

"One who sprinkles the lustral water shall wash his garments, and anyone who comes in contact with this water shall be unclean until evening. **22** Moreover, whatever the unclean person touches becomes unclean itself, and anyone who touches it becomes unclean until evening."

CHAPTER 20

Death of Miriam.   **1** The whole Israelite community arrived in the desert of Zin in the first month,* and the people settled at Kadesh. It was here that Miriam died, and here that she was buried.

Water Famine at Kadesh.   **2** As the community had no water, they held a council against Moses and Aaron. **3** The people contended with Moses, exclaiming, "Would that we too had perished with our kinsmen in the LORD's presence! **4** Why have you brought the LORD's community into this desert where we and our livestock are dying? **5** Why did you lead us out of Egypt, only to bring us to this wretched place which has neither grain nor figs nor vines nor pomegranates? Here there is not even water to drink!" **6** But Moses and Aaron went away from the assembly to the entrance of the meeting tent, where they fell prostrate.

Sin of Moses and Aaron.   Then the glory of the LORD appeared to them, **7** and the LORD said to Moses, **8** "Take the staff and assemble the community, you and your brother Aaron, and in their presence order the rock to yield its waters. From the rock you shall bring forth water for the community and their livestock to drink." **9** So Moses took the staff from its place before the LORD, as he was ordered. **10** He and Aaron assembled the community in front of the rock, where he said to them,ᵛ "Listen to me, you rebels! Are we to bring water for you out of this rock?" **11** ʷThen, raising his hand, Moses struck the rock twice* with his staff, and water gushed out in abundance for the community and their livestock to drink. **12** *But the LORD said to Moses and Aaron, "Because you were not faithful to me in showing forth my sanctity before the Israelites, you shall not lead this community into the land I will give them."

13 These are the waters of Meribah,ˣ where the Israelites contended against the LORD, and where he revealed his sanctity among them.

Edom's Refusal.   **14** From Kadesh Moses sent men to the king of Edom with the message: "Your brother Israel* has this to say: You know of all the hardships that have befallen us, **15** how our fathers went down to Egypt, where we stayed a long time, how the Egyptians maltreated us and our fathers, **16** and how, when we cried to the LORD,ʸ he heard our cry and sent an angel who led us out of Egypt. Now here we are at the town of Kadesh at the edge of your territory. **17** Kindly let us pass through your country. We will not cross any fields or vineyards, nor drink any well water, but we will go straight along the royal road* without turning to the right or to the left, until we have passed through your territory."

18 But Edom answered him, "You shall not pass through here; if you do, I will advance against you with the sword." **19** The Israelites insisted, "We want only to go up along the highway. If we or our livestock drink any of your water, we will pay for it. Surely there is no harm in merely letting us march through." **20** But Edom still said, "No, you shall not pass through,"ᶻ and advanced against them with a large and heavily armed force. **21** Therefore, since Edom refused to let them pass through their territory, Israel detoured around them.

Death of Aaron.   **22** ᵃSetting out from Kadesh, the whole Israelite community came to Mount Hor.* **23** There at Mount Hor, on the border of the land of Edom, the LORD said to

---

v Ex 17, 5f.
w Ps 78, 15f; Wis 11, 4;
   1 Cor 10, 4.
x Nm 27, 14: Ex 17, 7.
y Ex 2, 23.
z Jgs 11, 17.
a 21f: Nm 33, 37.

*

20, 1: The first month: we would expect the mention also of the day and of the year (after the exodus) when this took place; cf similar dates in Nm 1, 1; 10, 11; 33, 38; Dt 1, 3. Here the full date seems to have been lost. Probably the Israelites arrived in Kadesh in the third year after the exodus. Cf Dt 1, 46. The desert of Zin: a barren region with a few good oases, southwest of the Dead Sea. See note on Nm 13, 21.

20, 11: Twice: perhaps because he had not sufficient faith to work the miracle with the first blow. Cf v 12.

20, 12f: The sin of Moses and Aaron consisted in doubting God's mercy toward the ever-rebellious people. In showing forth my sanctity: God's sacred power and glory: an allusion to the name of the place, Kadesh, which means "sanctified, sacred." Meribah means "contention." Cf Ex 17, 7.

20, 14: Your brother Israel: the Edomites were descended from Esau, the brother of Jacob. Their country, to the southeast of the Dead Sea, was also known as Seir; cf Gn 25, 24ff; 36, 1. 8f.

20, 17: The royal road: an important highway, running north and south along the plateau east of the Dead Sea. In ancient times it was much used by caravans and armies; later it was improved by the Romans, and large stretches of it are still clearly recognizable.

20, 22: Mount Hor: not definitively identified, but probably to be sought in the vicinity of Kadesh. According to Dt 10, 6, Aaron died at Moserah (cf "Moseroth" in Nm 33, 30f), which is apparently the name of the region in which Mount Hor is situated.

Moses and Aaron, **24** "Aaron is about to be taken to his people; he shall not enter the land I am giving to the Israelites, because you both rebelled against my commandment at the waters of Meribah. **25** Take Aaron and his son Eleazar and bring them up on Mount Hor.^b **26** Then strip Aaron of his garments and put them on his son Eleazar; for there Aaron shall be taken in death."

27 Moses did as the LORD commanded. When they had climbed Mount Hor in view of the whole community, **28** Moses stripped Aaron of his garments and put them on his son Eleazar. Then Aaron died there on top of the mountain.^c When Moses and Eleazar came down from the mountain, **29** all the community understood that Aaron had passed away; and for thirty days the whole house of Israel mourned him.

CHAPTER 21

Victory over Arad. **1** When the Canaanite king of Arad,* who lived in the Negeb,^d heard that the Israelites were coming along the way of Atharim, he engaged them in battle and took some of them captive. **2** Israel then made this vow to the LORD: "If you deliver this people into my hand, I will doom their cities."^e **3** Later, when the LORD heeded Israel's prayer and delivered up the Canaanites,^f they doomed them and their cities. Hence that place was named Hormah.*

The Bronze Serpent. **4** From Mount Hor they set out on the Red Sea road, to bypass the land of Edom. But with their patience worn out by the journey, **5** the people complained^g against God and Moses, "Why have you brought us up from Egypt to die in this desert, where there is no food or water? We are disgusted with this wretched food!"*

6 In punishment the LORD sent among the people saraph* serpents, which bit^h the people so that many of them died. **7** Then the people came to Moses and said, "We have sinned in complaining against the LORD and you. Pray the LORD to take the serpents from us." So Moses prayed for the people, **8** and the LORD said to Moses, "Make a saraph and mount it on a pole, and if anyone who has been bitten looks at it, he will recover."* **9** Moses accordingly made a bronze serpent* and mounted it on a pole, and whenever anyone who had been bitten by a serpent looked at the bronze serpent, he recovered.ⁱ

Journey around Moab. **10** The Israelites moved on and encamped in Oboth.^j **11** Setting out from Oboth, they encamped in Iyeabarim* in the desert fronting Moab on the east. **12** Set-

ting out from there, they encamped in the Wadi Zered. **13** Setting out from there, they encamped on the other side of the Arnon, in the desert that extends from the territory of the Amorites; for the Arnon forms Moab's boundary with the Amorites. **14** Hence it is said in the "Book of the Wars of the LORD"* :

"Waheb in Suphah and the wadies,
15 Arnon and the wadi gorges
That reach back toward the site of Ar
and slant to the border of Moab."

16 From there they went to Beer,* where there was the well of which the LORD said to Moses, "Bring the people together, and I will give them water." **17** Then it was that Israel sang this song:

"Spring up, O well!—so sing to it—
18 The well that the princes sank,
that the nobles of the people dug,
with their scepters and their staffs."

From Beer they went to Mattanah, **19** from Mattanah to Nahaliel, from Nahaliel to Bamoth, **20** from Bamoth to the cleft in the plateau of Moab at the headland of Pisgah that overlooks Jeshimon.*

---

b 25f: Dt 32, 50.
c Nm 33, 38.
d Nm 33, 40.
e Jos 6, 17; Jgs 1, 17.
f Nm 14, 45.
g Nm 11, 6; Ex 16, 3.

h Dt 8, 15; Wis 16, 5; 1 Cor 10, 9.
i Wis 16, 6f. 10; Jn 3, 14f.
j Nm 33, 43f.

---

*

21, 1–3: The account of this episode seems to be a later insertion here, for Nm 21, 4, belongs logically immediately after Nm 20, 29. Perhaps this is the same event as that mentioned in Jgs 1, 16f.

21, 3: Hormah: related to the Hebrew word herem, meaning "doomed." See notes on Nm 14, 45; 18, 14.

21, 5: This wretched food: apparently the manna is meant.

21, 6: Saraph: the Hebrew name for a certain species of venomous snakes; the word probably signifies "the fiery one," these snakes being so called from the burning effect of their poisonous bite.

21, 8: If anyone who has been bitten looks at it, he will recover: "and as Moses lifted up the serpent in the desert, even so must the Son of Man be lifted up, that those who believe in him may not perish, but may have life everlasting" (Jn 3, 14f).

21, 9: King Hezekiah, in his efforts to abolish idolatry, "smashed the bronze serpent which Moses had made" (2 Kgs 18, 4).

21, 11: Iye-abarim: probably means "the ruins in the Abarim (Mountains)" See note on Nm 27, 12.

21, 14: The "Book of the Wars of the Lord": an ancient collection of Israelite songs, now lost. Waheb in Suphah: since neither place is mentioned elsewhere, it is quite uncertain whether these dubious Hebrew words are even to be considered as place names; some Hebrew words apparently lost must have preceded this phrase.

21, 16: Beer: means a well.

21, 20: Jeshimon: "the wasteland"; in 1 Sm 23, 19. 24, and 26, 1. 3, this is the desert of Judah, on the western side of the Dead Sea, but here and in Nm 23, 28, it seems to refer to the southern end of the Jordan valley where Beth-jeshimoth was situated.

Victory over Sihon. 21 Now Israel sent men to Sihon, king of the Amorites, with the message, 22 "Let us pass through your country. We will not turn aside into any field or vineyard, nor will we drink any well water, but we will go straight along the royal road until we have passed through your territory." 23 Sihon,[k] however, would not let Israel pass through his territory, but mustered all his forces and advanced into the desert against Israel. When he reached Jahaz, he engaged Israel in battle. 24 But Israel defeated him at the point of the sword, and took possession of his land from the Arnon to the Jabbok and as far as the country of the Ammonites, whose boundary was at Jazer. 25 [l]Israel seized all the towns here and settled in these towns of the Amorites, in Heshbon and all its dependencies. 26 Now Heshbon was the capital of Sihon, king of the Amorites, who had fought against the former king of Moab and had seized all his land from Jazer to the Arnon. 27 That is why the poets say:

"Come to Heshbon, let it be rebuilt,
    let Sihon's capital be firmly constructed.
28 For fire went forth from Heshbon
    and a blaze from the city of Sihon;
It consumed the cities of Moab
    and swallowed up the high places of the
    Arnon.
29 Woe to you, O Moab!
    You are ruined, O people of Chemosh!*
He let his sons become fugitives
    and his daughters be taken captive by the
    Amorite king Sihon.
30 Their plowland is ruined from Heshbon to
    Dibon;
    Ar is laid waste; fires blaze as far as
    Medeba."

31 When Israel had settled in the land of the Amorites, 32 Moses sent spies to Jazer; Israel then captured it with its dependencies and dispossessed the Amorites who were there.

Victory over Og. 33 [m]Then they turned and went up along the road to Bashan. But Og, king of Bashan, advanced against them with all his people to give battle at Edrei. 34 The LORD, however, said to Moses, "Do not be afraid of him; for into your hand I will deliver him with all his people and his land. Do to him as you did to Sihon, king of the Amorites, who lived in Heshbon."[n] 35 So they struck him down with his sons and all his people, until not a survivor was left to him, and they took possession of his land.

CHAPTER 22

1 Then the Israelites moved on and encamped in the plains of Moab* on the other side of the Jericho stretch of the Jordan.

III: On the Plains of Moab

Balaam Summoned. 2 Now Balak, son of Zippor, saw all that Israel did to the Amorites. 3 Indeed, Moab feared the Israelites greatly because of their numbers, and detested them. 4 So Moab said to the elders of Midian, "Soon this horde will devour all the country around us as an ox devours the grass of the field." And Balak, Zippor's son, who was king of Moab at that time, 5 sent messengers to Balaam, son of Beor, at Pethor on the Euphrates, in the land of the Amawites, summoning him with these words, "A people has come here from Egypt who now cover the face of the earth and are settling down opposite us! 6 Please come and curse this people for us;* they are stronger than we are. We may then be able to defeat them and drive them out of the country. For I know that whoever you bless is blessed and whoever you curse is cursed." 7 Then the elders of Moab and of Midian left with the divination fee in hand and went to Balaam. When they had given him Balak's message, 8 he said to them in reply, "Stay here overnight, and I will give you whatever answer the LORD gives me." So the princes of Moab lodged with Balaam.

9 Then God came to Balaam and said, "Who are these men visiting you?" 10 Balaam answered God, "Balak, son of Zippor, king of Moab, sent me the message: 11 'This people that came here from Egypt now cover the face of the earth. Please come and lay a curse on them for us; we may then be able to give them battle and drive them out.'" 12 But God said to Balaam, "Do not go with them and do not curse this people, for they are blessed." 13 The next morning Balaam arose and told the princes of Balak, "Go back to your own country, for the LORD has refused to let me go with you." 14 So the princes of Moab went back to Balak with the report, "Balaam refused to come with us."

Second Appeal to Balaam. 15 Balak again sent princes, who were more numerous and more distinguished than the others. 16 On

---

k Dt 2, 32; Jgs 11, 20.   m Dt 3, 1ff.
l 25f; Jos 21, 39; Jgs 11,   n Ps 136, 17ff.
26.

*

21, 29: Chemosh: the chief god of the Moabites, and mentioned as such in the famous inscription of Mesha, king of Moab, who was the contemporary of the dynasty of Omri in Israel. Cf 1 Kgs 11, 7. 33; 2 Kgs 23, 13; Jer 48, 7. 13.

22, 1: The plains of Moab: the lowlands to the northeast of the Dead Sea, between the Jordan and the foothills below Mount Nebo. Here the Israelites remained until they crossed the Jordan, as told in Jos 1–4. Jericho lay to the west of the Jordan.

22, 6: Curse this people for us: Balak believed that if Balaam forecast an evil omen for Israel, this evil would come to pass, as if by magic. Balaam was a soothsayer or foreteller; cf Jos 13, 22.

coming to Balaam they told him, "This is what Balak, son of Zippor, has to say: Please do not refuse to come to me. **17** I will reward you very handsomely and will do anything you ask of me. Please come and lay a curse on this people for me." **18** *o*But Balaam replied to Balak's officials, "Even if Balak gave me his house full of silver and gold, I could not do anything, small or great, contrary to the command of the LORD, my God. **19** But, you too shall stay here overnight, till I learn what else the LORD may tell me."

20 That night God came to Balaam and said to him, "If these men have come to summon you, you may go with them; yet only on the condition that you do exactly as I tell you." **21** So the next morning when Balaam arose, he saddled his ass, and went off with the princes of Moab.

The Talking Ass. **22** But now the anger of God flared up* at him for going, and the angel of the LORD stationed himself on the road to hinder him as he was riding along on his ass, accompanied by two of his servants. **23** When the ass saw the angel of the LORD standing on the road with sword drawn, she turned off the road and went into the field, and Balaam had to beat her to bring her back on the road. **24** Then the angel of the LORD took his stand in a narrow lane between vineyards with a stone wall on each side. **25** When the ass saw the angel of the LORD there, she shrank against the wall; and since she squeezed Balaam's leg against it, he beat her again. **26** The angel of the LORD then went ahead, and stopped next in a passage so narrow that there was no room to move either to the right or to the left. **27** When the ass saw the angel of the LORD there, she cowered under Balaam. So, in anger, he again beat the ass with his stick.

28 *p*But now the LORD opened the mouth of the ass, and she asked Balaam, "What have I done to you that you should beat me these three times?" **29** "You have acted so willfully against me," said Balaam to the ass, "that if I but had a sword at hand, I would kill you here and now." **30** But the ass said to Balaam, "Am I not your own beast, and have you not always ridden upon me until now? Have I been in the habit of treating you this way before?" "No," replied Balaam.

31 Then the LORD removed the veil from Balaam's eyes, so that he too saw the angel of the LORD standing on the road with sword drawn; and he fell on his knees and bowed to the ground. **32** But the angel of the LORD said to him, "Why have you beaten your ass these three times? It is I who have come armed to hinder you because this rash journey of yours is directly opposed to me. **33** When the ass saw

me, she turned away from me these three times. If she had not turned away from me, I would have killed you; her I would have spared." **34** Then Balaam said to the angel of the LORD, "I have sinned. Yet I did not know that you stood against me to oppose my journey. Since it has displeased you, I will go back home." **35** But the angel of the LORD said to Balaam, "Go with the men; but you may say only what I tell you." So Balaam went on with the princes of Balak.

36 When Balak heard that Balaam was coming, he went out to meet him at the boundary city Ir-Moab on the Arnon at the end of the Moabite territory. **37** And he said to Balaam, "I sent an urgent summons to you! Why did you not come to me? Did you think I could not reward you?" **38** Balaam answered him, "Well, I have come to you after all. But what power have I to say anything? I can speak only what God puts in my mouth." **39** Then Balaam went with Balak, and they came to Kiriath-huzoth. **40** Here Balak slaughtered oxen and sheep, and sent portions to Balaam and to the princes who were with him.

The First Oracle. **41** The next morning Balak took Balaam up on Bamoth-baal, and from there he saw some of the clans.

CHAPTER 23

1 Then Balaam said to Balak, "Build me seven altars, and prepare seven bullocks and seven rams for me here." **2** So he did as Balaam had ordered, offering a bullock and a ram on each altar. And Balak said to him, "I have erected the seven altars, and have offered a bullock and a ram on each." **3** Balaam then said to him, "Stand here by your holocaust while I go over there. Perhaps the LORD will meet me, and then I will tell you whatever he lets me see." He went out on the barren height, **4** and God met him. **5** When he had put an utterance in Balaam's mouth, the LORD said to him, "Go back to Balak, and speak accordingly." **6** So he went back to Balak, who was still standing by his holocaust together with all the princes of Moab. **7** Then Balaam gave voice to his oracle:

---

o Nm 24, 13.   q Nm 22, 6.
p 2 Pt 2, 16.

*

22, 22: **The anger of God flared up:** not merely because Balaam was going to Balak, for he had God's permission for the journey (v 20), but perhaps because he was tempted by avarice to curse Israel against God's command. "They have followed the way of Balaam, son of Bosor, who loved the wages of wrongdoing" (2 Pt 2, 15); "and have rushed on thoughtlessly into the error of Balaam for the sake of gain" (Jude 11). Cf v 32 and compare Ex 4, 18–26.

23, 7: **Aram:** the ancient name of the region later known as Syria. **The Eastern Mountains:** the low ranges in the Syrian

From Aram* has Balak brought me here,
  Moab's king, from the Eastern
    Mountains:*q
"Come and lay a curse for me on Jacob,
  come and denounce Israel."
8 How can I curse whom God has not cursed?
  How denounce whom the LORD has not
    denounced?
9 For from the top of the crags I see him,
  from the heights I behold him.
  Here is a people that lives apart*
    and does not reckon itself among the
      nations.
10 Who has ever counted the dust of Jacob,
  or numbered Israel's wind-borne
    particles?*
  May I die the death of the just,
    may my descendants be as many as theirs!

11 "What have you done to me?" cried Balak to Balaam. "It was to curse my foes that I brought you here; instead, you have even blessed them." 12 Balaam replied, "Is it not what the LORD puts in my mouth that I must repeat with care?"

The Second Oracle.   13 Then Balak said to him, "Please come with me to another place* from which you can see only some and not all of them, and from there curse them for me." 14 So he brought him to the lookout field on the top of Pisgah, where he built seven altars and offered a bullock and a ram on each of them. 15 Balaam then said to Balak, "Stand here by your holocaust, while I seek a meeting over there." 16 Then the LORD met Balaam, and having put an utterance in his mouth, he said to him, "Go back to Balak, and speak according-ly." 17 So he went back to Balak, who was still standing by his holocaust together with the princes of Moab. When Balak asked him, "What did the LORD say?" 18 Balaam gave voice to his oracle:

Be aroused, O Balak, and hearken;
  give ear to my testimony, O son of
    Zippor!
19 God is not man that he should speak falsely,
  nor human, that he should change his
    mind.
  Is he one to speak and not act,
    to decree and not fulfill?
20 It is a blessing I have been given to
    pronounce;
  a blessing which I cannot restrain.
21 Misfortune is not observed in Jacob,
  nor misery* seen in Israel.
  The LORD, his God, is with him;
    with him is the triumph of his King.
22 It is God who brought him out of Egypt,*r
  a wild bull of towering might.*
23 No, there is no sorcery against Jacob,
  nor omen against Israel.
  It shall yet be said of Jacob,

and of Israel, "Behold what God has
  wrought!"
24 Here is a people that springs up like a
    lioness,
  and stalks forth like a lion;
  It rests not till it has devoured its prey
    and has drunk the blood of the slain.*s

25 "Even though you cannot curse them," said Balak to Balaam, "at least do not bless them." 26 But Balaam answered Balak, "Did I not warn you that I must do all that the LORD tells me?"

The Third Oracle.   27 Then Balak said to Balaam, "Come, let me bring you to another place; perhaps God will approve of your cursing them for me from there." 28 So he took Balaam to the top of Peor, that overlooks Jeshimon. 29 Balaam then said to him, "Here build me seven altars; and here prepare for me seven bullocks and seven rams." 30 And Balak did as Balaam had ordered, offering a bullock and a ram on each altar.

CHAPTER 24

1 Balaam, however, perceiving that the LORD was pleased to bless Israel, did not go aside as before to seek omens, but turned his gaze toward the desert. 2 When he raised his eyes and saw Israel encamped, tribe by tribe, the spirit of God came upon him, 3 and he gave voice to his oracle:

The utterance of Balaam, son of Beor,
  the utterance of the man whose eye is
    true,
4 The utterance of one who hears what God
    says,
  and knows what the Most High knows,
  Of one who sees what the Almighty sees,
    enraptured, and with eyes unveiled:
5 How goodly are your tents, O Jacob;
  your encampments, O Israel!
6 They are like gardens beside a stream,
  like the cedars planted by the LORD.

---

r Nm 24, 8.   s Nm 24, 9; Gn 49, 9.

*

desert near the Euphrates and Balaam's town of Pethor; cf Nm 22, 5.

23, 9: A people that lives apart: Israel, as the chosen people of God, occupied a unique place among the nations, from which they kept themselves aloof.

23, 10: The dust of Jacob . . . Israel's wind-borne particles: the Israelites will be as numerous as dust in a desert sandstorm. May I . . . as many as theirs: a formula by which Balaam swears he is speaking the truth; he sees the reward of virtue in having numerous descendants.

23, 13: To another place: Balak thought that if Balaam would view Israel from a different site, he could forecast a different kind of omen.

23, 21: Misfortune . . . misery: Balaam admits that he is unable to predict any evils for Israel.

23, 22: A wild bull of towering might: the reference is to Israel, rather than to God.

7 His wells shall yield free-flowing waters,
    he shall have the sea within reach;
    His king shall rise higher than. . . .
    and his royalty shall be exalted.
8 It is God who brought him out of Egypt,
    a wild bull of towering might.
    He shall devour the nations like grass,
    their bones he shall strip bare.[t]
9 He lies crouching like a lion,
    or like a lioness; who shall arouse him?
    Blessed is he who blesses you,
    and cursed is he who curses you![u]

10 Balak beat his palms* together in a blaze of anger at Balaam and said to him, "It was to curse my foes that I summoned you here; yet three times now you have even blessed them instead![v] **11** Be off at once, then, to your home. I promised to reward you richly, but the LORD has withheld the reward from you!" **12** Balaam replied to Balak, "Did I not warn the very messengers whom you sent to me, **13** 'Even if Balak gave me his house full of silver and gold, I could not of my own accord do anything, good or evil, contrary to the command of the LORD'? Whatever the LORD says I must repeat.[w]

The Fourth Oracle. **14** "But now that I am about to go to my own people, let me first warn you what this people will do to your people in the days to come." **15** Then Balaam gave voice to his oracle:

    The utterance of Balaam, son of Beor,
        the utterance of the man whose eye is true,
16 The utterance of one who hears what God says,
    and knows what the Most High knows,
    Of one who sees what the Almighty sees,
        enraptured and with eyes unveiled.
17 I see him, though not now;
    I behold him, though not near:
    A star shall advance from Jacob,
    and a staff* shall rise from Israel,
    That shall smite the brows of Moab,[x]
    and the skulls of all the Shuthites,
18 Till Edom is dispossessed,
    and no fugitive is left in Seir.
    Israel shall do valiantly,
19   and Jacob shall overcome his foes.

20 Upon seeing Amalek, Balaam gave voice to his oracle:

    First* of the peoples was Amalek,
    but his end is to perish forever.[y]

21 Upon seeing the Kenites,* he gave voice to his oracle:

    Your abode is enduring, O smith,
    and your nest is set on a cliff;
22 Yet destined for burning—
    even as I watch—are your inhabitants.

23 Upon seeing . . . he gave voice to his oracle:

    *Alas, who shall survive of Ishmael,
24   to deliver his people from the hands of the Kittim?
    When they have conquered Asshur and conquered Eber,
    He too shall perish forever.

25 Then Balaam set out on his journey home; and Balak also went his way.

CHAPTER 25

Worship of Baal of Peor. **1** While Israel was living at Shittim,* the people degraded themselves by having illicit relations with the Moabite women.[z] **2** These then invited the people to the sacrifices of their god, and the people ate of the sacrifices[a] and worshiped their god. **3** When Israel thus submitted to the rites of Baal of Peor,[b] the LORD's anger flared up against Israel, **4** [c]and he said to Moses, "Gather all the leaders of the people, and hold a public execution* of the guilty ones before the LORD, that his blazing wrath may be turned away from Israel." **5** So Moses told the Israelite judges, "Each of you shall kill those of his men who have submitted to the rites of Baal of Peor."

---

t Nm 23, 22.
u Nm 23, 24; Gn 12, 3; 27, 29; 49, 9.
v Nm 23, 11.
w Nm 22, 18.
x 2 Sm 8, 2.
y Ex 17, 14; 1 Sm 15, 3.
z Nm 31, 16.
a Ex 34, 15f.
b Ps 106, 28; Hos 9, 10.
c Dt 4, 3.

---

*

24, 10: Balak beat his palms: a sign of disclaiming any responsibility for paying the promised reward.

24, 17: A star . . . a staff: many of the Fathers have understood this as a Messianic prophecy, although it is not referred to anywhere in the New Testament; in this sense the star is Christ himself, just as he is the staff from Israel; cf Is 11, 1. But it is doubtful whether this passage is to be connected with the "star of the Magi" in Mt 2, 1–12. The Shuthites: mentioned in other documents of this period as nomads on the borded of Palestine.

24, 20: First: literally "the beginning." Amalek was an aboriginal people in Palestine and therefore considered as of great antiquity. There is a deliberate contrast here between the words first and end.

24, 21: The Kenites lived in high strongholds in the mountains of southern Palestine and the Sinai Peninsula, and were skilled in working the various metals found in their territory. Their name is connected, at least by popular etymology, with the Hebrew word for "smith"; of similar sound is the Hebrew word for "nest"—hence the play on words in the present passage.

24, 23f: The translation of this short oracle is based on a reconstructed text and is rather uncertain. Ishmael: the survival of Ishmael is indicated in Gn 17, 20; 21, 13. 18.

25, 1: Shittim: the full name was Abel-shittim, a locality at the foot of the mountains in the northeastern corner of the plains of Moab (Nm 33, 49). Illicit relations: perhaps as part of the licentious worship of Baal of Peor.

25, 4: Hold a public execution: the same phrase occurs in 2 Sm 21, 6–14, where the context shows that at least a part of the penalty consisted in being denied honorable burial. In both passages, dismemberment as a punishment for the breaking of covenant pledges is a current understanding of the phrase.

Zeal of Phinehas.

6 Yet a certain Israelite came and brought in a Midianite woman* to his clansmen in the view of Moses and of the whole Israelite community, while they were weeping at the entrance of the meeting tent. **7** *d*When Phinehas, son of Eleazar, son of Aaron the priest, saw this, he left the assembly, and taking a lance in hand, **8** followed the Israelite into his retreat where he pierced the pair of them, the Israelite and the woman. Thus the slaughter of Israelites was checked; **9** but only after twenty-four thousand had died.

10 Then the LORD said to Moses, **11** "Phinehas, son of Eleazar, son of Aaron the priest, has turned my anger from the Israelites by his zeal for my honor* among them; that is why I did not put an end to the Israelites for the offense to my honor. **12** *e*Announce, therefore, that I hereby give him my pledge of friendship, **13** which shall be for him and for his descendants after him the pledge of an everlasting priesthood, because he was zealous on behalf of his God and thus made amends for the Israelites."

14 *The Israelite slain with the Midianite woman was Zimri, son of Salu, prince of an ancestral house of the Simeonites. **15** The slain Midianite woman was Cozbi, daughter of Zur, who was head of a clan, an ancestral house, in Midian.

Vengeance on the Midianites.

16 *The LORD then said to Moses, **17** *f*"Treat the Midianites as enemies and crush them, **18** for they have been your enemies by their wily dealings with you as regards Peor and as regards their kinswoman Cozbi, the daughter of the Midianite prince, who was killed at the time of the slaughter because of Peor."

CHAPTER 26

The Second Census.

19 After the slaughter* **1** the LORD said to Moses and Eleazar, son of Aaron the priest, **2** "Take a census, by ancestral houses, throughout the community of the Israelites of all those of twenty years or more who are fit for military service in Israel."*g* **3** So on the plains of Moab along the Jericho stretch of the Jordan, Moses and the priest Eleazar registered **4** those of twenty years or more, as the LORD had commanded Moses.

The Israelites who came out of the land of Egypt were as follows:

5 *h*Of Reuben, the first-born of Israel, the Reubenites by clans were: through Hanoch the clan of the Hanochites, through Pallu the clan of the Palluites, **6** through Hezron the clan of the Hezronites, through Carmi the clan of the Carmites. **7** These were the clans of the Reu-

benites, of whom forty-three thousand seven hundred and thirty men were registered.

8 From Pallu descended Eliab, **9** and the descendants of Eliab were Dathan and Abiram*i*—the same Dathan and Abiram, councilors of the community, who revolted against Moses and Aaron [like Korah's band when it rebelled against the LORD]. **10** The earth opened its mouth and swallowed them as a warning [Korah too and the band that died when the fire consumed two hundred and fifty men. **11** The descendants of Korah, however, did not die out].

12 The Simeonites by clans were: through Nemuel* the clan of the Nemuelites, through Jamin the clan of the Jaminites, through Jachin the clan of the Jachinites, **13** through Sohar the clan of the Soharites, through Shaul the clan of the Shaulites. **14** These were the clans of the Simeonites, of whom twenty-two thousand two hundred men were registered.

15 The Gadites by clans were: through Zephon the clan of the Zephonites, through Haggi the clan of the Haggites, through Shuni the clan of the Shunites, **16** through Ozni the clan of the Oznites, through Eri the clan of the Erites, **17** through Arod the clan of the Arodites, through Areli the clan of the Arelites. **18** These were the clans of the Gadites, of whom forty thousand five hundred men were registered.

19 The sons of Judah who died in the land of Canaan were Er and Onan.*j* **20** The Judahites by clans were: through Shelah the clan of the Shelahites, through Perez the clan of the Perezites, through Zerah the clan of the Zerahites. **21** The Perezites were: through Hezron the clan of the Hezronites, through Hamul the clan of the Hamulites. **22** These were the clans of Judah, of whom seventy-six thousand five hundred men were registered.

23 The Issacharites by clans were: through

d Ps 106, 30.
e 12f: Sir 45, 23f; Ps 106, 31; 1 Mc 2, 26. 54.
f 17f: Nm 31, 2-12.
g Nm 1, 2f.
h 5f: 1 Chr 5, 3.
i 9f: Nm 16, 1. 32.
j Gn 38, 7. 10; 46, 12; 1 Chr 2, 3.

---

*

25, 6: Midianite woman: at this time the Midianites were leagued with the Moabites in opposing Israel; cf Nm 22, 4. 7. Balaam had induced both the Midianites (Nm 31, 16) and the Moabites (Rv 2, 14) to lure the Israelites to the obscene rites of Baal of Peor. They were weeping: on account of the plague that had struck them; cf v 8.

25, 11: For my honor: by taking vengeance on those who had made Baal of Peor a rival of the Lord.

25, 14f: The nobility of the slain couple is mentioned in order to stress the courage of Phinehas in punishing them. The zeal of Phinehas became proverbial; cf Ps 106, 30; Sir 45, 23; 1 Mc 2, 26. 54.

25, 16ff: The account of the execution of this command is given in Nm 31, 1–18.

26, 19: This is the last verse of Ch 25.

26, 12: Nemuel: so also in Gn 46, 10; 1 Chr 4, 24. In Ex 6, 15, the same man is called "Jemuel"; it is uncertain which form is correct.

Tola the clan of the Tolaites, through Puvah the clan of the Puvahites, **24** through Jashub the clan of the Jashubites, through Shimron the clan of the Shimronites. **25** These were the clans of Issachar, of whom sixty-four thousand three hundred men were registered.

26 The Zebulunites by clans were: through Sered the clan of the Seredites, through Elon the clan of the Elonites, through Jahleel the clan of the Jahleelites. **27** These were the clans of the Zebulunites, of whom sixty thousand five hundred men were registered.

28 The sons of Joseph were Manasseh, and Ephraim. **29** The Manassehites by clans were: through Machir the clan of the Machirites, through Gilead, a descendant of Machir, the clan of the Gileadites. **30** The Gileadites were: through Abiezer the clan of the Abiezrites, through Helek the clan of the Helekites, **31** through Asriel the clan of the Asrielites, through Shechem the clan of the Shechemites, **32** through Shemida the clan of the Shemida-ites, through Hepher the clan of the Hepherites. **33** ᵏZelophehad, son of Hepher, had no sons, but only daughters, whose names were Mahlah, Noah, Hoglah, Milcah and Tirzah. **34** These were the clans of Manasseh, of whom fifty-two thousand seven hundred men were registered.

35 The Ephraimites by clans were: through Shuthelah the clan of the Shuthelahites, through Becher the clan of the Bechrites, through Tahan the clan of the Tahanites. **36** The Shuthelahites were: through Eran the clan of the Eranites. **37** These were the clans of the Ephraimites, of whom thirty-two thousand five hundred men were registered.

These were the descendants of Joseph by clans.

38 The Benjaminites by clans were: through Bela the clan of the Belaites, through Ashbel the clan of the Ashbelites, through Ahiram the clan of the Ahiramites, **39** through Shupham the clan of the Shuphamites, through Hupham the clan of the Huphamites. **40** The descendants of Bela were Arad and Naaman: through Arad the clan of the Aradites, through Naaman the clan of the Naamanites. **41** These were the Benjami-nites by clans, of whom forty-five thousand six hundred men were registered.

42 The Danites by clans were: through Shu-ham the clan of the Shuhamites. These were the clans of Dan, **43** of whom sixty-four thousand four hundred men were registered.

44 The Asherites by clans were: through Im-nah the clan of the Imnites, through Ishvi the clan of the Ishvites, through Beriah the clan of the Beriites, **45** through Heber the clan of the Heberites, through Malchiel the clan of the Mal-chielites. **46** The name of Asher's daughter was Serah. **47** These were the clans of Asher, of

whom fifty-three thousand four hundred men were registered.

48 The Naphtalites by clans were: through Jahzeel the clan of the Jahzeelites, through Guni the clan of the Gunites, **49** through Jezer the clan of the Jezerites, through Shillem the clan of the Shillemites. **50** These were the clans of Naphtali, of whom forty-five thousand four hundred men were registered.

51 These six hundred and one thousand sev-en hundred and thirty were the Israelites who were registered.

Allotment of the Land. **52** *The LORD said to Moses, **53** ˡ"Among these groups the land shall be divided as their heritage in keeping with the number of individuals in each group. **54** ᵐTo a large group you shall assign a large heritage, to a small group a small heritage, each group receiving its heritage in proportion to the number of men registered in it. **55** But the land shall be divided by lot, as the heritage of the various ancestral tribes. **56** As the lot falls shall each group, large or small, be assigned its heri-tage."

Census of the Levites. **57** The Levites registered by clans were: through Gershon the clan of the Gershonites, through Kohath the clan of the Kohathites, through Merari the clan of the Merarites. **58** These also were clans of Levi: the clan of the Libnites, the clan of the Hebronites, the clan of the Mahlites, the clan of the Mushites, the clan of the Korahites.

Among the descendants of Kohath was Am-ram, **59** whose wife was named Jochebed. She also was of the tribe of Levi, born to the tribe in Egypt. To Amram she bore Aaron and Moses and their sister Miriam. **60** To Aaron were born Nadab and Abihu, Eleazar and Ithamar. **61** But Nadab and Abihu died when they offered pro-fane fire before the LORD.

62 The total number of male Levites one month or more of age, who were registered, was twenty-three thousand. ⁿ They were not regis-tered with the other Israelites, however, for no heritage was given them among the Israelites.

63 These, then, were the men registered by Moses and the priest Eleazar in the census of the Israelites taken on the plains of Moab along the

---

k Nm 27, 1; 36, 11; Jos 17, 3.
l Jos 11, 23.
m Nm 33, 54; 35, 8.
n Nm 3, 39.

*

26, 52–56: The division of Canaan among the various tribes and clans and families was determined partly by the size of each group and partly by lot. Perhaps the lots determined the respective locality of each tribal land and the section re-served for each clan, while the relative size of the allotted locality and section depended on the numerical strength of each group. The Hebrews considered the outcome of the drawing of lots as an expression of God's will; cf Acts 1, 23–26.

Jericho stretch of the Jordan. **64** Among them there was not a man of those who had been registered by Moses and the priest Aaron in the census of the Israelites taken in the desert of Sinai. **65** *o* For the LORD had told them that they would surely die in the desert, and not one of them was left except Caleb, son of Jephunneh, and Joshua, son of Nun.

CHAPTER 27

Zelophehad's Daughters. **1** Zelophehad, son of Hepher, son of Gilead, son of Machir, son of Manasseh, son of Joseph, had daughters named Mahlah, Noah, Hoglah, Milcah and Tirzah.*p* They came forward, **2** and standing in the presence of Moses, the priest Eleazar, the princes, and the whole community at the entrance of the meeting tent, said: **3** "Our father died in the desert. Although he did not join those who banded together against the LORD* [in Korah's band], he died for his own sin without leaving any sons. **4** But why should our father's name be withdrawn from his clan merely because he had no son? Let us, therefore, have property among our father's kinsmen."

Laws Concerning Heiresses. **5** *When Moses laid their case before the LORD, **6** the LORD said to him, **7** "The plea of Zelophehad's daughters is just; you shall give them hereditary property among their father's kinsmen, letting their father's heritage pass on to them. **8** Therefore, tell the Israelites: If a man dies without leaving a son, you shall let his heritage pass on to his daughter; **9** if he has no daughter, you shall give his heritage to his brothers; **10** if he has no brothers, you shall give his heritage to his father's brothers; **11** if his father had no brothers, you shall give his heritage to his nearest relative in his clan, who shall then take possession of it." This is the legal norm for the Israelites, as the LORD commanded Moses.*q*

Joshua To Succeed Moses. **12** The LORD said to Moses, "Go up here into the Abarim Mountains* and view the land that I am giving to the Israelites.*r* **13** When you have viewed it, you too shall be taken to your people, as was your brother Aaron,*s* **14** because in the rebellion of the community in the desert of Zin you both rebelled against my order to manifest my sanctity to them by means of the water."*t* [This is the water of Meribah of Kadesh in the desert of Zin.]

15 Then Moses said to the LORD, **16** "May the LORD, the God of the spirits of all mankind,* set over the community a man **17** who shall act as their leader in all things, to guide them in all their actions; that the LORD's community may

not be like sheep without a shepherd." **18** And the LORD replied to Moses, "Take Joshua, son of Nun,*u* a man of spirit,* and lay your hand upon him. **19** Have him stand in the presence of the priest Eleazar and of the whole community, and commission him before their eyes. **20** Invest him with some of your own dignity, that the whole Israelite community may obey him. **21** He shall present himself to the priest Eleazar, to have him seek out for him the decisions of the Urim* in the LORD's presence; and as he directs, Joshua, all the Israelites with him, and the community as a whole shall perform all their actions."

22 Moses did as the LORD had commanded him. Taking Joshua and having him stand in the presence of the priest Eleazar and of the whole community, **23** he laid his hands on him and gave him his commission, as the LORD had directed through Moses.

CHAPTER 28

General Sacrifices. **1** The LORD said to Moses, **2** "Give the Israelites this commandment: At the times I have appointed, you shall be careful to present me the food offerings that are offered to me as sweet-smelling oblations.

Each Morning and Evening. **3** *v* "You shall tell them therefore: This is the oblation which you shall offer to the LORD: two unblem-

---

o Nm 14, 22ff. 29.
p Nm 26, 33; Jos 17, 3.
q Jer 32, 6-9.
r Dt 3, 27; 32, 49; 34, 1.
s 13f: Nm 20, 12. 24.
t Dt 32, 51.
u Dt 34, 9.
v 3-8: Ex 29, 38-42.

*

27, 3: He did not join . . . against the Lord: had he done so, he and his heirs could have rightly been deprived of the privilege of receiving a portion in the Promised Land.

27, 5–11: The purpose of this law, as also that of the related laws in Nm 36, 2–10 (heiresses to marry within the same tribe), Dt 25, 5–10 (levirate marriage), and Lv 25, 10 (return of property in the jubilee year), was to keep the landed property within the proper domain of each tribe.

27, 12: The Abarim Mountains: the range on the eastern side of the Dead Sea.

27, 16: The God of the spirits of all mankind: the sense is either that God knows the character and abilities of all men and therefore knows best whom to appoint (cf Acts 1, 24), or, more probably, that God is Master of life and death and therefore can call Moses from this world whenever he wishes; cf the same phrase in Nm 16, 22, where "spirit" evidently means "the life principle."

27, 18: A man of spirit: literally, "a man in whom there is spirit": one who has the qualities of a good leader—courage, prudence, and strength of will. Cf Gn 41, 38; Dt 34, 9.

27, 21: The Urim: certain sacred objects which the Hebrew priests employed to ascertain the divine will, probably by obtaining a positive or negative answer to a given question. The full expression was "the Urim and Thummim"; cf Ex 28, 30; Lv 8, 8; Dt 33, 8; Ezr 2, 63; Neh 7, 65. Joshua was ordinarily not to receive direct revelations from God as Moses had received them.

28, 3: The established holocaust: "the tamid holocaust," the technical term for the daily sacrifice.

ished yearling lambs each day as the established holocaust,* **4** offering one lamb in the morning and the other during the evening twilight, **5** each with a cereal offering of one tenth of an ephah of fine flour mixed with a fourth of a hin of oil of crushed olives.* **6** This is the established holocaust that was offered at Mount Sinai as a sweet-smelling oblation to the LORD. **7** And as the libation for the first lamb, you shall pour out to the LORD in the sanctuary* a fourth of a hin of wine. **8** The other lamb, to be offered during the evening twilight, you shall offer with the same cereal offering and the same libation as in the morning, as a sweet-smelling oblation to the LORD.

On the Sabbath. **9** "On the sabbath day you shall offer two unblemished yearling lambs, with their cereal offering, two tenths of an ephah of fine flour mixed with oil, and with their libations. **10** Each sabbath there shall be the sabbath holocaust in addition to the established holocaust and its libation.

At the New Moon Feast. **11** "On the first of each month* you shall offer as a holocaust to the LORD two bullocks, one ram, and seven unblemished yearling lambs, **12** with three tenths of an ephah of fine flour mixed with oil as the cereal offering for each bullock, two tenths of an ephah of fine flour mixed with oil as the cereal offering for the ram, **13** and one tenth of an ephah of fine flour mixed with oil as the cereal offering for each lamb, that the holocaust may be a sweet-smelling oblation to the LORD. **14** Their libations shall be half a hin of wine for each bullock, a third of a hin for the ram, and a fourth of a hin for each lamb. This is the new moon holocaust for every new moon of the year. **15** Moreover, one goat shall be sacrificed as a sin offering to the LORD. These are to be offered in addition to the established holocaust and its libation.

At the Passover. **16** "On the fourteenth day* of the first month falls the Passover of the LORD,w **17** and the fifteenth day of this month is the pilgrimage feast. For seven days unleavened bread is to be eaten. **18** On the first of these days you shall hold a sacred assembly, and do no sort of work.x **19** As an oblation you shall offer a holocaust to the LORD, which shall consist of two bullocks, one ram, and seven yearling lambs that you are sure are unblemished, **20** with their cereal offerings of fine flour mixed with oil, offering three tenths of an ephah for each bullock, two tenths for the ram, **21** and one tenth for each of the seven lambs; **22** and offer one goat as a sin offering in atonement for yourselves. **23** These offerings you shall make in addition to the established morning holo-

caust: **24** you shall make exactly the same offerings each day for seven days as food offerings, in addition to the established holocaust with its libation, for a sweet-smelling oblation to the LORD. **25** On the seventh day you shall hold a sacred assembly, and do no sort of work.y

At Pentecost. **26** "On the day of first fruits,* on your feast of Weeks,z when you present to the LORD the new cereal offering, you shall hold a sacred assembly, and do no sort of work. **27** You shall offer as a sweet-smelling holocaust to the LORD two bullocks, one ram, and seven yearling lambs that you are sure are unblemished, **28** with their cereal offerings of fine flour mixed with oil; offering three tenths of an ephah for each bullock, two tenths for the ram, **29** and one tenth for each of the seven lambs. **30** Moreover, one goat shall be offered as a sin offering in atonement for yourselves. **31** You shall make these offerings, together with their libations, in addition to the established holocaust with its cereal offering.

CHAPTER 29

On New Year's Day. **1** "On the first day of the seventh month* you shall hold a sacred assembly, and do no sort of work; it shall be a day on which you sound the trumpet.a **2** You shall offer as a sweet-smelling holocaust to the LORD one bullock, one ram, and seven unblemished yearling lambs, **3** with their cereal offerings of fine flour mixed with oil; offering three tenths of an ephah for the bullock, two tenths for the ram, **4** and one tenth for each of the seven lambs. **5** Moreover, one goat shall be offered as a sin offering in atonement for yourselves. **6** These are to be offered in addition to the

---

w Ex 12, 18; Lv 23, 5;　　　23, 8.
Dt 16, 1.　　　　　　　　z Ex 34, 22.
x Ex 12, 16; Lv 23, 7.　　a Nm 10, 10; Lv 23, 24.
y Ex 12, 16; 13, 6; Lv

*

28, 5: Oil of crushed olives: this oil, made in a mortar, was purer and more expensive than oil extracted in the olive press.

28, 7: In the sanctuary: according to Sir 50, 15, it was at the base of the altar.

28, 11: On the first of each month: literally, "at the new moons"; beginning on the evening when the crescent of the new moon first appeared.

28, 16: On the fourteenth day: toward evening at the end of this day; cf Ex 12, 6. 18.

28, 26: The day of first fruits: a unique term for this feast, which is usually called "the feast of Weeks"; it was celebrated as a thanksgiving for the wheat harvest seven weeks after the barley harvest (Passover). In the time of Christ it was commonly known by the Greek word "Pentecost," that is, "fiftieth" (day after the Passover); see note on Lv 23, 16.

29, 1: The first day of the seventh month: (about September-October) is now the Jewish New Year's Day. In the older calendar the year began with the first of Nisan (March-April); cf Ex 12, 2.

ordinary new moon holocaust with its cereal offering, and in addition to the established holocaust with its cereal offering, together with the libations prescribed for them, as a sweet-smelling oblation to the LORD.

On the Day of Atonement.

7 "On the tenth day of this seventh month* you shall hold a sacred assembly, and mortify yourselves, and do no sort of work.*b* 8 You shall offer as a sweet-smelling holocaust to the LORD one bullock, one ram, and seven yearling lambs that you are sure are unblemished, 9 with their cereal offerings of fine flour mixed with oil; offering three tenths of an ephah for the bullock, two tenths for the ram, 10 and one tenth for each of the seven lambs. 11 Moreover, one goat shall be sacrificed as a sin offering. These are to be offered in addition to the atonement sin offering,* the established holocaust with its cereal offering, and their libations.

On the Feast of Booths.*

12 "On the fifteenth day of the seventh month you shall hold a sacred assembly,*c* and do no sort of work; then, for seven days following, you shall celebrate a pilgrimage feast to the LORD. 13 You shall offer as a sweet-smelling holocaust to the LORD thirteen bullocks,* two rams, and fourteen yearling lambs that are unblemished, 14 with their cereal offerings of fine flour mixed with oil; offering three tenths of an ephah for each of the thirteen bullocks, two tenths for each of the two rams, 15 and one tenth for each of the fourteen lambs. 16 Moreover, one goat shall be sacrificed as a sin offering. These are to be offered in addition to the established holocaust with its cereal offering and libation.

17 "On the second day you shall offer twelve bullocks, two rams, and fourteen unblemished yearling lambs, 18 with their cereal offerings and libations as prescribed for the bullocks, rams and lambs in proportion to their number, 19 as well as one goat for a sin offering, besides the established holocaust with its cereal offering and libation.

20 "On the third day you shall offer eleven bullocks, two rams, and fourteen unblemished yearling lambs, 21 with their cereal offerings and libations as prescribed for the bullocks, rams and lambs in proportion to their number, 22 as well as one goat for a sin offering, besides the established holocaust with its cereal offering and libation.

23 "On the fourth day you shall offer ten bullocks, two rams, and fourteen unblemished yearling lambs, 24 with their cereal offerings and libations as prescribed for the bullocks, rams and lambs in proportion to their number, 25 as well as one goat for a sin offering, besides

the established holocaust with its cereal offering and libation.

26 "On the fifth day you shall offer nine bullocks, two rams, and fourteen unblemished yearling lambs, 27 *d*with their cereal offerings and libations as prescribed for the bullocks, rams and lambs in proportion to their number, 28 as well as one goat for a sin offering, besides the established holocaust with its cereal offering and libation.

29 "On the sixth day you shall offer eight bullocks, two rams, and fourteen unblemished yearling lambs, 30 with their cereal offerings and libations as prescribed for the bullocks, rams and lambs in proportion to their number, 31 as well as one goat for a sin offering, besides the established holocaust with its cereal offering and libation.

32 "On the seventh day you shall offer seven bullocks, two rams, and fourteen unblemished yearling lambs, 33 with their cereal offerings and libations as prescribed for the bullocks, rams and lambs in proportion to their number, 34 as well as one goat for a sin offering, besides the established holocaust with its cereal offering and libation.

35 "On the eighth day*e* you shall hold a solemn meeting,* and do no sort of work. 36 You shall offer up in holocaust as a sweet-smelling oblation to the LORD one bullock, one ram, and seven unblemished yearling lambs, 37 with their cereal offerings and libations as prescribed for the bullocks, rams and lambs in proportion to their number, 38 as well as one goat for a sin offering, besides the established holocaust with its cereal offering and libation.

39 "These are the offerings you shall make to the LORD on your festivals, besides whatever holocausts, cereal offerings, libations, and peace offerings you present as your votive or free-will offerings."

---

b Lv 16, 29; 23, 27f. 32.   d Nm 29, 30. 37.
c Lv 23, 34f.   e Lv 23, 36; Jn 7, 37.

---

*

29, 7: The tenth day of this seventh month: the Day of Atonement. Mortify yourselves: literally, "afflict your souls," that is, with fasting.

29, 11: The atonement sin offering: the bullock prescribed in Lv 16, 11f.

29, 12: This feast of Booths celebrating the vintage harvest was the most popular of all and therefore had the most elaborate ritual. See note on Lv 23, 34.

29, 13: Thirteen bullocks: the number of bullocks sacrificed before the octave day was seventy, arranged on a descending scale so that the number on the seventh day was the sacred number seven.

29, 35: A solemn meeting: the Hebrew word is the technical term for the closing celebration of the three major feasts of the Passover, Pentecost and Booths, or of other special feasts that lasted for a week. Cf Lv 23, 36; Dt 16, 8; 2 Chr 7, 9; Neh 8, 18.

CHAPTER 30

1 Moses then gave the Israelites these instructions, just as the LORD had ordered him.

Validity and Annulment of Vows. **2** Moses said to the heads of the Israelite tribes, "This is what the LORD has commanded: **3** When a man makes a vow to the LORD or binds himself under oath to a pledge* of abstinence, he shall not violate his word, but must fulfill exactly the promise he has uttered.ƒ

4 "When a woman, while still a maiden in her father's house, makes a vow to the LORD, or binds herself to a pledge, **5** if her father learns of her vow or the pledge to which she bound herself and says nothing to her about it, then any vow or any pledge she has made remains valid. **6** But if on the day he learns of it her father expresses to her his disapproval, then any vow or any pledge she has made becomes null and void; and the LORD releases her from it, since her father has expressed to her his disapproval.

7 "If she marries while under a vow or under a rash pledge to which she bound herself, **8** and her husband learns of it, yet says nothing to her that day about it, then the vow or pledge she had made remains valid. **9** But if on the day he learns of it her husband expresses to her his disapproval, he thereby annuls the vow she had made or the rash pledge to which she had bound herself, and the LORD releases her from it. **10** The vow of a widow or of a divorced woman, or any pledge to which such a woman binds herself, is valid.

11 "If it is in her husband's house* that she makes a vow or binds herself under oath to a pledge, **12** and her husband learns of it yet says nothing to express to her his disapproval, then any vow or any pledge she has made remains valid. **13** But if on the day he learns of them her husband annuls them, then whatever she has expressly promised in her vow or in her pledge becomes null and void; since her husband has annulled them, the LORD releases her from them.

14 "Any vow or any pledge that she makes under oath to mortify herself, her husband can either allow to remain valid or render null and void. **15** But if her husband, day after day, says nothing at all to her about them, he thereby allows as valid any vow or any pledge she has made; he has allowed them to remain valid, because on the day he learned of them he said nothing to her about them. **16** If, however, he countermands them* some time after he first learned of them, he is responsible for her guilt.''

17 These are the statutes which the LORD prescribed through Moses concerning the relationship between a husband and his wife, as well as between a father and his daughter while she is still a maiden in her father's house.

CHAPTER 31

Extermination of the Midianites. **1** The LORD said to Moses,* **2** "Avenge the Israelites on the Midianites, and then you shall be taken to your people.'' **3** So Moses told the people, "Select men from your midst and arm them for war, to attack the Midianites and execute the LORD's vengeance on them. **4** From each of the tribes of Israel you shall send a band of one thousand men to war.'' **5** From the clans of Israel, therefore, a thousand men of each tribe were levied, so that there were twelve thousand men armed for war. **6** Moses sent them out on the campaign, a thousand from each tribe, with Phinehas, son of Eleazar, the priest for the campaign, who had with him the sacred vessels and the trumpets for sounding the alarm. **7** They waged war against the Midianites, as the LORD had commanded Moses, and killed every male among them. **8** Besides those slain in battle, they killed the five Midianite kings:* Evi, Rekem, Zur, Hur and Reba; and they also executed Balaam, son of Beor, with the sword. **9** But the Israelites kept the women of the Midianites with their little ones as captives, and all their herds and flocks and wealth as spoil, **10** while they set on fire all the towns where they had settled and all their encampments. **11** Then they took all the booty, with the people and beasts they had captured, and brought the captives, together with the spoils and booty, **12** to Moses and the priest Eleazar and to the Israelite community at their camp on the plains of Moab, along the Jericho stretch of the Jordan.

Treatment of the Captives. **13** When Moses and the priest Eleazar, with all the princes of the community, went outside the camp to meet them, **14** Moses became angry with the officers of the army, the clan and company commanders, who were returning from combat. **15** "So you have spared all the women!'' he exclaimed. **16** "Why, they are the very

---

ƒ Dt 23, 22; Eccl 5, 3f.   g 2 Pt 2, 15; Rv 2, 14.

30, 3: A vow ... a pledge: here the former signifies the doing of some positive good deed, in particular the offering of some sacrifice; the latter signifies the abstaining from some otherwise licit action or pleasure; cf v 14.

30, 11: In her husband's house: after her marriage. This contrasts with the case given in vv 7ff.

30, 16: He countermands them: he prevents their fulfillment. Since he has first allowed the vows to remain valid, he can no longer annul them.

31, 1ff: The narrative of Israel's relations with Midian, which was interrupted after Nm 25, 18, is now resumed.

31, 8: The five Midianite kings: they are called "Midianite princes, Sihon's vassals" in Jos 13, 21.

ones who on Balaam's advice prompted the unfaithfulness of the Israelites toward the LORD in the Peor affair, g which began the slaughter of the LORD's community. 17 *Slay, therefore, every male child and every woman who has had intercourse with a man. 18 But you may spare and keep for yourselves all girls who had no intercourse with a man.

Purification after Combat. 19 "Moreover, you shall stay outside the camp for seven days, and those of you who have slain anyone or touched anyone slain in battle shall purify yourselves on the third and on the seventh day. This applies both to you and to your captives. 20 You shall also purify every article of cloth, leather, goats' hair, or wood."

21 Eleazar the priest told the soldiers who had returned from combat: "This is what the law, as prescribed by the LORD to Moses, ordains: 22 Whatever can stand fire, such as gold, silver, bronze, iron, tin and lead, 23 you shall put into the fire, that it may become clean; however, it must also be purified with lustral water.* But whatever cannot stand fire you shall put into the water. 24 On the seventh day you shall wash your clothes, and then you will again be clean. After that you may enter the camp."

Division of the Booty. 25 The LORD said to Moses: 26 "With the help of the priest Eleazar and of the heads of the ancestral houses, count up all the human captives and the beasts that have been taken; 27 then divide them evenly,* giving half to those who took active part in the war by going out to combat, and half to the rest of the community. 28 You shall levy a tax for the LORD on the warriors who went out to combat: one out of every five hundred persons, oxen, asses and sheep 29 in their half of the spoil you shall turn over to the priest Eleazar as a contribution to the LORD. 30 From the Israelites' half you shall take one out of every fifty persons, and the same from the different beasts, oxen, asses and sheep, and give them to the Levites, who have charge of the LORD's Dwelling." 31 So Moses and the priest Eleazar did this, as the LORD had commanded Moses.

Amount of Booty. 32 This booty, what was left of the loot which the soldiers had taken, amounted to six hundred and seventy-five thousand sheep, 33 seventy-two thousand oxen, 34 sixty-one thousand asses, 35 and thirty-two thousand girls who were still virgins.

36 The half that fell to those who had gone out to combat was: three hundred and thirty-seven thousand five hundred sheep, 37 of which six hundred and seventy-five fell as tax to the LORD; 38 thirty-six thousand oxen, of which seventy-two fell as tax to the LORD; 39 thirty

thousand five hundred asses, of which sixty-one fell as tax to the LORD; 40 and sixteen thousand persons, of whom thirty-two fell as tax to the LORD. 41 The taxes contributed to the LORD, Moses gave to the priest Eleazar, as the LORD had commanded him.

42 The half for the other Israelites, which fell to the community when Moses had taken it from the soldiers, was: 43 three hundred and thirty-seven thousand five hundred sheep, 44 thirty-six thousand oxen, 45 thirty thousand five hundred asses, 46 and sixteen thousand persons. 47 From this, the Israelites' share, Moses, as the LORD had ordered, took one out of every fifty, both of persons and of beasts, and gave them to the Levites, who had charge of the LORD's Dwelling.

Gifts of the Officers. 48 Then the officers who had been clan and company commanders of the army came up to Moses 49 and said to him, "Your servants have counted up the soldiers under our command, and not one is missing. 50 *So, to make atonement for ourselves before the LORD, each of us will bring as an offering to the LORD some gold article he has picked up, such as an anklet, a bracelet, a ring, an earring, or a necklace." 51 Moses and the priest Eleazar accepted this gold from them, all of it in well-wrought articles. 52 The gold that they gave as a contribution to the LORD amounted in all to sixteen thousand seven hundred and fifty shekels. This was from the clan and company commanders; 53 what the common soldiers had looted each one kept for himself. 54 Moses, then, and the priest Eleazar accepted the gold from the clan and company commanders, and put it in the meeting tent as a memorial for the Israelites before the LORD.

CHAPTER 32

Request of Gad and Reuben. 1 Now the Reubenites and Gadites had a very large number of livestock. Noticing that the land of Jazer and

---

31, 17: There are later references to Midian in Jgs 6–8; 1 Kgs 11, 18; Is 60, 6. The present raid was only against those Midianites who were dwelling at this time near the encampment of the Israelites.

31, 23: Lustral water: water mixed with the ashes of the red heifer as prescribed in Nm 19, 9.

31, 27: Divide them evenly: for a similar division of the booty into two equal parts, between those who engaged in the fray and those who stayed with the baggage, cf 1 Sm 30, 24. But note that here the tax on the booty of the non-combatants is ten times as much as that on the soldier's booty.

31, 50: The precise nature and use of some of these articles of gold is not certain.

32, 1: Gilead: the name of the western part of the plateau east of the Jordan, sometimes signifying the whole region from the Yarmuk to the Jordan, sometimes only the northern part of this region, and sometimes, as here, only its southern part. Jazer lay to the east of southern Gilead.

of Gilead* was grazing country, **2** they came to Moses and the priest Eleazar and to the princes of the community and said, **3** *"The region of Ataroth, Dibon, Jazer, Nimrah, Heshbon, Elealeh, Sebam, Nebo and Baal-meon, **4** which the LORD has laid low before the community of Israel, is grazing country. Now, since your servants have livestock," **5** they continued, "if we find favor with you, let this land be given to your servants as their property. Do not make us cross the Jordan."

Moses' Rebuke. **6** But Moses answered the Gadites and Reubenites: "Are your kinsmen, then, to engage in war, while you remain here? **7** Why do you wish to discourage the Israelites from crossing to the land the LORD has given them? **8** That is just what your fathers did when I sent them from Kadesh-barnea to reconnoiter the land[h] **9** They went up to the Wadi Eshcol and reconnoitered the land, then so discouraged the Israelites that they would not enter the land the LORD had given them. **10** [i]At that time the wrath of the LORD flared up, and he swore, **11** 'Because they have not followed me unreservedly, none of these men of twenty years or more who have come up from Egypt shall ever see this country I promised under oath to Abraham and Isaac and Jacob, **12** [j]except the Kenizzite* Caleb, son of Jephunneh, and Joshua, son of Nun, who have followed the LORD unreservedly.' **13** So in his anger with the Israelites the LORD made them wander in the desert forty years, until the whole generation that had done evil in the sight of the LORD had died out. **14** And now here you are, a brood of sinners, rising up in your fathers' place to add still more to the LORD's blazing wrath against the Israelites. **15** If you turn away from following him, he will make them stay still longer in the desert, and so you will bring about the ruin of this whole nation."

Counter Proposal. **16** But they were insistent with him: "We wish only to build sheepfolds here for our flocks, and towns for our families; **17** but we ourselves will march as troops in the van of the Israelites,[k] until we have led them to their destination. Meanwhile our families can remain here in the fortified towns, safe from attack by the natives. **18** We will not return to our homes until every one of the Israelites has taken possession of his heritage, **19** [l]and will not claim any heritage with them once we cross the Jordan, so long as we receive a heritage for ourselves on this eastern side of the Jordan."

Agreement Reached. **20** *Moses said to them in reply: "If you keep your word to march as troops in the LORD's vanguard **21** and to

cross the Jordan in full force before the LORD until he has driven his enemies out of his way **22** and the land is subdued before him, then you may return here, quit of every obligation to the LORD and to Israel, and this region shall be your possession before the LORD.[m] **23** But if you do not do this, you will sin against the LORD, and you can be sure that you will not escape the consequences of your sin. **24** Build the towns, then, for your families, and the folds for your flocks, but also fulfill your express promise."

25 The Gadites and Reubenites answered Moses, "Your servants will do as you command, my lord. **26** [n]While our wives and children, our herds and other livestock remain in the towns of Gilead, **27** all your servants will go across as armed troops to battle before the LORD, just as your lordship says."

28 Moses, therefore, gave this order in their regard to the priest Eleazar, to Joshua, son of Nun, and to the heads of the ancestral tribes of the Israelites: **29** "If all the Gadites and Reubenites cross the Jordan with you as combat troops before the LORD, you shall give them Gilead as their property when the land has been subdued before you. **30** But if they will not go across with you as combat troops before the LORD, you shall bring their wives and children and livestock across before you into Canaan, and they shall have their property with you in the land of Canaan."

31 To this the Gadites and Reubenites replied, "We will do what the LORD has commanded us, your servants. **32** We ourselves will go across into the land of Canaan as troops before the LORD, but we will retain our hereditary property on this side of the Jordan." **33** So Moses gave them [* the Gadites and Reubenites, as well as half the tribe of Manasseh, son of Joseph, the kingdom of Sihon, king of the

h 8f: Nm 13, 31ff; Dt 1, 22.
i 10f: Dt 1, 34f.
j Nm 14, 24; Dt 1, 36.
k Jos 4, 12f.
l Jos 13, 8.
m Jos 1, 15.
n Jos 1, 14.
o Dt 3, 12; 29, 7; Jos 12, 6; 13, 8.

*

32, 3: The places named in this verse, as well as the additional ones given in vv 34–38, were all in the former kingdom of Sihon, that is, in the region between the Jabbok and the Arnon. Cf Nm 21, 23f; Jos 13, 19–21. 24–27.

32, 12: Kenizzite: a member of the clan of Kenaz, which, according to Gn 36, 11. 15. 42, was Edomitic; hence, although Caleb belonged to the tribe of Judah (Nm 13, 6; 34, 19), he must have had Edomite blood in his veins; cf also Jos 14, 6. 14.

32, 20ff: Since the ark of the Lord was borne into battle with the Israelite army, the vanguard was said to march before the Lord.

32, 33: The preceding is concerned solely with the two tribes of Gad and Reuben and with the land of the former kingdom of Sihon; hence it seems probable that the sudden reference here to the half-tribe of Manasseh and to their territory in Bashan, the former kingdom of Og, is a later addition to the text.

Amorites, and the kingdom of Og, king of Bashan,] the land with its towns and the districts that surrounded them. *o*

34 The Gadites rebuilt the fortified towns of Dibon, Ataroth, Aroer, **35** Atroth-shophan, Jazer, Jogbehah, **36** Beth-nimrah and Beth-haran, and they built sheepfolds. **37** The Reubenites rebuilt Heshbon, Elealeh, Kiriathaim, **38** Nebo, Baal-meon [names to be changed!],* and Sibmah. These towns, which they rebuilt, they called by their old names.

Other Conquests. **39** The descendants of Machir, son of Manasseh, invaded Gilead and captured it, driving out the Amorites who were there. **40** [Moses gave Gilead to Machir,*p* son of Manasseh, and he settled there.] **41** Jair,*q* a Manassehite clan, campaigned against the tent villages, captured them and called them Havvoth-jair. **42** Nobah also campaigned against Kenath, captured it with its dependencies and called it Nobah after his own name.

CHAPTER 33

Stages on the Journey. **1** The following are the stages by which the Israelites journeyed up by companies from the land of Egypt under the guidance of Moses and Aaron.* **2** By the LORD's command Moses recorded the starting places of the various stages. The starting places of the successive stages were:

3 *They set out from Rameses in the first
    month,
    on the fifteenth day of the first month.
On the Passover morrow the Israelites went
    forth
    in triumph, in view of all Egypt,
4 While the Egyptians buried their first-born
    all of whom the LORD had struck down;
    on their gods, too, the LORD executed
    judgments.*r*

From Egypt to Sinai. **5** Setting out from Rameses, the Israelites camped at Succoth. **6** Setting out from Succoth, they camped at Etham near the edge of the desert. **7** Setting out from Etham, they turned back to Pi-hahiroth, which is opposite Baalzephon, and they camped opposite Migdol.*s* **8** Setting out from Pi-hahiroth, they crossed over through the sea into the desert,*t* and after a three days' journey in the desert of Etham, they camped at Marah. **9** Setting out from Marah, they came to Elim, where there were twelve springs of water and seventy palm trees, and they camped there. *u* **10** Setting out from Elim, they camped beside the Red Sea. **11** Setting out from the Red Sea, they camped in the desert of Sin. **12** Setting out from the desert of Sin, they camped at Dophkah. **13** Setting out from Dophkah, they camped at Alush.

14 Setting out from Alush, they camped at Rephidim, where there was no water for the people to drink.*v* **15** Setting out from Rephidim, they camped in the desert of Sinai. *w*

From Sinai to Kadesh. **16** Setting out from the desert of Sinai, they camped at Kibroth-hattaavah. **17** Setting out from Kibroth-hattaavah, they camped at Hazeroth.*x* **18** Setting out from Hazeroth, they camped at Rithmah. **19** Setting out from Rithmah, they camped at Rimmon-perez. **20** Setting out from Rimmon-perez, they camped at Libnah. **21** Setting out from Libnah, they camped at Rissah. **22** Setting out from Rissah, they camped at Kehelathah. **23** Setting out from Kehelathah, they camped at Mount Shepher. **24** Setting out from Mount Shepher, they camped at Haradah. **25** Setting out from Haradah, they camped at Makheloth. **26** Setting out from Makheloth, they camped at Tahath. **27** Setting out from Tahath, they camped at Terah. **28** Setting out from Terah, they camped at Mithkah. **29** Setting out from Mithkah, they camped at Hashmonah. **30** *Setting out from Hashmonah,—

From Mount Hor to Ezion-geber. They camped at Moseroth. **31** Setting out from Moseroth, they camped at Bene-jaakan. **32** Setting out from Bene-jaakan, they camped at Mount Gidgad. **33** Setting out from Mount Gidgad, they camped at Jotbathah. **34** Setting out from Jotbathah, they camped at Abronah. **35** Setting

---

p Dt 3, 15.   u Ex 15, 27.
q Dt 3, 14.   v Ex 17, 1.
r 4f: Ex 12, 12. 29. 37.   w Ex 19, 2.
s Ex 14, 2.   x 17f: Nm 11, 34f.
t Ex 15, 22.

*

32, 38: The phrase in brackets is a gloss, warning the reader either to change the order of the preceding names, or, more probably, to read some other word, such as bosheth, "shame," for Baal. They called by their old names: literally, "they called by their names" (see Textual Notes); however, some understand the current Hebrew text to mean, "they called by new names."

33, 1ff: This list of camping sites was drawn up by Moses, as v 2 expressly states. However, in its present form it probably includes some glosses. Moreover, a comparison with the more detailed accounts of the journey as given elsewhere shows that this is not complete. It records just forty camping sites, not counting the starting place, Rameses, and the terminus, the plains of Moab. This number, which corresponds exactly to the forty years of wandering in the desert, is probably a schematic device. Besides, it seems that in its present form the order of some of these names has been disturbed. Several names listed here are not recorded elsewhere.

33, 3f: These two verses were probably borrowed from some ancient song celebrating the exodus from Egypt.

33, 30–36: Moseroth is mentioned in Dt 10, 6 (in the form of "Moserah"), as the place where Aaron died. It must therefore have been close to Mount Hor; cf Nm 20, 22ff. It seems very probable that the section vv 36b–41a stood originally immediately after v 30a.

out from Abronah, they camped at Ezion-geber. 36 Setting out from Ezion-geber,—

From Kadesh to Mount Hor.

They camped in the desert of Zin, at Kadesh.y 37 Setting out from Kadesh, they camped at Mount Hor on the border of the land of Edom. 38 [Aaron the priest ascended Mount Horz at the LORD's command, and there he died in the fortieth year from the departure of the Israelites from the land of Egypt, on the first day of the fifth month. 39 Aaron was a hundred and twenty-three years old when he died on Mount Hor. 40 *Now, when the Canaanite king of Arad, who lived in the Negeb in the land of Canaan, heard that the Israelites were coming. . . .] 41 Setting out from Mount Hor,—

From Ezion-geber to the Plains of Moab.*

They camped at Zalmonah. 42 Setting out from Zalmonah, they camped at Punon. 43 Setting out from Punon, they camped at Oboth. 44 Setting out from Oboth, they camped at Iye-abarim on the border of Moab. 45 Setting out from Iye-abarim, they camped at Dibon-gad. 46 Setting out from Dibon-gad, they camped at Almon-diblathaim. 47 Setting out from Almon-diblathaim, they camped in the Abarim Mountains opposite Nebo. 48 Setting out from the Abarim Mountains, they camped on the plains of Moab along the Jericho stretch of the Jordan. 49 Their camp along the Jordan on the plains of Moab extended from Beth-jeshimoth to Abel-shittim.

Conquest and Division of Canaan.

50 The LORD spoke to Moses on the plains of Moab beside the Jericho stretch of the Jordan and said to him: 51 "Tell the Israelites: When you go across the Jordan into the land of Canaan, 52 drive out all the inhabitants of the land before you; destroy all their stone figures and molten images, and demolish all their high places.a

53 "You shall take possession of the land and settle in it, for I have given you the land as your property. 54 You shall apportion the land among yourselves by lot, clan by clan, assigning a large heritage to a large group and a small heritage to a small group.b Wherever anyone's lot falls, there shall his property be within the heritage of his ancestral tribe.

55 "But if you do not drive out the inhabitants of the land before you, those whom you allow to remain will become as barbs in your eyes and thorns in your sides, and they will harass you in the country where you live,c 56 and I will treat you as I had intended to treat them."

CHAPTER 34

The Boundaries. 1 The LORD said to Moses, 2 "Give the Israelites this order: When you enter the land of Canaan, this is the territory that shall fall to you as your heritage—the land of Canaan with its boundaries:

3 "Your southern boundary shall be at the desert of Zin along the border of Edom;d on the east it shall begin at the end of the Salt Sea, 4 and turning south of the Akrabbim Pass, it shall cross Zin, and extend south of Kadesh-barnea to Hazar-addar; thence it shall cross to Azmon,e 5 and turning from Azmon to the Wadi of Egypt, shall terminate at the Sea.f

6 "For your western boundary you shall have the Great Sea* with its coast; this shall be your western boundary.

7 "The following shall be your boundary on the north: from the Great Sea you shall draw a line to Mount Hor,* 8 and shall continue it from Mount Hor to Labo in the land of Hamath, with the boundary extending through Zedad. 9 Thence the boundary shall reach to Ziphron and terminate at Hazar-enan. This shall be your northern boundary.

10 "For your eastern boundary you shall draw a line from Hazar-enan to Shepham. 11 From Shepham the boundary shall go down to Ar-Baal, east of Ain, and descending further, shall strike the ridge on the east side of the Sea of Chinnereth; 12 thence the boundary shall continue along the Jordan and terminate with the Salt Sea.

"This is the land that shall be yours, with the boundaries that surround it."

13 Moses also gave this order to the Israelites: "This is the land, to be apportioned among you by lot, which the LORD has commanded to be given to the nine and one half tribes. 14 For all the ancestral houses of the tribe of Reuben, and the ancestral houses of the tribe of Gad, as well as half of the tribe of Manasseh, have already received their heritage; 15 these two and one half tribes have received their heritage on the eastern side of the Jericho stretch of the Jordan, toward the sunrise."

y 36f: Nm 20, 1. 22.
z Nm 20, 25; Dt 32, 50.
a Ex 23, 31; 34, 13; Dt 7, 5; 12, 3.
b Nm 26, 53ff.
c Jos 23, 13; Jgs 2, 3.
d Jos 15, 1f.
e Jos 15, 3.
f Jos 15, 4.

*

33, 40: The verse begins the same account of the victory over Arad as is given in Nm 21, 1ff, where it also follows the account of Aaron's death.

33, 41b–49: It seems that this section stood originally immediately after v 36a.

34, 6: The Great Sea: the Mediterranean.

34, 7f: Mount Hor: different from the one where Aaron died; cf Nm 20, 22; 33, 37f.

Supervisors of the Allotment.   16 The
LORD said to Moses, 17 "These are the names
of the men who shall apportion the land among
you: Eleazar the priest, and Joshua, son of Nun,
18 *g* and one prince from each of the tribes
whom you shall designate for this task.
19 These shall be as follows:

from the tribe of Judah: Caleb, son of
   Jephunneh;
20 from the tribe of Simeon: Samuel, son of
   Ammihud;
21 from the tribe of Benjamin: Elidad, son of
   Chislon;
22 from the tribe of Dan: Bukki, son of Jogli;
23 from the tribe of Manasseh: Hanniel, son of
   Ephod; and
24 from the tribe of Ephraim: Kemuel, son of
   Shiphtan, for the descendants of Joseph;
25 from the tribe of Zebulun: Elizaphan, son of
   Parnach;
26 from the tribe of Issachar: Paltiel, son of
   Azzan;
27 from the tribe of Asher: Ahihud, son of
   Shelomi;
28 from the tribe of Naphtali: Pedahel, son of
   Ammihud."

29 These are they whom the LORD commanded
to assign the Israelites their heritage in the land
of Canaan.

CHAPTER 35

Cities for the Levites.   1 The LORD gave
these instructions to Moses on the plains of
Moab beside the Jericho stretch of the Jordan:
2 *h* "Tell the Israelites that out of their hereditary property they shall give the Levites cities
for homes, as well as pasture lands around the
cities. 3 The cities shall serve them to dwell in,
and the pasture lands shall serve their herds and
flocks and other animals. 4 The pasture lands of
the cities to be assigned the Levites shall extend
a thousand cubits from the city walls in each
direction. 5 Thus you shall measure out two
thousand cubits outside the city along each
side—east, south, west and north—with the city
lying in the center. This shall serve them as the
pasture lands of their cities.

6 *i* "Now these are the cities you shall give
to the Levites: the six cities of asylum which you
must establish as places where a homicide can
take refuge, and in addition forty-two other cities— 7 a total of forty-eight cities with their
pasture lands to be assigned the Levites. 8 *In
assigning the cities from the property of the
Israelites, take more from a larger group and
fewer from a smaller one, so that each group
will cede cities to the Levites in proportion to its
own heritage."

Cities of Asylum.   9 The LORD said to Mo-
ses, 10 "Tell the Israelites: When you go
across the Jordan into the land of Canaan,
11 select for yourselves cities *j* to serve as cities
of asylum, where a homicide who has killed
someone unintentionally may take refuge.
12 These cities shall serve you as places of
asylum from the avenger of blood,* so that a
homicide shall not be put to death unless he is
first tried before the community. 13 Six cities
of asylum shall you assign: 14 three beyond the
Jordan, and three in the land of Canaan.
15 These six cities of asylum shall serve not
only the Israelites but all the resident or transient
aliens among them, so that anyone who has
killed another unintentionally may take refuge
there.

Murder and Manslaughter.   16 *"If a
man strikes another with an iron instrument and
causes his death, he is a murderer and shall be
put to death. *k* 17 If a man strikes another with
a death-dealing stone in his hand and causes his
death, he is a murderer and shall be put to death.
18 If a man strikes another with a death-dealing
club in his hand and causes his death, he is a
murdered and shall be put to death. 19 The
avenger of blood may execute the murderer,
putting him to death on sight.

20 "If a man pushes another out of hatred,
or after lying in wait for him he throws something
at him, and causes his death, *l* 21 or if he strikes
another out of enmity and causes his death, he
shall be put to death as a murderer. The avenger
of blood may execute the murderer on sight.

22 *m* "However, if a man pushes another accidentally and not out of enmity, or if without
lying in wait for him he throws some object at
him, 23 or without seeing him throws a
death-dealing stone which strikes him and
causes his death, although he was not his enemy
nor seeking to harm him: 24 then the community, deciding the case between the slayer and the
avenger of blood in accordance with these
norms, 25 shall free the homicide from the
avenger of blood and shall remand him to the
city of asylum where he took refuge; *n* and he
shall stay there until the death of the high priest
who has been anointed with sacred oil. 26 If the

---

g Nm 1, 4.
h Jos 14, 3f; 21, 2.
i Dt 4, 41f; Jos 20, 2.
j 10ff: Dt 19, 2; Jos 20,
   2ff.

k Ex 21, 12; Lv 24, 17.
l Ex 21, 14; Dt 19, 11.
m Jos 20, 3.
n Jos 20, 6.

---

*

35, 8: This provision was hardly observed in the actual
assignment of the levitical cities as narrated in Jos 21.

35, 12: The avenger of blood: one of the close relatives of
the slain (2 Sm 14, 7) who, as executor of public justice, had
the right and duty to take the life of the murderer; cf Dt 19, 6.
12; Jos 20, 3. 5. 9.

35, 16–25: Here, as also in Dt 19, 1–13, there is a casuistic
development of the original law as stated in Ex 21, 12ff.

homicide of his own accord leaves the bounds of the city of asylum where he has taken refuge, **27** and the avenger of blood finds him beyond these bounds and kills him, the avenger incurs no blood-guilt; **28** the homicide was bound to stay in his city of asylum until the death of the high priest. Only after the death of the high priest may the homicide return to his own district.

29 "These shall be norms for you and all your descendants, wherever you live, for rendering judgment.

Witnesses. **30** "Whenever someone kills another, the evidence of witnesses is required for the execution of the murderer.*o* The evidence of a single witness is not sufficient for putting a person to death.

No Indemnity. **31** "You shall not accept indemnity in place of the life of a murderer who deserves the death penalty; he must be put to death. **32** Nor shall you accept indemnity to allow a refugee to leave his city of asylum and again dwell elsewhere in the land before the death of the high priest. **33** You shall not desecrate the land where you live. Since bloodshed desecrates the land, the land can have no atonement for the blood shed on it except through the blood of him who shed it. **34** Do not defile the land in which you live and in the midst of which I dwell;*p* for I am the LORD who dwells; in the midst of the Israelites."

CHAPTER 36

Property of Heiresses. **1** The heads of the ancestral houses in the clan of descendants of Gilead, son of Machir, son of Manasseh—one of the Josephite clans—came up and laid this plea before Moses and the priest Eleazar and before the princes who were the heads of the ancestral houses of the other Israelites. **2** They said: "The LORD commanded you, my lord, to apportion the land by lot among the Israelites;*q* and you, my lord, were also commanded by the LORD to give the heritage of our kinsman Zelophehad to his daughters. **3** But if they marry into one of the other Israelite tribes, their heritage will be withdrawn from our ancestral heritage and will be added to that of the tribe into which they marry; thus the heritage that fell to us by lot will be diminished. **4** When the Israelites celebrate the jubilee year,* the heritage of these women will be permanently added to that of the tribe into which they marry and will be withdrawn from that of our ancestral tribe."

5 *So Moses gave this regulation to the Israelites according to the instructions of the LORD: "The tribe of the Josephites are right in what they say. **6** This is what the LORD commands

with regard to the daughters of Zelophehad: They may marry anyone they please, provided they marry into a clan of their ancestral tribe, **7** so that no heritage of the Israelites will pass from one tribe to another, but all the Israelites will retain their own ancestral heritage. **8** Therefore, every daughter who inherits property in any of the Israelite tribes shall marry someone belonging to a clan of her own ancestral tribe, in order that all the Israelites may remain in possession of their own ancestral heritage. **9** Thus, no heritage can pass from one tribe to another, but all the Israelite tribes will retain their own ancestral heritage."

10 The daughters of Zelophehad obeyed the command which the LORD had given to Moses. **11** Mahlah, Tirzah, Hoglah, Milcah and Noah, Zelophehad's daughters, married relatives on their father's side **12** within the clans of the descendants of Manasseh, son of Joseph; hence their heritage remained in the tribe of their father's clan.

Conclusion. **13** These are the commandments and decisions which the LORD prescribed for the Israelites through Moses, on the plains of Moab beside the Jericho stretch of the Jordan.

---

o Dt 17, 6; 19, 15; Jn 8, 17; 2 Cor 13, 1; 1 Tm 5, 19.　　p Ex 29, 45.　　q Nm 26, 55; 27, 6; Jos 17, 3f.

36, 4: Before the jubilee year various circumstances, such as divorce, could make such property revert to its original tribal owners; but in the jubilee year it became irrevocably attached to its new owners.

36, 5-9: This is a supplement to the law given in Nm 27, 5-11.

The Book of
DEUTERONOMY

The fifth and last book of the Pentateuch is called Deuteronomy, meaning "second law." In reality, what it contains is not a new law but a partial repetition, completion and explanation of the law proclaimed on Mount Sinai. The historical portions of the book are also a résumé of what is related elsewhere in the Pentateuch. The chief characteristic of this book is its vigorous oratorical style. In a series of eloquent discourses Moses presents the theme of covenant renewal in a vital religious framework. He exhorts, corrects and threatens his people, appealing to their past glory, their historic mission and the promise of future triumph. His aim is to enforce among the Israelites the Lord's claim to their obedience, loyalty and love. The events contained in the Book of Deuteronomy took place in the plains of Moab (Dt 1, 5) between the end of the wanderings in the desert (Dt 1, 3) and the crossing of the Jordan River (Jos 4, 19), a period of no more than forty days. The Book of Deuteronomy, written after the Israelites had for centuries been resident in the Land of Promise, takes the form of a testament of Moses, the great leader and legislator, to his people on the eve of his death. At the time of our Lord's coming, it shared with the Psalms a preeminent religious influence among the Old Testament books. The Savior quoted passages of Deuteronomy in overcoming the threefold temptation of Satan in the desert (Mt 4; Dt 6, 13. 16; 8, 3; 10, 20), and in explaining to the lawyer the first and greatest commandment (Mt 22, 35–39; Dt 6, 4).

The book is divided as follows:
   I. Historical Review and Exhortation (Dt 1, 1—4, 43).
   II. God and His Covenant (Dt 4, 44—11, 32).
   III. Exposition of the Law (Dt 12, 1—26, 19).
   IV. Final Words of Moses (Dt 27, 1—34, 12).

I: Historical Review and Exhortation

CHAPTER 1

Introduction. 1 These are the words which Moses spoke to all Israel beyond the Jordan [* in the desert, in the Arabah, opposite Suph, between Paran and Tophel, Laban, Hazeroth and Dizahab; **2** it is a journey of eleven days from Horeb to Kadesh-barnea by way of the highlands of Seir].

3 In the fortieth year, on the first day of the eleventh month, Moses spoke to the Israelites all the commands that the LORD had given him in their regard. **4** After he had defeated Sihon, king of the Amorites, who lived in Heshbon,[a] and Og, king of Bashan, who lived in Ashtaroth and in Edrei, **5** Moses began to explain the law in the land of Moab beyond the Jordan, as follows:

Departure from Horeb. 6 "The LORD, our God, said to us at Horeb, 'You have stayed long enough at this mountain. **7** *Leave here

and go to the hill country of the Amorites and to all the surrounding regions,[b] the land of the Canaanites in the Arabah, the mountains, the foothills, the Negeb and the seacoast; to Lebanon, and as far as the Great River [the Euphrates]. **8** I have given that land over to you.[c] Go now and occupy the land I swore to your fathers, Abraham, Isaac and Jacob, I would give to them and to their descendants.'

Appointment of Elders. 9 "At that time I said to you, 'Alone, I am unable to carry you.* **10** The LORD, your God, has so multiplied you

---

a Dt 3, 2; Nm 21, 21-35.
b Nm 13, 29.
c Gn 12, 7; 15, 18; 17,

7f; 28, 13f.
d Dt 10, 22; Gn 15, 5.

*

1, 1: The local setting of all these discourses is in the land of Moab beyond the Jordan (cf v 5), also known as the plains of Moab (Nm 36, 13).

1, 7: The Amorites and the Canaanites formed the principal part of the pre-Israelite population of Palestine. The foothills: the hills on the western slope of the Judean mountain range. The Arabah: the valley of the Jordan and the depression south of the Dead Sea. The Negeb: the arid land in southern Palestine.

1, 9: Carry you; cf v 31.

that you are now as numerous as the stars in the sky.[d] **11** May the LORD, the God of your fathers, increase you a thousand times over, and bless you as he promised! **12** But how can I alone bear the crushing burden that you are, along with your bickering? **13** [e]Choose wise, intelligent and experienced men from each of your tribes, that I may appoint them as your leaders.' **14** You answered me, 'We agree to do as you have proposed.' **15** So I took outstanding men of your tribes, wise and experienced, and made them your leaders as officials over thousands, over hundreds, over fifties and over tens, and other tribal officers. **16** I charged your judges at that time, 'Listen to complaints among your kinsmen, and administer true justice to both parties even if one of them is an alien.[f] **17** In rendering judgment, do not consider who a person is; give ear to the lowly and to the great alike, fearing no man, for judgment is God's. Refer to me any case that is too hard for you and I will hear it.' **18** Thereupon I gave you all the commands you were to fulfill.

The Twelve Scouts. **19** "Then, in obedience to the command of the LORD, our God, we set out from Horeb and journeyed through the whole desert, vast and fearful as you have seen,[g] in the direction of the hill country of the Amorites. We had reached Kadesh-barnea **20** when I said to you, 'You have come to the hill country of the Amorites, which the LORD, our God, is giving us. **21** The LORD, your God, has given this land over to you. Go up and occupy it, as the LORD, the God of your fathers, commands you. Do not fear or lose heart.' **22** [h]Then all of you came up to me and said, 'Let us send men ahead to reconnoiter the land for us and report to us on the road we must follow and the cities we must take.' **23** Agreeing with the proposal, I chose twelve men from your number, one from each tribe. **24** They set out into the hill country as far as the Wadi Eshcol, and explored it. **25** Then, taking along some of the fruit of the land, they brought it down to us and reported, 'The land which the LORD, our God, gives us is good.'

Threats of Revolt. **26** "But you refused to go up,[i] and after defying the command of the LORD, your God, **27** you set to murmuring in your tents,* 'Out of hatred for us the LORD has brought us up out of the land of Egypt,[j] to deliver us into the hands of the Amorites and destroy us. **28** What shall we meet with up there? Our kinsmen have made us fainthearted by reporting that the people are stronger and taller than we, and their cities are large and fortified to the sky; besides, they saw the Anakim there.'[k] **29** "But I said to you, 'Have no dread or fear

of them. **30** The LORD, your God, who goes before you, will himself fight for you, just as he took your part before your very eyes in Egypt, **31** as well as in the desert, where you saw how the LORD, your God, carried you, as a man carries his child, all along your journey until you arrived at this place.' **32** Despite this, you would not trust the LORD, your God, **33** who journeys before you to find you a resting place—by day in the cloud, and by night in the fire, to show the way you must go.[l] **34** When the LORD heard your words, he was angry; **35** and he swore, 'Not one man of this evil generation shall look upon the good land I swore to give to your fathers,[m] **36** except Caleb,* son of Jephunneh; he shall see it. For to him and to his sons I will give the land he trod upon, because he has followed the LORD unreservedly.'

37 "The LORD was angered against me also on your account, and said, 'Not even you shall enter there,[n] **38** but your aide Joshua,[o] son of Nun, shall enter. Encourage him, for he is to give Israel its heritage. **39** Your little ones, who you said would become booty, and your children, who as yet do not know good from bad —they shall enter; to them I will give it, and they shall occupy it.[p] **40** But as for yourselves: turn about and proceed into the desert on the Red Sea road.'

Unsuccessful Invasion. **41** [q]"In reply you said to me, 'We have sinned against the LORD. We will go up ourselves and fight, just as the LORD, our God, commanded us.' And each of you girded on his weapons, making light of going up into the hill country. **42** But the LORD said to me, 'Warn them: Do not go up and fight, lest you be beaten down before your enemies, for I will not be in your midst.' **43** I gave you this warning but you would not listen. In defiance of the LORD's command you arrogantly marched off into the hill country. **44** Then the Amorites living there came out against you and, like bees, chased you, cutting you down in Seir as far as Hormah. **45** On your return you wept before the LORD, but he did not listen to your cry or give ear to you. **46** That is why you had to stay as long as you did at Kadesh.

e 13ff: Ex 18, 21-25.
f 16f: Ex 18, 26; 2 Chr
   19, 6f; Prv 24, 23; Jn
   7, 24; Jas 2, 9.
g Dt 8, 15; 32, 10.
h 22-28: Nm 13, 2-34.
i Dt 9, 23.
j Dt 9, 28; Nm 14, 1-4;
   Ps 106, 25.
k Dt 9, 1f.
l Ex 13, 21; Nm 10, 33f;

14, 14.
m 34ff: Nm 14, 22f.
   28-38; Jos 14, 9.
n Dt 4, 21; 34, 4; Nm
   20, 12.
o Dt 31, 3. 7; Nm 27,
   18ff; 34, 17.
p 39f: Nm 14, 31.
q 41-45: Nm 14, 40.
   42-45.

*

1, 27: In your tents: among yourselves.

1, 36: Except Caleb: Joshua also was allowed to enter, but he is not referred to here because special mention is made of him in v 38 as the successor of Moses.

CHAPTER 2

Northward along Edom.   1 "When we did turn and proceed into the desert on the Red Sea road,[r] as the LORD had commanded me, we circled around the highlands of Seir for a long time. 2 Finally the LORD said to me, 3 'You have wandered round these highlands long enough; turn and go north. 4 Give this order to the people: You are now about to pass through the territory of your kinsmen, the descendants of Esau, who live in Seir. Though they are afraid of you, be very careful 5 not to come in conflict with them, for I will not give you so much as a foot of their land, since I have already given Esau possession of the highlands of Seir. 6 You shall purchase from them with silver the food you eat and the well water you drink. 7 The LORD, your God, has blessed you in all your undertakings; he has been concerned about your journey through this vast desert. It is now forty years that he has been with you, and you have never been in want.'[s]

Along Moab.   8 "Then we left behind us the Arabah route, Elath, Ezion-geber, and Seir, where our kinsmen, the descendants of Esau, live; and we went on toward the desert of Moab.[t] 9 And the LORD said to me, 'Do not show hostility to the Moabites or engage them in battle, for I will not give you possession of any of their land, since I have given Ar to the descendants of Lot as their own.[u] 10 [Formerly the Emim lived there, a people strong and numerous and tall like the Anakim;[v] 11 like them they were considered Rephaim. It was the Moabites who called them Emim. 12 In Seir, however, the former inhabitants were the Horites;[w] the descendants of Esau dispossessed them, clearing them out of the way and taking their place, just as the Israelites have done in the land of their heritage which the LORD has given them.] 13 Get ready, then, to cross the Wadi Zered.'[x] So we crossed it. 14 Thirty-eight years had elapsed between our departure from Kadesh-barnea and that crossing; in the meantime the whole generation of soldiers had perished from the camp, as the LORD had sworn they should.[y] 15 For it was the LORD's hand that was against them, till he wiped them out of the camp completely.

Along Ammon.   16 "When at length death had put an end to all the soldiers among the people, 17 the LORD said to me, 18 'You are now about to leave Ar and the territory of Moab behind. 19 As you come opposite the Ammonites,[z] do not show hostility or come in conflict with them, for I will not give you possession of any land of the Ammonites, since I have given it to the descendants of Lot as their own.

20 [This also was considered a country of the Rephaim from its former inhabitants, whom the Ammonites called Zamzummim; 21 a people strong and numerous and tall like the Anakim. But these, too, the LORD cleared out of the way for the Ammonites, who ousted them and took their place. 22 He had done the same for the descendants of Esau, who dwell in Seir, by clearing the Horites out of their way, so that the descendants of Esau have taken their place down to the present. 23 So also the Caphtorim,* migrating from Caphtor, cleared away the Avvim, who once dwelt in villages as far as Gaza, and took their place.]

Defeat of Sihon.   24 "'Advance now across the Wadi Arnon.[a] I now deliver into your hands Sihon, the Amorite king of Heshbon, and his land. Begin the occupation; engage him in battle. 25 This day I will begin to put a fear and dread of you into every nation under the heavens, so that at the mention of your name they will quake and tremble before you.'

26 "So I sent messengers from the desert of Kedemoth to Sihon, king of Heshbon, with this offer of Peace: 27 'Let me pass through your country by the highway; I will go along it without turning aside to the right or to the left. 28 For the food I eat which you will supply, and for the water you give me to drink, you shall be paid in silver. Only let me march through, 29 as the descendants of Esau who dwell in Seir[b] and the Moabites who dwell in Ar have done, until I cross the Jordan into the land which the LORD, our God, is about to give us.' 30 But Sihon, king of Heshbon, refused to let us pass through his land, because the LORD, your God, made him stubborn in mind and obstinate in heart that he might deliver him up to you, as indeed he has now done.

31 "Then the LORD said to me, 'Now that I have already begun to hand over to you Sihon and his land, begin the actual occupation.' 32 So Sihon and all his people advanced against us to join battle at Jahaz; 33 but since the LORD, our God, had delivered him to us, we defeated him and his sons and all his people.[c] 34 At that time we seized all his cities and doomed* them all, with their men, women and children; we left

r Dt 1, 40; Nm 14, 25;
  21, 4.
s Dt 8, 2ff.
t Jgs 11, 18.
u Gn 19, 36f.
v Dt 1, 28.
w Gn 36, 20f.
x Nm 21, 12.

y Nm 14, 29. 33. 35.
z Gn 19, 38.
a Nm 21, 13; Jgs 11,
  19-22.
b Dt 2, 5. 8f; Jgs 11, 17.
c Dt 29, 7; Nm 21, 23-32.
d Dt 3, 6; 29, 7f.

*———————————————

2, 23: The Caphtorim: members of one of the groups of sea peoples who invaded the coast of Egypt and the southern part of Palestine about 1200 B.C. Caphtor: the ancient name of the island of Crete. Cf Am 9, 7.

2, 34: Doomed: see notes on Nm 18, 14; 21, 3.

no survivor.*d* **35** Our only booty was the live-stock and the loot of the captured cities. **36** From Aroer on the edge of the Wadi Arnon and from the city in the wadi itself, as far as Gilead,*e* no city was too well fortified for us to whom the LORD had delivered them up. **37** However, in obedience to the command of the LORD, our God, you did not encroach upon any of the Ammonite land, neither the region bordering on the Wadi Jabbok, nor the cities of the highlands.*f*

CHAPTER 3

Defeat of Og.   **1** "Then we turned and pro-ceeded toward Bashan. But Og, king of Ba-shan,*g* advanced against us with all his people to give battle at Edrei. **2** The LORD, however, said to me,*h* 'Do not be afraid of him, for I have delivered him into your hand with all his people and his land. Do to him as you did to Sihon, king of the Amorites, who lived in Heshbon.' **3** And thus the LORD, our God, delivered into our hands Og, king of Bashan, with all his people. We defeated him so completely that we left him no survivor. **4** At that time we captured all his cities, none of them eluding our grasp, the whole region of Argob, the kingdom of Og in Bashan: sixty cities in all, **5** to say nothing of the great number of unwalled towns. All the cities were fortified with high walls and gates and bars. **6** *i*As we had done to Sihon, king of Heshbon, so also here we doomed all the cities, with their men, women and children; **7** but all the livestock and the loot of each city we took as booty for ourselves.

8 "And so at that time we took from the two kings of the Amorites beyond the Jordan the territory from the Wadi Arnon to Mount Her-mon **9** [which is called Sirion by the Sidonians and Senir by the Amorites], **10** comprising all the cities of the plateau and all Gilead and all the cities of the kingdom of Og in Bashan including Salecah and Edrei. **11** [Og, king of Bashan, was the last remaining survivor of the Rephaim. He had a bed of iron,* nine regular cubits long and four wide, which is still preserved in Rab-bah of the Ammonites.]

Allotment of the Conquered Lands.
12 *j*"When we occupied the land at that time, I gave Reuben and Gad the territory from Aroer, on the edge of the Wadi Arnon, halfway up into the highlands of Gilead, with the cities therein. **13** The rest of Gilead and all of Bashan, the kingdom of Og, the whole Argob region, I gave to the half-tribe of Manasseh. [All this region of Bashan was once called a land of the Rephaim. **14** Jair, a Manassehite clan,*k* took all the region of Argob as far as the border of the Geshurites and Maacathites, and called it after his own

name Bashan Havvoth-jair, the name it bears today.] **15** To Machir I gave Gilead, **16** and to Reuben and Gad the territory from Gilead to the Wadi Arnon—including the wadi bed and its banks—and to the Wadi Jabbok, which is the border of the Ammonites, **17** as well as the Arabah with the Jordan and its eastern banks from Chinnereth to the Salt Sea of the Arabah, under the slopes of Pisgah.*l*

18 "At that time I charged them* as follows: 'The LORD, your God, has given you this land as your own. But all you troops equipped for battle must cross over in the vanguard of your brother Israelites.*m* **19** Only your wives and children, as well as your livestock, of which I know you have a large number, shall remain behind in the towns I have given you,*n* **20** until the LORD has settled your kinsmen as well, and they too possess the land which the LORD, your God, will give them on the other side of the Jordan.*o* Then you may all return to the posses-sions I have given you.'

21 "It was then that I instructed Joshua, 'Your eyes have seen all that the LORD, your God, has done to both these kings; so, too, will the LORD do to all the kingdoms which you will encounter over there. **22** Fear them not, for the LORD, your God, will fight for you.'

Refusal to Moses.   **23** "And it was then that I besought the LORD, **24** 'O LORD God, you have begun to show to your servant your great-ness and might. For what god in heaven or on earth can perform deeds as mighty as yours? **25** Ah, let me cross over and see this good land beyond the Jordan, this fine hill country, and the Lebanon!' **26** But the LORD was angry with me on your account and would not hear me.*p* 'Enough!' the LORD said to me. 'Speak to me no more of this. **27** Go up to the top of Pisgah and look out to the west, and to the north, and to the south, and to the east. Look well, for you shall not cross this Jordan.*q* **28** Commission Joshua,*r* and encourage and strengthen him, for he shall cross at the head of this people and shall put them in possession of the land you are to see.' **29** This was while we were in the ravine opposite Beth-peor.

---

e Dt 3, 12; Jos 13, 9.   13.
  16; Jgs 11, 26.   l Dt 4, 49; Jos 12, 3.
f Nm 21, 24; Jos 12, 2.   m Jos 1, 14; 4, 12.
g Dt 29, 6; Nm 21, 33.   n Nm 32, 1. 4; Jos 1, 14.
h 2f; Nm 21, 34f.   o Nm 32, 4.
i Ps 135, 10ff.   p Dt 4, 21.
j 12f: Nm 32, 29. 32f;   q Dt 34, 4; Nm 27, 12f.
  Jos 13, 8. 29.   r Dt 1, 38; 31, 7; Nm 27,
k Nm 32, 41; Jos 13, 11.   22f.
*

3, 11: Bed of iron: some translate, "a sarcophagus of ba-salt."

3, 18: I charged them: the words which follow were spoken to the men of Reuben and Gad (cf Nm 32).

Wed week 3 Lent (26 mar 0 3)

CHAPTER 4

Verses 1 & 5-9

Advantages of Fidelity.

1 "Now, Israel, hear the statutes and decrees which I am teaching you to observe, that you may live, and may enter in and take possession of the land which the LORD, the God of your fathers, is giving you. **2** In your observance of the commandments of the LORD, your God,[s] which I enjoin upon you, you shall not add to what I command you nor subtract from it. **3** You have seen with your own eyes what the LORD did at Baal-peor:[t] the LORD, your God, destroyed from your midst everyone that followed the Baal of Peor; **4** but you, who clung to the LORD, your God, are all alive today. **5** Therefore, I teach you the statutes and decrees as the LORD, my God, has commanded me, that you may observe them in the land you are entering to occupy. **6** Observe them carefully, for thus will you give evidence of your wisdom and intelligence to the nations, who will hear of all these statutes and say, 'This great nation is truly a wise and intelligent people.' **7** [u]For what great nation is there that has gods so close to it as the LORD, our God, is to us whenever we call upon him? **8** Or what great nation has statutes and decrees that are as just as this whole law which I am setting before you today?

Revelation at Horeb.

9 "However, take care and be earnestly on your guard not to forget the things which your own eyes have seen, nor let them slip from your memory as long as you live, but teach them to your children[v] and to your children's children: **10** *There was the day on which you stood before the LORD, your God, at Horeb, and he said to me,[w] 'Assemble the people for me; I will have them hear my words, that they may learn to fear me as long as they live in the land and may so teach their children.' **11** You came near and stood at the foot of the mountain,[x] which blazed to the very sky with fire and was enveloped in a dense black cloud. **12** Then the LORD spoke to you from the midst of the fire.[y] You heard the sound of the words, but saw no form; there was only a voice. **13** He proclaimed to you his covenant, which he commanded you to keep: the ten commandments, which he wrote on two tablets of stone. **14** The LORD charged me at that time to teach you the statutes and decrees which you are to observe over in the land you will occupy.

Danger of Idolatry.

15 "You saw no form at all on the day the LORD spoke to you at Horeb from the midst of the fire.[z] Be strictly on your guard, therefore, **16** not to degrade yourselves by fashioning an idol to represent any figure, whether it be the form of a man or of a woman,[a] **17** of any animal on the earth or of any bird that flies in the sky, **18** of anything that crawls on the ground or of any fish in the waters under the earth. **19** And when you look up to the heavens and behold the sun or the moon or any star among the heavenly hosts, do not be led astray into adoring them and serving them.[b] These the LORD, your God, has let fall to the lot of all other nations under the heavens; **20** but you he has taken and led out of that iron foundry,* Egypt, that you might be his very own people, as your are today.[c] **21** Since the LORD was angered against me on your account[d] and swore that I should not cross the Jordan nor enter the good land which he is giving you as a heritage, **22** I myself shall die in this country without crossing the Jordan; but you will cross over and take possession of that good land.[e] **23** Take heed, therefore, lest, forgetting the covenant which the LORD, your God, has made with you, you fashion for yourselves against his command an idol in any form whatsoever.[f] **24** For the LORD, your God, is a consuming fire, a jealous God.

God's Fidelity.

25 "When you have children and grandchildren, and have grown old* in the land, should you then degrade yourselves by fashioning an idol in any form and by this evil done in his sight provoke the LORD, your God, **26** I call heaven and earth this day to witness against you, that you shall all quickly perish from the land which you will occupy when you cross the Jordan. You shall not live in it for any length of time but shall be promptly wiped out. **27** The LORD will scatter you among the nations, and there shall remain but a handful of you among the nations to which the LORD will lead you.[g] **28** There you shall serve gods fashioned by the hands of man out of wood and stone, gods which can neither see nor hear, neither eat nor smell.[h] **29** Yet there too you shall seek the LORD, your God; and you shall indeed find him when you search after him with

s Dt 13, 1.
t Nm 25, 3-9.
u 2 Sm 7, 23.
v Dt 11, 19; Ps 78, 3-6.
w Heb 12, 18f.
x Ex 19, 17f.
y Dt 4, 33. 36; 5, 4.
z Ex 24, 12; 31, 18; 34, 28.

a Dt 5, 8; Ex 20, 4.
b Dt 17, 3; Jb 31, 26ff.
c 1 Kgs 8, 51; Jer 11, 4.
d Dt 1, 37; 3, 26.
e Dt 3, 27.
f Dt 4, 16.
g 27f: Dt 28, 36. 62. 64.
h Ps 135, 15ff; Is 44, 9.
i Jer 29, 13.

*

4, 10: Beginning here and continuing on for several verses (at least to the end of v 14) is the "reminiscence," the account of the things that the Israelites should recall and teach their children.

4, 20: Egypt is called an iron foundry, or furnace for smelting iron, because God allowed the Israelites to be afflicted there for the sake of their spiritual purification; the same expression for Egypt occurs also in 1 Kgs 8, 51; Jer 11, 4; compare the expression, "the furnace of affliction," in Is 48, 10.

4, 25: Grown old: Israel will lose the freshness of its youthful fervor.

your whole heart and your whole soul.[i] **30** In your distress, when all these things shall have come upon you, you shall finally return to the LORD, your God, and heed his voice. **31** Since the LORD, your God, is a merciful God, he will not abandon and destroy you, nor forget the covenant which under oath he made with your fathers.[j]

Proofs of God's Love.

32 "Ask now of the days of old, before your time, ever since God created man upon the earth; ask from one end of the sky to the other: Did anything so great ever happen before? Was it ever heard of? **33** Did a people ever hear the voice of God speaking from the midst of fire, as you did, and live?[k] **34** Or did any god venture to go and take a nation for himself from the midst of another nation, by testings,* by signs and wonders,[l] by war, with his strong hand and outstretched arm, and by great terrors, all of which the LORD, your God, did for you in Egypt before your very eyes? **35** All this you were allowed to see that you might know the LORD is God and there is no other. **36** Out of the heavens he let you hear his voice to discipline you; on earth he let you see his great fire, and you heard him speaking out of the fire. **37** For love of your fathers he chose their descendants and personally led you out of Egypt by his great power, **38** driving out of your way nations greater and mightier than you, so as to bring you in and to make their land your heritage, as it is today. **39** This is why you must now know, and fix in your heart, that the LORD is God in the heavens above and on earth below, and that there is no other.[m] **40** You must keep his statutes and commandments which I enjoin on you today, that you and your children after you may prosper, and that you may have long life on the land which the LORD, your God, is giving you forever."[n]

Cities of Refuge.

41 [o]Then Moses set apart three cities in the region east of the Jordan, **42** that a homicide might take refuge there if he unwittingly killed his neighbor to whom he had previously borne no malice, and that he might save his life by fleeing to one of these cities: **43** Bezer in the desert, in the region of the plateau, for the Reubenites; Ramoth in Gilead for the Gadites; and Golan in Bashan for the Manassehites.

II: God and His Covenant

Introduction.

44 This is the law which Moses set before the Israelites. **45** These are the ordinances, statutes and decrees which he proclaimed to them when they had come out of Egypt **46** and were beyond the Jordan in the ravine opposite Beth-peor, in the land of Sihon,

king of the Amorites, who dwelt in Hishbon and whom Moses and the Israelites defeated after coming out of Egypt. **47** They occupied his land and the land of Og, king of Bashan, as well—the land of these two kings of the Amorites in the region east of the Jordan: **48** from Aroer on the edge of the Wadi Arnon to Mount Sion* (that is, Hermon) **49** and all the Arabah east of the Jordan, as far as the Arabah Sea under the slopes of Pisgah.[p]

CHAPTER 5

The Covenant at Horeb.

1 Moses summoned all Israel and said to them, "Hear, O Israel, the statutes and decrees which I proclaim in your hearing this day, that you may learn them and take care to observe them. **2** The LORD, our God, made a covenant with us at Horeb;[q] **3** not with our fathers did he make this covenant, but with us, all of us who are alive here this day. **4** The LORD spoke with you face to face on the mountain from the midst of the fire. **5** [r]Since you were afraid of the fire and would not go up the mountain, I stood between the LORD and you at that time, to announce to you these words of the LORD:

The Decalogue.

6 [s]I, the LORD, am your God, who brought you out of the land of Egypt,[t] that place of slavery. **7** [u]You shall not have other gods besides me. **8** You shall not carve idols for yourselves[v] in the shape of anything in the sky above or on the earth below or in the waters beneath the earth; **9** *you shall not bow down before them or worship them. For I, the LORD, your God, am a jealous God,[w] inflicting punishments for their fathers' wickedness on the children of those who hate me, down to the third and fourth generation **10** but bestowing mercy, down to the thousandth generation,[x] on the children of those who love me and keep my commandments.

---

j Dt 31, 8.
k Dt 4, 36; 5, 24. 26; Ex 20, 19.
l Dt 7, 19; 26, 8; 29, 2; Ex 7, 3; 15, 3-10; Jer 32, 21.
m Dt 4, 35.
n Dt 6, 2f; 12, 28.
o 41ff: Dt 19, 2-13; Nm 35, 6-29; Jos 20, 8; 21, 27. 36f; 1 Chr 6, 71. 80.
p Dt 3, 17.
q Dt 28, 69.
r Ex 24, 2.
s 6-21: Ex 20, 2-17.
t Ps 81, 11.
u Ps 81, 10.
v Dt 27, 15; Lv 26, 1; Ps 97, 7.
w Ex 34, 14.
x Dt 7, 9; Ex 20, 6.

*

4, 34: Testings: the demonstrations of God's power as in the ten great plagues of Egypt; cf Dt 7, 19; 29, 2.

4, 48: Sion: another name for Mount Hermon, besides those mentioned in Dt 3, 9.

5, 9f: God does not punish us for another's sins, but because of the solidarity of human society, the good or evil deeds of one generation may make their effects felt even in later generations. Yet note how God's mercy allows the good effects of virtue to last much longer than the bad effects of vice: a thousand generations compared to three or four.

11 'You shall not take the name of the LORD, your God, in vain.*y* For the LORD will not leave unpunished him who takes his name in vain.

12 'Take care to keep holy the sabbath day as the LORD, your God, commanded you. **13** Six days you may labor and do all your work; **14** but the seventh day is the sabbath of the LORD, your God.*z* No work may be done then, whether by you, or your son or daughter, or your male or female slave, or your ox or ass or any of your beasts, or the alien who lives with you. Your male and female slave should rest as you do. **15** For remember that you too were once slaves in Egypt,*a* and the LORD, your God, brought you from there with his strong hand and outstretched arm. That is why the LORD, your God, has commanded you to observe the sabbath day.

16 *b*'Honor your father and your mother, as the LORD, your God, has commanded you, that you may have a long life and prosperity in the land which the LORD, your God, is giving you.

17 *c*'You shall not kill.

18 'You shall not commit adultery.

19 'You shall not steal.

20 'You shall not bear dishonest witness against your neighbor.

21 'You shall not covet your neighbor's wife.

'You shall not desire your neighbor's house or field, nor his male or female slave, nor his ox or ass, nor anything that belongs to him.'

Moses as Mediator.   **22** "These words, and nothing more, the LORD spoke with a loud voice to your entire assembly on the mountain from the midst of the fire and the dense cloud. He wrote them upon two tablets of stone and gave them to me. **23** But when you heard the voice from the midst of the darkness, while the mountain was ablaze with fire, you came to me in the person of all your tribal heads and elders, **24** and said, 'The LORD, our God, has indeed let us see his glory and his majesty! We have heard his voice from the midst of the fire*d* and have found out today that a man can still live after God has spoken with him. **25** But why should we die now? Surely this great fire will consume us. If we hear the voice of the LORD, our God, any more, we shall die.*e* **26** For what mortal has heard, as we have, the voice of the living God speaking from the midst of fire, and survived? **27** Go closer, you, and hear all that the LORD, our God, will say, and then tell us what the LORD, our God, tells you; we will listen and obey.'*f*

28 "The LORD heard your words as you were speaking to me and said to me, 'I have heard the words these people have spoken to you, which are all well said.*g* **29** Would that they might always be of such a mind, to fear me and to keep all my commandments! Then they and their descendants would prosper forever. **30** Go, tell them to return to their tents. **31** Then you wait here near me and I will give you all the commandments, the statutes and decrees you must teach them, that they may observe them in the land which I am giving them to possess.'

32 "Be careful, therefore, to do as the LORD, your God, has commanded you, not turning aside to the right or to the left, **33** but following exactly the way prescribed for you by the LORD, your God, that you may live and prosper, and may have long life in the land which you are to occupy.*h*

CHAPTER 6

1 "These then are the commandments, the statutes and decrees*i* which the LORD, your God, has ordered that you be taught to observe in the land into which you are crossing for conquest, **2** so that you and your son and your grandson may fear the LORD, your God, and keep, throughout the days of your lives, all his statutes and commandments*j* which I enjoin on you, and thus have long life. **3** Hear then, Israel, and be careful to observe them, that you may grow and prosper the more, in keeping with the promise of the LORD, the God of your fathers, to give you a land flowing with milk and honey.

The Great Commandment.   **4** *"Hear, O Israel! The LORD is our God, the LORD alone!*k* **5** Therefore, you shall love the LORD, your God, with all your heart, and with all your soul, and with all your strength.*l* **6** Take to heart these words which I enjoin on you today. **7** Drill them into your children.*m* Speak of them at home and abroad, whether you are busy or at rest. **8** Bind them at your wrist as a sign* and let them be as a pendant on your forehead.*n*

---

y Mt 5, 33.
z Gn 2, 2; Ex 20, 8; 23, 12; Heb 4, 4.
a Dt 15, 15; 16, 12; 24, 18. 22.
b Sir 3, 2-16; Mt 15, 4; Mk 7, 10; Lk 18, 20; Eph 6, 2.
c Dt 4; Mt 5, 21. 27; Lk 18, 20; Jas 2, 11.
d Dt 4, 33.
e Dt 18, 16.
f Ex 20, 19.
g Dt 18, 17.
h Dt 4, 40.
i Dt 4, 1; 5, 31; 12, 1.
j Dt 4, 40; 5, 29; 10, 12f.
k Mk 12, 29.
l Dt 10, 12; 11, 13; Mt 22, 37; Mk 12, 30; Lk 10, 27.
m 6f: Dt 4, 9; 11, 18; 32, 46.
n Dt 11, 18; Ex 13, 9. 16; Mt 23, 5.

---

*

6, 4f: This passage contains the basic principle of the whole Mosaic law, the keynote of the Book of Deuteronomy: since the Lord alone is God, we must love him with an undivided heart. Christ cited these words as "the greatest and the first commandment," embracing in itself the whole law of God (Mt 22, 37f and parallels).

6, 8: Bind them . . . as a sign: these injunctions were probably meant merely in a figurative sense; cf Ex 13, 9. 16. However, the later Jews understood them literally, and tied on their wrists and foreheads "phylacteries," boxes containing strips of parchment on which the words were inscribed; cf Mt 23, 5.

9 Write them on the doorposts of your houses and on your gates.o

Fidelity in Prosperity.

10 "When the LORD, your God, brings you into the land which he swore to your fathers, Abraham, Isaac and Jacob, that he would give you, a land with fine, large cities that you did not build,p **11** with houses full of goods of all sorts that you did not garner, with cisterns that you did not dig, with vineyards and olive groves that you did not plant; and when, therefore, you eat your fill, **12** qtake care not to forget the LORD, who brought you out of the land of Egypt, that place of slavery. **13** rThe LORD, your God, shall you fear; him shall you serve,* and by his name shall you swear. **14** You shall not follow other gods, such as those of the surrounding nations, **15** lest the wrath of the LORD, your God, flare up against you and he destroy you from the face of the land;s for the LORD, your God, who is in your midst, is a jealous God.

16 t"You shall not put the LORD, your God, to the test, as you did at Massah. **17** But keep the commandments of the LORD, your God, and the ordinances and statutes he has enjoined on you. **18** Do what is right and good in the sight of the LORD, that you may, according to his word, prosper, and may enter in and possess the good land which the LORD promised on oath to your fathers, **19** thrusting all your enemies out of your way.u

Instruction to Children.

20 "Later on, when your son asks you what these ordinances, statutes and decrees meanv which the LORD, our God, has enjoined on you, **21** you shall say to your son, 'We were once slaves of Pharaoh in Egypt, but the LORD brought us out of Egypt with his strong handw **22** and wrought before our eyes signs and wonders, great and dire, against Egypt and against Pharaoh and his whole house. **23** He brought us from there to lead us into the land he promised on oath to our fathers, and to give it to us. **24** Therefore, the LORD commanded us to observe all these statutes in fear of the LORD, our God, that we may always have as prosperous and happy a life as we have today; **25** and our justice before the LORD, our God, is to consist in carefully observing all these commandments he has enjoined on us.'

CHAPTER 7

Destruction of Pagans.

1 "When the LORD, your God, brings you into the land which you are to enter and occupy, and dislodges great nations before you—the Hittites, Girgashites, Amorites, Canaanites, Perizzites, Hivites and Jebusites:x seven nations more numerous and powerful than you— **2** and when the LORD, your God, delivers them up to you and you defeat them, you shall doom them. Make no covenant with themy and show them no mercy. **3** You shall not intermarry with them, neither giving your daughters to their sons nor taking their daughters for your sons.z **4** For they would turn your sons from following me to serving other gods, and then the wrath of the LORD would flare up against you and quickly destroy you.

5 "But this is how you must deal with them:a Tear down their altars, smash their sacred pillars, chop down their sacred poles,* and destroy their idols by fire. **6** For you are a people sacred to the LORD, your God; he has chosen you from all the nations on the face of the earth to be a people peculiarly his own.b **7** It was not because you are the largest of all nations that the LORD set his heart on you and chose you, for you are really the smallest of all nations. **8** It was because the LORD loved you and because of his fidelity to the oath he had sworn to your fathers, that he brought you out with his strong hand from the place of slavery, and ransomed you from the hand of Pharaoh, king of Egypt. **9** cUnderstand, then, that the LORD, your God, is God indeed, the faithful God who keeps his merciful covenant down to the thousandth generation toward those who love him and keep his commandments, **10** but who repays with destruction the person who hates him; he does not dally with such a one, but makes him personally pay for it. **11** You shall therefore carefully observe the commandments, the statutes and the decrees which I enjoin on you today.

Blessings of Obedience.

12 d"As your reward for heeding these decrees and observing them carefully, the LORD, your God, will keep with you the merciful covenant which he promised on oath to your fathers. **13** He will love and bless and multiply you; he will bless the fruit of your womb and the produce of your soil, your grain and wine and oil, the issue of your herds and the young of your flocks, in the land which he swore to your fathers he would give you.e **14** You will be blessed above all peoples; no

o Dt 11, 20.
p 10f: Jos 24, 13.
q Dt 5, 6.
r Dt 10, 20; Mt 4, 10; Lk 4, 8.
s 14f: Dt 8, 19; 11, 16. 28.
t Nm 20, 1-13.
u Ex 23, 27; 34, 11.
v Ex 12, 26; 13, 14.
w Ex 20, 2.
x Ex 23, 23; 33, 2.
y Ex 34, 12.
z 3f: Ex 34, 16; 1 Kgs 11, 1f.
a Dt 12, 3; Ex 34, 13.
b Dt 14, 2; 26, 18; Ex 19, 6.
c 9f: Dt 5, 9f.
d 12-16: Dt 28, 1-14; Ex 23, 22-26; Lv 26, 3-13.
e Dt 30, 9.

6, 13: Him shall you serve: here, to "serve" God means especially to "worship" him; in this sense it is quoted by our Lord (Mt 4, 10) as an argument against worshiping the devil.
7, 5: Sacred pillars ... poles: see note on Ex 34, 13.

man or woman among you shall be childless nor shall your livestock be barren. **15** The LORD will remove all sickness from you; he will not afflict you with any of the malignant diseases that you know from Egypt, but will leave them with all your enemies.

16 "You shall consume all the nations which the LORD, your God, will deliver up to you. You are not to look on them with pity, lest you be ensnared into serving their gods. **17** Perhaps you will say to yourselves,*f* 'These nations are greater than we. How can we dispossess them?' **18** But do not be afraid of them. Rather, call to mind what the LORD, your God, did to Pharaoh and to all Egypt: **19** the great testings which your own eyes have seen, the signs and wonders, his strong hand and outstretched arm with which the LORD, your God, brought you out.*g* The same also will he do to all the nations of whom you are now afraid. **20** Moreover, the LORD, your God, will send hornets among them, until the survivors who have hidden from you are destroyed.*h* **21** Therefore, do not be terrified by them, for the LORD, your God, who is in your midst, is a great and awesome God. **22** He will dislodge these nations before you little by little. You cannot exterminate them all at once, lest the wild beasts become too numerous for you.*i* **23** The LORD, your God, will deliver them up to you and will rout them utterly until they are annihilated.*j* **24** He will deliver their kings into your hand, that you may make their names perish from under the heavens. No man will be able to stand up against you,*k* till you have put an end to them. **25** The images of their gods you shall destroy by fire. Do not covet the silver or gold on them, nor take it for yourselves, lest you be ensnared by it; for it is an abomination to the LORD, your God. **26** You shall not bring any abominable thing into your house, lest you be doomed with it; loathe and abhor it utterly as a thing that is doomed.

CHAPTER 8

God's Care.   **1** "Be careful to observe all the commandments*l* I enjoin on you today, that you may live and increase, and may enter in and possess the land which the LORD promised on oath to your fathers. **2** Remember how for forty years now the LORD, your God, has directed all your journeying in the desert,*m* so as to test you by affliction and find out whether or not it was your intention to keep his commandments. **3** He therefore let you be afflicted with hunger, and then fed you with manna,*n* a food unknown to you and your fathers, in order to show you that not by bread alone* does man live, but by every word that comes forth from the mouth of the LORD. **4** The clothing did not fall from you in tatters, nor did your feet swell these forty

years.*o* **5** So you must realize that the LORD, your God, disciplines you even as a man disciplines his son.

Danger of Prosperity.   **6** "Therefore, keep the commandments of the LORD, your God, by walking in his ways and fearing him. **7** For the LORD, your God, is bringing you into a good country,*p* a land with streams of water, with springs and fountains welling up in the hills and valleys, **8** a land of wheat and barley, of vines and fig trees and pomegranates, of olive trees and of honey, **9** a land where you can eat bread without stint and where you will lack nothing, a land whose stones contain iron and in whose hills you can mine cooper. **10** But when you have eaten your fill, you must bless the LORD, your God, for the good country he has given you. **11** Be careful not to forget the LORD, your God, by neglecting his commandments and decrees and statutes which I enjoin on you today: **12** lest, when you have eaten your fill, and have built fine houses and lived in them, **13** and have increased your herds and flocks, your silver and gold, and all your property, **14** you then become haughty of heart and unmindful of the LORD, your God, who brought you out of the land of Egypt, that place of slavery; **15** who guided you through the vast and terrible desert with its saraph serpents and scorpions, its parched and waterless ground; who brought forth water for you from the flinty rock*q* **16** and fed you in the desert with manna, a food unknown to your fathers, that he might afflict you and test you, but also make you prosperous in the end. **17** Otherwise, you might say to yourselves,*r* 'It is my own power and the strength of my own hand that has obtained for me this wealth.' **18** Remember then, it is the LORD, your God, who gives you the power to acquire wealth, by fulfilling, as he has now done, the covenant which he swore to your fathers. **19** But if you forget the LORD, your God, and follow other gods, serving and worshiping them,*s* I forewarn you this day that you will perish utterly. **20** Like the nations which the LORD destroys before you, so shall you too perish for not heeding the voice of the LORD, your God.

---

f 17f: Dt 1, 28ff.
g Dt 4, 34.
h Ex 23, 28ff.
i Ex 23, 29f.
j Dt 7, 2.
k Dt 11, 25.
l Dt 4, 1; 6, 1.
m Dt 2, 7; 29, 4; Am 2, 10.
n Ex 16, 12-15. 35; Nm 11, 6-9; Mt 4, 4; Lk 4, 4.
o Dt 29, 4; Neh 9, 21.
p Dt 11, 10ff.
q Wis 11, 4.
r Dt 9, 4.
s Dt 4, 25f; 30, 18.

8, 3: Not by bread alone, etc.: quoted by our Lord in Mt 4, 4. The sense is: God takes care of those who love him even when natural means seem to fail them.

CHAPTER 9

Unmerited Success. 1 "Hear, O Israel! You are now about to cross the Jordan to enter in and dispossess nations greater and stronger than yourselves, having large cities fortified to the sky,^{t} 2 the Anakim, a people great and tall.^{u} You know of them and have heard it said of them, 'Who can stand up against the Anakim?' 3 Understand, then, today that it is the LORD, your God, who will cross over before you as a consuming fire; he it is who will reduce them to nothing and subdue them before you, so that you can drive them out and destroy them quickly, as the LORD promised you.^{v} 4 After the LORD, your God, has thrust them out of your way, do not say to yourselves, 'It is because of my merits that the LORD has brought me in to possess this land';^{w} for it is really because of the wickedness of these nations that the LORD is driving them out before you. 5 No, it is not because of your merits or the integrity of your heart that you are going in to take possession of their land; but the LORD, your God, is driving these nations out before you on account of their wickedness and in order to keep the promise which he made on oath to your fathers, Abraham, Isaac and Jacob. 6 Understand this, therefore: it is not because of your merits that the LORD, your God, is giving you this good land to possess, for you are a stiff-necked people.

The Golden Calf. 7 "Bear in mind and do not forget how you angered the LORD, your God, in the desert. From the day you left the land of Egypt until you arrived in this place, you have been rebellious toward the LORD.^{x} 8 At Horeb you so provoked the LORD that he was angry enough to destroy you,^{y} 9 when I had gone up the mountain to receive the stone tablets of the covenant which the LORD made with you.^{z} Meanwhile I stayed on the mountain forty days and forty nights without eating or drinking, 10 till the LORD gave me the two tablets of stone inscribed, by God's own finger,^{a} with a copy of all the words that the LORD spoke to you on the mountain from the midst of the fire on the day of the assembly. 11 Then, at the end of the forty days and forty nights, when the LORD had given me the two stone tablets of the covenant, 12 he said to me,^{b} 'Go down from here now, quickly, for your people whom you have brought out of Egypt have become depraved; they have already turned aside from the way I pointed out to them and have made for themselves a molten idol. 13 I have seen how stiff-necked this people is,' the LORD said to me. 14 'Let me be, that I may destroy them and blot out their name from under the heavens. I will then make of you a nation mightier and greater than they.'

15 "When I had come down again from the blazing, fiery mountain, with the two tablets of the covenant in both my hands,^{c} 16 I saw how you had sinned against the LORD, your God: you had already turned aside from the way which the LORD had pointed out to you by making for yourselves a molten calf! 17 Raising the two tablets with both hands I threw them from me and broke them before your eyes.^{d} 18 Then, as before, I lay prostrate before the LORD for forty days and forty nights without eating or drinking, because of all the sin you had committed in the sight of the LORD and the evil you had done to provoke him.^{e} 19 For I dreaded the fierce anger of the LORD against you: his wrath would destroy you.^{f} Yet once again the LORD listened to me. 20 With Aaron, too, the LORD was deeply angry, and would have killed him had I not prayed for him also at that time. 21 Then, taking the calf, the sinful object you had made, and fusing it with fire, I ground it down to powder as fine as dust, which I threw into the wadi that went down the mountainside.^{g}

22 "At Taberah, at Massah, and at Kibroth-hattaavah likewise, you provoked the LORD to anger.^{h} 23 And when he sent you up from Kadesh-barnea to take possession of the land he was giving you, you rebelled against this command of the LORD, your God, and would not trust or obey him.^{i} 24 Ever since I have known you, you have been rebels against the LORD.

25 "Those forty days, then, and forty nights, I lay prostrate before the LORD, because he had threatened to destroy you. 26 This was my prayer to him: O Lord GOD, destroy not your people, the heritage which your majesty has ransomed and brought out of Egypt with your strong hand. 27 Remember your servants, Abraham, Isaac and Jacob. Look not upon the stubbornness of this people nor upon their wickedness and sin, 28 lest the people from whose land you have brought us say, 'The LORD was not able to bring them into the land he promised them'; or 'Out of hatred for them he brought them out to slay them in the desert,'^{j} 29 They are, after all, your people and your heritage, whom you have brought out by your great power and with your outstretched arm.^{k}

---

t Dt 1, 28; 4, 38.
u Nm 13, 33.
v Dt 31, 3; Ex 23, 27.
w Dt 8, 17.
x Dt 31, 27; Ex 14, 11; Nm 14, 11.
y Ex 32, 4; Ps 106, 19.
z Ex 24, 12. 18; 34, 28.
a Ex 31, 18.
b 12ff: Ex 32, 7-10.
c Ex 32, 15.
d 16f: Ex 32, 19.
e Ex 32, 31; 34, 28.
f Dt 10, 10; Ex 32, 10.
g Ex 32, 20.
h Ex 17, 7; Nm 11, 1ff. 34.
i Nm 14, 1-4; Ps 106, 24f.
j Nm 14, 14ff.
k Dt 4, 20; Ex 6, 6f.

CHAPTER 10

1 "At that time the LORD said to me, 'Cut two tablets of stone like the former;[l] then come up the mountain to me. Also make an ark of wood. 2 I will write upon the tablets the commandments that were on the former tablets that you broke, and you shall place them in the ark.' 3 So I made an ark of acacia wood, and cut two tablets of stone like the former, and went up the mountain carrying the two tablets.[m] 4 [n]The LORD then wrote on them, as he had written before, the ten commandments which he spoke to you on the mountain from the midst of the fire on the day of the assembly. After the LORD had given them to me, 5 I turned and came down the mountain, and placed the tablets in the ark I had made.[o] There they have remained, in keeping with the command the LORD gave me.

6 [The Israelites set out from Beeroth Benejaakan[p] for Moserah, where Aaron died and was buried, his son Eleazar succeeding him in the priestly office. 7 From there they set out for Gudgodah, and from Gudgodah for Jotbathah,[q] a region where there is water in the wadies.]

8 "At that time the LORD set apart the tribe of Levi to carry the ark of the covenant of the LORD,[r] to be in attendance before the LORD and minister to him, and to give blessings in his name, as they have done to this day. 9 For this reason, Levi has no share in the heritage with his brothers;[s] the LORD himself is his heritage, as the LORD, your God, has told him.

10 "After I had spent these other forty days and forty nights on the mountain, and the LORD had once again heard me and decided not to destroy you, 11 he said to me, 'Go now and set out at the head of your people,[t] that they may enter in and occupy the land which I swore to their fathers I would give them.'

The Lord's Majesty. 12 "And now, Israel, what does the LORD, your God, ask of you but to fear the LORD, your God and follow his ways exactly, to love and serve the LORD, your God, with all your heart and all your soul,[u] 13 to keep the commandments and statutes of the LORD which I enjoin on you today for your own good? 14 Think! The heavens, even the highest heavens,* belong to the LORD, your God, as well as the earth and everything on it.[v] 15 Yet in his love for your fathers the LORD was so attached to them as to choose you, their descendants, in preference to all other peoples, as indeed he has now done.[w] 16 Circumcise your hearts,* therefore, and be no longer stiffnecked. 17 For the LORD, your God, is the God of gods, the LORD of lords, the great God, mighty and awesome, who has no favorites, accepts no bribes;[x] 18 who executes justice for the orphan and the widow, and befriends the alien, feeding and clothing him. 19 So you too must befriend the alien, for you were once aliens yourselves in the land of Egypt.[y] 20 The LORD, your God, shall you fear, and him shall you serve; hold fast to him and swear by his name.[z] 21 He is your glory, he, your God, who has done for you those great and terrible things which your own eyes have seen. 22 Your ancestors went down to Egypt seventy strong,[a] and now the LORD, your God, has made you as numerous as the stars of the sky.

CHAPTER 11

The Wonders of the Lord. 1 "Love the LORD, your God, therefore, and always heed his charge: his statutes, decrees and commandments. 2 It is not your children, who have not known it from experience, but you yourselves who must now understand the discipline of the LORD, your God; his majesty, his strong hand and outstretched arm; 3 the signs and deeds he wrought among the Egyptians, on Pharaoh, king of Egypt, and on all his land;[b] 4 what he did to the Egyptian army and to their horses and chariots, engulfing them in the water of the Red Sea as they pursued you,[c] and bringing ruin upon them even to this day; 5 what he did for you in the desert until you arrived in this place; 6 and what he did to the Reubenites Dathan and Abiram, sons of Eliab, when the ground opened its mouth and swallowed them up out of the midst of Israel, with their families and tents and every living thing that belonged to them.[d] 7 With your own eyes you have seen all these great deeds that the LORD has done. 8 Keep all the commandments, then, which I enjoin on you today, that you may be strong enough to enter in and take possession of the land into which you are crossing, 9 and that you may have long life on the land which the LORD swore to your

---

l Ex 34, 1.
m Ex 34, 4.
n Ex 20, 1-17; 34, 28.
o Ex 40, 20; 1 Kgs 8, 9.
p Nm 33, 31.
q Nm 33, 32f.
r Nm 3, 6; 6, 23-27; 16, 9.
s Nm 18, 20.
t Ex 32, 34; 33, 1.
u Dt 6, 2. 5.
v Neh 9, 6.
w Dt 7, 6ff.

x 2 Chr 19, 7; Jb 34, 19; Wis 6, 7; Acts 10, 34; Rom 2, 11; Gal 2, 6.
y Ex 22, 21; 23, 9; Lv 19, 33f.
z Dt 6, 13; Mt 4, 10; Lk 4, 8.
a Gn 46, 27; Ex 1, 5; Acts 7, 14.
b Dt 6, 22; Ps 78, 42-51.
c Ex 14, 26ff; 15, 9; Pss 78, 53; 106, 11.
d Nm 16, 31ff.

*

10, 14: Even the highest heavens: literally, "and the heavens of the heavens"; compare the phrase, "the third heaven," in 2 Cor 12, 2.

10, 16: Circumcise your hearts: cf Dt 30, 6; Jer 4, 4; Rom 2, 29. The "uncircumcised heart" (Lv 26, 41; Jer 9, 25; Ez 44, 7. 9) is closed and unreceptive to divine grace and guidance, just as "uncircumcised ears" (Jer 6, 10) are closed to sound, and "uncircumcised lips" (Ex 6, 12. 30) do not open well in speech.

fathers he would give to them and their descendants, a land flowing with milk and honey.

The Gift of Rain.   **10** "For the land which you are to enter and occupy is not like the land of Egypt from which you have come, where you would sow your seed and then water it by hand, as in a vegetable garden. **11** *e*No, the land into which you are crossing for conquest is a land of hills and valleys that drinks in rain from the heavens, **12** a land which the LORD, your God, looks after; his eyes are upon it continually from the beginning of the year to the end. **13** *If, then, you truly heed my commandments which I enjoin on you today, loving and serving the LORD, your God, with all your heart and all your soul,*f* **14** I will give the seasonal rain to your land, the early rain* and the late rain, that you may have your grain, wine and oil to gather in; **15** and I will bring forth grass in your fields for your animals.*g* Thus you may eat your fill. **16** But be careful lest your heart be so lured away that you serve other gods and worship them.*h* **17** For then the wrath of the LORD will flare up against you and he will close up the heavens, so that no rain will fall, and the soil will not yield its crops, and you will soon perish from the good land he is giving you.

Reward of Fidelity.   **18** *i*"Therefore, take these words of mine into your heart and soul. Bind them at your wrist as a sign, and let them be a pendant on your forehead. **19** Teach them to your children, speaking of them at home and abroad, whether you are busy or at rest. **20** And write them on the doorposts of your houses and on your gates, **21** so that, as long as the heavens are above the earth, you and your children may live on in the land which the LORD swore to your fathers he would give them.

22 "For if you are careful to observe all these commandments I enjoin on you, loving the LORD, your God, and following his ways exactly, and holding fast to him, **23** the LORD will drive all these nations out of your way,*j* and you will dispossess nations greater and mightier than yourselves. **24** *k*Every place where you set foot shall be yours: from the desert and from Lebanon, from the Euphrates River to the Western Sea,* shall be your territory. **25** None shall stand up against you; the LORD, your God, will spread the fear and dread of you through any land where you set foot, as he promised you.*l*

A Blessing and a Curse.   **26** *m*"I set before you here, this day, a blessing and a curse: **27** a blessing for obeying the commandments of the LORD, your God, which I enjoin on you today; **28** a curse if you do not obey the commandments of the LORD, your God, but turn aside from the way I ordain for you today, to

follow other gods, whom you have not known. **29** When the LORD, your God, brings you into the land which you are to enter and occupy, then you shall pronounce the blessing on Mount Gerizim,*n* the curse* on Mount Ebal. **30** [Are they not beyond the Jordan, on the other side of the western road in the country of the Canaanites who live in the Arabah, opposite the Gilgal beside the terebinth of Moreh?] **31** For you are about to cross the Jordan to enter and occupy the land which the LORD, your God, is giving you. When therefore, you take possession of it and settle there, **32** be careful to observe all the statutes and decrees that I set before you today.

III: *Exposition of the Law*

CHAPTER 12

One Sanctuary.   **1** "These are the statutes and decrees which you must be careful to observe in the land which the LORD, the God of your fathers, has given you to occupy, as long as you live on its soil. **2** Destroy without fail every place on the high mountains, on the hills, and under every leafy tree where the nations you are to dispossess worship their gods.*o* **3** Tear down their altars, smash their sacred pillars, destroy by fire their sacred poles, and shatter the idols of their gods, that you may stamp out the remembrance of them in any such place.

4 "That is not how you are to worship the LORD, your God. **5** Instead,*p* you shall resort to the place which the LORD, your God, chooses out of all your tribes and designates as his dwelling **6** and there you shall bring your holocausts and sacrifices, your tithes and personal contributions, your votive and freewill offerings, and the firstlings of your herds and flocks. **7** There, too, before the LORD, your God, you and your families shall eat and make merry over all your undertakings, because the LORD, your God, has

---

e 11f: Dt 8, 7.
f 13f: Dt 10, 12; Lv 26, 4.
g Ps 104, 14.
h 16f: Dt 4, 25f; 6, 14.
i 18-21: Dt 6, 6-9.
j Dt 7, 1; 9, 1.
k Ex 23, 31.
l Dt 2, 25; 7, 24; Ex 23, 27.

m 26ff: Dt 28, 2-45; 30, 1. 15. 19.
n Dt 27, 12f.
o 2f: Dt 7, 5; Ex 23, 24; 34, 13.
p 5-7. 11f: Dt 14, 22-26; 15, 19f; 16, 2. 10f. 14f; 26, 2.

---

*

11, 13ff: As often in the Prophets, the discourse passes into the words of God himself. Cf Dt 7, 4; 17, 3; 28, 20; 29, 4f.

11, 14: The early rain: the rains which begin in October or November and continue intermittently throughout the winter. The late rain: the heavy showers of March and April. In Palestine the crops are sown in the autumn and reaped in the spring.

11, 24: The Western Sea: the Mediterranean.

11, 29: You shall pronounce the blessing . . . the curse: for the full ceremony, see chapters 27 and 28. Gerizim . . . Ebal: adjacent mountains in Samaria with a deep ravine between them. Their summits command an excellent view of the entire country.

blessed you. **8** You shall not do as we are now doing; here, everyone does what seems right to himself, **9** since you have not yet reached your resting place, the heritage which the LORD, your God, will give you. **10** But after you have crossed the Jordan and dwell in the land which the LORD, your God, is giving you as a heritage, when he has given you rest from all your enemies round about and you live there in security, **11** then to the place which the LORD, your God, chooses as the dwelling place for his name you shall bring all the offerings I command you: your holocausts and sacrifices, your tithes and personal contributions, and every special offering you have vowed to the LORD. **12** You shall make merry before the LORD, your God, with your sons and daughters, your male and female slaves, as well as with the Levite who belongs to your community but has no share of his own in your heritage. **13** Take care not to offer up your holocausts in any place you fancy, **14** but offer them up in the place which the LORD chooses from among your tribes; there you shall make whatever offerings I enjoin upon you.

Profane and Sacred Meals.

15 "However, in any of your communities you may slaughter and eat to your heart's desire as much meat as the LORD, your God, has blessed you with; and the unclean as well as the clean may eat it, as they do the gazelle or the deer. **16** Only, you shall not partake of the blood, but must pour it out on the ground like water. q **17** Moreover, you shall not, in your own communities, partake of your tithe of grain or wine or oil, of the first-born of your herd or flock, of any offering you have vowed, of your freewill offerings, or of your personal contributions. **18** These you must eat before the LORD, your God, in the place he chooses, along with your son and daughter, your male and female slave, and the Levite who belongs to your community; and there, before the LORD, you shall make merry over all your undertakings. **19** Take care, also, that you do not neglect the Levite as long as you live in the land. r

20 "After the LORD, your God, has enlarged your territory, as he promised you, s when you wish meat for food,* you may eat it at will, to your heart's desire; **21** and if the place which the LORD, your God, chooses for the abode of his name is too far, you may slaughter in the manner I have told you any of your herd or flock that the LORD has given you, and eat it to your heart's desire in your own community. **22** You may eat it as you would the gazelle or the deer: the unclean and the clean eating it alike. **23** But make sure that you do not partake of the blood; for blood is life, and you shall not consume this seat of life with the flesh. **24** Do not partake of the blood, therefore, but pour it out on the

ground like water. **25** Abstain from it, that you and your children after you may prosper for doing what is right in the sight of the LORD. **26** However, any sacred gifts or votive offerings that you may have, you shall bring with you to the place which the LORD chooses, **27** and there you must offer both the flesh and the blood of your holocausts on the altar of the LORD, your God; of your other sacrifices the blood indeed must be poured out against the altar of the LORD, your God, t but their flesh may be eaten. **28** Be careful to heed all these commandments I enjoin on you, that you and your descendants may always prosper for doing what is good and right in the sight of the LORD, your God.

Pagan Rites.

29 "When the LORD, your God, removes the nations from your way as you advance to dispossess them, be on your guard! Otherwise, once they have been wiped out before you and you have replaced them and are settled in their land, **30** you will be lured into following them. Do not inquire regarding their gods, 'How did these nations worship their gods? I, too, would do the same.' **31** You shall not thus worship the LORD, your God, because they offered to their gods every abomination that the LORD detests, even burning their sons and daughters to their gods. u

CHAPTER 13

Penalties for Idolatry.

1 "Every command that I enjoin on you, you shall be careful to observe, neither adding to it nor subtracting from it.

2 "If there arises among you a prophet or a dreamer* who promises you a sign or wonder, **3** urging you to follow other gods, whom you have not known, and to serve them: even though the sign or wonder he has foretold you comes to pass, **4** pay no attention to the words of that prophet or that dreamer; for the LORD, your God, is testing you to learn whether you really love him with all your heart and with all your soul. **5** The LORD, your God, shall you follow, and him shall you fear; his commandment shall you observe, and his voice shall you heed, serving him and holding fast to him alone. **6** v But

---

q Dt 15, 23; Gn 9, 4; Lv
    3, 17.
r Dt 14, 27.
s Dt 19, 8; Gn 28, 14;
    Ex 34, 24.

t Lv 17, 11.
u Lv 18, 21; Jer 7, 31.
v 6-10. 14: Dt 6, 14; 17,
    2-7.

*

12, 20: Meat for food: as on special feasts. Meat was not eaten every day in Israel, even by the wealthy.

13, 2. 4. 6: Dreamer: a false prophet who pretended to have received revelations from God in his dreams; of Jer 23, 25–32; Zec 10, 2. But dreams could also be a channel of true prophecy (Nm 12, 6; Jl 3, 1) and of genuine revelations (Gn 20, 3. 6; 31, 10. 24; 37, 5. 9; Mt 1, 20; 2, 12f. 19; etc.)

that prophet or that dreamer shall be put to death, because, in order to lead you astray from the way which the LORD, your God, has directed you to take, he has preached apostasy from the LORD, your God, who brought you out of the land of Egypt and ransomed you from that place of slavery. Thus shall you purge the evil from your midst.

7 "If your own full brother, or your son or daughter, or your beloved wife, or your intimate friend, entices you secretly to serve other gods, whom you and your fathers have not known, 8 gods of any other nation, near at hand or far away, from one end of the earth to the other: 9 do not yield to him or listen to him, nor look with pity upon him, to spare or shield him, 10 but kill him. Your hand shall be the first raised to slay him; the rest of the people shall join in with you. 11 You shall stone him to death, because he sought to lead you astray from the LORD, your God, who brought you out of the land of Egypt, that place of slavery. 12 And all Israel, hearing of it, shall fear and never again do such evil as this in your midst.

13 "If, in any of the cities which the LORD, your God, gives you to dwell in, you hear it said 14 that certain scoundrels have sprung up among you and have led astray the inhabitants of their city to serve other gods whom you have not known, 15 you must inquire carefully into the matter and investigate it thoroughly. If you find that it is true and an established fact that this abomination has been committed in your midst, 16 ^wyou shall put the inhabitants of that city to the sword, dooming the city and all life that is in it, even its cattle, to the sword. 17 Having heaped up all its spoils in the middle of its square, you shall burn the city with all its spoils as a whole burnt offering to the LORD, your God. Let it be a heap of ruins forever, never to be rebuilt. 18 You shall not retain anything that is doomed, that the blazing wrath of the LORD may die down and he may show you mercy and in his mercy for you may multiply you as he promised your fathers on oath; 19 because you have heeded the voice of the LORD, your God, keeping all his commandments which I enjoin on you today, doing what is right in his sight.

CHAPTER 14

Pagan Mourning Rites. 1 "You are children of the LORD, your God. You shall not gash yourselves nor shave the hair above your foreheads for the dead.^x 2 For you are a people sacred to the LORD, your God, who has chosen you from all the nations on the face of the earth to be a people peculiarly his own.^y

Clean and Unclean Animals. 3 "You shall not eat any abominable thing.^z 4 ^aThese

are the animals you may eat: the ox, the sheep, the goat, 5 the red deer, the gazelle, the roe deer, the ibex, the addax, the oryx,* and the mountain sheep. 6 Any animal that has hoofs you may eat, provided it is cloven-footed and chews the cud. 7 But you shall not eat any of the following that only chew the cud or only have cloven hoofs: the camel, the hare and the rock badger, which indeed chew the cud, but do not have hoofs and are therefore unclean for you; 8 and the pig, which indeed has hoofs and is cloven-footed, but does not chew the cud and is therefore unclean for you. Their flesh you shall not eat, and their dead bodies you shall not touch. ^b

9 "Of the various creatures that live in the water, whatever has both fins and scales you may eat, 10 but all those that lack either fins or scales you shall not eat; they are unclean for you.

11 "You may eat all clean birds. 12 But you shall not eat any of the following: the eagle, the vulture, the osprey, 13 the various kites and falcons, 14 all the various species of crows, 15 the ostrich, the nightjar, the gull, the various species of hawks, 16 the owl, the screech owl, the ibis, 17 the desert owl, the buzzard, the cormorant, 18 the stork, the various species of herons, the hoopoe, and the bat. 19 *All winged insects, too, are unclean for you and shall not be eaten. 20 But you may eat any clean winged creatures.

21 "You must not eat any animal that has died of itself, for you are a people sacred to the LORD, your God.^c But you may give it to an alien who belongs to your community, and he may eat it, or you may sell it to a foreigner.

"You shall not boil a kid in its mother's milk.*

Tithes. 22 "Each year you shall tithe all the produce that grows in the field you have sown;^d 23 then in the place which the LORD, your God, chooses as the dwelling place of his name^e you shall eat in his presence your tithe of the grain, wine and oil, as well as the firstlings of your herd and flock, that you may learn always to

---

w 16f: Jos 6, 18. 24; 7, 26; 8, 28.
x Lv 19, 28.
y Dt 7, 6.
z Ez 4, 14; Acts 10, 14.
a 4-20; Lv 11, 2-23.

b Lv 11, 26.
c Ex 22, 30; 23, 19; 34, 26.
d Lv 27, 30.
e 23f: Dt 12, 5ff.

*

14, 5: The gazelle, the addax, the oryx: species of antelopes. The ibex: a species of wild goat.

14, 19f: The apparent contradiction is to be resolved in the light of Lv 11, 20–23; the unclean winged insects are those that walk on the ground; the clean winged creatures are those that leap on the ground, such as certain species of locusts.

14, 21: Boil a kid in its mother's milk: see note on Ex 23, 19.

fear the LORD, your God. **24** If, however, the journey is too much for you and you are not able to bring your tithe, because the place which the LORD, your God, chooses for the abode of his name is too far for you, considering how the LORD has blessed you,* **25** you may exchange the tithe for money and, with the purse of money in hand, go to the place which the LORD, your God, chooses. **26** You may then exchange the money for whatever you desire, oxen or sheep, wine or strong drink, or anything else you would enjoy, and there before the LORD, your God, you shall partake of it and make merry with your family. **27** But do not neglect the Levite who belongs to your community, for he has no share in the heritage with you.*f*

28 "At the end of every third year you shall bring out all the tithes of your produce for that year and deposit them in community stores, **29** that the Levite who has no share in the heritage with you, and also the alien, the orphan and the widow who belong to your community, may come and eat their fill;*g* so that the LORD, your God, may bless you in all that you undertake.

CHAPTER 15

Debts and the Poor. **1** "At the end of every seven-year period* you shall have a relaxation of debts,*h* **2** which shall be observed as follows. Every creditor shall relax his claim on what he has loaned his neighbor; he must not press his neighbor, his kinsman, because a relaxation in honor of the LORD has been proclaimed. **3** You may press a foreigner, but you shall relax the claim on your kinsman for what is yours.*i* **4** Nay, more! since the LORD, your God, will bless you abundantly in the land he will give you to occupy as your heritage, there should be no one of you in need. **5** If you but heed the voice of the LORD, your God, and carefully observe all these commandments which I enjoin on you today, **6** you will lend to many nations, and borrow from none;*j* you will rule over many nations, and none will rule over you, since the LORD, your God, will bless you as he promised. **7** If one of your kinsmen in any community is in need in the land which the LORD, your God, is giving you, you shall not harden your heart nor close your hand to him in his need. **8** Instead, you shall open your hand to him and freely lend him enough to meet his need.*k* **9** Be on your guard lest, entertaining the mean thought that the seventh year, the year of relaxation, is near, you grudge help to your needy kinsman and give him nothing; else he will cry to the LORD against you and you will be held guilty. **10** When you give to him, give freely and not with ill will; for the LORD, your God, will bless you for this in all your works and undertakings. **11** The needy will never be

lacking* in the land; that is why I command you to open your hand to your poor and needy kinsman in your country.*l*

Hebrew Slaves. **12** "If your kinsman, a Hebrew man or woman, sells himself to you, he is to serve you for six years, but in the seventh year you shall dismiss him from your service, a free man.*m* **13** When you do so, you shall not send him away empty-handed, **14** but shall weight him down with gifts from your flock and threshing floor and wine press, in proportion to the blessing the LORD, your God, has bestowed on you. **15** For remember that you too were once slaves in the land of Egypt, and the LORD, your God, ransomed you. That is why I am giving you this command today.*n* **16** If, however, he tells you that he does not wish to leave you, because he is devoted to you and your household, since he fares well with you, **17** you shall take an awl and thrust it through his ear* into the door, and he shall then be your slave forever.*o* Your female slave, also, you shall treat in the same way. **18** You must not be reluctant to let your slave go free, since the service he has given you for six years was worth twice a hired man's salary; then also the LORD, your God, will bless you in everything you do.

Firstlings. **19** *p* "You shall consecreate to the LORD, your God, all the male firstlings of your herd and of your flock. You shall not work the firstlings of your cattle, nor shear the firstlings of your flock. **20** Year after year you and your family shall eat them before the LORD, your God, in the place he chooses.*q* **21** If, however, a firstling is lame or blind or has any other serious defect, you shall not sacrifice it to the LORD, your God, **22** but in your own communities you may eat it, the unclean and the clean eating it alike, as you would a gazelle or a deer. **23** Only, you shall not partake of its blood,

f Dt 12, 12. 19.
g 28f: Dt 26, 12.
h Neh 10, 31.
i Dt 23, 20.
j Dt 28, 12f.
k Lv 25, 35; Sir 29, 1f;
　Mt 5, 42.
l Dt 15, 8; Sir 29, 12.

m Ex 21, 2; Jer 34, 14.
n Dt 5, 15.
o 16f: Ex 21, 5f.
p Ex 13, 11.
q Dt 14, 23.
r 21ff: Dt 12, 15f; Lv 22,
　20.

*

14, 24:　Considering how the Lord has blessed you: should the Israelite farmer be blessed with an abundant harvest, a tenth of this would be too much to transport for a great distance.

15, 1:　At the end of every seven-year period: in every seventh, or sabbatical, year Cf Dt 15, 9; 31, 10; and compare Jer 34, 14 with Dt 15, 12. A relaxation of debts: it is uncertain whether a full cancellation of debts is meant, or merely a suspension of payment on them or on their interest among the Israelites. Cf Ex 23, 11 where the same Hebrew root is used of a field that is "let lie fallow" in the sabbatical year.

15, 11:　The needy will never be lacking: compare the words of Christ, "The poor you have always with you" (Mt 26, 11).

15, 17:　His ear: cf Ex 21, 6 and the note there.

which must be poured out on the ground like water.[r]

CHAPTER 16

Feast of the Passover. 1 "Observe the month of Abib* by keeping the Passover of the LORD, your God,[s] since it was in the month of Abib that he brought you by night out of Egypt. 2 You shall offer the Passover sacrifice from your flock or your herd to the LORD, your God, in the place which he chooses as the dwelling place of his name. 3 [t]You shall not eat leavened bread with it. For seven days you shall eat with it only unleavened bread, the bread of affliction, that you may remember as long as you live the day of your departure from the land of Egypt; for in frightened haste you left the land of Egypt. 4 Nothing leavened may be found in all your territory for seven days, and none of the meat which you sacrificed on the evening of the first day shall be kept overnight for the next day.

5 "You may not sacrifice the Passover in any of the communities which the LORD, your God, gives you; 6 only at the place which he chooses as the dwelling place of his name, and in the evening at sunset, on the anniversary of your departure from Egypt, shall you sacrifice the Passover. 7 You shall cook and eat it at the place the LORD, your God, chooses; then in the morning you may return to your tents. 8 For six days you shall eat unleavened bread, and on the seventh there shall be a solemn meeting in honor of the LORD, your God; on that day you shall not do any sort of work.

Feast of Weeks. 9 [u]"You shall count off seven weeks, computing them from the day when the sickle is first put to the standing grain. 10 You shall then keep the feast of Weeks* in honor of the LORD, your God, and the measure of your own freewill offering shall be in proportion to the blessing the LORD, your God, has bestowed on you. 11 In the place which the LORD, your God, chooses as the dwelling place of his name,[v] you shall make merry in his presence together with your son and daughter, your male and female slave, and the Levite who belongs to your community, as well as the alien, the orphan and the widow among you. 12 Remember that you too were once slaves in Egypt, and carry out these statutes carefully.

Feast of Booths. 13 [w]"You shall celebrate the feast of Booths for seven days, when you have gathered in the produce from your threshing floor and wine press.* 14 You shall make merry at your feast,[x] together with your son and daughter, your male and female slave, and also the Levite, the alien, the orphan and the widow who belong to your community. 15 For

seven days you shall celebrate this pilgrim feast in honor of the LORD, your God, in the place which he chooses; since the LORD, your God, has blessed you in all your crops and in all your undertakings, you shall do naught but make merry.

16 "Three times a year,[y] then, every male among you shall appear before the LORD, your God, in the place which he chooses: at the feast of Unleavened Bread, at the feast of Weeks, and at the feast of Booths. No one shall appear before the LORD empty-handed, 17 but each of you with as much as he can give, in proportion to the blessings which the LORD, your God, has bestowed on you.

Judges. 18 "You shall appoint judges and officials throughout your tribes to administer true justice for the people in all the communities which the LORD, your God, is giving you. 19 You shall not distort justice; you must be impartial.[z] You shall not take a bribe; for a bribe blinds the eyes even of the wise and twists the words even of the just. 20 Justice and justice alone shall be your aim, that you may have life and may possess the land which the LORD, your God, is giving you.

Pagan Worship. 21 *"You shall not plant a sacred pole of any kind of wood beside the altar of the LORD, your God, which you will build;[a] 22 nor shall you erect a sacred pillar,* such as the LORD, your God, detests.

CHAPTER 17

1 "You shall not sacrifice to the LORD, your God, from the herd or from the flock an animal with any serious defect;[b] that would be an abomination to the LORD, your God.

2 [c]"If there is found among you, in any one of the communities which the LORD, your God, gives you, a man or a woman who does evil in

---

s 1-8: Ex 12, 2-20; 23, 15; Nm 28, 16ff. 24f.
t 3f: Ex 13, 6f; 34, 18.
u 9-12: Lv 23, 15-21.
v Dt 12, 5. 7. 12. 18.
w 13-15: Ex 23, 16; Lv 23, 34-43; Nm 29, 12-38.
x Dt 16, 11.
y Ex 23, 14f. 17; 34, 23; 2 Chr 8, 13.
z Dt 1, 17; Ex 23, 8.
a 1 Kgs 14, 15; 2 Chr 33, 3.
b Lv 22, 20.
c 2-7: Dt 13, 6-15.

*
16, 1: Abib: "ear of grain, ripe grain," the name of the month in which the barley harvest fell, corresponding to our March and April; at a later period this month received the Babylonian name of "Nisan."
16, 10: Feast of Weeks: later known more commonly as "Pentecost."
16, 13: See note on Lv 23, 34.
16, 21–17, 7: This section seems to be out of its proper place, since it interrupts the natural sequence of the laws for the judges (Dt 16, 18–20 and 17, 8–13). It probably belongs to the similar section, Dt 12, 29—14, 2.
16, 21f: Sacred pole . . . sacred pillar; see note on Ex 34, 13.

the sight of the LORD, your God, and transgresses his covenant, **3** by serving other gods, or by worshiping the sun or the moon or any of the host of the sky, against my command;[d] **4** and if, on being informed of it, you find by careful investigation that it is true and an established fact that this abomination has been committed in Israel; **5** you shall bring the man (or woman) who had done the evil deed out to your city gates* and stone him to death. **6** The testimony of two or three witnesses is required for putting a person to death;[e] no one shall be put to death on the testimony of only one witness. **7** At the execution, the witnesses are to be the first to raise their hands against him; afterward all the people are to join in.[f] Thus shall you purge the evil from your midst.

Judges. **8** "If in your own community there is a case at issue which proves too complicated for you to decide, in a matter of bloodshed or of civil rights or of personal injury, you shall then go up to the place which the LORD, your God, chooses, **9** to the levitical priests or to the judge who is in office at that time. They shall study the case and then hand down to you their decision.[g] **10** According to this decision that they give you in the place which the LORD chooses, you shall act, being careful to do exactly as they direct. **11** You shall carry out the directions they give you and the verdict they pronounce for you, without turning aside to the right or to the left from the decision they hand down to you. **12** Any man who has the insolence to refuse to listen to the priest* who officiates there in the ministry of the LORD, your God, or to the judge, shall die. Thus shall you purge the evil from your midst. **13** And all the people, on hearing of it, shall fear, and never again be so insolent.

The King. **14** "When you have come into the land which the LORD, your God, is giving you, and have occupied it and settled in it, should you then decide to have a king over you like all the surrounding nations,[h] **15** you shall set that man over you as your king whom the LORD, your God, chooses.[i] He whom you set over you as king must be your kinsman; a foreigner, who is no kin of yours, you may not set over you. **16** But he shall not have a great number of horses;* nor shall he make his people go back again to Egypt to acquire them, against the LORD's warning that you must never go back that way again.[j] **17** Neither shall he have a great number of wives, lest his heart be estranged,[k] nor shall he accumulate a vast amount of silver and gold. **18** When he is enthroned in his kingdom, he shall have a copy of this law made from the scroll that is in the custody of the levitical priests.[l] **19** He shall keep it with him

and read it all the days of his life that he may learn to fear the LORD, his God, and to heed and fulfill all the words of this law and these statutes. **20** Let him not become estranged from his countrymen through pride, nor turn aside to the right or to the left from these commandments. Then he and his descendants will enjoy a long reign in Israel.

CHAPTER 18

Priests. **1** "The whole priestly tribe of Levi shall have no share in the heritage with Israel; they shall live on the oblations of the LORD and the portions due to him.[m] **2** Levi shall have no heritage among his brothers; the LORD himself is his heritage, as he has told him. **3** The priests shall have a right to the following things from the people: from those who are offering a sacrifice, whether the victim is from the herd or from the flock, the priest shall receive the shoulder, the jowls and the stomach. **4** You shall also give him the first fruits of your grain and wine and oil,[n] as well as the first fruits of the shearing of your flock; **5** for the LORD, your God, has chosen him and his sons out of all your tribes to be always in attendance to minister in the name of the LORD.

6 "When a Levite goes from one of your communities anywhere in Israel in which he ordinarily resides, to visit, as his heart may desire, the place which the LORD chooses, **7** he may minister there in the name of the LORD, his God, like all his fellow Levites who are in attendance there before the LORD, **8** He shall then receive the same portions to eat as the rest, along with his monetary offerings and heirlooms.

Prophets. **9** "When you come into the land which the LORD, your God, is giving you, you shall not learn to imitate the abominations of the

---

d Dt 4, 19.
e Dt 19, 15; Nm 35, 30; Mt 18, 16; Jn 8, 17; 2 Cor 13, 1.
f Dt 13, 10.
g Dt 21, 5; 2 Chr 19, 8.
h 1 Sm 8, 5. 19f.
i 1 Sm 9, 16; 10, 24; 16, 12.
j Dt 28, 68; 1 Kgs 4, 26;

k 1 Kgs 11; 3f; Neh 13, 26.
l Dt 31, 9. 26.
m Nm 18, 8f. 20-24; 1 Cor 9, 13.
n Nm 18, 12; 2 Chr 31, 5.
o Dt 12, 29ff; Lv 18, 26-30.

*

17, 5: Out to your city gates: outside the gates in an unclean place; cf Lv 24, 14; Nm 15, 36; Acts 7, 58; Heb 13, 12.

17, 12: The priest: the high priest; the judge: a layman. The former presided over the court in cases which directly concerned religion, the latter in cases of a more secular nature; cf 2 Chr 19, 8–11.

17, 16: Horses: chariotry for war. The Lord's warning: the same warning is also referred to in Dt 28, 68, although it is not mentioned explicitly elsewhere in the Pentateuch. We know from other sources that Egypt used to export war horses to Palestine. The danger envisioned here is that some king might make Israel a vassal of Egypt for the sake of such military aid.

peoples there.*o* **10** Let there not be found among you anyone who immolates his son or daughter*p* in the fire,* nor a fortune-teller, soothsayer, charmer, diviner, **11** or caster of spells, nor one who consults ghosts and spirits or seeks oracles from the dead. **12** Anyone who does such things is an abomination to the LORD, and because of such abominations the LORD, your God, is driving these nations out of your way.*q* **13** You, however, must be altogether sincere toward the LORD, your God. **14** Though these nations whom you are to dispossess listen to their soothsayers and fortune-tellers, the LORD, your God, will not permit you to do so.

15 "A prophet like me* will the LORD, your God, raise up for you from among your own kinsmen; to him you shall listen.*r* **16** This is exactly what you requested of the LORD, your God, at Horeb on the day of the assembly, when you said, 'Let us not again hear the voice of the LORD, our God, nor see this great fire any more, lest we die.'*s* **17** And the LORD said to me, 'This was well said. **18** I will raise up for them a prophet like you from among their kinsmen, and will put my words into his mouth; he shall tell them all that I command him. **19** If any man will not listen to my words which he speaks in my name, I myself will make him answer for it.*t* **20** But if a prophet presumes to speak in my name*u* an oracle that I have not commanded him to speak, or speaks in the name of other gods, he shall die.'

21 "If you say to yourselves, 'How can we recognize an oracle which the LORD has spoken?', **22** know that, even though a prophet speaks in the name of the LORD, if his oracle is not fulfilled or verified, it is an oracle which the LORD did not speak. The prophet has spoken it presumptuously, and you shall have no fear of him.

CHAPTER 19

Cities of Refuge. **1** "When the LORD, your God, removes the nations whose land he is giving you, and you have taken their place and are settled in their cities and houses, **2** *v*you shall set apart three cities* in the land which the LORD, your God, is giving you to occupy. **3** You shall thereby divide into three regions the land which the LORD, your God, will give you as a heritage, and so arrange the routes that every homicide will be able to find a refuge.

4 "It is in the following case that a homicide may take refuge in such a place to save his life: when someone unwittingly kills his neighbor to whom he had previously borne no malice.*w* **5** For example, if he goes with his neighbor to a forest to cut wood, and as he swings his ax to fell a tree, its head flies off the handle and hits his neighbor a mortal blow, he may take refuge

in one of these cities to save his life. **6** Should the distance be too great, the avenger of blood* may in the heat of his anger pursue the homicide and overtake him and strike him dead, even though he does not merit death since he had previously borne the slain man no malice. **7** That is why I order you to set apart three cities.

8 *x*"But if the LORD, your God, enlarges your territory, as he swore to your fathers, and gives you all the land he promised your fathers he would give **9** in the event that you carefully observe all these commandments which I enjoin on you today, loving the LORD, your God, and ever walking in his ways: then add three cities to these three. **10** Thus, in the land which the LORD, your God, is giving you as a heritage, innocent blood will not be shed and you will not become guilty of bloodshed.

11 *y*"However, if someone lies in wait for his neighbor out of hatred for him, and rising up against him, strikes him mortally, and then takes refuge in one of these cities, **12** the elders of his own city shall send for him and have him taken from there, and shall hand him over to be slain by the avenger of blood. **13** Do not look on him with pity, but purge from Israel the stain of shedding innocent blood, that you may prosper.

Removal of Landmarks. **14** "You shall not move your neighbor's landmarks erected by

---

p 10f: Lv 18, 21; 19, 31; 20, 27; 1 Sm 28, 7; 2 Kgs 17, 17; 21, 6.
q Dt 9, 4.
r Jn 1, 45; 6, 14; Acts 3, 22; 7, 37.
s Ex 20, 19.
t Acts 3, 23.
u 20. 22: Dt 13, 2ff.
v Dt 4, 41ff; Ex 21, 13;

w Dt 4, 42; Nm 35, 15; Jos 20, 3. 5.
x Gn 15, 18-21; 28, 14; Ex 23, 31; 34, 24.
y 11ff: Ex 21, 12. 14; Nm 35, 20f.
z Dt 27, 17; Prv 23, 10; Hos 5, 10.

---

*

18, 10f: Immolates his son or daughter in the fire: to Molech. See note on Lv 18, 21. Such human sacrifices are classed here with other pagan superstitions because they were believed to possess magical powers for averting a calamity; cf 2 Kgs 3, 27. Three other forms of superstition are listed here: augury (by a fortune-teller, a soothsayer or a diviner); black magic (by a charmer . . . or caster of spells); and necromancy (by one who consults ghosts and spirits or seeks oracles from the dead).

18, 15: A prophet like me: from the context (opposition to the pagan soothsayers) it seems that Moses is referring in general to all the true prophets who were to succeed him. But since Christ is the Great Prophet in whom the prophetic office finds its fulfillment and completion, this passage was understood in a special Messianic sense both by the Jews (Jn 6, 14; 7, 40) and by the Apostles (Acts 3, 22; 7, 37).

19, 2: Set apart three cities: the Israelites were to have at least six cities of refuge, three in the land east of the Jordan and three in the land of Canaan west of the Jordan (Nm 35, 9–34); but since the three cities east of the Jordan had now been appointed (Dt 4, 41–43), reference is made here only to the three west of the Jordan. The execution of this command is narrated in Jos 20.

19, 6: The avenger of blood: see note on Nm 35, 12.

your forefathers in the heritage you receive in the land which the LORD, your God, is giving you to occupy.[z]

False Witnesses.

15 "One witness alone shall not take the stand against a man in regard to any crime or any offense of which he may be guilty; a judicial fact shall be established only on the testimony of two or three witnesses.[a]

16 "If an unjust witness takes the stand against a man to accuse him of a defection from the law, **17** the two parties in the dispute shall appear before the LORD in the presence of the priests or judges in office at that time;[b] **18** and if after a thorough investigation the judges find that the witness is a false witness and has accused his kinsman falsely, **19** you shall do to him as he planned to do to his kinsman.[c] Thus shall you purge the evil from your midst. **20** The rest, on hearing of it, shall fear, and never again do a thing so evil among you. **21** Do not look on such a man with pity. Life for life, eye for eye, tooth for tooth, hand for hand, and foot for foot![d]

CHAPTER 20

Courage in War.

1 "When you go out to war against your enemies and you see horses and chariots and an army greater than your own, do not be afraid of them, for the LORD, your God, who brought you up from the land of Egypt, will be with you.

2 "When you are about to go into battle, the priest shall come forward and say to the soldiers: **3** 'Hear, O Israel! Today you are going into battle against your enemies. Be not weakhearted or afraid; be neither alarmed nor frightened by them. **4** For it is the LORD, your God, who goes with you to fight for you against your enemies and give you victory.'[e]

5 "Then the officials shall say to the soldiers,[f] 'Is there anyone who has built a new house and not yet had the housewarming? Let him return home, lest he die in battle and another dedicate it. **6** Is there anyone who has planted a vineyard and never yet enjoyed its fruits? Let him return home, lest he die in battle and another enjoy its fruits in his stead. **7** Is there anyone who has betrothed a woman and not yet taken her as his wife? Let him return home, lest he die in battle and another take her to wife.'[g] **8** In fine, the officials shall say to the soldiers, 'Is there anyone who is afraid and weakhearted?[h] Let him return home, lest he make his fellows as fainthearted as himself.'

9 "When the officials have finished speaking to the soldiers, military officers shall be appointed over the army.

Cities of the Enemy.

10 "When you march up to attack a city, first offer it terms of peace. **11** If it agrees to your terms of peace and opens its gates to you, all the people to be found in it shall serve you in forced labor. **12** But if it refuses to make peace with you and instead offers you battle, lay siege to it, **13** and when the LORD, your God, delivers it into your hand, put every male in it to the sword; **14** but the women and children and livestock and all else in it that is worth plundering you may take as your booty, and you may use this plunder of your enemies which the LORD, your God, has given you.[i]

15 "That is how you shall deal with any city at a considerable distance from you, which does not belong to the peoples of this land. **16** But in the cities of those nations which the LORD, your God, is giving you as your heritage, you shall not leave a single soul alive. **17** You must doom them all—the Hittites, Amorites, Canaanites, Perizzites, Hivites and Jebusites[j]—as the LORD, your God, has commanded you, **18** lest they teach you to make any such abominable offerings as they make to their gods, and you thus sin against the LORD, your God.

Trees of a Besieged City.

19 "When you are at war with a city and have to lay siege to it for a long time before you capture it, you shall not destroy its trees by putting an ax to them. You may eat their fruit, but you must not cut down the trees. After all, are the trees of the field men, that they should be included in your siege? **20** However, those trees which you know are not fruit trees you may destroy, cutting them down to build siegeworks with which to reduce the city that is resisting you.

CHAPTER 21

Expiation of Untraced Murder.

1 "If the corpse of a slain man* is found lying in the open on the land which the LORD, your God, is giving you to occupy, and it is not known who killed him, **2** your elders and judges shall go out and measure the distances to the cities that are in the

a Dt 17, 6; Nm 35, 30;   Mt 18, 16; Jn 8, 17;   2 Cor 13, 1.
b Dt 17, 8f.
c 18f: Dn 13, 61f.
d Ex 21, 23f; Lv 24, 20;   Mt 5, 38.
e Dt 1, 30; 3, 22; Jos

23, 10.
f 5ff: 1 Mc 3, 56.
g Dt 24, 5.
h Jgs 7, 3.
i 13f: Nm 31, 7. 9. 11;   Jos 22, 8.
j 16f: Dt 7, 1f; Jos 10, 40;   11, 14.

*

21, 1–9: This paragraph is best read immediately after Dt 19, 21. The slain man may not necessarily have been murdered; he may have been killed by a wild beast. But the blood of the slain cries out to God from the soil where it was shed; cf Gn 4, 10. Therefore a religious ceremony of propitiation is here prescribed in order to avert God's anger on the community.

neighborhood of the corpse. **3** When it is established which city is nearest the corpse, the elders of that city shall take a heifer that has never been put to work as a draft animal under a yoke, **4** and bringing it down to a wadi with an ever-flowing stream at a place that has not been plowed or sown, they shall cut the heifer's throat there in the wadi.* **5** The priests, the descendants of Levi, shall also be present, for the LORD, your God, has chosen them to minister to him and to give blessings in his name, and every case of dispute or violence must be settled by their decision.*k* **6** Then all the elders of that city nearest the corpse shall wash their hands* over the heifer whose throat was cut in the wadi, **7** and shall declare, 'Our hands did not shed this blood,* and our eyes did not see the deed. **8** Absolve, O LORD, your people Israel, whom you have ransomed, and let not the guilt of shedding innocent blood remain in the midst of your people Israel.' Thus they shall be absolved from the guilt of bloodshed, **9** and you shall purge from your midst the guilt of innocent blood, that you may prosper for doing what is right in the sight of the LORD.

Marriage with a Female Captive.

10 "When you go out to war against your enemies and the LORD, your God, delivers them into your hand, so that you take captives, **11** if you see a comely woman among the captives and become so enamored of her that you wish to have her as wife, **12** you may take her home to your house. But before she may live there, she must shave her head* and pare her nails **13** and lay aside her captive's garb. After she has mourned her father and mother for a full month, you may have relations with her, and you shall be her husband and she shall be your wife. **14** However, if later on you lose your liking for her, you shall give her her freedom, if she wishes it; but you shall not sell her or enslave her, since she was married to you under compulsion.

Rights of the First-born.

15 "If a man with two wives loves one and dislikes the other; and if both bear him sons, but the first-born is of her whom he dislikes: **16** when he comes to bequeath his property to his sons he may not consider as his first-born the son of the wife he loves, in preference to his true first-born, the son of the wife whom he dislikes. **17** On the contrary, he shall recognize as his first-born the son of her whom he dislikes, giving him a double share of whatever he happens to own, since he is the first fruits of his manhood, and to him belong the rights of the first-born.

The Incorrigible Son.

18 "If a man has a stubborn and unruly son who will not listen to

his father or mother, and will not obey them even though they chastise him, **19** his father and mother shall have him apprehended and brought out to the elders at the gate* of his home city, **20** where they shall say to those city elders, 'This son of ours is a stubborn and unruly fellow who will not listen to us; he is a glutton and a drunkard.' **21** Then all his fellow citizens shall stone him to death. Thus shall you purge the evil from your midst, and all Israel, on hearing of it, shall fear.

Corpse of a Criminal.

22 "If a man guilty of a capital offense is put to death and his corpse hung on a tree,* **23** it shall not remain on the tree overnight.*l* You shall bury it the same day; otherwise, since God's curse rests on him who hangs on a tree,* you will defile the land which the LORD, your God, is giving you as an inheritance.

CHAPTER 22

Care for Lost Animals.

1 "You shall not see your kinsman's ox or sheep driven astray without showing concern about it; see to it that it is returned to your kinsman.*m* **2** If this kinsman does not live near you, or you do not know who he may be, take it to your own place and keep it with you until he claims it; then give it back to him. **3** You shall do the same with his ass, or his garment, or anything else which your kinsman loses and you happen to find; you may not be unconcerned about them. **4** You shall not see your kinsman's ass or ox foundering on the

---

k Dt 19, 17.   m 1-4: Ex 23, 4f.
l Gal 3, 13.
*

21, 4: They shall cut the heifer's throat there in the wadi: its blood is to be carried away by the stream, signifying thereby the removal of the human blood from the soil. This is not a sacrifice but a symbolic action; the priests are present merely as official witnesses.

21, 6: Wash their hands: a symbolic gesture in protestation of one's own innocence when human blood is unjustly shed; cf Mt 27, 24.

21, 7: This blood: the blood of the slain man as symbolized by the heifer's blood.

21, 12f: Shave her head . . . : these symbolic actions are meant to signify the purification of the woman from her pagan defilement or perhaps the end of her period of mourning for her previous husband.

21, 19: The gate: in the city walls. This open space served as the forum for the administration of justice. Cf Dt 22, 15; 25, 7; Ru 4, 1f. 11; Is 29, 21; Am 5, 10. 12. 15.

21, 22: Hung on a tree: some understand, "impaled on a stake." In any case the hanging or impaling was not the means used to execute the criminal; he was first put to death by the ordinary means, stoning, and his corpse was then exposed on high as a salutary warning for others. Cf Jos 8, 29; 10, 26; 1 Sm 31, 10; 2 Sm 21, 9.

21, 23: God's curse rests on him who hangs on a tree: St. Paul quotes these words in Gal 3, 13, where he applies them to the crucified Savior, who "redeemed us from the curse of the law, becoming a curse for us."

road without showing concern about it; see to it that you help him lift it up.

Various Precepts.

5 "A woman shall not wear an article proper to a man, nor shall a man put on a woman's dress; for anyone who does such things is an abomination to the LORD, your God.

6 "If, while walking along, you chance upon a bird's nest with young birds or eggs in it, in any tree or on the ground, and the mother bird is sitting on them, you shall not take away the mother bird along with her brood; **7** you shall let her go, although you may take her brood away. It is thus that you shall have prosperity and a long life.

8 "When you build a new house, put a parapet around the roof; otherwise, if someone falls off, you will bring blood-guilt upon your house.

9 *n* "You shall not sow your vineyard with two different kinds of seed; if you do, its produce shall become forfeit,* both the crop you have sown and the yield of the vineyard. **10** You shall not plow with an ox and an ass harnessed together. **11** You shall not wear cloth of two different kinds of thread, wool and linen, woven together.

12 "You shall put twisted cords* on the four corners of the cloak that you wrap around you. *o*

Crimes against Marriage.

13 "If a man, after marrying a woman and having relations with her, comes to dislike her, **14** and makes monstrous charges against her and defames her by saying, 'I married this woman, but when I first had relations with her I did not find her a virgin,' **15** the father and mother of the girl shall take the evidence of her virginity* and bring it to the elders at the city gate. **16** There the father of the girl shall say to the elders, 'I gave my daughter to this man in marriage, but he has come to dislike her, **17** and now brings monstrous charges against her, saying: I did not find your daughter a virgin. But here is the evidence of my daughter's virginity!' And they shall spread out the cloth before the elders of the city. **18** Then these city elders shall take the man and chastise him,* **19** besides fining him one hundred silver shekels, which they shall give to the girl's father, because the man defamed a virgin in Israel. Moreover, she shall remain his wife, and he may not divorce her as long as he lives.

20 "But if this charge is true, and evidence of the girl's virginity is not found, **21** they shall bring the girl to the entrance of her father's house and there her townsmen shall stone her to death, because she committed a crime against Israel by her unchasteness in her father's house. Thus shall you purge the evil from your midst.

22 "If a man is discovered having relations with a woman who is married to another, both the man and the woman with whom he has had relations shall die. *p* Thus shall you purge the evil from your midst.

23 "If within the city a man comes upon a maiden who is betrothed,* and has relations with her, **24** you shall bring them both out to the gate of the city and there stone them to death: the girl because she did not cry out for help though she was in the city, and the man because he violated his neighbor's wife. Thus shall you purge the evil from your midst.

25 "If, however, it is in the open fields that a man comes upon such a betrothed maiden, seizes her and has relations with her, the man alone shall die. **26** You shall do nothing to the maiden, since she is not guilty of a capital offense. This case is like that of a man who rises up against his neighbor and murders him: **27** it was in the open fields that he came upon her, and though the betrothed maiden may have cried out for help, there was no one to come to her aid.

28 *q* "If a man comes upon a maiden that is not betrothed, takes her and has relations with her, and their deed is discovered, **29** the man who had relations with her shall pay the girl's father fifty silver shekels and take her as his wife, because he has deflowered her. Moreover, he may not divorce her as long as he lives.

CHAPTER 23

1 "A man shall not marry his father's wife,* nor shall he dishonor his father's bed.

Membership in the Community.

2 "No one whose testicles have been crushed or whose penis has been cut off, may be admitted into the community of the Lord. **3** No child of an incestuous union may be admitted into the community of the LORD, nor any descendant of his even to the tenth generation. **4** *r* No Ammonite or Moabite may ever be admitted into the community of the LORD, nor any descendants of theirs even to the tenth generation, **5** *s* because they would not succor you with food and water on your journey after you left Egypt, and because

---

n 9. 11: Lv 19, 19. q 28f: Ex 22, 16.
o Nm 15, 38; Mt 23, 5. r Neh 13, 1f.
p Lv 20, 10; Jn 8, 4f. s Nm 24, 10.

*

22, 9: Become forfeit: to the sanctuary; cf Lv 19, 19; Jos 6, 19.

22, 12: Twisted cords: referred to as "tassels" on "violet cords" in Nm 15, 38. See note there.

22, 15: The evidence of her virginity: the bridal garment or sheet stained with a little blood from the first nuptial relations.

22, 18: Chastise him: flog him, as prescribed in Dt 25, 1–3.

22, 23: A maiden who is betrothed: a girl who is married but not yet brought to her husband's home and whose marriage is therefore still unconsummated.

23, 1: Father's wife: stepmother. Dishonor: cf Dt 27, 20.

Moab hired Balaam, son of Beor, from Pethor in Aram Naharaim, to curse you; **6** though the LORD, your God, would not listen to Balaam and turned his curse into a blessing for you, because he loves you. **7** Never promote their peace and prosperity as long as you live. **8** ᵗBut do not abhor the Edomite, since he is your brother, nor the Egyptian, since you were an alien in his country. **9** Children born to them may in the third generation be admitted into the community of the LORD.

Cleanliness in Camp.

10 "When you are in camp during an expedition against your enemies, you shall keep yourselves from everything offensive. **11** If one of you becomes unclean because of a nocturnal emission, he shall go outside the camp, and not return until, **12** toward evening, he has bathed in water; then, when the sun has set, he may come back into the camp. **13** Outside the camp you shall have a place set aside to be used as a latrine. **14** You shall also keep a trowel in your equipment and with it, when you go outside to ease nature, you shall first dig a hole and afterward cover up your excrement. **15** Since the LORD, your God, journeys along within your camp to defend you and to put your enemies at your mercy, your camp must be holy; otherwise, if he sees anything indecent in your midst, he will leave your company.

Various Precepts.

16 "You shall not hand over to his master a slave who has taken refuge from him with you. **17** Let him live with you wherever he chooses, in any one of your communities* that pleases him. Do not molest him.

18 *"There shall be no temple harlot among the Israelite women, nor a temple prostitute among the Israelite men.ᵘ **19** You shall not offer a harlot's fee or a dog's price as any kind of votive offering in the house of the LORD, your God; both these things are an abomination to the LORD, your God.

20 "You shall not demand interest from your countrymen on a loan of money or of food or of anything else on which interest is usually demanded.ᵛ **21** You may demand interest from a foreigner, but not from your countryman, so that the LORD, your God, may bless you in all your undertakings on the land you are to enter and occupy.

22 "When you make a vow to the LORD, your God, you shall not delay in fulfilling it; otherwise you will be held guilty, for the LORD, your God, is strict in requiring it of you. **23** Should you refrain from making a vow, you will not be held guilty. **24** But you must keep your solemn word and fulfill the votive offering you have freely promised to the LORD.

25 "When you go through your neighbor's vineyard, you may eat as many of his grapes as you wish, but do not put them in your basket. **26** When you go through your neighbor's grainfield, you may pluck some of the ears with your hand, but do not put a sickle to your neighbor's grain.

CHAPTER 24

Marriage Laws.

1 "When a man,* after marrying a woman and having relations with her, is later displeased with her because he finds in her something indecent,* and therefore he writes out a bill of divorce and hands it to her, thus dismissing her from his house: **2** if on leaving his house she goes and becomes the wife of another man, **3** and the second husband, too, comes to dislike her and dismisses her from his house by handing her a written bill of divorce; **4** or if this second man who has married her, dies; then her former husband, who dismissed her, may not again take her as his wife after she has become defiled. That would be an abomination before the LORD, and you shall not bring such guilt upon the land which the LORD, your God, is giving you as a heritage.

5 ʷ"When a man is newly wed, he need not go out on a military expedition, nor shall any public duty be imposed on him. He shall be exempt for one year for the sake of his family, to bring joy to the wife he has married.

Justice, Equity and Charity.

6 *"No one shall take a hand mill or even its upper stone as

---

t Gn 25, 24ff.
u 1 Kgs 14, 24; 22, 46;
2 Kgs 23, 7.
v Ex 22, 25; Lv 25, 37;
Lk 6, 34f.
w Dt 20, 7.

---

*

23, 17: In any one of your communities: from this it would seem that the slave in question is a fugitive from a foreign country.

23, 18f: The pagans believed that they could enter into special relationship with their gods and goddesses by having sexual relations with the pagan priests and priestesses who prostituted themselves for this purpose. The money paid for this was considered a sort of votive offering made to the pagan sanctuary. Such abominations were naturally forbidden in Israel. A dog's price: the money paid the pagan priest for his indecent service.

24, 1–4: This law is directly concerned only with forbidding divorced couples to remarry each other, and indirectly with checking hasty divorces, by demanding sufficient cause and certain legal formalities. Divorce itself is taken for granted and tolerated as an existing custom whose evils this law seeks to lessen. Cf Dt 22, 19. 29; Mal 2, 14ff. Christ gave the authentic interpretation of this law: "Moses, by reason of the hardness of your heart, permitted you to put away your wives; but it was not so from the beginning" (Mt 19, 8f).

24, 1: Something indecent: a rather indefinite phrase, meaning perhaps "immodest conduct." At the time of Christ the rabbis differed in opinion concerning the sufficient grounds for divorce; cf Mt 19, 3.

24, 6: Since the Israelites ground their grain into flour only in sufficient quantity for their current need, to deprive a debtor a pledge for debt, for he would be taking the debtor's sustenance as a pledge.

7 "If a any man is caught kidnaping a fellow Israelite in order to enslave him and sell him, the kidnaper shall be put to death. *x* Thus shall you purge the evil from your midst.

8 *y* "In an attack of leprosy you shall be careful to observe exactly and to carry out all the directions of the levitical priests. Take care to act in accordance with the instructions I have given them. **9** *z* Remember what the LORD, your God, did to Miriam on the journey after you left Egypt.

10 * "When you make a loan of any kind to your neighbor, you shall not enter his house to receive a pledge from him, **11** but shall wait outside until the man to whom you are making the loan brings his pledge outside to you. **12** If he is a poor man, you shall not sleep in the mantle he gives as a pledge, **13** but shall return it to him at sunset that he himself may sleep in it. *a* Then he will bless you, and it will be a good deed of yours before the LORD, your God.

14 "You shall not defraud a poor and needy hired servant, whether he be one of your own countrymen or one of the aliens who live in your communities. **15** You shall pay him each day's wages before sundown on the day itself, since he is poor and looks forward to them. *b* Otherwise he will cry to the LORD against you, and you will be held guilty.

16 "Fathers shall not be put to death for their children, nor children for their fathers; only for his own guilt shall a man be put to death. *c*

17 "You shall not violate the rights of the alien or of the orphan, nor take the clothing of a widow as a pledge. *d* **18** For, remember, you were once slaves in Egypt, and the LORD, your God, ransomed you from there; that is why I command you to observe this rule.

19 *e* "When you reap the harvest in your field and overlook a sheaf there, you shall not go back to get it; let it be for the alien, the orphan or the widow, that the LORD, your God, may bless you in all your undertakings. **20** When you knock down the fruit of your olive trees, you shall not go over the branches a second time; let what remains be for the alien, the orphan and the widow. **21** When you pick your grapes, you shall not go over the vineyard a second time; let what remains be for the alien, the orphan, and the widow. **22** For remember that you were once slaves in Egypt; that is why I command you to observe this rule.

CHAPTER 25

1 "When men have a dispute and bring it to court, and a decision is handed down to them acquitting the innocent party and condemning the guilty party, **2** if the latter deserves stripes,

the judge shall have him lie down and in his presence receive the number of stripes his guilt deserves. **3** Forty stripes* may be given him, but no more; *f* lest, if he were beaten with more stripes than these, your kinsman should be looked upon as disgraced because of the severity of the beating.

4 * "You shall not muzzle an ox when it is treading out grain. *g*

Levirate Marriage. **5** "When brothers live together* and one of them dies without a son, the widow of the deceased shall not marry anyone outside the family; but her husband's brother shall go to her and perform the duty of a brother-in-law by marrying her. *h* **6** *i* The first-born son she bears shall continue the line of the deceased brother, that his name may not be blotted out from Israel. **7** If, however, a man does not care to marry his brother's wife, she shall go up to the elders at the gate and declare, 'My brother-in-law does not intend to perform his duty toward me and refuses to perpetuate his brother's name in Israel.' **8** Thereupon the elders of his city shall summon him and admonish him. If he persists in saying, 'I am not willing to marry her,' **9** *his sister-in-law, in the presence of the elders, shall go up to him and strip his sandal from his foot and spit in his face, saying publicly, 'This is how one should be treated who will not build up his brother's family!' **10** And his lineage shall be spoken of in Israel as 'the family of the man stripped of his sandal.'

---

x Ex 21, 16.
y Lv 13, 1-14.
z Nm 12, 10-15.
a Ex 22, 26.
b 14f: Lv 19, 13; Tb 4, 15; Sir 34, 25f; Jer 22, 13.
c 2 Kgs 14, 6; 2 Chr 25, 4; Ez 18, 20.
d Ex 22, 22; 23, 9.
e 19ff: Lv 19. 9f; 23, 22.
f 2 Cor 11, 24.
g 1 Cor 9, 9; 1 Tm 5, 18.
h Mt 22, 24; Mk 12, 19; Lk 20, 28.
i 6-9; Ru 4, 5-10.

*

of his hand mill was virtually equivalent to condemning him to starve to death.

24, 10f: The debtor had the right to select the pledge that the creditor demanded as a guarantee for his loan.

25, 3: Forty stripes: a relatively mild punishment in ancient times. Later Jewish practice limited the number to thirty-nine; cf 2 Cor 11, 24.

25, 4: St Paul argues from this verse that a laborer has the right to live on the fruits of his labor; cf 1 Cor 9, 9; 1 Tm 5, 18.

25, 5: When brothers live together: when relatives of the same clan, though married, hold their property in common. It was only in this case that the present law was to be observed, since one of its purposes was to keep the property of the deceased within the same clan. Such a marriage of a widow with her brother-in-law is known as a "levirate" marriage from the Latin word levir, meaning "a husband's brother."

25, 9f: The penalty decreed for a man who refuses to comply with this law of family loyalty is public disgrace (the widow is to spit in his face) and the curse of poverty; sandals were proverbially a man's cheapest possession (cf Am 2, 6; 8, 6), and therefore "a man without sandals" was the poorest of the poor. Some commentators, however, connect this symbolic act with the ceremony mentioned in Ru 4, 7f.

Various Precepts. 11 "When two men are fighting and the wife of one intervenes to save her husband from the blows of his opponent, if she stretches out her hand and seizes the latter by his private parts, 12 you shall chop off her hand without pity.

13 "You shall not keep two differing weights in your bag, one large and the other small;*j* 14 nor shall you keep two different measures in your house, one large and the other small. 15 But use a true and just weight, and a true and just measure, that you may have a long life on the land which the LORD, your God, is giving you. 16 Everyone who is dishonest in any of these matters is an abomination to the LORD, your God.

17 *Bear in mind what Amalek did to you on the journey after you left Egypt,*k* 18 how without fear of any god he harassed you along the way, weak and weary as you were, and cut off at the rear all those who lagged behind. 19 Therefore, when the LORD, your God, gives you rest from all your enemies round about in the land which he is giving you to occupy as your heritage, you shall blot out the memory of Amalek from under the heavens.*l* Do not forget!

CHAPTER 26

Thanksgiving for the Harvest. 1 "When you have come into the land which the LORD, your God, is giving you as a heritage, and have occupied it and settled in it, 2 you shall take some first fruits*m* of the various products of the soil which you harvest from the land which the LORD, your God, gives you, and putting them in a basket, you shall go to the place which the LORD, your God, chooses for the dwelling place of his name. 3 There you shall go to the priest in office at that time and say to him, 'Today I acknowledge to the LORD, my God, that I have indeed come into the land which he swore to our fathers he would give us.' 4 The priest shall then receive the basket from you and shall set it in front of the altar of the LORD, your God. 5 Then you shall declare before the LORD, your God, 'My father was a wandering Aramean* who went down to Egypt with a small household and lived there as an alien.*n* But there he became a nation great, strong and numerous. 6 *o*When the Egyptians maltreated and oppressed us, imposing hard labor upon us, 7 we cried to the LORD, the God of our fathers, and he heard our cry and saw our affliction, our toil and our oppression. 8 He brought us out of Egypt with his strong hand and outstretched arm, with terrifying power, with signs and wonders;*p* 9 and bringing us into this country, he gave us this land flowing with milk and honey.*q* 10 Therefore, I have now brought you the first fruits of the products of the soil which you, O

LORD, have given me.' And having set them before the LORD, your God, you shall bow down in his presence. 11 Then you and your family, together with the Levite and the aliens who live among you, shall make merry over all these good things which the LORD, your God, has given you.*r*

Prayer with the Tithes. 12 "When you have finished setting aside all the tithes of your produce in the third year,*s* the year of the tithes, and you have given them to the Levite,* the alien, the orphan and the widow, that they may eat their fill in your own community, 13 you shall declare before the LORD, your God, 'I have purged my house of the sacred portion and I have given it to the Levite,* the alien, the orphan and the widow, just as you have commanded me. In this I have not broken or forgotten any of your commandments: 14 *I have not eaten any of the tithe as a mourner; I have not brought any of it out as one unclean; I have not offered any of it to the dead. I have thus hearkened to the voice of the LORD, my God, doing just as you have commanded me. 15 Look down, then, from heaven, your holy abode, and bless your people Israel and the soil you have given us in the land flowing with milk and honey which you promised on oath to our fathers.'

The Covenant. 16 "This day the LORD, your god, commands you to observe these statutes and decrees. Be careful, then, to observe them with all your heart and with all your soul. 17 Today you are making this agreement with the LORD: he is to be your God and you are to walk in his ways and observe his statutes, commandments and decrees, and to hearken to his voice.*t* 18 And today the LORD is making this agreement with you: you are to be a people peculiarly his own,*u* as he promised you; and provided you keep all his commandments, 19 he will then raise you high in praise and renown and glory above all other nations he has

---

j 13ff: Lv 19, 35f; Prv 16, 11; Ez 45, 10; Ml 6, 11.	3, 9; Nm 20, 15f.
	p Ex 12, 51.
	q Ex 3, 8.
k Ex 17, 8.	r Dt 12, 7. 12.
l Ex 17, 14; 1 Sm 15, 2f.	s Dt 14, 28f.
m Ex 23, 19; 34, 26.	t Ex 24, 7.
n Gn 46, 6f; Acts 7, 14f.	u 18f: Dt 7, 6; 14, 2; 28,
o 6f: Ex 1, 8-22; 2, 23ff;	1; Ex 19, 5.

* ———

25, 17–19: This attack on Israel by Amalek is not mentioned elsewhere in the Old Testament, although it probably was connected with the battle mentioned in Ex 17, 8. A campaign against Amalek was carried out by Saul; cf 1 Sm 15.

26, 5: Aramean: either in reference to the origin of the patriarchs from Aram Naharaim (cf Gn 24, 10; 25, 20; 28, 5; 31, 20. 24), or merely in the sense of "nomad," in the same way as "Arab" was later used; cf Jer 3, 2.

26, 12: And you have given them to the Levite . . . : as prescribed in Dt 14, 28f.

26, 14: These are allusions to pagan religious practices.

made, and you will be a people sacred to the LORD, your God, as he promised.''

IV: Final Words of Moses

CHAPTER 27

Ceremonies. 1 Then Moses, with the elders of Israel, gave the people this order: "Keep all these commandments which I enjoin on you today. 2 On the day you cross the Jordan into the land which the LORD, your God, is giving you, set up some large stones and coat them with plaster. 3 Also write on them,^{v} at the time you cross, all the words of this law, that you may thus enter into the land flowing with milk and honey, which the LORD, your God, and the God of your fathers, is giving you as he promised you. 4 When, moreover, you have crossed the Jordan, besides setting up on Mount Ebal these stones concerning which I command you today, and coating them with plaster, 5 you shall also build to the LORD, your God, an altar made of stones that no iron tool has touched.^{w} 6 You shall make this altar of the LORD, your God, with undressed stones, and shall offer on it holocausts to the LORD, your God. 7 You shall also sacrifice peace offerings and eat them there, making merry before the LORD, your God. 8 On the stones* you shall inscribe all the words of this law very clearly.''

9 Moses, with the levitical priests, then said to all Israel: "Be silent, O Israel, and listen! This day you have become the people of the LORD, your God.^{x} 10 You shall therefore hearken to the voice of the LORD, your God, and keep his commandments and statutes which I enjoin on you today.''

11 That same day Moses gave the people this order: 12 "When you cross the Jordan, Simeon, Levi, Judah, Issachar, Joseph and Benjamin shall stand on Mount Gerizim^y to pronounce blessings over the people, 13 while Reuben, Gad, Asher, Zebulun, Dan and Naphtali shall stand on Mount Ebal to pronounce curses.

The Twelve Curses. 14 "The Levites shall proclaim aloud to all the men of Israel: 15 'Cursed be the man who makes a carved or molten idol^z—an abomination to the LORD, the product of a craftsman's hands—and sets it up in secret!' And all the people shall answer, 'Amen!'*

16 'Cursed be he who dishonors his father or his mother!'^{a} And all the people shall answer, 'Amen!'

17 'Cursed be he who moves his neighbor's landmarks!'^{b} And all the people shall answer, 'Amen!'

18 'Cursed be he who misleads a blind man

on his way!'^{c} And all the people shall answer, 'Amen!'

19 'Cursed be he who violates the rights of the alien, the orphan or the widow!'^{d} And all the people shall answer, 'Amen!'

20 'Cursed be he who has relations with his father's wife, for he dishonors his father's bed!'^{e} And all the people shall answer, 'Amen!'

21 'Cursed be he who has relations with any animal!'^{f} And all the people shall answer, 'Amen!'

22 'Cursed be he who has relations with his sister or his half-sister!'^{g} And all the people shall answer, 'Amen!'

23 'Cursed be he who has relations with his mother-in-law!'^{h} And all the people shall answer, 'Amen!'

24 'Cursed be he who slays his neighbor in secret!'^{i} And all the people shall answer, 'Amen!'

25 'Cursed be he who accepts payment for slaying an innocent man!' And all the people shall answer, 'Amen!'

26 'Cursed be he who fails to fulfill any of the provisions of this law!'^{j} And all the people shall answer, 'Amen!'

CHAPTER 28*

Blessings for Obedience. 1 "Thus, then,^{k} shall it be:^{l} if you continue to heed the voice of the LORD, your God, and are careful to observe all his commandments which I enjoin on you today, the LORD, your God, will raise you high above all the nations of the earth.^{m} 2 When you hearken to the voice of the LORD, your God, all these blessings will come upon you and overwhelm you:

3 "May you be blessed in the city,
  and blessed in the country!
4 "Blessed be the fruit of your womb,
  the produce of your soil and the offspring
    of your livestock,
  the issue of your herds and the young of
    your flocks!^{n}

---

v Jos 8, 32.
w Ex 20, 25; Jos 8, 31.
x Dt 26, 17ff.
y 12f: Dt 11, 29; Jos 8, 33f.
z Ex 20, 4. 23; Lv 19, 4; Wis 14, 8.
a Dt 21, 18-21; Ex 21, 17; Lv 20, 9.
b Dt 19, 14.
c Lv 19, 14.
d Dt 24, 17; Ex 22, 21f.
e Dt 22; 23, 1; Lv 18, 8;

20, 11.
20, 15.
f Ex 22, 18; Lv 18, 23; 20, 15.
g Lv 18, 9; 20, 17.
h Lv 18, 17; 20, 14.
i Ex 20, 13; 21, 12; Nm 35, 20f.
j Gal 3, 10.
k 1-68: Lv 26, 1-45.
l 1-14: Dt 7, 12-16.
m Dt 26, 19.
n Dt 7, 13; 30. 9.

---

*

27, 8: On the stones: cf vv 3f; not the stones of the altar.

27, 15–26: Amen: see note on Nm 5, 22.

28, 1–69: This chapter would read better immediately after chapter 26.

5 "Blessed be your grain bin and your
kneading bowl!

6 "May you be blessed in your coming in,
and blessed in your going out!*

Victory and Prosperity. 7 "The LORD will beat down before you the enemies that rise up against you; though they come out against you from but one direction, they will flee before you in seven.* 8 The LORD will affirm his blessing upon you, on your barns and on all your undertakings, blessing you in the land that the LORD, your God, gives you. 9 Provided that you keep the commandments of the LORD, your God, and walk in his ways, he will establish you as a people sacred to himself, as he swore to you;*o* 10 so that, when all the nations of the earth see you bearing the name of the LORD,* they will stand in awe of you.*p* 11 The LORD will increase in more than goodly measure the fruit of your womb, the offspring of your livestock, and the produce of your soil, in the land which he swore to your fathers he would give you. 12 The LORD will open up for you his rich treasure house of the heavens, to give your land rain in due season, blessing all your undertakings, so that you will lend to many nations and borrow from none.*q* 13 The LORD will make you the head, not the tail,* and you will always mount higher and not decline, as long as you obey the commandments of the LORD, your God, which I order you today to observe carefully; 14 not turning aside to the right or to the left from any of the commandments which I now give you, in order to follow other gods and serve them.

Curses for Disobedience. 15 "But if you do not hearken to the voice of the LORD, your God,*r* and are not careful to observe all his commandments which I enjoin on you today, all these curses shall come upon you and overwhelm you:

16 "May you be cursed in the city,
and cursed in the country!

17 "Cursed be your grain bin and your
kneading bowl!

18 "Cursed be the fruit of your womb,
the produce of your soil and the offspring
of your livestock,
the issue of your herds and the young of
your flocks!

19 "May you be cursed in your coming in,
and cursed in your going out!

Sickness and Defeat. 20 "The LORD will put a curse on you, defeat and frustration in every enterprise you undertake, until your are speedily destroyed and perish for the evil you have done in forsaking me. 21 The LORD will bring a pestilence upon you that will persist until he has exterminated you from the land you are entering to occupy. 22 The LORD will strike you with wasting and fever, with scorching, fiery drought, with blight and searing wind, that will plague you until you perish. 23 The sky over your heads will be like bronze and the earth under your feet like iron.*s* 24 For rain the LORD will give your land powdery dust, which will come down upon you from the sky until you are destroyed. 25 The LORD will let you be beaten down before your enemies; though you advance against them from one direction, you will flee before them in seven, so that you will become a terrifying example to all the kingdoms of the earth.*t* 26 Your carcasses will become food for all the birds of the air and for the beasts of the field, with no one to frighten them off. 27 The LORD will strike you with Egyptian boils*u* and with tumors, eczema and the itch, until you cannot be cured. 28 And the LORD will strike you with madness, blindness and panic, 29 so that even at midday you will grope like a blind man in the dark, unable to find your way.

Despoilment. "You will be oppressed and robbed continually, with no one to come to your aid. 30 Though you betroth a wife, another man will have her. Though you build a house, you will not live in it. Though you plant a vineyard, you will not enjoy its fruits. 31 Your ox will be slaughtered before your eyes, and you will not eat of its flesh. Your ass will be stolen in your presence, but you will not recover it. Your flocks will be given to your enemies, with no one to come to your aid. 32 Your sons and daughters will be given to a foreign nation while you look on and grieve for them in constant helplessness. 33 A people whom you do not know will consume the fruit of your soil and of all your labor, and you will be oppressed and crushed at all times without surcease, 34 until you are driven mad by what your eyes must look upon. 35 *The LORD will strike you with malignant boils of which you cannot be cured, on

---

o Dt 26, 18; Ex 19, 5f. Mal 2, 2.
p Dt 2, 25; 11, 25. s 22f: Lv 26, 19.
q Dt 15, 6. t Lv 26, 17. 37.
r Bar 1, 20; Dn 9, 11; u Ex 9, 9ff.

*

28, 6: In your coming in . . . in your going out: at the beginning and end of every action, or in all actions in general.

28, 7. 25: From but one direction . . . in seven: in one compact mass, contrasted with many scattered groups.

28, 10: You bearing the name of the Lord: literally, "The LORD'S name is called over you," an expression signifying ownership and protection. Cf 2 Sm 12, 28; 1 Kgs 8, 43; Is 4, 1; 63, 19; Jer 7, 10f; 14, 9; 15, 16; 25, 29; Am 9, 12.

28, 13: The head, not the tail: in the honorable position as leader. Cf Is 9, 14; 19, 15.

28, 35: This verse is best read with v 27.

your knees and legs, and from the soles of your feet to the crown of your head.

Exile. 36 *v*"The LORD will bring you, and your king whom you have set over you, to a nation which you and your fathers have not known, and there you will serve strange gods of wood and stone, 37 and will call forth amazement, reproach and barbed scorn from all the nations to which the LORD will lead you.

Fruitless Labors. 38 "Though you spend much seed on your field, you will harvest but little, for the locusts will devour the crop.*w* 39 Though you plant and cultivate vineyards, you will not drink or store up the wine, for the grubs will eat the vines clean.*x* 40 Though you have olive trees throughout your country, you will have no oil for ointment, for your olives will drop off unripe.*y* 41 Though you beget sons and daughters, they will not remain with you, but will go into captivity.*z* 42 Buzzing insects will infest all your trees and the crops of your soil. 43 The alien residing among you will rise higher and higher above you, while you sink lower and lower. 44 He will lend to you, not you to him. He will become the head, you the tail.

45 "All these curses will come upon you, pursuing you and overwhelming you, until you are destroyed, because you would not hearken to the voice of the LORD, your God, nor keep the commandments and statutes he gave you. 46 They will light on you and your descendants as a sign and a wonder* for all time. 47 Since you would not serve the LORD, your God, with joy and gratitude for abundance of every kind, 48 therefore in hunger and thirst, in nakedness and utter poverty, you will serve the enemies whom the LORD will send against you. He will put an iron yoke on your neck, until he destroys you.

Invasion and Siege. 49 *a*"The LORD will raise up against you a nation from afar, from the end of the earth, that swoops down like an eagle, a nation whose tongue you do not understand, 50 a nation of stern visage, that shows neither respect for the aged nor pity for the young. 51 They will consume the offspring of your livestock and the produce of your soil, until you are destroyed; they will leave you no grain or wine or oil, no issue of your herds or young of your flocks, until they have brought about your ruin. 52 They will besiege you in each of your communities, until the great, unscalable walls you trust in come tumbling down all over your land. They will so besiege you in every community throughout the land which the LORD, your God, has given you, 53 that in the distress of the siege to which your enemy sub-

jects you, you will eat the fruit of your womb, the flesh of your own sons and daughters*b* whom the LORD, your God, has given you. 54 The most refined and fastidious man among you will begrudge his brother and his beloved wife and his surviving children 55 any share in the flesh of his children that he himself is using for food when nothing else is left him in the straits of the siege to which your enemy will subject you in all your communities. 56 The most refined and delicate woman among you, so delicate and refined that she would not venture to set the sole of her foot on the ground, will begrudge her beloved husband and her son and daughter 57 the afterbirth that issues from her womb and the infant she brings forth when she secretly uses them for food for want of anything else, in the straits of the siege to which your enemy will subject you in your communities.

Plagues. 58 "If you are not careful to observe every word of the law which is written in this book, and to revere the glorious and awesome name of the LORD, your God, 59 he will smite you and your descendants with severe and constant blows, malignant and lasting maladies. 60 He will again afflict you with all the diseases of Egypt* which you dread, and they will persist among you.*c* 61 Should there be any kind of sickness or calamity not mentioned in this book of the law, that too the LORD will bring upon you until you are destroyed. 62 Of you who were numerous as the stars in the sky,*d* only a few will be left, because you would not hearken to the voice of the LORD, your God.

Exile. 63 "Just as the LORD once took delight in making you grow and prosper,*e* so will he now take delight in ruining and destroying you, and you will be plucked out of the land you are now entering to occupy. 64 The LORD will scatter you among all the nations from one end of the earth to the other,*f* and there you will serve strange gods of wood and stone, such as you and your fathers have not known. 65 Among these nations you will find no repose, not a foot of ground to stand upon, for

v 1 Kgs 9, 7ff; 2 Chr 7, 20ff; 33, 11; 36, 6. 20.
w Ml 6, 15; Hg 1, 6.
x Zep 1, 13.
y Mi 6, 15.
z Lam 1, 5.
a 49-52: Jer 5, 15ff; Bar 4, 15f.
b Lv 26, 29; 2 Kgs 6, 28f; Jer 19, 9; Lam 4, 10;
Bar 2. 3.
c Dt 28, 27.
d Dt 1, 10; Jer 42, 2.
e Dt 30, 9.
f Lv 26, 33.

28, 46: A sign and a wonder: an ominous example, attracting attention; cf Dt 29, 21–28.

28, 60: He will again afflict you with all the diseases of Egypt: such as the Lord had promised to remove from his people; cf Dt 7, 15.

28, 65: Wasted eyes: worn out and disappointed in their longing gaze.

there the LORD will give you an anguished heart and wasted eyes* and a dismayed spirit. **66** You will live in constant suspense and stand in dread both day and night, never sure of your existence. **67** In the morning you will say, 'Would that it were evening!' and in the evening you will say, 'Would that it were morning!' for the dread that your heart must feel and the sight that your eyes must see. **68** The LORD will send you back in galleys* to Egypt, to the region I told you that you were never to see again;⁸ and there you will offer yourselves for sale to your enemies as male and female slaves, but there will be no buyer.''

69 These are the words of the covenant which the LORD ordered Moses to make with the Israelites in the land of Moab, in addition to the covenant which he made with them at Horeb.

CHAPTER 29

Past Favors Recalled. **1** Moses summoned all Israel and said to them, "You have seen all that the LORD did in the land of Egypt before your very eyes to Pharaoh and all his servants and to all his land; **2** the great testings your own eyes have seen, and those great signs and wonders.ʰ **3** But not even at the present day has the LORD yet given you a mind to understand, or eyes to see, or ears to hear.* **4** 'I led you for forty years in the desert.ⁱ Your clothes did not fall from you in tatters nor your sandals from your feet; **5** bread was not your food, nor wine or beer your drink. Thus you should know that I, the LORD, am your God.' **6** ʲWhen we came to this place, Sihon, king of Heshbon, and Og, king of Bashan, came out to engage us in battle, but we defeated them **7** and took over their land, which we then gave as a heritage to the Reubenites, Gadites, and half the tribe of Manasseh.ᵏ **8** Keep the terms of this covenant, therefore, and fulfill them, that you may succeed in whatever you do.

All Israel Bound to the Covenant.

9 "You are all now standing before the LORD, your God—your chiefs and judges, your elders and officials, and all of the men of Israel, **10** together with your wives and children and the aliens who live in your camp, down to those who hew wood and draw water for you— **11** that you may enter into the covenant of the LORD, your God, which he concluded with you today under this sanction of a curse;* **12** so that he may now establish you as his people and he may be your God, as he promised you and as he swore to your fathers Abraham, Isaac and Jacob. **13** But it is not with you alone that I am making this covenant, under this sanction of a curse; **14** it is just as much with those who are not here among us* today as it is with those of

us who are now here present before the LORD, our God.

Warning against Idolatry. **15** "You know in what surroundings we lived in the land of Egypt and what we passed by in the nations we traversed, **16** and you saw the loathsome idols of wood and stone, of gold and silver, that they possess. **17** Let there be, then, no man or woman, no clan or tribe among you, who would now turn away their hearts from the LORD, our God, to go and serve these pagan gods! Let there be no root that would bear such poison and wormwood among you! **18** If any such person, upon hearing the words of this curse, should beguile himself into thinking that he can safely persist in his stubbornness of heart, as though to sweep away both the watered soil and the parched ground,* **19** the LORD will never consent to pardon him. Instead, the LORD's wrath and jealousy will flare up against that man, and every curse mentioned in this book will alight on him. The LORD will blot out his name from under the heavens **20** and will single him out from all the tribes of Israel for doom, in keeping with all the curses of the covenant inscribed in this book of the law.

Punishment for Infidelity. **21** "Future generations, your own descendants who will rise up after you, as well as the foreigners who will come here from far-off lands, when they see the calamities of this land and the ills with which the LORD has smitten it— **22** all its soil being nothing but sulphur and salt, a burnt-out waste, unsown and unfruitful, without a blade of grass, destroyed like Sodom and Gomorrah,ˡ Admah and Zeboiim, which the LORD overthrew in his furious wrath— **23** they and all the nations will ask, 'Why has the LORD dealt thus with this land? Why this fierce outburst of wrath?'ᵐ **24** And the answer will be, 'Because they forsook the covenant which the LORD, the God of their fathers, had made with them when he brought them out of the land of Egypt,

---

g Hos 8, 13; 9, 3.
h Dt 4, 34; Ex 19, 4.
i Dt 8, 2. 4.
j Dt 2, 24. 32; 3, 1; Nm 21, 33ff.
k Dt 3, 16; Nm 32, 33.
l Gn 14, 10f; 19, 24f.
m 23f: 1 Kgs 9, 8f; Jer 22, 8f.

---

*

28, 68: In galleys: in the ships of the Phoenician slave traders (Ez 27, 13; Jl 4, 6; Am 1, 9), who also dealt with Egypt (Is 23, 3).

29, 3: Eyes to see . . . ears to hear: with inner, spiritual discernment. Cf Mt 13, 43.

29, 11: Sanction of a curse: the present pact binds under penalty of the curses mentioned in this book. Cf v 20.

29, 14: Not here among us: this includes their descendants.

29, 18: To sweep away both the watered soil and the parched ground: apparently a proverb signifying that such an unfaithful Israelite will cause God to punish the good with the wicked, to root out the good plants growing in irrigated soil, together with the worthless plants growing in the dry ground.

25 and they went and served other gods and adored them, gods whom they did not know and whom he had not let fall to their lot: **26** that is why the LORD was angry with this land and brought on it all the imprecations listed in this book; **27** in his furious wrath and tremendous anger the LORD uprooted them from their soil and cast them out into a strange land,*n* where they are today.' **28** [Both what is still hidden* and what has already been revealed concern us and our descendants forever, that we may carry out all the words of this law.]

CHAPTER 30

Mercy for the Repentant. **1** "When all these things which I have set before you, the blessings and the curses, are fulfilled in you,*o* and from among whatever nations the LORD, your God, may have dispersed you, you ponder them in your heart: **2** then, provided that you and your children return to the LORD, your God, and heed his voice with all your heart and all your soul,*p* just as I now command you, **3** the LORD, your God, will change your lot; and taking pity on you, he will again gather you from all the nations wherein he has scattered you. **4** Though you may have been driven to the farthest corner of the world, even from there will the LORD, your God, gather you; even from there will he bring you back. **5** The LORD, your God, will then bring you into the land which your fathers once occupied, that you too may occupy it, and he will make you more prosperous and numerous than your fathers. **6** The LORD, your God, will circumcise your hearts* and the hearts of your descendants,*q* that you may love the LORD, your God, with all your heart and all your soul, and so may live. **7** But all those curses the LORD, your God, will assign to your enemies and the foes who persecuted you. **8** You, however, must again heed the LORD's voice and carry out all his commandments which I now enjoin on you. **9** Then the LORD, your God, will increase in more than goodly measure the returns from all your labors, the fruit of your womb, the offspring of your livestock, and the produce of your soil;*r* for the LORD, your God, will again take delight in your prosperity, even as he took delight in your fathers', **10** if only you heed the voice of the LORD, your God, and keep his commandments and statutes that are written in this book of the law, when you return to the LORD, your God, with all your heart and all your soul.

God's Command Clear. **11** *"For this command which I enjoin on you today is not too mysterious and remote for you. **12** It is not up in the sky, that you should say, 'Who will go up in the sky to get it for us and tell us of it, that

we may carry it out?' **13** Nor is it across the sea, that you should say, 'Who will cross the sea to get it for us and tell us of it, that we may carry it out?' **14** No, it is something very near to you, already in your mouths* and in your hearts; you have only to carry it out.

The Choice before Israel. **15** "Here, then, I have today set before you life and prosperity, death and doom. **16** If you obey the commandments of the LORD, your God, which I enjoin on you today, loving him, and walking in his ways, and keeping his commandments, statutes and decrees, you will live and grow numerous, and the LORD, your God, will bless you in the land you are entering to occupy. **17** If, however, you turn away your hearts and will not listen, but are led astray and adore and serve other gods, **18** I tell you now that you will certainly perish; you will not have a long life on the land which you are crossing the Jordan to enter and occupy. **19** I call heaven and earth today to witness against you:*s* I have set before you life and death, the blessing and the curse.*t* Choose life, then, that you and your descendants may live, **20** by loving the LORD, your God, heeding his voice, and holding fast to him. For that will mean life for you, a long life for you to live on the land which the LORD swore he would give to your fathers Abraham, Isaac and Jacob."

CHAPTER 31

The Lord's Leadership. **1** When Moses had finished speaking these words to all Israel, **2** he said to them, "I am now one hundred and twenty years old*u* and am no longer able to move about freely; besides, the LORD has told me that I shall not cross this Jordan. **3** It is the LORD your God, who will cross before you; he will destroy these nations before you, that you may supplant them.*v* [It is Joshua who will cross before you, as the LORD promised.] **4** *w*The LORD will deal with them just as he

---

n Dn 9, 11-14.
o Dt 11, 26ff.
p 2f; Neh 1, 9.
q Dt 6, 5.
r Dt 28, 11.

s Dt 4, 26.
t Dt 11, 26ff; 28, 2. 15.
u Dt 34, 7; Nm 20, 12.
v Dt 9, 3.
w Nm 21, 21-35.

---

*

29, 28: What is still hidden: the events of the future. What has already been revealed: God's law and the punishments in store for those who break it. Leave the future to God; our business is to keep his law.

30, 6: Circumcise your hearts: see note on Dt 10, 16.

30, 11-14: God has revealed his will so clearly that ignorance of his law can be no excuse. St Paul in Rom 10, 6-9, applies these words to the ease with which we can come to faith and salvation in Christ.

30, 14: In your mouths: that you may readily talk about it; cf Dt 6, 7; 11, 19. And in your hearts: that you may easily remember it; cf Dt 6, 6; 11, 18.

dealt with Sihon and Og, the kings of the Amorites whom he destroyed, and with their country. **5** When, therefore, the LORD delivers them up to you, you must deal with them exactly as I have ordered you.[x] **6** Be brave and steadfast; have no fear or dread of them, for it is the LORD, your God, who marches with you; he will never fail you or forsake you."[y]

Call of Joshua.   **7** Then Moses summoned Joshua and in the presence of all Israel said to him,[z] "Be brave and steadfast, for you must bring this people into the land which the LORD swore to their fathers he would give them; you must put them in possession of their heritage. **8** It is the LORD who marches before you; he will be with you and will never fail you or forsake you. So do not fear or be dismayed."

The Reading of the Law.   **9** When Moses had written down this law, he entrusted it to the livitical priests who carry the ark of the covenant of the LORD, and to all the elders of Israel, **10** giving them this order: "On the feast of Booths,[a] at the prescribed time in the year of relaxation* which comes at the end of every seven-year period, **11** when all Israel goes to appear before the LORD, your God, in the place which he chooses, you shall read this law* aloud in the presence of all Israel. **12** Assemble the people—men, women and children, as well as the aliens who live in your communities—that they may hear it and learn it, and so fear the LORD, your God, and carefully observe all the words of this law. **13** Their children also, who do not know it yet, must hear it and learn it, that they too may fear the LORD, your God, as long as you live on the land which you will cross the Jordan to occupy."

Commission of Joshua.   **14** The LORD said to Moses, "The time is now approaching for you to die. Summon Joshua, and present yourselves at the meeting tent that I may give him his commission." So Moses and Joshua went and presented themselves at the meeting tent.* **15** And the LORD appeared at the tent in a column of cloud, which stood still at the entrance of the tent.

A Command to Moses.   **16** The LORD said to Moses, "Soon you will be at rest with your fathers, and then this people will take to rendering wanton worship to the strange gods among whom they will live in the land they are about to enter.[b] They will forsake me and break the covenant which I have made with them. **17** At that time my anger will flare up against them; I will forsake them and hide my face from them, so that they will become a prey to be devoured, and many evils and troubles will befall them. At

that time they will indeed say, 'Is it not because our God is not among us that these evils have befallen us?' **18** Yet I will be hiding my face from them at that time only because of all the evil they have done in turning to other gods. **19** Write out this song,[c] then, for yourselves. Teach it to the Israelites and have them recite it, so that this song may be a witness for me against the Israelites. **20** For when I have brought them into the land flowing with milk and honey which I promised on oath to their fathers, and they have eaten their fill and grown fat, if they turn to other gods and serve them, despising me and breaking my covenant; **21** then, when many evils and troubles befall them, this song, which their descendants will not have forgotten to recite, will bear witness against them. For I know what they are inclined to do even at the present time, before I have brought them into the land which I promised on oath to their fathers." **22** So Moses wrote this song that same day, and he taught it to the Israelites.

Commission of Joshua.   **23** Then the LORD commissioned Joshua, son of Nun, and said to him, "Be brave and steadfast, for it is you who must bring the Israelites into the land which I promised them on oath.[d] I myself will be with you."

The Law Placed in the Ark.   **24** When Moses had finished writing out on a scroll the words of the law in their entirety, **25** he gave the Levites[e] who carry the ark of the covenant of the LORD this order: **26** "Take this scroll of the law and put it beside the ark of the covenant of the LORD, your God, that there it may be a witness against you. **27** For I already know how rebellious and stiff-necked you will be. Why, even now, while I am alive among you, you have been rebels against the LORD! How much more, then, after I am dead! **28** [f]Therefore, assemble all your tribal elders and your officials before me, that I may speak these words for them to hear, and so may call heaven and earth to witness against them. **29** [g]For I know that after my death you are sure to become corrupt and to turn aside from the way along which I directed you, so that evil will befall you in some future age because you have done evil in the

---

x Dt 7, 2.
y Dt 20, 3f.
z 7f: Jos 1, 6f. 9.
a 10f: Dt 16, 13ff.
b Jgs 2, 12. 17.

c Dt 31, 21; 32, 1-43.
d Dt 31, 7f; Jos 1, 5ff.
e 24f: Dt 31, 9.
f Dt 32, 1-43.
g Jgs 2, 19.

31, 10: The year of relaxation: cf Dt 15, 1ff and the note there.

31, 11ff: Reading the law not only instructed the people but also consoled them by the assurance of the divine goodness.

31, 14f. 23: V 23 is best read immediately after v 15; perhaps the original order was vv 7-8. 14-15. 23.

LORD's sight, and provoked him by your deeds."

The Song of Moses.

30 Then Moses recited the words of this song from beginning to end, for the whole assembly of Israel to hear:

CHAPTER 32

A

1 Give ear, O heavens, while I speak;*
    let the earth hearken to the words of my
      mouth!
2 May my instruction soak in like the rain,
    and my discourse permeate like the dew,
  Like a downpour upon the grass,
    like a shower upon the crops:
3 For I will sing the LORD's renown.
  Oh, proclaim the greatness of our God!
4 The Rock—how faultless are his deeds,
    how right all his ways!
  A faithful God, without deceit,
    how just and upright he is!*h*

5 Yet basely has he been treated by his
    degenerate children,
  a perverse and crooked race!*i*
6 Is the LORD to be thus repaid by you,
  O stupid and foolish people?
  Is he not your father who created you?
  Has he not made you and established
    you?*j*

7 Think back on the days of old,
    reflect on the years of age upon age.
  Ask your father and he will inform you,
    ask your elders and they will tell you:*k*
8 When the Most High assigned the nations
    their heritage,
    when he parceled out the descendants of
      Adam,*l*
  He set up the boundaries of the peoples
    after the number of the sons of God;*
9 While the LORD's own portion was Jacob,
  His hereditary share was Israel.*m*

10 He found them in a wilderness,
    a wasteland of howling desert.
  He shielded them and cared for them,
    guarding them as the apple of his eye.*n*

11 As an eagle incites its nestlings forth
    by hovering over its brood,
  So he spread his wings to receive them
    and bore them up on his pinions.*o*
12 The LORD alone was their leader,
    no strange god was with him.
13 He had them ride triumphant over the
    summits of the land*
    and live off the products of its fields,
  Giving them honey to suck from its rocks
    and olive oil from its hard, stony ground;

14 Butter from its cows and milk from its
    sheep,
  with the fat of its lambs and rams;
  Its Bashan* bulls and its goats,
    with the cream of its finest wheat;
    and the foaming blood of its grapes you
      drank.

B

15 [So Jacob ate his fill,]
    the darling* grew fat and frisky;
    you became fat and gross and gorged.
  They spurned the God who made them
    and scorned their saving Rock.*p*
16 They provoked him with strange gods
    and angered him with abominable idols.*q*

17 They offered sacrifice to demons, to
    "no-gods,"
    to gods whom they had not known before,
  To newcomers just arrived,
    of whom their fathers had never stood in
      awe.
18 You were unmindful of the Rock that begot
    you,
  You forgot the God who gave you birth.*r*
19 When the LORD saw this, he was filled with
    loathing
    and anger toward his sons and daughters.
20 "I will hide my face from them," he said,
    "and see what will then become of them.
  What a fickle race they are,
    sons with no loyalty in them!*s*
21 "Since they have provoked me with their
    'no god'
    and angered me with their vain idols,
  I will provoke them with a 'no-people';
    with a foolish nation I will anger them.*t*

22 "For by my wrath a fire is enkindled

---

h Ps 92, 15; Rv 15, 3.
i Dt 31, 29; Ps 78, 8; Lk
  9, 41.
j Ex 4, 22; Is 63, 16; 64,
  8; Jer 31, 9.
k Dt 4, 32; Ps 44, 2.
l Gn 10, 1-32; Acts 17,
  26.
m Ex 19, 5; Ps 33, 12.

n Dt 8, 15; Jer 2, 6; Zec
  2, 8.
o Ex 19, 4.
p Dt 31, 20.
q Nm 25, 2f; Ps 78, 58.
r Jer 2, 32.
s Dt 31, 17.
t Rom 10, 19.
u Lam 4, 11.

*

32, 1–43: In the style of the great prophets, the speaker is often God himself. The whole song is a poetic sermon, having for its theme God's benefits to Israel (vv 1–14) and Israel's ingratitude and idolatry in turning to the gods of the pagans, which sins will be punished by the pagans themselves (vv 15–29); in turn, the foolish pride of the pagans will be punished, and the Lord's honor will be vindicated (vv 30–43).

32, 8: The sons of God: the angels; cf Jb 1, 6; 2, 1; 38, 7; Ps 89, 7f. Here the various nations are portrayed as having their respective guardian angels. Cf Dn 10, 20f; 12, 1.

32, 13: The land: Canaan.

32, 14: Bashan: a fertile grazing land east of the Jordan, famous for its strong cattle. Cf Ps 22, 13; Ez 39, 18; Am 4, 1.

32, 15: The darling: a probable meaning of the Hebrew word yeshurun, a term of endearment for "Israel." Cf Dt 33, 5. 26; Is 44, 2.

that shall rage to the depths of the
　　netherworld,
Consuming the earth with its yield,
　　and licking with flames the roots of the
　　mountains. *u*

23 I will spend on them woe upon woe
　　and exhaust all my arrows against them:

24 "Emaciating hunger and consuming fever
　　and bitter pestilence,
And the teeth of wild beasts I will send
　　among them,
　　with the venom of reptiles gliding in the
　　dust.

25 "Snatched away by the sword in the street
　　and by sheer terror at home
Shall be the youth and the maiden alike,
　　the nursing babe as well as the hoary old
　　man. *v*

26 "I would have said, 'I will make an end of
　　them
　　and blot out their name from men's
　　memories,'
27 Had I not feared the insolence of their
　　enemies,
　　feared that these foes would mistakenly
　　boast,
'Our own hand won the victory;
　　the LORD had nothing to do with it.'"

28 For they are a people devoid of reason,*
　　having no understanding.
29 If they had insight they would realize what
　　happened,
　　they would understand their future and
　　say,

C

30 "How could one man rout a thousand,
　　or two men put ten thousand to flight,
Unless it was because their Rock sold them
　　and the LORD delivered them up?"
31 Indeed, their "rock" is not like our Rock,
　　and our foes are under condemnation.

32 They are a branch of Sodom's vine-stock,
　　from the vineyards of Gomorrah.
Poisonous are their grapes and bitter their
　　clusters.
33 Their wine is the venom of dragons
　　and the cruel poison of cobras.

34 "Is not this preserved in my treasury,
　　sealed up in my storehouse,
35 Against the day of vengeance and requital,
　　against the time they lose their footing?"
Close at hand is the day of their disaster,
　　and their doom is rushing upon them!

36 Surely, the LORD shall do justice for his
　　people;
　　on his servants he shall have pity.

When he sees their strength failing,
　　and their protected and unprotected* alike
　　disappearing, *w*

37 He will say, "Where are their gods *x*
　　whom they relied on as their 'rock'?
38 Let those who ate the fat of your sacrifices
　　and drank the wine of your libations
Rise up now and help you!
　　Let them be your protection!

39 "Learn then that I, I alone, am God,
　　and there is no god beside me.
It is I who bring both death and life,
　　I who inflict wounds and heal them,
　　and from my hand there is no rescue. *y*
40 "To the heavens I raise my hand and swear:
　　As surely as I live forever,

41 I will sharpen my flashing sword,
　　and my hand shall lay hold of my quiver.

"With vengeance I will repay my foes
　　and require those who hate me.
42 I will make my arrows drunk with blood,
　　and my sword shall gorge itself with
　　flesh—
With the blood of the slain and the captured,
　　Flesh from the heads of the enemy
　　leaders."

43 Exult with him, you heavens,
　　glorify him, all you angels of God;
For he avenges the blood of his servants
　　and purges his people's land.

44 So Moses, together with Joshua, son of
Nun, went and recited all the words of this song
for the people to hear.

Final Appeal. 45 When Moses had finished
speaking all these words to all Israel, 46 he
said, *z* "Take to heart all the warning which I
have now given you and which you must im-
press on your children, that you may carry out
carefully every word of this law. 47 For this is
no trivial matter for you; rather, it means your
very life, since it is by this means that you are
to enjoy a long life on the land which you will
cross the Jordan to occupy."

Moses to View Canaan. 48 On that very
day the LORD said to Moses, 49 "Go up on

---

v Lv 26, 25.
w 2 Mc 7, 6.
x 37f: Jgs 10, 14; Jer 2,
　28.

y Dt 4, 35; Tb 13, 2; Wis
　16, 13.
z Dt 4, 9.
a Nm 27, 12; 33, 47f.

*

32, 28–35: The reference is to the pagan nations, not to
Israel.

32, 36: *Their protected and unprotected:* the meaning of
the Hebrew is uncertain; according to some, the idea is "slaves
and freemen."

Mount Nebo, here in the Abarim Mountains [it is in the land of Moab facing Jericho], and view the land of Canaan, which I am giving to the Israelites as their possession.*a* **50** Then you shall die on the mountain you have climbed, and shall be taken to your people, just as your brother Aaron died on Mount Hor and there was taken to his people;*b* **51** because both of you broke faith with me among the Israelites at the waters of Meribath-kadesh in the desert of Zin by failing to manifest my sanctity among the Israelites.*c* **52** You may indeed view the land at a distance, but you shall not enter that land which I am giving to the Israelites."*d*

CHAPTER 33

Blessing upon the Tribes. **1** This is the blessing which Moses, the man of God, pronounced upon the Israelites before he died. **2** He said:

"The LORD came from Sinai*
and dawned on his people from Seir;
He shone forth from Mount Paran
and advanced from Meribath-kadesh,
While at his right hand a fire blazed forth
and his wrath devastated the nations.*e*
3 But all his holy ones were in his hand;*
they followed at his feet
and he bore them up on his pinions.
4 A law he gave to us;
he made the community of Jacob his
domain,*f*
5 and he became king of his darling,*
When the chiefs of the people assembled
and the tribes of Israel came together.
6 "May Reuben live and not die out,*g*
but let his men be few."*

7 The following is for Judah. He said:
"The LORD hears the cry of Judah;
you will bring him to his people.*
His own hands defend his cause
and you will be his help against his
foes."*h*

8 Of Levi he said:
"To Levi belong your Thummim,
to the man of your favor your Urim;*
For you put him to the test at Massah
and you contended with him at the waters
of Meribah.*i*
9 He said of his father, 'I regard him not';
his brothers he would not acknowledge,
and his own children he refused to
recognize.
Thus the Levites keep your words,
and your covenant they uphold.*
10 They promulgate your decisions to Jacob
and your law to Israel.
They bring the smoke of sacrifice to your
nostrils,
and burnt offerings to your altar.*j*

11 Bless, O LORD, his possessions
and accept the ministry of his hands.
Break the backs of his adversaries
and of his foes, that they may not rise."

12 Of Benjamin he said:
"Benjamin is the beloved of the LORD,
who shelters him all the day,
while he abides securely at his breast."*k*

13 Of Joseph he said:*l*
"Blessed by the LORD is his land
with the best of the skies above
and of the abyss crouching beneath;
14 With the best of the produce of the year,
and the choicest sheaves of the months;
15 With the finest gifts of the age-old
mountains
and the best from the timeless hills;
16 With the best of the earth and its fullness,
and the favor of him who dwells in the
bush.*
These shall come upon the head of Joseph
and upon the brow of the prince among
his brothers,
17 The majestic bull, his father's first-born,
whose horns are those of the wild ox
With which to gore the nations,
even those at the ends of the earth."
[These are the myriads of Ephraim,
and these the thousands of Manasseh.]

18 Of Zebulun he said:*m*
"Rejoice, O Zebulun, in your pursuits,
and you, Issachar, in your tents!
19 You who invite the tribes to the mountains

---

b Nm 20, 24ff. 28; 27, 13;
  33, 38.
c Nm 20, 12; 27, 14.
d Dt 3, 27; 34, 4.
e Ex 19, 18. 20; Jgs 5,
  4f.
f Jn 1, 17; 7, 19.
g Gn 49, 3f.
h Gn 49, 8-12.
i Gn 49, 5; Ex 17, 7; 28,
  30; Nm 20, 13.
j Ex 30, 7f.
k Gn 49, 27.
l 13-17: Gn 49, 22-26.
m 18f: Gn 49, 13ff.

---

*

33, 2–5. 26–29: These verses seem to form an independent hymn describing, in the form of a theophany, the conquest of Canaan. The first section of this hymn (vv 2–5) serves here as an introduction to the various "blessings"; the second section (vv 26–29), as their conclusion.

33, 3: His holy ones were in his hand: the Israelites were protected by the Lord.

33, 5. 26: The darling: see note on Dt 32, 15.

33, 6: In keeping with the other blessings, probably this verse was once introduced by the phrase, "Of Reuben he said." It is to be noted that there is no blessing here for Simeon.

33, 7: Bring him to his people: this probably refers to the isolated position of the tribe of Judah during the conquest of the Promised Land (cf Jgs 1, 17–19); according to some commentators the reference is to the divided kingdom.

33, 8: Thummim . . . Urim: see note on Ex 28, 30.

33, 9: The reference is probably to the Levites' slaughter of their brethren after the affair of the golden calf in the desert; cf Ex 32, 27–29.

33, 16: Him who dwells in the bush: a title given to the Lord because of his appearance to Moses in the burning bush; cf Ex 3.

33, 19: The abundance of the seas: perhaps the wealth that

where feasts are duly held,
Because you suck up the abundance of the
seas*
and the hidden treasures of the sand.''

20 Of Gad he said:[n]
''Blessed be he who has made Gad so
vast!
He lies there like a lion
that has seized the arm and head of the
prey.
21 He saw that the best should be his
when the princely portion* was assigned,
while the heads of the people were
gathered.
He carried out the justice of the LORD
and his decrees respecting Israel.''[o]

22 Of Dan he said:
''Dan is a lion's whelp,[p]
that springs forth from Bashan!''*

23 Of Naphtali he said:
''Naphtali is enriched with favors
and filled with the blessings of the LORD;
The lake* and south of it are his
possession!''[q]

24 Of Asher he said:[r]
''More blessed than the other sons be Asher!
May he be the favorite among his brothers,
as the oil of his olive trees runs over his
feet!*
25 May your bolts be of iron and bronze;
may your strength endure through all your
days!''

26 ''There is no god like the God of the
darling,
who rides the heavens in his power,
and rides the skies in his majesty;
27 He spread out the primeval tent;
he extended the ancient canopy.
He drove the enemy out of your way
and the Amorite he destroyed.
28 Israel has dwelt securely,
and the fountain of Jacob has been
undisturbed.
In a land of grain and wine,
where the heavens drip with dew.[s]
29 How fortunate you are, O Israel!
Where else is a nation victorious in the
LORD?
The LORD is your saving shield,
and his sword is your glory.
Your enemies fawn upon you,
as you stride upon their heights.''[t]

CHAPTER 34

Death and Burial of Moses. 1 Then Moses went up from the plains of Moab to Mount Nebo,[u] the headland of Pisgah which faces Jericho, and the LORD showed him all the land—

Gilead, and as far as Dan, 2 all Naphtali, the land of Ephraim and Manasseh, all the land of Judah as far as the Western Sea, 3 the Negeb, the circuit of the Jordan with the lowlands at Jericho, city of palms, and as far as Zoar. 4 The LORD then said to him, ''This is the land[v] which I swore to Abraham, Isaac and Jacob that I would give to their descendants. I have let you feast your eyes upon it, but you shall not cross over.'' 5 So there, in the land of Moab, Moses, the servant of the LORD, died[w] as the LORD had said; 6 and he was buried in the ravine opposite Beth-peor in the land of Moab, but to this day no one knows the place of his burial.
7 Moses was one hundred and twenty years old[x] when he died, yet his eyes were undimmed and his vigor unabated. 8 For thirty days the Israelites wept for Moses in the plains of Moab, till they had completed the period of grief and mourning for Moses.
9 Now Joshua, son of Nun,[y] was filled with the spirit of wisdom, since Moses had laid his hands upon him; and so the Israelites gave him their obedience, thus carrying out the LORD's command to Moses.
10 [z]Since then no prophet has arisen in Israel like Moses, whom the LORD knew face to face. 11 [a]He had no equal in all the signs and wonders the LORD sent him to perform in the land of Egypt against Pharaoh and all his servants and against all his land, 12 and for the might and the terrifying power that Moses exhibited in the sight of all Israel.

---

n 20f: Gn 49, 19.
o Nm 32, 1. 5. 16-19.
  31f; Jos 1, 12-15;
  1 Chr 5, 18-22.
p Gn 49, 16f.
q Gn 49, 21; Jos 19,
  32-39.
r 24f: Gn 49, 20.
s Gn 27, 28.
t Dt 4, 7f.

u Dt 3, 27.
v Dt 3, 27; 32, 52; Gn
  12, 7; 15, 18.
w Dt 32, 50.
x Dt 31, 2.
y Nm 27, 18. 23; Jos 1,
  17.
z Ex 33, 11.
a Dt 4, 34.

*

---

comes from sea-borne trade or from fishing. The hidden treasures of the sand: possibly an allusion to the valuable purple dye extracted from certain marine shells found on the coast of northern Palestine.
33, 21: The princely portion: Moses gave the tribe of Gad their land on the east of the Jordan only on condition that they would help the other tribes conquer the land west of the river; cf Nm 32; Jos 22.
33, 22: The sense is, ''May he leap up like a lion of Bashan''; the heavily wooded hills of Bashan were notorious for their lions, but the tribe of Dan was not settled in this region.
33, 23: The lake: the Lake of Gennesaret on which the land of this tribe bordered.
33, 24: The land of the tribe of Asher was covered with olive groves.

The Book of

JOSHUA

The Book of Joshua derives its name from the successor of Moses, with whose deeds it is principally concerned. The purpose of the book is to demonstrate God's fidelity in giving to the Israelites the land he had promised them for an inheritance (Gn 15, 18ff; Jos 1, 2ff; 21, 41ff; 23, 14ff).

Their occupation of the country is begun with the crossing of the Jordan and the conquest of Jericho (ch 1–6), in both of which the Lord intervenes on their behalf. This is followed by a first foothold on the Palestinian mountain range, at Ai, Bethel and Gibeon (ch 7–9), and two sweeping campaigns against the city states in the south of the country (ch 10) and in the north (ch 11), with a summary in ch 12. The broad claim to total sovereignty thus established is spelled out by a combined list of tribal boundaries and of the towns contained within each area or administrative district (ch 13–19), including cities of asylum and cities for the Levites (ch 20, 21). The book closes with a narrative about the tribes east of the Jordan (ch 22), a warning speech by Joshua (ch 23), and a renewal at Shechem (ch 24) of the covenant with the Lord, already affirmed there near the beginning (8, 30–35) of the conquest.

Like the books which precede it, the Book of Joshua was built up by a long and complex process of editing traditional materials. Both Jewish and Christian believers have always regarded it as inspired.

The entire history of the conquest of the Promised Land is a prophecy of the spiritual conquest of the world through the church under the leadership of Jesus the Messiah.

The Book of Joshua may be divided as follows:
I. Conquest of Canaan (Jos 1, 1–12, 24).
II. Division of the Land (Jos 13, 1–21, 45).
III. Return of the Transjordan Tribes and Joshua's Farewell (Jos 22, 1–24, 33).

I: Conquest of Canaan

CHAPTER 1

Divine Promise of Assistance.   **1** After Moses, the servant of the LORD, had died, the LORD said to Moses' aid Joshua, son of Nun: **2** "My servant Moses is dead. So prepare to cross the Jordan here, with all the people, into the land I will give the Israelites. **3** As I promised Moses, I will deliver to you every place where you set foot. **4** *Your domain is to be all the land of the Hittites, from the desert and from Lebanon east to the great river Euphrates and west to the Great Sea.*[a] **5** No one can withstand you while you live. I will be with you as I was with Moses:[b] I will not leave you nor forsake you. **6** Be firm and steadfast, so that you may give this people possession of the land which I swore to their fathers I would give them. **7** Above all, be firm and steadfast, taking care to observe the entire law which my servant Moses enjoined on you. Do not swerve from it either to the right or to the left, that you may

succeed wherever you go. **8** Keep this book of the law on your lips. Recite it by day and by night, that you may observe carefully all that is written in it; then you will successfully attain your goal. **9** I command you: be firm and steadfast! Do not fear nor be dismayed, for the LORD, your God, is with you wherever you go."[c]

10 So Joshua commanded the officers of the people: **11** "Go through the camp and instruct the people, 'Prepare your provisions, for three days from now you shall cross the Jordan here, to march in and take possession of the land which the LORD, your God, is giving you.'"[d]

The Transjordan Tribes.   **12** Joshua reminded the Reubenites, the Gadites, and the half-tribe of Manasseh: **13** "Remember what Moses, the servant of the LORD, commanded

---

a 3f: Jos 14, 9; Gn 15,
18; Dt 11, 24.
b Dt 31, 8; Heb 13, 5.
c 7. 9: Dt 31, 7f.
d Dt 11, 31.

*

1, 4: The ideal frontiers are given: in the south the desert of Sinai, in the north the Lebanon range, in the east the Euphrates, and in the west the Great Sea, the Mediterranean.

you when he said, The LORD, your God, will permit you to settle in this land.'' **14** Your wives, your children, and your livestock shall remain in the land Moses gave you here beyond the Jordan.*e* But all the warriors among you must cross over armed ahead of your kinsmen and you must help them **15** until the LORD has settled your kinsmen, and they like you possess the land which the LORD, your God, is giving them. Afterward you may return and occupy your own land, which Moses, the servant of the LORD, has given you east of the Jordan.''*f* **16** "We will do all you have commanded us," they answered Joshua, "and we will go wherever you send us. We will obey you as completely as we obeyed Moses. **17** But may the LORD, your God, be with you as he was with Moses. **18** If anyone rebels against your orders and does not obey every command you give him, he shall be put to death. But be firm and steadfast.''

CHAPTER 2

Spies Saved by Rahab.   **1** Then Joshua, son of Nun, secretly sent out two spies from Shittim, saying, "Go, reconnoiter the land and Jericho.'' When the two reached Jericho, they went into the house of a harlot* named Rahab,*g* where they lodged. **2** But a report was brought to the king of Jericho that some Israelites had come there that night to spy out the land. **3** So the king of Jericho sent Rahab the order, "Put out the visitors who have entered your house, for they have come to spy out the entire land.'' **4** The woman*h* had taken the two men and hidden them, so she said, "True, the men you speak of came to me, but I did not know where they came from. **5** At dark, when it was time for the gate to be shut, they left, and I do not know where they went. You will have to pursue them immediately to overtake them.'' **6** Now, she had led them to the roof, and hidden them among her stalks of flax spread out* there. **7** But the pursuers set out along the way to the fords of the Jordan, and once they had left, the gate was shut.

8 Before the spies fell asleep, Rahab* came to them on the roof **9** and said: "I know that the LORD has given you the land, that a dread of you had come upon us, and that all the inhabitants of the land are overcome with fear of you.*i* **10** For we have heard how the LORD dried up the waters of the Red Sea before you when you came out of Egypt,*j* and how you dealt with Sihon and Og, the two kings of the Amorites beyond the Jordan, whom you doomed to destruction. **11** At these reports, we are disheartened; everyone is discouraged because of you, since the LORD, your God, is God in heaven above and on earth below.*k* **12** Now then,

swear to me by the LORD that, since I am showing kindness to you, you in turn will show kindness to my family;*l* and give me an unmistakable token **13** that you are to spare my father and mother, brothers and sisters, and all their kin, and save us from death.'' **14** "We pledge our lives for yours,'' the men answered her. "If you do not betray this errand of ours, we will be faithful in showing kindness to you when the LORD gives us the land.''

15 Then she let them down through the window with a rope; for she lived in a house built into the city wall.* **16** "Go up into the hill country,'' she suggested to them, "that your pursuers may not find you. Hide there for three days, until they return; then you may proceed on your way.'' **17** The men answered her, "This is how we will fulfill the oath you made us take: **18** When we come into the land, tie this scarlet cord in the window through which you are letting us down; and gather your father and mother, your brothers and all your family into your house. **19** Should any of them pass outside the doors of your house, he will be responsible for his own death, and we shall be guiltless. But we shall be responsible if anyone in the house with you is harmed. **20** If, however, you betray this errand of ours, we shall be quit of the oath you have made us take.'' **21** "Let it be as you say,'' she replied, and bade them farewell. When they were gone, she tied the scarlet cord in the window.

22 They went up into the hills, where they stayed three days until their pursuers, who had sought them all along the road without finding them, returned. **23** Then the two came back down from the hills, crossed the Jordan to Joshua, son of Nun, and reported all that had befallen them. **24** They assured Joshua, "The LORD has delivered all this land into our power; in-

---

e Nm 32, 26.
f Jos 22, 4; Dt 3, 20.
g Mt 1, 5; Jas 2, 25.
h Jos 6, 17.
i Ex 15, 15f; 23, 27.

j Jos 4, 23; Ex 14, 21; Nm 21, 23-26. 33ff.
k Dt 4, 39.
l Jos 2, 18; 6, 23. 25.

---

*

2, 1:   Harlot: this is the regular equivalent of the Hebrew word, but perhaps it is used here of Rahab in the broader sense of a woman who kept a public house. Joshua's spies hoped to remain undetected at such an inn.

2, 6:   Stalks of flax spread out: to dry in the sun, after they had been soaked in water, according to the ancient process of preparing flax for linen-making. In the Near East the flax harvest occurs near the time of the feast of the Passover (Jos 4, 19; 5, 10); cf Ex 9, 31.

2, 8–11:   Rahab's faith and good works are praised in the New Testament; cf Heb 11, 31; Jas 2, 25.

2, 15:   A house built into the city wall: such houses, which used the city wall for their own inner walls, have been found at ancient sites. The upper story of Rahab's house was evidently higher than the city wall. It was through the window of such a house that St. Paul escaped from Damascus; cf Acts 9, 25; 2 Cor 11, 33.

deed, all the inhabitants of the land are overcome with fear of us.''

CHAPTER 3

Preparations for Crossing the Jordan.

1 Early the next morning, Joshua*m* moved with all the Israelites from Shittim to the Jordan, where they lodged before crossing over. **2** Three days later the officers went through the camp **3** and issued these instructions to the people: ''When you see the ark of the covenant of the LORD, your God, which the levitical priests will carry, you must also break camp and follow it, **4** that you may know the way to take, for you have not gone over this road before. But let there be a space of two thousand cubits between you and the ark. Do not come nearer to it.'' **5** Joshua also said to the people, ''Sanctify yourselves, for tomorrow the LORD will perform wonders among you.'' **6** And he directed the priests to take up the ark of the covenant and go on ahead of the people; and they did so.

7 Then the LORD said to Joshua, ''Today I will begin to exalt you in the sight of all Israel, that they may know I am with you, as I was with Moses.*n* **8** Now command the priests carrying the ark of the covenant to come to a halt in the Jordan when they reach the edge of the waters.''

9 So Joshua said to the Israelites, ''Come here and listen to the words of the LORD, your God.'' **10** He continued: ''This is how you will know that there is a living God in your midst, who at your approach will dispossess the Canaanites, Hittites, Hivites, Perizzites, Girgashites, Amorites and Jebusites.*o* **11** The ark of the covenant of the LORD of the whole earth will precede you into the Jordan. **12** [Now choose twelve men,*p* one from each of the tribes of Israel.] **13** When the soles of the feet of the priests carrying the ark of the LORD, the Lord of the whole earth, touch the water of the Jordan, it will cease to flow; for the water flowing down from upstream will halt in a solid bank.''

The Crossing Begun.

14 The people struck their tents to cross the Jordan, with the priests carrying the ark of the covenant ahead of them. **15** No sooner had these priestly bearers of the ark waded into the waters at the edge of the Jordan, which overflows all its banks during the entire season of the harvest,* **16** than the waters flowing from upstream halted, backing up in a solid mass*q* for a very great distance indeed, from Adam, a city in the direction of Zarethan; while those flowing downstream toward the Salt Sea of the Arabah disappeared entirely.* Thus the people crossed over opposite Jericho. **17** While all Israel crossed over on dry ground, the priests carrying the ark of the covenant of the LORD remained motionless on dry ground in the bed of the Jordan*r* until the whole nation had completed the passage.

CHAPTER 4

Memorial Stones.

1 After the entire nation had crossed the Jordan, the LORD said to Joshua, **2** ''Choose twelve men*s* from the people, one from each tribe, **3** and instruct them to take up twelve stones from this spot in the bed of the Jordan where the priests have been standing motionless.*t* Carry them over with you, and place them where you are to stay tonight.''

4 Summoning the twelve men whom he had selected from among the Israelites, one from each tribe, **5** Joshua said to them: ''Go to the bed of the Jordan in front of the ark of the LORD, your God; lift to your shoulders one stone apiece, so that they will equal in number the tribes of the Israelites. **6** In the future, these are to be a sign among you. When your children ask you what these stones mean to you, **7** you shall answer them, 'The waters of the Jordan ceased to flow before the ark of the covenant of the LORD when it crossed the Jordan.'*u* Thus these stones are to serve as a perpetual memorial to the Israelites.'' **8** The twelve Israelites did as Joshua had commanded: they took up as many stones from the bed of the Jordan as there were tribes of the Israelites, and carried them along to the camp site, where they placed them, according to the LORD's direction. **9** Josua also had twelve stones set up in the bed of the Jordan on the spot where the priests stood who were carrying the ark of the covenant. They are there to this day.

10 *The priests carrying the ark remained in the bed of the Jordan until everything had been done that the LORD had commanded Joshua to tell the people. The people crossed over quick-

m Jos 2, 1.
n Jos 1, 5; 4, 14.
o Ex 33, 2; Dt 7, 1.
p Jos 4, 2. 4.
q Ps 114, 3.

r Jos 4, 7. 22.
s Jos 3, 12.
t Jos 3, 13; 4, 8f; Dt 27, 2.
u Jos 3, 13. 16.

*

3, 15: Season of the harvest: toward the end of March and the beginning of April, when the grain and other crops that grew during the rainy season of winter were reaped. The crossing took place ''on the tenth day of the first month'' of the Hebrew year, which began with the first new moon after the spring equinox; cf Jos 4, 19. At this time of the year the Jordan would be swollen as a result of the winter rains and the melting snow of Mount Hermon.

3, 16: The sudden damming of the river could have been caused by a landslide, as has happened on other occasions. The miraculous character of this event would not thereby be removed because God, who foretold it (Jos 3, 13), also caused it to take place at precisely the right moment (Jos 3, 15), whether or not he used natural forces to accomplish his will.

4, 10–18: After the digression about the two sets of memorial stones, the author resumes the narrative by briefly repeating the story of the crossing, which he had already told in Jos 3, 14–17.

ly, **11** and when all had reached the other side, the ark of the LORD, borne by the priests, also crossed to its place in front of them. **12** The Reubenites, Gadites, and half-tribe of Manasseh, armed, marched in the vanguard of the Israelites, as Moses had ordered.^{v} **13** About forty thousand troops equipped for battle passed over before the LORD to the plains of Jericho.

14 That day the LORD exalted Joshua in the sight of all Israel,^{w} and thenceforth during his whole life they respected him as they had respected Moses.

15 Then the LORD said to Joshua, **16** "Command the priests carrying the ark of the commandments to come up from the Jordan."^{x} **17** Joshua did so, **18** and when the priests carrying the ark of the covenant of the LORD had come up from the bed of the Jordan, as the soles of their feet regained the dry ground, the waters of the Jordan resumed their course and as before overflowed all its banks.

19 The people came up from the Jordan on the tenth day of the first month, and camped in Gilgal on the eastern limits of Jericho. **20** At Gilgal Joshua set up the twelve stones which had been taken from the Jordan, **21** saying to the Israelites, "In the future, when the children among you ask their fathers what these stones mean, **22** you shall inform them, 'Israel crossed the Jordan here on dry ground.' **23** For the LORD, your God, dried up the waters of the Jordan in front of you until you crossed over, just as the LORD, your God, had done at the Red Sea, which he dried up in front of us until we crossed over;^{y} **24** in order that all the peoples of the earth may learn that the hand of the LORD is mighty, and that you may fear the LORD, your God, forever."

CHAPTER 5

Rites at Gilgal. **1** When all the kings of Amorites to the west of the Jordan and all the kings of the Canaanites by the sea heard that the LORD had dried up the waters of the Jordan before the Israelites until they crossed over, they were disheartened and lost courage at their approach.

2 On this occasion the LORD said to Joshua, "Make flint knives and circumcise the Israelite nation for the second time." **3** So Joshua made flint knives and circumcised the Israelites at Gibeath-haaraloth,* **4** under these circumstances: Of all the people who came out of Egypt, every man of military age had died in the desert^z during the journey after they left Egypt. **5** Though all the men who came out were circumcised, none of those born in the desert during the journey after the departure from Egypt were circumcised. **6** Now the Israelites had wandered forty years in the desert, until all the

warriors among the people that came forth from Egypt died off because they had not obeyed the command of the LORD.^{a} For the LORD swore^b that he would not let them see the land flowing with milk and honey which he had promised their fathers he would give us. **7** ^{c}It was the children whom he raised up in their stead whom Joshua circumcised, for these were yet with foreskins, not having been circumcised on the journey. **8** When the rite had been performed, the whole nation remained in camp where they were, until they recovered. **9** Then the LORD said to Joshua, "Today I have removed the reproach of Egypt from you."^{d} Therefore the place is called Gilgal* to the present day.

10 ^{e}While the Israelites were encamped at Gilgal on the plains of Jericho, they celebrated the Passover on the evening of the fourteenth of the month.* **11** On the day after the Passover they ate of the produce of the land in the form of unleavened cakes and parched grain. On that same day **12** after the Passover on which they ate of the produce of the land, the manna ceased. No longer was there manna for the Israelites, who that year ate of the yield of the land of Canaan.^{f}

Siege at Jericho. **13** *While Joshua was near Jericho, he raised his eyes and saw one who stood facing him, drawn sword in hand.^{g} Joshua went up to him and asked, "Are you one of us or of our enemies?" **14** He replied, "Neither. I am the captain of the host of the LORD and I have just arrived." Then Joshua fell prostrate to the ground in worship, and said to him, "What has my lord to say to his servant?" **15** The captain of the host of the LORD replied to Joshua, "Remove your sandals from your feet, for the place on which you are standing is holy."^{h} And Joshua obeyed.

---

v Dt 3, 18.
w Jos 3, 7.
x Jos 3, 6.
y Ex 14, 21.
z Nm 14, 29; 26, 64f; Dt 2, 16; Ps 106, 26; 1 Cor 10, 5.
a Nm 14, 29.
b Heb 3, 11. 17.
c Dt 1, 39.
d Jos 4, 19.
e Ex 12, 6; Lv 23, 5; Nm 9, 3-5.
f Ex 16, 35.
g Ex 23, 20.
h Ex 3, 5; Acts 7, 33.

5, 3: Gibeath-haaraloth: "Hill of the Foreskins."

5, 9: The place is called Gilgal: by popular etymology, because of the similarity of sound with the Hebrew word gallothi, "I have removed." Gilgal probably means "(the place of) the circle of standing stones." Cf Jos 4, 4–8.

5, 10: The month: the first month of the year, later called Nisan; see note on Jos 3, 15. The crossing of the Jordan occurred, therefore, about the same time of the year as did the equally miraculous crossing of the Red Sea; cf Ex 12–14.

5, 13–6, 26: The account of the siege of Jericho embraces: (1) the command of the Lord, through his angel, to Joshua (Jos 5, 13–6, 5); (2) Joshua's instructions to the Israelites, with a brief summary of how these orders were carried out (Jos 6, 6–11); (3) a description of the action on each of the first six days (Jos 6, 12–14); (4) the events on the seventh day (Jos 6, 15–26).

CHAPTER 6

1 Now Jericho was in a state of siege because of the presence of the Israelites, so that no one left or entered. **2** And to Joshua the LORD said, ''I have delivered Jericho and its king into your power. **3** Have all the soldiers circle the city, marching once around it. Do this for six days, **4** [i]with seven priests carrying ram's horns ahead of the ark. On the seventh day march around the city seven times, and have the priests blow the horns. **5** When they give a long blast on the ram's horns and you hear that signal, all the people shall shout aloud. The wall of the city will collapse, and they will be able to make a frontal attack.''

6 Summoning the priests, Joshua, son of Nun, then ordered them to take up the ark of the covenant with seven of the priests carrying ram's horns in front of the ark of the LORD. **7** And he ordered the people to proceed in a circle around the city, with the picked troops marching ahead of the ark of the LORD. **8** At this order they proceeded, with the seven priests who carried the ram's horns before the LORD blowing their horns, and the ark of the covenant of the LORD following them. **9** In front of the priests with the horns marched the picked troops; the rear-guard followed the ark, and the blowing of horns was kept up continually as they marched. **10** But the people had been commanded by Joshua not to shout or make any noise or outcry until he gave the word: only then were they to shout. **11** So he had the ark of the LORD circle the city, going once around it, after which they returned to camp for the night.

12 Early the next morning, Joshua had the priests take up the ark of the LORD. **13** The seven priests bearing the ram's horns marched in front of the ark of the LORD, blowing their horns. Ahead of these marched the picked troops, while the rear guard followed the ark of the LORD, and the blowing of horns was kept up continually. **14** On this second day they again marched around the city once before returning to camp; and for six days in all they did the same.

15 On the seventh day, beginning at daybreak, they marched around the city seven times in the same manner; on that day only did they march around the city seven times. **16** The seventh time around, the priests blew the horns and Joshua said to the people, ''Now shout, for the LORD has given you the city **17** and everything in it.[j] It is under the LORD's ban. Only the harlot Rahab and all who are in the house with her are to be spared, because she hid the messengers we sent. **18** [k]But be careful not to take, in your greed, anything that is under the ban;* else you will bring upon the camp of Israel this ban and the misery of it. **19** All silver and gold, and the articles of bronze or iron, are sacred to the LORD. They shall be put in the treasury of the LORD.''

The Fall of Jericho. **20** As the horns blew, the people began to shout. When they heard the signal horn, they raised a tremendous shout. The wall collapsed,* and the people stormed the city in a frontal attack and took it.[l] **21** They observed the ban by putting to the sword all living creatures[m] in the city: men and women, young and old, as well as oxen, sheep and asses.

22 Joshua directed the two men who had spied out the land, ''Go into the harlot's house and bring out the woman with all her kin, as you swore to her you would do.''[n] **23** The spies entered and brought out Rahab, with her father, mother, brothers, and all her kin.[o] Her entire family they led forth and placed them outside the camp of Israel. **24** The city itself they burned with all that was in it,[p] except the silver, gold, and articles of bronze and iron, which were placed in the treasury of the house of the LORD. **25** *Because Rahab the harlot had hidden the messengers whom Joshua had sent to reconnoiter Jericho, Joshua spared her with her family and all her kin, who continue in the midst of Israel to this day.

26 [q]On that occasion Joshua imposed the oath: Cursed before the LORD be the man who attempts to rebuild this city, Jericho. He shall lose his first-born when he lays its foundation, and he shall lose his youngest son when he sets up its gates.*

27 Thus the LORD was with Joshua so that his fame spread throughout the land.[r]

CHAPTER 7

Defeat at Ai. **1** But the Israelites violated the ban; Achan, son of Carmi, son of Zerah, son of Zara of the tribe of Judah, took goods that

---

i Nm 10, 8f.
j Jos 2, 4; Dt 20, 17; Heb 11, 31.
k Jos 7, 12. 25; Dt 13, 18.
l 2 Mc 12, 15; Heb 11, 30.
m Dt 7, 2.
n Jos 2, 14.
o Jos 2, 13; Heb 11, 31.
p Jos 8, 2.
q 1 Kgs 16, 34.
r Jos 1, 5.
s Jos 6, 18; 22, 20; 1 Chr 2, 7.

6, 18: That is under the ban: that is doomed to destruction; see notes on Lv 27, 29; Nm 18, 14; 21, 3.

6, 20: The wall collapsed: by the miraculous intervention of God. The blowing of the horns and the shouting of the people were a customary feature of ancient warfare, here intended by God as a test of the people's obedience and of their faith in his promise; cf Heb 11, 30.

6, 25: From Mt 1, 5, we learn that Rahab married Salmon of the tribe of Judah and thus became the great-great-grandmother of David, Christ's ancestor; cf Ru 4, 18–22.

6, 26: He shall lose his first-born . . . its gates: this curse was fulfilled when Hiel rebuilt Jericho as a fortified city during the reign of Ahab, king of Israel, cf 1 Kgs 16, 34. Till then Jericho was merely an unwalled village; cf Jos 18, 12. 21; Jgs 3, 13; 2 Sm 10, 5.

were under the ban,[s] and the anger of the LORD flared up against the Israelites.

2 Joshua next sent men from Jericho to Ai, which is near Bethel on its eastern side, with instructions to go up and reconnoiter the land. When they had explored Ai, **3** they returned to Joshua and advised, "Do not send all the people up; if only about two or three thousand go up, they can overcome Ai. The enemy there are few; you need not call for an effort from all the people." **4** About three thousand of the people made the attack, but they were defeated by those at Ai, **5** who killed some thirty-six of them. They pressed them back across the clearing in front of the city gate till they broke ranks, and defeated them finally on the descent, so that the confidence of the people melted away like water.

6 Joshua, together with the elders of Israel, rent his garments and lay prostrate before the ark of the LORD until evening; and they threw dust on their heads. **7** "Alas, O Lord GOD," Joshua prayed, "why did you ever allow this people to pass over the Jordan, delivering us into the power of the Amorites, that they might destroy us? Would that we had been content to dwell on the other side of the Jordan. **8** Pray, Lord, what can I say, now that Israel has turned its back to its enemies? **9** When the Canaanites and the other inhabitants of the land hear of it, they will close in around us and efface our name from the earth. What will you do for your great name?"

10 The LORD replied to Joshua: "Stand up. Why are you lying prostrate? **11** [t]Israel has sinned: they have violated the covenant which I enjoined on them. They have stealthily taken goods subject to the ban, and have deceitfully put them in their baggage. **12** If the Israelites cannot stand up to their enemies, but must turn their back to them, it is because they are under the ban.[u] I will not remain with you unless you remove from among you whoever has incurred the ban. **13** Rise, sanctify the people.[v] Tell them to sanctify themselves before tomorrow, for the LORD, the God of Israel, says: You are under the ban, O Israel. You cannot stand up to your enemies until you remove from among you whoever has incurred the ban. **14** In the morning you must present yourselves by tribes. The tribe which the LORD designates shall come forward by clans; the clan which the LORD designates shall come forward by families; the family which the LORD designates shall come forward one by one. **15** He who is designated as having incurred the ban shall be destroyed by fire, with all that is his, because he has violated the covenant of the LORD and has committed a shameful crime in Israel."

Achan's Guilt and Punishment. **16** Early the next morning Joshua had Israel come forward by tribes, and the tribe of Judah was designated.* **17** Then he had the clans of Judah come forward, and the clan of Zerah was designated. He had the clan of Zerah[w] come forward by families, and Zabdi was designated. **18** Finally he had that family come forward one by one, and Achan, son of Carmi, son of Zabdi, son of Zerah of the tribe of Judah, was designated. **19** Joshua said to Achan, "My son, give to the LORD, the God of Israel, glory and honor by telling me what you have done; do not hide it from me." **20** Achan answered Joshua, "I have indeed sinned against the LORD, the God of Israel. This is what I have done: **21** Among the spoils, I saw a beautiful Babylonian mantle, two hundred shekels of silver, and a bar of gold fifty shekels in weight; in my greed I took them. They are now hidden in the ground inside my tent, with the silver underneath." **22** The messengers whom Joshua sent hastened to the tent and found them hidden there, with the silver underneath. **23** They took them from the tent, brought them to Joshua and all the Israelites, and spread them out before the LORD.

24 Then Joshua and all Israel took Achan, son of Zerah, with the silver, the mantle, and the bar of gold, and with his sons and daughters, his ox, his ass and his sheep, his tent, and all his possessions, and led them off to the Valley of Achor. **25** Joshua said, "The LORD bring upon you today the misery with which you have afflicted us!"[x] And all Israel stoned him to death **26** and piled a great heap of stones over him, which remains to the present day.[y] Then the anger of the LORD relented. That is why the place is called the Valley of Achor* to this day.

CHAPTER 8

Capture of Ai. **1** The LORD then said to Joshua, "Do not be afraid or dismayed. Take all the army with you and prepare to attack Ai.[z] I have delivered the king of Ai into your power, with his people, city, and land. **2** Do to Ai and its king what you did to Jericho and its king; except that you may take its spoil and livestock as booty.[a] Set an ambush behind the city."

---

t Jos 6, 17-19.
u Jos 6, 18.
v Jos 3, 5; Lv 20, 7;
　1 Sm 16, 5.
w Nm 26, 20.
x Jos 6, 18; 22, 20;

1 Chr 2, 7.
y Jos 8, 29.
z Jos 2, 24.
a Jos 6, 21. 24; Dt 20, 14.

---

*

7, 16ff: Was designated: probably by means of the Urim and Thummim; cf 1 Sm 14, 38–42. See note on Ex 28, 30.

7, 26: Achor: "misery, affliction." The reference is to the saying of Joshua in v 25, with an allusion also to the similar-sounding name of Achan.

3 So Joshua and all the soldiers prepared to attack Ai. Picking out thirty thousand warriors,* Joshua sent them off by night **4** with these orders: "See that you ambush the city from the rear, at no great distance; then all of you be on the watch. **5** The rest of the people and I will come up to the city, and when they make a sortie against us as they did the last time, we will flee from them. **6** They will keep coming out after us until we have drawn them away from the city, for they will think we are fleeing from them as we did the last time. When this occurs, **7** rise from ambush and take possession of the city, which the LORD, your God, will deliver into your power. **8** When you have taken the city, set it afire in obedience to the LORD's command. These are my orders to you." **9** Then Joshua sent them away. They went to the place of ambush, taking up their position to the west of Ai, toward Bethel. Joshua, however, spent that night in the plain.

10 Early the next morning Joshua mustered the army and went up to Ai at its head, with the elders of Israel. **11** When all the troops he led were drawn up in position before the city, they pitched camp north of Ai, on the other side of the ravine. **12** [He took about five thousand men and set them in ambush between Bethel and Ai, west of the city.] **13** Thus the people took up their stations, with the main body north of the city and the ambush west of it, and Joshua waited overnight among his troops. **14** The king of Ai saw this, and he and all his army came out very early in the morning to engage Israel in battle at the descent toward the Arabah, not knowing that there was an ambush behind the city. **15** Joshua and the main body of the Israelites fled in seeming defeat toward the desert, **16** till the last of the soldiers in the city had been called out to pursue them. **17** Since they were drawn away from the city, with every man engaged in this pursuit of Joshua and the Israelites, not a soldier remained in Ai [or Bethel], and the city was open and unprotected.

18 Then the LORD directed Joshua, "Stretch out the javelin in your hand toward Ai, for I will deliver it into your power." Joshua stretched out the javelin in his hand toward the city, **19** and as soon as he did so, the men in ambush rose from their post, rushed in, captured the city, and immediately set it on fire. **20** By the time the men of Ai looked back, the smoke from the city was already sky-high. Escape in any direction was impossible, because the Israelites retreating toward the desert now turned on their pursuers; **21** for when Joshua and the main body of Israelites saw that the city had been taken from ambush and was going up in smoke, they struck back at the men of Ai. **22** Since those in the city came out to intercept them, the men of Ai were hemmed in by Israelites on either side, who cut them down without any fugitives or survivors[b] **23** except the king, whom they took alive and brought to Joshua.

24 All the inhabitants of Ai who had pursued the Israelites into the desert were slain by the sword there in the open, down to the last man. Then all Israel returned and put to the sword those inside the city. **25** There fell that day a total of twelve thousand men and women, the entire population of Ai. **26** [c]Joshua kept the javelin in his hand stretched out until he had fulfilled the doom on all the inhabitants of Ai. **27** However, the Israelites took for themselves as booty the livestock and the spoil of that city, according to the command of the LORD issued to Joshua. **28** Then Joshua destroyed the place by fire, reducing it to an everlasting mound of ruins, as it remains today.[d] **29** He had the king of Ai hanged on a tree until evening;[e] then at sunset Joshua ordered the body removed from the tree and cast at the entrance of the city gate, where a great heap of stones was piled up over it, which remains to the present day.

Altar on Mount Ebal.   **30** *Later Joshua built an altar to the LORD, the God of Israel, on Mount Ebal, **31** of unhewn stones on which no iron tool had been used,[f] in keeping with the command to the Israelites of Moses, the servant of the LORD, as recorded in the book of the law. On this altar they offered holocausts and peace offerings to the LORD. **32** There, in the presence of the Israelites, Joshua inscribed upon the stones a copy of the law written by Moses.[g] **33** And all Israel, stranger and native alike, with their elders, officers and judges, stood on either side of the ark facing the levitical priests who were carrying the ark of the covenant of the LORD.[h] Half of them were facing Mount Gerizim and half Mount Ebal, thus carrying out the instructions of Moses, the servant of the LORD, for the blessing of the people of Israel on this first occasion. **34** [i]Then were read aloud all the words of the law, the blessings and the curses, exactly as written in the book of the law. **35** [j]Every single word that Moses had commanded, Joshua read aloud to the entire com-

---

b Dt 7, 2.
c Ex 17, 11ff.
d Dt 13, 16.
e Jos 10, 26f; Dt 21, 22f;
   Jn 19, 31.
f Ex 20, 24f; Dt 27, 5f.

g Dt 27, 2. 8.
h Jos 3, 3; Dt 11, 27;
   27, 12; 31, 9. 12.
i Dt 28, 2-68; 30, 19; 31,
   11; Neh 8, 2f.
j Dt 31, 12.

*

8, 3: Thirty thousand warriors: this figure of the Hebrew text, which seems extremely high, may be due to a copyist's error; some manuscripts of the Septuagint have "three thousand," which is the number of the whole army in the first, unsuccessful attack (Jos 7, 4); the variant reading in v 12 mentions "five thousand."

8, 30–35: These ceremonies were prescribed in Dt 11, 29, and Dt 27, 2–26. See notes on those passages.

munity, including the women and children, and the strangers who had accompanied Israel.

CHAPTER 9

Confederacy against Israel. 1 When the news reached the kings west of the Jordan, in the mountain regions and in the foothills, and all along the coast of the Great Sea as far as Lebanon: Hittites, Amorites, Canaanites, Perizzites, Hivites and Jebusites,k 2 they all formed an alliance to launch a common attack against Joshua and Israel.

The Gibeonite Deception. 3 On learning what Joshua had done to Jericho and Ai, the inhabitants of Gibeonl 4 put into effect a device of their own. They chose provisions for a journey, making use of old sacks for their asses, and old wineskins, torn and mended. 5 They wore old, patched sandals and shabby garments; and all the bread they took was dry and crumbly. 6 Thus they journed to Joshua in the camp at Gilgal, where they said to him and to the men of Israel, "We have come from a distant land to propose that you make an alliance with us."m 7 But the men of Israel replied to the Hivites,* "You may be living in land that is ours. How, then, can we make an alliance with you?" 8 But they answered Joshua, "We are your servants." Then Joshua asked them, "Who are you? Where do you come from?" 9 They answered him, "Your servants have come from a far-off land, because of the fame of the LORD, your God. For we have heard reports of all that he did in Egyptn 10 and all that he did to the two kings of the Amorites beyond the Jordan,o Sihon, king of Heshbon, and Og, king of Bashan, who lived in Ashtaroth. 11 So our elders and all the inhabitants of our country said to us, 'Take along provisions for the journey and go to meet them. Say to them: We are your servants; we propose that you make an alliance with us.' 12 This bread of ours was still warm when we brought it from home as provisions the day we left to come to you, but now it is dry and crumbled. 13 Here are our wineskins, which were new when we filled them, but now they are torn. Look at our garments and sandals, which are worn out from the very long journey." 14 Then the Israelite princes partook of their provisions, without seeking the advice of the LORD.p 15 So Joshua made an alliance with them and entered into an agreement to spare them,q which the princes of the community sealed with an oath.

Gibeonites Made Vassals. 16 Three days after the agreement was entered into, the Israelites learned that these people were from nearby, and would be living in Israel. 17 The third day on the road, the Israelites came to their cities of Gibeon, Chephirah, Beeroth and Kiriath-jearim, 18 but did not attack them, because the princes of the community had sworn to them by the LORD, the God of Israel. When the entire community grumbled against the princes, 19 these all remonstrated with the people, "We have sworn to them by the LORD, the God of Israel, and so we cannot harm them. 20 Let us therefore spare their lives and so deal with them that we shall not be punished for the oath we have sworn to them." 21 Thus the princes recommended that they be let live, as hewers of wood and drawers of water* for the entire community; and the community did as the princes advised them.

22 Joshua summoned the Gibeonites and said to them, "Why did you lie to us and say that you lived at a great distance from us, when you will be living in our very midst? 23 For this are you accursed: every one of you shall always be a slave [hewers of wood and drawers of water] for the house of my God." 24 They answered Joshua, "Your servants were fully informed of how the LORD, your God, commanded his servant Moses that you be given the entire land and that all its inhabitants be destroyed before you. Since, therefore, at your advance, we were in great fear for our lives, we acted as we did.r 25 And now that we are in your power, do with us what you think fit and right." 26 *Joshua did what he had decided: while he saved them from being killed by the Israelites, 27 at the same time he made them, as they still are, hewers of wood and drawers of water for the community and for the altar of the LORD, in the place of the LORD's choice.s

CHAPTER 10

The Siege of Gibeon. 1 Now Adonizedek, king of Jerusalem, heard that, in the capture and destruction of Ai, Joshua had done to that city and its king as he had done to Jericho and its king.t He heard also that the inhabitants of Gibeon had made their peace with Israel,

---

k Jos 3, 10; Ex 3, 8. 17;　　p Nm 27, 21.
　　23, 23; Dt 1, 7.　　　　　q Jos 11, 19; 2 Sm 21, 2.
l Jos 6, 21. 24; 11, 19.　　r Ex 23, 27f; Dt 7, 1f.
m Ex 23, 32; Dt 7, 2.　　　s Dt 12, 5.
n Jos 2, 10.　　　　　　　t Jos 9, 15; 6, 21. 24; 8,
o Nm 21. 25. 33.　　　　　　26-29.

*

9, 7: The Hivites: apparently the Gibeonites belonged to this larger ethnic group (cf also Jos 11, 19), although in 2 Sm 21, 2 they are classed as Amorites; both groups are listed among the seven nations in Canaan whom the Israelites were to exterminate; cf Dt 7, 1f.

9, 21: Hewers of wood and drawers of water: proverbial terms for the lowest social class in the Israelite community; cf Dt 29, 10f.

9, 26f: Later on, Saul violated the immunity of the Gibeonites, but David vindicated it; cf 2 Sm 21, 1–9.

remaining among them, **2** and that there was great fear abroad, because Gibeon was large enough for a royal city, larger even than the city of Ai, and all its men were brave. **3** So Adonizedek, king of Jerusalem, sent for Hoham, king of Hebron, Piram, king of Jarmuth, Japhia, king of Lachish, and Debir, king of Eglon, **4** to come to his aid for an attack on Gibeon, since it had concluded peace with Joshua and the Israelites.*u* **5** The five Amorite kings, of Jerusalem, Hebron, Jarmuth, Lachish and Eglon,* united all their forces and marched against Gibeon, where they took up siege positions. **6** Thereupon, the men of Gibeon sent an appeal to Joshua in his camp at Gilgal: "Do not abandon your servants. Come up here quickly and save us. Help us, because all the Amorite kings of the mountain country have joined forces against us."*v*

Joshua's Victory.

7 So Joshua marched up from Gilgal with his picked troops and the rest of his soldiers. **8** Meanwhile the LORD said to Joshua, "Do not fear them, for I have delivered them into your power. Not one of them will be able to withstand you." **9** And when Joshua made his surprise attack upon them after an all-night march from Gilgal, **10** the LORD threw them into disorder before him. The Israelites inflicted a great slaughter on them at Gibeon and pursued them down the Beth-horon slope, harassing them as far as Azekah and Makkedah.

11 While they fled before Israel along the descent from Beth-horon, the LORD hurled great stones from the sky* above them all the way to Azekah, killing many.*w* More died from these hailstones than the Israelites slew with the sword. **12** On this day, when the LORD delivered up the Amorites to the Israelites,

Joshua prayed to the LORD,
and said in the presence of Israel:
Stand still, O sun, at Gibeon,
O moon, in the valley of Aijalon!
13 And the sun stood still,
and the moon stayed,
while the nation took vengeance on its
foes.*x*

Is this not recorded* in the Book of Jashar? The sun halted in the middle of the sky; not for a whole day did it resume its swift course. **14** Never before or since was there a day like this, when the LORD obeyed the voice of a man; for the LORD fought for Israel. **15** [Then Joshua and all Israel returned to the camp at Gilgal.]

Execution of Amorite Kings.

16 Meanwhile the five kings who had fled, hid in a cave at Makkedah. **17** When Joshua was told that the five kings had been discovered hiding in a cave at Makkedah, **18** he said, "Roll large stones to the mouth of the cave and post men over it to guard them. **19** But do not remain there yourselves. Pursue your enemies, and harry them in the rear. Do not allow them to escape to their cities, for the LORD, your God, has delivered them into your power."

20 Once Joshua and the Israelites had finally inflicted the last blows in this very great slaughter, and the survivors had escaped from them into the fortified cities, **21** all the army returned safely to Joshua and the camp at Makkedah, no man uttering a sound against the Israelites. **22** Then Joshua said, "Open the mouth of the cave and bring out those five kings to me." **23** Obediently, they brought out to him from the cave the five kings, of Jerusalem, Hebron, Jarmuth, Lachish and Eglon. **24** When they had done so, Joshua summoned all the men of Israel and said to the commanders of the soldiers who had marched with him, "Come forward and put your feet on the necks of these kings." They came forward and put their feet upon their necks. **25** Then Joshua said to them, "Do not be afraid or dismayed, be firm and steadfast. This is what the LORD will do to all the enemies against whom you fight." **26** *y*Thereupon Joshua struck and killed them, and hanged them on five trees, where they remained hanging until evening. **27** At sunset they were removed from the trees at the command of Joshua and cast into the cave where they had hidden; over the mouth of the cave large stones were placed, which remain until this very day.

Conquest of Southern Canaan.

28 *z*Makkedah, too, Joshua captured and put to the sword at that time. He fulfilled the doom on the city, on its king, and on every person in it, leaving no survivors. Thus he did to the king of Makkedah what he had done to the king of Jericho. **29** Joshua then passed on with all Israel from Makkedah to Libnah, which he attacked. **30** Libnah also, with its king, the LORD

---

u Jos 9, 15.   Heb 3, 11.
v Jos 9, 6.   y 26f: Jos 8, 29; Dt 21,
w Jb 38, 22.   22f.
x Sir 46, 4; Is 28, 21;   z Jos 6, 21.

*

10, 5: Hebron . . . Eglon: these four cities were to the south and southwest of Jerusalem.

10, 11: Great stones from the sky: the hailstones mentioned in the next sentence.

10, 13: Is this not recorded: the reference is to the preceding, poetic passage. Evidently the Book of Jashar, like the Book of the Wars of the Lord (Nm 21, 14), recounted in epic style the exploits of Israel's early heroes. The sun halted: though it is widely supposed that this passage describes in popular language and according to external appearances a miraculous lengthening of the day, it is equally probable that Joshua's prayer was rather for an abrupt obscuration of the sun, which would impede his enemies in their flight homeward and also prevent them from rallying their forces; this request would have been answered by the hailstorm (cf Sir 46, 5) and by a darkness relieved only twenty-four hours later, well into the next day.

death. **18** Joshua waged war against all these kings for a long time. **19** With the exception of the Hivites who lived in Gibeon, no city made peace with the Israelites; all were taken in battle. *h* **20** For it was the design of the LORD to encourage them to wage war against Israel, that they might be doomed to destruction and thus receive no mercy, but be exterminated, as the LORD had commanded Moses. *i*

21 *At that time Joshua penetrated the mountain regions and exterminated the Anakim in Hebron, *j* Debir, Anab, the entire mountain region of Judah, and the entire mountain region of Israel. Joshua fulfilled the doom on them and on their cities, **22** so that no Anakim were left in the land of the Israelites. However, some survived in Gaza, in Gath, and in Ashdod. **23** *k* Thus Joshua captured the whole country, just as the LORD had foretold to Moses. Joshua gave it to Israel as their heritage, apportioning it among the tribes. And the land enjoyed peace.*

CHAPTER 12*

Lists of Conquered Kings. **1** The kings of the land east of the Jordan, from the River Arnon to Mount Hermon, including all the eastern section of the Arabah, whom the Israelites conquered and whose lands they occupied, were: **2** *l* First, Sihon, king of the Amorites, who lived in Heshbon. His domain extended from Aroer, which is on the bank of the Wadi Arnon, to include the wadi itself, and the land northward through half of Gilead to the Wadi Jabbok, **3** as well as the Arabah from the eastern side of the Sea of Chinnereth, as far south as the eastern side of the Salt Sea of the Arabah in the direction of Beth-jeshimoth, *m* to a point under the slopes of Pisgah. **4** Secondly, Og, king of Bashan, a survivor of the Rephaim, who lived at Ashtaroth and Edrei. *n* **5** He ruled over Mount Hermon, Salecah, and all Bashan as far as the boundary of the Geshurites and Maacathites, and over half of Gilead as far as the territory of Sihon, king of Heshbon. **6** After Moses, the servant of the LORD, and the Israelites conquered them, he assigned their land to the Reubenites, the Gadites, and the half-tribe of Manasseh, as their property. *o*

7 This is a list of the kings whom Joshua and the Israelites conquered west of the Jordan and whose land, from Baal-gad in the Lebanon valley to Mount Halak which rises toward Seir, Joshua apportioned to the tribes of Israel. **8** It included the mountain regions and foothills, the Arabah, the slopes, the desert, and the Negeb, belonging to the Hittites, Amorites, Canaanites, Perizzites, Hivites and Jebusites. **9** They were the kings of Jericho, *p* Ai (which is near Bethel), **10** Jerusalem, Hebron, **11** Jarmuth, Lachish, *q*

12 Eglon, Gezer, *r* **13** Debir, Geder, *s* **14** Hormah, Arad, **15** Libnah, Adullam, *t* **16** Makkedah, Bethel, *u* **17** Tappuah, Hepher, *v* **18** Aphek, Lasharon, *w* **19** Madon, Hazor, *x* **20** Shimron, Achshaph, *y* **21** Taanach, Megiddo, *z* **22** Kedesh, Jokneam (at Carmel), *a* **23** and Dor (in Naphath-dor), the foreign king at Gilgal, *b* **24** and the king of Tirzah, thirty-one kings in all.

II: Division of the Land

CHAPTER 13

Division of Land Commanded. **1** When Joshua was old and advanced in years, the LORD said to him: *c* "Though now you are old and advanced in years, a very large part of the land still remains to be conquered. **2** This additional land includes all Geshur* and all the districts of the Philistines **3** (from the stream adjoining Egypt to the boundary of Ekron in the north is reckoned Canaanite territory, though held by the five lords of the Philistines in Gaza, Ashdod, Ashkelon, Gath and Ekron); also where the Avvim are in the south; *d* **4** all the land of the Canaanites from Mearah of the Sidonians to Aphek, and the boundaries of the Amorites; **5** and the Gebalite territory; and all the Lebanon on the east, from Baal-gad at the foot of Mount Hermon to Labo in the land of Hamath. **6** At the advance of the Israelites I will drive out all the Sidonian inhabitants of the mountain regions between Lebanon and Misrephoth-maim; *e* at

h Jos 9, 3. 7. 15.
i Dt 2, 30; 20, 16f.
j Jos 15, 13f; Nm 13, 22;
  Dt 1, 28.
k Jos 14, 1-19, 51; Nm
  34, 2-12.
l 2-5: Nm 21, 21-26.
  33ff.
m Jos 13, 20.
n Jos 13, 11f.
o Nm 32, 33; Dt 3, 12f.
p Jos 6, 2; 8, 23.
q 10f; Jos 10, 23.
r Jos 10, 23. 33.

s Jos 10, 38f; 15, 36.
t Jos 10, 29f; 15, 35.
u Jos 8, 17; 10, 28.
v Jos 15, 34.
w Jos 15, 53.
x Jos 11, 1. 10.
y Jos 11, 1.
z Jos 17, 11.
a Jos 19, 37.
b Jos 11, 2.
c Jos 23, 1.
d Jgs 3, 3.
e Jos 11, 8.

---

*

11, 21ff: Most of the land assigned to the tribe of Judah was not conquered by it till the early period of the Judges. See note on Jgs 1, 1–36.

11, 23: The land enjoyed peace: of a limited and temporary nature. Many of the individual tribes had still to fight against the remaining Canaanites; cf Jos 15, 13–17; 17, 12f. This verse forms the conclusion to the first part of the book. Cf note on Jos 12, 1–24.

12, 1–24: This chapter, inserted between the two principal parts of the book (chapters 1–11 and 13–21), resembles the lists of conquered cities which are inscribed on monuments of the Egyptian and Assyrian monarchs. Perhaps it was copied here from some such public Israelite record.

13, 2: Geshur: not to be confused with the large Aramaean district of the same name in Bashan (vv 11–13; Dt 3, 14); here it is a region to the south of the Philistine country, since vv 2–5 list the unconquered lands along the coast from south to north; cf also 1 Sm 27, 8.

least include these areas in the division of the Israelite heritage, just as I have commanded you. **7** Now, therefore, apportion among the nine tribes and the half-tribe of Manasseh the land which is to be their heritage.''

The Eastern Tribes.   **8** *f*Now the other half of the tribe of Manasseh, as well as the Reubenites and Gadites, had received their heritage which Moses, the servant of the LORD, had given them east of the Jordan: **9** from Aroer on the bank of the Wadi Arnon and the city in the wadi itself, through the tableland of Medeba and Dibon, **10** with the rest of the cities of Sihon, king of the Amorites, who reigned in Heshbon, to the boundary of the Ammonites; **11** also Gilead and the territory of the Geshurites and Maacathites, all Mount Hermon, and all Bashan as far as Salecah, **12** the entire kingdom in Bashan of Og, a survivor of the Rephaim, who reigned at Ashtaroth and Edrei. Though Moses conquered and occupied these territories, **13** the Israelites did not dislodge the Geshurites and Maacathites, so that Geshur and Maacath survive in the midst of Israel to this day. **14** *g*However, to the tribe of Levi Moses assigned no heritage since, as the LORD had promised them, the LORD, the God of Israel, is their heritage.

Reuben.   **15** *h*What Moses gave to the Reubenite clans: *i* **16** Their territory reached from Aroer, on the bank of the Wadi Arnon, and the city in the wadi itself, through the tableland about Medeba, **17** to include Heshbon and all its towns which are on the tableland, Dibon, Bamoth-baal, Beth-baal-meon, **18** Jahaz, Kedemoth, Mephaath, **19** Kiriathaim, Sibmah, Zereth-shahar on the knoll within the valley, **20** Beth-peor, the slopes of Pisgah, Beth-jeshimoth, **21** and the other cities of the tableland and, generally, of the kingdom of Sihon. This Amorite king, who reigned in Heshbon, Moses had killed, with his vassals, the princes of Midian, who were settled in the land: Evi, Rekem, Zur, Hur and Reba; *j* **22** and among their slain followers the Israelites put to the sword also the soothsayer Balaam, son of Beor. *k* **23** The boundary of the Reubenites was the bank of the Jordan. These cities and their villages were the heritage of the clans of the Reubenites.

Gad.   **24** *l*What Moses gave to the Gadite clans: **25** Their territory included Jazer, all the cities of Gilead, and half the land of the Ammonites as far as Aroer, toward Rabbah **26** (that is, from Heshbon to Ramath-mizpeh and Betonim, and from Mahanaim to the boundary of Lodebar); **27** and in the Jordan valley: Beth-haram, Beth-nimrah, Succoth, Zaphon, the other part of the kingdom of Sihon, king of Heshbon,

with the bank of the Jordan to the southeastern tip of the Sea of Chinnereth. **28** These cities and their villages were the heritage of the clans of the Gadites.

Manasseh.   **29** *m*What Moses gave to the clans of the half-tribe of Manasseh: **30** Their territory included Mahanaim, all of Bashan, the entire kingdom of Og, king of Bashan, and all the villages of Jair, which are sixty cities in Bashan *n* **31** Half of Gilead, with Ashtaroth and Edrei, once the royal cities of Og in Bashan, fell to the descendants of Machir, son of Manasseh, for half the clans descended from Machir.

32 These are the portions which Moses gave when he was in the plains of Moab, beyond the Jordan east of Jericho. **33** However, Moses gave no heritage to the tribe of Levi, since the LORD himself, the God of Israel, is their heritage. *o*

CHAPTER 14

The Western Tribes.   **1** Here follow the portions which the Israelites received in the land of Canaan. *p* Eleazar the priest, Joshua, son of Nun, and the heads of families in the tribes of the Israelites determined **2** their heritage by lot, in accordance with the instructions the LORD had given through Moses concerning the remaining nine and a half tribes. *q* **3** For to two and a half tribes Moses had already given a heritage beyond the Jordan; and though the Levites were given no heritage among the tribes, *r* **4** the descendants of Joseph formed two tribes, Manasseh and Ephraim. The Levites themselves received no share of the land except cities to live in, with their pasture lands for the cattle and flocks. *s*

5 Thus, in apportioning the land, did the Israelites carry out the instructions of the LORD to Moses.

Caleb's Portion.   **6** *t*When the Judahites came up to Joshua in Gilgal, the Kenizzite Caleb, son of Jephunneh, said to him: ''You know what the LORD said to the man of God, Moses, about you and me in Kadesh-barnea. **7** *u*I was forty years old when the servant of the LORD, Moses, sent me from Kadesh-barnea to reconnoiter the land; and I brought back to him a

---

f Jos 12, 6; Nm 32, 33.
g Jos 14, 3f; Nm 18, 20-24.
h 15-31; Dt 3, 12-17.
i 15-23; Nm 21, 25-31; 32, 37f.
j Nm 21, 24; 31, 8; Dt 3, 10.
k Nm 31, 8.
l 24-28: Nm 32, 34ff.
m 29-31: Nm 32, 39ff.
n Nm 32, 41.
o Jos 18, 7; Nm 18, 20.
p Jos 17, 4; 21, 1; Nm 34, 17f.
q Nm 26, 55; 33, 54; 34, 13.
r Jos 13, 8. 14. 33.
s Jos 21, 3-40; Gn 48, 5.
t Nm 14, 24. 30; 32, 12; Dt 1, 36. 38.
u Nm 14, 6-9.

conscientious report. **8** *v*My fellow scouts who went up with me discouraged the people, but I was completely loyal to the LORD, my God. **9** On that occasion Moses swore this oath, "The land where you have set foot shall become your heritage and that of your descendants forever, because you have been completely loyal to the LORD, my God." **10** Now, as he promised, the LORD has preserved me while Israel was journeying through the desert, for the forty-five years since the LORD spoke thus to Moses; and although I am now eighty-five years old, *w* **11** I am still as strong today as I was the day Moses sent me forth, with no less vigor whether for war or for ordinary tasks. *x* **12** Give me, therefore, this mountain region which the LORD promised me that day, as you yourself heard. True, the Anakim are there, with large fortified cities, but if the LORD is with me I shall be able to drive them out, as the LORD promised." *y* **13** Joshua blessed Caleb, son of Jephunneh, and gave him Hebron as his heritage. *z* **14** Therefore Hebron remains the heritage of the Kenizzite Caleb, son of Jephunneh, to the present day, because he was completely loyal to the LORD, the God of Israel. **15** Hebron was formerly called Kiriatharba, for Arba, the greatest among the Anakim. *a* And the land enjoyed peace.

CHAPTER 15

Boundaries of Judah. 1 The lot for the clans of the Judahite tribe fell in the extreme south toward the boundary of Edom, the desert of Zin in the Negeb. *b* **2** *c*The boundary there ran from the bay that forms the southern end of the Salt Sea, **3** southward below the pass of Akrabbim, across through Zin, up to a point south of Kadesh-barnea, across to Hezron, and up to Addar; from there, looping around Karka, **4** it crossed to Azmon and then joined the Wadi of Egypt before coming out at the sea. [This is your southern boundary.] **5** The eastern boundary was the Salt Sea as far as the mouth of the Jordan.

6 *d*The northern boundary climbed from the bay where the Jordan meets the sea, up to Beth-hoglah, and ran north of Beth-arabah, up to Eben-Bohan-ben-Reuben. **7** Thence it climbed to Debir, north of the vale of Achor, *e* in the direction of the Gilgal that faces the pass of Adummim, on the south side of the wadi; from there it crossed to the waters of En-shemesh and emerged at En-rogel. **8** Climbing again to the Valley of Ben-Hinnom* on the southern flank of the Jebusites [that is, Jerusalem], the boundary rose to the top of the mountain at the northern end of the Valley of Rephaim, *f* which bounds the Valley of Hinnom on the west. **9** From the top of the mountain it ran to the fountain of waters of Nephtoah, *g* extended

to the cities of Mount Ephron, and continued to Baalah, or Kiriath-jearim. **10** From Baalah the boundary curved westward to Mount Seir and passed north of the ridge of Mount Jearim (that is, Chesalon); thence it descended to Bethshemesh, and ran across to Timnah. **11** It then extended along the northern flank of Ekron, continued through Shikkeron, and across to Mount Baalah, thence to include Jabneel, before it came out at the sea. **12** The western boundary was the Great Sea and its coast. This was the complete boundary of the clans of the Judahites.

Conquest by Caleb. 13 *h*As the LORD had commanded, Joshua gave Caleb, son of Jephunneh, *i* a portion among the Judahites, namely, Kiriath-arba (Arba was the father of Anak), that is, Hebron. **14** *j*And Caleb drove out from there the three Anakim, the descendants of Anak: Sheshai, Ahiman and Talmai. **15** From there he marched up against the inhabitants of Debir, *k* which was formerly called Kiriath-sepher. **16** Caleb said, "I will give my daughter Achsah in marriage to the one who attacks Kiriath-sepher and captures it." **17** *Othniel, son of Caleb's brother Kenaz, captured it, and so Caleb gave him his daughter Achsah in marriage. **18** On the day of her marriage to Othniel, she induced him to ask her father for some land. Then, as she alighted from the ass, Caleb asked her, "What is troubling you?" **19** She answered, "Give me an additional gift! Since you have assigned to me land in the Negeb, give me also pools of water." So he gave her the upper and the lower pools.

Cities of Judah. 20 *This is the heritage of the clans of the tribe of Judahites: **21** The cities

v Nm 13, 31ff; 14, 24;	d Jos 18, 18f. 22.
32, 12; Dt 1, 36.	e Jos 7, 26; 18, 16ff.
w Nm 14, 30.	2 Sm 17, 17.
x Sir 46, 1ff.	f Jos 18, 16.
y Jos 11, 21.	g Jos 18, 15.
z Jos 10, 36f; 15, 13-19;	h 13-19: Jgs 1, 10-15.
21, 11f.	i Jos 14, 13ff.
a Jgs 1, 10.	j Nm 13, 22; Jgs 1, 20.
b Nm 34, 3.	k Jos 10, 38.
c 2-4: Nm 34, 3ff.	

*

15, 8: The Valley of Ben-hinnom: the southern limit of Jerusalem. Ben-hinnom means "son of Hinnom." The place was also called Valley of Hinnom, in Hebrew ge-hinnom, whence the word "Gehenna" is derived.

15, 17–19: The story of Othniel is told again in Jgs 1, 13–15; cf also Jgs 3, 9–11.

15, 20–62: This elaborate list of the cities of Judah was probably taken from a document made originally for administrative purposes; the cities are divided into four provincial districts, some of which have further subdivisions. For similar lists of the cities of Judah, cf Jos 19, 2–7; 1 Chr 4, 28–32; Neh 11, 25–30. This list has suffered in transmission, so that the totals given in vv 32 and 36 are not exact, and some of the names are probably misspelled; many of the cities cannot be identified.

of the tribe of the Judahites in the extreme southern district toward Edom were: Kabzeel, Eder, Jagur, **22** Kinah, Dimonah, Adadah, **23** Kedesh, Hazor and Ithnan; **24** Ziph, Telem, Bealoth, **25** Hazor-hadattah, and Kerioth-hezron (that is, Hazor); **26** Amam, Shema, Moladah, **27** Hazar-gaddah, Heshmon, Beth-pelet, **28** Hazar-shual, Beer-sheba, and Biziothiah, **29** Baalah, Iim, Ezem, **30** Elto-lad, Chesil, Hormah, **31** Ziklag,*l* Madmannah, Sansannah, **32** Lebaoth, Shilhim and En-rimmon; a total of twenty-nine cities with their villages.

33 In the foothills:* Eshtaol, Zorah, Ashnah, **34** Zanoah, Engannim, Tappuah, Enam, **35** Jarmuth, Adullam, Socoh, Azekah, **36** Shaaraim, Adithaim, Gederah, and Gederothaim; fourteen cities and their villages. **37** Zenan, Hadashah, Migdal-gad, **38** Dilean, Mizpeh, Joktheel, **39** Lachish, Bozkath, Eglon, **40** Cabbon, Lahmam, Chitlish, **41** Gederoth, Beth-dagon, Naamah and Makkedah; sixteen cities and their villages. **42** Libnah, Ether, Ashan, **43** Iphtah, Ashnah, Nezib, **44** Keilah, Achzib and Mareshah; nine cities and their villages. **45** Ekron and its towns and villages; **46** from Ekron to the sea, all the towns that lie alongside Ashdod and their villages; **47** Ashdod and its towns and villages; Gaza and its towns and villages, as far as the Wadi of Egypt and the coast of the Great Sea.

48 In the mountain regions: Shamir, Jattir, Socoh, **49** Dannah, Kiriath-sannah (that is, Debir), **50** Anab, Eshtemoh, Anim, **51** Goshen, Holon and Giloh; eleven cities and their villages. **52** Arab, Dumah, Eshan, **53** Janim, Beth-tappuah, Aphekah, **54** Humtah, Kiriath-arba (that is, Hebron), and Zior; nine cities and their villages. **55** Maon, Carmel, Ziph, Juttah, **56** Jezreel, Jokdeam, Zanoah, **57** Kain, Gibbeah and Timnah; ten cities and their villages. **58** Halhul, Beth-zur, Gedor, **59** Ma-arath, Beth-anoth and Eltekon; six cities and their villages. Tekoa, Ephrathah (that is, Bethlehem), Peor, Etam, Kulom, Tatam, Zores, Karim, Gallim, Bether and Manoko; eleven cities and their villages. **60** Kiriath-baal (that is, Kiriath-jearim) and Rabbah: two cities and their villages.*m*

61 In the desert:* Beth-arabah, Middin, Secacah, **62** Nibshan, Ir-hamelah and Engedi; six cities and their villages. **63** [But the Jebusites who lived in Jerusalem the Judahites could not drive out; so the Jebusites dwell in Jerusalem beside the Judahites to the present day.*n*]

CHAPTER 16

The Joseph Tribes.   **1** The lot that fell to the Josephites* extended from the Jordan at Jericho to the waters of Jericho east of the desert; then the boundary went up from Jericho to the heights at Bethel.* **2** Leaving Bethel for Luz,

it crossed the ridge to the border of the Archites at Ataroth, **3** and descended westward to the border of the Japhletites, to that of Lower Beth-horon, and to Gezer, ending thence at the sea.*o*

Ephraim.   **4** Within the heritage of Manasseh and Ephraim, sons of Joseph, **5** the dividing line* for the heritage of the clans of the Ephraimites ran from east of Ataroth-addar to Upper Beth-horon*p* **6** and thence to the sea. From Michmethath*q* on the north, their boundary curved eastward around Taanath-shiloh, and continued east of it to Janoah; **7** from there it descended to Ataroth and Naarah, and skirting Jericho, it ended at the Jordan. **8** From Tappuah*r* the boundary ran westward to the Wadi Kanah and ended at the sea. This was the heritage of the clans of the Ephraimites, **9** including the villages that belonged to each city set aside for the Ephraimites within the territory of the Manassehites.*s* **10** But they did not drive out the Canaanites living in Gezer,*t* who live on within Ephraim to the present day, though they have been impressed as laborers.

CHAPTER 17

Manasseh.   **1** Now as for the lot that fell to the tribe of Manasseh*u* as the first-born of Joseph: since his eldest son, Machir, the father of Gilead, was a warrior, who had already obtained Gilead and Bashan, **2** *v*the allotment was now made to the other descendants of Manasseh, the clans of Abiezer, Helek, Asriel, Shechem, Hepher and Shemida, the other male children of Manasseh, son of Joseph.

3 Furthermore, Zelophehad, son of Hepher,*w* son of Gilead, son of Machir, son of Manasseh, had had no sons, but only daughters, whose names were Mahlah, Noah, Hoglah, Milcah, and Tirzah. **4** These presented them-

---

l 1 Sm 27, 6.
m Jos 18, 14.
n Jgs 1, 21; 2 Sm 5, 6.
o Jos 10, 10. 33.
p Jos 18, 13.
q Jos 17, 7.
r Jos 17, 7.
s Jos 17, 9.
*

t Jgs 1, 29.
u Gn 41, 51; 46, 20; 48, 18; 50, 23; Nm 26, 29; Dt 3, 13. 15.
v Nm 26, 29-32.
w Nm 26, 33; 27, 1; 36, 2.
x Nm 27, 6f; 36, 2.

15, 33: In the foothills: see note on Dt 1, 7.

15, 61: In the desert: in the Jordan rift near the Dead Sea.

16, 1–17, 18: The boundaries and cities of Judah, the most important tribe, having been given, the land of the next most important group, the two Josephite tribes of Ephraim and Manasseh, is now described, though it was separated from Judah by the territories of Benjamin (Jos 18, 11–20) and Dan (Jos 19, 40–48).

16, 1–3: This line formed the southern boundary of Ephraim and the northern boundaries of Benjamin and of Dan.

16, 5: The dividing line: separating Ephraim from Manasseh. Ephraim's northern border (v 5) is given in an east-to-west direction; its eastern border (v 6f) in a north-to-south direction.

selves to Eleazar the priest, to Joshua, son of Nun, and to the princes, saying, "The LORD commanded Moses to give us a heritage among our kinsmen." So in obedience to the command of the LORD a heritage was given to each of them among their father's kinsmen.[x] **5** Thus ten shares fell to Manasseh apart from the land of Gilead and Bashan beyond the Jordan,[y] **6** since these female descendants of Manasseh received each a portion among his sons. The land of Gilead fell to the rest of the Manassehites.

7 Manasseh bordered on Asher.* From Michmethath, near Shechem, another boundary ran southward to include the natives of En-Tappuah, **8** because the district of Tappuah belonged to Manasseh, although Tappuah itself was an Ephraimite city on the border of Manasseh. **9** This same boundary continued down to the Wadi Kanah.[z] The cities that belonged to Ephraim from among the cities of Manasseh were those to the south of the wadi; thus the territory of Manasseh ran north of the wadi and ended at the sea. **10** The land on the south belonged to Ephraim and that on the north to Manasseh; with the sea as their common boundary, they reached Asher on the north and Issachar on the east.

11 [a]Moreover, in Issachar and in Asher Manasseh was awarded Beth-shean[b] and its towns, Ibleam and its towns, Dor and its towns and the natives there, Endor and its towns and natives, Taanach and its towns and natives, and Megiddo and its towns and natives [the third is Naphath-dor]. **12** Since the Manassehites could not conquer these cities, the Canaanites persisted in this region. **13** When the Israelites grew stronger they impressed the Canaanites as laborers, but they did not drive them out.

Protest of Joseph Tribes. **14** The descendants of Joseph said to Joshua, "Why have you given us only one lot and one share as our heritage?[c] Our people are too many, because of the extent to which the LORD has blessed us." **15** Joshua answered them, "If you are too many, go up to the forest and clear out a place for yourselves there in the land of the Perizzites and Rephaim, since the mountain regions of Ephraim are so narrow." **16** For the Josephites said, "Our mountain regions are not enough for us; on the other hand, the Canaanites living in the valley region all have iron chariots, in particular those in Beth-shean and its towns, and those in the valley of Jezreel."[d] **17** Joshua therefore said to Ephraim and Manasseh, the house of Joseph, "You are a numerous people and very strong. You shall have not merely one share, **18** for the mountain region which is now forest shall be yours when you clear it. Its adjacent land shall also be yours if, despite their

strength and iron chariots, you drive out the Canaanites."

CHAPTER 18

1 After they had subdued the land, the whole community of the Israelites assembled at Shiloh, where they set up the meeting tent.[e]

The Seven Remaining Portions. **2** Seven tribes among the Israelites had not yet received their heritage. **3** Joshua therefore said to the Israelites, "How much longer will you put off taking steps to possess the land which the LORD, the God of your fathers, has given you? **4** Choose three men from each of your tribes; I will commission them to begin a survey of the land, which they shall describe for purposes of inheritance. When they return to me, **5** you shall divide it into seven parts. Judah is to retain its territory in the south,[f] and the house of Joseph its territory in the north. **6** You shall bring here to me the description of the land in seven sections. I will then cast lots for you here before the LORD, our God. **7** For the Levites have no share among you,[g] because the priesthood of the LORD is their heritage; while Gad, Reuben, and the half-tribe of Manasseh have already received the heritage east of the Jordan which Moses, the servant of the LORD, gave them."

8 When those who were to map out the land were ready for the journey, Joshua instructed them to survey the land, prepare a description of it, and return to him; then he would cast lots for them there before the LORD in Shiloh. **9** So they went through the land, listed its cities in writing in seven sections, and returned to Joshua in the camp at Shiloh. **10** Joshua then divided up the land for the Israelites into their separate shares, casting lots for them before the LORD in Shiloh.

Benjamin. **11** One lot fell to the clans of the tribe of Benjaminites. The territory allotted them lay between the descendants of Judah and those of Joseph. **12** [h]Their northern boundary*

---

y Jos 13, 30f.
z Jos 16, 8f.
a 1 Chr 7, 29.
b 11ff: Jgs 1, 27f.
c Jos 16, 4; Gn 48, 19f.
22.
d Jgs 6, 33.
e Jos 19, 51.
f Jos 15, 1—17, 18.
g Jos 13, 8. 33.
h Jos 16, 1.

---

*

17, 7: Manasseh bordered on Asher: only at the extreme northwestern section of Manasseh's territory. The boundary given in the following sentences (vv 7–10) is a more detailed description of the one already mentioned in Jos 16, 5ff, as separating Manasseh from Ephraim.

18, 12–20: Benjamin's northern boundary (vv 12f) corresponded to part of the southern boundary of Ephraim (Jos 16, 1f). Their western border (v 14) was the eastern border of Dan (cf Jos 19, 40–47). Their southern boundary (vv 15–19) corresponded to part of the northern boundary of Judah (Jos 15, 6–9).

began at the Jordan and went over the northern flank of Jericho, up westward into the mountains, till it reached the desert of Beth-aven. **13** From there it crossed over to the southern flank of Luz (that is, Bethel). Then it ran down to Ataroth-addar, on the mountaintop south of Lower Beth-horon. *i* **14** For the western border, the boundary line swung south from the mountaintop opposite Beth-horon till it reached Kiriath-baal (that is, Kiriath-jearim), which city belonged to the Judahites. This was the western boundary. **15** The southern boundary began at the limits of Kiriath-jearim and projected to the spring at Nephtoah. **16** It went down to the edge of the mountain on the north of the Valley of Rephaim, where it faces the Valley of Ben-hinnom; and continuing down the Valley of Hinnom along the southern flank of the Jebusites, reached En-rogel. *j* **17** Inclining to the north, it extended to En-shemesh, and thence to Geliloth, opposite the pass of Adummim. Then it dropped to Eben-Bohan-ben-Reuben, **18** across the northern flank of the Arabah overlook, down into the Arabah. *k* **19** From there the boundary continued across the northern flank of Beth-hoglah and extended to the northern tip of the Salt Sea, at the southern end of the Jordan. This was the southern boundary. **20** The Jordan bounded it on the east. This was how the heritage of the clans of the Benjaminites was bounded on all sides.

21 Now the cities belonging to the clans of the tribe of the Benjaminites were: Jericho, Beth-hoglah, Emek-keziz, **22** Beth-arabah, Zemaraim, Bethel, **23** Avvim, Parah, Ophra, **24** Chepharammoni, Ophni and Geba; twelve cities and their villages. **25** Also Gibeon, Ramah, Beeroth, **26** Mizpeh, Chephirah, Mozah, **27** Rekem, Irpeel, Taralah, **28** Zela, Haeleph, the Jebusite city (that is, Jerusalem), Gibeah and Kiriath; fourteen cities and their villages. This was the heritage of the clans of Benjaminites.

CHAPTER 19

Simeon.   **1** The second lot fell to Simeon. The heritage of the clans of the tribe of Simeonites lay within that of the Judahites. **2** *l*For their heritage they received Beer-sheba, Shema, Moladah, **3** Hazar-shual, Balah, Ezem, **4** Eltolad, Bethul, Hormah, **5** Ziklag, Beth-marcaboth, Hazar-susah, **6** Beth-lebaoth and Sharuhen; thirteen cities and their villages. **7** Also En-rimmon, Ether and Ashan; four cities and their villages, **8** besides all the villages around these cities as far as Baalath-beer (that is, Ramoth-negeb). This was the heritage of the clans of the tribe of the Simeonites. **9** This heritage of the Simeonites was within the confines of the Judahites; for since the portion of the latter was

too large for them, the Simeonites obtained their heritage within it.

Zebulun.   **10** *The third lot fell to the clans of the Zebulunites. The limit of their heritage was at Sarid. **11** Their boundary went up west . . . and through Mareal, reaching Dabbe-sheth and the wadi that is near Jokneam. **12** From Sarid eastward it ran to the district of Chisloth-tabor, on to Daberath, and up to Japhia. **13** From there it continued eastward to Gath-hepher and to Eth-kazin, extended to Rimmon, and turned to Neah. **14** Skirting north of Hannathon, the boundary ended at the valley of Iphtahel. **15** Thus, with Kattath, Nahalal, Shimron, Idalah and Bethlehem, there were twelve cities and their villages **16** to comprise the heritage of the clans of the Zebulunites.

Issachar.   **17** *The fourth lot fell to Issachar. The territory of the clans of the Issacharites **18** included Jezreel, Chesulloth, Shunem, **19** Hapharaim, Shion, Anaharath, **20** Rabbith, Kishion, Ebez, **21** Remeth, En-gannim, En-haddah and Beth-pazzez. **22** The boundary reached Tabor, Shahazumah and Beth-shemesh, ending at the Jordan. These sixteen cities and their villages **23** were the heritage of the clans of the Issacharites.

Asher.   **24** *The fifth lot fell to the clans of the tribe of the Asherites. **25** Their territory include Helkath, Hali, Beten, Achshaph, **26** Allammelech, Amad and Mishal, and reached Carmel on the west, and Shihor-libnath. **27** In the other direction, it ran eastward of Beth-dagon, reached Zebulun and the valley of Iphtahel; then north of Beth-emek and Neiel, it extended to Cabul, **28** Mishal, Abdon, Rehob, *m* Hammon and Kanah, near Greater Sidon. **29** Then the boundary turned back to Ramah and to the fortress city of Tyre; thence it cut

---

i Jos 16, 2f. 5; Gn 28, 19.   l 2-8: 1 Chr 4, 28-33.
j Jos 15, 7f.   m 28f: Jgs 1, 31.
k Jos 15, 6.
*

19, 10–16: Zebulun's territory was in the central section of the Plain of Esdraelon and of southern Galilee; it was bounded on the south by Manasseh, on the southeast by Issachar, on the northeast and north by Naphtali, and on the west by Asher. The site of the later city of Nazareth was within its borders. Bethlehem of Zebulun was, of course, distinct from the city of the same name in Judah. Twelve cities: apparently seven of the names are missing from v 15, unless some of the places mentioned in vv 12–14 are to be included in the number.

19, 17–23: Issachar's land was on the eastern watershed of the Plain of Esdraelon, but also included the southeastern end of the Galilean mountains. It was surrounded by Manasseh on the south and east, by Naphtali on the north, and by Zebulun on the west. Jezreel (v 18) dominated the plain to which it gave its name, the later form of which was Esdraelon.

19, 24–31: Asher inherited the western slope of the Galilean hills as far as the sea, with Manasseh to the south, Zebulun and Naphtali to the east, and Phoenicia to the north.

back to Hosah and ended at the sea. Thus, with Mahalab, Achzib, **30** Ummah, Acco, Aphek and Rehob, there were twenty-two cities and their villages **31** to comprise the heritage of the clans of the tribe of the Asherites.

Naphtali. **32** *The sixth lot fell to the Naphtalites. The boundary of the clans of the Naphtalites **33** extended from Heleph, from the oak at Zaanannim to Lakkum, including Adami-nekeb and Jabneel, and ended at the Jordan. **34** In the opposite direction, westerly, it ran through Aznoth-tabor and from there extended to Hukkok; it touched Zebulun on the south, Asher on the west, and the Jordan on the east. **35** The fortified cities were Ziddim, Zer, Hammath, Rakkath, Chinnereth, **36** Adamah, Ramah, Hazor, **37** Kedesh, Edrei, En-hazor, **38** Yiron, Migdal-el, Horem, Beth-anath and Beth-shemesh;[n] nineteen cities and their villages, **39** to comprise the heritage of the clans of the tribe of the Naphtalites.

Dan. **40** *The seventh lot fell to the clans of the tribe of Danites. **41** Their heritage was the territory of Zorah, Eshtaol, Ir-shemesh, **42** Shaalabbin, Aijalon, Ithlah,[o] **43** Elon, Timnah, Ekron, **44** Eltekoh, Gibbethon, Baalath, **45** Jehud, Bene-berak, Gath-rimmon, **46** Me-jarkon and Rakkon, with the coast at Joppa. **47** [p]But the territory of the Danites was too small for them; so the Danites marched up and attacked Leshem,* which they captured and put to the sword. Once they had taken possession of Leshem, they renamed the settlement after their ancestor Dan. **48** These cities and their villages were the heritage of the clans of the tribe of the Danites.

Joshua's City. **49** When the last of them had received the portions of the land they were to inherit, the Israelites assigned a heritage in their midst to Joshua, son of Nun. **50** In obedience to the command of the LORD, they gave him the city which he requested, Timnah-serah[q] in the mountain region of Ephraim. He rebuilt the city and made it his home.

51 These are the final portions into which Eleazar the priest, Joshua, son of Nun, and the heads of families in the tribes of the Israelites divided the land by lot in the presence of the LORD, at the door of the meeting tent in Shiloh.

CHAPTER 20

Cities of Asylum. **1** The LORD said to Joshuah:* **2** ''Tell the Israelites to designate the cities of which I spoke to them through Moses,[r] **3** to which one guilty of accidental and unintended homicide may flee for asylum from the avenger of blood. **4** To one of these cities the killer shall flee, and standing at the entrance of the city gate, he shall plead his case before the elders, who must receive him and assign him a place in which to live among them. **5** Though the avenger of blood pursues him, they are not to deliver up the homicide who slew his fellow man unintentionally and not out of previous hatred. **6** Once he has stood judgment before the community, he shall live on in that city till the death of the high priest who is in office at the time. Then the killer may go back home to his own city from which he fled.''[s]

List of Cities. **7** So they set apart Kedesh in Galilee in the mountain region of Naphtali, Shechem in the mountain region of Ephraim, and Kiriath-arba (that is, Hebron) in the mountain region of Judah.[t] **8** And beyond the Jordan east of Jericho they designated Bezer on the open tableland in the tribe of Reuben, Ramoth in Gilead in the tribe of Gad, and Golan in Bashan in the tribe of Manasseh.[u] **9** These were the designated cities[v] to which any Israelite or stranger living among them who had killed a person accidentally might flee to escape death at the hand of the avenger of blood, until he could appear before the community.

CHAPTER 21

Levitical Cities. **1** The heads of the Levite families* came up to Eleazar the priest, to Joshua, son of Nun, and to the heads of families of the other tribes of the Israelites[w] **2** at Shiloh in the land of Canaan, and said to them, ''The LORD commanded, through Moses, that cities

---

n Jgs 1, 33.
o Jgs 1, 35.
p Jgs 18, 27-29.
q Jos 24, 30; Jgs 2, 9.
r Ex 21, 13; Nm 35, 10-14; Dt 4, 41-43; 19, 2-9.
s Nm 35, 12. 24f.
t Jos 15, 13; 19, 37; 21, 21.
u Jos 21, 27. 36f.
v Nm 35, 15.
w Ex 6, 16-19; Nm 3, 17-20.
x Nm 35, 2.

19, 32-39: Naphtali received eastern Galilee; Asher was to the west and Zebulun and Issachar were to the south, while the upper Jordan and Mount Hermon formed the eastern border. Part of the tribe of Dan later on occupied the northern extremity of Naphtali's lands, at the sources of the Jordan (v 47).

19, 40-46: The original territory of Dan was a small enclave between Judah, Benjamin, Ephraim and the Philistines.

19, 47: Leshem: called Laish in Jgs 18, where the story of the migration of the Danites is told at greater length.

20, 1-9: The laws concerning the cities of refuge are given in Nm 35, 9-28; Dt 19, 1-13; see notes on Nm 35, 16-25; Dt 19, 2.

21, 1: The order to establish special cities for the Levites is given in Nm 35, 1-8. The forty-eight cities listed here were hardly the exclusive possession of the Levites; at least the more important of them, such as Hebron, Shechem and Ramoth in Gilead, were certainly peopled for the most part by the tribe in whose territory they were situated. But in all these cities the Levites had special property rights which they did not possess in other cities; cf Lv 25, 32ff.

be given us to dwell in, with pasture lands for our livestock.''ˣ **3** Out of their own heritage, in obedience to this command of the LORD, the Israelites gave the Levites the following cities with their pasture lands.

4 When the first lot among the Levites fell to the clans of the Kohathites, the descendants of Aaron the priest obtained thirteen cities by lot from the tribes of Judah, Simeon and Benjamin. **5** The rest of the Kohathites obtained ten cities by lot from the clans of the tribe of Ephraim, from the tribe of Dan, and from the half-tribe of Manasseh. **6** The Gershonites obtained thirteen cities by lot from the clans of the tribe of Issachar, from the tribe of Asher, from the tribe of Naphtali, and from the half-tribe of Manasseh. **7** The clans of the Merarites obtained twelve cities from the tribes of Reuben, Gad and Zebulun. **8** These cities with their pasture lands the Israelites allotted to the Levites in obedience to the LORD's command through Moses.ʸ

Cities of the Priests. 9 ᶻFrom the tribes of the Judahites and Simeonites they designated the following cities, **10** and assigned them to the descendants of Aaron in the Kohathite clan of the Levites, since the first lot fell to them: **11** first, Kiriatharba (Arba was the father of Anak), that is, Hebron, in the mountain region of Judah, with the adjacent pasture lands, **12** although the open country and villages belonging to the city had been given to Caleb, son of Jephunneh, as his property.ᵃ **13** Thus to the descendants of Aaron the priest were given the city of asylum for homicides at Hebron, with its pasture lands; also, Libnah with its pasture lands, **14** Jattir with its pasture lands, Eshtemoa with its pasture lands, **15** Holon with its pasture lands, Debir with its pasture lands, **16** Ashan with its pasture lands, Juttah with its pasture lands, and Bethshemesh with its pasture lands: nine cities from the two tribes mentioned. **17** From the tribe of Benjamin they obtained the four cities of Gibeon with its pasture lands, Geba with its pasture lands, **18** Anathothᵇ with its pasture lands, and Almon with its pasture lands. **19** These cities which with their pasture lands belonged to the priestly descendants of Aaron, were thirteen in all.

Cities of the Other Kohathites. 20 ᶜThe rest of the Kohathite clans among the Levites obtained by lot, from the tribe of Ephraim, four cities. **21** They were assigned, with its pasture lands, the city of asylum for homicides at Shechem in the mountain region of Ephraim; also Gezer with its pasture lands, **22** Kibzaim with its pasture lands, and Beth-horon with its pasture lands. **23** From the tribe of Dan they obtained the four cities of Elteke with its pasture lands, Gibbethon with its pasture lands, **24** Ai-

jalon with its pasture lands, and Gath-rimmon with its pasture lands; **25** and from the half-tribe of Manasseh the two cities of Taanach with its pasture lands and Ibleam with its pasture lands. **26** These cities which with their pasture lands belonged to the rest of the Kohathite clans were ten in all.

Cities of the Gershonites. 27 ᵈThe Gershonite clan of the Levites received from the half-tribe of Manasseh two cities: the city of asylum for homicides at Golan with its pasture lands; and also Beth-Astharoth with its pasture lands. **28** From the tribe of Issachar they obtained the four cities of Kishion with its pasture lands, Daberath with its pasture lands, **29** Jarmuth with its pasture lands, and Engannim with its pasture lands; **30** from the tribe of Asher, the four cities of Mishal with its pasture lands, Abdon with its pasture lands, **31** Helkath with its pasture lands, and Rehob with its pasture lands; **32** and from the tribe of Naphtali, three cities: the city of asylum for homicides at Kedesh in Galilee, with its pasture lands; also Hammath with its pasture lands, and Rakkath with its pasture lands. **33** These cities which with their pasture lands belonged to the Gershonite clans were thirteen in all.

Cities of the Merarites. 34 ᵉThe Merarite clans, the last of the Levites, received from the tribe of Zebulun the four cities of Jokneam with its pasture lands, Kartah with its pasture lands, **35** Rimmon with its pasture lands, and Nahalal with its pasture lands; **36** also, across the Jordan, from the tribe of Reuben, four cities: the city of asylum for homicides at Bezer with its pasture lands, Jahaz with its pasture lands, **37** Kedemoth with its pasture lands, and Mephaath with its pasture lands; **38** and from the tribe of Gad a total of four cities: the city of asylum for homicides at Ramoth in Gilead with its pasture lands, also Mahanaim with its pasture lands, **39** Heshbon with its pasture lands, and Jazer with its pasture lands. **40** The cities which were allotted to the Merarite clans, the last of the Levites, were therefore twelve in all.

41 Thus the total number of citiesᶠ within the territory of the Israelites which, with their pasture lands, belonged to the Levites, was forty-eight. **42** With each and every one of these cities went the pasture lands round about it.

43 And so the LORD gave Israel all the land he had sworn to their fathers he would give them.ᵍ Once they had conquered and occupied it, **44** the LORD gave them peace on every side, just as he had promised their fathers. Not one of

y Nm 35, 2.
z 9-19: 1 Chr 6, 54-60.
a Jos 14, 14; 15, 13.
b Jer 1, 1.
c 20-26: 1 Chr 6, 66-70.
d 27-33: 1 Chr 6, 71-76.
e 34-38: 1 Chr 6, 77-81.
f Nm 35, 7.
g Gn 12, 7; 13, 15; 15, 18; 26, 3; 28, 4. 13.

their enemies could withstand them; the LORD brought all their enemies under their power. **45** Not a single promise[h] that the LORD made to the house of Israel was broken; every one was fulfilled.

III.: Return of the Transjordan Tribes and Joshua's Farewell

CHAPTER 22

The Eastern Tribes Dismissed. **1** At that time Joshua summoned the Reubenites, the Gadites, and the half-tribe of Manasseh **2** and said to them:[i] "You have done all that Moses, the servant of the LORD, commanded you, and have obeyed every command I gave you. **3** For many years now you have not once abandoned your kinsmen, but have faithfully carried out the commands of the LORD, your God. **4** Since, therefore, the LORD, your God, has settled your kinsmen as he promised them, you may now return to your tents beyond the Jordan; to your own land, which Moses, the servant of the LORD, gave you.[j] **5** But be very careful to observe the precept and law which Moses, the servant of the LORD, enjoined upon you: love the LORD, your God;[k] follow him faithfully; keep his commandments; remain loyal to him; and serve him with your whole heart and soul." **6** Joshua then blessed them and sent them away to their own tents.

7 (For, to half the tribe of Manasseh Moses had assigned land in Bashan;[l] and to the other half Joshuah had given a portion along with their kinsmen west of the Jordan.) What Joshua said to them when he sent them off to their tents with his blessing was, **8** "Now that you are returning to your own tents with great wealth, with very numerous livestock, with silver, gold, bronze and iron, and with a very large supply of clothing, divide these spoils of your enemies with your kinsmen there."[m] **9** So the Reubenites, the Gadites, and the half-tribe of Manasseh left the other Israelites at Shiloh in the land of Canaan and returned to the land of Gilead, their own property, which they had received according to the LORD's command through Moses.[n]

The Altar beside the Jordan. **10** When the Reubenites, the Gadites, and the half-tribe of Manasseh came to the region of the Jordan in the land of Canaan, they built there at the Jordan a conspicuously large altar. **11** The other Israelites heard the report[o] that the Reubenites, the Gadites, and the half-tribe of Manasseh had built an altar in the region of the Jordan facing the land of Canaan,* across from them, **12** and therefore they assembled their whole community at Shiloh to declare war on them.*

Accusation of the Western Tribes. **13** First, however, they sent to the Reubenites, the Gadites, and the half-tribe of Manasseh in the land of Gilead an embassy consisting of Phinehas, son of Eleazar the priest,[p] **14** and ten princes, one from every tribe of Israel, each one being both prince and military leader of his ancestral house. **15** When these came to the Reubenites, the Gadites, and the half-tribe of Manasseh in the land of Gilead, they said to them: **16** [q]"The whole community of the LORD sends this message: What act of treachery is this you have committed against the God of Israel? You have seceded from the LORD this day, and rebelled against him by building an altar of your own! **17** For the sin of Peor, a plague came upon the community of the LORD.[r] **18** We are still not free of that; must you now add to it? You are rebelling against the LORD today and by tomorrow he will be angry with the whole community of Israel! **19** If you consider the land you now possess unclean,* cross over to the land the LORD possesses, where the Dwelling of the LORD stands,[s] and share that with us. But do not rebel against the LORD, nor involve us in rebellion, by building an altar of your own in addition to the altar of the LORD, our God. **20** When Achan, son of Zerah,[t] violated the ban, did not wrath fall upon the entire community of Israel? Though he was but a single man, he did not perish alone* for his guilt!"

Reply of the Eastern Tribes. **21** The Reubenites, the Gadites, and the half-tribe of Manasseh replied to the military leaders of the Israelites: "The LORD is the God of gods. **22** The LORD, the God of gods,* knows and

---

h Jos 23, 14f.
i Jos 1, 16f; Nm 32, 20ff;
  Dt 3, 18ff.
j Jos 1, 13; 13, 8; Nm
  32, 33.
k Dt 6, 5f. 17; 10, 12;
  11, 1. 13. 22.
l Jos 17, 5.
m Nm 31, 27.

n Jos 18, 1; Nm 32, 1.
  26. 29.
o Dt 13, 13ff.
p Ex 6, 25; Sir 45, 28.
q Lv 17, 8f.
r Nm 25, 3f; Dt 4, 3.
s Jos 18, 1.
t Jos 7, 1. 5.

---

*

22, 11: In the region of the Jordan facing the land of Canaan: on the eastern side of the Jordan valley. The river itself formed the boundary between these eastern tribes and the rest of the tribes who lived in what was formerly Canaan—though the term Canaan could also be used of both sides of the Jordan valley (cf v 10). The Transjordan tribes naturally built their altar in their own territory.

22, 12: To declare war on them: the western Israelites considered this altar, which seemed to violate the customary unity of the sanctuary (cf Lv 17, 1–9; Dt 12, 4–14), as a sign of secession and dangerous to national unity. The motives for the war were political as well as religious.

22, 19: Unclean: not sanctified by the Dwelling of the Lord.

22, 20: Achan . . . did not perish alone: his guilt caused the failure of the first attack on Ai (Jos 7, 4–23); this fact is adduced as an argument for the solidarity and mutual responsibility of all the Israelites.

22, 22: The Lord, the God of gods: the Hebrew, which cannot be adequately rendered in English here, adds to the

Israel shall know. If now we have acted out of rebellion or treachery against the LORD, our God, **23** and if we have built an altar of our own to secede from the LORD, or to offer holocausts, grain offerings or peace offerings upon it, the LORD himself will exact the penalty. **24** We did it rather out of our anxious concern lest in the future your children should say to our children: 'What have you to do with the LORD, the God of Israel? **25** For the LORD has placed the Jordan as a boundary between you and us. You descendants of Reuben and Gad have no share in the LORD.' Thus your children would prevent ours from revering the LORD. **26** So we decided to guard our interests by building this altar of our own: not for holocausts or for sacrifices, **27** ᵘbut as evidence for you on behalf of ourselves and our descendants, that we have the right to worship the LORD in his presence with our holocausts, sacrifices, and peace offerings. Now in the future your children cannot say to our children, "You have no share in the LORD." **28** Our thought was, that if in the future they should speak thus to us or to our descendants, we could answer: 'Look at the model of the altar of the LORD which our fathers made, not for holocausts or for sacrifices, but to witness* between you and us.' **29** Far be it from us to rebel against the LORD or to secede now from the LORD by building an altar for holocaust, grain offering, or sacrifice in addition to the altar of the LORD, our God, which stands before his Dwelling."

30 When Phinehas the priest and the princes of the community, the military leaders of the Israelites, heard what the Reubenites, the Gadites and the Manassehites had to say, they were satisfied. **31** Phinehas, son of Eleazar the priest, said to the Reubenites, the Gadites and the Manassehites, "Now we know that the LORD is with us. Since you have not committed this act of treachery against the LORD, you have kept the Israelites free from punishment by the LORD."

32 Phinehas, son of Eleazar the priest, and the princes returned from the Reubenites and the Gadites in the land of Gilead to the Israelites in the land of Canaan, and reported the matter to them. **33** The report satisfied the Israelites, who blessed God and decided against declaring war on the Reubenites and Gadites or ravaging the land they occupied.

34 The Reubenites and the Gadites gave the altar its name* as a witness among them that the LORD is God.

CHAPTER 23

Joshua's Final Plea. **1** Many years later, after the LORD had given the Israelites rest from all their enemies round about them, and when

Joshua was old and advanced in years,ᵛ **2** he summoned all Israel (including their elders, leaders, judges and officers) and said to them: "I am old and advanced in years. **3** You have seen all that the LORD, your God, has done for you against all these nations; for it has been the LORD, your God, himself who fought for you. **4** ʷBear in mind that I have apportioned among your tribes as their heritage the nations that survive [as well as those I destroyed] between the Jordan and the Great Sea in the west. **5** The LORD, your God, will drive them out and dislodge them at your approach, so that you will take possession of their land as the LORD, your God, promised you. **6** Therefore strive hard to observe and carry out all that is written in the book of the law of Moses, not straying from it in any way,ˣ **7** or mingling with these nations while they survive among you. You must not invoke their gods, or swear by them, or serve them, or worship them,ʸ **8** but you must remain loyal to the LORD, your God, as you have been to this day. **9** At your approach the LORD has driven out large and strong nations, and to this day no one has withstood you. **10** One of you puts to flight a thousand, because it is the LORD, your God, himself who fights for you,ᶻ as he promised you. **11** Take great care, however, to love the LORD, your God. **12** For if you ever abandon him and ally yourselves with the remnant of these nations while they survive among you, by intermarrying and intermingling with them,ᵃ **13** know for certain that the LORD, your God, will no longer drive these nations out of your way. Instead they will be a snare and a trap for you, a scourge for your sides and thorns for your eyes, until you perish from this good land which the LORD, your God, has given you.

14 "Today, as you see, I am going the way of all men.* So now acknowledge with your whole heart and soul that not one of all the promises the LORD, your God, made to you has remained unfulfilled. Every promise has been fulfilled for you, with not one single exception. **15** ᵇBut just as every promise the LORD, your

---

u Dt 12, 5f. 17f.
v Jos 13, 1.
w Jos 13, 2-7; 14, 2; 18, 10; Ps 78, 55.
x Jos 1, 7.
y Dt 7, 2ff.
z Ex 14, 14; Lv 26, 8; Dt 3, 22.
a Ex 34, 16; Dt 7, 3.
b Lv 26, 14-39; Dt 28, 15-68.

---

*

divine name Yahweh ("the LORD") two synonymous words for "God," el and elohim. The repetition of these three sacred words adds force to the protestations of fidelity and innocence.

22, 28: To witness: far from being destined to form a rival sanctuary, the model of the altar was intended by the eastern tribes solely as a means of teaching their children to be faithful to the one true sanctuary beyond the Jordan.

22, 34: The name of this altar was the Hebrew word for "witness," ᶜ ed.

23, 14: Going the way of all men: drawing near to death, the inevitable goal of all; cf 1 Kgs 2, 1f.

23, 15: Every threat: mentioned especially in Dt 28, 15–68.

God, made to you as has been fulfilled for you, so will he fulfill every threat,* even so far as to exterminate you from this good land which the LORD, your God, has given you. **16** If you transgress the covenant of the LORD, your God, which he enjoined on you, serve other gods and worship them, the anger of the LORD will flare up against you and you will quickly perish from the good land which he has given you.''

CHAPTER 24

Reminder of the Divine Goodness.

1 Joshua gathered together all the tribes of Israel at Shechem, summoning their elders, their leaders, their judges and their officers. When they stood in ranks before God, **2** Joshua addressed all the people: ''Thus says the LORD, the God of Israel: In times past your fathers, down to Terah,*c* father of Abraham and Nahor, dwelt beyond the River* and served other gods. **3** But I brought your father Abraham from the region beyond the River and led him through the entire land of Canaan.*d* I made his descendants numerous, and gave him Isaac. **4** To Isaac I gave Jacob and Esau.*e* To Esau I assigned the mountain region of Seir in which to settle, while Jacob and his children went down to Egypt.

5 ''Then I sent Moses and Aaron, and smote Egypt with the prodigies which I wrought in her midst.*f* **6** Afterward I led you out of Egypt, and when you reached the sea, the Egyptians pursued your fathers to the Red Sea with chariots and horsemen.*g* **7** Because they cried out to the LORD,*h* he put darkness between your people and the Egyptians, upon whom he brought the sea so that it engulfed them. After you witnessed what I did to Egypt, and dwelt a long time in the desert, **8** *i*I brought you into the land of the Amorites who lived east of the Jordan. They fought against you, but I delivered them into your power. You took possesion of their land, and I destroyed them [the two kings of the Amorites] before you. **9** *j*Then Balak, son of Zippor, king of Moab, prepared to war against Israel. He summoned Balaam, son of Beor, to curse you; **10** *k*but I would not listen to Balaam. On the contrary, he had to bless you, and I saved you from him. **11** Once you crossed the Jordan*l* and came to Jericho, the men of Jericho fought against you, but I delivered them also into your power. **12** And I sent the hornets* ahead of you which drove them [the Amorites, Perizzites, Canaanites, Hittites, Girgashites, Hivites and Jebusites] out of your way; it was not your sword or your bow.*m*

13 ''I gave you a land which you had not tilled and cities which you had not built, to dwell in; you have eaten of vineyards and olive groves which you did not plant.*n*

14 *o*''Now, therefore, fear the LORD and serve him completely and sincerely. Cast out the gods your fathers served beyond the River and in Egypt, and serve the LORD. **15** *p*If it does not please you to serve the LORD, decide today whom you will serve, the gods your fathers served* beyond the River or the gods of the Amorites in whose country you are dwelling. As for me and my household, we will serve the LORD.''

Renewal of the Covenant.

16 But the people answered, ''Far be it from us to forsake the LORD for the service of other gods. **17** For it was the LORD, our God, who brought us and our fathers up out of the land of Egypt, out of a state of slavery. He performed those great miracles before our very eyes and protected us along our entire journey and among all the peoples through whom we passed. **18** At our approach the LORD drove out [all the peoples, including] the Amorites who dwelt in the land. Therefore we also will serve the LORD, for he is our God.''

19 Joshua in turn said to the people, ''You may not be able* to serve the LORD, for he is a holy God; he is a jealous God*q* who will not forgive your transgressions or your sins. **20** If, after the good he has done for you, you forsake the LORD and serve strange gods, he will do evil to you and destroy you.''

21 But the people answered Joshua, ''We will still serve the LORD.'' **22** Joshua therefore said to the people, ''You are your own witnesses that you have chosen to serve the LORD.'' They replied, ''We are, indeed!'' **23** ''Now, therefore, put away the strange gods that are among you and turn your hearts to the LORD, the God of Israel.'' **24** Then the people promised Joshua, ''We will serve the LORD, our God, and obey his voice.''

25 So Joshua made a covenant with the people that day and made statutes and ordinances for them at Shechem, **26** which he recorded in the book of the law of God. Then he took a large

---

c Gn 11, 26. 31; 31, 53.
d Gn 12, 1; Acts 7, 2-4.
e Gn 25, 24ff; 36, 8; 46,
  1. 6; Acts 7, 15.
f Ex 3, 10; 7, 14-12, 30.
g Ex 12, 37. 51; 14, 9.
h Ex 14, 10. 20. 27f.
i Nm 21, 21-35.
j Nm 22, 2-5.
k Nm 23, 1-24, 25.
l Jos 3, 14; 6, 1.

m Jos 11, 20; Ex 23, 28;
  Dt 7, 20.
n Dt 6, 10f.
o Dt 10, 12; 1 Sm 7, 3;
  12, 24; Tb 14, 9.
p Dt 30, 15-19.
q Ex 20, 5; 23, 21; 34,
  14; Lv 19, 2.
r Gn 28, 18; 31, 45; Jgs
  9, 6.

---

*

24, 2: Beyond the River: east of the Euphrates; cf Gn 11, 28–31.

24, 12: the hornets: see note on Ex 23, 28.

24, 15: The gods your fathers served: Abraham's ancestors were polytheists.

24, 19: You may not be able: fidelity to God's service is not easy, and therefore those who take such solemn obligations on themselves must be ever vigilant against human weakness.

stone and set it up there under the oak that was in the sanctuary of the LORD.ʳ **27** And Joshua said to all the people, "This stone shall be our witness,ˢ for it has heard all the words which the LORD spoke to us. It shall be a witness against you, should you wish to deny your God." **28** Then Joshua dismissed the people, each to his own heritage.ᵗ

Death of Joshua.

29 ᵘAfter these events, Joshua, son of Nun, servant of the LORD, died at the age of a hundred and ten. **30** He was buried within the limits of his heritage at Timnath-serahᵛ in the mountain region of Ephraim north of Mount Gaash. **31** Israel served the LORD during the entire lifetime of Joshua and that of the elders who outlived Joshua and knew all that the LORD had done for Israel. **32** ʷThe bones of Joseph,* which the Israelites had brought up from Egypt, were buried in Shechem in the plot of ground Jacob had bought from the sons of Hamor, father of Shechem, for a hundred pieces of money. This was a heritage of the descendants of Joseph. **33** When Eleazar, son of Aaron, also died, he was buried on the hill which had been given to his son Phinehasˣ in the mountain region of Ephraim.

s Gn 31, 48. 52; Dt 31,
　19. 21. 26.
t Jgs 2, 6.
u 29ff: Jgs 2, 7ff.
v Jos 19, 50: Jgs 2, 9.
w Gn 33, 19; 50, 24; Ex
　13, 19.
x Jos 22, 13.

24, 32:　The bones of Joseph: the mummified body of Joseph (Gn 50, 25f), which the Israelites took with them as they left Egypt (Ex 13, 19), was fittingly buried at the ancient city of Shechem, near the border between the two Josephite tribes of Ephraim and Manasseh.

The Book of

JUDGES

The Book of Judges derives its title from the twelve heroes of Israel whose deeds it records. They were not magistrates, but military leaders sent by God to aid and to relieve his people in time of external danger. They exercised their activities in the interval of time between the death of Joshua and the institution of the monarchy in Israel. Six of them—Othniel, Ehud, Barak, Gideon, Jephtah and Samson—are treated in some detail and have accordingly been styled the Major Judges. The other six, of whose activities this book preserves but a summary record, are called the Minor Judges. There were two other judges, whose judgeships are described in 1 Samuel—Eli and Samuel, who seem to have ruled the entire nation of Israel just before the institution of the monarchy. The twelve judges of the present book, however, very probably exercised their authority, sometimes simultaneously, over one or another tribe of Israel, never over the entire nation.

The purpose of the book is to show that the fortunes of Israel depended upon the obedience or disobedience of the people to God's law. Whenever they rebelled against him, they were oppressed by pagan nations; when they repented, he raised up judges to deliver them (cf Jgs 2, 10–23).

The accounts of various events, whether written shortly after their occurrence or orally transmitted, were later skillfully unified according to the moral purpose of the redactor sometime during the Israelite monarchy.

The book is divided as follows:

I. Palestine after the Death of Joshua (Jgs 1, 1–3, 6).

II. Stories of the Judges (Jgs 3, 7–16, 31).

III. The Tribes of Dan and Benjamin in the Days of the Judges (Jgs 17, 1–21, 25).

I: Palestine After the Death of Joshua

CHAPTER 1

Pagan Survivors in Palestine.   **1** After the death of Joshua* the Israelites consulted the LORD, asking, "Who shall be first among us to attack the Canaanites and to do battle with them?"[a] **2** The LORD answered, "Judah shall attack: I have delivered the land into his power." **3** Judah then said to his brother Simeon, "Come up with me into the territory allotted to me, and let us engage the Canaanites in battle. I will likewise accompany you into the territory allotted to you." So Simeon went with him.

4 When the forces of Judah attacked, the LORD delivered the Canaanites and Perizzites into their power, and they slew ten thousand of them in Bezek. **5** It was in Bezek that they came upon Adonibezek and fought against him. When they defeated the Canaanites and Perizzites, **6** Adonibezek fled. They set out in pursuit, and when they caught him, cut off his thumbs and his big toes. **7** At this Adonibezek said, "Seventy kings, with their thumbs and big toes cut off, used to pick up scraps under my table. As I have done, so has God repaid me." He was brought to Jerusalem, and there he died. **8** [The Judahites fought against Jerusalem and captured it, putting it to the sword; then they destroyed the city by fire.]

9 [b]Afterward the Judahites went down to fight against the Canaanites who lived in the mountain region, in the Negeb, and in the foothills, **10** [c]Judah also marched against the Canaanites who dwelt in Hebron, which war formerly called Kiriath-arba, and defeated Sheshai, Ahiman and Talmai.[d] **11** From there they marched against the inhabitants of Debir, which was formerly called Kiriath-sepher. **12** And Caleb said, "I will give my daughter Achsah in marriage to the one who attacks Kiriath-sepher and captures it." **13** [e]Othniel, son

a Jgs 20, 18; Nm 27, 21.   c Jos 15, 13-19.
b Jos 10, 40; 11, 16; 12,   d Nm 13, 22; Jos 14, 15.
8.   e Jgs 3, 9.

1, 1–36: This chapter summarizes events most of which occurred shortly after the death of Joshua. Perhaps because they were planned and inaugurated by him, they are also attributed to him in the last half of the preceding book (Jos 14—22).

of Caleb's younger brother Kenaz, captured it; so Caleb gave him his daughter Achsah in marriage. **14** On the day of her marriage to Othniel she induced him to ask her father for some land. Then, as she alighted from the ass, Caleb asked her, "What is troubling you?" **15** "Give me an additional gift," she answered. "Since you have assigned land in the Negeb to me, give me also pools of water." So Caleb gave her the upper and the lower pool. **16** The descendants of the Kenite, Moses' father-in-law,* came up with the Judahites from the city of palms to the desert at Arad [which is in the Negeb]. But they later left and settled among the Amalekites.*f*

17 *g*Judah then went with his brother Simeon, and they defeated the Canaanites who dwelt in Zephath. After having doomed the city to destruction, they renamed it Hormah. **18** *h*Judah, however, did not occupy Gaza with its territory, Ashkelon with its territory, or Ekron with its territory. **19** *i*Since the LORD was with Judah, he gained possession of the mountain region. Yet he could not dislodge those who lived on the plain, because they had iron chariots. **20** As Moses had commanded, Hebron was given to Caleb, who then drove from it the three sons of Anak.*j*

21 *The Benjaminites did not dislodge the Jebusites who dwelt in Jerusalem, with the result that the Jebusites live in Jerusalem beside the Benjaminites to the present day.*k*

22 The house of Joseph, too, marched up against Bethel, and the LORD was with them. **23** The house of Joseph had a reconnaissance made of Bethel, which formerly was called Luz.*l* **24** The scouts saw a man coming out of the city and said to him, "Show us a way into the city, and we will spare you." **25** He showed them a way into the city, which they then put to the sword; but they let the man and his whole clan go free. **26** He then went to the land of the Hittites, where he built a city and called it Luz, as it is still called.

27 Manasseh did not take possession of Beth-shean with its towns or of Taanach with its towns. Neither did he dislodge the inhabitants of Dor and its towns, those of Ibleam and its towns, or those of Megiddo and its towns.*m* The Canaanites kept their hold in this district. **28** When the Israelites grew stronger, they impressed the Canaanites as laborers, but did not drive them out. **29** Similarly, the Ephraimites did not drive out the Canaanites living in Gezer, and so the Canaanites live in Gezer in their midst.*n*

30 Zebulun did not dislodge the inhabitants of Kitron or those of Nahalol; the Canaanites live among them, but have become forced laborers.

31 *o*Nor did Asher drive out the inhabitants of Acco or those of Sidon, or take possession of Mahaleb, Achzib, Helbah, Aphik or Rehob. **32** The Asherites live among the Canaanite natives of the land, whom they have not dislodged.

33 *p*Naphtali did not drive out the inhabitants of Beth-shemesh or those of Beth-anath, and so they live among the Canaanite natives of the land. However, the inhabitants of Beth-shemesh and Beth-anath have become forced laborers for them.

34 The Amorites hemmed in the Danites in the mountain region, not permitting them to go down into the plain.*q* **35** The Amorites had a firm hold in Harheres, Aijalon and Shaalbim, but as the house of Joseph gained the upper hand, they were impressed as laborers.

36 The territory of the Amorites extended from the Akrabbim pass to Sela and beyond.

CHAPTER 2

Infidelities of the Israelites. **1** *r*An angel of the LORD went up from Gilgal to Bochim and said, "It was I who brought you up from Egypt and led you into the land which I promised on oath to your fathers. I said that I would never break my covenant with you, **2** but that you were not to make a pact with the inhabitants of this land, and you were to pull down their altars. Yet you have not obeyed me.*s* What did you mean by this? **3** For now I tell you, I will not clear them out of your way; they shall oppose you and their gods shall become a snare for you."*t*

4 When the angel of the LORD had made these threats to all the Israelites, the people wept aloud; **5** and so that place came to be called Bochim.* They offered sacrifice there to the LORD.

6 *u*When Joshua dismissed the people, each Israelite went to take possession of his own hereditary land. **7** The people served the LORD during the entire lifetime of Joshua, and of those elders who outlived Joshua and who had seen all the great work which the LORD had done for

f Jgs 4, 11; Nm 10, 29-32.
g Nm 21, 3.
h Jos 11, 22.
i Jos 17, 16ff.
j Jos 14, 9. 13; 15, 14.
k Jos 15, 63.
l Gn 28, 19; 35, 6; 48, 3; Jos 18, 13.
m 27f: Jos 17, 11ff.
n Jos 16, 10.
o 31f: Jos 19, 24-31.
p Jos 19, 32-39.
q Jos 19, 47f.
r 1ff: Jgs 6, 8ff.
s Ex 34, 12f. 15; Dt 7, 2. 5; 21, 2f.
t Nm 33, 55; Jos 23, 13.
u 6-9: Jos 24, 28-31.

*

1, 16: Moses' father-in-law: Reuel; cf Nm 10, 29-32 and note. City of palms: Jericho (cf Dt 34, 3), or a town in the Negeb.

1, 21: According to Jos 18, 16, Jerusalem was assigned to the tribe of Benjamin. But it was not actually taken from the Jebusites until David captured it (2 Sm 5, 6-9) and made it his capital, outside the tribal organization.

2, 5: Bochim: the Hebrew word for "weepers."

Israel. **8** Joshua, son of Nun, the servant of the LORD, was a hundred and ten years old when he died; **9** and they buried him within the borders of his heritage at Timnath-heres in the mountain region of Ephraim north of Mount Gaash.ᵛ

10 But once the rest of that generation were gathered to their fathers, and a later generation arose that did not know the LORD, or what he had done for Israel, **11** the Israelites offended the LORD by serving the Baals.*ʷ **12** Abandoning the LORD, the God of their fathers, who had led them out of the land of Egypt, they followed the other gods of the various nations around them, and by their worship of these gods provoked the LORD.

13 Because they had thus abandoned him and served Baal and the Ashtaroth,* **14** the anger of the LORD flared up against Israel, and he delivered them over to plunderers who despoiled them. He allowed them to fall into the power of their enemies round about whom they were no longer able to withstand. **15** Whatever they undertook, the LORD turned into disaster for them, as in his warning he had sworn he would do, till they were in great distress.ˣ **16** Even when the LORD raised up judges to deliver them from the power of their despoilers, **17** they did not listen to their judges, but abandoned themselves to the worship of other gods. They were quick to stray from the way their fathers had taken, and did not follow their example of obedience to the commandments of the LORD. **18** Whenever the LORD raised up judges for them, he would be with the judge and save them from the power of their enemies as long as the judge lived; it was thus the LORD took pity on their distressful cries of affliction under their oppressors. **19** But when the judge died, they would relapse and do worse than their fathers, following other gods in service and worship, relinquishing none of their evil practices or stubborn conduct.ʸ

20 ᶻIn his anger toward Israel the LORD said, "Inasmuch as this nation has violated my covenant which I enjoined on their fathers, and has disobeyed me, **21** I for my part will not clear away for them any more of the nations which Joshua left when he died." **22** Through these nations the Israelites were to be made to prove whether or not they would keep to the way of the LORD and continue in it as their fathers had done; **23** therefore the LORD allowed them to remain instead of expelling them immediately, or delivering them into the power of Israel.

CHAPTER 3

1 The following are the nations which the LORD allowed to remain, so that through them he might try all those Israelites who had no experience of the battles with Canaan **2** [just to instruct, by training them in battle, those genera-

tions only of the Israelites who would not have had that previous experience]: **3** ᵃthe five lords of the Philistines;* and all the Canaanites, the Sidonians, and the Hivites who dwell in the mountain region of Lebanon between Baal-hermon and the entrance to Hamath. **4** These served to put Israel to the test, to determine whether they would obey the commandments the LORD had enjoined on their fathers through Moses. **5** Besides, the Israelites were living among the Canaanites, Hittites, Amorites, Perizzites, Hivites and Jebusites. **6** In fact, they took their daughters in marriage, and gave their own daughters to their sons in marriage, and served their gods.

II: Stories of the Judges

Othniel. **7** ᵇBecause the Israelites had offended the LORD by forgetting the LORD, their God, and serving the Baals and the Asherahs,* **8** the anger of the LORD flared up against them, and he allowed them to fall into the power of Cushan-rishathaim, king of Aram Naharaim, whom they served for eight years. **9** But when the Israelites cried out to the LORD, he raised up for them a savior, Othniel, son of Caleb's younger brother Kenaz, who rescued them. **10** The spirit of the LORD came upon him, and he judged Israel.ᶜ When he went out to war, the LORD delivered Cushan-risha-thaim, king of Aram, into his power, so that he made him subject. **11** The land then was at rest for forty years,ᵈ until Othniel, son of Kenaz, died.

Ehud. **12** Again the Israelites offended the LORD, who because of this offense strengthened Eglon, king of Moab, against Israel. **13** In alliance with the Ammonites and Amalekites, he attacked and defeated Israel, taking possession of the city of palms. **14** The Israelites then served Eglon, king of Moab, for eighteen years.

---

v Jos 19, 50.
w 11. 14; Jgs 3, 7f; 4, 1f; 6, 1; 10, 6f; 13, 1.
x Dt 28, 15-68.
y Jgs 3, 12; 4, 1; 6, 1; 8, 33.
z 20f: Jos 23, 16.
a Jos 13, 2-6.
b Jgs 2, 11ff.
c Jgs 6, 34; 11, 29; 13, 25; 14, 6. 19; 15, 14.
d Jgs 5, 31; 8, 28.

---

*

2, 11: Baals: the chief god of the Canaanites and the Phoenicians was called "Baal," a word meaning "lord." He was honored by various titles, hence the plural form here, equivalent to "the pagan gods."

2, 13: Ashtaroth: the Canaanite Phoenician goddess of love and fertility was Astarte. The plural form used here refers to her various titles and images and is equivalent to "goddesses."

3, 3: The Philistines; non-Semitic invaders, who gave their name to all Palestine, although they occupied only its southwestern plains. Their confederation embraced the five leading cities of Gaza, Ashkelon, Ashdod, Gath and Ekron.

3, 7: Asherahs: elsewhere rendered "sacred poles." See note on Ex 34, 13 and on Dt 7, 5. Here the word seems to mean "goddesses."

15 But when the Israelites cried out to the LORD, he raised up for them a savior, the Benjaminite Ehud, son of Gera, who was left-handed. It was by him that the Israelites sent their tribute to Eglon, king of Moab. **16** Ehud made himself a two-edged dagger a foot long, and wore it under his clothes over his right thigh. **17** He presented the tribute to Eglon, king of Moab, who was very fat, **18** and after the presentation went off with the tribute bearers. **19** He returned, however, from where the idols are, near Gilgal, and said, "I have a private message for you, O king." And the king said, "Silence!" Then when all his attendants had left his presence, **20** and Ehud went in to him where he sat alone in his cool upper room, Ehud said, "I have a message from God for you." So the king rose from his chair, **21** and then Ehud with his left hand drew the dagger from his right thigh, and thrust it into Eglon's belly. **22** The hilt also went in after the blade, and the fat closed over the blade because he did not withdraw the dagger from his body.

23 Then Ehud went out into the hall, shutting the doors of the upper room on him and locking them. **24** When Ehud had left and the servants came, they saw that the doors of the upper room were locked, and thought, "He must be easing himself in the cool chamber." **25** They waited until they finally grew suspicious. Since he did not open the doors of the upper room, they took the key and opened them. There on the floor, dead, lay their lord!

26 During their delay Ehud made good his escape and, passing the idols, took refuge in Seirah. **27** On his arrival he sounded the horn in the mountain region of Ephraim, and the Israelites went down from the mountains with him as their leader. **28** "Follow me," he said to them, "for the LORD has delivered your enemies the Moabites into your power." So they followed him down and seized the fords of the Jordan leading to Moab, permitting no one to cross.[e] **29** On that occasion they slew about ten thousand Moabites, all of them strong and valiant men. Not a man escaped. **30** Thus was Moab brought under the power of Israel at that time; and the land had rest for eighty years.

Shamgar.   **31** After him there was Shamgar, son of Anath, who slew six hundred Philistines with an oxgoad. He, too, rescued Israel.

CHAPTER 4

Deborah and Barak.   **1** After Ehud's death, however, the Israelites again offended the LORD. **2** So the LORD allowed them to fall into the power of the Canaanite king, Jabin, who reigned in Hazor.[f] The general of his army was Sisera, who dwelt in Harosheth-ha-goiim.

3 But the Israelites cried out to the LORD; for with his nine hundred iron chariots he sorely oppressed the Israelites for twenty years.

4 At this time the prophetess Deborah, wife of Lappidoth, was judging Israel. **5** She used to sit under Deborah's palm tree, situated between Ramah and Bethel in the mountain region of Ephraim, and there the Israelites came up to her for judgment. **6** She sent and summoned Barak, son of Abinoam,[g] from Kedesh of Naphtali. "This is what the LORD, the God of Israel, commands," she said to him; "go, march on Mount Tabor, and take with you ten thousand Naphtalites and Zebulunites. **7** I will lead Sisera, the general of Jabin's army, out to you at the Wadi Kishon,[h] together with his chariots and troops, and will deliver them into your power." **8** But Barak answered her, "If you come with me, I will go; if you do not come with me, I will not go." **9** "I will certainly go with you," she replied, "but you shall not gain the glory in the expedition on which you are setting out, for the LORD will have Sisera fall into the power of a woman." So Deborah joined Barak and journeyed with him to Kedesh.

10 Barak summoned Zebulun and Naphtali to Kedesh, and ten thousand men followed him. Deborah also went up with him.[i] **11** *Now the Kenite Heber had detached himself from his own people, the descendants of Hobab, Moses' brother-in-law,[j] and had pitched his tent by the terebinth of Zaanannim, which was near Kedesh.

12 It was reported to Sisera that Barak, son of Abinoam, had gone up to Mount Tabor. **13** So Sisera assembled from Harosheth-hagoiim at the Wadi Kishon all nine hundred of his iron chariots and all his forces. **14** Deborah then said to Barak, "Be off, for this is the day on which the LORD has delivered Sisera into your power. The LORD marches before you." So Barak went down Mount Tabor, followed by his ten thousand men. **15** And the LORD put Sisera[k] and all his chariots and all his forces to rout before Barak. Sisera himself dismounted from his chariot and fled on foot. **16** Barak, however, pursued the chariots and the army as far as Harosheth-ha-goiim. The entire army of Sisera fell beneath the sword, not even one man surviving.

17 *Sisera, in the meantime, had fled on foot

---

e Jgs 4, 7. 14; 7, 9. 15.
f Jos 11, 1. 10; Ps 83,
   10; 1 Sm 12, 9.
g Heb 11, 32.

h Jgs 5, 21; Ps 83, 10.
i Jgs 5, 18.
j Nm 10, 29.
k Ps 83, 10.

*

4, 11: Most of the Kenites occupied a district in the southern part of Judah (Jgs 1, 16). A group of them, however, had detached themselves and settled in lower Galilee.

4, 17–22: It is to be noted that the sacred author merely records the fact of the murder of Sisera. We must not construe this as approval of Jael's action.

to the tent of Jael, wife of the Kenite Heber,
since Jabin, king of Hazor, and the family of the
Kenite Heber were at peace with one another.
18 Jael went out to meet Sisera and said to him,
"Come in, my lord, come in with me; do not be
afraid." So he went into her tent, and she covered him with a rug. **19** He said to her, "Please
give me a little water to drink. I am thirsty."
But she opened a jug of milk for him to drink,
and then covered him over.[l] **20** "Stand at the
entrance of the tent," he said to her. "If anyone
comes and asks, 'Is there someone here?' say,
'No!' " **21** Instead Jael, wife of Heber, got a
tent peg and took a mallet in her hand. While
Sisera was sound asleep, she stealthily approached him and drove the peg through his
temple down into the ground, so that he perished in death.[m] **22** Then when Barak came in
pursuit of Sisera, Jael went out to meet him and
said to him, "Come, I will show you the man
you seek." So he went in with her, and there lay
Sisera dead, with the tent peg through his temple.

23 Thus on that day God humbled the Canaanite king, Jabin, before the Israelites;
24 their power weighed ever heavier upon him,
till at length they destroyed the Canaanite king
Jabin.

CHAPTER 5

Canticle of Deborah. **1** On that day Deborah [and Barak, son of Abinoam] sang this
song:

2 Of chiefs who took the lead in Israel,*
of noble deeds by the people who bless
the LORD,
3 Hear, O kings! Give ear, O princes!
I to the LORD will sing my song,
my hymn to the LORD, the God of Israel.

4 O LORD, when you went out from Seir,
when you marched from the land of
Edom,
The earth quaked and the heavens were
shaken,
while the clouds sent down showers.
5 Mountains trembled
in the presence of the LORD, the One of
Sinai,[n]
in the presence of the LORD, the God of
Israel.[o]

6 In the days of Shamgar, son of Anath,[p]
in the days of slavery caravans ceased;
Those who traveled the roads
went by roundabout paths.
7 Gone was freedom beyond the walls
gone indeed from Israel.

When I, Deborah, rose,
when I rose, a mother in Israel,

8 New gods* were their choice;
then the war was at their gates.
Not a shield could be seen, nor a lance,
among forty thousand in Israel!

9 My heart is with the leaders of Israel,
nobles of the people who bless the LORD;
10 They who ride on white asses,
seated on saddlecloths as they go their
way;
11 Sing of them to the strains of the harpers at
the wells,
where men recount the just deeds of the
LORD,
his just deeds that brought freedom to
Israel.

12 Awake, awake, Deborah!
awake, awake, strike up a song.
Strength! arise, Barak,
make despoilers your spoil, son of
Abinoam.
13 Then down came the fugitives with the
mighty,
the people of the LORD came down for me
as warriors.

14 From Ephraim, princes were in the valley;*
behind you was Benjamin, among your
troops.
From Machir came down commanders,
from Zebulun wielders of the marshal's
staff.

15 With Deborah were the princes of Issachar;
Barak, too, was in the valley, his course
unchecked.

Among the clans of Reuben
great were the searchings of heart.[q]
16 Why do you stay beside your hearths
listening to the lowing of the herds?
Among the clans of Reuben
great were the searchings of heart!

17 Gilead, beyond the Jordan, rests;
why does Dan spend his time in ships?
Asher, who dwells along the shore,

---

l Jgs 5, 25.
m Jgs 5, 26.
n Dt 33, 2; 2 Sm 22, 8; Pss 18, 8; 68, 9.
o Ex 19, 16; Dt 4, 11; Ps 97, 5.
p Jgs 3, 31.
q Jgs 4, 14.

---

*

5, 2–31: This canticle is an excellent example of early Hebrew poetry, even though some of its verses are now obscure.

5, 8: New gods: pagan deities; cf Dt 32, 16–18. God punished the idolatry of the Israelites by leaving them relatively unarmed before the attacks of their enemies, who had better weapons, made of iron; cf 1 Sm 13, 19–22.

5, 14–22: Praise for the tribes which formed the Israelite league against Sisera: Ephraim, Benjamin, Manasseh (represented by Machir), Zebulun, Issachar, and Naphtali (led by Barak), The tribes of Reuben, Gad (Gilead), Dan, and Asher are chided for their lack of co-operation. The more distant tribes of Judah and Simeon are not mentioned.

is resting in his coves.

18 Zebulum is the people defying death;
    Naphtali, too, on the open heights! [r]

19 The kings came and fought;
    then they fought, those kings of Canaan,
At Taanach by the waters of Megiddo;
    no silver booty did they take. [s]

20 From the heavens the stars, too, fought;*
    from their courses they fought against
    Sisera. [t]

21 The Wadi Kishon swept them away;
    a wadi . . . , the Kishon. [u]

22 Then the hoofs of the horses pounded,
    with the dashing, dashing of his steeds.

23 "Curse Meroz,"* says the LORD,
    "hurl a curse at its inhabitants!
For they came not to my help,
    as warriors to the help of the LORD."

24 Blessed among women be Jael,
    blessed among tent-dwelling women. [v]

25 He asked for water, she gave him milk; [w]
    in a princely bowl she offered curds.

26 With her left hand she reached for the peg,
    with her right, for the workman's mallet.

She hammered Sisera, crushed his head;
    she smashed, stove in his temple.

27 At her feet he sank down, fell, lay still;
    down at her feet he sank and fell;
where he sank down, there he fell, slain.

28 From the window peered down and wailed
    the mother of Sisera, from the lattice:
"Why is his chariot so long in coming?
    why are the hoofbeats of his chariots
    delayed?"

29 The wisest of her princesses answers her,
    and she, too, keeps answering herself:

30 They must be dividing the spoil they took:
    there must be a damsel or two for each
    man,
Spoils of dyed cloth as Sisera's spoil,
    an ornate shawl or two for me in the
    spoil."

31 May all your enemies perish thus, O LORD! [x]
    but your friends be as the sun rising in its
    might!

And the land was at rest for forty years.

CHAPTER 6

The Call of Gideon.   **1** The Israelites offended the LORD, who therefore delivered them into the power of Midian for seven years, **2** so that Midian held Israel subject. For fear of Midian the Israelites established the fire signals on the mountains, the caves for refuge, and the strongholds. **3** And it used to be that when the Israelites had completed their sowing, Midian, Amalek and the Kedemites would come up, [y] **4** encamp opposite them, and destroy the produce of the land as far as the outskirts of Gaza, leaving no sustenance in Israel, nor sheep, oxen or asses. **5** For they would come up with their livestock, and their tents would become as numerous as locusts; and neither they nor their camels could be numbered, when they came into the land to lay it waste. **6** Thus was Israel reduced to misery by Midian, and so the Israelites cried out to the LORD.

7 When Israel cried out to the LORD because of Midian, **8** [z] he sent a prophet to the Israelites who said to them, "The LORD, the God of Israel, says: I led you up from Egypt; I brought you out of the place of slavery. **9** I rescued you from the power of Egypt and of all your other oppressors. I drove them out before you and gave you their land. **10** And I said to you: I, the LORD, am your God; you shall not venerate the gods of the Amorites in whose land you are dwelling. But you did not obey me."

11 Then the angel of the LORD came and sat under the terebinth in Ophrah that belonged to Joash the Abiezrite. While his son Gideon was beating out wheat in the wine press to save it from the Midianites, **12** the angel of the LORD appeared to him and said, "The LORD is with you, O champion!" **13** "My LORD," Gideon said to him, "if the LORD is with us, why has all this happened to us? Where are his wondrous deeds of which our fathers told us when they said, 'Did not the LORD bring us up from Egypt?' For now the LORD has abandoned us and has delivered us into the power of Midian." **14** The LORD turned to him and said, "Go with the strength you have and save Israel from the power of Midian. It is I who send you." **15** But he answered him, "Please, my lord, how can I save Israel? My family is the meanest in Manasseh, and I am the most insignificant in my father's house." **16** "I shall be with you," the LORD said to him, "and you will cut down Midian to the last man." **17** He answered him, "If I find favor with you, give me a sign that you are speaking with me. **18** Do not depart from here, I pray you, until I come back to you and bring out my offering and set it before you." He answered, "I will await your return."

---

r Jgs 4, 10.
s Jgs 1, 27; Jos 17, 11.
t Jgs 4, 15; Jos 10, 14.
u Jgs 4, 7. 13.
v Jgs 4, 17; Jdt 13, 17;
   Lk 1, 28. 42.
w 25f: Jgs 4, 19. 21.
x Ps 83, 10-19.
y 3f: Jgs 7, 12; Dt 28,
   30ff.
z 8ff: Jgs 2, 1f; 10, 11-14.

*

5, 20f: It would seem that nature aided the Hebrews in some way. Perhaps the torrential rains swelled the waters of Kishon, which then overwhelmed the Canaanites.

5, 23: Meroz: an unknown locality in which Hebrews probably resided, since its inhabitants are cursed for their failure to proffer aid.

19 So Gideon went off and prepared a kid and an ephah of flour in the form of unleavened cakes. Putting the meat in a basket and the broth in a pot, he brought them out to him under the terebinth and presented them. **20** The angel of God said to him, "Take the meat and unleavened cakes and lay them on this rock; then pour out the broth."*a* When he had done so, **21** the angel of the LORD stretched out the tip of the staff he held, and touched the meat and unleavened cakes. Thereupon a fire came up from the rock which consumed the meat and unleavened cakes, and the angel of the LORD disappeared from sight. **22** *b*Gideon, now aware that it had been the angel of the LORD, said, "Alas, Lord, GOD, that I have seen the angel of the LORD face to face!" **23** The LORD answered him, "Be calm, do not fear. You shall not die." **24** So Gideon built there an altar to the LORD and called it Yahweh-shalom.* To this day it is still in Ophrah of the Abiezrites.

25 That same night the LORD said to him, "Take the seven-year-old spare bullock and destroy your father's altar to Baal and cut down the sacred pole* that is by it. **26** You shall build, instead, the proper kind of altar to the LORD, your God, on top of this stronghold. Then take the spare bullock and offer it as a holocaust on the wood from the sacred pole you have cut down." **27** So Gideon took ten of his servants and did as the LORD had commanded him. But through fear of his family and of the townspeople, he would not do it by day, but did it at night. **28** Early the next morning the townspeople found that the altar of Baal had been destroyed, the sacred pole near it cut down, and the spare bullock offered on the altar that was built. **29** They asked one another, "Who did this?" Their inquiry led them to the conclusion that Gideon, son of Joash, had done it. **30** So the townspeople said to Joash, "Bring out your son that he may die, for he was destroyed the altar of Baal and has cut down the sacred pole that was near it." **31** But Joash replied to all who were standing around him, "Do you intend to act in Baal's stead, or be his champion? If anyone acts for him, he shall be put to death by morning. If he whose altar has been destroyed is a god, let him act for himself!" **32** So on that day Gideon was called Jerubbaal,* because of the words, "Let Baal take action against him, since he destroyed his altar."*c*

33 Then all Midian and Amalek and the Kedemites mustered and crossed over into the valley of Jezreel, where they encamped. **34** The spirit of the LORD enveloped Gideon; he blew the horn that summoned Abiezer to follow him. **35** He sent messengers, too, throughout Manasseh, which also obeyed his summons; through Asher, Zebulun and Naphtali, likewise, he sent messengers and these tribes advanced to

meet the others. **36** Gideon said to God, "If indeed you are going to save Israel through me, as you promised, **37** I am putting this woolen fleece on the threshing floor. If dew comes on the fleece alone, while all the ground is dry, I shall know that you will save Israel through me, as you promised." **38** That is what took place. Early the next morning he wrung the dew from the fleece, squeezing out of it a bowlful of water. **39** Gideon then said to God, "Do not be angry with me if I speak once more. Let me make just one more test with the fleece. Let the fleece alone be dry, but let there be dew on all the ground." **40** That night God did so; the fleece alone was dry, but there was dew on all the ground.

CHAPTER 7

Defeat of Midian. **1** Early the next morning Jerubbaal*d* (that is, Gideon) encamped by Enharod with all his soldiers. The camp of Midian was in the valley north of Gibeath-hammoreh. **2** The LORD said to Gideon, "You have too many soldiers with you for me to deliver Midian into their power, lest Israel vaunt itself against me and say, 'My own power brought me the victory.' **3** Now proclaim to all the soldiers, 'If anyone is afraid or fearful, let him leave.' "*e* When Gideon put them to this test on the mountain, twenty-two thousand of the soldiers left, but ten thousand remained. **4** The LORD said to Gideon, "There are still too many soldiers. Lead them down to the water and I will test them for you there. If I tell you that a certain man is to go with you, he must go with you. But no one is to go if I tell you he must not." **5** *When Gideon led the soldiers down to the water, the LORD said to him, "You shall set to one side everyone who laps up the water as a dog does with its tongue; to the other, everyone who kneels down to drink." **6** Those who lapped up the water raised to their mouths by hand numbered three hundred, but all the rest of the soldiers knelt down to drink the water. **7** The LORD said to Gideon, "By means of the three hundred who lapped up the water I will save you

---

a Jgs 13, 19.
b 22f: Gn 32, 31; Dt 5, 24ff.
c 1 Sm 12, 11.
d Jgs 6, 32.
e Dt 20, 8.

*

6, 24: Yahweh-shalom: Hebrew for "the LORD is peace," a reference to the Lord's words, "Be calm," literally, "Peace be to you!"

6, 25: The sacred pole: see note on Ex 34, 13.

6, 32: Jerubbaal: similar in sound to the Hebrew words meaning, "Let Baal take action."

7, 5: The Lord desired not numerous but reliable soldiers. Those who drank from their hands were alert, standing ready to resist attack, whereas the others were careless and undependable. The cowardly soldiers had already been dismissed (v 3); cf Dt 20, 8.

and will deliver Midian into your power. So let all the other soldiers go home." **8** Their horns, and such supplies as the soldiers had with them, were taken up, and Gideon ordered the rest of the Israelites to their tents, but kept the three hundred men. Now the camp of Midian was beneath him in the valley.

9 That night the LORD said to Gideon, "Go, descend on the camp, for I have delivered it up to you. **10** If you are afraid to attack, go down to the camp with your aide Purah. **11** When you hear what they are saying, you will have the courage to descend on the camp." So he went down with his aide Purah to the outposts of the camp. **12** The Midianites, Amalekites, and all the Kedemites lay in the valley, as numerous as locusts. Nor could their camels be counted, for these were as many as the sands on the seashore. **13** *When Gideon arrived, one man was telling another about a dream. "I had a dream," he said, "that a round loaf of barley bread was rolling into the camp of Midian. It came to our tent and struck it, and as it fell it turned the tent upside down." **14** "This can only be the sword of the Israelite Gideon, son of Joash," the other replied. "God has delivered Midian and all the camp into his power." **15** When Gideon heard the description and explanation of the dream, he prostrated himself. Then returning to the camp of Israel, he said, "Arise, for the LORD has delivered the camp of Midian into your power."

16 He divided the three hundred men into three companies, and provided them all with horns and with empty jars and torches inside the jars. **17** "Watch me and follow my lead," he told them. "I shall go to the edge of the camp, and as I do, you must do also. **18** When I and those with me blow horns, you too must blow horns all around the camp and cry out, 'For the LORD and for Gideon!' " **19** So Gideon and the hundred men who were with him came to the edge of the camp at the beginning of the middle watch,* just after the posting of the guards. They blew the horns and broke the jars they were holding. **20** All three companies blew horns and broke their jars. They held the torches in their left hands, and in their right the horns they were blowing, and cried out, "A sword for the LORD and Gideon!" **21** They all remained standing in place around the camp, while the whole camp fell to running and shouting and fleeing. **22** But the three hundred men kept blowing the horns, and throughout the camp the LORD set the sword of one against another.*f* The army fled as far as Beth-shittah in the direction of Zarethan, near the border of Abel-meholah at Tabbath.

23 The Israelites were called to arms from Naphtali, from Asher, and from all Manasseh, and they pursued Midian. **24** Gideon also sent messengers throughout the mountain region of Ephraim to say, "Go down to confront Midian, and seize the water courses against them as far as Beth-barah, as well as the Jordan." So all the Ephraimites were called to arms, and they seized the water courses as far as Beth-barah, and the Jordan as well. **25** *g*They captured the two princes of Midian, Oreb and Zeeb, killing Oreb at the rock of Oreb and Zeeb at the wine press of Zeeb. Then they pursued Midian and carried the heads of Oreb and Zeeb to Gideon beyond the Jordan.

CHAPTER 8

1 But the Ephraimites said to him, "What have you done to us, not calling us when you went to fight against Midian?" And they quarrelled bitterly with him. **2** "What have I accomplished now in comparison with you?" he answered them. "Is not the gleaning of Ephraim better than the vintage of Abiezer?*h* **3** Into your power God delivered the princes of Midian, Oreb and Zeeb. What have I been able to do in comparison with you?" When he said this, their anger against him subsided.

4 When Gideon reached the Jordan and crossed it with his three hundred men, they were exhausted and famished. **5** So he said to the men of Succoth, "Will you give my followers some loaves of bread? They are exhausted, and I am pursuing Zebah and Zalmunna, kings of Midian." **6** But the princes of Succoth replied, "Are the hands of Zebah and Zalmunna already in your possession, that we should give food to your army?"* **7** Gideon said, "Very well; when the LORD has delivered Zebah and Zalmunna into my power, I will grind your flesh in with the thorns and briers of the desert." **8** He went up from there to Penuel and made the same request of them, but the men of Penuel answered him as had the men of Succoth. **9** So to the men of Penuel, too, he said, "When I return in triumph, I will demolish this tower."

10 Now Zebah and Zalmunna were in Karkor with their force of about fifteen thousand men; these were all who were left of the whole Kedemite army, a hundred and twenty thousand swordsmen having fallen. **11** Gideon went up

---

f 22f: Ps 83, 10; Is 9, 4.   10, 26.
g Jgs 8, 3; Ps 83, 12; Is   h Jg 6, 34.

*

7, 13: The barley loaf represents the agricultural Hebrews while the tent refers to the nomadic Midianites. The overthrow of the tent indicates the victory of the Hebrews over their Midianite oppressors.

7, 19: At the beginning of the middle watch: about two hours before midnight. The ancient Hebrews divided the night into three watches of about four hours each. At the beginning of a watch the sentinels were changed.

8, 6: Are the hands . . . in your possession . . .?: i.e., can you already boast of victory? The hands as well as the heads of slain enemies were cut off and counted as trophies; cf 2 Sm 4, 8; 2 Kgs 10, 7f; and the Ugaritic Anath Epic, V AB, II 10ff.

the route of the nomads east of Nobah and Jogbehah, and attacked the camp when it felt secure. **12** Zebah and Zalmunna fled. He pursued them and took the two kings of Midian, Zebah and Zalmunna, captive, throwing the entire army into panic.

13 Then Gideon, son of Joash, returned from battle by the pass of Heres. **14** He captured a young man of Succoth, who upon being questioned listed for him the seventy-seven princes and elders of Succoth. **15** So he went to the men of Succoth and said, "Here are Zebah and Zalmunna, with whom you taunted me, 'Are the hands of Zebah and Zalmunna already in your possession, that we should give food to your weary followers?'" **16** He took the elders of the city, and thorns and briers of the desert, and ground these men of Succoth into them. **17** He also demolished the tower of Penuel and slew the men of the city.

18 Then he said to Zebah and Zalmunna, "Where now are the men you killed at Tabor?" "They all resembled you," they replied. "They appeared to be princes." **19** "They were my brothers, my mother's sons," he said. "As the LORD lives, if you had spared their lives, I should not kill you." **20** Then he said to his first-born, Jether, "Go, kill them." Since Jether was still a boy, he was afraid and did not draw his sword. **21** Zebah and Zalmunna said, "Come, kill us yourself, for a man's strength is like the man." So Gideon stepped forward and killed Zebah and Zalmunna. He also took the crescents that were on the necks of their camels.

22 The Israelites then said to Gideon, "Rule over us—you, your son, and your son's son—for you rescued us from the power of Midian." **23** But Gideon answered them, "I will not rule over you, nor shall my son rule over you. The LORD must rule over you."

24 Gideon went on to say, "I should like to make a request of you. Will each of you give me a ring from his booty?" (For being Ishmaelites,* the enemy had gold rings.) **25** "We will gladly give them," they replied, and spread out a cloak into which everyone threw a ring from his booty. **26** The gold rings that he requested weighed seventeen hundred gold shekels, in addition to the crescents and pendants, the purple garments worn by the kings of Midian, and the trappings that were on the necks of their camels. **27** Gideon made an ephod out of the gold and placed it in his city Ophrah. However, all Israel paid idolatrous homage to it there, and caused the ruin of Gideon and his family.

28 Thus was Midian brought into subjection by the Israelites; no longer did they hold their heads high. And the land had rest for forty years, during the lifetime of Gideon.

Gideon's Son Abimelech.

29 Then Jerubbaal, son of Joash, went back home to stay. **30** *i*Now Gideon had seventy sons, his direct descendants, for he had many wives. **31** His concubine* who lived in Shechem also bore him a son, whom he named Abimelech. **32** At a good old age Gideon, son of Joash, died and was buried in the tomb of his father Joash in Ophrah of the Abiezrites. **33** But after Gideon was dead, the Israelites again abandoned themselves to the Baals, making Baal of Berith* their god **34** and forgetting the LORD, their God, who had delivered them from the power of their enemies all around them. **35** Nor were they grateful to the family of Jerubbaal [Gideon] for all the good he had done for Israel.

CHAPTER 9

1 Abimelech, son of Jerubbaal, went to his mother's kinsmen in Shechem,*j* and said to them and to the whole clan to which his mother's family belonged, **2** "Put this question to all the citizens of Shechem: 'Which is better for you: that seventy men, or all Jerubbaal's sons, rule over you, or that one man rule over you?' You must remember that I am your own flesh and bone." **3** When his mother's kin repeated these words to them on his behalf, all the citizens of Shechem sympathized with Abimelech, thinking, "He is our kinsman." **4** They also gave him seventy silver shekels from the temple of Baal of Berith, with which Abimelech hired shiftless men and ruffians as his followers. **5** He then went to his ancestral house in Ophrah, and slew his brothers, the seventy sons of Jerubbaal, on one stone. Only the youngest son of Jerubbaal, Jotham, escaped, for he was hidden. **6** Then all the citizens of Shechem and all Beth-millo came together and proceeded to make Abimelech king by the terebinth at the memorial pillar in Shechem.

7 When this was reported to him, Jotham went to the top of Mount Gerizim, and standing there, cried out to them in a loud voice: "Hear me, citizens of Shechem, that God may then hear you! **8** Once the trees went to anoint a king over themselves. So they said to the olive tree, 'Reign over us.'*k* **9** But the olive tree answered

---

i Jgs 9, 2. 5.   k Jgs 8, 22f.
j Jgs 8, 31.

---

*

8, 24: Ishmaelites: here as in Gn 37, 25–28, the designation is not ethnic; it refers rather to their status as nomads.

8, 31: Concubine: a wife of secondary rank.

8, 33: Baal of Berith: one of the titles of Baal as worshiped by the Canaanites of Shechem, meaning "the lord of the covenant."

9, 9: Whereby men and gods are honored: oil was used in the worship both of the true God and of false gods; it was prescribed in the worship of Yahweh (Lv 2, 1. 6. 15; 24, 2). It was also used to consecrate prophets, priests and kings (Ex 30, 25. 30; 1 Sm 10, 1; 16, 13).

them, 'Must I give up my rich oil, whereby men and gods are honored,* and go to wave over the trees?' **10** Then the trees said to the fig tree, 'Come; you reign over us!' **11** But the fig tree answered them, 'Must I give up my sweetness and my good fruit, and go to wave over the trees?' **12** Then the trees said to the vine, 'Come you, and reign over us.' **13** But the vine answered them, 'Must I give up my wine that cheers gods* and men, and go to wave over the trees?' **14** Then all the trees said to the buckthorn, 'Come; you reign over us!' **15** But the buckthorn replied to the trees, 'If you wish to anoint me king over you in good faith, come and take refuge in my shadow. Otherwise, let fire come from the buckthorn and devour the cedars of Lebanon.'

16 *"Now then, if you have acted in good faith and honorably in appointing Abimelech your king, if you have dealt well with Jerubbaal and with his family, and if you have treated him as he deserved— **17** for my father fought for you at the risk of his life when he saved you from the power of Midian; **18** but you have risen against his family this day and have killed his seventy sons upon one stone, and have made Abimelech, the son of his handmaid,ⁱ king over the citizens of Shechem, because he is your kinsman— **19** if, then, you have acted in good faith and with honor toward Jerubbaal and his family this day, rejoice in Abimelech and may he in turn rejoice in you. **20** But if not, let fire come forth from Abimelech to devour the citizens of Shechem and Beth-millo, and let fire come forth from the citizens and from Beth-millo to devour Abimelech." **21** Then Jotham went in flight to Beer, where he remained for fear of his brother Abimelech.

22 When Abimelech had ruled Israel for three years, **23** God put bad feelings between Abimelech and the citizens of Shechem, who rebelled against Abimelech. **24** This was to repay the violence done to the seventy sons of Jerubbaal and to avenge their blood upon their brother Abimelech, who killed them, and upon the citizens of Shechem, who encouraged him to kill his brothers. **25** The citizens of Shechem then set men in ambush for him on the mountaintops, and these robbed all who passed them on the road. But it was reported to Abimelech.

26 Now Gaal, son of Ebed, came over to Shechem with his kinsmen. The citizens of Shechem put their trust in him, **27** and went out into the fields, harvested their grapes and trod them out. Then they held a festival and went to the temple of their god, where they ate and drank and cursed Abimelech. **28** Gaal, son of Ebed, said, "Who is Abimelech? And why should we of Shechem serve him? Were not the son of Jerubbaal and his lieutenant Zebul once subject to the men of Hamor, father of She-

chem?ᵐ Why should we serve him? **29** Would that this people were entrusted to my command! I would depose Abimelech. I would say to Abimelech, 'Get a larger army and come out!' "

30 At the news of what Gaal, son of Ebed, had said, Zebul, the ruler of the city, was angry **31** and sent messengers to Abimelech in Arumah with the information: "Gaal, son of Ebed, and his kinsmen have come to Shechem and are stirring up the city against you. **32** Now rouse yourself; set an ambush tonight in the fields, you and the men who are with you. **33** Promptly at sunrise tomorrow morning, make a raid on the city. When he and his followers come out against you, deal with him as best you can."

34 During the night Abimelech advanced with all his soldiers and set up an ambush for Shechem in four companies. **35** Gaal, son of Ebed, went out and stood at the entrance of the city gate. When Abimelech and his soldiers rose from their place of ambush, **36** Gaal saw them and said to Zebul, "There are men coming down from the hilltops!" But Zebul answered him, "You see the shadow of the hills as men." **37** But Gaal went on to say, "Men are coming down from the region of Tabbur-Haares, and one company is coming by way of Elon-Meonenim." **38** Zebul said to him, "Where now is the boast you uttered, 'Who is Abimelech that we should serve him?' Are these not the men for whom you expressed contempt? Go out now and fight with them." **39** So Gaal went out at the head of the citizens of Shechem and fought against Abimelech. **40** But Abimelech routed him, and he fled before him; and many fell slain right up to the entrance of the gate. **41** Abimelech returned to Arumah, but Zebul drove Gaal and his kinsmen from Shechem, which they had occupied.

42 The next day, when the people were taking the field, it was reported to Abimelech, **43** who divided the men he had into three companies, and set up an ambush in the fields. He watched till he saw the people leave the city, and then rose against them for the attack. **44** Abimelech and the company with him dashed in and stood by the entrance of the city gate, while the other two companies rushed upon all who were in the field and attacked them. **45** That entire day Abimelech fought

---

ⁱ Jgs 8, 31.　　　　　　　　ᵐ Gn 34, 2. 6.

*

9, 13: Cheers gods: wine was used in the libations both of the Temple of Jerusalem and of pagan temples.

9, 16: Just as the noble trees refused the honor of royalty and were made subject to a mean plant, so did Abimelech of less noble birth than the seventy sons of Gideon now tyrannize over the people.

9, 45: Sowing the site with salt: a severe measure, which was a symbol of desolation, and even more, since it actually rendered the ground barren and useless.

against the city, and captured it. He then killed its inhabitants and demolished the city, sowing the site with salt.*

46 When they heard of this, all the citizens of Migdal-shechem went into the crypt of the temple of El-berith. **47** It was reported to Abimelech that all the citizens of Migdal-shechem were gathered together. **48** So he went up Mount Zalmon with all his soldiers, took his ax in his hand, and cut down some brushwood. This he lifted to his shoulder, then said to the men with him, "Hurry! Do just as you have seen me do." **49** So all the men likewise cut down brushwood, and following Abimelech, placed it against the crypt. Then they set the crypt on fire over their heads, so that every one of the citizens of Migdal-shechem, about a thousand men and women, perished.

50 Abimelech proceeded to Thebez, which he invested and captured. **51** Now there was a strong tower in the middle of the city, and all the men and women, in a word all the citizens of the city, fled there, shutting themselves in and going up to the roof of the tower. **52** Abimelech came up to the tower and fought against it, advancing to the very entrance of the tower to set it on fire. **53** But a certain woman cast the upper part of a millstone down on Abimelech's head, and it fractured his skull.*n* **54** He immediately called his armor-bearer and said to him, "Draw your sword and dispatch me, lest they say of me that a woman killed me."*o* So his attendant ran him through and he died. **55** When the Israelites saw that Abimelech was dead, they all left for their homes.

56 Thus did God requite the evil Abimelech had done to his father in killing his seventy brothers. **57** God also brought all their wickedness home to the Shechemites, for the curse of Jotham, son of Jerubbaal, overtook them.

CHAPTER 10

Tola. **1** After Abimelech there rose to save Israel the Issacharite Tola, son of Puah, son of Dodo, a resident of Shamir in the mountain region of Ephraim. **2** When he had judged Israel twenty-three years, he died and was buried in Shamir.

Jair. **3** Jair the Gileadite came after him and judged Israel twenty-two years. **4** He had thirty sons who rode on thirty saddle-asses* and possessed thirty cities in the land of Gilead; these are called Havvoth-jair to the present day.*p* **5** Jair died and was buried in Kamon.

Oppression by the Ammonites. **6** The Israelites again offended the LORD, serving the Baals and Ashtaroths, the gods of Aram, the gods of Sidon, the gods of Moab, the gods of

the Ammonites, and the gods of the Philistines. Since they had abandoned the LORD and would not serve him, **7** the LORD became angry with Israel and allowed them to fall into the power of [the Philistines and] the Ammonites. **8** For eighteen years they afflicted and oppressed the Israelites in Bashan, and all the Israelites in the Amorite land beyond the Jordan in Gilead. **9** The Ammonites also crossed the Jordan to fight against Judah, Benjamin, and the house of Ephraim, so that Israel was in great distress.

10 Then the Israelites cried out to the LORD, "We have sinned against you; we have forsaken our God and have served the Baals." **11** *q*The LORD answered the Israelites: "Did not the Egyptians, the Amorites,*r* the Ammonites, the Philistines, **12** the Sidonians, the Amalekites, and the Midianites oppress you?*s* Yet when you cried out to me, and I saved you from their grasp, **13** you still forsook me and worshiped other gods. Therefore I will save you no more. **14** Go and cry out to the gods you have chosen; let them save you now that you are in distress." **15** But the Israelites said to the LORD, "We have sinned. Do to us whatever you please. Only save us this day." **16** And they cast out the foreign gods from their midst and served the LORD, so that he grieved over the misery of Israel.

17 The Ammonites had gathered for war and encamped in Gilead, while the Israelites assembled and encamped in Mizpah.*t* **18** And among the people the princes of Gilead said to one another, "The one who begins the war against the Ammonites shall be leader of all the inhabitants of Gilead."*u*

CHAPTER 11

Jephthah. **1** There was a chieftain, the Gileadite Jephthah, born to Gilead of a harlot. **2** Gilead's wife had also borne him sons, and on growing up the sons of the wife had driven Jephthah away, saying to him, "You shall inherit nothing in our family, for you are the son of another woman." **3** So Jephthah had fled from his brothers and had taken up residence in the land of Tob. A rabble had joined company with him, and went out with him on raids.

4 Some time later, the Ammonites warred on Israel. **5** When this occurred the elders of Gilead went to bring Jephthah from the land of Tob. **6** "Come," they said to Jephthah, "be our

---

n 2 Sm 11, 21.
o 1 Sm 31, 4; 1 Chr 10, 4.
p Dt 3, 14.
q 11-14: Jgs 2, 1ff; 6, 8ff.
r Nm 21, 21-32.
s Jgs 6, 3.
t Jgs 11, 29.
u Jgs 11, 5-11.

*

10, 4: Saddle-asses: a sign of rank and wealth; cf Jgs 5, 10; 12, 14.

commander that we may be able to fight the Ammonites." **7** "Are you not the ones who hated me and drove me from my father's house?" Jephthah replied to the elders of Gilead. "Why do you come to me now, when you are in distress?" **8** The elders of Gilead said to Jephthah, "In any case, we have now come back to you; if you go with us to fight against the Ammonites, you shall be the leader of all of us who dwell in Gilead." **9** Jephthah answered the elders of Gilead, "If you bring me back to fight against the Ammonites and the LORD delivers them up to me, I shall be your leader." **10** The elders of Gilead said to Jephthah, "The LORD is witness between us that we will do as you say."

11 So Jephthah went with the elders of Gilead, and the people made him their leader and commander.*v* In Mizpah, Jephthah settled all his affairs before the LORD. **12** Then he sent messengers to the king of the Ammonites to say, "What have you against me that you come to fight with me in my land?" **13** He answered the messengers of Jephthah, "Israel took away my land from the Arnon to the Jabbok and the Jordan when they came up from Egypt.*w* Now restore the same peaceably."

14 Again Jephthah sent messengers to the king of the Ammonites, **15** saying to him, "This is what Jephthah says: Israel did not take the land of Moab or the land of the Ammonites.*x* **16** For when they came up from Egypt, Israel went through the desert to the Red Sea and came to Kadesh. **17** Israel then sent messengers to the king of Edom saying, 'Let me pass through your land.' But the king of Edom did not give consent. They also sent to the king of Moab, but he too was unwilling. So Israel remained in Kadesh.*y* **18** Then they went through the desert, and by-passing the land of Edom and the land of Moab, went east of the land of Moab and encamped across the Arnon.*z* Thus they did not go through the territory of Moab, for the Arnon is the boundary of Moab. **19** *a*Then Israel sent messengers to Sihon, king of the Amorites, king of Heshbon. Israel said to him, 'Let me pass through your land to my own place.' **20** But Sihon refused to let Israel pass through his territory. On the contrary, he gathered all his soldiers, who encamped at Jahaz and fought Israel. **21** But the LORD, the God of Israel, delivered Sihon and all his men into the power of Israel, who defeated them and occupied all the land of the Amorites dwelling in that region, **22** the whole territory from the Arnon to the Jabbok, from the desert to the Jordan. **23** If now the LORD, the God of Israel, has cleared the Amorites out of the way of his people, are you to dislodge Israel? **24** Should you not possess that which your god Chemosh* gave you to possess, and should we not possess all that the LORD, our God, has cleared out for us?*b* **25** Again, are you any better than Balak, son of Zippor, king of Moab? Did he ever quarrel with Israel, or did he war against them*c* **26** when Israel occupied Heshbon and its villages, Aroer and its villages, and all the cities on the banks of the Arnon?*d* Three hundred years have passed; why did you not recover them during that time? **27** I have not sinned against you, but you wrong me by warring against me. Let the LORD, who is judge, decide this day between the Israelites and the Ammonites!" **28** But the king of the Ammonites paid no heed to the message Jephthah sent him.

Jephthah's Vow. **29** The spirit of the LORD came upon Jephthah. He passed through Gilead and Manasseh, and through Mizpah-Gilead as well, and from there he went on to the Ammonites. **30** *Jephthah made a vow to the LORD. "If you deliver the Ammonites into my power," he said, **31** "whoever comes out of the doors of my house to meet me when I return in triumph from the Ammonites shall belong to the LORD. I shall offer him up as a holocaust."

32 Jephthah then went on to the Ammonites to fight against them, and the LORD delivered them into his power, **33** so that he inflicted a severe defeat on them, from Aroer to the approach of Minnith (twenty cities in all) and as far as Abel-keramim. Thus were the Ammonites brought into subjection by the Israelites. **34** When Jephthah returned to his house in Mizpah, it was his daughter who came forth, playing the tambourines and dancing. She was an only child: he had neither son nor daughter besides her. **35** When he saw her, he rent his garments and said, "Alas, daughter, you have struck me down and brought calamity upon me. For I have made a vow to the LORD and I cannot retract."*e* **36** "Father," she replied, "you have made a vow to the LORD. Do with me as you have vowed, because the LORD has wrought

---

v Jgs 10, 18.
w Nm 21, 13. 24ff.
x Dt 2, 9. 19.
y Nm 20, 1. 14. 18-21; Dt 1, 46.
z Nm 21, 4. 11. 13; 22, 36; Dt 2, 8.
a 19-22: Nm 21, 21-26;

b Nm 21, 29; 1 Kgs 11, 7.
c Nm 22, 2; Jos 24, 9; Mi 6, 5.
d Nm 21, 25; Dt 2, 36.
e Nm 30, 3.

*

11, 24: Chemosh: the chief god of the Moabites—not of the Ammonites, whose leading deity was called Molech or Milcom; cf Nm 21, 29; 1 Kgs 11, 7; 2 Kgs 23, 13. The error is probably due to an ancient copyist. Jephthah argues from the viewpoint of his adversaries, the Ammonites, that they were entitled to all the land they had conquered with the aid of their god. It does not necessarily follow that Jephthah himself believed in the actual existence of this pagan god.

11, 30–40: The text clearly implies that Jephthah vowed a human sacrifice, according to the custom of his pagan neighbors; cf 2 Kgs 3, 27. The inspired author merely records the fact; he does not approve of the action.

vengeance for you on your enemies the Ammonites.'' **37** Then she said to her father, ''Let me have this favor. Spare me for two months, that I may go off down the mountains to mourn my virginity* with my companions.'' **38** ''Go,'' he replied, and sent her away for two months. So she departed with her companions and mourned her virginity on the mountains. **39** At the end of the two months she returned to her father, who did to her as he had vowed. She had not been intimate with man. It then became a custom in Israel **40** for Israelite women to go yearly to mourn the daughter of Jephthah the Gileadite for four days of the year.

CHAPTER 12

The Shibboleth Incident. **1** The men of Ephraim gathered together and crossed over to Zaphon. They said to Jephthah, ''Why do you go on to fight with the Ammonites without calling us to go with you? We will burn your house over you.''*f* **2** Jephthah answered them, ''My soldiers and I were engaged in a critical contest with the Ammonites. I summoned you, but you did not rescue me from their power. **3** When I saw that you would not effect a rescue, I took my life in my own hand and went on to the Ammonites, and the LORD delivered them into my power. Why, then, do you come up against me this day to fight with me?''

4 Then Jephthah called together all the men of Gilead and fought against Ephraim, whom they defeated; for the Ephraimites had said, ''You of Gilead are Ephraimite fugitives in territory belonging to Ephraim and Manasseh.'' **5** The Gileadites took the fords of the Jordan toward Ephraim. When any of the fleeing Ephraimites said, ''Let me pass,'' the men of Gilead would say to him, ''Are you an Ephraimite?'' If he answered, ''No!'' **6** they would ask him to say ''Shibboleth.''* If he said ''Sibboleth,'' not being able to give the proper pronunciation, they would seize him and kill him at the fords of the Jordan. Thus forty-two thousand Ephraimites fell at that time.

7 After having judged Israel for six years, Jephthah the Gileadite died and was buried in his city in Gilead.

Ibzan. **8** After him Ibzan of Bethlehem judged Israel. **9** He had thirty sons. He also had thirty daughters married outside the family, and he brought in as wives for his sons thirty young women from outside the family. After having judged Israel for seven years, **10** Ibzan died and was buried in Bethlehem.

Elon. **11** After him the Zebulunite Elon judged Israel. When he had judged Israel for ten

years, **12** the Zebulunite Elon died and was buried in Elon in the land of Zebulun.

Abdon. **13** After him the Pirathonite Abdon, son of Hillel, judged Israel. **14** He had forty sons and thirty grandsons who rode on seventy saddle-asses. After having judged Israel for eight years, **15** the Pirathonite Abdon, son of Hillel, died and was buried in Pirathon in the land of Ephraim on the mountain of the Amalekites.

CHAPTER 13

The Birth of Samson. **1** The Israelites again offended the LORD, who therefore delivered them into the power of the Philistines for forty years.*g* **2** There was a certain man from Zorah, of the clan of the Danites, whose name was Manoah. His wife was barren and had borne no children. **3** An angel of the LORD appeared to the woman and said to her, ''Though you are barren and have had no children, yet you will conceive and bear a son.*h* **4** Now, then, be careful to take no wine or strong drink and to eat nothing unclean. **5** As for the son you will conceive and bear, no razor shall touch his head,*i* for this boy is to be consecrated* to God from the womb. It is he who will begin the deliverance of Israel from the power of the Philistines.''

6 The woman went and told her husband, ''A man of God came to me; he had the appearance of an angel of God, terrible indeed. I did not ask him where he came from, nor did he tell me his name. **7** But he said to me, 'You will be with child and will bear a son. So take neither wine nor strong drink, and eat nothing unclean. For the boy shall be consecrated to God from the womb, until the day of his death.' '' **8** Manoah then prayed to the LORD. ''O LORD, I beseech you,'' he said, ''may the man of God whom you sent, return to us to teach us what to do for the boy who will be born.''

9 God heard the prayer of Manoah, and the

---

f Jgs 8, 1.
g Jgs 10, 6.
h 3f: 1 Sm 1, 20; Lk 1, 31.
i Nm 6, 5.

11, 37: Mourn my virginity: to bear children was woman's greatest pride; to be childless was regarded as a great misfortune. Hence Jephthah's daughter asks permission to mourn the fact that she will be put to death before she can bear children.

12, 6: Shibboleth: "an ear of grain." But this Hebrew word can also mean "flood water" as in Ps 69, 3. 16. Apparently the Gileadites engaged the Ephraimites in conversation about the "flood water" of the Jordan. Differences in enunciating the initial sibilant of the Hebrew word betrayed different tribal affinities.

13, 5: Consecrated: In Hebrew, nazir. Samson therefore was for life to be under the nazirite vow, which obliged him to abstain from drinking wine or having his hair cut; cf Nm 6, 2–8.

angel of God came again to the woman as she was sitting in the field. Since her husband Manoah was not with her, **10** the woman ran in haste and told her husband. "The man who came to me the other day has appeared to me," she said to him; **11** so Manoah got up and followed his wife. When he reached the man, he said to him, "Are you the one who spoke to my wife?" "Yes," he answered. **12** Then Manoah asked, "Now, when that which you say comes true, what are we expected to do for the boy?" **13** The angel of the LORD answered Manoah, "Your wife is to abstain from all the things of which I spoke to her. **14** She must not eat anything that comes from the vine, nor take wine or strong drink, nor eat anything unclean. Let her observe all that I have commanded her." **15** Then Manoah said to the angel of the LORD, "Can we persuade you to stay, while we prepare a kid for you?" **16** But the angel of the LORD answered Manoah, "Although you press me, I will not partake of your food. But if you will, you may offer a holocaust to the LORD." Not knowing that it was the angel of the LORD, **17** Manoah said to him, "What is your name, that we may honor you when your words come true?" **18** The angel of the LORD answered him,[j] "Why do you ask my name, which is mysterious?"* **19** [k]Then Manoah took the kid with a cereal offering and offered it on the rock to the LORD, whose works are mysteries. While Manoah and his wife were looking on, **20** as the flame rose to the sky from the altar, the angel of the LORD ascended in the flame of the altar. When Manoah and his wife saw this, they fell prostrate to the ground; **21** but the angel of the LORD was seen no more by Manoah and his wife. Then Manoah, realizing that it was the angel of the LORD, **22** said to his wife, "We will certainly die, for we have seen God."[l] **23** But his wife pointed out to him, "If the LORD had meant to kill us, he would not have accepted a holocaust and cereal offering from our hands! Nor would he have let us see all this just now, or hear what we have heard."

24 The woman bore a son and named him Samson.[m] The boy grew up and the LORD blessed him; **25** the spirit of the LORD first stirred him in Mahaneh-dan, which is between Zorah and Eshtaol.

CHAPTER 14

Marriage of Samson. **1** Samson went down to Timnah and saw there one of the Philistine women.* **2** On his return he told his father and mother, "There is a Philistine woman I saw in Timnah whom I wish you to get as a wife for me." **3** His father and mother said to him, "Can you find no wife among your kinsfolk or among all our people, that you must go and take

a wife from the uncircumcised Philistines?" But Samson answered his father, "Get her for me, for she pleases me." **4** [n]Now his father and mother did not know that this had been brought about by the LORD, who was providing an opportunity against the Philistines; for at that time they had dominion over Israel.

5 *So Samson went down to Timnah with his father and mother. When they had come to the vineyards of Timnah, a young lion came roaring to meet him. **6** But the spirit of the LORD came upon Samson, and although he had no weapons, he tore the lion in pieces as one tears a kid. **7** However, on the journey to speak for the woman, he did not mention to his father or mother what he had done. **8** Later, when he returned to marry the woman who pleased him, he stepped aside to look at the remains of the lion and found a swarm of bees and honey in the lion's carcass. **9** So he scooped the honey out into his palms and ate it as he went along. When he came to his father and mother, he gave them some to eat, without telling them that he had scooped the honey from the lion's carcass.

10 His father also went down to the woman, and Samson gave a banquet there, since it was customary for the young men to do this. **11** When they met him, they brought thirty men to be his companions.* **12** Samson said to them, "Let me propose a riddle to you. If within the seven days of the feast you solve it for me successfully, I will give you thirty linen tunics and thirty sets of garments. **13** But if you cannot answer it for me, you must give me thirty tunics and thirty sets of garments." "Propose your riddle," they responded; "we will listen to it." **14** So he said to them,

> "Out of the eater came forth food,
>   and out of the strong came forth
>   sweetness."

After three days' failure to answer the riddle, **15** they said on the fourth day to Samson's

---

j Gn 32, 29.
k 19f: Jgs 6, 19ff.
l 21f: Jgs 6, 22f.

m Heb 11, 32.
n Jgs 15, 11.

---

*

13, 18: Mysterious: incomprehensible, above human understanding. Hence, the angel speaks in the name of the Lord himself, to whom Manoah at once offers a sacrifice.

14, 1–3: Marriages were arranged by the parents of the bridegroom as well as of the bride; cf Gn 24, 2–8; 34, 3–6. The Mosaic law specified only seven pagan nations, not including the Philistines, in the prohibition against mixed marriages; cf Dt 7, 1–4. But national and religious sentiment was against any marriage with a non-Israelite; cf Gn 28, 1f; 1 Kgs 11, 1–10.

14, 5ff: Although Samson was accompanied by his parents on the journey to Timnah, v 7 implies that he was not near them when he tore the lion in pieces.

14, 11: Companions: known at a later period as "the friends of the bridegroom" (1 Mc 9, 39; Mk 2, 19), the best man and his fellows. Here they are Philistines (v 16), appointed by the family of the bride, who would also have several bridesmaids; cf Mt 25, 1–13.

wife, "Coax your husband to answer the riddle for us, or we will burn you and your family. Did you invite us here to reduce us to poverty?" **16** At Samson's side, his wife wept and said, "You must hate me; you do not love me, for you have proposed a riddle to my countrymen, but have not told me the answer." He said to her, "If I have not told it even to my father or my mother, must I tell it to you?" **17** But she wept beside him during the seven days the feast lasted. On the seventh day, since she importuned him, he told her the answer, and she explained the riddle to her countrymen.

18 On the seventh day, before the sun set, the men of the city said to him,

> "What is sweeter than honey,
>   and what is stronger than a lion?"

He replied to them,

> "If you had not plowed with my heifer,
>   you would not have solved my riddle."

19 The spirit of the LORD came upon him, and he went down to Ashkelon, where he killed thirty of their men and despoiled them; he gave their garments to those who had answered the riddle. Then he went off to his own family in anger, **20** and Samson's wife was married to the one who had been best man at his wedding. *o*

CHAPTER 15

Samson Defeats the Philistines. **1** After some time, in the season of the wheat harvest, Samson visited his wife, bringing a kid. But when he said, "Let me be with my wife in private," her father would not let him enter, **2** saying, "I thought it certain you wished to repudiate her; so I gave her to your best man. Her younger sister is more beautiful than she; you may have her instead." **3** Samson said to them, "This time the Philistines cannot blame me if I harm them." **4** So Samson left and caught three hundred foxes. Turning them tail to tail, he tied between each pair of tails one of the torches he had at hand. **5** He then kindled the torches and set the foxes loose in the standing grain of the Philistines, thus burning both the shocks and the standing grain, and the vineyards and olive orchards as well.

6 *p*When the Philistines asked who had done this, they were told, "Samson, the son-in-law of the Timnite, because his wife was taken and given to his best man." So the Philistines went up and destroyed her and her family by fire. **7** Samson said to them, "If this is how you act, I will not stop until I have taken revenge on you." **8** And with repeated blows, he inflicted a great slaughter on them. Then he went down and remained in a cavern of the cliff of Etam. **9** The Philistines went up and, from a camp in Judah, deployed against Lehi. **10** When the men of Judah asked, "Why have you come up against us?" they answered, "To take Samson prisoner; to do to him as he has done to us." **11** Three thousand men of Judah went down to the cavern in the cliff of Etam and said to Samson, "Do you not know that the Philistines are our rulers? Why, then, have you done this to us?" He answered them, "As they have done to me, so have I done to them." **12** They said to him, "We have come to take you prisoner, to deliver you over to the Philistines." Samson said to them, "Swear to me that you will not kill me yourselves." **13** "No," they replied, "we will certainly not kill you but will only bind you and deliver you over to them." *q* So they bound him with two new ropes and brought him up from the cliff. **14** When he reached Lehi, and the Philistines came shouting to meet him: the spirit of the LORD came upon him: the ropes around his arms became as flax that is consumed by fire and his bonds melted away from his hands. **15** Near him was the fresh jawbone of an ass; he reached out, grasped it, and with it killed a thousand men. **16** Then Samson said,

> "With the jawbone of an ass
>   I have piled them in a heap;
> With the jawbone of an ass
>   I have slain a thousand men."

17 As he finished speaking he threw the jawbone from him; and so that place was named Ramath-lehi.* **18** Being very thirsty, he cried to the LORD and said, "You have granted this great victory by the hand of your servant. Must I now die of thirst or fall into the hands of the uncircumcised?" **19** Then God split the cavity in Lehi, and water issued from it, which Samson drank till his spirit returned and he revived. Hence that spring in Lehi is called En-hakkore* to this day.

20 Samson judged Israel for twenty years in the days of the Philistines. *r*

CHAPTER 16

1 Once Samson went to Gaza, where he saw a harlot and visited her. **2** Informed that Samson had come there, the men of Gaza surrounded him with an ambush at the city gate all night long. And all the night they waited, saying, "Tomorrow morning we will kill him." **3** Samson rested there until midnight. Then he rose, seized the doors of the city gate and the two gateposts, and tore them loose, bar and all. He hoisted them on his shoulders and carried

---

o Jgs 15, 2. 6.   q Jgs 16, 11f.
p Jgs 14, 20.   r Jgs 16, 31.

15, 17: Ramath-lehi: "heights of the jawbone."
15, 19: En-hakkore: "the spring of him who cries out," an allusion to Samson's cry in v 18.

them to the top of the ridge opposite Hebron.

Samson and Delilah.   4 After that he fell
in love with a woman in the Wadi Sorek whose
name was Delilah. 5 The lords of the Philistines
came to her and said, "Beguile him and find out
the secret of his great strength, and how we may
overcome and bind him so as to keep him helpless. We will each give you eleven hundred
shekels of silver."

6 So Delilah said to Samson, "Tell me the
secret of your great strength and how you may
be bound so as to be kept helpless." 7 "If they
bind me with seven fresh bowstrings which
have not dried," Samson answered her, "I shall
be as weak as any other man." 8 So the lords
of the Philistines brought her seven fresh bowstrings which had not dried, and she bound him
with them. 9 She had men lying in wait in the
chamber and so she said to him, "The Philistines are upon you, Samson!" But he snapped
the strings as a thread of tow is severed by a
whiff of flame;s and the secret of his strength
remained unknown.

10 Delilah said to Samson, "You have
mocked me and told me lies. Now tell me how
you may be bound." 11 "If they bind me tight
with new ropes, with which no work has been
done," he answered her, "I shall be as weak as
any other man."t 12 So Delilah took new ropes
and bound him with them. Then she said to him,
"The Philistines are upon you, Samson!" For
there were men lying in wait in the chamber.
But he snapped them off his arms like thread.

13 Delilah said to Samson again, "Up to
now you have mocked me and told me lies. Tell
me how you may be bound." He said to her, "If
you weave my seven locks of hair into the web
and fasten them with the pin, I shall be as weak
as any other man." 14 So while he slept, Delilah wove his seven locks of hair into the web,
and fastened them in with the pin. Then she
said, "The Philistines are upon you, Samson!"
Awakening from his sleep, he pulled out both
the weaver's pin and the web.

15 Then she said to him, "How can you say
that you love me when you do not confide in
me? Three times already you have mocked me,
and not told me the secret of your great
strength!" 16 She importuned him continually
and vexed him with her complaints till he was
deathly weary of them. 17 So he took her completely into his confidence and told her, "No
razor has touched my head,u for I have been
consecrated to God from my mother's womb. If
I am shaved, my strength will leave me, and I
shall be as weak as any other man!" 18 When
Delilah saw that he had taken her completely
into his confidence, she summoned the lords of
the Philistines, saying, "Come up this time, for
he has opened his heart to me." So the lords of

the Philistines came and brought up the money
with them. 19 She had him sleep on her lap,
and called for a man who shaved off his seven
locks of hair. Then she began to mistreat him,
for his strength had left him. 20 When she said,
"The Philistines are upon you, Samson!", and
he woke from his sleep, he thought he could
make good his escape as he had done time and
again, for he did not realize that the LORD had
left him. 21 But the Philistines seized him and
gouged out his eyes. Then they brought him
down to Gaza and bound him with bronze fetters, and he was put to grinding in the prison.
22 But the hair of his head began to grow as
soon as it was shaved off.

The Death of Samson.   23 vThe lords of
the Philistines assembled to offer a great sacrifice to their god Dagon* and to make merry.
They said,

> "Our god has delivered into our power
>   Samson our enemy."

25 When their spirits were high, they said,
"Call Samson that he may amuse us." So they
called Samson from the prison, and he played
the buffoon before them. 24 When the people
saw him, they praised their god. For they said,

> "Our god has delivered into our power
>   our enemy, the ravager of our land,
>   the one who has multiplied our slain."

Then they stationed him between the columns. 26 Samson said to the attendant who was
holding his hand, "Put me where I may touch
the columns that support the temple and may
rest against them." 27 The temple was full of
men and women: all the lords of the Philistines
were there, and from the roof about three thousand men and women looked on as Samson
provided amusement. 28 Samson cried out to
the LORD and said, "O Lord GOD, remember
me! Strengthen me, O God, this last time that
for my two eyes I may avenge myself once and
for all on the Philistines." 29 Samson grasped
the two middle columns on which the temple
rested and braced himself against them, one at
his right hand, the other at his left. 30 And
Samson said, "Let me die with the Philistines!"
He pushed hard, and the temple fell upon the
lords and all the people who were in it. Those
he killed at his death were more than those he
had killed during his lifetime.

31 All his family and kinsmen went down
and bore him up for burial in the grave of his

---

s Jgs 15, 14.   v 1 Sm 5, 2-5.
t Jgs 15, 13.   w Jgs 15, 20.
u Jgs 13, 5.
*

16, 23: Dagon was originally a Mesopotamian deity, whom
the Philistines came to worship as their own god of grain.

father Manoah between Zorah and Eshtaol. He had judged Israel for twenty years.[w]

III: The Tribes of Dan and Benjamin in the Days of the Judges

CHAPTER 17

Micah and the Levite. 1 There was a man in the mountain region of Ephraim whose name was Micah. 2 He said to his mother, "The eleven hundred shekels of silver over which you pronounced a curse in my hearing when they were taken from you, are in my possession. It was I who took them; so now I will restore them to you." 3 When he restored the eleven hundred shekels of silver to his mother, she took two hundred of them and gave them to the silversmith, who made of them a carved idol* overlaid with silver.[x] 4 Then his mother said, "May the LORD bless my son! I have consecrated the silver to the LORD as my gift in favor of my son, by making a carved idol overlaid with silver." It remained in the house of Micah. 5 Thus the layman Micah had a sanctuary. He also made an ephod and household idols,[y] and consecrated one of his sons, who became his priest. 6 In those days there was no king in Israel; everyone did what he thought best.[z]

7 There was a young Levite who had resided within the tribe of Judah at Bethlehem of Judah. 8 From that city he set out to find another place of residence. On his journey he came to the house of Micah in the mountain region of Ephraim. 9 Micah said to him, "Where do you come from?" He answered him, "I am a Levite from Bethlehem in Judah, and am on my way to find some other place of residence." 10 "Stay with me," Micah said to him. "Be father and priest to me,[a] and I will give you ten silver shekels a year, a set of garments, and your food." 11 So the young Levite decided to stay with the man, to whom he became as one of his own sons. 12 *Micah consecrated the young Levite, who became his priest, remaining in his house. 13 Therefore Micah said, "Now I know that the LORD will prosper me, since the Levite has become my priest."

CHAPTER 18

Migration of the Danites. 1 At that time there was no king in Israel.[b] Moreover the tribe of Danites were in search of a district to dwell in, for up to that time they had received no heritage among the tribes of Israel.*

2 So the Danites sent from their clan a detail of five valiant men of Zorah and Eshtaol, to reconnoiter the land and scout it. With their instructions to go and scout the land, they trav-

eled as far as the house of Micah in the mountain region of Ephraim, where they passed the night. 3 Near the house of Micah, they recognized the voice* of the young Levite[c] and turned in that direction. "Who brought you here and what are you doing here?" they asked him. "What is your interest here?" 4 "This is how Micah treats me," he replied to them. "He pays me a salary and I am his priest."[d] 5 They said to him, "Consult God, that we may know whether the undertaking we are engaged in will succeed." 6 The priest said to them, "Go and prosper: the LORD is favorable to the undertaking you are engaged in."

7 So the five men went on and came to Laish. They saw that the people dwelling there lived securely after the manner of the Sidonians, quiet and trusting, with no lack of any natural resources. They were distant from the Sidonians and had no contact with other people. 8 When the five returned to their kinsmen in Zorah and Eshtaol and were asked for a report, 9 they replied, "Come, let us attack them, for we have seen the land and it is very good. Are you going to hesitate? Do not be slothful about beginning your expedition to possess the land. 10 Those against whom you go are a trusting people, and the land is ample. God has indeed given it into your power: a place where no natural resource is lacking."

11 So six hundred men of the clan of the Danites, fully armed with weapons of war, set out from where they were in Zorah and Eshtaol, 12 and camped in Judah, up near Kiriath-jearim; hence to this day the place, which lies west of Kiriath-jearim, is called Mahaneh-dan.[e] 13 From there they went on to the mountain region of Ephraim and came to the house of Micah. 14 The five men who had gone to reconnoiter the land of Laish said to their kinsmen, "Do you know that in these houses there are an ephod, household idols, and a carved idol overlaid with silver?[f] Now decide what you must do!" 15 So turning in that direction, they went to the house of the young Levite at the home of Micah and greeted him. 16 The six

x Ex 20, 4; Lv 19, 4.   c Jgs 17, 7.
y Jgs 18, 14. 17.   d Jgs 17, 10.
z Jgs 18, 1; 21, 25.   e Jgs 13, 25.
a Jgs 18, 19.   f Jgs 17, 4f.
b Jos 19, 40-48.

*

17, 3: Idol: an image, not of a pagan god, but of the Lord. The Mosaic law forbade the making of an image even of the true God.

17, 12f: According to Nm 18, 1–7 only those Levites who were descended from Aaron could be consecrated as priests.

18, 1: The tribe of Dan had been assigned a territory with definite limits in central Palestine. However they were unable to gain possession of the better portion of their land (Jgs 1, 34). So they now seek territory elsewhere in Palestine.

18, 3: Recognized the voice: perhaps they noticed the peculiar pronunciation of his south Hebrew dialect.

hundred men girt with weapons of war, who were Danites, stood by the entrance of the gate, and the priest stood there also. **17** Meanwhile the five men who had gone to reconnoiter the land went up and entered the house of Micah. **18** When they had gone in and taken the ephod, the household idols, and the carved idol overlaid with silver, the priest said to them, "What are you doing?" **19** They said to him, "Be still: put your hand over your mouth. Come with us and be our father and priest. *g* Is it better for you to be priest for the family of one man or to be priest for a tribe and a clan in Israel?" **20** The priest, agreeing, took the ephod, household idols, and carved idol and went off in the midst of the band. **21** As they turned to depart, they placed their little ones, their livestock, and their goods at the head of the column.

22 The Danites had already gone some distance, when those in the houses near that of Micah took up arms and overtook them. **23** They called to the Danites, who turned about and said to Micah, "What do you want, that you have taken up arms?" **24** "You have taken my god, which I made, and have gone off with my priest as well," he answered. "What is left for me? How, then, can you ask me what I want?" **25** The Danites said to him, "Let us hear no further sound from you, lest fierce men fall upon you and you and your family lose your lives." **26** The Danites then went on their way, and Micah, seeing that they were stronger than he, returned home.

27 Having taken what Micah had made, and the priest he had had, they attacked Laish, a quiet and trusting people; they put them to the sword and destroyed their city by fire. **28** No one came to their aid, since the city was far from Sidon and they had no contact with other people. The Danites then rebuilt the city, which was in the valley that belongs to Beth-rehob, and lived there. **29** They named it Dan after their ancestor Dan, son of Israel. However, the name of the city was formerly Laish. **30** The Danites set up the carved idol for themselves, and Jonathan, son of Gershom, son of Moses, and his descendants were priests for the tribe of the Danites until the time of the captivity of the land.* **31** They maintained the carved idol Micah had made as long as the house of God was in Shiloh.

CHAPTER 19

The Levite from Ephraim. **1** At that time, when there was no king in Israel, *h* there was a Levite residing in remote parts of the mountain region of Ephraim who had taken for himself a concubine from Bethlehem of Judah. **2** His concubine was unfaithful to him and left him for her father's house in Bethlehem of Judah, where

she stayed for some four months. **3** Her husband then set out with his servant and a pair of asses, and went after her to forgive her and take her back. She brought him into her father's house, and on seeing him, the girl's father joyfully made him welcome. **4** He was detained by the girl's father, and so he spent three days with this father-in-law of his, eating and drinking and passing the night there. **5** *On the fourth day they rose early in the morning and he prepared to go. But the girl's father said to his son-in-law, "Fortify yourself with a little food; you can go later on." **6** So they stayed and the two men ate and drank together. Then the girl's father said to the husband, "Why not decide to spend the night here and enjoy yourself?" **7** The man still made a move to go, but when his father-in-law pressed him he went back and spent the night there.

8 On the fifth morning he rose early to depart, but the girl's father said, "Fortify yourself and tarry until the afternoon." When he and his father-in-law had eaten, **9** and the husband was ready to go with his concubine and servant, the girl's father said to him, "It is already growing dusk. Stay for the night. See, the day is coming to an end. Spend the night here and enjoy yourself. Early tomorrow you can start your journey home." **10** The man, however, refused to stay another night; he and his concubine set out with a pair of saddled asses, and traveled till they came opposite Jebus, which is Jerusalem. **11** Since they were near Jebus with the day far gone, the servant said to his master, "Come, let us turn off to this city of the Jebusites and spend the night in it." **12** But his master said to him, "We will not turn off to a city of foreigners, who are not Israelites, but will go on to Gibeah. *i* **13** Come," he said to his servant, "let us make for some other place, either Gibeah or Ramah, to spend the night." *j* **14** So they continued on their way till the sun set on them when they were abreast of Gibeah of Benjamin.

15 *There they turned off to enter Gibeah for the night. *k* The man waited in the public square of the city he had entered, but no one offered them the shelter of his home for the night. **16** In the evening, however, an old man came from his work in the field; he was from the mountain region of Ephraim, though he lived among the

---

g Jgs 17, 10.   j Jos 18, 25.
h Jgs 17, 6.   k Jgs 20, 4.
i Jgs 1, 21.

*

18, 30: Until . . . land: about the year 734 B.C., when the Assyrian emperor Tiglath-pileser III subjected northern Palestine.

19, 5–9: Such importuning of guests to prolong their stay at the home of their host is characteristic of Oriental hospitality.

19, 15: Private hospitality was the customary means of providing comfort to travelers where public facilities were so rare.

Benjaminite townspeople of Gibeah. **17** When he noticed the traveler in the public square of the city, the old man asked where he was going, and whence he had come. **18** He said to him, "We are traveling from Bethlehem of Judah far up into the mountain region of Ephraim, where I belong. I have been to Bethlehem of Judah and am now going back home; but no one has offered us the shelter of his house. **19** We have straw and fodder for our asses, and bread and wine for the woman and myself and for our servant; there is nothing else we need." **20** "You are welcome," the old man said to him, "but let me provide for all your needs, and do not spend the night in the public square." **21** So he led them to his house and provided fodder for the asses. Then they washed their feet, and ate and drank.*l*

The Outrage at Gibeah. **22** *m*While they were enjoying themselves, the men of the city, who were corrupt,* surrounded the house and beat on the door. They said to the old man whose house it was, "Bring out your guest, that we may abuse him." **23** The owner of the house went out to them and said, "No, my brothers; do not be so wicked. Since this man is my guest, do not commit this crime. **24** Rather let me bring out my maiden daughter or his concubine. Ravish them, or do whatever you want with them; but against the man you must not commit this wanton crime." **25** When the men would not listen to his host, the husband seized his concubine and thrust her outside to them. They had relations with her and abused her all night until the following dawn, when they let her go. **26** Then at daybreak the woman came and collapsed at the entrance of the house in which her husband was a guest, where she lay until the morning. **27** When her husband rose that day and opened the door of the house to start out again on his journey, there lay the woman, his concubine, at the entrance of the house with her hands on the threshold. **28** He said to her, "Come, let us go"; but there was no answer. So the man placed her on an ass and started out again for home.

29 *On reaching home, he took a knife to the body of his concubine, cut her into twelve pieces, and sent them throughout the territory of Israel. **30** *n*Everyone who saw this said, "Nothing like this has been done or seen from the day the Israelites came up from the land of Egypt to this day. Take note of it, and state what you propose to do."

CHAPTER 20

Assembly of Israelites. **1** So all the Israelites came out as one man: from Dan to Beer-she-ba,* and from the land of Gilead, the community was gathered to the LORD at Mizpah. **2** The leaders of all the people and all the tribesmen of Israel, four hundred thousand foot soldiers who were swordsmen, presented themselves in the assembly of the people of God. **3** Meanwhile, the Benjaminites heard that the Israelites had gone up to Mizpah. The Israelites asked to be told how the crime had taken place, **4** and the Levite, the husband of the murdered woman, testified: "My concubine and I went into Gibeah of Benjamin*o* for the night. **5** *p*But the citizens of Gibeah rose up against me by night and surrounded the house in which I was. Me they attempted to kill, and my concubine they abused so that she died. **6** *q*So I took my concubine and cut her up and sent her through every part of the territory of Israel, because of the monstrous crime they had committed in Israel. **7** *Now that you are all here, O Israelites, state what you propose to do."*r* **8** All the people rose as one man to say, "None of us is to leave for his tent or return to his home. **9** Now as for Gibeah, this is what we will do: We will proceed against it by lot, **10** taking from all the tribes of Israel ten men for every hundred, a hundred for every thousand, a thousand for every ten thousand, and procuring supplies for the soldiers who will go to deal fully and suitably with Gibeah of Benjamin for the crime it committed in Israel."

11 When, therefore, all the men of Israel without exception were leagued together against the city, **12** *the tribes of Israel sent men throughout the tribe of Benjamin to say, "What is this evil which has occurred among you? **13** Now give up these corrupt men of Gibeah, that we may put them to death and thus purge the evil from Israel." But the Benjaminites refused to accede to the demand of their brothers, the Israelites. **14** Instead, the Benjaminites assembled from their other cities to Gibeah, to do battle with the Israelites. **15** The number of the

---

l Gn 18, 4; 24, 32; 43, 24.
m 22-25: Gn 19, 4-9.
n Hos 9, 9; 10, 9.
o Jgs 19, 14f.
p Jgs 19, 22-27.
q Jgs 19, 29.
r Jgs 19, 30.

*

19, 22: Who were corrupt: literally "sons of Belial," indicating extreme perversion; cf Gn 19, 4–8. This crime and its punishment made the name Gibeah proverbial as a place of shameful wickedness; cf Hos 9, 9; 10, 9.

19, 29: A drastic means for arousing the tribes to avenge the unheard of crime of the Benjaminites.

20, 1: From Dan to Beer-sheba: from north to south. The land of Gilead: all the territory east of the Jordan.

20, 7: The Israelites were asked to decide at once what action to take concerning this crime; cf 2 Sm 16, 20. The Levite undoubtedly addressed the tribal heads who would speak in behalf of the multitude.

20, 12: Before the crime at Gibeah was punished, the Benjaminites were invited to join their brethren, the Israelites, in punishing the crime. Since they failed to respond, special messengers were sent asking them to deliver up the guilty ones. They replied by gathering their forces for combat.

Benjaminite swordsmen from the other cities on that occasion was twenty-six thousand, in addition to the inhabitants of Gibeah. **16** Included in this total were seven hundred picked men who were left-handed, every one of them able to sling a stone at a hair without missing. **17** Meanwhile the other Israelites who, without Benjamin, mustered four hundred thousand swordsmen ready for battle, **18** moved on to Bethel and consulted God. When the Israelites asked who should go first in the attack on the Benjaminites,ˢ the LORD said, "Judah shall go first."* **19** The next day the Israelites advanced on Gibeah with their forces.

War with Benjamin. **20** On the day the Israelites drew up in battle array at Gibeah for the combat with Benjamin, **21** the Benjaminites came out of the city and felled twenty-two thousand men of Israel. **23** Then the Israelites went up and wept before the LORD until evening. "Shall I again engage my brother Benjamin in battle?" they asked the LORD; and the LORD answered that they should. **22** But though the Israelite soldiers took courage and again drew up for combat in the same place as on the previous day, **24** when they met the Benjaminites for the second time, **25** once again the Benjaminites who came out of Gibeah against them felled eighteen thousand Israelites, all of them swordsmen. **26** So the entire Israelite army went up to Bethel, where they wept and remained fasting before the LORD until evening of that day, besides offering holocausts and peace offerings before the LORD. **27** ᵗWhen the Israelites consulted the LORD (for the ark of the covenant of God was there in those days, **28** and Phinehas, son of Eleazar, son of Aaron, was ministering to him in those days), and asked, "Shall I go out again to battle with Benjamin, my brother, or shall I desist?" the LORD said, "Attack! for tomorrow I will deliver him into your power." **29** ᵘSo Israel set men in ambush around Gibeah.*

30 The Israelites went up against the Benjaminites for the third time and formed their line of battle at Gibeah as on other occasions. **31** The Benjaminites went out to meet them, and in the beginning they killed off about thirty of the Israelite soldiers in the open field, just as on the other occasions. **32** Therefore the Benjaminites thought, "We are defeating them as before"; not realizing that disaster was about to overtake them. The Israelites, however, had planned the flight so as to draw them away from the city onto the highways. They were drawn away from the city onto the highways, of which the one led to Bethel, the other to Gibeon. **33** And then all the men of Israel rose from their places. They re-formed their ranks at Baal-tamar, and the Israelites in ambush rushed from

their place west of Gibeah, **34** ten thousand picked men from all Israel, and advanced against the city itself. In a fierce battle, **35** the LORD defeated Benjamin before Israel; and on that day the Israelites killed twenty-five thousand one hundred men of Benjamin, all of them swordsmen.

36 To the Benjaminites it had looked as though the enemy were defeated, for the men of Israel gave ground to Benjamin, trusting in the ambush they had set at Gibeah. **37** But then the men in ambush made a sudden dash into Gibeah, overran it, and put the whole city to the sword. **38** Now, the other Israelites had agreed with the men in ambush on a smoke signal they were to send up from the city. **39** And though the men of Benjamin had begun by killing off some thirty of the men of Israel, under the impression that they were defeating them as surely as in the earlier fighting, the Israelites wheeled about to resist **40** as the smoke of the signal column began to rise up from the city. It was when Benjamin looked back and saw the whole city in flames against the sky **41** that the men of Israel wheeled about. Therefore the men of Benjamin were thrown into confusion, for they realized the disaster that had overtaken them. **42** They retreated before the men of Israel in the direction of the desert, with the fight being pressed against them. In their very midst, meanwhile, those who had been in the city were spreading destruction. **43** The men of Benjamin had been surrounded, and were now pursued to a point east of Gibeah, **44** while eighteen thousand of them fell, warriors to a man. **45** The rest turned and fled through the desert to the rock Rimmon.ᵛ But on the highways the Israelites picked off five thousand men among them, and chasing them up to Gidom, killed another two thousand of them there. **46** Those of Benjamin who fell on that day were in all twenty-five thousand swordsmen, warriors to a man. **47** But six hundred others who turned and fled through the desert reached the rock Rimmon, where they remained for four months.

48 The men of Israel withdrew through the territory of the Benjaminites, putting to the sword the inhabitants of the cities, the livestock, and all they chanced upon. Moreover they de-

---

s Jgs 1, 1f.　　　u 29–46: Jos 8, 4–24.
t 1 Sm 4, 3f.　　　v Jgs 21, 13.

*

20, 18: Judah shall go first: the same response as in Jgs 1, 1f, but without the assurance of immediate success. Only after the Israelites were punished at the hands of the Benjaminites for their own grossness, and had performed penance, did they succeed in punishing the latter for their part in the crime of rape and murder, by gaining the victory over them.

20, 29–46: This stratagem proved more useful to the Israelites than force, as in the siege of Ai (Jos 8, 3–21). In the parallel accounts the first (vv 29–35) is a summary of the second (vv 36–46).

stroyed by fire all the cities they came upon.

CHAPTER 21

Wives for the Survivors. **1** Now the men of Israel* had sworn at Mizpah that none of them would give his daughter in marriage to anyone from Benjamin. **2** So the people went to Bethel and remained there before God until evening, raising their voices in bitter lament.[w] **3** They said, "LORD, God of Israel, why has it come to pass in Israel that today one tribe of Israel should be lacking?" **4** Early the next day the people built an altar there and offered holocausts and peace offerings. **5** Then the Israelites asked, "Are there any among all the tribes of Israel who did not come up to the LORD for the assembly?" For they had taken a solemn oath that anyone who did not go up to the LORD at Mizpah should be put to death without fail.[x]

6 *The Israelites were disconsolate over their brother Benjamin and said, "Today one of the tribes of Israel has been cut off. **7** What can we do about wives for the survivors, since we have sworn by the LORD not to give them any of our daughters in marriage?" **8** And when they asked whether anyone among the tribes of Israel had not come up to the LORD in Mizpah, they found that none of the men of Jabesh-gilead had come to the encampment for the assembly. **9** A roll call of the army established that none of the inhabitants of that city were present. **10** The community, therefore, sent twelve thousand warriors with orders to go to Jabesh-gilead and put those who lived there to the sword, including the women and children. **11** They were told to include under the ban* all males and every woman who was not still a virgin.[y] **12** Finding among the inhabitants of Jabesh-gilead four hundred young virgins, who had had no relations with men, they brought them to the camp at Shiloh in the land of Canaan. **13** [z]Then the whole community sent a message to the Benjaminites at the rock Rimmon, offering them peace. **14** When Benjamin returned at that time, they gave them as wives the women of Jabesh-gilead whom they had spared; but these proved to be not enough for them.

15 The people were still disconsolate over Benjamin because the LORD had made a breach* among the tribes of Israel. **16** And the elders of the community said, "What shall we do for wives for the survivors? For every woman in Benjamin has been put to death." **17** They said, "Those of Benjamin who survive must have heirs, else one of the Israelite tribes will be wiped out. **18** *Yet we cannot give them any of our daughters in marriage, because the Israelites have sworn, 'Cursed be he who gives a woman to Benjamin!' " **19** Then they thought of the yearly feast of the LORD at Shiloh, north of Bethel, east of the highway that goes up from Bethel to Shechem, and south of Lebonah. **20** And they instructed the Benjaminites, "Go and lie in wait in the vineyards. **21** When you see the girls of Shiloh come out to do their dancing, leave the vineyards and each of you seize one of the girls of Shiloh for a wife, and go to the land of Benjamin. **22** When their fathers or their brothers come to complain to us, we shall say to them, 'Release them to us as a kindness, since we did not take a woman apiece in the war. Had you yourselves given them these wives, you would now be guilty.' "

23 The Benjaminites did this; they carried off a wife for each of them from their raid on the dancers, and went back to their own territory, where they rebuilt and occupied the cities. **24** Also at that time the Israelites dispersed; each of them left for his own heritage in his own clan and tribe.

25 *In those days there was no king in Israel; everyone did what he thought best.[a]

---

w Jgs 20, 26.   z Jgs 20, 47.
x Jgs 20, 8ff.   a Jgs 17, 6; 18, 1; 19, 1.
y Nm 31, 17.

---

*

21, 1–3: The anger of the Israelites led them to destroy their brethren, the Benjaminites. Having realized their goal, however, they were soon filled with dismay, and sought to restore the tribe they had all but exterminated.

21, 6–9: This account is summarized in the parallel passage in vv 2–5.

21, 11: Under the ban; see note on Nm 21, 3.

21, 15: Had made a breach: what is here attributed to God was in reality the free and deliberate act of the Israelites and happened only by the permissive will of God. The ancients attributed to the first primary cause what is more directly due to secondary causes.

21, 18: Regardless of the serious consequences of their vow, the Israelites considered themselves obliged to fulfill it; cf Jgs 11, 31. 35f. 39.

21, 25: Cf Jgs 17, 6; 18, 1; 19, 1. The verse gives the reason why the lawlessness of the period of judges, and the events described herein, were possible.

The Book of

RUTH

The Book of Ruth is named after the Moabite woman who was joined to the Israelite people by her marriage with the influential Boaz of Bethlehem.

The book contains a beautiful example of filial piety, pleasing to the Hebrews especially because of its connection with King David, and useful both to Hebrews and to Gentiles. Its aim is to demonstrate the divine reward for such piety even when practiced by a stranger. Ruth's piety (Ru 2, 11), her spirit of self-sacrifice, and her moral integrity were favored by God with the gift of faith and an illustrious marriage whereby she became the ancestress of David and of Christ. In this, the universality of the messianic salvation is foreshadowed.

In the Greek and Latin canons the Book of Ruth is placed just after Judges, to which it is closely related because of the time of its action, and just before Samuel, for which it is an excellent introduction, since it traces the ancestry of the Davidic dynasty. One might characterize the literary form of this book as dramatic, since about two-thirds of it is in dialogue. Yet there is every indication that, as tradition has always held, it contains true history.

There is no certainty about the author of the book. It was written long after the events had passed (Ru 4, 7), which took place "in the time of the judges" (Ru 1, 1).

CHAPTER 1

Naomi in Moab. **1** Once in the time of the judges* there was a famine in the land; so a man from Bethlehem of Judah departed with his wife and two sons to reside on the plateau of Moab. **2** The man was named Elimelech, his wife Naomi, and his sons Mahlon and Chilion; they were Ephrathites from Bethlehem of Judah. Some time after their arrival on the Moabite plateau, **3** Elimelech, the husband of Naomi, died, and she was left with her two sons, **4** who married Moabite women, one named Orpah, the other Ruth. When they had lived there about ten years, **5** both Mahlon and Chilion died also, and the woman was left with neither her two sons nor her husband. **6** She then made ready to go back from the plateau of Moab because word reached her there that the LORD had visited his people and given them food.

7 She and her two daughters-in-law left the place where they had been living. Then as they were on the road back to the land of Judah, **8** Naomi said to her two daughters-in-law, "Go back, each of you, to your mother's house!* May the LORD be kind to you as you were to the departed and to me! **9** May the LORD grant each of you a husband and a home in which you will find rest." She kissed them good-by, but they wept with loud sobs, **10** and told her they would return with her to her people. **11** "Go back, my daughters!" said Naomi. "Why should you come with me? Have I other sons in

my womb who may become your husbands?* **12** Go back, my daughters! Go, for I am too old to marry again. And even if I could offer any hopes, or if tonight I had a husband or had borne sons, **13** would you then wait and deprive yourselves of husbands until those sons grew up? No, my daughters! my lot is too bitter for you, because the LORD has extended his hand against me." **14** Again they sobbed aloud and wept; and Orpah kissed her mother-in-law good-by, but Ruth stayed with her.

15 "See now!" she said, "your sister-in-law has gone back to her people and her god. Go back after your sister-in-law!" **16** *But Ruth said, "Do not ask me to abandon or forsake you! for wherever you go I will go, wherever you lodge I will lodge, your people shall be my people, and your God my God. **17** Wherever

---
*

1, 1f: In the time of the judges: three generations before the end of the period of Judges; cf Ru 4, 21f. Bethlehem of Judah: to distinguish it from the town of the same name in the tribe of Zebulun (Jos 19, 15). Ephrathites from Bethlehem: belonging to a Judean clan which settled in Bethlehem; cf 1 Sm 17, 12; 1 Chr 2, 50f; 4, 4.

1, 8: Mother's house: the women's part of the dwelling; cf Jgs 4, 17; Song 3, 4.

1, 11: Have I other sons . . . husbands?: Naomi insisted that her daughters-in-law remain in their own country only for the sake of posterity. If she had had other sons, the levirate law would have obliged them to marry the widows of her deceased sons to perpetuate the names of the deceased; cf Gn 38, 8; Dt 25, 5f.

1, 16f: An example of heroic fidelity and piety. Ruth's decision, confirmed with an oath, to adhere to her mother-in-law impelled her to abandon her country and its pagan worship.

you die I will die, and there be buried. May the LORD do so and so to me, and more besides, if aught but death separates me from you!" **18** Naomi then ceased to urge her, for she saw she was determined to go with her.

The Return to Bethlehem. **19** So they went on together till they reached Bethlehem. On their arrival there, the whole city was astir over them, and the women asked, "Can this be Naomi?" **20** *a*But she said to them, "Do not call me Naomi.* Call me Mara, for the Almighty has made it very bitter for me. **21** I went away with an abundance, but the LORD has brought me back destitute. Why should you call me Naomi, since the LORD has pronounced against me and the Almighty has brought evil upon me?" **22** Thus it was that Naomi returned with the Moabite daughter-in-law, Ruth, who accompanied her back from the plateau of Moab. They arrived in Bethlehem at the beginning of the barley harvest.*

CHAPTER 2

The Meeting. **1** Naomi had a prominent kinsman named Boaz, *b* of the clan of her husband Elimelech. **2** Ruth the Moabite said to Naomi, "Let me go and glean ears of grain* in the field of anyone who will allow me that favor." *c* Naomi said to her, "Go, my daughter," **3** and she went. The field she entered to glean after the harvesters happened to be the section belonging to Boaz of the clan of Elimelech. **4** Boaz himself came from Bethlehem and said to the harvesters, "The LORD be with you!"* and they replied, "The LORD bless you!" **5** Boaz asked the overseer of his harvesters, "Whose girl is this?" **6** The overseer of the harvesters answered, "She is the Moabite girl who returned from the plateau of Moab with Naomi. *d* **7** She asked leave to gather the gleanings into sheaves after the harvesters; and ever since she came this morning she has remained here until now, with scarcely a moment's rest."

8 Boaz said to Ruth, "Listen, my daughter! Do not go to glean in anyone else's field; you are not to leave here. Stay here with my women servants. **9** Watch to see which field is to be harvested, and follow them; I have commanded the young men to do you no harm. When you are thirsty, you may go and drink from the vessels the young men have filled." **10** Casting herself prostrate upon the ground, she said to him, "Why should I, a foreigner, be favored with your notice?" **11** *e*Boaz answered her: "I have had a complete account of what you have done for your mother-in-law after your husband's death; you have left your father and your mother and the land of your birth, and have come to a people whom you did not know previ-

ously. **12** May the LORD reward what you have done! May you receive a full reward from the LORD, the God of Israel, under whose wings you have come for refuge." **13** She said, "May I prove worthy of your kindness, my lord: you have comforted me, your servant, with your consoling words; would indeed that I were a servant of yours!" **14** At mealtime Boaz said to her, "Come here and have some food; dip your bread in the sauce." Then as she sat near the reapers, he handed her some roasted grain and she ate her fill and had some left over. **15** She rose to glean, and Boaz instructed his servants to let her glean among the sheaves themselves without scolding her, **16** and even to let drop some handfuls and leave them for her to glean without being rebuked.

17 She gleaned in the field until evening, and when she beat out what she had gleaned it came to about an ephah of barley, **18** which she took into the city and showed to her mother-in-law. Next she brought out and gave her what she had left over from lunch. **19** So her mother-in-law said to her, "Where did you glean today? Where did you go to work? May he who took notice of you be blessed!" Then she told her mother-in-law with whom she had worked. "The man at whose place I worked today is named Boaz," she said. **20** *f*"May he be blessed by the LORD, who is ever merciful to the living and to the dead," Naomi exclaimed to her daughter-in-law; and she continued, "He is a relative of ours, one of our next of kin."* **21** "He even told me," added Ruth the Moabite, "that I should stay with his servants until they complete his entire harvest." **22** "You would do well, my dear," Naomi rejoined, "to go out with his servants; for in someone else's field you might be insulted." **23** So she stayed

---

a Ex 15, 23.   d Ru 1, 22.
b Ru 3, 2. 12; 4, 21; Mt   e Ru 1, 14-17.
  1, 5.   f Ru 3, 9.
c Dt 24, 19.

*

1, 20f: Naomi: means "amiable" or "pleasant," suggesting God's favor toward her. The Almighty has brought evil upon me: the ancients regarded adversity as a punishment from God for personal sin, as if good and evil were always repaid in a temporal and material manner.

1, 22: Barley harvest: early April. This circumstance favored the events of the narrative that follow.

2, 2: Let me go and glean . . . grain: even the poor, the widow, the stranger, and the orphan had a right to glean at harvest time; cf Lv 19, 9f, 23, 22; Dt 24, 19–22.

2, 4: The Lord be with you: courtesy and religious feeling characterize the salutations of the Hebrews. This greeting is used in the Christian liturgy.

2, 20: One of our next of kin: literally "our redeemer," a near relative of the same clan who had the right and duty to restore the land which an impoverished kinsman had alienated (Lv 25, 25–28), and to marry the widow of a relative who had died without male offspring so as to raise up posterity to his name (Dt 25, 5–10).

gleaning with the servants of Boaz until the end of the barley and wheat harvests.

CHAPTER 3

Ruth Again Presents Herself.　When she was back with her mother-in-law, **1** Naomi said to her, "My daughter, I must seek a home for you that will please you. **2** *g*Now is not Boaz, with whose servants you were, a relative of ours? This evening he will be winnowing barley at the threshing floor. **3** So bathe and anoint yourself; then put on your best attire and go down to the threshing floor. Do not make yourself known to the man before he has finished eating and drinking. **4** But when he lies down, take note of the place where he does so. Then go, uncover a place at his feet,* and lie down. He will tell you what to do." **5** "I will do whatever you advise," Ruth replied. **6** So she went down to the threshing floor and did just as her mother-in-law had instructed her.

7 Boaz ate and drank to his heart's content. Then when he went and lay down at the edge of the sheaves, she stole up, uncovered a place at his feet, and lay down. **8** In the middle of the night, however, the man gave a start and turned around to find a woman lying at his feet. **9** He asked, "Who are you?" And she replied, "I am your servant Ruth. Spread the corner of your cloak over me,* for you are my next of kin." **10** He said, "May the LORD bless you, my daughter! You have been even more loyal now than before in not going after the young men, whether poor or rich.*h* **11** So be assured, daughter, I will do for you whatever you say; all my townspeople know you for a worthy woman. **12** *i*Now, though indeed I am closely related to you, you have another relative still closer.* **13** Stay as you are for tonight, and tomorrow, if he wishes to claim you, good! let him do so. But if he does not wish to claim you, as the LORD lives, I will claim you myself. Lie there until morning."*j* **14** So she lay at his feet until morning, but rose before men could recognize one another. Boaz said, "Let it not be known that this woman came to the threshing floor." **15** Then he said to her, "Take off your cloak and hold it out." When she did so, he poured out six measures of barley, helped her lift the bundle,*k* and left for the city.

16 Ruth went home to her mother-in-law, who asked, "How have you fared, my daughter?" So she told her all the man had done for her, **17** and concluded, "He gave me these six measures of barley because he did not wish me to come back to my mother-in-law empty-handed!" **18** Naomi then said, "Wait here, my daughter, until you learn what happens, for the man will not rest, but will settle the matter today."

CHAPTER 4

Boaz Marries Ruth.　**1** Boaz went and took a seat at the gate;* and when he saw the closer relative*l* of whom he had spoken come along, he called to him by name, "Come and sit beside me!" And he did so. **2** Then Boaz picked out ten of the elders* of the city and asked them to sit nearby. When they had done this, **3** he said to the near relative: "Naomi, who has come back from the Moabite plateau, is putting up for sale the piece of land that belonged to our kinsman Elimelech. **4** *So I thought I would inform you, bidding you before those here present, including the elders of my people, to put in your claim for it if you wish to acquire it as next of kin.*m* But if you do not wish to claim it, tell me so, that I may be guided accordingly, for no one has a prior claim to yours, and mine is next." He answered, "I will put in my claim."

5 *Boaz continued, "Once you acquire the field from Naomi, you must take also Ruth the Moabite,*n* the widow of the late heir, and raise up a family for the departed on his estate." **6** The near relative replied, "I cannot exercise my claim lest I depreciate my own estate. Put in a claim yourself in my stead, for I cannot exercise my claim." **7** Now it used to be the custom in Israel that, to make binding a contract of redemption or exchange, one party would take off his sandal* and give it to the other. This was the form of attestation in Israel. **8** So the near relative, in saying to Boaz, "Acquire it for yourself," drew off his sandal. **9** Boaz then

---

g Ru 1.
h Dt 25, 5.
i Ru 4, 1.
j Ru 4, 5; Dt 25, 5.
k Ru 2, 17.
l Ru 3, 12.
m Lv 25, 25.
n Ru 3, 13; Dt 25, 5.

*

3, 4: Uncover a place at his feet . . . : confident of the virtue of Ruth and Boaz, Naomi advises this unusual expedient to her daughter-in-law for the purpose of introducing her claim.

3, 9: Spread the corner of your cloak over me: be my protector by marrying me according to the duty of a near kinsman; cf Dt 25, 5; Ez 16, 8.

3, 12: Relative still closer: who had a prior right and duty to marry Ruth.

4, 1: Took a seat at the gate: i.e., of the city, where business affairs were settled.

4, 2: Ten of the elders: to serve as judges in legal matters as well as witnesses of the settlement of business affairs; cf Dt 25, 7–9.

4, 4: Poverty had obliged Naomi to sell the land of her deceased husband. The law permitted the nearest kinsman to redeem the land and thus preserve the family patrimony; cf Lv 25, 25.

4, 5f: The heir of Elimelech's field had died without children (Ru 1, 5). The nearest of kin could now redeem the land but he must also take Ruth, the widow of the late heir, to wife to perpetuate the family of the deceased; cf Dt 25, 5f. The first male child of such a marriage would be the legal son of Mahlon and grandson of Elimelech.

4, 7: Take off his sandal . . . : by this act the near relative renounced his legal right, both to the field of Elimelech and to the marriage with Ruth. The custom mentioned in Dt 25, 6 is somewhat different.

said to the elders and to all the people, "You are witnesses today that I have acquired from Naomi all the holdings of Elimelech, Chilion and Mahlon. **10** I also take Ruth the Moabite, the widow of Mahlon, as my wife, in order to raise up a family for her late husband on his estate, so that the name of the departed may not perish among his kinsmen and fellow citizens. Do you witness this today?" **11** *o*All those at the gate, including the elders, said, "We do so. May the LORD make this wife come into your house like Rachel and Leah, who between them built up the house of Israel. May you do well in Ephrathah and win fame in Bethlehem. **12** *p*With the offspring the LORD will give you from this girl, may your house become like the house of Perez, who Tamar bore to Judah."*

13 Boaz took Ruth. When they came together as man and wife, the LORD enabled her to conceive and she bore a son. **14** Then the women said to Naomi, "Blessed is the LORD who has not failed to provide you today with an heir! May he become famous in Israel! **15** He will be your comfort and the support of your old age, for his mother is the daughter-in-law who loves you. She is worth more to you than seven sons!" **16** Naomi took the child, placed him on her lap,* and became his nurse. **17** And the neighbor women gave him his name,*q* at the news that a grandson had been born to Naomi. They called him Obed. He was the father of Jesse, the father of David.*

18 *r*These are the descendants of Perez: Perez was the father of Hezron,*s* **19** Hezron was the father of Ram, Ram was the father of Amminadab, **20** *t*Amminadab was the father of Nahshon, Nahshon was the father of Salmon, **21** Salmon was the father of Boaz, Boaz was the father of Obed, **22** *u*Obed was the father of Jesse, and Jesse became the father of David.

---

o Gn 29, 31-30, 24; 35, 19.
p Gn 38, 29.
q Lk 1, 58.
r 18-22: 1 Chr 2, 4-15;

Mt 1, 3-6.
s Gn 46, 12; 1 Chr 4, 1.
t Ex 6, 23; Nm 1, 7.
u 1 Sm 16, 10-13.

4, 12: Perez, whom Tamar bore to Judah: the right which Judah unwittingly satisfied for his daughter-in-law Tamar (Gn 38), Boaz willingly rendered to Ruth.

4, 16: Placed him on her lap: took him as her own; cf Gn 30, 3; 48, 12; Nm 11, 12.

4, 17: The father of Jesse, the father of David: indicating the place of Obed, Jesse and David in the line of Judah and the ancestry of Christ, the Messiah; cf Mt 1, 5f.

THE HISTORICAL BOOKS

The historical books include 1 and 2 Samuel, 1 and 2 Kings, 1 and 2 Chronicles, Ezra, Nehemiah, 1 and 2 Maccabees. To these are added the special literary group of Tobit, Judith and Esther.

The books of Tobit, Judith, and 1 and 2 Maccabees, as well as parts of Esther, are called deuterocanonical: they are not contained in the Hebrew canon but have been accepted by the Catholic Church as canonical and inspired.

By means of a series of episodes involving the persons of Samuel, Saul, and David, a century of history unfolds in 1 and 2 Samuel from the close of the period of Judges to the rise and establishment of the monarchy in Israel. Most important is God's promise to David of a lasting dynasty (2 Sm 7), from which royal messianism in the Bible developed.

In 1 and 2 Kings the religious history of Israel extends another four centuries, from the last days of David to the Babylonian captivity and the destruction of Jerusalem (587 B.C.). The various sources for these books are woven into a uniform pattern based on the principle of fidelity to Yahweh for rulers and people alike. The sequence of regnal chronicles in both books is interrupted by a cycle of traditions surrounding the prophets Elijah (1 Kgs) and Elisha (2 Kgs).

Chronicles, Ezra and Nehemiah form a historical work, uniform in style and basic ideas. Chronicles records the long period from the reign of Saul to the return from exile, not so much with exactitude of detail as with concern for the meaning of the facts which demonstrate God's intervention in history. The Ezra-Nehemiah chronicle constitutes the most important source for the formation of the Jewish religious community after the Babylonian exile; the two persons most responsible for the reorganization of Jewish life were Ezra and Nehemiah.

1 and 2 Maccabees contain independent accounts of partially identical events which accompanied the attempted suppression of Judaism in Palestine in the second century B.C. Vigorous reaction to this attempt established for a time the religious and political independence of the Jews. 1 Maccabees portrays God as the eternal benefactor of the Jews and their unfailing source of help. The people are required to be devoted to his exclusive worship and to observe exactly the law he has given them. 2 Maccabees, besides supplementing the former volume, gives a theological interpretation of the history of the period and contains teaching on the resurrection from the dead, intercession of the saints, and suffrages for the dead.

Tobit, Judith, and Esther are examples of free composition—the religious novel used for purposes of edification and instruction. Interest in whatever historical data these books may contain is merely intensified by the addition of vivid details. Judith is a lesson in Providence: a pious reflection on the annual Passover observance to convey the reassurance that God is still the master of history who saves Israel from her enemies. Esther's purpose is the glorification of the Jewish people and the explanation of the origin, significance, and date of the feast of Purim. It is a literary development of the principle of reversal of fortune through punishment of the prosperous rich and reward for the virtuous who are oppressed.

Samuel to Maccabees demonstrates that before as well as during the millennium of history with which it is concerned, Israel was a covenanted people, bound to Yahweh, Lord of the universe, by the ties of faith and obedience. This required observance of the law and worship in his temple, the consequent rewards of which were divine favor and protection. In this way these books anticipate and prepare for the coming of him who would bring type and prophecy to fulfillment, history to term, and holiness to perfection: Christ, the Son of David and the promised Messiah.

The Books of

SAMUEL

Originally but one book, the scroll of Samuel was early divided into two. The Greek translators called these the first and second Books of Kingdoms, a title St. Jerome later modified to "Kings." The Hebrew title, "Samuel," alludes to the leading figure in the first book, who was responsible for the enthronement of David. It is David's history that the second book recounts.

This sacred work thus comprises the history of about a century, describing the close of the age of the Judges and the beginnings of monarchy in Israel under Saul and David. It is not a complete and continuous history, nor a systematic account of the period, but rather a series of episodes centered around the persons of Samuel, Saul and David, the principal figures leading up to the establishment of the royal dynasty of David.

The final editor is unknown, nor are we certain of the time at which the various strands of the narrative were put together, though one may think of the period, perhaps late in the seventh century B.C., when the other volumes of the "Former Prophets," from Joshua through Kings, were built into a more or less continuous historical corpus. The Samuel-Saul-David narratives clearly depend on several written sources: a Samuel cycle, two sets of stories about Saul and David, and a family history of David. This last (2 Sm 9–20; 1 Kgs 1–2), one of the most vivid historical narratives surviving from ancient times, probably originated early in the reign of Solomon.

One of the most significant theological contributions of the Old Testament is found in 2 Samuel 7, the oracle of Nathan. David is here promised an eternal dynasty, and this becomes the basis for the development of royal messianism throughout the Bible. With this promise to David one should compare 1 Chr 17; Pss 89, 20–38 and 132, 11ff; Acts 2, 30; and Heb 1, 5.

The contents of this work may be divided as follows:
I. History of the Last Judges, Eli and Samuel (1 Sm 1, 1–7, 17).
II. Establishment of the Monarchy in Israel (1 Sm 8, 1–12, 25).
III. Saul and David (1 Sm 13, 1–2 Sm 2, 7).
IV. The Reign of David (2 Sm 2, 8–20, 26).
V. Appendixes (2 Sm 21, 1–24, 25).

THE FIRST BOOK OF SAMUEL

I: History of the Last Judges, Eli and Samuel

CHAPTER 1

Elkanah and His Family at Shiloh.
1 There was a certain man from Rama-thaim, Elkanah by name, a Zuphite from the hill country of Ephraim. He was the son of Jeroham, son of Elihu, son of Tohu, son of Zuph, an Ephraimite.[a] **2** He had two wives, one named Hannah, the other Peninnah; Peninnah had children, but Hannah was childless. **3** This man regularly went on pilgrimage from his city to worship the LORD of hosts and to sacrifice to him at Shiloh, where the two sons of Eli, Hophni and Phine-

has, were ministering as priests of the LORD.[b] **4** When the day came for Elkanah to offer sacrifice, he used to give a portion each to his wife Peninnah and to all her sons and daughters, **5** but a double portion to Hannah because he loved her, though the LORD had made her barren.[c] **6** Her rival, to upset her, turned it into a constant reproach to her that the LORD had left her barren.[d] **7** This went on year after year; each time they made their pilgrimage to the sanctuary of the LORD, Peninnah would approach her, and Hannah would weep and refuse to eat. **8** Her husband Elkanah used to ask her:

---

a 1 Chr 6, 19f.   c Dt 21, 15ff.
b Ex 23, 14-17; 34, 23;   d Gn 16, 4f.
  Dt 16, 16; Jgs 21, 19.   e Ru 4, 15.

"Hannah, why do you weep, and why do you refuse to eat? Why do you grieve? Am I not more to you than ten sons?"[e]

Hannah's Prayer.

9 Hannah rose after one such meal at Shiloh, and presented herself before the LORD; at the time, Eli the priest was sitting on a chair near the doorpost of the LORD's temple. **10** In her bitterness she prayed to the LORD, weeping copiously, **11** and she made a vow, promising: "O LORD of hosts, if you look with pity on the misery of your handmaid, if you remember me and do not forget me, if you give your handmaid a male child, I will give him to the LORD* for as long as he lives; neither wine nor liquor shall he drink, and no razor shall ever touch his head."[f] **12** As she remained long at prayer before the LORD, Eli watched her mouth, **13** for Hannah was praying silently; though her lips were moving, her voice could not be heard. Eli, thinking her drunk, **14** said to her, "How long will you make a drunken show of yourself? Sober up from your wine!" **15** "It isn't that, my lord," Hannah answered. "I am an unhappy woman. I have had neither wine nor liquor; I was only pouring out my troubles to the LORD. **16** Do not think your handmaid a ne'er-do-well; my prayer has been prompted by my deep sorrow and misery." **17** Eli said, "Go in peace, and may the God of Israel grant you what you have asked of him." **18** She replied, "Think kindly of your maidservant," and left. She went to her quarters, ate and drank with her husband, and no longer appeared downcast. **19** Early the next morning they worshiped before the LORD, and then returned to their home in Ramah.

Hannah Bears a Son.

When Elkanah had relations with his wife Hannah, the LORD remembered her. **20** She conceived, and at the end of her term bore a son whom she called Samuel, since she had asked* the LORD for him. **21** The next time her husband Elkanah was going up with the rest of his household to offer the customary sacrifice to the LORD and to fulfill his vows, **22** Hannah did not go, explaining to her husband, "Once the child is weaned, I will take him to appear before the LORD and to remain there forever; I will offer him as a perpetual nazirite." **23** Her husband Elkanah answered her: "Do what you think best; wait until you have weaned him. Only, may the LORD bring your resolve to fulfillment!" And so she remained at home and nursed her son until she had weaned him.

Samuel is Offered to God.

24 Once he was weaned, she brought him up with her, along with a three-year-old bull, an ephah* of flour, and a skin of wine, and presented him at the

temple of the LORD in Shiloh. **25** After the boy's father had sacrificed the young bull, Hannah, his mother, approached Eli **26** and said: "Pardon, my lord! As you live, my lord, I am the woman who stood near you here, praying to the LORD. **27** I prayed for this child, and the LORD granted my request. **28** Now I, in turn, give him to the LORD; as long as he lives, he shall be dedicated to the LORD." She left him there;* **1** and as she worshiped the LORD, she said:

CHAPTER 2

"My heart exults in the LORD,*
  my horn* is exalted in my God.
I have swallowed up my enemies;
  I rejoice in my victory.[g]
2 There is no Holy One like the LORD;
  there is no Rock like our God.[h]

3 "Speak boastfully no longer,
  nor let arrogance issue from your
    mouths.*
For an all-knowing God is the LORD,
  a God who judges deeds.[i]
4 The bows of the mighty are broken,
  while the tottering gird on strength.[j]
5 The well-fed hire themselves out for bread,
  while the hungry batten on spoil.
The barren wife bears seven sons,
  while the mother of many languishes.
6 "The LORD puts to death and gives life;
  he casts down to the nether world; he
    raises up again.[k]
7 The LORD makes poor and makes rich,
  he humbles, he also exalts.
8 He raises the needy from the dust;
  from the ash heap he lifts up the poor,
To seat them with nobles

---

f Nm 6, 1-5; Jgs 13, 2-5; 16, 17; Lk 1, 15.
g Dt 33, 17; 2 Sm 22, 3; Ps 18, 2; Is 61, 10; Lk 1, 47. 69
h 2 Sm 22, 3; Ps 18, 2.
i Ps 75, 4.
j Is 40, 29.
k Dt 32, 39; Tb 4, 19; Jb 5, 11; Ps 30, 4; Wis 16, 13; Lk 1, 52.
l Jb 9, 6; 38, 6; Ps 104, 5; 121, 3.

---

*

1, 11: Give him to the Lord: some ancient texts call Samuel a nazir in this context; see note on Nm 6, 1ff.

1, 20: Since she had asked: this explanation would be more directly appropriate for the name Saul, which means "asked"; Samuel means "name of God."

1, 24: An ephah: a little more than a bushel.

1, 1: And . . . said: this belongs to ch 2.

2, 1–10: A hymn attributed to Hannah, the mother of Samuel, as her thanksgiving to God because she has borne a son despite her previous sterility. She praises God as the helper of the weak (1ff), who casts down the mighty and raises up the lowly (3ff), and who alone is the source of true strength (8ff); the hymn ends with a prayer for the king (v 10). This canticle has several points of resemblance with our Lady's Magnificat.

2, 1: Horn: the symbol of strength; cf Pss 18, 3; 75, 5; 89, 18; 112, 9.

2, 3: Speak . . . mouths: addressed to the enemies mentioned in v 1.

and make a glorious throne their
heritage.[l]
He gives to the vower his vow,
　　and blesses the sleep of the just.

"For the pillars of the earth are the LORD's,
　　and he has set the world upon them.
9 He will guard the footsteps of his faithful
　　　ones,
　　but the wicked shall perish in the
　　　darkness.
For not by strength does man prevail;
10　　the LORD's foes shall be shattered.
The Most High in heaven thunders;
　　The LORD judges the ends of the earth.
Now may he give strength to his king
　　and exalt the horn of his anointed!"[m]

11 When Elkanah returned home to Ramah,
the child remained in the service of the LORD
under the priest Eli.

Wickedness of Eli's Sons.
12 Now the
sons of Eli were wicked; they had respect neither for the LORD **13** nor for the priests' duties
toward the people. When someone offered a
sacrifice, the priest's servant would come with
a three-pronged fork, while the meat was still
boiling,[n] **14** and would thrust it into the basin,
kettle, caldron, or pot. Whatever the fork
brought up, the priest would keep. That is how
all the Israelites were treated who came to the
sanctuary at Shiloh. **15** In fact, even before the
fat was burned, the priest's servant would come
and say to the man offering the sacrifice, "Give
me some meat to roast for the priest. He will not
accept boiled meat from you, only raw meat."
16 And if the man protested to him, "Let the
fat be burned first as is the custom, then take
whatever you wish," he would reply, "No,
give it to me now, or else I will take it by
force."[o] **17** Thus the young men sinned grievously in the presence of the LORD; they treated
the offerings to the LORD with disdain.

The Lord Rewards Hannah.
18 Mean-
while the boy Samuel, girt with a linen apron,*
was serving in the presence of the LORD. **19** His
mother used to make a little garment for him,
which she would bring him each time she went
up with her husband to offer the customary sacrifice. **20** And Eli would bless Elkanah and his
wife, as they were leaving for home. He would
say, "May the LORD repay you with children
from this woman for the gift she has made to the
LORD!" **21** The LORD favored Hannah so that
she conceived and gave birth to three more sons
and two daughters, while young Samuel grew
up in the service of the LORD.[p]

Eli's Futile Rebuke.
22 When Eli was
very old, he heard repeatedly how his sons were
treating all Israel [and that they were having

relations with the women serving at the entry of
the meeting tent.]* **23** So he said to them:
"Why are you doing such things? **24** No, my
sons, you must not do these things! It is not a
good report that I hear the people of the LORD
spreading about you. **25** If a man sins against
another man, one can intercede for him with the
LORD; but if a man sins against the LORD, who
can intercede for him?" But they disregarded
their father's warning, since the LORD had decided on their death. **26** Meanwhile, young
Samuel was growing in stature and in worth in
the estimation of the LORD and of men.[q]

Doom of Eli's House.*
27 A man of God
came to Eli and said to him: "This is what the
LORD says: 'I went so far as to reveal myself to
your father's family when they were in Egypt as
slaves to the house of Pharaoh. **28** I chose them
out of all the tribes of Israel to be my priests,
to go up to my altar, to burn incense, and to
wear the ephod* before me; and I assigned all
the oblations of the Israelites to your father's
family.[r] **29** Why do you keep a greedy eye on
my sacrifices and on the offerings which I have
prescribed? And why do you honor your sons in
preference to me, fattening yourselves with the
choicest part of every offering of my people
Israel?' **30** [s]This, therefore, is the oracle of the
LORD, the God of Israel: 'I said in the past that
your family and your father's family should
minister in my presence forever. But now,' the
LORD declares, 'away with this! for I will honor
those who honor me, but those who spurn me
shall be accursed. **31** Yes, the time is coming
when I will break your strength and the strength
of your father's family, so that no man in your
family shall reach old age. **32** You shall witness

---

m Ps 98, 9.
n 13-15: Ex 29, 27f; Lv
　7, 29-36; Dt 18, 3.
o Lv 3, 3ff.
p 1 Sm 3, 19.

q Lk 2, 52.
r 1 Sm 23, 9; 30, 7f; Jgs
　17, 5.
s 30f: 2 Sm 22, 26;
　1 Kgs 2, 27; Ps 18, 25.

*

2, 18: Linen apron: called in Hebrew "ephod," but not the
same as the high priest's ephod (Ex 28, 6–14) or the ephod
used in divination (v 28). Samuel wore a simple apron such as
was worn by the priests (1 Sm 22, 18), and on one occasion
also by David (2 Sm 6, 14).

2, 22: The bracketed words, which recall Ex 38, 8, are a
gloss in the received text; they are lacking in the oldest Greek
translation, and in a Hebrew manuscript from Qumran.

2, 27-36: These verses propose the punishment of Eli from
a point of view contemporary with the reform of Josiah (2 Kgs
23, 9; cf v 36); they hint at the events recorded in 1 Sm 22,
18–23 and 1 Kgs 2, 27. The older story of this divine warning
is that in 1 Sm 3, 11–14.

2, 28: Ephod: a portable container, presumably of cloth, for
the lots used in ritual consultation of God during the days of
the Judges (Jgs 17, 5; 18, 14–15) and down into the time of
David (1 Sm 14, 3ff; 23, 6ff; 30, 7f). The ephod of the high
priest described in Ex 28, 6ff becomes a garment upon which
a breastpiece of decision symbolizes, but no longer serves for,
such consultation. The Exodus text codifies a later form of the
tradition.

as a disappointed rival all the benefits enjoyed by Israel, but there shall never be an old man in your family. 33 I will permit some of your family to remain at my altar, to wear out their eyes in consuming greed; but the rest of the men of your family shall die by the sword. 34 You shall have a sign in what will happen to your two sons, Hophni and Phinehas: both shall die on the same day.[t] 35 I will choose a faithful priest who shall do what I have in heart and mind. I will establish a lasting house for him which shall function in the presence of my anointed forever. 36 Then whoever is left of your family will come to grovel before him for a piece of silver or a loaf of bread, and will say: Appoint me, I beg you, to a priestly function, that I may have a morsel of bread to eat.' "[u]

a type of discernment for a call to modern vocation

CHAPTER 3

Revelation to Samuel. 1 During the time young Samuel was minister to the LORD under Eli, a revelation of the LORD was uncommon* and vision infrequent. 2 One day Eli was asleep in his usual place. His eyes had lately grown so weak that he could not see. 3 The lamp of God was not yet extinguished, and Samuel was sleeping in the temple of the LORD where the ark of God was.[v] 4 The LORD called to Samuel, who answered, "Here I am." 5 He ran to Eli and said, "Here I am. You called me." "I did not call you," Eli said. "Go back to sleep." So he went back to sleep. 6 Again the LORD called Samuel, who rose and went to Eli. "Here I am," he said. "You called me." But he answered, "I did not call you, my son. Go back to sleep."

7 At that time Samuel was not familiar with the LORD, because the LORD had not revealed anything to him as yet. 8 The LORD called Samuel again, for the third time. Getting up and going to Eli, he said, "Here I am. You called me." Then Eli understood that the LORD was calling the youth. 9 So he said to Samuel, "Go to sleep, and if you are called, reply, 'Speak, LORD, for your servant is listening.' " When Samuel went to sleep in his place, 10 the LORD came and revealed his presence, calling out as before, "Samuel, Samuel!" Samuel answered, "Speak, for your servant is listening." 11 The LORD said to Samuel: "I am about to do something in Israel that will cause the ears of everyone who hears it to ring. 12 On that day I will carry out in full against Eli everything I threatened against his family. 13 I announce to him that I am condemning his family once and for all, because of this crime: though he knew his sons were blaspheming God, he did not reprove them.[w] 14 Therefore, I swear to the family of Eli that no sacrifice or offering will ever expiate its crime." 15 Samuel then slept until morning,

when he got up early and opened the doors of the temple of the LORD. He feared to tell Eli the vision, 16 but Eli called to him, "Samuel, my son!" He replied, "Here I am." 17 Then Eli asked, "What did he say to you? Hide nothing from me! May God do thus and so to you* if you hide a single thing he told you." 18 So Samuel told him everything, and held nothing back. Eli answered, "He is the LORD. He will do what he judges best."

Samuel Acknowledged as Prophet.

19 Samuel grew up, and the LORD was with him, not permitting any word of his to be without effect.[x] 20 [y]Thus all Israel from Dan to Beer-sheba came to know that Samuel was an accredited prophet of the LORD. 21 The LORD continued to appear at Shiloh; he manifested himself to Samuel at Shiloh through his word, 1 *and Samuel spoke to all Israel.

CHAPTER 4

Defeat of the Israelites. At that time, the Philistines gathered for an attack on Israel. Israel went out to engage them in battle and camped at Ebenezer, while the Philistines camped at Aphek. 2 The Philistines then drew up in battle formation against Israel. After a fierce struggle Israel was defeated by the Philistines, who slew about four thousand men on the battlefield. 3 When the troops retired to the camp, the elders of Israel said, "Why has the LORD permitted us to be defeated today by the Philistines? Let us fetch the ark of the LORD from Shiloh that it may go into battle among us and save us from the grasp of our enemies."

Loss of the Ark. 4 So the people sent to Shiloh and brought from there the ark of the LORD of hosts, who is enthroned upon the cherubim.* The two sons of Eli, Hophni and Phinehas, were with the ark of God.[z] 5 When the ark of the LORD arrived in the camp, all Israel shouted so loudly that the earth resounded. 6 The Philistines, hearing the noise of shouting, asked, "What can this loud shouting in the

---

t 1 Sm 4, 11.
u 2 Kgs 23, 9.
v Ex 25, 22; 27, 20f; Lv 24, 2. 4; 2 Chr 13, 11.
w 1 Sm 2, 27-36.
x 1 Sm 2, 21.
y Jgs 20, 1.
z Ex 25, 22.

---
*

3, 1: Uncommon: prophetic communications from God were almost unknown.

3, 17: May God do thus and so to you: the Biblical writers avoid repeating for us the specific terms of a curse as the speaker would have uttered it.

3, 1: And . . . Israel: this belongs to ch 4.

4, 4: Enthroned upon the cherubim: this title of the Lord seems to have originated in the sanctuary at Shiloh; it represents the divine Majesty as seated upon a throne on which he can be borne through the heavens by winged creatures somewhat as in the visions of Ez 1 and 10.

camp of the Hebrews mean?'' On learning that the ark of the LORD had come into the camp, **7** the Philistines were frightened. They said, ''Gods have come to their camp.'' They said also, ''Woe to us! This has never happened before. **8** Woe to us! Who can deliver us from the power of these mighty gods?* These are the gods that struck the Egyptians with various plagues and with pestilence. **9** Take courage and be manly, Philistines; otherwise you will become slaves to the Hebrews, as they were your slaves. So fight manfully!'' **10** The Philistines fought and Israel was defeated; every man fled to his own tent. It was a disastrous defeat, in which Israel lost thirty thousand foot soldiers. *a* **11** The ark of God was captured, and Eli's two sons, Hophni and Phinehas, were among the dead. *b*

Death of Eli. **12** A Benjaminite fled from the battlefield and reached Shiloh that same day, with his clothes torn and his head covered with dirt. *c* **13** When he arrived, Eli was sitting in his chair beside the gate, watching the road, for he was troubled at heart about the ark of God. The man, however, went into the city to divulge his news, which put the whole city in an uproar. **14** Hearing the outcry of the men standing near him, Eli inquired, ''What does this commotion mean?'' **15** (Eli was ninety-eight years old, and his eyes would not focus, so that he could not see.) **16** The man quickly came up to Eli and said, ''It is I who have come from the battlefield; I fled from there today.'' He asked, ''What happened, my son?'' **17** And the messenger answered: ''Israel fled from the Philistines; in fact, the troops suffered heavy losses. Your two sons, Hophni and Phinehas, are among the dead, and the ark of God has been captured.'' **18** At this mention of the ark of God, Eli fell backward from his chair into the gateway; since he was an old man and heavy, he died of a broken neck. He had judged Israel for forty years.

19 His daughter-in-law, the wife of Phinehas, was with child and at the point of giving birth. When she heard the news concerning the capture of the ark and the deaths of her father-in-law and her husband, she was seized with the pangs of labor, and gave birth. **20** She was about to die when the women standing around her said to her, ''Never fear! You have given birth to a son.'' Yet she neither answered nor paid any attention. *d* **21** [She named the child Ichabod, saying, ''Gone is the glory from Israel,'' with reference to the capture of the ark of God and to her father-in-law and her husband.] **22** She said, ''Gone is the glory from Israel,'' because the ark of God had been captured. *e*

CHAPTER 5

The Ark in the Temple of Dagon. **1** *f* The Philistines, having captured the ark of God, transferred it from Ebenezer to Ashdod. **2** They then took the ark of God and brought it into the temple of Dagon, placing it beside Dagon. **3** When the people of Ashdod rose early the next morning, Dagon was lying prone on the ground before the ark of the LORD. So they picked Dagon up and replaced him. **4** But the next morning early, when they arose, Dagon lay prone on the ground before the ark of the LORD, his head and hands broken off and lying on the threshold, his trunk alone intact. **5** For this reason, neither the priests of Dagon nor any others who enter the temple of Dagon tread on the threshold of Dagon in Ashdod to this very day; they always step over it.

The Ark is Carried About. **6** Now the LORD dealt severely with the people of Ashdod. He ravaged and afflicted the city and its vicinity with hemorrhoids; he brought upon the city a great and deadly plague of mice* that swarmed in their ships and overran their fields. *g* **7** On seeing how matters stood, the men of Ashdod decided, ''The ark of the God of Israel must not remain with us, for he is handling us and our god Dagon severely.'' **8** So they summoned all the Philistine lords and inquired of them, ''What shall we do with the ark of the God of Israel?'' The men of Gath replied, ''Let them move the ark of the God of Israel on to us.'' **9** So they moved the ark of the God of Israel to Gath! But after it had been brought there, the LORD threw the city into utter turmoil: he afflicted its inhabitants, young and old, and hemorrhoids broke out on them. **10** The ark of God was next sent to Ekron; but as it entered that city, the people there cried out, ''Why have they brought the ark of the God of Israel here to kill us and our kindred?'' **11** Then they, too, sent a summons to all the Philistine lords and pleaded: ''Send away the ark of God of Israel. Let it return to its own place, that it may not kill us and our kindred.'' A deadly panic had seized the whole city, since the hand of God had been very heavy upon it. **12** Those who escaped death

---

a Ps 78, 61.
b 1 Sm 2, 34.
c Jos 7, 6; 2 Sm 1, 2;
  Jer 7, 12.
d 1 Sm 14, 3; Gn 35,

16ff.
e Ps 78, 61.
f 1-5: Jgs 16, 23-30; Is
  45, 5f. 20f.
g Ps 78, 66.

*

4, 8: These mighty gods: the Philistines, who were polytheists, are represented as supposing the Israelites honored several gods.

5, 6: Hemorrhoids ... mice: a double calamity fell upon them—a plague of mice or rats, and a severe epidemic of pestilential tumors, probably the bubonic plague.

were afflicted with hemorrhoids, and the outcry from the city went up to the heavens.

CHAPTER 6

The Ark To Be Returned.   **1** The ark of the LORD had been in the land of the Philistines seven months **2** when they summoned priests and fortune-tellers to ask, "What shall we do with the ark of the LORD? Tell us what we should send back with it." **3** They replied: "If you intend to send away the ark of the God of Israel, you must not send it alone, but must, by all means, make amends to him through a guilt offering.* Then you will be healed, and will learn why he continues to afflict you." **4** When asked further, "What guilt offering should be our amends to him?", they replied:

"Five golden hemorrhoids and five golden mice to correspond to the number of Philistine lords, since the same plague has struck all of you and your lords. **5** Therefore, make images of the hemorrhoids and of the mice that are infesting your land and give them as a tribute to the God of Israel. Perhaps then he will cease to afflict you, your gods, and your land. **6** Why should you become stubborn, as the Egyptians and Pharaoh were stubborn? Was it not after he had dealt ruthlessly with them that the Israelites were released and departed?[h] **7** So now set to work and make a new cart. Then take two milch cows that have not borne the yoke; hitch them to the cart, but drive their calves indoors away from them.[i] **8** You shall next take the ark of the LORD and place it on the cart, putting in a box beside it the golden articles that you are offering, as amends for your guilt. Start it on its way, and let it go. **9** Then watch! If it goes up to Beth-shemesh along the route to his own territory, he has brought this great calamity upon us; if not, we will know it was not he who struck us, but that an accident happened to us."

The Ark in Beth-shemesh.   **10** They acted upon this advice. Taking two milch cows, they hitched them to the cart but shut up their calves indoors. **11** Then they placed the ark of the LORD on the cart, along with the box containing the golden mice and the images of the hemorrhoids. **12** The cows went straight for the route to Beth-shemesh and continued along this road, mooing as they went, without turning right or left. The Philistine lords followed them as far as the border of Beth-shemesh. **13** The people of Beth-shemesh were harvesting the wheat in the valley. When they looked up and spied the ark, they greeted it with rejoicing. **14** The cart came to the field of Joshua the Beth-shemite and stopped there. At a large stone in the field, the wood of the cart was split up and the cows were offered as a holocaust to

the LORD.[j] **15** The Levites, meanwhile, had taken down the ark of God and the box beside it, in which the golden articles were, and had placed them on the great stone. The men of Beth-shemesh also offered other holocausts and sacrifices to the LORD that day. **16** After witnessing this, the five Philistine lords returned to Ekron the same day.

Guilt Offering.   **17** The golden hemorrhoids the Philistines sent back as a guilt offering to the LORD were as follows: one for Ashdod, one for Gaza, one for Ashkelon, one for Gath, and one for Ekron. **18** The golden mice, however, corresponded to the number of all the cities of the Philistines belonging to the five lords, including fortified cities and open villages. The large stone on which the ark of the LORD was placed is still in the field of Joshua the Beth-shemite at the present time.

Penalty for Irreverence.   **19** The descendants of Jeconiah did not join in the celebration with the inhabitants of Beth-shemesh when they greeted the ark of the LORD, and seventy of them were struck down. The people went into mourning at this great calamity with which the LORD had afflicted them. **20** The men of Beth-shemesh asked, "Who can stand in the presence of this Holy One? To whom shall he go from us?" **21** They then sent messengers to the inhabitants of Kiriath-jearim, saying, "The Philistines have returned the ark of the LORD; come down and get it."

CHAPTER 7

1 So the inhabitants of Kiriath-jearim came for the ark of the LORD and brought it into the house of Abinadab on the hill, appointing his son Eleazar as guardian of the ark of the LORD.

Religious Reform.   **2** From the day the ark came to rest in Kiriath-jearim a long time, twenty years, elapsed, and the whole Israelite population turned to the LORD. **3** Samuel said to them: "If you wish with your whole heart to return to the LORD, put away your foreign gods and your Ashtaroth, devote yourselves to the LORD, and worship him alone. Then he will deliver you from the power of the Philistines."[k] **4** So the Israelites put away their Baals and Ashtaroth, and worshiped the LORD alone. **5** Samuel then gave orders, "Gather all Israel

---

h Ex 7, 14; 8, 15; 9, 34.
i Nm 19, 2; Dt 21, 3;
  2 Sm 6, 3.
j 2 Sm 24, 21ff.

k 1 Sm 12, 10. 20. 24;
  Jos 24, 23; Jgs 6,
  6-10; 10, 10-16.
l 1 Sm 10, 17; Jgs 20, 1.

*

6, 3: A guilt offering: a propitiatory offering customary after unwitting transgression of the ordinances of God regarding holy things or property rights; cf Lv 6, 1ff.

to Mizpah, that I may pray to the LORD for you."[l] **6** When they were gathered at Mizpah, they drew water and poured it out on the ground* before the LORD, and they fasted that day, confessing, "We have sinned against the LORD." It was at Mizpah that Samuel began to judge the Israelites.[m]

Rout of the Philistines. **7** When the Philistines heard that the Israelites had gathered at Mizpah, their lords went up against Israel. Hearing this, the Israelites became afraid of the Philistines **8** and said to Samuel, "Implore the LORD our God unceasingly for us, to save us from the clutches of the Philistines."[n] **9** Samuel therefore took an unweaned lamb and offered it entire as a holocaust to the LORD.[o] He implored the LORD for Israel, and the LORD heard him. **10** While Samuel was offering the holocaust, the Philistines advanced to join battle with Israel. That day, however, the LORD thundered loudly against the Philistines, and threw them into such confusion that they were defeated by Israel. **11** Thereupon the Israelites sallied forth from Mizpah and pursued the Philistines, harrying them down beyond Bethcar. **12** Samuel then took a stone and placed it between Mizpah and Jeshanah; he named it Ebenezer,* explaining, "To this point has the LORD helped us." **13** Thus were the Philistines subdued, never again to enter the territory of Israel, for the LORD was severe with them as long as Samuel lived.[p] **14** The cities from Ekron to Gath which the Philistines had taken from Israel were restored to them. Israel also freed the territory of these cities from the dominion of the Philistines. Moreover there was peace between Israel and the Amorites.

15 Samuel judged Israel as long as he lived. **16** He made a yearly journey, passing through Bethel, Gilgal and Mizpah and judging Israel at each of these sanctuaries. **17** Then he used to return to Ramah, for that was his home. There, too, he judged Israel and built an altar to the LORD.[q]

II: Establishment of the Monarchy in Israel

CHAPTER 8*

Request for a King. **1** In his old age Samuel appointed his sons judges over Israel. **2** His first-born was named Joel, his second son, Abijah; they judged at Beer-sheba. **3** His sons did not follow his example but sought illicit gain and accepted bribes, perverting justice.[r] **4** Therefore all the elders of Israel came in a body to Samuel at Ramah **5** and said to him, "Now that you are old, and your sons do not

follow your example, appoint a king over us, as other nations have, to judge us."[s]

God Grants the Request. **6** Samuel was displeased when they asked for a king to judge them. He prayed to the LORD, however, **7** who said in answer: "Grant the people's every request. It is not you they reject, they are rejecting me as their king.[t] **8** As they have treated me constantly from the day I brought them up from Egypt to this day, deserting me and worshiping strange gods, so do they treat you too. **9** Now grant their request; but at the same time, warn them solemnly and inform them of the rights of the king who will rule them."

The Rights of a King. **10** Samuel delivered the message of the LORD in full to those who were asking him for a king. **11** He told them: "The rights of the king who will rule you will be as follows: He will take your sons and assign them to his chariots and horses, and they will run before his chariot.[u] **12** He will also appoint from among them his commanders of groups of a thousand and of a hundred soldiers. He will set them to do his plowing and his harvesting, and to make his implements of war and the equipment of his chariots.[v] **13** He will use your daughters as ointment-makers, as cooks, and as bakers. **14** He will take the best of your fields, vineyards, and olive groves, and give them to his officials.[w] **15** He will tithe your crops and your vineyards, and give the revenue to his eunuchs and his slaves. **16** He will take your male and female servants, as well as your best oxen and your asses, and use them to do his work. **17** He will tithe your flocks and you yourselves will become his slaves.[x] **18** When this takes place, you will complain

m Jgs 20, 26; Ps 22, 14; Lam 2, 19.
n Ex 17, 9-13.
o 9f: 2 Sm 22, 14f; Sir 46, 16ff.
p Jgs 3, 30; 8, 28; 11, 33.
q 1 Sm 9, 12; 14, 35.
r Ex 23, 8; Dt 16, 19; Prv 17, 23.
s 5f: Dt 17, 14f; Hos 13, 10; Acts 13, 21.
t 7f: 1 Sm 12, 1. 12f; Jgs 8, 22f; 10, 13; 1 Kgs 9, 9.
u 1 Sm 10, 25; Dt 17, 14-20; 1 Kgs 12.
v 2 Sm 15, 1; 1 Kgs 1, 5.
w 1 Sm 22, 7; 1 Kgs 21, 1-24; Ez 46, 18.
x 1 Kgs 12, 4.

7, 6: Poured it out on the ground: for the symbolism, cf 2 Sm 14, 14.

7, 12: Ebenezer: or eben ha-ezer, means "stone of help."

8, 1: From this chapter on, the First Book of Samuel gives us two and sometimes three viewpoints on most of the events with which it is concerned, such as the appointment of Saul as king, the reasons for his downfall, his relationship with David, even the circumstances of Saul's death (1 Sm 31; 2 Sm 1). The choice of Saul as king is seen, in ch 8, followed by 10, 17–27 and ch 12, as motivated by the people's defection from the proper service of God; this later editorial approach incorporates not only narratives with which it is consistent, but also early traditions (9, 1–10. 16; ch 11) which portray the events and their motivation quite differently.

against the king whom you have chosen, but on that day the LORD will not answer you.''

Persistent Demand.
19 The people, however, refused to listen to Samuel's warning and said, "Not so! There must be a king over us. ʸ **20** We too must be like other nations, with a king to rule us and to lead us in warfare and fight our battles.'' **21** When Samuel had listened to all the people had to say, he repeated it to the LORD, **22** *who then said to him, "Grant their request and appoint a king to rule them.'' Samuel thereupon said to the men of Israel, "Each of you go to his own city.''

CHAPTER 9

Sat week's last time
1–4 and 17–19

1 There was a stalwart man from Benjamin named Kish, who was the son of Abiel, son of Zeror, son of Becorath, son of Aphiah, a Benjaminite. ᶻ **2** He had a son named Saul, who was a handsome young man. There was no other Israelite handsomer than Saul; he stood head and shoulders above the people. ᵃ

The Lost Asses.
3 Now the asses of Saul's father, Kish, had wandered off. Kish said to his son Saul, "Take one of the servants with you and go out and hunt for the asses.'' **4** Accordingly they went through the hill country of Ephraim, and through the land of Shalishah. Not finding them there, they continued through the land of Shaalim without success. They also went through the land of Benjamin, but they failed to find the animals. **5** When they came to the land of Zuph, Saul said to the servant who was with him, "Come, let us turn back, lest my father forget about the asses and become anxious about us.'' **6** The servant replied, "Listen! There is a man of God in this city, a man held in high esteem; all that he says is sure to come true. Let us go there now! Perhaps he can tell us how to accomplish our errand.'' **7** ᵇBut Saul said to his servant, "If we go, what can we offer the man? There is no bread in our bags, and we have no present to give the man of God. What have we?'' **8** Again the servant answered Saul, "I have a quarter of a silver shekel.* If I give that to the man of God, he will tell us our way.'' **10** Saul then said to his servant, "Well said! Come on, let us go!'' And they went to the city where the man of God lived.

Quest for Samuel's Aid.
11 ᶜAs they were going up the ascent to the city, they met some girls coming out to draw water and inquired of them, "Is the seer in town?'' **9** ᵈ(In former times in Israel, anyone who sent to consult God used to say, "Come, let us go to the seer.'' For he who is now called prophet was formerly called seer.)* **12** ᵉThe girls answered, "Yes, there—straight ahead. Hurry now; just

today he came to the city, because the people have a sacrifice today on the high place.* **13** When you enter the city, you may reach him before he goes up to the high place to eat. The people will not eat until he arrives; only after he blesses the sacrifice will the invited guests eat. Go up immediately, for you should find him right now.''

Samuel's Revelation about Saul.
14 So they went up to the city. As they entered it, Samuel was coming toward them on his way to the high place. **15** The day before Saul's arrival, the LORD had given Samuel the revelation:ᶠ **16** "At this time tomorrow I will send you a man from the land of Benjamin whom you are to anoint as commander of my people Israel. He shall save my people from the clutches of the Philistines, for I have witnessed their misery and accepted their cry for help.''ᵍ **17** When Samuel caught sight of Saul, the LORD assured him, "This is the man of whom I told you; he is to govern my people.'' **18** Saul met Samuel in the gateway and said, "Please tell me where the seer lives.'' **19** Samuel answered Saul: "I am the seer. Go up ahead of me to the high place and eat with me today. In the morning, before dismissing you, I will tell you whatever you wish. **20** As for the asses you lost three days ago, do not worry about them, for they have been found. Whom does Israel desire ardently if not you and your father's family?'' **21** Saul replied: "Am I not a Benjaminite, of one of the smallest tribes of Israel, and is not my clan the least among the clans of the tribe of Benjamin? Why say such things to me?''ʰ

22 Samuel then took Saul and his servant and brought them to the room, where he placed them at the head of the guests, of whom there were about thirty. **23** He said to the cook, "Bring the portion I gave you and told you to put aside.'' **24** So the cook took up the leg and what went

---

y 1 Sm 10, 19.
z 1 Sm 14, 51; 1 Chr 8, 33.
a 1 Sm 10, 23.
b 7f: Nm 22, 7; 1 Kgs 14, 3; 2 Kgs 4, 42; 5, 15; 8, 8f.
c Gn 24, 11ff; Ex 2, 16.

d Sir 46, 15.
e 1 Sm 7, 17; 16, 2. 5; 20, 6. 29; Dt 12, 13; 1 Kgs 3, 2. 4.
f Acts 13, 21.
g 1 Sm 10, 1.
h 1 Sm 15, 17.

---

*

9, 8: A quarter of a silver shekel: about a tenth of an ounce of silver.

9, 9: This verse is a later explanation of the term seer, first used in the text in 1 Sm 9, 11.

9, 12: On the high place: the local sanctuary on the top of a hill, where the sacrifice was offered and the sacrificial meal eaten.

9, 24: And what went with it: a slight change would give "and the fatty tail" as perhaps the original reading. Sheep in the Near East are exceptionally fat-tailed, and such a portion would be thought a special delicacy by the Hebrews. However, the ritual legislation as we know it (Lv 3, 9) would require that the fat tail be burned on the altar. If this general rule was later than the time of Samuel, the present text may have been

with it,* and placed it before Saul. Samuel said: "This is a reserved portion that has been set before you. Eat, for it was kept for you until your arrival; I explained that I was inviting some guests." Thus Saul dined with Samuel that day. **25** When they came down from the high place into the city, a mattress was spread for Saul on the roof, **26** and he slept there.

Saul's Anointing. At daybreak Samuel called to Saul on the roof, "Get up, and I will start you on your journey." Saul rose, and he and Samuel went outside the city together. **27** As they were approaching the edge of the town, Samuel said to Saul, "Tell the servant to go on ahead of us, but stay here yourself for the moment, that I may give you a message from God."

CHAPTER 10

1 Then, from a flask he had with him, Samuel poured oil on Saul's head; he also kissed him, saying: "The LORD anoints you commander over his heritage. You are to govern the LORD's people Israel, and to save them from the grasp of their enemies roundabout. *i*

"This will be the sign for you that the LORD has anointed you commander over his heritage: **2** When you leave me today, you will meet two men near Rachel's tomb* at Zelah in the territory of Benjamin, who will say to you, 'The asses you went to look for have been found. Your father is no longer worried about the asses, but is anxious about you and says, What shall I do about my son?'*j* **3** Farther on, when you arrive at the terebinth of Tabor, you will be met by three men going up to God at Bethel; one will be bringing three kids, another three loaves of bread, and the third a skin of wine. **4** They will greet you and offer you two wave offerings of bread, which you will take from them. **5** *k*After that you will come to Gibeath-elohim, where there is a garrison of the Philistines.* As you enter that city, you will meet a band of prophets, in a prophetic state, coming down from the high place, preceded by lyres, tambourines, flutes and harps. **6** The spirit of the LORD will rush upon you, and you will join them in their prophetic state and will be changed into another man.*l* **7** When you see these signs fulfilled, do whatever you judge feasible, because God is with you. **8** *m*Now go down ahead of me to Gilgal, for I shall come down to you, to offer holocausts and to sacrifice peace offerings. Wait seven days until I come to you; I shall then tell you what you must do."*

Fulfillment of the Signs. **9** As Saul turned to leave Samuel, God gave him another heart. That very day all these signs came to pass. . . . **10** *When they were going from there to Gibe-

ah, a band of prophets met him, and the spirit of God rushed upon him, so that he joined them in their prophetic state.*n* **11** When all who had known him previously saw him in a prophetic state among the prophets, they said to one another, "What has happened to the son of Kish? Is Saul also among the prophets?"*o* **12** And someone from that district added, "And who is their father?" Thus the proverb arose, "Is Saul also among the prophets?" **13** When he came out of the prophetic state, he went home.

Silence about the Kingship. **14** Saul's uncle inquired of him and his servant, "Where have you been?" Saul replied, "To look for the asses. When we could not find them, we went to Samuel." **15** Then Saul's uncle said, "Tell me, then, what Samuel said to you." **16** Saul said to his uncle, "He assured us that the asses had been found." But he mentioned nothing to him of what Samuel had said about the kingship.

Saul Chosen King by Lot. **17** Samuel called the people together to the LORD at Mizpah*p* **18** and addressed the Israelites: "Thus says the LORD, the God of Israel, 'It was I who brought Israel up from Egypt and delivered you from the power of the Egyptians and from the power of all the kingdoms that oppressed you.'*q* **19** But today you have rejected your God, who delivers you from all your evils and calamities, by saying to him, 'Not so, but you must appoint a king over us.' Now, therefore, take your stand before the LORD according to tribes and families."*r* **20** So Samuel had had all the tribes of Israel come forward, and the tribe of Benjamin was chosen. **21** Next he had the tribe of Benja-

---

i 1 Sm 9, 16f; 24, 7; Jgs
9, 9; 1 Kgs 1, 39; Acts
13, 21.
j Jer 31, 15; Mk 14, 13.
k 5f: 1 Sm 13, 3; 16, 13;
19, 20f.
l 1 Sm 11, 6; 16, 13; Jgs
14, 6. 19; 15, 14;
2 Kgs 3, 15.

m 1 Sm 13, 8; Lv 3, 1.
n 1 Sm 19, 20-24; Nm
11, 25.
o 1 Sm 19, 24.
p 1 Sm 7, 5.
q Ex 20, 2; Lv 11, 45;
25, 38; Nm 15, 41; Dt
5, 6; Jgs 6, 8f.
r 1 Sm 8, 19.

---

*

retouched so as not to seem to contravene it. A Qumran text has "the festive (leg)" here.

10, 2: Here, as in Jer 31, 15, Rachel's tomb is placed north of Jerusalem. Later tradition understood Gn 35, 19f in the sense given by Mt 2, 16ff, and placed the tomb at Bethlehem, farther south.

10, 5: A garrison of the Philistines: the Hebrew word for "garrison" has been explained alternatively to mean a pillar erected to mark the Philistine occupation, or an inspector or officer for the collection of taxes. In a prophetic state: in an ecstatic condition due to strong feelings of religious enthusiasm induced by a communal observance, possibly accompanied by music and dancing.

10, 8: By inserting this verse, with its seven days, an editor has prepared for one narrative of the rejection of Saul (1 Sm 13, 8–15) in the very context of Saul's anointing.

10, 10: The story has here been abridged by omitting the fulfillment of the first two signs given by Samuel (1 Sm 10, 2ff).

min come forward in clans, and the clan of Matri was chosen, and finally Saul, son of Kish, was chosen. But they looked for him in vain. **22** ˢAgain they consulted the LORD, "Has he come here?" The LORD answered, "He is hiding among the baggage." **23** They ran to bring him from there; and when he stood among the people, he was head and shoulders above all the crowd.ᵗ **24** Samuel said to all the people, "Do you see the man whom the LORD has chosen? There is none like him among all the people!" Then all the people shouted, "Long live the king!"ᵘ

25 Samuel next explained to the people the law of royalty* and wrote it in a book, which he placed in the presence of the LORD. This done, Samuel dismissed the people, each to his own place.ᵛ **26** Saul also went home to Gibeah, accompanied by warriors whose hearts the LORD had touched. **27** But certain worthless men said, "How can this fellow save us?" They despised him and brought him no present.ʷ

CHAPTER 11

Defeat of the Ammonites. **1** About a month later,* Nahash the Ammonite went up and laid siege to Jabesh-gilead. All the men of Jabesh begged Nahash, "Make a treaty with us, and we will be your subjects."ˣ **2** But Nahash the Ammonite replied, "This is my condition for a treaty with you: I must gouge out every man's right eye, that I may thus bring ignominy on all Israel." **3** The elders of Jabesh said to him: "Give us seven days to send messengers throughout the territory of Israel. If no one rescues us, we will surrender to you." **4** When the messengers arrived at Gibeah of Saul, they related the news to the people, all of whom wept aloud. **5** Just then Saul came in from the field, behind his oxen. "Why are the people weeping?" he asked. The message of the inhabitants of Jabesh was repeated to him. **6** As he listened to this report, the spirit of God rushed upon him and he became very angry.ʸ **7** Taking a yoke of oxen, he cut them into pieces, which he sent throughout the territory of Israel by couriers with the message, "If anyone does not come out to follow Saul [and Samuel], the same as this will be done to his oxen!" In dread of the LORD, the people turned out to a man.ᶻ **8** When he reviewed them in Bezek, there were three hundred thousand Israelites and seventy thousand Judahites.

9 To the messengers who had come he said, "Tell the inhabitants of Jabesh-gilead that tomorrow, while the sun is hot, they will be rescued." The messengers came and reported this to the inhabitants of Jabesh, who were jubilant, **10** and said to Nahash, "Tomorrow we will surrender to you, and you may do whatever you please with us." **11** On the appointed day, Saul arranged his troops in three companies and invaded the camp during the dawn watch. They slaughtered Ammonites until the heat of the day; by then the survivors were so scattered that no two were left together.

Saul Accepted as King. **12** *The people then said to Samuel: "Who questioned whether Saul should rule over us? Hand over the men and we will put them to death."ᵃ **13** But Saul broke in to say, "No man is to be put to death this day, for today the LORD has saved Israel."ᵇ **14** Samuel said to the people, "Come, let us go to Gilgal to inaugurate the kingdom there." **15** So all the people went to Gilgal, where, in the presence of the LORD, they made Saul king. They also sacrificed peace offerings there before the LORD, and Saul and all the Israelites celebrated the occasion with great joy.

CHAPTER 12

Samuel's Integrity. **1** Samuel addressed all Israel: "I have granted your request in every respect," he said. "I have set a king over youᶜ **2** and now the king is your leader. As for me, I am old and gray, and have sons among you. I have lived with you from my youth to the present day. **3** Here I stand! Answer me in the presence of the LORD and of his anointed. Whose ox have I taken? Whose ass have I taken? Whom have I cheated? Whom have I oppressed? From whom have I accepted a bribe and overlooked his guilt? I will make restitution to you."ᵈ **4** They replied, "You have neither cheated us, nor oppressed us, nor accepted anything from anyone." **5** So he said to them, "The LORD is witness against you this day, and his anointed as well, that you have found nothing in my possession." "He is witness," they agreed.

---

s 1 Sm 30, 24.
t 1 Sm 9, 2; 16, 7.
u 2 Sm 16, 16; 1 Kgs 1, 25; 2 Kgs 11, 12.
v 1 Sm 8, 11; Dt 17, 14-20.
w 1 Sm 11, 12.
x 1 Sm 12, 12; 31, 11.
y 1 Sm 16, 13; Jgs 14, 6.
19.
z 1 Kgs 11, 30; 2 Kgs 13, 18.
a 1 Sm 10, 27.
b 2 Sm 19, 23.
c 1 Sm 8, 7. 9. 22.
d Ex 20, 17; 23, 8; Nm 16, 15; Dt 16, 19; Sir 46, 19.

10, 25: The law of royalty: the charter defining the rights of the king.

11, 1: About a month later: there is ancient evidence for a longer introduction to this campaign. The time indication here may refer to its earlier stages rather than to the events of ch 10.

11, 12–14: With these verses, an editor has harmonized the account of the acknowledgment of Saul as king at Mizpah (1 Sm 10, 17–24) with the public acclamation at Gilgal (1 Sm 11, 15) after the defeat of the Ammonites (1 Sm 11, 1–11). The Greek text of 1 Sm 11, 15 reads "and Samuel anointed Saul as king," instead of they made Saul king.

Samuel Upbraids the People. 6 Continuing, Samuel said to the people: "The LORD is witness, who appointed Moses and Aaron, and who brought your fathers up from the land of Egypt. e 7 Now, therefore, take your stand, and I shall arraign you before the LORD, and shall recount for you all the acts of mercy the LORD has done for you and your fathers. 8 When Jacob and his sons went to Egypt and the Egyptians oppressed them, your fathers appealed to the LORD, who sent Moses and Aaron to bring them out of Egypt, and he gave them this place to live in. f 9 But they forgot the LORD their God; and he allowed them to fall into the clutches of Sisera, the captain of the army of Jabin, king of Hazor, into the grasp of the Philistines, and into the grip of the king of Moab, who made war against them. g 10 Each time they appealed to the LORD and said, 'We have sinned in forsaking the LORD and worshiping Baals and Ashtaroth; but deliver us now from the power of our enemies, and we will worship you.' h 11 Accordingly, the LORD sent Jerubbaal, Barak, Jephthah, and Samson; he delivered you from the power of your enemies on every side, so that you were able to live in security. i 12 Yet, when you saw Nahash, king of the Ammonites, advancing against you, you said to me, 'Not so, but a king must rule us,' even though the LORD your God is your king. j

Warnings for People and King.
13 "Now you have the king you want, a king the LORD has given you. k 14 If you fear the LORD and worship him, if you are obedient to him and do not rebel against the LORD's command, if both you and the king who rules you follow the LORD your God—well and good. 15 But if you do not obey the LORD and if you rebel against his command, the LORD will deal severely with you and your king, and destroy you. 16 Now then, stand ready to witness the great marvel the LORD is about to accomplish before your eyes. 17 Are we not in the harvest time for wheat? Yet I shall call to the LORD, and he will send thunder and rain. Thus you will see and understand how greatly the LORD is displeased that you have asked for a king." l 18 Samuel then called to the LORD, and the LORD sent thunder and rain that day.

Assistance Promised. As a result, all the people dreaded the LORD and Samuel. 19 They said to Samuel, "Pray to the LORD your God for us, your servants, that we may not die for having added to all our other sins the evil of asking for a king." 20 "Do not fear," Samuel answered them. "It is true you have committed all this evil; still, you must not turn from the LORD, but must worship him with your whole heart. 21 Do not turn to meaningless idols which can

neither profit nor save; they are nothing. m 22 For the sake of his own great name the LORD will not abandon his people, since the LORD himself chose to make you his people. n 23 As for me, far be it from me to sin against the LORD by ceasing to pray for you and to teach you the good and right way. o 24 But you must fear the LORD and worship him faithfully with your whole heart; keep in mind the great things he has done among you. 25 If instead you continue to do evil, both you and your king shall perish."

III: Saul and David

CHAPTER 13

1 [Saul was . . . years old when he became king and he reigned . . . (two) years over Israel.]*

Saul Offers Sacrifice. 2 Saul chose three thousand men of Israel, of whom two thousand remained with him in Michmash and in the hill country of Bethel, and one thousand were with Jonathan in Gibeah of Benjamin. He sent the rest of the people back to their tents. 3 Now Jonathan overcame the Philistine garrison* which was in Gibeah, and the Philistines got word of it. Then Saul sounded the horn throughout the land, with a proclamation, "Let the Hebrews hear!" p 4 Thus all Israel learned that Saul had overcome the garrison of the Philistines and that Israel had brought disgrace upon the Philistines; and the soldiers were called up to Saul in Gilgal. 5 The Philistines also assembled for battle, with three thousand chariots, six thousand horsemen, and foot soldiers as numerous as the sands of the seashore. Moving up against Israel, they encamped in Michmash, east of Beth-aven. 6 Some Israelites, aware of the danger and of the difficult situation, hid themselves in caves, in thickets, among rocks,

---

e Mi 6, 4.
f Gn 46, 5; Ex 1, 11; 2, 23ff.
g Jgs 3, 12ff; 4, 2f; 10, 7; 13, 1.
h 1 Sm 7, 3f.
i Jgs 6, 14. 32; 11, 1.
j 1 Sm 8, 6f. 19; 11, 1f; Jgs 8, 23.
k 1 Sm 8, 7.
l Ex 9, 23. 28ff; 1 Kgs 18, 1.
m Dt 32, 37ff.
n Jer 14, 21; Ex 20, 9; Dn 3, 34.
o Ex 32, 11.
p 1 Sm 14, 1-15; Jgs 3, 27; 6, 34; 2 Sm 20, 1f.
q 1 Sm 14, 22.

---

*

13, 1: A formula like that of 2 Sm 5, 4 was introduced here at some time; but the age of Saul when he became king remains a blank, and the two years assigned for his reign in the received text cannot be correct. Tradition (Acts 13, 21) offers the round number, "forty years."

13, 3–4: The Philistine garrison: see note on 1 Sm 10, 5. Let the Hebrews hear: a different reading of these verses, based on the Greek, would yield: "And the Philistines heard that the Hebrews (or: the slaves) had revolted. Saul in the meantime sounded the trumpet throughout all the land (v 4), and all Israel heard that Saul. . . ."

in caverns, and in cisterns,*q* **7** and other Hebrews passed over the Jordan into the land of Gad and Gilead. Saul, however, held out at Gilgal, although all his followers were seized with fear.* **8** He waited seven days—the time Samuel had determined. When Samuel did not arrive at Gilgal, the men began to slip away from Saul.*r* **9** He then said, ''Bring me the holocaust and peace offerings,'' and he offered up the holocaust.

King Saul Reproved.

10 He had just finished this offering when Samuel arrived. Saul went out to greet him, **11** and Samuel asked him, ''What have you done?'' Saul replied: ''When I saw that the men were slipping away from me, since you had not come by the specified time, and with the Philistines assembled at Michmash, **12** I said to myself, 'Now the Philistines will come down against me at Gilbal, and I have not yet sought the LORD's blessing.' So in my anxiety I offered up the holocaust.'' **13** Samuel's response was: ''You have been foolish! Had you kept the command the LORD your God gave you, the LORD would now establish your kingship in Israel as lasting; **14** but as things are, your kingdom shall not endure. The LORD has sought out a man after his own heart and has appointed him commander of his people, because you broke the LORD's command.''*s*

Philistine Invasion.

15 Then Samuel set out from Gilgal and went his own way; but the rest of the people went up after Saul to meet the soldiers, going from Gilgal to Gibeah of Benjamin. Saul then numbered the soldiers he had with him, who were about six hundred.*t* **16** Saul, his son Jonathan, and the soldiers they had with them were now occupying Geba of Benjamin, and the Philistines were encamped at Michmash. **17** Meanwhile, raiders left the camp of the Philistines in three bands.*u* One band took the Ophrah road toward the district of Shual; **18** another turned in the direction of Beth-horon; and the third took the road for Geba that overlooks the Valley of the Hyenas toward the desert.

Disarmament of Israel.

19 Not a single smith was to be found in the whole land of Israel, for the Philistines had said, ''Otherwise the Hebrews will make swords or spears.''*v* **20** All Israel, therefore, had to go down to the Philistines to sharpen their plowshares, mattocks, axes, and sickles. **21** The price for the plowshares and mattocks was two-thirds of a shekel, and a third of a shekel for sharpening the axes and for setting the ox-goads. **22** And so on the day of battle neither sword nor spear could be found in the possession of any of the soldiers

with Saul or Jonathan. Only Saul and his son Jonathan had them.

Jonathan's Exploit.

23 An outpost of the Philistines had pushed forward to the pass of Michmash.*w*

CHAPTER 14

1 One day Jonathan, son of Saul, said to his armor-bearer, ''Come, let us go over to the Philistine outpost on the other side.'' But he did not inform his father.*x* **2** (Saul's command post was under the pomegranate tree near the threshing floor on the outskirts of Geba; those with him numbered about six hundred men. **3** Ahijah, son of Ahitub, brother of Ichabod, who was the son of Phinehas, son of Eli, the priest of the LORD at Shiloh, was wearing the ephod.) Nor did the soldiers know that Jonathan had gone.*y* **4** Flanking the ravine through which Jonathan intended to get over to the Philistine outpost there was a rocky crag on each side, one called Bozez, the other Seneh. **5** One crag was to the north, toward Michmash, the other to the south, toward Geba. **6** Jonathan said to his armor-bearer: ''Come, let us go over to that outpost of the uncircumcised. Perhaps the LORD will help us, because it is no more difficult for the LORD to grant victory through a few than through many.''*z* **7** His armor-bearer replied, ''Do whatever you are inclined to do; I will match your resolve.'' **8** Jonathan continued: ''We shall go over to those men and show ourselves to them. **9** If they say to us, ''Stay there until we can come to you,' we shall stop where we are; we shall not go up to them. **10** But if they say, 'Come up to us,' we shall go up, because the LORD has delivered them into our grasp. That will be our sign.'' **11** Accordingly, the two of them appeared before the outpost of the Philistines, who said, ''Look, some Hebrews are coming out of the holes where they have been hiding.'' **12** The men of the outpost called to Jonathan and his armor-bearer. ''Come up here,'' they said, ''and we will teach you a lesson.'' So Jonathan said to his armor-bearer, ''Climb up after me, for the LORD has delivered them into the grasp of Israel.'' **13** Jonathan clambered up with his armor-bearer behind him; as the Philistines turned to flee him, he cut them down, and his armor-bearer followed him and

r 1 Sm 10, 8.
s 1 Sm 25, 30; 2 Sm 7, 15f; Ps 78, 70; Acts 13, 22.
t 1 Sm 14, 2.
u 1 Sm 14, 15.
v Jgs 5, 8.
w 1 Sm 14, 15.
x 1 Sm 13, 3.
y 1 Sm 2, 28; 4, 21; 14, 18; 23, 9; 30, 7.
z 1 Sm 17, 26. 36. 47; Sir 39, 18; 1 Mc 3, 19.

*

13, 7–15: These verses, like 1 Sm 10, 8, anticipate the rejection of Saul; a different occasion and motivation for this are given in ch 15, resumed in 1 Sm 28, 17f.

finished them off. **14** In this first exploit Jonathan and his armor-bearer slew about twenty men within half a furlong. **15** Then panic spread to the army and to the countryside, and all the soldiers, including the outpost and the raiding parties, were terror-stricken. The earth also shook, so that the panic was beyond human endurance.

Rout of the Philistines.

16 The lookouts of Saul in Geba of Benjamin saw that the enemy camp had scattered and were running about in all directions. **17** Saul said to those around him, "Count the troops and find out if any of us are missing." When they had investigated, they found Jonathan and his armor-bearer missing. **18** Saul then said to Ahijah, "Bring the ephod* here." (Ahijah was wearing the ephod in front of the Israelites at that time.) **19** While Saul was speaking to the priest, the tumult in the Philistine camp kept increasing. So he said to the priest, "Withdraw your hand." **20** And Saul and all his men shouted and rushed into the fight, where the Philistines, wholly confused, were thrusting swords at one another.ᵃ **21** In addition, the Hebrews who had previously sided with the Philistines and had gone up with them to the camp, turned to join the Israelites under Saul and Jonathan.ᵇ **22** Likewise, all the Israelites who were hiding in the hill country of Ephraim, on hearing that the Philistines were fleeing, pursued them in the rout.ᶜ **23** Thus the LORD saved Israel that day.

Saul's Oath.

The battle continued past Beth-horon;* **24** the whole people, about ten thousand combatants, were with Saul, and there was scattered fighting in every town in the hill country of Ephraim. And Saul swore a very rash oath that day, putting the people under this ban: "Cursed be the man who takes food before evening, before I am able to avenge myself on my enemies." So none of the people tasted food. **25** Indeed, there was a honeycomb lying on the ground, **26** and when the soldiers came to the comb the swarm had left it; yet no one would raise a hand to his mouth from it, because the people feared the oath.

Violation of the Oath.

27 Jonathan, who had not heard that his father had put the people under oath, thrust out the end of the staff he was holding and dipped it into the honey. Then he raised it to his mouth and his eyes lit up. **28** At this one of the soldiers spoke up: "Your father put the people under a strict oath, saying, 'Cursed be the man who takes food this day!' As a result the people are weak." **29** Jonathan replied: "My father brings trouble to the land. Look how bright my eyes are from this small taste of honey I have had. **30** What is more, if

the people had eaten freely today of their enemy's booty when they came across it, would not the slaughter of the Philistines by now have been the greater for it?"

Use of Flesh with Blood Forbidden.

31 After the Philistines were routed that day from Michmash to Aijalon, the people were completely exhausted. **32** So they pounced upon the spoil and took sheep, oxen and calves, slaughtering them on the ground and eating the flesh with blood.ᵈ **33** Informed that the people were sinning against the LORD by eating the flesh with blood, Saul said: "You have broken faith. Roll a large stone here for me." **34** He continued: "Mingle with the people and tell each of them to bring his ox or his sheep to me. Slaughter it here and then eat, but you must not sin against the LORD by eating the flesh with blood." So everyone brought to the LORD whatever ox he had seized, and they slaughtered them there; **35** and Saul built an altar to the LORD—this was the first time he built an altar to the LORD.ᵉ

Jonathan in Danger of Death.

36 Then Saul said, "Let us go down in pursuit of the Philistines by night, to plunder among them until daybreak and to kill them all off." They replied, "Do what you think best." But the priest said, "Let us consult God." **37** So Saul inquired of God: "Shall I go down in pursuit of the Philistines? Will you deliver them into the power of Israel?" But he received no answer on this occasion.ᶠ **38** Saul then said, "Come here, all officers of the army. We must investigate and find out how this sin was committed today. **39** As the LORD lives who has given victory to Israel, even if my son Jonathan has committed it, he shall surely die!" But none of the people answered him. **40** So he said to all Israel, "Stand on one side, and I and my son Jonathan will stand on the other." The people responded, "Do what you think best."ᵍ **41** And Saul said

a Jgs 7, 22.
b 1 Sm 29, 4.
c 1 Sm 13, 6.
d 1 Sm 15, 19. 21; Lv 3, 17; 7, 26f; 17, 10-14; Acts 15, 20. 29.
e 1 Sm 7, 17; Jgs 6, 24.
f 1 Sm 28, 6. 15.
g Jos 7, 13ff.
h 1 Sm 28, 6; Ex 28, 30; Dt 33, 8.

14, 18: Ephod: to be used in consulting God; see note on v 41, and that on 1 Sm 2, 28, above.

14, 23: Past Beth-horon: this is a textual correction influenced by 1 Sm 13, 18; the received Hebrew text refers to Bethel (Bethaven), but the effect of the victory would seem to have been that the main ridge of mountains in the territories of Benjamin and Ephraim was cleared of Philistines.

14, 41: The Urim and Thummim, or sacred lots, were a device for ascertaining the will of God; they ceased to be used after the time of David. The material and the shape of these objects, and the manner in which they were used, are unknown. They gave a "yes" or "no" answer to specific questions.

to the LORD, the God of Israel: "Why did you not answer your servant this time? If the blame for this resides in me or my son Jonathan, LORD, God of Israel, respond with Urim; but if this guilt is in your people Israel, respond with Thummim."* Jonathan and Saul were designated, and the people went free.[h] **42** Saul then said, "Cast lots between me and my son Jonathan." And Jonathan was designated. **43** Saul said to Jonathan, "Tell me what you have done." Jonathan replied, "I only tasted a little honey from the end of the staff I was holding. Am I to die for this?" **44** Saul said, "May God do thus and so to me if you do not indeed die, Jonathan!"[i]

Rescue of Jonathan. **45** But the army said to Saul: "Is Jonathan to die, though it was he who brought Israel this great victory? This must not be! As the LORD lives, not a single hair of his head shall fall to the ground, for God was with him in what he did today!" Thus the soldiers were able to rescue* Jonathan from death.[j] **46** After that Saul gave up the pursuit of the Philistines, who returned to their own territory.

Wars and Victories. **47** After taking over the kingship of Israel, Saul waged war on all their surrounding enemies—Moab, the Ammonites, Aram, Bethrehob, the king of Zobah, and the Philistines. Wherever he turned, he was successful[k] **48** and fought bravely. He defeated Amalek and delivered Israel from the hands of those who were plundering them.

Saul's Family. **49** The sons of Saul were Jonathan, Ishvi,* and Malchishua; his two daughters were named, the elder, Merob, and the younger, Michal.[l] **50** Saul's wife, who was named Ahinoam, was the daughter of Ahimaaz. The name of his general was Abner, son of Saul's uncle, Ner; **51** Kish, Saul's father, and Ner, Abner's father, were sons of Abiel.[m]

52 An unremitting war was waged against the Philistines during Saul's lifetime. When Saul saw any strong or brave man, he took him into his service.

CHAPTER 15

1 Samuel said to Saul: "It was I the LORD sent to anoint you king over his people Israel. Now, therefore, listen to the message of the LORD. **2** This is what the LORD of hosts has to say: 'I will punish what Amalek did to Israel when he barred his way as he was coming up from Egypt.[n] **3** Go, now, attack Amalek, and deal with him and all that he has under the ban.* Do not spare him, but kill men and women, children and infants, oxen and sheep, camels and asses.'"[o]

Disobedience of Saul. **4** Saul alerted the soldiers, and at Telaim reviewed two hundred thousand foot soldiers and ten thousand men of Judah.* **5** Saul went to the city of Amalek, and after setting an ambush in the wadi, **6** [p]warned the Kenites: "Come! Leave Amalek and withdraw, that I may not have to destroy you with them, for you were kind to the Israelites when they came up from Egypt." After the Kenites left, **7** Saul routed Amalek from Havilah to the approaches of Shur, on the frontier of Egypt.[q] **8** He took Agag, king of Amalek, alive, but on the rest of the people he put into effect the ban of destruction by the sword. **9** He and his troops spared Agag and the best of the fat sheep and oxen, and the lambs. They refused to carry out the doom on anything that was worthwhile, dooming only what was worthless and of no account.

Saul Is Reproved. **10** Then the LORD spoke to Samuel: **11** "I regret* having made Saul king, for he has turned from me and has not kept my command." At this Samuel grew angry and cried out to the LORD all night. **12** Early in the morning he went to meet Saul, but was informed that Saul had gone to Carmel, where he erected a trophy in his own honor, and that on his return he had passed on and gone down to Gilgal. **13** When Samuel came to him, Saul greeted him: "The LORD bless you! I have kept the command of the LORD." **14** But Samuel asked, "What, then, is the meaning of this bleating of sheep that comes to my ears, and the lowing of oxen that I hear?" **15** Saul replied: "They were brought from Amalek. The men spared the best sheep and oxen to sacrifice to the LORD, your God; but we have carried out the ban on the rest." **16** Samuel said to Saul: "Stop! Let me tell you what the LORD said to

---

i 1 Sm 3, 17; Ru 1, 17.
j 2 Sm 14, 11; 1 Kgs 1, 52.
k 2 Sm 1, 22; 8, 2-5.
l 1 Sm 18, 20. 25; 31, 2; 1 Chr 8, 33; 9, 39; 10, 2.
m 1 Sm 9, 1.
n Ex 17, 8-10. 16; Dt 25, 17ff.
o 1 Sm 27, 8; 30, 17; Ex 17, 16; Nm 24, 20.
p Nm 24, 21.
q 1 Sm 27, 8.

*

14, 45: Rescue: the Hebrew word used is that for the "redemption" of the first-born (Ex 13, 13ff).

14, 49: Ishvi: known also as Ishbaal, in 2 Sm 2, 8 and elsewhere. The name may once have read "Ishyo" here.

15, 3: Under the ban: in such wars of extermination, all things (men, cities, beasts, etc.) were to be blotted out; nothing could be reserved for private use. The interpretation of God's will here attributed to Samuel is in keeping with the abhorrent practices of blood revenge prevalent among pastoral, seminomadic peoples such as the Hebrews had recently been: The slaughter of the innocent has never been in conformity with the will of God.

15, 4: The numbers here are not realistic; compare 1 Sm 14, 24 above.

15, 11: I regret: God manifests "regret" when, offended by men, he takes away his benefits, graces and favors. It is not God, but men, who change, to their own detriment.

me last night.'' ''Speak!'' he replied. **17** Samuel then said: ''Though little in your own esteem, are you not leader of the tribes of Israel? The LORD anointed you king of Israel[r] **18** and sent you on a mission, saying, 'Go and put the sinful Amalekites under a ban of destruction. Fight against them until you have exterminated them.'[s] **19** Why then have you disobeyed the LORD? You have pounced on the spoil, thus displeasing the LORD.''[t] **20** Saul answered Samuel: ''I did indeed obey the LORD and fulfill the mission on which the LORD sent me. I have brought back Agag, and I have destroyed Amalek under the ban. **21** But from the spoil the men took sheep and oxen, the best of what had been banned, to sacrifice to the LORD their God in Gilgal.''[u] **22** [v]But Samuel said:

> ''Does the LORD so delight in holocausts and sacrifices
>> as in obedience to the command of the LORD?
> Obedience is better than sacrifice,
>> and submission than the fat of rams.*
23 For a sin like divination is rebellion,
>> and presumption is the crime of idolatry.
> Because you have rejected the command of the LORD,
>> he, too, has rejected you as a ruler.''

Saul Asks Forgiveness. **24** Saul replied to Samuel: ''I have sinned, for I have disobeyed the command of the LORD and your instructions. In my fear of the people, I did what they said.[w] **25** Now forgive my sin, and return with me, that I may worship the LORD.'' **26** But Samuel said to Saul, ''I will not return with you, because you rejected the command of the LORD and the LORD rejects you as king of Israel.''[x] **27** As Samuel turned to go, Saul seized a loose end of his mantle, and it tore off.[y] **28** So Samuel said to him: ''The LORD has torn the kingdom of Israel from you this day, and has given it to a neighbor of yours, who is better than you.[z] **29** The Glory of Israel neither retracts nor repents, for he is not man that he should repent.''[a] **30** But he answered: ''I have sinned, yet honor me now before the elders of my people and before Israel. Return with me that I may worship the LORD your God.'' **31** And so Samuel returned with him, and Saul worshiped the LORD.

Agag Is Cut Down. **32** Afterward Samuel commanded, ''Bring Agag, king of Amalek, to me.'' Agag came to him struggling and saying, ''So it is bitter death!'' **33** And Samuel said,

> ''As your sword has made women childless,
>> so shall your mother be childless among women.''

Then he cut Agag down before the LORD in Gilgal.[b]

34 Samuel departed for Ramah, while Saul went up to his home in Gibeah of Saul. **35** Never again, as long as he lived, did Samuel see Saul. Yet he grieved over Saul, because the LORD regretted having made him king of Israel.[c]

CHAPTER 16

Samuel Sent to Bethlehem. **1** [d]The LORD said to Samuel: ''How long will you grieve for Saul, whom I have rejected as king of Israel? Fill your horn with oil, and be on your way. I am sending you to Jesse of Bethlehem, for I have chosen my king from among his sons.''* **2** But Samuel replied: ''How can I go? Saul will hear of it and kill me.'' To this the LORD answered: ''Take a heifer along and say, 'I have come to sacrifice to the LORD.' **3** Invite Jesse to the sacrifice, and I myself will tell you what to do; you are to anoint for me the one I point out to you.''

4 Samuel did as the LORD had commanded him. When he entered Bethlehem, the elders of the city came trembling to meet him and inquired, ''Is your visit peaceful, O seer?'' **5** He replied: ''Yes! I have come to sacrifice to the LORD. So cleanse yourselves and join me today for the banquet.'' He also had Jesse and his sons cleanse themselves and invited them to the sacrifice.[e] **6** As they came, he looked at Eliab and thought, ''Surely the LORD's anointed is here before him.'' **7** But the LORD said to Samuel: ''Do not judge from his appearance or from his lofty stature, because I have rejected him. Not as man sees does God see, because man sees the appearance but the LORD looks into the heart.''[f] **8** [g]Then Jesse called Abinadab and presented him before Samuel, who said, ''The LORD has not chosen him.'' **9** Next Jesse presented Shammah, but Samuel said, ''The LORD has not chosen this one either.'' **10** In the same way

r 1 Sm 9, 21.
s 1 Sm 28, 18.
t 1 Sm 14, 32.
u Lv 27, 28.
v Prv 21, 3; Hos 6, 6; Am 5, 21-25; Zec 10, 2; Mt 9, 13; 12, 7; Heb 10, 9.
w 1 Sm 26, 21.
x 1 Kgs 11, 11. 30f.
y 1 Sm 24, 6.
z 1 Sm 28, 17; 2 Sm 7, 15f.
a Nm 23, 19.
b Ex 21, 23.
c Gn 6, 6.
d 1 Kgs 1, 39; Ru 4, 17-22; 1 Chr 11, 3; Is 11, 1; Lk 2, 4.
e 1 Sm 9, 12f; 20, 26; Ex 19, 10; Jb 1, 5.
f 1 Sm 10, 23f; 1 Chr 28, 9; Prv 15, 11; Jer 17, 10; 20, 12; Lk 16, 15; Acts 1, 24.
g 8ff: 1 Sm 17, 12f; 1 Chr 2, 13ff.

*
15, 22: Samuel is disapproving, not of sacrifices in general, but of merely external sacrifices offered in defiance of God's commandment and without heartfelt obedience.

16, 1: The anointing here prepared for is unknown to David's brother Eliab in the next chapter (1 Sm 17, 28), and David is twice anointed after Saul's death (2 Sm 2, 4; 5, 3).

Jesse presented seven sons before Samuel, but Samuel said to Jesse, "The LORD has not chosen any one of these." **11** Then Samuel asked Jesse, "Are these all the sons you have?" Jesse replied, "There is still the youngest, who is tending the sheep." Samuel said to Jesse, "Send for him; we will not begin the sacrificial banquet until he arrives here."[h] **12** Jesse sent and had the young man brought to them. He was ruddy, a youth handsome to behold and making a splendid appearance. The LORD said, "There—anoint him, for this is he!"[i] **13** Then Samuel, with the horn of oil in hand, anointed him in the midst of his brothers; and from that day on, the spirit of the LORD rushed upon David. When Samuel took his leave, he went to Ramah.[j]

Saul's Spirit of Melancholy.

14 [k]The spirit of the LORD had departed from Saul, and he was tormented by an evil spirit sent by the LORD.* **15** So the servants of Saul said to him: "Please! An evil spirit from God is tormenting you. **16** If your lordship will order it, we, your servants here in attendance on you, will look for a man skilled in playing the harp. When the evil spirit from God comes over you, he will play and you will feel better." **17** Saul then told his servants, "Find me a skillful harpist and bring him to me." **18** [l]A servant spoke up to say: "I have observed that one of the sons of Jesse of Bethlehem is a skillful harpist. He is also a stalwart soldier, besides being an able speaker, and handsome. Moreover, the LORD is with him."*

David Made Armor-Bearer.

19 Accordingly, Saul dispatched messengers to ask Jesse to send him his son David, who was with the flock. **20** Then Jesse took five loaves of bread, a skin of wine, and a kid, and sent them to Saul by his son David.[m] **21** Thus David came to Saul and entered his service. Saul became very fond of him, made him his armor-bearer,[n] **22** and sent Jesse the message, "Allow David to remain in my service, for he meets with my approval." **23** Whenever the spirit from God seized Saul, David would take the harp and play, and Saul would be relieved and feel better, for the evil spirit would leave him.

CHAPTER 17

The Challenge of Goliath.

1 The Philistines rallied their forces for battle at Socoh in Judah and camped between Socoh and Azekah at Ephes-dammim. **2** Saul and the Israelites also gathered and camped in the Vale of the Terebinth, drawing up their battle line to meet the Philistines. **3** The Philistines were stationed on one hill and the Israelites on an opposite hill, with a valley between them.

4 A champion named Goliath of Gath came out from the Philistine camp; he was six and a half feet tall. **5** He had a bronze helmet on his head and wore a bronze corselet of scale armor weighing five thousand shekels, **6** and bronze greaves, and had a bronze scimitar* slung from a baldric. **7** The shaft of his javelin was like a weaver's heddle-bar, and its iron head weighed six hundred shekels.* His shield-bearer went before him.[o] **8** He stood and shouted to the ranks of Israel: "Why come out in battle formation? I am a Philistine, and you are Saul's servants. Choose one of your men, and have him come down to me. **9** If he beats me in combat and kills me, we will be your vassals; but if I beat him and kill him, you shall be our vassals and serve us." **10** The Philistine continued: "I defy the ranks of Israel today. Give me a man and let us fight together." **11** Saul and all the men of Israel, when they heard this challenge of the Philistine, were dismayed and terror-stricken.

David Comes to the Camp.*

12 [David was the son of an Ephrathite named Jesse, who was from Bethlehem in Judah. He had eight sons, and in the days of Saul was old and well on in years.[p] **13** The three oldest sons of Jesse had followed Saul to war; these three sons who had gone off to war were named, the first-born Eliab, the second son Abinadab, and the third Shammah. **14** David was the youngest. While the three oldest had joined Saul, **15** David would go and come from Saul to tend his father's sheep at Bethlehem.[q]

---

h 1 Sm 17, 15. 28. 34; 2 Sm 7, 8.	16, 1; 17, 27ff.
i 1 Sm 9, 2.	n 1 Sm 18, 2.
j 1 Sm 10, 6; 11, 6; Jgs 3, 10; 9, 9; Sir 46, 13.	o 2 Sm 21, 19; 1 Chr 11, 23; 20, 5.
k 1 Sm 18, 10f.	p 1 Sm 16, 1. 10; Ru 1, 2.
l 2 Sm 17, 8.	q 1 Sm 18, 2; 2 Sm 7, 8.
m 1 Sm 9, 7f; 10, 4. 27;	

*

16, 14: An evil spirit sent by the Lord: the Lord permitted Saul to be tormented with violent fits of rage.

16, 18: Of the two traditions which describe the coming of David into Saul's service, the oldest Greek translation retains only the one comprised in 1 Sm 16, 14–23; 17, 1–11. 32–54. This effort at consistency is not in accord with the character of the rest of the book; see note on 1 Sm 8, 1. Though square brackets are used in this edition to indicate the passages lacking in the oldest translation, this is meant only to help the reader follow one account at a time. Both are equally a part of the inspired text, as are also the various amplifications and retouchings of the narrative given within brackets in chs 18 and 19.

17, 6: Scimitar: the Hebrew word for this is rather rare, and the nature of the weapon was in doubt until recent years. It is not the same as the sword of v 45.

17, 7: Six hundred shekels: over 15 pounds.

17, 12–31: An alternative account of how David came to undertake the combat with the Philistine is here inserted; it is continued in 1 Sm 17, 55—18, 6. See note on 1 Sm 16, 18.

16 [Meanwhile the Philistine came forward and took his stand morning and evening for forty days.

17 [Now Jesse said to his son David: "Take this ephah of roasted grain and these ten loaves for your brothers, and bring them quickly to your brothers in the camp. **18** Also take these ten cheeses for the field officer. Greet your brothers and bring home some token from them. **19** Saul, and they, and all Israel are fighting against the Philistines in the Vale of the Terebinth." **20** Early the next morning, having left the flock with a shepherd, David set out on his errand, as Jesse had commanded him. He reached the barricade of the camp just as the army, on their way to the battleground, were shouting their battle cry.ʳ **21** The Israelites and the Philistines drew up opposite each other in battle array. **22** David entrusted what he had brought to the keeper of the baggage and hastened to the battle line where he greeted his brothers.ˢ **23** While he was talking with them, the Philistine champion, by name Goliath of Gath, came up from the ranks of the Philistines and spoke as before, and David listened. **24** When the Israelites saw the man, they all retreated before him, very much afraid. **25** The Israelites had been saying: "Do you see this man coming up? He comes up to insult Israel. If anyone should kill him, the king would give him great wealth, and his daughter as well, and would grant exemption to his father's family in Israel."ᵗ **26** David now said to the men standing by: "What will be done for the man who kills this Philistine and frees Israel of the disgrace? Who is this uncircumcised Philistine in any case, that he should insult the armies of the living God?"ᵘ **27** They repeated the same words to him and said, "That is how the man who kills him will be rewarded." **28** When Eliab, his oldest brother, heard him speaking with the men, he grew angry with David and said: "Why did you come down? With whom have you left those sheep in the desert meanwhile? I know your arrogance and your evil intent. You came down to enjoy the battle!" **29** David replied, "What have I done now?—I was only talking." **30** Yet he turned from him to another and asked the same question; and everyone gave him the same answer as before. **31** The words that David had spoken were overheard and reported to Saul, who sent for him.]

David Fights Goliath. **32** Then David spoke to Saul: "Let your majesty not lose courage. I am at your service to go and fight this Philistine." **33** But Saul answered David, "You cannot go up against this Philistine and fight with him, for you are only a youth, while he has been a warrior from his youth." **34** ᵛThen David told Saul: "Your servant used

to tend his father's sheep, and whenever a lion or bear came to carry off a sheep from the flock, **35** I would go after it and attack it and rescue the prey from its mouth. If it attacked me, I would seize it by the jaw, strike it, and kill it. **36** Your servant has killed both a lion and a bear, and this uncircumcised Philistine will be as one of them, because he has insulted the armies of the living God." **37** David continued: "The LORD, who delivered me from the claws of the lion and the bear, will also keep me safe from the clutches of this Philistine." Saul answered David, "Go! the LORD will be with you."ʷ

Preparation for the Encounter. **38** Then Saul clothed David in his own tunic, putting a bronze helmet on his head and arming him with a coat of mail. **39** David also girded himself with Saul's sword over the tunic. He walked with difficulty, however, since he had never tried armor before. He said to Saul, "I cannot go in these, because I have never tried them before." So he took them off. **40** Then, staff in hand, David selected five smooth stones from the wadi and put them in the pocket of his shepherd's bag. With his sling also ready to hand, he approached the Philistine.

David's Victory. **41** With his shield-bearer marching before him, the Philistine also advanced closer and closer to David. **42** When he had sized David up, and seen that he was youthful, and ruddy, and handsome in appearance, he held him in contempt. **43** The Philistine said to David, "Am I a dog that you come against me with a staff?" Then the Philistine cursed David by his gods **44** and said to him, "Come here to me, and I will leave your flesh for the birds of the air and the beasts of the field."ˣ **45** David answered him: "You come against me with sword and spear and scimitar, but I come against you in the name of the LORD of hosts, the God of the armies of Israel that you have insulted. **46** Today the LORD shall deliver you into my hand; I will strike you down and cut off your head. This very day I will leave your corpse and the corpses of the Philistine army for the birds of the air and the beasts of the field; thus the whole land shall learn that Israel has a God. **47** All this multitude, too, shall learn that it is not by sword or spear that the LORD saves. For the battle is the LORD's, and he shall deliver you into our hands."ʸ

48 The Philistine then moved to meet David

r 1 Sm 26, 5.
s 1 Sm 25, 13.
t 1 Sm 18, 17; Jos 15, 16.
u 1 Sm 18, 25; Jgs 15, 18; 2 Kgs 19, 4; Is 37, 4.
v 34f: Jgs 14, 6; Sir 47, 3.
w Prv 28, 1.
x Dt 28, 26; Is 18, 6; Jer 15, 3.
y 1 Sm 14, 6; Ps 33, 16.

at close quarters, while David ran quickly toward the battle line in the direction of the Philistine. **49** David put his hand into the bag and took out a stone, hurled it with the sling, and struck the Philistine on the forehead. The stone embedded itself in his brow, and he fell prostrate on the ground. **50** [Thus David overcame the Philistine with sling and stone; he struck the Philistine mortally, and did it without a sword.]*z* **51** Then David ran and stood over him; with the Philistine's own sword [which he drew from its sheath] he dispatched him and cut off his head.*a*

Flight of the Philistines. When they saw that their hero was dead, the Philistines took to flight. **52** Then the men of Israel and Judah, with loud shouts, went in pursuit of the Philistines to the approaches of Gath and to the gates of Ekron, and Philistines fell wounded along the road from Shaaraim as far as Gath and Ekron. **53** On their return from the pursuit of the Philistines, the Israelites looted their camp. **54** *b*David took the head of the Philistine and brought it to Jerusalem; but he kept Goliath's armor in his own tent.*

David Presented to Saul. **55** [When Saul saw David go out to meet the Philistine, he asked his general Abner, "Abner, whose son is that youth?" Abner replied, "As truly as your majesty is alive, I have no idea." **56** And the king said, "Find out whose son the lad is." **57** So when David returned from slaying the Philistine, Abner took him and presented him to Saul. David was still holding the Philistine's head. **58** Saul then asked him, "Whose son are you, young man?" David replied, "I am the son of your servant Jesse of Bethlehem."

CHAPTER 18

David and Jonathan. **1** [By the time David finished speaking with Saul, Jonathan had become as fond of David as if his life depended on him; he loved him as he loved himself.*c* **2** Saul laid claim to David that day and did not allow him to return to his father's house.*d* **3** And Jonathan entered into a bond with David, because he loved him as himself. **4** Jonathan divested himself of the mantle he was wearing and gave it to David, along with his military dress, and his sword, his bow and his belt.*e* **5** David then carried out successfully every mission on which Saul sent him. So Saul put him in charge of his soldiers, and this was agreeable to the whole army, even to Saul's own officers.]

Saul's Jealousy. **6** At the approach of Saul and David (on David's return after slaying the Philistine), women came out from each of the cities of Israel to meet King Saul, singing and dancing, with tambourines, joyful songs, and sistrums.*f* **7** The women played and sang:

> "Saul has slain his thousands,
> and David his ten thousands."*g*

8 Saul was very angry and resentful of the song, for he thought: "They give David ten thousands, but only thousands to me. All that remains for him is the kingship." **9** [And from that day on, Saul was jealous of David.

10 [*h* The next day an evil spirit from God came over Saul, and he raged in his house. David was in attendance, playing the harp as at other times, while Saul was holding his spear. **11** Saul poised the spear, thinking to nail David to the wall, but twice David escaped him.] **12** Saul then began to fear David, [because the LORD was with him, but had departed from Saul himself.] **13** Accordingly, Saul removed him from his presence by appointing him a field officer. So David led the people on their military expeditions, **14** and prospered in all his enterprises, for the LORD was with him. **15** Seeing how successful he was, Saul conceived a fear of David; **16** on the other hand, all Israel and Judah loved him, since he led them on their expeditions.*i*

17 [Saul said to David, "There is my older daughter, Merob, whom I will give you in marriage if you become my champion and fight the battles of the LORD." Saul had in mind, "I shall not touch him; let the Philistines strike him."*j* **18** But David answered Saul: "Who am I? And who are my kin or my father's clan in Israel that I should become the king's son-in-law?" **19** However, when it was time for Saul's daughter Merob to be given to David, she was given in marriage to Adriel the Meholathite instead.]*k* **20** Now Saul's daughter Michal loved David, and it was reported to Saul, who was pleased at this,*l* **21** for he thought, "I will offer her to him to become a snare for him, so that the Philistines may strike him." [Thus for the second time Saul said to David, "You shall become my son-in-law today."] **22** Saul then ordered his servants to speak to David privately

z Sir 47, 4; 1 Mc 4, 30.
a 1 Sm 21, 10.
b 1 Sm 31, 9.
c 1 Sm 19, 1-7; 20, 17;
 23, 16; 2 Sm 1, 26; 9,
 1.
d 1 Sm 16, 21; 17, 15.
e 1 Sm 16, 21; 17, 15.
f Ex 15, 20f; Jgs 11, 34;
 Jdt 15, 12.
g 1 Sm 21, 12; 29, 5; Sir
 47, 6f.
h 10f: 1 Sm 16, 14; 19,
 9f; 20, 33; 22, 6; 26, 8.
i 2 Sm 5, 2.
j 1 Sm 14, 49; 17, 25.
k 1 Sm 21, 8; 24, 16.
l 1 Sm 14, 49; 25, 44;
 26, 23; 2 Sm 3, 13.

*

17, 54: At the time supposed by this narrative, Jerusalem was still Jebusite, and David had no military tent of his own; the verse is a later gloss.

and to say: "The king is fond of you, and all his officers love you. You should become the king's son-in-law." **23** But when Saul's servants mentioned this to David, he said: "Do you think it easy to become the king's son-in-law? I am poor and insignificant." **24** When his servants reported to him the nature of David's answer, **25** Saul commanded them to say this to David: "The king desires no other price for the bride than the foreskins of one hundred Philistines, that he may thus take vengeance on his enemies." Saul intended in this way to bring about David's death through the Philistines. *m* **26** When the servants reported this offer to David, he was pleased with the prospect of becoming the king's son-in-law. [Before the year was up,] **27** David made preparations and sallied forth with his men and slew two hundred Philistines. He brought back their foreskins and counted them out before the king, that he might thus become the king's son-in-law. So Saul gave him his daughter Michal in marriage. **28** Saul thus came to recognize that the LORD was with David; besides, his own daughter Michal loved David. **29** Therefore Saul feared David all the more [and was his enemy ever after].

30 [The Philistine chiefs continued to make forays, but each time they took the field, David was more successful against them than any other of Saul's officers, and as a result acquired great fame.]

CHAPTER 19

Persecution of David. **1** Saul discussed his intention of killing David with his son Jonathan and with all his servants. But Saul's son Jonathan, who was very fond of David, *n* **2** told him: "My father Saul is trying to kill you. Therefore, please be on your guard tomorrow morning; get out of sight and remain in hiding. **3** I, however, will go out and stand beside my father in the countryside where you are, and will speak to him about you. If I learn anything, I will let you know."

4 Jonathan then spoke well of David to his father Saul, saying to him: "Let not your majesty sin against his servant David, for he has committed no offense against you, but has helped you very much by his deeds. **5** When he took his life in his hands and slew the Philistine, and the LORD brought about a great victory for all Israel through him, you were glad to see it. Why, then, should you become guilty of shedding innocent blood by killing David without cause?" *o* **6** Saul heeded Jonathan's plea and swore, "As the LORD lives, he shall not be killed." **7** So Jonathan summoned David and repeated the whole conversation to him. Jonathan then brought David to Saul, and David served him as before.

8 When war broke out again, David went out to fight against the Philistines and inflicted a great defeat upon them, putting them to flight. **9** *p* Then an evil spirit from the LORD came upon Saul as he was sitting in his house with spear in hand and David was playing the harp nearby. **10** Saul tried to nail David to the wall with the spear, but David eluded Saul, so that the spear struck only the wall, and David got away safe.

11 The same night, Saul sent messengers to David's house to guard it, that he might kill him in the morning. David's wife Michal informed him, "Unless you save yourself tonight, tomorrow you will be killed."* **12** Then Michal let David down through a window, and he made his escape in safety. *q* **13** Michal took the household idol and laid it in the bed, putting a net of goat's hair at its head and covering it with a spread. *r* **14** When Saul sent messengers to arrest David, she said, "He is sick." **15** Saul, however, sent the messengers back to see David and commanded them, "Bring him up to me in the bed, that I may kill him." **16** But when the messengers entered, they found the household idol in the bed, with the net of goat's hair at its head. **17** Saul therefore asked Michal: "Why did you play this trick on me? You have helped my enemy to get away!" Michal answered Saul: "He threatened me, 'Let me go or I will kill you.'"

David and Samuel in Ramah. **18** Thus David got safely away; he went to Samuel in Ramah, informing him of all that Saul had done to him. Then he and Samuel went to stay in the sheds. **19** When Saul was told that David was in the sheds near Ramah, **20** he sent messengers to arrest David. But when they saw the band of prophets, presided over by Samuel, in a prophetic frenzy, they too fell into the prophetic state. *s* **21** Informed of this, Saul sent other messengers, who also fell into the prophetic state. For the third time Saul sent messengers, but they too fell into the prophetic state.

Saul among the Prophets. **22** Saul then went to Ramah himself. Arriving at the cistern of the threshing floor on the bare hilltop, he inquired, "Where are Samuel and David?", and was told, "At the sheds near Ramah." **23** As he set out from the hilltop toward the sheds, the spirit of God came upon him also,

---

m 1 Sm 17, 26; Gn 34, 12.
n 1 Sm 18, 1; 20, 1ff.
o Dt 19, 10; Ps 119, 109.
p 9f: 1 Sm 16, 14; 18, 10f.
q Jos 2, 15; Acts 9, 25; 2 Cor 11, 33.
r Gn 31, 19; Jos 17, 5; 18, 14, 18. 20.
s 1 Sm 10, 5f. 10; Nm 11, 25.

*

19, 11: This story in all probability originally followed 1 Sm 18, 29, placing the episode of David's escape on the night of his marriage with Michal.

and he continued on in a prophetic condition until he reached the spot. At the sheds near Ramah **24** he, too, stripped himself of his garments and he, too, remained in the prophetic state in the presence of Samuel; all that day and night he lay naked. That is why they say, "Is Saul also among the prophets?"[t]

CHAPTER 20

David Consults with Jonathan. **1** David fled from the sheds near Ramah, and went to Jonathan. "What have I done?" he asked him. "What crime or what offense does your father hold against me that he seeks my life?"[u] **2** Jonathan answered him: "Heaven forbid that you should die! My father does nothing, great or small, without disclosing it to me. Why, then, should my father conceal this from me? This cannot be so!" **3** But David replied: "Your father is well aware that I am favored with your friendship, so he has decided, 'Jonathan must not know of this lest he be grieved.' Nevertheless, as the LORD lives and as you live, there is but a step between me and death." **4** Jonathan then said to David, "I will do whatever you wish." **5** David answered: "Tomorrow is the new moon, which I should in fact dine with the king. Let me go and hide in the open country until evening.[v] **6** If it turns out that your father misses me, say, 'David urged me to let him go on short notice to his city Bethlehem, because his whole clan is holding its seasonal sacrifice there.' **7** If he says, 'Very well,' your servant is safe. But if he becomes quite angry, you can be sure he has planned some harm. **8** [w]Do this kindness for your servant because of the LORD's bond between us, into which you brought me: if I am guilty, kill me yourself! Why should you give me up to your father?" **9** But Jonathan answered: "Not I! If ever I find out that my father is determined to inflict injury upon you, I will certainly let you know." **10** David then asked Jonathan, "Who will tell me if your father gives you a harsh answer?"

Mutual Agreement. **11** [Jonathan replied to David, "Come, let us go out into the field." When they were out in the open country together, **12** Jonathan said to David: "As the LORD, the God of Israel, lives, I will sound out my father about this time tomorrow. Whether he is well disposed toward David or not, I will send you the information. **13** [x]Should it please my father to bring any injury upon you, may the LORD do thus and so to Jonathan if I do not apprise you of it and send you on your way in peace. May the LORD be with you even as he was with my father. **14** Only this: if I am still alive, may you show me the kindness of the LORD. But if I die, **15** never withdraw your

kindness from my house. And when the LORD exterminates all the enemies of David from the surface of the earth, **16** the name of Jonathan must never be allowed by the family of David to die out from among you, or the LORD will make you answer for it." **17** And in his love for David, Jonathan renewed his oath to him, because he loved him as his very self.]

18 Jonathan then said to him: "Tomorrow is the new moon; and you will be missed, since your place will be vacant. **19** On the following day you will be missed all the more. Go to the spot where you hid on the other occasion and wait near the mound there.[y] **20** On the third day of the month I will shoot arrows, as though aiming at a target. **21** I will then send my attendant to go and recover the arrows. If in fact I say to him, 'Look, the arrow is this side of you; pick it up,' come, for you are safe. As the LORD lives, there will be nothing to fear. **22** But if I say to the boy, 'Look, the arrow is beyond you,' go, for the LORD sends you away. **23** However, in the matter which you and I have discussed, the LORD shall be between you and me forever." **24** So David hid in the open country.

On the day of the new moon, when the king sat at table to dine, **25** taking his usual place against the wall, Jonathan sat facing him, while Abner sat at the king's side, and David's place was vacant. **26** [z]Saul, however, said nothing that day, for he thought, "He must have become unclean by accident, and not yet have been cleansed."* **27** On the next day, the second day of the month, David's place was vacant. Saul inquired of his son Jonathan, "Why has the son of Jesse not come to table yesterday or today?" **28** Jonathan answered Saul: "David urgently asked me to let him go to his city, Bethlehem. **29** 'Please let me go,' he begged, 'for we are to have a clan sacrifice in our city, and my brothers insist on my presence. Now, therefore, if you think well of me, give me leave to visit my brothers.' That is why he has not come to the king's table." **30** But Saul was extremely angry with Jonathan and said to him: "Son of a rebellious woman, do I not know that, to your own shame and to the disclosure of your mother's shame, you are the companion of Jesse's son? **31** Why, as long as the son of Jesse lives upon the earth, you cannot make good your claim to the kingship! So send for him, and bring him to me, for he is doomed."[a] **32** But Jonathan asked his father Saul: "Why should he

---

t 1 Sm 10, 10ff.   2 Sm 9, 1-13; 21, 7.
u 1 Sm 19, 1-7, 11-17 y 1 Sm 19, 1-7.
v Nm 10, 10; 28, 11-15. z 1 Sm 16, 5; Lv 7, 20f;
w 8f: 1 Sm 23, 17f.   15, 1ff.
x 13-16: 1 Sm 24, 22f; a 2 Sm 12, 5.

*

20, 26: The meal on the first day of the month would have religious overtones, and a ritual impurity (Lv 15, 16; Dt 23, 10ff) would bar David from sharing in it.

die? What has he done?'' **33** At this Saul brandished his spear to strike him, and thus Jonathan learned that his father was resolved to kill David.[b] **34** Jonathan sprang up from the table in great anger and took no food that second day of the month, for he was grieved on David's account, since his father had railed against him.

Jonathan's Farewell.

35 The next morning Jonathan went out into the field with a little boy for his appointment with David. **36** There he said to the boy, "Run and fetch the arrow." And as the boy ran, he shot an arrow beyond him in the direction of the city. **37** When the boy made for the spot where Jonathan had shot the arrow, Jonathan called after him, "The arrow is farther on!" **38** Again he called to his lad, "Hurry, be quick, don't delay!" Jonathan's boy picked up the arrow and brought it to his master. **39** The boy knew nothing; only Jonathan and David knew what was meant. **40** Then Jonathan gave his weapons to this boy of his and said to him, "Go, take them to the city." **41** When the boy had left, David rose from beside the mound and prostrated himself on the ground three times before Jonathan in homage. They kissed each other and wept aloud together. **42** [c]At length Jonathan said to David, "Go in peace, in keeping with what we two have sworn by the name of the LORD; 'The LORD shall be between you and me, and between your posterity and mine forever.' "

CHAPTER 21

1 Then David departed on his way, while Jonathan went back into the city.

The Holy Bread.

2 David went to Ahimelech, the priest of Nob, who came trembling to meet him and asked, "Why are you alone? Is there no one with you?"[d] **3** David answered the priest: "The king gave me a commission and told me to let no one know anything about the business on which he sent me or the commission he gave me. For that reason I have arranged a meeting place with my men. **4** [e]Now what have you on hand? Give me five loaves, or whatever you can find." **5** But the priest replied to David, "I have no ordinary bread on hand, only holy bread; if the men have abstained from women, you may eat some of that."* **6** David answered the priest: "We have indeed been segregated from women as on previous occasions. Whenever I go on a journey, all the young men are consecrated—even for a secular journey. All the more so today, when they are consecrated at arms!" **7** So the priest gave him holy bread, for no other bread was on hand except the showbread which had been removed from the LORD's presence and replaced by fresh bread when it was taken away.[f] **8** One of Saul's

servants was there that day, detained before the LORD; his name was Doeg the Edomite, and he was Saul's chief henchman.

The Sword of Goliath.

9 David then asked Ahimelech: "Do you have a spear or a sword on hand? I brought along neither my sword nor my weapons, because the king's business was urgent." **10** The priest replied: "The sword of Goliath the Philistine, whom you killed in the Vale of the Terebinth, is here [wrapped in a mantle] behind an ephod. If you wish to take that, take it; there is no sword here except that one." David said: "There is none to match it. Give it to me!"[g]

David a Fugitive.

11 That same day David took to flight from Saul, going to Achish, king of Gath.[h] **12** But the servants of Achish said, "Is this not David, the king of the land? During their dances do they not sing,

'Saul has slain his thousands,
   but David his ten thousands'?"[i]

13 David took note of these remarks and became very much afraid of Achish, king of Gath. **14** So, as they watched, he feigned insanity and acted like a madman in their hands, drumming on the doors of the gate and drooling onto his beard. **15** Finally Achish said to his servants: "You see the man is mad. Why did you bring him to me? **16** Do I not have enough madmen, that you bring in this one to carry on in my presence? Should this fellow come into my house?"

CHAPTER 22

1 David left Gath and escaped to the cave of Adullam. When his brothers and the rest of his family heard about it, they came down to him there.[j] **2** He was joined by all those who were in difficulties or in debt, or who were embittered, and he became their leader. About four hundred men were with him.

3 From there David went to Mizpeh of Moab and said to the king of Moab, "Let my father and mother stay with you, until I learn what God will do for me." **4** He left them with the king

b 1 Sm 18, 11.
c 2 Sm 9, 1; 21, 7.
d Is 10, 32; Mk 2, 26.
e Lv 24, 5. 9.
f 1 Sm 22, 9; Lv 24, 5-9;
  Mt 12, 3f; Mk 2, 26;

Lk 6, 3ff.
g 1 Sm 17, 51, 54.
h 1 Sm 27, 2; 29, 5.
i 1 Sm 18, 7; 29, 5.
j 2 Sm 23, 13; Ps 63; Mi
  1, 15.

21, 5f: From women: the high priest, willing to distribute the holy bread to David and his men, requires that they be free from ritual uncleanness, associated in Old Testament times (Lv 15, 18) with the marriage act. David's answer supposes the discipline of a military campaign under the conditions of "holy war" (Dt 23, 10).

22, 4–5: Refuge: seemingly connected with the cave complex spoken of in v 1.

of Moab, and they stayed with him as long as David remained in the refuge.*

5 But the prophet Gad said to David: "Do not remain in the refuge. Leave, and go to the land of Judah." And so David left and went to the forest of Hereth.

Doeg Betrays Ahimelech. **6** Now Saul heard that David and his men had been located. At the time he was sitting in Gibeah under a tamarisk tree on the high place, holding his spear, while all his servants were standing by. *k* **7** So he said to them: "Listen, men of Benjamin! Will the son of Jesse give all of you fields and vineyards? Will he make each of you an officer over a thousand or a hundred men, *l* **8** that you have all conspired against me and no one tells me that my son has made an agreement with the son of Jesse? None of you shows sympathy for me or discloses to me that my son has stirred up my servant to be an enemy against me, as is the case today." **9** *m*Then Doeg the Edomite, who was standing with the officers of Saul, spoke up: "I saw the son of Jesse come to Ahimelech, son of Ahitub, in Nob. **10** He consulted the LORD for him and gave him supplies, and the sword of Goliath the Philistine as well."

Slaughter of the Priests. **11** At this the king sent a summons to Ahimelech the priest, son of Ahitub, and to all his family who were priests in Nob; and they all came to the king. **12** Then Saul said, "Listen, son of Ahitub!" He replied, "Yes, my lord." **13** Saul asked him, "Why did you conspire against me with the son of Jesse by giving him food and a sword and by consulting God for him, that he might rebel against me and become my enemy, as is the case today?" **14** Ahimelech answered the king: "And who among all your servants is as loyal as David, the king's son-in-law, captain of your bodyguard, and honored in your own house? **15** Is this the first time I have consulted God for him? No indeed! Let not the king accuse his servant or anyone in my family of such a thing. Your servant knows nothing at all, great or small, about the whole matter." **16** But the king said, "You shall die, Ahimelech, with all your family." **17** The king then commanded his henchmen standing by: "Make the rounds and kill the priests of the LORD, for they assisted David. They knew he was a fugitive and yet failed to inform me." But the king's servants refused to lift a hand to strike the priests of the LORD. *n*

18 The king therefore commanded Doeg, "You make the rounds and kill the priests!" So Doeg the Edomite went from one to the next and killed the priests himself, slaying on that day eighty-five who wore the linen ephod. **19** Saul

also put the priestly city of Nob to the sword, including men and women, children and infants, and oxen, asses and sheep.

Abiathar Escapes. **20** One son of Ahimelech, son of Ahitub, named Abiathar, escaped and fled to David. *o* **21** When Abiathar told David that Saul had slain the priests of the LORD, **22** David said to him: "I knew that day, when Doeg the Edomite was there, that he would surely tell Saul. I am responsible for the death of all your family. **23** Stay with me. Fear nothing; he that seeks your life must seek my life also. You are under my protection."

CHAPTER 23

Keilah Liberated. **1** David received information that the Philistines were attacking Keilah and plundering the threshing floors. *p* **2** So he consulted the LORD, inquiring, "Shall I go and defeat these Philistines?" The LORD answered, "Go, for you will defeat the Philistines and rescue Keilah." *q* **3** But David's men said to him: "We are afraid here in Judah. How much more so if we go to Keilah against the forces of the Philistines!" **4** Again David consulted the LORD, who answered, "Go down to Keilah, for I will deliver the Philistines into your power." **5** David then went with his men to Keilah and fought with the Philistines. He drove off their cattle and inflicted a severe defeat on them, and thus rescued the inhabitants of Keilah.

6 Abiathar, son of Ahimelech, who had fled to David, went down with David to Keilah, taking the ephod with him. *r*

Flight from Keilah. **7** When Saul was told that David had entered Keilah, he said: "God has put him in my grip. Now he has shut himself in, for he has entered a city with gates and bars." **8** Saul then called all the people to war, in order to go down to Keilah and besiege David and his men. **9** When David found out that Saul was planning to harm him, he said to the priest Abiathar, "Bring forward the ephod." *s* **10** David then said: "O LORD God of Israel, your servant has heard a report that Saul plans to come to Keilah, to destroy the city on my account. **11** Will they hand me over? And now: will Saul come down as your servant has heard? O LORD God of Israel, tell your servant." The LORD answered, "He will come down." **12** David then asked, "Will the citizens of Keilah deliver me and my men into the grasp of Saul?" And the LORD answered, "Yes." **13** So

k Ps 52.
l 1 Sm 8, 14.
m 9f: 1 Sm 21, 2-10.
n 1 Sm 2, 31. 33; 21, 7.
o 1 Sm 23, 6; 30, 7;

1 Kgs 2, 28f.
p Jos 15, 44.
q 1 Sm 28, 6.
r 1 Sm 22, 20; 30, 7.
s 1 Sm 2, 28.

David and his men, about six hundred in number, left Keilah and wandered from place to place. When Saul was informed that David had escaped from Keilah, he abandoned the expedition.

David and Jonathan in Horesh.

14 David now lived in the refuges in the desert, or in the barren hill country near Ziph. Though Saul sought him continually, the LORD did not deliver David into his grasp. **15** David was apprehensive because Saul had come out to seek his life; but while he was at Horesh in the barrens near Ziph, **16** Saul's son, Jonathan, came down there to David and strengthened his resolve in the LORD.ᵗ **17** He said to him: "Have no fear, my father Saul shall not lay a hand to you. You shall be king of Israel and I shall be second to you. Even my father Saul knows this." **18** They made a joint agreement before the LORD in Horesh, where David remained, while Jonathan returned to his home.ᵘ

Treachery of the Ziphites.

19 Some of the Ziphites went up to Saul in Gibeah and said, "David is hiding among us, now in the refuges, and again at Horesh, or on the hill of Hachilah, south of the wasteland.ᵛ **20** Therefore, whenever the king wishes to come down, let him do so. It will be our task to deliver him into the king's grasp." **21** Saul replied: "The LORD bless you for your sympathy toward me.ʷ **22** Go now and make sure once more! Take note of the place where he sets foot" (for he thought, perhaps they are playing some trick on me). **23** "Look around and learn in which of all the various hiding places he is holding out. Then come back to me with sure information, and I will go with you. If he is in the region, I will search him out among all the families of Judah." **24** So they went off to Ziph ahead of Saul. At this time David and his men were in the desert below Maon, in the Arabah south of the wasteland.ˣ

Escape from Saul.

25 When Saul and his men came looking for him, David got word of it and went down to the gorge in the desert below Maon. Saul heard of this and pursued David into the desert below Maon. **26** As Saul moved along one rim of the gorge, David and his men took to the other. David was in anxious flight to escape Saul, and Saul and his men were attempting to outflank David and his men in order to capture them, **27** when a messenger came to Saul, saying, "Come quickly, because the Philistines have invaded the land." **28** Saul interrupted his pursuit of David and went to meet the Philistines. This is how that place came to be called the Gorge of Divisions.

CHAPTER 24

David Spares Saul.

1 David then went up from there and stayed in the refuges behind Engedi. **2** And when Saul returned from the pursuit of the Philistines, he was told that David was in the desert near Engedi. **3** So Saul took three thousand picked men from all Israel and went in search of David and his men in the direction of the wild goat crags. **4** When he came to the sheepfolds along the way, he found a cave, which he entered to ease nature. David and his men were occupying the inmost recesses of the cave.ʸ

5 David's servants said to him, "This is the day of which the LORD said to you, 'I will deliver your enemy into your grasp; do with him as you see fit.'" So David moved up and stealthily cut off an end of Saul's mantle. **6** Afterward, however, David regretted that he had cut off an end of Saul's mantle.ᶻ **7** He said to his men, "The LORD forbid that I should do such a thing to my master, the LORD's anointed, as to lay a hand on him, for he is the LORD's anointed."ᵃ **8** With these words David restrained his men and would not permit them to attack Saul. Saul then left the cave and went on his way. **9** David also stepped out of the cave, calling to Saul, "My lord the king!" When Saul looked back, David bowed to the ground in homage **10** and asked Saul: "Why do you listen to those who say, 'David is trying to harm you'? **11** You see for yourself today that the LORD just now delivered you into my grasp in the cave. I had some thought of killing you, but I took pity on you instead. I decided, 'I will not raise a hand against my lord, for he is the LORD's anointed and a father to me.' **12** Look here at this end of your mantle which I hold. Since I cut off an end of your mantle and did not kill you, see and be convinced that I plan no harm and no rebellion. I have done you no wrong, though you are hunting me down to take my life.ᵇ **13** The LORD will judge between me and you, and the LORD will exact justice from you in my case. I shall not touch you. **14** The old proverb says, 'From the wicked comes forth wickedness.' So I will take no action against you. **15** Against whom are you on campaign, O king of Israel? Whom are you pursuing? A dead dog, or a single flea! **16** The LORD will be the judge; he will decide between me and you. May he see this, and take my part, and grant me justice beyond your reach!"ᶜ

t 1 Sm 18, 1.
u 1 Sm 18, 3; 20, 8.
v 1 Sm 26, 1-3; Ps 54.
w 2 Sm 2, 5.
x 1 Sm 25, 2.
y Ps 57.

z 1 Sm 15, 27.
a 1 Sm 10, 1; 31, 4;
  2 Sm 1, 14.
b Rom 12, 19.
c 1 Sm 18, 19. 31; 26,
  19; Pss 35, 1ff; 43, 1.

Saul's Remorse. **17** When David finished saying these things to Saul, Saul answered, "Is that your voice, my son David?" And he wept aloud. **18** Saul then said to David: "You are in the right rather than I; you have treated me generously, while I have done you harm. **19** Great is the generosity you showed me today, when the LORD delivered me into your grasp and you did not kill me. **20** For if a man meets his enemy, does he send him away unharmed? May the LORD reward you generously for what you have done this day. **21** And now, since I know that you shall surely be king and that sovereignty over Israel shall come into your possession,*d* **22** swear to me by the LORD that you will not destroy my descendants and that you will not blot out my name and family."*e* **23** David gave Saul his oath and Saul returned home, while David and his men went up to the refuge.

CHAPTER 25

Death of Samuel. **1** Samuel died, and all Israel gathered to mourn him; they buried him at his home in Ramah.*f*

Nabal and Abigail. **2** Then David went down to the desert of Maon. There was a man of Maon who had property in Carmel; he was very wealthy, owning three thousand sheep and a thousand goats. At this time he was present for the shearing of his flock in Carmel.*g* **3** The man was named Nabal, his wife, Abigail. The woman was intelligent and attractive, but Nabal himself, a Calebite, was harsh and ungenerous in his behavior.*h* **4** When David heard in the desert that Nabal was shearing his flock, **5** he sent ten young men, instructing them: "Go up to Carmel. Pay Nabal a visit and greet him in my name. **6** Say to him, 'Peace be with you, my brother, and with your family, and with all who belong to you. **7** I have just heard that shearers are with you. Now, when your shepherds were with us, we did them no injury, neither did they miss anything all the while they were in Carmel. **8** Ask your servants and they will tell you so. Look kindly on these young men, since we come at a festival time. Please give your servants and your son David whatever you can manage.' "

9 When David's young men arrived, they delivered this message fully to Nabal in David's name, and then waited. **10** But Nabal answered the servants of David: "Who is David? Who is the son of Jesse? Nowadays there are many servants who run away from their masters. **11** Must I take my bread, my wine, my meat that I have slaughtered for my own shearers, and give them to men who come from I know not where?" **12** So David's young men retraced

their steps and on their return reported to him all that had been said. **13** Thereupon David said to his men, "Let everyone gird on his sword." And so everyone, David included, girded on his sword. About four hundred men went up after David, while two hundred remained with the baggage.

14 But Nabal's wife Abigail was informed of this by one of the servants, who said: "David sent messengers from the desert to greet our master, but he flew at them screaming. **15** Yet these men were very good to us. We were done no injury, neither did we miss anything all the while we were living among them during our stay in the open country. **16** For us they were like a rampart night and day the whole time we were pasturing the sheep near them. **17** Now, see what you can do, for you must realize that otherwise evil is in store for our master and for his whole family. He is so mean that no one can talk to him." **18** Abigail quickly got together two hundred loaves, two skins of wine, five dressed sheep, five seahs of roasted grain, a hundred cakes of pressed raisins, and two hundred cakes of pressed figs, and loaded them on asses. **19** She then said to her servants, "Go on ahead; I will follow you." But she did not tell her husband Nabal.

20 As she came down through a mountain defile riding on an ass, David and his men were also coming down from the opposite direction. When she met them, **21** David had just been saying: "Indeed, it was in vain that I guarded all this man's possessions in the desert, so that he missed nothing. He has repaid good with evil. **22** May God do thus and so to David, if by morning I leave a single male alive among all those who belong to him."*i* **23** As soon as Abigail saw David, she dismounted quickly from the ass and, falling prostrate on the ground before David, did him homage. **24** As she fell at his feet she said: "My lord, let the blame be mine. Please let your handmaid speak to you, and listen to the words of your handmaid. **25** Let not my lord pay attention to that worthless man Nabal, for he is just like his name. Fool is his name,* and he acts the fool. I, your handmaid, did not see the young men whom my lord sent. **26** Now, therefore, my lord, as the LORD lives, and as you live, it is the LORD who has kept you from shedding blood and from avenging yourself personally. May your enemies and those who seek to harm my lord become as

---

d 1 Sm 26, 25.
e 2 Sm 9, 1ff.
f 1 Sm 28, 3; Sir 46, 13-20.
g 1 Sm 23, 24; Jos 15,
55.
h 1 Sm 27, 3; Jos 14, 6; 1 Chr 2, 42. 45.
i 1 Kgs 16, 11; 21, 21; 2 Kgs 9, 8.

25, 25: Fool is his name: Nabal in Hebrew means "a fool."

25, 26: Abigail anticipates that some misfortune will shortly overtake Nabal, as in fact it does (vv 37–38).

Nabal!* 27 Accept this present, then, which your maidservant has brought for my lord, and let it be given to the young men who follow my lord. 28 Please forgive the transgression of your handmaid, for the LORD shall certainly establish a lasting dynasty for my lord, because your lordship is fighting the battles of the LORD, and there is no evil to be found in you your whole life long. 29 If anyone rises to pursue you and to seek your life, may the life of my lord be bound in the bundle of the living* in the care of the LORD your God; but may he hurl out the lives of your enemies as from the hollow of a sling.*j* 30 And when the LORD carries out for my lord the promise of success he has made concerning you, and appoints you as commander over Israel,*k* 31 you shall not have this as a qualm or burden on your conscience, my lord, for having shed innocent blood or for having avenged yourself personally. When the LORD confers this benefit on your lordship, remember your handmaid.'' 32 David said to Abigail: ''Blessed be the LORD, the God of Israel, who sent you to meet me today. 33 Blessed be your good judgment and blessed be you yourself, who this day have prevented me from shedding blood and from avenging myself personally. 34 Otherwise, as the LORD, the God of Israel, lives, who has restrained me from harming you, if you had not come so promptly to meet me, by dawn Nabal would not have had a single man or boy left alive.'' 35 David then took from her what she had brought him and said to her: ''Go up to your home in peace! See, I have granted your request as a personal favor.''

Nabal's Death.   36 When Abigail came to Nabal, there was a drinking party in his house like that of a king, and Nabal was merry because he was very drunk. So she told him nothing at all before daybreak the next morning. 37 But then, when Nabal had become sober, his wife told him what had happened. At this his courage died within him, and he became like a stone. 38 About ten days later the LORD struck him and he died. 39 On hearing that Nabal was dead, David said: ''Blessed be the LORD, who has requited the insult I received at the hand of Nabal, and who restrained his servant from doing evil, but has punished Nabal for his own evil deeds.''

David Marries Abigail and Ahinoam.
David then sent a proposal of marriage to Abigail. 40 When David's servants came to Abigail in Carmel, they said to her, ''David has sent us to you that he may take you as his wife.'' 41 Rising and bowing to the ground, she answered, ''Your handmaid would become a slave to wash the feet of my lord's servants.'' 42 She got up immediately, mounted an ass, and fol-

lowed David's messengers, with her five maids following in attendance upon her. She became his wife, 43 *l*and David also married Ahinoam of Jezreel. Thus both of them were his wives; but Saul gave David's wife Michal, Saul's own daughter, to Palti, son of Laish, who was from Gallim.*m*

CHAPTER 26

Saul's Life Again Spared.   1 *n*Men from Ziph came to Saul in Gibeah, reporting that David was hiding on the hill of Hachilah at the edge of the wasteland. 2 So Saul went off down to the desert of Ziph with three thousand picked men of Israel, to search for David in the desert of Ziph. 3 Saul camped beside the road on the hill of Hachilah, at the edge of the wasteland. David, who was living in the desert, saw that Saul had come into the desert after him 4 and sent out scouts, who confirmed Saul's arrival. 5 David himself then went to the place where Saul was encamped and examined the spot where Saul and Abner, son of Ner, the general, had their sleeping quarters. Saul's were within the barricade, and all his soldiers were camped around him.*o* 6 David asked Ahimelech the Hittite, and Abishai, son of Zeruiah and brother of Joab, ''Who will go down into the camp with me to Saul?'' Abishai replied, ''I will.''*p* 7 So David and Abishai went among Saul's soldiers by night and found Saul lying asleep within the barricade, with his spear thrust into the ground at his head and Abner and his men sleeping around him.

8 Abishai whispered to David: ''God has delivered your enemy into your grasp this day. Let me nail him to the ground with one thrust of the spear; I will not need a second thrust!''*q* 9 But David said to Abishai, ''Do not harm him, for who can lay hands on the LORD's anointed and remain unpunished? 10 As the LORD lives,'' David continued, ''it must be the LORD himself who will strike him, whether the time comes for him to die, or he goes out and perishes in battle. 11 But the LORD forbid that I touch his anointed! Now take the spear which is at his head and the water jug, and let us be on our way.'' 12 So David took the spear and the water jug from

j Ps 69, 28.
k 1 Sm 13, 14; 2 Sm 3, 10.
l 1 Sm 27, 3.
m 1 Sm 18, 20; 27, 3; 30, 5; 2 Sm 3, 2. 13ff;

1 Chr 3, 1.
n 1f: 1 Sm 23, 19f; Ps 54.
o 1 Sm 17, 20.
p 1 Chr 2, 16.
q 1 Sm 18, 11; 19, 10.

*

25, 29: The bundle of the living: the figure is perhaps taken from the practice of tying up valuables in a kerchief or bag for safekeeping. Abigail desires that David enjoy permanent peace and security, but that his enemies be subject to constant agitation and humiliation like a stone whirled about, cast out of the sling, and thereafter disregarded.

their place at Saul's head, and they got away without anyone's seeing or knowing or awakening. All remained asleep, because the LORD had put them into a deep slumber.

David Taunts Abner. 13 Going across to an opposite slope, David stood on a remote hilltop at a great distance from Abner, son of Ner, and the troops. 14 He then shouted, "Will you not answer, Abner?" And Abner answered, "Who is it that calls me?" 15 David said no to Abner: "Are you not a man whose like does not exist in Israel? Why, then, have you not guarded your lord the king when one of his subjects went to kill the king, your lord? 16 This is no creditable service you have performed. As the LORD lives, you people deserve death because you have not guarded your lord, the LORD's anointed. Go, look: where are the king's spear and the water jug that was at his head?"

Saul Admits His Guilt. 17 Saul recognized David's voice and asked, "Is that your voice, my son David?" David answered, "Yes, my lord the king." 18 He continued: "Why does my lord pursue his servant? What have I done? What evil do I plan? 19 Please, now, let my lord the king listen to the words of his servant. If the LORD has incited you against me, let an offering appease him; but if men, may they be cursed before the LORD, because they have exiled me so that this day I have no share in the LORD's inheritance,* but am told: 'Go, serve other gods!'ʳ 20 Do not let my blood flow to the ground far from the presence of the LORD. For the king of Israel has come out to seek a single flea as if he were hunting partridge in the mountains." 21 Then Saul said: "I have done wrong. Come back, my son David, I will not harm you again, because you have held my life precious today. Indeed, I have been a fool and have made a serious mistake." 22 But David answered: "Here is the king's spear. Let an attendant come over to get it. 23 The LORD will reward each man for his justice and faithfulness. Today, though the LORD delivered you into my grasp, I would not harm the LORD's anointed.ˢ 24 As I valued your life highly today, so may the LORD value my life highly and deliver me from all difficulties." 25 Then Saul said to David: "Blessed are you, my son David! You shall certainly succeed in whatever you undertake." David went his way, and Saul returned to his home.ᵗ

CHAPTER 27

Refuge among Philistines. 1 But David said to himself: "I shall perish some day at the hand of Saul. I have no choice but to escape to the land of the Philistines; then Saul will give up

his continuous search for me throughout the land of Israel, and I shall be out of his reach." 2 Accordingly, David departed with his six hundred men and went over to Achish, son of Maoch, king of Gath.ᵘ 3 David and his men lived in Gath with Achish; each one had his family, and David had his two wives, Ahinoam from Jezreel and Abigail, the widow of Nabal from Carmel.ᵛ 4 When Saul was told that David had fled to Gath, he no longer searched for him.

In Ziklag. 5 David said to Achish: "If I meet with your approval, let me have a place to live in one of the country towns. Why should your servant live with you in the royal city?" 6 That same day Achish gave him Ziklag, which has, therefore, belonged to the kings of Judah* up to the present time.ʷ 7 In all, David lived a year and four months in the country of the Philistines.ˣ

Raids on Israel's Foes. 8 David and his men went up and made raids on the Geshurites, Girzites, and Amalekites—peoples living in the land between Telam, on the approach to Shur, and the land of Egypt.ʸ 9 In attacking the land David would not leave a man or woman alive, but would carry off sheep, oxen, asses, camels, and clothes. On his return he brought these to Achish, 10 who asked, "Whom did you raid this time?" And David answered, "The Negeb of Judah," or "The Negeb of Jarahmeel," or "The Negeb of the Kenites."ᶻ 11 But David would not leave a man or woman alive to be brought to Gath, fearing that they would betray him by saying, "This is what David did." This was his custom as long as he lived in the country of the Philistines. 12 And Achish trusted David, thinking, "He must certainly be detested by his people Israel. I shall have him as my vassal forever."

CHAPTER 28

1 In those days the Philistines mustered their military forces to fight against Israel. So Achish said to David, "You realize, of course, that you and your men must go out on campaign with me to Jezreel." 2 David answered Achish, "Good! Now you shall learn what your servant

---

r 1 Sm 24, 16.   w 1 Sm 30, 1.
s 1 Sm 18, 20.   x 1 Sm 29, 3.
t 1 Sm 24, 21.   y 1 Sm 15, 3. 7.
u 1 Sm 21, 11-16.   z 1 Sm 30, 14. 29; 1 Chr
v 1 Sm 25, 3. 44; 30, 3ff;   2, 9. 25. 42.
  2 Sm 2, 3.

26, 19: The Lord's inheritance; the land of Israel (Dt 32, 8f), under the Lord's special protection, where he could be freely worshiped.

27, 6: Has . . . belonged to the kings of Judah: as a personal holding, outside the system of tribal lands; Jerusalem, when taken by David, had a similar status (2 Sm 5, 7–9).

can do.'' Then Achish said to David, ''I shall appoint you my permanent bodyguard.''

3 Now Samuel had died and, after being mourned by all Israel, was buried in his city, Ramah. Meanwhile Saul had driven mediums and fortune-tellers out of the land.*a*

Saul in Dismay.   **4** The Philistine levies advanced to Shunem and encamped. Saul, too, mustered all Israel; they camped on Gilboa. **5** When Saul saw the camp of the Philistines, he was dismayed and lost heart completely. **6** He therefore consulted the LORD; but the LORD gave no answer, whether in dreams or by the Urim or through prophets.*b* **7** Then Saul said to his servants, ''Find me a woman who is a medium, to whom I can go to seek counsel through her.'' His servants answered him, ''There is a woman in Endor who is a medium.''*c*

The Witch of Endor.   **8** So he disguised himself, putting on other clothes, and set out with two companions. They came to the woman by night, and Saul said to her, ''Tell my fortune through a ghost; conjure up for me the one I ask you to.''*d* **9** But the woman answered him, ''You are surely aware of what Saul has done, in driving the mediums and fortune-tellers out of the land. Why, then, are you laying snares for my life, to have me killed?'' **10** But Saul swore to her by the LORD, ''As the LORD lives, you shall incur no blame for this.'' **11** Then the woman asked him, ''Whom do you want me to conjure up?'' and he answered, ''Samuel.''

Samuel Appears.   **12** When the woman saw Samuel, she shrieked at the top of her voice and said to Saul, ''Why have you deceived me? You are Saul!''* **13** But the king said to her, ''Have no fear. What do you see?'' The woman answered Saul, ''I see a preternatural being rising from the earth.'' **14** ''What does he look like?'' asked Saul. And she replied, ''It is an old man who is rising, clothed in a mantle.'' Saul knew that it was Samuel, and so he bowed face to the ground in homage.

Saul's Doom.   **15** Samuel then said to Saul, ''Why do you disturb me by conjuring me up?'' Saul replied: ''I am in great straits, for the Philistines are waging war against me and God has abandoned me. Since he no longer answers me through prophets or in dreams, I have called you to tell me what I should do.''*e* **16** To this Samuel said: ''But why do you ask me, if the LORD has abandoned you and is with your neighbor?*f* **17** The LORD has done to you what he foretold through me: he has torn the kingdom from your grasp and has given it to your neighbor David. **18** ''Because you disobeyed the LORD's di-

rective and would not carry out his fierce anger against Amalek, the LORD has done this to you today.*g* **19** Moreover, the LORD will deliver Israel, and you as well, into the clutches of the Philistines. By tomorrow you and your sons will be with me, and the LORD will have delivered the army of Israel into the hands of the Philistines.''*h*

Saul's Despair.   **20** Immediately Saul fell full length on the ground, for he was badly shaken by Samuel's message. Moreover, he had no bodily strength left, since he had eaten nothing all that day and night. **21** Then the woman came to Saul, and seeing that he was quite terror-stricken, said to him: ''Remember, your maidservant obeyed you: I took my life in my hands and fulfilled the request you made of me. **22** Now you, in turn, please listen to your maidservant. Let me set something before you to eat, so that you may have strength when you go on your way.'' **23** But he refused, saying, ''I will not eat.'' However, when his servants joined the woman in urging him, he listened to their entreaties, got up from the ground, and sat on a couch. **24** The woman had a stall-fed calf in the house, which she now quickly slaughtered. Then taking flour, she kneaded it and baked unleavened bread. **25** She set the meal before Saul and his servants, and they ate. Then they stood up and left the same night.

CHAPTER 29

David's Aid Rejected.   **1** Now the Philistines had mustered all their forces in Aphek, and the Israelites were encamped at the spring of Harod near Jezreel.*i* **2** As the Philistine lords were marching their groups of a hundred and a thousand, David and his men were marching in the rear guard with Achish. **3** The Philistine chiefs asked, ''What are those Hebrews doing here?'' And Achish answered them: ''Why, that is David, the officer of Saul, king of Israel. He has been with me now for a year or two, and I have no fault to find with him from the day he

---

a 1 Sm 25, 1; Sir 46, 20.
b 1 Sm 14, 37. 41; Ex 28, 30; Lv 8, 8.
c Lv 19, 31; 20, 27; Dt 18, 10ff; 1 Chr 10, 13f; Acts 16, 16.
d 1 Kgs 14, 2.
e Sir 46, 20.
f 1 Sm 15, 27f.
g 1 Sm 15, 18f. 26.
h 1 Sm 31, 2-6; Sir 46, 20.
i 1 Sm 4, 1.
j 1 Sm 27, 7.

*

28, 12: Human beings cannot communicate at will with the souls of the dead. God may, however, permit a departed soul to appear to the living and even to disclose things unknown to them. Saul's own prohibition of necromancy and divination (v 3) was in keeping with the consistent teaching of the Old Testament. If we are to credit the reality of the apparition to Saul, it was due, not to the summons of the witch, but to God's will; the woman merely furnished the occasion.

came over to me until the present.''*j* **4** But the Philistine chiefs were angered at this and said to him: "Send that man back! Let him return to the place you picked out for him. He must not go down into battle with us, lest during the battle he become our enemy. For how else can he win back his master's favor, if not with the heads of these men of ours?*k* **5** Is this not the David of whom they sing during their dances,

> 'Saul has slain his thousands,
>> but David his ten thousands'?''*l*

6 So Achish summoned David and said to him: "As the LORD lives, you are honest, and I should be pleased to have you active with me in the camp, for I have found nothing wrong with you from the day of your arrival to this day. But you are not welcome to the lords. **7** Withdraw peaceably, now, and do nothing that might displease the Philistine lords." **8** But David said to Achish: "What have I done? Or what have you against your servant from the first day I have been with you to this day, that I cannot go to fight against the enemies of my lord the king?" **9** "You know," Achish answered David, "that you are acceptable to me. But the Philistine chiefs have determined you are not to go up with us to battle. **10** So the first thing tomorow, you and your lord's servants who came with you, go to the place I picked out for you. Do not decide to take umbrage at this; you are as acceptable to me as an angel of God. But make an early morning start, as soon as it grows light, and be on your way." **11** So David and his men left early in the morning to return to the land of the Philistines. The Philistines, however, went on up to Jezreel.

CHAPTER 30

Ziklag in Ruins.

1 Before David and his men reached Ziklag on the third day, the Amalekites had raided the Negeb and Ziklag, had stormed the city, and had set it on fire.*m* **2** They had taken captive the women and all who were in the city, young and old, killing no one; they had carried them off when they left. **3** David and his men arrived at the city to find it burned to the ground and their wives, sons and daughters taken captive. **4** Then David and those who were with him wept aloud until they could weep no more. **5** David's two wives, Ahinoam of Jezreel and Abigail, the widow of Nabal from Carmel, had also been carried off with the rest.*n* **6** Now David found himself in great difficulty, for the men spoke of stoning him, so bitter were they over the fate of their sons and daughters. But with renewed trust in the LORD his God, **7** *o*David said to Abiathar, the priest, son of Ahimelech, "Bring me the ephod!" When Abiathar brought him the ephod, **8** David inquired of the LORD, "Shall I pursue these raiders? Can I overtake them?" The LORD answered him, "Go in pursuit, for you shall surely overtake them and effect a rescue."

Raid of the Amalekites.

9 So David went off with his six hundred men and came as far as the Wadi Besor, where those who were to remain behind halted. **10** David continued the pursuit with four hundred men, but two hundred were too exhausted to cross the Wadi Besor and remained behind. **11** An Egyptian was found in the open country and brought to David. He was provided with food, which he ate, and given water to drink; **12** a cake of pressed figs and two cakes of pressed raisins were also offered to him. When he had eaten, he revived; he had not taken food nor drunk water for three days and three nights. **13** Then David asked him, "To whom do you belong, and where do you come from?" He replied: "I am an Egyptian, the slave of an Amalekite. My master abandoned me because I fell sick three days ago today. **14** We raided the Negeb of the Cherethites, the territory of Judah, and the Negeb of Caleb; and we set Ziklag on fire."*p* **15** David then asked him, "Will you lead me down to this raiding party?" He answered, "Swear to me by God that you will not kill me or deliver me to my master, and I will lead you to the raiding party." **16** He did lead them, and there were the Amalekites scattered all over the ground, eating, drinking, and in a festive mood because of all the rich booty they had taken from the land of the Philistines and from the land of Judah.

The Booty Recovered.

17 From dawn to sundown David attacked them, putting them under the ban so that none escaped except four hundred young men, who mounted their camels and fled.*q* **18** David recovered everything the Amalekites had taken, and rescued his two wives. **19** Nothing was missing, small or great, booty or sons or daughters, of all that the Amalekites had taken. David brought back everything. **20** Moreover, David took all the sheep and oxen, and as they drove them before him, they shouted, "This is David's spoil."

Division of the Spoils.

21 When David came to the two hundred men who had been too exhausted to follow him, and whom he had left behind at the Wadi Besor, they came out to meet David and the men with him. On nearing them David greeted them. **22** But all the stingy and worthless men among those who had accompa-

---

k 1 Chr 12, 19f.
l 1 Sm 18, 6f; 21, 11.
m 1 Sm 27, 6. 10; 1 Chr 12, 21.
n 1 Sm 25, 42; 27, 3; 30, 5.
o 7f: 1 Sm 2, 28; 23, 6; Ex 28, 30.
p 1 Sm 27, 10; Ez 25, 16.
q 1 Sm 15, 3; Jos 6, 17; Jgs 7, 12.

nied David spoke up to say, "Since they did not accompany us, we will not give them anything from the booty, except to each man his wife and children. Let them take those along and be on their way." **23** But David said: "You must not do this, my brothers, after what the LORD has given us. He has protected us and delivered into our grip the band that came against us. **24** Who could agree with this proposal of yours? Rather, the share of the one who goes down to battle and that of the one who remains with the baggage shall be the same; they shall share alike."*r* **25** And from that day forward he made it a law and a custom in Israel, as it still is today.*s*

David's Gifts to Judah.
26 When David came to Ziklag, he sent part of the spoil to the elders of Judah, city by city, saying, "This is a gift to you from the spoil of the enemies of the LORD": **27** to those in Bethel, to those in Ramoth-negeb, to those in Jattir, **28** to those in Aroer, to those in Siphmoth, to those in Eshtemoa, **29** to those in Racal, to those in the Jerahmeelite cities, to those in the Kenite cities,*t* **30** to those in Hormah, to those in Borashan, to those in Athach, **31** to those in Hebron, and to all the places frequented by David and his men.

CHAPTER 31

Death of Saul and His Sons.
1 *u*As they pressed their attack on Israel, with the Israelites fleeing before them and falling mortally wounded on Mount Gilboa, **2** the Philistines pursued Saul and his sons closely, and slew Jonathan, Abinadab, and Malchishua, sons of Saul.*v* **3** The battle raged around Saul, and the archers hit him; he was pierced through the abdomen. **4** Then Saul said to his armor-bearer, "Draw your sword and run me through, lest these uncircumcised come and make sport of me." But his armor-bearer, badly frightened, refused to do it. So Saul took his own sword and fell upon it.*w* **5** *x*When the armor-bearer saw that Saul was dead, he too fell upon his sword and died with him.* **6** Thus Saul, his three sons, and his armor-bearer died together on that same day.

7 When the Israelites on the slope of the valley and those along the Jordan saw that the men of Israel had fled and that Saul and his sons were dead, they too abandoned their cities and fled. Then the Philistines came and lived in those cities.

8 The day after the battle the Philistines came to strip the slain, and found Saul and his three sons lying on Mount Gilboa. **9** They cut off Saul's head and stripped him of his armor, and then sent the good news throughout the land of the Philistines to their idols and to the people.*y* **10** They put his armor in the temple of Astarte, but impaled his body on the wall of Bethshan.

Burial of Saul.
11 *z*When the inhabitants of Jabesh-gilead heard what the Philistines had done to Saul, **12** all their warriors set out, and after marching throughout the night, removed the bodies of Saul and his sons from the wall of Beth-shan, and brought them to Jabesh, where they cremated them.* **13** Then they took their bones and buried them under the tamarisk tree in Jabesh, and fasted for seven days.

---

r 1 Sm 17, 22; 25, 13.   1 Chr 10, 4.
s Nm 31, 27.   x 1 Sm 10, 1; 26, 9;
t 1 Sm 27, 10.   2 Mc 14, 42.
u 1-13: 1 Chr 10, 1-12;   y 1 Sm 17, 54; 2 Sm 1,
  2 Sm 1, 1-16; 4, 4.   20; 2 Mc 15, 35.
v 1 Sm 14, 49; 28, 19;   z 11ff: 1 Sm 11, 1-11;
  1 Chr 10, 2f.   2 Sm 2, 4-7.
w 1 Sm 24, 7; Jgs 9, 54;

*

31, 5: This report of the suicidal act of Saul is presented as a part of his downfall, to be judged accordingly.

31, 12: Cremated them: cremation was not normally practiced in Israel, though it was known in the country from pre-Israelite times.

The Second Book of

SAMUEL

CHAPTER 1

Report of Saul's Death.   **1** After the death of Saul, David returned from his defeat of the Amalekites and spent two days in Ziklag.*a* **2** On the third day a man came from Saul's camp, with his clothes torn and dirt on his head. Going to David, he fell to the ground in homage. **3** David asked him, "Where do you come from?" He replied, "I have escaped from the Israelite camp." **4** "Tell me what happened," David bade him. He answered that the soldiers had fled the battle and that many of them had fallen and were dead, among them Saul and his son Jonathan. **5** Then David said to the youth who was reporting to him, "How do you know that Saul and his son Jonathan are dead?" **6** *b*The youthful informant replied: "It was by chance that I found myself on Mount Gilboa and saw Saul leaning on his spear, with chariots and horsemen closing in on him. **7** He turned around and, seeing me, called me to him. When I said, 'Here I am,' **8** he asked me, 'Who are you?' and I replied, 'An Amalekite.' **9** Then he said to me, 'Stand up to me, please, and finish me off, for I am in great suffering, yet fully alive.' **10** So I stood up to him and dispatched him, for I knew that he could not survive his wound. I removed the crown from his head and the armlet from his arm and brought them here to my lord."

11 David seized his garments and rent them, and all the men who were with him did likewise.*c* **12** They mourned and wept and fasted until evening for Saul and his son Jonathan, and for the soldiers of the LORD of the clans of Israel, because they had fallen by the sword.*d* **13** Then David said to the young man who had brought him the information, "Where are you from?" He replied, "I am the son of an Amalekite immigrant." **14** David said to him, "How is it that you were not afraid to put forth your hand to desecrate the LORD's anointed?"*e* **15** David then called one of the attendants and said to him, "Come, strike him down"; and the youth struck him a mortal blow. **16** Meanwhile David said to him, "You are responsible for your own death, for you testified against yourself when you said, 'I dispatched the LORD's anointed.'"

Elegy for Saul and Jonathan.   **17** Then David chanted this elegy for Saul and his son

Jonathan, **18** which is recorded in the Book of Jashar to be taught to the Judahites. He sang:*f*

19 "Alas! the glory of Israel, Saul,
    slain upon your heights;
how can the warriors have fallen!

20 "Tell it not in Gath,
    herald it not in the streets of Ashkelon,
Lest the Philistine maidens rejoice,
    lest the daughters of the strangers exult!*g*
21 Mountains of Gilboa,
    may there be neither dew nor rain upon
      you,
    nor upsurgings of the deeps!*
Upon you lie begrimed the warriors' shields,
    the shield of Saul, no longer anointed
    with oil.*h*

22 "From the blood of the slain,
    from the bodies of the valiant,
The bow of Jonathan did not turn back,
    or the sword of Saul return unstained.*i*
23 Saul and Jonathan, beloved and cherished,
    separated neither in life nor in death,
    swifter than eagles, stronger than lions!
24 Women of Israel, weep over Saul,
    who clothed you in scarlet and in finery,
    who decked your attire with ornaments of
      gold.

25 "How can the warriors have fallen—
    in the thick of the battle,
    slain upon your heights!
26 "I grieve for you, Jonathan my brother!
    most dear have you been to me;
More precious have I held love for you
    than love for women.*j*

27 "How can the warriors have fallen,
    the weapons of war have perished!'"

---

a 1 Sm 30, 17-20; 31,   105, 15.
   1-13.   f Jos 10, 13.
b 6-10: 2 Sm 4, 10;   g Jgs 16, 23; 1 Sm 31, 9;
   1 Sm 31, 1-4; 1 Chr   Mi 1, 10.
   10, 1-4.   h Gn 27, 28.
c 2 Sm 13, 31.   i 1 Sm 14, 47.
d 1 Sm 31, 13.   j 1 Sm 18, 1; 1 Mc 9, 21.
e 1 Sm 10, 1; 24, 7; Ps.

*

1, 21: **Upsurgings of the deeps:** this reading attempts to recover from an unintelligible Hebrew phrase the poetic parallel to dew and rain. The sense would be a wish that the mountain should have neither moisture from above nor water from springs or wells.

CHAPTER 2

David Anointed King. 1 After this David inquired of the LORD, "Shall I go up into one of the cities of Judah?" The LORD replied to him, "Yes." Then David asked, "Where shall I go?" He replied, "To Hebron." 2 So David went up there accompanied by his two wives, Ahinoam of Jezreel and Abigail, the widow of Nabal of Carmel. k 3 David also brought up his men with their families, and they dwelt in the cities near Hebron. 4 Then the men of Judah came there and anointed David king of the Judahites. l

A report reached David that the men of Jabesh-gilead had buried Saul. 5 So David sent messengers to the men of Jabesh-gilead and said to them: "May you be blessed by the LORD for having done this kindness to your lord Saul in burying him. 6 And now may the LORD be kind and faithful to you. I, too, will be generous to you for having done this. 7 Take courage, therefore, and prove yourselves valiant men, for though your lord Saul is dead, the Judahites have anointed me their king."

IV: The Reign of David

Ishbaal King of Israel. 8 Abner, son of Ner, Saul's general, took Ishbaal, son of Saul, and brought him over to Mahanaim, m 9 where he made him king over Gilead, the Ashurites, Jezreel, Ephraim, Benjamin, and the rest of Israel. 10 Ishbaal, son of Saul, was forty years old when he became king over Israel, and he reigned for two years. The Judahites alone followed David. 11 In all, David spent seven years and six months in Hebron as king of the Judahites. n

Combat near Gibeon. 12 Now Abner, son of Ner, and the servants of Ishbaal, Saul's son, left Mahanaim for Gibeon. 13 Joab, son of Zeruiah, and David's servants also set out and met them at the pool of Gibeon. And they sat down, one group on one side of the pool and the other on the opposite side. 14 Then Abner said to Joab, "Let the young men rise and perform for us." Joab replied, "All right!" 15 So they rose and were counted off: twelve of the Benjaminites of Ishbaal, son of Saul, and twelve of David's servants. 16 Then each one grasped his opponent's head and thrust his sword into his opponent's side, and all fell down together.* And so that place, which is in Gibeon, was named the Field of the Sides.

Death of Asahel. 17 After a very fierce battle that day, Abner and the men of Israel were defeated by David's servants. 18 The three sons of Zeruiah were there—Joab, Abishai, and Asahel. Asahel, who was as fleet of foot as a gazelle in the open field, o 19 set out after Abner, turning neither right nor left in his pursuit. p 20 Abner turned around and said, "Is that you, Asahel?" He replied, "Yes." 21 Abner said to him, "Turn right or left; seize one of the young men and take what you can strip from him." But Asahel would not desist from his pursuit. 22 Once more Abner said to Asahel: "Stop pursuing me! Why must I strike you to the ground? How could I face your brother Joab?" q 23 Still he refused to stop. So Abner struck him in the abdomen with the heel of his javelin, and the weapon protruded from his back. He fell there and died on the spot. And all who came to the place where Asahel had fallen and died, came to a halt. 24 Joab and Abishai, however, continued the pursuit of Abner. The sun had gone down when they came to the hill of Ammah which lies east of the valley toward the desert near Geba.

Truce between Joab and Abner. 25 Here the Benjaminites rallied around Abner, forming a single group, and made a stand on the hilltop. 26 Then Abner called to Joab and said: "Must the sword destroy to the utmost? Do you not know that afterward there will be bitterness? How much longer will you refrain from ordering the people to stop the pursuit of their brothers?" 27 Joab replied, "As God lives, if you had not spoken, the soldiers would not have been withdrawn from the pursuit of their brothers until morning." 28 Joab then sounded the horn, and all the soldiers came to a halt, pursuing Israel no farther and fighting no more. 29 Abner and his men marched all night long through the Arabah, crossed the Jordan, marched all through the morning, and came to Mahanaim. 30 Joab, after interrupting the pursuit of Abner, assembled all the men. Besides Asahel, nineteen other servants of David were missing. 31 But David's servants had fatally wounded three hundred and sixty men of Benjamin, followers of Abner. 32 They took up Asahel and buried him in his father's tomb in Bethlehem. Joab and his men made an all-night march, and dawn found them in Hebron.

CHAPTER 3

1 There followed a long war between the house of Saul and that of David, in which David grew stronger, but the house of Saul weaker.

---

k 1 Sm 25, 42f.
l 1 Sm 31, 11ff.
m 1 Sm 14, 50.
n 2 Sm 5, 5; 1 Kgs 2, 11.

o 2 Sm 23, 24: 1 Chr 2, 16.
p 1 Chr 27, 7.
q 2 Sm 3, 27f. 30.

---

*

2, 16: The nature of this gruesome game is not clear, and the place name is variously given in the older texts.

Sons Born in Hebron. 2 ^rSons were born to David in Hebron: his first-born, Amnon, of Ahinoam from Jezreel; 3 the second, Chileab, of Abigail the widow of Nabal of Carmel; the third, Absalom, son of Maacah the daughter of Talmai, king of Geshur;^s 4 the fourth, Adonijah, son of Haggith; the fifth, Shephatiah, son of Abital;^t 5 and the sixth, Ithream, of David's wife Eglah. These were born to David in Hebron.

Ishbaal and Abner Quarrel. 6 During the war between the house of Saul and of David, Abner was gaining power in the house of Saul. 7 Now Saul had had a concubine, Rizpah, the daughter of Aiah. And Ishbaal, son of Saul, said to Abner, "Why have you been intimate with my father's concubine?"^u 8 Enraged at the words of Ishbaal, Abner said, "Am I a dog's head in Judah? At present I am doing a kindness to the house of your father Saul, to his brothers and his friends, by keeping you out of David's clutches; yet this day you charge me with a crime involving a woman! 9 May God do thus and so to Abner if I do not carry out for David what the LORD swore to him^v — 10 that is, take away the kingdom from the house of Saul and establish the throne of David over Israel and over Judah from Dan to Beersheba."^w 11 In his fear of Abner, Ishbaal was no longer able to say a word to him.

Abner and David Reconciled. 12 Then Abner sent messengers to David in Telam, where he was at the moment, to say, "Make an agreement with me, and I will aid you by bringing all Israel over to you." 13 He replied, "Very well, I will make an agreement with you. But one thing I require of you. You must not appear before me unless you bring back Michal, Saul's daughter, when you come to present yourself to me."^x 14 At the same time David sent messengers to Ishbaal, son of Saul, to say, "Give me my wife Michal, whom I espoused by paying a hundred Philistine foreskins." 15 Ishbaal sent for her and took her away from her husband Paltiel, son of Laish,^y 16 who followed her weeping as far as Bahurim. But Abner said to him, "Go back!" And he turned back.

17 Abner then said in discussion with the elders of Israel: "For a long time you have been seeking David as your king. 18 Now take action, for the LORD has said of David, 'By my servant David I will save my people Israel from the grasp of the Philistines and from the grasp of all their enemies.' " 19 Abner also spoke personally to Benjamin, and then went to make his own report to David in Hebron concerning all that would be agreeable to Israel and to the whole house of Benjamin. 20 When Abner, accompanied by twenty men, came to David in Hebron, David prepared a feast for Abner and for the men who were with him. 21 Then Abner said to David, "I will now go to assemble all Israel for my lord the king, that they may make an agreement with you; you will then be king over all whom you wish to rule." So David bade Abner farewell, and he went away in peace.

Death of Abner. 22 Just then David's servants and Joab were coming in from an expedition, bringing much plunder with them. Abner, having been dismissed by David, was no longer with him in Hebron but had gone his way in peace. 23 When Joab and the whole force he had with him arrived, he was informed, "Abner, son of Ner, came to David; he has been sent on his way in peace." 24 So Joab went to the king and said: "What have you done? Abner came to you. Why did you let him go peacefully on his way? 25 Are you not aware that Abner came to deceive you and to learn the ins and outs of all that you are doing?" 26 Joab then left David, and without David's knowledge sent messengers after Abner, who brought him back from the cistern of Sirah. 27 When Abner returned to Hebron, Joab took him aside within the city gate as though to speak with him privately. There he stabbed him in the abdomen, and he died in revenge for the killing of Joab's brother Asahel.^z 28 Later David heard of it and said: "Before the LORD, I and my kingdom are forever innocent.^a 29 May the full responsibility for the death of Abner, son of Ner, be laid to Joab and to all his family. May the men of Joab's family never be without one suffering from a discharge, or a leper, or one unmanly, one falling by the sword, or one in need of bread!" 30 [Joab and his brother Abishai had lain in wait for Abner because he killed their brother Asahel in battle at Gibeon.]

David Mourns Abner. 31 Then David said to Joab and to all the people who were with him, "Rend your garments, gird yourselves with sackcloth, and mourn over Abner." King David himself followed the bier.^b 32 When they had buried Abner in Hebron, the king wept aloud at the grave of Abner, and the people also wept. 33 And the king sang this elegy over Abner:

"Would Abner have died like a fool?
34 Your hands were not bound with chains,
   nor your feet placed in fetters;
As men fall before the wicked, you fell."

And all the people continued to weep for him.

r 2-5: 1 Chr 3, 14.
s 2 Sm 13, 37; 15, 8.
t 1 Kgs 1, 5.
u 2 Sm 21, 8ff.
v Ru 1, 17.
w 2 Sm 5, 2; 1 Sm 25,
30.
x 1 Sm 18, 20-27.
y 1 Sm 25, 44.
z 1 Kgs 2, 5. 32.
a 28. 30: 2 Sm 2, 22f.
b 2 Sm 21, 10.

X TO REX ·
a shepherd King

35 Then they went to console David with food while it was still day. But David swore, "May God do thus and so to me if I eat bread or anything else before sunset."*c* **36** All the people noted this with approval, just as they were pleased with everything that the king did. **37** So on that day all the people and all Israel came to know that the king had no part in the killing of Abner, son of Ner. **38** The king then said to his servants: "You must recognize that a great general has fallen today in Israel. **39** Although I am the anointed king, I am weak this day, and these men, the sons of Zeruiah, are too ruthless for me. May the LORD requite the evildoer in accordance with his evil deed."*d*

CHAPTER 4

Death of Ishbaal. **1** When Ishbaal, son of Saul, heard that Abner had died in Hebron, he ceased to resist and all Israel was alarmed. **2** Ishbaal, son of Saul, had two company leaders named Baanah and Rechab, sons of Rimmon the Beerothite, of the tribe of Benjamin. [Beeroth, too, was ascribed to Benjamin:*e* **3** the Beerothites fled to Gittaim, where they have been resident aliens to this day.*f* **4** Jonathan, son of Saul, had a son named Meribbaal* with crippled feet. He was five years old when the news about Saul and Jonathan came from Jezreel, and his nurse took him up and fled. But in their hasty flight, he fell and became lame.]*g* **5** The sons of Rimmon the Beerothite, Rechab and Baanah, came into the house of Ishbaal during the heat of the day, while he was taking his siesta. **6** The portress of the house had dozed off while sifting wheat, and was asleep. So Rechab and his brother Baanah slipped past **7** and entered the house while Ishbaal was lying asleep in his bedroom. They struck and killed him, and cut off his head. Then, taking the head, they traveled on the Arabah road all night long.

The Murder Avenged. **8** They brought the head of Ishbaal to David in Hebron and said to the king: "This is the head of Ishbaal, son of your enemy Saul, who sought your life. Thus has the LORD this day avenged my lord the king on Saul and his posterity." **9** But David replied to Rechab and his brother Baanah, sons of Rimmon the Beerothite: "As the LORD lives, who rescued me from all difficulty, **10** in Ziklag I seized and put to death the man who informed me of Saul's death, thinking himself the bearer of good news for which I ought to give him a reward.*h* **11** How much more now, when wicked men have slain an innocent man in bed at home, must I hold you responsible for his death and destroy you from the earth!" **12** So at a command from David, the young men killed them and cut off their hands and feet, hanging them up near the pool in Hebron. But he took the head of Ishbaal and buried it in Abner's grave in Hebron.*i*

CHAPTER 5
1—3 about the King *1st Reading*

David King of Israel. **1** *j*All the tribes of Israel came to David in Hebron and said: "Here we are, your bone and your flesh. **2** In days past, when Saul was our king, it was you who led the Israelites out and brought them back. And the LORD said to you, 'You shall shepherd my people Israel and shall be commander of Israel.' "*k* **3** When all the elders of Israel came to David in Hebron, King David made an agreement with them there before the LORD, and they anointed him king of Israel. **4** David was thirty years old when he became king, and he reigned for forty years: **5** seven years and six months in Hebron over Judah, and thirty-three years in Jerusalem over all Israel and Judah.*l*

Capture of Zion.* **6** *m*Then the king and his men set out for Jerusalem against the Jebusites who inhabited the region. David was told, "You cannot enter here: the blind and the lame will drive you away!" which was their way of saying, "David cannot enter here."*n* **7** But David did take the stronghold of Zion, which is the City of David. **8** On that day David said: "All who wish to attack the Jebusites must strike at them through the water shaft. The lame and the blind shall be the personal enemies of David." That is why it is said, "The blind and the lame shall not enter the palace."*o* **9** David then dwelt in the stronghold, which was called the City of David; he built up the area from Millo to the palace.*p* **10** David grew steadily more powerful, for the LORD of hosts was with him.*q* **11** *r*Hiram, king of Tyre, sent ambassadors to David; he furnished cedar wood, as well as carpenters and masons, who built a palace for David.*s* **12** And David knew that the LORD had

c Ru 1, 17.
d Ps 28, 4; Is 3, 11.
e 2 Sm 4, 3; Jos 9, 17f.
f Jos 18, 25.
g 2 Sm 9, 3; 19, 25.
h 2 Sm 1, 6-10. 14. 16.
i Dt 21, 22f; 1 Sm 31, 10.
j 1ff: 1 Chr 11, 1ff.
k 2 Sm 3, 10; Dt 17, 15;
   1 Sm 18, 16.
l 2 Sm 2, 11; 1 Kgs 2, 11;

1 Chr 3, 4.
m 6-10: 1 Chr 11, 4-9.
n Jos 15, 63; Jgs 1, 19.
   21; Is 29, 3.
o Lv 21, 18; Mt 21, 14f.
p 1 Kgs 3, 1; 11, 27.
q Pss 78, 70ff. 89; 132,
   13.
r 11-25: 1 Chr 14, 1-16.
s 11f: 1 Kgs 5, 15; 1 Chr
   14, 1f.

4, 4: Saul's grandson Meribbaal is the subject of ch 9 below. The text of this verse may owe its present place to the fact that pre-Christian copies of the Books of Samuel tended to confuse his name with that of his uncle Ishbaal, Saul's son and successor, a principal figure in chapters 2–4.

5, 6–12: David's most important military exploit, the taking of Jerusalem, is here presented before his battles with the Philistines, vv 17–25, which were earlier in time. The sense of vv 6 and 8 is in doubt.

established him as king of Israel and had exalted his rule for the sake of his people Israel.

David's Family in Jerusalem.

13 [t]David took more concubines and wives in Jerusalem after he had come from Hebron, and more sons and daughters were born to him in Jerusalem. **14** These are the names of those who were born to him in Jerusalem: Shammua, Shobab, Nathan, Solomon, **15** Ibhar, Elishua, Nepheg, Japhia, **16** Elishama, Baaliada, and Eliphelet.

Rout of the Philistines.

17 When the Philistines heard that David had been anointed king of Israel, they all took the field in search of him. On hearing this, David went down to the refuge.* **18** The Philistines came and overran the valley of Rephaim.* **19** David inquired of the LORD, "Shall I attack the Philistines—will you deliver them into my grip?" The LORD replied to David, "Attack, for I will surely deliver the Philistines into your grip." **20** David then went to Baal-perazim,* where he defeated them. He said, "The LORD has scattered my enemies before me like waters that have broken free." That is why the place is called Baal-perazim. **21** They abandoned their gods there, and David and his men carried them away. **22** But the Philistines came up again and overran the valley of Rephaim. **23** So David inquired of the LORD, who replied: "You must not attack frontally, but circle their rear and meet them before the mastic trees. **24** When you hear a sound of marching* in the tops of the mastic trees, act decisively, for the LORD will have gone forth before you to attack the camp of the Philistines." **25** David obeyed the LORD's command and routed the Philistines from Gibeon as far as Gezer.

CHAPTER 6

The Ark Brought to Jerusalem.

1 [u]David again assembled all the picked men of Israel, thirty thousand in number. **2** Then David and all the people who were with him set out for Baala of Judah to bring up from there the ark of God, which bears the name of the LORD of hosts enthroned above the cherubim.[v] **3** The ark of God was placed on a new cart and taken away from the house of Abinadab on the hill. Uzzah and Ahio, sons of Abinadab, guided the cart,[w] **4** with Ahio walking before it, **5** while David and all the Israelites made merry before the LORD with all their strength, with singing and with citharas, harps, tambourines, sistrums and cymbals.[x] **6** When they came to the threshing floor of Nodan, Uzzah reached out his hand to the ark of God and steadied it, for the oxen were making it tip. **7** But the LORD was angry with Uzzah; God struck him on that spot, and

he died there before God. **8** David was disturbed because the LORD had vented his anger on Uzzah. (The place has been called Perez-uzzah down to the present day.)[y] **9** David feared the LORD that day and said, "How can the ark of the LORD come to me?" **10** So David would not have the ark of the LORD brought to him in the City of David, but diverted it to the house of Obededom the Gittite.

11 The ark of the LORD remained in the house of Obededom the Gittite for three months, and the LORD blessed Obededom and his whole house.[z] **12** [a]When it was reported to King David that the LORD had blessed the family of Obededom and all that belonged to him, David went to bring up the ark of God from the house of Obededom into the City of David amid festivities. **13** As soon as the bearers of the ark of the LORD had advanced six steps, he sacrificed an ox and a fatling. **14** Then David, girt with a linen apron, came dancing before the LORD with abandon,[b] **15** as he and all the Israelites were bringing up the ark of the LORD with shouts of joy and to the sound of the horn. **16** As the ark of the LORD was entering the City of David, Saul's daughter Michal looked down through the window and saw King David leaping and dancing before the LORD, and she despised him in her heart. **17** [c]The ark of the LORD was brought in and set in its place within the tent David had pitched for it. Then David offered holocausts and peace offerings before the LORD. **18** When he finished making these offerings, he blessed the people in the name of the LORD of hosts. **19** He then distributed among all the people, to each man and each woman in the entire multitude of Israel, a loaf of bread, a cut of roast meat, and a raisin cake. With this, all the people left for their homes.

20 When David returned to bless his own family, Saul's daughter Michal came out to meet him and said, "How the king of Israel has honored himself today, exposing himself to the view of the slave girls of his followers, as a

---

t 13-16: 1 Chr 3, 5-8; 14, 3-7.
u 1-11: 1 Chr 13, 1-14.
v Ex 25, 10; Jos 15, 9; Ps 132, 8ff; 1 Chr 1, 4.
w 1 Sm 4, 3f; 6, 7f; 7, 1; Dn 3, 55.
x Pss 68, 25f; 150, 3. 5.

y 1 Kgs 8, 1.
z 1 Chr 26. 4.
a 12-23: 1 Chr 15, 1-29; Ps 24, 7-10.
b 1 Sm 2, 18.
c 17ff: Lv 1, 1-17; 3, 1-17; 1 Chr 16, 1ff.
d 1 Chr 16, 43.

*

5, 17: Refuge: probably near Adullam (1 Sm 22, 1-5).

5, 18-25: The successive defeats of the Philistines in the valley of Rephaim southwest of Jerusalem had the effect of blocking their access to the mountain ridge near Gibeon, and confining them to their holdings on the coast and in the foothills beyond Gezer to the west and south.

5, 20: Baal-perazim: means approximately "the lord of scatterings."

5, 24: Sound of marching: the wind in the treetops suggestive of the Lord's footsteps.

commoner might do!''*d* **21** But David replied to Michal: ''I was dancing before the LORD. As the LORD lives, who preferred me to your father and his whole family when he appointed me commander of the LORD's people, Israel, not only will I make merry before the LORD,*e* **22** but I will demean myself even more. I will be lowly in your esteem, but in the esteem of the slave girls you spoke of I will be honored.'' **23** And so Saul's daughter Michal was childless to the day of her death.

CHAPTER 7

David's Concern for the Ark. **1** *f*When King David was settled in his palace, and the LORD had given him rest from his enemies on every side,*g* **2** he said to Nathan the prophet, ''Here I am living in a house of cedar, while the ark of God dwells in a tent!''*h* **3** Nathan answered the king, ''Go, do whatever you have in mind, for the LORD is with you.''*i* **4** But that night the LORD spoke to Nathan and said: **5** ''Go, tell my servant David, 'Thus says the LORD: Should you build me a house to dwell in?*j* **6** I have not dwelt in a house from the day on which I led the Israelites out of Egypt to the present, but I have been going about in a tent under cloth. **7** In all my wanderings everywhere among the Israelites, did I ever utter a word to any one of the judges whom I charged to tend my people Israel, to ask: Why have you not built me a house of cedar?'

The Lord's Promises. **8** ''Now then, speak thus to my servant David, 'The LORD of hosts has this to say:* It was I who took you from the pasture and from the care of the flock to be commander of my people Israel.*k* **9** I have been with you wherever you went, and I have destroyed all your enemies before you. And I will make you famous like the great ones of the earth.*l* **10** I will fix a place for my people Israel; I will plant them so that they may dwell in their place without further disturbance. Neither shall the wicked continue to afflict them as they did of old, **11** since the time I first appointed judges over my people Israel. I will give you rest from all your enemies. The LORD also reveals to you that he will establish a house for you.*m* **12** *n*And when your time comes and you rest with your ancestors, I will raise up your heir after you, sprung from your loins, and I will make his kingdom firm. **13** It is he who shall build a house for my name. And I will make his royal throne firm forever. **14** I will be a father to him, and he shall be a son to me. And if he does wrong, I will correct him with the rod of men and with human chastisements; **15** but I will not withdraw my favor from him as I withdrew it from your predecessor Saul, whom I

removed from my presence.*o* **16** Your house and your kingdom shall endure forever before me; your throne shall stand firm forever.' ''*p* **17** Nathan reported all these words and this entire vision to David.

King David's Prayer. **18** Then King David went in and sat before the LORD and said, ''Who am I, Lord GOD, and who are the members of my house, that you have brought me to this point?*q* **19** Yet even this you see as too little, Lord GOD; you have also spoken of the house of your servant for a long time to come: this too you have shown to man,* Lord GOD! **20** What more can David say to you? You know your servant, Lord GOD! **21** For your servant's sake and as you have had at heart, you have brought about this entire magnificent disclosure to your servant. **22** And so—

''Great are you, Lord GOD! There is none like you and there is no God but you, just as we have heard it told.*r* **23** What other nation on earth is there like your people Israel, which God has led, redeeming it as his people; so that you have made yourself renowned by doing this magnificent deed, and by doing awe-inspiring things as you have cleared nations and their gods out of the way of your people, which you redeemed for yourself from Egypt?*s* **24** *t*You have established for yourself your people Israel as yours forever, and you, LORD, have become their God. **25** And now, LORD God, confirm for all time the prophecy you have made concerning your servant and his house, and do as you have promised. **26** Your name will be forever great,

e 1 Sm 13, 14; 15, 28.
f 1-29: 1 Chr 17, 1-27.
g 1 Kgs 5, 4.
h Dt 12, 10; 25, 19.
i Ps 132, 1-5.
j 1 Kgs 5, 17; 8, 16. 27; 1 Chr 22, 8; 28, 3; Is 66, 1; Acts 7, 48.
k 1 Sm 16, 13; 17, 15-20; Ps 78, 70f; Am 7, 14.
l Ps 89, 27.
m 2 Sm 23, 5; 1 Kgs 2, 4-24.
n 12ff: 1 Kgs 5, 19, 8, 19; 1 Chr 22, 10; 2 Chr 7,

18; Ps 89, 5, 27f. 30. 37f; Lk 1, 32; Heb 1, 5.
o 2 Sm 23, 5; 1 Sm 13, 14; 15, 26. 28; 2 Kgs 19, 34; 1 Chr 17, 11-14; Ps 89, 34.
p 2 Sm 23, 5; Dn 2, 45; 1 Mc 2, 57; Mk 11, 10; Lk 1, 32f; Heb 1, 8.
q 1 Chr 17, 16.
r Ex 15, 11; Is 45, 5.
s Dt 4, 7. 34.
t 24f: Ex 6, 7; Dt 7, 6; 26, 17; 29, 12.

*

7, 8–16: The prophecy to David contained in these verses is cited again, in poetic form, in Ps 89, 20–38, and alluded to in Ps 132. The promise regarding the people of Israel, vv 10–11, is a part of the promise to David at least as old as the composition of this chapter of Samuel, where it is anticipated in vv 6–7, and alluded to in David's thanksgiving, vv 23–24; it applies to the people an expression used of David in Ps 89, 23. The prophecy to David is the basis for Jewish expectation of a messiah, son of David, which Jesus Christ fulfilled in a transcendent way; cf Acts 2, 30; Heb 1, 5.

7, 19: This too you have shown to man: the text as transmitted has, rather, ''and this is instruction for (or: the law of) mankind.'' The author of Chronicles (1 Chr 17, 17) saw approximately the same phrase, which he endeavored to fit into the context in a quite different sense. The above is conjectural; cf Dt 5, 24.

when men say, 'The LORD of hosts is God of Israel,' and the house of your servant David stands firm before you. **27** It is you, LORD of hosts, God of Israel, who said in a revelation to your servant, 'I will build a house for you.' Therefore your servant now finds the courage to make this prayer to you. **28** And now, Lord GOD, you are God and your words are truth; you have made this generous promise to your servant. *u* **29** Do, then, bless the house of your servant that it may be before you forever; for you, Lord GOD, have promised, and by your blessing the house of your servant shall be blessed forever.''

CHAPTER 8

Summary of David's Wars.

1 *v*After this David attacked the Philistines and conquered them, wresting . . .* from the Philistines. **2** He also defeated Moab and then measured them with a line, making them lie down on the ground. He told off two lengths of line for execution, and a full length* to be spared. Thus the Moabites became tributary to David. **3** *w*Next David defeated Hadadezer, son of Rehob, king of Zobah, when he went to reestablish his dominion at the Euphrates River.* **4** David captured from him one thousand seven hundred horsemen and twenty thousand foot soldiers. And he hamstrung all the chariot horses, preserving only enough for a hundred chariots.*y* **5** When the Arameans of Damascus came to the aid of Hadadezer, king of Zobah, David slew twenty-two thousand of them. **6** David then placed garrisons in Aram of Damascus, and the Arameans became subjects, tributary to David. The LORD brought David victory in all his undertakings. **7** David also took away the golden shields used by Hadadezer's servants and brought them to Jerusalem. [These Shishak, king of Egypt, took away when he came to Jerusalem in the days of Rehoboam, son of Solomon.] **8** From Tebah and Berothai, towns of Hadadezer, King David removed a very large quantity of bronze. **9** When Toi, king of Hamath, heard that David had defeated all the forces of Hadadezer, **10** he sent his son Hadoram to King David to greet him and to congratulate him for his victory over Hadadezer in battle, because Toi had been in many battles with Hadadezer. Hadoram also brought with him articles of silver, gold, and bronze. **11** These, too, King David consecrated to the LORD, together with the silver and gold he had taken from every nation he had conquered: **12** from Edom and Moab, from the Ammonites, from the Philistines, from the Amalekites, and from the plunder of Hadadezer, son of Rehob, king of Zobah.

13 On his return,* David became famous for having slain eighteen thousand Edomites in the Salt Valley;*z* **14** after which he placed garrisons in Edom. Thus all the Edomites became David's subjects, and the LORD brought David victory in all his undertakings.

David's Officials.

15 *a*David reigned over all Israel, judging and administering justice to all his people. **16** Joab, son of Zeruiah, was in command of the army. Jehoshaphat, son of Ahilud, was chancellor. **17** Zadok, son of Ahitub, and Ahimelech, son of Abiathar, were priests. Shawsha was scribe. **18** Benaiah, son of Jehoiada, was in command of the Cherethites and Pelethites. And David's sons were priests. *b*

CHAPTER 9

David and Meribbaal.

1 David asked, ''Is there any survivor of Saul's house to whom I may show kindness for the sake of Jonathan?''*c* **2** Now there was a servant of the family of Saul named Ziba. He was summoned to David, and the king asked him, ''Are you Ziba?'' He replied, ''Your servant.''*d* **3** Then the king inquired, ''Is there any survivor of Saul's house to whom I may show God's kindness?'' Ziba answered the king, ''There is still Jonathan's son, whose feet are crippled.''*e* **4** The king said to him, ''Where is he?'' and Ziba answered, ''He is in the house of Machir, son of Ammiel, in Lodebar.''*f* **5** So King David sent for him and had him brought from the house of Machir, son of Ammiel, in Lodebar. **6** When Meribbaal, son of Jonathan, son of Saul, came to David, he fell prostrate in homage. David said, ''Meribbaal,'' and he answered, ''Your servant.'' **7** ''Fear not,'' David said to him, ''I will surely be kind to you for the sake of your father Jonathan. I will restore to you all the lands of your grandfather Saul, and you shall always eat at my table.'' **8** Bowing low, he answered, ''What is your servant that you

---

u Nm 23, 19; Jn 17, 17.
v 1-18: 1 Chr 18, 1-17.
w 3-8: 2 Sm 10, 15-19.
x 2 Sm 10, 6; 1 Kgs 11, 23.
y Jos 11, 6. 9.
z 2 Kgs 14, 7.
a 15-18: 2 Sm 20, 23-26; 1 Kgs 4, 1-6; 1 Chr

18, 14-17.
b 2 Sm 15, 18; 20, 7. 23; 23, 20.
c 2 Sm 21, 7; 1 Sm 18, 1-4; 20, 8ff. 15f. 42.
d 2 Sm 16, 1-4; 19, 27.
e 2 Sm 4, 4.
f 2 Sm 17, 27.
g 1 Sm 24, 15.

*

8, 1:   Wresting . . .: the Hebrew text here gives ''the bridle of the cubit''; 1 Chr 18, 1 understood ''Gath and its dependent villages''; others implausibly read ''dominion of the capital city.''

8, 2:   Two lengths . . . a full length: usually taken to mean that two-thirds of them were executed; but it could mean that two-thirds were spared, if the line was used full length in their case but doubled on itself to make ''two lines'' for those to be put to death.

8, 13:   On his return: possibly to Jerusalem, after the revolt of Absalom, a circumstance which this catalogue of victories would avoid mentioning. 1 Chr 18, 13 attributes the defeat of the Edomites to Abishai.

should pay attention to a dead dog like me?''g
9 The king then called Ziba, Saul's attendant,
and said to him: ''I am giving your lord's son
all that belonged to Saul and to all his family.
10 You and your sons and servants must till the
land for him. You shall bring in the produce,
which shall be food for your lord's family to eat.
But Meribbaal, your lord's son, shall always eat
at my table.'' Ziba, who had fifteen sons and
twenty servants, **11** said to the king, ''Your
servant shall do just as my lord the king has
commanded him.'' And so Meribbaal ate at
David's table like one of the king's sons.h
12 Meribbaal had a young son whose name was
Mica; and all the tenants of Ziba's family
worked for Meribbaal.i **13** But Meribbaal lived
in Jerusalem, because he always ate at the
king's table. He was lame in both feet.j

CHAPTER 10

Insult of the Ammonites. 1 kSome time
later* the king of the Ammonites died, and his
son Hanun succeeded him as king. **2** David
thought, ''I will be kind to Hanun, son of Nahash, as his father was kind to me.'' So David
sent his servants with condolences to Hanun for
the loss of his father. But when David's servants
entered the country of the Ammonites, **3** the
Ammonite princes said to their lord Hanun:
''Do you think that David is honoring your father by sending men with condolences? Is it not
rather to explore the city, to spy on it, and to
overthrow it, that David has sent his messengers
to you?'' **4** Hanun, therefore, seized David's
servants and, after shaving off half their beards
and cutting away the lower halves of their garments at the buttocks, sent them away.l
5 When he was told of it, King David sent out
word to them, since the men were quite
ashamed. ''Stay in Jericho until your beards
grow,'' he said, ''and then come back.''

Ammonites Defeated. 6 *In view of the
offense they had given to David, the Ammonites sent for and hired twenty thousand Aramean
foot soldiers from Beth-rehob and Zobah, as
well as the king of Maacah with one thousand
men, and twelve thousand men from Tob.m
7 On learning this, David sent out Joab with the
entire levy of trained soldiers.n **8** The Ammonites came out and drew up in battle formation at
the entrance of their city gate, while the Arameans of Zobah and Rehob and the men of Tob and
Maacah remained apart in the open country.
9 When Joab saw the battle lines drawn up
against him, both front and rear, he made a
selection from all the picked troops of Israel and
arrayed them against the Arameans. **10** He
placed the rest of the soldiers under the command of his brother Abishai, who arrayed them

against the Ammonites. **11** Joab said, ''If the
Arameans are stronger than I, you shall help
me. But if the Ammonites are stronger than you,
I will come to help you. **12** Be brave; let us
prove our valor for the sake of our people and
the cities of our God; the LORD will do what he
judges best.'' **13** When Joab and the soldiers
who were with him approached the Arameans
for battle, they fled before him. **14** The Ammonites, seeing that the Arameans had fled,
also fled from Abishai and withdrew into the
city. Joab then ceased his attack on the Ammonites and returned to Jerusalem.

Arameans Defeated. 15 oThen the Arameans responded to their defeat by Israel with
a full mustering of troops; **16** Hadadezer sent
for and enlisted Arameans from beyond the Euphrates. They came to Helam, with Shobach,
general of Hadadezer's army, at their head.
17 On receiving this news, David assembled all
Israel, crossed the Jordan, and went to Helam.
The Arameans drew up in formation against
David and fought with him. **18** But the Arameans gave way before Israel, and David's men
killed seven hundred charioteers and forty thousand of the Aramean foot soldiers. Shobach,
general of the army, was struck down and died
on the field. **19** All of Hadadezer's vassal
kings, in view of their defeat by Israel, then
made peace with the Israelites and became their
subjects. And the Arameans were afraid to give
further aid to the Ammonites.

CHAPTER 11

David's Sin. 1 At the turn of the year,*
when kings go out on campaign, David sent out
Joab along with his officers and the army of
Israel, and they ravaged the Ammonites and
besieged Rabbah. David, however, remained in
Jerusalem.p **2** One evening David rose from his
siesta and strolled about on the roof of the palace. From the roof he saw a woman bathing,
who was very beautiful. **3** David had inquiries
made about the woman and was told, ''She is

---

h 2 Sm 19, 29.
i 1 Chr 8, 34.
j 2 Sm 21, 7.
k 1-19: 1 Chr 19, 1-19.
l Is 20, 4.
m 2 Sm 8, 3; 1 Sm 14,
 47.

n 2 Sm 11, 1.
o 15-19: 2 Sm 8, 3-8;
 1 Chr 9, 16-19.
p 2 Sm 10, 7; 1 Chr 20,
 1.
q 2 Sm 23, 39.

*

10, 1: Some time later: early in the reign of David, since
Hanun's father had been ruling in Ammon at the beginning of
Saul's reign (1 Sm 11) and Solomon was as yet unborn (2 Sm
11, 1; 12, 24).

10, 6–9: A Hebrew text from Qumran (4Q Sam*) comes
closer in these verses to what is given in 1 Chr 19, 6–9. The
scene of the conflict is more likely Rabbath-Ammon, with Jose-
phus (Ant., vii, 123), than Madeba, as in 1 Chr; compare ch 11.

11, 1: At the turn of the year: in the spring.

Bathsheba, daughter of Eliam, and wife of [Joab's armor-bearer] Uriah the Hittite."[q] **4** Then David sent messengers and took her. When she came to him, he had relations with her, at a time when she was just purified after her monthly period. She then returned to her house.[r] **5** But the woman had conceived, and sent the information to David, "I am with child."

6 David therefore sent a message to Joab, "Send me Uriah the Hittite." So Joab sent Uriah to David. **7** When he came, David questioned him about Joab, the soldiers, and how the war was going, and Uriah answered that all was well. **8** David then said to Uriah, "Go down to your house and bathe your feet." Uriah left the palace, and a portion was sent out after him from the king's table. **9** But Uriah slept at the entrance of the royal palace with the other officers of his lord, and did not go down to his own house. **10** David was told that Uriah had not gone home. So he said to Uriah, "Have you not come from a journey? Why, then, did you not go down to your house?" **11** Uriah answered David, "The ark and Israel and Judah are lodged in tents, and my lord Joab and your majesty's servants are encamped in the open field. Can I go home to eat and to drink and to sleep with my wife? As the LORD lives and as you live, I will do no such thing."[s] **12** Then David said to Uriah, "Stay here today also, I shall dismiss you tomorrow." So Uriah remained in Jerusalem that day. On the day following, **13** David summoned him, and he ate and drank with David, who made him drunk. But in the evening he went out to sleep on his bed among his lord's servants, and did not go down to his home. **14** The next morning David wrote a letter to Joab which he sent by Uriah. **15** In it he directed: "Place Uriah up front, where the fighting is fierce. Then pull back and leave him to be struck down dead." **16** So while Joab was besieging the city, he assigned Uriah to a place where he knew the defenders were strong. **17** When the men of the city made a sortie against Joab, some officers of David's army fell, and among them Uriah the Hittite died.

18 Then Joab sent David a report of all the details of the battle, **19** instructing the messenger, "When you have finished giving the king all the details of the battle, **20** the king may become angry and say to you: 'Why did you go near the city to fight? Did you not know that they would shoot from the wall above? **21** Who killed Abimelech, son of Jerubbaal? Was it not a woman who threw a millstone down on him from the wall above, so that he died in Thebez? Why did you go near the wall?' Then you in turn shall say, 'Your servant Uriah the Hittite is also dead.' "[t] **22** The messenger set out, and on his

arrival he relayed to David all the details as Joab had instructed him.* **23** He told David: "The men had us at a disadvantage and came out into the open against us, but we pushed them back to the entrance of the city gate. **24** Then the archers shot at your servants from the wall above, and some of the king's servants died, among them your servant Uriah." **25** David said to the messenger: "This is what you shall convey to Joab: 'Do not be chagrined at this, for the sword devours now here and now there. Strengthen your attack on the city and destroy it.' Encourage him."

26 When the wife of Uriah heard that her husband had died, she mourned her lord. **27** But once the mourning was over, David sent for her and brought her into his house. She became his wife and bore him a son. But the LORD was displeased with what David had done.

CHAPTER 12

Nathan's Parable. **1** *The LORD sent Nathan to David, and when he came to him, he said: "Judge this case for me! In a certain town there were two men, one rich, the other poor.[u] **2** The rich man had flocks and herds in great numbers. **3** But the poor man had nothing at all except one little ewe lamb that he had bought. He nourished her, and she grew up with him and his children. She shared the little food he had and drank from his cup and slept in his bosom. She was like a daughter to him. **4** Now, the rich man received a visitor, but he would not take from his own flocks and herds to prepare a meal for the wayfarer who had come to him. Instead he took the poor man's ewe lamb and made a meal of it for his visitor." **5** David grew very angry with that man and said to Nathan: "As the LORD lives, the man who has done this merits death! **6** He shall restore the ewe lamb four-fold because he has done this and has had no pity."[v]

David's Punishment. **7** Then Nathan said to David: "You are the man! Thus says the LORD God of Israel: 'I anointed you king of Israel. I rescued you from the hand of Saul.[w] **8** I gave you your lord's house and your lord's wives for your own. I gave you the house of Israel and of Judah. And if this were not

---

r Lv 15, 19.
s 1 Sm 4, 3f.
t Jgs 9, 50-54.
u Sir 47, 1.
v Ex 21, 37; Lk 19, 8.
w 1 Sm 16, 13.

*

11, 22: After this verse, the Greek text, which is here the older form, has David, angry with Joab, repeat exactly the questions Joab had foreseen in vv 20ff. In v 24 of our oldest Greek text, the messenger specifies that about eighteen men were killed.

12, 1–4: This utterance of Nathan is in regular lines in Hebrew, resembling English blank verse.

enough, I could count up for you still more.
9 Why have you spurned the LORD and done
evil in his sight? You have cut down Uriah the
Hittite with the sword; you took his wife as your
own, and him you killed with the sword of the
Ammonites. **10** Now, therefore, the sword
shall never depart from your house, because you
have despised me and have taken the wife of
Uriah to be your wife.'ˣ **11** Thus says the
LORD: 'I will bring evil upon you out of your
own house. I will take your wives while you live
to see it, and will give them to your neighbor.
He shall lie with your wives in broad daylight.ʸ
12 You have done this deed in secret, but I will
bring it about in the presence of all Israel, and
with the sun looking down.' "

David's Repentance.   **13** Then David said
to Nathan, "I have sinned against the LORD."
Nathan answered David: "The LORD on his part
has forgiven your sin: you shall not die.ᶻ **14** But
since you have utterly spurned the LORD by this
deed, the child born to you must surely die."
15 Then Nathan returned to his house.

The LORD struck the child that the wife of
Uriah had borne to David, and it became desperately ill. **16** David besought God for the child.
He kept a fast, retiring for the night to lie on the
ground clothed in sackcloth. **17** The elders of
his house stood beside him urging him to rise
from the ground; but he would not, nor would
he take food with them. **18** On the seventh day,
the child died. David's servants, however, were
afraid to tell him that the child was dead, for
they said: "When the child was alive, we spoke
to him, but he would not listen to what we said.
How can we tell him the child is dead? He may
do some harm!" **19** But David noticed his servants whispering among themselves and realized that the child was dead. He asked his servants, "Is the child dead?" They replied,
"Yes, he is." **20** Rising from the ground, David washed and anointed himself, and changed
his clothes. Then he went to the house of the
LORD and worshiped. He returned to his own
house, where at his request food was set before
him, and he ate. **21** His servants said to him:
"What is this you are doing? While the child
was living, you fasted and wept and kept vigil;
now that the child is dead, you rise and take
food." **22** He replied: "While the child was
living, I fasted and wept, thinking, 'Perhaps the
LORD will grant me the child's life.' **23** But
now he is dead. Why should I fast? Can I bring
him back again? I shall go to him, but he will
not return to me."ᵃ **24** Then David comforted
his wife Bathsheba. He went and slept with her;
and she conceived and bore him a son, who was
named Solomon. The LORD loved him **25** and
sent the prophet Nathan to name him Jedidiah,
on behalf of the LORD.

Ammonite War Ends.   **26** ᵇJoab fought
against Rabbah of the Ammonites and captured
this royal city. **27** He sent messengers to David
with the word: "I have fought against Rabbah
and have taken the water-city. **28** Therefore,
assemble the rest of the soldiers, join the siege
against the city and capture it, lest it be I that
capture the city and it be credited to me." **29** So
David assembled the rest of the soldiers and
went to Rabbah. When he had fought against it
and captured it, **30** he took the crown from
Milcom's head. It weighed a talent,* of gold
and precious stones; it was placed on David's
head. He brought out immense booty from the
city, **31** and also led away the inhabitants,
whom he assigned to work with saws, iron
picks, and iron axes, or put to work at the brick-
mold. This is what he did to all the Ammonite
cities. David and all the soldiers then returned
to Jerusalem.

CHAPTER 13

The Crime of Amnon.   **1** Some time later
the following incident occurred. David's son
Absalom had a beautiful sister named Tamar,
and David's son Amnon loved her.ᶜ **2** He was
in such straits over his sister Tamar that he
became sick; since she was a virgin, Amnon
thought it impossible to carry out his designs
toward her. **3** Now Amnon had a friend named
Jonadab, son of David's brother Shimeah, who
was very clever.ᵈ **4** He asked him, "Prince,
why are you so dejected morning after morning?
Why not tell me?" So Amnon said to him, "I
am in love with Tamar, my brother Absalom's
sister." **5** Then Jonadab replied, "Lie down on
your bed and pretend to be sick. When your
father comes to visit you, say to him, 'Please let
my sister Tamar come and encourage me to take
food. If she prepares something appetizing in
my presence, for me to see, I will eat it from her
hand.' " **6** So Amnon lay down and pretended
to be sick. When the king came to visit him,
Amnon said to the king, "Please let my sister
Tamar come and prepare some fried cakes before my eyes, that I may take nourishment from
her hand."

7 David then sent home a message to Tamar,
"Please go to the house of your brother Amnon
and prepare some nourishment for him." **8** Tamar went to the house of her brother Amnon,
who was in bed. Taking dough and kneading it,

x 2 Sm 13, 28f; 18, 14.   a Jb 7, 9.
y 2 Sm 16, 11.· 22.   b 26-31: 1 Chr 20, 1-3.
z 1 Kgs 21, 29; Pss 32,   c 2 Sm 3, 2f; 1 Chr 3, 9.
   5; 50, 6; Sir 47, 11.   d 1 Sm 21, 21.

*

12, 30: Weighed a talent: since this would be more than 75
pounds, some commentators picture the idol's crown as dis-
playing a single precious stone of large size, which David took
to wear; but the text does not say this.

she twisted it into cakes before his eyes and fried the cakes. **9** Then she took the pan and set out the cakes before him. But Amnon would not eat; he said, "Have everyone leave me." When they had all left him, **10** Amnon said to Tamar, "Bring the nourishment into the bedroom, that I may have it from your hand." So Tamar picked up the cakes she had prepared and brought them to her brother Amnon in the bedroom. **11** But when she brought them to him to eat, he seized her and said to her, "Come! Lie with me, my sister!" **12** But she answered him, "No, my brother! Do not shame me! That is an intolerable crime in Israel. Do not commit this insensate deed.*e* **13** Where would I take my shame? And you would be a discredited man in Israel. So please, speak to the king; he will not keep me from you."*f*

14 Not heeding her plea, he overpowered her; he shamed her and had relations with her. **15** Then Amnon conceived an intense hatred for her, which far surpassed the love he had had for her. "Get up and leave," he said to her. **16** She replied, "No, brother, because to drive me out would be far worse than the first injury you have done me." He would not listen to her, **17** but called the youth who was his attendant and said, "Put her outside, away from me, and bar the door after her." **18** Now she had on a long tunic, for that is how maiden princesses dressed in olden days. When his attendant put her out and barred the door after her, **19** Tamar put ashes on her head and tore the long tunic in which she was clothed. Then, putting her hands to her head, she went away crying loudly. **20** Her brother Absalom said to her: "Has your brother Amnon been with you? Be still now, my sister; he is your brother. Do not take this affair to heart." But Tamar remained grief-stricken and forlorn in the house of her brother Absalom. **21** King David, who got word of the whole affair, became very angry. He did not, however, spark the resentment of his son Amnon, whom he favored because he was his firstborn. **22** Absalom, moreover, said nothing at all to Amnon, although he hated him for having shamed his sister Tamar.

Absalom's Plot.   **23** After a period of two years Absalom had shearers in Baalhazor near Ephraim, and he invited all the princes. **24** Absalom went to the king and said: "Your servant is having shearers. Please, your majesty, come with all your retainers to your servant." **25** But the king said to Absalom, "No, my son, all of us should not go lest we be a burden to you." And though Absalom urged him, he refused to go and began to bid him goodbye. **26** Absalom then said, "If you will not come yourself, please let my brother Amnon come to us." The king asked him, "Why should he go to you?"

27 At Absalom's urging, however, he sent Amnon and all the other princes with him. Absalom prepared a banquet fit for royalty. **28** *g*But he had instructed his servants: "Now watch! When Amnon is merry with wine and I say to you, 'Kill Amnon,' put him to death. Do not be afraid, for it is I who order you to do it. Be resolute and act manfully."

Death of Amnon.   **29** When the servants did to Amnon as Absalom had commanded, all the other princes rose, mounted their mules, and fled. **30** While they were still on the road, a report reached David that Absalom had killed all the princes and that not one of them had survived. **31** The king stood up, rent his garments, and then lay on the ground. All his servants standing by him also rent their garments.*h* **32** But Jonadab, son of David's brother Shimeah, spoke up: "Let not my lord think that all the young princes have been killed! Amnon alone is dead, for Absalom was determined on this ever since Amnon shamed his sister Tamar. **33** So let not my lord the king put faith in the report that all the princes are dead. Amnon alone is dead." **34** Meanwhile, Absalom had taken flight. Then the servant on watch looked about and saw a large group coming down the slope from the direction of Bahurim. He came in and reported this, telling the king that he had seen some men coming down the mountainside from the direction of Bahurim. **35** So Jonadab said to the king: "There! The princes have come. It is as your servant said." **36** No sooner had he finished speaking than the princes came in, weeping aloud. The king, too, and all his servants wept very bitterly. **37** But Absalom, who had taken flight, went to Talmai, son of Ammihud, king of Geshur,*i* **38** and stayed in Geshur for three years.

Efforts for Absalom's Return.   **39** The king continued during all that time to mourn over his son; but his longing reached out for Absalom as he became reconciled to the death of Amnon.

CHAPTER 14

1 When Joab, son of Zeruiah, observed how the king felt toward Absalom, **2** he sent to Tekoa and brought from there a gifted woman, to whom he said: "Pretend to be in mourning. Put on mourning apparel and do not anoint yourself with oil, that you may appear to be a woman who has been long in mourning for a departed one. **3** Then go to the king and speak to him in this manner." And Joab instructed her what to say.

---

e Lv 18, 9; 20, 17; Dt 27, 22.
f Gn 34, 7.
g 28f: 2 Sm 12, 10.
h 2 Sm 1, 11.
i 2 Sm 3, 3; 15, 8.

4 So the woman of Tekoa went to the king and fell prostrate to the ground in homage, saying, "Help, your majesty!" **5** *j*The king said to her, "What do you want?" She replied: "Alas, I am a widow; my husband is dead. **6** Your servant had two sons, who quarreled in the field. There being no one to part them, one of them struck his brother and killed him. **7** Then the whole clan confronted your servant and demanded: 'Give up the one who killed his brother. We must put him to death for the life of his brother whom he has slain; we must extinguish the heir also.' Thus they will quench my remaining hope* and leave my husband neither name nor posterity upon the earth."*k* **8** The king then said to the woman: "Go home. I will issue a command on your behalf." **9** The woman of Tekoa answered him, "Let me and my family be to blame, my lord king; you and your throne are innocent." **10** Then the king said, "If anyone says a word to you, have him brought to me, and he shall not touch you again." **11** But she went on to say, "Please, your majesty, keep in mind the LORD your God, that the avenger of blood may not go too far in destruction and that my son may not be done away with." He replied, "As the LORD lives, not a hair of your son shall fall to the ground."

12 The woman continued, "Please let your servant say still another word to my lord the king." He replied, "Speak." **13** So the woman said: "Why, then, do you think of this same kind of thing against the people of God? In pronouncing as he has, the king shows himself guilty, for not bringing back his own banished son. **14** We must indeed die; we are then like water that is poured out on the ground and cannot be gathered up. Yet, though God does not bring back life, he does take thought how not to banish* anyone from him.*l* **15** And now, if I have presumed to speak of this matter to your majesty, it is because the people have given me cause to fear. And so your servant thought: 'Let me speak to the king. Perhaps he will grant the petition of his maidservant. **16** For the king must surely consent to free his servant from the grasp of one who would seek to destroy me and my son as well from God's inheritance.'" **17** And the woman concluded: "Let the word of my lord the king provide a resting place;* indeed, my lord the king is like an angel of God, evaluating good and bad. The LORD your God be with you."*m*

18 The king answered the woman, "Now do not conceal from me anything I may ask you!" The woman said, "Let my lord the king speak." **19** So the king asked, "Is Joab involved with you in all this?" And the woman answered: "As you live, my lord the king, it is just as your majesty has said, and not otherwise. It was your servant Joab who instructed me and

told your servant all these things she was to say. **20** Your servant Joab did this to come at the issue in a roundabout way. But my lord is as wise as an angel of God, so that he knows all things on earth."

Absalom's Return. **21** Then the king said to Joab: "I hereby grant this request. Go, therefore, and bring back young Absalom." **22** Falling prostrate to the ground in homage and blessing the king, Joab said, "This day I know that I am in good favor with you, my lord the king, since the king has granted the request of his servant." **23** Joab then went off to Geshur and brought Absalom to Jerusalem. **24** But the king said, "Let him go to his own house; he shall not appear before me." So Absalom went off to his house and did not appear before the king.

25 In all Israel there was not a man who could so be praised for his beauty as Absalom, who was without blemish from the sole of his foot to the crown of his head. **26** When he shaved his head—which he used to do at the end of every year, because his hair became too heavy for him—the hair weighed two hundred shekels according to the royal standard. **27** Absalom had three sons born to him, besides a daughter named Tamar, who was a beautiful woman.*n*

Absalom Is Pardoned. **28** Absalom lived in Jerusalem for two years without appearing before the king. **29** Then he summoned Joab to send him to the king, but Joab would not come to him. Although he summoned him a second time, Joab refused to come. **30** He therefore instructed his servants: "You see Joab's field that borders mine, on which he has barley. Go, set it on fire." And so Absalom's servants set the field on fire.*o* Joab's farmhands came to him with torn garments and reported to him what had been done. **31** At this, Joab went to Absalom in his house and asked him, "Why have your servants set my field on fire?" **32** Absalom answered Joab: "I was summoning you to come here, that I may send you to the king to say: 'Why did I come back from Geshur? I would be better off if I were still there!' Now, let me appear before the king. If I am guilty, let him

---

j 5f: 2 Kgs 6, 26f.
k Nm 35, 19.
l Jb 7, 9; 14, 7-12; Ps 88, 5, 11ff.
m 17. 20: 1 Sm 29, 9.
n 2 Sm 18, 18.
o Jgs 15, 4f.

*

14, 7: Hope: literally, "glowing coal." The image is similar to that of the lighted lamp, e.g., Ps 89, 17, to keep alive the ancestral name.

14, 14: How not to banish: a possible allusion to the religious institution of cities of refuge for involuntary murderers; see Nm 35, 9–15.

14, 17: A resting place: cf Ps 95, 11; Heb 3, 7—4, 11. The reference here is to a return home for Absalom to Israel.

put me to death.'' **33** Joab went to the king and reported this. The king then called Absalom, who came to him and in homage fell on his face to the ground before the king. Then the king kissed him.

CHAPTER 15

Absalom's Plot. **1** After this Absalom provided himself with chariots, horses, and fifty henchmen.p **2** Moreover, Absalom used to rise early and stand alongside the road leading to the gate. If someone had a lawsuit to be decided by the king, Absalom would call to him and say, ''From what city are you?'' And when he replied, ''Your servant is of such and such a tribe of Israel,'' **3** Absalom would say to him, ''Your suit is good and just, but there is no one to hear you in the king's name.'' **4** And he would continue: ''If only I could be appointed judge in the land! Then everyone who has a lawsuit to be decided might come to me and I would render him justice.'' **5** Whenever a man approached him to show homage, he would extend his hand, hold him, and kiss him. **6** By behaving in this way toward all the Israelites who came to the king for judgment, Absalom was stealing away the loyalties of the men of Israel.

Conspiracy in Hebron. **7** After a period of four years, Absalom said to the king: ''Allow me to go to Hebron and fulfill a vow I made to the LORD. **8** For while living in Geshur in Aram, your servant made this vow: 'If the LORD ever brings me back to Jerusalem, I will worship him in Hebron.' ''q **9** The king wished him a safe journey, and he went off to Hebron. **10** Then Absalom sent spies throughout the tribes of Israel to say, ''When you hear the sound of the horn, declare Absalom king in Hebron.'' **11** Two hundred men had accompanied Absalom from Jerusalem. They had been invited and went in good faith, knowing nothing of the plan. **12** Absalom also sent to Ahithophel the Gilonite, David's counselor, an invitation to come from his town, Giloh, for the sacrifices he was about to offer. So the conspiracy gained strength, and the people with Absalom increased in numbers.r

David Flees Jerusalem. **13** An informant came to David with the report, ''The Israelites have transferred their loyalty to Absalom.''s **14** At this, David said to all his servants who were with him in Jerusalem: ''Up! Let us take flight, or none of us will escape from Absalom. Leave quickly, lest he hurry and overtake us, then visit disaster upon us and put the city to the sword.'' **15** The king's officers answered him, ''Your servants are ready, whatever our lord the king chooses to do.'' **16** Then the king set out, accompanied by his entire household, except for ten concubines whom he left behind to take care of the palace.t **17** As the king left the city, with all his officers accompanying him, they halted opposite the ascent of the Mount of Olives, at a distance, **18** while the whole army marched past him.u

David and Ittai. As all the Cherethites and Pelethites, and the six hundred men of Gath who had accompanied him from that city, were passing in review before the king, **19** he said to Ittai the Gittite: ''Why should you also go with us? Go back and stay with the king, for you are a foreigner and you, too, are an exile from your own country. **20** You came only yesterday, and shall I have you wander about with us today, wherever I have to go? Return and take your brothers with you, and may the LORD be kind and faithful to you.'' **21** But Ittai answered the king, ''As the LORD lives, and as my lord the king lives, your servant shall be wherever my lord the king may be, whether for death or for life.''v **22** So the king said to Ittai, ''Go, then, march on.'' And Ittai the Gittite, with all his men and all the dependents that were with him, marched on. **23** Everyone in the countryside wept aloud as the last of the soldiers went by, and the king crossed the Kidron Valley with all the soldiers moving on ahead of him by way of the Mount of Olives, toward the desert.

David and the Priests. **24** Zadok, too [with all the Levite bearers of the ark of the covenant of God], and Abiathar brought the ark of God to a halt until the soldiers had marched out of the city. **25** Then the king said to Zadok: ''Take the ark of God back to the city. If I find favor with the LORD, he will bring me back and permit me to see it and its lodging. **26** But if he should say, 'I am not pleased with you,' I am ready; let him do to me as he sees fit.''w **27** The king also said to the priest Zadok: ''See to it that you and Abiathar return to the city in peace, and both your sons with you, your own son Ahimaaz, and Abiathar's son Jonathan. **28** Remember, I shall be waiting at the fords near the desert until I receive information from you.'' **29** So Zadok and Abiathar took the ark of God back to Jerusalem and remained there.

30 As David went up the Mount of Olives, he wept without ceasing. His head was covered, and he was walking barefoot. All those who were with him also had their heads covered and were weeping as they went.x **31** When David

p 1 Sm 8, 11; 1 Kgs 1, 5.   v Ru 1, 16.
q 2 Sm 3, 3; 13, 37.   w 2 Sm 16, 10.
r 2 Sm 16, 23.   x 2 Sm 19, 5; Mi 1, 8.
s Ps 3.   y 2 Sm 16, 23; 17, 14.
t 2 Sm 16, 21f; 20, 3.   23.
u 2 Sm 8, 18.

was informed that Ahithophel was among the conspirators with Absalom, he said, "O LORD, turn the counsel of Ahithophel to folly!"[y]

David and Hushai. 32 When David reached the top, where men used to worship God, Hushai the Archite was there to meet him, with rent garments and dirt upon his head.[z] 33 David said to him: "If you come with me, you will be a burden to me. 34 But if you return to the city and say to Absalom, 'Let me be your servant, O king; I was formerly your father's servant, but now I will be yours,' you will undo for me the counsel of Ahithophel.[a] 35 You will have the priests Zadok and Abiathar there with you. If you hear anything from the royal palace, you shall report it to the priests Zadok and Abiathar, 36 who have there with them both Zadok's son Ahimaaz and Abiathar's son Jonathan. Through them you shall send on to me whatever you hear." 37 So David's friend Hushai went into the city of Jerusalem as Absalom was about to enter it.

CHAPTER 16

David and Ziba. 1 David had gone a little beyond the top when Ziba, the servant of Meribbaal, met him with saddled asses laden with two hundred loaves of bread, an ephah of cakes of pressed raisins, an ephah of summer fruits, and a skin of wine.[b] 2 The king said to Ziba, "What do you plan to do with these?" Ziba replied: "The asses are for the king's household to ride on. The bread and summer fruits are for your servants to eat, and the wine for those to drink who are weary in the desert." 3 Then the king said, "And where is your lord's son?" Ziba answered the king, "He is staying in Jerusalem, for he said, 'Now the Israelites will restore to me my father's kingdom.' "[c] 4 The king therefore said to Ziba, "So! Everything Meribbaal had is yours." Then Ziba said: "I pay you homage, my lord the king. May I find favor with you!"[d]

David and Shimei. 5 As David was approaching Bahurim, a man named Shimei, the son of Gera of the same clan as Saul's family, was coming out of the place, cursing as he came.[e] 6 He threw stones at David and at all the king's officers, even though all the soldiers, including the royal guard, were on David's right and on his left. 7 Shimei was saying as he cursed: "Away, away, you murderous and wicked man! 8 The LORD has requited you for all the bloodshed in the family of Saul,* in whose stead you became king, and the LORD has given over the kingdom to your son Absalom. And now you suffer ruin because you are a murderer." 9 Abishai, son of Zeruiah, said to

the king: "Why should this dead dog curse my lord the king? Let me go over, please, and lop off his head."[f] 10 But the king replied: "What business is it of mine or of yours, sons of Zeruiah, that he curses? Suppose the LORD has told him to curse David; who then will dare to say, 'Why are you doing this?' "[g] 11 Then the king said to Abishai and to all his servants: "If my own son, who came forth from my loins, is seeking my life, how much more might this Benjaminite do so? Let him alone and let him curse, for the LORD has told him to.[h] 12 Perhaps the LORD will look upon my affliction and make it up to me with benefits for the curses he is uttering this day." 13 David and his men continued on the road, while Shimei kept abreast of them on the hillside, all the while cursing and throwing stones and dirt as he went.[i] 14 The king and all the soldiers with him arrived at the Jordan tired out, and stopped there for a rest.

Absalom's Counselors. 15 In the meantime Absalom, accompanied by Ahithophel, entered Jerusalem with all the Israelites. 16 When David's friend Hushai the Archite came to Absalom, he said to him: "Long live the king! Long live the king!"[j] 17 But Absalom asked Hushai: "Is this your devotion to your friend? Why did you not go with your friend?" 18 Hushai replied to Absalom: "On the contrary, I am his whom the LORD and all this people and all Israel have chosen, and with him I will stay. 19 Furthermore, as I was in attendance upon your father, so will I be before you. Whom should I serve, if not his son?"[k] 20 Then Absalom said to Ahithophel, "Offer your counsel on what we should do." 21 Ahithophel replied to Absalom: "Have relations with your father's concubines, whom he left behind to take care of the palace. When all Israel hears how odious you have made yourself to your father, all your partisans will take courage."[l] 22 So a tent was pitched on the roof for Absalom, and he visited his father's concubines in view of all Israel.[m]

Counsel of Ahithophel. 23 Now the counsel given by Ahithophel at that time was as though one had sought divine revelation. Such

z 2 Sm 16, 16.
a 2 Sm 16, 19.
b 2 Sm 4, 4; 9, 1-13; 19, 18. 25.
c 2 Sm 19, 26f.
d 2 Sm 19, 30.
e 2 Sm 3, 16; 19, 17. 22f; 1 Kgs 2, 8.
f 2 Sm 19, 23. 29; 1 Sm 24, 15; 26, 6.
g 2 Sm 15, 25f; 19, 23.
h 2 Sm 12, 11.
i 2 Sm 19, 19-24.
j 2 Sm 15, 32-37.
k 2 Sm 15, 34.
l 2 Sm 15, 16; 20, 3.
m 2 Sm 12, 11f.
n 2 Sm 15, 12. 31; 17, 23.

* 16, 8: Bloodshed . . . Saul: refers to the episode recounted in 2 Sm 21, 1–14.

was all his counsel both to David and to Absalom.[n]

CHAPTER 17

1 Ahithophel went on to say to Absalom: "Please let me choose twelve thousand men, and be off in pursuit of David tonight. **2** If I come upon him when he is weary and discouraged, I shall cause him to panic. When all the people with him flee, I shall strike down the king alone. **3** Then I can bring back the rest of the people to you, as a bride returns to her husband. It is the death of only one man you are seeking; then all the people will be at peace." **4** This plan was agreeable to Absalom and to all the elders of Israel.

Counsel of Hushai. **5** Then Absalom said, "Now call Hushai the Archite also; let us hear what he too has to say." **6** When Hushai came to Absalom, Absalom said to him: "This is what Ahithophel proposed. Shall we follow his proposal? If not, speak up." **7** Hushai replied to Absalom, "This time Ahithophel has not given good counsel." **8** And he went on to say: "You know that your father and his men are warriors, and that they are as fierce as a bear in the wild robbed of her cubs. Moreover, since your father is skilled in warfare, he will not spend the night with the people.[o] **9** Even now he lies hidden in one of the caves or in some other place. And if some of our soldiers should fall at the first attack, whoever hears of it will say, 'Absalom's followers have been slaughtered.' **10** Then even the brave man with the heart of a lion will lose courage. For all Israel knows that your father is a warrior and that those who are with him are brave.

11 "This is what I counsel: Let all Israel from Dan to Beer-sheba, who are as numerous as the sands by the sea, be called up for combat; and go with them yourself. **12** We can then attack him wherever we find him, settling down upon him as dew alights on the ground. None shall survive—neither he nor any of his followers. **13** And if he retires into a city, all Israel shall bring ropes to that city and we can drag it into the gorge, so that not even a pebble of it can be found." **14** Then Absalom and all the Israelites pronounced the counsel of Hushai the Archite better than that of Ahithophel. For the LORD had decided to undo Ahithophel's good counsel, in order thus to bring Absalom to ruin.[p]

David Told of the Plan. **15** Then Hushai said to the priests Zadok and Abiathar: "This is the counsel Ahithophel gave Absalom and the elders of Israel, and this is what I counseled. **16** So send a warning to David immediately, not to spend the night at the fords near the desert, but to cross over without fail. Otherwise

the king and all the people with him will be destroyed." **17** Now Jonathan and Ahimaaz were staying at En-rogel, since they could not risk being seen entering the city. A maidservant was to come with information for them, and they in turn were to go and report to King David. **18** But an attendant saw them and informed Absalom. They sped on their way and reached the house of a man in Bahurim who had a cistern in his courtyard. They let themselves down into this, **19** and the housewife took the cover and spread it over the cistern, strewing ground grain on the cover so that nothing could be noticed. **20** When Absalom's servants came to the woman at the house, they asked, "Where are Ahimaaz and Jonathan?" The woman replied, "They went by a short while ago toward the water." They searched, but found no one, and so returned to Jerusalem. **21** As soon as they left, Ahimaaz and Jonathan came up out of the cistern and went on to inform King David. They said to him: "Leave! Cross the water at once, for Ahithophel has given the following counsel in regard to you." **22** So David and all his people moved on and crossed the Jordan. By daybreak, there was no one left who had not crossed.

23 When Ahithophel saw that his counsel was not acted upon, he saddled his ass and departed, going to his home in his own city. Then, having left orders concerning his family, he hanged himself. And so he died and was buried in his father's tomb.[q]

24 Now David had gone to Mahanaim when Absalom crossed the Jordan accompanied by all the Israelites. **25** Absalom had put Amasa in command of the army in Joab's place. Amasa was the son of an Ishmaelite named Ithra, who had married Abigail, daughter of Jesse and sister of Joab's mother Zeruiah.[r] **26** Israel and Absalom encamped in the territory of Gilead.

27 When David came to Mahanaim, Shobi, son of Nahash from Rabbah of the Ammonites, Machir, son of Ammiel from Lodebar, and Barzillai, the Gileadite from Rogelim,[s] **28** brought couches, coverlets, basins and earthenware, as well as wheat, barley, flour, roasted grain, beans, lentils,[t] **29** honey, butter and cheese from the flocks and herds, for David and those who were with him to eat; for they said, "The people have been hungry and tired and thirsty in the desert."

CHAPTER 18

Preparation for Battle. **1** After mustering the troops he had with him, David placed offi-

o Hos 13, 8.
p 2 Sm 15, 31.
q 2 Sm 15, 31; 16, 23.
r 2 Sm 19, 14; 20, 4-13.
s 2 Sm 9, 4; 19, 32;
　1 Kgs 2, 7.
t 2 Sm 19, 32; Ezr 2, 61.

cers in command of groups of a thousand and groups of a hundred. **2** David then put a third part of the soldiers under Joab's command, a third under command of Abishai, son of Zeruiah and brother of Joab, and a third under command of Ittai the Gittite. The king then said to the soldiers, "I intend to go out with you myself." **3** But they replied: "You must not come out with us. For if we should flee, we shall not count; even if half of us should die, we shall not count. You are equal to ten thousand of us. Therefore it is better that we have you to help us from the city." **4** So the king said to them, "I will do what you think best"; and he stood by the gate as all the soldiers marched out in units of a hundred and of a thousand. **5** But the king gave this command to Joab, Abishai and Ittai: "Be gentle with young Absalom for my sake." All the soldiers heard the king instruct the various leaders with regard to Absalom.

Defeat of Absalom.
6 David's army then took the field against Israel, and a battle was fought in the forest near Mahanaim. **7** The forces of Israel were defeated by David's servants, and the casualties there that day were heavy—twenty thousand men. **8** The battle spread out over that entire region, and the thickets consumed more combatants that day than did the sword.

Death of Absalom.
9 Absalom unexpectedly came up against David's servants. He was mounted on a mule, and, as the mule passed under the branches of a large terebinth, his hair caught fast in the tree. He hung between heaven and earth while the mule he had been riding ran off. **10** Someone saw this and reported to Joab that he had seen Absalom hanging from a terebinth. **11** Joab said to his informant: "If you saw him, why did you not strike him to the ground on the spot? Then it would have been my duty to give you fifty pieces of silver and a belt." **12** But the man replied to Joab: "Even if I already held a thousand pieces of silver in my two hands, I would not harm the king's son, for the king charged you and Abishai and Ittai in our hearing to protect the youth Absalom for his sake. **13** Had I been disloyal and killed him, the whole matter would have come to the attention of the king, and you would stand aloof." **14** Joab replied, "I will not waste time with you in this way." And taking three pikes in hand, he thrust for the heart of Absalom, still hanging from the tree alive.[u] **15** Next, ten of Joab's young armor-bearers closed in on Absalom, and killed him with further blows. **16** Joab then sounded the horn, and the soldiers turned back from the pursuit of the Israelites, because Joab called on them to halt.[v] **17** Absalom was taken up and cast into a deep pit in the forest,

and a very large mound of stones was erected over him. And all the Israelites fled to their own tents.[w] **18** During his lifetime Absalom had taken a pillar and erected it for himself in the King's Valley, for he said, "I have no son to perpetuate my name." The pillar which he named for himself is called Yad-abshalom to the present day.[x]

David Told of Absalom's Death.
19 Then Ahimaaz, son of Zadok, said, "Let me run to take the good news to the king that the LORD has set him free from the grasp of his enemies." **20** But Joab said to him: "You are not the man to bring the news today. On some other day you may take the good news, but today you would not be bringing good news, for in fact the king's son is dead." **21** Then Joab said to a Cushite, "Go, tell the king what you have seen." The Cushite bowed to Joab and sped away. **22** But Ahimaaz, son of Zadok, said to Joab again, "Come what may, permit me also to run after the Cushite." Joab replied: "Why do you want to run, my son? You will receive no reward." **23** But he insisted, "Come what may, I want to run." Joab said to him, "Very well." Ahimaaz sped off by way of the Jordan plain and outran the Cushite.

24 Now David was sitting between the two gates, and a lookout mounted to the roof of the gate above the city wall, where he looked about and saw a man running all alone. **25** The lookout shouted to inform the king, who said, "If he is alone, he has good news to report." As he kept coming nearer, **26** the lookout spied another runner. From his place atop the gate he cried out, "There is another man running by himself." And the king responded, "He, too, is bringing good news." **27** Then the lookout said, "I notice that the first one runs like Ahimaaz, son of Zadok." The king replied, "He is a good man; he comes with good news."[y] **28** Then Ahimaaz called out and greeted the king. With face to the ground he paid homage to the king and said, "Blessed be the LORD your God, who has delivered up the men who rebelled against my lord the king." **29** But the king asked, "Is the youth Absalom safe?" And Ahimaaz replied, "I saw a great disturbance when the king's servant Joab sent your servant on, but I do not know what it was." **30** The king said, "Step aside and remain in attendance here." So he stepped aside and remained there. **31** When the Cushite came in, he said, "Let my lord the king receive the good news that this day the LORD has taken your part, freeing you from the grasp of all who rebelled against you." **32** But the king asked the Cushite, "Is young

u 2 Sm 12, 10; 13, 28f.
v 2 Sm 20, 23-26.
w Jos 7, 26; 8, 29; 10,

27.
x 2 Sm 14, 27.
y 2 Kgs 9, 20.

Absalom safe?'' The Cushite replied, ''May the enemies of my lord the king and all who rebel against you with evil intent be as that young man!''

CHAPTER 19

1 The king was shaken, and went up to the room over the city gate to weep. He said as he wept, ''My son Absalom! My son, my son Absalom! If only I had died instead of you, Absalom, my son, my son!''

Joab Reproves David. 2 Joab was told that the king was weeping and mourning for Absalom; 3 and that day's victory was turned into mourning for the whole army when they heard that the king was grieving for his son. 4 The soldiers stole into the city that day like men shamed by flight in battle. 5 Meanwhile the king covered his face and cried out in a loud voice, ''My son Absalom! Absalom! My son, my son!''z 6 Then Joab went to his residence and said: ''Though they saved your life and your sons' and daughters' lives, also the lives of your wives and those of your concubines, you have put all your servants to shame today 7 by loving those who hate you and hating those who love you. For you have shown today that officers and servants mean nothing to you. Indeed I am now certain that if Absalom were alive today and all of us dead, you would think that more suitable. 8 Now then, get up! Go out and speak kindly to your servants. I swear by the LORD that if you do not go out, not a single man will remain with you overnight, and this will be a far greater disaster for you than any that has afflicted you from your youth until now.'' 9 So the king stepped out and sat at the gate. When all the people were informed that the king was sitting at the gate, they came into his presence.

The Reconciliation. Now the Israelites had fled to their separate tents, 10 but throughout the tribes of Israel all the people were arguing among themselves, saying to one another: ''The king delivered us from the clutches of our enemies, and it was he who rescued us from the grip of the Philistines. But now he has fled from the country before Absalom, 11 and Absalom, whom we anointed over us, died in battle. Why, then, should you remain silent about restoring the king to his palace?'' When the talk of all Israel reached the king, 12 David sent word to the priests Zadok and Abiathar: ''Say to the elders of Judah: 'Why should you be last to restore the king to his palace? 13 You are my brothers, you are my bone and flesh. Why should you be last to restore the king?' 14 Also say to Amasa: 'Are you not my bone and flesh? May God do thus and so to me, if you do not become my general permanently in place of

Joab.' ''a 15 He won over all the Judahites as one man, and so they summoned the king to return, with all his servants.

David and Shimei. 16 When the king, on his return, reached the Jordan, Judah had come to Gilgal to meet him and to escort him across the Jordan. 17 Shimei, son of Gera, the Benjaminite from Bahurim, hurried down with the Judahites to meet King David,b 18 accompanied by a thousand men from Benjamin. Ziba, too, the servant of the house of Saul, accompanied by his fifteen sons and twenty servants, hastened to the Jordan before the king.c 19 dThey crossed over the ford to bring the king's household over and to do whatever he wished. When Shimei, son of Gera, crossed the Jordan, he fell down before the king 20 and said to him: ''May my lord not hold me guilty, and may he not remember and take to heart the wrong that your servant did the day my lord the king left Jerusalem. 21 For your servant knows that he has done wrong. Yet realize that I have been the first of the whole house of Joseph to come down today to meet my lord the king.'' 22 But Abishai, son of Zeruiah, countered: ''Shimei must be put to death for this. He cursed the LORD's anointed.'' 23 David replied: ''What has come between you and me, sons of Zeruiah, that you would create enmity for me this day? Should anyone die today in Israel? Am I not aware that today I am king of Israel?''e 24 Then the king said to Shimei, ''You shall not die.'' And the king gave him his oath.

David and Meribbaal. 25 Meribbaal, son of Saul, also went down to meet the king. He had not washed his feet nor trimmed his mustache nor washed his clothes from the day the king left until he returned safely. 26 When he came from Jerusalem to meet the king, the king asked him, ''Why did you not go with me, Meribbaal?''f 27 He replied: ''My lord the king, my servant betrayed me. For your servant, who is lame, said to him, 'Saddle the ass for me, that I may ride on it and go with the king.'g 28 But he slandered your servant before my lord the king. But my lord the king is like an angel of God. Do what you judge best. 29 For though my father's entire house deserved only death from my lord the king, yet you placed your servant among the guests at your table. What right do I still have to make further appeal to the king?''h 30 But the king said to him: ''Why do you go on talking? I say, 'You and

---

z 2 Sm 15, 30.
a 2 Sm 17, 25; 20, 4.
b 2 Sm 16, 5-13.
c 2 Sm 16, 1-4; 19, 25-31.
d 19ff: 2 Sm 16, 13; Ex 22, 27; 1 Kgs 2, 8.
e 2 Sm 16, 9f; 1 Sm 11, 13; 1 Kgs 2, 8. 38. 46.
f 2 Sm 16, 3.
g 2 Sm 9, 2-13; Dt 21, 12f.
h 2 Sm 9, 9ff.
i 2 Sm 16, 4.

Ziba shall divide the property.' '' *i* **31** Meribb-aal answered the king, "Indeed let him have it all, now that my lord the king has returned safely to his palace."

David and Barzillai. **32** Barzillai the Gile-adite also came down from Rogelim and escort-ed the king to the Jordan for his crossing, taking leave of him there. *j* **33** It was Barzillai, a very old man of eighty and very wealthy besides, who had provisioned the king during his stay in Mahanaim. **34** The king said to Barzillai, "Cross over with me, and I will provide for your old age as my guest in Jerusalem." **35** But Barzillai answered the king: "How much longer have I to live, that I should go up to Jerusalem with the king? **36** I am now eighty years old. Can I distinguish between good and bad? Can your servant taste what he eats and drinks, or still appreciate the voices of singers and song-stresses? Why should your servant be any fur-ther burden to my lord the king? **37** In escorting the king across the Jordan, your servant is doing little enough! Why should the king give me this reward? **38** Please let your servant go back to die in his own city by the tomb of his father and mother. Here is your servant Chimham. Let him cross over with my lord the king. Do for him whatever you will." **39** Then the king said to him, "Chimham shall come over with me, and I will do for him as you would wish. And any-thing else you would like me to do for you, I will do." **40** Then all the people crossed over the Jordan, but the king remained; he kissed Barzil-lai and bade him Godspeed as he returned to his own district. **41** Finally the king crossed over to Gilgal, accompanied by Chimham.

Israel and Judah Quarrel. All the people of Judah and half of the people of Israel had escorted the king across. **42** But all these Israel-ites began coming to the king and saying, "Why did our brothers the Judahites steal you away and escort the king and his household across the Jordan, along with all David's men?" **43** All the Judahites replied to the men of Israel: "Be-cause the king is our relative. Why are you angry over this affair? Have we had anything to eat at the king's expense? Or have portions from his table been given to us?" **44** The Israelites answered the Judahites: "We have ten shares in the king. Also, we are the first-born rather than you. Why do you slight us? Were we not first to speak of restoring the king?" Then the Judah-ites in turn spoke even more fiercely than the Israelites. *k*

CHAPTER 20

Sheba's Rebellion. **1** Now a rebellious in-dividual from Benjamin named Sheba, the son of Bichri, happened to be there. He sounded the horn and cried out,

> "We have no portion in David,
>> nor any share in the son of Jesse.
> Every man to his tent, O Israel!" *l*

2 So all the Israelites left David for Sheba, son of Bichri. But from the Jordan to Jerusalem the Judahites remained loyal to their king. **3** When King David came to his palace in Jerusalem, he took the ten concubines whom he had left be-hind to take care of the palace and placed them in confinement. He provided for them, but had no further relations with them. And so they remained in confinement to the day of their death, lifelong widows. *m*

Amasa's Death. **4** Then the king said to Amasa: "Summon the Judahites for me within three days. Then present yourself here." *n* **5** Accordingly Amasa set out to summon Ju-dah, but delayed beyond the time set for him by David. **6** Then David said to Abishai: "Sheba, son of Bichri, may now do us more harm than Absalom did. Take your lord's servants and pursue him, lest he find fortified cities and take shelter while we look on." **7** So Joab and the Cherethites and Pelethites and all the warriors marched out behind Abishai from Jerusalem to campaign in pursuit of Sheba, son of Bichri. *o* **8** *They were at the great stone in Gibeon when Amasa met them. Now Joab had a belt over his tunic, from which was slung, in its sheath near his thigh, a sword that could be drawn with a downward movement. *p* **9** And Joab asked Am-asa, "How are you, my brother?" With his right hand Joab held Amasa's beard as if to kiss him. **10** And since Amasa was not on his guard against the sword in Joab's other hand, Joab stabbed him in the abdomen with it, so that his entrails burst forth to the ground, and he died without receiving a second thrust. Then Joab and his brother Abishai pursued Sheba, son of Bichri. *q* **11** One of Joab's attendants stood by Amasa and said, "Let him who favors Joab and is for David follow Joab." **12** Amasa lay cov-ered with blood in the middle of the highroad, and the man noticed that all the soldiers were stopping. So he removed Amasa from the road to the field and placed a garment over him, because all who came up to him were stopping. **13** When he had been removed from the road, everyone went on after Joab in pursuit of Sheba, son of Bichri.

j 2 Sm 17, 27ff; 1 Kgs 2,   n 2 Sm 17, 25; 19, 14.
    7; Ezr 2, 61.   o 2 Sm 8, 18.
k 1 Kgs 11, 31.   p 2 Sm 2, 13.
l 1 Kgs 12, 16.   q 1 Kgs 2, 5.
m 2 Sm 15, 16; 16, 20ff.

*

20, 8: The text of this verse is quite uncertain.

Joab Pursues Sheba. 14 Sheba passed through all the tribes of Israel to Abel Beth-maacah. Then all the Bichrites assembled and they too entered the city after him. 15 So David's servants came and besieged him in Abel Beth-maacah. They threw up a mound against the city, and all the soldiers who were with Joab began battering the wall to throw it down. 16 Then a wise woman from the city stood on the outworks and called out, "Listen, listen! Tell Joab to come here, that I may speak with him." 17 When Joab had come near her, the woman said, "Are you Joab?" And he replied, "Yes." She said to him, "Listen to what your maidservant has to say." He replied, "I am listening." 18 Then she went on to say: "There is an ancient saying,* 'Let them ask if they will in Abel'[r] 19 or in Dan whether loyalty is finished or ended in Israel.' You are seeking to beat down a city that is a mother in Israel. Why do you wish to destroy the inheritance of the LORD?" 20 Joab answered, "Not at all, not at all! I do not wish to destroy or to ruin anything. 21 That is not the case at all. A man named Sheba, son of Bichri, from the hill country of Ephraim has rebelled against King David. Surrender him alone, and I will withdraw from the city." Then the woman said to Joab, "His head shall be thrown to you across the wall." 22 She went to all the people with her advice, and they cut off the head of Sheba, son of Bichri, and threw it out to Joab. He then sounded the horn, and they scattered from the city to their own tents, while Joab returned to Jerusalem to the king.

David's Officials. 23 Joab was in command of the whole army of Israel. Banaiah, son of Jehoiada, was in command of the Cherethites and Pelethites.[s] 24 Adoram was in charge of the forced labor. Jehoshaphat, son of Ahilud, was the chancellor. 25 Shawsha was the scribe. Zadok and Abiathar were priests.[t] 26 Ira the Jairite was also David's priest.

V: APPENDIXES

CHAPTER 21

Gibeonite Vengeance. 1 During David's reign there was a famine for three successive years. David had recourse to the LORD, who said, "There is bloodguilt on Saul and his family because he put the Gibeonites to death."[u] 2 So the king called the Gibeonites and spoke to them. (Now the Gibeonites were not Israelites, but survivors of the Amorites; and although the Israelites had given them their oath, Saul had attempted to kill them off in his zeal for the men of Israel and Judah.)[v] 3 David said to the Gibeonites, "What must I do for you and how

must I make atonement, that you may bless the inheritance of the LORD?" 4 The Gibeonites answered him, "We have no claim against Saul and his house for silver or gold, nor is it our place to put any man to death in Israel." Then he said, "I will do for you whatever you propose." 5 They said to the king, "As for the man who was exterminating us and who intended to destroy us that we might have no place in all the territory of Israel, 6 let seven men from among his descendants be given to us, that we may dismember them before the LORD in Gibeon, on the LORD's mountain." The king replied, "I will give them up." 7 The king, however, spared Meribbaal, son of Jonathan, son of Saul, because of the LORD's oath that formed a bond between David and Saul's son Jonathan.[w] 8 But the king took Armoni and Meribbaal, the two sons that Aiah's daughter Rizpah had borne to Saul, and the five sons of Saul's daughter Merob that she had borne to Adriel, son of Barzillai the Meholathite,[x] 9 and surrendered them to the Gibeonites. They then dismembered them on the mountain before the LORD. The seven fell at the one time; they were put to death during the first days of the harvest—that is, at the beginning of the barley harvest.

10 Then Rizpah, Aiah's daughter, took sackcloth and spread it out for herself on the rock from the beginning of the harvest until rain came down on them from the sky, fending off the birds of the sky from settling on them by day, and the wild animals by night.[y] 11 When David was informed of what Rizpah, Aiah's daughter, the concubine of Saul, had done, 12 he went and obtained the bones of Saul and of his son Jonathan from the citizens of Jabesh-gilead, who had carried them off secretly from the public square of Beth-shan, where the Philistines had hanged them at the time they killed Saul on Gilboa.[z] 13 When he had brought up from there the bones of Saul and of his son Jonathan, the bones of those who had been dismembered were also gathered up. 14 Then the bones of Saul and of his son Jonathan were buried in the tomb of his father Kish at Zela in the territory of Benjamin. After all that the king commanded had been carried out, God granted relief to the land.[a]

Exploits in Philistine Wars. 15 There was another battle between the Philistines and Israel. David went down with his servants and

---

r Gn 49, 16.
s 2 Sm 8, 16ff; 23, 20.
t 2 Sm 8, 17f.
u 2 Sm 24, 13.
v Jos 9, 3-27.
w 2 Sm 9, 13; 1 Sm 18,

3; 20, 8ff. 15f. 42.
x 2 Sm 3, 7.
y 2 Sm 3, 31; 12, 16.
z 1 Sm 31, 10-13.
a 2 Sm 24, 25.

*

20, 18f: The proverbial expression here has been poorly transmitted, and its sense is doubtful.

fought the Philistines, but David grew tired. **16** Dadu, one of the Rephaim, whose bronze spear weighed three hundred shekels, was about to take him captive. Dadu was girt with a new sword and planned to kill David, **17** but Abishai, son of Zeruiah, came to his assistance and struck and killed the Philistine. Then David's men swore to him, "You must not go out to battle with us again, lest you quench the lamp of Israel."[b]

18 [c]After this there was another battle with the Philistines in Gob. On that occasion Sibbecai, from Husha, killed Saph, one of the Rephaim.[d] **19** [e]There was another battle with the Philistines in Gob, in which Elhanan, son of Jair from Bethlehem, killed Goliath of Gath, who had a spear with a shaft like a weaver's heddle-bar. **20** There was another battle at Gath in which there was a man of large stature with six fingers on each hand and six toes on each foot—twenty-four in all. He too was one of the Rephaim. **21** And when he insulted Israel, Jonathan, son of David's brother Shimei, killed him.[f] **22** These four were Rephaim in Gath, and they fell at the hands of David and his servants.

CHAPTER 22

Song of Thanksgiving.*

1 David sang the words of this song to the LORD when the LORD had rescued him from the grasp of all his enemies and from the hand of Saul.[g] **2** This is what he sang:[h]

A

I

"O LORD, my rock, my fortress, my
    deliverer,
3 my God, my rock of refuge!
My shield, the horn of my salvation,*
    my stronghold, my refuge,
    my savior, from violence you keep me
    safe.[i]
4 'Praised be the LORD,' I exclaim,
    and I am safe from my enemies.

II

5 "The breakers of death surged round about
    me,*
    the floods of perdition overwhelmed me;
6 The cords of the nether world enmeshed me,
    the snares of death overtook me.
7 In my distress I called upon the LORD
    and cried out to my God;
From his temple* he heard my voice,
    and my cry reached his ears.

III

8 "The earth swayed and quaked;*

    the foundations of the heavens trembled
    and shook when his wrath flared up.
9 Smoke rose from his nostrils,
    and a devouring fire from his mouth;
    he kindled coals into flame.
10 He inclined the heavens and came down,
    with dark clouds under his feet.[j]
11 He mounted a cherub* and flew,
    borne on the wings of the wind.[k]
12 He made darkness the shelter about him,
    with spattering rain and thickening clouds.
13 From the brightness of his presence
    coals were kindled to flame.

14 "The LORD thundered from heaven;
    the Most High gave forth his voice.
15 He sent forth arrows to put them to flight;
    he flashed lightning and routed them.[l]
16 Then the wellsprings of the sea appeared,
    the foundations of the earth were laid
    bare,
At the rebuke of the LORD,
    at the blast of the wind of his wrath.

17 "He reached out from on high and grasped
    me;
    he drew me out of the deep waters.[m]
18 He rescued me from my mighty enemy,
    from my foes, who were too powerful for
    me.
19 They attacked me on my day of calamity,
    but the LORD came to my support.

---

b 1 Kgs 11, 36; 15, 4;
   2 Kgs 8, 19.
c 18-22: 1 Chr 20, 4-8.
d 2 Sm 23, 27.
e 19f: 1 Sm 17, 4. 7.
f 2 Sm 13, 3.
g Ps 18, 1.
h 2-51: Ps 18, 3-51.
i 1 Sm 2, 1f.
j Ps 144, 5.
k Ex 25, 1ff.
l Ps 144, 6.
m Ps 144, 7.

22, 1–51: This song of thanksgiving is also given, with a few small variants, in Ps 18. In both places it is attributed to David. Two main sections can be distinguished. In the first part, after an introductory stanza of praise to God (2–4), David describes the peril he was in (5–7), and then poetically depicts, under the form of a theophany, God's intervention in his behalf (8–20), concluding with an acknowledgment of God's justice (21–31). In the second part, God is praised for having prepared the psalmist for war (32–35), given him victory over his enemies (36–39), whom he put to flight (40–43), and bestowed on him dominion over many peoples (44–46). The entire song ends with paean of grateful praise (47–51).

22, 3: The horn of my salvation: my strong savior. The horn, the dreadful weapon of an enraged bull, was a symbol of strength; cf Lk 1, 69.

22, 5f: These verses are to be understood figuratively.

22, 7: His temple: his heavenly abode.

22, 8ff: God's intervention is graphically portrayed under the figures of an earthquake (vv 8. 16) and a thunderstorm (vv 9–15); cf Jgs 5, 4f; Pss 29; 97, 2–6; Hb 3.

22, 11: He mounted a cherub: since God makes the winds his messengers, or "angels" (Ps 104, 4), he is spoken of poetically as riding on the clouds, or on the angelic creatures called "cherubim." His earthly throne above the ark of the covenant was likewise associated with two winged cherubim; cf Ex 37, 7ff. In both senses the Lord is enthroned upon the cherubim; cf Pss 79, 2; 99, 1.

20 He set me free in the open,
    and rescued me, because he loves me.

IV

21 "The LORD rewarded me according to my
    justice;
    according to the cleanness of my hands he
    requited me.
22 For I kept the ways of the LORD
    and was not disloyal to my God.
23 For his ordinances were all present to me,
    and his statutes I put not from me;
24 But I was wholehearted toward him,
    and I was on my guard against guilt.
25 And the LORD requited me according to my
    justice,
    according to my innocence in his sight.

26 n"Toward the faithful you are faithful;*
    toward the wholehearted you are
    wholehearted;
27 Toward the sincere you are sincere;
    but toward the crooked you are astute.
28 You save lowly people,
    though on the lofty your eyes look down.
29 You are my lamp,* O LORD!
    O my God, you brighten the darkness
    about me.
30 For with your aid I run against an armed
    band,
    and by the help of my God I leap over a
    wall.
31 God's way is unerring;
    the promise of the LORD is fire-tried;
    he is a shield to all who take refuge in
    him."o

B

I

32 "For who is God except the LORD?
    Who is a rock save our God?
33 The God who girded me with strength
    and kept my way unerring;
34 Who made my feet swift as those of hinds
    and set me on the heights;*
35 Who trained my hands for war
    till my arms could bend a bow of brass.

II

36 "You have given me your saving shield,
    and your help has made me great.
37 You made room for my steps;
    unwavering was my stride.
38 I pursued my enemies and destroyed them,
    nor did I turn again till I made an end of
    them.
39 I smote them and they did not rise;
    they fell beneath my feet.

III

40 "You girded me with strength for war;

    you subdued my adversaries beneath me.
41 My enemies you put to flight before me
    and those who hated me I destroyed.
42 They cried for help—but no one saved them;
    to the LORD—but he answered them not.
43 I ground them fine as the dust of the earth;
    like the mud in the streets I trampled
    them down.

IV

44 "You rescued me from the strife of my
    people;
    you made me head over nations.
    A people I had not known became my
    slaves;
45 as soon as they heard me, they obeyed.
46 The foreigners fawned and cringed before
    me;
    they staggered forth from their
    fortresses."

C

47 "The LORD live! And blessed be my Rock!
    Extolled be my God, Rock of my
    salvation.
48 O God, who granted me vengeance,
    who made peoples subject to me
49 and helped me escape from my enemies,
    Above my adversaries you exalt me
    and from the violent man you rescue me.
50 Therefore will I proclaim you, O LORD,
    among the nations,
    and I will sing praise to your name,p
51 You who gave great victories to your king
    and showed kindness to your anointed,
    to David and his posterity forever."

CHAPTER 23

The Last Words of David*

1 These are the last words of David:
    "The utterance of David, son of Jesse;
    the utterance of the man God raised up,
    Anointed of the God of Jacob,
    favorite of the Mighty One of Israel.q
2 The spirit of the LORD spoke through me;
    his word was on my tongue.r
3 The God of Israel spoke;
    of me the Rock of Israel said,
    'He that rules over men in justice,

---

n 26f: 1 Sm 2, 30.   q 1 Kgs 2, 3-9; Sir 47, 8.
o Prv 30, 5.   r Is 59, 21; Jer 1, 9.
p Ps 22, 23; Rom 15, 9.   s Ps 72, 1-4.

*

22, 26f: Men are treated by God in the same way they treat
him and their fellow men.

22, 29: My lamp: a figure of life and happiness; cf 1 Kgs 11,
36.

22, 34: The heights: a natural stronghold safe from attack;
cf Ps 62, 3; Hb 3, 19.

23, 1–7: The text of this short composition in the spirit of
the wisdom writers (Prv 30, 1–6) is difficult in places; it views
David's career in retrospect.

that rules in the fear of God,[s].
4 Is like the morning light at sunrise
    on a cloudless morning,
    making the greensward sparkle after
      rain.'[t]
5 Is not my house firm before God?
    He has made an eternal covenant with me,
      set forth in detail and secured.[u]
    Will he not bring to fruition
      all my salvation and my every desire?
6 But the wicked are all like thorns to be cast
    away;
      they cannot be taken up by hand.[v]
7 He who wishes to touch them
    must arm himself with iron and the shaft
      of a spear,
    and they must be consumed by fire.''

David's Warriors.   **8** These are the names of David's warriors.* Ishbaal, son of Hachamoni, was the first of the Three. It was he who brandished his battle-ax over eight hundred slain in a single encounter.[w] **9** Next to him, among the Three warriors, was Eleazar, son of Dodo the Ahohite. He was with David at Ephesdammim when the Philistines assembled there for battle. The Israelites had retreated,[x] **10** but he stood his ground and fought the Philistines until his hand grew tired and became cramped, holding fast to the sword. The LORD brought about a great victory on that day; the soldiers turned back after Eleazar, but only to strip the slain. **11** Next to him was Shammah, son of Agee the Hararite. The Philistines had assembled at Lehi, where there was a plot of land full of lentils. When the soldiers fled from the Philistines,[y] **12** he took his stand in the middle of the plot and defended it. He slew the Philistines, and the LORD brought about a great victory. Such were the deeds of the Three warriors.

13 During the harvest three of the Thirty went down to David in the cave of Adullam, while a Philistine clan was encamped in the Vale of Rephaim.[z] **14** At that time David was in the refuge, and there was a garrison of Philistines in Bethlehem. **15** Now David had a strong craving and said, "Oh, that someone would give me a drink of water from the cistern that is by the gate of Bethlehem!" **16** So the Three warriors broke through the Philistine camp and drew water from the cistern that is by the gate of Bethlehem. But when they brought it to David he refused to drink it, and instead poured it out to the LORD, **17** saying: "The LORD forbid that I do this! Can I drink the blood of these men who went at the risk of their lives?" So he refused to drink it.

18 Abishai, brother of Joab, son of Zeruiah, was at the head of the Thirty. It was he who brandished his spear over three hundred slain. He was listed among the Thirty **19** and commanded greater respect than the Thirty, becom-

ing their leader. However, he did not attain to the Three.

20 Benaiah, son of Jehoiada, a stalwart from Kabzeel, was a man of great achievements. It was he who slew the two lions in Moab. He also went down and killed the lion in the cistern at the time of the snow.[a] **21** It was he, too, who slew an Egyptian of large stature. Although the Egyptian was armed with a spear, he went against him with a club and wrested the spear from the Egyptian's hand, then killed him with his own spear. **22** Such were the deeds performed by Benaiah, son of Jehoiada. He was listed among the Thirty warriors **23** and commanded greater respect than the Thirty. However, he did not attain to the Three. David put him in command of his bodyguard.[b] **24** Asahel,* brother of Joab. . . .[c]

Among the Thirty were: Elhanan, son of Dodo, from Bethlehem; **25** Shammah from En-harod; Elika from En-harod; **26** Helez from Beth-pelet; Ira, son of Ikkesh, from Tekoa; **27** Abiezer from Anathoth; Sibbekai from Hushah;[d] **28** Zalmon from Ahoh; Maharai from Netophah; **29** Heled, son of Baanath, from Netophah; Ittai, son of Ribai, from Gibeah of the Benjaminites; **30** Benaiah from Pirathon; Hiddai from Nahale-gaash; **31** Abibaal from Beth-arabah; Azmaveth from Bahurim; **32** Eliahba from Shaalbon; Jashen the Gunite; Jonathan, **33** son of Shammah the Hararite; Ahiam, son of Sharar the Hararite; **34** Eliphelet, son of Ahasbai, from Beth-maacah; Eliam, son of Ahithophel, from Gilo; **35** Hezrai from Carmel; Paarai the Arbite; **36** Igal, son of Nathan, from Zobah; Bani the Gadite; **37** Zelek the Ammonite; Naharai from Beeroth, armor-bearer of Joab, son of Zeruiah; **38** Ira from Jattir; Gareb from Jattir; **39** Uriah the Hittite—thirty-seven in all.[e]

---

t Jgs 5, 31; Ps 72, 6.
u 2 Sm 7, 11. 15f; Ps
  89, 30; Is 55, 3.
v Dt 13, 14.
w 8-39: 1 Chr 11, 41; 27,
  1-15.
x 1 Sm 17, 1.
y Jgs 15, 9.

z 1 Sm 22, 1; Mi 1, 15.
a 2 Sm 8, 18; 20, 23;
  Jgs 14, 6; 1 Kgs 2,
  29f.
b 1 Sm 22, 14.
c 2 Sm 2, 18-23.
d 2 Sm 21, 18.
e 2 Sm 11, 3f.

*

23, 8ff: There are thirty-seven warriors in all mentioned in this list. First there are the Three warriors most noted for singlehanded exploits (vv 8–12). Then comes the story of a daring adventure by three unnamed members of the larger group (vv 13–17). Next come the commanders of the king's bodyguard, Abishai (vv 18–19) and Benaiah (vv 20–23), with whom must be counted Asahel (v 24) and Joab (vv 18. 24. 37), and finally the group of the Thirty (vv 24–39).

23, 24: A more complete notice about Asahel, who died early in his career (2 Sm 2, 16–23), is to be presumed lost at this point. Elhanan is the first of the Thirty.

CHAPTER 24

Census of the People. 1 *The LORD's anger against Israel flared again,*f* and he incited David against the Israelites by prompting him to number Israel and Judah. 2 Accordingly the king said to Joab and the leaders of the army who were with him, "Tour all the tribes in Israel from Dan to Beer-sheba and register the people, that I may know their number." 3 But Joab said to the king: "May the LORD your God increase the number of people a hundredfold for your royal majesty to see it with his own eyes. But why does it please my lord the king to order a thing of this kind?" 4 The king, however, overruled Joab and the leaders of the army, so they left the king's presence in order to register the people of Israel. 5 Crossing the Jordan, they began near Aroer, south of the city in the wadi, and went in the direction of Gad, toward Jazer. 6 They continued on to Gilead and to the district below Mount Hermon. Then they proceeded to Dan; from there they turned toward Sidon, 7 going to the fortress of Tyre and to all the cities of the Hivites and Canaanites, and ending up at Beer-sheba in the Negeb of Judah. 8 Thus they toured the whole country, reaching Jerusalem again after nine months and twenty days. 9 Joab then reported to the king the number of people registered: in Israel, eight hundred thousand men fit for military service; in Judah, five hundred thousand.

The Pestilence. 10 Afterward, however, David regretted having numbered the people, and said to the LORD: "I have sinned grievously in what I have done.*g* But now, LORD, forgive the guilt of your servant, for I have been very foolish."* 11 When David rose in the morning, the LORD had spoken to the prophet Gad, David's seer, saying: 12 "Go and say to David, 'This is what the LORD says: I offer you three alternatives; choose one of them, and I will inflict it on you.' " 13 Gad then went to David to inform him. He asked: "Do you want a three years' famine to come upon your land, or to flee from your enemy three months while he pursues you, or to have a three days' pestilence in your land? Now consider and decide what I must reply to him who sent me."*h* 14 David answered Gad: "I am in very serious difficulty. Let us fall by the hand of God, for he is most merciful; but let me not fall by the hand of man." 15 Thus David chose the pestilence. Now it was the time of the wheat harvest when the plague broke out among the people. [The LORD then sent a pestilence over Israel from morning until the time appointed, and seventy thousand of the people from Dan to Beer-sheba died.] 16 But when the angel stretched forth his hand toward Jerusalem to destroy it, the LORD

regretted the calamity and said to the angel causing the destruction among the people, "Enough now! Stay your hand." The angel of the LORD was then standing at the threshing floor of Araunah the Jebusite.*i* 17 When David saw the angel who was striking the people, he said to the LORD: "It is I who have sinned; it is I, the shepherd, who have done wrong. But these are sheep; what have they done? Punish me and my kindred."*

Sacrifice of Atonement. 18 On the same day Gad went to David and said to him, "Go up and build an altar to the LORD on the threshing floor of Araunah the Jebusite." 19 Following Gad's bidding, David went up as the LORD had commanded. 20 Now Araunah looked down and noticed the king and his servants coming toward him while he was threshing wheat. So he went out and paid homage to the king, with face to the ground. 21 Then Araunah asked, "Why does my lord the king come to his servant?" David replied, "To buy the threshing floor from you, to build an altar to the LORD, that the plague may be checked among the people." 22 *j*But Araunah said to David: "Let my lord the king take and offer up whatever he may wish. Here are oxen for holocausts, and threshing sledges and the yokes of the oxen for wood. 23 All this does Araunah give to the king." Araunah then said to the king, "May the LORD your God accept your offering." 24 The king, however, replied to Araunah, "No, I must pay you for it, for I cannot offer to the LORD my God holocausts that cost nothing." So David bought the threshing floor and the oxen for fifty silver shekels. 25 Then David built an altar there to the LORD, and offered holocausts and peace offerings. The LORD granted relief to the country, and the plague was checked in Israel.

---

f 1-25: 1 Chr 21, 1-27.
g 1 Sm 24, 6; 1 Chr 21, 7.
h 2 Sm 21, 1.
i Ex 12, 23; 2 Kgs 19, 35.
j 22f: 1 Sm 6, 14; 1 Kgs 19, 21.

*

24, 1ff: This story was probably joined at one time to 2 Sm 21, 1–14.

24, 10: The narrative supposes that since the people belonged to the Lord rather than to the king, only the Lord should know their exact number.

24, 17: Before this verse a Qumran manuscript (4Q Sam*a*) gives the fuller text of 1 Chr 21, 16, an alternative to the words "When David saw the angel who was striking the people."

The Books of

KINGS

The two Books of Kings were originally, like 1 and 2 Samuel, a single historical work. In conjunction with the Books of Samuel, they extend the consecutive history of Israel from the birth of Samuel to the destruction of Jerusalem in 587 B.C. This combined work is designed as a religious history; hence in Kings the temple, which is the chosen site for the worship of Yahweh, occupies the center of attention.

The Books of Kings show clearly the theological bent of a Deuteronomic editor. In them, as already in Judges, material from various sources, such as the "book of the acts of Solomon" (1 Kgs 11, 41) and the "book of the chronicles of the kings of Israel" (1 Kgs 14, 19), is forged into structural unity by an editor whose principal interest is in the fidelity to Yahweh of rulers and people. The reigns of individual kings are adapted to an editorial framework consisting of a presentation and an obituary notice for each, in stereotyped formulas. In between, the achievements of the king are reported—above all, his fidelity or lack of fidelity to Yahweh. The faithful prosper; the unfaithful pay for their defections. Since this is basically a narrative of sin and retribution, it would not be inappropriate to entitle the Books of Kings "The Rise and Fall of the Israelite Monarchy."

Without minimizing the complexity of the process by which this material was transmitted for many centuries, one may speak of two editions of the Books: the first at some time between 621 B.C. and 597 B.C. and the second, final edition during the Exile; probably shortly after Jehoiachin was released from his Babylonian Prison (561 B.C.)

1 Kings carries the history of Israel from the last days and death of David to the accession in Samaria of Ahaziah, son of Ahab, near the end of the reign of Jehoshaphat, king of Judah. Judgment is passed on Ahaziah's reign but the details are given only later, in 2 Kings. We should note the two large cycles of traditions which grew up around the great prophetic figures of Elijah and Elisha, the former in 1 Kings and the latter chiefly in 2 Kings. These cycles, which interrupt the sequence of regnal chronicles, were very probably preserved and transmitted by the prophetic communities to which there are references in the same traditions. The Elijah cycle is the more important since it dramatically underscores Israel's critical struggle with the religion of Canaan.

The principal divisions of the Books of Kings are:
  I. The Reign of Solomon (1 Kgs 1, 1–11, 43).
  II. Judah and Israel to the Time of Ahab (1 Kgs 12, 1–16, 34).
  III. Stories of the Prophets (1 Kgs 17, 1–22, 54).
  IV. The Kingdoms of Israel and Judah (2 Kgs 1, 1–17, 41).
  V. The Kingdom of Judah after 721 B.C. (2 Kgs 18, 1–25, 30).

THE FIRST BOOK OF KINGS

I: The Reign of Solomon

CHAPTER 1

1 When King David was old and advanced in years, though they spread covers over him he could not keep warm. **2** His servants therefore said to him, "Let a young virgin be sought to attend you, lord king, and to nurse you. If she sleeps with your royal majesty, you will be kept warm." **3** So they sought for a beautiful girl throughout the territory of Israel, and found Abishag the Shunamite, whom they brought to the king. **4** The maiden, who was very beautiful, nursed the king and cared for him, but the king did not have relations with her.

Ambition of Adonijah.   **5** Adonijah, son of Haggith, began to display his ambition to be king. He acquired chariots, drivers, and fifty henchmen. **6** Yet his father never rebuked him or asked why he was doing this. Adonijah was also very handsome, and next in age to Absalom by the same mother. **7** He conferred with Joab, son of Zeruiah, and with Abiathar the priest, and they supported him. **8** However, Zadok the priest, Benaiah, son of Jehoiada, Nathan the prophet, and Shimei and his companions, the pick of David's army, did not side with Adonijah. **9** When he slaughtered sheep, oxen, and fatlings at the stone Zoheleth, near En-rogel,* Adonijah invited all his brothers, the king's sons, and all the royal officials of Judah. **10** But he did not invite the prophet Nathan, or Benaiah, or the pick of the army, or his brother Solomon.

Solomon Proclaimed King. **11** Then Nathan said to Bathsheba, Solomon's mother: "Have you not heard that Adonijah, son of Haggith, has become king without the knowledge of our lord David? **12** Come now, let me advise you so that you may save your life and that of your son Solomon. **13** Go, visit King David, and say to him, 'Did you not, lord king, swear to your handmaid: Your son Solomon shall be king after me and shall sit upon my throne? Why, then, has Adonijah become king?' **14** And while you are still there speaking to the king, I will come in after you and confirm what you have said."

15 So Bathsheba visited the king in his room, while Abishag the Shunamite was attending him because of his advanced age. **16** Bathsheba bowed in homage to the king, who said to her, "What do you wish?" **17** She answered him: "My lord, you swore to me your handmaid by the LORD, your God, that my son Solomon should reign after you and sit upon your throne. **18** But now Adonijah has become king, and you, my lord king, do not know it. **19** He has slaughtered oxen, fatlings, and sheep in great numbers; he has invited all the king's sons, Abiathar the priest, and Joab, the general of the army, but not your servant Solomon. **20** Now, my lord king, all Israel is waiting for you to make known to them who is to sit on the throne after your royal majesty.* **21** If this is not done, when my lord the king sleeps with his fathers, I and my son Solomon will be considered criminals."

22 While she was still speaking to the king, the prophet Nathan came in. **23** When he had been announced, the prophet entered the king's presence and, bowing to the floor, did him homage. **24** Then Nathan said: "Have you decided, my lord king, that Adonijah is to reign after you and sit on your throne? **25** He went down today and slaughtered oxen, fatlings, and sheep in great numbers; he invited all the king's sons, the commanders of the army, and Abiathar the priest, and they are eating and drinking in his company and saying, 'Long live King Adoni-

jah!' **26** But me, your servant, he did not invite; nor Zadok the priest, nor Benaiah, son of Jehoiada, nor your servant Solomon. **27** Was this done by my royal master's order without my being told who was to succeed to your majesty's kingly throne?"

28 King David answered, "Call Bathsheba here." When she re-entered the king's presence and stood before him, **29** the king swore, "As the LORD lives, who has delivered me from all distress, **30** this very day I will fulfill the oath I swore to you by the LORD, the God of Israel, that your son Solomon should reign after me and should sit upon my throne in my place." **31** Bowing to the floor in homage to the king, Bathsheba said, "May my lord, King David, live forever!" **32** Then King David summoned Zadok the priest, Nathan the prophet, and Benaiah, son of Jehoiada. When they had entered the king's presence, **33** he said to them: "Take with you the royal attendants. Mount my son Solomon upon my own mule and escort him down to Gihon. **34** There Zadok the priest and Nathan the prophet are to anoint him king of Israel, and you shall blow the horn and cry, 'Long live King Solomon!' **35** When you come back in his train, he is to go and sit upon my throne and reign in my place. I designate him ruler of Israel and of Judah." **36** In answer to the king, Benaiah, son of Jehoiada, said: "So be it! May the LORD, the God of my lord the king, so decree! **37** As the LORD has been with your royal majesty, so may he be with Solomon, and exalt his throne even more than that of my lord, King David!"

38 So Zadok the priest, Nathan the prophet, Benaiah, son of Jehoiada, and the Cherethites and Pelethites* went down, and mounting Solomon on King David's mule, escorted him to Gihon. **39** Then Zadok the priest took the horn of oil from the tent and anointed Solomon. They blew the horn and all the people shouted, "Long live King Solomon!" **40** Then all the people went up after him, playing flutes and rejoicing so much as to split open the earth with their shouting.

41 Adonijah and all the guests who were with him heard it, just as they ended their banquet. When Joab heard the sound of the horn, he asked, "What does this uproar in the city mean?" **42** As he was speaking, Jonathan, son

*

1, 9: En-rogel: the modern Job's Well southeast of Jerusalem. It marked the ancient boundary between the tribes of Benjamin and Judah (Jos 15, 7; 18, 16). Here David's men sought information about Absalom's revolt (2 Sm 17, 17).

1, 20: At this time, neither law nor the right of primogeniture, but the will of the ruling monarch, determined succession to the throne.

1, 38: Cherethites and Pelethites: mercenaries in David's bodyguard. They became part of his retinue after he defeated the Philistines and established himself in Jerusalem; cf 2 Sm 8, 18; 15, 18; 20, 23.

of Abiathar the priest, arrived. "Come," said Adonijah, "you are a man of worth and must bring good news." **43** "On the contrary!" Jonathan answered him. "Our lord, King David, has made Solomon king. **44** The king sent with him Zadok the priest, Nathan the prophet, Benaiah, son of Jehoiada, and the Cherethites and Pelethites, and they mounted him upon the king's own mule. **45** Zadok the priest and Nathan the prophet anointed him king at Gihon, and they went up from there rejoicing, so that the city is in an uproar. That is the noise you heard. **46** Besides, Solomon took his seat on the royal throne, **47** and the king's servants went in and paid their respects to our lord, King David, saying, 'May God make Solomon more famous than you and exalt his throne more than your own!' And the king in his bed worshiped God, **48** and this is what he said: 'Blessed be the LORD, the God of Israel, who has this day seated one of my sons upon my throne, so that I see it with my own eyes.'"

49 All the guests of Adonijah left in terror, each going his own way. **50** Adonijah, in fear of Solomon, also left; he went and seized the horns of the altar.* **51** It was reported to Solomon that Adonijah, in his fear of King Solomon, had seized the horns of the altar and said, "Let King Solomon first swear that he will not kill me, his servant, with the sword." **52** Solomon answered, "If he proves himself worthy, not a hair shall fall from his head. But if he is found guilty of crime, he shall die." **53** King Solomon sent to have him brought down from the altar, and he came and paid homage to the king. Solomon then said to him, "Go to your home."

CHAPTER 2

David's Last Instructions and Death.

1 When the time of David's death drew near,* he gave these instructions to his son Solomon: **2** "I am going the way of all mankind. Take courage and be a man. **3** Keep the mandate of the Lord, your God, following his ways and observing his statutes, commands, ordinances, and decrees as they are written in the law of Moses, that you may succeed in whatever you do, wherever you turn,*a* **4** and the LORD may fulfill the promise he made on my behalf when he said, 'If your sons so conduct themselves that they remain faithful to me with their whole heart and with their whole soul, you shall always have someone of your line on the throne of Israel.'*b* **5** You yourself know what Joab, son of Zeruiah, did to me when he slew the two generals of Israel's armies, Abner, son of Ner, and Amasa, son of Jether. He took revenge for the blood of war in a time of peace, and put blood shed without provocation on the belt about my waist

and on the sandal on my foot.*c* **6** Act with the wisdom you possess; you must not allow him to go down to the grave in peaceful old age.

7 "But be kind to the sons of Barzillai the Gileadite, and have them eat at your table. For they received me kindly when I was fleeing your brother Absalom.*d*

8 "You also have with you Shimei, son of Gera, the Benjaminite of Bahurim, who cursed me balefully when I was going to Mahanaim. Because he came down to meet me at the Jordan, I swore to him by the LORD that I would not put him to the sword.*e* **9** But you must not let him go unpunished. You are a prudent man and will know how to deal with him to send down his hoary head in blood to the grave."

10 David rested with his ancestors and was buried in the City of David.*f* **11** The length of David's reign over Israel was forty years: he reigned seven years in Hebron and thirty-three years in Jerusalem.*g*

The Kingdom Made Secure. **12** When Solomon was seated on the throne of his father David, with his sovereignty firmly established, **13** Adonijah, son of Haggith, went to Bathsheba, the mother of Solomon. "Do you come as a friend?" she asked. "Yes," he answered, **14** and added, "I have something to say to you." She replied, "Say it." **15** So he said: "You know that the kingdom was mine, and all Israel expected me to be king. But the kingdom escaped me and became my brother's, for the LORD gave it to him. **16** But now there is one favor I would ask of you. Do not refuse me." And she said, "Speak on." **17** He said, "Please ask King Solomon, who will not refuse you, to give me Abishag the Shunamite for my wife."* **18** "Very well," replied Bathsheba, "I will speak to the king for you."

19 Then Bathsheba went to King Solomon to speak to him for Adonijah, and the king stood

---

a Dt 17, 19.
b 2 Sm 7, 11-16; Ps 132, 11f.
c 2 Sm 3, 27; 20, 10.
d 2 Sm 19, 33ff.
e 2 Sm 16, 5; 19, 19.
f Acts 2, 29.
g 1 Chr 29, 27.

*

1, 50: Horns of the altar: the protuberances on each of the four corners of the altar were surrounded with a special degree of holiness (Ex 27, 2; 29, 12), and constituted a place of asylum for transgressors of the law (Ex 21, 13f; 1 Kgs 2, 28).

2, 1-6. 8-9: Solomon is expected to remove from his father's family the imputation of blood guilt brought upon it by Joab in the unwarranted killings of Abner (2 Sm 3, 27-29) and Amasa (2 Sm 19, 9-10); and likewise to punish Shimei for his curse, the effects of which David had pledged himself not to avenge in person (2 Sm 19, 21-23). The standards of morality presumed in these verses are far from the Christian ones.

2, 17. 22-25: Abishag had been the concubine of King David (1 Kgs 1, 4). His successor, Solomon, inherited his father's harem. When Adonijah requested Abishag as his wife, he was subtly undermining the security of Solomon's throne and exposing himself to the suspicion of insurrection that would cost him his life; cf 2 Sm 3, 6-11; 16, 22.

up to meet her and paid her homage. Then he sat down upon his throne, and a throne was provided for the king's mother, who sat at his right. 20 "There is one small favor I would ask of you," she said. "Do not refuse me." "Ask it, my mother," the king said to her, "for I will not refuse you." 21 So she said, "Let Abishag the Shunamite be given to your brother Adonijah for his wife." 22 "And why do you ask Abishag the Shunamite for Adonijah?" King Solomon answered his mother. "Ask the kingdom for him as well, for he is my elder brother and has with him Abiathar the priest and Joab, son of Zeruiah." 23 And King Solomon swore by the LORD: "May God do thus and so to me, and more besides, if Adonijah has not proposed this at the cost of his life. 24 And now, as the LORD lives, who has seated me firmly on the throne of my father David and made of me a dynasty as he promised, this day shall Adonijah be put to death." 25 Then King Solomon sent Benaiah, son of Jehoiada, who struck him dead.

26 The king said to Abiathar the priest: "Go to your land in Anathoth. Though you deserve to die, I will not put you to death this time, because you carried the ark of the Lord GOD before my father David and shared in all the hardships my father endured." 27 So Solomon deposed Abiathar from his office of priest of the LORD, thus fulfilling the prophecy which the LORD had made in Shiloh about the house of Eli. *h*

28 When the news came to Joab, who had sided with Adonijah, though not with Absalom, he fled to the tent of the LORD and seized the horns of the altar. 29 King Solomon was told that Joab had fled to the tent of the LORD and was at the altar. He sent Benaiah, son of Jehoiada, with the order, "Go, strike him down." 30 Benaiah went to the tent of the LORD and said to him, "The king says, 'Come out.'" But he answered, "No! I will die here." Benaiah reported to the king, "This is what Joab said to me in reply." 31 The king answered him: "Do as he has said. Strike him down and bury him, and you will remove from me and from my family the blood which Joab shed without provocation. 32 The LORD will hold him responsible for his own blood, because he struck down two men better and more just than himself, and slew them with the sword without my father David's knowledge: Abner, son of Ner, general of Israel's army, and Amasa, son of Jether, general of Judah's army. *i* 33 Joab and his descendants shall be responsible forever for their blood. But there shall be the peace of the LORD forever for David, and his descendants, and his house, and his throne." 34 Benaiah, son of Jehoiada, went back, struck him down and killed him; he was buried in his house in the desert. 35 The king appointed Benaiah, son of

Jehoiada, over the army in his place, and put Zadok the priest in place of Abiathar.

36 Then the king summoned Shimei and said to him: "Build yourself a house in Jerusalem and live there. Do not go anywhere else. 37 For if you leave, and cross the Kidron Valley, be certain you shall die without fail. You shall be responsible for your own blood." 38 Shimei answered the king: "I accept. Your servant will do just as the king's majesty has said." So Shimei stayed in Jerusalem for a long time. 39 But three years later, two of Shimei's servants ran away to Achish, son of Maacah, king of Gath, and Shimei was informed that his servants were in Gath. 40 So Shimei rose, saddled his ass, and went to Achish in Gath in search of his servants, whom he brought back. 41 When Solomon was informed that Shimei had gone from Jerusalem to Gath, and had returned, 42 the king summoned Shimei and said to him: "Did I not have you swear by the LORD to your clear understanding of my warning that, if you left and went anywhere else, you should die without fail? And you answered, 'I accept and obey.' 43 Why, then, have you not kept the oath of the LORD and the command that I gave you?" 44 And the king said to Shimei: "You know in your heart the evil that you did to my father David. Now the LORD requites you for your own wickedness. 45 But King Solomon shall be blessed, and David's throne shall endure before the LORD forever." 46 The king then gave the order to Benaiah, son of Jehoiada, who struck him dead as he left.

CHAPTER 3

Wisdom of Solomon. 1 With the royal power firmly in his grasp, Solomon allied himself by marriage with Pharaoh, king of Egypt. The daughter of Pharaoh, whom he married, he brought to the City of David, until he should finish building his palace, and the temple of the LORD, and the wall around Jerusalem. *j*

2 However, the people were sacrificing on the high places, for up to that time no temple had been built to the name of the LORD. 3 Solomon loved the LORD, and obeyed the statutes of his father David; yet he offered sacrifice and burned incense on the high places.

4 The king went to Gibeon to sacrifice there, because that was the most renowned high place. Upon its altar Solomon offered a thousand holocausts. 5 In Gibeon the LORD appeared to Solomon in a dream at night. God said, "Ask something of me and I will give it to you." 6 Solomon answered: "You have shown great favor to your servant, my father David, because

---

h 1 Sm 2, 31.
i 2 Sm 3, 27; 20, 10.
j 1 Kgs 7, 8; 2 Chr 1, 1.

he behaved faithfully toward you, with justice and an upright heart; and you have continued this great favor toward him, even today, seating a son of his on his throne. **7** O Lord, my God, you have made me, your servant, king to succeed my father David; but I am a mere youth, not knowing at all how to act. **8** I serve you in the midst of the people whom you have chosen, a people so vast that it cannot be numbered or counted. **9** Give your servant, therefore, an understanding heart to judge your people and to distinguish right from wrong. For who is able to govern this vast people of yours?"*k*

10 The Lord was pleased that Solomon made this request. **11** So God said to him: "Because you have asked for this—not for a long life for yourself, nor for riches, nor for the life of your enemies, but for understanding so that you may know what is right— **12** I do as you requested. I give you a heart so wise and understanding that there has never been anyone like you up to now, and after you there will come no one to equal you. **13** In addition, I give you what you have not asked for, such riches and glory that among kings there is not your like.*l* **14** And if you follow me by keeping my statutes and commandments, as your father David did, I will give you a long life."

15 When Solomon awoke from his dream, he went to Jerusalem, stood before the ark of the covenant of the Lord, offered holocausts and peace offerings, and gave a banquet for all his servants.

Solomon's Judgment.

16 Later, two harlots came to the king and stood before him. **17** One woman said: "By your leave, my lord, this woman and I live in the same house, and I gave birth in the house while she was present. **18** On the third day after I gave birth, this woman also gave birth. We were alone in the house; there was no one there but us two. **19** This woman's son died during the night; she smothered him by lying on him. **20** Later that night she got up and took my son from my side, as I, your handmaid, was sleeping. Then she laid him in her bosom, after she had laid her dead child in my bosom. **21** I rose in the morning to nurse my child, and I found him dead. But when I examined him in the morning light, I saw it was not the son whom I had borne."

22 The other woman answered, "It is not so! The living one is my son, the dead one is yours." But the first kept saying, "No, the dead one is your child, the living one is mine!" Thus they argued before the king.

23 Then the king said: "One woman claims, 'This, the living one, is my child, and the dead one is yours.' The other answers, 'No! The dead one is your child; the living one is mine.'" **24** The king continued, "Get me a sword."

When they brought the sword before him, **25** he said, "Cut the living child in two, and give half to one woman and half to the other." **26** The woman whose son it was, in the anguish she felt for it, said to the king, "Please, my lord, give her the living child—please do not kill it!" The other, however, said, "It shall be neither mine nor yours. Divide it!" **27** The king then answered, "Give the first one the living child! By no means kill it, for she is the mother."

28 When all Israel heard the judgment the king had given, they were in awe of him, because they saw that the king had in him the wisdom of God for giving judgment.

CHAPTER 4

Chief Officers of the Kingdom.

1 Solomon was king over all Israel, **2** and these were the officials he had in his service:

Azariah, son of Zadok, priest;
3 Elihoreph and Ahijah, sons of Shisha, scribes;
Jehoshaphat, son of Ahilud, chancellor;
4 [Benaiah, son of Jehoiada, commander of the army;
Zadok and Abiathar, priests;]
5 Azariah, son of Nathan, chief of the commissaries;
Zabud, son of Nathan, companion to the king;
6 Ahishar, major-domo of the palace; and Adoniram, son of Abda, superintendent of the forced labor.

Solomon's Royal State.

7 *Solomon had twelve commissaries for all Israel who supplied food for the king and his household, each having to provide for one month in the year. **8** Their names were:

the son of Hur in the hill country of Ephraim;
9 the son of Deker in Makaz, Shaalbim, Beth-shemesh, Elon and Beth-hanan;
10 the son of Hesed in Arubboth, as well as in Socoh and the whole region of Hepher;
11 the son of Abinadab, who was married to Solomon's daughter Taphath, in all the Naphath-dor;
12 Baana, son of Ahilud, in Taanach and Megiddo, and beyond Jokmeam, and in all Bethshean, and in the country around Zarethan below Jezreel from Beth-shean to Abelmeholah;
13 the son of Geber in Ramoth-Gilead, having charge of the villages of Jair, son of

---

k 2 Chr 1, 10.   l Wis 7, 11; Mt 6, 29.

*

4, 7–19: The administration of the kingdom thus initiated by Solomon continued in its main features for the duration of the monarchy in Israel and Judah.

Manasseh, in Gilead; and of the district of Argob in Bashan—sixty large walled cities with gates barred with bronze; **14** Ahinadab, son of Iddo, in Mahanaim; **15** Ahimaaz, who was married to Basemath, another daughter of Solomon, in Naphtali; **16** Baana, son of Hushai, in Asher and along the rocky coast; **17** Jehoshaphat, son of Paruah, in Issachar; **18** Shimei, son of Ela, in Benjamin; **19** Geber, son of Uri, in the land of Gilead, the land of Sihon, king of the Amorites, and of Og, king of Bashan.

There was one prefect besides, in the king's own land.*

CHAPTER 5

7 These commissaries, one for each month, provided food for King Solomon and for all the guests at the royal table. They left nothing unprovided. **8** For the chariot horses and draft animals also, each brought his quota of barley and straw to the required place.

20 *Judah and Israel were as numerous as the sands by the sea; they ate and drank and made merry. **1** Solomon ruled over all the kingdoms from the River to the land of the Philistines, down to the border of Egypt; they paid Solomon tribute and were his vassals as long as he lived. _m_

2 Solomon's supplies for each day were thirty kors of fine flour, sixty kors of meal, **3** ten fatted oxen, twenty pasture-fed oxen, and a hundred sheep, not counting harts, gazelles, roebucks, and fatted fowl.

4 He ruled over all the land west of the Euphrates, from Tiphsah to Gaza, and over all its kings, and he had peace on all his borders round about. **5** Thus Judah and Israel lived in security, every man under his vine or under his fig tree from Dan to Beer-sheba, as long as Solomon lived.

6 Solomon had four thousand stalls for his twelve thousand chariot horses. _n_

9 _o_ Moreover, God gave Solomon wisdom and exceptional understanding and knowledge, as vast as the sand on the seashore. **10** Solomon surpassed all the Cedemites and all the Egyptians in wisdom. **11** He was wiser than all other men—than Ethan the Ezrahite, or Heman, Chalcol, and Darda, the musicians—and his fame spread throughout the neighboring nations. **12** Solomon also uttered three thousand proverbs, and his songs numbered a thousand and five. _p_ **13** He discussed plants, from the cedar on Lebanon to the hyssop growing out of the wall, and he spoke about beasts, birds, reptiles, and fishes. **14** Men came to hear Solomon's wisdom from all nations, sent by all the kings of the earth who had heard of his wisdom.

Preparations for the Temple. **15** When Hiram, king of Tyre, heard that Solomon had been anointed king in place of his father, he sent an embassy to him; for Hiram had always been David's friend. **16** Solomon sent back this message to Hiram: **17** "You know that my father David, because of the enemies surrounding him on all sides, could not build a temple in honor of the LORD, his God, until such a time as the LORD should put these enemies under the soles of his feet. **18** But now the LORD, my God, has given me peace on all sides. There is no enemy or threat of danger. **19** So I propose to build a temple in honor of the LORD, my God, as the LORD predicted to my father David when he said: 'It is your son whom I will put upon your throne in your place who shall build the temple in my honor.' _q_ **20** Give orders, then, to have cedars from the Lebanon cut down for me. My servants shall accompany yours, since you know that there is no one among us who is skilled in cutting timber like the Sidonians, and I will pay you whatever you say for your servants' salary."

21 When he had heard the words of Solomon, Hiram was pleased and said, "Blessed be the LORD this day, who has given David a wise son to rule this numerous people." **22** Hiram then sent word to Solomon, "I agree to the proposal you sent me, and I will provide all the cedars and fir trees you wish. **23** My servants shall bring them down from the Lebanon to the sea, and I will arrange them into rafts in the sea and bring them wherever you say. There I will break up the rafts, and you shall take the lumber. You, for your part, shall furnish the provisions I desire for my household."

24 So Hiram continued to provide Solomon with all the cedars and fir trees he wished; **25** while Solomon every year gave Hiram twenty thousand kors of wheat to provide for his household, and twenty thousand measures of pure oil. **26** The LORD, moreover, gave Solomon wisdom as he promised him, and there was peace between Hiram and Solomon, since they were parties to a treaty.

27 King Solomon conscripted thirty thousand workmen from all Israel. **28** He sent them to the Lebanon each month in relays of ten thousand, so that they spent one month in the Lebanon and two months at home. Adoniram

---

m Sir 47, 15f; 2 Chr 9, 26.
n 2 Chr 9, 25f.
o 9-14; Sir 47, 16f.

p 1 Kgs 3, 12.
q 2 Sm 7, 13; 1 Chr 22, 10.

*

4, 19: One prefect . . . in the king's own land: the royal territory of Judah had its own peculiar administration different from that of the twelve districts which had to supply the king and his household with a month's provisions of food each year (v 7).

5, 20: This verse belongs to ch 4.

was in charge of the draft. **29** Solomon had seventy thousand carriers and eighty thousand stonecutters in the mountain, **30** in addition to three thousand three hundred overseers, answerable to Solomon's prefects for the work, directing the people engaged in the work. **31** By order of the king, fine, large blocks were quarried to give the temple a foundation of hewn stone. **32** Solomon's and Hiram's builders, along with the Gebalites, hewed them out, and prepared the wood and stones for building the temple.

CHAPTER 6

Building of the Temple.   **1** In the four hundred and eightieth year from the departure of the Israelites from the land of Egypt, in the fourth year of Solomon's reign over Israel, in the month of Ziv, which is the second month, the construction of the temple of the LORD* was begun.ʳ

2 The temple which King Solomon built for the LORD was sixty cubits long, twenty wide, and twenty-five high. **3** The porch in front of the temple was twenty cubits from side to side, along the width of the nave, and ten cubits deep in front of the temple. **4** Splayed windows with trellises were made for the temple, **5** and adjoining the wall of the temple, which enclosed the nave and the sanctuary, an annex of several stories was built. **6** Its lowest story was five cubits wide, the middle one six cubits wide, the third seven cubits wide, because there were offsets along the outside of the temple so that the beams would not be fastened into the walls of the temple. **7** (The temple was built of stone dressed at the quarry, so that no hammer, axe, or iron tool was to be heard in the temple during its construction.) **8** The entrance to the lowest floor of the annex was at the right side of the temple, and stairs with intermediate landings led up to the middle story and from the middle story to the third. **9** When the temple was built to its full height, it was roofed in with rafters and boards of cedar. **10** The annex, with its lowest story five cubits high, was built all along the outside of the temple, to which it was joined by cedar beams.

11 This word of the LORD* came to Solomon: **12** "As to this temple you are building —if you observe my statutes, carry out my ordinances, keep and obey all my commands, I will fulfill toward you the promise I made to your father David.ˢ **13** ʲI will dwell in the midst of the Israelites and will not forsake my people Israel."

14 When Solomon finished building the temple, **15** its walls were lined from floor to ceiling beams with cedar paneling, and its floor was laid with fir planking. **16** At the rear of the temple a space of twenty cubits was set off by cedar partitions from the floor to the rafters, enclosing the sanctuary, the holy of holies. **17** The nave, or part of the temple in front of the sanctuary, was forty cubits long. **18** The cedar in the interior of the temple was carved in the form of gourds and open flowers; all was of cedar, and no stone was to be seen.

19 In the innermost part of the temple* was located the sanctuary to house the ark of the LORD's covenant, **20** twenty cubits long, twenty wide, and twenty high.* **21** Solomon overlaid the interior of the temple with pure gold. He made in front of the sanctuary a cedar altar, overlaid it with gold, and looped it with golden chains. **22** The entire temple was overlaid with gold so that it was completely covered with it; the whole altar before the sanctuary was also overlaid with gold. **23** In the sanctuary were two cherubim, each ten cubits high, made of olive wood. **24** Each wing of a cherub measured five cubits so that the space from wing tip to wing tip of each was ten cubits. **25** The cherubim were identical in size and shape, **26** and each was exactly ten cubits high. **27** The cherubim were placed in the inmost part of the temple, with their wings spread wide, so that one wing of each cherub touched a side wall while the other wing, pointing toward the middle of the room, touched the corresponding wing of the second cherub. **28** The cherubim, too, were overlaid with gold.

29 The walls on all sides of both the inner and the outer rooms had carved figures of cherubim, palm trees, and open flowers. **30** The floor of both the inner and the outer rooms was overlaid with gold. **31** At the entrance of the sanctuary, doors of olive wood were made; the

---

r 2 Chr 3, 1.   t 1 Chr 22, 9f.
s 2 Sm 7, 13.

6, 1: Construction of the temple of the Lord is here paralleled in importance with the founding of the nation after the departure from Egypt. In both, God is the central figure who chose Israel as his people, and now chooses the place where his temple should be built (Dt 12, 4–18. 26). The year is given in a round number, 480, which corresponds to twelve generations. The fourth year of Solomon's reign: c. 968 B.C.

6, 11ff: The word of the Lord . . . my people Israel: the oracle, which came as a climax at the completion of the work, was an expression of God's acceptance and approval. Nevertheless the fulfillment of God's promises to David and his royal descendants will depend on their observance of his ordinances and commands.

6, 19: The innermost part of the temple: the sanctuary or holy of holies reserved exclusively for the Lord. Here through his presence he dwelt as on a throne between the cherubim above the ark of the covenant (2 Kgs 6, 23–28; 2 Chr 3, 10–13). See note on Ex 25, 18ff.

6, 20: Twenty (cubits) high: it is usually supposed that the holy of holies was of this height because it had a raised floor, five cubits above the floor level of the nave, rather than a dropped ceiling. The building was twenty-five cubits high (v 2) according to the reading here followed.

doorframes had beveled posts. **32** The two doors were of olive wood, with carved figures of cherubim, palm trees, and open flowers. The doors were overlaid with gold, which was also molded to the cherubim and the palm trees. **33** The same was done at the entrance to the nave, where the doorposts of olive wood were rectangular. **34** The two doors were of fir wood; each door was banded by a metal strap, front and back, **35** and had carved cherubim, palm trees, and open flowers, over which gold was evenly applied.

36 The inner court was walled off by means of three courses of hewn stones and one course of cedar beams.

37 The foundations of the LORD's temple were laid in the month of Ziv **38** in the fourth year, and it was completed in all particulars, exactly according to plan, in the month of Bul, the eighth month, in the eleventh year. Thus it took Solomon seven years to build it.

CHAPTER 7

Building of the Palace.   **1** His own palace Solomon completed after thirteen years of construction.ᵘ **2** He built the hall called the Forest of Lebanon one hundred cubits long, fifty wide, and thirty high; it was supported by four rows of cedar columns, with cedar capitals upon the columns. **3** Moreover, it had a ceiling of cedar above the beams resting on the columns; these beams numbered forty-five, fifteen to a row. **4** There were three window frames at either end, with windows in strict alignment. **5** The posts of all the doorways were rectangular, and the doorways faced each other, three at either end. **6** The porch of the columned hall he made fifty cubits long and thirty wide. The porch extended the width of the columned hall, and there was a canopy in front. **7** He also built the vestibule of the throne where he gave judgment—that is, the tribunal; it was paneled with cedar from floor to ceiling beams. **8** His living quarters were in another court, set in deeper than the tribunal and of the same construction. A palace like this tribunal was built for Pharaoh's daughter, whom Solomon had married.ᵛ

9 All these buildings were of fine stones, hewn to size and trimmed front and back with a saw, from the foundation to the bonding course. **10** (The foundation was made of fine, large blocks, some ten cubits and some eight cubits. **11** Above were fine stones hewn to size, and cedar wood.) **12** The great court was enclosed by three courses of hewn stones and a bonding course of cedar beams. So also were the inner court of the temple of the LORD and the temple porch.

Furnishing of the Temple.   **13** King Solomon had Hiram brought from Tyre. **14** He was a bronze worker, the son of a widow from the tribe of Naphtali; his father had been from Tyre. He was endowed with skill, understanding, and knowledge of how to produce any work in bronze. He came to King Solomon and did all his metal work.

15 Two hollow bronze columns* were cast, each eighteen cubits high and twelve cubits in circumference; their metal was of four fingers' thickness.ʷ **16** There were also two capitals cast in bronze, to place on top of the columns, each of them five cubits high. **17** Two pieces of network with a chainlike mesh were made to cover the (nodes of the) capitals on top of the columns, one for each capital. **18** Four hundred pomegranates were also cast; two hundred of them in a double row encircled the piece of network on each of the two capitals. **19** The capitals on top of the columns were finished wholly in a lotus pattern **20** above the level of the nodes and their enveloping network. **21** The columns were then erected adjacent to the porch of the temple, one to the right, called Jachin, and the other to the left, called Boaz. **22** Thus the work on the columns was completed.

23 *The sea was then cast; it was made with a circular rim, and measured ten cubit across, five in height, and thirty in circumference.ˣ **24** Under the brim, gourds encircled it, ten to the cubit all the way around; the gourds were in two rows and were cast in one mold with the sea. **25** This rested on twelve oxen, three facing north, three facing west, three facing south, and three facing east, with their haunches all toward the center, where the sea was set upon them. **26** It was a handbreadth thick, and its brim resembled that of a cup, being lily-shaped. Its capacity was two thousand measures.

27 Ten stands were also made of bronze, each four cubits long, four wide, and three high. **28** When these stands were constructed, panels were set within the framework. **29** On the panels between the frames there were lions, oxen, and cherubim; and on the frames likewise, above and below the lions and oxen, there were wreaths in relief.

30 Each stand had four bronze wheels and bronze axles. **32** The four wheels were below the paneling, and the axle-trees of the wheels and the stand were of one piece. Each wheel was

---

u 1 Kgs 9, 10.   w Jer 52, 21.
v 1 Kgs 3, 1.   x 2 Chr 4, 2.

*

7, 15–21: The two hollow bronze columns, Jachin and Boaz (2 Chr 3, 17), stood free to the right and left of the temple porch. The names are related to God's power (Boaz) founding (Jachin) the temple and his people.

7, 23–26: The sea . . . rested on twelve oxen: this was a large circular tank containing about twelve thousand gallons of water.

a cubit and a half high. **33** The wheels were constructed like chariot wheels; their axles, fellies, spokes, and hubs were all cast.

The four legs of each stand had cast braces, which were under the basin; they had wreaths on each side. **34** These four braces, extending to the corners of each stand, were of one piece with the stand.

35 On top of the stand there was a raised collar half a cubit high, with supports and panels which were of one piece with the top of the stand. **31** This was surmounted by a crown one cubit high within which was a rounded opening to provide a receptacle a cubit and a half in depth. There was carved work at the opening, on panels that were angular, not curved. **36** On the surfaces of the supports and on the panels, wherever there was a clear space, cherubim, lions, and palm trees were carved, as well as wreaths all around. **37** This was how the ten stands were made, all of the same casting, the same size, the same shape. **38** Ten bronze basins were then made, each four cubits in diameter with a capacity of forty measures, one basin for the top of each of the ten stands. **39** The stands were placed, five on the south side of the temple and five on the north. The sea was placed off to the southeast from the south side of the temple.

40 When Hiram made the pots, shovels, and bowls, he therewith completed all his work for King Solomon in the temple of the LORD: **41** two columns, two nodes for the capitals on top of the columns, two pieces of network covering the nodes for the capitals on top of the columns, **42** four hundred pomegranates in double rows on both pieces of network that covered the two nodes of the capitals where they met the columns, **43** ten stands, ten basins on the stands, **44** one sea, twelve oxen supporting the sea, **45** pots, shovels, and bowls. All these articles which Hiram made for King Solomon in the temple of the LORD were of burnished bronze. **46** The king had them cast in the neighborhood of the Jordan, in the clayey ground between Succoth and Zarethan. **47** Solomon did not weigh all the articles because they were so numerous; the weight of the bronze, therefore, was not determined.

48 Solomon had all the articles made for the interior of the temple of the LORD: the golden altar; the golden table on which the showbread lay; **49** the lampstands of pure gold, five to the right and five to the left before the sanctuary, with their flowers, lamps, and tongs of gold; **50** basins, snuffers, bowls, cups, and fire pans of pure gold; and hinges of gold for the doors of the inner room, or holy of holies, and for the doors of the outer room, the nave.

51 When all the work undertaken by King Solomon in the temple of the LORD was completed, he brought in the dedicated offerings of his father David, putting the silver, gold, and other articles in the treasuries of the temple of the LORD.[y]

CHAPTER 8

Dedication of the Temple. **1** At the order of Solomon, the elders of Israel and all the leaders of the tribes, the princes in the ancestral houses of the Israelites, came to King Solomon in Jerusalem, to bring up the ark of the LORD's covenant from the City of David [which is Zion].[z] **2** All the men of Israel assembled before King Solomon during the festival in the month of Ethanim (the seventh month). **3** When all the elders of Israel had arrived, the priests took up the ark; **4** they carried the ark of the LORD and the meeting tent with all the sacred vessels that were in the tent. (The priests and Levites carried them.)

5 King Solomon and the entire community of Israel present for the occasion sacrificed before the ark sheep and oxen too many to number or count. **6** *The priests brought the ark of the covenant of the LORD to its place beneath the wings of the cherubim in the sanctuary, the holy of holies of the temple. **7** The cherubim had their wings spread out over the place of the ark, sheltering the ark and its poles from above. **8** The poles were so long that their ends could be seen from that part of the holy place adjoining the sanctuary; however, they could not be seen beyond. (They have remained there to this day.) **9** There was nothing in the ark but the two stone tablets which Moses had put there at Horeb, when the LORD made a covenant with the Israelites at their departure from the land of Egypt.[a]

10 When the priests left the holy place, the cloud filled the temple of the LORD **11** so that the priests could no longer minister because of the cloud, since the LORD's glory had filled the temple of the LORD. **12** Then Solomon said, "The LORD intends to dwell in the dark cloud;[b] **13** I have truly built you a princely house, a dwelling where you may abide forever."

14 The king turned and greeted the whole community of Israel as they stood. **15** He said to them: "Blessed be the LORD, the God of

---

y 2 Chr 5, 1.   a Ex 34, 27; Heb 9, 4.
z 2 Chr 5, 2.   b 2 Chr 6, 1.

*

8, 6–9: The transfer of the ark of the covenant into the newly constructed temple building, and the oracle of God's acceptance (1 Kgs 9, 3–9), and his act of possession (1 Kgs 8, 10–13), constituted the temple's solemn dedication, and made of it the abiding dwelling of God among his people for which David had hoped (2 Sm 6, 12–15; 7, 1–3). The concurrence of the feast of Booths marks an appropriate transition of God's dwelling among nomadic tribes to his permanent abode among a settled people.

Israel, who with his own mouth made a promise to my father David and by his hand has brought it to fulfillment. It was he who said, **16** 'Since the day I brought my people Israel out of Egypt, I have not chosen a city out of any tribe of Israel for the building of a temple to my honor; but I choose David to rule my people Israel.' **17** When my father David wished to build a temple to the honor of the LORD, the God of Israel,*c* **18** the Lord said to him, 'In wishing to build a temple to my honor, you do well. **19** It will not be you, however, who will build the temple; but the son who will spring from you, he shall build the temple to my honor.' **20** And now the LORD has fulfilled the promise that he made: I have succeeded my father David and sit on the throne of Israel, as the LORD foretold, and I have built this temple to honor the LORD, the God of Israel. **21** I have provided in it a place for the ark in which is the covenant of the LORD, which he made with our fathers when he brought them out of the land of Egypt.''

Solomon's Prayer. **22** Solomon stood before the altar of the LORD in the presence of the whole community of Israel, and stretching forth his hands toward heaven, **23** he said, ''LORD, God of Israel, there is no God like you in heaven above or on earth below; you keep your covenant of kindness with your servants who are faithful to you with their whole heart. **24** You have kept the promise you made to my father David, your servant. You who spoke that promise, have this day, by your own power, brought it to fulfillment. **25** Now, therefore, LORD, God of Israel, keep the further promise you made to my father David, your servant, saying, 'You shall always have someone from your line to sit before me on the throne of Israel, provided only that your descendants look to their conduct so that they live in my presence, as you have lived in my presence.'*d* **26** Now, LORD, God of Israel, may this promise which you made to my father David, your servant, be confirmed.

27 ''Can it indeed be that God dwells among men on earth? If the heavens and the highest heavens cannot contain you, how much less this temple which I have built! **28** Look kindly on the prayer and petition of your servant, O LORD, my God, and listen to the cry of supplication which I, your servant, utter before you this day. **29** May your eyes watch night and day over this temple, the place where you have decreed you shall be honored; may you heed the prayer which I, your servant, offer in this place. **30** Listen to the petitions of your servant and of your people Israel which they offer in this place. Listen from your heavenly dwelling and grant pardon.

31 ''If a man sins against his neighbor and is required to take an oath sanctioned by a curse, when he comes and takes the oath before your altar in this temple, **32** listen in heaven; take action and pass judgment on your servants. Condemn the wicked and punish him for his conduct, but acquit the just and establish his innocence.

33 *''If your people Israel sin against you and are defeated by an enemy, and if then they return to you, praise your name, pray to you, and entreat you in this temple, **34** listen in heaven and forgive the sin of your people Israel, and bring them back to the land you gave their fathers.

35 ''If the sky is closed, so that there is no rain, because they have sinned against you and you afflict them, and if then they repent of their sin, and pray, and praise your name in this place, **36** listen in heaven and forgive the sin of your servant and of your people Israel, teaching them the right way to live and sending rain upon this land of yours which you have given to your people as their heritage.

37 ''If there is famine in the land or pestilence; or if blight comes, or mildew, or a locust swarm, or devouring insects; if an enemy of your people besieges them in one of their cities; whatever plague or sickness there may be, **38** if then any one [of your entire people Israel] has remorse of conscience and offers some prayer or petition, stretching out his hands toward this temple, **39** listen from your heavenly dwelling place and forgive. You who alone know the hearts of all men, render to each one of them according to his conduct; knowing their hearts, so treat them **40** that they may fear you as long as they live on the land you gave our fathers.

41 ''To the foreigner, likewise, who is not of your people Israel, but comes from a distant land to honor you **42** (since men will learn of your great name and your mighty hand and your outstretched arm), when he comes and prays toward this temple, **43** listen from your heavenly dwelling. Do all that the foreigner asks of you, that all the peoples of the earth may know your name, may fear you as do your people Israel, and may acknowledge that this temple which I have built is dedicated to your honor.

44 ''Whatever the direction in which you may send your people forth to war against their enemies, if they pray to you, O LORD, toward the city you have chosen and the temple I have built in your honor, **45** listen in heaven to their prayer and petition, and defend their cause.

46 ''When they sin against you (for there is no man who does not sin), and in your anger

---

c 2 Sm 7, 5.   e 2 Chr 6, 36; Eccl 7, 20;
d 2 Sm 7, 12.   1 Jn 1, 8.
*

8, 33–34. 46–53: These references to deportation of Israelites to a hostile land are an expansion of Solomon's prayer dating from the Babylonian exile four centuries later.

against them you deliver them to the enemy, so that their captors deport them to a hostile land, far or near,*e* **47** may they repent in the land of their captivity and be converted. If then they entreat you in the land of their captors and say, 'We have sinned and done wrong; we have been wicked'; **48** if with their whole heart and soul they turn back to you in the land of the enemies who took them captive, pray to you toward the land you gave their fathers, the city you have chosen, and the temple I have built in your honor, **49** listen from your heavenly dwelling. **50** Forgive your people their sins and all the offenses they have committed against you, and grant them mercy before their captors, so that these will be merciful to them. **51** For they are your people and your inheritance, whom you brought out of Egypt, from the midst of an iron furnace.

52 "Thus may your eyes be open to the petition of your servant and to the petition of your people Israel. Hear them whenever they call upon you, **53** because you have set them apart among all the peoples of the earth for your inheritance, as you declared through your servant Moses when you brought our fathers out of Egypt, O Lord GOD."

54 When Solomon finished offering this entire prayer of petition to the LORD, he rose from before the altar of the LORD, where he had been kneeling with his hands outstretched toward heaven. **55** He stood and blessed the whole community of Israel, saying in a loud voice: **56** "Blessed be the LORD who has given rest to his people Israel, just as he promised. Not a single word has gone unfulfilled of the entire generous promise he made through his servant Moses. **57** May the LORD, our God, be with us as he was with our fathers and may he not forsake us nor cast us off. **58** May he draw our hearts to himself, that we may follow him in everything and keep the commands, statutes, and ordinances which he enjoined on our fathers. **59** May this prayer I have offered to the LORD, our God, be present to him day and night, that he may uphold the cause of his servant and of his people Israel as each day requires, **60** that all the peoples of the earth may know the LORD is God and there is no other. **61** You must be wholly devoted to the LORD, our God, observing his statutes and keeping his commandments, as on this day."

62 The king and all Israel with him offered sacrifices before the LORD. **63** Solomon offered as peace offerings to the LORD twenty-two thousand oxen and one hundred twenty thousand sheep. Thus the king and all the Israelites dedicated the temple of the LORD. **64** On that day the king consecrated the middle of the court facing the temple of the LORD; he offered there the holocausts, the cereal offerings, and the fat

of the peace offerings, because the bronze altar before the LORD was too small to hold these offerings.

65 On this occasion Solomon and all the Israelites, who had assembled in large numbers from Labo of Hamath to the wadi of Egypt, celebrated the festival before the LORD, our God, for seven days. **66** On the eighth day he dismissed the people, who bade the king farewell and went to their homes, rejoicing and happy over all the blessings the LORD had given to his servant David and to his people Israel.

CHAPTER 9

Promise and Warning to Solomon.

1 After Solomon finished building the temple of the LORD, the royal palace, and everything else that he had planned, **2** the LORD appeared to him a second time, as he had appeared to him in Gibeon.*f* **3** The LORD said to him: "I have heard the prayer of petition which you offered in my presence. I have consecrated this temple which you have built; I confer my name upon it forever, and my eyes and my heart shall be there always. **4** As for you, if you live in my presence as your father David lived, sincerely and uprightly, doing just as I have commanded you, keeping my statutes and decrees, **5** I will establish your throne of sovereignty over Israel forever, as I promised your father David when I said, 'You shall always have someone from your line on the throne of Israel.'*g* **6** But if you and your descendants ever withdraw from me, fail to keep the commandments and statutes which I set before you, and proceed to venerate and worship strange gods, **7** I will cut off Israel from the land I gave them and repudiate the temple I have consecrated to my honor. Israel shall become a proverb and a byword among all nations, **8** and this temple shall become a heap of ruins. Every passerby shall catch his breath in amazement, and ask, 'Why has the LORD done this to the land and to this temple?'*h* **9** Men will answer: 'They forsook the LORD, their God, who brought their fathers out of the land of Egypt; they adopted strange gods which they worshiped and served. That is why the LORD has brought down upon them all this evil.'"

Other Acts of the King.

10 After the twenty years during which Solomon built the two houses, the temple of the LORD and the palace of the king— **11** Hiram, king of Tyre, supplying Solomon with all the cedar wood, fir wood, and gold he wished—King Solomon gave Hiram twenty cities in the land of Galilee.

f 1 Kgs 3, 5; 11, 9; 2 Chr   g 2 Sm 7, 12-16.
  7, 12.   h Dt 29, 23; Jer 22, 8.

12 Hiram left Tyre to see the cities Solomon had given him, but was not satisfied with them. **13** So he said, "What are these cities you have given me, my brother?" And he called them the land of Cabul, as they are called to this day. **14** Hiram, however, had sent King Solomon one hundred and twenty talents of gold.*

15 This is an account of the forced labor which King Solomon levied in order to build the temple of the LORD, his palace, Millo,* the wall of Jerusalem, Hazor, Megiddo, Gezer **16** (Pharaoh king of Egypt, had come up and taken Gezer and, after destroying it by fire and slaying all the Canaanites living in the city, had given it as dowry to his daughter, Solomon's wife; **17** Solomon then rebuilt Gezer), Lower Beth-horon, **18** Baalath, Tamar in the desert of Judah, **19** all his cities for supplies, cities for chariots and for horses, and whatever else Solomon decided should be built in Jerusalem, in Lebanon, and in the entire land under his dominion. **20** All the non-Israelite people who remained in the land, descendants of the Amorites, Hittites, Perizzites, Hivites, and Jebusites **21** whose doom the Israelites had been unable to accomplish, Solomon conscripted as forced laborers, as they are to this day. **22** But Solomon enslaved none of the Israelites, for they were his fighting force, his ministers, commanders, adjutants, chariot officers, and charioteers. **23** The supervisors of Solomon's works who policed the people engaged in the work numbered five hundred and fifty.

24 As soon as Pharaoh's daughter went up from the City of David to her palace, which he had built for her, Solomon built Millo.

25 Three times a year Solomon used to offer holocausts and peace offerings on the altar which he had built to the LORD, and to burn incense before the LORD; and he kept the temple in repair.

26 King Solomon also built a fleet at Eziongeber, which is near Elath on the shore of the Red Sea in the land of Edom.* **27** In this fleet Hiram placed his own expert seamen with the servants of Solomon. **28** They went to Ophir, and brought back four hundred and twenty talents of gold to King Solomon.

CHAPTER 10

Visit of the Queen of Sheba.   **1** The queen of Sheba,* having heard of Solomon's fame, came to test him with subtle questions.[i] **2** She arrived in Jerusalem with a very numerous retinue, and with camels bearing spices, a large amount of gold, and precious stones. She came to Solomon and questioned him on every subject in which she was interested. **3** King Solomon explained everything she asked about,

and there remained nothing hidden from him that he could not explain to her.

4 When the queen of Sheba witnessed Solomon's great wisdom, the palace he had built, **5** the food at his table, the seating of his ministers, the attendance and garb of his waiters, his banquet service, and the holocausts he offered in the temple of the LORD, she was breathless. **6** "The report I heard in my country about your deeds and your wisdom is true," she told the king. **7** "Though I did not believe the report until I came and saw with my own eyes, I have discovered that they were not telling me the half. Your wisdom and prosperity surpass the report I heard. **8** Happy are your men, happy these servants of yours, who stand before you always and listen to your wisdom. **9** Blessed be the LORD, your God, whom it has pleased to place you on the throne of Israel. In his enduring love for Israel, the LORD has made you king to carry out judgment and justice." **10** Then she gave the king one hundred and twenty gold talents, a very large quantity of spices, and precious stones. Never again did anyone bring such an abundance of spices as the queen of Sheba gave to King Solomon.

11 Hiram's fleet, which used to bring gold from Ophir, also brought from there a large quantity of cabinet* wood and precious stones. **12** With the wood the king made supports for the temple of the LORD and for the palace of the king, and harps and lyres for the chanters. No more such wood was brought or seen to the present day.

13 King Solomon gave the queen of Sheba everything she desired and asked for, besides such presents as were given her from Solomon's royal bounty. Then she returned with her servants to her own country.

Solomon's Wealth.   **14** The gold that Solomon received every year weighed six hundred and sixty-six gold talents, **15** in addition to what came from the Tarshish fleet, from the traffic of merchants, and from all the kings of Arabia and the governors of the country.

---

i 2 Chr 9, 1; Mt 12, 42;   Lk 11, 31.

*

9, 14: One hundred and twenty talents of gold: approximately three million six hundred thousand dollars.

9, 15: Millo: probably means a filling, and may refer to an artificial earthwork or platform of stamped ground south of the temple area. It was begun by David (2 Sm 5, 9); cf 1 Kgs 9, 24; 11, 27.

9, 26: Ezion-geber . . . Edom: the first mention of maritime commerce in the Israelite kingdom (to which the land of Edom was subject after its conquest by King David; cf 2 Sm 8, 14).

10, 1: Queen of Sheba: women rulers among the Arabs are recorded in eighth-century-B.C. Assyrian inscriptions. Sheba was for centuries the leading principality in what is now the Yemen.

10, 11f: Cabinet: an unknown wood, probably fragrant.

16 Moreover, King Solomon made two hundred shields of beaten gold (six hundred gold shekels went into each shield)^j **17** and three hundred bucklers of beaten gold (three minas of gold went into each buckler); and he put them in the hall of the Forest of Lebanon. **18** The king also had a large ivory throne made, and overlaid it with refined gold. **19** The throne had six steps, a back with a round top, and an arm on each side of the seat. Next to each arm stood a lion; **20** and twelve other lions stood on the steps, two to a step, one on either side of each step. Nothing like this was produced in any other kingdom. **21** In addition, all King Solomon's drinking vessels were of gold, and all the utensils in the hall of the Forest of Lebanon were of pure gold. There was no silver, for in Solomon's time it was considered worthless. **22** The king had a fleet of Tarshish ships* at sea with Hiram's fleet. Once every three years the fleet of Tarshish ships would come with a cargo of gold, silver, ivory, apes, and monkeys. **23** Thus King Solomon surpassed in riches and wisdom all the kings of the earth. **24** And the whole world sought audience with Solomon, to hear from him the wisdom which God had put in his heart. **25** Each one brought his yearly tribute: silver or gold articles, garments, weapons, spices, horses and mules.

26 Solomon collected chariots and drivers; he had one thousand four hundred chariots and twelve thousand drivers; these he allocated among the chariot cities and to the king's service in Jerusalem.^k **27** The king made silver as common in Jerusalem as stones, and cedars as numerous as the sycamores of the foothills. **28** Solomon's horses were imported from Cilicia, where the king's agents purchased them. **29** A chariot imported from Egypt cost six hundred shekels, a horse one hundred and fifty shekels; they were exported at these rates to all the Hittite and Aramean kings.

CHAPTER 11

The Sins of Solomon. 1 *King Solomon loved many foreign women besides the daughter of Pharaoh (Moabites, Ammonites, Edomites, Sidonians, and Hittites),^l **2** from nations with which the LORD had forbidden the Israelites to intermarry, "because," he said, "they will turn your hearts to their gods."^m **3** But Solomon fell in love with them. He had seven hundred wives of princely rank and three hundred concubines, and his wives turned his heart.

4 When Solomon was old his wives had turned his heart to strange gods, and his heart was not entirely with the LORD, his God, as the heart of his father David had been. **5** By adoring Astarte, the goddess of the Sidonians, and Milcom, the idol of the Ammonites, **6** Solomon did evil in the sight of the LORD; he did not follow him unreservedly as his father David had done. **7** Solomon then built a high place to Chemosh, the idol of Moab, and to Molech, the idol of the Ammonites, on the hill opposite Jerusalem. **8** He did the same for all his foreign wives who burned incense and sacrificed to their gods. **9** The LORD, therefore, became angry with Solomon, because his heart was turned away from the LORD, the God of Israel, who had appeared to him twice^n **10** (for though the LORD had forbidden him this very act of following strange gods, Solomon had not obeyed him).

11 So the LORD said to Solomon: "Since this is what you want, and you have not kept my covenant and my statutes which I enjoined on you, I will deprive you of the kingdom and give it to your servant. **12** I will not do this during your lifetime, however, for the sake of your father David; it is your son whom I will deprive.^o **13** Nor will I take away the whole kingdom. I will leave your son one tribe for the sake of my servant David and of Jerusalem, which I have chosen."

14 The LORD then raised up an adversary to Solomon: Hadad the Edomite, who was of the royal line in Edom. **15** Earlier, when David had conquered Edom, Joab, the general of the army, while going to bury the slain, put to death every male in Edom.^p **16** Joab and all Israel remained there six months until they had killed off every male in Edom. **17** Meanwhile, Hadad, who was only a boy, fled toward Egypt with some Edomite servants of his father. **18** They left Midian and passing through Paran, where they picked up additional men, they went into Egypt to Pharaoh, king of Egypt, who gave Hadad a house, appointed him rations, and assigned him land.

19 Hadad won great favor with Pharaoh, so

---

j 1 Kgs 14, 26.
k 2 Chr 1, 14.
l Dt 17, 17; Sir 47, 19f.
m Ex 34, 16.
n 1 Kgs 9, 2.
o 1 Kgs 12, 15.
p 2 Sm 8, 14.

*

10, 22: Tarshish ships: large, strong vessels for long voyages. Tarshish was the ancient Tartessus, a Phoenician colony in southern Spain, the name of which denotes a center for smelting metallic ore.

11, 1–3. 7: The glorious rise of Solomon, his piety and wisdom, administrative skill and wealth, the extension of his kingdom, his prestige among neighboring rulers, his reign of peace, above all his friendship with God—these are now eclipsed by his sins of intermarriage with great numbers of pagan wives and the consequent forbidden worship of their gods (Ex 34, 11–16; Dt 7, 1–5). His construction of temples in their honor merited the punishment of loss of a united kingdom to his posterity, and the opposition of adversaries to himself (vv 14. 23–27). Hadad the Edomite rebelled against Solomon at the beginning of his reign (v 25). Rezon of Syria established a new kingdom in Dàmascus; Jeroboam of Israel constituted the greatest threat because of his revolt from within. This threefold threat culminated in the breakup of Solomon's kingdom.

that he gave him in marriage the sister of Queen Tahpenes, his own wife. **20** Tahpenes' sister bore Hadad a son, Genubath. After his weaning, the queen kept him in Pharaoh's palace, where he then lived with Pharaoh's own sons. **21** When Hadad in Egypt heard that David rested with his ancestors and that Joab, the general of the army, was dead, he said to Pharaoh, "Give me leave to return to my own country." **22** Pharaoh said to him, "What do you lack with me, that you are seeking to return to your own country?" "Nothing," he said, "but please let me go!"

23 God raised up against Solomon another adversary, in Rezon, the son of Eliada, who had fled from his lord, Hadadezer, king of Zobah, **24** when David defeated them with slaughter. Rezon gathered men about him and became leader of a band, went to Damascus, settled there, and became king in Damascus. **25** He was an enemy of Israel as long as Solomon lived; this added to the harm done by Hadad, who made a rift in Israel by becoming king over Edom.

26 Solomon's servant Jeroboam, son of Nebat, an Ephraimite from Zeredah with a widowed mother, Zeruah, also rebelled against the king.*q* **27** This is why he rebelled. King Solomon was building Millo, closing up the breach of his father's City of David. **28** Jeroboam was a man of means, and when Solomon saw that he was also an industrious young man, he put him in charge of the entire labor force of the house of Joseph. **29** At that time Jeroboam left Jerusalem, and the prophet Ahijah the Shilonite met him on the road. The two were alone in the area, and the prophet was wearing a new cloak.*r* **30** Ahijah took off his new cloak, tore it into twelve pieces, **31** and said to Jeroboam:

"Take ten pieces for yourself; the LORD, the God of Israel, says: 'I will tear away the kingdom from Solomon's grasp and will give you ten of the tribes.*s* **32** One tribe shall remain to him for the sake of David my servant, and of Jerusalem, the city I have chosen out of all the tribes of Israel. **33** The ten I will give you because he has forsaken me and has worshiped Astarte, goddess of the Sidonians, Chemosh, god of Moab, and Milcom, god of the Ammonites; he has not followed my ways or done what is pleasing to me according to my statutes and my decrees, as his father David did. **34** Yet I will not take any of the kingdom from Solomon himself, but will keep him a prince as long as he lives for the sake of my servant David, whom I chose, who kept my commandments and statutes. **35** But I will take the kingdom from his son and will give it to you—that is, the ten tribes. **36** I will give his son one tribe, that my servant David may always have a lamp before me in Jerusalem, the city in which I choose to

be honored. **37** I will take you; you shall reign over all that you desire and shall become king of Israel. **38** If, then, you heed all that I command you, follow my ways, and please me by keeping my statutes and my commandments like my servant David, I will be with you. I will establish for you, as I did for David, a lasting dynasty; I will give Israel to you. **39** I will punish David's line for this, but not forever.' "

40 When Solomon tried to have Jeroboam killed for his rebellion, he escaped to King Shishak, in Egypt, where he remained until Solomon's death.

41 The rest of the acts of Solomon, with all his deeds and his wisdom, are recorded in the book of the chronicles of Solomon. **42** The time that Solomon reigned in Jerusalem over all Israel was forty years. **43** Solomon rested with his ancestors; he was buried in his father's City of David, and his son Rehoboam succeeded him as king.

II: Judah and Israel to the Time of Ahab

CHAPTER 12

Secession of Israel. **1** Rehoboam went to Shechem,* where all Israel had come to proclaim him king.*t* **3** They said to Rehoboam: **4** "Your father put on us a heavy yoke. If you now lighten the harsh service and the heavy yoke your father imposed on us, we will serve you." **5** "Come back to me in three days," he answered them. When the people had departed, **6** King Rehoboam consulted the elders who had been in his father's service while he was alive, and asked, "What answer do you advise me to give this people?" **7** They replied, "If today you will be the servant of this people and submit to them, giving them a favorable answer, they will be your servants forever." **8** But he ignored the advice the elders had given him, and consulted the young men who had grown up with him and were in his service. **9** He said to them, "What answer do you advise me to give this people, who have asked me to lighten the yoke my father imposed on them?" **10** The young men who had grown up with him replied, "This is what you must say to this people who have asked you to lighten the yoke your father put on them: 'My little finger is thicker than my father's body. **11** Whereas my father put a

q 2 Chr 13, 6.   s 1 Kgs 12, 15.
r 1 Kgs 14, 2; 2 Chr 10,   t 2 Chr 10, 1.
   15

*

12, 1: Shechem: chief city of the northern tribes, where a covenant of fidelity had previously been made between the Lord and his people and a stone of witness had been erected in memory of the event (Jos 24, 25ff).

heavy yoke on you, I will make it heavier. My father beat you with whips, but I will beat you with scorpions.' ''

12 On the third day all Israel came back to King Rehoboam, as he had instructed them to do. **13** Ignoring the advice the elders had given him, the king gave the people a harsh answer. **14** He said to them, as the young men had advised: "My father put on you a heavy yoke, but I will make it heavier. My father beat you with whips, but I will beat you with scorpions." **15** The king did not listen to the people, for the LORD brought this about to fulfill the prophecy he had uttered to Jeroboam, son of Nebat, through Ahijah the Shilonite. *u*

16 When all Israel saw that the king did not listen to them, the people answered the king:

"What share have we in David?*
We have no heritage in the son of Jesse.
To your tents, O Israel!
Now look to your own house, David."

So Israel went off to their tents, **17** but Rehoboam reigned over the Israelites who lived in the cities of Judah. **18** King Rehoboam then sent out Adoram, superintendent of the forced labor, but all Israel stoned him to death. Rehoboam managed to mount his chariot to flee to Jerusalem, **19** and Israel went into rebellion against David's house to this day. **2** Jeroboam, son of Nebat, who was still in Egypt, where he had fled from King Solomon, returned from Egypt as soon as he learned this. **20** When all Israel heard that Jeroboam had returned, they summoned him to an assembly and made him king over all Israel. None remained loyal to David's house except the tribe of Judah alone.

21 On his arrival in Jerusalem, Rehoboam gathered together all the house of Judah and the tribe of Benjamin—one hundred eighty thousand seasoned warriors—to fight against the house of Israel, to restore the kingdom to Rehoboam, son of Solomon. **22** *v*However, the LORD spoke to Shemaiah, a man of God: **23** "Say to Rehoboam, son of Solomon, king of Judah, and to the house of Judah and to Benjamin, and to the rest of the people: **24** 'Thus says the LORD: You must not march out to fight against your brother Israelites. Let every man return home, for I have brought this about.' '' They accepted this message of the LORD and gave up the expedition accordingly.

25 Jeroboam built up Shechem in the hill country of Ephraim and lived there. Then he left it and built up Penuel.

Religious Rebellion.*   **26** Jeroboam thought to himself: "The kingdom will return to David's house. **27** If now this people go up to offer sacrifices in the temple of the LORD in Jerusalem, the hearts of this people will return

to their master, Rehoboam, king of Judah, and they will kill me." **28** After taking counsel, the king made two calves of gold and said to the people: "You have been going up to Jerusalem long enough. Here is your God, O Israel, who brought you up from the land of Egypt." *w* **29** And he put one in Bethel, the other in Dan.* **30** This led to sin, because the people frequented these calves in Bethel and in Dan. **31** He also built temples on the high places and made priests from among the people who were not Levites. *x* **32** Jeroboam established a feast in the eighth month on the fifteenth day of the month to duplicate in Bethel the pilgrimage feast of Judah, with sacrifices to the calves he had made; and he stationed in Bethel priests of the high places he had built.

Message of the Prophet from Judah.
33 Jeroboam ascended the altar he built in Bethel on the fifteenth day of the eighth month, the month in which he arbitrarily chose to establish a feast for the Israelites; he was going to offer sacrifice.

CHAPTER 13

1 A man of God came from Judah to Bethel by the word of the LORD, while Jeroboam was standing at the altar to offer sacrifice. **2** He cried out against the altar the word of the LORD: "O altar, altar, the LORD says, 'A child shall be born to the house of David, Josiah by name, who shall slaughter upon you the priests of the high places who offer sacrifice upon you, and he shall burn human bones upon you.' '' *y* **3** He gave a sign that same day and said: "This is the sign that the LORD has spoken: The altar shall break up and the ashes on it shall be strewn about."

4 When King Jeroboam heard what the man of God was crying out against the altar, he

---

u 1 Kgs 11, 12. 31.   x 2 Chr 11, 15.
v 22-24; 2 Chr 11, 2ff.   y 2 Kgs 23, 16.
w Tb 1, 5; Ex 32, 8.

* 12, 16: What share have we in David: even in David's time the northern tribes seemed ready to withdraw from Judah (2 Sm 20, 1). The unreasonable attitude of Rehoboam toward them intensified the discontent caused by the oppression of Solomon (v 4) and thus precipitated the establishment of a rival monarchy (v 20).

12, 26–32: Jeroboam feared reunification of the divided kingdom through worship in the single temple in Jerusalem. To prevent this he encouraged shrines on the high places, and appointed false priests to supplement those of levitical descent. The golden bullocks he installed in two of his sanctuaries, though probably intended as bearers of the invisible Divine Majesty, quickly became occasions for idolatry. Thus Jeroboam caused Israel to sin, and sealed his doom and that of his royal house (1 Kgs 13, 34; 14, 7–14).

12, 29: Bethel and Dan: at the southern and northern boundaries of the separate kingdom of Israel, where sanctuaries had existed in the past (Gn 12, 8; 13, 3; 18, 10–22; 25, 1–16; Jgs 18, 1–31).

stretched forth his hand from the altar and said, "Seize him!" But the hand he stretched forth against him withered, so that he could not draw it back. **5** Moreover, the altar broke up and the ashes from it were strewn about—the sign the man of God had given as the word of the LORD. **6** Then the king appealed to the man of God. "Entreat the LORD, your God," he said, "and intercede for me that I may be able to withdraw my hand." So the man of God entreated the LORD, and the king recovered the normal use of his hand. **7** "Come home with me for some refreshment," the king invited the man of God, "and I will give you a present." **8** "If you gave me half your kingdom," the man of God said to the king, "I would not go with you, nor eat bread or drink water in this place. **9** For I was instructed by the word of the LORD not to eat bread or drink water and not to return by the way I came." **10** So he departed by another road and did not go back the way he had come to Bethel.

11 There was an old prophet living in the city, whose sons came and told him all that the man of God had done that day in Bethel. When they repeated to their father the words he had spoken to the king, **12** the father asked them, "Which way did he go?" And his sons pointed out to him the road taken by the man of God who had come from Judah. **13** Then he said to his sons, "Saddle the ass for me." When they had saddled it, he mounted **14** and followed the man of God, whom he found seated under a terebinth. When he asked him, "Are you the man of God who came from Judah?" he answered, "Yes." **15** Then he said, "Come home with me and have some bread." **16** "I cannot go back with you, and I cannot eat bread or drink water with you in this place," he answered, **17** "for I was told by the word of the LORD neither to eat bread nor drink water here, and not to go back the way I came." **18** But he said to him, "I, too, am a prophet like you, and an angel told me in the word of the LORD to bring you back with me to my house and to have you eat bread and drink water." He was lying to him, however.

19 So he went back with him, and ate bread and drank water in his house. **20** But while they were sitting at table, the LORD spoke to the prophet who had brought him back, **21** and he cried out to the man of God who had come from Judah: "The LORD says, 'Because you rebelled against the command of the LORD and did not keep the command which the LORD, your God, gave you, **22** but returned and ate bread and drank water in the place where he told you to do neither, your corpse shall not be brought to the grave of your ancestors.'"

23 After he had eaten bread and drunk water, the ass was saddled for him, and he again **24** set

out. But a lion met him on the road, and killed him. His corpse lay sprawled on the road, and the ass remained standing by it, and so did the lion. **25** Some passersby saw the body lying in the road, with the lion standing beside it, and carried the news to the city where the old prophet lived. **26** On hearing it, the prophet who had brought him back from his journey said: "It is the man of God who rebelled against the command of the LORD. He has delivered him to a lion, which mangled and killed him, as the LORD predicted to him." **27** Then he said to his sons, "Saddle the ass for me." When they had saddled it, **28** he went off and found the body lying in the road with the ass and the lion standing beside it. The lion had not eaten the body nor had it harmed the ass. **29** The prophet lifted up the body of the man of God and put it on the ass, and brought it back to the city to mourn over it and to bury it. **30** He laid the man's body in his own grave, and they mourned over it: "Alas, my brother!" **31** After he had buried him, he said to his sons, "When I die, bury me in the grave where the man of God is buried. Lay my remains beside his. **32** For the word of the LORD which he proclaimed against the altar in Bethel and against all the shrines on the high places in the cities of Samaria shall certainly come to pass."

33 Jeroboam did not give up his evil ways after this event, but again made priests for the high places from among the common people. Whoever desired it was consecrated and became a priest of the high places. **34** This was a sin on the part of the house of Jeroboam for which it was to be cut off and destroyed from the earth.

CHAPTER 14

Death of Abijah. **1** At that time Abijah, son of Jeroboam, took sick. **2** So Jeroboam said to his wife, "Get ready and disguise yourself so that none will recognize you as Jeroboam's wife. Then go to Shiloh, where you will find the prophet Ahijah. It is he who predicted my reign over this people.ᶻ **3** Take along ten loaves, some cakes, and a jar of preserves, and go to him. He will tell you what will happen to the child." **4** The wife of Jeroboam obeyed. She made the journey to Shiloh and entered the house of Ahijah who could not see because age had dimmed his sight.

5 The LORD had said to Ahijah: "Jeroboam's wife is coming to consult you about her son, for he is sick. This is what you must tell her. When she comes, she will be in disguise." **6** So Ahijah, hearing the sound of her footsteps as she entered the door, said, "Come in, wife of Jeroboam. Why are you in disguise? I have been commissioned to give you bitter news. **7** Go, tell Jeroboam, 'This is what the LORD, the God of Israel, says: I exalted you from among the people and made you ruler of my people Israel. **8** I deprived the house of David of the kingdom and gave it to you. Yet you have not been like my servant David, who kept my commandments and followed me with his whole heart, doing only what pleased me. **9** You have done worse than all who preceded you: you have gone and made for yourself strange gods and molten images to provoke me; but me you have cast behind your back. **10** Therefore, I am bringing evil upon the house of Jeroboam: I will cut off every male in Jeroboam's line, whether slave or freeman in Israel, and will burn up the house of Jeroboam completely, as though dung were being burned. *a* **11** When one of Jeroboam's line dies in the city, dogs will devour him; when one of them dies in the field, he will be devoured by the birds of the sky. For the LORD has spoken!' *b* **12** So leave; go home! As you step inside the city, the child will die, **13** and all Israel will mourn him and bury him, for he alone of Jeroboam's line will be laid in the grave, since in him alone of Jeroboam's house has something pleasing to the LORD, the God of Israel, been found. **14** Today, at this very moment, the LORD will raise up for himself a king of Israel who will destroy the house of Jeroboam. **15** The LORD will strike Israel like a reed tossed about in the water and will pluck out Israel from this good land which he gave their fathers, scattering them beyond the River, because they made sacred poles for themselves and thus provoked the LORD. **16** He will give up Israel because of the sins Jeroboam has committed and caused Israel to commit.''

17 So Jeroboam's wife started back; when she reached Tirzah and crossed the threshold of her house, the child died. **18** He was buried with all Israel mourning him, as the LORD had prophesied through his servant the prophet Ahijah.

19 The rest of the acts of Jeroboam, with his warfare and his reign, are recorded in the book of the chronicles of the kings of Israel. **20** The length of Jeroboam's reign was twenty-two years. He rested with his ancestors, and his son Nadab succeeded him as king.

Reign of Rehoboam.   **21** Rehoboam, son of Solomon, reigned in Judah. He was forty-one years old when he became king, and he reigned seventeen years in Jerusalem, the city in which, out of all the tribes of Israel, the LORD chose to be honored. His mother was the Ammonite named Naamah. *c*

22 Judah did evil in the sight of the LORD, and by their sins angered him even more than their fathers had done. **23** They, too, built for themselves high places, pillars, and sacred poles, upon every high hill and under every green tree. **24** There were also cult prostitutes in the land. Judah imitated all the abominable practices of the nations whom the LORD had cleared out of the Israelites' way.

25 In the fifth year of King Rehoboam, Shishak, king of Egypt, attacked Jerusalem.* **26** He took everything, including the treasures of the temple of the LORD and those of the royal palace, as well as all the gold shields made under Solomon. *d* **27** To replace them, King Rehoboam had bronze shields made, which he entrusted to the officers of the guard on duty at the entrance of the royal palace. **28** Whenever the king visited the temple of the LORD, those on duty would carry the shields, and then return them to the guardroom.

29 The rest of the acts of Rehoboam, with all that he did, are recorded in the book of the chronicles of the kings of Judah. **30** There was constant warfare between Rehoboam and Jeroboam. **31** Rehoboam rested with his ancestors; he was buried with them in the City of David. His mother was the Ammonite named Naamah. His son Abijam succeeded him as king.

CHAPTER 15

Reign of Abijam.   **1** In the eighteenth year of King Jeroboam, son of Nebat, Abijam became king of Judah; *e* **2** he reigned three years in Jerusalem. His mother's name was Maacah, daughter of Abishalom. **3** He imitated all the sins his father had committed before him, and his heart was not entirely with the LORD, his God, like the heart of his grandfather David. **4** Yet for David's sake the LORD, his God, gave him a lamp in Jerusalem, raising up his son after him and permitting Jerusalem to endure; **5** because David had pleased the LORD and did not disobey any of his commands as long as he lived, except in the case of Uriah the Hittite. *f*

7 The rest of Abijam's acts, with all that he did, are written in the book of the chronicles of the kings of Judah. *g* **6** There was war between Abijam and Jeroboam. **8** Abijam rested with his ancestors; he was buried in the City of Da-

---

a 1 Kgs 15, 29.   e 2 Chr 13, 1f.
b 1 Kgs 16, 4.   f 2 Sm 11, 4.
c 2 Chr 12, 13.   g 2 Chr 13, 2.
d 1 Kgs 10, 16.

*

14, 25: In the fifth year . . . Shishak, king of Egypt, attacked Jerusalem: c. 926 B.C. According to 2 Chr 12, 1–12, the repentance of King Rehoboam and of the princes of Israel after the warning of the prophet Shemaiah diverted the actual attack on Jerusalem. Shishak, however, carried off the treasures of the temple of the Lord and of the king's palace (2 Chr 12, 9). A bas-relief of this Pharaoh in the temple of Aman at Karnak commemorates his conquest of some hundred and fifty Palestinian and Trans-Jordanian cities and towns.

vid, and his son Asa succeeded him as king.

Reign of Asa.

9 In the twentieth year of Jeroboam, king of Israel, Asa, king of Judah, began to reign; **10** he reigned forty-one years in Jerusalem. His grandmother's name was Maacah, daughter of Abishalom. **11** Asa pleased the LORD like his forefather David, **12** banishing the temple prostitutes from the land and removing all the idols his father had made. **13** He also deposed his grandmother Maacah from her position as queen mother, because she had made an outrageous object for Asherah. Asa cut down this object and burned it in the Kidron Valley. **14** The high places did not disappear; yet Asa's heart was entirely with the LORD as long as he lived. **15** He brought into the temple of the LORD his father's and his own votive offerings of silver, gold, and various utensils.

16 There was war between Asa and Baasha, king of Israel, as long as they both reigned. **17** Baasha, king of Israel, attacked Judah and fortified Ramah to prevent communication with Asa, king of Judah.ʰ **18** Asa then took all the silver and gold remaining in the treasuries of the temple of the LORD and of the royal palace. Entrusting them to his ministers, King Asa sent them to Ben-hadad, son of Tabrimmon, son of Hezion, king of Aram,* resident in Damascus. He said: **19** "There is a treaty between you and me, as there was between your father and my father. I am sending you a present of silver and gold. Go, break your treaty with Baasha, king of Israel, that he may withdraw from me." **20** Ben-hadad agreed with King Asa and sent the leaders of his troops against the cities of Israel. They attacked Ijon, Dan, Abel-beth-maacah, and all Chinnereth, besides all the land of Naphtali. **21** When Baasha heard of it, he left off fortifying Ramah, and stayed in Tirzah. **22** Then King Asa summoned all Judah without exception, and they carried away the stones and beams with which Baasha was fortifying Ramah. With them King Asa built Geba of Benjamin and Mizpeh.

23 The rest of the acts of Asa, with all his valor and accomplishments, and the cities he built, are written in the book of the chronicles of the kings of Judah. In his old age, Asa had an infirmity in his feet. **24** He rested with his ancestors; he was buried in his forefather's City of David, and his son Jehoshaphat succeeded him as king.ⁱ

Reign of Nadab.

25 In the second year of Asa, king of Judah, Nadab, son of Jeroboam, became king of Israel; he reigned over Israel two years. **26** He did evil in the LORD's sight, imitating his father's conduct and the sin which he had caused Israel to commit. **27** Baasha, son of Ahijah, of the house of Issachar, plotted against him and struck him down at Gibbethon of the Philistines, which Nadab and all Israel were besieging. **28** Baasha killed him in the third year of Asa, king of Judah, and reigned in his stead. **29** Once he was king, he killed off the entire house of Jeroboam, not leaving a single soul to Jeroboam but destroying him utterly, according to the warning which the LORD had pronounced through his servant, Ahijah the Shilonite,ʲ **30** because of the sins Jeroboam committed and caused Israel to commit, by which he provoked the LORD, the God of Israel, to anger.

31 The rest of the acts of Nadab, with all that he did, are written in the book of the chronicles of the kings of Israel. **32** [There was war between Asa and Baasha, king of Israel, as long as they lived.]

Reign of Baasha.

33 In the third year of Asa, king of Judah, Baasha, son of Ahijah, began his twenty-four-year reign over Israel in Tirzah. **34** He did evil in the LORD'S sight, imitating the conduct of Jeroboam and the sin he had caused Israel to commit.

CHAPTER 16

1 The LORD spoke against Baasha to Jehu, son of Hanani, and said: **2** "Inasmuch as I lifted you up from the dust and made you ruler of my people Israel, but you have imitated the conduct of Jeroboam and have caused my people Israel to sin, provoking me to anger by their sins, **3** I will destroy you, Baasha, and your house;ᵏ **4** I will make your house like that of Jeroboam, son of Nebat. If anyone of Baasha's line dies in the city, dogs shall devour him; if he dies in the field, he shall be devoured by the birds of the sky."ˡ

5 The rest of the acts of Baasha, with all his valor and accomplishments, are written in the book of the chronicles of the kings of Israel.ᵐ **6** Baasha rested with his ancestors; he was buried in Tirzah, and his son Elah succeeded him as king. **7** [Through the prophet Jehu, son of Hanani, the LORD had threatened Baasha and his house, because of all the evil Baasha did in the sight of the LORD, provoking him to anger by his evil deeds, so that he became like the house of Jeroboam; and because he killed Nadab.]

---

h 2 Chr 16, 1.   k 1 Kgs 21, 22.
i 2 Chr 17, 1.   l 1 Kgs 14, 11.
j 1 Kgs 14, 10; 21, 22.   m 2 Chr 16, 1.

*

15, 18: Ben-hadad . . . king of Aram: Ben-hadad I, third successor of Rezon, who had thrown off the yoke of the Israelites during the reign of Solomon and become king of Aram (11, 23f).

Reign of Elah. 8 In the twenty-sixth year of Asa, king of Judah, Elah, son of Baasha, began his two-year reign over Israel in Tirzah. 9 His servant Zimri, commander of half his chariots, plotted against him. As he was in Tirzah, drinking to excess in the house of Arza, superintendent of his palace in Tirzah, 10 Zimri entered; he struck and killed him in the twenty-seventh year of Asa, king of Judah, and reigned in his place.[n] 11 Once he was seated on the royal throne, he killed off the whole house of Baasha, not sparing a single male relative or friend of his. 12 Zimri destroyed the entire house of Baasha, as the LORD had prophesied to Baasha through the prophet Jehu, 13 because of all the sins which Baasha and his son Elah committed and caused Israel to commit, provoking the LORD, the God of Israel, to anger by their idols.

14 The rest of the acts of Elah, with all that he did, are written in the book of the chronicles of the kings of Israel.

Reign of Zimri. 15 In the twenty-seventh year of Asa, king of Judah, Zimri reigned seven days in Tirzah. The army was besieging Gibbethon of the Philistines 16 when they heard that Zimri had formed a conspiracy and had killed the king. So that day in the camp all Israel proclaimed Omri, general of the army, king of Israel. 17 Omri marched up from Gibbethon, accompanied by all Israel, and laid siege to Tirzah. 18 When Zimri saw the city was captured, he entered the citadel of the royal palace and burned down the palace over him. He died 19 because of the sins he had committed, doing evil in the sight of the LORD by imitating the sinful conduct of Jeroboam, thus causing Israel to sin.

20 The rest of the acts of Zimri, with the conspiracy he carried out, are written in the book of the chronicles of the kings of Israel.

21 At that time the people of Israel were divided, half following Tibni, son of Ginath, to make him king, and half for Omri. 22 The partisans of Omri prevailed over those of Tibni, son of Ginath. Tibni died and Omri became king.

Reign of Omri. 23 In the thirty-first year of Asa, king of Judah, Omri became king; he reigned over Israel twelve years, the first six of them in Tirzah. 24 He then bought the hill of Samaria from Shemer for two silver talents and built upon the hill, naming the city he built Samaria after Shemer, the former owner. 25 But Omri did evil in the LORD's sight beyond any of his predecessors. 26 He closely imitated the sinful conduct of Jeroboam, son of Nebat, causing Israel to sin and to provoke the LORD, the God of Israel, to anger by their idols.

27 The rest of the acts of Omri, with all his valor and accomplishments, are written in the

book of the chronicles of the kings of Israel. 28 Omri rested with his ancestors; he was buried in Samaria, and his son Ahab succeeded him as king.

Reign of Ahab. 29 In the thirty-eighth year of Asa, king of Judah, Ahab, son of Omri, became king of Israel; he reigned over Israel in Samaria for twenty-two years. 30 Ahab, son of Omri, did evil in the sight of the LORD more than any of his predecessors. 31 It was not enough for him to imitate the sins of Jeroboam, son of Nebat. He even married Jezebel, daughter of Ethbaal, king of the Sidonians, and went over to the veneration and worship of Baal. 32 Ahab erected an altar to Baal in the temple of Baal which he built in Samaria, 33 and also made a sacred pole. He did more to anger the LORD, the God of Israel, than any of the kings of Israel before him.

34 [o]During his reign, Hiel from Bethel rebuilt Jericho. He lost his first-born son, Abiram, when he laid the foundation, and his youngest son, Segub, when he set up the gates, as the LORD had foretold through Joshua, son of Nun.

III: Stories of the Prophets

CHAPTER 17

Drought Predicted by Elijah. 1 Elijah the Tishbite,* from Tishbe in Gilead, said to Ahab: "As the LORD, the God of Israel, lives, whom I serve, during these years there shall be no dew or rain except at my word."[p] 2 The LORD then said to Elijah: 3 "Leave here, go east and hide in the Wadi Cherith, east of the Jordan. 4 You shall drink of the stream, and I have commanded ravens to feed you there." 5 So he left and did as the LORD had commanded. He went and remained by the Wadi Cherith, east of the Jordan. 6 Ravens brought him bread and meat in the morning, and bread and meat in the evening, and he drank from the stream.

Elijah and the Widow. 7 After some time, however, the brook ran dry, because no rain had fallen in the land. 8 So the LORD said to him: 9 "Move on to Zarephath of Sidon and stay

---

n 2 Kgs 9, 31.   p Sir 48, 3; Jas 5, 17.
o Jos 6, 26.

*

17, 1: Elijah the Tishbite: one of the most important figures in Old Testament history. As his name indicates ("Yahweh is my God"), Elijah was the successful leader in the struggle to preserve the knowledge and worship of Yahweh against the encroaching worship of Baal introduced into Israel by Jezebel, the Tyrian wife of Ahab. The Elijah cycle of narratives includes, besides the above struggle, miracle stories, denunciations of kings, and a preparation for the prophet's role as eschatological forerunner of the "great day of the Lord"; cf Mal 3, 23–24; Mt 17, 10–13; Lk 1, 17.

there. I have designated a widow there to provide for you.'' **10** He left and went to Zarephath. As he arrived at the entrance of the city, a widow was gathering sticks there; he called out to her, ''Please bring me a small cupful of water to drink.''*q* **11** She left to get it, and he called out after her, ''Please bring along a bit of bread.'' **12** ''As the LORD, your God, lives,'' she answered, ''I have nothing baked; there is only a handful of flour in my jar and a little oil in my jug. Just now I was collecting a couple of sticks, to go in and prepare something for myself and my son; when we have eaten it, we shall die.'' **13** ''Do not be afraid,'' Elijah said to her. ''Go and do as you propose. But first make me a little cake and bring it to me. Then you can prepare something for yourself and your son. **14** For the LORD, the God of Israel, says, 'The jar of flour shall not go empty, nor the jug of oil run dry, until the day when the LORD sends rain upon the earth.' '' **15** She left and did as Elijah had said. She was able to eat for a year, and he and her son as well; **16** the jar of flour did not go empty, nor the jug of oil run dry, as the LORD had foretold through Elijah.

17 Some time later the son of the mistress of the house fell sick, and his sickness grew more severe until he stopped breathing. **18** So she said to Elijah, ''Why have you done this to me, O man of God? Have you come to me to call attention to my guilt and to kill my son?'' **19** ''Give me your son,'' Elijah said to her. Taking him from her lap, he carried him to the upper room where he was staying, and laid him on his own bed. **20** He called out to the LORD: ''O LORD, my God, will you afflict even the widow with whom I am staying by killing her son?'' **21** Then he stretched himself out upon the child three times and called out to the LORD: ''O LORD, my God, let the life breath return to the body of this child.'' **22** The LORD heard the prayer of Elijah; the life breath returned to the child's body and he revived. **23** Taking the child, Elijah brought him down into the house from the upper room and gave him to his mother. ''See!'' Elijah said to her, ''your son is alive.'' **24** ''Now indeed I know that you are a man of God,'' the woman replied to Elijah. ''The word of the LORD comes truly from your mouth.''

CHAPTER 18

Elijah and the Prophets of Baal. **1** Long afterward, in the third year, the LORD spoke to Elijah. ''Go, present yourself to Ahab,'' he said, ''that I may send rain upon the earth.'' **2** So Elijah went to present himself to Ahab.

3 Now the famine in Samaria was bitter, **4** and Ahab had summoned Obadiah, his vizier, who was a zealous follower of the LORD. When

Jezebel was murdering the prophets of the LORD, Obadiah took a hundred prophets, hid them away fifty each in two caves, and supplied them with food and drink. **5** Ahab said to Obadiah, ''Come, let us go through the land to all sources of water and to all the streams. We may find grass and save the horses and mules, so that we shall not have to slaughter any of the beasts.'' **6** Dividing the land to explore between them, Ahab went one way by himself, Obadiah another way by himself.

7 As Obadiah was on his way, Elijah met him. Recognizing him, Obadiah fell prostrate and asked, ''Is it you, my lord Elijah?'' **8** ''Yes,'' he answered. ''Go tell your master, 'Elijah is here!' '' **9** But Obadiah said, ''What sin have I committed, that you are handing me over to Ahab to have me killed? **10** As the LORD, your God, lives, there is no nation or kingdom where my master has not sent in search of you. When they replied, 'He is not here,' he made each kingdom and nation swear they could not find you. **11** And now you say, 'Go tell your master: Elijah is here!' **12** After I leave you, the spirit of the LORD will carry you to some place I do not know, and when I go to inform Ahab and he does not find you, he will kill me. Your servant has revered the LORD from his youth. **13** Have you not been told, my lord, what I did when Jezebel was murdering the prophets of the LORD—that I hid a hundred of the prophets of the LORD, fifty each in two caves, and supplied them with food and drink? **14** And now you say, 'Go tell your master: Elijah is here!' He will kill me!'' **15** Elijah answered, ''As the LORD of hosts lives, whom I serve, I will present myself to him today.''

16 So Obadiah went to meet Ahab and informed him. Ahab came to meet Elijah, **17** and when he saw Elijah, said to him, ''Is it you, you disturber of Israel?'' **18** ''It is not I who disturb Israel,'' he answered, ''but you and your family, by forsaking the commands of the LORD and following the Baals. **19** Now summon all Israel to me on Mount Carmel, as well as the four hundred and fifty prophets of Baal and the four hundred prophets of Asherah who eat at Jezebel's table.'' **20** So Ahab sent to all the Israelites and had the prophets assemble on Mount Carmel.

21 Elijah appealed to all the people and said, ''How long will you straddle the issue? If the LORD is God, follow him; if Baal, follow him.'' The people, however, did not answer him. **22** So Elijah said to the people, ''I am the only surviving prophet of the LORD, and there are four hundred and fifty prophets of Baal. **23** Give us two young bulls. Let them choose one, cut it into pieces, and place it on the wood, but start no fire. I shall prepare the other and place it on the wood, but shall start no fire. **24** You shall call on your gods, and I will call on the LORD. The God who answers with fire is God.'' All the people answered, ''Agreed!''

25 Elijah then said to the prophets of Baal, ''Choose one young bull and prepare it first, for there are more of you. Call upon your gods, but do not start the fire.'' **26** Taking the young bull that was turned over to them, they prepared it and called on Baal from morning to noon, saying, ''Answer us, Baal!'' But there was no sound, and no one answering. And they hopped around the altar they had prepared. **27** When it was noon, Elijah taunted them: ''Call louder, for he is a god and may be meditating, or may have retired, or may be on a journey. Perhaps he is asleep and must be awakened.'' **28** They called out louder and slashed themselves with swords and spears, as was their custom, until blood gushed over them. **29** Noon passed and they remained in a prophetic state until the time for offering sacrifice. But there was not a sound; no one answered, and no one was listening.

30 Then Elijah said to all the people, ''Come here to me.'' When they had done so, he repaired the altar of the LORD which had been destroyed. **31** He took twelve stones, for the number of tribes of the sons of Jacob, to whom the LORD had said, ''Your name shall be Israel.'' **32** He built an altar in honor of the LORD with the stones, and made a trench around the altar large enough for two seahs of grain. **33** When he had arranged the wood, he cut up the young bull and laid it on the wood. **34** ''Fill four jars with water,'' he said, ''and pour it over the holocaust and over the wood.'' ''Do it again,'' he said, and they did it again. ''Do it a third time,'' he said, and they did it a third time. **35** The water flowed around the altar, and the trench was filled with the water.

36 At the time for offering sacrifice, the prophet Elijah came forward and said, ''LORD, God of Abraham, Isaac, and Israel, let it be known this day that you are God in Israel and that I am your servant and have done all these things by your command. **37** Answer me, LORD! Answer me, that this people may know that you, LORD, are God and that you have brought them back to their senses.'' **38** The LORD's fire came down and consumed the holocaust, wood, stones, and dust, and it lapped up the water in the trench. **39** Seeing this, all the people fell prostrate and said, ''The LORD is God! The LORD is God!'' **40** Then Elijah said to them, ''Seize the prophets of Baal. Let none of them escape!'' They were seized, and Elijah had them brought down to the brook Kishon and there he slit their throats.

41 Elijah then said to Ahab, ''Go up, eat and drink, for there is the sound of a heavy rain.''

42 So Ahab went up to eat and drink, while Elijah climbed to the top of Carmel, crouched down to the earth, and put his head between his knees. **43** ''Climb up and look out to sea,'' he directed his servant, who went up and looked, but reported, ''There is nothing.'' Seven times he said, ''Go, look again!'' **44** And the seventh time the youth reported, ''There is a cloud as small as a man's hand rising from the sea.'' Elijah said, ''Go and say to Ahab, 'Harness up and leave the mountain before the rain stops you.' '' **45** In a trice, the sky grew dark with clouds and wind, and a heavy rain fell. Ahab mounted his chariot and made for Jezreel. **46** But the hand of the LORD was on Elijah, who girded up his clothing and ran before Ahab as far as the approaches to Jezreel.

CHAPTER 19

Flight to Horeb. **1** Ahab told Jezebel all that Elijah had done—that he had put all the prophets to the sword. **2** Jezebel then sent a messenger to Elijah and said, ''May the gods do thus and so to me if by this time tomorrow I have not done with your life what was done to each of them.'' **3** Elijah was afraid and fled for his life, going to Beer-sheba of Judah. He left his servant there **4** and went a day's journey into the desert, until he came to a broom tree and sat beneath it. He prayed for death: ''This is enough, O LORD! Take my life, for I am no better than my fathers.'' **5** He lay down and fell asleep under the broom tree, but then an angel touched him and ordered him to get up and eat. **6** He looked and there at his head was a hearth cake and a jug of water. After he ate and drank, he lay down again, **7** but the angel of the LORD came back a second time, touched him, and ordered, ''Get up and eat, else the journey will be too long for you!'' **8** He got up, ate and drank; then strengthened by that food, he walked forty days and forty nights to the mountain of God, Horeb.

9 There he came to a cave, where he took shelter. But the word of the LORD came to him, ''Why are you here, Elijah?'' **10** He answered: ''I have been most zealous for the LORD, the God of hosts, but the Israelites have forsaken your covenant, torn down your altars, and put your prophets to the sword. I alone am left, and they seek to take my life.'' **11** *Then the LORD

19, 11ff: Compare these divine manifestations to Elijah with those to Moses (Ex 19, 1–23; 33, 21ff; 34, 5) on the same Mount Horeb (Sinai) (Dt 4, 10–15). Though various phenomena, such as wind, storms, earthquakes, fire (Ex 19, 18f), herald the divine presence, they do not constitute the presence itself which, like the tiny whispering sound, is imperceptible and bespeaks the spirituality of God. It was fitting that Elijah, whose mission it was to reestablish the covenant and restore the pure faith, should have returned to Horeb where the covenant was

said, ''Go outside and stand on the mountain before the LORD; the LORD will be passing by.'' A strong and heavy wind was rending the mountains and crushing rocks before the LORD—but the LORD was not in the wind. After the wind there was an earthquake—but the LORD was not in the earthquake. 12 After the earthquake there was fire—but the LORD was not in the fire. After the fire there was a tiny whispering sound. 13 When he heard this, Elijah hid his face in his cloak and went and stood at the entrance of the cave. A voice said to him, ''Elijah, why are you here?'' 14 He replied, ''I have been most zealous for the LORD, the God of hosts. But the Israelites have forsaken your covenant, torn down your altars, and put your prophets to the sword. I alone am left, and they seek to take my life.''r 15 *''Go, take the road back to the desert near Damascus,'' the LORD said to him. ''When you arrive, you shall anoint Hazael as king of Aram. 16 Then you shall anoint Jehu, son of Nimshi, as king of Israel, and Elisha, son of Shaphat of Abel-meholah, as prophet to succeed you.s 17 If anyone escapes the sword of Hazael, Jehu will kill him. If he escapes the sword of Jehu, Elisha will kill him. 18 Yet I will leave seven thousand men in Israel—all those who have not knelt to Baal or kissed him.''t

Call of Elisha.* 19 Elijah set out, and came upon Elisha, son of Shaphat, as he was plowing with twelve yoke of oxen; he was following the twelfth. Elijah went over to him and threw his cloak over him. 20 Elisha left the oxen, ran after Elijah, and said, ''Please, let me kiss my father and mother goodbye, and I will follow you.'' ''Go back!'' Elijah answered. ''Have I done anything to you?'' 21 Elisha left him and, taking the yoke of oxen, slaughtered them; he used the plowing equipment for fuel to boil their flesh, and gave it to his people to eat. Then he left and followed Elijah as his attendant.

CHAPTER 20

Ahab's Victories over Ben-hadad.

1 Ben-hadad, king of Aram, gathered all his forces, and accompanied by thirty-two kings with horses and chariotry, proceeded to invest and attack Samaria. 2 He sent couriers to Ahab, king of Israel, within the city, 3 and said to him, ''This is Ben-hadad's message: 'Your silver and gold are mine, and your wives and your promising sons are mine.' '' 4 The king of Israel answered, ''As you say, my lord king, I and all I have are yours.'' 5 But the couriers came again and said, ''This is Ben-hadad's message: 'I sent you word to give me your silver and gold, your wives and your sons. 6 Now, however, at this time tomorrow I will send my servants to

you, and they shall ransack your house and the houses of your servants. They shall seize and take away whatever they consider valuable.' ''

7 The king of Israel then summoned all the elders of the land and said: ''Understand clearly that this man wants to ruin us. When he sent to me for my wives and sons, my silver and my gold, I did not refuse him.'' 8 All the elders and all the people said to him, ''Do not listen. Do not give in.'' 9 Accordingly he directed the couriers of Ben-hadad, ''Say to my lord the king, 'I will do all that you demanded of your servant the first time. But this I cannot do.' '' The couriers left and reported this. 10 Ben-hadad then sent him the message, ''May the gods do thus and so to me if there is enough dust in Samaria to make handfuls for all my followers.'' 11 The king of Israel replied, ''Tell him, 'It is not for the man who is buckling his armor to boast as though he were taking it off.' '' 12 Ben-hadad was drinking in the pavilions with the kings when he heard this reply. ''Prepare the assault,'' he commanded his servants; and they made ready to storm the city.

13 Then a prophet came up to Ahab, king of Israel, and said: ''The LORD says, 'Do you see all this huge army? When I deliver it up to you today, you will know that I am the LORD.' '' 14 But Ahab asked, ''Through whom will it be delivered up?'' He answered, ''The LORD says, 'Through the retainers of the governors of the provinces.' '' Then Ahab asked, ''Who is to attack?'' He replied, ''You are.'' 15 So Ahab called up the retainers of the governors of the provinces, two hundred thirty-two of them. Behind them he mustered all the Israelite soldiery, who numbered seven thousand. 16 They marched out at noon, while Ben-hadad was drinking heavily in the pavilions with the thirty-two kings who were his allies. 17 When the retainers of the governors of the provinces marched out first, Ben-hadad received word that some men had marched out of Samaria. 18 He answered, ''Whether they have come out for peace or for war, in any case take them alive.'' 19 But when these had come out of the city

r Rom 11, 3.　　　　　　t Rom 11, 4.
s 2 Kgs 9, 2.

*

revealed to Moses and through him to the Israelite people (Ex 3, 1–4. 17; 33, 18—34, 9). Moses and Elijah appeared with Christ at the time of his transfiguration (Mt 17, 1–9; Mk 9, 1–7; Lk 9, 28–36).

19, 15–17: Elijah himself carried out only the third of the commissions entrusted to him (vv 19–21); Elisha was deputed to perform the first in person (2 Kgs 8, 7–19), and the second through one of his followers (2 Kgs 9, 1–10).

19, 19–21: Elijah's act of throwing his mantle over the shoulders of Elisha expressed the divine call to share the prophetic mission. Elisha's prompt response through destruction of his plow and oxen is an example of total obedience and detachment from his former manner of living in order to promote the glory of God.

—the soldiers of the governors of the provinces with the army following them— **20** each of them struck down his man. The Arameans fled with Israel pursuing them, while Ben-hadad, king of Aram, escaped on a chariot steed. **21** The king of Israel went out, took the horses and chariots, and inflicted a severe defeat on Aram.

22 Then the prophet went up to the king of Israel and said to him: "Go, regroup your forces. Mark well what you do, for at the beginning of the year* the king of Aram will attack you." **23** On the other hand, the servants of the king of Aram said to him: "Their gods are gods of mountains. That is why they defeated us. But if we fight them on level ground, we shall be sure to defeat them. **24** This is what you must do: Take the kings from their posts and put prefects in their places. **25** Mobilize an army as large as the army that has deserted you, horse for horse, chariot for chariot. Let us fight them on level ground, and we shall surely defeat them." He took their advice and did this.

26 At the beginning of the year, Ben-hadad mobilized Aram and went up to Aphek to fight against Israel. **27** The Israelites, too, were called to arms and supplied with provisions; then they went out to engage the foe. The Israelites, encamped opposite them, seemed like a couple of small flocks of goats, while Aram covered the countryside. **28** A man of God came up and said to the king of Israel: "The LORD says, 'Because Aram has said the LORD is a god of mountains, not a god of plains, I will deliver up to you all this large army, that you may know I am the LORD.'" **29** They were encamped opposite each other for seven days. On the seventh day battle was joined, and the Israelites struck down one hundred thousand foot soldiers of Aram in one day. **30** The survivors, twenty-seven thousand of them, fled into the city of Aphek, and there the wall collapsed. Ben-hadad, too, fled, and took refuge within the city, in an inside room.

31 His servants said to him: "We have heard that the kings of the land of Israel are merciful kings. Allow us, therefore, to garb ourselves in sackcloth, with cords around our heads, and go out to the king of Israel. Perhaps he will spare your life." **32** So they dressed in sackcloth girded at the waist, and wearing cords around their heads, they went to the king of Israel. "Your servant Ben-hadad pleads for his life," they said. "Is he still alive?" the king asked. "He is my brother." **33** Hearing this as a good omen, the men quickly took him at his word and said, "Ben-hadad is your brother." He answered, "Go and get him." When Ben-hadad came out to him, the king had him mount his chariot. **34** Ben-hadad said to him, "I will restore the cities which my father took from your

father, and you may make yourself bazaars in Damascus, as my father did in Samaria." "On these terms," Ahab replied, "I will set you free." So he made an agreement with him and then set him free.

35 One of the guild prophets was prompted by the LORD to say to his companion, "Strike me." But he refused to strike him. **36** Then he said to him, "Since you did not obey the voice of the LORD, a lion will kill you when you leave me." When they parted company, a lion came upon him and killed him. **37** The prophet met another man and said, "Strike me." The man struck him a blow and wounded him. **38** The prophet went on and waited for the king on the road, having disguised himself with a bandage over his eyes. **39** As the king was passing, he called out to the king and said, "Your servant went into the thick of the battle, and suddenly someone turned and brought me a man and said, 'Guard this man. If he is missing, you shall have to pay for his life with your life or pay out a talent of silver.' **40** But while your servant was looking here and there, the man disappeared." The king of Israel said to him, "That is your sentence. You have decided it yourself." **41** He immediately removed the bandage from his eyes, and the king of Israel recognized him as one of the prophets. **42** He said to him: "The LORD says, 'Because you have set free the man I doomed to destruction, your life shall pay for his life, your people for his people.'" Disturbed and angry, the king of Israel went off homeward and entered Samaria.ᵘ

CHAPTER 21

Seizure of Naboth's Vineyard. **1** Some time after this, as Naboth the Jezreelite had a vineyard in Jezreel next to the palace of Ahab, king of Samaria, **2** Ahab said to Naboth, "Give me your vineyard to be my vegetable garden, since it is close by, next to my house. I will give you a better vineyard in exchange, or, if you prefer, I will give you its value in money." **3** "The LORD forbid," Naboth answered him, "that I should give you my ancestral heritage." **4** Ahab went home disturbed and angry at the answer Naboth the Jezreelite had made to him: "I will not give you my ancestral heritage." Lying down on his bed, he turned away from food and would not eat.

5 His wife Jezebel came to him and said to him, "Why are you so angry that you will not eat?" **6** He answered her, "Because I spoke to Naboth the Jezreelite and said to him, 'Sell me your vineyard, or, if you prefer, I will give you

---

u 1 Kgs 22, 35.

*

20, 22: At the beginning of the year: in the spring.

a vineyard in exchange.' But he refused to let me have his vineyard.'' 7 "A fine ruler over Israel you are indeed!'' his wife Jezebel said to him. "Get up. Eat and be cheerful. I will obtain the vineyard of Naboth the Jezreelite for you.''

8 So she wrote letters in Ahab's name and, having sealed them with his seal, sent them to the elders and to the nobles who lived in the same city with Naboth. 9 This is what she wrote in the letters: "Proclaim a fast and set Naboth at the head of the people. 10 Next, get two scoundrels to face him and accuse him of having cursed God and king. Then take him out and stone him to death.'' 11 His fellow citizens—the elders and the nobles who dwelt in his city—did as Jezebel had ordered them in writing, through the letters she had sent them. 12 They proclaimed a fast and placed Naboth at the head of the people. 13 Two scoundrels came in and confronted him with the accusation, "Naboth has cursed God and king.'' And they led him out of the city and stoned him to death. 14 Then they sent the information to Jezebel that Naboth had been stoned to death.

15 When Jezebel learned that Naboth had been stoned to death, she said to Ahab, "Go on, take possession of the vineyard of Naboth the Jezreelite which he refused to sell you, because Naboth is not alive, but dead.'' 16 On hearing that Naboth was dead, Ahab started off on his way down to the vineyard of Naboth the Jezreelite, to take possession of it.

17 But the LORD said to Elijah the Tishbite: 18 "Start down to meet Ahab, king of Israel, who rules in Samaria. He will be in the vineyard of Naboth, of which he has come to take possession. 19 *ᵛ This is what you shall tell him, 'The LORD says: After murdering, do you also take possession? For this, the LORD says: In the place where the dogs licked up the blood of Naboth, the dogs shall lick up your blood, too.' '' 20 *"Have you found me out, my enemy?'' Ahab said to Elijah. "Yes,'' he answered. "Because you have given yourself up to doing evil in the LORD's sight, 21 I am bringing evil upon you: I will destroy you and will cut off every male in Ahab's line, whether slave or freeman, in Israel.ʷ 22 I will make your house like that of Jeroboam, son of Nebat, and like that of Baasha, son of Ahijah, because of how you have provoked me by leading Israel into sin.''ˣ 23 (Against Jezebel, too, the LORD declared, "The dogs shall devour Jezebel in the district of Jezreel.'')ʸ 24 "When one of Ahab's line dies in the city, dogs will devour him; when one of them dies in the field, the birds of the sky will devour him.'' 25 Indeed, no one gave himself up to the doing of evil in the sight of the LORD as did Ahab, urged on by his wife Jezebel. 26 He became completely abominable by following idols, just as the Amorites had done,

whom the LORD drove out before the Israelites. 27 When Ahab heard these words, he tore his garments and put on sackcloth over his bare flesh. He fasted, slept in the sackcloth, and went about subdued. 28 Then the LORD said to Elijah the Tishbite, 29 "Have you seen that Ahab has humbled himself before me? Since he has humbled himself before me, I will not bring the evil in his time. I will bring the evil upon his house during the reign of his son.''ᶻ

CHAPTER 22

Campaign against Ramoth-gilead.

1 Three years passed without war between Aram and Israel.ᵃ 2 In the third year, however, King Jehoshaphat of Judah came down to the king of Israel, 3 who said to his servants, "Do you not know that Ramoth-gilead is ours and we are doing nothing to take it from the king of Aram?'' 4 He asked Jehoshaphat, "Will you come with me to fight against Ramoth-gilead?'' Jehoshaphat answered the king of Israel, "You and I are as one, and your people and my people, your horses and my horses as well.'' 5 Jehoshaphat also said to the king of Israel, "Seek the word of the LORD at once.''

6 The king of Israel gathered together the prophets, about four hundred of them, and asked, "Shall I go to attack Ramoth-gilead or shall I refrain?'' "Go up,'' they answered. "The LORD will deliver it over to the king.'' 7 But Jehoshaphat said, "Is there no other prophet of the LORD here whom we may consult?'' 8 The king of Israel answered, "There is one other through whom we might consult the LORD, Micaiah, son of Imlah; but I hate him because he prophesies not good but evil about me.'' Jehoshaphat said, "Let not your majesty speak of evil against you.''

9 So the king of Israel called an official and said to him, "Get Micaiah, son of Imlah, at once.'' 10 The king of Israel and King Jehoshaphat of Judah were seated, each on his throne,

---

v 1 Kgs 22, 38. y 2 Kgs 9, 36.
w 2 Kgs 9, 8. z 2 Kgs 9, 26.
x 1 Kgs 15, 29; 16, 3. a 2 Chr 18, 1.
*

21, 19: The response of Ahab to this divine judgment is described in v 27, and the consequences are given in vv 28–29, and in 2 Kgs 9, 21–26.

21, 20–26: In these verses the Judean editor of the Books of Kings substitutes, for the message of Elijah prepared for in v 19, a sweeping and definitive judgment against the whole family of Ahab in the same terms as were used against the families of Jeroboam I (1 Kgs 14, 9–11) and Baasha (1 Kgs 16, 2–4). This judgment is the fruit of later theological reflection; it is not occasioned directly by the crime against Naboth, but by the idolatry of Ahab and Jezebel. The judgment on Jezebel herself (v 23) may have been uttered by Elijah during the Naboth episode; it finds its fulfillment in 2 Kgs 9, 36–37. Still another theological explanation for the death of Ahab is given by the north Israelite writer of 1 Kgs 20, 35–42 above.

clothed in their robes of state on a threshing floor at the entrance of the gate of Samaria, and all the prophets were prophesying before them. **11** Zedekiah, son of Chenaanah, made himself horns of iron and said, "The LORD says, 'With these you shall gore Aram until you have destroyed them.' " **12** The other prophets prophesied in a similar vein, saying: "Go up to Ramoth-gilead; you shall succeed. The LORD will deliver it over to the king."

13 The messenger who had gone to call Micaiah said to him, "Look now, the prophets are unanimously predicting good for the king. Let your word be the same as any of theirs; predict good." **14** "As the LORD lives," Micaiah answered, "I shall say whatever the LORD tells me."

15 When he came to the king, the king said to him, "Micaiah, shall we go to fight against Ramoth-gilead, or shall we refrain?" "Go up," he answered, "you shall succeed! The LORD will deliver it over to the king." **16** But the king answered him, "How many times must I adjure you to tell me nothing but the truth in the name of the LORD?" **17** So Micaiah said:

"I see all Israel
    scattered on the mountains,
    like sheep without a shepherd,
and the LORD saying, 'These have no
        master!
Let each of them go back home in peace.' "

18 The king of Israel said to Jehoshaphat, "Did I not tell you he prophesies not good but evil about me?" **19** *Micaiah continued: "Therefore hear the word of the LORD: I saw the LORD seated on his throne, with the whole host of heaven standing by to his right and to his left. **20** The LORD asked, 'Who will deceive Ahab, so that he will go up and fall at Ramoth-gilead?' And one said this, another that, **21** until one of the spirits came forth and presented himself to the LORD, saying, 'I will deceive him.' The LORD asked, 'How?' **22** He answered, 'I will go forth and become a lying spirit in the mouths of all his prophets.' The LORD replied, 'You shall succeed in deceiving him. Go forth and do this.' **23** So now, the LORD has put a lying spirit in the mouths of all these prophets of yours, but the LORD himself has decreed evil against you."

24 Thereupon Zedekiah, son of Chenaanah, came up and slapped Micaiah on the cheek, saying, "Has the spirit of the LORD, then, left me to speak with you?" **25** "You shall find out," Micaiah replied, "on that day when you retreat into an inside room to hide." **26** The king of Israel then said, "Seize Micaiah and take him back to Amon, prefect of the city, and to Joash, the king's son, **27** and say, 'This is the king's order: Put this man in prison and feed him scanty rations of bread and water until I return

in safety.' " **28** But Micaiah said, "If ever you return in safety, the LORD has not spoken through me."*

29 The king of Israel and King Jehoshaphat of Judah went up to Ramoth-gilead, **30** and the king of Israel said to Jehoshaphat, "I will disguise myself and go into battle, but you put on your own clothes." So the king of Israel disguised himself and entered the fray. **31** In the meantime the king of Aram had given his thirty-two chariot commanders the order, "Do not fight with anyone at all except the king of Israel." **32** When the chariot commanders saw Jehoshaphat, they cried out, "That must be the king of Israel!" and shifted to fight him. But Jehoshaphat shouted his battle cry, **33** and the chariot commanders, aware that he was not the king of Israel, gave up pursuit of him. **34** Someone, however, drew his bow at random, and hit the king of Israel between the joints of his breast-plate. He ordered his charioteer, "Rein about and take me out of the ranks, for I am disabled." **35** The battle grew fierce during the day, and the king, who was propped up in his chariot facing the Arameans, died in the evening. The blood from his wound flowed to the bottom of the chariot.ᵇ **36** At sunset a cry went through the army, "Every man to his city, every man to his land, **37** for the king is dead!" So they went to Samaria, where they buried the king. **38** When the chariot was washed at the pool of Samaria, the dogs licked up his blood and harlots bathed there, as the LORD had prophesied.ᶜ

39 The rest of the acts of Ahab, with all that he did, including the ivory palace and all the cities he built, are recorded in the book of the chronicles of the kings of Israel. **40** Ahab rested with his ancestors, and his son Ahaziah succeeded him as king.

Reign of Jehoshaphat. **41** Jehoshaphat, son of Asa, began to reign over Judah in the fourth year of Ahab, king of Israel. **42** Jehoshaphat was thirty-five years old when he began to reign, and reigned twenty-five years in Jerusalem. His mother's name was Azubah, daughter of Shilhi. **43** He followed all the ways of his father Asa unswervingly, doing what was right in the LORD's sight. **44** Nevertheless, the high places did not disappear, and the people continued to sacrifice and to burn incense on the high

---

b 1 Kgs 20, 42.   c 1 Kgs 21, 19.
*

22, 19–23: The prophet Micaiah uses as a last resort to deter Ahab from his foolhardy design of fighting against Ramoth-gilead the literary device of describing false prophets as messengers of a lying spirit which God, after holding counsel with his angels, permits to deceive them.
22, 28: A note in the Hebrew text after this verse attributes to Micaiah ben Imlah the first words of the book of a different Micaiah, the minor prophet of Moresheth.

places. **45** Jehoshaphat also made peace with the king of Israel. **46** The rest of the acts of Jehoshaphat, with his prowess, what he did and how he fought, are recorded in the book of the chronicles of the kings of Judah.

47 He removed from the land the rest of the cult prostitutes who had remained in the reign of his father Asa. **48** There was no king in Edom, but an appointed regent. **49** Jehoshaphat made Tarshish ships to go to Ophir for gold; but in fact the ships did not go, because they were wrecked at Ezion-geber. **50** Then Ahaziah, son of Ahab, said to Jehoshaphat, "Let my servants accompany your servants in the ships." But Jehoshaphat would not agree. **51** Jehoshaphat rested with his ancestors; he was buried in his forefathers' City of David. His son Jehoram succeeded him as king.

Reign of Ahaziah.

52 Ahaziah, son of Ahab, began to reign over Israel in Samaria in the seventeenth year* of Jehoshaphat, king of Judah; he reigned two years over Israel. **53** He did evil in the sight of the Lord, behaving like his father, his mother, and Jeroboam, son of Nebat, who caused Israel to sin. **54** He served and worshiped Baal, thus provoking the Lord, the God of Israel, just as his father had done.

22, 52: Seventeenth year: so the present Hebrew text. More consistent with 2 Kgs 1, 17 would be a date in the twenty-fourth year of Jehoshaphat for Ahab's death; see note on 2 Kgs 1, 1.

The Second Book of

KINGS

I: The Kingdoms of Israel and Judah

CHAPTER 1

Ahaziah Consults Baalzebub. **1** After Ahab's death, Moab rebelled against Israel.*a* **2** Ahaziah had fallen through the lattice of his roof terrace at Samaria and had been injured. So he sent out messengers with the instructions: "Go and inquire of Baalzebub,* the god of Ekron, whether I shall recover from this injury."

3 Meanwhile, the angel of the LORD said to Elijah the Tishbite: "Go, intercept the messengers of Samaria's king, and ask them, 'Is it because there is no God in Israel that you are going to inquire of Baalzebub, the god of Ekron?' **4** For this, the LORD says: 'You shall not leave the bed upon which you lie; instead, you shall die.'" And with that, Elijah departed. **5** The messengers then returned to Ahaziah, who asked them, "Why have you returned?" **6** "A man came up to us," they answered, "who said to us, 'Go back to the king who sent you and tell him: The LORD says, Is it because there is no God in Israel that you are sending to inquire of Baalzebub, the god of Ekron? For this you shall not leave the bed upon which you lie; instead, you shall die.'" **7** The king asked them, "What was the man like who came up to you and said these things to you?" **8** "Wearing a hairy garment,"* they replied, "with a leather girdle about his loins." "It is Elijah the Tishbite!" he exclaimed.*b*

Death of Two Captains. **9** Then the king sent a captain with his company of fifty men after Elijah. The prophet was seated on a hilltop when he found him. "Man of God," he ordered, "the king commands you to come down." **10** "If I am a man of God," Elijah answered the captain, "may fire come down from heaven and consume you and your fifty men." And fire came down from heaven and consumed him and his fifty men.*c* **11** Ahaziah sent another captain with his company of fifty men after Elijah. "Man of God," he called out to Elijah, "the king commands you to come down immediately." **12** "If I am a man of God," Elijah answered him, "May fire come down from heaven and consume you and your

fifty men." And divine fire* came down from heaven, consuming him and his fifty men.

Death of the King. **13** Again, for the third time, Ahaziah sent a captain with his company of fifty men. When the third captain arrived, he fell to his knees before Elijah, pleading with him. "Man of God," he implored him, "let my life and the lives of these fifty men, your servants, count for something in your sight! **14** Already fire has come down from heaven, consuming two captains with their companies of fifty men. But now, let my life mean something to you!" **15** Then the angel of the LORD said to Elijah, "Go down with him; you need not be afraid of him."

16 So Elijah left and went down with him and stated to the king: "Thus says the LORD: 'Because you sent messengers to inquire of Baalzebub, the god of Ekron, you shall not leave the bed upon which you lie; instead you shall die.'"*d*

17 Ahaziah died in fulfillment of the prophecy of the LORD spoken by Elijah. Since he had no son, his brother Joram* succeeded him as king, in the second year of Jehoram, son of Jehoshaphat, king of Judah. **18** The rest of the acts of Ahaziah are recorded in the book of chronicles of the kings of Israel.

---

a 2 Kgs 3, 4-27.   9, 54f.
b Zec 13, 4.
c Lv 10, 2; Sir 48, 3f; Lk   d Sir 48, 6.

---

*

1, 2: Baalzebub: in this form, "Baal of flies." The name in the Hebrew text is a derisive alteration of Baalzebul, "Prince Baal." The best New Testament evidence supports the latter form in Mt. 10, 25; Lk 11, 15. Later associations with Aramaic beeldebaba, "enemy," gave the ancient name its connotation of "devil."

1, 8: Hairy garment: a sign of ascetical and prophetic calling, imitated by John the Baptizer; see Mt 3, 4; Mk 1, 6.

1, 12: Divine fire: literally, "fire of God," which in Hebrew sounds quite like man of God. The play on words is the basis for Elijah's alleged retort. This story was told among the people to enhance the dignity of the prophet and to reflect the power of God whom he served. The mercy which God extends even to the wicked is described in Wis 11, 17–12, 22, and the prophet Elijah was well aware of it (1 Kgs 21, 28f).

1, 17: Joram: in the Second Book of Kings the name Joram (yoram), alternately Jehoram (yehoram), appears in numerous passages to designate both the king of Judah, son and successor of Jehoshaphat (848–841 B.C.), and the contemporary king of Israel, son of Ahab (852–841 B.C.). For the convenience of the reader in distinguishing these two kings, the longer form, Jehoram, is used to designate the king of Judah and the shorter form, Joram, to designate the king of Israel. See note on 2 Kgs 3, 1.

CHAPTER 2

Elijah and Elisha. 1 When the LORD was about to take Elijah up to heaven in a whirlwind, he and Elisha were on their way from Gilgal.* 2 "Stay here, please," Elijah said to Elisha. "The LORD has sent me on to Bethel." "As the LORD lives, and as you yourself live," Elisha replied, "I will not leave you." So they went down to Bethel, 3 where the guild prophets went out to Elisha and asked him, "Do you know that the LORD will take your master from over you today?" "Yes, I know it," he replied. "Keep still."

4 Then Elijah said to him, "Stay here, please, Elisha, for the LORD has sent me on to Jericho." "As the LORD lives, and as you yourself live," Elisha replied, "I will not leave you." 5 They went on to Jericho, where the guild prophets approached Elisha and asked him, "Do you know that the LORD will take your master from over you today?" "Yes, I know it," he replied. "Keep still."

6 Elijah said to Elisha, "Please stay here; the LORD has sent me on to the Jordan." "As the LORD lives, and as you yourself live," Elisha replied, "I will not leave you." And so the two went on together. 7 Fifty of the guild prophets followed, and when the two stopped at the Jordan, stood facing them at a distance. 8 Elijah took his mantle, rolled it up and struck the water, which divided, and both crossed over on dry ground.[e]

Elisha Succeeds Elijah. 9 When they had crossed over, Elijah said to Elisha, "Ask for whatever I may do for you, before I am taken from you." Elisha answered, "May I receive a double portion of your spirit."* 10 "You have asked something that is not easy," he replied. "Still, if you see me taken up from you, your wish will be granted; otherwise not."[f] 11 As they walked on conversing, a flaming chariot and flaming horses came between them, and Elijah went up to heaven in a whirlwind.[g] 12 When Elisha saw it happen he cried out, "My father!* my father! Israel's chariots and drivers!" But when he could no longer see him, Elisha gripped his own garment and tore it in two.[h]

13 Then he picked up Elijah's mantle which had fallen from him, and went back and stood at the bank of the Jordan.[i] 14 Wielding the mantle which had fallen from Elijah, he struck the water in his turn and said, "Where is the LORD, the God of Elijah?" When Elisha struck the water it divided and he crossed over.

15 The guild prophets in Jericho, who were on the other side, saw him and said, "The spirit of Elijah rests on Elisha." They went to meet him, bowing to the ground before him.

16 "Among your servants are fifty brave men," they said. "Let them go in search of your master. Perhaps the spirit of the LORD has carried him away to some mountain or some valley." "Do not send them," he answered.[j] 17 However, they kept urging him, until he was embarrassed and said, "Send them." So they sent the fifty men, who searched for three days without finding him. 18 When they returned to Elisha in Jericho, where he was staying, he said to them, "Did I not tell you not to go?"

Healing of the Water. 19 Once the inhabitants of the city complained to Elisha, "The site of the city is fine indeed, as my lord can see, but the water is bad and the land unfruitful." 20 "Bring me a new bowl," Elisha said, "and put salt into it." When they had brought it to him, 21 he went out to the spring and threw salt into it, saying, "Thus says the LORD, 'I have purified this water. Never again shall death or miscarriage spring from it.' " 22 And the water has stayed pure even to this day, just as Elisha prophesied.

The Prophet's Curse. 23 *From there Elisha went up to Bethel. While he was on the way, some small boys came out of the city and jeered at him. "Go up, baldhead," they shouted, "go up, baldhead!" 24 The prophet turned and saw them, and he cursed them in the name of the LORD. Then two she-bears came out of the woods and tore forty-two of the children to pieces. 25 From there he went to Mount Carmel, and thence he returned to Samaria.

---

e Ex 14, 16. 22.
f Nm 11, 17. 25.
g Gn 5, 24; 1 Mc 2, 58; Acts 1, 9.
h 2 Kgs 13, 14; Sir 48, 9. 12.
i 1 Kgs 19, 19.
j 1 Kgs 18, 12.

*

2, 1: Gilgal: commonly identified with Jiljulieh, about seven miles north of Bethel, and different from the Gilgal in Dt 11, 30 near Shechem, and that in Jos 4 and 5, passim, near Jericho.

2, 9: Double portion of your spirit: as the first-born son inherited a double portion of his father's property (Dt 21, 17), so Elisha asks to inherit from Elijah his spirit of prophecy in the degree befitting his principal disciple. In Nm 11, 17. 25, God bestows some of the spirit of Moses on others.

2, 12: My father: a religious title accorded prophetic leaders; cf 2 Kgs 6, 21; 8, 9. Israel's chariots and drivers: Elijah was worth more than a whole army in defending Israel and the true religion. King Joash of Israel uses the same phrase of Elisha himself (2 Kgs 13, 14).

2, 23f: This story, like the one about Elijah and the captains (ch 1), is preserved for us in Scripture to convey a popular understanding of the dignity of the prophet. Told in popular vein, it becomes a caricature, in which neither Elisha nor the bears behave in character. See note on 2 Kgs 1, 12 and the contrasting narrative in ch 4.

CHAPTER 3

Campaign of Joram against Moab.

1 Joram, son of Ahab, became king of Israel in Samaria [in the eighteenth year of Jehoshaphat, king of Judah, and he reigned for twelve years].* **2** He did evil in the LORD's sight, though not as much as his father and mother. He did away with the pillar of Baal, which his father had made, **3** but he still clung to the sin to which Jeroboam, son of Nebat, had lured Israel; this he did not give up.

4 Now Mesha, king of Moab, who raised sheep, used to pay the king of Israel as tribute a hundred thousand lambs and the wool of a hundred thousand rams. **5** But when Ahab died, the king of Moab had rebelled against the king of Israel. **6** Joram as king mustered all Israel, and when he set out on a campaign from Samaria, **7** he sent the king of Judah the message: "The king of Moab is in rebellion against me. Will you join me in battle against Moab?" "I will," he replied. "You and I shall be as one, your people and mine, and your horses and mine as well."[k] **8** They discussed the route for their attack, and settled upon the route through the desert of Edom.

9 So the king of Israel set out, accompanied by the king of Judah and the king of Edom. After their roundabout journey of seven days the water gave out for the army and for the animals with them. **10** "Alas!" exclaimed the king of Israel. "The LORD has called together these three kings to put them in the grasp of Moab." **11** But the king of Judah asked, "Is there no prophet of the LORD here through whom we may inquire of the LORD?" One of the officers of the king of Israel replied, "Elisha, son of Shaphat, who poured water on the hands of Elijah, is here."[l] **12** "He has the word of the LORD," the king of Judah agreed. So the kings of Israel, Judah, and Edom went down to Elisha. **13** "What do you want with me?" Elisha asked the king of Israel. "Go to the prophets of your father and to the prophets of your mother." "No," the king of Israel replied. "The LORD has called these three kings together to put them in the grasp of Moab." **14** Then Elisha said, "As the LORD of hosts lives, whom I serve, were it not that I respect the king of Judah, I should neither look at you nor notice you at all.[m] **15** Now get me a minstrel."

When the minstrel played, the power of the LORD came upon Elisha **16** and he announced: "Thus says the LORD, 'Provide many catch basins in this wadi.' **17** For the LORD says, 'Though you will see neither wind nor rain, yet this wadi will be filled with water for you, your livestock, and your pack animals to drink.' **18** And since the LORD does not consider this enough, he will also deliver Moab into your

grasp. **19** You shall destroy every fortified city, fell every fruit tree, stop up all the springs, and ruin every fertile field with stones."[n]

20 In the morning, at the time of the sacrifice, water came from the direction of Edom and filled the land.[o] **21** Meanwhile, all Moab heard that the kings had come to give them battle; every man capable of bearing arms was called up and stationed at the border. **22** Early that morning, when the sun shone on the water, the Moabites saw the water at a distance as red as blood.* **23** "This is blood!" they exclaimed. "The kings have fought among themselves and killed one another. Quick! To the spoils, Moabites!" **24** But when they reached the camp of Israel, the Israelites rose up and attacked the Moabites, who fled from them. They ranged through the countryside striking down the Moabites, and **25** destroying the cities; each of them cast stones onto every fertile field till they had loaded it down; all the springs they stopped up and every useful tree they felled. Finally only Kir-hareseth* was left behind its stone walls, and the slingers had surrounded it and were attacking it.[p] **26** When he saw that he was losing the battle, the king of Moab took seven hundred swordsmen to break through to the king of Aram, but he failed. **27** So he took his first-born, his heir apparent, and offered him as a holocaust upon the wall. The wrath against

---

k 1 Kgs 22, 4.
l 1 Kgs 22, 7.
m 1 Kgs 18, 15.
n Dt 20, 19.

o 1 Kgs 18, 29.
p Jb 5, 23.
q Jgs 11, 30f.

*

3, 1: The sequence of the reigns between Ahab and Jehu of Israel may be reconstructed as follows: Jehoshaphat of Judah outlived Ahab by a short time, so that Ahaziah of Israel was his contemporary. Jehoram of Judah succeeded his father Jehoshaphat while Ahaziah of Israel was still alive. Jehoram (Joram) of Israel became king, following his brother Ahaziah, in the second year of Jehoram of Judah (2 Kgs 1, 17); this is one datum on which the earliest Greek evidence and the standard Hebrew text are in agreement.

The two Jehorams were contemporary for much of their reigns; Jehoram of Judah was succeeded by Ahaziah something more than a year before Jehu did away with the rulers of both kingdoms (2 Kgs 9, 1–29).

The Moabite campaign of 2 Kgs 3, 4–27 is thus best placed under the two Kings Jehoram, before the Edomite rebellion mentioned in 2 Kgs 8, 20. In the received Hebrew text, Jehoshaphat has been made the Judahite protagonist in the campaign against Moab as a tribute to his piety; this assimilates the story of 2 Kgs 3 to that of 1 Kgs 22, but creates difficulties in the chronology which the extant data leave party unresolved. An older practice for stories of the Israelite kings was to leave them and their fellow kings without identification by name; cf 2 Kgs 6, 8—7, 20. The name of Jehoshaphat has been omitted from a number of places in 2 Kgs 3—8, in this translation; cf 1 Kgs 22, 51.

3, 22: Red as blood: possibly caused by the red sandstone of the Wadi Zered (Dt 2, 13), south of Moab.

3, 25: Kir-hareseth: modern Kerak, east of the Dead Sea; cf Is 16, 7. 11; Jer 48, 31. 36.

3, 27: The wrath against Israel: probably the wrath of Chemosh, the Moabite god to whom the child was offered. He was feared by the Israelites who lost heart on foreign soil.

Israel* was so great that they gave up the siege and returned to their own land. *q*

CHAPTER 4

The Widow's Oil.   **1** *r*A certain woman, the widow of one of the guild prophets, complained to Elisha: "My husband, your servant, is dead. You know that he was a God-fearing man, yet now his creditor has come to take my two children as his slaves."* **2** "How can I help you?" Elisha answered her. "Tell me what you have in the house." "This servant of yours has nothing in the house but a jug of oil," she replied. **3** "Go out," he said, "borrow vessels from all your neighbors—as many empty vessels as you can. **4** Then come back and close the door on yourself and your children; pour the oil into all the vessels, and as each is filled, set it aside." **5** She went and did so, closing the door on herself and her children. As they handed her the vessels, she would pour in oil. **6** When all the vessels were filled, she said to her son, "Bring me another vessel." "There is none left," he answered her. And then the oil stopped. **7** She went and told the man of God, who said, "Go and sell the oil to pay off your creditor; with what remains, you and your children can live."

Elisha and the Shunammite.   **8** One day Elisha came to Shunem, where there was a woman of influence, who urged him to dine with her. Afterward, whenever he passed by, he used to stop there to dine. **9** So she said to her husband, "I know that he is a holy man of God. Since he visits us often, **10** let us arrange a little room on the roof and furnish it for him with a bed, table, chair, and lamp, so that when he comes to us he can stay there." **11** Some time later Elisha arrived and stayed in the room overnight. **12** Then he said to his servant Gehazi, "Call this Shunammite woman." He did so, and when she stood before Elisha, **13** he told Gehazi, "Say to her, 'You have lavished all this care on us; what can we do for you? Can we say a good word for you to the king or to the commander of the army?'" She replied, "I am living among my own people." **14** Later Elisha asked, "Can something be done for her?" "Yes!" Gehazi answered. "She has no son, and her husband is getting on in years." **15** "Call her," said Elisha. When she had been called, and stood at the door, **16** Elisha promised, "This time next year you will be fondling a baby son." "Please, my lord," she protested, "you are a man of God; do not deceive your servant."*s* **17** Yet the woman conceived, and by the same time the following year she had given birth to a son, as Elisha promised.

18 The day came when the child was old enough to go out to his father among the reap-

ers.*t* **19** "My head hurts!" he complained to his father. "Carry him to his mother," the father said to a servant. **20** The servant picked him up and carried him to his mother; he stayed with her until noon, when he died in her lap. **21** The mother took him upstairs and laid him on the bed of the man of God. Closing the door on him, she went out **22** and called to her husband, "Let me have a servant and a donkey. I must go quickly to the man of God, and I will be back." **23** "Why are you going to him today?" he asked. "It is neither the new moon nor the sabbath." But she bade him good-bye, **24** and when the donkey was saddled, said to her servant: "Lead on! Do not stop my donkey unless I tell you to." **25** She kept going till she reached the man of God on Mount Carmel. When he spied her at a distance, the man of God said to his servant Gehazi: "There is the Shunammite! **26** Hurry to meet her, and ask if all is well with her, with her husband, and with the boy." "Greetings,"* she replied. **27** But when she reached the man of God on the mountain, she clasped his feet. Gehazi came near to push her away, but the man of God said: "Let her alone, she is in bitter anguish; the LORD hid it from me and did not let me know." **28** "Did I ask my lord for a son?" she cried out. "Did I not beg you not to deceive me?" **29** "Gird your loins," Elisha said to Gehazi, "take my staff with you and be off; if you meet anyone, do not greet him,* and if anyone greets you, do not answer. Lay my staff upon the boy." **30** But the boy's mother cried out: "As the LORD lives and as you yourself live, I will not release you." So he started to go back with her.

31 *u*Meanwhile, Gehazi had gone on ahead and had laid the staff upon the boy, but there was no sound or sign of life. He returned to meet Elisha and informed him that the boy had not awakened. **32** When Elisha reached the house, he found the boy lying dead. **33** He went in, closed the door on them both, and prayed to the LORD.*v* **34** Then he lay upon the child on the bed, placing his mouth upon the child's mouth, his eyes upon the eyes, and his hands upon the hands. As Elisha stretched himself over the child, the body became warm. **35** He arose, paced up and down the room, and then once

---

r 1 Kgs 17, 8-16.   u 31-36; Acts 20, 10ff.
s Gn 18, 10.   v 1 Kgs 17, 21-23.
t 1 Kgs 17, 17-24.   w Heb 11, 35.

*

4, 1: His creditor ... slaves: Hebrew law permitted the selling of wife and children as chattels for debt; cf. Ex 21, 7; Am 2, 6; 8, 6; Is 50.

4, 26: Greetings: the conventional answer to Gehazi's question, which tells him nothing.

4, 29: Do not greet him: the profuse exchange of compliments among Orientals meeting and greeting one another consumed time. Urgency necessitated their omission, as our Lord counseled his disciples (Lk 10, 4).

more lay down upon the boy, who now sneezed seven times and opened his eyes.ʷ **36** Elisha summoned Gehazi and said, "Call the Shunammite." She came at his call, and Elisha said to her, "Take your son." **37** She came in and fell at his feet in gratitude; then she took her son and left the room.

The Poisoned Stew. **38** When Elisha returned to Gilgal, there was a famine in the land. Once, when the guild prophets were seated before him, he said to his servant, "Put the large pot on, and make some vegetable stew for the guild prophets." **39** Someone went out into the field to gather herbs and found a wild vine, from which he picked a clothful of wild gourds. On his return he cut them up into the pot of vegetable stew without anybody's knowing it. **40** The stew was poured out for the men to eat, but when they began to eat it, they exclaimed, "Man of God, there is poison in the pot!" And they could not eat it. **41** "Bring some meal," Elisha said. He threw it into the pot and said, "Serve it to the people to eat." And there was no longer anything harmful in the pot.

Multiplication of Loaves. **42** A man came from Baal-shalishah bringing the man of God twenty barley loaves made from the first-fruits, and fresh grain in the ear. "Give it to the people to eat," Elisha said. **43** But his servant objected, "How can I set this before a hundred men?" "Give it to the people to eat," Elisha insisted. "For thus says the LORD, 'They shall eat and there shall be some left over.'" **44** And when they had eaten, there was some left over, as the LORD had said.

CHAPTER 5

Cure of Naaman. **1** Naaman, the army commander of the king of Aram, was highly esteemed and respected by his master, for through him the LORD had brought victory to Aram. But valiant as he was, the man was a leper. **2** Now the Arameans had captured from the land of Israel in a raid a little girl, who became the servant of Naaman's wife. **3** "If only my master would present himself to the prophet in Samaria," she said to her mistress, "he would cure him of his leprosy." **4** Naaman went and told his lord just what the slave girl from the land of Israel had said. **5** "Go," said the king of Aram. "I will send along a letter to the king of Israel." So Naaman set out, taking along ten silver talents, six thousand gold pieces, and ten festal garments. **6** To the king of Israel he brought the letter, which read: "With this letter I am sending my servant Naaman to you, that you may cure him of his leprosy."

7 When he read the letter, the king of Israel tore his garments and exclaimed: "Am I a god with power over life and death, that this man should send someone to me to be cured of leprosy? Take note! You can see he is only looking for a quarrel with me!"ˣ **8** When Elisha, the man of God, heard that the king of Israel had torn his garments, he sent word to the king: "Why have you torn your garments? Let him come to me and find out that there is a prophet in Israel."

9 Naaman came with his horses and chariots and stopped at the door of Elisha's house. **10** The prophet sent him the message: "Go and wash seven times in the Jordan, and your flesh will heal, and you will be clean."ʸ **11** But Naaman went away angry, saying, "I thought that he would surely come out and stand there to invoke the LORD his God, and would move his hand over the spot, and thus cure the leprosy. **12** Are not the rivers of Damascus, the Abana and the Pharpar, better than all the waters of Israel? Could I not wash in them and be cleansed?"* With this, he turned about in anger and left.

13 But his servants came up and reasoned with him. "My father," they said, "if the prophet had told you to do something extraordinary, would you not have done it? All the more now, since he said to you, 'Wash and be clean,' should you do as he said." **14** So Naaman went down and plunged into the Jordan seven times at the word of the man of God. His flesh became again like the flesh of a little child, and he was clean.ᶻ

15 He returned with his whole retinue to the man of God. On his arrival he stood before him and said, "Now I know that there is no God in all the earth, except in Israel. Please accept a gift from your servant."

16 "As the LORD lives whom I serve, I will not take it," Elisha replied; and despite Naaman's urging, he still refused. **17** Naaman said: "If you will not accept, please let me, your servant, have two mule-loads of earth,* for I will no longer offer holocaust or sacrifice to any other god except to the LORD. **18** But I trust the LORD will forgive your servant this: when my master enters the temple of Rimmon to worship there, then I, too, as his adjutant, must bow down in the temple of Rimmon. May the LORD

---

x Gn 30, 2; 1 Sm 2, 6;   y Jn 9, 7.
  Jn 5, 21.   z Lk 4, 27.

*

5, 12: **Wash in them and be cleansed:** typical of the ambiguity in ritual healing or cleanliness. The muddy waters of the Jordan are no match hygienically for the mountain spring waters of Damascus; ritually, it is the other way around.

5, 17: **Two mule-loads of earth:** Israelite earth on which to erect in Aram an altar to the God of Israel.

forgive your servant this." **19** "Go in peace,"* Elisha said to him.

20 Naaman had gone some distance when Gehazi, the servant of Elisha, the man of God, thought to himself: "My master was too easy with this Aramean Naaman, not accepting what he brought. As the LORD lives, I will run after him and get something out of him." **21** So Gehazi hurried after Naaman. Aware that someone was running after him, Naaman alighted from his chariot to wait for him. "Is everything all right?" he asked. **22** "Yes," Gehazi replied, "but my master sent me to say, 'Two young men have just come to me, guild prophets from the hill country of Ephraim. Please give them a talent of silver and two festal garments.' " **23** "Please take two talents," Naaman said, and pressed them upon him. He tied up these silver talents in bags and gave them, with the two festal garments, to two of his servants, who carried them before Gehazi. **24** When they reached the hill, Gehazi took what they had, carried it into the house, and sent the men on their way.

25 He went in and stood before Elisha his master, who asked him, "Where have you been, Gehazi?" He answered, "Your servant has not gone anywhere." **26** But Elisha said to him: "Was I not present in spirit when the man alighted from his chariot to wait for you? Is this a time to take money or to take garments, olive orchards or vineyards, sheep or cattle, male or female servants? **27** The leprosy of Naaman shall cling to you and your descendants forever." And Gehazi left Elisha, a leper white as snow. *a*

CHAPTER 6

Recovery of the Lost Ax. **1** The guild prophets once said to Elisha: "There is not enough room for us to continue to live here with you. **2** Let us go to the Jordan, where by getting one beam apiece we can build ourselves a place to live." "Go," Elisha said. **3** "Please agree to accompany your servants," one of them requested. "Yes, I will come," he replied.

4 So he went with them, and when they arrived at the Jordan they began to fell trees. **5** While one of them was felling a tree trunk, the iron axhead slipped into the water. "O master," he cried out, "it was borrowed!" **6** "Where did it fall?" asked the man of God. When he pointed out the spot, Elisha cut off a stick, threw it into the water, and brought the iron to the surface. **7** "Pick it up," he said. And the man reached down and grasped it.

Aramean Ambush. **8** When the king of Aram was waging war on Israel, he would make plans with his servants to attack a particular

place. **9** But the man of God would send word to the king of Israel, "Be careful! Do not pass by this place, for Aram will attack there." **10** So the king of Israel would send word to the place which the man of God had indicated, and alert it; then they would be on guard. This happened several times.

11 Greatly disturbed over this, the king of Aram called together his officers. "Will you not tell me," he asked them, "who among us is for the king of Israel?" **12** "No one, my lord king," answered one of the officers. "The Israelite prophet Elisha can tell the king of Israel the very words you speak in your bedroom." **13** "Go, find out where he is," he said, "so that I may take him captive."

Blinded Aramean Soldiers. Informed that Elisha was in Dothan, **14** he sent there a strong force with horses and chariots. They arrived by night and surrounded the city. **15** Early the next morning, when the attendant of the man of God arose and went out, he saw the force with its horses and chariots surrounding the city. "Alas!" he said to Elisha. "What shall we do, my lord?" **16** "Do not be afraid," Elisha answered. "Our side outnumbers theirs." **17** Then he prayed, "O LORD, open his eyes, that he may see." And the LORD opened the eyes of the servant, so that he saw the mountainside filled with horses and fiery chariots around Elisha. *b*

18 When the Arameans came down to get him, Elisha prayed to the LORD, "Strike this people blind, I pray you." And in answer to the prophet's prayer the LORD struck them blind. **19** Then Elisha said to them: "This is the wrong road, and this is the wrong city. Follow me! I will take you to the man you want." And he led them to Samaria. **20** When they entered Samaria, Elisha prayed, "O LORD, open their eyes that they may see." The LORD opened their eyes, and they saw that they were inside Samaria. **21** When the king of Israel saw them, he asked, "Shall I kill them, my father?" **22** "You must not kill them," replied Elisha. "Do you slay those whom you have taken captive with your sword or bow?* Serve them bread and water. Let them eat and drink, and then go back to their master." **23** The king spread a great feast for them. When they had eaten and

---

a Ex 4, 6; Nm 12, 10.   b 2 Kgs 7, 6; Ps 67, 18.
*

5, 19: **Go in peace:** Elisha understands and approves the situation of Naaman who, though a proselyte as regards belief in and worship of the God of Israel, is required by his office to assist his master, the king, worshiping in the pagan temple of Rimmon.

6, 22: **With your sword or bow:** since the king would not slay prisoners who had surrendered to his power, much less should he slay prisoners captured by God's power. By Oriental custom they became guests within Samaria's walls.

drunk he sent them away, and they went back to their master. No more Aramean raiders came into the land of Israel.

Siege of Samaria. 24 After this, Ben-hadad, king of Aram, mustered his whole army and laid seige to Samaria. 25 Because of the seige the famine in Samaria was so severe that an ass's head sold for eighty pieces of silver, and a fourth of a kab of wild onion for five pieces of silver.

26 One day, as the king of Israel was walking on the city wall, a woman cried out to him, "Help, my lord king!" 27 "No," he replied, "the LORD help you! Where could I find help for you: from the threshing floor or the winepress?" 28 Then the king asked her, "What is your trouble?" She replied: "This woman said to me, 'Give up your son that we may eat him today; then tomorrow we will eat my son.'ᶜ 29 So we boiled my son and ate him. The next day I said to her, 'Now give up your son that we may eat him.' But she hid her son." 30 When the king heard the woman's words, he tore his garments. And as he was walking on the wall, the people saw that he was wearing sackcloth underneath, next to his skin.ᵈ

31 "May God do thus and so to me," the king exclaimed, "if the head of Elisha, son of Shaphat, stays on him today!" 32 Meanwhile, Elisha was sitting in his house in conference with the elders. The king had sent a man ahead before he himself should come to him. Elisha had said to the elders: "Do you know that this son of a murderer is sending someone to cut off my head? When the messenger comes, see that you close the door and hold it fast against him. His master's footsteps are echoing behind him." 33 While Elisha was still speaking, the king came down to him and said, "This evil is from the LORD. Why should I trust in the LORD any longer?"

CHAPTER 7

1 Elisha said: "Hear the word of the LORD! Thus says the LORD, 'At this time tomorrow a seah of fine flour will sell for a shekel, and two seahs of barley for a shekel, in the market* of Samaria.'" 2 But the adjutant on whose arm the king leaned, answered the man of God, "Even if the LORD were to make windows in heaven, how could this happen?" "You shall see it with your own eyes," Elisha said, "but you shall not eat of it."ᵉ

The Lepers at the Gate. 3 At the city gate were four lepers who were deliberating, "Why should we sit here until we die?ᶠ 4 If we decide to go into the city, we shall die there, for there is famine in the city. If we remain here, we shall die too. Come, let us desert to the camp of the

Arameans. If they spare us, we live; if they kill us, we die." 5 At twilight they left for the Arameans; but when they reached the edge of the camp, no one was there. 6 ᵍThe LORD had caused the army of the Arameans to hear the sound of chariots and horses, the din of a large army, and they had reasoned among themselves, "The king of Israel has hired the kings of the Hittites and the kings of the borderlands* to fight us." 7 Then in the twilight they fled, abandoning their tents, their horses, and their asses, the whole camp just as it was, and fleeing for their lives.

8 After the lepers reached the edge of the camp, they went first into one tent, ate and drank, and took silver, gold, and clothing from it, and went out and hid them. Back they came into another tent, took things from it, and again went out and hid them. 9 Then they said to one another: "We are not doing right. This is a day of good news, and we are keeping silent. If we wait until morning breaks, we shall be blamed. Come, let us go and inform the palace."

10 They came and summoned the city gatekeepers. "We went to the camp of the Arameans," they said, "but no one was there—not a human voice, only the horses and asses tethered, and the tents just as they were left." 11 The gatekeepers announced this and it was reported within the palace. 12 Though it was night, the king got up; he said to his servants: "Let me tell you what the Arameans have done to us. Knowing that we are in famine, they have left their camp to hide in the field, hoping to take us alive and enter our city when we leave it." 13 One of his servants, however, suggested: "Since those who are left in the city are not better off than all the throng that has perished, let some of us take five of the abandoned horses and send scouts to investigate."

End of the Siege. 14 They took two chariots, and horses, and the king sent them to reconnoiter the Aramean army. "Go and find out," he ordered. 15 They followed the Arameans as far as the Jordan, and the whole route was strewn with garments and other objects that the Arameans had thrown away in their haste. The messengers returned and told the king.

16 The people went out and plundered the camp of the Arameans; and then a seah of fine flour sold for a shekel and two seahs of barley for a shekel, as the LORD had said.

---

c Dt 28, 53-57.
d 1 Kgs 20, 31; 21, 27.
e 2 Kgs 7, 17; Ps 78, 23;
  Is 24, 18.
f Lv 13, 46.
g 6f: 2 Kgs 6, 17; 19, 35f;
  2 Sm 5. 24.

*

7, 1: Market: literally "gate," the principal place of trading in ancient walled cities in time of peace.

7, 6: Kings of the borderlands: from Musur in Anatolia rather than Egypt.

17 The king put in charge of the gate the officer who was his adjutant; but the people trampled him to death at the gate, just as the man of God had predicted when the king visited him. **18** Thus was fulfilled the prophecy of the man of God to the king, "Two seahs of barley will sell for a shekel, and one seah of fine flour for a shekel at this time tomorrow at the gate of Samaria." **19** The adjutant had answered the man of God, "Even if the LORD were to make windows in heaven, how could this happen?" And Elisha has replied, "You shall see it with your own eyes, but you shall not eat of it." **20** And that is what happened to him, for the people trampled him to death at the gate.

CHAPTER 8

Prediction of Famine. **1** Elisha once said to the woman whose son he had restored to life: "Get ready! Leave with your family and settle wherever you can, because the LORD has decreed a seven-year famine which is coming upon the land."*h* **2** The woman got ready and did as the man of God said, setting out with her family and settling in the land of the Philistines for seven years. **3** At the end of the seven years, the woman returned from the land of the Philistines and went out to the king to claim her house and her field. **4** The king was talking with Gehazi, the servant of the man of God. "Tell me," he said, "all the great things that Elisha has done." **5** Just as he was relating to the king how his master had restored a dead person to life, the very woman whose son Elisha had restored to life came to the king to claim her house and field. "My lord king," Gehazi said, "this is the woman, and this is that son of hers whom Elisha restored to life." **6** The king questioned the woman, and she told him her story. With that the king placed an official* at her disposal, saying, "Restore all her property to her, with all that the field produced from the day she left the land until now."

Death of Ben-hadad Foretold. **7** Elisha came to Damascus at a time when Ben-hadad, king of Aram, lay sick. When he was told that the man of God had come there, **8** the king said to Hazael, "Take a gift with you and go call on the man of God. Have him consult the LORD as to whether I shall recover from this sickness." **9** Hazael went to visit him, carrying a present, and with forty camel loads of the best goods of Damascus. On his arrival, he stood before the prophet and said, "Your son Ben-hadad, king of Aram, has sent me to ask you whether he will recover from his sickness." **10** "Go and tell him," Elisha answered, "that he will surely recover. However, the LORD has showed me that he will in fact die." **11** Then he stared him

down until Hazael became ill at ease. The man of God wept, **12** and Hazael asked, "Why are you weeping, my lord?" Elisha replied, "Because I know the evil that you will inflict upon the Israelites. You will burn their fortresses, you will slay their youth with the sword, you will dash their little children to pieces, you will rip open their pregnant women."*i*

13 Hazael exclaimed, "How can a dog like me, your servant,* do anything so important?" "The LORD has showed you to me as king over Aram," replied Elisha.*j*

14 Hazael left Elisha and returned to his master. "What did Elisha tell you?" asked Ben-hadad. "He told me that you would surely recover," replied Hazael. **15** The next day, however, Hazael took a cloth, dipped it in water, and spread it over the king's face, so that he died. And Hazael reigned in his stead.

Reign of Jehoram of Judah. **16** In the fifth year of Joram, son of Ahab, king of Israel, Jehoram,* son of Jehoshaphat, king of Judah, became king. **17** *k*He was thirty-two years old when he began to reign, and he reigned eight years in Jerusalem. **18** He conducted himself like the kings of Israel of the line of Ahab, since the sister of Ahab was his wife; and he did evil in the LORD's sight. **19** Even so, the LORD was unwilling to destroy Judah, because of his servant David. For he had promised David that he would leave him a lamp in the LORD's presence for all time.*l* **20** During Jehoram's reign, Edom revolted against the sovereignty of Judah and chose a king of its own. **21** Thereupon Jehoram with all his chariots crossed over to Zair. He arose by night and broke through the Edomites when they had surrounded him and the commanders of his chariots. Then his army fled homeward. **22** To this day Edom has been in revolt against the rule of Judah. Libnah also revolted at that time.*m* **23** The rest of the acts of Jehoram, with all that he did, are recorded in the book of the chronicles of the kings of Judah. **24** Jehoram rested with his ancestors and was buried with them in the City of David. His son Ahaziah succeeded him as king.

h 2 Kgs 4, 36.   l 2 Sm 7, 11-16; 21, 17;
i 2 Kgs 13, 7.   1 Kgs 11, 36; 15, 4;
j 2 Kgs 15, 16; 1 Kgs 19,   2 Chr 21, 7.
   15.   m Gn 27, 40; 2 Chr 21,
k 17ff: 2 Chr 21, 5ff.   8ff.
*

8, 6: An official: Literally "eunuch," and perhaps actually so in this instance.

8, 13: A dog . . . your servant: Hazael feigns humility (1 Sm 24, 14; 2 Sm 9, 8), without attending to the crimes he would commit after usurping the royal power as the prophet predicts. Anything so important: literally "a great deed" for a patriotic Syrian.

8, 16: Jehoram of Judah succeeded his father Jehoshaphat during the reign of Ahaziah of Israel. See note on 2 Kgs 3, 1.

Accession of Ahaziah. **25** Ahaziah, son of Jehoram, king of Judah, became king in the twelfth year of Joram,* son of Ahab, king of Israel. **26** He was twenty-two years old when he began his reign, and he reigned one year in Jerusalem. His mother's name was Athaliah; she was the daughter of Omri, king of Israel. **27** He conducted himself like the house of Ahab, doing evil in the LORD's sight as they did, since he was related to them by marriage. **28** He joined Joram, son of Ahab, in battle against Hazael, king of Aram, at Ramoth-gilead, where the Arameans wounded Joram.[n] **29** King Joram returned to Jezreel to be healed of the wounds which the Arameans had inflicted on him at Ramah in his battle against Hazael, king of Aram. Then Ahaziah, son of Jehoram, king of Judah, went down to Jezreel to visit him there in his illness.

CHAPTER 9

Anointing of Jehu. **1** The prophet Elisha called one of the guild prophets and said to him: "Gird your loins, take this flask of oil with you, and go to Ramoth-gilead.[o] **2** When you get there, look for Jehu, son of Jehoshaphat, son of Nimshi. Enter and take him away from his companions into an inner chamber.[p] **3** From the flask you have, pour oil on his head, and say, 'Thus says the LORD: I anoint you king over Israel.' Then open the door and flee without delay."[q] **4** The young man (the guild prophet) went to Ramoth-gilead. **5** When he arrived, the commanders of the army were in session. "I have a message for you, commander," he said. "For which one of us?" asked Jehu. "For you, commander," he answered. **6** Jehu got up and went into the house. Then the young man poured the oil on his head and said, "Thus says the LORD, the God of Israel: 'I anoint you king over the people of the LORD, over Israel. **7** *You shall destroy the house of Ahab your master; thus will I avenge the blood of my servants the prophets, and the blood of all the other servants of the LORD shed by Jezebel, **8** [r]and by all the rest of the family of Ahab. I will cut off every male in Ahab's line, whether slave or freeman in Israel. **9** I will deal with the house of Ahab as I dealt with the house of Jeroboam, son of Nebat, and with the house of Baasha, son of Ahijah. **10** Dogs shall devour Jezebel at the confines of Jezreel, so that no one can bury her.' " Then he opened the door and fled.

11 When Jehu rejoined his master's servants, they asked him, "Is all well? Why did that madman come to you?" "You know that kind of man and his talk," he replied. **12** But they said, "Not at all! Come, tell us." So he told them what the young man had said to him, and finally, "Thus says the LORD: 'I anoint you

king over Israel.' " **13** At once each took his garment, spread it under Jehu on the bare steps, blew the trumpet, and cried out, "Jehu is king!"[s]

14 [t]Thus Jehu, son of Jehoshaphat, son of Nimshi, formed a conspiracy against Joram. Joram, with all Israel, had been besieging Ramoth-gilead against Hazael, king of Aram, **15** but had returned to Jezreel to be healed of the wounds the Arameans had inflicted on him in the battle against Hazael, king of Aram.

Murder of Joram. "If you are truly with me," Jehu said, "see that no one escapes from the city to report in Jezreel." **16** Then Jehu mounted his chariot and drove to Jezreel, where Joram lay ill and Ahaziah, king of Judah, had come to visit him.

17 The watchman standing on the tower in Jezreel saw the troop of Jehu coming and reported, "I see chariots." "Get a driver," Joram said, "and send him to meet them and to ask whether all is well." **18** So a driver went out to meet him and said, "The king asks whether all is well." "What does it matter to you how things are?" Jehu said. "Get behind me." The watchman reported to the king, "The messenger has reached them, but is not returning."

19 Joram sent a second driver, who went to them and said, "The king asks whether all is well." "What does it matter to you how things are?" Jehu replied. "Get behind me."

20 The watchman reported, "The messenger has reached them, but is not returning. The driving is like that of Jehu, son of Nimshi, in its fury." **21** "Prepare my chariot," said Joram. When they had done so, Joram, king of Israel, and Ahaziah, king of Judah, set out, each in his own chariot, to meet Jehu. They reached him near the field of Naboth the Jezreelite. **22** When Joram recognized Jehu, he asked, "Is all well, Jehu?" "How can all be well," Jehu replied, "as long as the many fornications and witchcrafts* of your mother Jezebel continue?" **23** Joram reined about and fled, crying to Ahaziah, "Treason, Ahaziah!" **24** But Jehu drew his bow and shot Joram between the shoulders, so that the arrow went through his heart and he

---

n 2 Kgs 9, 14f.   3f: 21, 21-24.
o 1 Kgs 21, 29; Hos 1, 4.   s Mt 21, 8.
p 1 Kgs 19, 16;   t 14f: 2 Kgs 8, 28f; 1 Kgs
q 1 Kgs 19, 16.   22, 3f.
r 8ff: 1 Kgs 14, 10f; 16,

---

*

8, 25: Twelfth year of Joram: i.e., of Israel, who probably reigned only eight years.

9, 7–10: The editors of the Books of Kings have here added to the prophet's message the same type of indictment and sanctions against the family of Ahab as were invoked against the dynasties of Jeroboam (1 Kgs 14, 10f), Baasha (1 Kgs 16, 3f), and Ahab on a previous occasion (1 Kgs 21, 21–24).

9, 22: Fornications and witchcrafts: the worship of foreign gods.

collapsed in his chariot. 25 ^uThen Jehu said to his adjutant Bidkar, ''Take him and throw him into the field of Naboth the Jezreelite. For I remember that when we were driving teams behind his father Ahab, the LORD delivered this oracle against him: 26 'As surely as I saw yesterday the blood of Naboth and the blood of his sons,' says the LORD, 'I will repay you for it in that very plot of ground, says the LORD.' So now take him into this plot of ground, in keeping with the word of the LORD.''

Death of Ahaziah. 27 ^vSeeing what was happening, Ahaziah, king of Judah, fled toward Beth-haggan. Jehu pursued him, shouting, ''Kill him too!'' And they pierced him as he rode through the pass of Gur near Ibleam. He continued his flight as far as Megiddo and died there. 28 His servants brought him in a chariot to Jerusalem and buried him in the tomb of his ancestors in the City of David. 29 Ahaziah had become king of Judah in the eleventh year of Joram, son of Ahab.

Death of Jezebel. 30 When Jezebel learned that Jehu had arrived in Jezreel, she shadowed her eyes, adorned her hair, and looked down from her window. 31 As Jehu came through the gate, she cried out, ''Is all well, Zimri, murderer of your master?''^w 32 Jehu looked up to the window and shouted, ''Who is on my side? Anyone?'' At this, two or three eunuchs looked down toward him. 33 ''Throw her down,'' he ordered. They threw her down, and some of her blood spurted against the wall and against the horses. Jehu rode in over her body 34 and, after eating and drinking, he said: ''Attend to that accursed woman and bury her; after all, she was a king's daughter.'' 35 But when they went to bury her, they found nothing of her but the skull, the feet, and the hands. 36 They returned to Jehu, and when they told him, he said, ''This is the sentence which the LORD pronounced through his servant Elijah the Tishbite: 'In the confines of Jezreel dogs shall eat the flesh of Jezebel.^x 37 The corpse of Jezebel shall be like dung in the field in the confines of Jezreel, so that no one can say: This was Jezebel.' ''

CHAPTER 10

Killing of Ahab's Descendants. 1 Ahab had seventy descendants in Samaria. Jehu prepared letters and sent them to the city rulers, to the elders, and to the guardians of Ahab's descendants in Samaria.^y 2 ''Since your master's sons are with you,'' he wrote, ''and you have the chariots, the horses, a fortified city, and the weapons, when this letter reaches you 3 decide which is the best and the fittest of your master's offspring, place him on his father's throne, and fight for your master's house.'' 4 They were overcome with fright and said, ''If two kings could not withstand him, how can we?'' 5 So the vizier and the ruler of the city, along with the elders and the guardians, sent this message to Jehu: ''We are your servants, and we will do everything you tell us. We will proclaim no one king; do whatever you think best.'' 6 So Jehu wrote them a second letter: ''If you are on my side and will obey me, count the heads of your master's sons and come to me in Jezreel at this time tomorrow.'' [The seventy princes were in the care of prominent men of the city, who were rearing them.]

7 When the letter arrived, they took the princes and slew all seventy of them, put their heads in baskets, and sent them to Jehu in Jezreel. 8 ''They have brought the heads of the princes,'' a messenger came in and told him. ''Pile them in two heaps at the entrance of the city until morning,'' he ordered. 9 Going out in the morning, he stopped and said to all the people: ''You are not responsible, and although I conspired against my lord and slew him, yet who killed all these? 10 Know that not a single word which the LORD has spoken against the house of Ahab shall go unfulfilled. The LORD has accomplished all that he foretold through his servant Elijah.''^z 11 Thereupon Jehu slew all who were left of the family of Ahab in Jezreel, as well as all his powerful supporters, intimates, and priests, leaving him no survivor.^a

Ahaziah's Kinsmen. 12 ^bThen he set out for Samaria, and at Beth-eked-haroim on the way, 13 he came across kinsmen of Ahaziah, king of Judah. ''Who are you?'' he asked. ''We are kinsmen of Ahaziah,'' they replied. ''We are going down to visit the princes and the family of the queen mother.'' 14 ''Take them alive,'' Jehu ordered. They were taken alive, forty-two in number, then slain at the pit of Beth-eked. Not one of them was spared.

Jehu in Samaria. 15 When he had left there, Jehu met Jehonadab, son of Rechab, on the road. He greeted him and asked, ''Are you sincerely disposed toward me, as I am toward you?'' ''Yes,'' replied Jehonadab. ''If you are,'' continued Jehu, ''give me your hand.'' Jehonadab gave him his hand, and Jehu drew him up into his chariot.^c 16 ''Come with me,'' he said, ''and see my zeal for the LORD.'' And he took him along in his own chariot.

17 When he arrived in Samaria, Jehu slew all

u 25f: 1 Kgs 21, 9-16.
v 27ff: 2 Chr 22, 7ff.
w 1 Kgs 16, 9ff.
x 1 Kgs 21, 23.
y Jgs 9, 5; 1 Kgs 15, 29; 16, 11.
z Hos 1, 4.
a Hos 1, 4.
b 12ff: 2 Chr 22, 8f.
c 1 Chr 2, 55; Jer 35, 1-11.

who remained there of Ahab's line, doing away with them completely and thus fulfilling the prophecy which the LORD had spoken to Elijah.

Baal's Temple Destroyed. 18 Jehu gathered all the people together and said to them: "Ahab served Baal to some extent, but Jehu will serve him yet more.*d* 19 Now summon for me all Baal's prophets, all his worshipers, and all his priests. See that no one is absent, for I have a great sacrifice for Baal. Whoever is absent shall not live." This Jehu did as a ruse, so that he might destroy the worshipers of Baal. 20 Jehu said further, "Proclaim a solemn assembly in honor of Baal." They did so, 21 and Jehu sent word of it throughout the land of Israel. All the worshipers of Baal without exception came into the temple of Baal, which was filled to capacity. 22 Then Jehu said to the custodian of the wardrobe, "Bring out the garments for all the worshipers of Baal." When he had brought out the garments for them,*e* 23 Jehu, with Jehonadab, son of Rechab, entered the temple of Baal and said to the worshipers of Baal, "Search and be sure that there is no worshiper of the LORD here with you, but only worshipers of Baal." 24 Then they proceeded to offer sacrifices and holocausts. Now Jehu had stationed eighty men outside with this warning, "If one of you lets anyone escape of those whom I shall deliver into your hands, he shall pay life for life." 25 As soon as he finished offering the holocaust, Jehu said to the guards and officers, "Go in and slay them. Let no one escape." So the guards and officers put them to the sword and cast them out. Afterward they went into the inner shrine of the temple of Baal, 26 took out the stele of Baal, and burned the shrine. 27 Then they smashed the stele of Baal, tore down the building, and turned it into a latrine, as it remains today.

28 Thus Jehu rooted out the worship of Baal from Israel. 29 However, he did not desist from the sins which Jeroboam, son of Nebat, had caused Israel to commit, as regards the golden calves at Bethel and at Dan.*f* 30 The LORD said to Jehu, "Because you have done well what I deem right, and have treated the house of Ahab as I desire, your sons to the fourth generation shall sit upon the throne of Israel."*g* 31 But Jehu was not careful to observe wholeheartedly the law of the LORD, the God of Israel, since he did not desist from the sins which Jeroboam caused Israel to commit.

32 *h*At that time the LORD began to dismember Israel. Hazael defeated the Israelites throughout their territory 33 east of the Jordan (all the land of Gilead, of the Gadites, Reubenites and Manassehites), from Aroer on the river Arnon up through Gilead and Bashan.

34 The rest of the acts of Jehu, his valor and all his accomplishments, are written in the book of the chronicles of the kings of Israel. 35 Jehu rested with his ancestors and was buried in Samaria. His son Jehoahaz succeeded him as king. 36 The length of Jehu's reign over Israel in Samaria was twenty-eight years.

CHAPTER 11

Rule of Athaliah. 1 When Athaliah, the mother of Ahaziah, saw that her son was dead, she began to kill off the whole royal family.*i* 2 But Jehosheba,* daughter of King Jehoram and sister of Ahaziah, took Joash, his son, and spirited him away, along with his nurse, from the bedroom where the princes were about to be slain. She concealed him from Athaliah, and so he did not die. 3 For six years he remained hidden in the temple of the LORD, while Athaliah ruled the land.

4 *j*But in the seventh year, Jehoiada summoned the captains of the Carians and of the guards. He had them come to him in the temple of the LORD, exacted from them a sworn commitment, and then showed them the king's son. 5 He gave them these orders: "This is what you must do: the third of you who come on duty on the sabbath shall guard the king's palace; 6 another third shall be at the gate Sur; and the last third shall be at the gate behind the guards. 7 The two of your divisions who are going off duty that week shall keep guard over the temple of the LORD for the king. 8 You shall surround the king, each with drawn weapons, and if anyone tries to approach the cordon, kill him; stay with the king, whatever he may do."

9 *k*The captains did just as Jehoiada the priest commanded. Each one with his men, both those going on duty for the sabbath and those going off duty that week, came to Jehoiada the priest. 10 *l*He gave the captains King David's spears and shields, which were in the temple of the LORD. 11 And the guards, with drawn weapons, lined up from the southern to the northern limit of the enclosure, surrounding the altar and the temple on the king's behalf. 12 Then Jehoiada led out the king's son and put the crown and the insignia upon him. They proclaimed him king and anointed him, clapping their hands and shouting, "Long live the king!"*m*

13 *n*Athaliah heard the noise made by the people, and appeared before them in the temple

---

d 1 Kgs 16, 30ff.
e 1 Kgs 16, 32.
f 1 Kgs 12, 28f.
g 2 Kgs 15, 12ff.
h Am 1, 3.
i Jgs 9, 5.

j 4-8: 2 Chr 23, 1-7.
k 9-12: 2 Chr 23, 8-11.
l 10ff: 2 Sm 8, 7; 1 Kgs 1, 33f.
m 2 Sm 1, 10.
n 13-16: 2 Chr 23, 12-15.

*

11, 2: Jehosheba was the wife of Jehoida, the high priest; cf 2 Chr 22, 11.

of the LORD. **14** When she saw the king standing by the pillar,* as was the custom, and the captains and trumpeters near him, with all the people of the land rejoicing and blowing trumpets, she tore her garments and cried out, "Treason, treason!" **15** Then Jehoiada the priest instructed the captains in command of the force: "Bring her outside through the ranks. If anyone follows her," he added, "let him die by the sword." He had given orders that she should not be slain in the temple of the LORD. **16** She was led out forcibly to the horse gate of the royal palace, where she was put to death.

17 *o*Then Jehoiada made a covenant between the LORD as one party and the king and the people as the other, by which they would be the LORD's people; and another covenant, between the king and the people. **18** Thereupon all the people of the land went to the temple of Baal and demolished it. They shattered its altars and images completely, and slew Mattan, the priest of Baal, before the altars. After appointing a detachment for the temple of the LORD, Jehoiada **19** with the captains, the Carians, the guards, and all the people of the land, led the king down from the temple of the LORD through the guards' gate to the palace, where Joash took his seat on the royal throne. **20** All the people of the land rejoiced and the city was quiet, now that Athaliah had been slain with the sword at the royal palace.

CHAPTER 12

Reign of Joash. **1** Joash was seven years old when he became king.*p* **2** Joash began to reign in the seventh year of Jehu, and he reigned forty years in Jerusalem. His mother, who was named Zibiah, was from Beer-sheba. **3** Joash did what was pleasing to the LORD as long as he lived, because the priest Jehoiada guided him. **4** Still, the high places did not disappear; the people continued to sacrifice and to burn incense there.

5 *q*For the priests Joash made this rule: "All the funds for sacred purposes that are brought to the temple of the LORD—the census tax, personal redemption money, and whatever funds are freely brought to the temple of the LORD— **6** the priests may take for themselves, each from his own clients. However, they must make whatever repairs on the temple may prove necessary." **7** Nevertheless, as late as the twenty-third year of the reign of King Joash, the priests had not made needed repairs on the temple. **8** Accordingly, King Joash summoned the priest Jehoiada and the other priests. "Why do you not repair the temple?" he asked them. "You must no longer take funds from your clients, but you shall turn them over for the repairs." **9** *r*So the priests agreed that they would neither take funds from the people nor make the repairs on the temple.

10 The priest Jehoiada then took a chest, bored a hole in its lid, and set it beside the stele, on the right as one entered the temple of the LORD. The priests who guarded the entry would put into it all the funds that were brought to the temple of the LORD. **11** When they noticed that there was a large amount of silver in the chest, the royal scribe [and the priest] would come up, and they would melt down all the funds that were in the temple of the LORD, and weigh them. **12** The amount thus realized they turned over to the master workmen in the temple of the LORD. They in turn would give it to the carpenters and builders working in the temple of the LORD, **13** and to the lumbermen and stone cutters, and for the purchase of the wood and hewn stone used in repairing the breaches, and for any other expenses that were necessary to repair the temple. **14** None of the funds brought to the temple of the LORD were used there to make silver cups, snuffers, basins, trumpets, or any gold or silver article. **15** Instead, they were given to the workmen, and with them they repaired the temple of the LORD. **16** Moreover, no reckoning was asked of the men who were provided with the funds to give to the workmen, because they held positions of trust. **17** The funds from guilt-offerings and from sin-offerings, however, were not brought to the temple of the LORD; they belonged to the priests.

18 *s*Then King Hazael of Aram mounted a siege against Gath. When he had taken it, Hazael decided to go on to attack Jerusalem.*t* **19** But King Jehoash of Judah took all the dedicated offerings presented by his forebears, Jehoshaphat, Jehoram, and Ahaziah, kings of Judah, as well as his own, and all the gold there was in the treasuries of the temple and the palace, and sent them to King Hazael of Aram, who then led his forces away from Jerusalem. **20** The rest of the acts of Joash, with all that he did, are recorded in the book of the chronicles of the kings of Judah. **21** Certain of his officials entered into a plot against him and killed him at Beth-millo. **22** Jozacar, son of Shimeath, and Jehozabad, son of Shomer, were the officials who killed him. He was buried in his forefathers' City of David, and his son Amaziah succeeded him as king.

CHAPTER 13

Reign of Jehoahaz of Israel. **1** In the twenty-third year of Joash, son of Ahaziah, king

---

o 17-20: 2 Chr 23, 16-21.   r 9-16: 2 Chr 24, 11-14.
p 1f: 2 Chr 24, 1f.   s 2 Kgs 8, 12.
q 5-8: 2 Chr 24, 5-10.   t 18-22: 2 Chr 24, 23-27.

*

11, 14: By the pillar: see note on 2 Chr 23, 13.

of Judah, Jehoahaz, son of Jehu, began his seventeen-year reign over Israel in Samaria. **2** He did evil in the LORD's sight, conducting himself like Jeroboam, son of Nebat, and not renouncing the sin he had caused Israel to commit. **3** The LORD was angry with Israel and for a long time left them in the power of Hazael, king of Aram, and of Ben-hadad, son of Hazael. **4** Then Jehoahaz entreated the LORD, who heard him, since he saw the oppression to which the king of Aram had subjected Israel.ᵘ **5** So the LORD gave Israel a savior,* and the Israelites, freed from the power of Aram, dwelt in their own homes as formerly. **6** Nevertheless, they did not desist from the sins which the house of Jeroboam had caused Israel to commit, but persisted in them. The sacred pole* also remained standing in Samaria.ᵛ **7** No soldiers were left to Jehoahaz, except fifty horsemen with ten chariots and ten thousand foot soldiers, since the king of Aram had destroyed them and trampled them like dust. **8** The rest of the acts of Jehoahaz, with all his valor and accomplishments, are recorded in the book of the chronicles of the kings of Israel. **9** Jehoahaz rested with his ancestors and was buried in Samaria. His son Joash succeeded him as king.

Reign of Joash of Israel.   **10** In the thirty-seventh year of Joash, king of Judah, Jehoash, son of Jehoahaz, began his sixteen-year reign over Israel in Samaria. **11** He did evil in the sight of the LORD; he did not desist from any of the sins which Jeroboam, son of Nebat, had caused Israel to commit, but persisted in them. **12** *[The rest of the acts of Joash, the valor with which he fought against Amaziah, king of Judah, and all his accomplishments, are recorded in the book of the chronicles of the kings of Israel.ʷ **13** Joash rested with his ancestors, and Jeroboam occupied the throne. Joash was buried with the kings of Israel in Samaria.]

14 When Elisha was suffering from the sickness of which he was to die, King Joash of Israel went down to visit him. "My father, my father!"* he exclaimed, weeping over him. "Israel's chariots and horsemen!"ˣ **15** "Take a bow and some arrows," Elisha said to him. When he had done so, **16** *Elisha said to the king of Israel, "Put your hand on the bow." As the king held the bow, Elisha placed his hands over the king's hands **17** and said, "Open the window toward the east." He opened it, Elisha said, "Shoot," and he shot. The prophet exclaimed, "The LORD's arrow of victory! The arrow of victory over Aram! You will completely conquer Aram at Aphec."

18 Then he said to the king of Israel, "Take the arrows," which he did. Elisha said to him, "Strike the ground!" He struck the ground three times and stopped. **19** Angry with him,

the man of God said: "You should have struck five or six times; you would have defeated Aram completely. Now, you will defeat Aram only three times."

20 Elisha died and was buried. At the time, bands of Moabites used to raid the land each year. **21** Once some people were burying a man, when suddenly they spied such a raiding band. So they cast the dead man into grave of Elisha, and everyone went off. But when the man came in contact with the bones of Elisha, he came back to life and rose to his feet.ʸ

22 King Hazael of Aram oppressed Israel during the entire reign of Jehoahaz. **23** But the LORD was merciful with Israel and looked on them with compassion because of his covenant with Abraham, Isaac, and Jacob. He was unwilling to destroy them or to cast them out from his presence.ᶻ **24** So when King Hazael of Aram died and his son Ben-hadad succeeded him as king, **25** Joash, son of Jehoahaz, took back from Ben-hadad, son of Hazael, the cities which Hazael had taken in battle from his father Jehoahaz. Joash defeated Ben-hadad three times, and thus recovered the cities of Israel.

CHAPTER 14

Amaziah of Judah.   **1** In the second year of Joash, son of Jehoahaz, king of Israel, Amaziah, son of Joash, king of Judah, began to reign. **2** ᵃHe was twenty-five years old when he became king, and he reigned twenty-nine years in Jerusalem. His mother, whose name was Jehoaddin, was from Jerusalem. **3** He pleased the LORD, yet not like his forefather David, since he did just as his father Joash had done. **4** Thus the high places did not disappear, but the people

---

u 2 Kgs 14, 26f.   y Sir 48, 14.
v Ex 34, 13.   z Dt 9, 27.
w 2 Kgs 14, 8-16.   a 2f: 2 Chr 25, 1f.
x 2 Kgs 2, 12.

*

13, 5: A savior: by this language, typical of the Book of Judges (Jgs 3, 9, 15), Jeroboam II of Israel is meant; cf 2 Kgs 14, 27.

13, 6: Sacred pole: see note on Ex 34, 13.

13, 12f: The conclusion to the reign of Joash is given again in 2 Kgs 14, 15f, where it is more appropriate.

13, 14: My father, my father: the king expresses here the same sentiments as those with which Elisha addressed Elijah.

13, 16–19: Symbolic acts similar to these are seen in Ex 17, 8ff; Jos 8, 18ff; Ez 4, 1ff.

14, 1f: In the second year . . . twenty-nine years in Jerusalem: the reigns of the kings of Judah between Athaliah and Ahaz are assigned too many years in all to correspond to the reigns in Israel from Jehu to the fall of Samaria. It seems probable that Amaziah was murdered as soon as his son Azaiah was old enough to rule, and that Amaziah's reign was nearer nineteen than twenty-nine years. The correlation, in 2 Kgs 15, 1, of the beginning of Azariah's reign with the 27th year of Jeroboam II can hardly be correct; and the sixteen-year reign of Joatham of Judah (2 Kgs 15, 33) consisted for the most part of a regency during the illness of his father (2 Kgs 15, 5).

continued to sacrifice and to burn incense on them. **5** *b*When Amaziah had the kingdom firmly in hand, he slew the officials who had murdered the king, his father. **6** But the children of the murderers he did not put to death, obeying the LORD's command written in the book of the law of Moses, "Fathers shall not be put to death for their children, nor shall children be put to death for their fathers; each one shall die for his own sin."*c*

7 Amaziah slew ten thousand Edomites in the Salt Valley, and took Sela in battle. He renamed it Joktheel, the name it has to this day.*d*

8 Then Amaziah sent messengers to Jehoash, son of Jehoahaz, son of Jehu, king of Israel, with this challenge, "Come, let us meet face to face."*e* **9** King Jehoash of Israel sent this reply to the king of Judah: "The thistle of Lebanon sent word to the cedar of Lebanon, 'Give your daughter to my son in marriage,' but an animal of Lebanon passed by and trampled the thistle underfoot. **10** You have indeed conquered Edom, and you have become ambitious. Enjoy your glory, but stay at home! Why involve yourself and Judah with you in misfortune and failure?"

11 But Amaziah would not listen. King Jehoash of Israel then advanced, and he and King Amaziah of Judah met in battle at Beth-shemesh of Judah. **12** Judah was defeated by Israel, and all the Judean soldiery fled homeward. **13** King Jehoash of Israel captured Amaziah, son of Jehoash, son of Ahaziah, king of Judah, at Beth-shemesh. He went on to Jerusalem where he tore down four hundred cubits of the city wall, from the Gate of Ephraim to the Corner Gate. **14** He took all the gold and silver and all the utensils there were in the temple of the LORD and in the treasuries of the palace, and hostages as well. Then he returned to Samaria. **15** The rest of the acts of Jehoash, his valor, and how he fought Amaziah, king of Judah, are recorded in the book of the chronicles of the kings of Israel.*f* **16** Jehoash rested with his ancestors; he was buried in Samaria with the kings of Israel. His son Jeroboam succeeded him as king.

17 Amaziah, son of Joash, king of Judah, survived Jehoash, son of Jehoahaz, king of Israel, by fifteen years.* **18** The rest of the acts of Amaziah are written in the book of the chronicles of the kings of Judah. **19** When a conspiracy was formed against him in Jerusalem, he fled to Lachish. But he was pursued to Lachish and killed there. **20** He was brought back on horses and buried with his ancestors in the City of David in Jerusalem. **21** Thereupon all the people of Judah took the sixteen-year-old Azariah* and proclaimed him king to succeed his father Amaziah.*g* **22** It was Azariah who rebuilt Elath

and restored it to Judah, after King Amaziah rested with his ancestors.

Jeroboam II of Israel. **23** In the fifteenth year of Amaziah, son of Joash, king of Judah, Jeroboam, son of Joash, king of Israel, began his forty-one-year reign in Samaria. **24** He did evil in the sight of the LORD; he did not desist from any of the sins which Jeroboam, son of Nebat, had caused Israel to commit. **25** He restored the boundaries of Israel from Labo-of-Hamath to the sea of the Arabah,* just as the LORD, the God of Israel, had prophesied through his servant, the prophet Jonah, son of Amittai, from Gath-hepher. **26** For the LORD saw the very bitter affliction of Israel, where there was neither slave nor freeman, no one at all to help Israel.*h* **27** Since the LORD had not determined to blot out the name of Israel from under the heavens, he saved them through Jeroboam, son of Joash. **28** The rest of the acts of Jeroboam, his valor and all his accomplishments, how he fought with Damascus and turned back Hamath from Israel, are recorded in the book of the chronicles of the kings of Israel. **29** Jeroboam rested with his ancestors, the kings of Israel, and his son Zechariah succeeded him as king.

CHAPTER 15

Azariah of Judah. **1** *i*Azariah, son of Amaziah, king of Judah, became king in the twenty-seventh year* of Jeroboam, king of Israel. **2** He was sixteen years old when he began to reign, and he reigned fifty-two years in Jerusalem. His mother, whose name was Jecholiah, was from Jerusalem. **3** He pleased the LORD just as his father Amaziah had done. **4** Yet the high places did not disappear; the people continued to sacrifice and to burn incense on them. **5** *j*The LORD afflicted the king, and he was a leper to the day of his death. He lived in a house apart, while Jotham, the king's son, was vizier and regent for the people of the land. **6** The rest of the acts of Azariah, and all his accomplishments, are recorded in the book of the chronicles of the kings of Judah. **7** Azariah rested with his ancestors, and was buried with them in

---

b 5f: 2 Chr 25, 3f.
c Dt 24, 16; Ez 18, 20.
d 2 Sm 8, 13f; 2 Chr 25, 11.
e 2 Kgs 13, 12; Jgs 9, 8-15.
f 2 Kgs 13, 12f.
g 2 Chr 26, 1f.
h 2 Kgs 13, 4f; 1 Kgs 14, 10.
i 1ff: 2 Chr 26, 3f.
j 5ff: 2 Chr 26, 21ff.

*

14, 17: See note on 2 Kgs 14, 1f.

14, 21: Azariah: also called Uzziah in many texts.

14, 25: Sea of the Arabah: the Dead Sea. Jonah: see note on Jon 1, 1.

15, 1: Twenty-seventh year: see note on 2 Kgs 14, 1f.

the City of David. His son Jotham succeeded him as king.

Zechariah of Israel. 8 In the thirty-eighth year of Azariah, king of Judah, Zechariah, son of Jeroboam, was king of Israel in Samaria for six months. 9 He did evil in the sight of the LORD as his fathers had done, and did not desist from the sins which Jeroboam, son of Nebat, had caused Israel to commit. 10 Shallum, son of Jabesh, conspired against Zechariah, attacked and killed him at Ibleam, and reigned in his place. 11 The rest of the acts of Zechariah are recorded in the book of the chronicles of the kings of Israel. 12 Thus the LORD's promise to Jehu, "Your descendants to the fourth generation shall sit upon the throne of Israel," was fulfilled. k

Shallum of Israel. 13 Shallum, son of Jabesh, became king in the thirty-ninth year of Uzziah, king of Judah; he reigned one month in Samaria. 14 Menahem, son of Gadi, came up from Tirzah to Samaria, where he attacked and killed Shallum, son of Jabesh, and reigned in his place. 15 The rest of the acts of Shallum, and the fact of his conspiracy, are recorded in the book of the chronicles of the kings of Israel. 16 At that time, Menahem punished Tappuah, all the inhabitants of the town and of its whole district, because on his way from Tirzah they did not let him in. He punished them even to ripping open all the pregnant women.

Menahem of Israel. 17 In the thirty-ninth year of Azariah, king of Judah, Menahem, son of Gadi, began his ten-year reign over Samaria. 18 He did evil in the sight of the LORD, not desisting from the sins which Jeroboam, son of Nebat, had caused Israel to commit. During his reign, 19 Pul,* king of Assyria, invaded the land, and Menahem gave him a thousand talents of silver to have his assistance in strengthening his hold on the kingdom. 20 Menahem secured the money to give to the king of Assyria by exacting it from all the men of substance in the country, fifty silver shekels from each. The king of Assyria did not remain in the country but withdrew. 21 The rest of the acts of Menahem, and all his accomplishments, are recorded in the book of the chronicles of the kings of Israel. 22 Menahem rested with his ancestors, and his son Pekahiah succeeded him as king.

Pekahiah of Israel. 23 In the fiftieth year of Azariah, king of Judah, Pekahiah, son of Menahem, began his two-year reign over Israel in Samaria. 24 He did evil in the sight of the LORD, not desisting from the sins which Jeroboam, son of Nebat, had caused Israel to commit. 25 His adjutant Pekah, son of Remaliah, who

had with him fifty men from Gilead, conspired against him, killed him within the palace stronghold in Samaria, and reigned in his place. 26 The rest of the acts of Pekahiah, and all his accomplishments, are recorded in the book of the chronicles of the kings of Israel.

Pekah of Israel. 27 In the fifty-second year of Azariah, king of Judah, Pekah, son of Remaliah, began his twenty-year reign over Israel in Samaria.* 28 He did evil in the sight of the LORD, not desisting from the sins which Jeroboam, son of Nebat, had caused Israel to commit. 29 During the reign of Pekah, king of Israel, Tiglath-pileser, king of Assyria, came and took Ijon, Abel-beth-maacah, Janoah, Kedesh, Hazor, all the territory of Naphtali, Gilead, and Galilee, deporting the inhabitants to Assyria. 30 Hoshea, son of Elah, conspired against Pekah, son of Remaliah; he attacked and killed him, and reigned in his place [in the twentieth year of Jotham, son of Uzziah]. 31 The rest of the acts of Pekah, and all his accomplishments, are recorded in the book of the chronicles of the kings of Israel.

Jotham of Judah. 32 ¹In the second year of Pekah, son of Remaliah, king of Israel, Jotham, son of Uzziah, king of Judah, began to reign. 33 He was twenty-five years old when he became king, and he reigned sixteen years in Jerusalem. His mother's name was Jerusha, daughter of Zadok. 34 He pleased the LORD, just as his father Uzziah had done. 35 Nevertheless the high places did not disappear and the people continued to sacrifice and to burn incense on them. It was he who built the Upper Gate* of the temple of the LORD. 36 The rest of the acts of Jotham, and all his accomplishments, are recorded in the book of the chronicles of the kings of Judah. 37 It was at that time that the LORD first loosed Rezin, king of Aram, and Pekah, son of Remaliah, against Judah. 38 Jotham rested with his ancestors and was buried with them in his forefather's City of David. His son Ahaz succeeded him as king.

---

k 2 Kgs 10, 30.   7-9.
l 32-38: 2 Chr 27, 1-4.

*

15, 19: Pul: the Babylonian throne name of the Assyrian Tiglathpileser III; cf 2 Kgs 15, 29.

15, 27: The twenty years here ascribed to Pekah are an impossibility; the calculation which made his reign, of five years at most, appear so long may have been based on the attempt to give Jotham of Judah a full sixteen-year reign independently of his regency. See 2 Kgs 16, 1 and the note on 2 Kgs 14, 1f.

15, 35: The Upper Gate: also the Gate of Benjamin; cf Jer 20, 2; Ez 9, 2.

CHAPTER 16

Ahaz of Judah. 1 *m*In the seventeenth year of Pekah, son of Remaliah, Ahaz, son of Jotham, king of Judah, began to reign. 2 Ahaz was twenty years old when he became king, and he reigned sixteen years in Jerusalem. He did not please the LORD, his God, like his forefather David, 3 but conducted himself like the kings of Israel, and even immolated his son by fire, in accordance with the abominable practice of the nations whom the LORD had cleared out of the way of the Israelites.*n* 4 Further, he sacrificed and burned incense on the high places, on hills, and under every leafy tree.*o*

5 Then Rezin, king of Aram, and Pekah, son of Remaliah, king of Israel, came up to Jerusalem to attack it. Although they besieged Ahaz, they were unable to conquer him.*p* 6 At the same time the king of Edom recovered Elath for Edom, driving the Judeans out of it. The Edomites then entered Elath, which they have occupied until the present.*q*

7 Meanwhile, Ahaz sent messengers to Tiglath-pileser, king of Assyria, with the plea: "I am your servant and your son. Come up and rescue me from the clutches of the king of Aram and the king of Israel, who are attacking me."*r* 8 Ahaz took the silver and gold that were in the temple of the LORD and in the palace treasuries and sent them as a present to the king of Assyria,*s* 9 who listened to him and moved against Damascus, which he captured. He deported its inhabitants to Kir and put Rezin to death.*

10 King Ahaz went to Damascus to meet Tiglath-pileser, king of Assyria. When he saw the altar in Damascus, King Ahaz sent to Uriah the priest a model of the altar and a detailed design of its construction. 11 Uriah the priest built an altar according to the plans which King Ahaz sent him from Damascus, and had it completed by the time the king returned home. 12 On his arrival from Damascus, the king inspected this altar, then went up to it and offered sacrifice on it, 13 burning his holocaust and cereal-offering, pouring out his libation, and sprinkling the blood of his peace-offerings on the altar.*t* 14 The bronze altar that stood before the LORD he brought from the front of the temple—that is, from the space between the new altar and the temple of the Lord—and set it on the north side of his altar. 15 *u*"Upon the large altar," King Ahaz commanded Uriah the priest, "burn the morning holocaust and the evening cereal-offering, the royal holocaust and cereal-offering, as well as the holocausts, cereal-offerings, and libations of the people. You must also sprinkle on it all the blood of holocausts and sacrifices. But the old bronze altar shall be mine for consultation."* 16 Uriah the priest did just as King Ahaz had commanded.

17 King Ahaz detached the frames from the bases and removed the lavers from them; he also took down the bronze sea from the bronze oxen that supported it, and set it on a stone pavement.*v* 18 In deference to the king of Assyria he removed from the temple of the LORD the emplacement which had been built in the temple for a throne, and the outer entrance for the king.* 19 The rest of the acts of Ahaz are recorded in the book of the chronicles of the kings of Judah.*w* 20 Ahaz rested with his ancestors and was buried with them in the City of David. His son Hezekiah succeeded him as king.

CHAPTER 17

Hoshea of Israel. 1 In the twelfth year of Ahaz, king of Judah, Hoshea, son of Elah, began his nine-year reign over Israel in Samaria. 2 He did evil in the sight of the LORD, yet not to the extent of the kings of Israel before him. 3 Shalmaneser,* king of Assyria, advanced against him, and Hoshea became his vassal and paid him tribute.*x* 4 But the king of Assyria found Hoshea guilty of conspiracy for sending envoys to the king of Egypt at Sais, and for failure to pay the annual tribute to his Assyrian overlord. 5 For this, the king of Assyria arrested and imprisoned Hoshea; he then occupied the whole land and attacked Samaria, which he besieged for three years. 6 In the ninth year of Hoshea, the king of Assyria* took Samaria, and deported the Israelites to Assyria, settling them in Halah, at the Habor, a river of Gozan, and in the cities of the Medes.*y*

7 This came about because the Israelites

---

m 1-4: 2 Chr 28, 1-4.
n Lv 18, 21.
o Dt 12, 2.
p 2 Chr 28, 5f.
q 2 Chr 28, 17.
r 2 Chr 28, 16.
s 2 Chr 28, 21.

t 2 Chr 28, 23.
u Ex 29, 38f; Nm 28, 3f.
v 2 Chr 28, 24.
w 2 Chr 28, 26f.
x 2 Kgs 18, 9; Tb 1, 2.
y 2 Kgs 18, 10f.

*

16, 9: Firmly dated events bearing on chapters 16 through 20 are: the fall of Damascus (16, 9) in 732 B.C., the fall of Samaria (18, 9–11) in 721 B.C., and Sennacherib's invasion of Judah (18, 13) in 701 B.C., which is equated both in Kgs and in Is 36, 1 with the 14th year of Hezekiah. These data make it necessary to credit Ahaz with at least a twenty-year reign, between 735 and c. 715 B.C., and to exclude the correlations between Hoshea of Israel and Hezekiah in chapter 18.

If the 14th-year correspondence for 701 B.C. is given up, other arrangements are possible. The alleged ages of Jotham (15, 33), Ahaz (16, 2), and Hezekiah (18, 2) at their successive accessions to the throne do not argue for an early date for Hezekiah; but one or more of these may be artificial. Azariah (15, 1–7; Is 6, 1) was still on the throne of Judah in 743 B.C.

16, 15: For consultation: perhaps the introduction into Judah of the Babylonian practice of omen sacrifices; cf Ez 21, 16.

16, 18: Emplacement . . . for a throne, and the outer entrance for the king: signs of sovereignty for the Hebrew kings.

17, 3: Shalmaneser: son and successor of Tiglath-pileser.

17, 6: The king of Assyria: Shalmaneser's successor and usurper, Sargon II.

sinned against the LORD, their God, who had brought them up from the land of Egypt, from under the domination of Pharaoh, king of Egypt, and because they venerated other gods. **8** They followed the rites of the nations whom the LORD had cleared out of the way of the Israelites [and the kings of Israel whom they set up]. **9** They adopted unlawful practices toward the LORD, their God. They built high places in all their settlements, the watchtowers as well as the walled cities. **10** They set up pillars and sacred poles for themselves on every high hill and under every leafy tree.ᶻ **11** There, on all the high places, they burned incense like the nations whom the LORD had sent into exile at their coming. They did evil things that provoked the LORD, **12** and served idols, although the LORD had told them, "You must not do this."

13 And though the LORD warned Israel and Judah by every prophet and seer, "Give up your evil ways and keep my commandments and statutes, in accordance with the entire law which I enjoined on your fathers and which I sent you by my servants the prophets," **14** ᵃthey did not listen, but were as stiff-necked as their fathers, who had not believed in the LORD, their God. **15** They rejected his statutes, the covenant which he had made with their fathers, and the warnings which he had given them. The vanity they pursued, they themselves became: they followed the surrounding nations whom the LORD had commanded them not to imitate.ᵇ **16** They disregarded all the commandments of the LORD, their God, and made for themselves two molten calves; they also made a sacred pole and worshiped all the host of heaven, and served Baal.ᶜ **17** ᵈThey immolated their sons and daughters by fire, practiced fortune-telling and divination, and sold themselves into evildoing in the LORD's sight, provoking him **18** till, in his great anger against Israel, the LORD put them away out of his sight. Only the tribe of Judah was left.

19 Even the people of Judah, however, did not keep the commandments of the LORD, their God, but followed the rites practiced by Israel. **20** So the LORD rejected the whole race of Israel. He afflicted them and delivered them over to plunderers, finally casting them out from before him. **21** When he tore Israel away from the house of David, they made Jeroboam, son of Nebat, king: he drove the Israelites away from the LORD, causing them to commit a great sin.ᵉ **22** The Israelites imitated Jeroboam in all the sins he committed, nor would they desist from them. **23** Finally, the LORD put Israel away out of his sight as he had foretold through all his servants, the prophets; and Israel went into exile from their native soil to Assyria, an exile lasting to the present.ᶠ

24 The king of Assyria brought people from Babylon, Cuthah, Avva, Hamath, and Sephar-

vaim, and settled them in the cities of Samaria in place of the Israelites. They took possession of Samaria and dwelt in its cities. **25** When they first settled there, they did not venerate the LORD, so he sent lions among them that killed some of their number. **26** A report reached the king of Assyria: "The nations whom you deported and settled in the cities of Samaria do not know how to worship the God of the land, and he has sent lions among them that are killing them, since they do not know how to worship the God of the land." **27** The king of Assyria gave the order, "Send back one of the priests whom I deported, to go there and settle, to teach them how to worship the God of the land." **28** So one of the priests who had been deported from Samaria returned and settled in Bethel, and taught them how to venerate the LORD.

29 But these peoples began to make their own gods in the various cities in which they were living; in the shrines on the high places which the Samarians had made, each people set up gods.ᵍ **30** Thus the Babylonians made Marduk and his consort; the men of Cuth made Nergal; the men of Hamath made Ashima; **31** the men of Avva made Nibhaz and Tartak; and the men of Sepharvaim immolated their children by fire to their city gods, King Hadad and his consort Anath. **32** They also venerated the LORD, choosing from their number priests for the high places, who officiated for them in the shrines on the high places.ʰ **33** But, while venerating the LORD, they served their own gods, following the worship of the nations from among whom they had been deported.

34 To this day they worship according to their ancient rites.* [They did not venerate the LORD nor observe the statutes and regulations, the law and commandments, which the LORD enjoined on the descendants of Jacob, whom he had named Israel.ⁱ **35** When he made a covenant with them, he commanded them: "You must not venerate other gods, nor worship them, nor serve them, nor offer sacrifice to them.ʲ **36** The LORD, who brought you up from the land of Egypt with great power and outstretched arm: him shall you venerate, him shall you worship, and to him shall you sacrifice. **37** You must be careful to observe forever the statutes and regulations, the law and command-

z Ex 23, 24; 34, 13; Dt 12, 2.
a Jer 25, 5; Dt 9, 13.
b Jer 2, 5.
c 1 Kgs 12, 28; Ex 34, 13; Dt 4, 19; 17, 2f.
d Lv 18, 21; Dt 18, 10.
e 1 Kgs 12, 19f; 12, 26-33.
f Jer 25, 9.
g Jn 4, 9.
h 1 Kgs 12, 31.
i Gn 32, 29.
j Ex 20, 3ff.

*

17, 34–40: They did not . . . earlier manner: this passage is an adaptation of language denouncing the Israelites to make it applicable to the later Samaritan sect of post-exilic times. The original bearing of the discourse (vv 13–15) can be seen by reading it between vv 22 and 23. Cf also 2 Kgs 18, 12.

ment, which he wrote for you, and you must not venerate other gods. **38** The covenant which I made with you, you must not forget; you must not venerate other gods. **39** But the LORD, your God, you must venerate; it is he who will deliver you from the power of all your enemies.'' **40** They did not listen, however, but continued in their earlier manner.] **41** Thus these nations venerated the LORD, but also served their idols. And their sons and grandsons, to this day, are doing as their fathers did.

II: The Kingdom of Judah after 721 B.C.

CHAPTER 18

Hezekiah.   **1** *k*In the third year of Hoshea, son of Elah, king of Israel, Hezekiah, son of Ahaz, king of Judah, began to reign. **2** He was twenty-five years old when he became king, and he reigned twenty-nine years in Jerusalem. His mother's name was Abi, daughter of Zechariah. **3** He pleased the LORD, just as his forefather David had done. **4** It was he who removed the high places, shattered the pillars, and cut down the sacred poles. He smashed the bronze serpent called Nehushtan which Moses had made, because up to that time the Israelites were burning incense to it.*l* **5** He put his trust in the LORD, the God of Israel; and neither before him nor after him was there anyone like him among all the kings of Judah. **6** Loyal to the LORD, Hezekiah never turned away from him, but observed the commandments which the LORD had given Moses. **7** The LORD was with him, and he prospered in all that he set out to do. He rebelled against the king of Assyria and did not serve him. **8** He also subjugated the watchtowers and walled cities of the Philistines, all the way to Gaza and its territory.

9 In the fourth year of King Hezekiah, which was the seventh year of Hoshea, son of Elah, king of Israel, Shalmaneser, king of Assyria, attacked Samaria, laid siege to it,* **10** *m*and after three years captured it. In the sixth year of Hezekiah, the ninth year of Hoshea, king of Israel, Samaria was taken. **11** The king of Assyria then deported the Israelites to Assyria and settled them in Halah, at the Habor, a river of Gozan, and in the cities of the Medes. **12** This came about because they had not heeded the warning of the LORD, their God, but violated his covenant, not heeding and not fulfilling the commandments of Moses, the servant of the LORD.*n*

Invasion of Sennacherib.   **13** *In the fourteenth year of King Hezekiah, Sennacherib,* king of Assyria, went on an expedition

against all the fortified cities of Judah and captured them.*o* **14** Hezekiah, king of Judah, sent this message to the king of Assyria at Lachish: ''I have done wrong. Leave me, and I will pay whatever tribute you impose on me.'' The king of Assyria exacted three hundred talents of silver and thirty talents of gold from Hezekiah, king of Judah. **15** Hezekiah paid him all the funds there were in the temple of the LORD and in the palace treasuries. **16** He broke up the door panels and the uprights of the temple of the LORD which he himself had ordered to be overlaid with gold, and gave the gold to the king of Assyria.*p*

17 The king of Assyria sent the general, the lord chamberlain, and the commander* from Lachish with a great army to King Hezekiah at Jerusalem. They went up, and on their arrival in Jerusalem, stopped at the conduit of the upper pool on the highway of the fuller's field.*q* **18** They called for the king, who sent out to them Eliakim, son of Hilkiah, the master of the palace; Shebnah the scribe; and the herald Joah, son of Asaph.*r* **19** The commander said to them, ''Tell Hezekiah, 'Thus says the great king, the king of Assyria: On what do you base this confidence of yours? **20** Do you think mere words substitute for strategy and might in war? On whom, then, do you rely, that you rebel against me? **21** This Egypt, the staff on which you rely, is in fact a broken reed which pierces the hand of anyone who leans on it. That is what Pharaoh, king of Egypt, is to all who rely on him.*s* **22** But if you say to me, We rely on the LORD, our God, is not he the one whose high places and altars Hezekiah has removed, commanding Judah and Jerusalem to worship before this altar in Jerusalem?'

23 ''Now, make a wager with my lord, the king of Assyria: I will give you two thousand horses if you can put riders on them. **24** How then can you repulse even one of the least servants of my lord, relying as you do on Egypt for chariots and horsemen? **25** Was it without the LORD's will that I have come up to destroy this

---

k 1ff: 2 Chr 28, 27; 29, 1f.   o 2 Chr 32, 1ff; Sir 48,
l Ex 23, 24; 34, 13; Nm   18; Is 36, 1.
   21, 9; Dt 12, 2; 2 Chr   p 1 Kgs 6, 20-22.
   31, 1; Wis 16, 6; Jn 3,   q 2 Chr 32, 9; Is 36, 1ff.
   14.   r Is 22, 13-25.
m 10f: 2 Kgs 17. 6; Tb 1,   s Is 30, 1-7; 31, 1-3; Ez
   2.   29, 6-7.
n 2 Kgs 17, 7-18.

*

18, 9:   See note on 2 Kgs 16, 9.

18, 13—20, 11:   Duplication of Is 36, 1—38, 8. 21. 22.

18, 13:   Sennacherib succeeded Sargon II as king of Assyria. His Judean campaign was waged in 701 B.C. See note on 2 Kgs 16, 9.

18, 17:   General, the lord chamberlain . . . commander: the text lists three major functionaries by their Assyrian titles, of which only the first, more nearly ''lord lieutenant,'' is military in origin; the commander was technically the king's chief butler.

place? The LORD said to me, 'Go up and destroy that land!' "

26 Then Eliakim, son of Hilkiah, and Shebnah and Joah said to the commander: "Please speak to your servants in Aramaic; we understand it. Do not speak to us in Judean within earshot of the people who are on the wall."

27 But the commander replied: "Was it to your master and to you that my lord sent me to speak these words? Was it not rather to the men sitting on the wall, who, with you, will have to eat their own excrement and drink their urine?"

28 Then the commander stepped forward and cried out in a loud voice in Judean, "Listen to the words of the great king, the king of Assyria. **29** Thus says the king: 'Do not let Hezekiah deceive you, since he cannot deliver you out of my hand. **30** Let not Hezekiah induce you to rely on the LORD, saying, The LORD will surely save us; this city will not be handed over to the king of Assyria. **31** Do not listen to Hezekiah, for the king of Assyria says: Make peace with me and surrender! Then each of you will eat of his own vine and of his own fig-tree, and drink the water of his own cistern, **32** until I come to take you to a land like your own, a land of grain and wine, of bread and orchards, of olives, oil and fruit syrup. Choose life, not death. Do not listen to Hezekiah when he would seduce you by saying, The LORD will rescue us. **33** Has any of the gods of the nations ever rescued his land from the hand of the king of Assyria? **34** Where are the gods of Hamath and Arpad? Where are the gods of Sepharvaim, Hena, and Avva? Where are the gods of the land of Samaria?[t] **35** Which of the gods for all these lands ever rescued his land from my hand? Will the LORD then rescue Jerusalem from my hand?' " **36** But the people remained silent and did not answer him one word, for the king had ordered them not to answer him.

37 Then the master of the palace, Eliakim, son of Hilkiah, Shebnah the scribe, and the herald Joah, son of Asaph, came to Hezekiah with their garments torn, and reported to him what the commander had said.

CHAPTER 19

Hezekiah and Isaiah. **1** [u]When King Hezekiah heard this, he tore his garments, wrapped himself in sackcloth, and went into the temple of the LORD. **2** He sent Eliakim, the master of the palace, Shebnah the scribe, and the elders of the priests, wrapped in sackcloth, to tell the prophet Isaiah, son of Amoz, **3** "Thus says Hezekiah: 'This is a day of distress, of rebuke, and of disgrace. Children are at the point of birth, but there is no strength to bring them forth.* **4** Perhaps the LORD, your God, will hear all the words of the commander, whom his

master, the king of Assyria, sent to taunt the living God, and will rebuke him for the words which the LORD, your God, has heard. So send up a prayer for the remnant that is here.' " **5** When the servants of King Hezekiah had come to Isaiah, **6** he said to them, "Tell this to your master: 'Thus says the LORD: Do not be frightened by the words you have heard, with which the servants of the king of Assyria have blasphemed me.[v] **7** I am about to put in him such a spirit that, when he hears a certain report, he will return to his own land, and there I will cause him to fall by the sword.' "

8 When the commander, on his return, heard that the king of Assyria had withdrawn from Lachish, he found him besieging Libnah. **9** The king of Assyria heard a report that Tirhakah, king of Ethiopia, had come out to fight against him. Again he sent envoys to Hezekiah with this message: **10** "Thus shall you say to Hezekiah, king of Judah: 'Do not let your God on whom you rely deceive you by saying that Jerusalem will not be handed over to the king of Assyria. **11** You have heard what the kings of Assyria have done to all other countries: they doomed them! Will you, then, be saved? **12** Did the gods of the nations whom my fathers destroyed save them? Gozan, Haran, Rezeph, or the Edenites in Telassar?[w] **13** Where are the king of Hamath, the king of Arpad, or the kings of the cities Sepharvaim, Hena and Avva?' "[x]

14 [y]Hezekiah took the letter from the hand of the messengers and read it; then he went up to the temple of the LORD, and spreading it out before him, **15** he prayed in the LORD's presence: "O LORD, God of Israel, enthroned upon the cherubim! You alone are God over all the kingdoms of the earth. You have made the heavens and the earth.[z] **16** Incline your ear, O LORD, and listen! Open your eyes, O LORD, and see! Hear the words of Sennacherib which he sent to taunt the living God. **17** Truly, O LORD, the kings of Assyria have laid waste the nations and their lands, **18** and cast their gods into the fire; they destroyed them because they were not gods, but the work of human hands, wood and stone.[a] **19** Therefore, O LORD, our God, save us from the power of this man, that all the kingdoms of the earth may know that you alone, O LORD, are God."[b]

Punishment of Sennacherib. **20** Then Isaiah, son of Amoz, sent this message to Hezekiah: "Thus says the LORD, the God of Israel,

t 2 Kgs 17, 24.
u 1-7: Is 37, 1-7.
v Is 10, 5-19.
w 2 Kgs 17, 6.
x 2 Kgs 18, 34.

y 14-19: 2 Chr 32, 20; Is 37, 14-20.
z Ex 25, 18.
a Jer 10, 3.
b 1 Kgs 18, 24.

19, 3: See note on Is 37, 3.

in answer to your prayer for help against Sennacherib, king of Assyria: I have listened!
21 This is the word the LORD has spoken concerning him:*

" 'She despises you, laughs you to scorn,
　　the virgin daughter Zion!
Behind you she wags her head,
　　daughter Jerusalem.
22 Whom have you insulted and blasphemed,
　　against whom have you raised your voice
And lifted up your eyes on high?
　　Against the Holy One of Israel!
23 Through your servants you have insulted the
　　LORD.
You said: With my many chariots
I climbed the mountain heights,
　　the recesses of Lebanon;
I cut down its lofty cedars,
　　its choice cypresses;
I reached the remotest heights,
　　its forest park.
24 I dug wells and drank water in foreign
　　lands;
I dried up with the soles of my feet
　　all the rivers of Egypt.

25 " 'Have you not heard?
Long ago I prepared it,
From days of old I planned it.
　　Now I have brought it to pass:
That you should reduce fortified cities
　　into heaps of ruins,
26 While their inhabitants, shorn of power,
　　are dismayed and ashamed,
Becoming like the plants of the field, like
　　the green growth,
like the scorched grass on the housetops.
27 I am aware whether you stand or sit;
　　I know whether you come or go,ᶜ
28 　　and also your rage against me.
Because of your rage against me
　　and your fury which has reached my ears,
I will put my hook in your nose
　　and my bit in your mouth,
　　and make you return the way you came.

29 " 'This shall be a sign for you:
this year you shall eat the aftergrowth,
　　next year, what grows of itself;
But in the third year, sow and reap,
　　plant vineyards and eat their fruit!
30 The remaining survivors of the house of
　　Judah
shall again strike root below
　　and bear fruit above.
31 For out of Jerusalem shall come a remnant,
　　and from Mount Zion, survivors.
　　The zeal of the LORD of hosts shall do
　　　　this.'

32 "Therefore, thus says the LORD concerning the king of Assyria: 'He shall not reach this city, nor shoot an arrow at it, nor come before it with a shield, nor cast up siege-works against

it. **33** He shall return by the same way he came, without entering the city, says the LORD. **34** I will shield and save this city for my own sake, and for the sake of my servant David.' "ᵈ

35 That night the angel of the LORD went forth and struck down one hundred and eighty-five thousand men in the Assyrian camp. Early the next morning, there they were, all the corpses of the dead.ᵉ **36** So Sennacherib, the king of Assyria, broke camp, and went back home to Nineveh.

37 When he was worshiping in the temple of his god Nisroch, his sons Adram-melech and Sharezer slew him with the sword and fled into the land of Ararat. His son Esar-haddon reigned in his stead.

CHAPTER 20

Hezekiah's Illness. **1** ᶠIn those days, when Hezekiah was mortally ill, the prophet Isaiah, son of Amoz, came and said to him: "Thus says the LORD: 'Put your house in order, for you are about to die; you shall not recover.' " **2** He turned his face to the wall and prayed to the LORD: **3** "O LORD, remember how faithfully and wholeheartedly I conducted myself in your presence, doing what was pleasing to you!" And Hezekiah wept bitterly.

4 Before Isaiah had left the central courtyard, the word of the LORD came to him: **5** "Go back and tell Hezekiah, the leader of my people: 'Thus says the LORD, the God of your forefather David: I have heard your prayer and seen your tears. I will heal you. In three days you shall go up to the LORD's temple; **6** I will add fifteen years to your life. I will rescue you and this city from the hand of the king of Assyria; I will be a shield to this city for my own sake, and for the sake of my servant David.' "

7 Isaiah then ordered a poultice of figs to be brought and applied to the boil, that he might recover. **8** Then Hezekiah asked Isaiah, "What is the sign that the LORD will heal me and that I shall go up to the temple of the LORD on the third day?" **9** Isaiah replied, "This will be the sign for you from the LORD that he will do what he has promised: Shall the shadow go forward or back ten steps?"

10 "It is easy for the shadow to advance ten steps," Hezekiah answered. "Rather, let it go back ten steps." **11** So the prophet Isaiah invoked the LORD, who made the shadow retreat

---

c Ps 139, 2f.
d 2 Sm 7, 12; Hos 1, 7.
e Sir 48, 21; 2 Chr 32,
21f; Is 37, 36-38;

1 Mc 7, 41; 2 Mc 8, 19.
f 1-9: 2 Chr 32, 24; Is
38, 1-8.

*

19, 21–31: vv 21–28 are addressed to Sennacherib, vv 29–31 to Judah.

the ten steps it had descended on the staircase to the terrace of Ahaz.

12 *At that time, when Merodach-baladan, son of Baladan, king of Babylon, heard that Hezekiah had been ill, he sent letters and gifts to him.g **13** Hezekiah was pleased at this, and therefore showed the messengers his whole treasury, his silver, gold, spices and fine oil, his armory, and all that was in his storerooms; there was nothing in his house or in all his realm that Hezekiah did not show them.

14 Then Isaiah the prophet came to King Hezekiah and asked him: "What did these men say to you? Where did they come from?" "They came from a distant land, from Babylon," replied Hezekiah. **15** "What did they see in your house?" the prophet asked. "They saw everything in my house," answered Hezekiah. "There is nothing in my storerooms that I did not show them."

16 Then Isaiah said to Hezekiah: "Hear the word of the LORD: **17** The time is coming when all that is in your house, and everything that your fathers have stored up until this day, shall be carried off to Babylon; nothing shall be left, says the LORD. **18** Some of your own bodily descendants shall be taken and made servants in the palace of the king of Babylon."

19 Hezekiah replied to Isaiah, "The word of the LORD which you have spoken is favorable." For he thought, "There will be peace and security in my lifetime."

20 The rest of the acts of Hezekiah, all his valor, and his construction of the pool and conduit* by which water was brought into the city, are written in the book of the chronicles of the kings of Judah.h **21** Hezekiah rested with his ancestors and his son Manasseh succeeded him as king.

CHAPTER 21

Reign of Manasseh.   **1** iManasseh was twelve years old when he began to reign, and he reigned fifty-five years in Jerusalem. His mother's name was Hephzibah. **2** He did evil in the sight of the LORD, following the abominable practices of the nations whom the LORD had cleared out of the way of the Israelites. **3** He rebuilt the high places which his father Hezekiah had destroyed. He erected altars to Baal, and also set up a sacred pole, as Ahab, king of Israel, had done. He worshiped and served the whole host of heaven.j **4** He built altars in the temple of the LORD, about which the LORD had said, "I will establish my name in Jerusalem"— **5** altars for the whole host of heaven, in the two courts of the temple.k

6 He immolated his son by fire. He practiced soothsaying and divination, and reintroduced the consulting of ghosts and spirits. He did much evil in the LORD's sight and provoked him to anger.

7 The Asherah idol he had made, he set up in the temple, of which the LORD had said to David and to his son Solomon: "In this temple and in Jerusalem, which I have chosen out of all the tribes of Israel, I shall place my name forever.l **8** I will not in future allow Israel to be driven off the land I gave their fathers, provided that they are careful to observe all I have commanded them, the entire law which my servant Moses enjoined upon them." **9** But they did not listen, and Manasseh misled them into doing even greater evil than the nations whom the LORD had destroyed at the coming of the Israelites.

10 Then the LORD spoke through his servants the prophets: **11** "Because Manasseh, king of Judah, has practiced these abominations and has done greater evil than all that was done by the Amorites before him, and has led Judah into sin by his idols,m **12** therefore thus says the LORD, the God of Israel: 'I will bring such evil on Jerusalem and Judah that, whenever anyone hears of it, his ears shall ring. **13** I will measure Jerusalem with the same cord as I did Samaria, and with the plummet I used for the house of Ahab. I will wipe Jerusalem clean as one wipes a dish, wiping it inside and out.n **14** I will cast off the survivors of my inheritance and deliver them into enemy hands, to become a prey and a booty for all their enemies, **15** because they have done evil in my sight and provoked me from the day their fathers came forth from Egypt until today.' "

16 In addition to the sin which he caused Judah to commit, Manasseh did evil in the sight of the LORD, shedding so much innocent blood as to fill the length and breadth of Jerusalem. **17** The rest of the acts of Manasseh, the sin he committed and all that he did, are written in the book of the chronicles of the kings of Judah.o **18** Manasseh rested with his ancestors and was buried in his palace garden, the garden of Uzza. His son Amon succeeded him as king.

Reign of Amon.   **19** pAmon was twenty-two years old when he began to reign, and he reigned two years in Jerusalem. His mother's name was Meshullemeth, daughter of Haruz of Jotbah. **20** He did evil in the sight of the LORD,

---

g 12f: Is 39, 1f; 2 Chr 32, 27ff.
h 2 Chr 32, 30; Sir 48, 17.
i 1-10: 2 Chr 33, 1-10.
j 2 Kgs 17, 16; 1 Kgs 18, 4; 16, 32f.
k Lv 18, 21.

l 2 Sm 7, 13; 1 Kgs 8, 16: 9, 3.
m 1 Kgs 21, 26; Jer 15, 4.
n Is 34, 11; Am 7, 7-9; Lam 2, 8.
o 2 Chr 33, 18ff.
p 19-26: 2 Chr 33, 21-25.

20, 12–19: Duplication of Is 39, 1–8.
20, 20: Pool and conduit: Hezekiah's tunnel; cf 2 Chr 32, 30.

as his father Manasseh had done. **21** He followed exactly the path his father had trod, serving and worshiping the idols his father had served. **22** He abandoned the Lord, the God of his fathers, and did not follow the path of the Lord. **23** Subjects of Amon conspired against him and slew the king in his palace, **24** but the people of the land then slew all who had conspired against King Amon, and proclaimed his son Josiah king in his stead. **25** The rest of the acts that Amon did are written in the book of the chronicles of the kings of Judah. **26** He was buried in his own grave in the garden of Uzza, and his son Josiah succeeded him as king.

CHAPTER 22

Reign of Josiah.   **1** ᑫJosiah was eight years old when he began to reign, and he reigned thirty-one years in Jerusalem. His mother's name was Jedidah, daughter of Adaiah of Bozkath. **2** He pleased the Lord and conducted himself unswervingly just as his ancestor David had done.

3 ʳIn his eighteenth year, King Josiah sent the scribe Shaphan,* son of Azaliah, son of Meshullam, to the temple of the Lord with orders to **4** ˢgo to the high priest Hilkiah and have him smelt down the precious metals that had been donated to the temple of the Lord, which the doorkeepers had collected from the people. **5** They were to be consigned to the master workmen in the temple of the Lord, who should then pay them out to the carpenters, builders, and lumbermen making repairs on the temple, **6** and for the purchase of wood and hewn stone for the temple repairs. **7** No reckoning was asked of them regarding the funds consigned to them, because they held positions of trust.

The Book of the Law.   **8** The high priest Hilkiah informed the scribe Shaphan, "I have found the book of the law in the temple of the Lord." Hilkiah gave the book to Shaphan, who read it. **9** Then the scribe Shaphan went to the king and reported, "Your servants have smelted down the metals available in the temple and have consigned them to the master workmen in the temple of the Lord." **10** The scribe Shaphan also informed the king that the priest Hilkiah had given him a book, and then read it aloud to the king. **11** When the king had heard the contents of the book of the law, he tore his garmentsʳ **12** and issued this command to Hilkiah the priest, Ahikam, son of Shaphan, Achbor, son of Micaiah, the scribe Shaphan, and the king's servant Asaiah: **13** "Go, consult the Lord for me, for the people, for all Judah, about the stipulations of this book that has been found, for the anger of the Lord has been set furiously

ablaze against us, because our fathers did not obey the stipulations of this book, nor fulfill our written obligations."

14 So Hilkiah the priest, Ahikam, Achbor, Shaphan, and Asaiah betook themselves to the Second Quarter in Jerusalem, where the prophetess Huldah resided. She was the wife of Shallum, son of Tikvah, son of Harhas, keeper of the wardrobe. When they had spoken to her, **15** she said to them, "Thus says the Lord, the God of Israel: 'Say to the man who sent you to me, **16** Thus says the Lord: I will bring upon this place and upon its inhabitants all the evil that is threatened in the book which the king of Judah has read. **17** Because they have forsaken me and have burned incense to other gods, provoking me by everything to which they turn their hands, my anger is ablaze against this place and it cannot be extinguished.'

18 "But to the king of Judah who sent you to consult the Lord, give this response: 'Thus says the Lord, the God of Israel: As for the threats you have heard, **19** because you were heartsick and have humbled yourself before the Lord when you heard my threats that this place and its inhabitants would become a desolation and a curse; because you tore your garments and wept before me; I in turn have listened, says the Lord. **20** I will therefore gather you to your ancestors; you shall go to your grave in peace, and your eyes shall not see all the evil I will bring upon this place.' " This they reported to the king.

CHAPTER 23

1 ᵘThe king then had all the elders of Judah and of Jerusalem summoned together before him. **2** The king went up to the temple of the Lord with all the men of Judah and all the inhabitants of Jerusalem: priests, prophets, and all the people, small and great. He had the entire contents of the book of the covenant that had been found in the temple of the Lord, read out to them. **3** Standing by the column, the king made a covenant before the Lord that they would follow him and observe his ordinances, statutes and decrees with their whole hearts and souls, thus reviving the terms of the covenant which were written in this book. And all the people stood as participants in the covenant.

4 Then the king commanded the high priest Hilkiah, his vicar, and the doorkeepers to re-

---

q 1f: 2 Chr 34, 1f.   t 11-20: 2 Chr 34, 19-28.
r 3-13: 2 Chr 34, 8-21.   u 1-5: 2 Chr 34, 29-33.
s 4-7: 2 Kgs 12, 11-16.   v 2 Chr 34, 3-5; Sir 49, 3.

*

22, 3: Shaphan: head of a prominent family in the reign of Josiah, secretary to the king, bearer and reader of the new-found book of the law (vv 3–13; 2 Chr 34, 8f. 15–20). He and his sons favored the reform of King Josiah and supported the prophet Jeremiah; cf Jer 26, 24.

move from the temple of the LORD all the objects that had been made for Baal, Asherah, and the whole host of heaven. He had these burned outside Jerusalem on the slopes of the Kidron and their ashes carried to Bethel. *v* **5** He also put an end to the pseudo-priests whom the kings of Judah had appointed to burn incense on the high places in the cities of Judah and in the vicinity of Jerusalem, as well as those who burned incense to Baal, to the sun, moon, and signs of the Zodiac, and to the whole host of heaven. *w* **6** From the temple of the LORD he also removed the sacred pole, to the Kidron Valley, outside Jerusalem; there he had it burned and beaten to dust, which was then scattered over the common graveyard. *x* **7** He tore down the apartments of the cult prostitutes* which were in the temple of the LORD, and in which the women wove garments for the Asherah. *y*

8 He brought in all the priests from the cities of Judah, and then defiled, from Geba to Beer-sheba, the high places where they had offered incense. He also tore down the high place of the satyrs, which was at the entrance of the Gate of Joshua, governor of the city, to the left as one enters the city gate. *z* **9** The priests of the high places could not function at the altar of the LORD in Jerusalem; but they, along with their relatives, ate the unleavened bread.

10 The king also defiled Topheth in the Valley of Ben-hinnom, so that there would no longer be any immolation of sons or daughters by fire* in honor of Molech. *a* **11** He did away with the horses which the kings of Judah had dedicated to the sun; these were at the entrance of the temple of the LORD, near the chamber of Nathan-melech the eunuch, which was in the large building.* The chariots of the sun he destroyed by fire. **12** He also demolished the altars made by the kings of Judah on the roof (the roof terrace of Ahaz), and the altars made by Manasseh in the two courts of the temple of the LORD. He pulverized them and threw the dust into the Kidron Valley. *b* **13** The king defiled the high places east of Jerusalem, south of the Mount of Misconduct,* which Solomon, king of Israel, had built in honor of Astarte, the Sidonian horror, of Chemosh, the Moabite horror, and of Milcom, the idol of the Ammonites. *c* **14** He broke to pieces the pillars, cut down the sacred poles, and filled the places where they had been with human bones. *d* **15** Likewise the altar which was at Bethel, the high place built by Jeroboam, son of Nebat, who caused Israel to sin—this same altar and high place he tore down, breaking up the stones and grinding them to powder, and burning the Asherah. *e*

16 When Josiah turned and saw the graves there on the mountainside, he ordered the bones taken from the graves and burned on the altar, and thus defiled it in fulfillment of the word of

the LORD which the man of God had proclaimed as Jeroboam was standing by the altar on the feast day. When the king looked up and saw the grave of the man of God who had proclaimed these words, **17** he asked, "What is that tombstone I see?" The men of the city replied, "It is the grave of the man of God who came from Judah and predicted the very things you have done to the altar of Bethel." **18** *f* "Let him be," he said, "let no one move his bones." So they left his bones undisturbed together with the bones of the prophet who had come from Samaria.*

19 Josiah also removed all the shrines on the high places near the cities of Samaria which the kings of Israel had erected, thereby provoking the LORD; he did the very same to them as he had done in Bethel. *g* **20** He slaughtered upon the altars all the priests of the high places that were at the shrines, and burned human bones upon them. Then he returned to Jerusalem.

21 The king issued a command to all the people to observe the Passover of the LORD, their God, as it was prescribed in that book of the covenant. *h* **22** No Passover such as this had been observed during the period when the Judges ruled Israel, or during the entire period of the kings of Israel and the kings of Judah, **23** until the eighteenth year of King Josiah, when this Passover of the LORD was kept in Jerusalem.

24 Further, Josiah did away with the consultation of ghosts and spirits, with the household gods, idols,* and all the other horrors to be seen in the land of Judah and in Jerusalem, so that he might carry out the stipulations of the law written in the book that the priest Helkiah had found in the temple of the LORD. *i*

25 Before him there had been no king who turned to the LORD as he did, with his whole

---

w Dt 17, 3ff.
x Dt 16, 21; 1 Kgs 14, 23.
y 1 Kgs 14, 24; Dt 23, 18f.
z Dt 12, 2f.
a Lv 18, 21.
b 2 Kgs 21, 5.
c 1 Kgs 11, 7.
d Dt 16, 21f; 1 Kgs 14, 23.
e 1 Kgs 12, 31f; 13, 32.
f 1 Kgs 13, 31.
g 2 Chr 34, 6f.
h Dt 16, 1-8; 2 Chr 35, 1ff. 18f.
i 2 Kgs 21, 6; Gn 31, 19; Dt 18, 11; Jgs 18, 14.
j Dt 6, 5.

---

*

23, 7: Cult prostitutes: of both sexes; cf 1 Kgs 14, 24.

23, 10: Topheth . . . by fire: condemned by Deuteronomic law and denounced by Jeremiah (Dt 12, 31; Jer 7, 29ff; Jer 19).

23, 11: Large building: to the west of the temple area (1 Chr 26, 18), named in the Hebrew by an Egyptian name for a similar construction.

23, 13: Mount of Misconduct: a paranomasia on "Mount of Olives" (in Hebrew Maschit/mishchee) as suggested by the Targum. Cf Vulgate, "Mount of Offense." Horror . . . idol: in all three phrases here the Hebrew uses a pejorative designation meaning "abomination."

23, 18: From Samaria: more narrowly, from Bethel; cf 1 Kgs 13, 31f.

23, 24: Household gods . . . idols: teraphim. See note on Gn 31, 19.

heart, his whole soul, and his whole strength, in accord with the entire law of Moses; nor could any after him compare with him.*j*

26 Yet, because of all the provocations that Manasseh had given, the LORD did not desist from his fiercely burning anger against Judah. **27** The LORD said: "Even Judah will I put out of my sight as I did Israel. I will reject this city, Jerusalem, which I chose, and the temple of which I said, 'There shall my name be.' "*k*

28 The rest of the acts of Josiah, with all that he did, are written in the book of the chronicles of the kings of Judah.*l* **29** In his time Pharaoh Neco, king of Egypt, went up toward the river Euphrates to the king of Assyria. King Josiah set out to confront him, but was slain at Megiddo at the first encounter.*m* **30** His servants brought his body on a chariot from Megiddo to Jerusalem, where they buried him in his own grave. Then the people of the land* took Jehoahaz, son of Josiah, anointed him, and proclaimed him king to succeed his father.

Reign of Jehoahaz.　　**31** Jehoahaz was twenty-three years old when he began to reign, and he reigned three months in Jerusalem. His mother, whose name was Hamutal, daughter of Jeremiah, was from Libnah.*n* **32** He did evil in the sight of the LORD, just as his forebears had done. **33** Pharaoh Neco took him prisoner at Riblah in the land of Hamath, thus ending his reign in Jerusalem. He imposed a fine upon the land of a hundred talents of silver and a talent of gold.* **34** Pharaoh Neco then appointed Eliakim, son of Josiah, king in place of his father Josiah; he changed his name to Jehoiakim. Jehoahaz he took away with him to Egypt, where he died. **35** Jehoiakim gave the silver and gold to Pharaoh, but taxed the land to raise the amount Pharaoh demanded. He exacted the silver and gold from the people of the land, from each proportionately, to pay Pharaoh Neco.

Reign of Jehoiakim.　**36** *o*Jehoiakim was twenty-five years old when he began to reign, and he reigned eleven years in Jerusalem. His mother's name was Zebidah, daughter of Pedaiah, from Rumah. **37** He did evil in the sight of the LORD, just as his forebears had done.

CHAPTER 24

1 *p*During his reign Nebuchadnezzar, king of Babylon, moved against him, and Jehoiakim became his vassal for three years. Then Jehoiakim turned and rebelled against him. **2** The LORD loosed against him bands of Chaldeans, Arameans, Moabites, and Ammonites; he loosed them against Judah to destroy it, as the LORD had threatened through his servants the prophets.*q* **3** This befell Judah because the LORD had stated that he would inexorably put

them out of his sight for the sins Manasseh had committed in all that he did; **4** and especially because of the innocent blood he shed, with which he filled Jerusalem, the LORD would not forgive.*r*

5 The rest of the acts of Jehoiakim, with all that he did, are written in the book of the chronicles of the kings of Judah.*s* **6** Jehoiakim rested with his ancestors, and his son Jehoiachin succeeded him as king. **7** The king of Egypt did not again leave his own land, for the king of Babylon had taken all that belonged to the king of Egypt from the wadi of Egypt to the Euphrates River.

Reign of Jehoiachin.　**8** Jehoiachin was eighteen years old when he began to reign, and he reigned three months* in Jerusalem. His mother's name was Nehushta, daughter of Elnathan of Jerusalem. **9** He did evil in the sight of the LORD, just as his forebears had done.

10 At that time the officials of Nebuchadnezzar, king of Babylon, attacked Jerusalem, and the city came under siege.*t* **11** Nebuchadnezzar, king of Babylon, himself arrived at the city while his servants were besieging it. **12** Then Jehoiachin, king of Judah, together with his mother, his ministers, officers, and functionaries, surrendered to the king of Babylon, who, in the eighth year of his reign, took him captive. **13** He carried off all the treasures of the temple of the LORD and those of the palace, and broke up all the gold utensils that Solomon, king of Israel, had provided in the temple of the LORD, as the LORD had foretold.*u* **14** He deported all Jerusalem: all the officers and men of the army, ten thousand in number, and all the craftsmen and smiths. None were left among the people of the land except the poor. **15** He deported Jehoiachin to Babylon, and also led captive from Jerusalem to Babylon the king's mother and wives, his functionaries, and the chief men of the land.*v* **16** The king of Babylon also led captive to Babylon all seven thousand men of the army, and a thousand craftsmen and smiths, all of them trained soldiers. **17** In place of Jehoiachin, the king of Babylon appointed his uncle Mattaniah king, and changed his name to Zedekiah.

---

k 2 Kgs 24, 2.	q 2 Kgs 23, 27.
l 2 Chr 35, 26f.	r 2 Kgs 21, 16.
m 2 Chr 35, 20-24.	s 2 Chr 36, 8.
n 2 Chr 36, 2f.	t 2 Chr 36, 10; Dn 1, 1f.
o 36f: 2 Chr 36, 4f.	u 2 Kgs 20, 17; Is 39, 6.
p 1-5: 2 Chr 36, 6ff.	v Est A, 3; 2, 6.

23, 30, 35: People of the land: in this period, the phrase referred to "landed gentry"; in later times it meant "the poor." Cf 2 Kgs 24, 14.

23, 33: A talent of gold: some manuscripts of the Greek and Syriac texts have "ten talents."

24, 8: He reigned three months: in the year 597 B.C.

Reign of Zedekiah. **18** Zedekiah was twenty-one years old when he became king, and he reigned eleven years in Jerusalem. His mother's name was Hamutal, daughter of Jeremiah of Libnah.ʷ **19** He also did evil in the sight of the LORD, just as Jehoiakim had done. **20** The LORD's anger befell Jerusalem and Judah till he cast them out from his presence. Thus Zedekiah rebelled against the king of Babylon.ˣ

CHAPTER 25

1 *ʸ In the tenth month of the ninth year of Zedekiah's reign, on the tenth day of the month, Nebuchadnezzar, king of Babylon, and his whole army advanced against Jerusalem, encamped around it, and built siege walls on every side. **2** The siege of the city continued until the eleventh year of Zedekiah. **3** On the ninth day of the fourth month, when famine had gripped the city, and the people had no more bread, **4** the city walls were breached. Then the king and all the soldiers left the city by night through the gate between the two walls which was near the king's garden. Since the Chaldeans had the city surrounded, they went in the direction of the Arabah. **5** But the Chaldean army pursued the king and overtook him in the desert near Jericho, abandoned by his whole army.

6 The king was therefore arrested and brought to Riblah to the king of Babylon, who pronounced sentence on him. **7** He had Zedekiah's sons slain before his eyes. Then he blinded Zedekiah, bound him with fetters, and had him brought to Babylon.

8 On the seventh day of the fifth month (this was in the nineteenth year of Nebuchadnezzar, king of Babylon), Nebuzaradan, captain of the bodyguard, came to Jerusalem as the representative of the king of Babylon. **9** He burned the house of the LORD, the palace of the king, and all the houses of Jerusalem; every large building was destroyed by fire.ᶻ **10** Then the Chaldean troops who were with the captain of the guard tore down the walls that surrounded Jerusalem.

11 Then Nebuzaradan, captain of the guard, led into exile the last of the people remaining in the city, and those who had deserted* to the king of Babylon, and the last of the artisans. **12** But some of the country's poor, Nebuzaradan, captain of the guard, left behind as vinedressers and farmers.

13 The bronze pillars that belonged to the house of the LORD, and the wheeled carts and the bronze sea in the house of the LORD, the Chaldeans broke into pieces; they carried away the bronze to Babylon.ᵃ **14** They took also the pots, the shovels, the snuffers, the bowls, the pans and all the bronze vessels used for service.ᵇ **15** The fire-holders and the bowls which were of gold or silver the captain of the guard

also carried off. **16** The weight in bronze of the two pillars, the bronze sea, and the wheeled carts, all of them furnishings which Solomon had made for the house of the LORD, was never calculated. **17** Each of the pillars was eighteen cubits high; a bronze capital five cubits high surmounted each pillar, and a network with pomegranates encircled the capital, all of bronze; and so for the other pillar, as regards the network.ᶜ

18 The captain of the guard also took Seraiah the high priest, Zephaniah the second priest, and the three keepers of the entry. **19** And from the city he took one courtier, a commander of soldiers, five men in the personal service of the king who were still in the city, the scribe of the army commander, who mustered the people of the land, and sixty of the common people still remaining in the city. **20** The captain of the guard, Nebuzaradan, arrested these and brought them to the king of Babylon at Riblah; **21** the king had them struck down and put to death in Riblah, in the land of Hamath. Thus was Judah exiled from her land.

Governorship of Gedaliah. **22** ᵈAs for the people whom he had allowed to remain in the land of Judah, Nebuchadnezzar, king of Babylon, appointed as their governor Gedaliah, son of Ahikam, son of Shaphan. **23** Hearing that the king of Babylon had appointed Gedaliah governor, all the army commanders with their men came to him at Mizpah: Ishmael, son of Nethaniah, Johanan, son of Kareah, Seraiah, son of Tanhumeth the Netophathite, and Jaazaniah, from Beth-maacah. **24** Gedaliah gave the commanders and their men his oath. "Do not be afraid of the Chaldean officials," he said to them. "Remain in the country and serve the king of Babylon, and all will be well with you."

25 But in the seventh month Ishmael, son of Nethaniah, son of Elishama, of royal descent, came with ten men, attacked Gedaliah and killed him, along with the Jews and Chaldeans who were in Mizpah with him. **26** Then all the people, great and small, left with the army commanders and went to Egypt for fear of the Chaldeans.

Release of Jehoiachin. **27** ᵉIn the thirty-seventh year of the exile of Jehoiachin, king

---

w 2 Chr 36, 9; Jer 37, 1f; 52, 1ff.
x 2 Kgs 22, 17; 23, 27.
y 1-21: Jer 39, 1-10; 52, 4-28.
z 2 Chr 36, 19; Ps 74, 7.
a 2 Kgs 16, 17; 1 Kgs 7, 15-39; 2 Chr 3, 15;
36, 18; Jer 27, 19.
b 1 Kgs 7, 48ff.
c 1 Kgs 7, 15; Jer 52, 21ff.
d 22-26: Jer 40, 5. 7-41, 1-3.
e 27-30: Jer 52, 31-34.

*

25, 1–30: This chapter parallels Jer 39 and 52; see notes to those parts of Jeremiah.

25, 11: Those who had deserted: perhaps on the advice of Jeremiah; cf Jer 38, 2f.

of Judah, on the twenty-seventh day of the twelfth month, Evil-merodach, king of Babylon, in the inaugural year of his own reign, raised up Jehoiachin, king of Judah, from prison. 28 He spoke kindly to him and gave him a throne higher than that of the other kings who were with him in Babylon. 29 Jehoiachin took off his prison garb and ate at the king's table as long as he lived. 30 The allowance granted him by the king was a perpetual allowance, in fixed daily amounts, for as long as he lived.

The First Book of

CHRONICLES

Originally the two books of Chronicles formed, with the Books of Ezra and Nehemiah, a single historical work, uniform in style and basic ideas. The Greek title, paraleipomena, means "things omitted, or passed over (in Samuel and Kings)." The Books of Chronicles, however, are more than a supplement to Samuel and Kings; a comparison of the two histories discloses striking differences in scope and purpose. The Books of Chronicles record in some detail the lengthy span from the reign of Saul to the return from the Exile. Unlike the exact science of history today, wherein factual accuracy and impartiality of judgment are the standards for estimating what is of permanent worth, ancient biblical history, with rare exceptions, was less concerned with reporting in precise detail all the facts of a situation than with explaining the meaning of those facts. Such history was primarily interpretative and, in the Old Testament, its purpose was to disclose the action of the living God in the affairs of men. For this reason we speak of it as "sacred history"; its writer's first concern was to bring out the divine or supernatural dimension in history.

This is apparent when we examine the primary objective of the Chronicler in compiling his work. In view of the situation which confronted the Jewish people at this time (the end of the fifth century B.C.), the Chronicler realized that Israel's political greatness was a thing of the past. It would be a people under God, or nothing. Yet Israel's past held the key to her future. The Chronicler proposed to establish and defend the legitimate claims of the Davidic monarchy in Israel's history, and to underscore the place of Jerusalem and its divinely established temple worship as the center of religious life for the Jewish community of his day. If Judaism was to survive and prosper, it would have to heed the lessons of the past and devoutly serve Yahweh in the place where he had chosen to dwell, the temple of Jerusalem. From the Chronicler's point of view, David's reign was the ideal to which all subsequent rule in Judah must aspire.

The Chronicler was much more interested in David's religious and cultic influence than in his political power. There is little of royal messianism in his book. He apparently regarded as something of the distant past the prophet Zechariah's abortive attempt to have the Davidic kingdom reestablished in the time of Zerubbabel at the end of the sixth century B.C. (Zec 6, 9–15). He saw David's primary importance as deriving from the establishment of Jerusalem and its temple as the center of the true worship of the Lord. Furthermore, he presented David as the one who had authorized the elaborate ritual (which, in point of fact, only gradually evolved in the temple built by Zerubbabel) and who had also appointed Levites to supervise the liturgical services there.

There are good reasons for believing that originally the Books of Ezra and Nehemiah formed the last part of a single literary work that began with 1 and 2 Chronicles. Some authors even regard Ezra himself as having been the anonymous Chronicler. In any case, the Chronicler's Hebrew as well as his religious and political outlook points to c. 400 B.C. as the time of composition of this work.

The Chronicler used sources in writing his history. Besides the canonical Books of Genesis, Exodus, Numbers, Joshua and Ruth, and especially the Books of Samuel and Kings, he cites the titles of many other works no longer extant. "The books of the kings of Israel," or "the books of the kings of Israel and Judah," "the history of Samuel the seer," "the history of Nathan the prophet," "the history of Gad the seer," "the commentary of the Books of Kings," are some of the documents mentioned as historical sources.

In addition, the Chronicler's work contains early preexilic material not found in the Books of Kings. At one time scholars discounted the value of this material, but modern research has shown that, even though the Chronicler may have at times treated the material rather freely, he derived it from authentic and reliable sources.

The principal divisions of 1 Chronicles are as follows:
I. Genealogical Tables (1, 1—9, 34).
II. The History of David (9, 35—29, 30).

I: Genealogical Tables

CHAPTER 1

From Adam to Abraham. 1 *a** Adam, Seth, Enosh, 2 *b*Kenan, Mahalalel, Jared, 3 Enoch, Methuselah, Lamech,*c* 4 Noah, Shem, Ham, and Japheth.*d* 5 *e*The descendants of Japheth were Gomer, Magog, Madai, Javan, Tubal, Meshech, and Tiras. 6 The descendants of Gomer were Ashkenaz, Riphath, and Togarmah. 7 The descendants of Javan were Elishah, Tarshis, the Kittim, and the Rodanim.

8 *f*The descendants of Ham were Cush, Mesraim, Put, and Canaan. 9 The descendants of Cush were Seba, Havilah, Sabta, Raama, and Sabteca. The descendants of Raama were Sheba and Dedan. 10 Cush became the father of Nimrod, who was the first to be a conqueror on the earth. 11 *g*Mesraim became the father of the Ludim, Anamim, Lehabim, Naphtuhim, 12 Pathrusim, Casluhim, and Caphtorim, from whom the Philistines sprang. 13 Canaan became the father of Sidon, his first-born, and Heth, 14 and the Jebusite, the Amorite, the Girgashite, 15 the Hivite, the Arkite, the Sinite, 16 the Arvadite, the Zemarite, and the Hamathite.

17 *h*The descendants of Shem were Elam, Asshur, Arpachshad, Lud, and Aram. The descendants of Aram were Uz, Hul, Gether, and Mash. 18 Arpachshad became the father of Shelah, and Shelah became the father of Eber. 19 Two sons were born to Eber; the first was named Peleg (for in his time the world was divided), and his brother was Joktan. 20 Joktan became the father of Almodad, Sheleph, Hazarmaveth, Jerah, 21 Hadoram, Uzal, Diklah, 22 Ebal, Abimael, Sheba, 23 Ophir, Havilah, and Jobab; all these were the sons of Joktan.

24 *i*Shem, Arpachshad, Shelah, 25 Eber, Peleg, Reu, 26 Serug, Nahor, Terah, 27 Abram, who was Abraham.*j*

From Abraham to Jacob. 28 The sons of Abraham were Isaac and Ishmael.*k* 29 These were their descendants:*l*

Nebaioth, the first-born of Ishmael, then Kedar, Adbeel, Mibsam, 30 Mishma, Dumah, Massa, Hadad, Tema, 31 Jetur, Naphish, and Kedemah. These were the descendants of Ishmael.

32 *m*The descendants of Keturah, Abraham's concubine: she bore Zimran, Jokshan, Medan, Midian, Ishbak, and Shuah. The sons of Jokshan were Sheba and Dedan. 33 The descendants of Midian were Ephah, Epher, Hanoch, Abida, and Eldaah. All these were the descendants of Keturah.

34 Abraham became the father of Isaac. The sons of Isaac were Esau and Israel.*n*

35 *o*The sons of Esau were Eliphaz, Reuel, Jeush, Jalam, and Korah. 36 The sons of Eliphaz were Teman, Omar, Zephi, Gatam, Kenaz, [Timna,] and Amalek. 37 The sons of Reuel were Nahath, Zerah, Shammah, and Mizzah.

38 *p*The descendants of Seir* were Lotan, Shobal, Zibeon, Anah, Dishon, Ezer, and Dishan. 39 The sons of Lotan were Hori and Homam; Timna was the sister of Lotan. 40 The sons of Shobal were Alian, Manahath, Ebal, Shephi, and Onam. The sons of Zibeon were Aiah and Anah. 41 The sons of Anah: Dishon. The sons of Dishon were Hemdan, Eshban, Ithran, and Cheran. 42 The sons of Ezer were Bilhan, Zaavan, and Jaakan. The sons of Dishan were Uz and Aran.

43 *q*The kings who reigned in the land of Edom before they had Israelite kings were the following: Bela, son of Beor, the name of whose city was Ninhabah. 44 When Bela died, Jobab, son of Zerah, from Bozrah, succeeded him.*r* 45 When Jobab died, Husham, from the land of the Temanites, succeeded him.*s* 46 Husham died and Hadad, son of Bedad, succeeded him. He overthrew the Midianites on the Moabite plateau, and the name of his city was Avith. 47 Hadad died and Samlah of Masrekah suc-

a 1 Chr 4, 25f; Gn 5, 3.
6. 9.
b 2ff: Gn 5, 9-32; 10, 2ff.
c Gn 4, 25.
d Gn 5, 32; 6, 10; 9, 18.
e 5ff: Gn 10, 2ff.
f Gn 10, 8.
g 11-16: Gn 10, 13-18.
h 17-23: Gn 10, 22-29; 11, 10-18.
i 24-27: Gn 11, 10-26; Lk 3, 34ff.
j Gn 17, 5; Neh 9, 7.
k Gn 16, 11. 15; 21, 2f;

Gal 4, 22f; Heb 11, 11.
l 29ff: Gn 25, 13-16.
m 32f: Gn 25, 1-4.
n Gn 21, 2f; 25, 19. 25f: 32, 28f; Mt 1, 2; Lk 3, 34.
o 35ff: Gn 36, 4f. 10-13. 15ff.
p 38-42: Gn 36, 20-28.
q 43-54: Gn 36, 31-43.
r Is 34, 6; 63, 1; Jer 49, 13. 22.
s Gn 36, 11; Jb 2, 11; Jer 49, 7. 20.

*

1, 1–9, 34: The Chronicler set as his task the retelling, from his particular viewpoint, of the story of God's people from the beginning to his own day. Since his primary interest was the history of David and the Davidic dynasty of Judah, he presents through mere genealogical lists a summary of what preceded the reign of Saul, David's predecessor in the kingdom. The sources for these genealogies are mostly the canonical Hebrew Scriptures that were already in their present form in his time. The cross references in this book indicate in each case the scriptural sources used.

1, 38: Seir: another name for Esau (v 35) or Edom (v 43).

ceeded him. **48** Samlah died and Shaul from Rehoboth-han-nahar succeeded him. **49** When Shaul died, Baalhanan, son of Achbor, succeeded him. **50** Baalhanan died and Hadad succeeded him. The name of his city was Pai, and his wife's name was Mehetabel. She was the daughter of Matred, who was the daughter of Mezahab. **51** *t*After Hadad died. . . .

These were the chiefs of Edom: the chiefs of Timna, Aliah, Jetheth, **52** Oholibamah, Elah, Pinon, **53** Kenaz, Teman, Mibzar, **54** Magdiel, and Iram were the chiefs of Edom.

CHAPTER 2

1 These were the sons of Israel: Reuben, Simeon, Levi, Judah, Issachar, Zebulun,*u* **2** Dan, Joseph, Benjamin, Naphtali, Gad, and Asher.*v*

Judah. **3** The sons of Judah* were: Er, Onan, and Shelah; these three were born to him of Bathshua, a Canaanite woman. But Judah's first-born, Er, was wicked in the sight of the LORD, so he killed him.*w* **4** Judah's daughter-in-law Tamar bore him Perez and Zerah, so that he had five sons in all.*x*

5 The sons of Perez were Hezron and Hamul.*y* **6** The sons of Zerah were Zimri, Ethan, Heman, Calcol, and Darda—five in all.*z* **7** The sons of Zimri: Carmi. The sons of Carmi: Achar, who brought trouble upon Israel by violating the ban.*a* **8** The sons of Ethan: Azariah. **9** The sons born to Hezron were Jerahmeel, Ram, and Chelubai.*b* *

10 *Ram became the father of Amminadab, and Amminadab became the father of Nahshon, a prince of the Judahites.*c* **11** *d*Nahshon became the father of Salma. Salma became the father of Boaz. **12** Boaz became the father of Obed. Obed became the father of Jesse. **13** *e*Jesse became the father of Eliab, his first-born, of Abinadab, the second son, Shimea, the third,*f* **14** Nethanel, the fourth, Raddai, the fifth, **15** Ozem, the sixth, and David, the seventh. **16** Their sisters were Zeruiah and Abigail. Zeruiah had three sons: Abishai, Joab, and Asahel.*g* **17** Abigail bore Amasa, whose father was Jether the Ishmaelite.*h*

18 *By his wife Azubah, Caleb, son of Hezron, became the father of a daughter, Jerioth. Her sons were Jesher, Shobab, and Ardon.*i* **19** When Azubah died, Caleb married Ephrath, who bore him Hur.*j* **20** Hur became the father of Uri, and Uri became the father of Bezalel.*k* **21** Then Hezron had relations with the daughter of Machir, the father of Gilead, having married her when he was sixty years old. She bore him Segub.*l* **22** Segub became the father of Jair,*m* who possessed twenty-three cities in the land of Gilead. **23** Geshur and Aram took from them the villages of Jair, that is, Kenath and its

towns, sixty cities in all, which had belonged to the sons of Machir, the father of Gilead.*n* **24** After the death of Hezron, Caleb had relations with Ephrathah, the widow of his father Hezron, and she bore him Ashhur, the father of Tekoa.*o*

25 The sons of Jerahmeel,* the first-born of Hezron, were Ram, the first-born, then Bunah, Oren, and Ozem, his brothers.*p* **26** Jerahmeel also had another wife, Atarah by name, who was the mother of Onam. **27** The sons of Ram, the first-born of Jerahmeel, were Maaz, Jamin, and Eker. **28** The sons of Onam were Shammai and Jada. The sons of Shammai were Nadab and Abishur. **29** Abishur's wife, who was named Abihail, bore him Ahban and Molid. **30** The sons of Nadab were Seled and Appaim. Seled died without sons. **31** The sons of Appaim: Ishi. The sons of Ishi: Sheshan. The sons of Sheshan: Ahlai.*q* **32** The sons of Jada, the brother of Shammai, were Jether and Jonathan. Jether died without sons. **33** The sons of Jonathan were Peleth and Zaza. These were the descendants of Jerahmeel. **34** Sheshan, who had no sons, only daughters, had an Egyptian slave named Jarha. **35** Sheshan gave his daughter in marriage to his slave Jarha, and she bore him Attai. **36** Attai became the father of Nathan. Nathan became the father of Zabad. **37** Zabad became the father of Ephlal. Ephlal became the

---

t 51-54: Gn 36, 40-43.	f 2 Chr 11, 18.
u Gn 29, 32-35; 30, 18.	g 2 Sm 2, 18.
20; 35, 23.	h 2 Sm 17, 25; 19, 14;
v Gn 30, 6. 8. 11. 13.	20, 4-13.
24; 35, 18. 24ff.	i 1 Chr 2, 18.
w 1 Chr 4, 21; Gn 38,	j 1 Chr 2, 24.
1-5; 46, 12.	k Ex 24, 14; 31, 2; 35,
x Gn 38, 7. 13-30; 46,	30; 2 Chr 1, 5.
12; Rv 4, 12. 18; Mt	l Nm 26, 29; 27, 1; 32,
1, 3.	32; Jos 13, 31; Jgs 5,
y Gn 46, 12.	14.
z 1 Kgs 5, 11.	m Nm 32, 41; 1 Kgs 4,
a Jos 7, 1. 18ff. 24f; 22,	13.
20.	n Dt 3, 14; Jos 13, 30;
b Rv 4, 19; Mt 1, 3.	Jgs 10, 4.
c Rv 4, 19; Mt 1, 4.	o 1 Chr 2, 19; 2 Sm 14,
d 11f: Nm 1, 7; Rv 4, 20f;	2; 2 Chr 11, 6.
Mt 1, 4f.	p 1 Sm 27, 10; 30, 29;
e 13ff: 1 Sm 16, 6-13;	Jb 32, 2.
17, 13f.	q 1 Chr 4, 20.

---

*

2, 3–4, 23: For two reasons, the Chronicler places the genealogy of the tribe of Judah before that of the other tribes, giving it also at greater length than the others: because of his interest in David and because in the Chronicler's time the people of God were almost exclusively Jews. Both David and the Jews were of the tribe of Judah.

2, 9: Chelubai: a variant form of the name Caleb (vv 18. 42), distinct from Chelub of 1 Chr 4, 11.

2, 10–17: Immediate ancestors of David. A similar list is given in Ru 4, 19–22; each list, independent of the other, derives from a common source.

2, 18–24: Descendants of Caleb. In 1 Chr 4, 15, as is often the case in the Pentateuch (Nm 13, 6; 14, 6, 30; 26, 65; etc.), Caleb is called son of Jephunneh. Here he is called son of Hezron, perhaps because the Calebites were reckoned as part of the clan of the Hezronites.

2, 25–41: The Jerahmeelites were a clan in the Negeb of Judah.

father of Obed. **38** Obed became the father of Jehu. Jehu became the father of Azariah. **39** Azariah became the father of Helez. Helez became the father of Eleasah. **40** Eleasah became the father of Sismai. Sismai became the father of Shallum. **41** Shallum became the father of Jekamiah. Jekamiah became the father of Elishama.

42 The descendants of Caleb,* the brother of Jerahmeel: [Mesha] his first-born, who was the father of Ziph. Then the sons of Mareshah, who was the father of Hebron. **43** The sons of Hebron were Korah, Tappuah, Rekem, and Shema. **44** Shema became the father of Raham, who was the father of Jorkeam. Rekem became the father of Shammai. **45** The sons of Shammai: Maon, who was the father of Beth-zur. **46** Ephah, Caleb's concubine, bore Haran, Moza, and Gazez. Haran became the father of Gazez. **47** The sons of Jahdai were Regem, Jotham, Geshan, Pelet, Ephah, and Shaaph. **48** Maacah, Caleb's concubine, bore Sheber and Tirhanah. **49** She also bore Shaaph, the father of Madmannah, Sheva, the father of Mach-benah, and the father of Gibea. Achsah was Caleb's daughter.

50 These were descendants of Caleb, sons of Hur,* the first-born of Ephrathah: Shobal, the father of Kiriath-jearim, **51** Salma, the father of Bethlehem, and Hareph, the father of Bethgader. **52** The sons of Shobal, the father of Kiriath-jearim, were Reaiah, half the Manahathites, **53** and the clans of Kiriath-jearim: the Ithrites, the Puthites, the Shumathites, and the Mishraites. From these the people of Zorah and the Eshtaolites derived. **54** The descendants of Salma were Bethlehem, the Netophathites, Atroth-beth-Joab, half the Manahathites, and the Zorites. **55** The clans of the Sopherim dwelling in Jabez were the Tirathites, the Shimeathites, and the Sucathites. They were the Kenites, who came from Hammath of the ancestor of the Rechabites.

CHAPTER 3

1 The following* were the sons of David who were born to him in Hebron: the first-born, Amnon, by Ahinoam of Jezreel; the second, Daniel,* by Abigail of Carmel; **2** the third, Absalom, son of Maacah, who was the daughter of Talmai, king of Geshur; the fourth, Adonijah, son of Haggith; **3** the fifth, Shephatiah, by Abital; the sixth, Ithream, by his wife Eglah. **4** Six in all were born to him in Hebron, where he reigned seven years and six months. Then he reigned thirty-three years in Jerusalem, **5** where the following were born to him: Shimea,* Shobab, Nathan, Solomon—four by Bathsheba, the daughter of Ammiel,* **6** Ibhar, Elishua, Eliphelet, **7** Nogah, Nepheg, Japhia,

8 Elishama, Eliada, and Eliphelet—nine. **9** All these were sons of David, in addition to other sons by concubines; and Tamar was their sister.

10 * The son of Solomon was Rehoboam, whose son was Abijah, whose son was Asa, whose son was Jehoshaphat, **11** whose son was Joram, whose son was Ahaziah, whose son was Joash, **12** whose son was Amaziah, whose son was Azariah, whose son was Jotham, **13** whose son was Ahaz, whose son was Hezekiah, whose son was Manasseh, **14** whose son was Amon, whose son was Josiah. **15** The sons of Josiah were: the first-born, Johanan; the second, Jehoiakim; the third, Zedekiah; the fourth, Shallum.* **16** The sons of Jehoiakim were: Jeconiah, his son; Zedekiah, his son.

17 The sons of Jeconiah* the captive were: Shealtiel, **18** Malchiram, Pedaiah, Shenazzar,* Jekamiah, Shama, and Nedabiah. **19** The sons of Pedaiah were Zerubbabel* and Shimei. The sons of Zerubbabel were Meshullam and Hananiah; Shelomith was their sister. **20** The sons of Meshullam were Hashubah, Ohel, Bere-

r   Jos 15, 16; Jgs 1, 12.
s   Jgs 18, 2.
t   Nm 24, 21; Jgs 1, 16; 4, 11; 1 Sm 15, 6.
u   1-4: 2 Sm 3, 2-5.
v   2 Sm 2, 11; 5, 5.
w   5-8: 2 Sm 5, 14ff.
x   2 Sm 5, 5.
y   2 Sm 13, 1f.
z   10-17: Mt 1, 7-12.
a   1 Kgs 11, 43; 14, 31; 15, 1. 8. 24; 2 Chr 9, 31; 12, 16; 13, 23; 17, 1.
b   1 Kgs 22, 51; 2 Chr 21, 1; 22, 1; 24, 1. 27.

c   2 Kgs 12, 21; 14, 21; 15, 7; 2 Chr 25, 1; 26, 1. 23; 27, 1.
d   2 Kgs 15, 38; 16, 20; 20, 21; 2 Chr 28, 1. 27; 32, 33.
e   2 Kgs 21, 18. 26; 2 Chr 33, 20. 25.
f   2 Kgs 23, 34; 24, 17; 2 Chr 36, 4. 10.
g   2 Kgs 24, 6. 17; 2 Chr 36, 8. 10.
h   17. 19; Ezr 2, 2; 3, 2. 8; 5, 2; Sir 49, 11; Hg 1, 1. 12. 14; Mt 1, 12f; Lk 3, 27.

*

2, 42–49: Another list, dating from preexilic times, of the Calebites, a clan that inhabited the south of Judah.

2, 50–55: The Hurites, a clan dwelling to the south and west of Jerusalem and related to the Calebites.

3, 1–9: David's sons.

3, 1: Daniel: called Chileab in 2 Sm 3, 3.

3, 5: Shimea: called Shammua in 2 Sm 5, 14. Ammiel: called Eliam in 2 Sm 11, 3.

3, 10–16: The kings of Judah from Solomon to the destruction of Jerusalem by the Babylonians.

3, 15: Shallum: the same as Jehoahaz, Josiah's successor; cf Jer 22, 11.

3, 17–24: The descendants of King Jechoniah up to the time of the Chronicler. If twenty-five years are allowed to each generation, the ten generations between Jechoniah and Anani (the last name on the list) would bring the birth of the latter to about 405 B.C.—an important item in establishing the approximate date of the Chronicler.

3, 18: Shenazzar: presumably the same as Sheshbazzar of Ezr 1, 8. 11; 5, 14ff, the prince of Judah who was the first Jewish governor of Judah after the exile. Both forms of the name probably go back to the Babylonian name Sin-ab-ussar signifying, "O [god] Sin, protect [our] father!"

3, 19: Zerubbabel: here called the son of Pedaiah, though elsewhere (Hg 1, 12. 14; 2, 2. 23; Ezr 3, 2. 8; 5, 2; Neh 12, 1) called son of Shealtiel. The latter term may merely mean that Zerubbabel succeeded Shealtiel as head of the house of David.

chiah, Hasadiah, Jushabhesed—five. **21** The sons of Hananiah were Pelatiah, Jeshaiah, Rephaiah, Arnan, Obadiah, and Shecaniah. **22** *The sons of Shecaniah were Shemiah, Hattush, Igal, Bariah, Neariah, Shaphat—six. **23** The sons of Neariah were Elioenai, Hizkiah, and Azrikam—three. **24** The sons of Elioenai were Hodaviah, Eliashib, Pelaiah, Akkub, Johanan, Delaiah, and Anani—seven.

CHAPTER 4

1 *The descendants of Judah were: Perez, Hezron, Carmi, Hur, and Shobal.* **2** Reaiah, the son of Shobal, became the father of Jahath, and Jahath became the father of Ahumai and Lahad. These were the clans of the Zorathites.

3 These were the descendants of Hareph, the father of Etam: Jezreel, Ishma, and Idbash; their sister was named Hazzelelponi. **4** Penuel was the father of Gedor, and Ezer the father of Hushah. These were the descendants of Hur, the first-born of Ephrathah, the father of Bethlehem.

5 Ashhur, the father of Tekoa, had two wives, Helah and Naarah.* **6** Naarah bore him Ahuzzam, Hepher, the Temenites and the Ahashtarites. These were the descendants of Naarah. **7** The sons of Helah were Zereth, Izhar, Ethnan, and Koz. **8** Koz became the father of Anub and Zobebah, as well as of the clans of Aharhel, son of Harum. **9** Jabez was the most distinguished of the brothers. His mother had named him Jabez, saying, "I bore him with pain." **10** Jabez prayed to the God of Israel: "Oh, that you may truly bless me and extend my boundaries! Help me and make me free of misfortune, without pain!" And God granted his prayer.

11 Chelub, the brother of Shuhah, became the father of Mehir, who was the father of Eshton. **12** Eshton became the father of Beth-rapha, Paseah, and Tehinnah, the father of the city of Nahash. These were the men of Recah.

13 The sons of Kenaz were Othniel and Seraiah. The sons of Othniel were Hathath and Meonothai;* **14** Meonothai became the father of Ophrah. Seraiah became the father of Joab, the father of Geharashim, so called because they were craftsmen. **15** The sons of Caleb, son of Jephunneh, were Ir, Elah, and Naam. The sons of Elah were . . . and Kenaz.* **16** The sons of Jehallelel were Ziph, Ziphah, Tiria, and Asarel. **17** The sons of Ezrah were Jether, Mered, Epher, and Jalon. Jether became the father of Miriam, Shammai, and Ishbah, the father of Eshtemoa. [. . . . . .]* **18** His (Mered's) Egyptian wife bore Jared, the father of Gedor, Heber, the father of Soco, and Jekuthiel, the father of Zanoah. These were the sons of Bithiah, the daughter of Pharaoh, whom Mered married. **19** The sons of his Jewish wife, the sister of

Naham, the father of Keilah, were Shimon the Garmite and Ishi the Maacathite. **20** The sons of Shimon were Amnon, Rinnah, Benhanan, and Tilon. The son of Ishi was Zoheth and the son of Zoheth. . . . . .

21 The descendants of Shelah, son of Judah, were: Er, the father of Lecah; Laadah, the father of Mareshah; the clans of the linen weavers' guild in Bethashbea;* **22** Jokim; the men of Cozeba; and Joash and Saraph, who held property in Moab, but returned to Bethlehem. [These are events of old.] **23** They were potters and inhabitants of Netaim and Gederah, where they lived in the king's service.

Simeon. **24** The sons of Simeon were Nemuel, Jamin, Jachin, Zerah, and Shaul,* **25** whose son was Shallum, whose son was Mibsam, whose son was Mishma. **26** The descendants of Mishma were his son Hammuel, whose son was Zaccur, whose son was Shimei. **27** Shimei had sixteen sons and six daughters. His brothers, however, did not have many sons, and as a result all their clans did not equal the number of the Judahites.

28 *They dwelt in Beer-sheba, Moladah, Hazar-shual, **29** Bilhah, Ezem, Tolad, **30** Bethuel, Hormah, Ziklag, **31** Bethmarcaboth, Hazar-susim, Bethbiri, and Shaaraim. Until David came to reign, these were their cities **32** and their villages. Etam, also, and Ain, Rimmon, Tochen, and Ashan—five cities, **33** together with all their outlying villages as far as Baal. Here is where they dwelt, and so it was inscribed of them in their family records.

34 Meshobab, Jamlech, Joshah, son of Amaziah, **35** Joel, Jehu, son of Joshibiah, son of Seraiah, son of Asiel, **36** Elioenai, Jaakobath, Jeshohaiah, Asaiah, Adiel, Jesimiel, Benaiah, **37** Ziza, son of Shiphi, son of Allon, son of Jedaiah, son of Shimri, son of Shemaiah— **38** these just named were princes in their clans, and their ancestral houses spread out to such an extent* **39** that they went to the approaches of Gedor,* east of the valley, seeking pasture for their flocks. **40** They found abundant and good pastures, and the land was spacious, quiet, and peaceful. **41** They who have just been listed by name set out during the reign of Hezekiah, king of Judah, and attacked the tents of Ham (for Hamites dwelt there formerly) and also the Me-

---

i Neh 3, 29.
j 1 Chr 2, 4f. 7. 9. 50; Gn 38, 29; 46, 12; Mt 1, 3.
k 1 Chr 2, 24.
l Jos 15, 17; Jgs 1, 13; 3, 9. 11.
m Nm 13, 6; 14, 6; 32, 12; Jos 14, 6. 14.
n 1 Sm 30, 28.
o 1 Chr 2, 3; Gn 38, 5; 46, 12; Nm 26, 20.
p Gn 46, 10; Ex 6, 15; Nm 26, 12f.
q 28-32: Jos 19, 2-8.
r Nm 1, 2.
s 2 Kgs 18, 1f; 2 Chr 29, 1.

4, 1–43: The southern tribes.

4, 39: Gedor: in the Greek, Gerar, no doubt correct.

unites who were there. They pronounced against them the ban that is still in force and dwelt in their place because they found pasture there for their flocks.[s]

42 Five hundred of them (the Simeonites) went to Mount Seir under the leadership of Pelatiah, Neariah, Rephaiah, and Uzziel, sons of Ishi. **43** They attacked the surviving Amalekites who had escaped, and have resided there to the present day.[t]

CHAPTER 5

Reuben. **1** *The sons of Reuben, the first-born of Israel. (He was indeed the first-born, but because he disgraced the couch of his father his birthright was given to the sons of Joseph, son of Israel, so that he is not listed in the family records according to birthright.[u] **2** Judah, in fact, became powerful among his brothers, so that the ruler came from him, though the birthright had been Joseph's.)[v] **3** The sons of Reuben, the first-born of Israel, were Hanoch, Pallu, Hezron, and Carmi.[w] **4** His son was Joel, whose son was Shemaiah, whose son was Gog, whose son was Shimei, **5** whose son was Micah, whose son was Reaiah, whose son was Baal, **6** whose son was Beerah, whom Tiglath-pileser, the king of Assyria, took into exile; he was a prince of the Reubenites.[x] **7** His brothers who belonged to his clans, when they were listed in the family records according to their descendants, were: Jeiel, the chief, and Zechariah, **8** and Bela, son of Azaz, son of Shema, son of Joel. The Reubenites lived in Aroer and as far as Nebo and Baalmeon;[y] **9** toward the east they dwelt as far as the desert which extends from the Euphrates River, for they had much livestock in the land of Gilead.[z] **10** During the reign of Saul they waged war with the Hagrites, and when they had defeated them they occupied their tents throughout the region east of Gilead.[a]

Gad. **11** The Gadites lived alongside them in the land of Bashan as far as Salecah.[b] **12** Joel was chief, Shapham was second in command, and Janai was judge in Bashan.[c] **13** Their brothers, corresponding to their ancestral houses, were: Michael, Meshullam, Sheba, Jorai, Jacan, Zia, and Eber—seven. **14** These were the sons of Abihail, son of Huri, son of Jaroah, son of Gilead, son of Michael, son of Jeshishai, son of Jahdo, son of Buz. **15** Ahi son of Abdiel, son of Guni, was the head of their ancestral houses. **16** They dwelt in Gilead, in Bashan and its towns, and in all the pasture lands of Sirion to the borders. **17** All were listed in the family records in the time of Jotham, king of Judah, and of Jeroboam, king of Israel.

18 The Reubenites, Gadites, and half-tribe of Manasseh were warriors, men who bore shield and sword and who drew the bow, trained in warfare—forty-four thousand seven hundred and sixty men fit for military service. **19** When they waged war against the Hagrites and against Jetur, Naphish, and Nodab,[d] **20** they received help so that they mastered the Hagrites and all who were with them. For during the battle they called on God, and he heard them because they had put their trust in him.[e] **21** Along with one hundred thousand men they also captured their livestock: fifty thousand camels, two hundred fifty thousand camels, two hundred fifty thousand sheep, and two thousand asses. **22** Many had fallen in battle, for victory is from God; and they took over their dwelling place until the time of the exile.[f]

East Manasseh. **23** The numerous members of the half-tribe of Manasseh lived in the land of Bashan as far as Baal-hermon, Senir, and Mount Hermon. **24** The following were the heads of their ancestral houses: Epher, Ishi, Eliel, Azriel, Jeremiah, Hodaviah, and Jahdiel—men who were warriors, famous men, and heads over their ancestral houses.

25 However, they offended the God of their fathers by lusting after the gods of the natives of the land, whom God had cleared out of their way.[g] **26** Therefore the God of Israel incited against them the anger of Pul,* king of Assyria, and of Tiglath-pileser, king of Assyria, who deported the Reubenites, the Gadites, and the half-tribe of Manasseh and brought them to Halah, Habor, and Hara, and to the river Gozan, where they have remained to this day.[h]

Levi.* **27** The sons of Levi were Gershon, Kohath, and Merari.[i] **28** The sons of Kohath were Amram, Izhar, Hebron, and Uzziel.[j] **29** The children of Amram were Aaron, Moses, and Miriam. The sons of Aaron were Nadab,

---

t Ex 17, 8. 14; Dt 25, 17ff; 1 Sm 14, 48; 15, 3. 7f; 2 Sm 8, 12.
u Gn 35, 22; 48, 5. 15-22; 49, 3f; Dt 33, 6.
v 1 Chr 28, 4; Gn 49, 8ff.
w Gn 46, 9; Ex 6, 14; Nm 26, 5f.
x 2 Kgs 15, 29.
y Jos 13, 9. 16f; Nm 32, 3. 38.
z Jos 22, 9.
a Ps 83, 6.
b Jos 13, 11. 24-28.

c Gn 46, 16.
d 1 Chr 1, 31; 5, 10; Gn 25, 15; Ps 83, 6.
e Dt 33, 20f.
f Nm 32, 39; Dt 3, 8ff; Jgs 3, 3.
g Ex 34, 14ff; 2 Kgs 17, 7.
h 2 Kgs 15, 9. 29; 17, 6.
i 1 Chr 6, 1; 23, 6; Gn 46, 11; Ex 6, 16; Nm 26, 57.
j 1 Chr 6, 3; Ex 6, 18.
k Ex 6, 20; Nm 26, 59f.

*

5, 1–26: The Transjordan tribes.

5, 26: Pul: the name which the Assyrian king Tiglath-pileser III (745–727 B.C.) took as king of Babylon.

5, 27–6, 66: The tribe of Levi. The list gives special prominence to Levi's son Kohath, from whom were descended both the Aaronite priests (1 Chr 5, 28–41) and the leading group of temple singers (1 Chr 6, 18–23).

Abihu, Eleazar, and Ithamar.*k* **30** *Eleazar, became the father of Phinehas. Phinehas became the father of Abishua. **31** Abishua became the father of Bukki. Bukki became the father of Uzzi. **32** Uzzi became the father of Zerahiah. Zerahiah became the father of Meraioth. **33** Meraioth became the father of Amariah. Amariah became the father of Ahitub. **34** Ahitub became the father of Zadok. Zadok became the father of Ahimaaz. **35** Ahimaaz became the father of Azariah. Azariah became the father of Johanan. **36** Johanan became the father of Azariah, who served as priest in the temple Solomon built in Jerusalem. **37** Azariah became the father of Amariah. Amariah became the father of Ahitub. **38** Ahitub became the father of Zadok. Zadok became the father of Shallum. **39** Shallum became the father of Hilkiah. Hilkiah became the father of Azariah. **40** Azariah became the father of Seraiah. Seraiah became the father of Jehozadak. **41** Jehozadak was one of those who went into the exile which the LORD inflicted on Judah and Jerusalem through Nebuchadnezzar.

CHAPTER 6

1 The sons of Levi were Gershon, Kohath, and Merari.*l* **2** The sons of Gershon were named Libni and Shimei.*m* **3** The sons of Kohath were Amram, Izhar, Hebron, and Uzziel.*n* **4** *o*The sons of Merari were Mahli and Mushi. The following were the clans of Levi, distributed according to their ancestors: **5** of Gershon: his son Libni, whose son was Jahath, whose son was Zimmah, **6** whose son was Joah, whose son was Iddo, whose son was Zerah, whose son was Jetherai.

7 The descendants of Kohath were: his son Amminadab, whose son was Korah, whose son was Assir, **8** whose son was Elkanah, whose son was Ebiasaph, whose son was Assir, **9** whose son was Tahath, whose son was Uriel, whose son was Uzziah, whose son was Shaul. **10** The sons of Elkanah were Amasai and Ahimoth, **11** whose son was Elkanah, whose son was Zophai, whose son was Nahath, **12** whose son was Eliab, whose son was Jeroham, whose son was Elkanah, whose son was Samuel. **13** The sons of Samuel were Joel, the firstborn, and Abijah, the second.

14 The descendants of Merari were Mahli, whose son was Libni, whose son was Shimei, whose son was Uzzah,*p* **15** whose son was Shimea, whose son was Haggiah, whose son was Asaiah.

16 The following were entrusted by David with the choir services* in the LORD'S house from the time when the ark had obtained a permanent resting place. **17** They served as singers before the Dwelling of the meeting tent until Solomon built the temple of the LORD in Jerusa-

lem, and they performed their services in an order prescribed for them. **18** Those who so performed are the following, together with their descendants.

Among the Kohathites: Heman, the chanter, son of Joel, son of Samuel, **19** son of Elkanah, son of Jeroham, son of Eliel, son of Toah, **20** son of Zuth, son of Elkanah, son of Mahath, son of Amasi, **21** son of Elkanah, son of Joel, son of Azariah, son of Zephaniah, **22** son of Tahath, son of Assir, son of Ebiasaph, son of Korah,*q* **23** son of Izhar, son of Kohath, son of Levi, son of Israel.

24 His brother Asaph stood at his right hand. Asaph was the son of Berechiah, son of Shimea, **25** son of Michael, son of Baaseiah, son of Malchijah, **26** son of Ethni, son of Zerah, son of Adaiah, **27** son of Ethan, son of Zimmah,*r* son of Shimei, **28** son of Jahath, son of Gershon, son of Levi.

29 Their brothers, the Merarites, stood at the left: Ethan, son of Kishi, son of Abdi, son of Malluch, **30** son of Hashabiah, son of Amaziah, son of Hilkiah, **31** son of Amzi, son of Bani, son of Shemer, **32** son of Mahli, son of Mushi, son of Merari, son of Levi.*s*

33 Their brother Levites were appointed to all other services of the Dwelling of the house of God.*t* **34** However, it was Aaron and his descendants who burnt the offerings on the altar of holocausts and on the altar of incense; they alone had charge of the holy of holies and of making atonement for Israel, as Moses, the servant of God, had ordained.*u*

35 These were the descendants of Aaron: his son Eleazer, whose son was Phinehas, whose son was Abishua, **36** whose son was Bukki, whose son was Uzzi, whose son was Zerahiah, **37** whose son was Meraioth, whose son was Amariah, whose son was Ahitub, **38** whose son was Zadok, whose son was Ahimaaz.

39 *The following were their dwelling places to which their encampment was limited. To the descendants of Aaron who belonged to the clan of the Kohathites, since the first lot fell

---

l 1 Chr 5, 27; 23, 6; Gn 46, 11; Ex 6, 16; Nm 26, 57.
m Ex 6, 17.
n Ex 6, 18; Nm 3, 19; 26, 59.
o 1 Chr 6, 14; Ex 6, 19; Nm 3, 20; 26, 58.

p 1 Chr 6, 4; Ex 6, 19; Nm 3, 20; 26, 58.
q Ex 6, 24.
r 1 Chr 6, 2. 5.
s Ex 6, 19; Nm 26, 58.
t 1 Chr 15, 17. 19; 16, 41f; 2 Chr 5, 12.
u 1 Chr 16, 39f.

---

*

5, 30–41: The line of preexilic priests. The list seems to be confused in vv 36ff, which repeat the names, mostly in inverse order, that occur in vv 34f. A similar but shorter list is given, with variations, in Ezr 7, 1–5.

6, 16–32: The origin of the choir services performed by the levitical families in the postexilic temple at the time of the Chronicler is here attributed to David, somewhat as all the laws in the Pentateuch are attributed to Moses.

6, 39–66: Regarding the nature of the rights of Levites in the cities assigned to them, see note on Jos 21, 1.

to them, **40** was assigned Hebron with its adjacent pasture lands in the land of Judah, **41** although the open country and the villages belonging to the city had been given to Caleb, the son of Jephunneh. **42** There were assigned to the descendants of Aaron: Hebron, a city of asylum, Libnah with its pasture lands, Jattir with its pasture lands, Eshtemoa with its pasture lands, **43** Holon with its pasture lands, Debir with its pasture lands, **44** Ashan with its pasture lands, Jetta with its pasture lands, and Beth-shemesh with its pasture lands. **45** Also from the tribe of Benjamin: Gibeon with its pasture lands, Geba with its pasture lands, Almon with its pasture lands, Anathoth with its pasture lands. In all, they had thirteen cities with their pasture lands. **49** The Israelites assigned these cities with their pasture lands to the Levites, **50** designating them by name and assigning them by lot from the tribes of the Judahites, Simeonites, and Benjaminites.

46 The other Kohathites obtained ten cities by lot for their clans from the tribe of Ephraim, from the tribe of Dan, and from the half-tribe of Manasseh. **47** The clans of the Gershonites obtained thirteen cities from the tribes of Issachar, Asher, and Naphtali, and from the half-tribe of Manasseh in Bashan. **48** The clans of the Merarites obtained twelve cities by lot from the tribes of Reuben, Gad, and Zebulun.

51 The clans of the Kohathites obtained cities by lot from the tribe of Ephraim. **52** They were assigned: Shechem in the mountain region of Ephraim, a city of asylum, with its pasture lands, Gezer with its pasture lands, **53** Kibzaim with its pasture lands, and Beth-horon with its pasture lands. **54** From the tribe of Dan: Elteke with its pasture lands, Gibbethon with its pasture lands, Aijalon with its pasture lands, and Gath-rimmon with its pasture lands. **55** From the half-tribe of Manasseh: Taanach with its pasture lands and Ibleam with its pasture lands. These belonged to the rest of the Kohathite clan.

56 The clans of the Gershonites received from the half-tribe of Manasseh: Golan in Bashan with its pasture lands and Ashtaroth with its pasture lands. **57** From the tribe of Issachar: Kedesh with its pasture lands, Daberath with its pasture lands, **58** Ramoth with its pasture lands, and Engannim with its pasture lands. **59** From the tribe of Asher: Mashal with its pasture lands, Abdon with its pasture lands, **60** Hilkath with its pasture lands, and Rehob with its pasture lands. **61** From the tribe of Naphtali: Kedesh in Galilee with its pasture lands, Hammon with its pasture lands, and Kiriathaim with its pasture lands.

62 The rest of the Merarites received from the tribe of Zebulun: Jokneam with its pasture lands, Kartah with its pasture lands, Rimmon with its pasture lands, and Tabor with its pasture

lands. **63** Across the Jordan at Jericho [that is, east of the Jordan] they received from the tribe of Reuben: Bezer in the desert with its pasture lands, Jahzah with its pasture lands, **64** Kedemoth with its pasture lands, and Mephaath with its pasture lands. **65** From the tribe of Gad: Ramoth in Gilead with its pasture lands, Mahanaim with its pasture lands, **66** Heshbon with its pasture lands, and Jazer with its pasture lands.

CHAPTER 7

Issachar.*   **1** The sons of Issachar were Tola, Puah, Jashub, and Shimron: four.[v] **2** The sons of Tola were Uzzi, Rephaiah, Jeriel, Jahmai, Ibsam, and Shemuel, warrior heads of the ancestral houses of Tola. Their kindred numbered twenty-two thousand six hundred in the time of David.[w] **3** The sons of Uzzi: Izarahiah. The sons of Izarahiah were Michael, Obadiah, Joel, and Isshiah. All five of these were chiefs. **4** Their kindred, by ancestral houses, numbered thirty-six thousand men in organized military troops, since they had more wives and sons **5** than their fellow tribesmen. In all the clans of Issachar there was a total of eighty-seven thousand warriors in their family records.

Benjamin.   **6** The sons of Benjamin were Bela, Becher, and Jediael—three.[x] **7** The sons of Bela were Ezbon, Uzzi, Uzziel, Jerimoth, and Iri—five. They were heads of their ancestral houses and warriors. Their family records listed twenty-two thousand and thirty-four. **8** The sons of Becher were Zemirah, Joash, Eliezer, Elioenai, Omri, Jeremoth, Abijah, Anathoth, and Alemeth—all these were sons of Becher.[y] **9** Their family records listed twenty thousand two hundred of their kindred who were heads of their ancestral houses and warriors. **10** The sons of Jediael: Bilhan. The sons of Bilhan were Jeush, Benjamin, Ehud, Chenaanah, Zethan, Tarshish, and Ahishahar. **11** All these were descendants of Jediael, heads of ancestral houses and warriors. They numbered seventeen thousand two hundred men fit for military service . . . Shupham and Hupham.[z]

Dan, Naphtali and Manasseh.   **12** [a]The sons of Dan: Hushim. **13** The sons of Naphtali were Jahziel, Guni, Jezer, and Shallum. These were descendants of Bilhah. **14** The sons of

v Gn 46, 13.
w Nm 26, 23f; Jgs 10, 1.
x 1 Chr 7, 6; Gn 46, 21; Nm 26, 38.
y 1 Chr 7, 8.
z Nm 26, 39.
a 12f: Gn 46, 24; Nm 26, 48f.
b 14-19: Nm 26, 29-32.
c Nm 26, 29; Jos 17, 1.

*
7, 1-40: The northern tribes.

Manasseh, whom his Aramean concubine bore:[b] she bore Machir, the father of Gilead.[c] **15** Machir took a wife whose name was Maacah; his sister's name was Molecheth. Manasseh's second son was named Zelophehad, but to Zelophehad only daughters were born.[d] **16** Maacah, Machir's wife, bore a son whom she named Peresh. He had a brother named Sheresh, whose sons were Ulam and Rakem. **17** The sons of Ulam: Bedan. These were the descendants of Gilead, the son of Machir, the son of Manasseh. **18** His sister Molecheth bore Ishhod, Abiezer, and Mahlah. **19** The sons of Shemida were Ahian, Shechem, Likhi, and Aniam.

Ephraim. **20** [e]The sons of Ephraim: Shuthelah, whose son was Bered, whose son was Tahath, whose son was Eleadah, whose son was Tahath, **21** whose son was Zabad, Ephraim's son Shuthelah, and Ezer and Elead, who were born in the land, were slain by the inhabitants of Gath because they had gone down to take away their livestock. **22** Their father Ephraim mourned a long time, but after his kinsmen had come and comforted him, **23** he visited his wife, who conceived and bore a son whom he named Beriah, since evil had befallen his house.[f] **24** He had a daughter, Sheerah, who built lower and upper Beth-horon and Uzzensheerah. **25** Zabad's son was Rephah, whose son was Resheph, whose son was Telah, whose son was Tahan, **26** whose son was Ladan, whose son was Ammihud, whose son was Elishama,[g] **27** whose son was Nun, whose son was Joshua.

28 Their property and their dwellings were in Bethel and its towns, Naaran to the east, Gezer and its towns to the west, and also Shechem and its towns as far as Ayyah and its towns.[h] **29** Manasseh, however, had possession of Beth-shean and its towns, Taanach and its towns, Megiddo and its towns, and Dor and its towns. In these dwelt the descendants of Joseph, the son of Israel.[i]

Asher. **30** The sons of Asher were Imnah, Iishvah, Ishvi, and Beriah; their sister was Serah.[j] **31** Beriah's sons were Heber and Malchiel, who was the father of Birzaith. **32** Heber became the father of Japhlet, Shomer, Hotham, and their sister Shua. **33** The sons of Japhlet were Pasach, Bimhal, and Ashvath; these were the sons of Japhlet. **34** The sons of Shomer were Ahi, Rohgah, Jehubbah, and Aram. **35** The sons of his brother Hotham were Zophah, Imna, Shelesh, and Amal. **36** The sons of Zophah were Suah, Harnepher, Shual, Beri, Imrah, **37** Bezer, Hod, Shamma, Shilshah, Ithran, and Beera. **38** The sons of Jether were Jephunneh, Pispa, and Ara. **39** The sons of Ulla

were Arah, Hanniel, and Rizia. **40** All these were descendants of Asher, heads of ancestral houses, distinguished men, warriors, and chiefs among the princes. Their family records numbered twenty-six thousand men fit for military service.

CHAPTER 8

Benjamin.* **1** Benjamin became the father of Bela, his first-born, Ashbel, the second son, Aharah, the third,[k] **2** Nohah, the fourth, and Rapha, the fifth. **3** The sons of Bela were Addar and Gera, the father of Ehud. **4** The sons of Ehud were Abishua, Naaman, Ahoah,[l] **5** Gera, Shephuphan, and Huram. **6** These were the sons of Ehud, family heads over those who dwelt in Geba and were deported to Manahath. **7** Also Naaman, Ahijah, and Gera. The last, who led them into exile, became the father of Uzza and Ahihud. **8** Shaharaim became a father on the Moabite plateau after he had put away his wives Hushim and Baara. **9** By his wife Hodesh he became the father of Jobab, Zibia, Mesha, Malcam, **10** Jeuz, Sachia, and Mirmah. These were his sons, family heads. **11** By Hushim he became the father of Abitub and Elpaal. **12** The sons of Elpaal were Eber, Misham, Shemed, who built Ono and Lod with its nearby towns,[m] **13** Beriah, and Shema. They were family heads of those who dwelt in Aijalon, and they put the inhabitants of Gath to flight. **14** Their brethren were Elpaal, Shashak, and Jeremoth. **15** Zebadiah, Arad, Eder, **16** Michael, Ishpah, and Joha were the sons of Beriah. **17** Zebadiah, Meshullam, Hizki, Heber, **18** Ishmerai, Izliah, and Jobab were the sons of Elpaal. **19** Jakim, Zichri, Zabdi, **20** Elienai, Zillethai, Eliel, **21** Adaiah, Beraiah, and Shimrath were the sons of Shimei. **22** Ishpan, Eber, Eliel, **23** Abdon, Zichri, Hanan, **24** Hananiah, Elam, Anthothijah, **25** Iphdeiah, and Penuel were the sons of Shashak. **26** Shamsherai, Shehariah, Athaliah, **27** Jaareshiah, Elijah, and Zichri were the sons of Jeroham. **28** These were family heads over their kindred, chiefs who dwelt in Jerusalem.

29 [n]In Gibeon dwelt Jeiel, the founder of Gibeon, whose wife's name was Maacah; **30** also his first-born son, Abdon, and Zur, Kish, Baal, Ner, Nadab, **31** Gedor, Ahio, Zecher, and Mikloth. **32** Mikloth became the

d Nm 26, 33; Jos 17, 3.
e Nm 26, 35.
f 1 Chr 8, 13.
g Nm 1, 10; 2, 18; 7, 48; 10, 22.
h Gn 12, 8; 1 Kgs 9, 16.
i Jos 17, 11.
j Gn 46, 17; Nm 26, 44ff.
k 1 Chr 7, 6; Gn 46, 21; Nm 26, 38ff.
l Jgs 3, 15.
m Neh 11, 35.
n 29-32: 1 Chr 9, 35-38.

8, 1–40: A second, variant list of the Benjaminites, with special prominence given to Saul's family (vv 33–40).

father of Shimeah. These, too, dwelt with their relatives in Jerusalem, opposite their fellow tribesmen. **33** *o*Ner became the father of Kish, and Kish became the father of Saul. Saul became the father of Jonathan, Malchishua, Abinadab, and Eshbaal.*p* **34** The son of Jonathan was Meribbaal, and Meribbaal became the father of Micah.*q* **35** The sons of Micah were Pithon, Melech, Tarea, and Ahaz. **36** Ahaz became the father of Jehoaddah, and Jehoaddah became the father of Alemeth, Azmaveth, and Zimri. Zimri became the father of Moza.*r* **37** Moza became the father of Binea, whose son was Raphah, whose son was Eleasah, whose son was Azel.*s* **38** Azel had six sons, whose names were Azrikam, his first-born, Ishmael, Sheariah, Azariah, Obadiah, and Hanan; all these were the sons of Azel. **39** The sons of Eshek, his brother, were Ulam, his first-born, Jeush, the second son, and Eliphelet, the third. **40** The sons of Ulam were combat archers, and many were their sons and grandsons: one hundred and fifty. All these were the descendants of Benjamin.

CHAPTER 9

1 Thus all Israel was inscribed in its family records which are recorded in the book of the kings of Israel.*t*

Now Judah had been carried in captivity to Babylon because of its rebellion. **2** *u**The first to settle again in their cities and dwell there were certain lay Israelites, the priests, the Levites, and the temple slaves.*v*

Jerusalemites. 3 In Jerusalem lived Judahites and Benjaminites; also Ephraimites and Manassehites. **4** Among the Judahites was Uthai, son of Ammihud, son of Omri, son of Imri, son of Bani, one of the descendants of Perez, son of Judah. **5** Among the Shelanites were Asaiah, the first-born, and his sons. **6** Among the Zerahites were Jeuel and six hundred and ninety of their brethren. **7** Among the Benjaminites were Sallu, son of Meshullam, son of Hodaviah, son of Hassenuah; **8** Ibneiah, son of Jeroham; Elah, son of Uzzi, son of Michri; Meshullam, son of Shephatiah, son of Reuel, son of Ibnijah. **9** Their kindred of various families were nine hundred and fifty-six. All those named were heads of their ancestral houses.

10 Among the priests were Jedaiah; Jehoiarib; Jachin; **11** Azariah, son of Hilkiah, son of Meshullam, son of Zadok, son of Meraioth, son of Ahitub, the ruler of the house of God; **12** Adaiah, son of Jeroham, son of Pashhur, son of Malchijah; Maasai, son of Adiel, son of Jahzerah, son of Meshullam, son of Meshillemith, son of Immer. **13** Their brethren, heads

of their ancestral houses, were one thousand seven hundred and sixty, valiant for the work of the service of the house of God.

14 Among the Levites were Shemaiah, son of Hasshub, son of Azrikam, son of Hashabiah, one of the descendants of Merari; **15** Bakbakkar; Heresh; Galal; Mattaniah, son of Mica, son of Zichri, a descendant of Asaph; **16** Obadiah, son of Shemaiah, son of Galal, a descendant of Jeduthun; and Berechiah, son of Asa, son of Elkanah, whose family lived in the villages of the Netophathites.

17 The gatekeepers were Shallum, Akkub, Talmon, Ahiman, and their brethren; Shallum was the chief. **18** Previously they had stood guard at the king's gate on the east side; now they became gatekeepers for the encampments of the Levites. **19** Shallum, son of Kore, son of Ebiasaph, a descendant of Korah, and his brethren of the same ancestral house of the Korahites had as their assigned task the guarding of the threshold of the tent, just as their fathers had guarded the entrance to the encampment of the LORD. **20** Phinehas, son of Eleazar, had been their chief in times past—the LORD be with him!*w* **21** Zechariah, son of Meshelemiah, guarded the gate of the meeting tent.*x* **22** In all, those who were chosen for gatekeepers at the threshold were two hundred and twelve. They were inscribed in the family records of their villages. David and Samuel the seer had established them in their position of trust. **23** Thus they and their sons kept guard over the gates of the house of the LORD, the house which was then a tent. **24** The gatekeepers were stationed at the four sides, to the east, the west, the north, and the south.*y* **25** Their kinsmen who lived in their own villages took turns in assisting them for seven-day periods,*z* **26** while the four chief gatekeepers were on constant duty. These were the Levites who also had charge of the chambers and treasures of the house of God. **27** At night they lodged about the house of God, for it was in their charge and they had the duty of opening it each morning.

28 Some of them had charge of the liturgical equipment, tallying it as it was brought in and taken out. **29** Others were appointed to take care of the utensils and all the sacred vessels, as well as the fine flour, the wine, the oil, the

---

o 33-38: 1 Chr 9, 39-44.
p 1 Chr 10, 2; 1 Sm 9, 1;
  14, 49. 51; 31, 2.
q 2 Sm 4, 4; 9, 6. 10.
  12.
r 1 Chr 9, 42.
s 1 Chr 9, 43.
t 2 Chr 16, 11; 20, 34;
  25, 26; 27, 7; 33, 18;

36, 8.
u 2-22: Neh 11, 3-19.
v Ezr 2, 70; 7, 7; Neh
  11, 3.
w Ex 6, 25; Nm 25, 7.
  11; Jgs 20, 28.
x 1 Chr 26, 2. 14.
y 1 Chr 26, 13.
z 2 Chr 23, 4f.

*
9, 2-34: The inhabitants of Jerusalem after the exile. A similar list, with many variants in the names, is given in Neh 11, 3-24.

frankincense, and the spices. **30** It was the sons of priests, however, who mixed the spiced ointments.ᵃ **31** ᵇMattithiah, one of the Levites, the first-born of Shallum the Koreite, was entrusted with preparing the cakes. **32** Benaiah the Kohathite, one of their brethren, was in charge of setting out the showbread each sabbath.ᶜ

33 These were the chanters and the gatekeepers, family heads over the Levites. They stayed in the chambers when free of duty, for day and night they had to be ready for service. **34** These were the levitical family heads over their kindred, chiefs who dwelt in Jerusalem.

II: The History of David

Genealogy of Saul. 35 ᵈIn Gibeon dwelt Jeiel, the founder of Gibeon, whose wife's name was Maacah. **36** His first-born son was Abdon; then came Zur, Kish, Baal, Ner, Nadab, **37** Gedor, Ahio, Zechariah, and Mikloth. **38** Mikloth became the father of Shimeam. These, too, with their brethren, dwelt opposite their brethren in Jerusalem. **39** Ner became the father of Kish, and Kish became the father of Saul. Saul became the father of Jonathan, Malchishua, Abinadab, and Eshbaal. **40** The son of Jonathan was Meribbaal, and Meribbaal became the father of Micah. **41** The sons of Micah were Pithon, Melech, Tahrea, and Ahaz. **42** Ahaz became the father of Jehoaddah, and Jehoaddah became the father of Alemeth, Azmaveth, and Zimri. Zimri became the father of Moza. **43** Moza became the father of Binea, whose son was Rephaiah, whose son was Eleasah, whose son was Azel. **44** Azel had six sons, whose names were Azrikam, his first-born, Ishmael, Sheariah, Azariah, Obadiah, and Hanan; these were the sons of Azel.

CHAPTER 10

His Death and Burial. 1 ᵉNow the Philistines were at war with Israel; the Israelites fled before the Philistines, and a number of them fell, slain on Mount Gilboa. **2** The Philistines pressed hard after Saul and his sons. When the Philistines had killed Jonathan, Abinadab, and Malchishua, sons of Saul, **3** the whole fury of the battle descended upon Saul. Then the archers found him, and wounded him with their arrows.

4 Saul said to his armor-bearer, "Draw your sword and thrust me through with it, that these uncircumcised may not come and maltreat me." But the armor-bearer, in great fear, refused. So Saul took his own sword and fell on it; **5** and seeing him dead, the armor-bearer also fell on his sword and died. **6** Thus, with Saul and his three sons, his whole house died at one time. **7** When all the Israelites who were in the valley

saw that Saul and his sons had died in the rout, they left their cities and fled; thereupon the Philistines came and occupied them.

8 On the following day, when the Philistines came to strip the slain, they found Saul and his sons where they had fallen on Mount Gilboa. **9** They stripped him, cut off his head, and took his armor; these they sent throughout the land of the Philistines to convey the good news to their idols and their people. **10** His armor they put in the house of their gods, but his skull they impaled on the temple of Dagon.

11 When all the inhabitants of Jabesh-gilead had heard what the Philistines had done to Saul, **12** its warriors rose to a man, recovered the bodies of Saul and his sons, and brought them to Jabesh. They buried their bones under the oak of Jabesh, and fasted seven days.ᶠ

13 *Thus Saul died because of his rebellion against the LORD in disobeying his command, and also because he had sought counsel of a necromancer,ᵍ **14** and had not rather inquired of the LORD. Therefore the LORD slew him, and transferred his kingdom to David, the son of Jesse.ʰ

CHAPTER 11

David Is Made King. 1 ⁱThen all Israel gathered about David in Hebron, and they said: "Surely, we are of the same bone and flesh as you. **2** Even formerly, when Saul was still the king, it was you who led Israel in all its battles. And now the LORD, your God, has said to you, 'You shall shepherd my people Israel and be ruler over them.'"ʲ **3** Then all the elders of Israel came to the king at Hebron, and there David made a covenant with them in the presence of the LORD; and they anointed him king over Israel, in accordance with the word of the LORD as revealed through Samuel.ᵏ

Jerusalem Captured. 4 Then David and all Israel went to Jerusalem, that is, Jebus, where the natives of the land were called Jebusites.ˡ **5** The inhabitants of Jebus said to David, "You shall not enter here." David nevertheless captured the fortress of Sion, which is the City

a Ex 30, 22-33.
b 31f: 1 Chr 23, 29; Lv 2, 1ff; 6, 13ff; 7, 11.
c Ex 25, 30; Lv 24, 5-8.
d 35-44: 1 Chr 8, 29-38.
e 1-12: 1 Sm 31, 1-13.
f 2 Sm 2, 5.
g Dt 18, 10ff; 1 Sm 13, 13f; 15, 3. 11. 26.
h 1 Sm 15, 28; 2 Sm 3, 9f.
i 1-9: 2 Sm 5, 1-10.
j 1 Sm 18, 5. 13-16. 30; 19, 8.
k 1 Sm 16, 1. 13; 2 Sm 2, 4.
l Jos 15, 8; Jgs 1, 21; 19, 10f.

*

10, 13f: The Chronicler's comment on why Saul met his tragic end: he had disobeyed the Lord's command given through the prophet Samuel (1 Sm 15, 3–9), and had sought counsel of a necromancer (1 Sm 28, 6–19), contrary to the Mosaic law against necromancy (Dt 18, 10f).

of David. **6** David said, "Whoever strikes the Jebusites first shall be made the chief commander." Joab, the son of Zeruiah, was the first to go up; and so he became chief.*m* **7** David took up his residence in the fortress, which thenceforth was called the City of David. **8** He rebuilt the city on all sides, from the Millo all the way around, while Joab restored the rest of the city.*n* **9** David became more and more powerful, for the LORD of hosts was with him.

David's Warriors. **10** *o*These were David's chief warriors who, together with all Israel, supported him in his reign in order to make him true king, even as the LORD had commanded concerning Israel. **11** Here is the list of David's warriors:

Ishbaal, the son of Hachamoni, chief of the Three.* He brandished his spear against three hundred, whom he slew in a single encounter. **12** Next to him Eleazar, the son of Dodo the Ahohite, one of the Three warriors.*p* **13** He was with David at Pasdammim, where the Philistines had massed for battle. The plowland was fully planted with barley, but its defenders were retreating before the Philistines.*q* **14** He made a stand on the sown ground, kept it safe, and cut down the Philistines. Thus the LORD brought about a great victory.

15 Three of the Thirty chiefs went down to the rock, to David, who was in the cave of Adullam while the Philistines were encamped in the valley of Rephaim.*r* **16** David was then in the stronghold, and a Philistine garrison was at Bethlehem. **17** David expressed a desire: "Oh, that someone would give me a drink from the cistern that is by the gate at Bethlehem!" **18** Thereupon the Three broke through the encampment of the Philistines, drew water from the cistern by the gate at Bethlehem, and carried it back to David. But David refused to drink it. Instead, he poured it out as a libation to the LORD, **19** saying, "God forbid that I should do such a thing! Could I drink the blood of these men who risked their lives?" For at the risk of their lives they brought it; and so he refused to drink it. Such deeds as these the Three warriors performed.

20 *s*Abishai, the brother of Joab. He was the chief of the Thirty;* he brandished his spear against three hundred, and slew them. Thus he had a reputation like that of the Three.*t* **21** He was twice as famous as any of the Thirty and became their commander, but he did not attain to the Three.

22 Benaiah, the son of Jehoiada, a valiant man of mighty deeds, from Kabzeel. He killed the two sons of Ariel of Moab, and also, on a snowy day, he went down and killed the lion in the cistern. **23** He likewise slew the Egyptian, a huge man five cubits tall. The Egyptian car-

ried a spear that was like a weaver's heddle-bar, but he came against him with a staff, wrested the spear from the Egyptian's hand, and killed him with his own spear. **24** Such deeds as these of Benaiah, the son of Jehoiada, gave him a reputation like that of the Three. **25** He was more famous than any of the Thirty, but he did not attain to the Three. David put him in charge of his bodyguard.*u*

26 Also these warriors: Asahel, the brother of Joab; Elhanan, son of Dodo, from Bethlehem;*v* **27** Shammoth, from En-harod; Helez, from Palti; **28** Ira, son of Ikkesh, from Tekoa; Abiezer, from Anathoth; **29** Sibbecai, from Husha; Ilai, from Ahoh;*w* **30** Maharai, from Netophah; Heled, son of Baanah, from Netophah;*x* **31** Ithai, son of Ribai, from Gibeah of Benjamin; Benaiah, from Pirathon;*y* **32** Hurai, from the valley of Gaash; Abiel, from Betharabah; **33** Azmaveth, from Bahurim; Eliahba, from Shaalbon; **34** Jashen the Gunite; Jonathan, son of Shagee, from Enharod; **35** Ahiam, son of Sachar, from Enharod; Elipheleth, son of **36** Ahasabi, from Bethmaacah; Ahijah, from Gilo; **37** Hezro, from Carmel; Naarai, the son of Ezbai; **38** Joel, brother of Nathan, from Rehob, the Gadite; **39** Zelek the Ammonite; Naharai, from Beeroth, the armor-bearer of Joab, son of Zeruiah; **40** Ira, from Jattir; Gareb, from Jattir; **41** Uriah the Hittite; Zabad, son of Ahlai, **42** and, in addition to the Thirty, Adina, son of Shiza, the Reubenite, chief of the tribe of Reuben; **43** Hanan, from Beth-maacah; Joshaphat the Mithnite; **44** Uzzia, from Ashterath; Shama and Jeiel, sons of Hotham, from Aroer; **45** Jediael, son of Shimri, and Joha, his brother, the Tizite; **46** Eliel the Mahavite; Jeribai and Joshaviah, sons of Elnaam; Ithmah, from Moab; **47** Eliel, Obed, and Jaasiel the Mezobian.

CHAPTER 12

David's Early Followers. **1** The following men came to David in Ziklag while he was still under banishment from Saul, son of Kish; they, too, were among the warriors who helped him in his battles.*z* **2** They were archers who

---

m 2 Sm 2, 13ff; 8, 16.
n 1 Kgs 9, 15. 24; 11, 27;
 2 Chr 32, 5.
o 10-41: 2 Sm 23, 8-39.
p 1 Chr 27, 4.
q 1 Sm 17, 1.
r 1 Chr 14, 9; 2 Sm 5, 18.
 22.
s 20f: 2 Sm 23, 18f.

t 1 Chr 18, 12; 1 Sm 26,
 6ff; 2 Sm 16, 9; 18, 2;
 21, 17.
u 2 Sm 8, 18; 20, 23.
v 1 Chr 2, 16; 27, 7.
w 1 Chr 27, 11.
x 1 Chr 27, 13.
y 1 Chr 27, 14.
z 1 Sm 27, 1-7.

*

11, 11f: The Three: the Chronicler names only two of them: Ishbaal and Eleazar. According to 2 Sm 23, 8–12, the Three were Ishbaal, Eleazar, and Shammah.

11, 20: The Thirty: listed by name in vv 26–47. The list given in 2 Sm 23, 8–39 often differs in names and spellings; for the numbers, see the note there.

could use either the right or the left hand, both in slinging stones and in shooting arrows with the bow. They were some of Saul's kinsmen, from Benjamin. **3** Ahiezer was their chief, along with Joash, both sons of Shemaah of Gibeah; also Jeziel and Pelet, sons of Azmaveth; Beracah; Jehu, from Anathoth;*a* **4** Ishmaiah the Gibeonite, a warrior on the level of the Thirty, and in addition to their number: **5** Jeremiah; Jahaziel; Johanan; Jozabad, from Gederah; **6** Eluzai; Jerimoth; Bealiah; Shemariah; Shephatiah the Haruphite; **7** Elkanah, Isshiah, Azarel, Joezer, and Ishbaal, who were Korahites; **8** Joelah, finally, and Zebadiah, sons of Jeroham, from Gedor.

9 Some of the Gadites also went over to David when he was at the stronghold in the wilderness. They were valiant warriors, experienced soldiers equipped with shield and spear, who bore themselves like lions, and were as swift as the gazelles on the mountains.*b* **10** Ezer was their chief, Obadiah was second, Eliab third, **11** Mishmannah fourth, Jeremiah fifth, **12** Attai sixth, Eliel seventh, **13** Johanan eighth, Elzabad ninth, **14** Jeremiah tenth, and Machbannai eleventh. **15** These Gadites were army commanders, the lesser placed over hundreds and the greater over thousands. **16** It was they who crossed over the Jordan when it was overflowing both its banks in the first month, and dispersed all who were in the valleys to the east and to the west.

17 Some Benjaminites and Judahites also came to David at the stronghold. **18** David went out to meet them and addressed them in these words: "If you come peacefully, to help me, I am of a mind to have you join me. But if you have come to betray me to my enemies though my hands have done no wrong, may the God of our fathers see and punish you."

19 Then spirit enveloped Amasai, the chief of the Thirty, who spoke:

"We are yours, O David,
    we are with you, O son of Jesse.
Peace, peace to you,
    and peace to him who helps you;
    your God it is who helps you."

So David received them and placed them among the leaders of his troops.

20 Men from Manasseh also deserted to David when he came with the Philistines to battle against Saul. However, he did not help the Philistines, for their lords took counsel and sent him home, saying, "At the cost of our heads he will desert to his master Saul." **21** As he was returning to Ziklag, therefore, these deserted to him from Manasseh: Adnah, Jozabad, Jediael, Michael, Jozabad, Elihu, and Zillethai, chiefs of thousands of Manasseh. **22** They helped David by taking charge of his troops, for they were

all warriors and became commanders of his army. **23** And from day to day men kept coming to David's help until there was a vast encampment, like an encampment of angels.

The Assembly at Hebron. **24** This is the muster of the detachments of armed troops that came to David at Hebron to transfer to him Saul's kingdom, as the LORD had ordained. **25** *Judahites bearing shields and spears: six thousand eight hundred armed troops. **26** Of the Simeonites, warriors fit for battle: seven thousand one hundred. **27** Of the Levites: four thousand six hundred, **28** along with Jehoiada, leader of the line of Aaron, with another three thousand seven hundred, **29** and Zadok, a young warrior, with twenty-two princes of his father's house. **30** Of the Benjaminites, the brethren of Saul: three thousand—until this time, most of them had held their allegiance to the house of Saul. **31** Of the Ephraimites: twenty thousand eight hundred warriors, men renowned in their ancestral houses. **32** Of the half-tribe of Manasseh: eighteen thousand, designated by name to come and make David king. **33** Of the Issacharites, their chiefs who were endowed with an understanding of the times and who knew what Israel had to do: two hundred chiefs, together with all their brethren under their command. **34** From Zebulun, men fit for military service, set in battle array with every kind of weapon for war: fifty thousand men rallying with a single purpose. **35** From Naphtali: one thousand captains, and with them, armed with shield and lance, thirty-seven thousand men. **36** Of the Danites, set in battle array: twenty-eight thousand six hundred. **37** From Asher, fit for military service and set in battle array: forty thousand. **38** From the other side of the Jordan, of the Reubenites, Gadites, and the half-tribe of Manasseh, men equipped with every kind of weapon of war: one hundred and twenty thousand.

39 All these soldiers, drawn up in battle order, came to Hebron with the resolute intention of making David king over all Israel. The rest of Israel was likewise of one mind to make David king. **40** They remained with David for three days, feasting and drinking, for their brethren had prepared for them. **41** Moreover, their neighbors from as far as Issachar, Zebulun, and Naphtali came bringing food on asses,

a 1 Chr 27, 12.   b Dt 33, 20.

12, 25–38: The Chronicler fills out the pageantry of joyous occasions in keeping with his much later appreciation of the significance of the event in the history of God's people: the numbers in attendance at David's crowning in Hebron (cf 2 Sm 5, 1ff) are recounted in the same spirit of enthusiasm which in v 23 compares David's band of desert freebooters to a numerous encampment of angels.

camels, mules, and oxen—provisions in great quantity of meal, pressed figs, raisins, wine, oil, oxen, and sheep. For there was rejoicing in Israel.

CHAPTER 13

Transfer of the Ark. 1 cAfter David had taken counsel with his commanders of thousands and of hundreds, that is to say, with every one of his leaders, 2 he said to the whole assembly of Israel: "If it seems good to you, and is so decreed by the LORD our God, let us summon the rest of our brethren from all the districts of Israel, and also the priests and the Levites from their cities with pasture lands, that they may join us;d 3 and let us bring the ark of our God here among us, for in the days of Saul we did not visit it." 4 And the whole assembly agreed to do this, for the idea was pleasing to all the people.

5 Then David assembled all Israel, from Shihor of Egypt* to Labo of Hamath, to bring the ark of God from Kiriath-jearim.e 6 David and all Israel went up to Baalah, that is, to Kiriath-jearim, of Judah, to bring back the ark of God, which was known by the name "LORD enthroned upon the cherubim."f 7 They transported the ark of God on a new cart from the house of Abinadab; Uzzah and Ahio were guiding the cart, 8 while David and all Israel danced before God with great enthusiasm, amid songs and music on lyres, harps, tambourines, cymbals, and trumpets.

9 As they reached the threshing floor of Chidon,* Uzzah stretched out his hand to steady the ark, for the oxen were upsetting it. 10 Then the LORD became angry with Uzzah and struck him; he died there in God's presence, because he had laid his hand on the ark. 11 David was disturbed because the LORD's anger had broken out against Uzzah. Therefore that place has been called Perez-uzza* even to this day.

12 David was now afraid of God, and he said, "How can I bring the ark of God with me?" 13 Therefore he did not take the ark back with him to the City of David, but he took it instead to the house of Obed-edom the Gittite. 14 The ark of God remained in the house of Obed-edom with his family for three months, and the LORD blessed Obed-edom's household and all that he possessed.g

CHAPTER 14

David in Jerusalem. 1 hHiram, king of Tyre, sent envoys to David along with masons and carpenters, and cedar wood to build him a house.i 2 David now understood that the LORD had truly confirmed him as king over Israel, for his kingdom was greatly exalted for the sake of his people Israel. 3 jDavid took other wives in Jerusalem and became the father of more sons and daughters. 4 These are the names of those who were born to him in Jerusalem: Shammua, Shobab, Nathan, Solomon, 5 Ibhar, Elishua, Elpelet, 6 Nogah, Nepheg, Japhia, 7 Elishama, Beeliada, and Eliphelet.

The Philistine Wars. 8 When the Philistines had heard that David was anointed king over all Israel, they went up in unison to seek him out. But when David heard of this, he marched out against them. 9 Meanwhile the Philistines had come and raided the valley of Rephaim.k 10 David inquired of God, "Shall I advance against the Philistines, and will you deliver them into my power?" The LORD answered him, "Advance, for I will deliver them into your power." 11 They advanced, therefore, to Baal-perazim, and David defeated them there. Then David said, "God has used me to break through my enemies just as water breaks through a dam." Therefore that place was called Baal-perazim. 12 The Philistines had left their gods there, and David ordered them to be burnt.l

13 Once again the Philistines raided the valley, 14 and again David inquired of God. But God answered him: "Do not try to pursue them, but go around them and come upon them from the direction of the mastic trees. 15 When you hear the sound of marching in the tops of the mastic trees, then go forth to battle, for God has already gone before you to strike the army of the Philistines." 16 David did as God commanded him, and they routed the Philistine army from Gibeon to Gezer.

17 Thus David's fame was spread abroad through every land, and the LORD made all the nations fear him.

CHAPTER 15

The Ark Brought to Jerusalem. 1 David built houses for himself in the City of David and prepared a place for the ark of God, pitching a tent for it there. 2 At that time he said, "No one may carry the ark of God except the Levites, for the LORD chose them to carry the ark of the

c 1-14: 2 Sm 6, 1-11.
d Nm 35, 1ff; Jos 14, 4; 21, 2ff.
e 1 Chr 15, 3; Jos 13, 3. 5; 1 Sm 6, 21; 7, 1f; 2 Sm 6, 1-11.
f Jos 15, 9; 18, 14; 1 Sm 4, 4; 7, 1.
g 1 Chr 26, 4f.
h 1-16: 2 Sm 5, 11-25.
i 1 Kgs 5, 1; 2 Chr 2, 3.
j 3-7: 1 Chr 3, 5-8; 2 Sm 5, 13-16.
k 1 Chr 11, 15.
l Dt 7, 5. 25.
m Nm 1, 50; 7, 9; Dt 10, 8; 31, 25; 1 Sm 6, 15; Jos 3, 8.

*

13, 5: Shihor of Egypt: the eastern branch of the Nile delta. Labo of Hamath: in southern Syria.

13, 9: Chidon: in 2 Sm 6, 6, Nodan.

13, 11: Perez-uzza: A Hebrew term meaning "the breaking out against Uzza."

LORD and to minister to him forever."[m] **3** Then David assembled all Israel in Jerusalem to bring the ark of the LORD to the place which he had prepared for it.[n] **4** David also called together the sons of Aaron and the Levites: **5** of the sons of Kohath, Uriel, their chief, and one hundred and twenty of his brethren; **6** of the sons of Merari, Asaiah, their chief, and two hundred and twenty of his brethren; **7** of the sons of Gershon, Joel, their chief, and one hundred and thirty of his brethren; **8** of the sons of Elizaphan, Shemaiah, their chief, and two hundred of his brethren; **9** of the sons of Hebron, Eliel, their chief, and eighty of his brethren; **10** of the sons of Uzziel, Amminadab, their chief, and one hundred and twelve of his brethren.

11 David summoned the priests Zadok and Abiathar, and the Levites Uriel, Asaiah, Joel, Shemaiah, Eliel, and Amminadab,[o] **12** and said to them: "You, the heads of the levitical families, must sanctify yourselves along with your brethren and bring the ark of the LORD, the God of Israel, to the place which I have prepared for it.[p] **13** Because you were not with us the first time, the wrath of the LORD our God burst upon us, for we did not seek him aright."[q] **14** Accordingly, the priests and the Levites sanctified themselves to bring up the ark of the LORD, the God of Israel. **15** The Levites bore the ark of God on their shoulders with poles, as Moses had ordained according to the word of the LORD[r]. **16** David commanded the chiefs of the Levites to appoint their brethren as chanters, to play on musical instruments, harps, lyres, and cymbals, to make a loud sound of rejoicing.[s] **17** Therefore the Levites appointed Heman, son of Joel, and, among his brethren, Asaph, son of Berechiah; and among the sons of Merari, their brethren, Ethan, son of Kushaiah;[t] **18** and, together with these, their brethren of the second rank: the gatekeepers Zechariah, Uzziel, Shemiramoth, Jehiel, Unni, Eliab, Benaiah, Maaseiah, Mattithiah, Eliphelehu, Mikneiah, Obededom, and Jeiel. **19** The chanters, Heman, Asaph, and Ethan, sounded brass cymbals. **20** Zechariah, Uzziel, Shemiramoth, Jehiel, Unni, Eliab, Maaseiah, and Benaiah played on harps set to "Alamoth."* **21** But Mattithiah, Eliphelehu, Mikneiah, Obed-edom, and Jeiel led the chant on lyres set to "the eighth." **22** Chenaniah was the chief of the Levites in the chanting; he directed the chanting, for he was skillful.[u] **23** Berechiah and Elkanah were gatekeepers before the ark. **24** The priests, Shebaniah, Joshaphat, Nethanel, Amasai, Zechariah, Benaiah, and Eliezer, sounded the trumpets before the ark of God. Obed-edom and Jeiel were also gatekeepers before the ark.[v]

25 [w]Thus David, the elders of Israel, and the commanders of thousands went to bring up the ark of the covenant of the LORD with joy from the house of Obed-edom. **26** While the Levites, with God's help, were bearing the ark of the covenant of the LORD, seven bulls and seven rams were sacrificed.[x] **27** David was clothed in a robe of fine linen, as were all the Levites who carried the ark, the singers, and Chenaniah, the leader of the chant; David was also wearing a linen ephod.[y] **28** Thus all Israel brought back the ark of the covenant of the LORD with joyful shouting, and to the sound of horns, trumpets, and cymbals, and the music of harps and lyres. **29** But as the ark of the covenant of the LORD was entering the City of David, Michal, daughter of Saul, looked down from her window, and when she saw King David leaping and dancing, she despised him in her heart.[z]

CHAPTER 16

1 [a]They brought in the ark of God and set it within the tent which David had pitched for it. Then they offered up holocausts and peace offerings to God.[b] **2** When David had finished offering up the holocausts and peace offerings, he blessed the people in the name of the LORD, **3** and distributed to every Israelite, to every man and to every woman, a loaf of bread, a piece of meat, and a raisin cake.

The Ministering Levites. **4** He now appointed certain Levites to minister before the ark of the LORD, to celebrate, thank, and praise the LORD, the God of Israel.[c] **5** Asaph was their chief, and second to him were Zechariah, Uzziel, Shemira-moth, Jehiel, Mattithiah, Eliab, Benaiah, Obed-edom, and Jeiel. These were to play on harps and lyres, while Asaph was to sound the cymbals, **6** and the priests Benaiah and Jahaziel were to be the regular trumpeters before the ark of the covenant of God.

7 Then, on that same day, David appointed Asaph and his brethren to sing for the first time these praises of the LORD:

8 *Give thanks to the LORD, invoke his
name;[d]

---

n 1 Chr 13, 5; 2 Sm 6, 15. 17.
o 1 Chr 16, 39; 2 Sm 8, 17; 15, 29. 35.
p 2 Chr 29, 5. 15. 34; 30, 3. 15. 24.
q 1 Chr 13, 3.
r Ex 25, 13ff; Nm 1, 50; 7, 9; 2 Chr 35, 3.
s 1 Chr 13, 8; 16, 5; 2 Chr 5, 12; 29, 25; Neh 12, 27.
t 1 Chr 6, 31-47; 25, 1-8.
u 1 Chr 26, 29.
v Nm 10, 8; Jos 6, 4ff.
w 25-29: 2 Sm 6, 12-16.
x 2 Sm 6, 17; 2 Chr 29, 21.
y 1 Sm 2, 18; 2 Sm 6, 14.
z 2 Sm 6, 20ff.
a 1-3: 2 Sm 6, 17ff.
b 1 Chr 15, 1.
c Sir 47, 9.
d 8-22: Ps 105, 1-15.

* ---

15, 20: Alamoth: a musical term (literally, "young women") of uncertain meaning, occurring also in Ps 46, 1, where it is rendered as virgins. Perhaps it may mean something like "soprano," whereas the term "eighth" (Hebrew sheminith, v 21) may then mean "bass"; cf Pss 6, 1; 12, 1.

16, 8–36: A hymn composed of parts, with textual variants,

make known among the nations his deeds.
9 Sing to him, sing his praise,
   proclaim all his wondrous deeds.
10 Glory in his holy name;
   rejoice, O hearts that seek the LORD!
11 Look to the LORD in his strength;
   seek to serve him constantly.
12 Recall the wondrous deeds that he has
     wrought,
   his portents, and the judgments he has
     uttered,
13 You descendants of Israel, his servants,
   sons of Jacob, his chosen ones!

14 He, the LORD, is our God;
   throughout the earth his judgments
     prevail.
15 He remembers forever his covenant
   which he made binding for a thousand
     generations—
16 Which he entered into with Abraham
   and by his oath to Isaac;
17 Which he established for Jacob by statute,
   for Israel as an everlasting covenant,
18 Saying, "To you will I give the land of
     Canaan
   as your alloted inheritance."

19 When they were few in number,
   a handful, and strangers there,
20 Wandering from nation to nation,
   from one kingdom to another people,
21 He let no one oppress them,
   and for their sake he rebuked kings:
22 "Touch not my anointed,
   and to my prophets do no harm."

23 *e*Sing to the LORD, all the earth,
   announce his salvation, day after day.
24 Tell his glory among the nations;
   among all peoples, his wondrous deeds.
25 For great is the LORD and highly to be
     praised;
   and awesome is he, beyond all gods.
26 For all the gods of the nations are things of
     nought,
   but the LORD made the heavens.
27 Splendor and majesty go before him;
   praise and joy are in his holy place.

28 Give to the LORD, you families of nations,
   give to the LORD glory and praise;
29 Give to the LORD the glory due his name!
   Bring gifts, and enter his presence;
   worship the LORD in holy attire.
30 Tremble before him, all the earth;
   he has made the world firm, not to be
     moved.

31 Let the heavens be glad and the earth
     rejoice;
   let them say among the nations: The LORD
     is king.
32 Let the sea and what fills it resound;

let the plains rejoice and all that is in
   them!
33 Then shall all the trees of the forest exult
   before the LORD, for he comes:
   he comes to rule the earth.

34 *f*Give thanks to the LORD, for he is good,
   for his kindness endures forever;
35 And say, "Save us, O God, our savior,
   gather us and deliver us from the nations,
   That we may give thanks to your holy name
   and glory in praising you."
36 Blessed be the LORD, the God of Israel,
   through all eternity!
   Let all the people say, Amen! Alleluia.

37 Then David left Asaph and his brethren there before the ark of the covenant of the LORD to minister before the ark regularly according to the daily ritual; 38 he also left there Obed-edom and sixty-eight of his brethren, including Obed-edom, son of Jeduthun, and Hosah, to be gatekeepers. *g*

39 But the priest Zadok and his priestly brethren he left before the Dwelling of the LORD on the high place at Gibeon, *h* 40 to offer holocausts to the LORD on the altar of holocausts regularly, morning and evening, and to do all that is written in the law of the LORD which he has decreed for Israel. *i* 41 With them were Heman and Jeduthun and the others who were chosen and designated by name to give thanks to the LORD, "because his kindness endures forever," *j* 42 with trumpets and cymbals for accompaniment, and instruments for the sacred chant. The sons of Jeduthun kept the gate. *k*

43 Then all the people departed, each to his own home, and David returned to bless his household. *l*

CHAPTER 17

The Oracle of Nathan. 1 *m*After David had taken up residence in his house, he said to Nathan the prophet, "See, I am living in a house of cedar, but the ark of the covenant of the LORD dwells under tentcloth." *n* 2 Nathan replied to David, "Do, therefore, whatever you desire, for God is with you."

3 But that same night the word of God came to Nathan: 4 "Go and tell my servant David, Thus says the LORD: It is not you who are to build a house for me to dwell in. *o* 5 For I have

---

e 23-33: Ps 96, 1-13.
f 34ff: Ps 106, 1. 47f.
g 1 Chr 15, 24.
h 1 Kgs 3, 4.
i Ex 29, 38-42; Lv 6, 9;
  Nm 28, 3. 6; 2 Chr 13,
  11.
j 2 Chr 5, 12; 7, 3. 6; 20,

21; Ezr 3, 11.
k 2 Chr 29, 27.
l 2 Sm 6, 19f.
m 1-27: 2 Sm 7, 1-29.
n 1 Chr 15, 1; 2 Sm 5,
  11.
o 1 Chr 28, 3; 1 Kgs 8,
  19.

*

from several Psalms; vv 8–22 = Ps 105, 1–15; vv 23–33 = Ps 96, 1–13; vv 34–36 = Ps 106, 1. 47f.

never dwelt in a house, from the time when I led Israel onward, even to this day, but I have been lodging in tent or pavilion **6** as long as I have wandered about with all of Israel. Did I ever say a word to any of the judges of Israel whom I commanded to guide my people, such as, 'Why have you not built me a house of cedar?' **7** Therefore, tell my servant David, Thus says the Lord of hosts: I took you from the pasture, from following the sheep, that you might become ruler over my people Israel.*p* **8** I was with you wherever you went, and I cut down all your enemies before you. I will make your name great like that of the greatest on the earth. **9** I will assign a place for my people Israel and I will plant them in it to dwell there henceforth undisturbed; nor shall wicked men ever again oppress them, as they did at first, **10** and during all the time when I appointed judges over my people Israel. And I will subdue all your enemies. Moreover, I declare to you that I, the Lord, will build you a house; **11** so that when your days have been completed and you must join your fathers, I will raise up your offspring after you who will be one of your own sons, and I will establish his kingdom.*q* **12** He it is who shall build me a house, and I will establish his throne forever.*r* **13** I will be a father to him, and he shall be a son to me, and I will not withdraw my favor from him as I withdrew it from him who preceded you;*s* **14** but I will maintain him in my house and in my kingdom forever, and his throne shall be firmly established forever.''

15 All these words and this whole vision Nathan related exactly to David.

David's Thanksgiving. **16** Then David came in and sat in the Lord's presence, saying: ''Who am I, O Lord God, and what is my family, that you should have brought me as far as I have come? **17** And yet, even this you now consider too little, O God! For you have made a promise regarding your servant's family reaching into the distant future, and you have looked on me as henceforth the most notable of men, O Lord God.*t* **18** What more can David say to you? You know your servant. **19** O Lord, for your servant's sake and in keeping with your purpose, you have done this great thing. **20** O Lord, there is no one like you and there is no God but you, just as we have always understood.*u* **21** ''Is there, like your people Israel, whom you redeemed from Egypt, another nation on earth whom a god went to redeem as his people? You won for yourself a name for great and awesome deeds by driving out the nations before your people.*v* **22** You made your people Israel your own forever, and you, O Lord, became their God. **23** Therefore, O Lord, may

the promise that you have uttered concerning your servant and his house remain firm forever. Bring about what you have promised, **24** that your renown as Lord of hosts, God of Israel, may be great and abide forever, while the house of David, your servant, is established in your presence.

25 ''Because you, O my God, have revealed to your servant that you will build him a house, your servant has made bold to pray before you.*w* **26** Since you, O Lord, are truly God and have promised this good thing to your servant, **27** and since you have deigned to bless the house of your servant, so that it will remain forever—since it is you, O Lord, who blessed it, it is blessed forever.''*x*

CHAPTER 18

David's Victories. **1** *y*After this, David defeated the Philistines and subdued them; and he took Gath and its towns away from the control of the Philistines. **2** He also defeated Moab, and the Moabites became his subjects, paying tribute.

3 David then defeated Hadadezer, king of Zobah toward Hamath, when the latter was on his way to set up his victory stele at the river Euphrates. **4** David took from him twenty thousand foot soldiers, one thousand chariots, and seven thousand horsemen. Of the chariot horses, David hamstrung all but one hundred.*z* **5** The Arameans of Damascus came to the aid of Hadadezer, king of Zobah, but David also slew twenty-two thousand of their men. **6** Then David set up garrisons in the Damascus region of Aram, and the Arameans became his subjects, paying tribute. Thus the Lord made David victorious in all his campaigns.

7 David took the golden shields that were carried by Hadadezer's attendants and brought them to Jerusalem. **8** He likewise took away from Tibhath and Cun, cities of Hadadezer, large quantities of bronze, which Solomon later used to make the bronze sea and the pillars and the vessels of bronze.*a* **9** When Tou, king of Hamath, heard that David had defeated the entire army of Hadadezer, king of Zobah, **10** he sent his son Hadoram to wish King David well and to congratulate him on having waged a victorious war against Hadadezer; for Hadadezer had been at war with Tou. He also sent David gold, silver and bronze utensils of every sort.*b* **11** These also King Da-

p 1 Sm 16, 11.
q 2 Sm 7, 12f.
r 1 Chr 22, 10; 28, 6. 10.
s 2 Sm 7, 14.
t 2 Sm 7, 19.
u Sir 36, 4.
v Dt 4, 7; 2 Sm 7, 23.
w 2 Sm 7, 27.

x Nm 22, 6.
y 1-13: 2 Sm 8, 1-14.
z 2 Sm 8, 4; Jos 11, 6.
9.
a 2 Sm 8, 8; 1 Kgs 7, 15. 23. 27.
b 2 Sm 8, 10.

vid consecrated to the LORD along with all the silver and gold that he had taken from the nations: from Edom, Moab, the Ammonites, the Philistines, and Amalek.

12 Abishai, the son of Zeruiah, also slew eighteen thousand Edomites in the Valley of Salt.*c* **13** He set up garrisons in Edom, and all the Edomites became David's subjects. Thus the LORD made David victorious in all his campaigns.

David's Officials. **14** *d*David reigned over all Israel and dispensed justice and right to all his people. **15** Joab, son of Zeruiah, was in command of the army; Jehoshaphat, son of Ahilud, was herald;*e* **16** Zadok, son of Ahitub, and Ahimelech, son of Abiathar, were priests;* Shavsha was scribe;*f* **17** Benaiah, son of Jehoiada, was in command of the Cherethites and the Pelethites; and David's sons were the chief assistants to the king.**g*

CHAPTER 19

Campaigns against Ammon.
1 *h*Afterward Nahash, king of the Ammonites, died and his son succeeded him as king. **2** David said, "I will show kindness to Hanun, the son of Nahash, for his father treated me with kindness." Therefore he sent envoys to him to comfort him over the death of his father. But when David's servants had entered the land of the Ammonites to comfort Hanun, **3** the Ammonite princes said to Hanun, "Do you think David is doing this—sending you these consolers—to honor your father? Have not his servants rather come to you to explore the land, spying it out for its overthrow?" **4** Thereupon Hanun seized David's servants and had them shaved and their garments cut off half-way at the hips. Then he sent them away. **5** When David was informed of what had happened to his men, he sent messengers to meet them, for the men had been greatly disgraced. "Remain at Jericho," the king told them, "until your beards have grown again; and then you may come back here."

6 When the Ammonites realized that they had put themselves in bad odor with David, Hanun and the Ammonites sent a thousand talents of silver to hire chariots and horsemen from Aram Naharaim, from Aram-maacah, and from Zobah. **7** They hired thirty-two thousand chariots along with the king of Maacah and his army, who came and encamped before Medeba. The Ammonites also assembled from their cities and came out for war. **8** When David heard of this, he sent Joab and his whole army of warriors against them. **9** The Ammonites marched out and lined up for battle at the gate of the city, while the kings who had

come to their help remained apart in the open field. **10** When Joab saw that there was a battle line both in front of and behind him, he chose some of the best fighters among the Israelites and set them in array against the Arameans;*i* **11** the rest of the army, which he placed under the command of his brother Abishai, then lined up to oppose the Ammonites.*j* **12** And he said: "If the Arameans prove too strong for me, you must come to my help; and if the Ammonites prove too strong for you, I will save you. **13** Hold steadfast and let us show ourselves courageous for the sake of our people and the cities of our God; then may the LORD do what seems best to him." **14** Joab therefore advanced with his men to engage the Arameans in battle; but they fled before him. **15** And when the Ammonites saw that the Arameans had fled, they also took to flight before his brother Abishai, and reentered the city. Joab then returned to Jerusalem.

16 Seeing themselves vanquished by Israel, the Arameans sent messengers to bring out the Arameans from the other side of the River, with Shophach, the general of Hadadezer's army, at their head. **17** When this was reported to David, he gathered all Israel together, crossed the Jordan, and met them. With the army of David drawn up to fight the Arameans, they gave battle. **18** But the Arameans fled before Israel, and David slew seven thousand of their chariot fighters and forty thousand of their foot soldiers; he also killed Shophach, the general of the army. **19** When the vassals of Hadadezer saw themselves vanquished by Israel, they made peace with David and became his subjects. After this, the Arameans refused to come to the aid of the Ammonites.

---

c 2 Sm 8, 13; 2 Kgs 14, 7.
d 14-17: 2 Sm 8, 15-18.
e 1 Chr 11, 6; 2 Sm 8, 16; 1 Kgs 4, 3.
f 1 Chr 24, 3. 6. 31; 2 Sm 8, 17.
g 1 Chr 11, 22; 2 Sm 8, 18; 1 Kgs 1, 38. 44.
h 1-19: 2 Sm 10, 1-19.
i 1 Chr 20, 23; 1 Kgs 2, 28. 34.
j 1 Chr 23, 18f.

18, 16: Zadok . . . and Ahimelech, son of Abiathar, were priests: as in the Chronicler's source, 2 Sm 8, 17. But according to 2 Sm 15, 24. 29. 35; 17, 15; 19, 11; 20, 25, and even 1 Chr 15, 11, it was Abiathar who shared the priestly office with Zadok, and he remained in this office even during the early years of Solomon's reign (1 Kgs 2, 26; 4, 4). Moreover, according to 1 Sm 22, 20; 23, 6; 30, 7, Ahimelech was the father, not the son, of Abiathar. If the text Ahimelech, son of Abiathar, is not due to a scribal change, one must assume that Abiathar had a son who was named after his grandfather and who shared the priestly office with his father during the last years of David's reign.

18, 17: David's sons were the chief assistants to the king: in the parallel passage, 2 Sm 8, 18, which was the Chronicler's source, David's sons were priests. The change is characteristic of the Chronicler, for whom only Aaron's descendants could be priests.

CHAPTER 20

1 At the beginning of the following year, the time when kings go to war, Joab led the army out in force, laid waste the land of the Ammonites, and went on to besiege Rabbah, while David himself remained in Jerusalem. When Joab had attacked Rabbah and destroyed it, 2 *k*David took the crown of Milcom from the idol's head. It was found to weigh a talent of gold; and it contained precious stones, which David wore on his own head. He also brought out a great amount of booty from the city. 3 He deported the people of the city and set them to work with saws, iron picks, and axes. Thus David dealt with all the cities of the Ammonites. Then he and his whole army returned to Jerusalem.

Victories over the Philistines.

4 *l*Afterward there was another battle with the Philistines, at Gezer. At that time, Sibbecai the Hushathite slew Sippai, one of the descendants of the Raphaim, and the Philistines were subdued.*m* 5 Once again there was war with the Philistines, and Elhanan, the son of Jair, slew Lahmi, the brother of Goliath* of Gath, whose spear shaft was like a weaver's heddle-bar.*n*

6 In still another battle, at Gath, they encountered a giant, also a descendant of the Raphaim, who had six fingers to each hand and six toes to each foot; twenty-four in all. 7 He defied Israel, and Jonathan, the son of Shimea, David's brother, slew him. 8 These were the descendants of the Raphaim of Gath who died at the hands of David and his servants.

CHAPTER 21

David's Census; the Plague.

1 *o*A satan* rose up against Israel, and he enticed David into taking a census of Israel.*p* 2 David therefore said to Joab and to the other generals of the army, "Go, find out the number of the Israelites from Beer-sheba to Dan, and report back to me that I may know their number." 3 But Joab replied: "May the LORD increase his people a hundredfold! My lord king, are not all of them my lord's subjects? Why does my lord seek to do this thing? Why will he bring guilt upon Israel?" 4 However, the king's command prevailed over Joab, who departed and traversed all of Israel, and then returned to Jerusalem. 5 Joab reported the result of the census to David: of men capable of wielding a sword, there were in all Israel one million one hundred thousand, and in Judah four hundred and seventy thousand. 6 Levi and Benjamin, however, he did not include in the census, for the king's command was repugnant to Joab.*q* 7 This command displeased God, who began to punish Israel. 8 Then David said to God, "I have sinned greatly in doing this thing. Take away your

servant's guilt, for I have acted very foolishly."

9 Then the LORD spoke to Gad, David's seer, in these words:*r* 10 "Go, tell David: Thus says the LORD: I offer you three alternatives; choose one of them, and I will inflict it on you." 11 Accordingly, Gad went to David and said to him: "Thus says the LORD: Decide now— 12 will it be three years of famine; or three months of fleeing your enemies, with the sword of your foes ever at your back; or three days of the LORD's own sword, a pestilence in the land, with the LORD's destroying angel in every part of Israel? Therefore choose: What answer am I to give him who sent me?" 13 Then David said to Gad: "I am in dire straits. But I prefer to fall into the hand of the LORD, whose mercy is very great, than into the hands of men."

14 Therefore the LORD sent pestilence upon Israel, and seventy thousand men of Israel died. 15 God also sent an angel to destroy Jerusalem; but as he was on the point of destroying it, the LORD saw and decided against the calamity, and said to the destroying angel, "Enough now! Stay your hand!"*s*

Ornan's Threshing Floor.

The angel of the LORD was then standing by the threshing floor of Ornan the Jebusite. 16 When David raised his eyes, he saw the angel of the LORD standing between earth and heaven, with a naked sword in his hand stretched out against Jerusalem. David and the elders, clothed in sackcloth, prostrated themselves face to the ground, 17 and David prayed to God: "Was it not I who ordered the census of the people? I am the one who sinned, I did this wicked thing. But these sheep, what have they done? O LORD, my God, strike me and my father's family, but do not afflict your people with this plague!"

18 Then the angel of the LORD commanded Gad to tell David to go up and erect an altar to the LORD on the threshing floor of Ornan the

---

k 2f: 2 Sm 12, 30f.
l 4-8: 2 Sm 21, 18-22.
m 1 Chr 11, 29; 27, 11.
n 1 Chr 11, 26; 1 Sm 17, 4. 23.
o 1-7: 2 Sm 24, 1-25.
p Zec 3, 1f.

q 1 Chr 27, 24; Nm 1, 49.
r 1 Chr 29, 29; 1 Sm 9, 9;
2 Chr 29, 25.
s Gn 6, 6; Ex 32, 14;
2 Sm 24, 16; Jon 3, 10.
t 2 Chr 3, 1.

*

20, 5: Elhanan . . . slew Lahmi, the brother of Goliath: the Chronicler thus solves the difficulty of the apparent contradiction between 1 Sm 17, 49ff (David killed Goliath) and 2 Sm 21, 19 (Elhanan killed Goliath).

21, 1: A satan: in the parallel passage of 2 Sm 24, 1, the Lord's anger. The change in the term reflects the changed theological outlook of postexilic Israel, when evil could no longer be attributed directly to God. At an earlier period the Hebrew word satan ("adversary," or, especially in a court of law, "accuser"), when not used of men, designated an angel who accused men before God (Jb 1, 6–12; 2, 1–7; Zec 3, 1f). Here, as in later Judaism (Wis 2, 24) and in the New Testament, satan, or the "devil" (from the Greek translation of the word), designates an evil spirit who tempts men to wrongdoing.

Jebusite.[t] **19** David went up at Gad's command, given in the name of the LORD. **20** While Ornan was threshing wheat, he turned around and saw the king, and his four sons who were with him, without recognizing them. **21** But as David came on toward him, he looked up and saw that it was David. Then he left the threshing floor and bowed down before David, his face to the ground. **22** David said to Ornan: "Sell me the ground of this threshing floor, that I may build on it an altar to the LORD. Sell it to me at its full price, that the plague may be stayed from the people." **23** But Ornan said to David: "Take it as your own, and let my lord the king do what seems best to him. See, I also give you the oxen for the holocausts, the threshing sledges for the wood, and the wheat for the cereal offering. I give it all to you." **24** But King David replied to Ornan: "No! I will buy it from you properly, at its full price. I will not take what is yours for the LORD, nor offer up holocausts that cost me nothing." **25** So David paid Ornan six hundred shekels of gold* for the place.

Altar of Holocausts.   **26** David then built an altar there to the LORD, and offered up holocausts and peace offerings. When he called upon the LORD, he answered him by sending down fire from heaven upon the altar of holocausts.[u] **27** Then the LORD gave orders to the angel to return his sword to its sheath.

28 Once David saw that the LORD had heard him on the threshing floor of Ornan the Jebusite, he continued to offer sacrifices there. **29** The Dwelling of the LORD, which Moses had built in the desert, and the altar of holocausts were at that time on the high place at Gibeon.[v] **30** But David could not go there to worship God, for he was fearful of the sword of the angel of the LORD. **1** Therefore David said, "This is the house of the LORD God, and this is the altar of holocausts for Israel."*[w]

CHAPTER 22

Material for the Temple.   **2** *David then ordered that all the aliens who lived in the land of Israel be brought together, and he appointed them stonecutters to hew out stone blocks for building the house of God.[x] **3** He also laid up large stores of iron to make nails for the doors of the gates, and clamps, together with so much bronze that it could not be weighed,[y] **4** and cedar trees without number. The Sidonians and Tyrians brought great stores of cedar logs to David,[z] **5** who said: "My son Solomon is young and immature; but the house that is to be built for the LORD must be made so magnificent that it will be renowned and glorious in all countries. Therefore I will make preparations for it."

Thus before his death David laid up materials in abundance.[a]

Charge to Solomon.   **6** Then he called for his son Solomon and commanded him to build a house for the LORD, the God of Israel. **7** [b]David said to Solomon: "My son, it was my purpose to build a house myself for the honor of the LORD, my God. **8** But this word of the LORD came to me: 'You have shed much blood, and you have waged great wars. You may not build a house in my honor, because you have shed too much blood upon the earth in my sight. **9** However, a son is to be born to you. He will be a peaceful man, and I will give him rest from all his enemies on every side. For Solomon shall be his name, and in his time I will bestow peace* and tranquility on Israel.[c] **10** It is he who shall build a house in my honor; he shall be a son to me, and I will be a father to him, and I will establish the throne of his kingship over Israel forever.'[d] **11** Now, my son, the LORD be with you, and may you succeed in building the house of the LORD your God, as he has said you shall. **12** May the LORD give you prudence and discernment when he brings you to rule over Israel, so that you keep the law of the LORD, your God. **13** Only then shall you succeed, if you are careful to observe the precepts and decrees which the LORD gave Moses for Israel. Be brave and steadfast; do not fear or lose heart.[e] **14** See,

u Lv 9, 24; Jgs 6, 21; 1 Kgs 18. 38; 2 Chr 7, 1; 2 Mc 2, 10ff.
v 1 Chr 16, 39; 1 Kgs 8, 4; 2 Chr 1, 8.
w 1 Chr 21, 18. 26. 28; 2 Chr 3, 1.
x 1 Kgs 5, 31f; 9, 20f; 2 Chr 2, 16f.
y 1 Chr 18, 8; 1 Kgs 7, 47.
z 1 Chr 10, 27; Ezr 3, 7.
a 1 Chr 29, 1.
b 7-10: 1 Chr 17, 1-14; 28, 2-7; 2 Sm 7, 1-16; 1 Kgs 5, 3ff; 8, 17-21.
c 2 Sm 12, 24.
d Heb 1, 5.
e 1 Chr 28, 7. 20; Dt 31, 6. 23; Jos 1, 6f. 9; 1 Kgs 2, 2f.
f 1 Chr 29, 2ff.

*

21, 25: Six hundred shekels of gold: about 10,000 dollars. According to 2 Sm 24, 24, David paid 50 shekels of silver, about 20 dollars, for Ornan's threshing floor; but for the Chronicler the site of the temple was much more precious than that.

21, 1: This belongs to ch 22.

22, 2ff: According to 1 Kgs 5, 15–32, it was Solomon who made the material preparations for building the temple, even though David had wished to do so (1 Kgs 5, 17ff). The Chronicler, however, sought to have David, who was Israel's ideal king, more closely connected with Israel's most sacred sanctuary, the temple of Jerusalem.

22, 9: The Hebrew word for peace, shalom, is reflected in the name Solomon, in Hebrew, Shelomo. A contrast is drawn here between Solomon, the peaceful man, and David, who waged great wars (v 8). David was prevented from building the temple, not only because all his time was taken up in waging war (1 Kgs 5, 17), but also because he shed much blood (v 8), and in the eyes of the Chronicler this made him ritually unfit for the task.

22, 14: A hundred thousand talents of gold: about 3,775 tons of gold. A million talents of silver: about 37,750 tons of silver. The fantastically exaggerated figures are intended merely to stress the inestimable value of the temple as the center of Israelite worship. More modest figures are given in

with great effort I have laid up for the house of the LORD a hundred thousand talents of gold,* a million talents of silver, and bronze and iron in such great quantities that they cannot be weighed. I have also stored up wood and stones, to which you must add.*f* 15 Moreover, you have available an unlimited supply of workmen, stonecutters, masons, carpenters, and every kind of craftsman 16 skilled in gold, silver, bronze, and iron. Set to work, therefore, and the LORD be with you!''

Charge to the Leaders. 17 David also commanded all of Israel's leaders to help his son Solomon: 18 ''Is not the LORD your God with you? Has he not given you rest on every side? Indeed, he has delivered the occupants of the land into my power, and the land is subdued before the LORD and his people.*g* 19 Therefore, devote your hearts and souls to seeking the LORD your God. Proceed to build the sanctuary of the LORD God, that the ark of the covenant of the LORD and God's sacred vessels may be brought into the house built in honor of the LORD.''*h*

CHAPTER 23

The Levitical Classes. 1 When David had grown old and was near the end of his days, he made his son Solomon king over Israel.*i* 2 He then gathered together all the leaders of Israel, together with the priests and the Levites.

3 The Levites thirty years old and above were counted, and their total number was found to be thirty-eight thousand men.*j* 4 Of these, twenty-four thousand were to direct the service of the house of the LORD, six thousand were to be officials and judges, 5 four thousand were to be gatekeepers, and four thousand were to praise the LORD with the instruments which David had devised for praise.*k* 6 David divided them into classes according to the sons of Levi: Gershon, Kohath, and Merari.*l*

7 To the Gershonites belonged Ladan and Shimei. 8 The sons of Ladan: Jehiel the chief, then Zetham and Joel; three in all.*m* 9 The sons of Shimei were Shelomoth, Haziel, and Haran; three. These were the heads of the families of Ladan. 10 The sons of Shimei were Jahath, Zizah, Jeush, and Beriah; these were the sons of Shimei, four in all. 11 Jahath was the chief and Zizah was second to him; but Jeush and Beriah had not many sons, and therefore they were classed as a single family, fulfilling a single office.

12 The sons of Kohath: Amram, Izhar, Hebron, and Uzziel; four in all.*n* 13 The sons of Amran were Aaron and Moses. Aaron was set apart to be consecrated as most holy, he and his sons forever, to offer sacrifice before the LORD,

to minister to him, and to bless his name forever.*o* 14 As for Moses, however, the man of God, his sons were counted as part of the tribe of Levi. 15 The sons of Moses were Gershon and Eliezer.*p* 16 The sons of Gershon: Shubael the chief.*q* 17 The sons of Eliezer were Rehabiah the chief—Eliezer had no other sons, but the sons of Rehabiah were very numerous. 18 The sons of Izhar: Shelomith the chief. 19 The sons of Hebron: Jeriah, the chief, Amariah, the second, Jahaziel, the third, and Jekameam, the fourth.*r* 20 The sons of Uzziel: Micah, the chief, and Isshiah, the second.*s*

21 The sons of Merari: Mahli and Mushi. The sons of Mahli: Eleazar and Kish.*t* 22 Eleazar died leaving no sons, only daughters; the sons of Kish, their kinsmen, married them.*u* 23 The sons of Mushi: Mahli, Eder, and Jeremoth; three in all.*v*

24 These were the sons of Levi according to their ancestral houses, the family heads as they were enrolled one by one according to their names. They performed the work of the service of the house of the LORD from twenty years of age upward,*w* 27 for David's final orders were to enlist the Levites from the time they were twenty years old.

25 David said: ''The LORD, the God of Israel, has given rest to his people, and has taken up his dwelling in Jerusalem.*x* 26 Henceforth the Levites need not carry the Dwelling or any of its furnishings or equipment.*y* 28 Rather, their duty shall be to assist the sons of Aaron in the service of the house of the LORD, having charge of the courts, the chambers, and the preservation of everything holy: they shall take part in the service of the house of God. 29 They shall also have charge of the showbread, of the fine flour for the cereal offering, of the wafers of unleavened bread, and of the baking and mixing, and of all measures of quantity and size.*z* 30 They must be present every morning to offer thanks and to praise the LORD, and likewise in the evening;*a* 31 and at every offering of holocausts to the LORD on sabbaths, new

g 1 Chr 23, 25; Jos 21, 44; 23, 1; 2 Sm 7, 1.
h 1 Kgs 8, 6. 21; 2 Chr 5, 7; 6, 11.
i 1 Chr 28, 5; 1 Kgs 1, 30.
j Nm 4, 3. 23. 30. 35. 39. 43. 47; 8, 23-26; 2 Chr 31, 17.
k 1 Chr 9, 22.
l 1 Chr 6, 1. 16-30; 26, 1-19; Ex 6, 16; Nm 3, 17; 26, 57.
m 1 Chr 26, 21f; 29, 8.
n 1 Chr 6, 23; Ex 6, 18; Nm 3, 19; 26, 23ff.
o 1 Chr 6, 49; Ex 6, 20; 28, 1; Nm 6, 23.
p Ex 2, 22; 18, 3f.

q 1 Chr 26, 24.
r 1 Chr 24, 23.
s 1 Chr 24, 24f.
t 1 Chr 6, 29; 24, 26. 28f; Ex 6, 19; Nm 3, 20. 33.
u 1 Chr 24, 28f.
v 1 Chr 6, 47; 24, 30.
w 2 Chr 31, 17; Ezr 3, 8.
x 1 Chr 22, 18; Ps 132, 13.
y 1 Chr 15, 15; 2 Chr 35, 3.
z 1 Chr 9, 29. 31f; Lv 2, 1. 4f; 24, 5-8.
a Nm 28, 3-8.
b Nm 28, 2-29. 39.

moons, and feast days, in such numbers as are prescribed, they must always be present before the Lord.[b] **32** They shall observe what is prescribed for them concerning the meeting tent, the sanctuary, and the sons of Aaron, their brethren, in the service of the house of the Lord.''[c]

CHAPTER 24

The Priestly Classes. **1** The descendants of Aaron also were divided into classes. The sons of Aaron were Nadab, Abihu, Eleazar, and Ithamar.[d] **2** Nadab and Abihu died before their father, leaving no sons; therefore only Eleazar and Ithamar served as priests.[e] **3** David, with Zadok, a descendant of Eleazar, and Ahimelech, a descendant of Ithamar, assigned the functions for the priestly service.[f] **4** But since the descendants of Eleazar were found to be more numerous than those of Ithamar, the former were divided into sixteen groups, and the latter into eight groups, each under its family head. **5** Their functions were assigned impartially by lot, for there were officers of the holy place, and officers of the divine presence, descended both from Eleazar and from Ithamar. **6** The scribe Shemaiah, son of Nethanel, a Levite, made a record of it in the presence of the king, and of the leaders, of Zadok the priest, and of Ahimelech, son of Abiathar,* and of the heads of the ancestral houses of the priests and of the Levites, listing two successive family groups from Eleazar before each one from Ithamar.[g]

7 [h]The first lot fell to Jehoiarib, the second to Jedaiah, **8** the third to Harim, the fourth to Seorim, **9** the fifth to Malchijah, the sixth to Mijamin, **10** the seventh to Hakkoz, the eighth to Abijah,[i] **11** the ninth to Jeshua, the tenth to Shecaniah, **12** the eleventh to Eliashib, the twelfth to Jakim, **13** the thirteenth to Huppah, the fourteenth to Ishbaal, **14** the fifteenth to Bilgah, the sixteenth to Immer, **15** the seventeenth to Hezir, the eighteenth to Happizzez, **16** the nineteenth to Pethahiah, the twentieth to Jehezkel, **17** the twenty-first to Jachin, the twenty-second to Gamul, **18** the twenty-third to Delaiah, the twenty-fourth to Maaziah. **19** This was the appointed order of their service when they functioned in the house of the Lord in keeping with the precepts given them by Aaron, their father, as the Lord, the God of Israel, had commanded him.[j]

Other Levites. **20** [k]Of the remaining Levites, there were Shubael, of the descendants of Amram, and Jehdeiah, of the descendants of Shubael; **21** Isshiah, the chief, of the descendants of Rehabiah; **22** Shelomith of the Izharites, and Jahath of the descendants of Shelomith.

23 The descendants of Hebron were Jeriah, the chief, Amariah, the second, Jahaziel, the third, Jekameam, the fourth. **24** The descendants of Uzziel were Micah; Shamir, of the descendants of Micah; **25** Isshiah, the brother of Micah; and Zechariah, a descendant of Isshiah. **26** The descendants of Merari were Mahli, Mushi, and the descendants of his son Uzziah. **27** The descendants of Merari through his son Uzziah: Shoham, Zaccur, and Ibri. **28** Descendants of Mahli were Eleazar, who had no sons, **29** and Jerahmeel, of the descendants of Kish. **30** The descendants of Mushi were Mahli, Eder, and Jerimoth.

These were the descendants of the Levites according to their ancestral houses. **31** They too, in the same manner as their relatives, the descendants of Aaron, cast lots in the presence of King David, Zadok, Ahimelech, and the heads of the priestly and levitical families; the more important family did so in the same way as the less important one.[l]

CHAPTER 25

The Singers. **1** David and the leaders of the liturgical cult set apart for service the descendants of Asaph, Heman, and Jeduthun, as singers of inspired song to the accompaniment of lyres and harps and cymbals.[m]

This is the list of those who performed this service: **2** *Of the sons of Asaph: Zaccur, Joseph, Nethaniah, and Asharelah, sons of Asaph, under the direction of Asaph, who sang inspired songs under the guidance of the king. **3** Of Jeduthun, these sons of Jeduthun: Gedaliah, Zeri, Jeshaiah, Shimei, Hashabiah, and Mattithiah; six, under the direction of their father Jeduthun, who sang inspired songs to the accompaniment of a lyre, to give thanks and praise to the Lord. **4** Of Heman, these sons of Heman: Bukkiah, Mattaniah, Uzziel, Shubael, and Jerimoth; Hananiah, Hanani, Eliathah, Giddal-

---

c Nm 3, 6-9; 18, 2-5.
d Ex 6, 23; Nm 3, 2ff;
  26, 60.
e Lv 10, 1-7. 12; Nm 3,
  2. 4.
f 1 Chr 18, 16; 2 Sm 8,
  17; 2 Chr 8, 14.
g 1 Chr 18, 16; 2 Sm 8,
  17.
h 7-10: 1 Chr 9, 10ff; Ezr

2, 36ff; Neh 7, 39ff;
  11, 10ff.
i Lk 1, 5.
j 2 Chr 23, 8.
k 20-31: 1 Chr 23, 7-23.
l 1 Chr 25, 8; 26, 13.
m 1 Chr 6, 31ff; 15, 16f.

---

* 24, 6: Ahimelech, son of Abiathar: see note on 1 Chr 18, 16.

25, 2–31: This list of twenty-four classes of temple singers balances the list of the twenty-four classes of priests (1 Chr 24, 4–19). The last nine names in 1 Chr 25, 4, which seem to form a special group, appear to have been originally fragments or incipits of hymns. With some slight changes in the vocalization, the names would mean: "Have mercy on me, O Lord," "Have mercy on me," "You are my God," "I magnify," "I extol the help of . . . ," "Sitting in adversity," "I have fulfilled," "He made abundant," and "Visions."

ti, Romamti-ezer, Joshbekashah, Mallothi, Hothir, and Mahazioth. 5 All these were the sons of Heman, the king's seer in divine matters; to enhance his prestige, God gave Heman fourteen sons and three daughters.[n] 6 All these, whether of Asaph, Jeduthun, or Heman, were under their fathers' direction in the singing in the house of the LORD to the accompaniment of cymbals, harps and lyres, serving in the house of God, under the guidance of the king.[o] 7 Their number, together with that of their brethren who were trained in singing to the LORD, all of them skilled men, was two hundred and eighty-eight. 8 They cast lots for their functions equally, young and old, master and pupil alike.[p]

9 The first lot fell to Asaph, the family of Joseph; he and his sons and his brethren were twelve. Gedaliah was the second; he and his brethren and his sons were twelve. 10 The third was Zaccur, his sons and his brethren: twelve. 11 The fourth fell to Izri, his sons, and his brethren: twelve. 12 The fifth was Nethaniah, his sons, and his brethren: twelve. 13 The sixth was Bukkiah, his sons, and his brethren: twelve. 14 The seventh was Jesarelah, his sons, and his brethren: twelve. 15 The eighth was Jeshaiah, his sons, and his brethren: twelve. 16 The ninth was Mattaniah, his sons, and his brethren: twelve. 17 The tenth was Shimei, his sons, and his brethren: twelve. 18 The eleventh was Uzziel, his sons, and his brethren: twelve. 19 The twelfth fell to Hashabiah, his sons, and his brethren: twelve. 20 The thirteenth was Shubael, his sons, and his brethren: twelve. 21 The fourteenth was Mattithiah, his sons, and his brethren: twelve. 22 The fifteenth fell to Jeremoth, his sons, and his brethren: twelve. 23 The sixteenth fell to Hananiah, his sons, and his brethren: twelve. 24 The seventeenth fell to Joshbekashah, his sons, and his brethren: twelve. 25 The eighteenth fell to Hanani, his sons, and his brethren: twelve. 26 The nineteenth fell to Mallothi, his sons, and his brethren: twelve. 27 The twentieth fell to Eliathah, his sons, and his brethren: twelve. 28 The twenty-first fell to Hothir, his sons, and his brethren: twelve. 29 The twenty-second fell to Giddalti, his sons, and his brethren: twelve. 30 The twenty-third fell to Mahazioth, his sons, and his brethren: twelve. 31 The twenty-fourth fell to Romamti-ezer, his sons, and his brethren: twelve.

CHAPTER 26

Classes of Gatekeepers. 1 [q]As for the classes of gatekeepers. Of the Korahites was Meshelemiah, the son of Kore, one of the sons of Abiasaph. 2 Meshelemiah's sons: Zechariah, the first-born, Jediael, the second son, Zeb-

adiah, the third, Jathniel, the fourth, 3 Elam, the fifth, Jehohanan, the sixth, Eliehoenai, the seventh. 4 Obed-edom's sons: Shemaiah, the first-born, Jehozabad, a second son, Joah, the third, Sachar, the fourth, Nethanel, the fifth, 5 Ammiel, the sixth, Issachar, the seventh, Peullethai, the eighth, for God blessed him. 6 To his son Shemaiah were born sons who ruled over their family, for they were warriors. 7 The sons of Shemaiah were Othni, Rephael, Obed, and Elzabad; also his brethren who were men of might, Elihu and Semachiah. 8 All these were of the sons of Obed-edom, who, together with their sons and their brethren, were mighty men, fit for the service. Of Obed-edom, sixty-two. 9 Of Meshelemiah, eighteen sons and brethren, mighty men.

10 Hosah, a descendant of Merari, had these sons: Shimri, the chief (for though he was not the first-born, his father made him chief),[r] 11 Hilkiah, the second son, Tebaliah, the third, Zechariah, the fourth. All the sons and brethren of Hosah were thirteen.

12 To these classes of gatekeepers, under their chief men, were assigned watches in the service of the house of the LORD, for each group in the same way. 13 They cast lots for each gate, the small and the large families alike. 14 When the lot was cast for the east side, it fell to Meshelemiah. Then they cast lots for his son Zechariah, a prudent counselor, and the north side fell to his lot.[s] 15 To Obededom fell the south side, and to his sons the storehouse. 16 To Hosah fell the west side with the Shallecheth gate at the ascending highway. For each family, watches were established. 17 On the east, six watched each day, on the north, four each day, on the south, four each day, and at the storehouse they were two and two; 18 as for the large building* on the west, there were four at the highway and two at the large building. 19 These were the classes of the gatekeepers, descendants of Kore and Merari.

Treasurers. 20 Their brother Levites superintended the stores for the house of God and the stores of votive offerings.[t] 21 Among the descendants of Ladan the Gershonite, the family heads were descendants of Jehiel: the descendants of Jehiel,[u] 22 [v]Zetham and his brother Joel, who superintended the treasures of the house of the LORD. 23 From the Amramites,

n 2 Chr 35, 15.
o 1 Chr 15, 16.
p 1 Chr 24, 31.
q 1 Chr 9, 19; 2 Chr 8, 14; 23, 19; 35, 15; Neh 12, 45.
r 1 Chr 16, 38.

s 1 Chr 9, 24.
t 1 Chr 28, 12; 1 Kgs 7, 51.
u 1 Chr 23, 7f; 29, 8.
v 22ff: 1 Chr 23, 8. 12 16.

*

26, 18: The large building (in the Hebrew text F
note on 2 Kgs 23, 11.

Izharites, Hebronites, and Uzzielites, **24** Shubael, son of Gershon, son of Moses, was chief superintendent over the treasures. **25** ʷHis associate pertained to Eliezer, whose son was Rehabiah, whose son was Jeshaiah, whose son was Joram, whose son was Zichri, whose son was Shelomith. **26** This Shelomith and his brethren superintended all the stores of the votive offerings dedicated by King David, the heads of the families, the commanders of thousands and of hundreds, and the commanders of the army,ˣ **27** from the booty they had taken in the wars, for the enhancement of the house of the LORD. **28** Also, whatever Samuel the seer, Saul, son of Kish, Abner, son of Ner, Joab, son of Zeruiah, and all others had consecrated, was under the charge of Shelomith and his brethren.

Magistrates.   **29** Among the Izharites, Chananiah and his sons were in charge of Israel's civil affairs as officials and judges.ʸ **30** Among the Hebronites, Hashabiah and his brethren, one thousand seven hundred police officers, had the administration of Israel on the western side of the Jordan in all the work of the LORD and in the service of the king.ᶻ **31** Among the Hebronites, Jerijah was their chief according to their family records. In the fortieth year of David's reign search was made, and there were found among them outstanding officers at Jazer of Gilead.ᵃ **32** His brethren were also police officers, two thousand seven hundred heads of families. King David appointed them to the administration of the Reubenites, the Gadites, and the half-tribe of Manasseh in everything pertaining to God and to the king.

CHAPTER 27

Army Commanders.* **1** This is the list of the Israelite family heads, commanders of thousands and of hundreds, and other officers who served the king in all that pertained to the divisions, of twenty-four thousand men each, that came and went month by month throughout the year.

2 Over the first division for the first month was Ishbaal, son of Zabdiel, and in his division were twenty-four thousand men; **3** a descendant of Perez, he was chief over all the commanders of the army for the first month. **4** Over the division of the second month was Eleazar, son of Dodo, from Ahoh, and in his division were twenty-four thousand men.ᵇ **5** ᶜThe third army commander, chief for the third month, was Benaiah, son of Jehoiada the priest, and in his division were twenty-four thousand men. Benaiah was a warrior among the Thirty over the Thirty. His son Ammizabad was division. **7** Fourth, for the fourth was Asahel, brother of Joab, and after

him his son Zebadiah, and in his division were twenty-four thousand men.ᵈ **8** Fifth, for the fifth month, was the commander Shamhuth, a descendant of Zerah, and in his division were twenty-four thousand men. **9** Sixth, for the sixth month, was Ira, son of Ikkesh, from Tekoa, and in his division were twenty-four thousand men. **10** Seventh, for the seventh month, was Helles, from Beth-pheleth, of the sons of Ephraim, and in his division were twenty-four thousand men. **11** Eighth, for the eighth month, was Sibbecai the Hushathite, a descendant of Zerah, and in his division were twenty-four thousand men.ᵉ **12** Ninth, for the ninth month, was Abiezer from Anathoth, of Benjamin, and in his division were twenty-four thousand men. **13** Tenth, for the tenth month, was Maharai from Netophah, a descendant of Zerah, and in his division were twenty-four thousand men. **14** Eleventh, for the eleventh month, was Benaiah the Pirathonite, of Ephraim, and in his division were twenty-four thousand men. **15** Twelfth, for the twelfth month, was Heldai the Netophathite, of the family of Othniel, and in his division were twenty-four thousand men.

Tribal Heads.   **16** Over the tribes of Israel, for the Reubenites the leader was Eliezer, son of Zichri; for the Simeonites, Shephatiah, son of Maacah; **17** for Levi, Hashabiah, son of Kemuel; for Aaron, Zadok; **18** for Judah, Eliab, one of David's brothers; for Issachar, Omri, son of Michael;ᶠ **19** for Zebulun, Ishmaiah, son of Obadiah; for Naphtali, Jeremoth, son of Azriel; **20** for the sons of Ephraim, Hoshea, son of Azaziah; for the half-tribe of Manasseh, Joel, son of Pedaiah; **21** for the half-tribe of Manasseh in Gilead, Iddo, son of Zechariah; for Benjamin, Jaasiel, son of Abner; **22** for Dan, Azarel, son of Jeroham. These were the commanders of the tribes of Israel.

23 David did not count those who were twenty years of age or younger, for the LORD had promised to multiply Israel like the stars of the heavens.ᵍ **24** Joab, son of Zeruiah, began to take the census, but he did not complete it, for because of it wrath fell upon Israel. Therefore

w 1 Chr 23, 17f; 24, 21.
x 2 Sm 8, 11.
y 1 Chr 23, 4.
z 1 Chr 27, 17; Neh 11, 15f.
a 1 Chr 23, 19; 29, 27; Jos 13, 25.
b 1 Chr 9, 37; 11, 12; 2 Sm 23, 9.
c 5f: 1 Chr 11, 22ff; 18, 17; 2 Sm 23, 20ff.
d 2 Sm 2, 18; 23, 24.
e 1 Chr 11, 29; 20, 4; 2 Sm 21, 18.
f 1 Chr 2, 13.
g 1 Chr 22, 17.
h 2 Sm 24, 10.

*

27, 1–15: This list of army commanders is similar to, but distinct from, the list of David's warriors as given in 1 Chr 11, 10–47. The schematic enumeration of the soldiers as presented here is, no doubt, artificial and grossly exaggerated (12 × 24,000 = 288,000 men!), unless the Hebrew word (eleph) for thousand is understood as designating a military unit of much smaller size; see note on 1 Chr 12, 25–38.

the number did not enter into the book of chronicles of King David.[h]

Overseers. **25** Over the treasures of the king was Azmaveth, the son of Adiel. Over the stores in the country, the cities, the villages, and the towers was Jonathan, son of Uzziah.[i] **26** Over the farm workers who tilled the soil was Ezri, son of Chelub. **27** Over the vineyards was Shimei from Ramah, and over their produce for the wine cellars was Zabdi the Shiphmite. **28** Over the olive trees and sycamores of the foothills was Baalhanan the Gederite, and over the stores of oil was Joash. **29** Over the cattle that grazed in Sharon was Shitrai the Sharonite, and over the cattle in the valleys was Shaphat, the son of Adlai; **30** over the camels was Obil the Ishmaelite; over the she-asses was Jehdeiah the Meronothite; **31** and over the flocks was Jaziz the Hagrite. All these were the overseers of King David's possessions.

David's Court. **32** Jonathan, David's uncle and a man of intelligence, was counselor and scribe; he and Jehiel, the son of Hachmoni, were tutors of the king's sons. **33** Ahithophel was also the king's counselor, and Hushai the Archite was the king's confidant.[j] **34** After Ahithophel* came Jehoiada, the son of Benaiah, and Abiathar. The commander of the king's army was Joab.

CHAPTER 28

The Assembly at Jerusalem. **1** David assembled at Jerusalem all the leaders of Israel, the heads of the tribes, the commanders of the divisions who were in the service of the king, the commanders of thousands and of hundreds, the overseers of all the king's estates and possessions, and his sons, together with the courtiers, the warriors, and every important man.[k] **2** [l]King David rose to his feet and said: "Hear me, my brethren and my people. It was my purpose to build a house of repose myself for the ark of the covenant of the LORD, the footstool for the feet of our God;* and I was preparing to build it. **3** But God said to me, 'You may not build a house in my honor, for you are a man who fought wars and shed blood.' **4** However, the LORD, the God of Israel, chose me from all my father's family to be king over Israel forever. For he chose Judah as leader, then one family of Judah, that of my father; and finally, among all the sons of my father, it pleased him to make me king over all Israel.[m] **5** And of all my sons—for the LORD has given me many sons—he has chosen my son Solomon to sit on the LORD's royal throne over Israel.[n] **6** For he said to me: 'It is your son Solomon who shall build my house and my courts, for I have chosen

him for my son, and I will be a father to him.[o] **7** I will establish his kingdom forever, if he perseveres in keeping my commandments and decrees as he keeps them now.' **8** Therefore in the presence of all Israel, the assembly of the LORD, and in the hearing of our God, I exhort you to keep and to carry out all the commandments of the LORD, your God, that you may continue to possess this good land and afterward leave it as an inheritance to your children forever.[p]

9 "As for you, Solomon, my son, know the God of your father and serve him with a perfect heart and a willing soul, for the LORD searches all hearts and understands all the mind's thoughts. If you seek him, he will let himself be found by you; but if you abandon him, he will cast you off forever.[q] **10** See, then! The LORD has chosen you to build a house as his sanctuary. Take courage and set to work."

Temple Plans Given to Solomon. **11** Then David gave to his son Solomon the pattern of the portico and of the building itself, with its storerooms, its upper rooms and inner chambers, and the room with the propitiatory.[r] **12** He provided also the pattern for all else that he had in mind by way of courts for the house of the LORD, with the surrounding compartments for the stores for the house of God and the stores of the votive offerings, **13** as well as for the divisions of the priests and Levites, for all the work of the service of the house of the LORD, and for all the liturgical vessels of the house of the LORD. **14** He specified the weight of gold to be used in the golden vessels for the various services and the weight of silver to be used in the silver vessels for the various services; **15** likewise for the golden lampstands and their lamps he specified the weight of gold for each lampstand and its lamps, and for the silver

---

i 2 Sm 23, 31.
j 2 Sm 15, 12. 32-37; 16, 16-19. 23; 17, 5-16. 23.
k 1 Chr 27, 2-22. 25-31; 11, 10ff.
l 2f: 1 Chr 17, 4; 22, 7ff; 2 Sm 7, 5; 1 Kgs 5, 3; Ps 132, 3-7.
m 1 Chr 17, 23; Gn 49,

8ff; 1 Sm 16, 6-13.
n 1 Chr 3, 1-9; 14, 3-7; 22, 9; 23, 1; Wis 9, 7.
o 1 Chr 17, 11ff; 22, 9f; 2 Sm 7, 12f.
p Dt 4, 5.
q 1 Chr 29, 17; 2 Chr 15, 2; 1 Kgs 8, 61.
r Ex 25, 9. 40;
s Ex 25, 31-37

---

*

27, 34: After Ahithophel: after his suicid Jehoiada then succeeded him as the king's [arbar]: see thar: the priest. The Chronicler does not n because he regards only the Zadokites as priests.

28, 2: The ark . . . the footstool . . . of our Go was invisibly enthroned upon the cherubim that were associated with the ark of the covenant at Shiloh and later in the Jerusalem temple, had the ark as his footstool; cf Pss 99, 5; 132, 7. The propitiatory (1 Chr 28, 11) and the chariot throne (1 Chr 28, 18) reflect the different circumstances of the postexilic community, for whom only the place of the ark was a focal point of worship, though the ark itself was no longer present.

lampstands he specified the weight of silver for each lampstand and its lamps, depending on the use to which each lampstand was to be put. *s* **16** He specified the weight of gold for each table to hold the showbread, and the silver for the silver tables; **17** the pure gold to be used for the forks and pitchers; the amount of gold for each golden bowl and the silver for each silver bowl; **18** the refined gold, and its weight, to be used for the altar of incense; and, finally, gold for what would suggest a chariot throne:* the cherubim that spread their wings and covered the ark of the covenant of the LORD. *t* **19** He had successfully committed to writing the exact specifications of the pattern, because the hand of the LORD was upon him.

20 Then David said to his son Solomon: "Be firm and steadfast; go to work without fear or discouragement, for the LORD God, my God, is with you. He will not fail you or abandon you before you have completed all the work for the service of the house of the LORD. *u* **21** The classes of the priests and Levites are ready for all the service of the house of God; they will help you in all your work with all those who are eager to show their skill in every kind of craftsmanship. Also the leaders and all the people will do everything that you command." *v*

CHAPTER 29

Offerings for the Temple.

1 King David then said to the whole assembly: "My son Solomon, whom alone God has chosen, is still young and immature; the work, however, is great, for this castle is not intended for man, but for the LORD God. *w* **2** For this reason I have stored up for the house of my God, as far as I was able, gold for what will be made of gold, silver for what will be made of silver, bronze for what will be made of bronze, iron for what will be made of iron, wood for what will be made of wood, onyx stones and settings for them, carnelian and mosaic stones, every other kind of precious stone, and great quantities of marble. *x* **3** But now, because of the delight I take in the house of my God, in addition to all that I stored up for the holy house, I give to the house of my God my personal fortune in gold and silver: **4** three thousand talents of Ophir gold, and seven thousand talents of refined silver, for overlaying the walls of the rooms, *y* **5** for the various utensils to be made of gold and silver, and for every work that is to be done by artisans. Now, who else is willing to contribute generously this day to the LORD?" *z*

6 Then the heads of the families, the leaders of the tribes of Israel, the commanders of thousands and of hundreds, and the overseers of the king's affairs came forward willingly *a* **7** and contributed for the service of the house of God

five thousand talents and ten thousand darics of gold, ten thousand talents of silver, eighteen thousand talents of bronze, and one hundred thousand talents of iron. *b* **8** Those who had precious stones gave them into the keeping of Jehiel the Gershonite for the treasury of the house of the LORD. *c* **9** The people rejoiced over these free-will offerings, which had been contributed to the LORD wholeheartedly. King David also rejoiced greatly. *d*

David's Prayer.

10 Then David blessed the LORD in the presence of the whole assembly, praying in these words:

"Blessed may you be, O LORD,
God of Israel our father,
from eternity to eternity.

11 "Yours, O LORD, are grandeur and power,
majesty, splendor, and glory.
For all in heaven and on earth is yours;
yours, O LORD, is the sovereignty;
you are exalted as head over all.

12 "Riches and honor are from you,
and you have dominion over all.
In your hand are power and might;
it is yours to give grandeur and strength
to all. *e*

13 Therefore, our God, we give you thanks
and we praise the majesty of your name."

14 "But who am I, and who are my people, that we should have the means to contribute so freely? For everything is from you, and we only give you what we have received from you. **15** For we stand before you as aliens: we are only your guests, like all our fathers. Our life on earth is like a shadow that does not abide. *f* **16** O LORD our God, all this wealth that we have brought together to build you a house in honor of your holy name comes from you and is entirely yours. **17** I know, O my God, that you put hearts to the test and that you take pleasure in uprightness. With a sincere heart I have willingly given all these things, and now with joy I have seen your people here present also giving to you generously. **18** O LORD, God of our fathers Abraham, Isaac, and Israel, keep such thoughts in the hearts and minds of your people

---

t Ex 25, 18-22; 30, 1-10;
  1 Kgs 6, 23-28.
u 1 Chr 22, 13. 16; Jos
  1, 5.
v Ex 36, 1-5.
w 1 Chr 22, 5; 28, 5.
x 1 Chr 22, 14.
y 2 Chr 9, 10; 1 Kgs 9,
  28; 10, 11.
z Ex 25, 2; 35, 5f.
a 1 Chr 27, 1. 25-31; 28,

1.
b Ezr 2, 69; 8, 27; Neh
  7, 70ff.
c 1 Chr 23, 8; 26, 21.
d 2 Kgs 12, 4.
e 2 Chr 20, 6; Wis 6, 3.
f Lv 25, 23; Wis 2, 5; 5,
  9.
g Ex 3, 6. 15f; 4. 5;
  1 Kgs 18, 36.

28, 18: Chariot throne: probably suggested by Ez 1, 4–24;
10, 1–22.